PACIFIC NORTHWEST CAMPING

The Complete Guide to More
Than 45,000 Campsites for
RVers, Car Campers, and Tenters
in Washington and Oregon

Tom Stienstra

Foghorn
Press
BOOKS BUILDING COMMUNITY™

ISBN 1-57354-037-4

9 781573 540377

52095

Foghorn Outdoors' guidebooks are available wherever books are sold. To find a retailer near you or to order, call 1-800-FOGHORN (364-4676) or (707) 773-4260 or visit the Foghorn Press Web site at www.foghorn.com. Foghorn Press titles are available to the book trade through Publishers Group West (800-788-3123) as well as through wholesalers.

Library of Congress ISSN Data:
April 1998
Pacific Northwest Camping
The Complete Guide to More Than 45,000 Campsites
for RVers, Car Campers, and Tenters in Washington and Oregon
Sixth Edition
ISSN: 1078-9588

> **Leave No Trace, Inc.,** is a program dedicated to maintaining the integrity of outdoor recreation areas through education and public awareness. Foghorn Press is a proud supporter of this program and its ethics.

The Foghorn Press Commitment

Foghorn Press is committed to the preservation of the environment. We promote Leave No Trace principles in our guidebooks.

Printed in the United States of America

PACIFIC NORTHWEST CAMPING

The Complete Guide to More Than 45,000 Campsites for RVers, Car Campers, and Tenters in Washington and Oregon

Tom Stienstra

Foghorn Press

BOOKS BUILDING COMMUNITY™

Dear Campers,

As part of an intense two-year effort, *Pacific Northwest Camping* has been rewritten, reworked, and redesigned in the attempt to make it the most accurate, easy-to-use, and comprehensive resource guidebook for campers in this region.

To make *Pacific Northwest Camping* the most up-to-date and accurate guidebook possible, every listing was reviewed by at least two resource experts. Hundreds of people were involved in polishing the final product.

We have incorporated dozens of suggestions inspired by requests from readers, and your comments are always welcome. Write to us at Foghorn Outdoors, 340 Bodega Avenue, Petaluma, CA 94952.

—T.S.

Chapter Reference Map

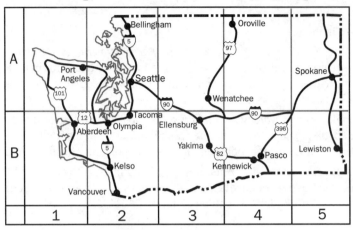

Washington map page 83

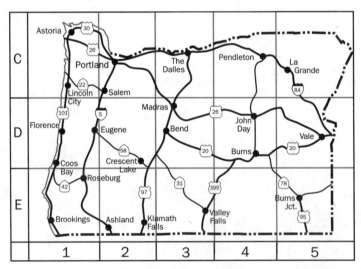

Oregon map page 337

Pacific Northwest Camping

The Complete Guide to More Than 45,000 Campsites for RVers, Car Campers, and Tenters in Washington and Oregon

Contents

How to Use This Book

You can search for your ideal camping spot in two ways:

1) If you know the name of the campground you'd like to visit, or the name of the corresponding geographical area (town name, national or state forest name, national or state park name, lake or river name, etc.), use the index beginning on page 608 to locate it and turn to the corresponding page. If you're looking for a specific campground name, you'll find that the page numbers of all campgrounds are listed in the index in boldfaced type.

2) If you'd like to camp in a particular part of a state and want to find out what camps are available there, use the Washington and Oregon state maps on page 83 and page 337, respectively. Find the area you'd like to camp in (such as A5 for Spokane, Washington or E2 for Ashland, Oregon), then turn to the corresponding page in the book.

Washington, pages 83–336 (maps A1–B5)

Oregon, pages 337–607 (maps C1–E5)

See the bottom of every page for a reference to corresponding maps.

Note to RV and Tent Campers

Those of you with recreational vehicles or tents will find *Pacific Northwest Camping* easy to use. Every camp listing that has RV and/or tent camping sites also has an easy-to-spot RV and/or tent camping symbol. Just flip the pages of the book and look for these symbols: **RV** or 🏕. Occasionally you'll find a campground listing that mentions RV sites but doesn't feature the RV symbol. This occurs in listings in which the access routes may not be safe for RVs.

Every effort has been made to ensure that the information in *Pacific Northwest Camping* is as up-to-date as possible. However, details such as fees and telephone numbers are subject to change. Please contact the campgrounds you plan to visit for current information.

Introduction

Going on a camping trip can be like trying to put hiking boots on an octopus. You've tried it too, eh? Instead of the relaxing, exciting sojourn that was intended, a camping trip can turn into a scenario called You Against The World. It can turn out to be about as easy as fighting an earthquake.

But it doesn't have to be that way and that's what this book is all about. If you give it a chance, it can put the mystery, excitement, and fun back into your camping vacations—and remove the fear of snarls, confusion, and occasional temper explosions of volcanic proportions that keep people at home, locked away from the action.

Mystery? There are hundreds of hidden, rarely used campgrounds listed and mapped in this book that you have never dreamed of. Excitement? At many of them you'll find the sizzle with the steak, the hike to a great lookout, the big fish at the end of the line. Fun? The how-to section of this book can help you take the futility out of your trips and put the fun back in. Add it up, put it in your cash register, and you can turn a camping trip into the satisfying adventure it's meant to be, whether it's just an overnight quicky or a month-long expedition.

It has been documented that 95 percent of American vacationers use only 5 percent of the available recreation areas. With this book, you can leave the herd to wander and be free, and join the inner circle, the 5 Percenters who know the great, hidden areas used by so few people. To join the 5 Percent Club, you should take a hard look at the maps for the areas you wish to visit and the corresponding listings of campgrounds. As you study the camps, you'll start to feel a sense of excitement building, a feeling that you are about to unlock a door and venture into a world that is rarely viewed. When you feel that excitement, act on it. Parlay that energy into a great trip.

The campground maps and listings can serve in two ways: 1) If you're on the road late in the day and you're stuck for a spot for the night, you can likely find one nearby; or 2) If you are planning in advance, you can tailor a vacation to fit exactly into your plans, rather than heading off, and hoping—maybe praying—it turns out all right.

For the latter, you may wish to obtain additional maps, particularly if you are venturing into areas governed by the U.S. Forest Service or Bureau of Land Management. Both are federal agencies that offer low-cost maps that detail all hiking trails, lakes, streams, and backcountry camps reached via logging roads. How to obtain these and other maps is described in the Resource Guide on pages 79 to 82.

Backcountry camps listed in this book are often in primitive and rugged settings but provide the sense of isolation that you may want for a trip. They also provide good jump-off points for backpacking trips, if that's your calling. These camps are also often free, and we have listed hundreds of them.

At the other end of the spectrum are the developed parks for RVs, parks that offer a home away from home with everything from full hookups to a grocery store and laundry room. These spots are just as important as the remote camps with no facilities. Instead of isolation, an RV park provides a place to shower and get outfitted for food and clean clothes. For RV cruisers, it's a place to stay in high style while touring the area. RV parks range in price from $8 to $20 per night, depending on location, and an advance deposit may be necessary in summer months.

Somewhere between the two extremes—the remote, unimproved camps and the lavish RV parks—are hundreds and hundreds of campgrounds that provide a compromise: beautiful settings and some facilities, with a small overnight fee. Piped water, vault toilets, and picnic tables tend to come with the territory, along with a fee that usually ranges from $7 to $15, with the higher-priced sites located near population centers. Because they offer a bit of both worlds, they are in high demand. Reservations are usually advised, and at state parks, particularly during the summer season, you can expect company. This doesn't mean you need to abandon them in hopes of a less confined environment. For one thing, most state parks have set up quotas so that you don't feel like you've been squeezed in with a shoehorn, and for another, the same parks are often uncrowded during the off-season or on weekdays.

Prior to your trip, you'll want to get organized, and that's where you must start putting socks on that giant octopus. The trick to organization for any task is breaking it down to its key components, then solving each element independent of the others. Remember the octopus. Grab a moving leg, jam on a boot, and make sure it's on tight before reaching for another leg. Do one thing at a time, in order, and all will get done quickly and efficiently.

In the stories that follow, we have isolated the different elements of camping, and you should do the same when planning for your trip. There are separate stories on each of the primary ingredients for a successful trip: 1) Food and cooking gear; 2) Clothing and weather protection; 3) Hiking and foot care and how to choose the right boots and socks; 4) Sleeping gear; 5) Combatting bugs and some common sense first-aid; 6) Catching fish, avoiding bears, and camp fun; 7) Outdoors with kids; and 8) Weather prediction. We've also included sections on boat-in and desert camping and ethics in the outdoors, as well as a camping gear checklist.

Now you can become completely organized for your trip in just one week, spending just a little time each evening. Getting organized is an unnatural act for many. By splitting up the tasks, you take the pressure out of planning and put the fun back in.

As a full-time outdoors writer, the question I get asked more than any other is, "Where are you going this week?" All of the answers are in this book.

Food and Cooking Gear

It was a warm, crystal clear day, the kind of day when if you had ever wanted to go skydiving, you would go skydiving. That was exactly the case for my old pal Foonsky, who had never before tried the sport. But a funny thing happened after he jumped out of the plane and pulled on the rip cord: His parachute didn't open.

In total free fall, Foonsky watched the earth below getting closer and closer. Not one to panic, he calmly pulled the rip cord on the emergency parachute. Again, nothing happened. No parachute, no nothing.

The ground was getting ever closer, and as he tried to search for a soft place to land, Foonsky detected a small object shooting up toward him, growing larger as it approached. It looked like a camper.

Figuring this was his last chance, Foonsky shouted as they passed in midair, "Hey, do you know anything about parachutes?"

The other fellow just yelled back as he headed off into space, "Do you know anything about lighting camping stoves?"

Well, Foonsky got lucky and his parachute opened. As for the other guy, well, he's probably in orbit like a NASA weather satellite. If you've ever had a mishap while lighting a camping stove, you know exactly what I'm talking about.

When it comes to camping, all gear is not created equal. Nothing is more important than lighting your stove easily and having it reach full heat without feeling like you're playing with a short

fuse to a miniature bomb. If your stove does not work right, your trip can turn into a disaster, regardless of how well you have planned the other elements. In addition, a bad stove will add an underlying sense of foreboding to your day. You will constantly have the inner suspicion that your darn stove is going to foul up again.

Camping Stoves

If you are buying a camping stove, remember this one critical rule: Do not leave the store with a new stove unless you have been shown exactly how to use it.

Know what you are getting. Many stores that specialize in outdoor recreation equipment now provide experienced campers/employees who will demonstrate the use of every stove they sell and, while they're at it, describe their respective strengths and weaknesses.

An innovation by Peak 1 is a two-burner backpacking stove, allowing you to boil water and heat a pot of food simultaneously. While that has long been standard for car campers using Coleman's legendary camp stove, it is previously unheard of for wilderness campers in high-elevation areas. Another recent invention is the flameless stove (no kidding), which allows campers to cook in a tent safely for the first time.

A stove that has developed a cultlike following is the little Sierra, which burns small twigs and pinecones, then uses a tiny battery-driven fan to develop increased heat and cooking ability. It's an excellent alternative for long-distance backpacking trips, as it solves the problem of carrying a fuel bottle, especially on expeditions for which large quantities of fuel would otherwise be needed. Some tinkering with the flame (a very hot one) is required, and they are legal and functional only in the alpine zone where dry wood is available. Also note that in years with high fire danger, the Forest Service will enact rules prohibiting open flames, and fires are also often prohibited above an elevation of 10,000 feet.

I prefer a small, lightweight stove that uses white gas so I can closely gauge fuel consumption. My pal Foonsky uses one with a butane bottle because it lights so easily. We have contests to see who can boil a pot of water faster, and the difference is usually negligible. Thus, other factors are important when choosing a stove.

Of these, ease of cleaning the burner is the most important. If you camp often, especially with a smaller stove, the burner holes will eventually become clogged. Some stoves have a built-in cleaning needle; a quick twist of the knob and you're in business. Others require disassembly and a protracted session using special cleaning tools. If a stove is difficult to clean, you will tend to put off doing it, and your stove will sputter and pant while you feel humiliated watching the cold pot of water sitting there.

Before making a purchase, have the salesperson show you how to clean the burner head. Except in the case of large, multiburner family camping stoves, which rarely require cleaning, this test can do more to determine the long-term value of a stove than any other factor.

Fuels for Camping Stoves

White gas and butane have long been the most popular camp fuels, but a newly developed fuel could dramatically change that.

LPG (liquid petroleum gas) comes in cartridges for easy attachment to a stove or lantern. At room temperature, LPG is delivered in a combustible gaseous form. When you shake the cartridge, the contents sound liquid; that is because under pressure, the gas liquefies, which is why it is so easy to use. Large amounts of fuel are compressed into small canisters.

While convenience has always been the calling card for LPG, recent innovations have allowed it to become a suitable choice for winter and high-altitude mountaineering expeditions, coming close to matching white gas performance specs. For several years now, MSR, Epi (Coleman), Coleman, Primus, Camping Gaz, Markill, and other makers have been mixing propanes, butanes, and isobutanes to improve performance capabilities.

Two important hurdles that stood in the way of LPG's popularity were recently leaped. Coleman, working in cooperation with the U.S. Postal Service, has developed a program in which three-packs of 170-gram Coleman Max fuel cartridges can be shipped by mail to any address or post office in the 50 states and Puerto Rico. Also, each Coleman Max fuel cartridge is now made of aluminum and comes with a special device that allows the consumer to safely puncture the cartridge once the fuel is gone and then toss it into any aluminum can recycling container.

The following details the benefits and drawbacks of other available fuels:

White gas: White gas is the most popular camp fuel, because it can be purchased at most outdoor recreation stores and many supermarkets, and is inexpensive and effective. It burns hot, has virtually no smell, and evaporates quickly when spilled. If you are caught in wet, miserable weather and can't get a fire going, you can use white gas as an emergency fire starter; however, if you do so, use it sparingly and never on an open flame.

White gas is a popular fuel both for car campers who use the large, two-burner stoves equipped with a fuel tank and a pump, and for hikers who carry a lightweight backpacking stove. On the latter, lighting can require priming with a gel called priming paste, which some people dislike. Another problem with white gas is that it can be extremely explosive.

As an example, I once almost burned my beard completely off in a mini explosion while lighting one of the larger stoves designed for car camping. I was in the middle of cooking dinner when the flame suddenly shut down. Sure enough, the fuel tank was empty, and after refilling it, I pumped the tank 50 or 60 times to regain pressure. When I lit a match, the sucker ignited from three feet away. The resulting explosion was like a stick of dynamite going off, and immediately the smell of burning beard was in the air. In a flash, my once thick, dark beard had been reduced to a mass of little yellow burned curlicues.

My error? After filling the tank, I forgot to shut the fuel cock off while pumping up the pressure in the tank. As a result, when I pumped the tank the stove burners were slowly producing the gas/air mixture, filling the air above the stove. Then, strike a match from even a few feet away and ka-boom!

Butane: That problem can be solved by using stoves that burn bottled butane fuel. Butane requires no pouring, pumping, or priming, and butane stoves are the easiest to light. Just turn a knob and light—that's it. On the minus side, because it comes in bottles, you never know precisely how much fuel you have left. And when a bottle is empty, you have a potential piece of litter. (Never litter. Ever.)

The other problem with butane is that it just plain does not work well in cold weather or when there is little fuel left in the cartridge. Since you cannot predict mountain weather in spring or fall, you can wind up using more fuel than originally projected. That can be frustrating, particularly if your stove starts wheezing when there are still several days left to go. In addition, with most butane cartridges, if there is any chance of the temperature falling below freezing, you often have to sleep with the cartridge to keep it warm, or forget about using it come morning.

Coleman Max Performance Fuel: This new fuel offers the most unique approach to solving the consistent burn challenge facing all pressurized gas cartridges: operating at temperatures at or below 0 degrees Fahrenheit. Using a standard propane/butane blend for high-octane performance, Coleman gets around the drop-off in performance other cartridges experience by utilizing a version of fuel injection. A hose inside the cartridge pulls liquid fuel into the stove where it vaporizes, a switch from the standard approach of pulling only a gaseous form of the fuel into a stove. By drawing liquid out of the cartridge, Coleman gets around the

Food and Cooking Gear   13

tendency of propane to burn off first and allows each cartridge to deliver a consistent mix of propane and butane to the stove's burners throughout the cartridge's life.

Butane/Propane: This blend offers higher octane performance than butane alone, solving the cold temperature doldrums somewhat. However, propane burns off before butane so there will be a performance drop as the fuel level in the cartridge lowers.

Propane: Now available for single-burner stoves using larger, heavier cartridges to accommodate higher pressures, propane offers the very best performance of any of the pressurized gas canister fuels.

Primus Tri-Blend: This blend is made up of 20 percent propane, 70 percent butane, and 10 percent isobutane and is designed to burn with more consistent heat and efficiency than standard propane/butane mixes.

Denatured alcohol: Though this fuel burns cleanly and quietly and is virtually explosion proof, it generates much less heat than pressurized or liquid gas fuels.

Kerosene: Never buy a stove that uses kerosene for fuel. Kerosene is smelly and messy, generates low heat, needs priming, and is virtually obsolete as a camp fuel in the United States. As a test, I once tried using a kerosene stove. I could scarcely boil a pot of water. In addition, some kerosene leaked out when the stove was packed, ruining everything it touched. The smell of kerosene never did go away. Kerosene remains popular in Europe only because most campers there haven't yet heard much about white gas. When they do, they will demand it.

Building Fires

One summer expedition took me to the Canadian wilderness in British Columbia for a 75-mile canoe trip on the Bowron Lake Circuit, a chain of 13 lakes, six rivers, and seven portages. It is one of the truly great canoe trips in the world, a loop that ends just a few hundred feet from its starting point. But at the first camp at Kibbee Lake, my stove developed a fuel leak at the base of the burner and the nuclear-like blast that followed just about turned Canada into a giant crater.

As a result, the final 70 miles of the trip had to be completed without a stove, cooking on open fires each night. The problem was compounded by the weather. It rained eight of the 10 days. Rain? In Canada, raindrops the size of silver dollars fall so hard they actually bounce on the lake surface. We had to stop paddling a few times in order to empty the rainwater out of the canoe. At the end of the day, we'd make camp and then face the test: Either make a fire or go to bed cold and hungry.

With an ax, at least we had a chance for success. As soaked as all the downed wood was, I was able to make my own fire-starting tinder from the chips of split logs; no matter how hard it rains, the inside of a log is always dry.

In miserable weather, matches don't stay lit long enough to get the tinder started. Instead, we used either a candle or the little waxlike fire-starter cubes that remain lit for several minutes. From those, we could get the tinder going. Then we added small, slender strips of wood that had been axed from the interior of the logs. When the flame reached a foot high, we added the logs, their dry interior facing in. By the time the inside of the logs had caught fire, the outside would be drying from the heat. It wasn't long before a royal blaze was brightening the rainy night.

That's a worst-case scenario, and hopefully you will never face anything like it. Nevertheless, being able to build a good fire and cook on it can be one of the more satisfying elements of a camping trip. At times, just looking into the flames can provide a special satisfaction at the end of a good day.

However, never expect to build a fire for every meal, or in some cases, even to build one at all. Many state and federal campgrounds have been picked clean of downed wood, or forest fire danger forces rangers to prohibit fires altogether during the fire season. In either case, you must use your camp stove or go hungry.

But when you can build a fire, and the resources for doing so are available, it will enhance the quality of your camping experience. Of the campgrounds listed in this book, those where you are permitted to build fires will usually have fire rings. In primitive areas where you can make your own fire, you should dig a ring eight inches deep, line the edges with rock, and clear all the needles and twigs in a five-foot radius. The next day, when the fire is dead, you can discard the rocks, fill over the black charcoal with dirt, then scatter pine needles and twigs over it. Nobody will even know you camped there. That's the best way I know to keep a secret spot a real secret.

When you start to build a campfire, the first thing you will notice is that no matter how good your intentions, your fellow campers will not be able to resist moving the wood around. Watch. You'll be getting ready to add a key piece of wood at just the right spot, and your companion will stick his mitts in, confidently believing he has a better idea. He'll shift the fire around and undermine your best thought-out plans.

So I enforce a rule on camping trips: One person makes the fire while everybody else stands clear or is involved with other camp tasks such as gathering wood, getting water, putting up tents, or planning dinner. Once the fire is going strong, then it's fair game; anyone adds logs at their discretion. But in the early, delicate stages of the campfire, it's best to leave the work to one person.

Before a match is ever struck, you should gather a complete pile of firewood. Then start small, with the tiniest twigs you can find, and slowly add larger twigs as you go, crisscrossing them like a miniature tepee. Eventually you will get to the big chunks that will produce high heat. The key is to get one piece of wood burning into another, which then burns into another, setting off what I call the "chain of flame." Conversely, single pieces of wood, set apart from each other, will not burn.

On a dry summer evening, at a campsite where plenty of wood is available, about the only way you can blow the deal is to get impatient and try to add the big pieces too quickly. Do that and you'll get smoke, not flames, and it won't be long before every one of your fellow campers is poking at your fire. It will drive you crazy, but they just won't be able to help it.

Cooking Gear

I like traveling light, and I've found that all I need for cooking is a pot, small frying pan, metal pot grabber, fork, knife, cup, and matches. If you want to keep the price of food low and also cook customized dinners each night, a small pressure cooker can be just the ticket. (See "Keeping the Price Down" on page 17.) I store all my gear in one small bag that fits into my pack. If I'm camping out of my four-wheel-drive rig, the little bag of cooking gear is easy to keep track of. Going simple, not complicated, is the key to keeping a camping trip on the right track.

You can get more elaborate by purchasing complete kits with plates, a coffeepot, large pots, and other cookware, but what really counts is having a single pot that makes you happy. It needs to be just the right size, not too big or small, and stable enough so it won't tip over, even if it is at a slight angle on a fire, full of water at a full boil. Mine is just six inches wide and four-and-a-half inches deep. It holds better than a quart of water and has served me well for several hundred camp dinners.

The rest of your cook kit is easy to complete. The frying pan should be small, light-gauge aluminum, Teflon-coated, with a fold-in handle so it's no hassle to store. A pot grabber is a great addition. It's a little aluminum gadget that clamps to the edge of pots and allows you to lift them and pour water with total control, without burning your fingers. For cleanup, take a plastic scrubber and a small bottle filled with dish cleaner, and you're in business.

A Sierra Cup, a wide aluminum cup with a wire handle, is an ideal item to carry because you can eat out of it as well as use it for drinking. This means no plates to scrub after dinner, so cleanup is quick and easy. In addition,

if you go for a hike, you can clip it to your belt with its handle.

If you want a more formal setup, complete with plates, glasses, silverware, and the like, you can end up spending more time preparing and cleaning up from meals than you do enjoying the country you are exploring. In addition, the more equipment you bring, the more loose ends you will have to deal with, and loose ends can cause plenty of frustration. If you have a choice, go simple.

And remember what Thoreau said: "A man is rich in proportion to what he can do without."

Food and Cooking Tricks

On a trip to the Bob Marshall Wilderness in western Montana, I woke up one morning, yawned, and said, "What've we got for breakfast?"

The silence was ominous. "Well," finally came the response, "we don't have any food left."

"What!?"

"Well, I figured we'd catch trout for meals every other night."

On the return trip, we ended up eating wild berries, buds, and, yes, even roots (not too tasty). When we finally landed the next day at a suburban pizza parlor, we nearly ate the wooden tables.

Running out of food on a camping trip can do more to turn reasonable people into violent grumps than any other event. There's no excuse for it, not when a system for figuring meals can be outlined with precision and little effort. You should not go out and buy a bunch of food, throw it in your rig, and head off for yonder. That leaves too much to chance. And if you've ever been in the woods and real hungry, you'll know it's worth taking a little effort to make sure a day or two of starvation will not occur. Here's a three-step solution:

1—Draw up a general meal-by-meal plan and make sure your companions like what's on it.

2—Tell your companions to buy any specialty items (like a special brand of coffee) on their own and not to expect you to take care of everything.

3—Put all the food on your living room floor and literally plan out every day of your trip, meal by meal, putting the food in plastic bags as you go. That way you will know exact food quotas and will not go hungry.

Fish for your dinner? There's one guarantee as far as that goes: If you expect to catch fish for meals, you will most certainly get skunked. If you don't expect to catch fish for meals, you will probably catch so many they'll be coming out of your ears. I've seen it a hundred times.

Keeping the Price Down

"There must be some mistake," I said with a laugh. "Who ever paid $750 for camp food?"

But the amount was as clear as the digital numbers on the cash register: $753.27.

"How is this possible?" I asked the clerk.

"Just add it up," she responded, irritated.

Then I started figuring. The freeze-dried backpack dinners cost $6 apiece. A small pack of beef jerky went for $2, the beef sticks for 75 cents, granola bars for 50 cents. Multiply it all by four

hungry men, including Foonsky, for 21 days. This food was to sustain us on a major expedition—four guys hiking 250 miles over three weeks from Mount Whitney to Yosemite Valley.

The dinners alone cost close to $500. Add in the usual goodies—jerky, granola bars, soup, dried fruit, oatmeal, Tang, candy, and coffee—and I felt like an earthquake had struck when I saw the tab.

A lot of campers have received similar shocks. In preparation for their trips, campers shop with enthusiasm. Then they pay the bill in horror.

Well, there are solutions, lots of them. You can eat gourmet style in the outback without having your wallet cleaned out. But it requires do-it-yourself cooking, more planning, and careful shopping. It also means transcending the push-button "I-want-it-now" attitude that so many people can't leave behind when they go to the mountains.

The secret is to bring along a small pressure cooker. A reader, Mike Bettinger of San Francisco, passed this tip on to me. Little pressure cookers weigh about two pounds, which may sound like a lot to backpackers and backcountry campers. But when three or four people are on a trip, it actually saves weight.

The key is that it allows campers to bring items that are difficult to cook at high altitudes, such as brown and white rice; red, black, pinto, and lima beans; and lentils. You pick one or more for a basic staple and then add a variety of freeze-dried ingredients to make a complete dish. Available are packets of meat, vegetables, onions, shallots, and garlic. Sun-dried tomatoes, for instance, reconstitute wonderfully in a pressure cooker. Add herbs, spices, and maybe a few rainbow trout and you will be eating better out of a backpack than most people do at home.

"In the morning, I have used the pressure cooker to turn dried apricots into apricot sauce to put on the pancakes we made with sourdough starter," Bettinger said. "The pressure cooker is also big enough for washing out cups and utensils. The days when backpacking meant eating terrible freeze-dried food are over. It doesn't take a gourmet cook to prepare these meals, only some thought beforehand."

Now when Foonsky, Mr. Furnai, Rambob, and I sit down to eat such a meal, we don't call it "eating." We call it "hodgepacking" or "time to pack your hodge." After a particularly long day on the trail, you can do some serious hodgepacking.

If your trip is a shorter one, say for a weekend, you can bring more fresh food to add some sizzle to the hodge. You can design a hot soup/stew mix that is good enough to eat at home.

Start by bringing a pot of water to a full boil, then adding pasta, ramen noodles, or macaroni. While it simmers, cut in a potato, carrot, onion, and garlic clove, and cook for about 10 minutes. When the vegetables have softened, add in a soup mix or two, maybe some cheese, and you are just about in business. But you can still ruin it and turn your hodge into slodge. Make sure you read the directions on the soup mix to determine cooking time. It can vary widely. In addition, make sure you stir the whole thing up; otherwise you will get these hidden dry clumps of soup mix that can taste like garlic sawdust.

How do I know? Well, it was up near Kearsage Pass in the Sierra Nevada, where, feeling half-starved, I dug into our nightly hodge. I will never forget that first bite—I damn near gagged to death. Foonsky laughed at me, until he took his first bite (a nice big one), then turned green.

Another way to trim food costs is to make your own beef jerky, the trademark staple of campers for more than 200 years. A tiny packet of beef jerky costs $2, and for that 250-mile expedition, I spent $150 on jerky alone. Never again. Now we make our own and get big strips of jerky that taste better than anything you can buy.

Foonsky settled on the following recipe, starting with a couple pieces of meat, lean top round, sirloin, or tri-tip. At home, cut it into 3/16-inch strips across the grain, trimming out the membrane, gristle, and fat. Marinate the strips for 24 hours in a glass dish. The fun begins in picking a marinade. Try two-thirds teriyaki sauce, one-third Worcestershire. You can customize the recipe by adding pepper, ground mustard, bay leaf, red wine vinegar, garlic, and, for the brave, Tabasco sauce. After a day or so, squeeze out each strip of meat with a rolling pin, lay them in rows on a cooling rack over a cookie sheet, and dry them in the oven at 125 degrees for 12 hours. Thicker pieces can take as long as 18 to 24 hours.

That's it. The hardest part is cleaning the cookie sheet when you're done. The easiest part is eating your own home-made jerky while sitting at a lookout on a mountain ridge. The do-it-yourself method for jerky may take a day or so, but it is cheaper and can taste better than any store-bought jerky.

If all this still doesn't sound like your

idea of a gourmet but low-cost camping meal, well, you are forgetting the main course: rainbow trout. Remember: If you don't plan on catching them for dinner, you'll probably snag more than you can finish in one night's hodgepacking.

Some campers go to great difficulties to cook their trout, bringing along frying pans, butter, grills, tinfoil, and more, but all you really need is some seasoned salt and a campfire.

Rinse the gutted trout, and while it's still wet, sprinkle on a good dose of seasoned salt, both inside and out. Clear any burning logs to the side of the campfire, then lay the trout right on the coals, turning it once so both sides are cooked. Sound ridiculous? Sound like you are throwing the fish away? Sound like the fish will burn up? Sound like you will have to eat the campfire ash? Wrong on all counts. The fish cooks perfectly, the ash doesn't stick, and after cooking trout this way, you may never fry trout again.

But if you can't convince your buddies, who may insist the trout should be fried, then make sure you have butter to fry them in, not oil. Also make sure you cook them all the way through, so the meat strips off the backbone in two nice, clean fillets. The fish should end up looking like Sylvester the Cat just drew it of his mouth, leaving only the head, tail, and a perfect skeleton.

You can supplement your eats with sweets, nuts, freeze-dried fruits, and drink mixes. In any case, make sure you keep the dinner menu varied. If you and your buddies look into your dinner cups and groan, "Ugh, not this again," you will soon start dreaming of cheeseburgers and french fries instead of hiking, fishing, and finding beautiful campsites.

If you are car camping and have a big ice chest, you can bring virtually anything to eat and drink. If you are on the trail and don't mind paying the price, the newest premade freeze-dried dinners provide another option.

Some of the biggest advances in the outdoors industry have come in the freeze-dried dinners now available to campers. Some of them are almost good enough to serve in restaurants. Sweet-and-sour pork over rice, tostadas, Burgundy chicken . . . it sure beats the poopy goop we used to eat, like the old, soupy chili mac dinners that tasted bad and looked so unlike "food" that consumption was near impossible, even for my dog, Rebel. Foonsky usually managed to get it down, however, but just barely.

To provide an idea of how to plan a menu, consider what my companions and I ate while hiking 250 miles on California's John Muir Trail:

• Breakfast—Instant soup, oatmeal (never get plain), one beef or jerky stick, coffee or hot chocolate.

• Lunch—One beef stick, two jerky sticks, one granola bar, dried fruit, half cup of pistachio nuts, Tang, one small bag of M&Ms.

• Dinner—Instant soup, one freeze-dried dinner, one milk bar, rainbow trout.

What was that last item? Rainbow trout? Right! Lest you plan on it, you can catch them every night.

Clothing and Weather Protection

What started as an innocent pursuit of a perfect campground evolved into one heck of a predicament for Foonsky and me.

We had parked at the end of a logging road and then bushwhacked our way down a canyon to a pristine trout stream. On my first cast, a little flip into the plunge pool of a waterfall, I caught a 16-inch rainbow trout, a real beauty that jumped three times. Magic stuff.

Then just across the stream, we saw it: The Perfect Camping Spot. On a sandbar on the edge of the forest, there lay a flat spot, high and dry above the river. Nearby was plenty of downed wood collected by past winter storms that we could use for firewood. And, of course, this beautiful trout stream was bubbling along just 40 yards from the site.

But nothing is perfect, right? To reach it, we had to wade across the river, although it didn't appear to be too difficult. The cold water tingled a bit, and the river came up surprisingly high, just above the belt. But it would be worth it to camp at The Perfect Spot.

Once across the river, we put on some dry clothes, set up camp, explored the woods, and fished the stream, catching several nice trout for dinner. But late that afternoon, it started raining. What? Rain in the summertime? Nature makes its own rules. By the next morning, it was still raining, pouring like a Yosemite waterfall from a solid gray sky.

That's when we noticed The Perfect Spot wasn't so perfect. The rain had raised the river level too high for us to wade back across. We were marooned, wet and hungry.

"Now we're in a heck of a predicament," said Foonsky, the water streaming off him.

Getting cold and wet on a camping trip with no way to warm up is not only unnecessary and uncomfortable, it can be a fast ticket to hypothermia, the number one killer of campers in the woods. By definition, hypothermia is a condition in which body temperature is lowered to the point where it causes illness. It is particularly dangerous because the afflicted are usually unaware it is setting in. The first sign is a sense of apathy, then a state of confusion, which can lead eventually to collapse (or what appears to be sleep), then death.

You must always have a way to get warm and dry in short order, regardless of any conditions you may face. If you have no way of getting dry, then you must take emergency steps to prevent hypothermia. Those steps are detailed in the first-aid section on page 38.

But you should never reach that point. For starters, always have spare sets of clothing tucked away, so no matter how cold and wet you might get, you have something dry to put on. On hiking trips, I always carry a second set of clothes, sealed to stay dry, in a plastic garbage bag. I keep a third set waiting back at the truck.

If you are car camping, your vehicle can

cause an illusory sense of security. But with an extra set of dry clothes stashed safely away, there is no illusion. The security is real. And remember, no matter how hot the weather is when you start your trip, always be prepared for the worst. Foonsky and I learned the hard way.

So both of us were soaking wet on that sandbar, and with no other choice, we tried holing up in the tent for the night. A sleeping bag with Quallofil™, or another polyester fiberfill, can retain warmth even when wet, because the fill is hollow and retains its loft. So as miserable as it was, we made it through the night.

The rain finally stopped the next day and the river dropped a bit, but it was still rolling big and angry. Using a stick as a wading staff, Foonsky crossed about 80 percent of the stream before he was dumped, but he made a jump for it and managed to scramble to the riverbank. He waved for me to follow. "No problem," I thought.

It took me 20 minutes to reach nearly the same spot where Foonsky had been dumped. The heavy river current was above my belt and pushing hard. Then, in the flash of an instant, my wading staff slipped on a rock. I teetered in the river current and was knocked over like a bowling pin. I became completely submerged. I went tumbling down the river, heading right toward the waterfall. While underwater, I looked up at the surface, and I can remember how close it seemed, yet how out of control I was. Right then, this giant hand appeared, and I grabbed it. It was Foonsky. If it wasn't for that hand, I would have sailed right over the waterfall.

My momentum drew Foonsky right into the river, and we scrambled in the current, but I suddenly sensed the river bottom under my knees. On all fours, the two of us clambered ashore. We were safe.

"Thanks ol' buddy," I said.

"Man, we're wet," he responded. "Let's get to the rig and get some dry clothes on."

The Art of Layering

The most important element in enjoying the outdoor experience in any condition is to stay dry and warm. There is no substitute. You must stay dry, and you must stay warm.

Thus comes the theory behind layering, which suggests that as your body temperature fluctuates or the weather shifts, you simply peel off or add available layers as needed—and have a waterproof shell available in case of rain.

The introduction of a new era of outdoor clothing has made it possible for the next generation of campers to turn choosing clothes into an art form. Like art, it comes much more expensive than throwing on a pair of blue jeans, a T-shirt, and some flannel, but for many it is worth the price.

In putting together your ideal layering system there are some general considerations. What you need to do is create a system that effectively combines elements of breathability, wicking, rapid drying, insulation, durability, wind-resistance, and water-repellence while still being lightweight and offering the necessary freedom of movement, all with just a few garments.

The basic intent of a base layer is to manage moisture. Your base layer will be the first article of clothing you put on, and the last to come off. Since your own skin will be churning out the perspiration, the goal of this "second skin" is to manage the moisture and move it away from you without trapping your body's heat. The only time that cotton should become a part of your base layer is if you wish to keep cool, not warm, such as in a hot desert climate where evaporative cooling becomes your friend, not your enemy.

That is why the best base layer available is from bicomponent knits, that is, blends of polyester and cotton, which work to provide wicking and insulative properties in one layer. The way it works is that the side facing your skin is water-hating, while the side away from your skin is water-loving; thus it pulls or "wicks" moisture through. You'll stay dry and happy, even with only one layer on, something not possible with old single-function weaves. The best include Thermax, Capilene, Driclime, Lifa, and Polartec 100.

Stretch fleece and microdenier pile also provide a good base layer, though they can be used as a second layer as well. Microdenier pile can be worn alone, or layered under or over other pieces, and it has excellent wicking capability as well as more windproof potential.

The next layer should be a light cotton shirt or a long-sleeved cotton/wool shirt, or both, depending on the coolness of the day. For pants, many just wear blue jeans when camping, but blue jeans can be hot, tight, and once wet, they tend to stay that way. Putting on wet blue jeans on a cold morning is a torturous way to start the day. I can tell you from experience since I have suffered that fate a number of times. A better choice are pants made from a cotton/canvas mix, which are available at outdoors stores. They are light, have a lot of give, and dry quickly. If the weather is quite warm, shorts that have some room to them can be the best choice.

Finally, you'll top the entire ensemble off with a thin windproof, water-resistant layer. You want this layer to breathe like crazy, yet not be so porous that rain runs through it like floodwaters through a leaking dike. Patagonia's Velocity shell is one of the best. Its outer fabric is DWR treated, and the coating is by Gore. Patagonia calls it Pneumatic (Gore now calls it Activent, while Marmot, Moonstone, and North Face all offer their own versions). Though condensation will still build up inside, it manages to get rid of enough moisture.

It is critical to know the difference between "water-resistant" and "waterproof." This is covered later in the chapter under the "Rain Gear" section.

But hey, why does anybody need all this fancy stuff just to go camping? Fair question. Like the introduction of Gore-Tex years ago, all this fabric and fiber mumbo jumbo has its skeptics, myself included. You don't have to opt for this aerobic function, fashion statement; it is unnecessary on many camping trips. But the fact is, when you venture into the outdoors, you must be ready for anything. And the truth is, the new era of outdoor clothing works and it works better than anything that has come before.

Regardless of what you choose, weather should never be a nuisance or cause discomfort, regardless of what you experience. Instead it should provide a welcome change of pace.

About Hats

One final word of advice: Always pack along a warm hat for those times when you need to seal in warmth. You lose a large percentage of heat through your head. I almost always wear a wide-brimmed hat, something like the legendary outlaws wore 150 years ago. There's actually logic behind it: My hat is made out of kangaroo skin (waterproof), is rigged with a lariat (can be cinched down when it's windy), and has a wide brim that keeps the tops of my ears from being sunburned (years ago, they once were burned to a red crisp on a trip where I was wearing a baseball hat). But to be honest, I like how it looks, kind of like my pal Waylon Jennings.

Vests and Parkas

In cold weather, you should take the layer system one step further with a warm vest and a parka jacket. Vests are especially useful because they provide warmth without the bulkiness of a parka. The warmest vests and parkas are either filled with down or Quallofil, or are made with a cotton/wool mix. Each has its respective merits and problems. Down fill provides the most warmth for the amount of weight, but becomes useless when wet, closely resembling a wet dishrag. Quallofil keeps much of its heat-retaining quality even when wet, but is expensive. Vests made of cotton/wool mixes are the most attractive and also are quite warm, but they can be as heavy as a ship's anchor when wet. Sometimes the answer is combining the two. One of my best camping companions wears a good-looking cotton/wool vest and a parka filled with Quallofil. The vest never gets wet, so weight is not a factor.

Rain Gear

One of the most miserable nights I ever spent in my life was on a camping trip where I didn't bring my rain gear or a tent. Hey, it was early August, the temperature had been in the 90s for weeks, and if anybody had said it was going to rain, I would have told them to consult a brain doctor. But rain it did. And as I got wetter and wetter, I kept saying to myself, "Hey, it's summer, it's not supposed to rain." Then I remembered one of the Ten Commandments of camping: Forget your rain gear and you can guarantee it will rain.

To stay dry, you need some form of water-repellent shell. It can be as simple as a $5 poncho made out of plastic or as elaborate as a Gore-Tex rain jacket and pants set that costs $300. What counts is not how much you spend, but how dry you stay.

The most important thing to realize is that waterproof and water-resistant are completely different things. In addition, there is no such thing as rain gear that is "waterproof" and "breathable" on equal planes. The more waterproof a jacket is, the less it breathes. Conversely, the more breathable a jacket is, the less waterproof it becomes.

If you wear water-resistant rain gear in a downpour, you'll get soaked. Water-resistant rain gear is appealing because it breathes and will keep you dry in the light stuff, such as mist, fog, even a little splash from a canoe paddle. But in rain? Forget it.

So what is the solution?

I've decided that the best approach is a set of fairly light but 100 percent waterproof rain gear. I recently bought a hooded jacket and pants from Coleman, and my assessment is that it is the most cost-efficient rain gear I've ever had. All I can say is, hey, it works: I stay dry, it doesn't weigh much, and it didn't cost a fortune.

You can also stay dry with any of the waterproof plastics and even heavy-duty rubber-coated outfits made for commercial fishermen. But these are uncomfortable during anything but a heavy rain. Because they are heavy and don't breathe, you'll likely get soaked anyway, even if it isn't raining hard—soaked, that is, from your own sweat.

On backpacking trips, I still stash a super lightweight water-repellent slicker for day hikes, and a poncho, which I throw over my pack at night to keep it dry. But otherwise, I never go anywhere—anywhere!—without my rain gear.

Some do just fine with a cheap poncho, and note that ponchos can serve other uses in addition to a raincoat. Ponchos can be used as a ground tarp, as a rain cover for supplies or a backpack, or can be roped up to trees in a pinch to provide a quick storm ceiling if you don't have a tent. The problem with ponchos is that in a hard rain, you just don't stay dry. First your legs get wet, then they get soaked. Then your arms follow the same pattern. If you're wearing cotton, you'll find that once part of the garment gets wet, the water will spread until, alas, you are dripping wet, poncho and all. Before long you start to feel like a walking refrigerator.

One high-cost option is buying a Gore-Tex rain jacket and pants. Gore-Tex is actually not a fabric, as is commonly believed, but a laminated film that coats a breathable fabric. The result is lightweight, water-repellent, breathable jackets and pants. They are perfect for campers, but they cost a fortune.

Some hiking buddies of mine have complained that the older Gore-Tex rain gear loses its water-repellent quality over time. However, manufacturers insist that this is the result of water seeping through seams, not leaks in the jacket. At each seam, tiny needles have pierced through the fabric, and as tiny as the holes are, water will find a way through. An application of Seam Lock, especially at major seams around the shoulders of a jacket, can usually fix the problem.

If you don't want to spend the big bucks for Gore-Tex rain gear, but want more rain protection than a poncho affords, a coated nylon jacket is the compromise that many choose. They are inexpensive, have the highest water-repellency of any rain gear, and are warm, providing a good outer shell for your layers of clothing. But they are not without fault. These jackets don't breathe at all, and if you zip them up tight, you can sweat like an Eskimo.

My brother Rambob gave me a nylon jacket prior to a mountain climbing expedition. I wore that $20 special all the way to the top with no complaints; it's warm and 100 percent waterproof. The one problem with nylon is when temperatures drop below freezing. It gets so stiff that it feels like you are wearing a straightjacket. But at $20, it seems like a treasure, especially compared to a $180 Gore-Tex jacket.

There's one more jacket-construction term to know: DWR, or durable water-repellent finish. All of the top-quality jackets these days are DWR-treated. The DWR causes water to bead up on the shell. When it wears off, even a once-waterproof jacket will feel like a wet dishrag.

Also note that ventilation is the key to coolness. The only ventilation on most shells is often the zipper. But waterproof jackets need additional openings. Look for mesh-backed pockets and underarm zippers, as well as cuffs, waists, and hems that can be adjusted to open wide. Storm flaps (the baffle over the zipper) that close with hook-and-loop material or snaps let you leave the zipper open for airflow into the jacket.

Other Gear ... and a Few Tips

What are the three items most commonly forgotten on a camping trip? A hat, sunglasses, and lip balm.

A hat is crucial, especially when you are visiting high elevations. Without one you are constantly exposed to everything nature can give you. The sun will dehydrate you, sap your energy, sunburn your head, and in worst cases, cause sunstroke. Start with a comfortable hat. Then finish with sunglasses, lip balm, and sunscreen for additional protection. They will help protect you from extreme heat.

To guard against extreme cold, it's a good idea to keep a pair of thin ski gloves stashed away with your emergency clothes, along with a wool ski cap. The gloves should be thick enough to keep your fingers from stiffening up, but pliable enough to allow full movement, so you don't have to take them off to complete simple tasks, like lighting a stove. An alternative to gloves are glovelets, which look like gloves with no fingers. In any case, just because the weather turns cold doesn't mean that your hands have to.

And if you fall into a river like Foonsky and I did, well, I hope you have a set of dry clothes waiting back at your rig. Oh, and a hand reaching out to you.

Hiking and Foot Care

We had set up a nice little camp in the woods, and my buddy, Foonsky, was strapping on his hiking boots, sitting against a big Douglas fir.

"New boots," he said with a grin. "But they seem pretty stiff."

We decided to hoof it down the trail for a few hours, exploring the mountain wildlands that are said to hide Bigfoot and other strange creatures. After just a short while on the trail, a sense of peace and calm seemed to settle in. The forest provides you the chance to be purified with clean air and the smell of trees, freeing you from all troubles.

But it wasn't long before a look of trouble was on Foonsky's face. And no, it wasn't from seeing Bigfoot.

"Got a hot spot on a toe," he said.

Immediately we stopped. He pulled off his right boot, then socks, and inspected the left side of his big toe. Sure enough, a blister had bubbled up, filled with fluid, but hadn't popped. From his medical kit, Foonsky cut a small piece of moleskin to fit over the blister, then taped it to hold it in place. A few minutes later, we were back on the trail.

A half hour later, there was still no sign of Bigfoot. But Foonsky stopped again and pulled off his other boot. "Another hot spot." On the little toe of his left foot was another small blister, over which he taped a Band-Aid to keep it from further chafing against the inside of his new boot.

In just a few days, ol' Foonsky, a strong, 6-foot-5, 200-plus pound guy, was walking around like a sore-hoofed horse that had been loaded with a month's worth of supplies and then ridden over sharp rocks. Well, it wasn't the distance that had done Foonsky in; it was those blisters. He had them on eight of his 10 toes and was going through Band-Aids, moleskin, and tape like he was a walking emergency ward. If he used any more tape, he would've looked like a mummy from an Egyptian tomb.

If you've ever been in a similar predicament, you know the frustration of wanting to have a good time, wanting to hike and explore the area where you have set up a secluded camp, only to be turned gimp-legged by several blisters. No one is immune—all are created equal before the blister god. You can be forced to bow to it unless you get your act together.

That means wearing the right style boots for what you have in mind and then protecting your feet with carefully selected socks. And then, if you are still so unfortunate as to get a blister or two, it means knowing how to treat them fast so they don't turn your walk into a sore-footed endurance test.

What causes blisters? In almost all cases, it is the simple rubbing of your foot against the rugged interior of your boot. That can be worsened by several factors:

1. A very stiff boot, or one in which your foot moves inside as you walk, instead of the boot flexing as if it were another layer of skin.

2. Thin, ragged, or dirty socks. This is the fastest route to blisters. Thin socks will allow your feet to move inside of your boots, ragged socks will allow

your skin to chafe directly against the boot's interior, and dirty socks will wrinkle and fold, also rubbing against your feet instead of cushioning them.

3. Soft feet. By themselves, soft feet will not cause blisters, but in combination with a stiff boot or thin socks, they can cause terrible problems. The best way to toughen up your feet is to go barefoot. In fact, some of the biggest, toughest-looking guys you'll ever see, from Hell's Angels to pro football players, have feet that are as soft as a baby's butt. Why? Because they never go barefoot and don't hike much.

Selecting the Right Boots

One summer I hiked 400 miles, including 250 miles in three weeks, along the crest of California's Sierra Nevada, and another 150 miles over several months in an earlier general training program. In that span, I got just one blister, suffered on the fourth day of the 250-miler. I treated it immediately and suffered no more. One key is wearing the right boot, and for me, that means a boot that acts as a thick layer of skin that is flexible and pliable to my foot. I want my feet to fit snugly in them, with no interior movement.

There are three kinds of boots: mountaineering boots, hiking boots, and canvas walking shoes. Select the right one for you or pay the consequences.

The stiffest of the lot is the mountaineering boot. These boots are often identified by mid-range tops, laces that extend almost as far as the toe area, and ankle areas that are as stiff as a board. The lack of "give" is what endears them to mountaineers. Their stiffness is preferred when rock climbing, walking off-trail on craggy surfaces, or

hiking down the edge of streambeds where walking across small rocks can cause you to turn your ankle. Because these boots don't give on rugged, craggy terrain, they reduce ankle injuries and provide better traction.

The drawback to stiff boots is that if you don't have the proper socks and your foot starts slipping around in the boot, you will get a set of blisters that would raise even Foonsky's eyebrows. But if you just want to go for a walk, or a good tromp with a backpack, then hiking shoes or backpacking boots will serve you better.

Canvas walking shoes are the lightest of all boots, designed for day walks or short backpacking trips. Some of the newer models are like rugged tennis shoes, designed with a canvas top for lightness and a lug sole for traction. These are perfect for people who like to walk but rarely carry a backpack. Because they are flexible, they are easy to break in, and with fresh socks they rarely cause blister problems. And because they are light, general hiking fatigue is greatly reduced.

On the negative side, because canvas shoes have shallow lug soles, traction can be far from good on slippery surfaces. In addition, they provide less than ideal ankle support, which can be a problem in rocky areas, such as along a stream where you might want to go trout fishing. Turn your ankle and your trip can be ruined.

My preference is for a premium backpacking boot, the perfect medium between the stiff mountaineering boot and the soft canvas hiking shoe. The deep lug bottom provides traction, the high ankle coverage provides support, yet the soft, waterproof leather body gives each foot a snug fit. Add it up and that means no blisters. On the negative side, they can be quite hot, weigh a ton, and, if they get wet, take days to dry.

There are a zillion styles, brands, and price ranges to choose from. If you wander about, comparing all their many features, you will get as confused as a kid in a toy store. Instead, go into the store with your mind clear about what you want, then find it and buy it. If you want the best, expect to spend $60 to $80 for canvas walking shoes, from $100 to $140 and sometimes more for hiking or mountaineering boots. This is one area where you don't want to scrimp, so try not to yelp about the high cost. Instead, walk out of the store believing you deserve the best, and that's exactly what you just paid for.

If you plan on using the advice of a shoe salesperson, first look at what kind of boots he is wearing. If he isn't even wearing boots, then any advice he might tender may not be worth a plug nickel. Most people I know who own quality boots, including salespeople, will wear them almost daily if their job allows, since boots are the best footwear available. However, even these well-meaning folks can offer sketchy advice. Every hiker I've ever met will tell you he wears the world's greatest boot.

Instead, enter the store with a precise use and style in mind. Rather than fish for suggestions, tell the salesperson exactly what you want, try two or three brands of the same style, and always try on both boots in a pair simultaneously so you know exactly how they'll feel. If possible, walk up and down stairs with them. Are they

too stiff? Are your feet snug yet comfortable, or do they slip? Do they have that "right" kind of feel when you walk?

If you get the right answers to those questions, then you're on your way to blister-free, pleasure-filled days of walking.

Socks

The poor gent was scratching his feet like ants were crawling over them. I looked closer. Huge yellow calluses had covered the bottom of his feet, and at the ball and heel, the calluses were about a quarter-inch thick, cracking and sore.

"I don't understand it," he said. "I'm on my feet a lot, so I bought a real good pair of hiking boots. But look what they've done to my feet. My feet itch so much I'm going crazy."

People can spend so much energy selecting the right kind of boot that they virtually overlook wearing the right kind of socks. One goes with the other.

Your socks should be thick enough to cushion your feet, as well as fit snugly. Without good socks, you might try to get the bootlaces too tight—and that's like putting a tourniquet on your feet. You should have plenty of clean socks on hand, or plan on washing what you have on your trip. As socks are worn, they become compressed, dirty, and damp. Any one of those factors can cause problems.

My camping companions believe I go overboard when it comes to socks, that I bring too many and wear too many. But it works, so that's where the complaints stop. So how many do I wear? Well, would you believe three socks on each foot? It may sound like overkill, but each has its purpose, and like I said, it works.

The interior sock is thin, lightweight, and made of polypropylene or silk synthetic materials designed to transport moisture away from your skin. With a poly interior sock, your foot stays dry when it sweats. Without a poly sock, your foot can get damp and mix with dirt, which can cause a "hot spot" to start on your foot. Eventually you get blisters, lots of them.

The second sock is for comfort and can be cotton, but a thin wool-based composite is ideal. Some made of the latter can wick moisture away from the skin, much like polypropylene does. If wool itches your feet, a thick cotton sock can be suitable, though cotton collects moisture and compacts more quickly than other socks. If you're on a short hike though, cotton will do just fine.

The exterior sock should be made of high-quality, thick wool—at least 80 percent wool. It will cushion your feet, provide that "just right" snug fit in your boot, and give you some additional warmth and insulation in cold weather. It is critical to keep the wool sock clean. If you wear a dirty wool sock over and over again, it will compact and lose its cushion and start wrinkling while you hike, then your feet will catch on fire from the blisters that start popping up.

A Few More Tips

If you are like most folks—that is, the bottom of your feet are rarely exposed and quite soft—you can take additional steps in their care. The best tip is keeping a fresh foot pad made of sponge rubber in your boot. Another cure for soft feet is to get out and walk or jog on a regular basis prior to your camping trip.

If you plan to use a foot pad and wear three socks, you will need to use these items when sizing boots. It is an unforgiving error to wear thin cotton socks when buying boots, then later trying to squeeze all this stuff, plus your feet, into them. There just won't be enough room.

The key to treating blisters is fast work at the first sign of a hot spot. But before you remove your socks, first check to see if the sock has a wrinkle in it, a likely cause of the problem. If so, either change socks or pull them tight, removing the tiny folds, after taking care of the blister. Cut a piece of moleskin to cover the offending toe, securing the moleskin with white medical tape. If moleskin is not available, small Band-Aids can do the job, but these have to be replaced daily, and sometimes with even more frequency. At night, clean your feet and sleep without socks.

Two other items that can help your walking is an Ace bandage and a pair of gaiters.

For sprained ankles and twisted knees, an Ace bandage can be like an insurance policy to get you back on the trail and out of trouble. Over the years, I have had serious ankle problems and have relied on a good wrap with a four-inch bandage to get me home. The newer bandages come with the clips permanently attached, so you don't have to worry about losing them.

Gaiters are leggings made of plastic, nylon, or Gore-Tex™ that fit from just below your knees, over your calves, and attach under your boots. They are of particular help when walking in damp areas, or in places where rain is common. As your legs brush against ferns or low-lying plants, gaiters will deflect the moisture. Without them, your pants will be soaking wet in short order.

Should your boots become wet, a good tip is never to try to force dry them. Some well-meaning folks will try to dry them quickly at the edge of a campfire or actually put the boots in an oven. While this may dry the boots, it can also loosen the glue that holds them together, ultimately weakening them until one day they fall apart in a heap.

A better bet is to treat the leather so the boots become water repellent. Silicone-based liquids are the easiest to use and least greasy of the treatments available.

A final tip is to have another pair of lightweight shoes or moccasins that you can wear around camp, and in the process give your feet the rest they deserve.

Sleeping Gear

One mountain night in the pines on an eve long ago, my dad, brother, and I had rolled out our sleeping bags and were bedded down for the night. After the pre-trip excitement, a long drive, an evening of trout fishing, and a barbecue, we were like three tired doggies who had played too much.

But as I looked up at the stars, I was suddenly wide awake. The kid was still wired. A half hour later? No change—wide awake.

And as little kids can do, I had to wake up ol' dad to tell him about it. "Hey, Dad, I can't sleep."

"This is what you do," he said. "Watch the sky for a shooting star and tell yourself that you cannot go to sleep until you see at least one. As you wait and watch, you will start getting tired, and it will be difficult to keep your eyes open. But tell yourself you must keep watching. Then you'll start to really feel tired. When you finally see a shooting star, you'll go to sleep so fast you won't know what hit you."

Well, I tried it that night and I don't even remember seeing a shooting star, I went to sleep so fast.

It's a good trick, and along with having a good sleeping bag, ground insulation, maybe a tent, or a few tricks for bedding down in a pickup truck or motor home, you can get a good night's sleep on every camping trip.

More than 20 years after that camping episode with my dad and brother, we made a trip to the planetarium at the Academy of Sciences in San Francisco to see a show on Halley's Comet. The lights dimmed, and the ceiling turned into a night sky, filled with stars and a setting moon. A scientist began explaining phenomena of the heavens.

After a few minutes, I began to feel drowsy. Just then, a shooting star zipped across the planetarium ceiling. I went into a deep sleep so fast it was like I was in a coma. I didn't wake up until the show was over, the lights were turned back on, and the people were leaving.

Feeling drowsy, I turned to see if ol' Dad had liked the show. Oh yeah? Not only had he gone to sleep too, but he apparently had no intention of waking up, no matter what. Just like a camping trip.

Sleeping Bags

Question: What could be worse than trying to sleep in a cold, wet sleeping bag on a rainy night without a tent in the mountains?

Answer: Trying to sleep in a cold, wet sleeping bag on a rainy night without a tent in the mountains when your sleeping bag is filled with down.

Water will turn a down-filled sleeping bag into a mushy heap. Many campers do not like a high-tech approach, but the state-of-the-art polyfiber sleeping bags can keep you warm even when wet. That factor, along with temperature rating and weight, is key when selecting a sleeping bag.

A sleeping bag is a shell filled with heat-retaining insulation. By itself, it is not warm. Your body provides the heat, and the sleeping bag's ability to retain that heat is what makes it warm or cold.

The old-style canvas bags are heavy, bulky, cold, and, when wet, useless. With other options available, their use is limited. Anybody who sleeps outdoors or backpacks should choose otherwise. Instead, buy and use a sleeping bag filled with down or one of the quality poly-fills. Down is light, warm, and aesthetically pleasing to those who don't think camping and technology mix. If you choose a down bag, be sure to keep it double wrapped in plastic garbage bags on your trip in order to keep it dry. Once wet, you'll spend your nights howling at the moon.

The polyfiber-filled bags are not necessarily better than those filled with down, but they can be. Their one key advantage is that even when wet, some poly-fills can retain up to 85 percent of your body heat. This allows you to sleep and get valuable rest even in miserable conditions. And my camping experience is that no matter how lucky you may be, there comes a time when you will get caught in an unexpected, violent storm and everything you've got will get wet, including your sleeping bag. That's when a poly-fill bag becomes priceless. You either have one and can sleep, or you don't have one and suffer. It is that simple. Of the synthetic fills, Quallofil made by Dupont is the industry leader.

But as mentioned, just because a sleeping bag uses a high-tech poly-fill doesn't necessarily make it a better bag. There are other factors.

The most important are a bag's temperature rating and weight. The temperature rating of a sleeping bag refers to how cold it can get before you start actually feeling cold. Many campers make the mistake of thinking, "I only camp in the summer, so a bag rated at 30 or 40 degrees should be fine." Later, they find out it isn't so fine, and all it takes is one cold night to convince them of that. When selecting the right temperature rating, visualize the coldest weather you might ever confront, and then get a bag rated for even colder weather.

For instance, if you are a summer camper, you may rarely experience a night in the low 30s or high 20s. A sleeping bag rated at 20 degrees would be appropriate, keeping you snug, warm, and asleep. For most campers, I advise bags rated at zero or 10 degrees.

If you buy a poly-filled sleeping bag, never leave it squished in your stuff sack between camping trips. Instead, keep it on a hanger in a closet or use it as a blanket. One thing that can reduce a poly-filled bag's heat-retaining qualities is if you lose the loft out of the tiny hollow fibers that make up the fill. You can avoid this with proper storage.

The weight of a sleeping bag can also be a key factor, especially for backpackers. When you have to carry your gear on your back, every ounce becomes important. To keep your weight to a minimum, sleeping bags that weigh just three pounds are available, although they are expensive. But if you hike much, it's worth the price. For an overnighter, you can get away with a four- or four-and-a-half-pound bag without much stress. However, bags weighing five pounds and up should be left back at the car.

I have two sleeping bags: a seven-pounder that feels like I'm in a giant sponge, and a little three-pounder. The heavy-duty model is for pickup truck camping in cold weather and doubles as a blanket at home. The lightweight bag is for hikes. Between the two, I'm set.

Insulation Pads

Even with the warmest sleeping bag in the world, if you just lay it down on the ground and try to sleep, you will likely get as cold as a winter cucumber. That is because the cold ground will suck the warmth right out of your body. The solution is to have a layer of insulation between you and the ground. For this, you can use a thin Insulite pad, a lightweight Therm-a-Rest inflatable pad, or an air mattress. Here is a capsule summary of all three:

• **Insulite pads:** They are light, inexpensive, roll up quick for transport, and can double as a seat pad at your camp. The negative side is that in one night, they will compress, making you feel like you are sleeping on granite.

• **Therm-a-Rest pads:** These are a real luxury, because they do everything an Insulite pad does, but also provide a cushion. The negative side is that they are expensive by comparison, and if they get a hole in them, they become worthless without a patch kit.

• **Air mattress:** These are okay for car campers, but their bulk, weight, and the amount of effort necessary to blow them up make them a nuisance.

A Few Tricks

When surveying a camp area, the most important consideration should be to select a good spot to sleep. Everything else is secondary. Ideally, you want a flat spot that is wind-sheltered, on ground soft enough to drive stakes into. Yeah, and I want to win the lottery, too.

Sometimes that ground will have a slight slope to it. In that case, always sleep with your head on the uphill side. If you sleep parallel to the slope, every time you roll over, you'll find yourself rolling down the hill. If you sleep with your head on the downhill side, you'll get a headache that feels like an ax is embedded in your brain.

When you've found a good spot, clear it of all branches, twigs, and rocks, of course. A good tip is to dig a slight indentation in the ground where your hip will fit. Since your body is not flat, but has curves and edges, it will not feel comfortable on flat ground. Some people even get severely bruised on the sides of their hips when sleeping on flat, hard ground. For that reason alone, they learn to hate camping. Instead, bring a spade, dig a little depression in the ground for your hip, and sleep well.

In wilderness, where leave-no-trace ethics should always be heeded, never dig such a depression. With a Therm-a-Rest pad, it will be unnecessary anyway.

After the ground is prepared, throw a ground cloth over the spot, which will keep much of the morning dew off you. In some areas, particularly where fog is a problem, morning dew can be heavy and get the outside of your sleeping bag quite wet. In that case, you need overhead protection, such as a tent or some kind of roof, like that of a poncho or tarp with its ends tied to trees.

Tents and Weather Protection

All it takes is to get caught in the rain once without a tent and you will never go anywhere without one again. A tent provides protection from rain, wind, and mosquito attacks. In exchange, you can lose a starry night's view, though some tents now even provide moon roofs.

A tent can be as complex as a four-season, tubular-jointed dome with a rain fly, or as simple as two ponchos snapped together and roped up to a tree. They can be as cheap as a $10 tube tent, which is nothing more than a hollow piece of plastic, or as expensive as a $500 five-person deluxe expedition dome model. They vary greatly in size, price, and put-up time. If you plan on getting a good one, then plan on doing plenty of shopping and asking lots of questions. The key ones are: Will it keep me dry? How hard is it to put up? Is it roomy enough? How much does it weigh?

With a little bit of homework, you can get the right answers to these questions.

• **Will it keep me dry?** On many one-person and two-person tents, the rain fly does not extend far enough to keep water off the bottom sidewalls of the tent. In a driving rain, water can also drip from the rain fly and to the bottom sidewalls of the tent. Eventually the water can leak through to the inside, particularly through the seams where the tent has been sewed together.

You must be able to stake out your rain fly so it completely covers all of the tent. If you are tent shopping and this does not appear possible, then don't buy the tent. To prevent potential leaks, use a seam waterproofer such as Seam Lock, a gluelike substance, to close potential leak areas on tent seams. For large umbrella tents, keep a patch kit handy.

Another way to keep water out of your tent is to store all wet garments outside the tent, under a poncho. Moisture from wet clothes stashed in the tent will condense on the interior tent walls. If you bring enough wet clothes in the tent, by the next morning you can feel like you're camping in a duck blind.

• **How hard is it to put up?** If a tent is difficult to erect in full sunlight, you can just about forget it at night. Some tents can go up in just a few minutes, without requiring help from another camper. This might be the kind of tent you want.

The way to compare put-up time of tents when shopping is to count the number of connecting points from the tent poles to the tent, and also the number of stakes required. The fewer, the better. Think simple. My tent has seven connecting points and, minus the rain fly, requires no stakes. It goes up in a few minutes. If you need a lot of stakes, it is a sure tip-off to a long put-up time. Try it at night or in the rain, and you'll be ready to cash your chips and go for broke.

Another factor is the tent poles themselves. Some small tents have poles that are broken into small sections that are connected by bungee cords. It takes only an instant to convert them to a complete pole.

Some outdoor shops have tents on display on their showroom floor. Before buying the tent, have the salesperson take the tent down and put it back up. If it takes him more than five minutes, or he says he "doesn't have time," then keep looking.

• **Is it roomy enough?** Don't judge the size of a tent on floor space alone. Some tents small on floor space can give the illusion of roominess with a high ceiling. You can be quite comfortable in them and snug.

But remember that a one-person or two-person tent is just that. A two-person tent has room for two people plus gear. That's it. Don't buy a tent expecting it to hold more than it is intended to.

- **How much does it weigh?** If you're a hiker, this becomes the preeminent question. If it's much more than six or seven pounds, forget it. A 12-pound tent is bad enough, but get it wet and it's like carrying a piano on your back. On the other hand, weight is scarcely a factor if you camp only where you can take your car. My dad, for instance, used to have this giant canvas umbrella tent that folded down to this neat little pack that weighed about 500 pounds.

Family Tents

It is always worth spending the time and money to purchase a tent you and your family will be happy with.

Though many good family tents are available for $125 to $175, particularly from Coleman, here is a synopsis of four of the best tents available anywhere, without regard to cost:

Sierra Designs Mondo 5CD

(800) 736-8551

$495

10.14 pounds

82 square feet / 20-square-foot vestibule / Inside peak height: 5 feet, 5 inches

If you've got a family that likes to head for distant camps, then this is your tent. It's light enough to pack along, yet big enough to accommodate a family of four. Using speed clips, this tent

is by far the easiest and quickest to set up of any family tent I've used. A generous rain fly and vestibule (new adjustment features allow various awning configurations) mean more than adequate protection from the elements, no matter how hard they are pelting down.

Kelty Domolite 6

(800) 423-2320

$350

16.4 pounds

81.5 square feet / Inside peak height: 5 feet, 7 inches

Using three 18-foot-long fiberglass poles, the Domolite boasts a sleek, low profile that slips the wind very nicely. Each pole slides easily through continuous pole sleeves, thanks to rubber-tipped ends, making set-up a snap. Kelty has an optional vestibule ($95) since without it, the tent is barely adequate shelter should you have to weather a deluge in cramped quarters. Floor seams are taped for added waterproofness. A great package.

Eureka! Space III

(800) 848-3673

$590

29 pounds

100 square feet / Inside peak height: 7 feet

This tent practically reeks of traditional design, and that's the beauty of it. It's a cabin tent by all appearances, with modern design applications intended to improve set-up convenience and make it essentially freestanding. The rigid side poles snap into four curved units that hook to a hub at the top of the tent and then attach to pins at each of the tent's four corners. From there it is a simple matter to hook the tent to the poles with clips attached to the tent body. Huge windows, a giant door, and high ceiling mean plenty of flow-through ventilation and wonderful interior space. At 29 pounds, you won't be wanting to move it around too much, but then who cares. With a tent like this, you're camping long-term anyway.

Quest Nomad

(800) 875-6901

$445

24.6 pounds

81 square feet + 50-square-foot screen porch / Inside peak height: 6 feet, 7 inches

If you are seeking bomb-proof construction, maximum insect protection, and ease of set-up coupled with plenty of space to spread out, then look no further. Using a patented Sportiva hub, the set-up is simplified as fiberglass poles extend like spider's legs, connecting into place with simple efficiency to rigid steel side poles. The screened porch makes this tent seem more like a mountain chalet. The tent's only weak point that I could find is a lack of tub floor. Puddles have a tendency to collect in many campgrounds I have frequented, and seams that rest on the ground, like the Nomad's, are an invitation to eventual leakage, even if well seam-sealed.

Bivouac Bags

If you like going solo and choose not to own a tent at all, a bivvy bag, short for bivouac bag, can provide the weather protection you require. A bivvy bag is a water-repellent shell in which your sleeping bag fits. It is light and tough, and for some is the perfect alternative

to a heavy tent. On the downside, however, there is a strange sensation when you try to ride out a rainy night in one. You can hear the rain hitting you, and sometimes even feel the pounding of the drops through the bivvy bag. It can be unsettling to try and sleep under such circumstances.

Pickup Truck Campers

If you own a pickup truck with a camper shell, you can turn it into a self-contained campground with a little work. This can be an ideal way to go: it's fast, portable, and you are guaranteed a dry environment.

But that does not necessarily mean it is a warm environment. In fact, without insulation from the metal truck bed, it can be like trying to sleep on an iceberg. That is because the metal truck bed will get as cold as the air temperature, which is often much colder than the ground temperature. Without insulation, it can be much colder in your camper shell than it would be on the open ground.

When I camp in my rig, I use a large piece of foam for a mattress and insulation. The foam measures four inches thick, 48 inches wide, and 76 inches long. It makes for a bed as comfortable as anything one might ask for. In fact, during the winter, if I don't go camping for a few weeks because of writing obligations, I sometimes will throw the foam on the floor, lay down the old sleeping bag, light a fire, and camp right in my living room. It's in my blood, I tell you.

RVs

The problems RVers encounter come from two primary sources: lack of privacy and light intrusion.

The lack of privacy stems from the natural restrictions of where a "land yacht" can go. Without careful use of the guide portion of this book, motor home owners can find themselves in parking lot settings, jammed in with plenty of neighbors. Because RVs often have large picture windows, you lose your privacy, causing some late nights; then, come daybreak, light intrusion forces an early wake-up. The result is you get shorted on your sleep. The answer is to always carry inserts to fit over the inside of your windows. This closes off the outside and retains your privacy. And if you don't want to wake up with the sun at daybreak, you don't have to. It will still be dark.

First Aid and Insect Protection

The mountain night could not have been more perfect, I thought as I lay in my sleeping bag.

The sky looked like a mass of jewels and the air tasted sweet and smelled of pines. A shooting star fireballed across the sky, and I remember thinking, "It just doesn't get any better."

Just then, as I was drifting into sleep, this mysterious buzz appeared from nowhere and deposited itself inside my left ear. Suddenly awake, I whacked my ear with the palm of my hand, hard enough to cause a minor concussion. The buzz disappeared. I pulled out my flashlight and shined it on my palm, and there, lit in the blackness of night, lay the squished intruder. A mosquito, dead amid a stain of blood.

Satisfied, I turned off the light, closed my eyes, and thought of the fishing trip planned for the next day. Then I heard them. It was a squadron of mosquitoes, flying landing patterns around my head. I tried to grab them with an open hand, but they dodged the assault and flew off. Just 30 seconds later another landed in my left ear. I promptly dispatched the invader with a rip of the palm.

Now I was completely awake, so I got out of my sleeping bag to retrieve some mosquito repellent. But while en route, several of the buggers swarmed and nailed me in the back and arms. Later, after applying the repellent and settling snugly again in my sleeping bag, the mosquitoes would buzz a few inches from my ear. After getting a whiff of the poison, they would fly off. It was like sleeping in a sawmill.

The next day, drowsy from little sleep, I set out to fish. I'd walked but 15 minutes when I brushed against a bush and felt this stinging sensation on the inside of my arm, just above the wrist. I looked down: A tick had his clamps in me. I ripped it out before he could embed his head into my skin.

After catching a few fish, I sat down against a tree to eat lunch and just watch the water go by. My dog, Rebel, sat down next to me and stared at the beef jerky I was munching as if it were a T-bone steak. I finished eating, gave him a small piece, patted him on the head, and said, "Good dog." Right then, I noticed an itch on my arm where a mosquito had drilled me. I unconsciously scratched it. Two days later, in that exact spot, some nasty red splotches started popping up. Poison oak. By petting my dog and then scratching my arm, I had transferred the oil residue of the poison oak leaves from Rebel's fur to my arm.

On returning back home, Foonsky asked me about the trip.

"Great," I said. "Mosquitoes, ticks, poison oak. Can hardly wait to go back."

"Sorry I missed out," he answered.

Mosquitoes, No-See-Ums, Gnats, and Horseflies

On a trip to Canada, Foonsky and I were fishing a small lake from the shore when suddenly a black horde of mosquitoes could be seen moving across the lake toward us. It was like when the French Army looked across the Rhine and saw the Wehrmacht coming. There was a buzz in the air.

We fought them off for a few minutes, then made a fast retreat to the truck and jumped in, content the buggers had been fooled. But somehow, still unknown to us, the mosquitoes gained entry to the truck. In 10 minutes, we squished 15 of them while they attempted to plant their oil derricks in our skin. Just outside the truck, the black horde waited for us to make a tactical error, like rolling down a window. It finally took a miraculous hailstorm to foil the attack.

When it comes to mosquitoes, no-see-ums, gnats, and horseflies, there are times when there is nothing you can do. However, in most situations you can muster a defense to repel the attack.

The first key with mosquitoes is to wear clothing too heavy for them to drill through. Expose a minimum of skin, wear a hat, and tie a bandanna around your neck, preferably one that has been sprayed with repellent. If you try to get by with just a cotton T-shirt, you will be declared a federal mosquito sanctuary.

So first your skin must be well covered, exposing only your hands and face. Second, you should have your companion spray your clothes with repellent. Third, you should dab liquid repellent directly on your skin.

Taking vitamin B1 and eating garlic are reputed to act as natural insect repellents, but I've met a lot of mosquitoes that are not convinced. A better bet is to examine the contents of the repellent in question. The key is the percentage of the ingredient non-diethyl-metatoluamide. That is the poison, and the percentage of it in the container must be listed and will indicate that brand's effectiveness. Inert ingredients are just excess fluids used to fill the bottles.

At night, the easiest way to get a good sleep without mosquitoes buzzing in your ear is to sleep in a bug-proof tent. If the nights are warm and you want to see the stars, new tent models are available that have a skylight covered with mosquito netting. If you don't like tents on summer evenings, mosquito netting rigged with an air space at your head can solve the problem. Otherwise prepare to get bit, even with the use of mosquito repellent.

If your problems are with no-see-ums or biting horseflies, then you need a slightly different approach.

No-see-ums are tiny black insects that look like nothing more than a sliver of dirt on your skin. Then you notice something stinging, and when you rub the area, you scratch up a little no-see-um. The results are similar to mosquito bites, making your skin itch, splotch, and, when you get them bad, swell. In addition to using the techniques described to repel mosquitoes, you should go one step further.

The problem is, no-see-ums are tricky little devils. Somehow they can actually get under your socks and around your ankles where they will bite to their heart's content all night long while you sleep, itch, sleep, and itch some more. The best solution is to apply a liquid repellent to your ankles, then wear clean socks.

Horseflies are another story. They are rarely a problem, but when they get their dander up, they can cause trouble you'll never forget.

One such episode occurred when Foonsky and I were paddling a canoe along the shoreline of a large lake. This giant horsefly, about the size of a fingertip, started dive-bombing the canoe. After 20 minutes, it landed on Foonsky's thigh. He immediately slammed it with an open hand, then let out a blood-curdling "yeeeee-ow!" that practically sent ripples across the lake. When Foonsky whacked it, the horsefly had somehow turned around and bit him in the hand, leaving a huge red welt.

In the next 10 minutes, that big fly strafed the canoe on more dive-bomb runs. I finally got my canoe paddle, swung it as if it was a baseball bat, and nailed that horsefly like I'd hit a home run. It landed about 15 feet from the boat, still alive and buzzing in the water. While I was trying to figure what it would take to kill this bugger, a large rainbow trout surfaced and snatched it out of the water, finally avenging the assault.

If you have horsefly or yellow jacket problems, you'd best just leave the area. One, two, or a few can be dealt with. More than that and your fun camping trip will be about as fun as being roped to a tree and stung by an electric shock rod.

On most trips, you will spend time doing everything possible to keep from getting bit by mosquitoes or no-see-ums. When that fails, you must know what to do next, and fast, if you are among those ill-fated campers who get big, red lumps from a bite inflicted from even a microscopic mosquito.

A fluid called After Bite or a dab of ammonia should be applied immediately to the bite. To start the healing process, apply a first-aid gel, not a liquid, such as Campho-Phenique.

A Discussion About DEET

What is DEET? You're not likely to find the word DEET on any repellent label. That's because DEET stands for N,N diethyl-m-toluamide. If the label contains this scientific name, the repellent contains DEET. Despite fears of DEET-associated health risks and the increased attention given natural alternatives, DEET-based repellents are still acknowledged as by far the best option when serious insect protection is required.

What are the health risks associated with using DEET? A number of deaths and a number of medical problems have been attributed in the press to DEET in recent years—events that those in the DEET community vehemently deny as being specifically DEET related, pointing to reams of scientific documentation as evidence. It does seem logical to assume that if DEET can peel paint, melt nylon, destroy plastic, wreck wood finishes, and damage fishing line, then it must be hell on the skin—perhaps worse.

On one trip, I had a small bottle of mosquito repellent in the same pocket as a Swiss army knife. Guess what happened? The mosquito repellent leaked a bit and literally melted the insignia right off the knife. DEET will also melt synthetic clothes. That is why in bad mosquito country, I'll expose a minimum of skin, just hands and face (with full beard), and apply the repellent only to the back of my hands and cheeks, perhaps wear a bandanna sprinkled with a few drops as well. That does the trick with a minimum of exposure to the repellent.

Although nothing definitive has been published, there is a belief among a growing number in the scientific community that repeated applications of products containing low percentages of DEET can be potentially dangerous. It is theorized that this actually puts consumers at a greater risk for absorbing high levels of DEET into the body than if they had just used one application of a 30 to 50 percent DEET product with an efficacy of four to six hours. Also being studied is the possibility that low levels of DEET, which might not otherwise be of toxicological concern, may become hazardous if they are formulated with solvents or dilutents (considered inert ingredients) that may enhance the absorption rate.

Are natural alternatives a safer choice? To imply that essential oils are completely safe because they are a "natural" product is not altogether accurate. Essential oils, while derived from plants that grow naturally, are chemicals too. Some are potentially hazardous if ingested, and most are downright painful if they find their way into the eyes or onto mucus membranes. For example, pennyroyal is perhaps the most toxic of the essential oils used to repel insects, and can be deadly if taken internally. Other oils used include citronella (perhaps the most common, it's extracted from an aromatic grass indigenous to Southern Asia), eucalyptus, cedarwood, and peppermint.

Three citronella-based products, Buzz Away (manufactured by Quantum), Avon's Skin-So-Soft, and Natrapel (manufactured by Tender), have received EPA registration and approval for sale as repellents for use in controlling mosquitoes, flies, gnats, and midges.

How effective are natural repellents? While there are numerous studies cited by those on the DEET and citronella sides of the fence, the average effective repelling time of a citronella product appears to range from 1.5 to two hours. Tests conducted at Cambridge University, England, comparing Natrapel to DEET-based Skintastic (a low-percentage DEET product) found citronella to be just as effective in repelling mosquitoes. The key here is effectiveness and the amount of time until reapplication.

Citronella products work for up to two hours and then require reapplication (the same holds true for other natural formulations). Products using a low-percentage level of DEET also require reapplication every two hours to remain effective. So, if you're going outside for only a short period in an environment where insect bites are more an irritant than a hazard, you would do just as well to "go natural."

What other chemical alternatives are there? Another line of defense against insects is the chemical permethrin, used on clothing, not on skin. Permethrin-based products are designed to repel and kill arthropods or crawling insects, making them a preferred repellent for ticks. The currently available civilian products will remain effective, repelling and killing mosquitoes, ticks, and chiggers, for two weeks and through two launderings.

Ticks

Ticks are nasty little vermin that will wait in ambush, jump on unsuspecting prey, and then crawl to a prime location before filling their bodies with their victim's blood.

I call them Dracula Bugs, but by any name they can be a terrible camp pest.

Ticks rest on grass and low plants and attach themselves to those who brush against the vegetation (dogs are particularly vulnerable). Typically, they are no more than 18 inches above ground, and if you stay on the trails, you can usually avoid them.

There are two common species of ticks. The common coastal tick is larger, brownish in color, and prefers to crawl around prior to putting its clamps on you. The latter habit can give you the creeps, but when you feel it crawling, you can just pick it off and dispatch it. The coastal tick's preferred destination is usually the back of your neck, just where the hairline starts. The other species, the wood tick, is small and black, and when he puts his clamps in, it's immediately painful. When a wood tick gets into a dog for a few days, it can cause a large red welt. In either case, ticks should be removed as soon as possible.

If you have hiked in areas infested with ticks, it is advisable to shower as soon as possible, washing your clothes immediately. If you just leave your clothes in a heap, a tick can crawl out and invade your home. They like warmth, and one way or another, they can end up in your bed. Waking up in the middle of the night with a tick crawling across your chest can really give you the creeps.

Once a tick has its clampers on you, you must decide how long it has been there. If it has been a short time, the most painless and effective method for removal is to take a pair of sharp tweezers and grasp the little devil, making certain to isolate the mouth area, then pull him out. Reader Johvin Perry sent in the suggestion to coat the tick with Vaseline, which will cut off its oxygen supply, after which it may voluntarily give up the hunt.

If the tick has been in longer, you may wish to have a doctor extract it. Some people will burn a tick with a cigarette, or poison it with lighter fluid, but this is not advisable. No matter how you do it, you must take care to remove all of it, especially its clawlike mouth.

The wound, however small, should then be cleansed and dressed. This is done by applying liquid peroxide, which cleans and sterilizes, and then applying a dressing coated with a first-aid gel such as First-Aid Cream, Campho-Phenique, or Neosporin.

Lyme disease, which can be transmitted by the bite of the deer tick, is rare but common enough to warrant some attention. To prevent tick bites, some people tuck their pant legs into their hiking socks and spray tick repellent, called Permamone, on their pants.

The first symptom of Lyme disease is that the bite area will develop a bright red, splotchy rash. Other possible early symptoms include headache, nausea, fever, and/or a stiff neck. If this happens, or if you have any doubts, you should see your doctor immediately. If you do get Lyme disease, don't panic. Doctors say it is easily treated in the early stages with simple antibiotics. If you are nervous about getting Lyme disease, carry a small plastic bag with you when you hike. If a tick manages to get his clampers into you, put it in the plastic bag after you pull it out. Then give it to your doctor for analysis, to see if the tick is a carrier of the disease.

During the course of my hiking and camping career, I have removed ticks from my skin hundreds of times without any problems. However, if you are really worried about ticks, you can purchase a tick removal kit from any outdoors store. These kits allow you to remove ticks in such a way that their toxins are guaranteed not to enter your bloodstream.

If you are particularly wary of ticks, or perhaps even have nightmares of them, then wear long pants that are tucked into the socks as well as long-sleeved shirts tucked securely into the pants and held with a belt. Clothing should be light in color, making it easier to spot ticks and tightly woven so ticks have trouble hanging on. On one hike with my mom, Eleanor, on the central coast, I brushed more than 100 ticks off my blue jeans in less than an hour, while she did not pick up a single one on her polyester pants.

Perform tick checks regularly, especially on the back of the neck. The combination of DEET insect repellents applied to the skin and permethrin repellents applied directly to clothing is considered to be the most effective line of defense against ticks.

Poison Oak

After a nice afternoon hike, about a five-miler, I was concerned about possible exposure to poison oak, so I immediately showered and put on clean clothes. Then I settled into a chair with my favorite foamy elixir to watch the end of a baseball game. The game went 18 innings; meanwhile, my dog, tired from the hike, went to sleep on my bare ankles.

A few days later I had a case of poison oak. My feet looked like they had been on fire and put out with an ice pick. The lesson? Don't always trust your dog, give him a bath as well, and beware of extra-inning ball games.

You can get poison oak only from direct contact with the oil residue from the leaves. It can be passed in a variety of ways, as direct as skin-to-leaf contact or as indirect as leaf to dog, dog to sofa, sofa to skin. Once you have it, there is little you can do but itch yourself to death. Applying Caladryl lotion or its equivalent can help because it contains antihistamines, which attack and dry the itch.

A tip that may sound crazy but seems to work is advised by my pal Furniss. You should expose the afflicted area to the hottest water you can stand, then suddenly immerse it in cold water. The hot water opens the skin pores and gets the "itch" out, and the cold water then quickly seals the pores.

In any case, you're a lot better off if you don't get poison oak to begin with. Remember the old Boy Scout saying: "Leaves of three, let them be." Also remember that poison oak can disguise itself. In the spring, it is green, then it gradually turns reddish in the summer. By fall, it becomes a bloody, ugly-looking red. In the winter, it loses its leaves altogether and appears to be nothing more than barren, brown sticks of small plant. However, at any time and in any form, skin contact can quickly lead to infection.

Some people are more easily afflicted than others, but if you are one of the lucky few who aren't, don't cheer too loudly. While some people can be exposed to the oil residue of poison oak with little or no effect, the body's resistance can gradually be worn down with repeated exposure. At one time, I could practically play in the stuff and the only symptom would be a few little bumps on the inside of my wrist. Now, over 15 years later, my resistance has broken down. If I merely rub against poison oak now, in a few days the exposed area can look like it was used for a track meet.

So regardless of whether you consider yourself vulnerable or not, you should take heed to reduce your exposure. That can be done by staying on trails when you hike and making sure your dog does the same. Remember, the worst stands of poison oak are usually brush-infested areas just off the trail. Protect yourself also by dressing so your skin is completely covered, wearing long-sleeved shirts, long pants, and boots. If you suspect you've been exposed, immediately wash your clothes, then wash yourself with aloc vera, rinsing with a cool shower.

And don't forget to give your dog a bath as well.

Sunburn

The most common injury suffered on camping trips is sunburn, yet some people wear it as a badge of honor, believing that it somehow enhances their virility. Well, it doesn't. Neither do suntans. And too much sun can lead to serious burns or sunstroke.

It is easy enough to avoid. Use a high-level sunscreen on your skin, apply lip balm with sunscreen, and wear sunglasses and a hat. If any area gets burned, apply first-aid cream, which will soothe and provide moisture for your parched, burned skin.

The best advice is not to get even a suntan. Those who do are involved in a practice that can be eventually ruinous to their skin and possibly lead to cancer.

A Word About Giardia and Cryptosporidium

You have just hiked in to your backwoods spot, you're thirsty and a bit tired, but you smile as you consider the prospects. Everything seems perfect—there's not a stranger in sight, and you have nothing to do but relax with your pals.

You toss down your gear, grab your cup and dip it into the stream, and take a long drink of that ice-cold mountain water. It seems crystal pure and sweeter than anything you've ever tasted. It's not till later that you find out it can be just like drinking a cup of poison.

Whether you camp in the wilderness or not, if you hike, you're going to get thirsty. And if your canteen runs dry, you'll start eyeing any water source. Stop! Do not pass Go. Do not drink.

By drinking what appears to be pure mountain water without first treating it, you can ingest a microscopic protozoan called *Giardia lamblia.* The pain of the ensuing abdominal cramps can make you feel like your stomach and intestinal tract are in a knot, ready to explode. With that comes long-term diarrhea that is worse than even a bear could imagine.

Doctors call the disease *giardiasis,* or Giardia for short, but it is difficult to diagnose. One friend of mine who contracted Giardia was told he might have stomach cancer before the proper diagnosis was made.

Drinking directly from a stream or lake does not mean you will get Giardia, but you are taking a giant chance. There is no reason to assume such a risk, potentially ruining your trip and enduring weeks of misery.

A lot of people are taking that risk. I made a personal survey of campers in the Yosemite National Park wilderness, and found that roughly only one in 20 were equipped with some kind of water-purification system. The result, according to the Public Health Service, is that an average of 4 percent of all backpackers and campers suffer giardiasis. According to the Parasitic Diseases Division of the Center for Infectious Diseases, the rates range from 1 percent to 20 percent across the country.

But if you get Giardia, you are not going to care about the statistics. "When I got Giardia, I just about wanted to die," said Henry McCarthy, a California camper. "For about 10 days, it was the most terrible thing I have ever experienced. And through the whole thing, I kept thinking, 'I shouldn't have drunk that water, but it seemed all right at the time.'"

That is the mistake most campers make. The stream might be running free, gurgling over boulders in the high country, tumbling into deep, oxygenated pools. It looks pure. Then in a few days, the problems suddenly start. Drinking untreated water from mountain streams is a lot like playing Russian roulette. Sooner or later, the gun goes off.

• **Filters:** There's really no excuse for going without a water filter: Handheld filters are getting more compact, lighter, easier to use, and often less expensive. Having to boil water or endure chemicals that leave a bad taste in the mouth has been all but eliminated.

With a filter, you just pump and drink. Filtering strains out microscopic contaminants, rendering the water clear and somewhat pure. How pure? That depends on the size of the filter's pores—what manufacturers call pore-size efficiency. A filter with a pore-size efficiency of one micron or smaller will remove protozoa like giardia and cryptosporidium, as well as parasitic eggs and larva, but it takes a pore-size efficiency of less than 0.4 microns to remove bacteria. All but one of the filters recommended here do that.

A good backcountry water filter weighs less than 20 ounces, is easy to grasp, simple to use, and a snap to clean and maintain. At the very least, buy one that will remove protozoa and bacteria. (A number of cheap, pocket-size filters remove only giardia and cryptosporidium. That, in my book, is risking your health to save money.) Consider the flow rate, too: A liter per minute is good.

All filters will eventually clog—it's a sign that they've been doing their job. If you force water through a filter that's becoming difficult to pump, you risk injecting a load of microbial nasties into your bottle. Some models can be backwashed, brushed, or, as with ceramic elements, scrubbed to extend their useful lives. And if the filter has a prefilter to screen out the big stuff, use it: It will give your filter a boost in mileage, which can then top out at about 100 gallons per disposable element. Any of the filters reviewed here will serve well on an outing into the wilds, providing you always play by the manufacturer's rules.

First Need Deluxe $70

The 15-ounce First Need Deluxe from General Ecology does something no other handheld filter will do: It removes protozoa, bacteria, and viruses without using chemicals. Such effectiveness is the result of a fancy three-stage matrix system. Unfortunately, if you drop the filter and unknowingly crack the cartridge, all the little nasties can get through. General Ecology's solution is to include a bottle of blue dye that indicates breaks. The issue hasn't scared off too many folks, though: the First Need has been around since 1982. Additional cartridges cost $30. A final note: The filter pumps smoothly and puts out more than a liter per minute. A favorite of mine.

Sweetwater Guardian +Plus $80

The Guardian was new in 1995 and quickly earned praise for its scant weight (11 ounces) and first-rate, fingertip-light pump action. The filter removes protozoa and bacteria—and chemicals, too, by way of the activated charcoal in the element. Add the four-ounce ViralGuard cartridge (included) and the Guardian protects against viruses, too, making it a suitable choice for international travel. At its lower price, the Guardian compares favorably with the more expensive PUR Explorer and MSR WaterWorks II.

PentaPure Oasis $35

The PentaPure Oasis Water Purification System from WTC/Ecomaster offers drinkable water with a twist: You squeeze and sip instead of pumping. Weighing 6.5 ounces, the system packages a three-stage filter inside a 21-ounce-capacity sport bottle with an angled and sealing drinking nozzle, ideal for mountain bikers. The filter removes and/or kills protozoa, bacteria, and viruses, so it's also suitable for world travel. It's certainly conve-nient: Just fill the bottle with untreated water, screw on the cap, give it a firm squeeze (don't expect the easy flow of a normal sport bottle; there's more work being done), and sip. The Oasis only runs into trouble if the water source is shallow; you'll need a cup for scooping.

Basic Designs Ceramic $32

The Basic Designs Ceramic Filter Pump weighs eight ounces and is as stripped-down a filter as you'll find. The pump is simple, easy to use, and quite reliable. The ceramic filter effectively removes protozoa and bacteria, making it ideal and cost-effective for backpacking—but it won't protect against viruses. Also, the filter element is too bulbous to work directly from a shallow water source; like the PentaPure, you'll have to contaminate a pot, cup, or bottle to transfer your unfiltered water. It's a great buy, though, for anyone worried only about giardia and cryptosporidium.

SweetWater WalkAbout $35

The WalkAbout is perfect for the day hiker or backpacker who obsesses on lightening the load. The filter weighs just 8.5 ounces, is easily cleaned in the field, and removes both protozoa and bacteria: a genuine bargain. There are some trade-offs, however, for its diminutiveness. Water delivery is a tad slow at just under a liter per minute, but redesigned filter cartridges ($12.50) are now good for up to 100 gallons. Although the WalkAbout is lighter and a bit more compact than SweetWater's Guardian (see above), I prefer the more expensive sibling because the Guardian can be effective against all waterborne dangers and its cartridges last twice as long.

MSR MiniWorks $59

Like the WalkAbout, the bargain-priced MiniWorks has a bigger and more expensive water-filtering brother. But in this case the differences are harder to discern: The new 14.3-ounce Mini-Works looks similar to the $140 WaterWorks II, and like the WaterWorks is fully field-maintainable while guarding against protozoa, bacteria, and chemicals. But the Mini is arguably the best-executed, easiest-to-use ceramic filter on the market, and it attaches directly to a standard one-quart Nalgene water bottle. Too bad it takes 90 seconds to filter that quart.

PUR Explorer $130

The Explorer offers protection from all the bad guys—viruses as well as protozoa and bacteria—by incorporating an iodine matrix into the filtration process. An optional carbon cartridge ($20) neutralizes the iodine's noxious taste. The Explorer is also considered a trusty veteran among water filters because of its smooth pumping action and nifty back-washing feature: With a quick twist, the device switches from filtering mode to self-cleaning mode. It may be on the heavy side (20 ounces) and somewhat pricey, but the Explorer works very well on iffy water anywhere.

Katadyn U.S.A.
Mini Filter $130

The Mini Filter is a much more compact version of Katadyn's venerable Pocket Filter. This one weighs just eight ounces, ideal for the minimalist backcountry traveler, and it effectively removes protozoa and bacteria. A palm-of-the-hand-size filter, however, makes it challenging to put any kind of power behind the pump's tiny handle,

and the filtered water comes through at a paltry half-liter per minute. It also requires more cleaning than most filters—though the good news is that the element is made of long-lasting ceramic. Ironically, one option lets you purchase the Mini Filter with a carbon element instead of the ceramic: The pumping is easier, the flow rate is better, and the price is way down ($99), but I'd only go that route if you'll be pumping from clear mountain streams.

MSR WaterWorks II
Ceramic $140

At 17.4 ounces the WaterWorks II isn't light, but for the same price as the Katadyn you get a better flow rate (90 seconds per liter), an easy pumping action, and—like the original Mini Filter—a long-lasting ceramic cartridge. This filter is a good match for the person who encounters a lot of dirty water—its three-stage filter weeds out protozoa, bacteria, and chemicals—and is mechanically inclined: The MSR can be completely disassembled afield for troubleshooting and cleaning. (If you're not so endowed, take the filter apart at home only, as the potential for confusion is somewhat high.) By the way, the company has corrected the clogging problem that plagued a previous version of the WaterWorks.

The big drawback with filters is that if you pump water from a mucky lake, the filter can clog in a few days. Therein lies the weakness. Once plugged up, it is useless and you have to replace it or take your chances.

One trick to extend the filter life is to fill your cook pot with water, let the sediment settle, then pump from there. As an added insurance policy, always have a spare filter canister on hand.

• **Boiling water:** Except for water filtration, this is the only treatment that you can use with complete confidence. According to the federal Parasitic Diseases Division, it takes a few minutes at a rolling boil to be certain you've killed *Giardia lamblia.* At high elevations, boil for three to five minutes. A side benefit is that you'll also kill other dangerous bacteria that live undetected in natural waters.

But to be honest, boiling water is a thorn for most people on backcountry trips. For one thing, if you boil water on an open fire, what should taste like crystal-pure mountain water tastes instead like a mouthful of warm ashes. If you don't have a campfire, it wastes stove fuel. And if you are thirsty *now,* forget it. The water takes hours to cool.

The only time boiling always makes sense, however, is when you are preparing dinner. The ash taste will disappear in whatever freeze-dried dinner, soup, or hot drink you make.

• **Water-purification pills:** Pills are the preference for most backcountry campers, and this can get them in trouble. At just $3 to $8 per bottle, which can figure up to just a few cents per canteen, they do come cheap. In addition, they kill most of the bacteria, regardless of whether you use iodine crystals or potable aqua iodine tablets.

The problem is they just don't always kill *Giardia lamblia,* and that is the one critter worth worrying about on your trip. That makes water-treatment pills unreliable and dangerous.

Another key element is the time factor. Depending on the water's temperature, organic content, and pH level, these pills can take a long time to do the job. A minimum wait of 20 minutes is advised. Most people don't like waiting that long, especially when they're hot and thirsty after a hike and thinking, "What the heck, the water looks fine."

And then there is the taste. On one trip, my water filter clogged and we had to use the iodine pills instead. It doesn't take long to get tired of the iodine-tinged taste of the water. Mountain water should be one of the greatest tasting beverages of the world, but the iodine kills that.

• **No treatment:** This is your last resort and, using extreme care, can be executed with success. One of my best hiking buddies, Michael Furniss, is a nationally renowned hydrologist, and on wilderness trips he has showed me the difference between "safe" and "dangerous" water sources.

Long ago, people believed that just finding water running over a rock used to be a guarantee of its purity. Imagine that. What we've learned is that the safe water sources are almost always small springs located in high, craggy mountain areas. The key is making sure no one has been upstream from where you drink.

Furniss mentioned that another potential problem in bypassing water treatment is that even in settings free of Giardia, you can still ingest other bacteria that can cause stomach problems.

The only sure way to beat the problem is to filter or boil your water before drinking, eating, or brushing your teeth. And the best way to prevent the spread of Giardia is to bury your waste products at least eight inches deep and 100 feet away from natural waters.

Hypothermia

No matter how well planned your trip might be, a sudden change in weather can turn it into a puzzle for which there are few answers. Bad weather or an accident can set in motion a dangerous chain of events.

Such a chain of episodes occurred for my brother Rambob and me on a fishing trip one fall day just below the snow line. The weather had suddenly turned very cold, and ice was forming along the shore of the lake. Suddenly, the canoe became terribly imbalanced and just that quick, it flipped. The little life vest seat cushions were useless, and using the canoe as a paddleboard, we tried to kick our way back to shore where my dad was going crazy at the thought of his two sons drowning before his eyes.

It took 17 minutes in that 38-degree water, but we finally made it to shore. When they pulled me out of the water, my legs were dead, not strong enough even to hold up my weight. In fact, I didn't feel so much cold as tired, and I just wanted to lie down and go to sleep.

I closed my eyes, and my brother-in-law, Lloyd Angal, slapped me in the face several times, then got me on my feet and pushed and pulled me about.

In the celebration over making it to shore, only Lloyd had realized that hypothermia was setting in. Hypothermia is the condition in which the temperature of the body is lowered to the point that it causes poor reasoning, apathy, and collapse. It can look like the afflicted person is just tired and needs to sleep, but that sleep can be the first step toward a coma.

Ultimately, my brother and I shared what little dry clothing remained. Then we began hiking around to get muscle movement, creating internal warmth. We ate whatever munchies were available because the body produces heat by digestion. But most important, we got our heads as dry as possible. More body heat is lost through wet hair than any other single factor.

A few hours later, we were in a pizza parlor replaying the incident, talking about how only a life vest can do the job of a life vest. We decided never again to rely on those little flotation seat cushions that disappear when the boat flips.

Almost by instinct we had done everything right to prevent hypothermia: Don't go to sleep, start a physical activity, induce shivering, put dry clothes on, dry your head, and eat something. That's how you fight hypothermia. In a dangerous situation, whether you fall in a lake or a stream or get caught unprepared in a storm, that's how you can stay alive.

After being in that ice-bordered lake for almost 20 minutes and then finally pulling ourselves to the shoreline, we discovered a strange thing. My canoe was flipped right-side up and almost all of its contents were lost: tackle box, flotation cushions, and cooler. But remaining was one paddle and one fishing rod, the trout rod my grandfather had given me for my 12th birthday.

Lloyd gave me a smile. "This means that you are meant to paddle and fish again," he said with a laugh.

Getting Unlost

You could not have been more lost. But there I was, a guy who is supposed to know about these things, transfixed by confusion, snow, and hoofprints from a big deer.

I discovered it is actually quite easy to get lost. If you don't get your bearings, getting found is the difficult part. This occurred on a wilderness trip where I'd hiked in to a remote lake and then set up a base camp for a deer hunt.

"There are some giant bucks up on that rim," confided Mr. Furnai, who lives near the area. "But it takes a mountain man to even get close to them."

That was a challenge I answered. After four-wheeling it to the trailhead, I tromped off with pack and rifle, gut-thumped it up 100 switchbacks over the rim, then followed a creek drainage up to a small but beautiful lake. The area was stark and nearly treeless, with bald granite broken only by large boulders. To keep from getting lost, I marked my route with piles of small rocks to act as directional signs for the return trip.

But at daybreak the next day, I stuck my head out of my tent and found eight inches of snow on the ground. I looked up into a gray sky filled by huge, cascading snowflakes. Visibility was about 50 yards, with fog on the mountain rim. "I better get out of here and get back to my truck," I said to myself. "If my truck gets buried at the trailhead, I'll never get out."

After packing quickly, I started down the mountain. But after 20 minutes, I began to get disoriented. You see, all the little piles of rocks I'd stacked to mark the way were now buried in snow, and I had only a smooth white blanket of snow to guide me. Everything looked the same, and it was snowing even harder now.

Five minutes later I started chewing on some jerky to keep warm, then suddenly stopped. Where was I? Where was the creek drainage? Isn't this where I was supposed to cross over a creek and start the switchbacks down the mountain?

Right then I looked down and saw the tracks of a huge deer, the kind Mr. Furnai had talked about. What a predicament: I was lost and snowed in, and seeing big hoofprints in the snow. Part of me wanted to abandon all safety and go after that deer, but a little voice in the back of my head won out. "Treat this as an emergency," it said.

The first step in any predicament is to secure your present situation, that is, to make sure it does not get any worse. I unloaded my rifle (too easy to slip, fall, and have a misfire), took stock of my food (three days worth), camp fuel (plenty), and clothes (rain gear keeping me dry). Then I wondered, "Where the hell am I?"

I took out my map, compass, and altimeter, then opened the map and laid it on the snow. It immediately began collecting snowflakes. I set the compass atop the map and oriented it to north. Because of the fog, there was no way to spot landmarks, such as prominent mountaintops, to verify my position. Then I checked the altimeter, which read 4,900 feet. Well, the elevation at my lake was 5,320 feet. That was critical information.

I scanned the elevation lines on the map and was able to trace the approximate area of my position, somewhere downstream from the lake, yet close to a 4,900-foot elevation. "Right here," I said, pointing to a spot on the map with a finger. "I should pick up the switchback trail down the mountain somewhere off to the left, maybe just 40 or 50 yards away."

Slowly and deliberately, I pushed through the light, powdered snow. In five minutes, I suddenly stopped. To the left, across a 10-foot depression in the snow, appeared a flat spot that veered off to the right. "That's it! That's the crossing."

In minutes, I was working down the switchbacks, on my way, no longer lost. I thought of the hoofprints I had seen, and now that I knew my position, I wanted to head back and spend the day hunting. Then I looked up at the sky, saw it filled with falling snowflakes, and envisioned my truck buried deep in snow. Alas, this time logic won out over dreams.

In a few hours, now trudging through more than a foot of snow, I was at my truck at a spot called Doe Flat, and next to it was a giant, all-terrain Forest Service vehicle and two rangers.

"Need any help?" I asked them.

They just laughed. "We're here to help you," one answered. "It's a good thing you filed a trip plan with our district office in Gasquet. We wouldn't have known you were out here."

"Winter has arrived," said the other. "If we don't get your truck out now, it will be stuck here until next spring. If we hadn't found you, you might have been here until the end of time."

They connected a chain from the rear axle of their giant rig to the front axle of my truck and started towing me out, back to civilization. On the way to pavement, I figured I had gotten some of the more important lessons of my life. Always file a trip plan and have plenty of food, fuel, and a camp stove you can rely on. Make sure your clothes, weather gear, sleeping bag, and tent will keep you dry and warm. Always carry a compass, altimeter, and map with elevation lines, and know how to use them, practicing in good weather to get the feel of it.

And if you get lost and see the hoofprints of a giant deer, well, there are times when it is best to pass them by.

Catching Fish, Avoiding Bears, and Having Fun

Feet tired and hot, stomachs hungry, we stopped our hike for lunch beside a beautiful little river pool that was catching the flows from a long but gentle waterfall. My brother Rambob passed me a piece of jerky. I took my boots off, then slowly dunked my feet into the cool, foaming water.

I was gazing at a towering peak across a canyon, when suddenly, Wham! There was a quick jolt at the heel of my right foot. I pulled my foot out of the water to find that, incredibly, a trout had bitten it.

My brother looked at me like I had antlers growing out of my head. "Wow!" he exclaimed. "That trout almost caught himself an outdoors writer!"

It's true that in remote areas trout sometimes bite on almost anything, even feet. On one high-country trip, I have caught limits of trout using nothing but a bare hook. The only problem is that the fish will often hit the splitshot sinker instead of the hook. Of course, fishing isn't usually that easy. But it gives you an idea of what is possible.

America's wildlands are home to a remarkable abundance of fish and wildlife. Deer browse with little fear of man, bears keep an eye out for your food, and little critters like squirrels and chipmunks are daily companions. Add in the fishing and you've got yourself a camping trip.

Your camping adventures will evolve into premium outdoor experiences if you can work in a few good fishing trips, avoid bear problems, and occasionally add a little offbeat fun with some camp games.

Trout and Bass

He creeps up on the stream as quiet as an Indian scout, keeping his shadow off the water. With his little spinning rod, he'll zip his lure within an inch or two of its desired mark, probing along rocks, the edges of riffles, pocket water, or wherever he can find a change in river habitat. Rambob is trout fishing, and he's a master at it.

In most cases, he'll catch a trout on his first or second cast. After that it's time to move up the river, giving no spot much more than five minutes due. Stick and move, stick and move, stalking the stream like a bobcat zeroing in on an unsuspecting rabbit. He might keep a few trout for dinner, but mostly he releases what he catches. Rambob doesn't necessarily fish for food. It's the feeling that comes with it.

Fishing can give you a sense of exhilaration, like taking a hot shower after being coated with dust. On your walk back to camp, the steps come easy. You suddenly understand what John Muir meant when he talked of developing a oneness with nature, because you have it. That's what fishing can provide.

You don't need a million dollars worth of fancy gear to catch fish. What you need is the right outlook, and that can be learned. That goes regardless of whether you are fishing for trout or bass, the two most popular fisheries in the United States. Your fishing tackle selection should be as simple and clutter-free as possible.

At home, I've got every piece of fishing tackle you might imagine, more than 30 rods and many tackle boxes, racks and cabinets filled with all kinds of stuff. I've got one lure that looks like a chipmunk and another that resembles a miniature can of beer with hooks. If I hear of something new, I want to try it and usually do. It's a result of my lifelong fascination with the sport.

But if you just want to catch fish, there's an easier way to go. And when I go fishing, I take that path. I don't try to bring everything. It would be impossible. Instead, I bring a relatively small amount of gear. At home I will scan my tackle boxes for equipment and lures, make my selections, and bring just the essentials. Rod, reel, and tackle will fit into a side pocket of my backpack or a small carrying bag.

So what kind of rod should be used on an outdoor trip? For most camper/anglers, I suggest the use of a light, multipiece spinning rod that will break down to a small size. One of the best deals on the fishing market is the six-piece Daiwa 6.5-foot pack rod, No. 6752. It retails for as low as $30, yet is made of a graphite/glass composite that gives it the quality of a much more expensive model. And it comes in a hard plastic carrying tube for protection. Other major rod manufacturers, such as Fenwick, offer similar premium rods. It's tough to miss with any of them.

The use of graphite/glass composites in fishing rods has made them lighter and more sensitive, yet stronger. The only downside to graphite as a rod material is that it can be brittle. If you rap your rod against something, it can crack or cause a weak spot. That weak spot can eventually snap when under even light pressure, like setting a hook or casting. Of course, a bit of care will prevent that from ever occurring.

If you haven't bought a fishing reel in some time, you will be surprised at the quality and price of micro spinning reels on the market. The reels come tiny and strong, with rear-control drag systems. Sigma, Shimano, Cardinal, Abu, and others all make premium reels. They're worth it. With your purchase, you've just bought a reel that will last for years and years.

The one downside to spinning reels is that after long-term use, the bail spring will weaken. The result is that after casting and beginning to reel, the bail will sometimes not flip over and allow the reel to retrieve the line. Then you have to do it by hand. This can be incredibly frustrating, particularly when stream fishing, where instant line pickup is essential. The solution is to have a new bail spring installed every few years. This is a cheap, quick operation for a tackle expert.

You might own a giant tackle box filled with lures, but on your fishing trip you are better off to fit just the essentials into a small container. One of the best ways to do that is to use the Plano Micro-Magnum 3414, a tiny two-sided tackle box for trout anglers that fits into a shirt pocket. In mine, I can fit 20 lures in one side of the box and 20 flies, splitshot, and snap swivels in the other. For bass lures, which are bigger, you need a slightly larger box, but the same principle applies.

There are more fishing lures on the market than you can imagine, but a few special ones can do the job. I make sure these are in my box on every trip. For trout, I carry a small black Panther Martin spinner with yellow spots, a small gold Kastmaster, a yellow Roostertail, a gold Z-Ray with red spots, a Super Duper, and a Mepps Lightning spinner.

You can take it a step further using insider's wisdom. My old pal Ed "the Dunk" showed me his trick of taking a tiny Dardevle spoon, then spray painting it flat black and dabbing five tiny red dots on it. It's a real killer, particularly in tiny streams where the trout are spooky.

The best trout catcher I've ever used on rivers is a small metal lure called a Met-L Fly. On days when nothing else works, it can be like going to a shooting gallery. The problem is that the lure is near impossible to find. Rambob and I consider the few we have remaining so valuable that if the lure is snagged on a rock, a cold swim is deemed mandatory for its retrieval. These lures are as hard to find in tackle shops as trout can be to catch without one.

For bass, you can also fit all you need into a small plastic tackle box. I have fished with many bass pros and all of them actually use just a few lures: a white spinner bait, a small jig called a Gits-It, a surface plug called a Zara Spook, and plastic worms. At times, like when the bass move into shoreline areas during the spring, shad minnow imitations like those made by Rebel or Rapala can be dynamite. My favorite is the one-inch blue-silver Rapala. Every spring, as the lakes begin to warm and the fish snap out of their winter ·doldrums, I like to float and paddle around in my small raft. I'll cast that little Rapala along the shoreline and catch and release hundreds of bass, bluegill, and sunfish. The fish are usually sitting close to the shoreline, awaiting my offering.

Fishing Tips

There's an old angler's joke about how you need to "think like a fish." But if you're the one getting zilched, you may not think it's so funny.

The irony is that it is your mental approach, what you see and what you miss, that often determines your fishing luck. Some people will spend a lot of money on tackle, lures, and fishing clothes, and that done, just saunter up to a stream or lake, cast out, and wonder why they are not catching fish. The answer is their mental outlook. They are not attuning themselves to their surroundings.

You must live on nature's level, not your own. Try this and you will become aware of things you never believed even existed. Soon you will see things that will allow you to catch fish. You can get a head start by reading about fishing, but to get your degree in fishing, you must attend the University of Nature.

On every fishing trip, regardless what you fish for, try to follow three hard-and-fast rules:

1. Always approach the fishing spot so you will be undetected.

2. Present your lure, fly, or bait in a manner so it appears completely natural, as if no line was attached.

3. Stick and move, hitting one spot, working it the best you can, then move to the next.

Here's a more detailed explanation.

Approach: No one can just walk up to a stream or lake, cast out, and start catching fish as if someone had waved a magic wand. Instead, give the fish credit for being smart. After all, they live there.

Your approach must be completely undetected by the fish. Fish can sense your presence through sight and sound, though this is misinterpreted by most people. By sight, this rarely means the fish actually see you; more likely, they will see your shadow on the water, or the movement of your arm or rod while casting. By sound, it doesn't mean they hear you talking, but that they will detect the vibrations of your footsteps along the shore, kicking a rock, or the unnatural plunking sound of a heavy cast hitting the water. Any of these elements can spook them off the bite. In order to fish undetected, you must walk softly, keep your shadow off the water, and keep your casting motion low. All of these keys become easier at sunrise or sunset, when shadows are on the water. At midday, a high sun causes a high level of light penetration in the water, which can make the fish skittish to any foreign presence.

Like hunting, you must stalk the spots. When my brother Rambob sneaks up on a fishing spot, he is like a burglar sneaking through an unlocked window.

Presentation: Your lure, fly, or bait must appear in the water as if no line was attached, so it looks as natural as possible. My pal Mo Furniss has skin-dived in rivers to watch what the fish see when somebody is fishing.

"You wouldn't believe it," he said. "When the lure hits the water, every trout within 40 feet, like 15, 20 trout, will do a little zigzag. They all see the lure and are aware something is going on. Meanwhile, onshore the guy casting doesn't get a bite and thinks there aren't any fish in the river."

If your offering is aimed at fooling a fish into striking, it must appear as part of its natural habitat, as if it is an insect just hatched or a small fish looking for a spot to hide. That's where you come in.

After you have snuck up on a fishing spot, you should zip your cast upstream, then start your retrieve as soon as it hits the water. If you let the lure sink to the bottom, then start the retrieve, you have no chance. A minnow, for instance, does not sink to the bottom then start swimming. On rivers, the retrieve should be more of a drift, as if the "minnow" was in trouble and the current was sweeping it downstream.

When fishing on trout streams, always hike and cast upriver, then retrieve as the offering drifts downstream in the current. This is effective because trout will sit almost motionless, pointed upstream, finning against the current. This way they can see anything coming their direction, and if a potential food morsel arrives, all they need to do is move over a few inches, open their mouths, and they've got an easy lunch. Thus you must cast upstream.

Conversely, if you cast downstream, your retrieve will bring the lure from behind the fish, where he cannot see it approaching. And I've never seen a trout that had eyes in its tail. In addition, when retrieving a downstream lure, the river current will tend to sweep your lure inshore to the rocks.

Finding spots: A lot of fishermen don't catch fish, and a lot of hikers never see any wildlife. The key is where they are looking.

The rule of the wild is that fish and wildlife will congregate wherever there is a distinct change in the habitat. This is where you should begin your search. To find deer, for instance, forget probing a thick forest, but look for where it breaks into a meadow or a clear-cut has splayed a stand of trees. That's where the deer will be.

In a river, it can be where a riffle pours into a small pool, a rapid that plunges into a deep hole and flattens, a big boulder in the middle of a long riffle, a shoreline point, a rock pile, a submerged tree. Look for the changes. Conversely, long, straight stretches of shoreline will not hold fish—the habitat is lousy.

On rivers, the most productive areas are often where short riffles tumble into small oxygenated pools. After sneaking up from the downstream side and staying low, you should zip your cast so the lure plops gently in the white water just above the pool. Starting your retrieve instantly, the lure will drift downstream and plunk into the pool. Bang! That's where the trout will hit. Take a few more casts, then head upstream to the next spot.

With a careful approach and lure presentation, and by fishing in the right spots, you have the ticket to many exciting days on the water.

Of Bears and Food

The first time you come nose-to-nose with a bear, it can make your skin quiver.

Even the sight of mild-mannered black bears, the most common bear in America, can send shock waves through your body. They range from 250 to 400 pounds and have large claws and teeth that are made to scare campers. When they bound, the muscles on their shoulders roll like ocean breakers.

Bears in camping areas are accustomed to sharing the mountains with hikers and campers. They have become specialists in the food-raiding business. As a result, you must be able to make a bear-proof food hang, or be able to scare the fellow off. Many campgrounds provide bear- and raccoon-proof food lockers. You can also stash your food in your vehicle, but that limits the range of your trip.

If you are staying at one of the easy backpack sites listed in this book, there will be no food lockers available. (The exceptions are the high Sierra camps in Yosemite National Park, where rangers have placed high wires for food hangs, the next best thing to food lockers.) Your car will not be there, either. The solution is to make a bear-proof food hang, suspending all of your food wrapped in a plastic garbage bag from a rope in midair, 10 feet from the trunk of a tree and 20 feet off the ground. (Counterbalancing two bags with a rope thrown over a tree limb is very effective, but finding an appropriate limb can be difficult.)

This is accomplished by tying a rock to a rope, then throwing it over a high but sturdy tree limb. Next, tie your food bag to the rope and hoist it in the air. When you are satisfied with the position of the food bag, tie off the end of the rope to another tree. In an area frequented by bears, a good food bag is a necessity—nothing else will do.

I've been there. On one trip, my pal Foonsky and my brother Rambob had left to fish, and I was stoking up an evening campfire when I felt the eyes of an intruder on my back. I turned around and this big bear was heading straight for our camp. In the next half hour, I scared the bear off twice, but then he got a whiff of something sweet in my brother's pack.

The bear rolled into camp like a semi truck, grabbed the pack, ripped it open, and plucked out the Tang and the Swiss Miss. The 350-pounder then sat astride a nearby log and lapped at the goodies like a thirsty dog drinking water.

Once a bear gets his mitts on your gear, he considers it his. I took two steps toward the pack and that bear jumped off the log and galloped across the camp right at me. Scientists say a man can't outrun a bear, but they've never seen how fast I can go up a granite block with a bear on my tail.

Shortly thereafter, Foonsky returned to find me perched on top of the rock, and demanded to know how I could let a bear get our Tang. It took all three of us, Foonsky, Rambob, and myself, charging at once and shouting like madmen, to clear the bear out of camp and send him off over the ridge. We learned never to let food sit unattended.

The Grizzly

When it comes to grizzlies, well, my friends, you need what we call an "attitude adjustment." Or that big ol' bear may just decide to adjust your attitude for you, making your stay at the park a short one.

Grizzlies are nothing like black bears. They are bigger, stronger, have little fear, and take what they want. Some people believe there are many different species of this critter, like Alaskan brown, silvertip, cinnamon, and Kodiak, but the truth is they are all grizzlies. Any difference in appearance has to do with diet, habitat, and life habits, not speciation. By any name, they all come big.

The first thing you must do is determine if there are grizzlies in the area where you are camping. That can usually be done by asking local rangers. If you are heading into Yellowstone or Glacier National Park, or the Bob Marshall Wilderness of Montana, well, you don't have to ask. They're out there, and they're the biggest and potentially most dangerous critters you could run into.

One general way to figure the size of a bear is from his footprint. Take the width of the footprint in inches, add one to it—and you'll have an estimated length of the bear in feet. For instance, a nine-inch footprint equals a 10-foot bear. Any bear that big is a grizzly, my friends. In fact, most grizzly footprints average about nine to 10 inches across, and black bears (though they may be brown in color) tend to have footprints only four and a half to six inches across.

If you are hiking in a wilderness area that may have grizzlies, it becomes a necessity to wear bells on your pack. That way, the bear will hear you coming and likely get out of your way. Keep talking, singing, or maybe even debating the country's foreign policy, but whatever, do not fall into a silent hiking vigil. And if a breeze is blowing in your face, you must make even more noise (a good excuse to rant and rave about the government's domestic affairs). Noise is important, because your smell will not be carried in the direction you are hiking. As a result, the bear will not smell you coming.

If a bear can hear you and smell you, it will tend to get out of the way and let you pass without your knowing it was even close by. The exception is if you are carrying fish or lots of sweets in your pack, or if you are wearing heavy, sweet deodorants or makeup. All of these are bear attractants.

Most encounters with grizzlies occur when hikers fall into a silent march in the wilderness with the wind in their faces, and they walk around a corner and right into a big, unsuspecting grizzly. If you do this and see a big hump just behind its neck, well, don't think twice: It's a grizzly.

And then what should you do? Get up a tree, that's what. Grizzlies are so big that their claws cannot support their immense weight, and thus they cannot climb trees. And although their young can climb, they rarely want to get their mitts on you.

If you do get grabbed, every instinct in your body will tell you to fight back. Don't believe it. Play dead. Go limp. Let the bear throw you around a little, because after awhile you become unexciting play material and the bear will get bored. My grandmother was grabbed by a grizzly in Glacier National Park and after a few tosses and hugs, was finally left alone to escape.

Some say it's a good idea to tuck your head under his chin, since that way, the bear will be unable to bite your head. I'll take a pass on that one. If you are taking action, any action, it's a signal that you are a force to be reckoned with, and he'll likely respond with more aggression. And bears don't lose many wrestling matches.

What grizzlies really like to do, believe it or not, is to pile a lot of sticks and leaves on you. Just let them, and keep perfectly still. Don't fight them; don't run. And when you have a 100 percent chance (not 98 or 99) to dash up a nearby tree, that's when you let fly. Once safely in a tree, you can hurl down insults and let your aggression out.

In a wilderness camp, there are special precautions you should take. Always hang your food at least 100 yards downwind of camp and get it high, 30 feet is reasonable. In addition, circle your camp with rope and hang the bells from your pack on it. Thus, if a bear walks into your camp, he'll run into the rope, the bells will ring, and everybody will have a chance to get up a tree before ol' griz figures out what's going on. Often, the unexpected ringing of bells is enough to send him off in search of a quieter environment.

You see, more often than not, grizzlies tend to clear the way for campers and hikers. So, be smart, don't act like bear bait, and always have a plan if you are confronted by one.

My pal Foonsky had such a plan during a wilderness expedition in Montana's northern Rockies. On our second day of hiking, we started seeing scratch marks on the trees, 13 to 14 feet off the ground.

"Mr. Griz made those," Foonsky said. "With spring here, the grizzlies are coming out of hibernation and using the trees like a cat uses a scratch board to stretch the muscles."

The next day, I noticed Foonsky had a pair of track shoes tied to the back of his pack. I just laughed.

"You're not going to outrun a griz," I said. "In fact, there's hardly any animal out here in the wilderness that man can outrun."

Foonsky just smiled.

"I don't have to outrun a griz," he said. "I just have to outrun you!"

Fun and Games

"Now what are we supposed to do?" the young boy asked his dad.

"Yeah, Dad, think of something," said another son.

Well, Dad thought hard. This was one of the first camping trips he'd taken with his sons and one of the first lessons he received was that kids don't appreciate the philosophic release of mountain quiet. They want action, and lots of it. With a glint in his eye, Dad searched around the camp and picked up 15 twigs, breaking them so each was four inches long. He laid them in three separate rows, three twigs in one row, five twigs in another, and seven in the other.

"OK, this game is called 3-5-7," said Dad. "You each take turns picking up sticks. You are allowed to remove all or as few as one twig from a row, but here's the catch: You can only pick from one row per turn. Whoever picks up the last stick left is the loser."

I remember this episode well because those two little boys were my brother Bobby, as in Rambobby, and me. And to this day, we still play 3-5-7 on campouts, with the winner getting to watch the loser clean the dishes. What I have learned in the span of time since that original episode is that it does not matter what your age is: Campers need options for camp fun.

Some evenings, after a long hike or ride, you are likely to feel too worn-out to take on a serious romp downstream to fish, or a climb up to a ridge for a view. That is especially true if you have been in the outback for a week or more. At that point a lot of campers will spend their time resting and gazing at a map of the area, dreaming of the next day's adventure, or just take a seat against a rock, watching the colors of the sky and mountain panorama change minute by minute. But kids in the push-button video era, and a lot of adults too, want more. After all, "I'm on vacation; I want some fun."

There are several options, like the 3-5-7 twig game, and they should be just as much a part of your pre-trip planning as arranging your gear.

For kids, plan on games, the more physically challenging the competition, the better. One of the best games is to throw a chunk of wood into a lake, then challenge the kids to hit it by throwing rocks. It wreaks havoc on the fishing, but it can keep kids totally absorbed for some time. Target practice with a wrist-rocket slingshot is also all-consuming for kids, firing rocks away at small targets like pinecones set on a log.

You can also set kids off on little missions near camp, such as looking for the footprints of wildlife, searching out good places to have a "snipe hunt," picking up twigs to get the evening fire started, or having them take the water purifier to a stream to pump some drinking water into a canteen. The latter is an easy, fun, yet important task that will allow kids to feel a sense of equality they often don't get at home.

For adults, the appeal should be more to the intellect. A good example is star and planet identification, and while you are staring into space, you're bound to spot a few asteroids, or shooting stars. A star chart can make it easy to locate and identify many distinctive stars and constellations, such as Pleiades (the Seven Sisters), Orion, and others from the zodiac, depending on the time of year. With a little research, this can add a unique perspective to your trip. You could point to Polaris, one of the most easily identified of all stars, and note that navigators in the 1400s used it to find their way. Polaris, of course, is the North Star and is at the end of the handle of the Little Dipper. Pinpointing Polaris is quite easy. First find the Big Dipper, then locate the outside stars of the ladle of the Big Dipper. They are called the "Pointer Stars" because they point right at Polaris.

A tree identification book can teach you a few things about your surroundings. It is also a good idea for one member of the party to research the history of the area you have chosen and another to research the geology. With shared knowledge, you end up with a deeper love of wild places.

Another way to add some recreation into your trip is to bring a board game, a number of which have been miniaturized for campers. The most popular are chess, checkers, and cribbage. The latter comes with an equally miniature set of playing cards. And if you bring those little cards, that opens a vast set of other possibilities. With kids along, for instance, just take the Queen of Clubs out of the deck and you can instantly play Old Maid.

But there are more serious card games and they come with high stakes. Such occurred on one high country trip where Foonsky, Rambob, and myself sat down for a late afternoon game of poker. In a game of seven-card stud, I caught a straight on the sixth card and felt like a dog licking on a T-bone. Already, I had bet several Skittles and peanut M&Ms on this promising hand.

Then I examined the cards Foonsky had face up. He was showing three sevens, and acting as happy as a grizzly with a pork chop, like he had a full house. He matched my bet of two peanut M&Ms, then raised me three SweetTarts, one Starburst, and one sour apple Jolly Rancher. Rambob folded, but I matched Foonsky's bet and hoped for the best as the seventh and final card was dealt.

Just after Foonsky glanced at that last card, I saw him sneak a look at my grape stick and beef jerky stash.

"I raise you a grape stick," he said.

Rambob and I both gasped. It was the highest bet ever made, equivalent to a million dollars laid down in Las Vegas. Cannons were going off in my chest. I looked hard at my cards. They looked good, but were they good enough?

Even with a great hand like I had, a grape stick was too much to gamble, my last one with 10 days of trail ahead of us. I shook my head and folded my cards. Foonsky smiled at his victory.

But I still had my grape stick.

Old Tricks Don't Always Work

Most people are born honest, but after a few camping trips, they usually get over it.

I remember some advice I got from Rambob, normally an honest soul, on one camping trip. A giant mosquito had landed on my arm and he alerted me to some expert advice.

"Flex your arm muscles," he commanded, watching the mosquito fill with my blood. "He'll get stuck in your arm, then he'll explode."

For some unknown reason, I believed him. We both proceeded to watch the mosquito drill countless holes in my arm.

Alas, the unknowing face sabotage from their most trusted companions on camping trips. It can arise at any time, usually in the form of advice from a friendly, honest-looking face, as if to say, "What? How can you doubt me?" After that mosquito episode, I was a little more skeptical of my dear old brother. Then, the next day, when another mosquito was nailing me in the back of the neck, out came this gem:

"Hold your breath," he commanded. I instinctively obeyed. "That will freeze the mosquito," he said, "then you can squish him."

But in the time I wasted holding my breath, the little bugger was able to fly off without my having the satisfaction of squishing him. When he got home, he probably told his family, "What a dummy I got to drill today!"

Over the years, I have been duped numerous times with dubious advice:

On a grizzly bear attack: "If he grabs you, tuck your head under the grizzly's chin, then he won't be able to bite you in the head." This made sense to me until the first time I looked face-to-face with a nine-foot grizzly, 40 yards away. In seconds, I was at the top of a tree, which suddenly seemed to make the most sense.

On coping with animal bites: "If a bear bites you in the arm, don't try to jerk it away. That will just rip up your arm. Instead force your arm deeper into his mouth. He'll lose his grip and will have to open it to get a firmer hold, and right then you can get away." I was told this in the Boy Scouts, and when I was 14, I had a chance to try it out when a friend's dog bit me after I tried to pet it. What happened? When I shoved my arm deeper into his mouth, he bit me about three extra times.

On cooking breakfast: "The bacon will curl up every time in a camp frying pan. So make sure you have a bacon stretcher to keep it flat." As a 12-year-old Tenderfoot, I spent two hours looking for the bacon stretcher until I figured out the camp leader had forgotten it. It wasn't for several years until I learned that there is no such thing.

On preventing sore muscles: "If you haven't hiked for a long time and you are facing a rough climb, you can keep from getting sore muscles in your legs, back, and shoulders by practicing the 'Dead Man's Walk.' Simply let your entire body go slack, and then take slow, wobbling steps. This will clear your muscles of lactic acid, which causes them to be so sore after a rough hike." Foonsky pulled this one on me. Rambob and I both bought it, then tried it while we were hiking up Mount Whitney, which requires a 6,000-foot elevation gain in six miles. In one 45-minute period, about 30 other hikers passed us and looked at us as if we were suffering from some rare form of mental aberration.

Catching Fish, Avoiding Bears, and Having Fun   61

Fish won't bite? No problem: "If the fish are not feeding or will not bite, persistent anglers can still catch dinner with little problem. Keep casting across the current, and eventually, as they hover in the stream, the line will feed across their open mouths. Keep reeling and you will hook the fish right in the side of the mouth. This technique is called 'lining.' Never worry if the fish will not bite, because you can always line 'em." Of course, heh, heh, heh, that explains why so many fish get hooked in the side of the mouth.

How to keep bears away: "To keep bears away, urinate around the borders of your campground. If there are a lot of bears in the area, it is advisable to go right on your sleeping bag." Yeah, surrrrrre.

What to do with trash: "Don't worry about packing out trash. Just bury it. It will regenerate into the earth and add valuable minerals." Bears, raccoons, skunks, and other critters will dig up your trash as soon as you depart, leaving one huge mess for the next camper. Always pack out everything.

Often the advice comes without warning. That was the case after a fishing trip with a female companion, when she outcaught me two-to-one, the third such trip in a row. I explained this to a shopkeeper, and he nodded, then explained why.

"The male fish are able to detect the female scent on the lure, and thus become aroused into striking."

Of course! That explains everything!

Getting Revenge

I was just a lad when Foonsky pulled the old snipe-hunt trick on me. It took nearly 30 years to get revenge.

You probably know about snipe hunting. That is where the victim is led out at night in the woods by a group, then is left holding a bag.

"Stay perfectly still and quiet," Foonsky explained. "You don't want to scare the snipe. The rest of us will go back to camp and let the woods settle down. Then when the snipe are least expecting it, we'll form a line and charge through the forest with sticks, beating bushes and trees, and we'll flush the snipe out right to you. Be ready with the bag. When we flush the snipe out, bag it. But until we start our charge, make sure you don't move or make a sound or you will spook the snipe and ruin everything."

I sat out there in the woods with my bag for hours, waiting for the charge. I waited, waited, and waited. Nothing happened. No charge, no snipe. It wasn't until well past midnight that I figured something was wrong. When I finally returned to camp, everybody was sleeping.

Well, I tell ya, don't get mad at your pals for the tricks they pull on you. Get revenge. Some 25 years later, on the last day of a camping trip, the time finally came.

"Let's break camp early," Foonsky suggested to Mr. Furnai and me. "Get up before dawn, eat breakfast, pack up, then be on the ridge to watch the sun come up. It will be a fantastic way to end the trip."

"Sounds great to me," I replied. But when Foonsky wasn't looking, I turned his alarm clock ahead three hours. So when the alarm sounded at the appointed 4:30 A.M. wake-up time, Mr. Furnai and I knew it was actually only 1:30 A.M.

Foonsky clambered out of his sleeping bag and whistled with a grin. "Time to break camp."

"You go ahead," I answered. "I'll skip breakfast so I can get a little more sleep. At the first sign of dawn, wake me up, and I'll break camp."

"Me, too," said Mr. Furnai.

Foonsky then proceeded to make some coffee, cook a breakfast, and eat it, sitting on a log in the black darkness of the forest, waiting for the sun to come up. An hour later, with still no sign of dawn, he checked his clock. It now read 5:30 a.m. "Any minute now we should start seeing some light," he said.

He made another cup of coffee, packed his gear, and sat there in the middle of the night, looking up at the stars, waiting for dawn. "Anytime now," he said. He ended up sitting there all night long.

Revenge is sweet. Prior to a fishing trip at a lake, I took Foonsky aside and explained that the third member of the party, Jimbobo, was hard of hearing and very sensitive about it. "Don't mention it to him," I advised. "Just talk real loud."

Meanwhile, I had already told Jimbobo the same thing. "Foonsky just can't hear very good."

We had fished less than 20 minutes when Foonsky got a nibble.

"GET A BITE?" shouted Jimbobo.

"YEAH!" yelled back Foonsky, smiling. "BUT I DIDN'T HOOK HIM!"

"MAYBE NEXT TIME!" shouted Jimbobo with a friendly grin.

Well, they spent the entire day yelling at each other from the distance of a few feet. They never did figure it out. Heh, heh, heh.

That is, I thought so, until we made a trip salmon fishing. I got a strike that almost knocked my fishing rod out of the boat. When I grabbed the rod, it felt like Moby Dick was on the other end. "At least a 25-pounder," I said. "Maybe bigger."

The fish dove, ripped off line, and then bulldogged. "It's acting like a 40-pounder," I announced, "Huge, just huge. It's going deep. That's how the big ones fight."

Some 15 minutes later, I finally got the "salmon" to the surface. It turned out to be a coffee can that Foonsky had clipped on the line with a snap swivel. By maneuvering the boat, he made the coffee can fight like a big fish.

This all started with a little old snipe hunt years ago. You never know what your pals will try next. Don't get mad. Get revenge!

Camping Options

Boat-in Seclusion

Most campers would never think of trading in their car, pickup truck, or RV for a boat, but people who go by boat on a camping trip enjoy virtually guaranteed seclusion and top-quality outdoor experiences.

Camping with a boat is a do-it-yourself venture in living under primitive circumstances. Yet at the same time you can bring along any luxury item you wish, from giant coolers, stoves, and lanterns to portable gasoline generators. Weight is almost never an issue.

In California, many outstanding boat-in campgrounds are available in beautiful surroundings. The best are on the shores of lakes accessible by canoe or skiff, and at offshore islands reached by saltwater cruisers. Several boat-in camps are detailed in this book.

If you want to take the adventure a step further and create your own boat-in camp, perhaps near a special fishing spot, this is a go-for-it deal that provides the best way possible to establish your own secret campsite. But most people who set out freelance style forget three critical items for boat-in camping: a shovel, a sunshade, and an ax. Here is why these items can make a key difference in your trip:

Shovel: Many lakes and virtually all reservoirs have steep, sloping banks. At reservoirs subject to drawdowns, what was lake bottom in the spring can be a campsite in late summer. If you want a flat area for a tent site, the only answer is to dig one out yourself. A shovel gives you that option.

Sunshade: The flattest spots to camp along lakes often have a tendency to support only sparse tree growth. As a result, a natural shield from sun and rain is rarely available. What? Rain in the summer? Oh yeah, don't get me started. A light tarp, set up with poles and staked ropes, solves the problem.

Ax: Unless you bring your own firewood, which is necessary at some sparsely wooded reservoirs, there is no substitute for a good, sharp ax. With an ax, you can almost always find dry firewood, since the interior of an otherwise wet log will be dry. When the weather turns bad is precisely when you will most want a fire. You may need an ax to get one going.

In the search to create your own personal boat-in campsite, you will find that the flattest areas are usually the tips of peninsulas and points, while the protected back ends of coves are often steeply sloped. At reservoirs, the flattest areas are usually near the mouths of the feeder streams and the points are quite steep. On rivers, there are usually sandbars on the inside of tight bends that make for ideal campsites.

Almost all boat-in campsites developed by government agencies are free of charge, but you are on your own. Only in extremely rare cases is piped water available.

Any way you go, by canoe, skiff, or power cruiser, you end up with a one-in-a-million campsite you can call your own.

Desert Outings

It was a cold, snowy day in Missouri when 10-year-old Rusty Ballinger started dreaming about the vast deserts of the West.

"My dad was reading aloud from a Zane Grey book called *Riders of the Purple Sage,*" Ballinger said. "He would get animated when he got to the passages about the desert. It wasn't long before I started to have the same feelings."

That was in 1947. Ballinger, now in his 60s, has spent a good part of his life exploring the West, camping along the way. "The deserts are the best part. There's something about the uniqueness of each little area you see," Ballinger said. "You're constantly surprised. Just the time of day and the way the sun casts a different color. It's like the lady you care about. One time she smiles, the next time she's pensive. The desert is like that. If you love nature, you can love the desert. After awhile, you can't help but love it."

A desert adventure is not just an anti-dote for a case of cabin fever in the winter. Whether you go by RV, pickup truck, car, or on foot, it provides its own special qualities.

If you go camping in the desert, your approach has to be as unique as the setting. For starters, don't plan on any campfires, but bring a camp stove instead. And unlike in the mountains, do not camp near a water hole. That's because an animal such as a badger, coyote, or desert bighorn might be desperate for water, and if you set up camp in the animal's way, you may be forcing a confrontation.

In some areas, there is a danger of flash floods. An intense rain can fall in one area, collect in a pool, then suddenly burst through a narrow canyon. If you are in its path, you could be injured or drowned. The lesson? Never camp in a gully.

"Some people might wonder, 'What good is this place?'" Ballinger said. "The answer is that it is good for looking at. It is one of the world's unique places."

Camp Ethics and Politics

The perfect place to set up a base camp turned out to be not so perfect. In fact, according to Doug Williams of California, it did not even exist.

Williams and his son, James, had driven deep into Angeles National Forest, prepared to set up camp and then explore the surrounding area on foot. But when they reached their destination, no campground existed.

"I wanted a primitive camp in a national forest where I could teach my son some basics," said the senior Williams. "But when we got there, there wasn't much left of the camp and it had been closed. It was obvious that the area had been vandalized."

It turned out not to be an isolated incident. A lack of outdoor ethics practiced by a few people using the nonsupervised campgrounds available on national forestland has caused the U.S. Forest Service to close a few of them, and make extensive repairs to others.

"There have been sites closed, especially in Angeles and San Bernardino national forests in Southern California," said David Flohr, regional campground coordinator for the Forest Service. "It's an urban type of thing, affecting forests near urban areas, and not just Los Angeles. They get a lot of urban users and they bring with them a lot of the same ethics they have in the city. They get drinking and they're not afraid to do things. They vandalize and run. Of course, it is a public facility, so they think nobody is getting hurt."

But somebody is getting hurt, starting with the next person who wants to use the campground. And if the ranger district budget doesn't have enough money to pay for repairs, the campground is then closed for the next arrivals. Just ask Doug and James Williams.

In an era of considerable fiscal restraint for the Forest Service, vandalized campgrounds could face closure instead of repair in the next few years. Williams had just a taste of it, but Flohr, as camping coordinator, gets a steady diet.

"It starts with behavior," Flohr said. "General rowdiness, drinking, partying, and then vandalism. It goes all the way from the felt tip pen things (graffiti) to total destruction, blowing up toilet buildings with dynamite. I have seen toilets destroyed totally with shotguns. They burn up tables, burn barriers. They'll burn up signs for firewood, even the shingles right off the roofs of the bathrooms. They'll shoot anything, garbage cans, signs. It can get a little hairy. A favorite is to remove the stool out of a toilet building. We've had people fall in the open hole."

The National Park Service had a similar problem some years back, especially with rampant littering. Park Director Bill Mott responded by creating an interpretive program that attempts to teach visitors the wise use of natural areas, and to have all park workers set examples by picking up litter and reminding others to do the same.

The Forest Service has responded with a similar program, with brochures available that detail the wise use of national forests. The four most popular brochures are titled: "Rules for Visitors to the National Forest," "Recreation on the National Forests," "Is the Water Safe?" and "Backcountry Safety Tips." These include details on campfires, drinking water from lakes or streams, hypothermia, safety, and outdoor ethics. They are available for free by writing to Public Affairs, U.S. Forest Service, 630 Sansome Street, San Francisco, CA 94111.

Flohr said even experienced campers sometimes cross over the ethics line unintentionally. The most common example, he said, is when campers toss garbage into the outhouse toilet, rather than packing it out in a plastic garbage bag.

"They throw it in the vault toilet bowls, which just fills them up," Flohr said. "That creates an extremely high cost to pump it. You know why? Because some poor guy has to pick that stuff out piece by piece. It can't be pumped."

At most backcountry sites, the Forest Service has implemented a program called "Pack it in, pack it out," even posting signs that remind all visitors to do so. But a lot of people don't do it, and others may even uproot the sign and burn it for firewood.

On a trip to a secluded lake near Carson Pass in the Sierra Nevada, I arrived at a small, little-known camp where the picnic table had been spray-painted and garbage had been strewn about. A pristine place, the true temple of God, had been defiled.

Then I remembered back 30 years to a story my dad told me: "There are two dogs inside of you," he said, "a good one, and a bad one. The one you feed is the one that will grow. Always try to feed the good dog."

Getting Along with Fellow Campers

The most important thing about a camping, fishing, or hunting trip is not where you go, how many fish you catch, or how many shots you fire. It often has little to do with how beautiful the view is, how easy the campfire lights, or how sunny the days are.

Oh yeah? Then what is the most important factor? The answer: The people you are with. It is that simple.

Who would you rather camp with? Your enemy at work or your dream mate in a good mood? Heh, heh. You get the idea. A camping trip is a fairly close-knit experience, and you can make lifetime friends or lifelong enemies in the process. That is why your choice of companions is so important. Your own behavior is equally consequential.

Yet most people spend more time putting together their camping gear than considering why they enjoy or hate the company of their chosen companions. Here are 10 rules of behavior for good camping mates:

1. No whining: Nothing is more irritating than being around a whiner. It goes right to the heart of adventure, since often the only difference between a hardship and an escapade is simply whether or not an individual has the spirit for it. The people who do can turn a rugged day in the outdoors into a cherished memory. Those who don't can ruin it with their incessant sniveling.

2. Activities must be agreed upon: Always have a meeting of the minds with your companions over the general game plan. Then everybody will possess an equal stake in the outcome of the trip. This is absolutely critical. Otherwise they will feel like merely an addendum to your trip, not an equal participant, and a whiner will be born (see No. 1).

3. Nobody's in charge: It is impossible to be genuine friends if one person is always telling another what to do, especially if the orders involve simple camp tasks. You need to share the space on the same emotional plane, and the only way to do that is to have a semblance of equality, regardless of differences in experience. Just try ordering your mate around at home for a few days. You'll quickly see the results, and they aren't pretty.

4. Equal chances at the fun stuff: It's fun to build the fire, fun to get the first cast at the best fishing spot, and fun to hoist the bagged food for a bear-proof food hang. It is not fun to clean the dishes, collect firewood, or cook every night. So obviously, there must be an equal distribution of the fun stuff and the not-fun stuff, and everybody on the trip must get a shot at the good and the bad.

5. No heroes: No awards are bestowed for achievement in the outdoors, yet some guys treat mountain peaks, big fish, and big game as if they are prizes in a trophy competition. Actually, nobody cares how wonderful you are, which is always a surprise to trophy chasers. What people care about is the heart of the adventure, the gut-level stuff.

6. Agree on a wake-up time: It is a good idea to agree on a general wake-up time before closing your eyes for the night, and that goes regardless of whether you want to sleep in late or get up at dawn. Then you can proceed on course regardless of what time you crawl out of your sleeping bag in the morning, without the risk of whining (see No. 1).

7. Think of the other guy: Be self-aware instead of self-absorbed. A good test is to count the number of times you say, "What do you think?" A lot of potential problems can be solved quickly by actually listening to the answer.

8. Solo responsibilities: There are a number of essential camp duties on all trips, and while they should be shared equally, most should be completed solo. That means that when it is time for you to cook, you don't have to worry about me changing the recipe on you. It means that when it is my turn to make the fire, you keep your mitts out of it.

9. Don't let money get in the way: Of course everybody should share equally in trip expenses, such as the cost of food, and it should be split up before you head out yonder. Don't let somebody pay extra, because that person will likely try to control the trip. Conversely, don't let somebody weasel out of paying their fair share.

10. Accordance on the food plan: Always have complete agreement on what you plan to eat each day. Don't figure that just because you like Steamboat's Sludge, everybody else will, too, especially youngsters. Always, always, always check for food allergies such as nuts, onions, or cheese, and make sure each person brings their own personal coffee brand. Some people drink only decaffeinated; others might gag on anything but Burma monkey beans.

Obviously, it is difficult to find companions who will agree on all of these elements. This is why many campers say that the best camping buddy they'll ever have is their mate, someone who knows all about them and likes them anyway.

Outdoors with Kids

How do you get a boy or girl excited about the outdoors? How do you compete with the television and remote control? How do you prove to a kid that success comes from persistence, spirit, and logic, which the outdoors teaches, and not from pushing buttons?

The answer is in the Ten Camping Commandments for Kids. These are lessons that will get youngsters excited about the outdoors, and will make sure adults help the process along, not kill it. Some are obvious, some are not, but all are important:

1. Take children to places where there is a guarantee of action. A good example is camping in a park where large numbers of wildlife can be viewed, such as squirrels, chipmunks, deer, and even bears. Other good choices are fishing at a small pond loaded with bluegill, or hunting in a spot where a kid can shoot a .22 at pinecones all day. Boys and girls want action, not solitude.

2. Enthusiasm is contagious. If you aren't excited about an adventure, you can't expect a child to be. Show a genuine zest for life in the outdoors, and point out everything as if it is the first time you have ever seen it.

3. Always, always, always be seated when talking to someone small. This allows the adult and child to be on the same level. That is why fishing in a small boat is perfect for adults and kids. Nothing is worse for youngsters than having a big person look down at them and give them orders. What fun is that?

4. Always *show* how to do something, whether it is gathering sticks for a campfire, cleaning a trout, or tying a knot. Never tell—always show. A button usually clicks to "off" when a kid is lectured. But they can learn behavior patterns and outdoor skills by watching adults, even when the adults are not aware they are being watched.

5. Let kids be kids. Let the adventure happen, rather than trying to force it within some preconceived plan. If they get sidetracked watching pollywogs, chasing butterflies, or sneaking up on chipmunks, let them be. A youngster can have more fun turning over rocks and looking at different kinds of bugs that sitting in one spot, waiting for a fish to bite.

6. Expect short attention spans. Instead of getting frustrated about it, use it to your advantage. How? By bringing along a bag of candy and snacks. Where there is a lull in the camp activity, out comes the bag. Don't let them know what goodies await, so each one becomes a surprise.

7. Make absolutely certain the child's sleeping bag is clean, dry, and warm. Nothing is worse than discomfort when trying to sleep, but a refreshing sleep makes for a positive attitude the next day. In addition, kids can become quite scared of animals at night. A parent should not wait for any signs of this, but always play the part of the outdoor guardian, the one who will "take care of everything."

8. Kids quickly relate to outdoor ethics. They will enjoy eating everything they kill, building a safe campfire, and picking up all their litter, and they will develop a sense of pride that goes with it. A good idea is to bring extra plastic garbage bags to pick up any trash you come across. Kids long remember when they do something right that somebody else has done wrong.

9. If you want youngsters hooked on the outdoors for life, take a close-up photograph of them holding up fish they have caught, blowing on the camp-fire, or completing other camp tasks. Young children can forget how much fun they had, but they never forget if they have a picture of it.

10. The least important word you can ever say to a kid is "I." Keep track of how often you are saying "Thank you" and "What do you think?" If you don't say them very often, you'll lose out. Finally, the most important words of all are: "I am proud of you."

Predicting Weather

Foonsky climbed out of his sleeping bag, glanced at the nearby meadow, and scowled hard.

"It doesn't look good," he said. "Doesn't look good at all."

I looked at my adventure companion of 20 years, noting his discontent. Then I looked at the meadow and immediately understood why: *"When the grass is dry at morning light, look for rain before the night."*

"How bad you figure?" I asked him.

"We'll know soon enough, I reckon," Foonsky answered. "Short notice, soon to pass. Long notice, long it will last."

When you are out in the wild, spending your days fishing and your nights camping, you learn to rely on yourself to predict the weather. It can make or break you. If a storm hits the unprepared, it can quash the trip and possibly endanger the participants. But if you are ready, a potential hardship can be an adventure.

You can't rely on TV weather forecasters, people who don't even know that when all the cows on a hill are facing north, it will rain that night for sure. God forbid if the cows are all sitting. But what do you expect from TV's talking heads?

Foonsky made a campfire, started boiling some water for coffee and soup, and we started to plan the day. In the process, I noticed the smoke of the campfire: It was sluggish, drifting and hovering.

"You notice the smoke?" I asked, chewing on a piece of homemade jerky.

"Not good," Foonsky said. "Not good."

He knew that sluggish, hovering smoke indicates rain.

"You'd think we'd have been smart enough to know last night that this was coming," Foonsky said. "Did you take a look at the moon or the clouds?"

"I didn't look at either," I answered. "Too busy eating the trout we caught." You see, if the moon is clear and white, the weather will be good the next day. But if there is a ring around the moon, the number of stars you can count inside the ring equals the number of days until the next rain. As for clouds, the high, thin clouds called cirrus indicate a change in the weather.

We were quiet for a while, planning our strategy, but as we did so, some terrible things happened: A chipmunk scampered past with his tail high, a small flock of geese flew by very low, and a little sparrow perched on a tree limb quite close to the trunk.

"We're in for trouble," I told Foonsky.

"I know, I know," he answered. "I saw 'em, too. And come to think of it, no crickets were chirping last night either."

"Damn, that's right!"

These are all signs of an approaching storm. Foonsky pointed at the smoke of the campfire and shook his head as if he had just been condemned. Sure enough, now the smoke was blowing toward the north, a sign of a south wind. *"When the wind is from the south, the rain is in its mouth."*

"We'd best stay hunkered down until it passes," Foonsky said.

I nodded. "Let's gather as much firewood now as we can, get our gear covered up, then plan our meals."

"Then we'll get a poker game going."

As we accomplished these camp tasks, the sky clouded up, then darkened. Within an hour, we had gathered enough firewood to make a large pile, enough wood to keep a fire going no matter how hard it rained. The day's meals had been separated out of the food bag, so it wouldn't have to be retrieved during the storm. We buttoned two ponchos together, staked two of the corners with ropes to the ground, and tied the other two with ropes to different tree limbs to create a slanted roof/shelter.

As the first raindrop fell with that magic sound on our poncho roof, Foonsky was just starting to shuffle the cards.

"Cut for deal," he said.

Just as I did so, it started to rain a bit harder. I pulled out another piece of beef jerky and started chewing on it. It was just another day in paradise. . . .

Weather lore can be valuable. Small signs provided by nature and wildlife can be translated to provide a variety of weather information. Here is the list I have compiled over the years:

When the grass is dry at morning light,

Look for rain before the night.

Short notice, soon to pass.

Long notice, long it will last.

When the wind is from the east,

'Tis fit for neither man nor beast.

When the wind is from the south,

The rain is in its mouth.

When the wind is from the west,

Then it is the very best.

Red sky at night, sailors' delight.

Red sky in the morning, sailors take warning.

When all the cows are pointed north,

Within a day rain will come forth.

Onion skins very thin, mild winter coming in.

Onion skins very tough, winter's going to be very rough.

When your boots make the squeak of snow,

Then very cold temperatures will surely show.

If a goose flies high, fair weather ahead.

If a goose flies low, foul weather will come instead.

A thick coat on a woolly caterpillar means a big, early snow is coming.

Chipmunks will run with their tails up before a rain.

Bees always stay near their hives before a rainstorm.

When the birds are perched on large limbs near tree trunks, an intense but short storm will arrive.

On the coast, if groups of seabirds are flying a mile inland, look for major winds.

If crickets are chirping very loud during the evening, the next day will be clear and warm.

If the smoke of a campfire at night rises in a thin spiral, good weather is assured for the next day.

If the smoke of a campfire at night is sluggish, drifting and hovering, it will rain the next day.

If there is a ring around the moon, count the number of stars inside the ring, and that is how many days until the next rain.

If the moon is clear and white, the weather will be good the next day.

High, thin clouds, or cirrus, indicate a change in the weather.

Oval-shaped lenticular clouds indicate high winds.

Two levels of clouds moving in different directions indicates changing weather soon.

Huge, dark billowing clouds called cumulonimbus, suddenly forming on warm afternoons in the mountains, mean that a short but intense thunderstorm with lightning can be expected.

When squirrels are busy gathering food for extended periods, it means good weather is ahead in the short term, but a hard winter is ahead in the long term.

And God forbid if all the cows are sitting down. . . .

Keep It Wild

"Enjoy America's country and leave no trace." That's the motto of the Leave No Trace organization, and we strongly support it. The following list was developed from the policies of Leave No Trace. For a free, pocket-sized, weatherproof card printed with these policies, as well as information that details how to minimize human impact on wild areas, phone Leave No Trace at (800) 332-4100.

Plan Ahead and Prepare

1. Learn about the regulations and issues that apply to the area you're visiting.

2. Avoid heavy-use areas.

3. Obtain all maps and permits.

4. Bring extra garbage bags to pack out any refuse you come across.

Keep the Wilderness Wild

1. Let nature's sound prevail. Avoid loud voices and noises.

2. Leave radios and tape players at home. At drive-in camping sites, never open car doors with music playing.

3. Careful guidance is necessary when choosing any games to bring for children. Most toys, especially any kind of gun toys with which children simulate shooting at each other, shouldn't be allowed on a camping trip.

4. Control pets at all times or leave them with a sitter at home.

5. Treat natural heritage with respect. Leave plants, rocks, and historical artifacts where you find them.

Respect Other Users

1. Horseback riders have priority over hikers. Step to the downhill side of the trail and talk softly when encountering horseback riders.

2. Hikers and horseback riders have priority over mountain bikers. When mountain bikers encounter other users, even on wide trails, they should pass at an extremely slow speed. On very narrow trails, they should dismount and get off to the side so the hiker or horseback rider can pass without having their trip disrupted.

3. Mountain bikes aren't permitted on most single-track trails and are expressly prohibited on all portions of the Pacific Crest Trail, in designated wilderness areas, and on most state park trails. Mountain bikers breaking these rules should be confronted and told to dismount and walk their bikes until they reach a legal area.

4. It's illegal for horseback riders to break off branches that may be in the path of wilderness trails.

5. Horseback riders on overnight trips are prohibited from camping in many areas and are usually required to keep stock animals in specific areas where they can do no damage to the landscape.

Travel Lightly

1. Visit the backcountry in small groups.

2. Below tree line, always stay on designated trails.

3. Don't cut across switchbacks.

4. When traveling cross-country where no trails are available, follow animal trails or spread out with your group so no new routes are created.

5. Read your map and orient yourself with landmarks, a compass, and an altimeter. Avoid marking trails with rock cairns, tree scars, or ribbons.

Camp with Care

1. Choose a preexisting, legal site. Restrict activities to areas where vegetation is compacted or absent.

2. Camp at least 75 steps (200 feet) from lakes, streams, and trails.

3. Always choose sites that won't be damaged by your stay.

4. Preserve the feeling of solitude by selecting camps that are out of view when possible.

5. Don't construct structures or furniture or dig trenches.

Campfires

1. Fire use can scar the backcountry. If a fire ring is not available, use a lightweight stove for cooking.

2. Where fires are permitted, use existing fire rings, away from large rocks or overhangs.

3. Don't char rocks by building new rings.

4. Gather sticks from the ground that are no larger than the diameter of your wrist.

5. Don't snap branches of live, dead, or downed trees, which can cause personal injury and also scar the natural setting.

6. Put the fire "dead out" and make sure it's cold before departing. Remove all trash from the fire ring.

7. Remember that some forest fires can be started by a campfire that appears to be out. Hot embers burning deep in the pit can cause tree roots to catch on fire and burn underground. If you ever see smoke rising from the ground, seemingly from nowhere, dig down and put the fire out.

Sanitation

If no refuse facility is available:

1. Deposit human waste in "cat holes" dug six to eight inches deep. Cover and disguise the cat hole when finished.

2. Deposit human waste at least 75 paces (200 feet) from any water source or camp.

3. Use toilet paper sparingly. When finished, carefully burn it in the cat hole, then bury it.

4. If no appropriate burial locations are available, such as in popular wilderness camps above tree line in hard granite settings—Devil's Punchbowl in the Siskiyou Wilderness is such an example—then all human refuse should be double-bagged and packed out.

5. At boat-in campsites, chemical toilets are required. Chemical toilets can also solve the problem of larger groups camping or long stays at one location where no facilities are available.

6. To wash dishes or your body, carry water away from the source and use small amounts of biodegradable soap. Scatter dishwater after all food particles have been removed.

7. Scour your campsites for even the tiniest piece of trash and any other evidence of your stay. Pack out all the trash you can, even if it's not yours. Finding cigarette butts, for instance, provides special irritation for most campers. Pick them up and discard them properly.

8. Never litter. Never. Or you become the enemy of all others.

Camping Gear Checklist

• Cooking Gear

Matches stored in zip-lock bags
Fire-starter cubes or candle
Camp stove
Camp fuel
Pot, pan, cup
Pot grabber
Knife, fork
Dish soap and scrubber
Salt, pepper, spices
Itemized food
Plastic spade

• Optional Cooking Gear

Ax or hatchet
Wood or charcoal for barbecue
Ice chest
Spatula
Grill
Tinfoil
Dustpan
Tablecloth
Whisk broom
Clothespins
Can opener

• Camping Clothes

Polypropylene underwear
Cotton shirt
Long-sleeved cotton/wool shirt
Cotton/canvas pants
Vest
Parka
Rain jacket, pants, or poncho
Hat
Sunglasses

• Optional Clothing

Seam Lock™
Shorts
Swimsuit
Gloves
Ski cap

• Hiking Gear

Quality hiking boots
Backup lightweight shoes
Polypropylene socks
Thick cotton socks
80 percent wool socks
Strong bootlaces
Innersole or foot cushion
Moleskin and medical tape
Gaiters
Water-repellent boot treatment

• Sleeping Gear

Sleeping bag
Insulite™ or Therm-a-Rest™ pad
Ground tarp
Tent

• Optional Sleeping Gear

Air pillow
Mosquito netting
Foam pad for truck bed
Windshield light screen for RV
Catalytic heater

• First Aid

Band-Aids
Sterile gauze pads
Roller gauze

Athletic tape
Moleskin
Thermometer
Aspirin
Ace bandage
Mosquito repellent
After-Bite™ or ammonia
Campho-Phenique™ gel
First-Aid Cream™
Sunscreen
Neosporin™
Caladryl™
Biodegradable soap
Towelettes
Tweezers

• Optional First Aid

Water purification system
Coins for emergency phone calls
Extra set of matches
Mirror for signaling

• Fishing/ Recreational Gear

Fishing rod
Fishing reel with fresh line
Small tackle box with lures,
    splitshot, snap swivels
Pliers
Knife

• Optional Recreation Gear

Stargazing chart
Tree identification handbook
Deck of cards
Backpacking cribbage board
Knapsack for each person

• Miscellaneous

Maps
Flashlight
Lantern and fuel
Nylon rope for food hang
Lip balm
Handkerchief
Camera and film
Plastic garbage bags
Toilet paper
Toothbrush and toothpaste
Compass
Watch
Feminine hygiene products

• Optional Miscellaneous

Binoculars
Notebook and pen
Towel

Resource Guide

WASHINGTON

Gifford Pinchot National Forest: Write to 10600 NE 51ˢᵗ Circle, Vancouver, WA 98682, or phone (360) 891-5045 or fax (360) 891-5000.

Olympic National Forest: Write to 1835 Black Lake Boulevard SW, Olympia, WA 98512, or phone (360) 956-2300 or fax (360) 956-2330.

Mount Baker–Snoqualmie National Forest: Write to 21905 64ᵗʰ Avenue West, Mountlake Terrace, WA 98043, or phone (425) 775-9702 or fax (425) 744-3255.

Colville National Forest: Write to 765 South Main Street, Colville, WA 99114, or phone (509) 684-3711 or fax (509) 684-7280.

Wenatchee National Forest: Write to 215 Melody Lane, Wenatchee, WA 98801-5933, or phone (509) 662-4335 or fax (509) 662-4368.

Okanogan National Forest: Write to 1240 Second Avenue South, Okanogan, WA 98840, or phone (509) 826-3275 or fax (509) 826-3789.

OREGON

Deschutes National Forest: Write to 1645 Highway 20 East, Bend, OR 97701, or phone (541) 388-2715 or fax (541) 383-5531.

Fremont National Forest: Write to 524 North G Street, Lakeview, OR 97630, or phone (541) 947-2151 or fax (541) 947-6399.

Malheur National Forest: Write to 431 Patterson Bridge Road, P.O Box 909, John Day, OR 97845, or phone (541) 575-1731 or fax (541) 575-3001.

Mount Hood National Forest: Write to 16400 Champion Way Sandy, OR 97035-7299, or phone (503) 668-1400 or fax (503) 668-1641.

Ochoco National Forest: Write to 3160 NE Third Street, Prineville, OR 97754, or phone (541) 416-6500 or fax (541) 416-6695.

Rogue River National Forest: Write to 333 West Eighth Street, Medford, OR 97501, or phone (541) 858-2200 or fax (541) 858-2220.

Siskiyou National Forest: Write to 200 NE Greenfield Road, Grants Pass, OR 97526, or phone (541) 471-6500 or fax (541) 471-6514.

Siuslaw National Forest: Write to 4077 Research Way, Corvallis, OR 97333, or phone (541) 750-7000 or fax (541) 750-7234.

Umatilla National Forest: Write to 2517 SW Hailey Avenue, Pendleton, OR 97801, or phone (541) 278-3716 or fax (541) 278-3730.

Umpqua National Forest: Write to 2900 NW Stewart Parkway, Roseburg, OR 97470, or phone (541) 672-6601 or fax (541) 957-3495.

Wallowa-Whitman National Forest: Write to 1550 Dewey Avenue, Baker City, OR 97814, or phone (541) 523-6391, (541) 426-4978, or fax (541) 523-1315.

Willamette National Forest: Write to P.O. Box 10607, Eugene, OR 97401, or phone (541) 465-6521 or fax (541) 465-6722.

Winema National Forest: Write to 2819 Dahlia Street, Klamath Falls, OR 97601, or phone (541) 883-6714 or fax (541) 883-6709.

STATE PARKS

The Washington and Oregon state parks systems provide many popular camping spots. Reservations are often a necessity during the summer months. The camps include drive-in, numbered sites, tent spaces, picnic tables, with showers and bathrooms provided nearby. Although some parks are well known, there are still some little-known gems in the State Parks systems where campers can get seclusion, even in the summer months.

Washington and Oregon have joined in sponsoring a central reservation system. Reservations can be made for 44 Washington and 25 Oregon state parks through Reservations Northwest at (800) 452-5687. Campgrounds under the system are clearly noted in the "reservations, fee" paragraph of their listings in this book. A nonrefundable reservation fee of $6 and the first night's fee will be required as an advanced deposit, charged to a MasterCard or Visa credit card. Under the system, reservations can be made throughout the year, up to 11 months in advance.

A Washington state parks central information number is available: (800) 233-0321. General information regarding Oregon state parks can be obtained by calling (800) 551-6949.

WASHINGTON

State Parks and Recreation Commission: Write to Public Affairs Office, 7150 Cleanwater Lane, P.O. Box 42650, Olympia, WA 98504-2650, or phone (360) 902-8562, (360) 902-8500, or fax (360) 664-8112.

Belfair State Park: Write to NE 410 Beck Road, Belfair, WA 98528-9426, or phone (360) 275-0668 or fax (360) 275-8734.

Birch Bay State Park: Write to 5105 Helwig Road, Blaine, WA 98230-9625, or phone (360) 371-2800.

Fort Canby State Park: Write to P.O. Box 488, Ilwaco, WA 98624-0488, or phone (360) 642-3078 or fax (360) 642-4216.

Fort Flagler State Park: Write to 10541 Flagler Road, Norland, WA 98358-9699, or phone (360) 385-1259 or fax (360) 379-1746.

Ike Kinswa State Park: Write to 873 Harmony Road, Silver Creek, WA 98585-9706, or phone (360) 983-3402 or fax (360) 983-3332.

Lake Chelan State Park: Write to 7544 South Lakeshore Drive, Chelan, WA 99755, or phone (509) 687-3710 or fax (509) 687-9656.

Moran State Park: Write to Star Route, Box 22, Eastsound, WA 98245-9603, or phone (360) 376-2326 or fax (360) 376-2360.

Lincoln Rock State Park: Write to 13253 Star Route 2, Wenatchee, WA 98802, or phone (509) 884-8702 or fax (509) 886-1704.

Pearrygin Lake State Park: Write to 861 Bear Creek Road, Winthrop, WA 98862-9710, or phone (509) 996-2370 or fax (509) 996-2630.

Steamboat Rock State Park: Write to P.O. Box 370, Electric City, WA 99123-0370, or phone (509) 633-1304 or fax (509) 633-1294.

Twin Harbors-Grayland Beach: Write Twin Harbors State Park, Westport, WA 98595-9801, or phone (360) 268-9717 or fax (360) 268-0372.

OREGON

State Parks and Recreation Division: Write to 1115 Commercial Street NE, Salem, OR 97310-1001, or phone (503) 378-6305 or fax (503) 378-6447.

State Parks, Portland Office: Write to 2501 Southwest First Avenue, Portland, OR 97201, or phone (503) 378-6305 or (503) 378-6447.

State Parks, Coos Bay Office: Write or phone the Portland Office.

State Parks, Central Oregon: Write to Central Oregon Service Center, Empire Corporate Park, Suite B1, 20300 Empire Avenue, Bend, OR 97701, or phone (541) 388-6211 or fax (541) 388-6391.

State Parks, Eastern Oregon Area: Write to 2034 Auburn, Baker City, OR 97814, or phone (541) 523-2499 extension 3 or fax (541) 523-2884.

NATIONAL PARKS

The national parks in Washington and Oregon are natural wonders, ranging from the spectacular Mount Rainier National Park to the lava-strewn Mount St. Helens National Monument to the often fog-bound Olympic National Park.

For information about each of the national parks in Washington and Oregon, contact the parks directly at the following numbers or addresses.

WASHINGTON

Olympic National Park: Write to 600 East Park Avenue, Port Angeles, WA 98362, or phone (360) 452-4501 or fax (360) 452-0335.

Mount St. Helens National Monument: Write to 42218 NE Yale Bridge Road, Amboy, WA 98601, or phone (360) 247-5473 or fax (360) 247-3901.

Mount Rainier National Park: Write to Tahoma Woods, Star Route, Ashford, WA 98304, or phone (360) 569-2211.

North Cascades National Park: Write to Ross Lake and Lake Chelan National Recreation Areas, 2105 State Route 20, Sedro Woolley, WA 98284, or phone (360) 856-5700 or fax (360) 856-1934.

Lake Roosevelt National Recreation Area: Write to 1008 Crest Drive, Coulee Dam, WA 99116-1259, or phone (509) 633-9441 or fax (509) 633-9332.

OREGON

Crater Lake National Park: Write to P.O. Box 7, Crater Lake, OR 97604, or phone (541) 594-2211 or fax (541) 594-2299.

Fort Clatsop National Memorial: Write to Route 3, Box 604-FC, Astoria, OR 97103, or phone (503) 861-2471 or fax (503) 861-2585.

John Day Fossil Beds National Monument: Write to HCR 82, Box 126, Kimberly, OR 97848, or phone (541) 987-2333 or fax (541) 987-2336.

Oregon Caves National Monument: Write to 19000 Caves Highway, Cave Junction, OR 97523, or phone (541) 592-2100 or fax (541) 592-3981.

DEPARTMENT OF NATURAL RESOURCES

The Department of Natural Resources manages about five million acres of public land in Washington. All of it is managed under the concept of "multiple use," designed to provide the greatest recreational opportunities while still protecting natural resources.

The campgrounds in these areas are among the most primitive, remote and least known of the camps listed in this book. The campsites are usually free and you are asked to remove all litter and trash from the area, leaving only your footprints behind.

In addition to maps of the area it manages, the Department of Natural Resources also has U.S. Geological Survey maps and U.S. Army Corps of Engineer maps. For information, write or phone:

Department of Natural Resources, Photo and Map Sales, P.O. Box 47031, Olympia, WA 98504-7031; (360) 902-1234 or (360) 902-1000 or (800) 527-3305.

BUREAU OF LAND MANAGEMENT

Oregon/Washington State Office: Write to P.O. Box 2965, Portland, OR 97208, or phone (503) 952-6002 or fax (503) 952-6308.

Burns District: Write to HC74-12533 Highway 20 West, Hines, OR 97738, or phone (541) 573-4400 or fax (541) 573-4411.

Coos Bay District: Write to 1300 Airport Lane, North Bend, OR 97459-2000, or phone (541) 756-0100 or fax (541) 756-9303.

Eugene District: Write to P.O. Box 10226, Eugene, OR 97440, or phone (541) 683-6600 or fax (541) 683-6981.

Lakeview District: Write to 1000 South Ninth Street, Lakeview, OR 97630, or phone (541) 947-2177 or fax (541) 947-2143.

Medford District: Write to 3040 Biddle Road, Medford, OR 97501, or phone (541) 770-2200 or fax (541) 770-2400.

Prineville District: Write to 185 East Fourth Street, Prineville, OR 97754, or phone (541) 447- 4115 or fax (541) 416-6700.

Roseburg District: Write to 777 NW Garden Valley Boulevard, Roseburg, OR 97470, or phone (541) 440-4930 or fax (541) 440-4948.

Salem District: Write to 1717 Fabry Road SW, Salem, OR 97306, or phone (503) 375-5646 or fax (503) 375-5622.

Vale District: Write to 100 Oregon Street, Vale, OR 97918, or phone (541) 473-3144 or fax (541) 473-6213.

Washington Campgrounds

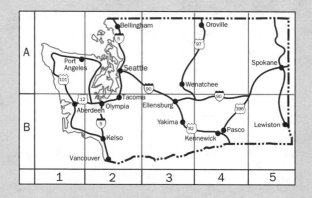

Map A1

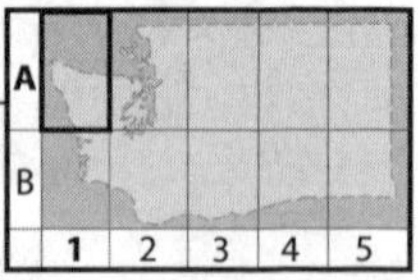

One inch equals approximately 20 miles.

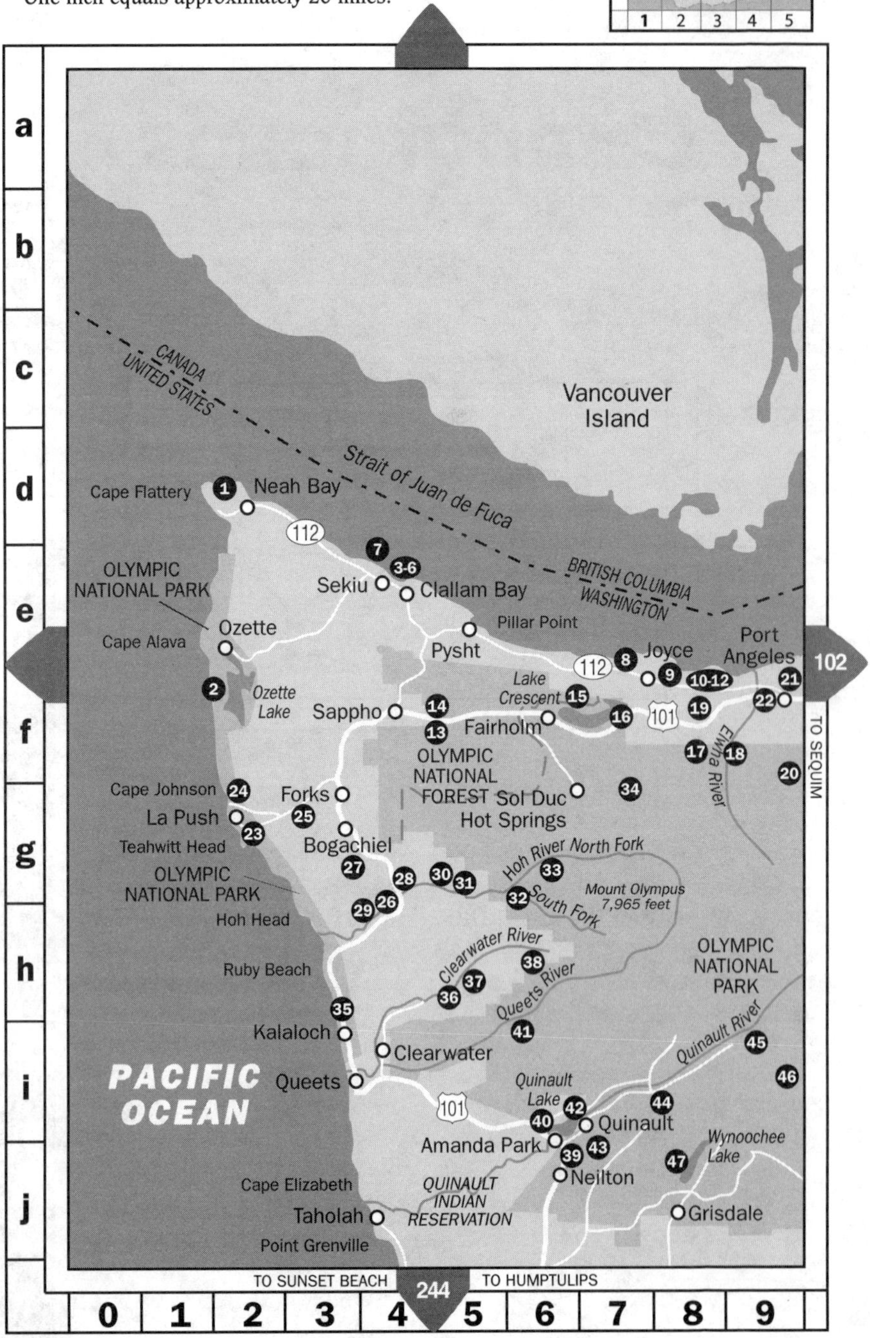

A
B
1 2 3 4 5

a

b

c

CANADA
UNITED STATES

Vancouver
Island

Strait of Juan de Fuca

d

Cape Flattery **1** Neah Bay

112

7

3-6

OLYMPIC
NATIONAL PARK

Sekiu Clallam Bay

BRITISH COLUMBIA
WASHINGTON

e

Cape Alava

Ozette

Pillar Point

Port
Angeles

102

Pysht

8 Joyce
9 **10-12**

112

21

2

Ozette
Lake

Sappho

14

Lake
Crescent **15**

101 **19**

22

TO SEQUIM

13 Fairholm

16

f

OLYMPIC
NATIONAL
FOREST Sol Duc
Hot Springs

17 **18**

Elwha River

20

Cape Johnson **24** Forks

34

La Push **23**

25

Teahwitt Head

Hoh River North Fork

g

OLYMPIC
NATIONAL PARK

Bogachiel

27

28 **30** **31**

33

Mount Olympus
7,965 feet

Hoh Head

29 **26**

32 South Fork

Ruby Beach

Clearwater River

OLYMPIC
NATIONAL
PARK

h

38

37

Queets River

36

Quinault River

35

41

45

Kalaloch

PACIFIC Queets

Clearwater

Quinault
Lake

46

i

OCEAN

101

42 **44**

40

Quinault

Wynoochee
Lake

Amanda Park

39 **43**

47

Cape Elizabeth

Neilton

j

Taholah

*QUINAULT
INDIAN
RESERVATION*

Grisdale

Point Grenville

TO SUNSET BEACH 244 TO HUMPTULIPS

0 1 2 3 4 5 6 7 8 9

Chapter A1 features:

---

❶ Tyee Motel and RV Park

Location: In Neah Bay; map A1, grid d2.

Campsites, facilities: There are 20 pull-through sites for trailers or RVs of any length. Electricity, piped water, and sewer hookups are provided. Bottled gas, sanitary services, toilets, a laundry room, and ice are available. A store and a cafe are located within one mile. Showers are available for an extra fee. Boat docks, launching facilities, and rentals are located across the street from the campground. Leashed pets and motorbikes are permitted.

Reservations, fees: Reservations are accepted. Sites are $15 per night. The campground is open year-round.

Contact: Phone the park at (360) 645-2223 or write to P.O. Box 193, Neah Bay, WA 98357.

Directions: From Interstate 5 at Olympia, north on U.S. 101 and drive 127 miles (five miles past the town of Port Angeles). Turn west on Highway 112 and drive 63 miles to the town of Neah Bay. The campground is located just off the highway in the middle of town.

Trip notes: For RVs and trailers only, this private, developed campground is located near the northwestern tip of the Olympic Peninsula. It's a fairly plain-looking park, with two long strips of spaces, but a few sites have ocean views. Fishing is excellent in this area. Recreation options include the world-renowned Makah Museum, which details the history of the Makah Indian tribe, and the half-mile hike to Cape Flattery, the northwestern tip of North America. Cape Flattery offers many hiking trails and opportunities for viewing whales, seals, and walrus. Nearby Makah Bay has a beautiful beach and is a popular spot for surfing.

❷ Ozette

Location: On Lake Ozette in Olympic National Park; map A1, grid f2.

Campsites, facilities: There are 14 sites for tents or RVs up to 21 feet long. Piped water, picnic tables, vault toilets, and fire grills are available. Leashed pets are permitted.

Reservations, fees: No reservations are accepted. There is no fee. The campground is open year-round.

Contact: Olympic National Park, 600 East Park Avenue, Port Angeles, WA 98362; (360) 452-4501 or fax (360) 452-0335.

Directions: From Interstate 5 at Olympia, turn north on U.S. 101 and drive 127 miles (five miles past the town of Port Angeles). Turn west on Highway 112 and drive to the town of Ozette. Turn on Hoko-Ozette Road and drive about 21 miles to the ranger station. The camp parking lot is a short distance on the right.

Trip notes: Very few people visit this site, set on the shore of Lake Ozette just a few miles from the Pacific Ocean. This is a boater's delight. The camp is remote and private with an isolated, mysterious feel to it.

❸ Van Ripers' Resort Hotel

Location: On Clallam Bay in Sekiu; map A1, grid e4.

Campsites, facilities: There are 150 sites with full or partial hookups for tents or RVs of any length; 60 are drive-through sites. Electricity, piped water, and picnic tables are provided. Sanitary services, toilets, showers, and ice are available. A store, a cafe, and laundry facilities are located within one mile. Firewood is available for an extra fee. Boat docks, launching facilities, and rentals are available in spring and summer. Leashed pets and motorbikes are permitted.

Reservations, fees: No reservations are accepted. Sites are $11–$16 per night. The campground is open from April to late September.

Contact: Phone the park at (360) 963-2334 or write to P.O. Box 246, Sekiu, WA 98381.

Directions: From Interstate 5 at Olympia, turn north on U.S. 101 and drive 127 miles (five miles past the town of Port Angeles). Turn west on Highway 112 and drive 53 miles to Sekiu. The campground is located off Highway 112, at the north end of Front Street.

Trip notes: Part of this campground is on the waterfront and the other part is on a hill overlooking the Strait of Juan de Fuca. The sites are graveled, many with ocean views. Hiking, fishing, and boating are among your options here, with salmon fishing being the principal draw. The beaches in the area are a mixture of sand and gravel, and rockhounding for agates and fossils is popular.

❹ Sam's Trailer and RV Park

Location: On Clallam Bay; map A1, grid e4.

Campsites, facilities: There are 10 tent sites and 20 sites for trailers or RVs of any length; 10 are drive-through sites. Electricity, piped water, sewer hookups, and picnic tables are provided. Sanitary services, toilets, showers, cable TV, and laundry facilities are available. Bottled gas, a store, a cafe, and ice are located within one mile. Boat docks, launching facilities, and rentals are located within two miles. Leashed pets and motorbikes are permitted

Reservations, fees: Reservations are accepted. Sites are $10–$15 per night. The campground is open year-round.

Contact: Phone the park at (360) 963-2402 or write to P.O. Box 45, Clallam Bay, WA 98326.

Directions: From Interstate 5 at Olympia, turn north on U.S. 101 and drive 127 miles (five miles past the town of Port Angeles). Turn west on Highway 112 and drive 43 miles to the town of Clallam Bay. The campground is on the right just as you come into town.

Trip notes: This is an alternative to Van Ripers' Resort Hotel, Olson's Resort, Surfside Resort, and Coho Resort and Trailer Park on Clallam Bay (see campground numbers 3, 5, 6, and 7). It's a family-oriented park, with grassy sites and many recreation options nearby. Beaches and shopping are within walking distance. Those wanting to visit Cape Flattery, Hoh Rain

Forest, or Port Angeles will find this a good central location.

⑤ Olson's Resort

Location: In Sekiu; map A1, grid e4.

Campsites, facilities: There are 30 tent sites and 100 sites for trailers or RVs of any length, 45 with full hookups and 10 with electric only. Picnic tables, piped water, sanitary services, toilets, showers, a laundry room, a store, and ice are available. A cafe, boat docks, launching facilities, and boat rentals are located within one mile. Leashed pets and motorbikes are permitted.

Reservations, fees: No reservations are accepted. Sites are $10–$14 per night. The campground is open year-round.

Contact: Phone the park at (360) 963-2311 or write to P.O. Box 216, Sekiu, WA 98381.

Directions: From Interstate 5 at Olympia, turn north on U.S. 101 and drive 127 miles (five miles past the town of Port Angeles). Turn west on Highway 112 and drive 53 miles to Sekiu. The campground is located off Highway 112, at the north end of Front Street.

Trip notes: This full-service camp is large and private. The marina nearby is salmon fishing headquarters. In fact, the resort caters to anglers, offering all-day salmon fishing trips and boat moorage. Chartered trips can be arranged by reservation. A tackle shop, cabins, and a motel are also available. See the trip notes for Van Ripers' (campground number 3) for details on the Sekiu area.

⑥ Surfside Resort

Location: In Sekiu; map A1, grid e4.

Campsites, facilities: There are 10 tent sites and 10 drive-through sites for trailers or RVs of any length. Electricity, piped water, sewer hookups, and picnic tables are provided. Sanitary services, cable TV, toilets, and showers are available. Bottled gas, a store, a cafe, a Laundromat, and ice are located within one mile. Boat docks, launching facilities, and rentals are located within two miles. Leashed pets and motorbikes are permitted.

Reservations, fees: Reservations are accepted. Sites are $10–$15 per night. The campground is open from May through September.

Contact: Surfside Resort, P.O. Box 39, Sekiu, WA 98381; (360) 963-2723.

Directions: From Interstate 5 at Olympia, turn north on U.S. 101 and drive 127 miles (five miles past the town of Port Angeles). Turn west on Highway 112 and drive 43 miles to the town of Clallam Bay. Continue about one mile west; the campground is located halfway between the towns of Sekiu and Clallam Bay.

Trip notes: This park is smaller, less crowded, and more secluded than many in the area. Campers can enjoy the park's private beach and panoramic views of the Strait of Juan de Fuca and Vancouver Island to the north. Nearby recreation options include marked hiking and bike trails, beachcombing, a full-service marina, and the finest fishing for miles.

⑦ Coho Resort and Trailer Park

Location: Near Sekiu; map A1, grid e4.

Campsites, facilities: There are 200 sites for tents, trailers, or RVs of any length. Electricity, piped water, sewer hookups, and cable TV are provided. Sanitary services, toilets, coin-operated showers, a cafe, laundry facilities, and ice are available. Bottled gas and a store are located within one mile. Boat docks, launching facilities, and rentals are available. Leashed pets and motorbikes are permitted.

Reservations, fees: No reservations are accepted. Sites are $12–$16 per night. The campground is open from April through September.

Contact: Coho Resort and Trailer Park, 15572 Highway 112, Sekiu, WA 98381; (360) 963-2333.

Directions: From Interstate 5 at Olympia, turn north on U.S. 101 and drive 127 miles (five miles past the town of Port Angeles). Turn west on Highway 112 and drive 44 miles. The campground is located about three-quarters of a mile east of Sekiu between mileposts 15 and 16.

Trip notes: This is one of several camps in the immediate area. A full-service marina nearby provides boating access. See the trip notes for Van Ripers' Resort Hotel, Olson's Resort, and Surfside Resort (campground numbers 3, 5, and 6) for information on the area.

❽ Whiskey Creek Beach

Location: On the Strait of Juan de Fuca; map A1, grid e7.

Campsites, facilities: There are 60 tent sites and 11 sites for trailers or RVs of any length, plus five cabins on the beach. Piped water and picnic tables are provided. Sanitary services and some sewer hookups are available. Launching facilities for small boats are on site. Leashed pets are permitted.

Reservations, fees: Reservations are accepted. Sites are $10 per night; cabins are $60 per night. The campground is open from May to late October.

Contact: Whiskey Creek Beach, P.O. Box 130, Joyce, WA 98343; (360) 928-3489 or fax (360) 928-3218.

Directions: From Interstate 5 at Olympia, turn north on U.S. 101 and drive 127 miles (five miles past the town of Port Angeles). Turn west on Highway 112 and drive 13 miles west. Turn north on Whiskey Creek Beach Road and continue 1.5 miles to the campground.

Trip notes: Located on the beach along the Strait of Juan de Fuca, this campground covers 400 acres and is popular with rockhounders. The setting is rustic, with one mile of beach access and five miles of hiking trails nearby. Five miles away is Olympic National Park, which offers numerous recreation possibilities. This camp is a good option if the national park camps are full.

❾ Carol's Crescent Beach

Location: On the Strait of Juan de Fuca; map A1, grid e8.

Campsites, facilities: There are 60 sites for tents, trailers, or RVs with full or partial hook-ups. Rest rooms, showers, a pay phone, a recreation field, and a laundry room are available. Leashed pets are permitted.

Reservations, fees: Reservations are recommended. Sites are $15–$25 per night. The campground is open year-round.

Contact: Carol's Crescent Beach, 2860 Crescent Beach Road, Port Angeles, WA 98362; (360) 928-3344.

Directions: From Interstate 5 at Olympia, go north on U.S. 101 and drive 127 miles (five miles past the town of Port Angeles). Turn west on Highway 112 and drive 10 miles to Camp Hayden Road (between mileposts 53 and 54). Drive northwest on Camp Hayden Road for four miles. The campground is located on the left, on the beach.

Trip notes: Set on a half-mile stretch of sandy beach, this campground makes a perfect weekend spot. Popular activities include swimming, fishing, and beachcombing. Numerous attractions and recreation options are available in Port Angeles.

❿ Lyre River

Location: On the Lyre River; map A1, grid e8.

Campsites, facilities: There are 11 primitive tent sites. Picnic tables, fire grills, tent pads, vault toilets, and piped water are provided. A roofed group shelter with a fireplace is available. Leashed pets are permitted.

Reservations, fees: No reservations are accepted. There is no fee. The campground is open year-round.

Contact: Department of Natural Resources, Olympic Region, 411 Tillicum Lane, Forks, WA 98331-9797; (360) 374-6131 or fax (360) 374-5446.

Directions: From Interstate 5 at Olympia, turn north on U.S. 101 and drive 127 miles (five miles past the town of Port Angeles). Turn west on Highway 112 and drive to milepost 46. Look to the right for a paved road between mileposts 46 and 47, then turn north and drive a half mile. The camp is on the left.

Trip notes: This prime spot is one of the rare free campgrounds on the Olympic Peninsula. Though quite primitive, it does offer piped water and an even more precious commodity in these parts—privacy. The camp is set along the Lyre River and is just a short distance from the ocean.

⑪ Lyre River RV Park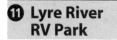

Location: Near the Lyre River; map A1, grid e8.

Campsites, facilities: There are 60 sites for tents, trailers, or RVs of any length; 30 are drive-through sites. Electricity, piped water, sewer hookups, and picnic tables are provided. Bottled gas, sanitary services, toilets, a store, laundry facilities, and ice are available. Showers and firewood are available for an extra fee. Leashed pets and motorbikes are permitted.

Reservations, fees: Reservations are accepted. Sites are $14–$25 per night. Group reservations are welcome with an advance deposit. The campground is open year-round.

Contact: Lyre River RV Park, 596 West Lyre River Road, Port Angeles, WA 98362; (360) 928-3436.

Directions: From Interstate 5 at Olympia, turn north on U.S. 101 and drive 127 miles (five miles past the town of Port Angeles). Turn west on Highway 112 and drive 15 miles. Turn right on West Lyre River Road and drive a half mile to the park.

Trip notes: This beautiful 80-acre camp is in a wooded area tucked between the Strait of Juan de Fuca and the Lyre River. Freshwater and saltwater beaches are available, giving the park a unique flavor. Kids can give their rods a try in the pond stocked with trout, while adult anglers can head for excellent fishing in the Lyre River and the strait. Tubing down the river is popular here, and bike and hiking trails are available nearby.

⑫ Salt Creek Recreation Area

Location: Near the Strait of Juan de Fuca; map A1, grid e8.

Campsites, facilities: There are 92 sites for tents, trailers, or RVs of any length. Picnic tables are provided. Sanitary services, toilets, showers, and a playground are available. Firewood is available for an extra fee. Leashed pets are permitted.

Reservations, fees: No reservations are accepted. Sites are $8–$10 per night. The campground is open year-round.

Contact: Salt Creek Recreation Area, 3506 Camp Hayden Road, Port Angeles, WA 98362; (360) 928-3441.

Directions: From Interstate 5 at Olympia, turn north on U.S. 101 and drive 127 miles (five miles past the town of Port Angeles). Turn west Highway 112 and drive six miles to Camp Hayden Road. Turn north and drive three miles to the campground.

Trip notes: Recreation options at this 192-acre park overlooking the Strait of Juan de Fuca include nearby hiking trails, swimming, fishing, horseshoes, and field sports. It's a good layover spot if you're planning to take the ferry out of Port Angeles to Victoria, British Columbia.

⑬ Bear Creek Motel and RV Park

Location: On Bear Creek; map A1, grid f5.

Campsites, facilities: There are eight tent sites and 20 drive-through sites for trailers or RVs of any length. Electricity, piped water, sewer hookups, and picnic tables are provided. Sanitary services, toilets, showers, a cafe, a laundry room, and firewood are available. Boat launching facilities are located within a half mile. Leashed pets are permitted.

Reservations, fees: No reservations are accepted. Sites are $15 per night. The campground is open year-round.

Contact: Bear Creek Motel and RV Park, P.O. Box 236, Beaver, WA 98305; (360) 327-3660.

Directions: From Interstate 5 at Olympia, turn north on U.S. 101 and drive about 163 miles north and west to the campground (located 15 miles northeast of Forks at milepost 205).

Trip notes: This quiet little spot is set where Bear Creek empties into the Soleduck River. It's private and developed, with a choice of sunny or shaded sites in a wooded setting. There are many recreation options in the area, including fishing, hunting, and nature and hiking trails leading to the ocean. Soleduck Hot Springs is 25 miles north and well worth the trip. A restaurant next to the camp serves family-style meals.

⑭ Klahowya

Location: On the Soleduck River in Olympic National Forest; map A1, grid f5.

Campsites, facilities: There are 25 tent sites and 30 sites for trailers or RVs up to 30 feet long. Picnic tables are provided. Piped water, vault and flush toilets, and wheelchair-accessible rest rooms are available. A boat ramp is nearby. Leashed pets are permitted.

Reservations, fees: No reservations are accepted. Sites are $7–$10 per night. The campground is open May to mid-October with full service. Limited service is available in the off-season.

Contact: Olympic National Forest, Soleduck Ranger District, Star Route 1, P.O. Box 5750, Forks, WA 98331; (360) 374-6522 or fax (360) 374-1250.

Directions: From Interstate 5 at Olympia, turn north on U.S. 101 and drive approximately 158 miles north and west to the campground, located 20 miles northeast of Forks.

Trip notes: Klahowya is a good choice if you don't want to venture far from U.S. 101, yet want to retain the feel of Olympic National Forest. Set along the headwaters of the Soleduck River, this 32-acre camp is pretty and wooded, with hiking trails in the area. Due to its close proximity to the highway, this is an extremely popular camp and fills up quickly in the summer.

⑮ Fairholm

Location: On Lake Crescent in Olympic National Park; map A1, grid f6.

Campsites, facilities: There are 87 sites for tents, trailers, or RVs up to 21 feet long. Picnic tables and fire grills are provided. A sanitary disposal station, rest rooms, drinking water, and wheelchair-accessible facilities are available. A store and a cafe are within one mile. Boat launching facilities are nearby on Lake Crescent. Leashed pets are permitted.

Reservations, fees: No reservations are accepted. Sites are $10 per night. The campground is open year-round, weather permitting.

Contact: Olympic National Park, 600 East Park Avenue, Port Angeles, WA 98362; (360) 452-4501 or fax (360) 452-0335.

Directions: From Interstate 5 at Olympia, turn north on U.S. 101 and drive approximately 122 miles to Port Angeles. Continue 26 miles west on U.S. 101, then turn right and drive one mile to the camp on North Shore Road.

Trip notes: This camp is set on the shore of Lake Crescent, a pretty lake situated within the boundary of Olympic National Park. It's less than a mile off U.S. 101 and gets heavy use during tourist months. A naturalist program is available in the summer. The elevation is 580 feet.

⑯ Log Cabin Resort

Location: On Lake Crescent in Olympic National Park; map A1, grid f7.

Campsites, facilities: There are 40 sites for trailers or RVs of any length. Electricity, piped water, sewer hookups, and picnic tables are provided. Sanitary services, toilets, a store, a cafe, laundry facilities, ice, and a playground are available. Showers and firewood are also available for an extra fee. Boat docks, launching facilities, and rentals are located in the campground at Lake Crescent. Leashed pets are permitted at specified sites.

Reservations, fees: Reservations are accepted. Sites are $27 per night. The campground is open from February 14 through December 24.

Contact: Log Cabin Resort, 3183 East Beach Road, Port Angeles, WA 98362; (360) 928-3325 or fax (360) 928-2088.

Directions: From Interstate 5 at Olympia, turn north on U.S. 101 and drive 122 miles to Port Angeles. Continue 18 miles northwest on U.S. 101, then turn right on East Beach

Road and drive three miles to the camp at Log Cabin Resort.

Trip notes: This pretty camp along the shore of Lake Crescent is a good spot for boaters, with many sites near the water with excellent views. Fishing and swimming are two options at this family oriented resort. A marked hiking trail traces the lake's shoreline.

⑰ Altaire

Location: On the Elwha River in Olympic National Park; map A1, grid f8.

Campsites, facilities: There are 30 sites for tents, trailers, or RVs up to 21 feet long. Picnic tables and fire grills are provided. Rest rooms and drinking water are available. Some facilities are wheelchair accessible. Leashed pets are permitted.

Reservations, fees: No reservations are accepted. Sites are $10 per night. The campground is open from June to September.

Contact: Olympic National Park, 600 East Park Avenue, Port Angeles, WA 98362; (360) 452-4501 or fax (360) 452-0335.

Directions: From Interstate 5 at Olympia, turn north on U.S. 101 and drive approximately 122 miles to Port Angeles. Continue nine miles west on U.S. 101, then turn left at the signed entrance road and drive four miles south along the Elwha River.

Trip notes: This camp set on the Elwha River about a mile from Lake Mills is a pretty and well-treed spot with easy highway access. It's a nice layover spot for a one-nighter before taking the ferry boat at Port Angeles to Victoria, British Columbia.

⑱ Elwha

Location: On the Elwha River in Olympic National Park; map A1, grid f8.

Campsites, facilities: There are 41 sites for tents, trailers, or RVs up to 21 feet long. Picnic tables and fire grills are provided. Rest rooms and drinking water are available. Some facilities are wheelchair accessible. Leashed pets are permitted.

Reservations, fees: No reservations are ac-

cepted. Sites are $10 per night. The campground is open year-round.

Contact: Olympic National Park, 600 East Park Avenue, Port Angeles, WA 98362; (360) 452-4501 or fax (360) 452-0335.

Directions: From Interstate 5 at Olympia, turn north on U.S. 101 and drive approximately 122 miles to Port Angeles. Continue nine miles west on U.S. 101, then turn right at the signed entrance road and drive three miles south along the Elwha River.

Trip notes: The Elwha River is the backdrop for this popular shorefront camp, with excellent hiking trails close by in Olympic National Park; check at one of the visitor centers for maps and backcountry information. Also see the trip notes for neighboring Altaire (campground number 18) for more information.

⑲ Elwha Resort and Campground

Location: On the Elwha River; map A1, grid f8.

Campsites, facilities: There are nine tent sites and four sites for trailers or RVs up to 32 feet long. Electricity, piped water, sewer hookups, and picnic tables are provided. Bottled gas, toilets, a store, a cafe, ice, and a playground are available. Sanitary services and laundry facilities are located within 10 miles. Showers and firewood are available for an extra fee. Boat docks and launching facilities are located eight miles away at the Elwha River. Pets and motorbikes are permitted.

Reservations, fees: Reservations are accepted. Sites are $8–$15 per night. The campground is open year-round.

Contact: Phone the park at (360) 457-7011 or write to 239521 Highway 101 West, Port Angeles, WA 98362.

Directions: From Interstate 5 at Olympia, turn north on U.S. 101 and drive 130 miles (eight miles past the town of Port Angeles) to the park at 239521 Highway 101 West.

Trip notes: Located at sea level next to the Elwha River, this small, private campground offers more seclusion than nearby camps. It has spacious, wooded sites in a pretty setting. Nearby recreation options include marked hiking trails, Lake Adwell, and Olympic National Park.

⑳ Heart o' the Hills

Location: In Olympic National Park; map A1, grid f9.

Campsites, facilities: There are 105 sites for tents, trailers, or RVs up to 21 feet long. Picnic tables are provided. Rest rooms, drinking water, and wheelchair-accessible facilities are available. Leashed pets are permitted.

Reservations, fees: No reservations are accepted. Sites are $10 per night. The campground is open year-round, weather permitting. (Access roads can be impassable in severe weather.)

Contact: Olympic National Park, 600 East Park Avenue, Port Angeles, WA 98362; (360) 452-4501 or fax (360) 452-0335.

Directions: From Interstate 5 at Olympia, turn north on U.S. 101 and drive approximately 122 miles to Port Angeles. Drive five miles south on Hurricane Ridge Road to the camp on the left.

Trip notes: Heart o' the Hills is nestled on the northern edge of Olympic National Park. You can drive deeper into the interior of the park on Hurricane Ridge Road and take one of numerous hiking trails. This camp is set at 1,807 feet. Evening naturalist programs are available in the summer.

㉑ Peabody Creek RV Park

Location: In Port Angeles; map A1, grid f9.

Campsites, facilities: There are 36 sites for trailers or RVs of any length. Electricity, piped water, and sewer hookups are provided. Bottled gas, sanitary services, toilets, ice, and laundry facilities are available. A store and a cafe are within one block. Showers are available for an extra fee. Boat docks, launching facilities, and rentals are located within 1.5 miles. Leashed pets are permitted.

Reservations, fees: Reservations are ac-

cepted. Sites are $19 per night. The campground is open year-round.

Contact: Phone the park at (800) 392-2361 or (360) 457-7092, or write to 127 South Lincoln, Port Angeles, WA 98362.

Directions: From Interstate 5 at Olympia, turn north on U.S. 101 and drive 122 miles to Port Angeles. Turn east at the intersection of Lincoln and Second Streets and drive 75 feet on Lincoln Street to the park.

Trip notes: This three-acre RV park is right in the middle of town but offers a wooded, streamside setting. Nearby recreation options include salmon fishing, an 18-hole golf course, marked biking trails, a full-service marina, and tennis courts. The park is within walking distance of shopping and ferry services.

㉒ Welcome Inn Trailer and RV Park

Location: Near Port Angeles; map A1, grid f9.

Campsites, facilities: There are 100 sites for tents, trailers, or RVs of any length. Electricity, piped water, sewer hookups, dump stations, and picnic tables are provided. Bottled gas, sanitary services, toilets, and laundry facilities are available. A store, a cafe, and ice are within one mile. Showers are available for an extra fee. Boat docks and launching facilities are located within one mile. Pets and motorbikes are permitted.

Reservations, fees: Reservations are accepted. Sites are $12–$18 per night. The campground is open year-round.

Contact: Phone the park at (360) 457-1553 or write to 1215 Highway 101 West, Port Angeles, WA 98363.

Directions: From Interstate 5 at Olympia, turn north on U.S. 101 and drive 122 miles to Port Angeles. Drive another 1.5 miles west on U.S. 101 to the park.

Trip notes: Welcome Inn is a privately developed campground for RVs and tent campers on an eight-acre site in the woods. Nearby recreation options include an 18-hole golf course, marked hiking trails, a full-service marina, and tennis courts. The park caters to tourists, offering arrangements for fishing charters and Victoria, British Columbia tours.

㉓ Mora

Location: Near the Pacific Ocean in Olympic National Park; map A1, grid g2.

Campsites, facilities: There are 94 sites for tents or RVs up to 21 feet long. Picnic tables and fire grills are provided. Drinking water, a sanitary disposal station, rest rooms, and wheelchair-accessible facilities are available. Leashed pets are permitted.

Reservations, fees: No reservations are accepted. Sites are $10 per night. The campground is open year-round..

Contact: Olympic National Park, 600 East Park Avenue, Port Angeles, WA 98362; (360) 452-4501 or fax (360) 452-0335.

Directions: From Interstate 5 at Olympia, turn north on U.S. 101 and drive approximately 175 miles to La Push Highway (two miles north of Forks). Turn west and drive 12 miles to the campground, making sure to follow the Mora Campground signs.

Trip notes: This is a good out-of-the-way choice near the Pacific Ocean and the Olympic Coast Marine Sanctuary at an elevation of 50 feet. The Soleduck River feeds into the ocean near here. A naturalist program is available during the summer.

㉔ Shoreline Resort and Ocean Park

Location: On the Pacific Ocean; map A1, grid g2.

Campsites, facilities: There are 62 drive-through sites for trailers or RVs of any length. Electricity, piped water, and sewer hookups are provided. Bottled gas, sanitary services, toilets, a store, and laundry facilities are available. A cafe and ice are located within one mile. Showers are available for an extra fee. Boat docks and launching facilities are located within one mile. Pets are permitted.

Reservations, fees: No reservations are ac-

cepted. Sites are $15 per night. The campground is open year-round.

Contact: Phone the park at (360) 374-6488 or write to P.O. Box 26, La Push, WA 98350.

Directions: From Interstate 5 at Olympia, turn north on U.S. 101 and drive approximately 178 miles to Forks. Turn west on La Push Road and drive 14 miles to the campground on the left.

Trip notes: This private, developed park is set along the Pacific Ocean and the coastal Dungeness National Wildlife Refuge. It offers such recreation options as fishing, beachcombing, boating, whale watching, and sunbathing.

㉕ Three Rivers Resort

Location: On the Soleduck River; map A1, grid g3.

Campsites, facilities: There are 11 sites for tents, trailers, or RVs of any length, 10 with full or partial hookups, plus five rental cabins. Picnic tables are provided. Bottled gas, toilets, a store, a cafe, laundry facilities, and ice are available. Electricity, piped water, sewer hookups, showers, and firewood are available for an extra fee. Leashed pets are permitted.

Reservations, fees: Reservations are accepted. Sites are $8–$12 per night; cabins are $35–$60 per night. The campground is open year-round.

Contact: Phone the park at (360) 374-5300 or write to 7764 La Push Road, Forks, WA 98331.

Directions: From Interstate 5 at Olympia, turn north on U.S. 101 and drive approximately 178 miles, almost to Forks. Turn west on La Push Road and drive nine miles to the campground.

Trip notes: This small, private camp set on the Soleduck River is pretty, with wooded, spacious sites. Beachcombing, hiking, and fishing are options here. The coastal Dungeness National Wildlife Refuge and Pacific Ocean are a short drive to the west. Hoh Rain Forest, a worthwhile side trip, is about 45 minutes away.

㉖ Hoh River Resort

Location: On the Hoh River; map A1, grid g4.

Campsites, facilities: There are 23 sites for tents, trailers, or RVs of any length. Electricity, piped water, sewer hookups, and picnic tables are provided. Flush toilets, a store, laundry facilities, and ice are available. Showers and firewood are available for an extra fee. Leashed pets and motorbikes are permitted.

Reservations, fees: Reservations are accepted. Sites are $10–$15 per night. The campground is open year-round.

Contact: Phone the park at (360) 374-5566 or write to 175443 Highway 101 South, Forks, WA 98331.

Directions: From Interstate 5 at Olympia, turn north on U.S. 101 and drive 178 miles to Forks. Continue 15 miles on U.S. 101 to the campground.

Trip notes: This is a nice camp along U.S. 101 with a choice of grassy or graveled shady sites. Marked hiking trails are in the area. It's a pleasant little park, with steelhead and salmon fishing available and elk hunting in season. Horseshoe pits and a recreation field are provided for campers.

㉗ Bogachiel State Park

Location: On the Bogachiel River; map A1, grid g4.

Campsites, facilities: There are two primitive tent sites, 34 developed tent sites, and six hookup sites for trailers or RVs up to 35 feet long. Picnic tables and fire grills are provided. A sanitary disposal station, rest rooms, coin-operated showers, and drinking water are available. A store and ice are located within one mile. A boat ramp is nearby. Leashed pets are permitted.

Reservations, fees: No reservations are accepted. Sites are $10–$15 per night. The campground is open year-round.

Contact: Washington State Parks Information Center, HC 80, P.O. Box 500, Forks, WA 98331; (800) 233-0321 or (360) 374-6356.

Directions: From Interstate 5 at Olympia, turn north on U.S. 101 and drive approximately 169 miles to the park on the left. It's located about six miles south of Forks.

Trip notes: This is a good base camp for salmon or steelhead fishing trips. The 119-acre park is set on the Bogachiel River, with marked hiking trails in the area. It can be noisy at times; there is a logging mill located directly across the river from the campground. Hunting is popular in the adjacent national forest.

㉘ Hoh Oxbow

Location: On the Hoh River; map A1, grid g4.

Campsites, facilities: There are seven sites for tents or small trailers. Picnic tables, fire grills, and tent pads are provided. Vault toilets and a hand boat launch are available, but there is no piped water. One site is wheelchair accessible. Firearms are prohibited. Leashed pets are permitted.

Reservations, fees: No reservations are accepted. There is no fee. The campground is open year-round.

Contact: Department of Natural Resources, Olympic Region, 411 Tillicum Lane, Forks, WA 98331-9797; (360) 374-6131 or fax (360) 374-5446.

Directions: From Interstate 5 at Olympia, turn north on U.S. 101 and drive approximately 175 miles to the campground between mileposts 176 and 177. The camp is east of the highway next to the river.

Trip notes: This is the most popular of the five camps on the Hoh River. It's primitive and close to the highway and the price is right. The adjacent boat launch makes this the camp of choice for anglers.

㉙ Cottonwood

Location: On the Hoh River; map A1, grid g4.

Campsites, facilities: There are nine sites for tents or small trailers. Picnic tables, fire grills, and tent pads are provided. Vault toilets, piped water, and a boat launch are available. Leashed pets are permitted.

Reservations, fees: No reservations are

accepted. There is no fee. The campground is open year-round.

Contact: Department of Natural Resources, Olympic Region, 411 Tillicum Lane, Forks, WA 98331-9797; (360) 374-6131 or fax (360) 374-5446.

Directions: From Interstate 5 at Olympia, turn north on U.S. 101 and drive approximately 175 miles to Oil City Road (between mileposts 177 and 178). Turn west and drive 2.3 miles. Turn left on Road H4060 (gravel) and drive one mile to the camp.

Trip notes: An alternative to Hoh Oxbow, Willoughby Creek, and Minnie Peterson (campground numbers 28, 30, and 31), this primitive camp is also set along the Hoh River. Like Hoh Oxbow, Cottonwood offers the bonus of a boat launch. Its location some distance from the highway almost insures fewer people.

⑳ Willoughby Creek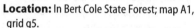

Location: In Bert Cole State Forest; map A1, grid g5.

Campsites, facilities: There are three campsites for tents or small trailers. Picnic tables, fire grills, and tent pads are provided. Vault toilets are available, but there is no piped water. Leashed pets are permitted.

Reservations, fees: No reservations are accepted. There is no fee. The campground is open year-round.

Contact: Department of Natural Resources, Olympic Region, 411 Tillicum Lane, Forks, WA 98331-9797; (360) 374-6131 or fax (360) 374-5446.

Directions: From Interstate 5 at Olympia, go north on U.S. 101 and drive approximately 175 miles to Hoh Rain Forest Road (between mileposts 178 and 179). Turn east and drive 3.5 miles to the camp on the right.

Trip notes: This little-known camp along Willoughby Creek and the Hoh River is tiny and rustic, with good fishing nearby. The area gets heavy rainfall. Other campground options in the vicinity are Hoh Oxbow, Cottonwood, and Minnie Peterson (campground numbers 28, 29, and 31).

㉛ Minnie Peterson

Location: On the Hoh River; map A1, grid g5.

Campsites, facilities: There are eight campsites for tents or small trailers. Picnic tables, fire grills, and tent pads are provided. Vault toilets and piped water are available. Firearms are prohibited. Leashed pets are permitted.

Reservations, fees: No reservations are accepted. There is no fee. The campground is open year-round.

Contact: Department of Natural Resources, Olympic Region, 411 Tillicum Lane, Forks, WA 98331-9797; (360) 374-6131 or fax (360) 374-5446.

Directions: From Interstate 5 at Olympia, turn north on U.S. 101 and drive approximately 175 miles to Hoh Rain Forest Road (between mileposts 178 and 179). Turn east and drive 4.5 miles to the camp on the left.

Trip notes: Not many folks know about this primitive camp, set on the Hoh River on the edge of the Hoh Rain Forest. It's quite pretty and forested, with nice riverside sites. Bring your rain gear.

㉜ South Fork Hoh

Location: In Bert Cole State Forest; map A1, grid g6.

Campsites, facilities: There are three campsites for tents or small trailers. Picnic tables, fire grills, and tent pads are provided. Vault toilets are available. There is no piped water, so bring your own. Leashed pets are permitted.

Reservations, fees: No reservations are accepted. There is no fee. The campground is open year-round.

Contact: Department of Natural Resources, Olympic Region, 411 Tillicum Lane, Forks, WA 98331-9797; (360) 374-6131 or fax (360) 374-5446.

Directions: From Interstate 5 at Olympia, turn north on U.S. 101 and drive approximately 175 miles. Turn east on Hoh Clearwater Mainline Road (milepost 176) and drive 6.5

miles. Turn left on Road H1000 and drive 7.5 miles to the camp on the right.

Trip notes: This rarely used camp set along the South Fork of the Hoh River is way out there. It's tiny and primitive but offers a guarantee of peace and quiet, something many U.S. 101 cruisers would cheerfully give a limb for after a few days of fighting crowds.

33 Hoh Rain Forest

Location: In Olympic National Park; map A1, grid g6.

Campsites, facilities: There are 89 sites for tents or RVs up to 21 feet long. Picnic tables and fire grills are provided. A sanitary disposal station, rest rooms, and drinking water are available. Facilities are wheelchair accessible. Leashed pets are permitted.

Reservations, fees: No reservations are accepted. Sites are $10 per night. The campground is open year-round.

Contact: Olympic National Park, 600 East Park Avenue, Port Angeles, WA 98362; (360) 452-4501 or fax (360) 452-0335.

Directions: From Interstate 5 at Olympia, turn north on U.S. 101 and drive approximately 178 miles to Forks. Continue 14 miles on U.S. 101, then 19 miles east along the Hoh River until you arrive at the campground.

Trip notes: This camp at a trailhead leading into the interior of Olympic National Park is located in the heart of a temperate, old growth rain forest. Hoh Oxbow, Cottonwood, Willoughby Creek, and Minnie Peterson are nearby (see campground numbers 28, 29, 30, and 31), set downstream on the Hoh River, outside national park boundaries. In the summer, there are evening naturalist programs, and there is a visitor center nearby. This is one of the most popular camps in the park.

34 Sol Duc

Location: On the Soleduck River in Olympic National Park; map A1, grid g7.

Campsites, facilities: There are 80 sites for tents or RVs up to 21 feet long. Picnic tables and fire grills are provided. A sanitary disposal station, rest rooms, drinking water, and wheelchair-accessible facilities are available. A store and a cafe are within one mile. Leashed pets are permitted.

Reservations, fees: No reservations are accepted. Sites are $10 per night. The campground is open from May to late October, with limited winter facilities.

Contact: Olympic National Park, 600 East Park Avenue, Port Angeles, WA 98362; (360) 452-4501 or fax (360) 452-0335.

Directions: From Interstate 5 at Olympia, turn north on U.S. 101 and drive approximately 122 miles to Port Angeles. Continue 27 miles on U.S. 101, then turn left at the Sol Duc turnoff and drive 12 miles to the camp.

Trip notes: This site is a nice hideaway, with Soleduck Hot Springs a highlight. The problem is that it's quite popular. The camp fills up quickly on weekends, and a fee is charged to use the hot springs, which have been fully developed since the early 1900s. The camp is set at 1,680 feet along the Soleduck River. A naturalist program is available in the summer months.

35 Kalaloch

Location: Near the Pacific Ocean in Olympic National Park; map A1, grid h3.

Campsites, facilities: There are 177 sites for tents or RVs up to 21 feet long. Picnic tables and fire grills are provided. Rest rooms, drinking water, wheelchair-accessible facilities, and a trailer sanitary station are available. A store and a restaurant are within one mile. Leashed pets are permitted in the campground.

Reservations, fees: No reservations are accepted. Sites are $10 per night. The campground is open year-round.

Contact: Olympic National Park, 600 East Park Avenue, Port Angeles, WA 98362; (360) 452-4501 or fax (360) 452-0335.

Directions: From Interstate 5 at Olympia, turn north on U.S. 101 and drive approximately 178 miles to Forks. Continue 25 miles on U.S. 101 to the campground.

Trip notes: This camp is located on a bluff above the beach, with some ocean-view sites. Like other camps set on the coast of the Olympic Peninsula, heavy rain in winter and spring is common, and it's often foggy in the summer. A naturalist program is offered in the summer months. There are several good hiking trails in the park; check out the visitor center for maps and information.

36 Coppermine Bottom

Location: On the Clearwater River; map A1, grid h5.

Campsites, facilities: There are nine campsites for tents or small trailers. Picnic tables, fire grills, and tent pads are provided. Vault toilets, a group shelter, and a hand boat launch are available. There is no piped water available. Leashed pets are permitted.

Reservations, fees: No reservations are accepted. There is no fee. The campground is open year-round.

Contact: Department of Natural Resources, Olympic Region, 411 Tillicum Lane, Forks, WA 98331-9797; (360) 374-6131 or fax (360) 374-5446.

Directions: From Interstate 5 at Olympia, turn north on U.S. 101 and drive approximately 150 miles to milepost 147, then turn north on Hoh Clearwater Mainline Road and drive 12.5 miles. Turn right on C-1010 (a graveled one-lane road) and drive 1.5 miles. The camp is on the left.

Trip notes: Few tourists ever visit this primitive, hidden campground with river dory launching facilities. It's set on the Clearwater River, a tributary of the Queets River, which runs to the ocean. The boat launch is a bonus, and makes this a perfect camp for anglers who want to avoid the usual U.S. 101 crowds.

37 Upper Clearwater

Location: On the Clearwater River; map A1, grid h5.

Campsites, facilities: There are nine sites for tents or small trailers. Picnic tables, fire grills, and tent pads are provided. Vault toilets, piped water, and a hand boat launch are available. Leashed pets are permitted.

Reservations, fees: No reservations are accepted. There is no fee. The campground is open year-round.

Contact: Department of Natural Resources, Olympic Region, 411 Tillicum Lane, Forks, WA 98331-9797; (360) 374-6131 or fax (360) 374-5446.

Directions: From Interstate 5 at Olympia, turn north on U.S. 101 and drive approximately 150 miles to milepost 147, then turn north on Hoh Clearwater Mainline Road. Drive 13 miles, then turn right on C-3000 (a gravel one-lane road) and drive 3.3 miles. The camp entrance is on the right.

Trip notes: Upper Clearwater is one of the three primitive camps set along the Clearwater River. It has river dory launching facilities. This is a great camp—it's pretty, unused by most tourists, has a boat ramp, piped water, and all other amenities, and, best of all, it's free.

38 Yahoo Lake

Location: In Bert Cole State Forest; map A1, grid h6.

Campsites, facilities: There are four tent sites at this primitive, hike-in camp. Pit toilets, a group shelter with a fireplace, and a boat dock are available. There is no piped water, so bring your own. Leashed pets are permitted.

Reservations, fees: No reservations are accepted. There is no fee. The campground is open year-round, weather permitting.

Contact: Department of Natural Resources, Olympic Region, 411 Tillicum Lane, Forks, WA 98331-9797; (360) 374-6131 or fax (360) 374-5446.

Directions: From Interstate 5 at Olympia, turn north on U.S. 101 and drive approximately 150 miles to milepost 147, then turn north on Hoh Clearwater Mainline Road. Drive 13 miles, then turn right on C-3000 (a graveled one-lane road) and drive four miles. Turn right on C-3100 (a graveled two-lane road), keep left, and continue on C-3100 another three-quarters of a mile to the trailhead. Hike in 500 feet to the camp.

Trip notes: This camp is located at about 2,000 feet on the edge of tiny Yahoo Lake in an idyllic setting that few people take advantage of. There are hiking trails in the area and fishing in the lake. If you're willing to take a little time to get here, this can be the camper's ideal getaway.

Willaby

Location: On Quinault Lake in Olympic National Forest; map A1, grid i6.

Campsites, facilities: There are 22 drive-in sites for tents, trailers, or RVs up to 16 feet long. Picnic tables are provided. Piped water, flush toilets, and electricity in the bathrooms are available. Boat docks, launching facilities, and rentals are available at nearby Quinault Lake. Leashed pets are permitted.

Reservations, fees: No reservations are accepted. Sites are $13 per night. The campground is open from mid-April to mid-November, weather permitting.

Contact: Olympic National Forest, Quinault Ranger District, P.O. Box 9, Quinault, WA 98575; (360) 288-2525.

Directions: From Interstate 5 north of Olympia, take exit 104 and drive west on Highway 8 for 27 miles to Elma (where Highway 8 becomes U.S. 12). Continue 25 miles on U.S. 12 to U.S. 101. Drive north on U.S. 101 for 45 miles to Quinault. Turn northeast on County Road 5 and drive 1.5 miles to the camp.

Trip notes: This 14-acre camp is set on the shore of Quinault Lake at 200 feet. The Quinault Rain Forest Nature Trail and the Quinault Loop National Recreation Trail are nearby. Quinault Lake covers about six square miles. This camp is concessionaire operated.

⑳ July Creek

Location: On Quinault Lake in Olympic National Park; map A1, grid i6.

Campsites, facilities: There are 29 walk-in tent sites. Picnic tables and fire grills are provided. Toilets and drinking water are available. Leashed pets are permitted.

Reservations, fees: No reservations are accepted. There is no fee. The campground is open year-round.

Contact: Olympic National Park, 600 East Park Avenue, Port Angeles, WA 98362; (360) 452-4501 or fax (360) 452-0335.

Directions: From Interstate 5 south of Olympia, take exit 88 and turn west on U.S. 12. Drive 46 miles, then turn north on U.S. 101 and drive 46 miles to the town of Amanda Park. Continue two miles north on U.S. 101, then turn right and drive two miles along the north shore of Quinault Lake to the camp.

Trip notes: This primitive camp on the north shore of Quinault Lake is set where July Creek empties into the lake. Full supplies are available on the south shore, which has a marina. This is a good choice for hikers looking to avoid crowds.

㊶ Queets

Location: On the Queets River in Olympic National Park; map A1, grid i6.

Campsites, facilities: There are 20 primitive tent sites. Picnic tables and fire grills are provided. Toilets are available, but there is no piped water. Rest rooms are wheelchair accessible. Pets are permitted.

Reservations, fees: No reservations are accepted. There is no fee. The campground is open year-round.

Contact: Olympic National Park, 600 East Park Avenue, Port Angeles, WA 98362; (360) 452-4501 or fax (360) 452-0335.

Directions: From Interstate 5 south of Olympia, take exit 88 and turn west on U.S. 12. Drive 46 miles, then turn north on U.S. 101 and drive 46 miles to the town of Amanda Park. Continue 19 miles north, then turn northeast on an unpaved road (there is a sign for the campground) and drive 14 miles along the Queets River. The campground is at the end of the road.

Trip notes: This primitive camp on the shore of the Queets River is a gem, if you don't mind bringing your own water or purifying river water. Since it's so close to the highway, the camp gets a fair amount of use, so try to arrive as early in the day as possible. A trailhead is available for hikes into the interior of Olympic National Park.

㊷ Gatton Creek

Location: On Quinault Lake in Olympic National Forest; map A1, grid i7.

Campsites, facilities: There are five tent sites and eight overflow RV sites (in a parking area). Picnic tables are provided. Vault toilets, wheelchair-accessible rest rooms, and firewood are available. Leashed pets are permitted.

Reservations, fees: No reservations are accepted. Sites are $10 per night. There is no charge for picnicking. The campground is open from May through October, weather permitting.

Contact: Olympic National Forest, Quinault Ranger District, P.O. Box 9, Quinault, WA 98575; (360) 288-2525.

Directions: From Interstate 5 south of Olympia, take exit 88 and turn west on U.S. 12. Drive 46 miles, then turn north on U.S. 101 and drive 45 miles to the South Shore Lake Quinault turnoff (County Road 5). Turn northeast and drive 3.5 miles to the camp on the shore of Quinault Lake.

Trip notes: This three-acre camp is set on the shore of Quinault Lake (elevation 200 feet) where Gatton Creek empties into it. The Quinault Rain Forest Nature Trail and the Quinault Loop National Recreation Trail are nearby. Quinault Lake covers about six square miles. This camp, like the others on the lake, is concessionaire operated.

㊸ Falls Creek

Location: On Quinault Lake in Olympic National Forest; map A1, grid i7.

Campsites, facilities: There are 11 tent sites and 20 sites for trailers or RVs up to 16 feet long. Picnic tables are provided. Piped

water, flush toilets, and electricity in the bathrooms are available. Some rest rooms are wheelchair accessible. Boat docks, launching facilities, and rentals are available at nearby Quinault Lake. Leashed pets are permitted.

Reservations, fees: No reservations are accepted. Sites are $10–$13 per night. The campground is open from Memorial Day through Labor Day.

Contact: Olympic National Forest, Quinault Ranger District, P.O. Box 9, Quinault, WA 98575; (360) 288-2525.

Directions: From Interstate 5 south of Olympia, take exit 88 and turn west on U.S. 12. Drive 46 miles, then turn north on U.S. 101 and drive 45 miles to the Quinault turnoff (County Road 5). Turn northeast and drive three miles to the camp on the shore of Quinault Lake.

Trip notes: This scenic five-acre camp is set at 200 feet, where Falls Creek empties into Quinault Lake. The Quinault Rain Forest Nature Trail and Quinault Loop National Recreation Trail are nearby. The camp is located adjacent to the Quinault Ranger Station and historic Lake Quinault Lodge.

㊹ Campbell Tree Grove

Location: On the Humptulips River in Olympic National Forest; map A1, grid i8.

Campsites, facilities: There are eight tent sites and three sites for trailers or RVs up to 16 feet long. Picnic tables are provided. Vault toilets and well water are available. Leashed pets are permitted.

Reservations, fees: No reservations are accepted. There is no fee. The campground is open year-round.

Contact: Olympic National Forest, Quinault Ranger District, P.O. Box 9, Quinault, WA 98575; (360) 288-2525 or fax (360) 352-2676.

Directions: From Interstate 5 south of Olympia, take exit 88 and turn west on U.S. 12. Drive 46 miles, then turn north on U.S. 101 and drive 22 miles to Humptulips. Turn north on Forest Service Road 22 and drive eight miles, then turn north on Forest Service Road 2204 and continue about 14 miles to the campground.

Trip notes: This 14-acre camp (elevation 1,100 feet) is located near trails leading into the Colonel Bob Wilderness; see a Forest Service map for more information. The West Fork of the Humptulips River runs near the camp. It's a prime base camp for a wilderness expedition. Fishing is an option here as well.

⑤ Graves Creek

Location: Near the Quinault River in Olympic National Park; map A1, grid i9.

Campsites, facilities: There are 30 sites for tents or RVs up to 21 feet long. Picnic tables, fire grills, drinking water, and rest rooms are available. The facilities are wheelchair accessible. Leashed pets are permitted.

Reservations, fees: No reservations are accepted. There is no fee. The campground is open year-round, with limited winter facilities.

Contact: Olympic National Park, 600 East Park Avenue, Port Angeles, WA 98362; (360) 452-4501 or fax (360) 452-0335.

Directions: From Interstate 5 south of Olympia, take exit 88 and turn west on U.S. 12. Drive 46 miles, then turn north on U.S. 101 and drive approximately 45 miles to the Quinault turnoff. Turn east and drive 15 miles. The campground and Graves Creek Ranger Station are located at road's end.

Trip notes: This camp located at an elevation of 540 feet is a short distance from a trailhead leading into the backcountry of Olympic National Park. See an Olympic National Park and Forest Service map for details. The Upper Quinault River is nearby, and there are lakes in the area.

⑥ Staircase

Location: On the North Fork of the Skokomish River in Olympic National Park; map A1, grid i9.

Campsites, facilities: There are 59 sites for tents or RVs up to 21 feet long. Picnic tables and fire grills are provided. Rest rooms, drinking water, and wheelchair-accessible facilities are available. Leashed pets are permitted in camp.

Reservations, fees: No reservations are accepted. Sites are $8 per night. The campground is open year-round.

Contact: Olympic National Park, 600 East Park Avenue, Port Angeles, WA 98362; (360) 452-4501 or fax (360) 452-0335;

Directions: From Interstate 5 at Olympia, go north on U.S. 101 and drive 37 miles to the town of Hoodsport. Turn west on Lake Cushman Road and drive 17 miles to the camp.

Trip notes: This camp is located on the Staircase Rapids of the North Fork of the Skokomish River, about one mile from where it empties into Lake Cushman. It's a take-your-pick spot. A major trailhead at the camp leads to the backcountry of Olympic National Park. See an Olympic National Park and Forest Service map for details. A beautiful two-mile loop trail runs along the river.

⑦ Coho

Location: On Wynoochee Lake in Olympic National Forest; map A1, grid j8.

Campsites, facilities: There are 58 sites for tents, trailers, or RVs up to 36 feet long. Picnic tables are provided. Flush toilets, piped water, and wheelchair-accessible rest rooms are available. Boat docks and launching facilities are available at Wynoochee Lake. Leashed pets are permitted.

Reservations, fees: No reservations are accepted. Sites are $5–$7 per night. The campground is open from May to mid-November.

Contact: Olympic National Forest, Hood Canal Ranger District, P.O. Box 68, Hoodsport, WA 98548; (360) 877-5254.

Directions: From Interstate 5 south of Olympia, take exit 88 and turn west on U.S. 8, which becomes U.S. 12 in 15 miles. Drive 36 miles to Montesano. Turn north on Wynoochee Valley Road, one mile west of Montesano, and drive 12 miles, then continue north for another 22 miles on Forest Service Road 22 to the camp on the west shore of Wynoochee Lake. A Forest Service map is essential.

Trip notes: This eight-acre camp is set on the shore of Wynoochee Lake at 900 feet. Points of interest include a working forest nature trail, Wynoochee Dam Viewpoint, and a 12-mile national recreation trail that goes around the lake. This is one of the most idyllic drive-to settings you could hope to find.

Map A2

Washington State Map .... *page 6*
One inch equals approximately 20 miles.

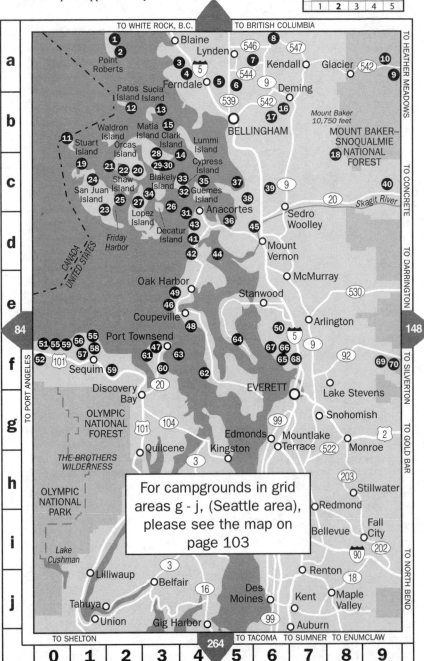

A | B | 1 2 3 4 5

TO WHITE ROCK, B.C.   TO BRITISH COLUMBIA

a TO HEATHER MEADOWS

Blaine
Lynden
Point Roberts
Ferndale
Kendall
Glacier (542)
544
546 547
Deming
9
539 542

b
Patos Island
Sucia Island
BELLINGHAM
Mount Baker 10,750 feet
MOUNT BAKER–SNOQUALMIE NATIONAL FOREST

Waldron Island
Matia Island
Clark Island
Lummi Island
Cypress Island

c TO CONCRETE
Stuart Island
Orcas Island
Shaw Island
Blakely Island
Guemes Island
San Juan Island
Anacortes
Skagit River
20
Sedro Woolley

d TO DARRINGTON
CANADA UNITED STATES
Friday Harbor
Lopez Island
Decatur Island
Mount Vernon
McMurray

e 84   148
Oak Harbor
Stanwood
530
Coupeville
Arlington

f TO PORT ANGELES   TO SILVERTON
Port Townsend
101
Sequim
Discovery Bay
92
9
5
EVERETT
Lake Stevens

g TO GOLD BAR
OLYMPIC NATIONAL FOREST
101   104
Quilcene
Kingston
Edmonds
Mountlake Terrace
Snohomish
Monroe
99
522
2

h
THE BROTHERS WILDERNESS
OLYMPIC NATIONAL PARK
203
Stillwater
Redmond

For campgrounds in grid areas g - j, (Seattle area), please see the map on page 103

i TO NORTH BEND
Lake Cushman
Bellevue
Fall City
202
90

j
Lilliwaup
Belfair
Renton
18
Tahuya
Union
Gig Harbor
16
Des Moines
Kent
Maple Valley
99
Auburn
3

TO SHELTON   264   TO TACOMA   TO SUMNER   TO ENUMCLAW

0 1 2 3 4 5 6 7 8 9

MAP A2-Seattle Area (inset)

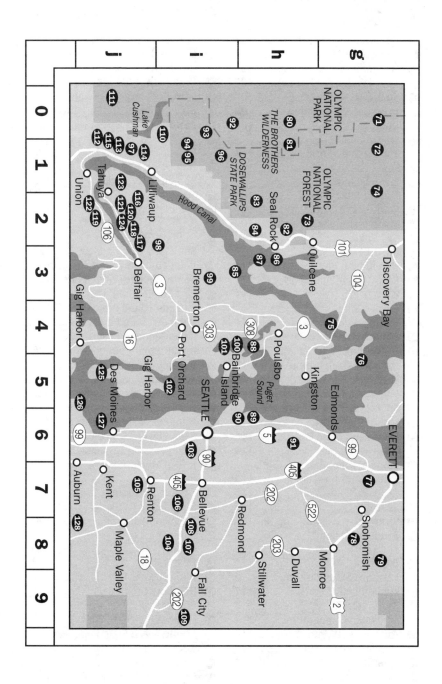

Chapter A2 features:

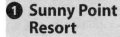 **① Sunny Point Resort**

Location: On Point Roberts; map A2, grid a2.

Campsites, facilities: There are approximately 25 spaces for tents and 50 sites for trailers or RVs. Rest rooms, showers, a public phone, and a recreation field are available. Leashed pets are permitted.

Reservations, fees: Reservations are recommended. Sites are $10–$17 per night. The campground is open year-round.

Contact: Phone the park at (360) 945-1986 or write to 1408 Gulf Road, Point Roberts, WA 98281.

Directions: The park is located on Point Roberts. From Bellingham, take Interstate 5 north through Blaine and the border customs to Highway 99N (British Columbia). Follow the signs for the Victoria Ferry to Highway 17. Turn south on Highway 17 through Twassen. Cross the U.S./Canada border (where Highway 17 becomes Tyee Road). Continue on Tyee Road, turn right on Gulf Road, and drive half a mile to the park on the right.

Trip notes: This pretty camp set on beautiful, remote Point Roberts is suitable for both trailers and tents. It's a bit smaller and more private than Whalen's RV Park (campground number 2). The campground is located only 2.5 blocks from the Pacific Ocean and just half a mile from Lighthouse Park. A golf course is nearby.

② Whalen's RV Park

Location: On Point Roberts; map A2, grid a2.

Campsites, facilities: There are 100 sites for tents and 65 sites for trailers or RVs of any length. Electricity, piped water, and picnic tables are provided. Flush toilets, sanitary services, firewood, and showers are available. A store, a cafe, a Laundromat, and ice are located within one mile. Boat docks and launching facilities are nearby. Pets are permitted.

Reservations, fees: Reservations are accepted. Sites are $15–$18 per night. The campground is open from May to late October.

Contact: Phone the park at (360) 945-2874, fax (360) 945-0934, or write to P.O. Box 985, Point Roberts, WA 98281.

Directions: From Bellingham, take Interstate 5 north through Blaine and border customs to Highway 99N (British Columbia). Drive 11 miles north on BC 99, then turn west on BC 10 and drive to Benson Road. Turn left and drive to Boundary Bay Road, then turn left and drive to Bay View Road. Turn left again and drive half a mile to the park on the left.

Trip notes: This little spot, a mix of woods and water, is known to few. It requires a roundabout drive into Canada to reach, and therefore is missed by most tourists. The park has grassy sites and lots of trees. A recreation field is provided for campers. Nearby recreational options include an 18-hole golf course, a full-service marina, and tennis courts.

❸ Birch Bay Resort

Location: On Birch Bay; map A2, grid a4.

Campsites, facilities: There are 64 drive-through sites for trailers or RVs of any length; 40 are full hookup sites. Electricity, piped water, sewer hookups, and picnic tables are provided. Flush toilets, sanitary services, showers, a recreation hall, satellite TV, and a laundry room are available. A store, a cafe, ice, and boat launching facilities are located within one mile. Leashed pets and motorbikes are permitted.

Reservations, fees: Reservations are accepted. Sites are $20 per night. The campground is open year-round.

Contact: Phone the park at (360) 371-7922 or write to 8080 Harbor View, Blaine, WA 98230.

Directions: From Interstate 5 south of Blaine, take exit 270 and drive four miles west on Birch Bay–Lynden Road, then 300 feet south on Harbor View to the park.

Trip notes: Good ocean access on Birch Bay is a highlight of this private campground, which is actually a large mobile home park with a few spaces for campers. Nearby recreational options include a full-service marina and tennis courts.

❹ Birch Bay State Park

Location: On Birch Bay; map A2, grid a4.

Campsites, facilities: There are 147 sites for tents or self-contained RVs, and 20 partial-hookup (water and electric) sites for trailers or RVs of any length. Picnic tables and fire grills are provided. Flush toilets, coin-operated showers, firewood, and a sanitary disposal station are available. A store, a restaurant, a Laundromat, and ice are located within one mile. Leashed pets are permitted.

Reservations, fees: Call Reservations Northwest at (800) 452-5687 ($6 reservation fee). Sites are $10–$16 per night, plus $5 for each extra vehicle per night. The campground is open year-round.

Contact: Phone (800) 233-0321 or (360) 371-2800, fax (360) 664-8112, or write to 5105 Helwig Road, Blaine, WA 98230.

Directions: From Interstate 5 at Blaine, drive 10 miles south and take the Grandview exit (exit 270). Turn right on Grandview Road and follow the signs for about seven miles. Turn right on Jackson Road and drive a quarter of a mile to Helwig Road. Turn left into the park.

Trip notes: Birch Bay State Park covers 193 acres and includes a mile-long beach. More than 100 different species of birds, many of which are migrating on the Pacific Flyway, can be seen here. Recreation options include the Terrell Marsh Interpretive Trail. Several 18-hole golf courses are located nearby.

❺ The Cedars RV Resort

Location: In Ferndale; map A2, grid a6.

Campsites, facilities: There are 117 sites for tents, trailers, or RVs of any length. Electricity, piped water, and cable, telephone, and sewer hookups are provided. Flush toilets, showers, laundry facilities, a playground, a pool, a small store, and ice are available. Small pets are permitted.

Reservations, fees: Reservations are accepted. Sites are $17–$26 per night. The campground is open year-round.

Contact: Phone the park at (360) 384-2622 or write to 6335 Portal Way, Ferndale, WA 98248.

Directions: From Interstate 5 at Ferndale, take exit 263 and drive one mile north on Portal Way to the campground.

Trip notes: An alternative to Windmill Inn and KOA Lynden (campground numbers 6 and 7), this campground provides more direct access from Interstate 5. It's a nice, clean camp with spacious sites and trees. A fishing pond, horseshoe pits, a game room, and a recreation field provide possible activities for campers. A golf course and riding stable are nearby options.

❻ Windmill Inn

Location: Near the Nooksack River; map A2, grid a5.

Campsites, facilities: There are eight sites for trailers or RVs of any length. Electricity, piped water, sewer, cable TV, and phone hookups, a park, and picnic tables are provided. Flush toilets, showers, bottled gas, a store, a cafe, a Laundromat, and ice are available within one mile. Boat launching facilities are located within 1.5 miles. Pets are permitted.

Reservations, fees: Reservations are accepted. Sites are $15 per night. The campground is open year-round.

Contact: Phone the park at (360) 354-3424 or write to 8022 Guide Meridian Road, Lynden, WA 98264.

Directions: From Interstate 5 at Bellingham, take exit 256 and drive 10 miles north on Highway 539 to the campground.

Trip notes: This nice little spot is set near the Nooksack River and Wiser Lake and is within 15 minutes of the Pacific Sound. Since it's the last stop before the border, the camp is used primarily as a layover for people heading up to Canada. The setting is quiet and pretty, with lots of trees and flowers. Area attractions include Mount Baker, the quaint little shops of Lynden, and the nearby Birch Bay area, which offers numerous recreation options.

❼ KOA Lynden

Location: In Lynden; map A2, grid a6.

Campsites, facilities: There are 80 tent sites and 100 sites for trailers or RVs of any length; 25 are drive-throughs. There are also 12 cabins. Electricity, piped water, sewer hookups, and picnic tables are provided. Flush toilets, bottled gas, sanitary services, showers, firewood, a recreation hall, store, a cafe, laundry facilities, ice, a playground, miniature golf, and a swimming pool are available. Boat rentals are available. Pets are permitted.

Reservations, fees: Reservations are accepted. Sites are $20–$27 per night. Cabins are $37 per night. The campground is open year-round.

Contact: Phone the park at (360) 354-4772, fax (360) 354-7050, or write to 8717 Line Road, Lynden, WA 98264.

Directions: From Interstate 5 at Bellingham, take exit 256 and drive 12 miles north on Highway 539, then turn east on Highway 546 (Badger Road) and drive three miles. Turn south on Line Road and drive one block to the campground.

Trip notes: A holdover spot for vacationers heading north to Canada via Highways 539 and 546, this campground is exceptionally clean and in a lovely setting, with pretty, grassy sites and lots of trees. There is a pond where campers can fish for trout. Tackle and boat rentals are available. Nearby recreational options include an 18-hole golf course and tennis courts.

❽ Sumas RV Park

Location: In Sumas; map A2, grid a7.

Campsites, facilities: There are 24 tent sites and 40 sites for trailers or RVs of any length; 12 are drive-throughs. Electricity, piped water, and picnic tables are provided. Flush toilets, sanitary services, showers, firewood, and a ballpark are available. A store, a cafe, a Laundromat, and ice are located within one mile. Pets and motorbikes are permitted.

Reservations, fees: Reservations are accepted. Sites are $10–$15 per night. The campground is open year-round.

Contact: Phone the park at (360) 988-8875 or write to 9600 Easterbrook Road, Sumas, WA 98295.

Directions: From Interstate 5 at Bellingham, take exit 256 and drive 12 miles, then turn north on Highway 546 (Badger Road) and drive 14 miles to Sumas. At the junction of Highway 9 and Cherry Street, turn south on Cherry Street and drive two blocks to the park on the left.

Trip notes: Located on the edge of the U.S./Canada border, this campground is a holdover spot to spend American dollars before heading into British Columbia. Set in the grassy flatlands, it has graveled sites and a few trees. Nearby recreation options include an 18-hole golf course and tennis courts.

9 Excelsior Group Camp

Location: Near the Nooksack River in Mount Baker–Snoqualmie National Forest; map A2, grid a9.

Campsites, facilities: There are two group sites only. Picnic tables, vault toilets, and fire grills are provided, but there is no piped water. Leashed pets are permitted.

Reservations, fees: Reservations are required for all groups; call (800) 280-CAMP/2267 for current fee information. The campground is open from May through September.

Contact: Mount Baker–Snoqualmie National Forest, Mount Baker Ranger District, 2105 State Route 20, Sedro-Woolley, WA 98284; (360) 856-5700 or fax (360) 856-1934.

Directions: From Interstate 5 at Bellingham, turn east on Highway 542 and drive 31 miles to Glacier. Continue 6.5 miles east on Highway 542 to the camp.

Trip notes: This campground is set near the Nooksack River less than a mile from Nooksack Falls and 1.5 miles from the site of the Excelsior Mine. There are numerous hiking trails available in the Mount Baker Wilderness, located to the east and south. Remember to bring your own water.

10 Douglas Fir

Location: On the Nooksack River in Mount Baker–Snoqualmie National Forest; map A2, grid a9.

Campsites, facilities: There are 30 sites for tents, trailers, or RVs up to 31 feet long. Picnic tables and fire grills are provided. Well water and vault toilets are available. A store, a cafe, a Laundromat, and ice are located within five miles. Leashed pets are permitted.

Reservations, fees: Reserve sites by calling (800) 280-CAMP ($8.65 reservation fee). Sites are $10 per night. The campground is open from May through September, with self-service access the remainder of the year.

Contact: Mount Baker–Snoqualmie National Forest, Mount Baker Ranger District, 2105 State Route 20, Sedro-Woolley, WA 98284; (360) 856-5700 or fax (360) 856-1934.

Directions: From Interstate 5 at Bellingham, turn east on Highway 542 and drive 31 miles to Glacier. Continue two miles northeast on Highway 542 to the campground.

Trip notes: Set along the Nooksack River, this camp is an alternative to Excelsior Group Camp (campground number 9). Fishing is available on the river, and there are hiking trails in the area. See the trip notes for the above camps for more information on the area.

11 Stuart Island Marine State Park

Location: Near San Juan Island; map A2, grid b1.

Campsites, facilities: There are 19 primitive, boat-in campsites. Picnic tables and piped water are provided. Pit toilets are available. Twenty-two buoys and floats are available for overnight moorage.

Reservations, fees: No reservations are accepted. Sites are $5–$11 per night. The campground is open from May 1 through Labor Day.

Contact: Phone (800) 233-0321, (360) 902-8563, or (360) 378-2044, or write to 6158 Lighthouse Road, Friday Harbor, WA 98250.

Directions: The park is on the north side of Stuart Island and is accessible only by boat. Stuart Island is located northwest of San Juan Island.

Trip notes: This is really stalking the unknown. Stuart Island is a remote little spot on the edge of Canadian waters that covers 153 acres and has excellent harbors for mooring. It's the western-most of the marine parks, making it a jump-off point for Limekiln, Sucia Island, Orcas Island, and San Juan Island parks. There is good fishing at nearby Reed and Provost Harbors. This park is very quiet and primitive, receiving little use even in the summer months.

⑫ Patos Island State Park

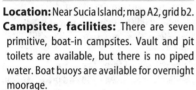

Location: Near Sucia Island; map A2, grid b2.
Campsites, facilities: There are seven primitive, boat-in campsites. Vault and pit toilets are available, but there is no piped water. Boat buoys are available for overnight moorage.
Reservations, fees: No reservations are accepted. Sites are $5 per night. The campground is open year-round.
Contact: Phone (800) 233-0321, (360) 902-8563, or (360) 378-2044, or write to 6158 Lighthouse Road, Friday Harbor, WA 98250.
Directions: The park is on the east side of Patos Island, which is 2.5 miles northwest of Sucia Island and five miles northwest of Orcas Island. It's accessible only by boat and is the northernmost of the coastal islands.
Trip notes: If you're going to get stranded on an island, this is not a bad choice, provided you like your companion. There are good hiking trails and excellent fishing opportunities here. It's tiny, primitive, and used by few.

⑬ Sucia Island Marine State Park

Location: Near Orcas Island; map A2, grid b3.
Campsites, facilities: There are 55 primitive, boat-in campsites. Picnic tables are provided and vault and composting toilets are available. Campers are asked to pack out their garbage. Boat buoys and floats are available for overnight moorage.
Reservations, fees: No reservations are accepted. Sites are $11 per night. The campground is open from May 1 through September.

Contact: Phone (800) 233-0321, (360) 902-8563, or (360) 378-2044, or write to 6158 Lighthouse Road, Friday Harbor, WA 98250.
Directions: The park is on the north side of Sucia Island, which is located 2.5 miles north of Orcas Island. It's accessible only by boat.
Trip notes: Here's a classic spot, with rocky outcrops for lookout points and good beach and fishing areas. Sucia Island covers 562 acres and provides opportunities for hiking, clamming, crabbing, canoeing, and scuba diving. Though primitive, the campground is beautiful and well worth the trip.

⑭ Clark Island State Park

Location: Near Orcas Island; map A2, grid c3.
Campsites, facilities: There are eight primitive, boat-in campsites. Vault toilets are available, but there is no piped water. Boat buoys are available for overnight moorage. No trash services are provided, so you must pack out your garbage.
Reservations, fees: No reservations are accepted. Sites are $5 per night. The campground is open year-round.
Contact: Phone (800) 233-0321, (360) 902-8563, or (360) 378-2044, or write to 6158 Lighthouse Road, Friday Harbor, WA 98250.
Directions: The campground, accessible only by boat, is on tiny Clark Island, located northeast of Orcas Island.
Trip notes: Clark Island State Park offers beautiful beaches with opportunities for scuba diving. Beachcombing and sunbathing are two other popular options. For just $5 a night, you can pretend you're on a deserted Caribbean island. Well, almost. There are excellent views of the other nearby islands from the campground.

⑮ Matia Island State Park

Location: Near Orcas Island; map A2, grid b3.
Campsites, facilities: There are six primitive, boat-in campsites. Composting toilets are

provided. There is a boat dock, and buoys and floats are available for overnight moorage.

Reservations, fees: No reservations are accepted. Sites are $5–$11 per night. The campground is open from May 1 through September.

Contact: Phone (800) 233-0321, (360) 902-8563, or (360) 378-2044, or write to 6158 Lighthouse Road, Friday Harbor, WA 98250.

Directions: The campground is located on the northeast side of Matia Island, which is 2.5 miles northeast of Orcas Island. It's accessible only by boat.

Trip notes: Campsites here are located just a short walk from the docking facilities, a big plus since many of the other island campgrounds don't have docks. Good fishing and beachcombing are among the highlights. Scuba diving is also popular.

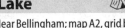 **⑯ Lily Lake**

Location: Near Bellingham; map A2, grid b6.

Campsites, facilities: There are six primitive, hike-in tent sites. Leashed pets are allowed.

Reservations, fees: No reservations are accepted. There is no fee. The campground is open year-round.

Contact: Department of Natural Resources, Northwest Region, 919 North Township Street, Sedro-Woolley, WA 98284-9395; (360) 856-3500.

Directions: From Interstate 5 south of Bellingham, take exit 240 and drive one-half mile north on Samish Lake Road. Turn left on Barrel Springs Road and drive one mile, then turn right on Road SW-C-1000 and drive 1.5 miles to the Blanchard Hill Trailhead. Hike 3.2 miles, then veer left and continue one-half mile to the campground.

Trip notes: This tiny, remote, hike-in campground is one of those that few people ever go to or even know about. Set on little Lily Lake, it's completely secluded and very primitive; you'll have to pack in everything you need and pack out everything that's left. This is a prime area for hiking, and the nearby trails are used by hikers and horse-packers alike.

⑰ Lizard Lake

Location: Near Bellingham; map A2, grid b6.

Campsites, facilities: There are three primitive, hike-in tent sites. Picnic tables, tent pads, fire grills, and vault toilets are available, but there is no piped water. Leashed pets are permitted.

Reservations, fees: No reservations are accepted. There is no fee. The campground is open year-round.

Contact: Department of Natural Resources, Northwest Region, 919 North Township Street, Sedro-Woolley, WA 98284-9395; (360) 856-3500.

Directions: From Interstate 5 south of Bellingham, take exit 240 and drive one-half mile north on Samish Lake Road. Turn left on Barrel Springs Road and drive one mile, then turn right on Road SW-C-1000 and drive 1.5 miles to the Blanchard Hill Trailhead. Hike 3.2 miles, then veer left and continue three-quarters of a mile to the campground.

Trip notes: Located just two-tenths of a mile down the trail from Lily Lake (campground number 16), this hike-in camp is even smaller and more isolated. It's set on Lizard Lake in a pretty, forested area. See the trip notes for Lily Lake for more information.

⑱ Hutchinson Creek

Location: Near the South Fork of the Nooksack River; map A2, grid b8.

Campsites, facilities: There are 11 sites for tents or small trailers. Picnic tables, fire grills, vault toilets, and tent pads are provided, but there is no piped water. A store is located within three miles. Leashed pets are permitted.

Reservations, fees: No reservations are accepted. There is no fee. The campground is open year-round.

Contact: Department of Natural Resources, Northwest Region, 919 North Township Street, Sedro-Woolley, WA 98284-9395; (360) 856-3500.

Directions: From Interstate 5 at Burlington, turn east on Highway 20 and drive seven miles.

Turn north on Highway 9 and drive 16 miles to Acme, just north of the Nooksack River Bridge. Turn east on Mosquito Lake Road and drive 2.5 miles, then turn right on a gravel road and continue for one-half mile to the campground.

Trip notes: This campground is set in the forest along Hutchinson Creek near the South Fork of the Nooksack River. Managed by the Department of Natural Resources, it's rustic, beautiful, primitive, and unknown to out-of-towners.

⑲ Posey Island State Park

Location: Near Roche Harbor; map A2, grid c1.

Campsites, facilities: There is one primitive, boat-in campsite. Fire rings and composting toilets are provided.

Reservations, fees: No reservations are accepted. The site is $5 per night. The campground is open year-round.

Contact: Phone (800) 233-0321, (360) 902-8563, or (360) 378-2044, or write to 6158 Lighthouse Road, Friday Harbor, WA 98250.

Directions: This little island is just north of Roche Harbor (on San Juan Island) and is accessible only by small boat.

Trip notes: If you want a beautiful little spot all to yourself, this is it—the smallest campground in Washington. It's difficult to get here, however. The best way is by skiff, just a short cruise from San Juan Island.

⑳ West Beach Resort

Location: On Orcas Island; map A2, grid c2.

Campsites, facilities: There are 62 sites for tents, trailers, or RVs. Rest rooms, showers, a sanitary dump, a public phone, laundry facilities, ice, a playground, and LP gas bottles are available. Also on site are a boat ramp, dock, marina, and rentals. Leashed pets are permitted.

Reservations, fees: Reservations are recommended. Sites are $15–$30 per night, plus $4 for each pet. The campground is open year-round.

Contact: West Beach Resort, Route 1, P.O. Box 510, Eastsound, WA 98245; (360) 376-2240, fax (360) 376-4746; e-mail: wstbeach @fidalgo.net.

Directions: From Bellingham, drive south on Interstate 5 past Mount Vernon and follow the signs to the San Juan Island's Ferry Terminals (about 45 minutes). Take the ferry from Anacortes to Orcas Island. From the ferry landing, turn left and drive for 11 miles on Horseshoe Highway to the entrance of town. There is a green sign that directs you left toward Moran State Park. Turn left and drive one-half mile to Enchanted Forest Road. Turn left again and drive to the end of Enchanted Forest Road and the resort.

Trip notes: Right on the beach, this resort offers salmon fishing, boating, and swimming. It's an excellent alternative to often-full Moran State Park and offers all the same recreation opportunities. The beaches at Orcas Island are prime spots for whale watching and sunset viewing.

㉑ Jones Island Marine State Park

Location: Near Orcas Island; map A2, grid c2.

Campsites, facilities: There are 21 primitive, boat-in campsites. Picnic tables and vault, composting, and pit toilets are provided. Boat buoys and floats are available for overnight moorage.

Reservations, fees: No reservations are accepted. Sites are $5–$11 per night. The campground is open from May through September.

Contact: Phone (360) 753-2027 or write to 6158 Lighthouse Road, Friday Harbor, WA 98250.

Directions: The campground is on tiny Jones Island, located one mile off the southwest tip of Orcas Island. It's accessible only by boat.

Trip notes: This small island is another hidden spot that gets little use. The campground is near the beach, so you don't have to carry your gear very far. The area offers good fishing and scuba diving. A note of caution: Raccoons have become pests and campers are advised to keep food well contained.

㉒ Blind Island State Park

Location: Near Shaw Island; map A2, grid c2.
Campsites, facilities: There are four primitive, boat-in campsites. Composting and pit toilets are provided, but there is no piped water. Boat buoys are available for overnight moorage.
Reservations, fees: No reservations are accepted. Sites are $5 per night. The campground is open year-round.
Contact: Phone (800) 233-0321, (360) 902-8563, or (360) 378-2044, or write to 6158 Lighthouse Road, Friday Harbor, WA 98250.
Directions: The campground is located just west of the Shaw Island ferry dock on little Blind Island, which is just north of Shaw Island. It's accessible only by boat.
Trip notes: This island has few trees and is known for its rocky shoreline. It's dangerous and ill-advised to try beaching cruiser-style boats. Bring a life raft to paddle ashore. Blind Island State Park is a designated natural area and is committed to conserving a natural environment in a minimally developed state. This is not a place to tromp around or throw big barbecues.

㉓ Griffin Bay

Location: On San Juan Island; map A2, grid c2.
Campsites, facilities: There is one primitive, boat-in campsite and three picnic sites. Piped water, picnic tables, and pit toilets are provided. Two boat buoys are available for overnight moorage.
Reservations, fees: No reservations are accepted. There is no fee. The campground is open year-round.
Contact: Department of Natural Resources, Northwest Region, 919 North Township Street, Sedro-Woolley, WA 98284-9395; (360) 856-3500.

Directions: Griffin Bay is on the southeast side of San Juan Island, south of Friday Harbor. It's accessible only by boat.
Trip notes: This is a tiny, remote camp that receives almost no use at all, yet it's located on one of the prettiest islands in the area. If you're one of the smart few who is willing to take the time to travel here, you're practically guaranteed a beautiful little spot all to yourself. The camp is within a few miles of the San Juan National Historic Park, a day-use area. There are several other state parks on the island as well.

㉔ Lakedale Campground

Location: On San Juan Island; map A2, grid c2.
Campsites, facilities: There are 70 tent sites and 25 sites for trailers or RVs up to 34 feet long; 12 are drive-throughs and 19 have partial hookups. There are also six group sites, three tent cabins, and six log cabins. Electricity, piped water, and picnic tables are provided. Toilets, a store, and ice are available. Showers and firewood are available for an extra fee. Boat docks and boat, bike, camping, and fishing gear rentals can be found on site. Leashed pets and motorbikes are permitted.
Reservations, fees: Reservations are accepted. Sites are $9–$23 per night for tent and RV campers, plus a $7 fee for an additional vehicle. Hike-in/bike-in sites are $5–$6, and log cabins are $110–$150 per night. The campground is open from April to late September.
Contact: Lakedale Campground, 2627 Roche Harbor, Friday Harbor, WA 98250; (800) 617-CAMP/2267 or (360) 378-2350, fax (360) 378-3355; Web site: www.lakedale.com.
Directions: From Interstate 5 at Burlington, turn west on Highway 20 and drive 12 miles, then turn north at the sign for Anacortes and drive to town. Take the ferry to Friday Harbor on San Juan Island. From the ferry landing, proceed two blocks on Spring Street, then turn right (northwest) on Second Street and drive one-half mile to Tucker Avenue (Roche

Harbor Road). Turn right (north) and continue 4.5 miles to the campground on the left.

Trip notes: This is a nice spot for visitors who want the solitude of an island camp, yet all the amenities of a privately run campground. Fishing, swimming, and boating are available at the Lakedale Lakes. Horseshoe pits and a grassy sports field are also on site.

㉕ Turn Island State Park

Location: Near Friday Harbor; map A2, grid c2.

Campsites, facilities: There are 12 primitive, boat-in campsites. Picnic tables are provided and vault and pit toilets are available. There is no piped water. Boat buoys are available for overnight moorage.

Reservations, fees: No reservations are accepted. Sites are $5 per night. The campground is open year-round.

Contact: Phone (800) 233-0321, (360) 902-8563, or (360) 378-2044, or write to 6158 Lighthouse Road, Friday Harbor, WA 98250.

Directions: Turn Island is located just east of Friday Harbor and San Juan Island. It's accessible only by boat.

Trip notes: This is one of about 30 campgrounds in the area that can be reached only by boat. Quiet, primitive, and beautiful, this spot offers good hiking trails and year-round angling for rockfish. There are pretty beaches for shell collectors. No cars are allowed, unless they float.

㉖ James Island State Park

Location: Near Decatur Island; map A2, grid c3.

Campsites, facilities: There are 13 primitive, boat-in campsites. Pit toilets are available. Boat floats and buoys are available for moorage off the east side of the island. A moorage dock on the west side of the island is open from May through September.

Reservations, fees: No reservations are accepted. Sites are $5–$11 per night from

May 1 through Labor Day; there is no fee the rest of the year. The campground is open year-round.

Contact: Phone (800) 233-0321, (360) 902-8563, or (360) 378-2044, or write to 6158 Lighthouse Road, Friday Harbor, WA 98250.

Directions: This island is east of Decatur Island on Rosario Strait and is only accessible by boat. The campground is on the east side of the island.

Trip notes: Small, hidden James Island provides good opportunities for hiking, fishing, and scuba diving. It's quiet and primitive, with lots of trees and a pretty beach for walking or sunbathing.

㉗ Spencer Spit State Park

Location: On Lopez Island; map A2, grid c3.

Campsites, facilities: There are 9 walk-in sites and 34 sites for tents or self-contained RVs up to 20 feet long. There are no hookups. Picnic tables and fire grills are provided. A sanitary disposal station and flush toilets are available. Boat docks are nearby. Some facilities are wheelchair accessible. Leashed pets are permitted.

Reservations, fees: Contact Reservations Northwest at (800) 452-5687 ($6 reservation fee). Sites are $10–$11 per night. The campground is open from March through October.

Contact: Phone (800) 233-0321, (360) 902-8563, or (360) 378-2044, or write to Route 2, P.O. Box 3600, Lopez, WA 98261.

Directions: From Interstate 5 south of Bellingham, take the Highway 20 exit and drive west through Anacortes to the ferry terminal. Take the ferry to the eastern shore of Lopez Island. You can then drive or walk in to the campground.

Trip notes: Spencer Spit State Park offers one of the few island campgrounds accessible to cars via a ferry boat ride. A long sliver of sand extends far into the water and provides good access to prime clamming areas. Picnicking, beachcombing, and sunbathing are some pleasant activities for campers looking for relaxation.

㉘ Moran State Park

Location: On Orcas Island; map A2, grid c3.

Campsites, facilities: There are 15 primitive hike-in/bike-in tent sites and 136 developed sites for tents or RVs up to 45 feet long. No hookups are available. Picnic tables and fire grills are provided. Flush toilets, showers, and firewood are available. Boat docks, fishing supplies, launching facilities, and boat rentals are located at the concession stand in the park. Some facilities are wheelchair accessible. Leashed pets are permitted.

Reservations, fees: Contact Reservations Northwest at (800) 452-5687 ($6 reservation fee). Sites are $5–$11 per night. The campground is open year-round.

Contact: Phone (800) 233-0321 or (360) 376-2326, or write to Star Route, Box 22, Eastsound, WA 98245.

Directions: From Interstate 5 at Burlington, turn west (exit 230) onto Highway 20 and drive through Anacortes to the ferry terminal. Take the ferry from Anacortes to Orcas Island. From the ferry landing, turn left and drive 13 miles on Horseshoe Highway to Moran State Park. Proceed to the campground registration booth and you will receive directions to your site.

Trip notes: This is a big, 5,175-acre park offering hiking trails and lake fishing. There are actually four separate campgrounds plus a primitive area. If you drive to the top of Mount Constitution, you'll have a view of Vancouver, Mount Baker, and the San Juan Islands. No RVs are allowed on this winding road. Nearby recreation options include a nine-hole golf course.

㉙ Doe Island State Park

Location: Near Orcas Island; map A2, grid c3.

Campsites, facilities: There are five primitive, boat-in campsites. Vault toilets are provided. Boat floats are available for moorage.

Reservations, fees: No reservations are accepted. Sites are $5–$11 per night. The campground is open year-round.

Contact: Phone (800) 233-0321 or (360)

902-8563, or write to 6158 Lighthouse Road, Friday Harbor, WA 98250.

Directions: This small, secluded island is just southeast of Orcas Island. It's accessible only by boat.

Trip notes: Doe Island has a rocky shoreline, which makes for an ideal fish habitat, and sure enough, the scuba diving and fishing are exceptional. Doe Island State Park is a tiny, primitive park that receives little use.

㉚ Obstruction Pass

Location: On Orcas Island; map A2, grid c3.

Campsites, facilities: There are nine primitive, hike-in campsites. Picnic tables are provided and vault toilets are available. There is no piped water. Two boat buoys are available for overnight moorage.

Reservations, fees: No reservations are accepted. There is no fee. The campground is open year-round.

Contact: Department of Natural Resources, Northwest Region, 919 North Township Street, Sedro-Woolley, WA 98284-9395; (360) 856-3500.

Directions: On Orcas Island at the town of Olga, travel east on Doe Bay Road for one-half mile, then take a right on Obstruction Pass Road and drive two-thirds of a mile. Keep right for one-third mile, then proceed straight for less than a mile to the parking area. Hike one-half mile to the campground.

Trip notes: It takes a ferry boat ride, a tricky drive, and then a half-mile walk to reach this campground, but that helps set it apart from others—you'll find a unique, primitive spot set in a forested area near the shore of Orcas Island with good hiking. Moran State Park (campground number 28) is a more developed alternative on this island, with many recreation options.

㉛ Pioneer Trails Campground

Location: On Fidalgo Island, in the San Juan Islands; map A2, grid d4.

Campsites, facilities: There are 91 sites for

tents or RVs, plus 24 covered wagons. Cable TV, rest rooms, showers, a public phone, and laundry facilities are provided. A recreation hall, a playground, and a sports field are available. If RV camping, pets are permitted.

Reservations, fees: Reservations are recommended. There is a two-night minimum. Sites are $17–$32 per night. The campground is open year-round.

Contact: Pioneer Trails Campground, 527 Miller Road, Anacortes, WA 98221; (360) 293-5355 or (888) 777-5355.

Directions: From Seattle, drive north on Interstate 5. Take exit 230 and travel west on Highway 20 for 12 miles. At the traffic signal, turn left (still Highway 20) and drive a half mile to Miller Road, then turn west. The ranch is located on Miller Road a quarter of a mile down on the right side. It's approximately 65 miles from Seattle.

Trip notes: This site offers resort camping in the beautiful San Juan Islands. Tall trees, breathtaking views, cascading waterfalls, and country hospitality can all be found here. Side trips include nearby Deception Pass State Park (eight minutes away) and ferries to Victoria, British Columbia. Horseback riding, horseshoes, wagon rides, a free 18-hole golf course, relaxing spas, and lake fishing are among the available activities.

32 Cypress Head

Location: On Cypress Island; map A2, grid c4.

Campsites, facilities: There are five primitive, boat-in campsites. Picnic tables and vault toilets are available. There is no piped water. Five boat buoys are available for overnight moorage.

Reservations, fees: No reservations are accepted. There is no fee. The campground is open year-round.

Contact: Department of Natural Resources, Northwest Region, 919 North Township Street, Sedro-Woolley, WA 98284-9395; (360) 856-3500 or fax (360) 856-2150.

Directions: This camp is set on the east shore of Cypress Island and is accessible only by boat. It's just south of Pelican Beach Campground.

Trip notes: Cypress Head is an alternative to Pelican Beach (campground number 33). Primitive but pretty, this camp is in a forested setting right on Puget Sound.

33 Pelican Beach

Location: On Cypress Island; map A2, grid c4.

Campsites, facilities: There are four primitive, boat-in campsites, plus picnic tables, a group shelter, and vault toilets. There is no piped water. Six buoys are available for overnight moorage.

Reservations, fees: No reservations are accepted. There is no fee. The campground is open year-round.

Contact: Department of Natural Resources, Northwest Region, 919 North Township Street, Sedro-Woolley, WA 98284-9395; (360) 856-3500 or fax (360) 856-2150.

Directions: This camp is set on the east shore of Cypress Island just north of Cypress Head and is accessible only by boat.

Trip notes: This forested island campground offers a group shelter, beach access, and hiking trails. The 1.2-mile trail to Eagle Cliff is a must. Like Cypress Head (campground number 32), this scenic camp is set on the oceanfront in a well-treed area.

34 Strawberry Island

Location: Near Cypress Island; map A2, grid c3.

Campsites, facilities: There are three primitive, boat-in campsites. Picnic tables are provided and vault toilets are available. There is no piped water.

Reservations, fees: No reservations are accepted. There is no fee. The campground is open year-round.

Contact: Department of Natural Resources, Northwest Region, 919 North Township Street, Sedro-Woolley, WA 98284-9395; (360) 856-3500 or fax (360) 856-2150.

Directions: This island is off the west coast of Cypress Island and is accessible only by small boat. Note: The Department of Natural Resources cautions that strong currents and submerged rocks can make landing difficult. They recommend anchoring your boat, then proceeding in a skiff or kayak.

Trip notes: This campground is rarely used because of the hazards of landing here (see the directions, above). If you can manage to land, however, you'll be rewarded with a pretty, forested camp and complete privacy.

🟥 Saddlebag Island State Park

Location: Near Guemes Island; map A2, grid c4.

Campsites, facilities: There are five primitive, boat-in campsites. Vault and pit toilets are available, but there is no piped water.

Reservations, fees: No reservations are accepted. Sites are $5 per night. The campground is open year-round.

Contact: Phone (800) 233-0321 or (360) 902-8563, or write to 6158 Lighthouse Road, Friday Harbor, WA 98250.

Directions: From Interstate 5 at Burlington, turn west on Highway 20 and proceed to Anacortes. Launch your boat and head north to Saddlebag Island, which is two miles northeast of Anacortes and east of Guemes Island. The camp is accessible only by boat.

Trip notes: Saddlebag Island State Park is a good cruise from Anacortes. The island is quiet and primitive, with a nice beach nearby for beachcombing and fine crabbing in the bay.

🟥 Bay View State Park

Location: On Padilla Bay; map A2, grid d5.

Campsites, facilities: There are three primitive sites, 67 sites for tents or self-contained RVs, and nine sites with full hookups for RVs up to 40 feet long. There is also one group tent camp for a maximum of 64 people. Picnic tables are provided. Flush toilets, piped water, a dump station, and coin-operated showers are available. A store and a Laundromat are eight miles away in Burlington. Leashed pets are permitted.

Reservations, fees: No reservations are ac-

cepted for family camping; sites are $10–$11 per night. Reservations are required for the group camp; there is a $25 reservation fee, plus $1 per person per night. The campground is open year-round.

Contact: Phone (800) 233-0321 or (360) 757-0227, or write to 1093 Bay View–Edison Road, Brighton, WA 98273.

Directions: From Interstate 5 at Burlington, take the Highway 20 exit (exit 230) and drive seven miles west toward Anacortes. Turn right (north) on Bay View–Edison Road and drive four miles to the park on the right.

Trip notes: This campground set on Padilla Bay has a large, grassy area for kids, making it a good choice for families. A nice day trip is to take the ferry at Anacortes to Lopez Island (there are several campgrounds there as well).

🟥 Larrabee State Park

Location: On Samish Bay; map A2, grid c5.

Campsites, facilities: There are eight primitive tent sites, 53 developed tent sites, and 26 sites for trailers or RVs up to 60 feet long. Picnic tables and fire grills are provided. Flush toilets, a sanitary disposal station, piped water, sewer hookups, showers, and firewood are available. Boat launching facilities can be found nearby. Leashed pets are permitted.

Reservations, fees: No reservations are accepted. Sites are $7–$16 per night. The campground is open year-round.

Contact: Phone (800) 233-0321 or (360) 676-2093, or write to 245 Chuckanut, Bellingham, WA 98225.

Directions: From Bellingham, drive seven miles south on Chuckanut Drive (Highway 11) to the park on the right.

Trip notes: This 2,683-acre state park is on Samish Bay in Puget Sound. Highlights include tide pools and nine miles of hiking trails, two routes going to small lakes. The park lies on a beautiful stretch of coastline and offers prime spots for wildlife viewing. A relatively short drive south will take you to Anacortes, where you can catch a ferry to Lopez Island.

⓷ Timberline RV Park

Location: Near Larrabee and Bay View State Parks; map A2, grid c5.

Campsites, facilities: There are 30 tent sites and 39 sites with full hookups and cable TV for trailers or RVs. Rest rooms, showers, a private phone, a laundry room, ice, LP gas bottles, a store, and a barbecue are available. There are also horseshoe pits, a recreation hall, a playground, and a sports field. Facilities are wheelchair accessible. Leashed pets are permitted.

Reservations, fees: Reservations are necessary. Sites are $10–$18 per night. The campground is open year-round.

Contact: Phone the park at (360) 826-3131.

Directions: From Bellingham, drive south on Interstate 5 for approximately 20 miles to exit 232 (Cook Road). Follow the road up and over the highway to the flashing light. Turn left on Cook Road. Drive four miles and turn left at the light onto Highway 20. Follow winding Highway 20 for 19 miles to Russell Road, then turn left. There is a sign for the campground just past mile marker 82. The camp is a quarter of a mile further up the hill on the left.

Trip notes: This rural RV park is just far enough off the main highway to be overlooked by most tourists. It is clean and has large sites and tall trees. Nearby attractions include Larrabee and Bay View State Parks. Both provide beach access and hiking opportunities.

⓸ Burlington KOA

Location: In Burlington; map A2, grid c6.

Campsites, facilities: There are 149 sites for tents, trailers, or RVs, plus six cabins. Rest rooms, showers, a sanitary dump, water, electricity, cable TV and sewer hookups, a public phone, a laundry room, limited groceries, ice, LP gas, and a barbecue are available. There is also a heated pool, a spa, horseshoes, a recreation hall, a game room, a playground, and a sports field. The facilities are wheelchair accessible. Leashed pets are permitted.

Reservations, fees: Reservations are necessary. Sites are $16–$25 per night.

Contact: Phone the park at (360) 724-5511 or write to 646 North Green Road, Burlington, WA 98233.

Directions: From Bellingham, drive south on Interstate 5 for approximately 20 miles to exit 232. Turn east and cross over the highway to the flashing light. Turn left on Cook Road, then turn left on Old Highway 99. The campground is about 3.5 miles farther on the right.

Trip notes: This is a typical KOA campground, complete with all the amenities. The sites are spacious and comfortable. It's an alternative to Creekside (campground number 40), with this one a little closer to the highway. Stream fishing is possible nearby.

⓹ Creekside Campground

Location: Near the Skagit River; map A2, grid c9.

Campsites, facilities: There are 28 sites for tents, trailers, or RVs up to 40 feet long. Electricity, piped water, sewer hookups, and picnic tables are provided. Flush toilets, sanitary services, a store, a laundry room, ice, a playground, and showers are available. A cafe is located within one mile. Leashed pets and motorbikes are permitted.

Reservations, fees: Reservations are recommended. Sites are $12.50–$20 per night. The campground is open year-round.

Contact: Phone (360) 826-3566 or write to 761 Baker Lake Road, Concrete, WA 98237.

Directions: From Interstate 5 south of Bellingham, take exit 232. Drive 4.4 miles on Cook Road, then turn left at the junction of Highway 20 and Cook Road and follow it for about 17 miles. Turn left on Baker Lake Road and drive a quarter mile to the camp.

Trip notes: This pretty, wooded campground is centrally located to nearby recreational opportunities at Baker Lake and the Skagit River. Trout fishing is excellent here. Tackle is available nearby. Horseshoe pits and a recreation hall are also available.

⑪ Anacortes RV Park

Location: In Anacortes; map A2, grid d4.

Campsites, facilities: There are 14 sites for tents and 16 sites for trailers or RVs of any length. Electricity, piped water, sewer hookups, and picnic tables are provided. Flush toilets, showers, a recreation hall, a laundry room, and a playground are available. A store and a cafe are located within one mile. Leashed pets and motorbikes are permitted.

Reservations, fees: Reservations are accepted. Sites are $12–$17 per night. The campground is open year-round.

Contact: Phone (360) 293-3700 or write to 1255 Highway 20, Anacortes, WA 98221.

Directions: From Interstate 5 at Burlington, turn west on Highway 20 and drive 12 miles to the Whidbey Island junction. At the Oak Harbor turnoff, continue 100 yards south on Highway 20 to the park on the left.

Trip notes: Covering six acres near the shoreline, this small, wooded park is not particularly scenic, but it is close to numerous recreation attractions. Tourists planning on taking the ferry to San Juan Island will find this a decent layover spot.

⑫ Deception Pass State Park

Location: On Whidbey Island; map A2, grid d4.

Campsites, facilities: There are five primitive tent sites and 246 developed sites for tents, trailers, or self-contained RVs up to 50 feet long. Picnic tables, fire pits, piped water, showers, flush toilets, and a sanitary disposal station are provided. A concession stand, a boat launch, boat rentals, buoys, and floats are available. The facilities are wheelchair accessible. Leashed pets are permitted.

Reservations, fees: No reservations are accepted. Sites are $5–$10 per night. The campground is open year-round, with limited winter services.

Contact: Phone (800) 233-0321, call the park at (360) 675-2417, or write to 5175 North State Highway 20, Oak Harbor, WA 98277.

Directions: From Interstate 5 at Burlington, turn west on Highway 20 and drive 12 miles. Take Highway 20 South and drive six miles, across the bridge at Deception Pass, to the park on the right.

Trip notes: This state park is located on beautiful Deception Pass on the west side of Whidbey Island. Recreation options include fishing and swimming at Pass Lake, a freshwater lake within the park. Fly-fishing for trout is a unique bonus for anglers. Scuba diving is also popular. There are several historic Civilian Conservation Corps buildings near the campground.

⑬ Washington Park

Location: In Washington Park; map A2, grid d4.

Campsites, facilities: There are 70 sites for tents and RVs, 46 with full or partial hookups, and one group site which can accommodate 30 people. Piped water, rest rooms, showers, a public phone, a playground, a recreation field, a dump station, and a laundry room are available. A day-use area is provided. A boat launch is also available. Leashed pets are permitted.

Reservations, fees: No reservations are accepted, except for city of Anacortes residents from April 15 to September 15. Sites are $12–$15 per night; the group site is $50 per night. The campground is open year-round.

Contact: Phone the park at (360) 293-1927 or write to P.O. Box 547, Anacortes, WA 98221.

Directions: From Bellingham, drive south on Interstate 5 for 30 miles. Take the Highway 20 exit west (Anacortes/San Juan Islands exit). Follow this road until it dead-ends, approximately 20 miles. Turn right on Commercial Avenue, then turn left on 12th Street and follow it until it dead-ends into the park (12th Street changes names several times, but keep following it).

Trip notes: Set in the woods, this city park has many hiking trails in addition to a 2.3-

mile paved trail for hikers and bicyclists. Picnic areas are also provided. The Washington State Ferry Terminals are located half a mile away, providing access to the San Juan Islands. This is a very popular camp, and it's a good idea to arrive early to claim your spot.

44 Hope Island State Park

Location: In Skagit Bay; map A2, grid d5.

Campsites, facilities: There are five primitive, boat-in campsites and one cabin, plus one pit toilet and one mooring buoy. No piped water is available.

Reservations, fees: No reservations are accepted. Sites are $5 per night. The campground is open year-round.

Contact: Phone (800) 233-0321 or (360) 675-2417, or write to 5175 Northstate Highway 20, Oak Harbor, WA 98277.

Directions: This little island is in Skagit Bay, two miles north of the entrance of Swinomish Bay. It's accessible only by private boat.

Trip notes: This site on the north side of Hope Island is a primitive alternative to the nearby and more developed Anacortes RV Park (campground number 41). The only catch is you must have a boat to reach it. Solitude is your reward, but the island has little to offer in the way of recreation besides beach access, where campers can sunbathe, walk, or scout for shells.

45 Riverbend Park

Location: On the Skagit River; map A2, grid d6.

Campsites, facilities: There are 25 tent sites and 95 drive-through sites for trailers or RVs of any length. Electricity, piped water, sewer and cable TV hookups, and picnic tables are provided. Flush toilets, sanitary services, showers, a laundry room, and a playground are available. A store, a cafe, ice, and a swimming pool are located within one mile. Pets are permitted.

Reservations, fees: Reservations are accepted. Sites are $6–$19 per night. The campground is open year-round.

Contact: Phone (360) 428-4044 or write to 305 West Stewart Road, Mount Vernon, WA 98273.

Directions: From Interstate 5 at Mount Vernon, take the College Way exit and drive one block west to Freeway Drive, then turn north and go a half mile to the park.

Trip notes: Riverbend Park is a pleasant layover spot for Interstate 5 travelers. While not particularly scenic, it's clean and spacious. Access to the Skagit River here is a high point. Nearby recreational options include a casino, an 18-hole golf course, marked bike trails, and tennis courts.

46 Fort Ebey State Park

Location: On Whidbey Island; map A2, grid e3.

Campsites, facilities: There are three primitive tent sites and 50 developed campsites for tents or self-contained RVs up to 70 feet long. Picnic tables and fire grills are provided. Sanitary disposal service, flush toilets, and coin-operated showers are available. Some facilities are wheelchair accessible. Leashed pets are permitted.

Reservations, fees: No reservations are accepted. Sites are $5–$10 per night. The campground is open from April through September.

Contact: Phone (800) 233-0321 or (360) 678-4636, or write to 395 North Fort Ebey Road, Coupeville, WA 98239.

Directions: From Interstate 5 at Burlington, take the Highway 20 exit and turn west. Drive approximately 23 miles southwest on Highway 20 to the park entrance on the right.

Trip notes: This park, located on the west side of Whidbey Island at Point Partridge, covers 228 acres and has access to a rocky beach that is good for hiking. Other options here include fishing and wildlife viewing. Fort Ebey is the site of a historic World War II bunker. There is also a freshwater lake nearby.

⑰ Fort Worden State Park

Location: Near Puget Sound; map A2, grid f3.
Campsites, facilities: There are three primitive, hike-in/bike-in tent sites and 80 sites for trailers or RVs up to 50 feet long. Picnic tables and fire grills are provided. Toilets, a laundry room, a store, a dinner restaurant, and conference facilities are available. Electricity, piped water, sewer hookups, showers, and firewood are available for an extra fee. Boat docks, buoys, floats, and launching facilities are nearby. Wheelchair-accessible facilities are available. Leashed pets are permitted.
Reservations, fees: Contact Reservations Northwest at (800) 452-5687 ($6 reservation fee). Sites are $5–$16 per night. The campground is open year-round.
Contact: Phone (800) 233-0321 or (360) 385-4730, or write to 200 Battery Way, Port Townsend, WA 98638.
Directions: This park is set on the northeastern tip of the Olympic Peninsula, at the northern end of Port Townsend. From Interstate 5 at Olympia, turn north on U.S. 101 and drive approximately 86 miles. Turn north on Highway 20 and drive about 13 miles to Port Townsend.
Trip notes: Highlights here include the great lookouts over the Strait of Juan de Fuca as it feeds into Puget Sound. This 433-acre park is at historic Fort Worden and includes buildings from the turn of the century. Nearby recreation options include marked hiking and biking trails and tennis courts. A ferry at Port Townsend will take you across the strait to Whidbey Island.

⑱ Fort Casey State Park

Location: On Whidbey Island; map A2, grid e4.
Campsites, facilities: There are three primitive tent sites and 35 developed campsites for tents or self-contained RVs up to 40 feet long. Picnic tables and fire grills are provided. Flush toilets and coin-operated showers are available. Some facilities are wheelchair accessible. Boat launching facilities are located in the park. Pets are permitted.
Reservations, fees: No reservations are accepted. Sites are $5–$10 per night. The campground is open year-round.
Contact: Phone (800) 233-0321 or (360) 678-4519, or write to 1280 Fort Casey, Coupeville, WA 98239.
Directions: From Interstate 5 at Burlington, take the Highway 20 exit and turn west. Drive approximately 35 miles to Coupeville. Continue south on Highway 20 for three miles to the park entrance on the right.
Trip notes: Fort Casey State Park is a good spot to set up a base camp for a fishing trip, with excellent rock fishing year-round and good salmon and steelhead fishing in season. This park covers 137 acres and is the site of a historic U.S. Defense Post. Another highlight is an underwater park for divers. You can also take a ferry from here to Port Townsend on the Olympic Peninsula.

⑲ Oak Harbor City Beach Park

Location: In Oak Harbor; map A2, grid e4.
Campsites, facilities: There are 56 sites for trailers or RVs of any length. Electricity, piped water, and picnic tables are provided. Sewer hookups, sanitary services, toilets, coin-operated showers, and a playground are available. Bottled gas, a store, a cafe, a Laundromat, and ice are located within one mile. Boat launching facilities are available at Oak Harbor. Leashed pets are permitted.
Reservations, fees: No reservations are accepted. Sites are $15 per night. The campground is open year-round.
Contact: Phone (360) 679-5551 or write to 865 Southeast Berrington Drive, Oak Harbor, WA 98277.
Directions: From Interstate 5 at Burlington, turn west on Highway 20 and drive 28 miles to the intersection of Highway 20 and Pioneer Way in the town of Oak Harbor, where Highway 20 becomes 80th SW Road. Continue on 80th SW/Becksma Drive about one block to the park on the left.

Trip notes: Fishing, swimming, boating, and sunbathing are all options at Oak Harbor City Beach Park. Nearby you'll find an 18-hole golf course, a full-service marina, and tennis courts. Fort Ebey and Fort Casey State Parks are both within a short drive and are excellent side trips.

50 Cedar Grove Shores

Location: On Lake Goodwin; map A2, grid e6.
Campsites, facilities: There are 48 sites for trailers or RVs. No tents are allowed. Electricity, piped water, sewer hookups, and picnic tables are provided. Flush toilets, showers, a laundry room, and firewood are available. Bottled gas, sanitary services, a store, a cafe, and ice are located within one mile. Boat docks, launching facilities, and rentals are within 1,000 feet on Lake Goodwin.
Reservations, fees: Reservations are accepted. Sites are $20–$24 per night. The campground is open year-round.
Contact: Phone (360) 652-7083 or write to 16529 52nd Avenue NW, Stanwood, WA 98292.
Directions: From Interstate 5 north of Everett, take exit 206 (Smokey Point), drive five miles west to Westlake Goodwin Road, then drive a half mile to park.
Trip notes: This wooded resort is set on the shore of Lake Goodwin near Wenberg State Park. Trout fishing and swimming are the highlights. Tent campers should try Lake Goodwin Resort (campground number 66). An 18-hole golf course is nearby.

51 KOA Port Angeles– Sequim

Location: Near Port Angeles; map A2, grid f0.
Campsites, facilities: There are 90 sites for tents, trailers, or RVs of any length; 45 are drive-throughs. Picnic tables are provided. There are also 12 cabins. Bottled gas, sanitary services, toilets, showers, a store, laundry facilities, ice, a playground, a recreation room, and a swimming pool are available. A cafe is located within two miles. Electricity, piped

water, sewer hookups, and firewood are available for an extra fee. Some facilities are wheelchair accessible. Leashed pets and motorbikes are permitted.
Reservations, fees: Reservations are accepted. Sites are $21–$27 per night; cabins are $37–$42 per night. The campground is open from April through October.
Contact: KOA Port Angeles–Sequim, 80 O'Brien Road, Port Angeles, WA 98362; (360) 457-5916 or fax (360) 417-0759.
Directions: From Interstate 5 at Olympia, turn north on U.S. 101 and drive 116 miles to O'Brien Road (located six miles southeast of Port Angeles). Turn left on O'Brien Road and drive half a block to the campground on the right.
Trip notes: This private, developed camp covering 41 acres in a country setting is a pleasant park, a typical KOA complete with pool, recreation hall, and playground. Horseshoe pits and a sports field are also available. Mini-golf, two 18-hole golf courses, marked hiking trails, and tennis courts are recreation options.

52 Elmer's Travel Trailer Park

Location: Near the Pacific Ocean; map A2, grid f0.
Campsites, facilities: There are 12 sites for trailers or RVs up to 31 feet long. Electricity, piped water, and sewer hookups are provided. Sanitary services and flush toilets are available. Bottled gas, a store, a cafe, and ice are within one mile.
Reservations, fees: No reservations are accepted. Sites are $14 per night. The campground is open year-round.
Contact: Phone (360) 457-4392 or write to 2442 East Highway 101, Port Angeles, WA 98362.
Directions: From Interstate 5 at Olympia, turn north on U.S. 101 and drive 120 miles to the park, located two miles east of Port Angeles.
Trip notes: Located at about 1,000 feet, this 10-acre camp is near the ocean, yet in an urban setting. It's hardly scenic, but will do as a lay-

over for U.S. 101 travelers. Nearby recreation options include an 18-hole golf course, marked hiking trails, and a full-service marina.

⑤③ Al's RV Trailer Park

Location: Near Port Angeles; map A2, grid f0.
Campsites, facilities: There are 31 sites for tents, trailers, or RVs up to 35 feet long. Electricity, piped water, and sewer hookups are provided. Bottled gas, cable TV, toilets, showers, a clubhouse, and laundry facilities are available. A store, a cafe, and ice are within one mile. Boat docks and launching facilities are located within two miles.
Reservations, fees: Reservations are accepted; phone (800) 357-1553. Sites are $14–$20 per night. The campground is open year-round.
Contact: Phone the park at (360) 457-9844 or write to 521 North Lees Creek Road, Port Angeles, WA 98362.
Directions: From Interstate 5 at Olympia, turn north on U.S. 101 and drive 122 miles to Port Angeles. Continue two miles west on U.S. 101, then turn left on Lees Creek Road and drive a half mile to park.
Trip notes: This is a good choice for motor home owners. The campground is set in the country at about 1,000 feet, yet is not far from the Strait of Juan de Fuca. Nearby recreation options include an 18-hole golf course and a full-service marina. Olympic National Park and the Victoria ferry are a short drive away.

⑤④ Dungeness Recreation Area

Location: Near the Strait of Juan de Fuca; map A2, grid f1.
Campsites, facilities: There are 66 sites for tents, trailers, or RVs of any length; five are pull-throughs. Picnic tables are provided. Sanitary services, toilets, and a playground are available. Showers and firewood are available for an extra fee. Leashed pets are permitted.

Reservations, fees: No reservations are accepted. Sites are $8–$10 per night. The campground is open from February to October, with facilities limited to day use in the winter.
Contact: Phone the park at (360) 683-5847 or write to 554 Voice of America Road, Sequim, WA 98382.
Directions: From Interstate 5 at Olympia, turn north on U.S. 101 and drive 105 miles to Sequim. Continue four miles west on U.S. 101, then turn right on Kitchen Dick Road and drive four miles to the park.
Trip notes: This park overlooks the Strait of Juan de Fuca and is set near the Dungeness National Wildlife Refuge. Nearby recreation options include marked hiking trails, fishing, and swimming. The toll ferry at Port Angeles can take you to Victoria, British Columbia.

⑤⑤ Rainbow's End

Location: On Sequim Bay; map A2, grid f1.
Campsites, facilities: There are 10 tent sites and 37 sites for trailers or RVs of any length. Electricity, piped water, sewer hookups, and cable TV are provided. Sanitary services, toilets, showers, bottled gas, and laundry facilities are available. A store, a cafe, and ice are located within one mile. Firewood is available for an extra fee. Leashed pets and motorbikes are permitted.
Reservations, fees: Reservations are accepted. Sites are $15–$21 per night. The campground is open year-round.
Contact: Phone the park at (360) 683-3863 or write to 261831 Highway 101, Sequim, WA 98382.
Directions: From Interstate 5 at Olympia, turn north on U.S. 101 and drive 105 miles to Sequim. At Sequim Avenue, drive two miles west on U.S. 101 to the park on the right.
Trip notes: Of the several camps on Sequim Bay, Rainbow's End is one of the nicest. The park is pretty and clean, with shaded, spacious sites, a pond, and a trout stream. Recreation seekers will find an 18-hole golf course, marked bike trails, a full-service marina, and tennis courts nearby.

56 Sunshine RV Park

Location: Near Sequim; map A2, grid f1.

Campsites, facilities: There are 20 sites for tents and 60 for trailers or RVs of any length. Electricity, piped water, sewer hookups, and picnic tables are provided. Toilets, showers, a recreation hall, and laundry facilities are available. Sanitary services, a store, and a cafe are located within one mile. Pets and motorbikes are permitted.

Reservations, fees: Reservations are accepted. Sites are $16–$18 per night. The campground is open year-round.

Contact: Phone the park at (360) 683-4769 or write to 259790 Highway 101 West, Sequim, WA 98382.

Directions: From Interstate 5 at Olympia, turn north on U.S. 101 and drive 105 miles to Sequim. At Sequim Avenue, drive four miles west on U.S. 101 to the park.

Trip notes: This six-acre, private camp is set at about 1,000 feet in a wooded area outside of Sequim. Though primarily an RV park, tents are permitted. It has paved, shaded sites, horseshoe pits, and a recreation hall, and is close to an 18-hole golf course and a full-service marina at Sequim Bay.

57 Sequim West RV Park

Location: Near the Dungeness River; map A2, grid f1.

Campsites, facilities: There are 27 drive-through sites with full hookups for trailers or RVs of any length. No tents are allowed. Electricity, piped water, cable TV and sewer hookups, and picnic tables are provided. Toilets, showers, laundry facilities, and ice are available. Bottled gas, a phone, sanitary services, a store, and a cafe are located within one mile. Leashed pets are permitted.

Reservations, fees: Reservations are accepted. Sites are $12–$18 per night. The campground is open year-round.

Contact: Sequim West RV Park, 740 West Washington Avenue, Sequim, WA 98382;

(360) 683-4144 or (800) 528-4527, fax (360) 683-6452.

Directions: From Interstate 5 at Olympia, turn north on U.S. 101 and drive 105 miles to Sequim. At Sequim Avenue, continue three-quarters of a mile west on U.S. 101 (Washington Avenue) to the park on the right.

Trip notes: This two-acre camp is near the Dungeness River and within 10 miles of Dungeness Spit State Park. It's a pleasant spot, with full facilities and an urban setting. An 18-hole golf course and a full-service marina at Sequim Bay are close by.

58 Sequim Bay Resort

Location: On Sequim Bay; map A2, grid f1.

Campsites, facilities: There are 43 sites for trailers or RVs of any length; 34 are pull-throughs. Electricity, piped water, and sewer and cable TV hookups are provided. Flush toilets and laundry facilities are available. Showers are available for an extra fee. Boat docks and launching facilities are located across the street from the resort. Leashed pets are permitted.

Reservations, fees: No reservations are accepted. Sites are $15.30 per night. The campground is open year-round.

Contact: Phone the park at (360) 681-3853 or write to 2634 West Sequim Bay Road, Sequim, WA 98382.

Directions: From Interstate 5 at Olympia, turn north on U.S. 101 and drive 102 miles to Whitefeather Way (located between mileposts 267 and 268, 2.5 miles east of Sequim). Turn north and drive one-half mile to West Sequim Bay Road. Turn west and drive one block to the park on the left.

Trip notes: This is Sequim Bay headquarters for salmon anglers. The camp is set in a wooded, hilly area, close to many activity centers, and with an 18-hole golf course nearby.

59 Sequim Bay State Park

Location: On Sequim Bay; map A2, grid f2.

Campsites, facilities: There are three primitive tent sites, 60 developed sites for tents or self-contained RVs, and 26 sites with full hookups for trailers or RVs up to 30 feet long. Picnic tables and fire grills are provided. A sanitary disposal station, toilets, drinking water, showers, and a playground are available. Boat docks, launching facilities, and moorage camping are available. Facilities are wheelchair accessible. Leashed pets are permitted.

Reservations, fees: Contact Reservations Northwest at (800) 452-5687. Sites are $5–$15 per night. The campground is open year-round.

Contact: Phone (800) 233-0321 or (360) 683-4235, or write to 269035 Highway 101, Sequim, WA 98382.

Directions: From Interstate 5 at Olympia, turn north on U.S. 101 and drive approximately 100 miles north to the park on the right. The entrance is located four miles southeast of the town of Sequim.

Trip notes: Marked hiking trails, tennis courts, and an underwater park for scuba divers are highlights of this 90-acre camp on Sequim Bay. Because of its unique location, the area gets far less rain than other spots on the Olympic Peninsula, which makes it popular with campers.

60 Old Fort Townsend State Park

Location: Near Quilcene; map A2, grid f3.
Campsites, facilities: There are three primitive tent sites and 40 sites for tents or RVs up to 40 feet long. Picnic tables and fire grills are provided. Flush toilets, coin-operated showers, a playground, and boat buoys are available. Firewood and showers are available for an extra fee. Leashed pets are permitted.

Reservations, fees: No reservations are accepted. Sites are $5–$10 per night. The campground is open year-round, with limited winter facilities.

Contact: Phone (800) 233-0321 or (360) 385-3595, or write to Route 1, Port Townsend, WA 98368.

Directions: From Interstate 5 at Olympia, turn north on U.S. 101 and drive approxi-

mately 86 miles. Turn north on Highway 20 and drive 10 miles to the park on the right, located three miles south of Port Townsend.

Trip notes: Built in 1859, this fort is one of the oldest remaining in the state. The campground has access to a good clamming beach, and visitors can also take a self-guided walking tour. Hiking and fishing are among other recreation options here.

61 Point Hudson Resort

Location: In Port Townsend; map A2, grid f3.
Campsites, facilities: There are 60 sites for trailers or RVs of any length (most are drive-throughs with full hookups). No tents are allowed. Flush toilets, a store, a cafe, three restaurants, laundry facilities, and ice are available. Showers are available for an extra fee. A 100-plus slip marina is on site.

Reservations, fees: Reservations are encouraged. Sites are $15–$18 per night. The campground is open year-round.

Contact: Phone (360) 385-2828 or write to 103 Hudson Street, Port Townsend, WA 98368.

Directions: From Interstate 5 at Olympia, turn north on U.S. 101 and drive 86 miles. Turn north on Highway 20 and drive 13 miles to Port Townsend. Turn north on Water Street and drive one-half mile, then turn west on Monroe Street and drive two blocks. Turn north on Jefferson Street and drive two blocks to the campground on the right.

Trip notes: Point Hudson Resort is located on the site of an old Coast Guard station in a wooded, hilly part of Port Townsend, a town known for its Victorian architecture. Fishing and boating are popular here, and nearby recreation possibilities include an 18-hole municipal golf course, a full-service marina, Old Fort Townsend State Park, Fort Flagler State Park, and Fort Worden State Park.

62 South Whidbey State Park

Location: On Whidbey Island; map A2, grid f4.
Campsites, facilities: There are six primi-

tive tent sites and 54 developed campsites for tents or self-contained RVs up to 45 feet long. Picnic tables and fire grills are provided. Sanitary disposal services, coin-operated showers, and toilets are available. Firewood can be obtained for an extra fee. Some facilities are wheelchair accessible. Leashed pets are permitted.

Reservations, fees: No reservations are accepted. Sites are $5–$10 per night. The campground is open from February 24 through October.

Contact: Phone (800) 233-0321 or (360) 321-4559, or write to 4128 Smugglers Cove Road, Freeland, WA 98429.

Directions: From Interstate 5 at Burlington, take the Highway 20 exit and turn west. Drive approximately 28 miles, past Coupeville, to the Highway 525 cutoff. Turn south on Highway 525 and drive eight miles (through Greenbank) to the park on the right.

Trip notes: Located on the southwest end of Whidbey Island, this wooded park covers 85 acres and provides opportunities for hiking, scuba diving, picnicking, and beachcombing along a sandy beach. There are spectacular views of Puget Sound and the Olympic Mountains.

63 Fort Flagler State Park

Location: Near Port Townsend; map A2, grid f4.

Campsites, facilities: There are 102 tent sites and 14 partial hookup (water and electric) sites for trailers or RVs up to 50 feet long. Picnic tables and fire grills are provided. Flush toilets, coin-operated showers, a sanitary dump station, a store, a cafe, boat buoys, floats, and a launch are available. Facilities are wheelchair accessible. Leashed pets are permitted.

Reservations, fees: Contact Reservations Northwest at (800) 452-5687 ($6 reservation fee). Sites are $10–$16 per night. The campground is open year-round, weather permitting.

Contact: Phone (800) 233-0321 or (360) 385-1259, or write to 10541 Flagler Road, Nordland, WA 98358.

Directions: From Interstate 5 at Olympia, take the U.S. 101 exit and turn north. Drive 86 miles north on U.S. 101, then turn right on Highway 20 and drive about seven miles. Turn right on Highway 19 and drive five miles, then turn left on Highway 116 and drive 14 miles to the park at the end of the road. The park is eight miles northeast of Hadlock.

Trip notes: Fort Flagler is a pretty, unique state park, set on an island east of Port Townsend. The campsites are right on the beach. Anglers like this spot for year-round rockfish and salmon fishing, and crabbing and clamming are good in season. The park offers an underwater park and is popular with scuba divers. Tours of Fort Flagler, which was built in 1898, are available. There is a youth hostel in the park.

64 Camano Island State Park

Location: Near Stanwood; map A2, grid f5.

Campsites, facilities: There is one primitive tent site and 87 developed campsites for tents or self-contained RVs up to 30 feet long. There is also one group camp for a maximum of 200 people. Picnic tables and fire grills are provided. Sanitary disposal service, flush toilets, coin-operated showers, and a playground are available. Firewood can be obtained for an extra fee. Boat launching facilities are located in the park. Leashed pets are permitted.

Reservations, fees: No reservations are accepted for family camping; sites are $5–$10 per night, plus $5 per extra vehicle per night. Reservations are required for the group camp; phone (360) 387-3031. The group camp base fee is $25, plus $1 per person per night. The campground is open year-round.

Contact: Phone (800) 233-0321 or (360) 387-3031, or write to 2269 South Lowell Point Road, Stanwood, WA 98292.

Directions: From Interstate 5 north of Everett, take exit 212 and drive west on Highway 532 to Stanwood. Continue 14 miles southeast to the park.

Trip notes: The campsites are quiet and private in this wooded park. Good inshore angling for rockfish is available year-round, and salmon fishing is also good in season. Clamming is excellent during low tides in June. An underwater park is provided for divers. There is also a self-guided nature trail.

⑥⑤ Wenberg State Park

Location: On Lake Goodwin; map A2, grid f6.

Campsites, facilities: There are 65 developed tent sites, and 10 sites for trailers or RVs up to 50 feet long. Picnic tables are provided. A sanitary disposal station, flush toilets, piped water, coin-operated showers, a store, and a playground are available. Boat launching facilities are located on Lake Goodwin. Leashed pets are permitted.

Reservations, fees: Contact Reservations Northwest at (800) 452-5687 ($6 reservation fee). Sites are $11–$16 per night. The campground is open year-round.

Contact: Phone (800) 233-0321 or (360) 652-7417, or write to 15430 East Lake Goodwin Road, Stanwood, WA 98292.

Directions: From Everett on Interstate 5, drive 12 miles north to exit 206 (Smokey Point), then west on Highway 531 for seven miles to the park on the right.

Trip notes: This state park is set along the shore of Lake Goodwin, where the trout fishing can be great. Power boats are allowed, and a seasonal concession stand provides food and fishing supplies. Lifeguards are on duty in the summer.

⑥⑥ Lake Goodwin Resort

Location: On Lake Goodwin; map A2, grid f6.

Campsites, facilities: There are 20 tent sites and 85 sites for trailers or RVs of any length; eight are drive-throughs. There is also one fully equipped cabin available. Electricity, piped water, sewer hookups, and picnic tables are provided. Flush toilets, bottled gas, sanitary services, a recreation hall, a store, a laundry room, ice, a playground, showers, and firewood are available. Boat docks, launching facilities, and rentals are nearby on Lake Goodwin.

Reservations, fees: Reservations are accepted. Sites are $15–$25 per night; cabins are $50 per night. The campground is open year-round.

Contact: Phone (360) 652-8169 or write to 4726 Lakewood Road, Stanwood, WA 98292.

Directions: From Interstate 5 north of Everett, take exit 206 (Smokey Point), then drive west for 5.5 miles to the park (follow the signs for Seven Lakes Area).

Trip notes: This private campground is set on Lake Goodwin, which is known for good trout fishing. Motorboats are permitted on the lake, and an 18-hole golf course is located nearby. Other activities include swimming in the lake, horseshoe pits, shuffleboard, and a recreation field.

⑥⑦ Kayak Point County Park

Location: On Puget Sound; map A2, grid f6.

Campsites, facilities: There are 32 sites with partial hookups, nine of them tent sites and 23 drive-throughs for trailers or RVs up to 25 feet long. Piped water and picnic tables are provided. Flush toilets and firewood are available. Boat docks and launching facilities are located in the park. Leashed pets are permitted.

Reservations, fees: No reservations are accepted. Sites are $15 per night. The campground is open year-round.

Contact: Phone (425) 339-1208 or (360) 652-7992.

Directions: From Everett, drive north on Interstate 5, then take exit 199 (Tulalip) at Marysville. The road winds for 13 miles through the Tulalip Indian Reservation, and then you'll see the park entrance on your left.

Trip notes: This large, wooded county park is set on the shore of Puget Sound, with an 18-hole golf course nearby.

68 Smokey Point RV Park

Location: Near Lake Goodwin; map A2, grid f7.

Campsites, facilities: There are 104 sites for trailers or RVs of any length with full hookups; 38 are drive-throughs. Piped water and picnic tables are provided. Flush toilets, sanitary services, showers, a recreation hall, a laundry room, a playground, electricity, bottled gas, ice, and sewer and cable TV hookups are available. Firewood, a store, and a cafe are located within one mile. Leashed pets are permitted.

Reservations, fees: Reservations are accepted. Sites are $18–$25 per night. The campground is open year-round.

Contact: Phone (360) 652-7300 or write to 17019 28th Drive NE, Arlington, WA 98223.

Directions: From Interstate 5 north of Everett, take exit 206 (Smokey Point). Drive west for half a block on 172nd Street to the park on the southwest corner.

Trip notes: Smokey Point RV Park is an ideal layover for RV cruisers heading up Interstate 5 and looking for a place to spend the night. It's located just off the freeway and is only five miles from the state park and resorts on Lake Goodwin. The park is pleasant and clean, with full facilities and spacious, shady sites. Marked bike trails are available nearby and use of an athletic club with swimming pool, sauna, and Jacuzzi is complimentary to park guests.

69 Turlo

Location: On the South Fork of the Stillaguamish River in Mount Baker–Snoqualmie National Forest; map A2, grid f9.

Campsites, facilities: There are 19 sites for tents or RVs up to 31 feet long. Picnic tables are provided. Vault toilets, piped water, and firewood are available. Some facilities are wheelchair accessible. A store, a cafe, and ice are located one mile away in Robe. Leashed pets are permitted.

Reservations, fees: Reserve sites by calling (800) 280-CAMP/2267 ($8.65 reservation

fee). Sites are $10 per night, plus $4 for each additional vehicle. The campground is open from mid-May to late September.

Contact: Mount Baker–Snoqualmie National Forest, Darrington Ranger District, 1405 Emmens Street, Darrington, WA 98241; (360) 436-1155.

Directions: From Interstate 5 at Everett, turn east on Highway 92 and drive approximately 15 miles to the town of Granite Falls. Continue 11 miles east on Highway 92 to the campground entrance on the right.

Trip notes: Set at 900 feet along the South Fork of the Stillaguamish River, Turlo is the westernmost camp located on this stretch of Highway 92. A Forest Service Public Information Center is nearby. Riverside campsites are available, and the fishing can be good here. A few hiking trails can be found in the area; see a Forest Service map or consult the nearby information center for trail locations.

70 Verlot

Location: On the South Fork of the Stillaguamish River in Mount Baker–Snoqualmie National Forest; map A2, grid f9.

Campsites, facilities: There are 26 sites for tents, trailers, or RVs up to 31 feet long. Picnic tables are provided. Flush toilets, firewood, and piped water are available. A store, a cafe, and ice are located within one mile. Pets are permitted on a six-foot leash.

Reservations, fees: Reserve sites by calling (800) 280-CAMP/2267 ($8.65 reservation fee). Sites are $10 per night, plus $4 for each additional vehicle. The campground is open from mid-May to late September.

Contact: Mount Baker–Snoqualmie National Forest, Darrington Ranger District, 1405 Emmens Street, Darrington, WA 98241; (360) 436-1155.

Directions: From Interstate 5 at Everett, turn east on Highway 92 and drive approximately 15 miles to the town of Granite Falls. Continue 11.6 miles east on Highway 92 to the campground entrance on the right.

Trip notes: This campground is set along the South Fork of the Stillaguamish River, a short distance from the Lake Twenty-Two Research Natural Area and the Maid of the Woods Trail. A Forest Service map details back roads and hiking trails. Fishing is another recreation option. Campsites with river views are available.

⑪ Deer Park

Location: Near Blue Mountain in Olympic National Park; map A2, grid g0.

Campsites, facilities: There are 18 tent sites. Picnic tables and fire grills are provided. Rest rooms and drinking water are available. Leashed pets are permitted.

Reservations, fees: No reservations are accepted. There is no fee. The campground is open from mid-June to late September, with limited winter facilities.

Contact: Olympic National Park, 600 East Park Avenue, Port Angeles, WA 98362; (360) 452-4501 or fax (360) 452-0335.

Directions: From Interstate 5 at Olympia, turn north on U.S. 101 and drive approximately 114 miles to Deer Park Road (about six miles southeast of Port Angeles). Turn left and drive 18 miles south to the campground.

Trip notes: This camp is set in the Olympic Peninsula's high country at 5,400 feet, just below 6,000-foot Blue Mountain. There are numerous trails in the area, including a major trailhead into the backcountry of Olympic National Park and the Buckhorn Wilderness.

⑫ Dungeness Forks

Location: On the Dungeness and Gray Wolf Rivers in Olympic National Forest; map A2, grid g1.

Campsites, facilities: There are 10 tent sites. Picnic tables are provided. Well water and vault toilets are available. Leashed pets are permitted.

Reservations, fees: No reservations are accepted. Sites are $8 per night. The campground is open from May through September.

Contact: Olympic National Forest, Quilcene Ranger District, P.O. Box 280, Quilcene, WA 98376; (360) 765-3368 or fax (360) 765-2202.

Directions: From Interstate 5 at Olympia, turn north on U.S. 101 and drive approximately 100 miles to Palo Alto Road (located three miles southeast of Sequim). Turn south and drive seven miles, then turn west on Forest Service Road 2880 and drive one mile to the campground. A Forest Service map is essential.

Trip notes: This pretty, wooded spot is nestled at the confluence of the Dungeness and Gray Wolf Rivers. It offers seclusion, yet easy access from the highway. If you want quiet, you'll find it here.

⑬ Falls View

Location: On the Big Quilcene River in Olympic National Forest; map A2, grid h2.

Campsites, facilities: There are 30 sites for tents, trailers, or RVs up to 21 feet long. Picnic tables are provided. Piped water, flush toilets, and wheelchair-accessible rest rooms are available. Leashed pets are permitted.

Reservations, fees: Reservations are accepted; phone (360) 796-4886. Sites are $10 per night. The campground is open from mid-May to mid-September.

Contact: Olympic National Forest, Quilcene Ranger District, P.O. Box 280, Quilcene, WA 98376; (360) 765-3368 or fax (360) 765-2202.

Directions: From Interstate 5 at Olympia, turn north on U.S. 101 and drive approximately 70 miles to the campground entrance (located about four miles south of Quilcene).

Trip notes: In spite of the rustic setting, this spot on the edge of the Olympic National Forest has a host of facilities and is very popular.

⑭ East Crossing

Location: In Olympic National Forest; map A2, grid g2.

Campsites, facilities: There are 10 sites for tents only. Picnic tables are provided. Well water and vault toilets are available. Leashed pets are permitted.

Reservations, fees: No reservations are accepted. Sites are $8 per night. The campground is open from May through September.

Contact: Olympic National Forest, Quilcene Ranger District, P.O. Box 280, Quilcene, WA 98376; (360) 765-3368 or fax (360) 765-2202.

Directions: From Interstate 5 at Olympia, turn north on U.S. 101 and drive approximately 100 miles to Palo Alto Road (located three miles southeast of Sequim). Turn south and drive eight miles, then turn south on Forest Service Road 2860 and drive two miles to the campground. A Forest Service map is essential.

Trip notes: An alternative to Dungeness Forks (campground number 72), this seven-acre camp is set at about 1,200 feet and offers some improvements, but it's still for individuals seeking an out-of-the-way spot.

75 Kitsap Memorial State Park

Location: On the Hood Canal; map A2, grid g4.

Campsites, facilities: There are 51 sites for tents or self-contained RVs up to 30 feet long. Picnic tables and fire grills are provided. A sanitary disposal service, toilets, and a playground are available. Showers and firewood can be obtained for an extra fee. Boat buoys are available. Leashed pets are permitted.

Reservations, fees: No reservations are accepted. Sites are $10 per night. The campground is open year-round.

Contact: Phone (800) 233-0321 or (360) 779-3205, or write to 202 NE Park Street, Poulsbo, WA 98370.

Directions: From Interstate 5 at Tacoma, turn north on Highway 16 and drive 44 miles. Continue north on Highway 3 for about eight miles to the park on the left. The entrance is located three miles south of the Hood Canal Bridge.

Trip notes: Kitsap Memorial State Park is a nice spot for tent campers along the Hood Canal. An 18-hole golf course and swimming, fishing, and hiking at nearby Anderson Lake Recreation Area are among the activities available. A short drive north will take you to historic Old Fort Townsend, an excellent day trip.

76 Captain's Landing

Location: In Hansville; map A2, grid g5.

Campsites, facilities: There are 22 drive-through sites for trailers or RVs of any length, plus a dispersed area for tent camping. Electricity, piped water, and sewer hookups are provided. Flush toilets, showers, a store, and ice are available. Boat docks, launching facilities, and boat rentals are located within one mile. Leashed pets are permitted.

Reservations, fees: Reservations are accepted. Sites are $18–$20 per night. The campground is open year-round.

Contact: Phone (360) 638-2257 or write to P.O. Box 113, Hansville, WA 98340.

Directions: From Interstate 5 at Tacoma, turn north on Highway 16 and drive about 42 miles. Highway 16 turns into Highway 3; continue north for 11 miles to Port Gamble. Turn southeast toward Kingston. About three miles northwest of Kingston is the turnoff for Hansville. Turn north and drive eight miles. The park is located in town.

Trip notes: Grassy, open sites make this a choice for tent campers. An 18-hole golf course and a full-service marina are close by.

77 Silver Lake RV Park

Location: On Silver Lake; map A2, grid g7.

Campsites, facilities: There are 110 sites for tents, trailers, or RVs. Electricity, piped water, and picnic tables are provided. Flush toilets, sanitary services, showers, propane, ice, and laundry facilities are available. Firewood, a store, and a cafe are located within one mile.

Reservations, fees: Reservations are accepted. Sites are $20–$27.50 per night. The campground is open year-round.

Contact: Phone (360) 337-8741 or write to 11621 Silver Lake Road, Everett, WA 98208.

Directions: From Interstate 5 at Everett, take exit 186 and head east to the intersection of 128th Street and Bothell-Everett Highway (also called Highway 527 or 19th Avenue SW). Turn left on 19th Avenue and drive to the first stop light. Turn left on Silver Lake Road and drive about a half mile to the park on the right.

Trip notes: Quiet, pretty Silver Lake RV Park is a good layover spot for travelers heading up Interstate 5. The wooded park is set along the shore of Silver Lake, a quiet lake with an 8 mph speed limit, plus good trout fishing and swimming opportunities. Tennis courts can be found nearby, and the park is close to shopping and Seattle.

78 Ferguson Park

Location: On Blackman's Lake; map A2, grid g8.

Campsites, facilities: There are about seven sites for tents and six sites for trailers or RVs. Rest rooms, showers, a sanitary dump, a public phone, limited groceries, a recreation hall, and a barbecue are available. A boat ramp is provided. No pets are allowed.

Reservations, fees: No reservations are accepted. Sites are $10–$15 per night. The campground is open year-round.

Contact: Phone City Hall at (360) 568-3115 or (360) 568-9686, or write to 116 Union Avenue, Snohomish, WA 98290.

Directions: From Everett, drive east on U.S. 2 for about 10 miles toward Monroe. Take the Snohomish Historical Society exit (Bickford Avenue), which turns into Avenue D. Take the first left after the blinking light into Ferguson Park. The turn is immediately before the shopping center.

Trip notes: Grassy, shaded sites can be found in this pretty city park set next to small Blackman's Lake. Recreational activities on the lake include swimming, boating (electric motors only), and trout fishing. A picnic and swimming park is located directly across the river from the camp.

79 Flowing Lake County Park

Location: Near Snohomish; map A2, grid g8.

Campsites, facilities: There are 10 tent sites and 32 drive-through sites for trailers or RVs up to 25 feet long. Electricity, piped water, sewer hookups, and picnic tables are provided. Flush toilets, sanitary services, firewood, a playground, boat docks, and launching facilities are available. Leashed pets are permitted.

Reservations, fees: No reservations are accepted. Sites are $10–$15 per night. The campground is open year-round for self-contained RVs, and from mid-May to late September for other campers.

Contact: Phone (360) 339-1208 or write to 3000 Rockefeller Avenue, Everett, WA 98201.

Directions: From Interstate 5 at Everett, turn east on U.S. 2 and drive to milepost 10. Turn left at the sign for 100th Street and Westwick Road. Drive five miles on 171st Street SE, then turn right on 48th Street SE and drive about one-half mile into the park at the end of the road.

Trip notes: This campground has a little something for everyone, including swimming, power boating, waterskiing, and good fishing on Flowing Lake.

80 Dosewallips

Location: On the Dosewallips River in Olympic National Park; map A2, grid h0.

Campsites, facilities: There are 30 tent sites. Picnic tables and fire grills are provided. Rest rooms, drinking water, and wheelchair-accessible facilities are available. Leashed pets are permitted.

Reservations, fees: No reservations are accepted. Sites are $10 per night. The campground is open from mid-May to late September.

Contact: Olympic National Park, 600 East Park Avenue, Port Angeles, WA 98362; (360) 452-4501 or fax (360) 452-0335.

Directions: From Interstate 5 at Olympia, go north on U.S. 101 and drive about 61 miles to a signed turnoff (located about one mile south of Brinnon). Turn west and drive 15 miles along the Dosewallips River to the camp.

Trip notes: Dosewallips is a more remote

option to Elkhorn and Collins (campground numbers 81 and 83). Set on the Dosewallips River at 1,540 feet, the camp provides a major trailhead into the backcountry of Olympic National Park. The trail follows the Dosewallips River over Anderson Pass, proceeds along the Quinault River, and ultimately reaches Quinault Lake.

⑧ Elkhorn

Location: On the Dosewallips River in Olympic National Forest; map A2, grid h1.

Campsites, facilities: There are 20 sites for tents, trailers, or RVs up to 21 feet long. Picnic tables are provided. Well water and vault toilets are available. Leashed pets are permitted.

Reservations, fees: Reservations are accepted; phone (360) 796-4886. Sites are $8 per night. The campground is open from mid-May through September.

Contact: Olympic National Forest, Quilcene Ranger District, P.O. Box 280, Quilcene, WA 98376; (360) 765-3368 or fax (360) 765-2202.

Directions: From Interstate 5 at Olympia, go north on U.S. 101 and drive 62 miles to Brinnon. Continue one mile north on U.S. 101, then turn left and drive 10 miles west on Dosewallips Road and Forest Service Road 2610 (the same road). The camp is on the left.

Trip notes: This eight-acre, wooded camp is set on the Dosewallips River at 600 feet, with river and fishing access. It's not far from Olympic National Park, a good side trip.

⑧ Rainbow Group Camp

Location: Near Quilcene in Olympic National Forest; map A2, grid h2.

Campsites, facilities: There are group tent sites only. Picnic tables and fire grills are provided. There is no piped water. Vault toilets are available. A store, a cafe, a Laundromat, and ice are within five miles. Leashed pets are permitted.

Reservations, fees: For reservation and fee information, call (360) 796-4886. Sites are $30 per night, plus $1 per person.

Contact: Olympic National Forest, Quilcene Ranger District, P.O. Box 280, Quilcene, WA 98376; (360) 765-3368 or fax (360) 765-2202.

Directions: From Interstate 5 at Olympia, go north on U.S. 101 and drive approximately 69 miles to the campground.

Trip notes: Rainbow Group Camp is in a rugged, primitive setting on the edge of Olympic National Forest, with backcountry access provided on Forest Service roads (a Forest Service map is advisable). This is an excellent layover spot for U.S. 101 cruisers. Olympic National Park is just a short drive away.

⑧ Collins

Location: On the Duckabush River in Olympic National Forest; map A2, grid h2.

Campsites, facilities: There are six tent sites and 10 sites for trailers or RVs up to 21 feet long. Picnic tables are provided. Well water and vault toilets are available. Leashed pets are permitted.

Reservations, fees: No reservations are accepted. There is no fee. The campground is open from mid-May through September.

Contact: Hood Canal Ranger District, Olympic National Forest, P.O. Box 68, Hoodsport, WA 98548; (360) 877-5254.

Directions: From Interstate 5 at Olympia, go north on U.S. 101 and drive approximately 59 miles. Turn left on Forest Service Road 2510 and drive five miles west. The camp is on the left.

Trip notes: Most tourists cruising U.S. 101 don't have a clue about this spot, yet it's not far from the highway. This four-acre camp is set on the Duckabush River at 200 feet. It has small, shaded sites, river access nearby, and plenty of fishing and hiking. Dosewallips State Park and Olympic National Park provide two side trips within easy driving distance.

⑧ Dosewallips State Park

Location: On Dosewallips Creek; map A2, grid h2.

Campsites, facilities: There are 88 sites for

tents, trailers, or RVs up to 60 feet long. Fire grills are provided. Showers, flush toilets, picnic tables, stoves, and drinking water are available. A recreation hall, a store, a cafe, and laundry facilities are within one mile. Electricity and sewer hookups are available for an extra fee. Facilities are wheelchair accessible. Leashed pets are permitted.

Reservations, fees: Contact Reservations Northwest at (800) 452-5687 ($6 reservation fee). Sites are $5–$16 per night. The campground is open year-round.

Contact: Phone (800) 233-0321 or (360) 796-4415, or write to P.O. Drawer K, Brinnon, WA 98320.

Directions: From Interstate 5 at Olympia, go north on U.S. 101 and drive 61 miles to the park. The entrance is located one mile south of Brinnon.

Trip notes: This 425-acre park is set on the shore of the Hood Canal at the mouth of Dosewallips Creek, which gets a fair run of steelhead in winter months. In Hood Canal, fishing for salmon and rockfish is popular. Beachcombers might consider clamming, but check with the Department of Health prior to harvesting any shellfish, due to seasonal and local conditions. This is a popular camp because it's set right off a major highway, so try to arrive early to insure a space.

85 Scenic Beach State Park

Location: On the Hood Canal; map A2, grid i3.

Campsites, facilities: There are two primitive tent sites and 50 sites for tents, trailers, or self-contained RVs up to 40 feet long. Picnic tables, piped water, fire grills, showers, a sanitary disposal station, and flush toilets are provided. The facilities are wheelchair accessible. Leashed pets are permitted.

Reservations, fees: Contact Reservations Northwest at (800) 452-5687 ($6 reservation fee). Sites are $5–$11 per night. The campground is open from April to mid-November.

Contact: Phone (800) 233-0321 or (360)

830-5079, or write to P.O. Box 7, Seabeck, WA 98380.

Directions: From Interstate 5 at Tacoma, turn north on Highway 16 and drive 30 miles to Bremerton. Continue north on Highway 3 for about nine miles and take the first Silverdale exit (Newberry Hill Road). Turn left and drive approximately three miles to the end of the road, then turn right on Seabeck Highway and follow it to Seabeck. Once in town, take the only road that follows the bay west, then turn right at the first street after the grade school. Continue 1.5 miles on the winding road to the park.

Trip notes: Scenic Beach is an exceptionally beautiful state park, with beach access and superb views of the Olympic Mountains. Beachcombing, oyster hunting, and salmon fishing are among your options. A public boat launch can be found one mile north at Misery Point. Wheelchair-accessible nature trails are available at the park.

86 Cove Trailer Park

Location: Near Dabob Bay; map A2, grid h3.

Campsites, facilities: There are six tent sites and 35 sites with full hookups (including cable TV) for trailers or RVs up to 38 feet long. Electricity, piped water, sewer hookups, and picnic tables are provided. Bottled gas, sanitary services, toilets, a store, laundry facilities, and ice are available. Showers are available for an extra fee. Boat docks and launching facilities are on the Hood Canal within one mile of the park. Leashed pets are permitted.

Reservations, fees: Reservations are accepted. Sites are $12.50 per night. The campground is open year-round.

Contact: Phone the park at (360) 796-4723 or write to 303075 Highway 101, Brinnon, WA 98320.

Directions: From Interstate 5 at Olympia, go north on U.S. 101 and drive 62 miles to Brinnon. Continue three miles north on U.S. 101. The camp is located between mileposts 303 and 304.

Trip notes: This five-acre private camp is in a rural setting, yet it's fully developed with the shore of Dabob Bay nearby. Sites are grassy and graveled with a few trees. Dosewallips State Park is a short drive away and a possible side trip.

⑧ Seal Rock

Location: On Dabob Bay in Olympic National Forest; map A2, grid h3.

Campsites, facilities: There are 40 sites for tents, trailers, or RVs up to 21 feet long. Picnic tables are provided. Piped water, flush toilets, and wheelchair-accessible facilities are available. Boat docks and launching facilities are nearby on the Hood Canal and in Dabob Bay. Leashed pets are permitted.

Reservations, fees: For reservation information, call (360) 796-4886. Sites are $10–$12 per night. The campground is open from mid-April through September.

Contact: Olympic National Forest, Quilcene Ranger District, P.O. Box 280, Quilcene, WA 98376; (360) 765-3368 or fax (360) 765-2202.

Directions: From Interstate 5 at Olympia, go north on U.S. 101 and drive 62 miles to Brinnon. Continue two miles north on U.S. 101. The camp is on the shore at Seal Rock.

Trip notes: Seal Rock is a 30-acre camp set along the shore near the mouth of Dabob Bay. The modern, developed setting provides a good spot for boat owners. This camp gets extremely crowded in the summer months, so reserve your site early.

⑧ Fay Bainbridge State Park

Location: On Bainbridge Island; map A2, grid h4.

Campsites, facilities: There are 10 primitive tent sites and 26 sites for tents or self-contained RVs up to 30 feet long. Picnic tables and fire grills are provided. Sanitary disposal service, piped water, coin-operated showers, toilets, and a playground are available. A store and a cafe are located within one mile. Fire-

wood can be obtained for an extra fee. Some facilities are wheelchair accessible. Boat docks and launching facilities are nearby. Leashed pets are permitted.

Reservations, fees: No reservations are accepted. Sites are $11 per night. The campground is open from April through August.

Contact: Phone (800) 233-0321 or (206) 842-3931, or write to 15546 Sunrise, Bainbridge Island, WA 98110.

Directions: From Interstate 5 at Tacoma, turn north on Highway 16 and drive 30 miles to the junction with Highway 3. Continue north on Highway 3 for about 18 miles, then turn south on Highway 305 and continue to the park at the southeast end of Bainbridge Island.

Trip notes: Set on the edge of Puget Sound, this camp provides all the recreation possibilities of a typical beach park. The primitive walk-in sites are heavily wooded, and the developed sites have great views of the sound. Clamming, diving, picnicking, beachcombing, and kite flying are popular pastimes here. On clear days, campers can enjoys views of Mount Rainier and Mount Baker to the east, and at night the park provides beautiful vistas of the lights of Seattle. In the winter months, there is excellent salmon fishing just offshore of the park.

⑧ Orchard Trailer Park

Location: In Seattle; map A2, grid h6.

Campsites, facilities: There are 10 sites for trailers or RVs of any length. Electricity, piped water, and sewer hookups are provided. A laundry room is available. Bottled gas, a store, a cafe, and ice are located within one mile. Pets are not permitted.

Reservations, fees: No reservations are accepted. Sites are $17 per night. The campground is open year-round.

Contact: Phone (206) 243-1210 or write to 4011 South 146th Street, Seattle, WA 98168.

Directions: From Interstate 5 in Seattle, take exit 154 (Burien) and drive one mile west to Highway 99. Continue north for three-quarters of a mile to South 146th Street, turn east (right), and drive to the trailer park.

Trip notes: Orchard Trailer Park is the smallest and most intimate of the motor home parks in the Seattle area. It's in an urban setting and makes a decent layover spot. An 18-hole golf course is nearby.

⑨⓪ Holiday Park Resort

Location: In Seattle; map A2, grid i6.
Campsites, facilities: There are 22 sites for trailers or RVs up to 32 feet long. Electricity, piped water, and sewer hookups are provided. Flush toilets, showers, a cafe, and a laundry room are available. Bottled gas, sanitary services, a store, and ice are located within one mile.
Reservations, fees: Reservations are accepted. Sites are $17 per night. The campground is open year-round.
Contact: Holiday Park Resort, 19250 Aurora Avenue North, Seattle, WA 98133; (206) 542-2760.
Directions: From Interstate 5 in Seattle, take the 176th Avenue exit and drive west to Aurora Avenue. Turn north and drive to 19250 Aurora Avenue North.
Trip notes: Be sure to reserve in advance; this camp is usually full. The downtown sights of Seattle are just a short drive away. Nearby recreation options include an 18-hole golf course, marked bike trails, and tennis courts.

⑨① Lake Pleasant RV Park

Location: On Lake Pleasant; map A2, grid h6.
Campsites, facilities: There are 196 sites for trailers or RVs. Cable TV, rest rooms, showers, a sanitary dump, a public phone, a laundry room, a playground, and LP gas are available. Facilities are wheelchair accessible. Leashed pets are permitted.
Reservations, fees: Reservations are recommended. Sites are $20 per night. The campground is open year-round.

Contact: Phone the park at (425) 487-1785 or (800) 742-0386, or write to 24025 Bothell Highway, SE, Bothell, WA 98021.
Directions: From Seattle, take Interstate 405 north for about 20 miles to exit 26. Follow the Bothell/Everett Highway over the freeway for about a mile. The park is marked by a large sign on the left side of the road.
Trip notes: Set on Lake Pleasant, this large, developed camp is geared primarily toward RVers. The setting is pretty, with lakeside sites and plenty of trees. Just off the highway, it's a very popular camp, so expect lots of company, especially in the summer. This is a good spot for a little trout fishing.

⑨② Lena Lake Walk-In

Location: Near the Hamma Hamma River in Olympic National Forest; map A2, grid i0.
Campsites, facilities: There are 29 primitive sites at this hike-In campground. There is no piped water. Vault toilets are available. Leashed pets are permitted.
Reservations, fees: No reservations are accepted. There is no fee for camping, but you must obtain a $25 annual Trail Park Pass or pay $3 a day to park at the trailhead. The campground is open year-round, weather permitting.
Contact: Olympic National Forest, Hood Canal Ranger District, P.O. Box 68, Hoodsport, WA 98548; (360) 877-5254 or fax (360) 352-2569.
Directions: From Interstate 5 at Olympia, go north on U.S. 101 and drive 37 miles to Hoodsport. Continue 14 miles north on U.S. 101, then head west for eight miles on Forest Service Road 25 to Lena Creek. Hike 3.2 miles to Lena Lake. Campsites are scattered around the lake.
Trip notes: You can't beat the price of this 135-acre camp set on Lena Lake. The hike in from Lena Creek to the campground is suitable for the entire family, and well worth it. The majority of weekend campers would rather not deal with the hassle, so this spot is rarely crowded. It's a lovely setting, too, with a pleasantly mild climate in summer.

⑨ Lena Creek

Location: On the Hamma Hamma River in Olympic National Forest; map A2, grid i0.

Campsites, facilities: There are 14 sites for tents, trailers, or RVs up to 21 feet long. Picnic tables are provided. Well water and vault toilets are available. Wheelchair-accessible rest rooms are available. Leashed pets are permitted.

Reservations, fees: No reservations are accepted. Sites are $8 per night. The campground is open from mid-May through September.

Contact: Olympic National Forest, Hood Canal Ranger District, P.O. Box 68, Hoodsport, WA 98548; (360) 877-5254 or fax (360) 352-2569.

Directions: From Interstate 5 at Olympia, go north on U.S. 101 and drive 37 miles to Hoodsport. Continue 14 miles north on U.S. 101, then turn left on Forest Service Road 25 and drive eight miles to the camp on the left.

Trip notes: This seven-acre camp is set where Lena Creek empties into the Hamma Hamma River. A trail from the camp leads three miles to Lena Lake and seven miles to Upper Lena Lake. A map of Olympic National Forest details the trail and road system. The camp is rustic with some improvements. If this camp is full, try the hike in to Lena Lake (see campground number 92)—with a little extra effort, you can camp for free.

⑨ Lilliwaup Creek

Location: On Lilliwaup Creek in Bert Cole State Forest; map A2, grid i1.

Campsites, facilities: There are 13 sites for tents or small trailers. Picnic tables, fire grills, and tent pads are provided. Vault toilets and piped water are available. Leashed pets are permitted.

Reservations, fees: No reservations are accepted. There is no fee. The campground is open year-round.

Contact: Department of Natural Resources, South Puget Sound Region, P.O. Box 68, Enumclaw, WA 98022-0068; (360) 825-1631.

Directions: From Interstate 5 at Olympia, go

north on U.S. 101 and drive 41 miles to Lilliwaup (four miles north of Hoodsport). Continue seven miles north on U.S. 101, then turn left on Jorsted Creek Road (Forest Service Road 24) and drive 6.5 miles west to the camp. It's on the right side of Lilliwaup Creek.

Trip notes: An alternative to Melbourne (campground number 95), this camp is also in a primitive, quiet setting, but has piped water. Lilliwaup Creek makes for a nice backdrop, and anglers will enjoy the fishing.

⑨ Melbourne

Location: On Melbourne Lake in Bert Cole State Forest; map A2, grid i1.

Campsites, facilities: There are five sites for tents or small trailers. Picnic tables, fire grills, and tent pads are provided. Vault toilets are available. There is no piped water, so bring your own. Firearms are prohibited. Leashed pets are permitted.

Reservations, fees: No reservations are accepted. There is no fee. The campground is open year-round.

Contact: Department of Natural Resources, South Puget Sound Region, P.O. Box 68, Enumclaw, WA 98022-0068; (360) 825-1631.

Directions: From Interstate 5 at Olympia, go north on U.S. 101 and drive 41 miles to Lilliwaup (four miles north of Hoodsport). Continue seven miles north on U.S. 101, then turn left on Jorsted Creek Road (Forest Service Road 24) and drive 5.5 miles. Turn left and travel on a gravel road for 1.7 miles, then bear left and drive three-quarters of a mile to the camp, which is on Melbourne Lake.

Trip notes: This primitive camp is on Melbourne Lake at about 1,000 feet in a little-known, rustic setting. If you want quiet, and don't mind a lack of facilities, this is a good drive-to option. Nearby Lilliwaup Creek (campground number 94) has piped water.

⑨ Hamma Hamma

Location: On the Hamma Hamma River in Olympic National Forest; map A2, grid i1.

Campsites, facilities: There are three tent sites and 12 sites for trailers or RVs up to 21 feet long. Picnic tables are provided. Hand-pumped water and vault toilets are available. Some facilities are wheelchair accessible. Leashed pets are permitted.

Reservations, fees: No reservations are accepted. Sites are $8 per night. The campground is open from May to mid-November.

Contact: Olympic National Forest, Hood Canal Ranger District, P.O. Box 68, Hoodsport, WA 98548; (360) 877-5254 or fax (360) 352-2569.

Directions: From Interstate 5 at Olympia, go north on U.S. 101 and drive 37 miles to Hoodsport. Continue 14 miles north on U.S. 101, then turn left on Forest Service Road 25 and drive 6.5 miles west to the camp on the left side of the road.

Trip notes: A good holdover for vacationers cruising U.S. 101, this camp is set on the Hamma Hamma River at about 600 feet. It's small and primitive, but can be preferable to the expensive developed camps on the U.S. 101 circuit.

⑨ Minerva Beach Mobile Village and RV Resort

Location: On the Hood Canal; map A2, grid j1.

Campsites, facilities: There are 20 tent sites and 23 sites for trailers or RVs. Cable TV, rest rooms, a public phone, a laundry room, limited groceries, ice, RV supplies, and LP gas are available. There are also horseshoe pits, a gift shop, and a recreation hall. Leashed pets are permitted.

Reservations, fees: Reservations are recommended. Sites are $15–$20 per night. The campground is open year-round.

Contact: Phone the park at (360) 877-5145 or write to North 21110 Highway 101, Shelton, WA 98584.

Directions: From Olympia, drive on Highway 104 west toward Aberdeen. Take the Shelton/Port Angeles exit. Turn right on U.S. 101 north. Drive about 20 miles and pass Potlatch State Park. Minerva Beach Mobile

Village and RV Resort is just past Potlatch on both sides. Access to the resort office is by the driveway on the left.

Trip notes: Located on the ocean, this is a perfect layover spot if you're cruising up or down U.S. 101. Recreational opportunities at this park include swimming and salmon fishing. Oysters, crabs, and clams are also available here. A good side trip is nearby Potlatch State Park.

⑨ Toonerville

Location: In Tahuya State Forest; map A2, grid i2.

Campsites, facilities: There are four sites for tents or small trailers. Picnic tables, fire grills, and tent pads are provided. Vault toilets are available, but there is no piped water. Leashed pets and motorbikes are permitted.

Reservations, fees: No reservations are accepted. There is no fee. Call for an update on seasonal closures. A map and brochure are available for $2; see the contact information below.

Contact: Department of Natural Resources, South Puget Sound Region, P.O. Box 68, Enumclaw, WA 98022-0068; (360) 825-1631 or fax (360) 825-1672.

Directions: From Interstate 5 at Tacoma, turn north on Highway 16 and drive 30 miles to Bremerton. Turn south on Highway 3 and drive nine miles southwest to the town of Belfair. From Belfair, take Highway 300 west for one-third of a mile, then bear left and continue for another 3.3 miles. Turn right on Belfair-Tahuya Road and drive one-half mile, then turn right on Elfendahl Pass Road for 2.5 miles (past the Tahuya four-wheel-drive trailhead). Continue straight through the intersection with Goat Ranch Road and drive 3.3 miles to the camp, which is on the left.

Trip notes: Primitive and rustic, this campground is managed by the Department of Natural Resources and has trails for use by hikers, horses, and motorbikes. It's a pretty, forested, and little-used spot. Be sure to bring your own water, because there is none to be found near here.

⑨ Green Mountain Camp

Location: In Tahuya State Forest; map A2, grid i3.

Campsites, facilities: There are 13 hike-in sites for tents only. Picnic tables, fire grills, and tent pads are provided. Vault toilets, hand-pumped water, and facilities for horses are available.

Reservations, fees: Reservations are required. There is no fee. Call the Department of Natural Resources (see the contact information below) for an update on seasonal closures and any gate information. A map and brochure are available for $2.

Contact: Department of Natural Resources, South Puget Sound Region, P.O. Box 68, Enumclaw, WA 98022-0068; (360) 825-1631 or fax (360) 825-1672.

Directions: From Silverdale on Highway 3, turn west on Newberry Hill Road and drive three miles. Turn left on Seabeck Highway and drive two miles, then turn right on Holly Road and travel four miles. Turn left on Tahuya Lake Road and drive one mile. At Green Mountain Road, the Department of Natural Resources provides a parking lot where your four-mile hike in will begin.

Trip notes: This is a prime spot, primitive but with hand-pumped water provided. The campground is operated by the Department of Natural Resources and is located in Tahuya State Forest. There are facilities for horses, as well as trails for motor biking, hiking, and horseback riding. The status changes, though; it's a good idea to call first.

⑩ Illahee State Park

Location: Near Bremerton; map A2, grid i4.

Campsites, facilities: There are eight primitive tent sites and 25 sites for tents or self-contained RVs up to 30 feet long. Picnic tables and fire grills are provided. A sanitary disposal service, toilets, and a playground are available. Showers and firewood can be ob-

tained for an extra fee. A Laundromat and ice are located within one mile. Some facilities are wheelchair accessible. Boat docks and launching facilities are available. Leashed pets are permitted.

Reservations, fees: No reservations are accepted. Sites are $5–$10 per night. The campground is open year-round.

Contact: Phone (800) 233-0321 or (360) 478-6460, or write to 3540 Bahia Vista, Bremerton, WA 98310.

Directions: From Interstate 5 at Tacoma, turn north on Highway 16 and drive 30 miles to Bremerton. Turn east on Highway 303 and continue three miles northeast, then take the east turnoff to the park on the right.

Trip notes: This 75-acre park is just three miles from civilization in Bremerton, yet virtually unknown to out-of-towners touring the area. The campsites are set in a pretty, forested area, and some are grassy. The park has a ball field, a playground, and beach access. The shoreline is fairly rocky, though there is a small sandy area for sunbathers. Clamming is popular here. A fishing pier and a moorage float are available for anglers.

⑪ Manchester State Park

Location: On Puget Sound; map A2, grid i4.

Campsites, facilities: There are 53 sites for tents or self-contained RVs up to 42 feet long. Picnic tables and fire grills are provided. Piped water, a sanitary disposal station, and toilets are available. Showers and firewood can be obtained for an extra fee. Some facilities are wheelchair accessible. Leashed pets are permitted.

Reservations, fees: Contact Reservations Northwest at (800) 452-5687 ($6 reservation fee). Sites are $5–$10 per night. The campground is open year-round, with limited winter facilities.

Contact: Phone (800) 233-0321 or (360) 871-4065, or write to P.O. Box 36, Manchester, WA 98353.

Directions: From Interstate 5 at Tacoma, take

the Highway 16 exit and head north to Bremerton. Take the Sedgwick exit off Highway 16 and follow the signs to the park.

Trip notes: Set on the edge of Point Orchard, this campground has excellent lookouts across Puget Sound. Manchester State Park has many good hiking trails, along with places for fishing and clamming. The camp gets relatively little use, especially in the off-season, so you're almost always guaranteed a spot. Group and day-use reservations are available.

102 Blake Island State Park

Location: Near Seattle; map A2, grid i5.

Campsites, facilities: There are 54 primitive, boat-in tent sites. Picnic tables and fire grills are provided. Piped water, portable toilets, showers, firewood, and a restaurant are available. Some facilities are wheelchair accessible. Boat buoys and floats are available. Leashed pets are permitted.

Reservations, fees: No reservations are accepted. Sites are $5–$10 per night. The campground is open year-round.

Contact: Phone (800) 233-0321 or (360) 731-0770, or write to P.O. Box 277, Manchester, WA 98353.

Directions: This little island is three miles west of Seattle and is accessible only by boat.

Trip notes: Located right in the middle of the massive Seattle metropolitan area on a small island, this camp offers a combination of primitive setting and developed facilities, including Tillicum Village, a restaurant serving northwest Indian fare. Good bottom fishing can be found off the reef. A three-quarter-mile nature trail and 15 miles of hiking trails are available.

103 Seattle Tacoma KOA

Location: In Kent; map A2, grid i6.

Campsites, facilities: There are 10 tent sites and 131 sites for trailers or RVs. Facilities include rest rooms, showers, water, electricity and sewer hookups, a sanitary dump, a public phone, a laundry room, limited groceries, ice, and RV supplies. A large playground, a game room, a heated swimming pool, and a recreation hall are also available. Facilities are wheelchair accessible. Leashed pets are permitted.

Reservations, fees: Reservations are recommended. Sites are $22–$28 per night. The campground is open year-round.

Contact: Phone the park at (800) 562-1892 or (253) 872-8652, or write to 5801 South 212th Street, Kent, WA 98032.

Directions: From Seattle, drive south on Interstate 5 to 188th Street (exit 152), then drive 50 feet on 188th Street. Turn east on Orillia Road and drive 2.5 miles to the campground on the right.

Trip notes: This is a popular urban campground, not far from the highway yet in a pleasant setting. The sites are spacious, with several pull-throughs to accommodate large RVs. A public golf course is located nearby. During the summer, a tour of Seattle can be taken from the campground.

104 Blue Sky RV Park

Location: Near Lake Sammamish State Park; map A2, grid i8.

Campsites, facilities: There are 51 sites for trailers or RVs. Cable TV, electricity, sewer hookups, rest rooms, showers, a public phone, and a laundry room are available. Facilities are wheelchair accessible. Leashed pets are permitted.

Reservations, fees: Reservations are recommended. Sites are $18.50 per night. The campground is open year-round.

Contact: Phone the park at (425) 222-7910 or write to 9002 302nd Avenue SE, Issaquah, WA 98027.

Directions: From Seattle, take Interstate 5 east to Highway 90. Turn east on Highway 90 and drive about 22 miles to exit 22 (Preston/Falls City exit). Turn right on Southeast 82nd Street and at the first stop sign, turn left on 302nd Avenue SE, and drive a short distance to the campground entrance at the end of the road.

Trip notes: Blue Sky RV Park is in an urban setting just outside of Seattle. It's a good off-the-beaten-path alternative to the crowded camps in the metro area, yet still only a short drive from the main attractions in the city. Nearby Lake Sammamish State Park provides more rustic recreation opportunities, including hiking and fishing.

105 Aqua Barn Ranch

Location: South of Seattle; map A2, grid j7.

Campsites, facilities: There are approximately 40 tent sites and 200 sites for trailers or RVs. Rest rooms, showers, a sanitary dump, a public phone, a laundry room, ice, a restaurant, and LP gas are available. Recreational facilities include horseshoe pits, a game room, an indoor heated swimming pool, and a playground. Some of the facilities are wheelchair accessible. Leashed pets are permitted.

Reservations, fees: Reservations are recommended. Sites are $16–$23 per night.

Contact: Phone (800) 284-2227 or (425) 255-4618, or write to 15227 SE Renton–Maple Valley Highway, Renton, WA 98058.

Directions: From Seattle, drive south on Interstate 5 for about 10 miles. Turn north on Highway 405 and take the Enumclaw/Maple Valley exit (exit 4), turning right on Highway 169/Maple Valley Road. Drive about three miles to the campground on the right.

Trip notes: This large park with spacious sites (grassy for tent campers) is an ideal layover spot for campers who want to avoid the metro-area crowds. You'll find all the amenities, including a pool and hot tub. Numerous recreation options are available in the Seattle area, just 20 minutes north.

106 Trailer Inns RV Park and Recreation Center

Location: Near Lake Sammamish State Park; map A2, grid i7.

Campsites, facilities: There are 104 sites for trailers or RVs of any length. Electricity, piped water, sewer hookups, and picnic tables are provided. Flush toilets, bottled gas, showers, a recreation hall, a swimming pool, a laundry room, ice, and a playground are available. Sanitary services, a store, and a cafe are available within one mile. Leashed pets and motorbikes are permitted.

Reservations, fees: Reservations are accepted. Sites are $19–$29 per night. The campground is open year-round.

Contact: Phone (206) 747-9181 or (509) 248-1142, or write to 15531 Southeast 37th Avenue, Bellevue, WA 98006.

Directions: From the junction of Interstate 405 and Interstate 90 in Bellevue, go east on Interstate 90 for two miles to exit 11A, then go south on the frontage road to the park.

Trip notes: This park with all the amenities is a haven for RV travelers, and it's close to Lake Sammamish State Park as well. Nearby recreation options include an 18-hole golf course, hiking trails, marked bike trails, and tennis courts.

107 Issaquah Village RV Park

Location: Near the Cascade Mountains; map A2, grid i8.

Campsites, facilities: There are 112 sites for trailers or RVs of any length. No tents are allowed. Cable TV, water, electricity, and sewer hookups, rest rooms, showers, a sanitary dump, a public phone, a laundry room, and LP gas are available. Picnic areas, a playground, and a recreation field are also provided. The facilities are wheelchair accessible. Leashed pets are permitted.

Reservations, fees: Reservations are recommended. Sites are $26–$28 per night. The campground is open year-round.

Contact: Phone the park at (800) 258-9233 or (425) 392-9233, or write to 650 First Avenue NE, Issaquah, WA 98027.

Directions: From Seattle, take Interstate 90 east for 17 miles to exit 17. Turn left and go under the freeway. Take the first right for a very short distance and keep bearing right. You'll end up paralleling the freeway. The park is on the left in about a quarter of a mile.

Trip notes: Though Issaquah Village RV Park doesn't allow tents, it's set in a beautiful environment ringed by the Cascade Mountains, making it a more scenic alternative to Blue Sky RV Park (campground number 104). Lake Sammamish State Park is just a few miles north.

108 Vasa Park Resort

Location: On Lake Sammamish; map A2, grid i8.

Campsites, facilities: There are 16 tent sites with partial hookups and six sites for trailers or RVs of any length with full hookups. Piped water, sewer hookups, and picnic tables are provided. Flush toilets, sanitary services, a playground, electricity, and showers are available. Bottled gas, firewood, a store, and a cafe are located within one mile. Boat launching facilities are at the resort on Lake Sammamish. Leashed pets are permitted.

Reservations, fees: Reservations are accepted. Sites are $15–$20 per night. The campground is open from mid-May to mid-October.

Contact: Phone (425) 746-3260 or write to 3560 West Lake Sammamish Parkway SE, Bellevue, WA 98008.

Directions: From Interstate 90 in Bellevue, take exit 13 and drive one mile north. The campground is on the west side of Lake Sammamish.

Trip notes: This is the most rustic of the parks in the immediate Seattle area. The resort is on Lake Sammamish, and the state park is at the south end of the lake. An 18-hole golf course, hiking trails, marked bike trails, and a riding stable are close by.

109 Snoqualmie River Campground

Location: On the Snoqualmie River; map A2, grid i9.

Campsites, facilities: There are approximately 80 tent sites and 50 sites for trailers or RVs of any length. Piped water and picnic tables are provided. Flush toilets, sanitary services, showers, and a playground are available. Electricity and firewood can be obtained for an extra fee. Bottled gas, a store, a cafe, and ice are located within two miles. Boat launching facilities are located within one-half mile. Leashed pets are permitted.

Reservations, fees: Reservations are accepted. Sites are $15–$18 per night. The campground is open from April to late October, as well as some off-season weekends (call first to verify).

Contact: Phone (425) 222-5545 or write to P.O. Box 16, Fall City, WA 98024.

Directions: From Interstate 5 at Seattle, turn east on Interstate 90 and drive 26 miles to exit 22 (Preston-Fall City). Turn north on Preston-Fall City Road and drive 4.5 miles, then turn east on SE 44th Place and drive one mile to the campground at the end of the road.

Trip notes: If you're in the Seattle area and stuck for a place for the night, this pretty 10-acre park set along the Snoqualmie River may be a welcome option. Activities include fishing, swimming, hiking, biking, and rafting. Nearby recreation options include several nine-hole golf courses. A worthwhile side trip is beautiful Snoqualmie Falls, 3.5 miles away in the famed "Twin Peaks" country.

110 Lake Cushman State Park

Location: On Lake Cushman; map A2, grid i0.

Campsites, facilities: There are 50 tent sites, 30 sites with full hookups for trailers or RVs up to 60 feet long, and two primitive sites. Picnic tables and fire grills are provided. Sanitary disposal services, piped water, rest rooms, showers, and wheelchair-accessible facilities are available. A store, a restaurant, and ice can be found within one mile. Firewood is available for an extra fee. Boat docks and launching facilities are located at nearby Lake Cushman. Leashed pets are permitted.

Reservations, fees: Contact Reservations

Northwest at (800) 452-5687 ($6 reservation fee). Sites are $10–$15 per night. The campground is open from April through October.

Contact: Phone (800) 233-0321 or (360) 877-5491, or write to P.O. Box 128, Hoodsport, WA 98548.

Directions: From Interstate 5 at Olympia, take the U.S. 101 exit and drive 37 miles north to Hoodsport. Turn west (left) on Highway 119 (Staircase Road) and continue seven miles to the park on the left.

Trip notes: Beach access and good trout fishing are highlights of this 603-acre camp on the shore of Lake Cushman. The 10-mile-long lake is surrounded by the Olympic Mountains, and an 18-hole golf course and marked hiking trails are nearby.

111 Brown Creek

Location: On Brown Creek in Olympic National Forest; map A2 grid j0.

Campsites, facilities: There are seven tent sites and 12 sites for trailers or RVs up to 25 feet long. Picnic tables are provided. Hand-pumped water and vault toilets are available. Leashed pets are permitted.

Reservations, fees: No reservations are accepted. Sites are $8 per night. The campground is open year-round.

Contact: Olympic National Forest, Hood Canal Ranger District, P.O. Box 68, Hoodsport, WA 94548; (360) 877-5254 or fax (360) 352-2569.

Directions: From Interstate 5 at Olympia, take exit 104 onto Highway 8 and drive for six miles. Head north on U.S. 101 for 23 miles. Go left on Skokomish Valley Road and drive five miles. Turn on Forest Service Road 23 and drive nine miles, then turn at Forest Service Road 2353 and drive for three-quarters of a mile. Turn onto Forest Service Road 2340 into the campground. A Forest Service map is essential.

Trip notes: Virtually unknown to outsiders, this camp is accessible to two-wheel-drive vehicles, but the road connects to a network of primitive, backcountry Forest Service roads.

The small campground (just six acres) is within the vast Olympic National Forest, which offers a plethora of opportunities for outdoors enthusiasts. Obtain a Forest Service map to expand your trip.

112 Potlatch State Park

Location: On the Hood Canal; map A2, grid j1.

Campsites, facilities: There are two primitive tent sites, 17 developed tent sites, and 18 drive-through sites with full hookups for trailers or RVs up to 60 feet long. Picnic tables, fire grills, and drinking water are provided. Sanitary disposal services and rest rooms with showers are available. Firewood is available for an extra fee. A boat launch is located at the park, and boat docks can be found nearby at the Hood Canal. Leashed pets are permitted.

Reservations, fees: No reservations are accepted. Sites are $5–$16 per night. The campground is open from late March through October.

Contact: Phone (800) 233-0321 or (360) 877-5361, or write to P.O. Box D, Hoodsport, WA 98548.

Directions: From Interstate 5 at Olympia, go north on U.S. 101 and drive 22 miles to Shelton. Continue north on U.S. 101 for 12 miles to the park, located along the shoreline of the Hood Canal.

Trip notes: Vacationers towing boats should consider this camp with spacious drive-through sites. The 57-acre park is set along the Hood Canal, where fishing, clamming, crabbing, and scuba diving should keep visitors busy. Marked hiking trails are located nearby.

113 Rest a While

Location: On the Hood Canal; map A2, grid j1.

Campsites, facilities: There are two tent sites and 90 sites for trailers or RVs of any length; 36 are pull-throughs. Electricity, piped water, and sewer and cable TV hookups are provided. Bottled gas, toilets, firewood, a recreation hall, a store, laundry facilities, and ice are available. A cafe is less than a mile from the park. Showers are available for an extra fee. Boat docks, launching facilities, boat rentals, and a private clamming beach are other amenities. Leashed pets and motorbikes are permitted.

Reservations, fees: Reservations are accepted. Sites are $17–$19 per night. The campground is open year-round.

Contact: Phone the park at (360) 877-9474 or write to N 27001 Highway 101, Hoodsport, WA 98548.

Directions: From Interstate 5 at Olympia, go north on U.S. 101 and drive 37 miles to Hoodsport. Continue 2.5 miles north on U.S. 101 to the camp located at milepost 329.

Trip notes: This seven-acre park, located at sea level on the Hood Canal, offers waterfront sites and a private beach for clamming and oyster gathering, not to mention plenty of opportunities to fish, boat, and scuba dive. It's an alternative to Potlatch State Park and Glen Ayr RV Park (campground numbers 112 and 115).

⑭ Big Creek

Location: Near Lake Cushman in Olympic National Forest; map A2, grid j1.

Campsites, facilities: There are 23 sites for tents or RVs up to 30 feet long. Sheltered picnic tables are provided. Well water, firewood (summer months), vault toilets, and wheelchair-accessible rest rooms are available. A boat dock and ramp are located at nearby Lake Cushman. Leashed pets are permitted.

Reservations, fees: No reservations are accepted. Sites are $6 per night. The campground is open from May through mid-November.

Contact: Olympic National Forest, Hood Canal Ranger District, P.O. Box 68, Hoodsport, WA 94548; (360) 877-5254 or fax (360) 352-2569.

Directions: From Interstate 5 at Olympia, go north on U.S. 101 and drive 37 miles to Hoodsport. Turn northwest on Highway 119

and drive nine miles to the T intersection. Turn left and the campground is on the right.

Trip notes: Big Creek is a good alternative to Staircase (see campground number 46 in Chapter A1) on the North Fork Skokomish River and Lake Cushman State Park (see campground number 110 in this chapter) on Lake Cushman, both of which get heavier use. The sites are large and well spaced over 30 acres.

⑮ Glen Ayr RV Park

Location: On the Hood Canal; map A2, grid j1.

Campsites, facilities: There are 45 sites for trailers or RVs of any length; nine are pull-throughs. Electricity, piped water, sewer hookups, and picnic tables are provided. Bottled gas, toilets, showers, cable TV, a recreation hall, and laundry facilities are available. A store, a cafe, and ice are within one mile. A boat dock is located across the street from the park. Leashed pets are permitted.

Reservations, fees: Reservations are accepted but not required. Sites are $21 per night for two people. The campground is open year-round.

Contact: Glen Ayr RV Park, N 25381 Highway 101, Hoodsport, WA 98548; (360) 877-9522; Web site: www.publiconline.com/glenayrcanal.

Directions: From Interstate 5 at Olympia, go north on U.S. 101 and drive 37 miles to Hoodsport. Continue one mile north on U.S. 101 to the park on the left.

Trip notes: This adult-oriented, fully developed, nine-acre park is located at sea level on the Hood Canal, where there are opportunities to fish and scuba dive. Salmon fishing is especially excellent. Swimming and boating are two other options. The park has a spa, a full-service marina, horseshoe pits, a recreation field, and a hotel.

⑯ Aldrich Lake

Location: On Aldrich Lake in Tahuya State Forest; map A2, grid j2.

Campsites, facilities: There are four primitive campsites for tents or small trailers. Picnic tables, fire grills, and tent pads are provided. Vault toilets and piped water are available. A hand launch for small boats is located at the lake. Leahed pets are permitted.

Reservations, fees: Call the park for an update on seasonal closures and any gate information. There is no fee. A map and brochure are available for $2; see the contact information below.

Contact: Department of Natural Resources, South Puget Sound Region, P.O. Box 68, Enumclaw, WA 98022-0068; (360) 825-1631 or fax (360) 825-1672.

Directions: From Interstate 5 at Tacoma, turn north on Highway 16 and drive 30 miles to Bremerton. Turn west on Highway 3 and drive nine miles to Belfair, then turn west on Highway 300 and proceed approximately 12 miles to the town of Tahuya. Turn north on Belfair-Tahuya Road and drive four miles, then turn left on Dewatto Road and drive two miles. Turn left again on Hobaj Lane and drive one-half mile, then turn right and drive two-thirds of a mile. Turn right again and drive 200 yards to the campground.

Trip notes: This campground on Aldrich Lake is managed by the Department of Natural Resources. Robbins Lake is nearby and has day-use facilities and a hand launch for small boats. To reach Robbins Lake, follow the directions above, except after turning left on Hobaj Lane and driving one-half mile, make another left and drive one mile to the lake.

⑪ Snooze Junction RV Park 🚐

Location: Near Belfair; map A2, grid J2.

Campsites, facilities: There are 36 sites for trailers or RVs of any length; 12 are drive-throughs with full hookups. Electricity, piped water, sewer hookups, and picnic tables are provided. Bottled gas, toilets, showers, and a recreation hall are available. A store, a cafe, a Laundromat, and ice are located within one mile. Boat docks and launching facilities are nearby. Leashed pets are permitted.

Reservations, fees: Reservations are accepted. Sites are $17.26–$19 per night. The campground is open year-round.

Contact: Phone (360) 275-2381 or write to P.O. Box 880, Belfair, WA 98528.

Directions: From Interstate 5 at Olympia, turn north on U.S. 101 and drive 22 miles to Shelton. Turn north on Highway 3 and drive approximately 24 miles to the town of Belfair. Turn left on Highway 300 and drive two miles northeast to Gladwin Beach Road (located between mileposts 1 and 2). Drive one-half mile left (west) to the campground on the right.

Trip notes: This is a good holdover spot for RV campers preparing to head north. It's a pleasant park, with ocean access and spacious sites. Fishing, swimming, an 18-hole golf course, and marked bike trails provide recreation options.

⑱ Belfair State Park 🚐 ⛺

Location: On the Hood Canal; map A2, grid J2.

Campsites, facilities: There are 137 sites for tents and 47 for trailers or RVs up to 75 feet long. Picnic tables and fire grills are provided. A sanitary disposal station, flush toilets, coin-operated showers, and a playground are available. A store and a restaurant are located within one mile. Electricity, piped water, and sewer hookups can be obtained for an extra fee. Some facilities are wheelchair accessible. Leashed pets are permitted.

Reservations, fees: Contact Reservations Northwest at (800) 452-5687 ($6 reservation fee). Sites are $10–$16 per night. The campground is open year-round.

Contact: Phone (800) 233-0321 or (360) 275-0668, or write to NE 410 Beck Road, Belfair, WA 98528.

Directions: From Interstate 5 at Tacoma, take the Highway 16 exit and drive northwest for 30 miles to Bremerton. Turn south on Highway 3 and continue nine miles to Belfair. Turn west and drive three miles on Highway 300 to the park on the left.

Trip notes: Tent campers will consider this a good alternative to Snooze Junction RV Park (campground number 117). Set along the edge of the Hood Canal, this park offers an unguarded saltwater swimming area, a sports area, and a few wooded campsites. Nearby recreation options include the town of Shelton, which boasts the Forest Festival in May and the Oysterfest in October, and the Puget Sound Naval Shipyard in Bremerton. Big Mission Creek and Little Mission Creek, both located in the park, are habitat for chum salmon during spawning season in the fall.

⑲ Twanoh State Park

Location: Near Union; map A2, grid j2.

Campsites, facilities: There are 38 tent sites and nine sites for trailers or RVs up to 35 feet long. Picnic tables and fire grills are provided. Flush toilets, a store, and a playground are available. Electricity, piped water, sewer hookups, showers, and firewood can be obtained for an extra fee. Some facilities are wheelchair accessible. Leashed pets are permitted.

Reservations, fees: No reservations are accepted. Sites are $5–$16 per night. The campground is open year-round, with limited winter facilities.

Contact: Phone (800) 233-0321 or (360) 275-2222, or write to P.O. Box 2520, Belfair, WA 98528.

Directions: From Interstate 5 at Olympia, go north on U.S. 101 and drive 32 miles. Turn east on Highway 106 and drive 10 miles (through the town of Union) to the park.

Trip notes: If you're cruising U.S. 101, this camp is only a short drive east off Highway 106. Often bypassed by visitors touring Washington, it's a prime recreation area, with opportunities for swimming, waterskiing, fishing, and boating on the beautiful Hood Canal. The water here is warmer because it's saltwater from the sound. Other amenities include a tennis court, horseshoe pits, and a concession stand.

⑳ Tahuya River Horse Camp

Location: On the Tahuya River in Tahuya State Forest; map A2, grid j2.

Campsites, facilities: There are nine primitive campsites for tents or small trailers. Picnic tables, fire grills, and tent pads are provided. Vault toilets, piped water, and equestrian facilities are available. Leashed pets and motorbikes are permitted.

Reservations, fees: Call the park for an update on seasonal closures and any gate information. There is no fee. A map and brochure are available for $2; see the contact information below.

Contact: Department of Natural Resources, South Puget Sound Region, P.O. Box 68, Enumclaw, WA 98022-0068; (360) 825-1631 or fax (360) 825-1672.

Directions: From Interstate 5 at Tacoma, turn north on Highway 16 and drive 30 miles to Bremerton. Turn south on Highway 3 and drive eight miles southwest to the town of Belfair. From Belfair, take Highway 300 west for one-third of a mile, then bear left and follow it for 3.3 miles. Turn right on Belfair-Tahuya Road and drive 1.7 miles, then turn right on Spillman Road and drive two miles. Turn left and drive three-quarters of a mile to the campground.

Trip notes: Set along the Tahuya River, Tahuya River Horse Camp is a good base for trips into Tahuya State Forest. The nearby trails can be used by hikers, horses, or motorbikes. Fishing is another recreation option here.

㉑ Howell Lake

Location: In Tahuya State Forest; map A2, grid j2.

Campsites, facilities: There are six campsites for tents or small trailers. Picnic tables, fire grills, and tent pads are provided. Vault toilets and piped water are available. A boat launch for small craft is located at Howell Lake. Leashed pets and motorbikes are permitted.

Reservations, fees: Call the park for an update on seasonal closures and any gate information. There is no fee. A map and brochure are available for $2; see the contact information below.

Contact: Department of Natural Resources, South Puget Sound Region, P.O. Box 68, Enumclaw, WA 98022-0068; (360) 825-1631 or fax (360) 825-1672.

Directions: From Interstate 5 at Tacoma, turn north on Highway 16 and drive 30 miles to Bremerton. Turn south on Highway 3 and drive eight miles southwest to the town of Belfair. From Belfair, take Highway 300 for one-third of a mile, then follow it left for another 3.3 miles. Turn right on Belfair-Tahuya Road and continue 4.5 miles to the campground.

Trip notes: Nestled along Lake Howell, this pretty spot managed by the Department of Natural Resources doesn't get a lot of use. But it's a great deal, with water, scenery, and a boat launch, plus trails for hikers, horses, and motorbikes—and very few people.

122 Robin Hood Village

Location: Near the Hood Canal; map A2, grid j2.

Campsites, facilities: There are four tent sites and 16 sites for trailers or RVs of any length. Electricity, piped water, sewer and cable TV hookups, and picnic tables are provided. Toilets, showers, a restaurant, a liquor store, and a laundry room are available. Bottled gas, sanitary services, a store, and ice can be found within one mile. Boat docks and launching facilities are located in the park. Leashed pets are permitted.

Reservations, fees: Reservations are accepted. Sites are $18 per night. The campground is open year-round.

Contact: Robin Hood Village, East 6780 Highway 106, Union, WA 98592; (360) 898-2163, fax (360) 898-2164.

Directions: From Interstate 5 at Tacoma, turn north on Highway 16 and drive 30 miles to the junction with Highway 3. Turn south-

west and drive eight miles to Belfair, then continue southwest on Highway 106 for 13 miles to the campground at East 6780 Highway 106.

Trip notes: This wooded park, an option near Toonerville Multiple Use Area and Howell Lake, has access to the Hood Canal. Nearby recreation options include an 18-hole golf course and a full-service marina.

123 Twin Lakes

Location: In Tahuya State Forest; map A2, grid j1.

Campsites, facilities: There are six primitive campsites for tents or small trailers. Picnic tables, fire grills, and tent pads are provided. Vault toilets are available, but there is no piped water. A hand launch for small boats can be found at the lake. Leashed pets are permitted.

Reservations, fees: Call the park for an update on seasonal closures and any gate information. There is no fee. A map and brochure are available for $2; see the contact information below.

Contact: Department of Natural Resources, South Puget Sound Region, P.O. Box 68, Enumclaw, WA 98022-0068; (360) 825-1631 or fax (360) 825-1672.

Directions: From Interstate 5 at Tacoma, turn north on Highway 16 and drive 30 miles to Bremerton. Turn south on Highway 3 and drive nine miles to the town of Belfair. From Belfair drive one-third of a mile on Highway 300, continue to follow it left for 3.3 miles, then turn right on Belfair-Tahuya Road. Drive one-half mile, then turn right on Elfendahl Pass Road and drive 2.5 miles. At Twin Lakes Road turn left and drive 1.7 miles, then turn right and drive one-half mile to the camp.

Trip notes: Little known, free, and quiet, this wooded campground is in Tahuya State Forest and managed by the Department of Natural Resources. The fishing can be decent, and other highlights include privacy, shady sites, lake views, and even a boat ramp. Don't forget to bring water.

124 Camp Spillman

Location: On the Tahuya River in Tahuya State Forest; map A2, grid j2.

Campsites, facilities: There are six primitive campsites for tents or small trailers. Picnic tables, fire grills, and tent pads are provided. Vault toilets and piped water are available. Leashed pets and motorbikes are permitted.

Reservations, fees: Call the park for an update on seasonal closures and any gate information. There is no fee. A map and brochure are available for $2; see the contact information below.

Contact: Department of Natural Resources, South Puget Sound Region, P.O. Box 68, Enumclaw, WA 98022-0068; (360) 825-1631 or fax (360) 825-1672.

Directions: From Interstate 5 at Tacoma, turn north on Highway 16 and drive 30 miles to Bremerton. Turn south on Highway 3 and drive nine miles to the town of Belfair. From Belfair drive one-third of a mile on Highway 300, continue to follow it left for 3.3 miles, then turn right on Belfair-Tahuya Road. Drive one-half mile, then turn right on Elfendahl Pass Road and drive 2.5 miles. At Twin Lakes Road turn left and drive two-thirds of a mile to the camp.

Trip notes: Camp Spillman is one of four campgrounds (along with Tahuya River Horse Camp, Howell Lake, and Twin Lakes; see campground numbers 120, 121, and 123) set in the immediate vicinity of Tahuya State Forest. This one sits along the Tahuya River, with wooded riverside sites and trails for hikers, horses, and motorbikes.

125 Gig Harbor RV Resort

Location: Near Tacoma; map A2, grid j5.

Campsites, facilities: There are 100 drive-through sites for trailers or RVs of any length. Electricity, piped water, and sewer hookups are provided. Bottled gas, cable TV, sanitary services, toilets, showers, a recreation hall, a store, a laundry room, ice, a playground, a sports field, and a heated swimming pool are available. Leashed pets are permitted.

Reservations, fees: Reservations are recommended in the summer. Sites are $22–$24 per night. The campground is open year-round.

Contact: Phone (800) 526-8311 or (253) 858-8138, or write to 9515 Burnham Drive NW, Gig Harbor, WA 98332.

Directions: From Interstate 5 in Tacoma, turn west on Highway 16 and drive 12 miles northwest. Take the North Rosedale exit. At the stop sign, turn right on Burnham Drive and proceed one mile to the campground on the left.

Trip notes: This is a popular layover spot for folks heading up to Bremerton. Just a short jaunt off the highway, it's pleasant, clean, and friendly. An 18-hole golf course, a full-service marina, and tennis courts are located nearby. Look for the great view of Mount Rainier from the end of the harbor.

126 Dash Point State Park

Location: Near Tacoma; map A2, grid j5.

Campsites, facilities: There are 110 tent sites and 28 sites for trailers or RVs up to 35 feet long. Water and electrical hookups are available. Picnic tables are provided. Flush toilets, a sanitary disposal station, a playground, electricity, piped water, showers, and firewood are available. Leashed pets are permitted.

Reservations, fees: Contact Reservations Northwest at (800) 452-5687 ($6 reservation fee). Sites are $5–$15 per night. The campground is open year-round.

Contact: Phone (800) 233-0321 or (253) 593-2206, or write to 5700 West Dash Point Road, Federal Way, WA 98003.

Directions: From Interstate 5 at Tacoma, drive five miles northeast on Highway 509 to the park on the right.

Trip notes: This urban state park has beach access, plus an 18-hole golf course and marked hiking trails nearby. Tacoma offers a variety of activities and attractions, including the Tacoma Art Museum (with a children's gallery); the Washington State Historical Society

Museum; the Seymour Botanical Conservatory at Wrights Park; Point Defiance Park, Zoo, and Aquarium; the Western Washington Forest Industries Museum; and the Fort Lewis Military Museum. The Old Town area along the waterfront has been renovated, and there are two public fishing piers there.

⓲ Saltwater State Park

Location: Near Seattle; map A2, grid j6.

Campsites, facilities: There are 52 sites for tents or self-contained RVs up to 50 feet long. Picnic tables and fire grills are provided. Flush toilets, a sanitary disposal station, showers, a playground, and firewood are available. A store, a restaurant, and ice are located within one mile. Some facilities are wheelchair accessible. Boat buoys are nearby on Puget Sound. Leashed pets are permitted.

Reservations, fees: No reservations are accepted. Sites are $10 per night. The campground is open from late March through early September.

Contact: Phone (800) 233-0321 or (206) 764-4128, or write to 25205 Eighth Place South, Des Moines, WA 98198.

Directions: From Interstate 5 at Seattle, drive eight miles south to Des Moines, then turn south on Highway 509 and drive two miles to the park on the left.

Trip notes: Set on the edge of Seattle and beautiful Puget Sound, Saltwater is a nice state park for tent or RV campers. Beaches offer clamming and picnic facilities, and scuba diving is a popular pastime. There are also foot trails that lead through Kent Smith Canyon. McSorely Creek runs through the park.

⓲ Game Farm Wilderness Park

Location: On the Stuck River in Auburn; map A2, grid j8.

Campsites, facilities: There are six group campsites for tents, trailers, and RVs, each with water and power hookups, a fire ring, and a picnic table. There are four sleeping units per site. Campers also have access to an open-air shelter during their stay. A dump station and rest rooms are located on site. Leashed pets are permitted.

Reservations, fees: Reservations are required and can be made up to one year in advance. Group sites are $25 per night. The campground is open from March through October.

Contact: City of Auburn Parks and Recreation Department, 25 West Main Street, Auburn, WA 98001; (253) 931-3043.

Directions: From Seattle, go south to Highway 18. Head east on Highway 18, and take the Auburn/Enumclaw exit. At the light, turn left onto Auburn Way South. Travel south approximately one mile to Howard Road. Exit to the right onto Howard Road. At the stop sign take a right onto R Street. Continue on R Street for approximately 1.5 miles to Stuck River Drive SE (just over the river). Turn left and drive one-quarter of a mile upriver to the left; the park is at 2401 Stuck River Road.

Trip notes: The Game Farm Wilderness Park is just minutes from downtown Auburn. Located along the scenic Stuck River, it was designed with group outings in mind. Mount Rainier, the Seattle waterfront, and the Cascade Mountains are all only a short drive away.

Map A3

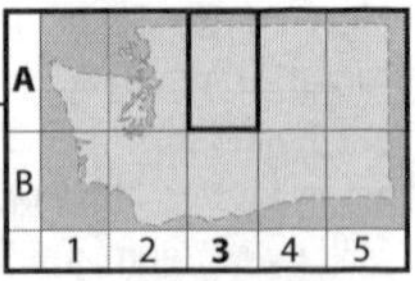

Washington State Map .... *page 6*
One inch equals approximately 20 miles.

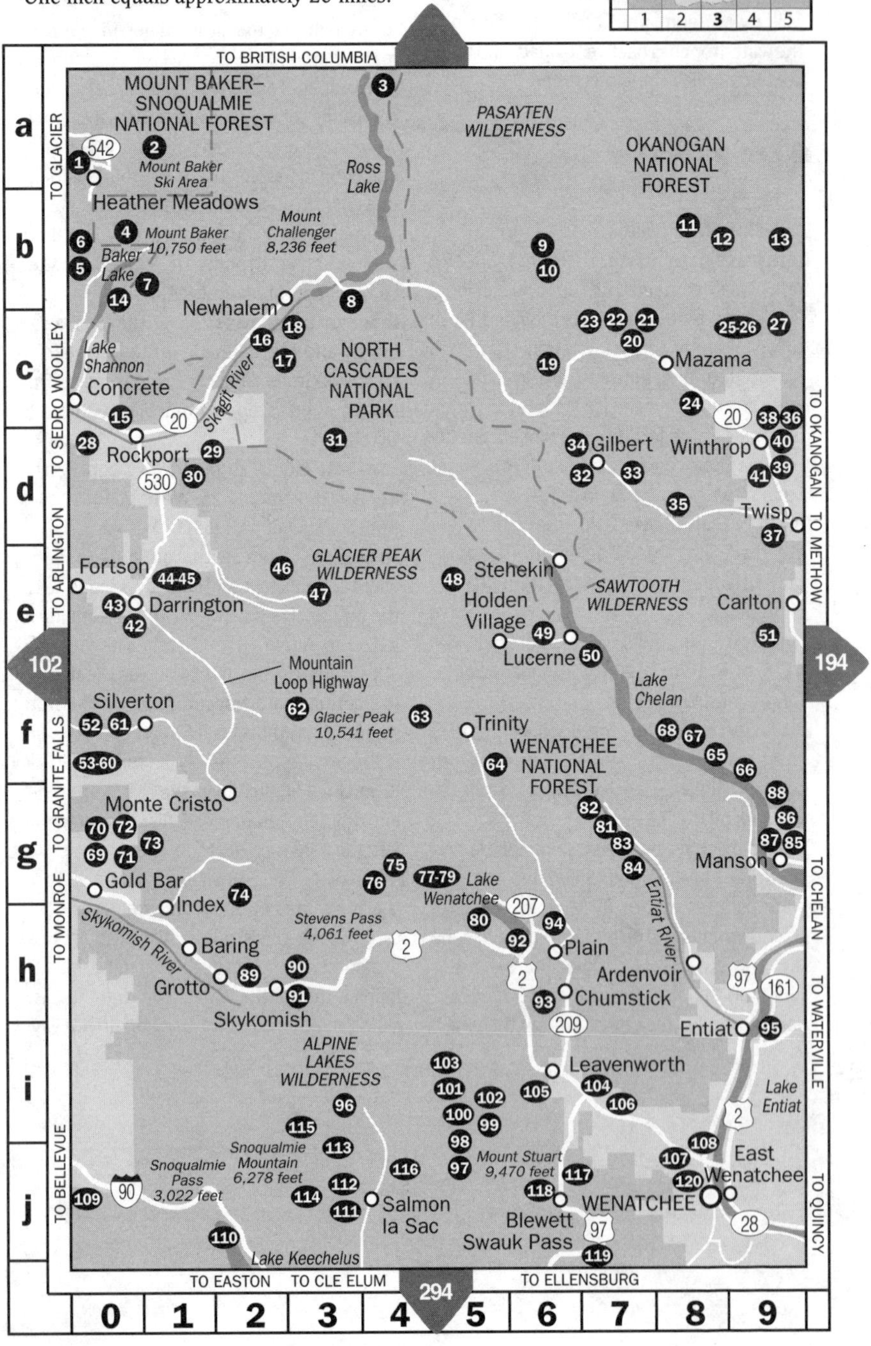

TO BRITISH COLUMBIA

a

TO GLACIER

MOUNT BAKER–
SNOQUALMIE
NATIONAL FOREST

PASAYTEN
WILDERNESS

OKANOGAN
NATIONAL
FOREST

Ross
Lake

❸

542

❷

❶

*Mount Baker
Ski Area*

Heather Meadows

*Mount
Challenger
8,236 feet*

b

❻

❹ *Mount Baker
10,750 feet*

❺

Baker
Lake

❼

❶❶

❶❷

❶❸

❾

❿

❽

❶❹

Newhalem

TO SEDRO WOOLLEY

Lake
Shannon

❶❻

❶❽

❶❼

NORTH
CASCADES
NATIONAL
PARK

❷❸ ❷❷ ❷❶

❷❿

❷❺-❷❻ ❷❼

c

❶❾

Mazama

Concrete

❶❺

20

Skagit River

❸❽ ❸❻

❷❹

20

❹❿

d

TO ARLINGTON

❷❽

Rockport

❷❾

530

❸❿

❸❶

❸❹ Gilbert

❸❷

❸❸

Winthrop

❹❶ ❸❾

TO OKANOGAN

TO METHOW

Twisp

❸❼

GLACIER PEAK
WILDERNESS

❹❽

Stehekin

❸❺

e

Fortson

❹❹-❹❺

❹❻

❹❼

Holden
Village

SAWTOOTH
WILDERNESS

Carlton

❺❶

102

❹❸

Darrington

❹❷

❹❾

Lucerne ❺❿

194

Mountain
Loop Highway

Lake
Chelan

f

TO GRANITE FALLS

Silverton

❺❷ ❻❶

❻❷ *Glacier Peak
10,541 feet* ❻❸

Trinity

❻❹

WENATCHEE
NATIONAL
FOREST

❻❽ ❻❼

❻❺

❻❻

❺❸-❻❿

❽❽

Monte Cristo

❽❻

g

TO MONROE

❼❿ ❼❷

❻❾ ❼❶

❼❸

Gold Bar

❼❹

❼❺

❼❻

❼❼-❼❾ Lake
Wenatchee

207

❽❷

❽❶

❽❸

❽❼ ❽❺

Manson

TO CHELAN

Index

❽❹

Entiat River

Stevens Pass
4,061 feet

❽❿

❾❹

Plain

h

Skykomish River

Baring

❾❿

❾❷

2

Ardenvoir

97

161

TO WATERVILLE

Grotto

❽❾

❾❶

2

❾❸ Chumstick

Entiat

❾❺

Skykomish

209

i

TO BELLEVUE

ALPINE
LAKES
WILDERNESS

❶❶❸

❾❻

❶❿❶

❶❿❸

❶❿❷

❶❿❺

Leavenworth

❶❿❹

❶❿❻

Lake
Entiat

2

❽ East
Wenatchee

❶❿❼ ❶❿❽

j

❶❶❺

❶❶❸

Snoqualmie
Mountain
6,278 feet

❶❶❷

❶❶❻

❶❿❿

❾❾

❾❽

❾❼

*Mount Stuart
9,470 feet*

❶❶❼

WENATCHEE

❶❶❽

❶❷❿

109

90

Snoqualmie
Pass
3,022 feet

❶❶❹

❶❶❶

Salmon
la Sac

Blewett
Swauk Pass

97

TO QUINCY

❶❶❿

Lake Keechelus

❶❶❾

28

TO EASTON   TO CLE ELUM   294   TO ELLENSBURG

0   1   2   3   4   5   6   7   8   9

Chapter A3 features:

❶ Silver Fir

Location: On the North Fork of the Nooksack River in Mount Baker–Snoqualmie National Forest; map A3, grid a0.

Campsites, facilities: There are 20 sites for tents, trailers, or RVs up to 21 feet long. Picnic tables and barbecue grills are provided. Well water, vault toilets, and a group picnic shelter are available. Leashed pets are permitted.

Reservations, fees: Sites can be reserved by calling (800) 280-CAMP/2267 ($8.65 reservation fee). Sites are $10 per night. The campground is open from May through September.

Contact: Mount Baker–Snoqualmie National Forest, Mount Baker Ranger District, 2105 State Route 20, Sedro-Woolley, WA 98284; (360) 856-5700 or fax (360) 856-1934.

Directions: From Interstate 5 at Bellingham, turn east on Highway 542 and drive 31 miles to Glacier. Continue east on Highway 542 for 12.5 miles to the campground on the right.

Trip notes: This campground is set on the North Fork of the Nooksack River, just a short distance from the North Fork Nooksack Research Natural Area. Fishing is available nearby, and, in the winter, the area becomes

a cross-country ski area. You're strongly advised to obtain a Forest Service map in order take maximum advantage of the recreational opportunities in the area.

❷ Hannegan

Location: On Ruth Creek in Mount Baker–Snoqualmie National Forest; map A3, grid a1.

Campsites, facilities: This is a very primitive area with no designated campsites and no piped water provided. There is one pit toilet. Leashed pets are permitted.

Reservations, fees: No reservations are accepted. There is no fee. The campground is open year-round, weather permitting.

Contact: Mount Baker–Snoqualmie National Forest, Mount Baker Ranger District, 2105 State Route 20, Sedro-Woolley, WA 98284; (360) 856-5700 or fax (360) 856-1934.

Directions: From Interstate 5 at Bellingham, turn east (left) on Highway 542 and drive 31 miles to Glacier. Continue 12.5 miles east on Highway 542, then turn east on Forest Service Road 32 and drive four miles to the campground at the end of the road. A Forest Service map is essential.

Trip notes: This quiet, rustic spot is set on Ruth Creek on the border of the Mount Baker Wilderness and at the trailhead leading into the Mount Baker Wilderness across Hannegan Pass. The trail extends into North Cascades National Park, where a permit is required for overnight stays. The free permit can be obtained at the Glacier Ranger Station. This is a perfect base camp for a wilderness backpacking expedition, and it is used primarily as such. Note: In the winter the campground may be accessible only on skis.

❸ Hozomeen

Location: On Ross Lake in Ross Lake National Recreation Area; map A3, grid a4.

Campsites, facilities: There are 122 sites for tents or RVs up to 22 feet long. Picnic tables and fireplaces are provided. Pit toilets, piped water, and a boat launch on Ross Lake are available. Leashed pets are permitted.

Reservations, fees: No reservations are accepted. There is no fee. The campground is open from late May to late October.

Contact: North Cascades National Park, 2105 State Route 20, Sedro-Woolley, WA 98284; (360) 856-5700.

Directions: This campground is accessible only through Canada. From the town of Hope, British Columbia, drive 38 miles south on Silver Skagit Road to the campground at the north end of Ross Lake. Much of the road is rough dirt.

Trip notes: Hozomeen is just inside the U.S./Canada border at the north end of Ross Lake. It takes quite an effort to get here, which tends to weed out all but the most stalwart campers. This is good news for those few, for they will find a quiet, uncrowded camp in a beautiful setting.

❹ Park Creek

Location: Near Baker Lake in Mount Baker–Snoqualmie National Forest; map A3, grid b0.

Campsites, facilities: There are 12 sites for tents or small RVs. Picnic tables are provided. Vault toilets are available, but there is no piped water. Boat docks, launching facilities, and rentals are nearby on Baker Lake. Leashed pets are permitted.

Reservations, fees: Reservations are required; call (800) 280-CAMP/2267 ($8.65 reservation fee). Sites are $6.50 per night. The campground is open from mid-May to early September.

Contact: Mount Baker–Snoqualmie National Forest, Mount Baker Ranger District, 2105 State Route 20, Sedro-Woolley, WA 98284; (360) 856-5700 or fax (360) 856-1934.

Directions: From Interstate 5 at Burlington, turn east on Highway 20 and drive approximately 24 miles to milepost 82. Turn north on Baker Lake Highway and drive about 19.5 miles, then take Forest Service Road 1144 about 200 yards northwest to the campground. A Forest Service map is essential.

Trip notes: This pretty camp, set at 800 feet amidst a heavily wooded area, is on Park Creek a short distance from the north shore of Baker Lake. It's primitive and small but still gets its fair share of use.

❺ Panorama Point

Location: On Baker Lake in Mount Baker–Snoqualmie National Forest; map A3, grid b0.

Campsites, facilities: There are 16 sites for tents, trailers, or RVs up to 21 feet long. Picnic tables are provided. Well water and vault toilets are available. A store and ice are located within one mile. A boat ramp is adjacent to the camp. Boat docks and rentals are nearby. Leashed pets are permitted.

Reservations, fees: Some sites can be reserved by calling (800) 280-CAMP/2267 ($8.65 reservation fee). Sites are $10 per night. The campground is open from May to mid-September.

Contact: Mount Baker–Snoqualmie National Forest, Mount Baker Ranger District, 2105 State Route 20, Sedro-Woolley, WA 98284; (360) 856-5700 or fax (360) 856-1934.

Directions: From Interstate 5 at Burlington, turn east on Highway 20 and drive approximately 22.5 miles to milepost 82. Turn north on Baker Lake Highway and drive about 18.5 miles to the campground entrance on the right.

Trip notes: Panorama Point is a well-maintained campground on the northwest shore of Baker Lake. The reservoir is one of the better fishing lakes in the area. The camp is true to its name, with incredible scenic views. Hiking trails are nearby.

❻ Boulder Creek

Location: Near Baker Lake in Mount Baker–Snoqualmie National Forest; map A3, grid b0.

Campsites, facilities: There are eight tent sites and two group sites. Picnic tables and fire grills are provided. Pit toilets are available, but there is no piped water. Boat docks and launching facilities are nearby on Baker Lake. Leashed pets are permitted.

Reservations, fees: Reservations are required for the group sites, and some family sites are reservable; phone (800) 280-CAMP/2267 ($8.65 family site reservation fee, $17.35 group reservation fee). Family sites are $6.50 per night; group sites are $40 per night. The campground is open from mid-May to early September.

Contact: Mount Baker–Snoqualmie National Forest, Mount Baker Ranger District, 2105 State Route 20, Sedro-Woolley, WA 98284; (360) 856-5700 or fax (360) 856-1934.

Directions: From Interstate 5 at Burlington, turn east on Highway 20 and drive approximately 22.5 miles to milepost 82. Turn north on Baker Lake Highway and drive about 17.4 miles to the campground on the right.

Trip notes: An alternative to Horseshoe Cove (campground number 14), this campground is set on Boulder Creek about one mile from the shore of Baker Lake. A boat launch is located at Panorama Point. Wild berries can be found in the area in season. The campground offers prime views of Mount Baker.

❼ Maple Grove

Location: On Baker Lake in Mount Baker–Snoqualmie National Forest; map A3, grid b0.

Campsites, facilities: There are five primitive tent sites which are only accessible by boat or on foot. Picnic tables are provided. There is no piped water. Boat launching facilities are located nearby on Baker Lake. Leashed pets are permitted.

Reservations, fees: No reservations are accepted. There is no fee. The campground is open year-round.

Contact: Mount Baker–Snoqualmie National Forest, Mount Baker Ranger District, 2105 State Route 20, Sedro-Woolley, WA 98284; (360) 856-5700 or fax (360) 856-1934.

Directions: From Interstate 5 at Burlington, turn east on Highway 20 and drive approximately 24 miles to milepost 82. Turn north on Baker Lake Highway and drive about 13 miles. Turn east (right) on Forest Service Road 1106 and drive across Baker Dam, where Forest Service Road 1106 becomes Forest Service Road 1107. Continue one-half mile to the parking area and the trailhead on the left. To reach the camp by boat, launch at one of the campgrounds on the west side of the lake (Horseshoe Cove, campground number 14, is the closest) or take trail 610 and walk in four miles to the camp. A Forest Service map is recommended.

Trip notes: Looking for a quiet spot on the edge of a lake? Except on summer weekends when there is a lot of water sports activity, here it is. This rustic campground is on the shore of Baker Lake and is hike-in or boat-in only. Privacy and great mountain views are your reward for the extra effort, and it's all free.

❽ Colonial Creek Campground

Location: On Diablo Lake in Ross Lake National Recreation Area; map A3, grid b3.

Campsites, facilities: There are 164 campsites for tents or RVs up to 32 feet long. Picnic tables and fireplaces are provided. Flush toilets, piped water, a sanitary dump station, and a boat ramp are available. Some facilities are wheelchair accessible. Leashed pets are permitted.

Reservations, fees: No reservations are accepted. Sites are $10 per night. The campground is open from mid-April to mid-October.

Contact: North Cascades Headquarters, 2105 State Route 20, Sedro-Woolley, WA 98284; (360) 856-5700.

Directions: From Interstate 5 at Burlington, take exit 230 and turn east on Highway 20. Drive 46 miles to Marblemount. Continue east on Highway 20 for 24 miles to the campground entrance.

Trip notes: Colonial Creek Campground (elevation 1,200 feet) sits along the shore of Diablo Lake in the Ross Lake National Recreation Area. The five-mile-long lake offers many hiking and fishing possibilities. A naturalist program is available during the summer months.

9 Harts Pass

Location: Near the Pasayten Wilderness in Okanogan National Forest; map A3, grid b6.

Campsites, facilities: There are five walk-in tent sites. Picnic tables and fire grills are provided. Vault toilets are available, but there is no piped water. No garbage service is provided, so trash must be packed out. Leashed pets are permitted.

Reservations, fees: No reservations are accepted. Overnight parking requires a $25 seasonal pass or $5 per night ($10 for three nights). The campground is open from mid-July to late September.

Contact: Okanogan National Forest, Methow Valley Visitor Center, P.O. Box 579, Winthrop, WA 98862; (509) 996-4000 or fax (509) 997-9770.

Directions: From Interstate 5 south of Bellingham, turn east on Highway 20 and drive approximately 120 miles to County Road 1163 (13 miles west of Winthrop). Turn left and drive northwest for seven miles to Lost

River, where the pavement ends and the road soon becomes Forest Road 5400. Drive 12.5 miles northwest on Forest Service Road 5400 and you'll arrive at the campground. Note: The road to Hart's Pass beyond Ballard Campground is closed to trailers.

Trip notes: This pretty little campground is near the Pasayten Wilderness, which offers 500 miles of trails leading to alpine meadows and glacier-fed lakes and streams, and along ridges to spectacular mountain heights. Contact the district ranger for details. The Pacific Crest Trail passes near the camp, and nearby Slate Peak, at 7,500 feet, offers a great view of the northern Cascade Range.

10 Meadows

Location: Near the Pacific Crest Trail in Okanogan National Forest; map A3, grid b6.

Campsites, facilities: There are 14 tent sites. Picnic tables and fire grills are provided. Vault toilets are available, but there is no piped water. No garbage service is provided, so trash must be packed out. Leashed pets are permitted.

Reservations, fees: No reservations are accepted. Overnight parking requires a $25 seasonal pass or $5 per night ($10 for three nights). The campground is open from mid-July to late September.

Contact: Okanogan National Forest, Methow Valley Visitor Center, P.O. Box 579, Winthrop, WA 98862; (509) 996-4000 or fax (509) 997-9770.

Directions: From Interstate 5 south of Bellingham, turn east on Highway 20 and drive approximately 120 miles to County Road 1163 (13 miles west of Winthrop). Turn left and drive northwest for seven miles, then drive 12.5 miles northwest on Forest Service Road 5400. Turn south on Forest Service Road 500 and drive one mile to the campground.

Trip notes: This campground is about one mile from Harts Pass and offers the same opportunities (see campground number 9 for more information). The camp is adjacent to the Pacific Crest Trail.

⑪ Honeymoon

Location: On Eightmile Creek in Okanogan National Forest; map A3, grid b8.

Campsites, facilities: There are six sites for tents, trailers, or small RVs. Picnic tables and fire grills are provided. Vault toilets are available, but there is no piped water. Garbage service is not provided, so trash must be packed out. Leashed pets are permitted.

Reservations, fees: No reservations are accepted. Overnight parking requires a $25 seasonal pass or $5 per night ($10 for three nights). The campground is open from June to late September.

Contact: Okanogan National Forest, Methow Valley Visitor Center, P.O. Box 579, Winthrop, WA 98862; (509) 996-4000 or fax (509) 997-9770.

Directions: From Interstate 5 south of Bellingham, turn east on Highway 20 and drive approximately 134 miles to Winthrop. Turn north on County Road 1213/West Chewuch Road and drive 6.5 miles, then continue north on Forest Service Road 51 for 2.5 miles. Turn northwest on Forest Service Road 5130/Eightmile Creek Road and drive nine miles to the campground.

Trip notes: This campground is set at 3,300 feet along Eightmile Creek. If you continue north seven miles to the end of Forest Service Road 5130, you'll reach a trailhead that provides access to the Pasayten Wilderness. See a Forest Service map for details. Why is it named Honeymoon? Well, seems a forest ranger and his bride chose this very spot to spend their wedding night.

⑫ Chewuch

Location: On the Chewuch River in Okanogan National Forest; map A3, grid b8.

Campsites, facilities: There are four tent sites. Fire grills are provided. Vault toilets are available. There is no piped water. No garbage service is provided, so trash must be packed out. Leashed pets are permitted.

Reservations, fees: No reservations are accepted. Overnight parking requires a $25 seasonal pass or $5 per night ($10 for three nights). The campground is open from June to late September.

Contact: Okanogan National Forest, Methow Valley Visitor Center, P.O. Box 579, Winthrop, WA 98862; (509) 996-4000 or fax (509) 997-9770.

Directions: From Interstate 5 south of Bellingham, turn east on Highway 20 and drive approximately 134 miles to Winthrop. Turn north on County Road 1213/West Chewuch Road and drive 6.5 miles, then continue northeast on Forest Service Roads 51 and 5160 for 8.5 miles to the campground.

Trip notes: Set along the Chewuch River, this campground is a more primitive option to nearby Falls Creek (campground number 27). Fishing is a highlight, and by traveling north, you can access trailheads that lead into the Pasayten Wilderness. See a Forest Service map for specific locations.

⑬ Camp 4

Location: On the Chewuch River in Okanogan National Forest; map A3, grid b9.

Campsites, facilities: There are five tent sites. Fire grills are provided. Vault toilets are available, but there is no piped water. No garbage service is provided, so trash must be packed out. Leashed pets are permitted.

Reservations, fees: No reservations are accepted. Overnight parking requires a $25 seasonal pass or $5 per night ($10 for three nights). The campground is open from June to late September.

Contact: Okanogan National Forest, Methow Valley Visitor Center, P.O. Box 579, Winthrop, WA 98862; (509) 996-4000 or fax (509) 997-9770.

Directions: From Interstate 5 south of Bellingham, turn east on Highway 20 and drive approximately 134 miles to Winthrop. Turn north on County Road 1213/West Chewuch Road and drive 6.5 miles, then continue northeast on Forest Service Road 51 for 11 miles to the campground.

Trip notes: Camp 4 is the smallest and most primitive of the three camps along the Chewuch River (the others are Chewuch and Falls Creek, campground numbers 12 and 27). There are three trailheads five miles north of camp: two at Lake Creek and another at Andrews Creek. They all have corrals, hitching rails, truck docks, and water for the stock. Trails leading into the Pasayten Wilderness leave from both locations. Contact the Forest Service for details.

⑭ Horseshoe Cove

Location: On Baker Lake in Mount Baker–Snoqualmie National Forest; map A3, grid b0.

Campsites, facilities: There are eight sites for tents only and 34 sites for tents, trailers, or RVs up to 25 feet long. Picnic tables are provided. Piped water and flush toilets are available. A boat ramp is adjacent to camp. Leashed pets are permitted.

Reservations, fees: Some sites can be reserved by calling (800) 280-CAMP/2267 ($8.65 reservation fee). Sites are $10 per night. The campground is open from May through September; one loop remains open through the off-season on a no service, no fee basis.

Contact: Mount Baker–Snoqualmie National Forest, Mount Baker Ranger District, 2105 State Route 20, Sedro-Woolley, WA 98284; (360) 856-5700 or fax (360) 856-1934.

Directions: From Interstate 5 at Burlington, turn east on Highway 20 and drive approximately 24 miles to milepost 82. Turn north on Baker Lake Highway and drive about 14.8 miles. Take Forest Service Road 1118 east for two miles to the campground. A Forest Service map is recommended.

Trip notes: Anglers will find good fishing at this campground set on the shore of 5,000-acre Baker Lake, where rainbow trout, kokanee salmon, cutthroat trout, and Dolly Varden trout await. Other highlights are swimming access from the campground and a boat ramp. Some hiking trails can be found nearby.

⑮ Rockport State Park

Location: Near the Skagit River; map A3, grid c0.

Campsites, facilities: There are three primitive tent sites, eight developed, walk-in tent sites, and 50 sites for trailers or RVs up to 60 feet long. There is also one group tent site. Picnic tables and fire grills are provided. Flush toilets, a sanitary disposal station, electricity, piped water, sewer hookups, showers, and firewood are available. Some facilities are wheelchair accessible. A store, gas, and ice are located within one mile. Leashed pets are permitted.

Reservations, fees: No reservations are accepted for the family sites, which are $5–$15 per night. For group site reservations, call (360) 853-8461; group sites are $25, plus $1 per person per night. The campground is open from April to late October.

Contact: Phone (360) 853-8461 or write to 5051 Highway 20, Concrete, WA 98237.

Directions: From Interstate 5 at Burlington, turn east on Highway 20 and drive 40 miles to Rockport. Continue one mile west on Highway 20 to the park.

Trip notes: This state park covers 457 acres and offers five miles of hiking trails and four adirondack (three-sided, roofed) shelters. The campground is set among old-growth Douglas firs and is near the Skagit River, a good steelhead stream.

⑯ Goodell Creek Campground

Location: On Goodell Creek and the Skagit River in Ross Lake National Recreation Area; map A3, grid c2.

Campsites, facilities: There are 21 campsites for tents or RVs up to 22 feet long and one group site. Picnic tables and fireplaces are provided. Pit toilets and piped water are available. Leashed pets are permitted.

Reservations, fees: No reservations are ac-

cepted for family camping; sites are $7 per night. Call (360) 873-4590, extension 16, for group site reservations and fee information. The campground is open year-round, but there are no services (and also no fee) in the winter.

Contact: North Cascades National Park Headquarters, 2105 State Route 20, Sedro-Woolley, WA 98284; (360) 856-5700.

Directions: From Interstate 5 at Burlington, take exit 230, turn east on Highway 20, and drive 46 miles to Marblemount. Continue 13 miles east on Highway 20 to the campground entrance.

Trip notes: Goodell Creek Campground is an alternative to the nearby and larger Newhalem Creek Campground (campground number 18). This one is set where Goodell Creek pours into the Skagit River in the Ross Lake National Recreation Area. It's a popular put in for raft trips downriver.

⑰ Marble Creek

Location: On Marble Creek in Mount Baker–Snoqualmie National Forest; map A3, grid c2.

Campsites, facilities: There are 24 sites for tents, trailers, or RVs up to 22 feet long. Picnic tables and fire grills are provided. Vault toilets are available, but there is no piped water. Leashed pets are permitted.

Reservations, fees: No reservations are accepted. There is no fee. The campground is open from mid-May to mid-September.

Contact: Mount Baker–Snoqualmie National Forest, Mount Baker Ranger District, 2105 State Route 20, Sedro-Woolley, WA 98284; (360) 856-5700 or fax (360) 856-1934.

Directions: From Interstate 5 at Burlington, take exit 230, turn east on Highway 20, and drive 46.6 miles to Marblemount. Turn east on County Road 3528 (Cascade River Road) and drive eight miles, then turn south on Forest Service Road 1530 and drive one mile to the campground on the right. A Forest Service map is recommended.

Trip notes: This primitive campground is set on Marble Creek. Continuing on Forest Service Road 1530 will take you up to Bush Lake.

A trailhead to Hidden Lake just inside the boundary of North Cascades National Park can be found about five miles from camp at the end of Forest Service Road 1540. See a Forest Service map for details.

⑱ Newhalem Creek Campground

Location: Near the Skagit River in Ross Lake National Recreation Area; map A3, grid c2.

Campsites, facilities: There are 128 sites for tents or RVs up to 32 feet long. Picnic tables and fireplaces are provided. Flush toilets, piped water, and a sanitary dump station are available. Some facilities are wheelchair accessible. Leashed pets are permitted.

Reservations, fees: No reservations are accepted. Sites are $10 per night. The campground is open from mid-May to mid-October.

Contact: North Cascades National Park Headquarters, 2105 State Route 20, Sedro-Woolley, WA 98284; (360) 856-5700.

Directions: From Interstate 5 at Burlington, take exit 230, turn east on Highway 20, and drive 46 miles to Marblemount. Continue 14 miles east on Highway 20 to the camp.

Trip notes: One of the newer camps in the Ross Lake National Recreation Area, this spot is set along the Skagit River west of Newhalem. Good hiking possibilities abound in the immediate area. Be sure to visit the North Cascades Visitor Center at the top of the hill from the campground.

⑲ Lone Fir

Location: On Early Winters Creek in Okanogan National Forest; map A3, grid c6.

Campsites, facilities: There are 27 sites for tents, trailers, or RVs up to 21 feet long. Piped water, fire grills, garbage service, and picnic tables are provided. Vault toilets are available. Leashed pets are permitted.

Reservations, fees: No reservations are accepted. Sites are $6–$8 per night. The campground is open from June to late September.

Contact: Okanogan National Forest, Methow Valley Visitor Center, P.O. Box 579, Winthrop,

WA 98862; (509) 996-4000 or fax (509) 997-9770.

Directions: From Interstate 5 south of Bellingham, turn east on Highway 20 and drive approximately 107 miles to the campground, located about 11 miles west of Mazama.

Trip notes: Lone Fir is set at 3,800 feet along the banks of Early Winters Creek. To the west is Washington Pass Overlook, which offers a spectacular view. Anglers can fish in the creek, and many hiking trails crisscross the area. A Forest Service map will provide details. A loop trail through the campground woods is wheelchair accessible for four-tenths of a mile. See the trip notes for Early Winters (campground number 20) for more information.

20 Early Winters

Location: On Early Winters Creek in Okanogan National Forest; map A3, grid c7.

Campsites, facilities: There are seven tent sites and six sites for tents, trailers, or RVs up to 24 feet long. Piped water, fire grills, garbage service, and picnic tables are provided. Vault toilets are available. There is a small store and snack bar in Mazama, about two miles away. Leashed pets are permitted.

Reservations, fees: No reservations are accepted. Sites are $6–$8 per night. The campground is open from June through September or October, weather permitting.

Contact: Okanogan National Forest, Methow Valley Visitor Center, P.O. Box 579, Winthrop, WA 98862; (509) 996-4000 or fax (509) 997-9770.

Directions: From Interstate 5 south of Bellingham, turn east on Highway 20 and drive approximately 118 miles to the campground.

Trip notes: The confluence of Early Winters Creek and the Methow River mark the site of this campground. Several hiking trails can be found in the area, including one that leads south to Cedar Creek Falls. Other possible side trips are Goat Wall to the north and the town of Winthrop to the south, which boasts a historical museum, a state fish hatchery, and

Pearrygin Lake State Park. Early Winters Information Center is adjacent to the camp and can provide detailed information.

21 Ballard

Location: Near the Methow River in Okanogan National Forest; map A3, grid c7.

Campsites, facilities: There are seven tent sites. Picnic tables and fire grills are provided. Vault toilets are available, but there is no piped water. No garbage service is provided, so trash must be packed out. Leashed pets are permitted.

Reservations, fees: No reservations are accepted. There is no fee. The campground is open from June through September or October, weather permitting.

Contact: Okanogan National Forest, Methow Valley Visitor Center, P.O. Box 579, Winthrop, WA 98862; (509) 996-4000 or fax (509) 997-9770.

Directions: From Interstate 5 south of Bellingham, turn east on Highway 20 and drive approximately 120 miles to County Road 1163. Turn left toward Mazama and drive northwest for seven miles to Lost River, where the pavement ends and the road soon becomes Forest Road 5400. Drive two miles northwest on Forest Service Road 5400 to the campground.

Trip notes: Ballard is located at an elevation of 2,600 feet, about half a mile from River Bend. Some facilities for horse packing are available at the Robinson Creek Trailhead near the campground, where there are several primitive sites. Numerous hiking trails can be found in the area, including one that heads west and eventually hooks up with the Pacific Crest Trail. See the trip notes for Early Winters (campground number 20) for area information.

22 River Bend

Location: On the Methow River in Okanogan National Forest; map A3, grid c7.

Campsites, facilities: There are five sites for tents, trailers, or RVs. Picnic tables and fire grills are provided, but there is no piped water. Vault toilets are available. Leashed pets are permitted.

Reservations, fees: No reservations are accepted. Overnight parking requires a $25 seasonal pass or $5 per night ($10 for three nights). The campground is open from June to late September.

Contact: Okanogan National Forest, Methow Valley Visitor Center, P.O. Box 579, Winthrop, WA 98862; (509) 996-4000 or fax (509) 997-9770.

Directions: From Interstate 5 south of Bellingham, turn east on Highway 20 and drive approximately 120 miles to County Road 1163. Turn left and drive northwest for seven miles, then travel 2.5 miles northwest on Forest Service Road 5400. Turn west on Forest Service Road 54060 and drive one-half mile to the campground.

Trip notes: This campground is located along the Methow River about two miles from the boundary of the Pasayten Wilderness. Several trails near the camp provide access to the wilderness, and another trail follows the Methow River west for about eight miles before hooking up with the Pacific Crest Trail near Azurite Peak; a Forest Service map will show you the options. If you're interested in traveling with pack animals or horses, a Forest Service camp nearby provides facilities. See the trip notes for Ballard (campground number 21) for further details.

㉓ Klipchuck

Location: On Early Winters Creek in Okanogan National Forest; map A3, grid c7.

Campsites, facilities: There are six tent sites and 40 sites for tents, trailers, or RVs up to 32 feet long. Piped water and picnic tables are provided. Flush and vault toilets are available. Leashed pets are permitted.

Reservations, fees: No reservations are accepted. Overnight parking requires a $25 seasonal pass or $5 per night ($10 for three nights). The campground is open from June to late September.

Contact: Okanogan National Forest, Methow

Valley Visitor Center, P.O. Box 579, Winthrop, WA 98862; (509) 996-4000 or fax (509) 997-9770.

Directions: From Interstate 5 south of Bellingham, turn east on Highway 20 and drive approximately 115 miles to Forest Service Road 300. Turn left at the sign for the campground and drive northwest one mile.

Trip notes: Located at an elevation of 3,000 feet along Early Winters Creek, Klipchuck provides hiking aplenty. A short loop trail from the camp leads about five miles up and over Delancy Ridge to Driveway Butte and down to the creek. Another trail starts nearby on Forest Service Road 200 (Sandy Butte–Cedar Creek Road) and goes two miles up Cedar Creek to lovely Cedar Creek Falls. Still another option is a two-mile trail along Early Winters Creek from the campground. See the trip notes for Early Winters (campground number 21) for more information.

㉔ Rocking Horse Ranch

Location: In the Methow River Valley; map A3, grid c8.

Campsites, facilities: There are 25 tent sites and 10 drive-through sites for trailers or RVs of any length. Electricity, piped water, sewer hookups, and picnic tables are provided. Flush toilets, sanitary services, showers, and firewood are available. Some facilities are wheelchair accessible. Leashed pets and motorbikes are permitted.

Reservations, fees: Reservations are accepted. Sites are $12–$15 per night. The campground is open from April to late October.

Contact: Phone (509) 996-2768 or write to Star Route, 18381 Highway 20, Winthrop, WA 98862.

Directions: From Interstate 5 at Burlington, turn east on Highway 20 and drive 123 miles to the campground, located nine miles northwest of Winthrop.

Trip notes: This ranch is set in the lovely Methow River Valley, which is flanked on both sides by national forest. There are numerous trails nearby and a horse stable at the ranch.

Owen Wister, who wrote the novel, *The Virginian*, lived in the nearby town of Winthrop at the turn of the century. Portions of the novel were based on his experiences in this area.

㉕ Nice

Location: On Eightmile Creek in Okanogan National Forest; map A3, grid c9.

Campsites, facilities: There are four tent sites. Picnic tables and fire grills are provided. Vault toilets are available, but there is no piped water. No garbage service is provided, so trash must be packed out. Leashed pets are permitted.

Reservations, fees: No reservations are accepted. Overnight parking requires a $25 seasonal pass or $5 per night ($10 for three nights). The campground is open from June to late September.

Contact: Okanogan National Forest, Methow Valley Visitor Center, P.O. Box 579, Winthrop, WA 98862; (509) 996-4000 or fax (509) 997-9770.

Directions: From Interstate 5 south of Bellingham, turn east on Highway 20 and drive approximately 134 miles to Winthrop. Turn north on County Road 1213/West Chewuch and drive 6.5 miles, then continue north on Forest Service Road 51 for three miles. Turn northwest on Forest Service Road 5130/Eightmile Creek Road and drive four miles to the campground.

Trip notes: Nice is along Eightmile Creek about four miles from Buck Lake. A trail leading into the Pasayten Wilderness can be found at the end of Forest Service Road 5130. Pearrygin Lake State Park is just a few miles to the south, near Winthrop.

㉖ Flat

Location: On Eightmile Creek in Okanogan National Forest; map A3, grid c9.

Campsites, facilities: There are 12 sites for tents, trailers, or RVs up to 15 feet long. Picnic tables and fire grills are provided, but there is no piped water. Vault toilets are available. Leashed pets are permitted.

Reservations, fees: No reservations are accepted. Overnight parking requires a $25 seasonal pass or $5 per night ($10 for three nights). The campground is open from June to late September.

Contact: Okanogan National Forest, Methow Valley Visitor Center, P.O. Box 579, Winthrop, WA 98862; (509) 996-4000 or fax (509) 997-9770.

Directions: From Interstate 5 south of Bellingham, turn east on Highway 20 and drive approximately 134 miles to Winthrop. Turn north on County Road 1213/West Chewuch Road and drive 6.5 miles, then continue three miles north on Forest Service Road 51. Turn northwest on Forest Service Road 5130/Eightmile Creek Road and proceed for two miles to the campground.

Trip notes: This campground is set along Eightmile Creek two miles from where it empties into the Chewuch River. Buck Lake is about three miles away. This is the closest of six camps to County Road 1213, which means it gets some of the heaviest use. Other options are Honeymoon, Nice, and Falls Creek (campground numbers 11, 25, and 27).

㉗ Falls Creek

Location: On the Chewuch River in Okanogan National Forest; map A3, grid c9.

Campsites, facilities: There are seven sites for tents, trailers, or RVs up to 18 feet long. Piped water and picnic tables are provided. Vault toilets are available. Leashed pets are permitted.

Reservations, fees: No reservations are accepted. Overnight parking requires a $25 seasonal pass or $5 per night ($10 for three nights). The campground is open from June to late September.

Contact: Okanogan National Forest, Methow Valley Visitor Center, P.O. Box 579, Winthrop, WA 98862; (509) 996-4000 or fax (509) 997-9770.

Directions: From Interstate 5 south of Bellingham, turn east on Highway 20 and drive approximately 134 miles to Winthrop. Turn north on County Road 1213/West

Chewuch Road and drive 6.5 miles, then continue north on Forest Service Roads 51 and 5160 for five miles to the campground.

Trip notes: Falls Creek is a quiet and pretty campground located at the confluence of its namesake, Falls Creek, and the Chewuch River, about a 20-minute drive out of Winthrop. Nearby Chewuch (campground number 12) and Camp 4 (campground number 13) don't have piped water, but this camp does. Highlights include fishing access and a wheelchair-accessible, 200-foot trail to a waterfall starting across the road from the campground.

28 Howard Miller Steelhead

Location: On the Skagit River; map A3, grid d0.

Campsites, facilities: There are 10 tent sites and 49 sites for trailers or RVs of any length; 11 are pull-throughs. Electricity, piped water, and picnic tables are provided. Flush toilets, sanitary services, showers, a clubhouse, a picnic shelter, adirondacks (three-sided, roofed shelters), and a playground are available. A store and ice are located within one mile. Boat launching facilities are located on the Skagit River. Leashed pets and motorbikes are permitted.

Reservations, fees: Reservations are recommended. Sites are $12–$16 per night. The campground is open year-round.

Contact: Phone (360) 853-8808 or write to P.O. Box 127, Rockport, WA 98283.

Directions: From Interstate 5 south of Bellingham, turn east on Highway 20 and drive 44 miles to Rockport. At the junction of Highway 20 and Rockport-Darrington Road (Highway 530), turn south and drive three blocks to the camp.

Trip notes: This grassy city park has access to the Skagit River, which has been designated a Wild and Scenic River. True to its name, the steelhead fishing here is good in season. Campsites at this pretty spot are sunny and spacious. A bald eagle sanctuary is located at the east end of the park; December through February is the best time to observe them.

29 Wilderness Village and RV Park

Location: Near the Skagit River; map A3, grid d1.

Campsites, facilities: There are 20 tent sites and 32 drive-through sites for trailers or RVs of any length. Electricity, cable TV, piped water, sewer hookups, and picnic tables are provided. Flush toilets, sanitary services, showers, a recreation hall, and a laundry room are available. A cafe and ice are located within one mile. Leashed pets are permitted.

Reservations, fees: Reservations are accepted. Sites are $10–$16 per night. The campground is open year-round.

Contact: Phone (360) 873-2571 or write to 5550 Highway 20, Rockport, WA 98283.

Directions: From Interstate 5 south of Bellingham, turn east on Highway 20 and drive 44 miles to Rockport. Continue five miles east on Highway 20. The park is between mileposts 102 and 103 on the right.

Trip notes: Located near the Skagit River, this park is cool and wooded, with nice, grassy sites and nearby access to the river and fishing. Horseshoe pits and a sports field offer recreation alternatives. Rockport State Park and hiking trails are nearby.

30 Clark's Skagit River Cabins and RVs

Location: On the Skagit River; map A3, grid d1.

Campsites, facilities: There are 48 sites for tents, trailers, and RVs, plus 23 cabins. Rest rooms, showers, a sanitary dump, a public phone, a laundry room, and a restaurant are available. Leashed pets are permitted.

Reservations, fees: Reservations are recommended. Sites are $10–$17 per night. Cabins range from $49–$109. There is a fee for pets. The campground is open year-round.

Contact: Phone the park at (800) 273-2606 or (360) 873-2250, or write to 5675 Highway 20, Rockport, WA 98283.

Directions: From Bellingham, take Interstate 5 south for about 20 miles. Take exit 232 and follow the road up and over the highway. At the light, turn left onto Cook Road. Drive four miles and turn left (east) onto Highway 20. Continue on Highway 20 for about 45 miles past Concrete and Rockport. The campground is located on the left between mileposts 103 and 104.

Trip notes: This beautiful camp is nestled in the trees along the Skagit River, where trout fishing and river walks keep visitors happy. Side trips include hiking trails among the glaciers and waterfalls close to the campground. There are also three hydroelectric plants nearby that offer tours. Recreational facilities include horseshoes and a sports field for volleyball, croquet, and badminton.

㉛ Mineral Park

Location: On the Cascade River in Mount Baker–Snoqualmie National Forest; map A3, grid d3.

Campsites, facilities: There are four tent sites. Picnic tables, fire rings, and vault toilets are provided, but there is no piped water. Leashed pets are permitted.

Reservations, fees: No reservation are necessary. There is no fee. The campground is open from mid-May to mid-September, weather permitting.

Contact: Mount Baker–Snoqualmie National Forest, Mount Baker Ranger District, 2105 State Route 20, Sedro-Woolley, WA 98284; (360) 856-5700 or fax (360) 856-1934.

Directions: From Interstate 5 south of Bellingham, turn east on Highway 20 and drive 46.6 miles. Turn east on County Road 3528 (Cascade River Road) and drive 15 miles to the campground.

Trip notes: Here's another classic, primitive, unknown camping area that can provide a jump-off for many adventures. This rustic site is set on the Cascade River and is near numerous trails leading into the Glacier Peak Wilderness. Fishing in the river can be quite good at times.

㉜ South Creek

Location: On the Twisp River in Okanogan National Forest; map A3, grid d7.

Campsites, facilities: There are four sites for tents or small trailers, plus a few sites with parking for RVs up to 30 feet in length. No piped water is available. Picnic tables and fire grills are provided. Vault toilets are available. No garbage service is provided, so trash must be packed out. Leashed pets are permitted.

Reservations, fees: No reservations are accepted. Overnight parking requires a $25 seasonal pass or $5 per night ($10 for three nights). The campground is open from late May to early September.

Contact: Okanogan National Forest, Methow Valley Visitor Center, P.O. Box 579, Winthrop, WA 98862; (509) 996-4000 or fax (509) 997-9770.

Directions: From Interstate 5 south of Bellingham, turn east on Highway 20 and drive approximately 145 miles to Twisp. Turn west on County Road 9114 and drive 11 miles, then continue west on Forest Service Roads 44 and 4440 for 11 miles to the campground.

Trip notes: Though small, quiet, and little known, South Creek Campground packs a wallop with good recreation options. It's set at the confluence of the Twisp River and South Creek at a major trailhead that accesses the Lake Chelan–Sawtooth Wilderness. See a Forest Service map for details. The campground also has horse facilities.

㉝ Poplar Flat

Location: On the Twisp River in Okanogan National Forest; map A3, grid d7.

Campsites, facilities: There are 16 sites for tents, trailers, or RVs up to 21 feet long. Piped water, fire grills, and picnic tables are provided. Vault toilets are available. Some facilities are wheelchair accessible. Leashed pets are permitted.

Reservations, fees: No reservations are accepted. Overnight parking requires a $25 seasonal pass or $5 per night ($10 for three nights). The campground is open from May to September.

Contact: Okanogan National Forest, Methow Valley Visitor Center, P.O. Box 579, Winthrop, WA 98862; (509) 996-4000 or fax (509) 997-9770.

Directions: From Interstate 5 south of Bellingham, turn east on Highway 20 and drive approximately 145 miles to Twisp. Turn west on County Road 9114 and drive 11 miles, then continue west on Forest Service Roads 44 and 4440 for 9.5 miles to the campground.

Trip notes: This campground is set at 2,900 feet along the Twisp River. Many trails in the area follow streams, some of them providing access to the Lake Chelan–Sawtooth Wilderness. Twisp River Horsecamp, across the river from the campground, has horse facilities.

34 Roads End

Location: On the Twisp River in Okanogan National Forest; map A3, grid d7.

Campsites, facilities: There are four sites for tents or small trailers. Vault toilets and firewood are available, but there is no piped water. Picnic tables and fire grills are provided. There is no garbage service, so trash must be packed out. Leashed pets are permitted.

Reservations, fees: No reservations are accepted. Overnight parking requires a $25 seasonal pass or $5 per night ($10 for three nights). The campground is open from late May to early September.

Contact: Okanogan National Forest, Methow Valley Visitor Center, P.O. Box 579, Winthrop, WA 98862; (509) 996-4000 or fax (509) 997-9770.

Directions: From Interstate 5 south of Bellingham, turn east on Highway 20 and drive approximately 145 miles to Twisp. Turn west on County Road 9114 and drive 11 miles, then continue west on Forest Service Roads 44 and 4440 for 13.5 miles to the campground.

Trip notes: Roads End is set along the Twisp River at a major trailhead that provides access to the Lake Chelan–Sawtooth Wilderness. The trail intersects with the Pacific Crest Trail about

nine miles from the camp. A Forest Service map is essential.

35 War Creek

Location: On the Twisp River in Okanogan National Forest; map A3, grid d8.

Campsites, facilities: There are 11 sites for tents, trailers, or RVs up to 21 feet long. Piped water, fire grills, and picnic tables are provided. Vault toilets and firewood are available. Leashed pets are permitted.

Reservations, fees: No reservations are accepted. Overnight parking requires a $25 seasonal pass or $5 per night ($10 for three nights). The campground is open from May to September.

Contact: Okanogan National Forest, Methow Valley Visitor Center, P.O. Box 579, Winthrop, WA 98862; (509) 996-4000 or fax (509) 997-9770.

Directions: From Interstate 5 south of Bellingham, turn east on Highway 20 and drive approximately 145 miles to Twisp. Turn west on County Road 9114 and drive 11 miles, then continue west on Forest Service Road 44 for 3.5 miles to the campground.

Trip notes: This campground is set along the Twisp River near the trailhead for Trail 408, which provides access to the Lake Chelan–Sawtooth Wilderness. Backpackers can take this path down into the Lake Chelan National Recreation Area, finishing the trip at the shore of Lake Chelan and the National Park Service outpost. It's a 15-mile trek, so contact the Forest Service for details. Also ask about the primitive trail which leads to a waterfall; use extreme caution on that trail.

36 Pearrygin Lake State Park

Location: On Pearrygin Lake; map A3, grid d9.

Campsites, facilities: There are 26 tent sites and 57 sites for tents or RVs of any length; 30 have full hookups and 27 have water-only hookups. Picnic tables and fire grills are provided. Flush toilets, sanitary services, electricity, piped water, sewer hookups, showers, and firewood are available. A store, a cafe, and ice are located within one mile. Some facilities are wheelchair accessible. Boat launching facilities are available. Leashed pets are permitted.

Reservations, fees: Contact Reservations Northwest at (800) 452-5687 ($6 reservation fee). Sites are $11–$16 per night. The campground is open form April through October.

Contact: Phone (800) 233-0321 or (509) 996-2370, or write to Route 1, P.O. Box 300, Winthrop, WA 98862.

Directions: From Interstate 5 south of Bellingham, turn east on Highway 20 and drive approximately 134 miles to Winthrop. Turn north on County Road 1631 and drive about four miles to the park on the right.

Trip notes: This 578-acre park is located in the beautiful Methow Valley, ringed by the North Cascade Mountains. The area is ideal for wildflower and wildlife viewing in the spring. The campground has access to a sandy beach and facilities for swimming, boating, fishing, and hiking. The sites are set close together and don't offer much privacy, but they are spacious and a variety of recreation options make it worth the crunch. In the winter there are opportunities for snowmobiling, cross-country skiing, and ice fishing. A nine-hole golf course is nearby.

37 River Bend Trailer Park

Location: Near the Methow River; map A3, grid d9.

Campsites, facilities: There are 10 tent sites and 86 sites for trailers or RVs of any length (30 are drive-throughs); 31 sites are on the riverfront. Picnic tables are provided. Flush toilets, sanitary services, firewood, a store, a laundry room, ice, a playground, electricity (30 and 50 watt), piped water, sewer hookups, and showers are available. Leashed pets and motorbikes are permitted.

Reservations, fees: Reservations are accepted. Sites are $14–$18 per night; call

for weekly rates. The campground is open year-round.

Contact: River Bend Trailer Park, 19961 Highway 20, Twisp, WA 98856; (509) 997-3500, (800) 686-4498, or fax (509) 997-3501; Web site: www.methow.com/riverbnd.

Directions: From Interstate 5 south of Bellingham, turn east on Highway 20 and drive approximately 140 miles to the campground, located two miles west of Twisp.

Trip notes: The shore of the Methow River skirts this campground. Trout fishing, river rafting, and swimming are popular here, and there is a nice separate area for tent campers set right along the river. The trip notes for KOA Methow River (campground number 39) detail the recreation possibilities available within 10 miles.

38 Derry's Resort

Location: On Pearrygin Lake; map A3, grid d9.

Campsites, facilities: There are 90 tent sites and 64 drive-through sites for trailers or RVs of any length. Electricity, piped water, sewer hookups, and picnic tables are provided. Flush toilets, bottled gas, showers, firewood, sanitary services, a store, a laundry room, ice, and a playground are available. A cafe is located within three miles. Boat docks, launching facilities, and rentals are available on Pearrygin Lake. Leashed pets and motorbikes are permitted.

Reservations, fees: Reservations are accepted. Sites are $14–$17 per night. The campground is open from mid-April to November.

Contact: Phone (509) 996-2322 or write to Route 1, P.O. Box 307, Winthrop, WA 98862.

Directions: From Interstate 5 south of Bellingham, turn east on Highway 20 and drive approximately 134 miles to Winthrop. Turn north on Riverside Avenue and drive one-tenth of a mile, then turn northeast on Bluff Street and drive 1.5 miles. Turn east on Pearrygin Lake Road and continue one mile to the resort on the right.

Trip notes: Pearrygin Lake is the backdrop for this exceptionally clean and pretty lakeshore campground with comfortable, shady sites. Fishing, swimming, and boating access is a short distance away. Other nearby recreation options include an 18-hole golf course, hiking trails, and a riding stable. See the trip notes for KOA Methow River (campground number 39) for more details on the area.

㉟ KOA Methow River– Winthrop

Location: On the Methow River; map A3, grid d9.

Campsites, facilities: There are 110 sites for tents, trailers, or RVs of any length; some drive-throughs are available. Piped water and picnic tables are provided. Flush toilets, electricity, firewood, sewer hookups, sanitary services, showers, a recreation hall, bike and video rentals, a store, a laundry room, ice, a playground, and a swimming pool are available. Bottled gas and a cafe are located within one mile. There is a courtesy shuttle to and from Winthrop. Leashed pets and motorbikes are permitted.

Reservations, fees: Reservations are accepted. Sites are $18–$23 per night. The campground is open from mid-April to November.

Contact: Phone (509) 996-2258, fax (509) 996-3848, or write to P.O. Box 305, Winthrop, WA 98862.

Directions: From Interstate 5 south of Bellingham, turn east on Highway 20 and drive approximately 134 miles to Winthrop. Continue one mile east on Highway 20. The camp is on the left, between mileposts 194 and 195.

Trip notes: Here's another campground set along the Methow River, which offers opportunities for fishing, boating, swimming, and rafting. The park has a free shuttle into Winthrop, an interesting town with many restored, turn-of-the-century buildings lining the main street, including the Shafer Museum,

which displays lots of period items. If you would like to observe wildlife, take a short, two-mile drive southeast out of Winthrop on County Road 9129, on the east side of the Methow River. Turn east on County Road 1631 into Davis Lake, and follow the signs to the Methow River Habitat Management Area Headquarters. Depending upon the time of year, you may see mule deer, porcupine, bobcat, mountain lion, snowshoe hare, black bear, red squirrel, and many species of birds. However, if you're looking for something tamer, other nearby recreation options include an 18-hole golf course and tennis courts.

㊵ Pine-Near Trailer Park

Location: On the Methow River; map A3, grid d9.

Campsites, facilities: There are 40 tent sites and 28 sites for trailers or RVs of any length; 14 are drive-throughs. Electricity, piped water, sewer hookups, and picnic tables are provided. Flush toilets, sanitary services, showers, and a laundry room are available. A store and a cafe are located within one mile. Leashed pets and motorbikes are permitted.

Reservations, fees: Reservations are accepted. Sites are $8–$14 per night. The campground is open year-round.

Contact: Phone (509) 996-2391 or write to Route 1, P.O. Box 400-32, Winthrop, WA 98862.

Directions: From Interstate 5 south of Bellingham, turn east on Highway 20 and drive approximately 134 miles to Winthrop. One block north of Riverside Drive, turn east on Castle Avenue and drive three blocks to the park on the left.

Trip notes: Not far from the Methow River, this camp is an adequate layover spot for Highway 20 cruisers and a good alternative camp to the more crowded sites at Pearrygin Lake. See the trip notes for KOA Methow River (campground number 39) for information on the various activities available in the Winthrop area.

⓬ Big Twin Lake Campground

Location: On Twin Lakes; map A3, grid d9.

Campsites, facilities: There are 35 tent sites and 68 sites for trailers or RVs of any length; 18 are drive-throughs. Electricity, piped water, sewer hookups, and picnic tables are provided. Flush toilets, sanitary services, showers, firewood, a laundry room, ice, and a playground are available. Boat docks, launching facilities, and rentals can be obtained on Big Twin Lake. Leashed pets and motorbikes are permitted.

Reservations, fees: Reservations are accepted. Sites are $10–$16 per night. The campground is open from April to late October.

Contact: Phone (509) 996-2650 or write to Big Twin Lake Road, Winthrop, WA 98862.

Directions: From Interstate 5 south of Bellingham, turn east on Highway 20 and drive approximately 134 miles to Winthrop. Continue three miles on Highway 20, then turn west on Big Twin Lake Road and drive two miles to the campground.

Trip notes: As the name implies, this campground is set along the shore of Twin Lakes. See the trip notes for KOA Methow River (campground number 39) for information on the various activities available in the Winthrop area.

⓫ Clear Creek

Location: On Clear Creek and the Sauk River in Mount Baker–Snoqualmie National Forest; map A3, grid e0.

Campsites, facilities: There are 12 sites for tents, trailers, or RVs up to 21 feet long. Picnic tables and fire grills are provided. Vault toilets and firewood are available. There is no piped water. Some facilities are wheelchair accessible. A store, a cafe, a Laundromat, and ice are located within four miles. Leashed pets are permitted.

Reservations, fees: Call the ranger district at (360) 436-1155 for reservation and fee information. The campground is open from late May to early September.

Contact: Mount Baker–Snoqualmie National

Forest, Darrington Ranger District, 1405 Emmens Street, Darrington, WA 98241; (360) 436-1155 or fax (360) 436-1309.

Directions: From Interstate 5 south of Bellingham, take exit 208 and head east on Highway 530. Drive 32 miles to Darrington, then drive 2.5 miles south on Forest Service Road 20 to the campground entrance on the left.

Trip notes: This nice, secluded spot doesn't get heavy use. It's set at the confluence of Clear Creek and the Sauk River, a designated Wild and Scenic River. A trail from camp leads about one mile up to Frog Lake.

⓭ Squire Creek County Park

Location: On Squire Creek; map A3, grid e0.

Campsites, facilities: There are 30 drive-through sites for trailers or RVs up to 25 feet long. Piped water, sewer hookups, and picnic tables are provided. Flush toilets, sanitary services, and firewood are available. A store is located a mile away in Darrington. Leashed pets are permitted.

Reservations, fees: No reservations are accepted. Sites are $10–$15 per night. The campground is open from mid-May to mid-September.

Contact: Phone (425) 339-1208 or write to 3000 Rockefeller Avenue, Everett, WA 98201.

Directions: From Interstate 5 south of Bellingham, take exit 208 and head east on Highway 530. Drive 32 miles to Darrington, then drive three miles on Highway 530 to the park on the left.

Trip notes: This wooded, low-cost RV park near the outback along Squire Creek is about three miles from the boundaries of the Boulder River Wilderness.

⓮ Cascade Kamloops Trout Farm/ RV Park

Location: In Darrington; map A3, grid e1.

Campsites, facilities: There are two tent

sites and 32 sites for trailers or RVs of any length. Electricity, piped water, sewer hook-ups, and picnic tables are provided. Flush toilets, sanitary services, showers, firewood, a laundry room, and a recreation hall are available. Bottled gas, a store, a cafe, and ice are located within one mile. Pets and motorbikes are permitted.

Reservations, fees: Reservations are accepted. Sites are $14–$16 per night. The campground is open year-round.

Contact: Phone (360) 436-1003 or write to P.O. Box 1205, Darrington, WA 98241.

Directions: From Interstate 5 south of Bellingham, take exit 208 and drive east on Highway 530 for about 30 miles to Darrington. In Darrington, turn right on Madison Street and drive about four blocks to Darrington Street. Turn right and drive two blocks to the park.

Trip notes: Campers will find a little bit of both worlds at this campground—a rustic quietness with all facilities available. A bonus is a nearby trout pond, which is stocked in season. No boats are allowed. Nearby recreation options include marked hiking trails and tennis courts.

45 William C. Dearinger

Location: On the Sauk River; map A3, grid e1.

Campsites, facilities: There are 12 sites for tents or small trailers. Picnic tables, fire grills, and tent pads are provided. Vault toilets and firewood are available, but there is no piped water. Leashed pets are permitted.

Reservations, fees: No reservations are accepted. There is no fee. The campground is open year-round.

Contact: Department of Natural Resources, Northwest Region, 411 Tillicum Lane, Forks, WA 98331-9797; (360) 856-3500.

Directions: From Interstate 5, take exit 208 and turn east on Highway 530. Drive 35 miles to Darrington. Continue one-third of a mile on Highway 530, then drive east on Mountain Loop Road for one-half mile. Continue straight

for five miles, then turn left and drive two-thirds of a mile on East Sauk Prairie Road. Stay right on Road SWD 5000 and drive 2.6 miles, then bear left for one mile. Bear left again on Road SWD 5400 and drive about 400 yards to the campground.

Trip notes: This secluded campground is on the Sauk River and is managed by the Department of Natural Resources. It may be a little difficult to reach, but that's why you'll probably be the only one here. It's pretty, with lots of trees and sites overlooking the river.

46 Buck Creek

Location: Near the Suiattle River in Mount Baker–Snoqualmie National Forest; map A3, grid e2.

Campsites, facilities: There are 29 tent sites and 10 sites for trailers or RVs up to 30 feet long. Picnic tables are provided. Vault toilets and firewood are available, but there is no piped water. Leashed pets are permitted.

Reservations, fees: Call the ranger district at (360) 436-1155 for reservation and fee information. The campground is open from late May to early September.

Contact: Mount Baker–Snoqualmie National Forest, Darrington Ranger District, 1405 Emmens Street, Darrington, WA 98241; (360) 436-1155 or fax (360) 436-1309.

Directions: From Interstate 5 south of Bellingham, take exit 208 and head east on Highway 530. Drive 32 miles to Darrington, then continue 7.5 miles on Highway 530 and turn right (southeast) on Forest Service Road 26. Drive 15.2 miles to the campground. A Forest Service map is essential. Note: In the past, Forest Service Road 26 has been closed due to flooding; it's a good idea to phone ahead for current conditions.

Trip notes: Quiet and remote, this primitive campground is set along Buck Creek near its confluence with the Suiattle River in the Glacier Peak Wilderness. There's a large (18 feet by 18 feet) adirondack shelter by the creek and stands of old growth timber. A zigzagging trail routed into the Glacier Peak

Wilderness is accessible about one mile west of camp. See a Forest Service map for specifics.

47 Sulphur Creek

Location: On the Suiattle River in Mount Baker–Snoqualmie National Forest; map A3, grid e3.

Campsites, facilities: There are 20 sites for tents, trailers, or RVs up to 15 feet long. Picnic tables and fire grills are provided. Downed wood can be gathered and used for firewood. Vault toilets are available. There is no piped water. Leashed pets are permitted.

Reservations, fees: Call the ranger district at (360) 436-1155 for reservation and fee information. The campground is open from June to early September.

Contact: Mount Baker–Snoqualmie National Forest, Darrington Ranger District, 1405 Emmens Street, Darrington, WA 98241; (360) 436-1155 or fax (360) 436-1309.

Directions: From Interstate 5 south of Bellingham, take exit 208 and head east on Highway 530. Drive 32 miles to Darrington, then continue 7.5 miles on Highway 530. Turn right on Forest Service Road 26 and drive 30 miles southeast to the campground on the right. A Forest Service map is advisable. Note: In the past, Forest Service Road 26 has been closed due to flooding; it's a good idea to phone ahead for current conditions.

Trip notes: Fishing access to the river across the road is a highlight of this campground set along the Suiattle River near the border of the Glacier Peak Wilderness. It's a good base camp for a wilderness expedition, with a horse ramp and a trailhead leading deep into the backcountry located about a mile south of the campground. The trail hooks up with the Pacific Crest Trail.

48 Holden Ballpark

Location: Near the Glacier Peak Wilderness in Wenatchee National Forest; map A3, grid e5.

Campsites, facilities: There are two primitive tent sites that are accessible only by boat or ferry. Picnic tables and fire rings are provided. One Wallowa (non-enclosed, platform) pit toilet is available, but there is no piped water. Be prepared to protect food from bears.

Reservations, fees: No reservations are accepted. There is no fee. The campground is open from mid-June to late September.

Contact: Wenatchee National Forest, Chelan Ranger District, 428 West Woodin Avenue, Chelan, WA 98816; (509) 682-2576 or fax (509) 682-9004.

Directions: From Interstate 5 at Everett, turn east on U.S. 2 and drive approximately 120 miles. Turn north on U.S. 97 and continue about 40 miles to Chelan. Take the ferry from there (another ferry is available at Fields Point Landing, a few miles northwest of Chelan) and proceed to Lucerne, 41 miles northwest of the town of Chelan. This spectacular voyage costs about $20 round-trip, depending on your destination. For more information call (509) 682-2224. From Lucerne, take the bus 12 miles west to Holden Village. The campground is at the end of the road.

Trip notes: Getting here is half the fun, with ferry boat rides provided by the Lake Chelan Boat Company that emphasize fun and education along with transportation. Several trails to lakes in the Glacier Peak Wilderness are accessible from a trail next to the campground, which is set along Railroad Creek. Since this area is on the eastern slope of the Cascade Range, it's drier than the western slopes and not as heavily forested. However, there is no shortage of glacier-fed streams and lakes in the area. See a Forest Service map for details. Less than a mile from the campground is the Holden Mine site, which was Washington's largest gold, copper, and zinc mine until it closed in 1957. Many of the buildings from the mining town have been preserved, and Holden Village offers housing and meals for travelers as space allows.

49 Domke Lake

Location: Near the Glacier Peak Wilderness in Wenatchee National Forest; map A3, grid e6.

Campsites, facilities: There are six tent sites accessible only by boat, ferry, or float plane. Picnic tables are provided. Pit toilets are available, but there is no piped water. Boat docks and rentals are nearby. Be prepared to protect food from bears.

Reservations, fees: No reservations are accepted. There is no fee for camping, but there is a $5 docking fee. The campground is open from May to late October.

Contact: Wenatchee National Forest, Chelan Ranger District, 428 West Woodin Avenue, Chelan, WA 98816; (509) 682-2576 or fax (509) 682-9004.

Directions: From Interstate 5 at Everett, turn east on U.S. 2 and drive approximately 120 miles. Turn north on U.S. 97 and continue about 40 miles to Chelan. Take the ferry from there (another ferry is available at Fields Point Landing, a few miles northwest of Chelan) and proceed to Lucerne, 41 miles northwest of the town of Chelan. This spectacular voyage costs about $20 round-trip, depending on your destination. For more information call (509) 682-2224. From Lucerne, hike, bike, or motorbike 2.5 miles on Trail 1280 to Domke Lake and the campground. The campground is also directly accessible by float plane. Call Chelan Airways at (509) 682-5555 for more information.

Trip notes: Little known and little used, this is a perfect jump-off for a wilderness backpacking trip. Domke Lake is about one mile long and one-half mile wide and offers good fishing by boat. Trails continue past the lake into the Glacier Peak Wilderness. See a Forest Service map for details.

50 Lucerne

Location: On Lake Chelan in Wenatchee National Forest; map A3, grid e7.

Campsites, facilities: There are two tent sites accessible only by boat, ferry, or float plane. Piped water, fire grills, and picnic tables are provided. Pit toilets are available. Boat docks are nearby.

Reservations, fees: No reservations are

accepted. There is no fee for camping, but there is a $5 docking fee. The campground is open from May to late October.

Contact: Wenatchee National Forest, Chelan Ranger District, 428 West Woodin Avenue, Chelan, WA 98816; (509) 682-2576 or fax (509) 682-9004.

Directions: From Interstate 5 at Everett, turn east on U.S. 2 and drive approximately 120 miles. Turn north on U.S. 97 and continue about 40 miles to Chelan. Take the ferry from there (another ferry is available at Fields Point Landing, a few miles northwest of Chelan) and proceed to Lucerne, 41 miles northwest of the town of Chelan. This spectacular voyage costs about $20 round-trip, depending on your destination. For more information call (509) 682-2224. The camp is in Lucerne. The campground is also directly accessible by float plane. Call Chelan Airways at (509) 682-5555 for more information.

Trip notes: This campground is set along the shore of 55-mile-long Lake Chelan, the second deepest lake in North America, with a depth of 1,500 feet. Mountains reaching to 8,000 feet flank each side of the lake. This is the only National Forest camp in the vicinity that offers piped water. Fishing, hiking, and boating are among your options here. See the trip notes for Holden (campground number 48) for information on the Holden Mine and Village.

51 Foggy Dew

Location: On Foggy Dew Creek in Okanogan National Forest; map A3, grid e9.

Campsites, facilities: There are 13 sites for tents, trailers, or RVs. Picnic tables and fire grills are provided. Vault toilets and firewood are available, but there is no piped water. No garbage service is provided, so trash must be packed out. Leashed pets are permitted.

Reservations, fees: No reservations are accepted. Overnight parking requires a $25 seasonal pass or $5 per night ($10 for three nights). The campground is open from late May to early September.

Contact: Okanogan National Forest, Methow Valley Visitor Center, P.O. Box 579, Winthrop, WA 98862; (509) 996-4000 or fax (509) 997-9770.

Directions: From Interstate 5 south of Bellingham, turn east on Highway 20 and drive approximately 145 miles to Twisp. Continue three miles east on Highway 20, then turn south on Highway 153 and drive 12 miles to County Road 1029. Turn south and drive one mile, then turn west on Forest Service Road 4340 and drive four miles to the campground.

Trip notes: This private, remote campground is set at the confluence of Foggy Dew Creek and the North Fork of Gold Creek. There are several trails nearby that provide access to various backcountry lakes and streams. To get to the trailheads, just follow the Forest Service roads near camp. Bicycles and motorbikes are allowed on Trails 417, 429, and 431. In the winter the area is open for both cross-country skiing and snowmobiling. See a Forest Service map for options.

---

⑤ Gold Basin

Location: On the South Fork of the Stillaguamish River in Mount Baker–Snoqualmie National Forest; map A3, grid f0.

Campsites, facilities: There are 10 tent sites and 83 sites for tents, trailers, or RVs up to 60 feet long. There is an overflow area available for group camping with three sites, each accommodating a maximum of 25 people. Picnic tables are provided. Vault toilets, piped water, and firewood are available. A store, a cafe, and ice are located within 2.5 miles. Some facilities are wheelchair accessible. Leashed pets are permitted.

Reservations, fees: Some sites can be reserved by calling (800) 280-CAMP/2267 ($8.65 reservation fee). Sites are $10 per night; group sites are $50 per night. The campground is open from mid-May to early September.

Contact: Mount Baker–Snoqualmie National Forest, Darrington Ranger District, 1405 Emmens Street, Darrington, WA 98241; (360) 436-1155 or fax (360) 436-1309.

Directions: From Interstate 5 at Everett, turn east on Highway 92 and drive about 15 miles to the town of Granite Falls. Continue 13.5 miles east on Highway 92 to the campground entrance on the left.

Trip notes: This is the largest campground in Mount Baker–Snoqualmie National Forest, and since it's loaded with facilities, it's a favorite with RVers. The campground is set at 1,100 feet along the South Fork of the Stillaguamish River, with riverside sites, easy access, and a wheelchair-accessible interpretive trail. Fishing and hiking are two options.

⑤ Beaver Plant Lake

Location: On Beaver Plant Lake; map A3, grid f0.

Campsites, facilities: There are six tent sites at this primitive, hike-in campground. Picnic tables, fire grills, and tent pads are provided. Portable vault toilets and firewood are available. There is no piped water. Leashed pets are permitted.

Reservations, fees: No reservations are accepted. There is no fee. The campground is open from mid-June through October.

Contact: Department of Natural Resources, Northwest Region, 919 North Township Street, Sedro-Woolley, WA 98284-9395; (360) 856-3500.

Directions: From Interstate 5 at Everett, turn east on Highway 92 and drive northeast to the town of Granite Falls. Turn north on Mountain Loop Highway and drive 15 miles. Turn south on Forest Service Road 4020 and drive 2.5 miles, then turn right on Forest Service Road 4021 and drive two miles to the Ashland Lakes Trailhead. From the trailhead, hike 1.5 miles to the campground.

Trip notes: This campground is on Beaver Plant Lake, one of four campgrounds detailed in the area (the others are Upper Ashland Lake, Lower Ashland Lake, and Twin Falls Lake, campground numbers 45, 55, and 61). Excellent hiking trails are a highlight of the region.

⑤④ Upper Ashland Lake

Location: Near Upper Ashland Lake; map A3, grid f0.

Campsites, facilities: There are six tent sites at this primitive, hike-in campground. Picnic tables, fire grills, and tent pads are provided. Portable vault toilets and firewood are available, but there is no piped water. Leashed pets are permitted.

Reservations, fees: No reservations are accepted. There is no fee. The campground is open from mid-June through October.

Contact: Department of Natural Resources, Northwest Region, 919 North Township Street, Sedro-Woolley, WA 98284-9395; (360) 856-3500.

Directions: From Interstate 5 at Everett, turn east on Highway 92 and drive northeast to the town of Granite Falls. Turn north on Mountain Loop Highway and drive 15 miles. Turn south on Forest Service Road 4020 and drive 2.5 miles, then turn right on Forest Service Road 4021 and drive two miles to the Ashland Lakes Trailhead. From the trailhead, hike two miles to the campground.

Trip notes: Reaching this primitive and very beautiful camp requires a short hike that's well worth the effort. The site is little known, so you can expect quiet and privacy. Several good hiking trails can be found near camp. A map available from the Department of Natural Resources is helpful.

⑤⑤ Lower Ashland Lake

Location: On Lower Ashland Lake; map A3, grid f0.

Campsites, facilities: There are six tent sites at this primitive, hike-in campground. Picnic tables, fire grills, and tent pads are provided. Vault toilets and firewood are available. There is no piped water. Leashed pets are permitted.

Reservations, fees: No reservations are accepted. There is no fee. The campground is open from mid-June through October.

Contact: Department of Natural Resources, Northwest Region, 919 North Township Street, Sedro-Woolley, WA 98284-9395; (360) 856-3500.

Directions: From Interstate 5 at Everett, turn east on Highway 92 and drive northeast to the town of Granite Falls. Turn north on Mountain Loop Highway and drive 15 miles. Turn south on Forest Service Road 4020 and drive 2.5 miles, then turn right on Forest Service Road 4021 and drive two miles to the Ashland Lakes Trailhead. From the trailhead, hike 2.5 miles to the campground.

Trip notes: This campground is on Lower Ashland Lake, set adjacent to Upper Ashland Lake; See the trip notes for campground number 54 for details.

⑤⑥ Esswine Group Camp

Location: In Mount Baker–Snoqualmie National Forest; map A3, grid f0.

Campsites, facilities: This is a specially designated group campground with four tent sites. Picnic tables are provided. Vault toilets and firewood are available, but there is no piped water. A store, a cafe, and ice are located within four miles. Leashed pets are permitted.

Reservations, fees: Reservations are required. The fee is $40 for the first night and $30 per night thereafter. The campground is open from mid-May to early September.

Contact: Mount Baker–Snoqualmie National Forest, Darrington Ranger District, 1405 Emmens Street, Darrington, WA 98241; (360) 436-1155 or fax (360) 436-1309.

Directions: From Interstate 5 at Everett, turn east on Highway 92 and drive about 15 miles to the town of Granite Falls. Continue 16 miles east on Highway 92 to the campground entrance on the left.

Trip notes: This small, quiet camp is a great place for a restful group getaway. The lack of piped water is the only drawback. Esswine is one of the few Forest Service campgrounds in the area that requires (or even accepts) reservations; get yours in early. Fishing access is available nearby. The Boulder River Wilderness is located to the north; see a Forest Service map for trailhead locations.

⑤⑦ Boardman Creek

Location: On the South Fork of the Stillaguamish River in Mount Baker–Snoqualmie National Forest; map A3, grid f0.

Campsites, facilities: There are eight tent sites and two sites for tents, trailers, or RVs of any length. Picnic tables are provided. Vault toilets and firewood are available, but there is no piped water. Leashed pets are permitted.

Reservations, fees: Call the ranger district at (360) 436-1155 for reservation, fee, and open period information.

Contact: Mount Baker–Snoqualmie National Forest, Darrington Ranger District, 1405 Emmens Street, Darrington, WA 98241; (360) 436-1155 or fax (360) 436-1309.

Directions: From Interstate 5 at Everett, turn east on Highway 92 and drive about 15 miles to the town of Granite Falls. Continue 16.5 miles east on Highway 92 to the campground entrance on the left.

Trip notes: Roomy sites and river access highlight this pretty riverside camp. The fishing is rumored to be excellent near here. Forest Service roads in the area will take you to several backcountry lakes, including Boardman Lake, Lake Evan, Clear Lake, and Ashland Lakes. Get a Forest Service map, set up your camp, and go for it.

⑤⑧ Coal Creek Bar Group Camp

Location: On the South Fork of the Stillaguamish River in Mount Baker–Snoqualmie National Forest; map A3, grid f0.

Campsites, facilities: There are two tent sites and two trailer sites. Picnic tables and fire grills are provided. Vault toilets and firewood are available. There is no piped water. Leashed pets are permitted.

Reservations, fees: Reservations are required. Sites are $40 per night for the entire

camp. The campground is open from mid-May to late September.

Contact: Mount Baker–Snoqualmie National Forest, Darrington Ranger District, 1405 Emmens Street, Darrington, WA 98241; (360) 436-1155 or fax (360) 436-1309.

Directions: From Interstate 5 at Everett, turn east on Highway 92 and drive about 15 miles to the town of Granite Falls. Continue 23.5 miles east on Highway 92 to the campground entrance.

Trip notes: A Forest Service map will unlock the beautiful country around this campground set along the South Fork of the Stillaguamish River near Coal Creek. Fishing access is available, and nearby Forest Service roads lead to Coal Lake and a trailhead that takes you to other backcountry lakes.

⑤⑨ Tulalip Millsite Group Camp

Location: On the South Fork of the Stillaguamish River in Mount Baker–Snoqualmie National Forest; map A3, grid f0.

Campsites, facilities: This is a specially designated group camp that will accommodate up to 80 people. Picnic tables and fire grills are provided. Vault toilets are available, but there is no piped water. Leashed pets are permitted.

Reservations, fees: Reservations are required. Sites are $50 per night. The campground is open from mid-May to late September.

Contact: Mount Baker–Snoqualmie National Forest, Darrington Ranger District, 1405 Emmens Street, Darrington, WA 98241; (360) 436-1155 or fax (360) 436-1309.

Directions: From Interstate 5 at Everett, turn east on Highway 92 and drive about 15 miles to the town of Granite Falls. Continue 18.5 miles east on Highway 92 to the campground entrance on the right.

Trip notes: Like Turlo, Verlot, Gold Basin, Esswine, Boardman Creek, Coal Creek Bar, and Red Bridge (see campground numbers 69 and 70 in Chapter A2, and 56, 57, 58, and 60 in this chapter), this campground is set along the

South Fork of the Stillaguamish River. A trailhead about one mile east of camp leads north into the Boulder River Wilderness. There are numerous creeks and streams that crisscross this area, providing good fishing prospects.

⑥⓪ Red Bridge

Location: On the South Fork of Stillaguamish River in Mount Baker–Snoqualmie National Forest; map A3, grid f0.

Campsites, facilities: There are two tent sites and 14 sites for tents, trailers, or RVs up to 31 feet long. Picnic tables are provided. Vault toilets are available, but there is no piped water. Some facilities are wheelchair accessible. Leashed pets are permitted.

Reservations, fees: Call the ranger district at (360) 436-1155 for reservation and fee information. The campground is open from late May to early September.

Contact: Mount Baker–Snoqualmie National Forest, Darrington Ranger District, 1405 Emmens Street, Darrington, WA 98241; (360) 436-1155 or fax (360) 436-1309.

Directions: From Interstate 5 at Everett, turn east on Highway 92 and drive about 15 miles to the town of Granite Falls. Continue 18 miles east on Highway 92 to the campground entrance.

Trip notes: Red Bridge is another classic spot, one of several in the vicinity, and a good base camp for a backpacking expedition. The campground is set at 1,300 feet on the South Fork of the Stillaguamish River near Mahardy Creek. It has pretty, riverside sites. A trailhead two miles east of camp leads to Granite Pass in the Boulder River Wilderness.

⑥① Twin Falls Lake

Location: On Twin Falls Lake; map A3, grid f0.

Campsites, facilities: There are five tent sites at this primitive, hike-in campground. Picnic tables are provided. Vault toilets and

firewood are available. There is no piped water. Leashed pets are permitted.

Reservations, fees: No reservations are accepted. There is no fee. The campground is open from mid-June through October.

Contact: Department of Natural Resources, Northwest Region, 919 North Township Street, Sedro-Woolley, WA 98284-9395; (360) 856-3500.

Directions: From Interstate 5 at Everett, turn east on Highway 92 and drive northeast to the town of Granite Falls. Turn north on Mountain Loop Highway and drive 15 miles. Turn south on Forest Service Road 4020 and drive 2.5 miles, then turn right on Forest Service Road 4021 and drive two miles to the Ashland Lakes Trailhead. Hike in four miles from the trailhead.

Trip notes: People willing to grunt a little will find good hiking, backpacking, and trout fishing at this site. It's a beautiful and secluded area, yet it's not a long drive from Seattle.

⑥② Bedal

Location: On the Sauk River in Mount Baker–Snoqualmie National Forest; map A3, grid f2.

Campsites, facilities: There are 19 sites for tents, trailers, or RVs up to 21 feet long. Picnic tables and a picnic shelter are provided. Vault toilets are available, but there is no piped water. Some facilities are wheelchair accessible. A Forest Service district office is nearby.

Reservations, fees: Call the ranger district at (360) 436-1155 for reservation and fee information. The campground is open from June to early September.

Contact: Mount Baker–Snoqualmie National Forest, Darrington Ranger District, 1405 Emmens Street, Darrington, WA 98241; (360) 436-1155 or fax (360) 436-1309.

Directions: From Interstate 5 at Everett, turn right (east) on Highway 530 and drive 33 miles to the junction of Highway 530 and Mountain Loop Highway (Forest Service Road 20) in Darrington. Turn right (south) on Forest Service Road 20 and drive 22 miles to the campground on the right. A Forest Service map is essential.

Trip notes: This campground, set at the confluence of the North and South Forks of the Sauk River, offers shaded sites, river views, and good fishing. It's a bit primitive, but you can't beat the price. North Fork Falls is about a mile up the North Fork of the Sauk from camp and worth the trip.

⓺ Phelps Creek

Location: On the Chiwawa River in Wenatchee National Forest; map A3, grid f4.

Campsites, facilities: There are seven tent sites. Picnic tables and fire grills are provided. Pit toilets are available, but there is no piped water. Horse facilities are nearby. Leashed pets are permitted.

Reservations, fees: No reservations are accepted. There is no fee. The campground is open from mid-June to mid-October.

Contact: Wenatchee National Forest, Lake Wenatchee Ranger District, 22976 Highway 207, Leavenworth, WA 98826; (509) 763-3103 or fax (509) 763-3211.

Directions: From Interstate 5 at Everett, turn east on U.S. 2 and drive approximately 87 miles. Turn north on Highway 207 and drive four miles, then turn east on Chiwawa Loop Road and drive 1.4 miles. Head north on Chiwawa Valley Road and Forest Service Road 6200 for 23.6 miles to the campground.

Trip notes: This campground is set at the confluence of Phelps Creek and the Chiwawa River. There's a key trailhead for backpackers and horseback riders nearby that provides access to the Glacier Peak Wilderness. It's advisable to obtain a Forest Service map.

⓸ Cottonwood

Location: On the Entiat River in Wenatchee National Forest; map A3, grid f5.

Campsites, facilities: There are 25 sites for tents or small RVs. Hand-pumped water, fire grills, and picnic tables are provided. Pit toilets are available. Leashed pets are permitted.

Reservations, fees: No reservations are accepted. Sites are $8 per vehicle per night. The campground is open from late June to mid-October.

Contact: Wenatchee National Forest, Entiat Ranger District, P.O. Box 476, Entiat, WA 98822; (509) 784-1511.

Directions: From Interstate 5 at Everett, turn east on U.S. 2 and drive approximately 120 miles. Turn north on U.S. 97A and drive 18.5 miles to County Road 371 (Entiat River Road). Turn northwest and drive 38 miles to the campground.

Trip notes: At 3,100 feet, this campground along the Entiat River is at a major trailhead leading into the Glacier Peak Wilderness. A Forest Service map details the backcountry. A bonus is good berry picking in season. Fishing is another alternative.

⓺ Deer Point

Location: On Lake Chelan in Wenatchee National Forest; map A3, grid f8.

Campsites, facilities: There are five tent sites accessible only by boat, ferry, or float plane. Picnic tables and fire rings are provided. Pit toilets are available, but there is no piped water. A floating dock can accommodate about eight boats. Be prepared to protect food from bears.

Reservations, fees: No reservations are accepted. There is no fee for camping, but there is a $5 docking fee. The campground is open from May to late October.

Contact: Wenatchee National Forest, Chelan Ranger District, 428 West Woodin Avenue, Chelan, WA 98816; (509) 682-2576 or fax (509) 682-9004.

Directions: From Interstate 5 at Everett, turn east on U.S. 2 and drive approximately 120 miles. Turn north on U.S. 97 and continue about 40 miles to Chelan. Take the ferry from there (another ferry is available at Fields Point Landing, a few miles northwest of Chelan) and proceed to Deer Point, 22 miles from Chelan. This spectacular voyage costs about $20 round-trip, depending on your destination. For more information call (509)

682-2224. The campground is also directly accessible by float plane. Call Chelan Airways at (509) 682-5555 for more information.

Trip notes: Here's another little-known spot set along the shore of Lake Chelan. If you want to camp on the remote east shore, this is one of three camps. The others are Prince Creek and Mitchell Creek (campground numbers 68 and 88). This is a good camp for anglers, because there isn't much to do but relax and wait for the fish to bite.

⑥⑥ Twenty-Five Mile Creek State Park

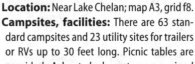

Location: Near Lake Chelan; map A3, grid f8.

Campsites, facilities: There are 63 standard campsites and 23 utility sites for trailers or RVs up to 30 feet long. Picnic tables are provided. A boat dock, rest rooms, piped water, electricity, and sewer hookups are available.

Reservations, fees: Contact Reservations Northwest at (800) 452-5687 ($6 reservation fee). Sites are $11–$16 per night. The campground is open from early April to late October.

Contact: Phone (800) 233-0321 or (509) 687-3710, or write Route 1, P.O. Box 142A, Chelan, WA 98816.

Directions: From Interstate 5 at Everett, turn east on U.S. 2 and drive approximately 120 miles. Turn north on U.S. 97 and continue about 40 miles to Chelan. Turn north on South Shore Road and drive 18 miles to the park at the end of the road.

Trip notes: This campground is located on Twenty-Five Mile Creek near where it empties into Lake Chelan. Fishing access is close by, and fishing supplies, a dock, and boat moorage are available. There is also a small wading area for kids. Forest Service Road 5900, which heads west from the park, accesses several trailheads leading into the Forest Service lands of the Chelan Mountains. Obtain a Forest Service map of Wenatchee National Forest for details.

⑥⑦ Graham Harbor

Location: On Lake Chelan in Wenatchee National Forest; map A3, grid f8.

Campsites, facilities: There are five tent sites accessible only by boat, ferry, or float plane. Picnic tables and fire rings are provided. Pit toilets are available, but there is no piped water. A floating dock can accommodate about 10 boats. Be prepared to protect food from bears.

Reservations, fees: No reservations are accepted. There is no fee for camping, but there is a $5 docking fee. The campground is open year-round.

Contact: Wenatchee National Forest, Chelan Ranger District, 428 West Woodin Avenue, Chelan, WA 98816; (509) 682-2576 or fax (509) 682-9004.

Directions: From Interstate 5 at Everett, turn east on U.S. 2 and drive approximately 120 miles. Turn north on U.S. 97 and continue about 40 miles to Chelan. Take the ferry from there (another ferry is available at Fields Point Landing, a few miles northwest of Chelan) and proceed to Graham Harbor Creek, 31 miles from Chelan. This spectacular voyage costs about $20 round-trip, depending on your destination. For more information call (509) 682-2224. Take the 8:30 A.M. ferry from Chelan, Manson, or Fields Point Landing and get off at Graham Harbor Creek, 31 miles from Chelan. See Holden (campground number 48) for additional ferry information. The campground is also directly accessible by float plane. Call Chelan Airways at (509) 682-5555 for more information.

Trip notes: This campground is set along Lake Chelan at the mouth of Graham Harbor Creek. It's one of the more remote and primitive campgrounds on giant Chelan. Fishing and boating are the main recreation attractions here.

⑥⑧ Prince Creek

Location: On Lake Chelan in Wenatchee National Forest; map A3, grid f8.

Campsites, facilities: There are six tent

sites accessible only by boat, ferry, or float plane. Picnic tables and fire rings are provided. Pit toilets are available, but there is no piped water. A floating dock can accommodate about three boats. Be prepared to protect food from bears.

Reservations, fees: No reservations are accepted. There is no fee for camping, but there is a $5 docking fee. The campground is open from May to mid-November.

Contact: Wenatchee National Forest, Chelan Ranger District, 428 West Woodin Avenue, Chelan, WA 98816; (509) 682-2576 or fax (509) 682-9004.

Directions: From Interstate 5 at Everett, turn east on U.S. 2 and drive approximately 120 miles. Turn north on U.S. 97 and continue about 40 miles to Chelan. Take the ferry from there (another ferry is available at Fields Point Landing, a few miles northwest of Chelan) and proceed to Prince Creek, 35 miles from Chelan. This spectacular voyage costs about $20 round-trip, depending on your destination. For more information call (509) 682-2224. The campground is also directly accessible by float plane. Call Chelan Airways at (509) 682-5555 for more information.

Trip notes: This camp is set along the shore of Lake Chelan at the mouth of Prince Creek. A trail from camp follows Prince Creek into the Lake Chelan–Sawtooth Wilderness, and then connects to a network of other trails— all of which lead to various lakes and streams. A Forest Service map shows details.

㉖ Wallace Falls State Park

Location: Near Gold Bar; map A3, grid g0.

Campsites, facilities: There are six tent sites. Picnic tables and fire grills are provided. Flush toilets and piped water are available. Some facilities are wheelchair accessible. Leashed pets are permitted.

Reservations, fees: No reservations are accepted. Sites are $10 per night, plus $5 per extra vehicle each night. The campground is open year-round.

Contact: Phone (800) 233-0321 or (360) 793-0420, or write to P.O. Box 106, Gold Bar, WA 98251.

Directions: From Interstate 5 at Everett, turn east on U.S. 2 and drive about 28 miles to the town of Gold Bar. Turn northeast at the sign for Wallace Falls State Park and proceed two miles to the park.

Trip notes: Seattle is loaded with people, but very few of them know of this tiny jewel nestled in the forest near the scenic Wallace Falls. The campground is located in a heavily treed area at the trailhead to the falls. The trail leads along the Wallace River and is a lovely hike.

㉗ Cutthroat Lakes

Location: On Bald Mountain; map A3, grid g0.

Campsites, facilities: There are 10 tent sites at this primitive, hike-in campground. Picnic tables, fire grills, and tent pads are provided. Portable vault toilets are available, but there is no piped water. Leashed pets are permitted.

Reservations, fees: No reservations are accepted. There is no fee. The campground is open from mid-June through October.

Contact: Department of Natural Resources, Northwest Region, 919 North Township Street, Sedro-Woolley, WA 98284-9395; (360) 856-3500.

Directions: From Interstate 5 at Everett, turn east on Highway 92 and drive about 15 miles to the town of Granite Falls. Continue 18 miles east on Highway 92 to Forest Service Road 4030. Turn south and drive for three miles to Forest Service Road 4032. Follow Road 4032 all the way to the end where the trailhead begins. The hike to Cutthroat Lakes is about four miles.

Trip notes: Reaching this spot requires following difficult directions, but it's worth the effort. You'll find beautiful lakeside camps, trout fishing, hiking, and few other campers. The "lakes" are actually small ponds, but they're very pretty.

⓱ Big Greider Lake

Location: On Big Greider Lake; map A3, grid g1.

Campsites, facilities: There are five tent sites at this primitive, hike-in campground. Picnic tables, fire grills, and tent pads are provided. Portable vault toilets and firewood are available, but there is no piped water. Leashed pets are permitted.

Reservations, fees: No reservations are accepted. There is no fee. The campground is open from mid-June through October.

Contact: Department of Natural Resources, Northwest Region, 919 North Township Street, Sedro-Woolley, WA 98284-9395; (360) 856-3500.

Directions: From Interstate 5 at Everett, turn east on U.S. 2 and drive 24 miles to Sultan. Continue one-half mile east, then turn north on Sultan Basin Road and drive 13.6 miles. Take the middle road (Road SLS 4000) for about 8.5 miles to the Greider Lake Trailhead. From the trailhead, hike 2.5 miles to the campground.

Trip notes: This primitive campground on Big Greider Lake is an alternative to Little Greider Lake Campground (see number 72), adjacent to Little Greider Lake. Hiking trails can be found nearby.

⓲ Little Greider Lake

Location: On Little Greider Lake; map A3, grid g1.

Campsites, facilities: There are nine tent sites at this primitive, hike-in campground. Picnic tables, fire grills, and tent pads are provided. Portable vault toilets and firewood are available. There is no piped water. Leashed pets are permitted.

Reservations, fees: No reservations are accepted. There is no fee. The campground is open from mid-June through October.

Contact: Department of Natural Resources, Northwest Region, 919 North Township Street, Sedro-Woolley, WA 98284-9395; (360) 856-3500.

Directions: From Interstate 5 at Everett, turn east on U.S. 2 and drive 24 miles to Sultan. Continue one-half mile east, then turn north on Sultan Basin Road and drive 13.6 miles. Take the middle road (Road SLS 4000) for about 8.5 miles to the Greider Lake Trailhead. From the trailhead, hike two miles to the campground.

Trip notes: This is prime country for hiking, backpacking, and trout fishing. The primitive, wooded campground is on Little Greider Lake.

⓳ Boulder Lake

Location: On Boulder Lake; map A3, grid g1.

Campsites, facilities: There are nine sites for tents at this primitive, hike-in campground. Picnic tables, fire grills, and tent pads are provided. Portable vault toilets and firewood are available. There is no piped water. Leashed pets are permitted.

Reservations, fees: No reservations are accepted. There is no fee. The campground is open from mid-June through October.

Contact: Department of Natural Resources, Northwest Region, 919 North Township Street, Sedro-Woolley, WA 98284-9395; (360) 856-3500.

Directions: From Interstate 5 at Everett, turn east on U.S. 2 and drive 24 miles to Sultan. Continue one-half mile east, then turn north on Sultan Basin Road and drive 13.6 miles. Take the middle road (Road SLS 4000) for about 8.5 miles to the Greider Lake Trailhead. Stay right on Road SLS 7000 and drive one mile to the Boulder Lake Trailhead. From the Boulder Lake Trailhead hike 3.8 miles to the campground.

Trip notes: This primitive, hike-in campground is on Boulder Lake. It's one of three hike-in camps in the immediate area: Little Greider Lake (campground number 72) and Big Greider Lake (campground number 71) are the other two. Hiking and fishing are two options.

⓴ Troublesome Creek

Location: On the North Fork of the Skykomish River in Mount Baker–Snoqualmie National Forest; map A3, grid g2.

Campsites, facilities: There are 24 sites for tents, trailers, or RVs up to 21 feet long and six walk-in tent sites. Picnic tables are provided. Piped water and vault toilets are available. Some facilities are wheelchair accessible. Leashed pets are permitted.

Reservations, fees: Some sites, including three that are wheelchair accessible, may be reserved by phoning (800) 280-CAMP/2267 ($8.65 reservation fee). Sites are $6.50–$10 per night. The campground is open from Memorial Day through Labor Day.

Contact: Mount Baker–Snoqualmie National Forest, Skykomish Ranger District, P.O. Box 305, Skykomish, WA 98288; (360) 677-2414.

Directions: From Interstate 5 at Everett, turn east on U.S. 2 and drive 36 miles to the town of Index. From there, drive 12 miles northeast on Forest Service Road 63 (Index-Galena Road) to the campground on the right.

Trip notes: Here's another one I bet you've never heard of. This campground is set along the North Fork of the Skykomish River. Highlights include a nature trail adjacent to the camp and good fishing in the river.

⓵ Soda Springs

Location: On the Little Wenatchee River in Wenatchee National Forest; map A3, grid g4.

Campsites, facilities: There are five tent sites. Picnic tables and fire grills are provided. Pit toilets are available, but there is no piped water.

Reservations, fees: No reservations are accepted. There is no fee. The campground is open from May to late October.

Contact: Wenatchee National Forest, Lake Wenatchee Ranger District, 22976 Highway 207, Leavenworth, WA 98826; (509) 763-3103 or fax (509) 763-3211.

Directions: From Interstate 5 at Everett, turn east on U.S. 2 and drive approximately 87 miles to Highway 207. Turn north and drive 10.5 miles, then turn west and drive 1.5 miles. Continue west on Forest Service Road 6500 and drive 6.4 miles to the campground.

Trip notes: This campground along Wenatchee River Road is a small, quiet, closer-to-civilization alternative to Tumwater (campground number 93), without piped water and with no trailer turnaround. There are some excellent hiking trails nearby.

⓶ Lake Creek

Location: On the Little Wenatchee River in Wenatchee National Forest; map A3, grid g4.

Campsites, facilities: There are eight tent sites. Picnic tables and fire grills are provided, but there is no piped water. Pit toilets are available.

Reservations, fees: No reservations are accepted. There is no fee. The campground is open from May to early November.

Contact: Wenatchee National Forest, Lake Wenatchee Ranger District, 22976 Highway 207, Leavenworth, WA 98826; (509) 763-3103 or fax (509) 763-3211.

Directions: From Interstate 5 at Everett, turn east on U.S. 2 and drive approximately 87 miles. Turn north on Highway 207 and drive 10.5 miles. Turn west on Forest Service Road 6500 and drive 10.5 miles to the campground.

Trip notes: Fishing can be excellent at this camp set in a remote and primitive spot along the Little Wenatchee River. Berry picking is a bonus in late summer.

⓷ Napeequa Crossing

Location: On the White River in Wenatchee National Forest; map A3, grid g5.

Campsites, facilities: There are five sites for tents, trailers, or RVs up to 30 feet long. Picnic tables and fire grills are provided. Pit toilets are available, but there is no piped water. Leashed pets are permitted.

Reservations, fees: No reservations are accepted. There is no fee. The campground is open from mid-May to late October.

Contact: Wenatchee National Forest, Lake Wenatchee Ranger District, 22976 Highway 207, Leavenworth, WA 98826; (509) 763-3103 or fax (509) 763-3211.

Directions: From Interstate 5 at Everett, turn east on U.S. 2 and drive approximately 87 miles. Turn north on Highway 207 and drive 10.5 miles. Head northwest on White River Road and Forest Service Road 6400 for 6.2 miles to the campground.

Trip notes: A trail from this camp on the White River heads east for about 3.5 miles to Twin Lakes in the Glacier Peak Wilderness. It's definitely worth the hike, with scenic views and marvelous wildlife and vegetation as your reward. Fishing access is available near camp.

78 White River Falls

Location: On the White River in Wenatchee National Forest; map A3, grid g5.

Campsites, facilities: There are five tent sites. Picnic tables and fire grills are provided. Pit toilets are available, but there is no piped water. Leashed pets are permitted.

Reservations, fees: No reservations are accepted. There is no fee. The campground is open from June to mid-October.

Contact: Wenatchee National Forest, Lake Wenatchee Ranger District, 22976 Highway 207, Leavenworth, WA 98826; (509) 763-3103 or fax 509) 763-3211.

Directions: From Interstate 5 at Everett, turn east on U.S. 2 and drive approximately 87 miles. Turn north on Highway 207 and drive 10.5 miles. Head northwest on White River Road and Forest Service Road 6400 for nine miles to the campground.

Trip notes: Though very primitive, this quiet and beautiful campground is a perfect spot for those seeking solitude in the wilderness. It's close to White River Falls on the White River, at a major trailhead that connects to a network of hiking trails into the Glacier Peak Wilderness.

79 Lake Wenatchee State Park

Location: On Lake Wenatchee; map A3, grid g5.

Campsites, facilities: There are two primitive tent sites and 197 developed sites for tents or self-contained RVs. Piped water, fire grills, and picnic tables are provided. Flush toilets, a sanitary disposal station, a store, ice, showers, firewood, a restaurant, a playground, and horse rentals are available. Some facilities are wheelchair accessible. Boat docks, launching facilities, and rentals are nearby. Leashed pets are permitted.

Reservations, fees: No reservations are accepted. Sites are $5–$10 per night. The campground is open year-round.

Contact: Phone (800) 233-0321 or (509) 763-3101, or write to Highway 207, Leavenworth, WA 98826.

Directions: From Interstate 5 at Everett, turn east on U.S. 2 and drive approximately 100 miles to Leavenworth. Turn north on Highway 207 and drive 22 miles to the park entrance.

Trip notes: Thanks to a nice location and drive-in sites that are spaced just right, you can expect plenty of company at this campground. The secluded campsites are near the Wenatchee River, which offers plenty of recreation opportunities, including groomed cross-country ski trails in winter.

80 Glacier View

Location: On Lake Wenatchee in Wenatchee National Forest; map A3, grid h5.

Campsites, facilities: There are 16 tent sites and four sites for very small RVs. Trailers are not recommended. Piped water, fire grills, and picnic tables are provided. Pit toilets and a boat launch are available. Leashed pets are permitted.

Reservations, fees: No reservations are ac-

cepted. Sites are $8 per night. The campground is open from May through September.

Contact: Wenatchee National Forest, Lake Wenatchee Ranger District, 22976 Highway 207, Leavenworth, WA 98826; (509) 763-3103 or fax 509) 763-3211.

Directions: From Interstate 5 at Everett, turn east on U.S. 2 and drive approximately 87 miles. Turn north on Highway 207 and drive 3.5 miles. Turn west on County Road 413 (Cedar Brae Road) and drive four miles, then continue west on Forest Service Road 6750 for 1.5 miles to the campground.

Trip notes: This campground on the southwestern shore of Lake Wenatchee is one of the quieter camps on the lake. It's a popular spot for boating, swimming, fishing, and waterskiing. There are also some good hiking trails in the area.

81 Silver Falls

Location: On the Entiat River in Wenatchee National Forest; map A3, grid g7.

Campsites, facilities: There are 30 sites for tents, trailers, or RVs up to 21 feet long, plus one group site. Hand-pumped water, fire grills, and picnic tables are provided. Vault toilets are available. Some facilities are wheelchair accessible. Pets are permitted.

Reservations, fees: Reservations are necessary for groups only. Single sites are $7.50 per vehicle per night; the group site is $60 a night. The campground is open from mid-May to mid-October.

Contact: Wenatchee National Forest, Entiat Ranger District, P.O. Box 476, Entiat, WA 98822; (509) 784-1511.

Directions: From Interstate 5 at Everett, turn east on U.S. 2 and drive approximately 120 miles. Turn north on U.S. 97-A and drive 18.5 miles to County Road 371 (Entiat River Road). Turn northwest and drive 30 miles. Turn on Forest Service Road 5100 and drive 5.5 miles to the campground.

Trip notes: This campground, an enchanted spot, is set at the confluence of Silver Creek and the Entiat River. A trail from camp leads one-half mile to the base of beautiful Silver Falls.

82 North Fork

Location: On the Entiat River in Wenatchee National Forest; map A3, grid g7.

Campsites, facilities: There are eight tent sites and one site for a small RV. Hand-pumped water, fire grills, and picnic tables are provided. Pit toilets are available. Leashed pets are permitted.

Reservations, fees: No reservations are accepted. Sites are $7 per vehicle per night. The campground is open from mid-June to mid-October.

Contact: Wenatchee National Forest, Entiat Ranger District, P.O. Box 476, Entiat, WA 98822; (509) 784-1511.

Directions: From Interstate 5 at Everett, turn east on U.S. 2 and drive approximately 120 miles. Turn north on U.S. 97-A and drive 18.5 miles to County Road 371 (Entiat River Road). Turn northwest and drive 34 miles to the campground.

Trip notes: One of seven campgrounds nestled along the Entiat River, North Fork is near the confluence of the Entiat and the North Fork of the Entiat River. Highlights of this pretty and shaded camp include river fishing access and Entiat Falls, which are nearby.

83 Lake Creek

Location: On the Entiat River in Wenatchee National Forest; map A3, grid g7.

Campsites, facilities: There are 18 tent sites. Hand-pumped water, picnic tables, and fire grills are provided. Vault toilets are available. Leashed pets are permitted.

Reservations, fees: No reservations are accepted. Sites are $8 per night. The campground is open from May to mid-October.

Contact: Wenatchee National Forest, Entiat Ranger District, P.O. Box 476, Entiat, WA 98822; (509) 784-1511.

Directions: From Interstate 5 at Everett, turn east on U.S. 2 and drive approximately 120 miles. Turn north on U.S. 97-A and drive 18.5 miles to County Road 371 (Entiat River Road). Turn northwest and drive 27 miles to the campground.

Trip notes: This camp is located at the confluence of Lake Creek and the Entiat River, at a trail crossroads. One trail heads northeast up to Lake Creek Basin in the Chelan Mountains, and several others head south and west into the Entiat Mountains. Consult a Forest Service map for more details on backcountry routes.

84 Fox Creek

Location: On the Entiat River in Wenatchee National Forest; map A3, grid g7.

Campsites, facilities: There are 16 tent sites. Hand-pumped water, fire grills, and picnic tables are provided. Vault toilets are available. Leashed pets are permitted.

Reservations, fees: No reservations are accepted. Sites are $6 per night. The campground is open from May to mid-October.

Contact: Wenatchee National Forest, Entiat Ranger District, P.O. Box 476, Entiat, WA 98822; (509) 784-1511.

Directions: From Interstate 5 at Everett, turn east on U.S. 2 and drive approximately 120 miles. Turn north on U.S. 97-A and drive 18.5 miles to County Road 371 (Entiat River Road). Turn northwest and drive 25 miles to the campground on the left.

Trip notes: Fishing access is a draw at this camp along the Entiat River near Fox Creek. During the winter, some of the snow-covered logging roads in the area are open for use by snowmobiles and cross-country skiers. Contact the Forest Service for details.

85 Lake Chelan State Park

Location: On Lake Chelan; map A3, grid g9.

Campsites, facilities: There are two primitive tent sites, 127 developed tent sites, and 17 sites with full hookups for trailers or RVs up to 30 feet. Picnic tables are provided. Flush toilets, a sanitary disposal station, a store, a restaurant, ice, a play-ground, electricity, piped water, sewer hookups, showers, a boat dock, and launching facilities are available. Some facilities are wheelchair accessible.

Reservations, fees: Contact Reservations Northwest at (800) 453-5687 ($6 reservation fee). Sites are $11–$16 per night. The campground is open from April through October.

Contact: Phone (800) 233-0321 or (509) 687-3710, or write to Route 1, P.O. Box 90, Chelan, WA 98816.

Directions: From Interstate 5 at Everett, turn east on U.S. 2 and drive approximately 120 miles. Turn north on U.S. 97 and continue toward the town of Chelan for about 35 miles. At the sign for Lake Chelan State Park, turn left and proceed northwest to the park, which is nine miles west of Chelan.

Trip notes: This is the recreation headquarters for Lake Chelan. The park provides boat docks and concession stands on the shore of the 55-mile lake. See the trip notes for Holden Ballpark, Domke Lake, Lucerne, Deer Point, Graham Harbor, and Prince Creek (campground numbers 48, 49, 50, 65, 67, and 68) for some of the recreation options available. Water sports include fishing, swimming, scuba diving, and waterskiing.

86 Kamei Resort

Location: On Lake Wapato; map A3, grid g9.

Campsites, facilities: There are 40 sites for tents, trailers, or RVs of any length. Electricity, piped water, sewer hookups, and picnic tables are provided. Flush toilets, showers, and ice are available. Boat docks, launching facilities, and rentals are nearby. Pets and motorbikes are permitted.

Reservations, fees: Reservations are accepted. Sites are $11–$12 per night. The campground is open from late April through July.

Contact: Phone (509) 687-3690 or write to Route 1, P.O. Box 238, Manson, WA 98831.

Directions: From Interstate 5 at Everett, turn east on U.S. 2 and drive approximately 120 miles. Turn north on U.S. 97 and continue 40 miles to the town of Chelan. Turn west on Highway 150 and drive seven miles, then turn north on Wapato Lake Road and drive three miles to the resort.

Trip notes: This resort is on Lake Wapato, about two miles from Lake Chelan. Note that this is a seasonal lake which closes midsummer. If you have an extra day, take the ferry boat ride on Lake Chelan, which is detailed in Holden (campground number 48). It's an adventure in itself.

87 Lakeview Park

Location: On Lake Chelan; map A3, grid g9.
Campsites, facilities: There are 30 sites for trailers or RVs of any length. The sites will also accommodate tents, but only families are permitted to tent camp. Electricity, piped water, and sewer hookups are provided. Flush toilets, sanitary services, and showers are available. Boat docks and launching facilities are located within one mile. Leashed pets are permitted.
Reservations, fees: Reservations are accepted. Sites are $10–$15 per night. The campground is open from April to November.
Contact: Phone (509) 687-3612 or write to P.O. Box 324, Manson, WA 98831.
Directions: From Interstate 5 at Everett, turn east on U.S. 2 and drive approximately 120 miles. Turn north on U.S. 97 and continue 40 miles to the town of Chelan. Turn west on Highway 150 and drive 5.2 miles northwest to the park on the right.
Trip notes: This developed park for RVs and trailers is set along the shore of Lake Chelan. It's a more commercial alternative to the primitive Forest Service campgrounds scattered around the lake. This resort has an interesting quirk: they'll accept tent campers, but only families with children. No couples or singles. Their reason? To discourage noise and parties, they say. No such restrictions for RVers, though.

88 Mitchell Creek

Location: On Lake Chelan in Wenatchee National Forest; map A3, grid g9.
Campsites, facilities: There are six tent sites accessible only by boat, ferry, or float plane. Picnic tables and fire rings are provided. Pit toilets are available, but there is no piped water. Boat docks are nearby.
Reservations, fees: No reservations are accepted. There is no fee for camping, but there is a $5 docking fee. The campground is open from May to late October.
Contact: Wenatchee National Forest, Chelan Ranger District, 428 West Woodin Avenue, Chelan, WA 98816; (509) 682-2576 or fax (509) 682-9004.
Directions: From Interstate 5 at Everett, turn east on U.S. 2 and drive approximately 120 miles. Turn north on U.S. 97 and continue about 40 miles to Chelan. Take the ferry from there (another ferry is available at Fields Point Landing, a few miles northwest of Chelan) and proceed to Mitchell Creek, 15 miles from Chelan. This spectacular voyage costs about $20 round-trip, depending on your destination. For more information call (509) 682-2224. The campground is also directly accessible by float plane. Call Chelan Airways at (509) 682-5555.
Trip notes: Primitive and remote Mitchell Creek Campground is nestled along the shore of Lake Chelan, where fishing, swimming, boating, hiking, and waterskiing keep visitors busy.

89 Money Creek Campground

Location: On the Skykomish River in Mount Baker–Snoqualmie National Forest; Map A3, grid h2.
Campsites, facilities: There are 24 sites for tents, trailers, or RVs up to 21 feet long. Picnic tables are provided. Vault toilets and piped water are available. A store, a cafe, and ice are located within 3.5 miles. Some sites are wheelchair accessible. Leashed pets are permitted.
Reservations, fees: Some sites can be reserved by phoning (800) 280-CAMP/2267 ($8.65 reservation fee). Sites are $10 per night, plus $6.50 for each additional vehicle. The campground is open from Memorial Day through Labor Day.

Contact: Mount Baker–Snoqualmie National Forest, Skykomish Ranger District, P.O. Box 305, Skykomish, WA 98288; (360) 677-2414 or fax (425) 744-3265.

Directions: From Interstate 5 at Everett, turn east on U.S. 2 and drive about 46 miles. Turn south on Old Cascade Highway and drive across the bridge to the campground.

Trip notes: Money Creek Campground is on the Skykomish River in an old-growth stand, with hiking trails a moderate driving distance away. Railroad buffs will be interested in the fact that the Burlington Northern rail runs along the western boundary of the campground.

90 Beckler River

Location: On the Beckler River in Mount Baker–Snoqualmie National Forest; map A3, grid h2.

Campsites, facilities: There are 27 sites for tents, trailers, or RVs up to 21 feet long. Picnic tables and fire grills are provided. Vault toilets and piped water are available. A store, a cafe, and ice are located within two miles. Some sites and facilities are wheelchair accessible. Leashed pets are permitted.

Reservations, fees: Some sites can be reserved by calling (800) 280-CAMP/2267 ($8.65 reservation fee). Sites are $10 per night. The campground is open from Memorial Day through Labor Day.

Contact: Mount Baker–Snoqualmie National Forest, Skykomish Ranger District, P.O. Box 305, Skykomish, WA 98288; (360) 677-2414 or fax (425) 744-3265.

Directions: From Interstate 5 at Everett, turn east on U.S. 2 and drive approximately 49 miles to Skykomish. Drive one-half mile east on U.S. 2, then 1.6 miles north on Forest Service Road 65 to the camp on the left.

Trip notes: Located on the Beckler River at an elevation of 900 feet, this camp has scenic riverside sites and good fishing prospects. The Skykomish Ranger Station is just a couple of miles away; the rangers will be happy to provide you with maps and answer any questions.

91 Miller River Group Camp

Location: Near the Alpine Lakes Wilderness in Mount Baker–Snoqualmie National Forest; map A3, grid h2.

Campsites, facilities: This is a group camp with 18 sites for tents, trailers, or RVs. Picnic tables and fire grills are provided. Vault toilets, piped water, a group barbecue, and a 24-foot group table are available. A store, a cafe, and ice are within five miles. Leashed pets are permitted.

Reservations, fees: Reserve sites by calling (800) 280-CAMP/2267 ($17.35 reservation fee). Sites are $35 for the first 50 people, and $1 for each additional camper to a limit of 100 people. The campground is open from mid-May to mid-September.

Contact: Mount Baker–Snoqualmie National Forest, Skykomish Ranger District, P.O. Box 305, Skykomish, WA 98288; (360) 677-2414 or fax (425) 744-3265.

Directions: From Interstate 5 at Everett, turn east on U.S. 2 and drive approximately 46 miles to Old Cascade Highway (about three miles west of Skykomish). Turn south and drive one mile, then turn on Forest Service Road 6410 and go two miles south to the campground.

Trip notes: This campground, located along the Miller River a short distance from the boundary of the Alpine Lakes Wilderness, is in prime mountain territory. If you continue another seven miles on Forest Service Road 6410, you'll get to a trailhead leading to Lake Dorothy and many other backcountry lakes. Be aware that there is a group limit of 12 people in wilderness areas. A Forest Service map is essential.

92 Nason Creek

Location: Near Lake Wenatchee in Wenatchee National Forest; map A3, grid h6.

Campsites, facilities: There are 29 tent sites and 41 sites for tents, trailers, or RVs up to 31 feet long. Piped water, fire grills, picnic tables, and flush toilets are provided. Boat launching facilities are nearby.

Reservations, fees: No reservations are accepted. Sites are $10 per night. The campground is open from May to late October.

Contact: Wenatchee National Forest, Lake Wenatchee Ranger District, 22976 Highway 207, Leavenworth, WA 98826; (509) 763-3103 or fax (509) 763-3211.

Directions: From Interstate 5 at Everett, turn east on U.S. 2 and drive approximately 87 miles to Highway 207 (one mile west of Winton). Turn north and drive 3.5 miles, then head west on Cedar Brae Road (County Road 413) for 100 yards to the campground.

Trip notes: This campground is on Nason Creek near Lake Wenatchee. Recreation activities include swimming, fishing, and waterskiing. Boat rentals, horseback riding, and golfing are nearby.

⑬ Tumwater

Location: Near the Alpine Lakes Wilderness in Wenatchee National Forest; map A3, grid h6.

Campsites, facilities: There are 84 sites for tents, trailers, or RVs up to 30 feet long, and one group site for up to 75 people. Piped water, fire grills, and picnic tables are provided. Flush toilets are available. Leashed pets are permitted.

Reservations, fees: Reserve the group site by phoning (800) 274-6104. Rates are $8 per night for single sites, and $50 for group sites. The campground is open from May to mid-October.

Contact: Wenatchee National Forest, Leavenworth Ranger District, 600 Sherbourne, Leavenworth, WA 98826; (509) 548-6977 or fax (509) 548-5817.

Directions: From Interstate 5 at Everett, turn east on U.S. 2 and drive approximately 93 miles to the campground, located 10 miles west of Leavenworth.

Trip notes: This large, popular camp provides a little bit of both worlds. It's a good layover for campers cruising U.S. 2. But there are also two Forest Service roads nearby, each

less than a mile long, which end at trailheads that provide access to the Alpine Lakes Wilderness. If you don't like to hike, no problem. The camp is on the Wenatchee River in Tumwater Canyon.

⑭ Midway Village Grocery and RV Park

Location: On the Wenatchee River; map A3, grid h6.

Campsites, facilities: There are 18 sites for trailers or RVs of any length. Electricity, piped water, sewer hookups, and picnic tables are provided. A store, showers, firewood, a cafe, a laundry room, ice, and a playground are available. Boat docks, launching facilities, and rentals are nearby. Leashed pets and motorbikes are permitted.

Reservations, fees: Reservations are accepted. Sites are $12 per night. The campground is open year-round.

Contact: Phone (509) 763-3344 or write to 14193 Chiwawa Loop Road, Leavenworth, WA 98826.

Directions: From Interstate 5 at Everett, turn east on U.S. 2 and drive approximately 88 miles to Highway 207 (one mile west of Winton). Turn north and drive four miles to the bridge over the Wenatchee River. Continue east for one mile to the park.

Trip notes: This private campground is a short distance from Lake Wenatchee State Park and is set along the Wenatchee River. Nearby recreation options include waterskiing, swimming, boating, fishing, hiking, and bike riding.

⑮ Entiat City Park

Location: On the Columbia River; map A3, grid h9.

Campsites, facilities: There are 50 tent sites and 31 sites for trailers or RVs. Electricity, piped water, and picnic tables are provided. Flush toilets, sanitary services, showers, a playground, bottled gas, a store, a cafe, a laundry room, and ice are available. Boat docks and launching facilities are nearby. Motorbikes are permitted.

Reservations, fees: Reservations are requested. Sites are $13–$16 per night. The campground is open from April to mid-September.

Contact: Phone (509) 784-1500 or write to P.O. Box 228, Entiat, WA 98822.

Directions: From Interstate 5 at Everett, turn east on U.S. 2 and drive approximately 120 miles to Wenatchee. Turn north on U.S. 97-A and drive 16 miles to Entiat. The park is set along the shore of Lake Entiat.

Trip notes: Lake Entiat is actually a dammed portion of the Columbia River. Rocky Reach Dam, located 10 miles south, is the closest to this campground. Access to nearby launching facilities makes this a good camping spot for boaters.

96 Fish Lake

Location: On Tucquala Lake in Wenatchee National Forest; map A3, grid i3.

Campsites, facilities: There are 15 tent sites. Picnic tables and fire grills are provided. Vault toilets are available, but there is no piped water. Leashed pets are permitted.

Reservations, fees: No reservations are accepted. There is no fee. The campground is open from July to October.

Contact: Wenatchee National Forest, Cle Elum Ranger District, West Second Street, Cle Elum, WA 98922; (509) 674-4411 or fax (509) 674-4794.

Directions: From Interstate 5 at Seattle, turn east on Interstate 90 and drive approximately 78 miles to Exit 80 (two miles before Cle Elum). Turn north on Bullfrog Road and drive four miles. Continue north on Highway 903 and drive about 20 miles to Forest Service Road 4330. Turn northeast and drive 11 miles to the campground. The access road is rough; no trailers are allowed.

Trip notes: This campground is way out there, and just a short jaunt to the Alpine Lakes Wilderness. There are numerous op-

portunities to access trails into the backcountry. The camp is nestled along the shore of tiny Tucquala Lake, a jewel near the headwaters of the Cle Elum River.

97 Eightmile

Location: Near the Alpine Lakes Wilderness in Wenatchee National Forest; map A3, grid i5.

Campsites, facilities: There are 45 sites for tents, trailers, or RVs up to 21 feet long. Hand-pumped water, fire grills, and picnic tables are provided. Vault toilets are available. Leashed pets are permitted.

Reservations, fees: Reserve group sites only by phoning (800) 274-6104. Rates are $8 per night for single sites, and $50 per night for group sites. The campground is open from mid-April to late October.

Contact: Wenatchee National Forest, Leavenworth Ranger District, 600 Sherbourne, Leavenworth, WA 98826; (509) 548-6977 or fax (509) 548-5817.

Directions: From Interstate 5 at Everett, turn east on U.S. 2 and drive approximately 103 miles to Leavenworth. Turn south on County Road 76 (Icicle River Road) and drive three miles. Turn west on Forest Service Road 7600 and drive four miles to the campground.

Trip notes: A key trailhead for backpackers providing access to many lakes and streams in the Alpine Lakes Wilderness is located at this campground set along Icicle and Eightmile Creeks.

98 Bridge Creek

Location: On Icicle Creek in Wenatchee National Forest; map A3, grid i5.

Campsites, facilities: There are six tent sites. Hand-pumped water, fire grills, and picnic tables are provided. Vault toilets and firewood are available. Leashed pets are permitted.

Reservations, fees: Reservations are required for groups only; phone (800) 274-6104. Single sites are $7–$8 per night, and group sites are $50 per night. The campground is open from mid-April to late October.

Contact: Wenatchee National Forest, Leavenworth Ranger District, 600 Sherbourne, Leavenworth, WA 98826; (509) 548-6977 or fax (509) 548-5817.

Directions: From Interstate 5 at Everett, turn east on U.S. 2 and drive approximately 103 miles to Leavenworth. Turn south on County Road 76 (Icicle River Road) and drive three miles. Turn northwest on Forest Service Road 7600 and drive 5.5 miles to campground.

Trip notes: This is a small, quiet spot along Icicle and Bridge Creeks. About one mile south of the camp at Eightmile Creek is a trail that accesses the Alpine Lakes Wilderness. See a Forest Service map for details.

99 Johnny Creek

Location: On Icicle Creek in Wenatchee National Forest; map A3, grid i5.

Campsites, facilities: There are 65 sites for tents, trailers, or RVs up to 30 feet long. Hand-pumped water, fire grills, and picnic tables are provided. Vault toilets are available. Leashed pets are permitted.

Reservations, fees: No reservations are accepted. Sites are $7–$8 per night. The campground is open from May to late October.

Contact: Wenatchee National Forest, Leavenworth Ranger District, 600 Sherbourne, Leavenworth, WA 98826; (509) 548-6977 or fax (509) 548-5817.

Directions: From Interstate 5 at Everett, turn east on U.S. 2 and drive approximately 103 miles to Leavenworth. Turn south on County Road 76 and drive three miles. Turn northwest on Forest Service Road 7600 and drive eight miles to campground.

Trip notes: This campground is set along Icicle and Johnny Creeks. See Bridge Creek (campground number 98) for area information.

100 Chatter Creek

Location: Near the Alpine Lakes Wilderness in Wenatchee National Forest; map A3, grid i5.

Campsites, facilities: There are nine tent

sites and three sites for tents, trailers, or RVs up to 21 feet long. Hand-pumped water, fire grills, and picnic tables are provided. Vault toilets are available. Leashed pets are permitted.

Reservations, fees: Reservations are required for group sites only. Rates are $7 per night for single sites, and $50 per night for group sites. The campground is open from May to late October.

Contact: Wenatchee National Forest, Leavenworth Ranger District, 600 Sherbourne, Leavenworth, WA 98826; (509) 548-6977 or fax (509) 548-5817.

Directions: From Interstate 5 at Everett, turn east on U.S. 2 and drive approximately 103 miles to Leavenworth. Turn south on County Road 76 (Icicle River Road) and drive three miles. Turn northwest on Forest Service Road 7600 and drive 12.5 miles to the campground.

Trip notes: Icicle and Chatter Creeks are the backdrop for this creekside campground. Trails lead out in several directions from the camp into the Alpine Lakes Wilderness.

101 Rock Island

Location: Near the Alpine Lakes Wilderness in Wenatchee National Forest; map A3, grid i5.

Campsites, facilities: There are 12 tent sites and 10 sites for tents, trailers, or RVs up to 21 feet long. Hand-pumped water, fire grills, and picnic tables are provided. Vault toilets are available. Leashed pets are permitted.

Reservations, fees: No reservations are accepted. Sites are $7 per night. The campground is open from May to late October.

Contact: Wenatchee National Forest, Leavenworth Ranger District, 600 Sherbourne, Leavenworth, WA 98826; (509) 548-6977 or fax (509) 548-5817.

Directions: From Interstate 5 at Everett, turn east on U.S. 2 and drive approximately 103 miles to Leavenworth. Turn south on County Road 76 (Icicle River Road) and drive three miles. Turn northwest on Forest Service Road 7600 and drive 14 miles to the campground.

Trip notes: Rock Island is one of several campgrounds in the immediate area along Icicle

Creek about a mile from the trailhead that takes hikers into the Alpine Lakes Wilderness. This is a pretty spot, with good fishing access.

⑩² Ida Creek

Location: On Icicle Creek in Wenatchee National Forest; map A3, grid i5.

Campsites, facilities: There are five tent sites and five sites for tents, trailers, or RVs up to 21 feet long. Hand-pumped water, fire grills, and picnic tables are provided. Vault toilets are available. Leashed pets are permitted.

Reservations, fees: No reservations are accepted. Sites are $7 per night. The campground is open from May to late October.

Contact: Wenatchee National Forest, Leavenworth Ranger District, 600 Sherbourne, Leavenworth, WA 98826; (509) 548-6977 or fax (509) 548-5817.

Directions: From Interstate 5 at Everett, turn east on U.S. 2 and drive approximately 103 miles to Leavenworth. Turn south on County Road 76 (Icicle River Road) and drive three miles. Turn northwest on Forest Service Road 7600 and drive 10 miles to the campground.

Trip notes: This campground is one of several small, quiet camps along Icicle and Ida Creeks, with similar recreation options to Chatter Creek and Rock Island (see campground numbers 100 and 101).

⑩³ Blackpine Creek Horse Camp

Location: Near the Alpine Lakes Wilderness in Wenatchee National Forest; map A3, grid i5.

Campsites, facilities: There are 14 sites for tents, trailers, or RVs up to 21 feet long. Hand-pumped water, fire grills, and picnic tables are provided. Vault toilets, firewood, and riding facilities are available. Leashed pets are permitted.

Reservations, fees: No reservations are accepted. Sites are $6 per night. The campground is open from mid-May to late October.

Contact: Wenatchee National Forest, Leavenworth Ranger District, 600 Sherbourne, Leavenworth, WA 98826; (509) 548-6977 or fax (509) 548-5817.

Directions: From Interstate 5 at Everett, turn east on U.S. 2 and drive approximately 103 miles to Leavenworth. Turn south on County Road 76 (Icicle River Road) and drive three miles. Turn northwest on Forest Service Road 7600 and drive 15 miles to the campground.

Trip notes: Blackpine Creek Horse Camp is set on Black Pine Creek near Icicle Creek, at a major trailhead leading into the Alpine Lakes Wilderness. It's one of seven rustic camps on the creek, with the distinction of being the only one with facilities for horses. For that reason, it's often used as a base camp for horse pack trips.

⑩⁴ Pine Village Resort/KOA Leavenworth

Location: Near the Wenatchee River; map A3, grid i6.

Campsites, facilities: There are 40 tent sites and 60 sites for trailers or RVs of any length; 22 are drive-throughs. Picnic tables are provided. Flush toilets, sanitary services, showers, firewood, a recreation hall, cable TV, a store, a laundry room, ice, a playground, a spa, a heated swimming pool, electricity, piped water, and sewer hookups are available. Bottled gas and a cafe are located within one mile. Pets and motorbikes are permitted.

Reservations, fees: Reservations are accepted. Sites are $23–$29 per night. The campground is open from April to November.

Contact: Phone (509) 548-7709, fax (509) 548-7709, or write to 11401 River Bend Drive, Leavenworth, WA 98826.

Directions: From Interstate 5 at Everett, turn east on U.S. 2 and drive approximately 103 miles to Leavenworth. Continue one-quarter mile east on U.S. 2 to River Bend Drive, then drive north one-half mile to the campground on the right.

Trip notes: This lovely resort is near the quaint "Bavarian Village" of Leavenworth, to which the park provides a free shuttle in the summer. The spectacularly scenic area is surrounded by the Cascade Mountains and set among ponderosa pines. The camp has access to the Wenatchee River, not to mention many luxurious extras, including a hot tub and heated pool. The park allows campfires and has firewood available. Nearby recreation options include an 18-hole golf course and hiking trails. Make a point to spend a day in Leavenworth if possible; it offers authentic German food and architecture along with music and art shows in the summer.

105 Icicle River RV Park

Location: On Icicle Creek; map A3, grid i6.

Campsites, facilities: There are 30 tent sites and 58 sites for trailers or RVs of any length; 14 are drive-throughs. Electricity, piped water, sewer hookups, and picnic tables are provided. Flush toilets and bottled gas are available. Showers and firewood are available for an extra fee. Pets and motorbikes are permitted.

Reservations, fees: Reservations are accepted. Sites are $20–$25 per night. The campground is open from April to late October.

Contact: Phone (509) 548-5420 or write to 7305 Icicle Road, Leavenworth, WA 98826.

Directions: From Interstate 5 at Everett, turn east on U.S. 2 and drive approximately 103 miles to Leavenworth. Take the Icicle Road exit and drive three miles southwest to the park on the left.

Trip notes: Icicle River RV Park is one of three campgrounds in the immediate area. The others are Pine Village Resort (campground number 104) and Chalet Trailer Park (campground number 106). This pretty, wooded spot is set along the Icicle River, where fishing and swimming are available. The park is exceptionally clean and scenic, and even has its own putting green. An 18-hole golf course and hiking trails are nearby.

106 Chalet Trailer Park

Location: On the Wenatchee River; map A3, grid i7.

Campsites, facilities: There are 29 sites for trailers or RVs of any length, and a grassy area for tents. Electricity, piped water, sewer and cable TV hookups, and picnic tables are provided. Flush toilets, sanitary services, propane, and showers are available. Bottled gas, a store, a cafe, a Laundromat, and ice can be found within one mile. Leashed pets and motorbikes are permitted.

Reservations, fees: Reservations are recommended. Sites are $18–$22 per night. The campground is open year-round.

Contact: Phone (800) 477-2697 or (509) 548-4578, or write to P.O. Box 293, Leavenworth, WA 98826.

Directions: From Interstate 5 at Everett, turn east on U.S. 2 and drive approximately 103 miles to Leavenworth. Turn south on Duncan Road and drive 150 feet to the campground on the right.

Trip notes: This park along the Wenatchee River near Leavenworth is within walking distance to the quaint Bavarian Village shops and restaurants. A pleasant grassy area is provided for tents. Nearby recreation options include an 18-hole golf course.

107 Wenatchee River County Park

Location: On the Wenatchee River in Chelan County; map A3, grid j7.

Campsites, facilities: There are 15 tent sites and 64 sites for trailers or RVs of any length; 24 are drive-throughs. Electricity, piped water, sewer hookups, and picnic tables are provided. Flush toilets, showers, sanitary services, and a playground are available. A store and ice are located within one mile. Boat launching facilities can be found within three miles. Leashed pets and motorbikes are permitted.

Reservations, fees: No reservations are accepted. Sites are $12.50–$16 per night. The campground is open year-round.

Contact: Phone (509) 662-2525 or write to P.O. Box 254, Monitor, WA 98836.

Directions: From Interstate 5 at Everett, turn east on U.S. 2 and drive approximately 116 miles to Monitor. The camp is just off the highway on the right.

Trip notes: This municipal park set along the Wenatchee River, with access nearby, is an excellent spot for fishing. It's the only option for tent campers in the immediate area.

108 Lincoln Rock State Park

Location: On Lake Entiat; map A3, grid i8.

Campsites, facilities: There are 27 sites for tents or self-contained RVs, and 67 sites with full hookups for trailers or RVs up to 65 feet long. Picnic tables and fire grills are provided. Flush toilets, a sanitary disposal station, a playground, showers, and firewood are available. Some facilities are wheelchair accessible. Boat docks and launching facilities are located on Lake Entiat. Leashed pets are permitted.

Reservations, fees: Contact Reservations Northwest at (800) 452-5687 ($6 reservation fee). Sites are $5–$14 per night. The campground is open year-round.

Contact: Phone (800) 233-0321 or (509) 884-8702, or write to Route 3, P.O. Box 3137, East Wenatchee, WA 98801.

Directions: From Interstate 5 at Everett, turn east on U.S. 2 and drive approximately 125 miles to the park. It's located seven miles north of Wenatchee on the east side of the highway.

Trip notes: An alternative to nearby Entiat City Park (campground number 95), this place is ideal for families with RVs or trailers. It's adjacent to the Rocky Reach Hydro Electric Dam along the shore of Lake Entiat. Water sports include swimming, boating, and waterskiing.

109 Tinkham

Location: On the Snoqualmie River in Mount Baker–Snoqualmie National Forest; map A3, grid j0.

Campsites, facilities: There are 48 sites for tents, trailers, or RVs up to 30 feet long. Picnic tables are provided. Vault toilets, firewood, and hand-pumped water are available. Some facilities are wheelchair accessible. Leashed pets are permitted.

Reservations, fees: Some sites can be reserved by calling (800) 280-CAMP/2267 ($8.65 reservation fee). Sites are $10 per night. The campground is open from mid-May to mid-September.

Contact: Mount Baker–Snoqualmie National Forest, North Bend Ranger District, 42404 SE North Bend Way, North Bend, WA 98045; (425) 888-1421.

Directions: From Interstate 5 at Seattle, turn east on Interstate 90 and take exit 42. Turn right on Forest Service Road 55 and drive 1.5 miles southeast to the campground. A Forest Service map is advisable.

Trip notes: Travelers heading west to Seattle will find this campground along the Snoqualmie River a good layover for the night. Not far north is the Alpine Lakes Wilderness, a spectacularly beautiful area. See a Forest Service map for trail locations. There are several ski areas to the east. Franklin Falls, a side trip worth taking, is also nearby.

110 Crystal Springs

Location: Near Kachess and Keechelus Lakes in Wenatchee National Forest; map A3, grid j2.

Campsites, facilities: There are 20 tent sites and six sites for tents, trailers, or RVs up to 21 feet long. Piped water, fire grills, and picnic tables are provided. Pit toilets and firewood are available. Boat docks and rentals are nearby. Leashed pets are permitted.

Reservations, fees: No reservations are accepted. Sites are $10 per vehicle per night, with a two-vehicle maximum. The campground is open from mid-May to mid-September.

Contact: Wenatchee National Forest, Cle Elum Ranger District, West Second Street,

Cle Elum, WA 98922; (509) 674-4411 or fax (509) 674-4794.

Directions: From Seattle, turn east on Interstate 90 and drive approximately 60.5 miles. Take Exit 62 to Forest Service Road 54 (about 8.5 miles west of Easton). Turn southwest and drive one-half mile to the campground.

Trip notes: This campground is just off Interstate 90 and a short drive from Kachess and Keechelus Lakes. Both lakes have boat ramps. For winter sports, there are also several snoparks in the area, which provide parking and access to Forest Service roads and open areas for snowmobiling and cross-country skiing. The Pacific West Ski Area is at the north end of Keechelus Lake.

111 Wish Poosh

Location: On Cle Elum Lake in Wenatchee National Forest; map A3, grid j3.

Campsites, facilities: There are 17 tent sites and 22 sites for tents, trailers, or RVs up to 21 feet long. Piped water, fire grills, and picnic tables are provided. Flush toilets, firewood, a restaurant, and ice are available. Boat docks and launching facilities are located on Cle Elum Lake. Leashed pets are permitted.

Reservations, fees: No reservations are accepted. Sites are $10 per vehicle per night, with a two-vehicle maximum. The campground is open mid-May to mid-September.

Contact: Wenatchee National Forest, Cle Elum Ranger District, West Second Street, Cle Elum, WA 98922; (509) 674-4411 or fax (509) 674-4794.

Directions: From Seattle, turn east on Interstate 90 and drive approximately 78 miles to exit 80 (two miles before Cle Elum). Turn north on Bullfrog Road and drive four miles. Continue on Highway 903 and drive about nine miles to the campground.

Trip notes: The shore of Cle Elum Lake is the site of this camp, where waterskiing, sailing, fishing, and swimming are among recreation possibilities. In the winter months, this is a popular area for cross-country skiing and snowshoeing.

112 Red Mountain

Location: On the Cle Elum River in Wenatchee National Forest; map A3, grid j3.

Campsites, facilities: There are 11 sites for tents. Picnic tables and fire grills are provided. Pit toilets and firewood are available, but there is no piped water. Leashed pets are permitted.

Reservations, fees: No reservations are accepted. Sites are $5 per vehicle per night, with a two-vehicle maximum. The campground is open from mid-May to mid-November.

Contact: Wenatchee National Forest, Cle Elum Ranger District, West Second Street, Cle Elum, WA 98922; (509) 674-4411 or fax (509) 674-4794.

Directions: From Seattle, turn east on Interstate 90 and drive approximately 78 miles to exit 80 (two miles before Cle Elum). Turn north on Bullfrog Road and drive four miles. Continue north on Highway 903 and drive about 13 miles to the campground.

Trip notes: This alternative to nearby Wish Poosh (campground number 111) has two big differences: there is no piped water and it's not on Cle Elum Lake. The camp is along the Cle Elum River a mile from the lake, just above where the river feeds into it. It has the same wintertime options as Wish Poosh.

113 Salmon La Sac

Location: On the Cle Elum River in Wenatchee National Forest; map A3, grid j3.

Campsites, facilities: There are 30 tent sites and 96 sites for tents, trailers, or RVs up to 21 feet long, plus one group site. A horse-use camp is also available. Piped water, fire grills, and picnic tables are provided. Flush toilets are available. Some facilities are wheelchair accessible. Leashed pets are permitted.

Reservations, fees: Some sites can be reserved by calling (800) 280-CAMP/2267 ($8.65 reservation fee for family sites and $17.35 for groups). Sites are $10 per vehicle per night, with a two-vehicle maximum; the group fee is $50 a night. The campground is open from late May to late September.

Contact: Wenatchee National Forest, Cle Elum Ranger District, West Second Street, Cle Elum, WA 98922; (509) 674-4411 or fax (509) 674-4794.

Directions: From Seattle, turn east on Interstate 90 and drive approximately 78 miles to exit 80 (two miles before Cle Elum). Turn north on Bullfrog Road and drive four miles. Continue north on Highway 903 and drive about 21 miles to the campground.

Trip notes: One of the most developed camps in the area, this is an ideal base camp for backpackers and day hikers. It's located along the Cle Elum River at a major trailhead, and hikers can follow creeks heading off in several directions, including into the Alpine Lakes Wilderness. Campground hosts will answer all your questions.

⑭ Kachess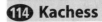

Location: On Kachess Lake in Wenatchee National Forest; map A3, grid j3.

Campsites, facilities: There are 133 tent sites and 50 sites for trailers or RVs up to 32 feet long. A group site is also available. Piped water, fire grills, and picnic tables are provided. Rest rooms and sanitary disposal stations are located at Kachess Lake. Some facilities are wheelchair accessible. Leashed pets are permitted but aren't allowed in swimming areas.

Reservations, fees: Some sites can be reserved by calling (800) 280-CAMP/2267 ($8.65 reservation fee for family sites and $17.35 for groups). Sites are $10 per vehicle per night, with a two-vehicle maximum; the group fee is $50. The campground is open from late May to mid-September.

Contact: Wenatchee National Forest, Cle Elum Ranger District, West Second Street, Cle Elum, WA 98922; (509) 674-4411 or fax (509) 674-4794.

Directions: From Seattle, turn east on Interstate 90 and drive approximately 59 miles to exit 62 on Forest Service Road 49. Turn northeast and drive five miles to the campground.

Trip notes: This is the only campground on the shore of Kachess Lake, and it's a winner. Recreation opportunities include waterskiing, fishing, hiking, and bicycling. A trail from camp heads north into the Alpine Lakes Wilderness; see a Forest Service map for details. A self-guided interpretive trail is also available. The Kachess Sno-Park is about a mile south of the campground and provides parking and access to Forest Service Roads and open areas ideal for snowmobiling and cross-country skiing.

⑮ Owhi

Location: On Cooper Lake in Wenatchee National Forest; map A3, grid j3.

Campsites, facilities: There are 28 walk-in tent sites. Picnic tables and fire grills are provided. Pit toilets are available, but there is no piped water. Boat docks and launching facilities are nearby. Leashed pets are permitted.

Reservations, fees: No reservations are accepted. Sites are $5 per vehicle per night, with a two-vehicle maximum. The campground is open from mid-June to mid-October.

Contact: Wenatchee National Forest, Cle Elum Ranger District, West Second Street, Cle Elum, WA 98922; (509) 674-4411 or fax (509) 674-4794.

Directions: From Seattle, turn east on Interstate 90 and drive approximately 78 miles to exit 80 (two miles before Cle Elum). Turn north on Bullfrog Road and drive four miles. Continue north on Highway 903 for 19 miles. Turn west on Forest Service Road 46. Proceed five miles to Forest Service Road 4616 and follow it for almost one mile. Turn left onto Spur Road 113 and drive about 300 yards to the campground. Campsites are located 100 to 300 feet from the parking lot.

Trip notes: This spot has everything. Well, everything but piped water. It's located on the shore of Cooper Lake, near the boundary of the Alpine Lakes Wilderness. A nearby trailhead provides access to several lakes in the wilderness and extends to the Pacific Crest Trail; see a Forest Service map for details. Fishing, swimming, and canoeing or nonmotorized boating are all popular at Cooper Lake.

⑯ Beverly

Location: On the North Fork of the Teanaway River in Wenatchee National Forest; map A3, grid j4.

Campsites, facilities: There are 13 tent sites and three sites for trailers or RVs up to 21 feet long. Picnic tables and fire grills are provided. Pit toilets are available, but there is no piped water. Leashed pets are permitted.

Reservations, fees: No reservations are accepted. There is no fee. The campground is open from June to mid-November.

Contact: Wenatchee National Forest, Cle Elum Ranger District, West Second Street, Cle Elum, WA 98922; (509) 674-4411 or fax (509) 674-4794.

Directions: From Seattle, turn east on Interstate 90 and drive approximately 80 miles to Cle Elum. Take exit 86 to County Road 970. Drive east for eight miles. Turn north on Teanaway River Road and drive 13 miles to the end of the paved road. Continue north on Forest Service Road 9737 and drive four miles to campground.

Trip notes: This primitive campground on the North Fork of the Teanaway River has good fishing, though it's primarily a hiker's camp, with several trails leading up nearby creeks and into the Alpine Lakes Wilderness. Self-issued permits are required for wilderness hiking.

⑰ Bonanza

Location: On Tronsen Creek in Wenatchee National Forest; map A3, grid j6.

Campsites, facilities: There are four tent sites and one site for tents, trailers, or RVs up to 15 feet long. Hand-pumped water, fire grills, and picnic tables are provided. Vault toilets are available. Leashed pets are permitted.

Reservations, fees: No reservations are accepted. There is no fee. The campground is open from mid-April to late November.

Contact: Wenatchee National Forest, Leavenworth Ranger District, 600 Sherbourne, Leavenworth, WA 98826; (509) 548-6977 or fax (509) 548-5817.

Directions: From Interstate 5 at Everett, turn east on U.S. 2 and drive approximately 103 miles to Leavenworth. Continue 4.5 miles on U.S. 2, then turn south on U.S. 97 and drive 13 miles to the campground.

Trip notes: This campground just off U.S. 97 along Tronsen Creek is used primarily as a layover spot, with few recreation options in the immediate area. Though it doesn't seem to have much to offer, it can become quite crowded, so plan to arrive early to guarantee a spot.

⑱ Blu Shastin RV Park

Location: Near Penshastin Creek; map A3, grid j6.

Campsites, facilities: There are 86 sites for tents, trailers, or RVs of any length; seven are drive-throughs. Electricity, piped water, sewer hookups, fire rings, and picnic tables are provided. Flush toilets, sanitary services, showers, a recreation hall, firewood, a laundry room, ice, a playground, horseshoes, badminton, volleyball, and a swimming pool are available. Bottled gas, a store, and a cafe are located within one mile. Leashed pets and motorbikes are permitted.

Reservations, fees: Reservations are recommended. Sites are $16–$20 per night. The campground is open year-round.

Contact: Phone (509) 548-4184 or (888) 548-4184 or write to 3300 Highway 97, Leavenworth, WA 98826.

Directions: From Interstate 5 at Everett, turn east on U.S. 2 and drive approximately 103 miles to Leavenworth. Continue three miles on U.S. 2 to the junction with U.S. 97, then turn south and drive seven miles to the park on the right.

Trip notes: This park is set in a mountainous area near Penshastin Creek. Gold panning in the river is a popular activity here, and rumor has it that the Penshastin is the best-producing river in the state. The camp has sites on the river bank and plenty of shade trees. A heated pool, a recreation field, and horseshoe pits provide possible activities in the park. Hiking trails and marked bike trails are nearby.

119 Swauk

Location: On Swauk Creek in Wenatchee National Forest; map A3, grid j6.

Campsites, facilities: There are 23 sites for tents, trailers, or RVs. Fire grills and picnic tables are provided. Pit toilets and firewood are available, but there is no piped water. Leashed pets are permitted.

Reservations, fees: No reservations are accepted. Sites are $8 per vehicle per night, with a two-vehicle maximum. The campground is open from mid-April to late September.

Contact: Wenatchee National Forest, Cle Elum Ranger District, West Second Street, Cle Elum, WA 98922; (509) 674-4411 or fax (509) 674-4794 .

Directions: From Seattle, turn east on Interstate 90 and drive approximately 80 miles to Cle Elum. Take exit 86 to County Road 970 and drive east 12 miles. Turn north on U.S. 97 and drive 10 miles to the campground.

Trip notes: Good fishing and some decent hiking trails can be found at this campground along Swauk Creek. It's a prime spot, particularly during winter months. About three miles east of the campground is Swauk Sno-Park, which provides a parking area and access to Forest Service roads and open areas for snowmobiling and cross-country skiing. Also near the sno-park on Forest Service Road 9716

is the Swauk Forest Discovery Trail. This interpretive trail is three miles long and explains how logging affects Forest Service management of the landscape.

120 Wenatchee Confluence State Park

Location: On the Columbia River; map A3, grid j8.

Campsites, facilities: There are eight developed tent sites and 51 hookup sites for trailers or RVs up to 65 feet long. Picnic tables, stoves, piped water, showers, flush toilets, and a sanitary disposal station are provided. A boat launch is available. The facilities are wheelchair accessible. Leashed pets are permitted.

Reservations, fees: Contact Reservations Northwest at (800) 452-5687 ($6 reservation fee). Sites are $11–$16 per night. The campground is open year-round.

Contact: Phone (800) 233-0321 or (509) 664-6373, or write to 333 Old Station Road, Wenatchee, WA 98801.

Directions: From Interstate 5 at Everett, turn east on U.S. 2 and drive approximately 121 miles to Wenatchee. The park is located at the north end of Wenatchee on Old Station Road.

Trip notes: This state park, just outside of Wenatchee on the Columbia River, provides a relaxing atmosphere and many activities. Recreation possibilities include fishing, swimming, boating, and waterskiing. Interpretive hiking trails are also available. Sports enthusiasts are provided with playing fields and tennis and basketball courts. Daroga State Park and Lake Chelan to the north offer side trip possibilities.

Map A4

Washington State Map .... *page 6*
One inch equals approximately 20 miles.

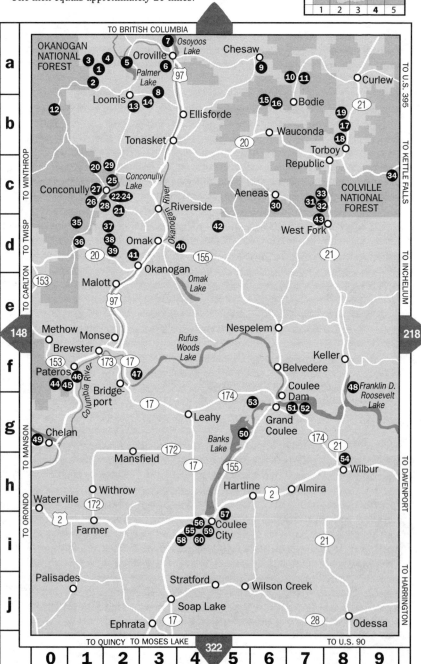

194

Chapter A4 features:

1 Toats Coulee

Location: On Toats Coulee Creek; map A4, grid a1.

Campsites, facilities: There are nine campsites for tents or small trailers. Picnic tables, fire grills, and tent pads are provided. Vault toilets are available. There is no piped water. Leashed pets are permitted.

Reservations, fees: No reservations are accepted. There is no fee. The campground is open year-round.

Contact: Department of Natural Resources, Northeast Region, P.O. Box 190, Colville, WA 99114-0190; (360) 902-1234, (509) 684-7474, or fax (509) 684-7484.

Directions: From Interstate 5 at Everett, turn east on U.S. 2 and drive 106 miles to the junction with U.S. 97. Turn north on U.S. 97 and drive 120 miles to Tonasket. Turn north on County Road 9437 and drive five miles, then head west to Loomis on County Road 9425. From Loomis, continue north on County Road 9425 for two miles, then turn left on Toats Coulee Road. Travel 5.5 miles to the lower camp. Continue 100 yards to the upper camp at the junction of Roads OMT 2000 and OMT 1000.

Trip notes: One of three little-known camps in the vicinity, this wooded spot is set along Toats Coulee Creek. Some moose are in the area. A road for snowmobile use follows the South Fork of Toats Coulee Creek, swinging south and then heading east along Cecil Creek. Contact the Department of Natural Resources for details.

❷ Cold Springs

Location: Near Cold Creek; map A4, grid a1.

Campsites, facilities: There are nine campsites for tents or small trailers. Picnic tables, fire grills, and tent pads are provided. Vault toilets and piped water, plus horse stalls and feeder boxes, are available. Leashed pets are permitted.

Reservations, fees: No reservations are accepted. There is no fee. The campground is open year-round.

Contact: Department of Natural Resources, Northeast Region, P.O. Box 190, Colville, WA 99114-0190; (360) 902-1234, (509) 684-7474, or fax (509) 684-7484.

Directions: From Interstate 5 at Everett, turn east on U.S. 2 and drive 106 miles to the junction with U.S. 97. Turn north on U.S. 97 and drive 120 miles to Tonasket. Turn north on County Road 9437 and drive five miles, then head west to Loomis on County Road 9425. From Loomis, continue north on County Road 9425 for two miles, then turn left on Toats Coulee Road. Travel 5.5 miles to the lower camp. Continue 100 yards to the upper camp at the junction of Roads OMT 2000 and OMT 1000. Take Road OMT 1000 for two miles to Cold Creek Road (gravel) and turn right. Travel one-half mile, keep right, and continue for two miles. Then keep left and drive two miles to the picnic area or three miles to the campground.

Trip notes: It's quite a drive to get here, but you'll be happy you made the effort to reach this pretty and forested camp, with sites near a small stream. Trails for horseback riding, hiking, and snowmobiling run through the area. Because the camp is little known and remote, it's advisable to obtain a map of the area from the Department of Natural Re-

sources. Don't be surprised if you see moose tromping around these parts.

❸ North Fork Nine Mile

Location: On the North Fork of Toats Coulee Creek; map A4, grid a1.

Campsites, facilities: There are 11 campsites for tents or small trailers. Picnic tables, fire grills, and tent pads are provided. Vault toilets and piped water are available. Leashed pets are permitted.

Reservations, fees: No reservations are accepted. There is no fee. The campground is open year-round.

Contact: Department of Natural Resources, Northeast Region, P.O. Box 190, Colville, WA 99114-0190; (360) 902-1234, (509) 684-7474, or fax (509) 684-7484.

Directions: From Interstate 5 at Everett, turn east on U.S. 2 and drive 106 miles to the junction with U.S. 97. Turn north on U.S. 97 and drive 120 miles to Tonasket. Turn north on County Road 9437 and go five miles, then head west to Loomis on County Road 9425. From Loomis, drive north on County Road 9425 for two miles, then turn left on Toats Coulee Road. Travel 5.5 miles to the lower camp. Continue 100 yards to the upper camp at the junction of Roads OMT 2000 and OMT 1000. Take Road OMT 1000 for 2.5 miles to the campground.

Trip notes: Northwestern moose frequent this campground in the forest along the North Fork of Toats Coulee Creek and Nine Mile Creek. It's advisable to obtain a map that details the area from the Department of Natural Resources.

❹ Chopaka Lake

Location: On Chopaka Lake; map A4, grid a2.

Campsites, facilities: There are 15 campsites for tents or small trailers. Picnic tables, fire grills, and tent pads are provided. Vault toilets, piped water, and boat launching facilities are available. Leashed pets are permitted.

Reservations, fees: No reservations are accepted. There is no fee. The campground is open year-round.

Contact: Department of Natural Resources, Northeast Region, P.O. Box 190, Colville, WA 99114-0190; (360) 902-1234, (509) 684-7474, or fax (509) 684-7484.

Directions: From Interstate 5 at Everett, turn east on U.S. 2 and drive 106 miles to the junction with U.S. 97. Turn north on U.S. 97 and drive 120 miles to Tonasket. Turn north on County Road 9437 and drive five miles, then head west to Loomis on County Road 9425. From Loomis, continue north on County Road 9425 for two miles, then turn left on Toats Coulee Road. Travel 1.5 miles, then turn right onto a steep, one lane road and drive 3.5 miles. Keep left and drive 1.5 miles, then turn right and drive two miles to the campground.

Trip notes: This campground provides a classic setting for the expert angler. It's nestled along the western shore of Chopaka Lake, which is stocked with Atlantic salmon. Only catch-and-release fly-fishing with barbless hooks is allowed.

⑤ Palmer Lake

Location: On Palmer Lake; map A4, grid a2.

Campsites, facilities: There are six campsites for tents or small trailers. Picnic tables, fire grills, and tent pads are provided. Vault toilets are available, but there is no piped water. Leashed pets are permitted.

Reservations, fees: No reservations are accepted. There is no fee. The campground is open year-round.

Contact: Department of Natural Resources, Northeast Region, P.O. Box 190, Colville, WA 99114-0190; (360) 902-1234, (509) 684-7474, or fax (509) 684-7484.

Directions: From Interstate 5 at Everett, turn east on U.S. 2 and drive 106 miles to the junction with U.S. 97. Turn north on U.S. 97 and drive 120 miles to Tonasket. Turn north on County Road 9437 and drive five miles, then head west to Loomis on County Road 9425. From Loomis, continue north on County Road 9425 for 8.5 miles, keep right, and you'll find the campground at the north end of the lake.

Trip notes: This shorefront camp is the only

one at Palmer Lake. An array of Washington wildlife call the area home. The winter range of the deer is in the Sinlahekin Valley to the south of Palmer Lake. There are numerous migration routes in the region. Wildlife (not for hunting) include the endangered Bighorn sheep, cougar, bald and golden eagles, black and brown bear, and grouse. See the trip notes for Chopaka Lake (campground number 4) for information on fishing for Atlantic salmon in nearby Chopaka Lake.

⑥ Sun Cove Resort

Location: On Wannacut Lake; map A4, grid a3.

Campsites, facilities: There are 22 tent sites and 28 drive-through sites for trailers or RVs of any length. Electricity, piped water, sewer hookups, and picnic tables are provided. Flush toilets, sanitary services, a recreation hall, a store, a cafe, a laundry room, ice, a playground, and a swimming pool are available, as are showers for an extra fee. Boat docks, launching facilities, and rentals are also available. Leashed pets are permitted.

Reservations, fees: Reservations are accepted. Sites are $16–$20 per night. The campground is open from late April through October.

Contact: Phone (509) 476-2223, fax (509) 476-2223, or write to 93 East Wannacut Lane, Oroville, WA 98844.

Directions: From Interstate 5 at Burlington, turn east on Highway 20 and drive 174 miles. Turn north on U.S. 97 and proceed 37 miles to Ellisford. Turn west on Loomis Highway and drive seven miles to Wannacut Lake Road. Turn north and drive five miles to the resort at the end of the road.

Trip notes: This beautiful resort, surrounded by trees and hills and set along the shore of Wannacut Lake, is a nice little spot that doesn't get much traffic. Fishing, swimming, boating, and hiking are all summertime options. The park provides full facilities, including a heated pool and a playground and recreation hall for kids.

❼ Osoyoos Lake State Park

Location: On Osoyoos Lake; map A4, grid a3.

Campsites, facilities: There are six primitive tent sites and 80 sites for tents or self-contained RVs up to 45 feet long. Picnic tables and fire grills are provided. Flush toilets, piped water, sanitary services, a store, a cafe, showers, firewood, and a playground are available. A Laundromat and ice are located within one mile. Boat launching facilities are nearby. Leashed pets are permitted.

Reservations, fees: Contact Reservations Northwest at (800) 452-5687 ($6 reservation fee). Sites are $5–$11 per night. The campground is open year-round.

Contact: Phone (800) 233-0321 or (509) 476-3321, or write to Route 1, P.O. Box 102 A, Oroville, WA 98844.

Directions: From Interstate 5 at Burlington, turn east on Highway 20 and drive 174 miles. Turn north on U.S. 97 and proceed 48 miles to Oroville. Continue one mile north on U.S. 97 to the park. Note: In the winter, sections of Highway 20 are closed; take an alternate route to U.S. 97.

Trip notes: This is a beautiful park near the Canadian border. Many years ago, the area was the site of the annual Okanogan (which means "rendezvous") of the Washington and British Columbia Indians. They would gather and share supplies of fish and game for the year. The park is located along the shore of Osoyoos Lake, where swimming, waterskiing, and fishing for trout and spiny rays are all possibilities. Osoyoos Lake is a winter nesting area for geese. An 18-hole golf course is nearby. Fishing gear and concessions are available at the park.

❽ Spectacle Lake Resort

Location: On Spectacle Lake; map A4, grid a3.

Campsites, facilities: There are 40 sites for tents, trailers, or RVs of any length. Electricity, piped water, sewer hookups, and picnic tables are provided. Flush toilets, bottled gas, sanitary services, showers, a store, a laundry room, ice, a playground, and a swimming pool are available. Boat docks, launching facilities, and rentals are also available. Leashed pets and motorbikes are permitted.

Reservations, fees: Reservations are accepted. Sites are $12–$14 per night. The campground is open from mid-April to late October.

Contact: Phone (509) 223-3433 or write to 10 McCammon Road, Tonasket, WA 98855.

Directions: From Interstate 5 at Burlington, turn east on Highway 20 and drive 174 miles. Turn north on U.S. 97 and drive 37 miles to Ellisford. Turn west on Loomis Highway and drive 7.7 miles. Turn south on Holmes Road and drive one-half mile to McCammon Road, then turn west and drive one block to the park at the end.

Trip notes: This pleasant resort on the shore of long, narrow Spectacle Lake has grassy, shaded sites. Recreation options include swimming, fishing, hunting, and horseback riding. A riding stable is nearby.

❾ Beth Lake

Location: On Beth Lake in Okanogan National Forest; map A4, grid a6.

Campsites, facilities: There are 17 sites for tents, trailers, or RVs up to 31 feet long, plus one multiple site. Piped water and picnic tables are provided. Vault toilets, a picnic area, and boat launching facilities are available. Leashed pets are permitted.

Reservations, fees: No reservations are accepted. Sites are $5 per vehicle per night. The campground is open from mid-May to mid-September.

Contact: Okanogan National Forest, Tonasket Ranger District, 1 West Winesap Avenue, Tonasket, WA 98855; (509) 486-2186 or fax (509) 486-5161.

Directions: From Interstate 5 south of Bellingham, turn east on Higway 20 and drive approximately 180 miles to Okanogan.

Turn north on Highway 97 and drive 20 miles to Tonasket. Continue 20 miles east on Highway 20 to County Road 4953, then drive north to Forest Service Road 32. Turn north and drive five miles. From there, drive northwest on County Road 9480 to the campground.

Trip notes: This campground can be found along little Beth Lake, which is adjacent to Beaver Lake. Side trip options in the area include Lost Lake, Bonaparte Lake, and several hiking trails, one of which leads up to the Mount Bonaparte Lookout.

⑩ Lost Lake

Location: On Lost Lake in Okanogan National Forest; map A4, grid a6.

Campsites, facilities: There are 12 single and six multiple sites for tents, trailers, or RVs up to 31 feet long. There is also one group unit available only by reservation. Piped water and picnic tables are provided. Vault toilets are available. Boat docks and launching facilities are nearby. Leashed pets are permitted.

Reservations, fees: Reservations are required for the group site. Single and multiple sites are $6 per vehicle per night; group rates are $40 for up to 25 people, $60 for 26 to 50 people, and $80 for 51 to 100 people. The campground is open from mid-May to mid-September.

Contact: Okanogan National Forest, Tonasket Ranger District, 1 West Winesap Avenue, Tonasket, WA 98855; (509) 486-2186 or fax (509) 486-5161.

Directions: From Interstate 5 south of Bellingham, turn east on Highway 20 and drive approximately 200 miles east and north to Tonasket. Continue 20 miles east on Highway 20 to County Road 4953, then drive north to Forest Service Road 32. Turn north and drive three miles, then turn northwest on Forest Service Road 33 and drive 6.5 miles to the campground.

Trip notes: This camp on the shore of Lost Lake keeps visitors happy with fishing, swimming, hiking, hunting, and horseback riding. The Big Tree Botanical Area is about a mile away.

⑪ Beaver Lake

Location: On Beaver Lake in Okanogan National Forest; map A4, grid a7.

Campsites, facilities: There are nine single and two multiple sites for tents, trailers, or RVs up to 21 feet long. Piped water and picnic tables are provided. Vault toilets are available. Leashed pets are permitted.

Reservations, fees: No reservations are accepted. Sites are $5 per vehicle per night. The campground is open from mid-May to mid-September.

Contact: Okanogan National Forest, Tonasket Ranger District, 1 West Winesap Avenue, Tonasket, WA 98855; (509) 486-2186 or fax (509) 486-5161.

Directions: From Interstate 5 south of Bellingham, turn east on Highway 20 and drive approximately 200 miles to Tonasket. Continue 20 miles east on Highway 20 to County Road 4953, then drive north to Forest Service Road 32. Turn north and drive five miles to the campground.

Trip notes: The southeastern shore of long, narrow Beaver Lake, one of several lakes in this area, is the home of this camp. Fishing, swimming, hunting, and hiking are all possibilities here. See the trip notes for Lost Lake and Bonaparte Lake (campground numbers 10 and 15) for information on the other lakes.

⑫ Tiffany Spring

Location: Near Tiffany Lake in Okanogan National Forest; map A4, grid b0.

Campsites, facilities: There are six tent sites for trailers or RVs up to 15 feet long. Picnic tables are provided. Vault toilets are available, but there is no piped water. No garbage service is provided, so trash must be packed out. Leashed pets are permitted.

Reservations, fees: No reservations are accepted. There is no fee. The campground is open from July to late September.

Contact: Okanogan National Forest, Tonasket Ranger District, 1 West Winesap Avenue, Tonasket, WA 98855; (509) 486-2186 or fax (509) 486-5161.

Directions: From Interstate 5 south of Bellingham, turn east on Highway 20 and drive approximately 180 miles east and north to Okanogan. Turn north on County Road 9229 and drive about 17.5 miles northwest to Conconully. Turn left on County Road 2017 and drive 1.5 miles southwest, then turn northwest on Forest Service Road 37 and drive 21 miles. Turn northeast on Forest Service Road 39 and proceed 7.5 miles to the campground.

Trip notes: Located at an elevation of 6,800 feet, this camp is less than a mile hike from Tiffany Lake. Tiffany Mountain rises 8,200 feet in the distance. There are some good hiking trails in the area. No other campgrounds are in the vicinity, and it's advisable to obtain a Forest Service map of the area.

⑬ Rainbow Resort

Location: On Spectacle Lake; map A4, grid b2.

Campsites, facilities: There are 10 tent sites and 40 sites for trailers or RVs of any length; 10 are drive-throughs. Electricity, piped water, sewer hookups, and picnic tables are provided. Flush toilets, showers, firewood, ice, boat docks, boat rentals, and launching facilities are available. Leashed pets and motorbikes are permitted.

Reservations, fees: Reservations are accepted. Sites are $16 per night. The campground is open from April through October.

Contact: Phone (509) 223-3700 or write to 761 Loomis Highway, Tonasket, WA 98855.

Directions: From Interstate 5 at Burlington, turn east on Highway 20 and drive 174 miles. Turn north on U.S. 97 and proceed 37 miles to Ellisford. Turn west on Loomis Highway and drive 9.5 miles to the resort on the left.

Trip notes: This resort on Spectacle Lake is an alternative to Spectacle Lake Resort (campground number 8), with pretty lake views and full facilities. Nearby activities include swimming, fishing, hunting, and tennis.

⑭ Spectacle Falls Resort

Location: On Spectacle Lake; map A4, grid b3.

Campsites, facilities: There are 10 tent sites and 28 drive-through sites for trailers or RVs of any length. Electricity, piped water, sewer hookups, and picnic tables are provided. Flush toilets, sanitary services, showers, ice, boat docks, launching facilities, and boat rentals are available. Leashed pets and motorbikes are permitted.

Reservations, fees: Reservations are accepted. Sites are $14 per night. The campground is open from mid-April to late July.

Contact: Spectacle Falls Resort, 879 Loomis Highway, Tonasket, WA 98855; (509) 223-4141; e-mail: jwalsh@nvinet.com.

Directions: From Interstate 5 at Burlington, turn east on Highway 20 and drive 174 miles. Turn north on U.S. 97 and drive 30 miles to Tonasket. Turn northwest on Loomis Highway and drive 15 miles to the resort.

Trip notes: Spectacle Falls Resort, on the shore of Spectacle Lake, is open only as long as fishing is allowed, which means an early closing in July. Be sure to phone ahead of time to verify whether they're open. Recreation options include hiking, swimming, fishing, horseback riding, and tennis. A riding stable is nearby.

⑮ Bonaparte Lake

Location: On Bonaparte Lake in Okanogan National Forest; map A4, grid b6.

Campsites, facilities: There are 15 single and 10 multiple sites for tents, trailers, or RVs up to 31 feet long, plus three bike-in/hike-in sites and one group site which can accommodate up to 30 people. Piped water, vault toilets, fire grills, and picnic tables are provided. Sanitary services, a store, a cafe, and ice can be found within one mile. Boat docks (including a wheelchair-accessible fishing dock) and launching facilities are also available. Leashed pets are permitted.

Reservations, fees: No reservations are accepted. For fee information, phone (509) 486-2186. The campground is open from mid-May to mid-September.

Contact: Okanogan National Forest, Tonasket Ranger District, 1 West Winesap Avenue, Tonasket, WA 98855; (509) 486-2186 or fax (509) 486-5161.

Directions: From Interstate 5 south of Bellingham, turn east on Highway 20 and drive approximately 180 miles to Okanogan. Turn north on Highway 97 and drive 30 miles to Tonasket. Continue 20 miles east on Highway 20 to County Road 4953, then drive north to Forest Service Road 32. Turn north and drive 5.5 miles to the campground.

Trip notes: This campground is located on the southern shore of Bonaparte Lake. See the trip notes for Bonaparte Lake Resort (campground number 16) for lake recreation information. There are several trails nearby that provide access to Mount Bonaparte Lookout. Consult a Forest Service map for details.

⑯ Bonaparte Lake Resort

Location: On Bonaparte Lake; map A4, grid b6.

Campsites, facilities: There are 10 tent sites and 35 sites for trailers or RVs of any length; some are drive-throughs. Electricity, piped water, sewer hookups, and picnic tables are provided. Flush toilets, bottled gas, sanitary services, showers, firewood, a recreation hall, a store, a cafe, a laundry room, ice, a playground, boat docks, launching facilities, and boat rentals are available. Leashed pets and motorbikes are permitted.

Reservations, fees: Reservations are accepted. Sites are $8–$12 per night. The campground is open from April through October.

Contact: Phone (509) 486-2828, fax (509) 486-1987, or write to 695 Bonaparte, Tonasket, WA 98855.

Directions: From Interstate 5 at Burlington, turn east on Highway 20 and drive 174 miles. Turn north on U.S. 97 and proceed 30 miles to Tonasket. Continue 20 miles east on Highway

20 to Bonaparte Road. Turn north and drive six miles to the resort on the left.

Trip notes: Fishing is popular at this resort on the southeast shore of Bonaparte Lake. Other recreational activities include hiking and hunting in the nearby Forest Service lands and snowmobiling and cross-country skiing in the winter.

⑰ Curlew Lake State Park

Location: On Curlew Lake; map A4, grid b8.

Campsites, facilities: There are five primitive tent sites, 57 developed tent sites, and 25 sites for trailers or RVs up to 30 feet long. Picnic tables are provided. Flush toilets, sanitary services, electricity, piped water, sewer hookups, showers, firewood, and boat launching facilities are available. Leashed pets are permitted.

Reservations, fees: No reservations are accepted. Sites are $10–$16 per night. The campground is open from April to late October.

Contact: Phone (800) 233-0321 or (509) 775-3592, or write to 974 Curlew Lake Street, Republic, WA 99166.

Directions: From Interstate 90 at Spokane, turn north on U.S. 395 and drive 87 miles. Turn west on Highway 20 and continue 34 miles to Highway 21 (two miles east of Republic). Turn north and drive 6.5 miles to the park entrance on the left.

Trip notes: Boredom is banned at this park on the eastern shore of Curlew Lake. Beach access, swimming, waterskiing, hiking, and excellent fishing for trout and bass are just some of the activities. Nearby recreation options include an 18-hole golf course, and in the winter, snowmobiling. The park is located in the heart of a historic gold-mining district, so you may want to bring along a pan and give it a whirl.

⑱ Tiffany's Resort

Location: On Curlew Lake; map A4, grid b8.

Campsites, facilities: There are four tent sites and 15 sites for trailers or RVs of any length. Electricity, piped water, sewer hookups, and picnic tables are provided. Flush toilets, showers, firewood, a store, a laundry room, ice, and a playground are available. Boat docks, launching facilities, and rentals are nearby. Pets and motorbikes are permitted.

Reservations, fees: Reservations are accepted. Sites are $16 per night. The campground is open from April to late October.

Contact: Tiffany's Resort, 1026 Tiffany Road, Republic, WA 99166; (509) 775-3152; Web site: www.quintessential.net.tiffres.

Directions: From Interstate 90 at Spokane, turn north on U.S. 395 and drive 87 miles. Turn west on Highway 20 and drive 34 miles to Highway 21 (two miles east of Republic). Turn north and drive 10 miles, then turn north on West Curlew Lake Road and drive five miles to the resort.

Trip notes: Tiffany's Resort is in a pretty, wooded setting along the western shore of Curlew Lake. Highlights include spacious sites, lake access, and good fishing. This is a smaller, more private alternative to Black's Beach Resort (campground number 19).

⑲ Black's Beach Resort

Location: On Curlew Lake; map A4, grid b8.

Campsites, facilities: There are 120 sites for trailers or RVs of any length; 60 are drive-throughs. Electricity, piped water, sewer hookups, and picnic tables are provided. Flush toilets, sanitary services, showers, a recreation hall, a store, a laundry room, ice, and a playground are available. Boat docks, launching facilities, and rentals are located at the resort. Leashed pets and motorbikes are permitted.

Reservations, fees: Reservations are accepted. Sites are $15–$17 per night. The campground is open from April through October; three winterized sites are open year-round.

Contact: Phone (509) 775-3989 or write to 848 Blacks Beach Road, Republic, WA 99166.

Directions: From Interstate 90 at Spokane, turn north on U.S. 395 and drive 87 miles.

Turn west on Highway 20 and continue 34 miles to Highway 21 (two miles east of Republic). Turn north and drive 10 miles, then turn north on West Curlew Lake Road and continue to the resort on the lake.

Trip notes: Here's another resort along Curlew Lake. This one is much larger, with beautiful waterfront sites and full facilities. Waterskiing, swimming, and fishing are all options.

⑳ Kerr

Location: On Salmon Creek in Okanogan National Forest; map A4, grid c1.

Campsites, facilities: There are 13 sites for tents, trailers, or RVs up to 21 feet long. Picnic tables and fire grills are provided. Vault toilets are available, but there is no piped water. No garbage service is provided, so trash must be packed out. Leashed pets are permitted.

Reservations, fees: No reservations are accepted. There is no fee. The campground is open from mid-May to mid-September.

Contact: Okanogan National Forest, Tonasket Ranger District, 1 West Winesap Avenue, Tonasket, WA 98855; (509) 486-2186 or fax (509) 486-5161.

Directions: From Interstate 5 south of Bellingham, turn east on Highway 20 and drive approximately 180 miles east and north to Okanogan. Turn north on County Road 9229 and drive about 17.5 miles northwest to Conconully. Turn northwest on County Road 2361 and drive two miles, then continue northwest on Forest Service Road 38 for two miles to the campground.

Trip notes: This camp is located at 3,100 feet along Salmon Creek, about four miles north of Conconully Lake, and is one of many campgrounds near the lake. Fishing prospects can be decent here, and there are numerous recreation options available at Conconully Lake.

㉑ Jack's RV Park and Motel

Location: Near Conconully Lake; map A4, grid c2.

Campsites, facilities: There are 57 sites for trailers or RVs of any length; 20 are drive-throughs. Electricity, piped water, cable TV and sewer hookups, and picnic tables are provided. Flush toilets, propane gas, showers, firewood, a laundry room, and a swimming pool are available. A store, a cafe, and ice are located within one mile. Boat docks, launching facilities, and rentals are nearby. Pets and motorbikes are permitted.

Reservations, fees: Reservations are accepted. Sites are $15 per night. The campground is open from mid-April through October, weather permitting.

Contact: Phone (509) 826-0132 or write to P.O. Box 98, Conconully, WA 98819.

Directions: From Interstate 5 south of Bellingham, turn east on Highway 20 and drive approximately 180 miles east and north to Okanogan. Turn north on Conconully Highway and drive about 17.5 miles northwest to Conconully. Turn east on Broadway Street and drive one block, then turn north on "A" Avenue and drive less than one block to the park on the right.

Trip notes: This park is in the town of Conconully, not far from Conconully Lake. A pool and horseshoe pits can be found in the park, and nearby recreation options include hiking trails and water sports at the lake.

㉒ Lazy Days RV Park

Location: Near Conconully Lake; map A4, grid c2.

Campsites, facilities: There are 43 drive-through sites for trailers or RVs of any length. Electricity, piped water, sewer hookups, and picnic tables are provided. Flush toilets, firewood, showers, a laundry room, cable TV, and ice are available. Bottled gas, sanitary services, a store, a cafe, and ice are located within one mile. Boat docks, launching facilities, and rentals are nearby. Leashed pets are permitted.

Reservations, fees: Reservations are accepted. Sites are $15 per night. The campground is open from April through October, weather permitting.

Contact: Phone (509) 826-0326 or write to P.O. Box 67, Conconully, WA 98819.

Directions: From Interstate 5 south of Bellingham, turn east on Highway 20 and drive approximately 180 miles east and north to Okanogan. Turn north on Conconully Highway and drive about 17.5 miles northwest to Conconully. Turn east on Silver Street and drive one block, then turn south on "A" Avenue and drive about half a block to the park on the right.

Trip notes: This park is in downtown Conconully, a short distance from the lake. The park is geared specifically toward RVs, with shaded grassy sites. Nearby activities include hiking trails and fishing, swimming, and boating at the lake.

㉓ Maple Flats RV Park and Resort

Location: On Conconully Lake; map A4, grid c2.

Campsites, facilities: There are six tent sites and 25 sites for trailers or RVs of any length with full hookups, including 50-amp electrical and cable TV; 12 sites are drive-throughs. Furnished cabins are also available. Electricity, piped water, sewer hookups, and picnic tables are provided. Flush toilets, showers, a laundry room, and a covered gazebo with electricity are available. Groceries, dining, dancing, propane, and boat, snowmobile, and jet ski rentals are located within two blocks. Boat docks and launching facilities are also nearby. Leashed pets and motorbikes are permitted.

Reservations, fees: Reservations are accepted. Sites are $10–$14 per night, plus an additional $2 for tent camping in sites already occupied by an RV. Call for cabin rental information. The campground is open year-round.

Contact: Phone (509) 826-4231 or write to 310 A Avenue, Conconully, WA 98819.

Directions: From Interstate 5 south of Bellingham, turn east on Highway 20 and drive approximately 180 miles east and north to Okanogan. Turn north on Conconully Highway and drive about 17.5 miles northwest to

Conconully. Turn east on Loomis Road and drive one block, then turn east on "A" Avenue and drive to the park on the right.

Trip notes: This campground on the shore of Conconully Lake is in a beautiful setting, surrounded by pine trees and mountains, with panoramic views. Nearby recreation options include hiking and biking on the many nature trails in the area, an 18-hole golf course (15 miles away), trout fishing in the well-stocked Upper and Lower Conconully Lakes, and, in the winter, snowmobiling and cross-country skiing.

㉔ Kozy Kabins and RV Park

Location: Near Conconully Lake; map A4, grid c2.

Campsites, facilities: There are six tent sites and 12 drive-through sites for trailers or RVs, half of which can accommodate a length of 20 feet. Electricity, piped water, sewer hookups, and picnic tables are provided. Flush toilets, showers, and firewood are available. Bottled gas, sanitary services, a store, a cafe, a Laundromat, and ice are located within one mile. Cabin rentals, boat docks, launching facilities, and boat rentals are nearby. Pets and motorbikes are permitted.

Reservations, fees: Reservations are accepted. Sites are $8–$12 per night; cabins are $35 per night. The campground is open year-round.

Contact: Phone (509) 826-6780 or write to P.O. Box 82, Conconully, WA 98819.

Directions: From Interstate 5 south of Bellingham, turn east on Highway 20 and drive approximately 180 miles east and north to Okanogan. Turn north on Conconully Highway and drive about 17.5 miles northwest to Conconully. The park is at the junction of "A" Avenue and Broadway.

Trip notes: This park is in Conconully not far from the lake. It's quiet, private, and secluded, with a small creek running through and plenty of greenery. A full-service marina is located close by. If you continue northeast of town on County Road 4015, the road will get a bit narrow for awhile, but will widen again when you enter the Sinlahekin Habitat Management Area, which is managed by the Department of Fish and Game. There are some primitive campsites in this valley, especially along the shores of the lakes in the area.

㉕ Conconully Lake Resort

Location: On Upper Conconully Lake; map A4, grid c2.

Campsites, facilities: There are 11 sites for trailers or RVs of any length with full hookups, plus some cabins. Electricity, piped water, sewer hookups, and picnic tables are provided. Flush toilets, showers, and ice are available. Bottled gas, sanitary services, a store, a cafe, and a Laundromat are located within one mile. Boat docks, launching facilities, and rentals are available. Pets and motorbikes are permitted.

Reservations, fees: Reservations are accepted. Sites are $16 per night; call for cabin fees. The campground is open from late April to late October.

Contact: Conconully Lake Resort, P.O. Box 131, Conconully, WA 98819; (509) 826-0813, (800) 850-0813, or fax (509) 826-0813; e-mail: leigh@televar.com.

Directions: From Interstate 5 south of Bellingham, turn east on Highway 20 and drive approximately 180 miles east and north to Okanogan. Turn north on Conconully Highway and drive about 17.5 miles northwest to Conconully. Turn east on Sinlahekin Road and continue one mile to the park on the right.

Trip notes: This resort is one of several in Conconully, set along the shore of Conconully Lake. No tents are permitted, but this is a prime vacation destination for RVers. Trout fishing, swimming, and boating are all options here.

㉖ Liar's Cove Resort

Location: On Conconully Lake; map A4, grid c1.

Campsites, facilities: There are 30 sites for tents, trailers, or RVs up to 50 feet long; 20 are drive-throughs. Electricity, piped water, sewer hookups, and picnic tables are provided. Flush toilets, showers, and ice are available. Bottled gas, sanitary services, a store, and a cafe are located within one mile. Boat docks, launching facilities, and rentals are nearby. Leashed pets and motorbikes are permitted.

Reservations, fees: Reservations are accepted. Sites are $15–$16 per night. The campground is open from April to early November.

Contact: Phone (800) 830-1288 or (509) 826-1288, or write to P.O. Box 72, Conconully, WA 98819.

Directions: From Interstate 5 south of Bellingham, turn east on Highway 20 and drive approximately 180 miles east and north to Okanogan. Turn north on Conconully Highway and drive about 16.5 miles northwest to the park on the left. It's located about one-quarter of a mile south of Conconully.

Trip notes: Roomy sites for RVs can be found at this camp on the shore of Conconully Lake. Tents are allowed, too. Fishing, swimming, boating, and hiking opportunities are located nearby.

㉗ Shady Pines Resort

Location: On Conconully Lake; map A4, grid c2.

Campsites, facilities: There are 23 sites for trailers or RVs of any length; 21 sites have full hookups. Electricity, piped water, sewer hookups, and picnic tables are provided. Flush toilets, ice, showers, and firewood are available. Bottled gas, sanitary services, a store, a cafe, and a Laundromat are located within one mile. Boat launching facilities and rentals are nearby. Leashed pets and motorbikes are permitted.

Reservations, fees: Reservations are accepted. Sites are $18–$19 per night. The campground is open from mid-April to late October.

Contact: Phone (800) 552-2287 or (509) 826-2287, or write to P.O. Box 44, Conconully, WA 98819.

Directions: From Interstate 5 south of

Bellingham, turn east on Highway 20 and drive approximately 180 miles east and north to Okanogan. Turn north on Conconully Highway and drive about 17.5 miles northwest to Conconully. Turn west on Broadway Street and drive one mile. The park is on the west shore of the lake.

Trip notes: This camp on Conconully Lake, near Conconully State Park, is an option if the state park campground is full, which occurs often in the summertime. See the trip notes for Kozy Kabins and RV Park and Conconully State Park (campground numbers 24 and 28) for area information.

㉘ Conconully State Park

Location: On Conconully Lake; map A4, grid c2.

Campsites, facilities: There are six primitive tent sites and 75 sites for tents or self-contained RVs up to 60 feet long. Piped water, fire grills, and picnic tables are provided. Flush toilets, a sanitary disposal station, showers, firewood, and a playground are available. A store, a cafe, a Laundromat, and ice are located within one mile. Boat launching facilities are nearby. Leashed pets are permitted.

Reservations, fees: No reservations are accepted. Sites are $5–$16 per night. The campground is open year-round, with limited winter facilities.

Contact: Phone (800) 233-0321 or (509) 826-7408, or write to P.O. Box 95, Conconully, WA 98819.

Directions: From Interstate 5 south of Bellingham, turn east on Highway 20 and drive approximately 185 miles east and north to Omak. Take the north Omak exit. At the base of the hill, turn right and proceed two miles until you reach Conconully Highway. Take another right and continue about 17 miles north to the park entrance.

Trip notes: Conconully State Park is set along Conconully Lake, where a boat launch, beach access, swimming, and fishing provide all sorts of water sports possibilities. Visitors can also explore a nice, half-mile nature trail, or take a trip to the Sinlahekin Habitat Management Area, which is accessible via County Road 4015. This route heads northeast along the shore of Conconully Lake on the other side of U.S. 97. The road is narrow at first, but then becomes wider as you enter the Habitat Management Area.

㉙ Sugarload

Location: On Sugarloaf Lake in Okanogan National Forest; map A4, grid c2.

Campsites, facilities: There are four tent sites and one site for a tent, trailer, or RV up to 21 feet long. Picnic tables are provided, but there is no piped water. No garbage service is provided, so trash must be packed out. Vault toilets and firewood are available. Boat launching facilities are available nearby. Leashed pets are permitted.

Reservations, fees: No reservations are accepted. There is no fee. The campground is open from mid-May to mid-September.

Contact: Okanogan National Forest, Tonasket Ranger District, 1 West Winesap Avenue, Tonasket, WA 98855; (509) 486-2186 or fax (509) 486-5161.

Directions: From Interstate 5 south of Bellingham, turn east on Highway 20 and drive approximately 180 miles east and north to Okanogan. Turn north on County Road 9229 and drive about 17.5 miles northwest to Conconully. Turn northwest on County Road 4015 and drive 4.5 miles to the campground.

Trip notes: At 2,400 feet, this campground on the shore of Sugarloaf Lake is the smallest, most private of the camps on the lake, and one of the least used. Conconully State Park and Information Center are nearby.

㉚ Lyman Lake

Location: On Lyman Lake in Okanogan National Forest; map A4, grid c6.

Campsites, facilities: There are four sites for tents, trailers, or RVs up to 31 feet long. Picnic tables and fire grills are provided. Vault toilets are available, but there is no piped water. No garbage service is provided, so trash must be packed out. Leashed pets are permitted.

Reservations, fees: No reservations are accepted. There is no fee. The campground is open from mid-May to mid-September.

Contact: Okanogan National Forest, Tonasket Ranger District, 1 West Winesap Avenue, Tonasket, WA 98855; (509) 486-2186 or fax (509) 486-5161.

Directions: From Interstate 5 south of Bellingham, turn east on Highway 20 and drive approximately 180 miles to Okanogan. Turn north on Highway 97 and drive 30 miles to Tonasket. Continue 12.5 miles east on Highway 20, then turn southeast on County Road 9455 and drive 13 miles. Turn south on County Road 3785 and proceed 2.5 miles to the campground entrance.

Trip notes: Little known and little used, this campground along the shore of Lyman Lake is an idyllic setting for those wanting solitude and quiet. The lake is quite small, but fishing is an option for patient anglers.

㉛ Swan Lake

Location: On Swan Lake in Colville National Forest; map A4, grid c7.

Campsites, facilities: There are 25 sites for tents, trailers, or RVs up to 31 feet long. Piped water, fire grills, and picnic tables are provided. Vault toilets, firewood, boat docks, and launching facilities are available. Internal combustion engines are prohibited on the lake. Leashed pets are permitted.

Reservations, fees: No reservations are accepted. Sites are $6 per night. The campground is open from May through September.

Contact: Colville National Forest, Republic Ranger District, Republic, WA 99166; (509) 775-3305 or fax (509) 775-7401.

Directions: From Spokane on Interstate 90, turn north on U.S. 395 and drive approximately 84 miles. Turn west on Highway 20 and drive 40 miles to Republic. Turn south on Highway 21 and drive seven miles, then turn southwest on Forest Service Road 53 (Scatter Creek Road) and proceed eight miles to the campground.

Trip notes: Scenic views greet visitors on the drive to and at this campground on the shore of Swan Lake, elevation 3,700 feet. A beautiful hiking trail circles the lake, and swimming, boating, fishing, mountain biking, and hiking are some of the possibilities here. It's a good out-of-the-way spot for RV cruisers seeking a rustic setting.

㉜ Long Lake

Location: On Long Lake in Colville National Forest; map A4, grid c7.

Campsites, facilities: There are 12 sites for tents, trailers, or RVs up to 21 feet long. Piped water, fire grills, and picnic tables are provided. Vault toilets and firewood are available. Launching facilities are nearby. No internal combustion engines are allowed on the lake, and fishing is restricted (fly-fishing only). Leashed pets are permitted.

Reservations, fees: No reservations are accepted. Sites are $5 per night. The campground is open from May through September.

Contact: Colville National Forest, Republic Ranger District, Republic, WA 99166; (509) 775-3305 or fax (509) 775-7401.

Directions: From Spokane on Interstate 90, turn north on U.S. 395 and drive approximately 84 miles. Turn west on Highway 20 and drive 40 miles to Republic. From Republic, drive seven miles south on Highway 21, then turn southwest on Forest Service Road 53 (Scatter Creek Road) and continue eight miles. Turn south on Forest Service Road 400 and drive 1.5 miles to the camp.

Trip notes: Long Lake is the third and smallest of the three lakes in this area (the others are Swan Lake and Ferry Lake). Expert anglers can get a quality angling experience here. A nice hiking trail circles the lake. The drive on Highway 21 south of Republic is particularly beautiful, with views of the Sanpoil River.

㉝ Ferry Lake

Location: On Ferry Lake in Colville National Forest; map A4, grid c7.

Campsites, facilities: There are nine sites for tents, trailers, or RVs up to 20 feet long. There is no piped water. Fire grills and picnic tables are provided. Vault toilets and firewood are available. Launching facilities are nearby. Internal combustion engines are prohibited on the lake. Leashed pets are permitted.

Reservations, fees: No reservations are accepted. There is no fee. The campground is open from May through September, weather permitting.

Contact: Colville National Forest, Republic Ranger District, Republic, WA 99166; (509) 775-3305 or fax (509) 775-7401.

Directions: From Spokane on Interstate 90, turn north on U.S. 395 and drive approximately 84 miles. Turn west on Highway 20 and drive 40 miles to Republic. From Republic, drive seven miles south on Highway 21, then turn southwest on Forest Service Road 53 (Scatter Creek Road) and go six miles. Turn north on Forest Service Road 5330 and drive one mile, then continue north on Forest Service Road 100 for 500 yards to the campground.

Trip notes: This is one of three fishing lakes within a four-square-mile area. The others are Swan Lake and Long Lake. See the trip notes for campground numbers 31 and 32 for area information.

㉞ Sherman Pass Overlook

Location: At Sherman Pass in Colville National Forest; map A4, grid c9.

Campsites, facilities: There are nine sites for tents, trailers, or RVs up to 24 feet long. Hand-pumped water, fire grills, and picnic tables are provided. Vault toilets are available. Leashed pets are permitted.

Reservations, fees: No reservations are accepted. There is no fee. The campground is open from mid-May to late September.

Contact: Colville National Forest, Kettle Falls Ranger District, 255 West 11th Street, Kettle Falls, WA 99141; (509) 738-6111 or fax (509) 738-7701.

Directions: From Spokane on Interstate 90, turn north on U.S. 395 and drive approximately 84 miles. Turn west on Highway 20 and drive 19.5 miles to the campground.

Trip notes: This roadside campground is located near Sherman Pass (5,575 feet), the highest pass in the state of Washington. Sherman Pass Scenic Byway is routed by there. Several trails passing through camp provide access to various peaks and vistas in the area. No other campgrounds are in the immediate vicinity.

③⑤ Loup Loup

Location: Near Loup Loup Ski Area in Okanogan National Forest; map A4, grid d1.

Campsites, facilities: There are 25 sites for tents, trailers, or RVs up to 21 feet long. Piped water and picnic tables are provided. Vault toilets are available. Leashed pets are permitted.

Reservations, fees: For reservation and fee information, phone (509) 997-2131. The campground is open from May through September, weather permitting.

Contact: Okanogan National Forest, Methow Valley Visitor Center, P.O. Box 579, Winthrop, WA 98862; (509) 997-4000 or fax (509) 997-9770; e-mail: fsinfor@methow.com.

Directions: From Interstate 5 south of Bellingham, turn east on Highway 20 and drive approximately 145 miles to Twisp. Continue 13 miles east on Highway 20, then turn north on Forest Service Road 42 and drive one mile to the campground.

Trip notes: At 4,200 feet, this campground is set next to the Loup Loup Ski Area, which has facilities for both downhill and cross-country skiing. It's just far enough off Highway 20 to be missed by many out-of-towners.

③⑥ J.R.

Location: On Frazier Creek in Okanogan National Forest; map A4, grid d1.

Campsites, facilities: There are six sites for tents, trailers, or RVs up to 16 feet long. Piped water and picnic tables are provided. Vault toilets are available. Leashed pets are permitted.

Reservations, fees: For reservation and fee

information, phone (509) 997-4000. The campground is open from late May to early September.

Contact: Okanogan National Forest, Methow Valley Visitor Center, P.O. Box 579, Winthrop, WA 98862; (509) 997-4000 or fax (509) 997-9770; e-mail: fsinfor@methow.com.

Directions: From Interstate 5 south of Bellingham, turn east on Highway 20 and drive approximately 145 miles to Twisp. Continue 12 miles east on Highway 20 to the campground.

Trip notes: This camp can be found along Frazier Creek near the Loup Loup summit and ski area. Some of the recreation possibilities in the surrounding area include fishing, hunting, cross-country skiing, snowmobiling, hiking, and bicycling. This is a good layover for travelers looking for a spot on Highway 20.

③⑦ Rock Lakes

Location: On Rock Lake; map A4, grid d2.

Campsites, facilities: There are eight sites for tents or small trailers. Picnic tables, fire grills, and tent pads are provided. Vault toilets are available, but there is no piped water. Leashed pets are permitted.

Reservations, fees: No reservations are accepted. There is no fee. The campground is open year-round.

Contact: Department of Natural Resources, Northeast Region, P.O. Box 190, Colville, WA 99114-0190; (509) 684-7474 or fax (509) 684-7484.

Directions: From Interstate 5 at Burlington, turn east on Highway 20 and drive 164 miles to Loup Loup Canyon Road (10 miles west of Okanogan). Turn right and drive five miles. Turn left on Rock Lakes Road and drive six miles, then turn left and drive 300 yards to the campground.

Trip notes: Trout fishing can be good at this campground set in a forested area along the shore of Rock Lake. There are some hiking trails in the area. A good bet is to combine a trip here with nearby Leader Lake (see campground number 39). Highway 20 east of Interstate 5 is a designated scenic route.

⊛ Rock Creek

Location: On Rock Creek and Loup Loup Creek; map A4, grid d2.

Campsites, facilities: There are six campsites for tents or small trailers. Picnic tables, fire grills, and tent pads are provided. Vault toilets and piped water are available. Leashed pets are permitted.

Reservations, fees: No reservations are accepted. There is no fee. The campground is open year-round.

Contact: Department of Natural Resources, Northeast Region, P.O. Box 190, Colville, WA 99114-0190; (509) 684-7474 or fax (509) 684-7484.

Directions: From Interstate 5 at Burlington, turn east on Highway 20 and drive 164 miles to Loup Loup Canyon Road (10 miles west of Okanogan). Turn right and drive four miles to the camp on the left.

Trip notes: This wooded campground is at the confluence of Rock and Loup Loup Creeks. A group shelter is available. It's advisable to obtain a map detailing the area from the Department of Natural Resources.

⊛ Leader Lake

Location: On Leader Lake; map A4, grid d2.

Campsites, facilities: There are 16 sites for tents or small trailers. Picnic tables, fire grills, and tent pads are provided. Pit toilets are available, but there is no piped water. Boat launching facilities are nearby. Leashed pets are permitted.

Reservations, fees: No reservations are accepted. There is no fee. The campground is open year-round.

Contact: Department of Natural Resources, Northeast Region, P.O. Box 190, Colville, WA 99114-0190; (509) 684-7474 or fax (509) 684-7484.

Directions: From Interstate 5 at Burlington, turn east on Highway 20 and drive 166 miles to Leader Lake Road (eight miles west of Okanogan). Turn right and drive 400 yards to the campground.

Trip notes: This primitive but pretty camp set along the shore of Leader Lake is just far enough off the beaten path to get missed by many travelers. The boat ramp is an added bonus, and trout fishing can be good in season.

⊛ Eastside Park and Campground

Location: On the Okanogan River; map A4, grid d4.

Campsites, facilities: There are 50 tent sites and 76 drive-through sites for trailers or RVs of any length. Electricity, piped water, sewer hookups, and picnic tables are provided. Flush toilets, sanitary services, showers, a swimming pool, and a playground are available. A store, a cafe, a Laundromat, and ice are located within one mile. Boat launching facilities are nearby. Leashed pets are permitted.

Reservations, fees: No reservations are accepted. Sites are $10–$12 per night. The campground is open from April to late October.

Contact: Phone (509) 826-1170 or write to P.O. Box 72, Omak, WA 98841.

Directions: From Interstate 5 south of Bellingham, turn east on Highway 20 and drive approximately 180 miles east and north to Okanogan. Turn north on U.S. 97 and drive six miles to Omak. Turn east on Highway 155 and drive three-tenths of a mile to the campground.

Trip notes: This city park is in the town of Omak, along the shore of the Okanogan River. Trout fishing is excellent here, and there is a boat ramp near the campground. Nearby recreation options include an 18-hole golf course, a pool, and a sports field.

⊛ American Legion Park

Location: On the Okanogan River; map A4, grid d3.

Campsites, facilities: There are 35 sites for trailers or RVs of any length. Piped water and picnic tables are provided. Flush toilets and showers are available. A store, a cafe, a Laundromat, and ice are located within one mile.

Reservations, fees: No reservations are accepted. Sites are $3–$5 per night. The campground is open year-round.

Contact: Phone (509) 422-3600 or write to Okanogan City Hall, Okanogan, WA 98840.

Directions: From Interstate 5 south of Bellingham, turn east on Highway 20 and drive approximately 180 miles east and north to Okanogan. Turn north on Highway 215 and drive one mile to the campground.

Trip notes: This city park is located along the shore of the Okanogan River in an urban setting. The sites are graveled and sunny. Anglers may want to try their hand at the excellent bass fishing here. There is a historical museum in town.

㊷ Crawfish Lake

Location: On Crawfish Lake in Okanogan National Forest; map A4, grid d5.

Campsites, facilities: There are 19 sites for tents, trailers, or RVs up to 31 feet long. Picnic tables and fire grills are provided. Vault toilets are available, but there is no piped water. No garbage service is provided, so trash must be packed out. Boat launching facilities are located on the lake. Leashed pets are permitted.

Reservations, fees: No reservations are accepted. There is no fee. The campground is open from mid-May to mid-September.

Contact: Okanogan National Forest, Tonasket Ranger District, 1 West Winesap Avenue, Tonasket, WA 98855; (509) 486-2186 or fax (509) 486-5161.

Directions: From Interstate 5 south of Bellingham, turn east on Highway 20 and drive approximately 180 miles to Okanogan. Turn north on U.S. 97 and drive 15 miles to Riverside. Turn east on County Road 9320 and drive 18 miles. (County Road 9320 becomes Forest Service Road 30.) Drive two miles on Forest Service Road 30; turn right on Forest Service Road 3000-100 and drive for a half mile to the campground.

Trip notes: This pretty, remote, and primitive camp is set at 4,500 feet along the shore of Crawfish Lake. Fishing and crawdad hunting are popular. For the latter, just put a small piece of chicken on a hook and wait 'til the little critters get their pinchers on it.

㊸ Ten Mile

Location: On the Sanpoil River in Colville National Forest; map A4, grid d7.

Campsites, facilities: There are nine sites for tents, trailers, or RVs up to 21 feet long. Picnic tables, vault toilets, and firewood are available. There is no piped water. Leashed pets are permitted.

Reservations, fees: No reservations are accepted. There is no fee. The campground is open from mid-May to mid-October.

Contact: Colville National Forest, Republic Ranger District, Republic, WA 99166; (509) 775-3305 or fax (509) 775-7401.

Directions: From Spokane on Interstate 90, turn north on U.S. 395 and drive approximately 84 miles. Turn west on Highway 20 and drive 40 miles to Republic. From Republic, drive 10 miles south on Highway 21 and to the campground entrance.

Trip notes: Located about nine miles from Swan Lake, Ferry Lake, and Long Lake, this campground along the Sanpoil River is a good choice for a multiday trip, visiting each of the lakes. There is fishing in the Sanpoil River, and a hiking trail leads west from camp for about 2.5 miles.

㊹ Whistlin' Pine Resort

Location: On Alta Lake; map A4, grid f0.

Campsites, facilities: There are 30 tent sites and nine sites for trailers or RVs up to 30 feet long. Cabins are also available for rental. Electricity, piped water, and picnic tables are provided. Flush toilets, showers, firewood, and ice are available. Sanitary services can be found within one mile. Boat docks, launching facilities, and rentals are nearby. Pets and motorbikes are permitted.

Reservations, fees: Reservations are accepted. Sites are $13–$18 per night; cabins are $40 per night. The campground is open from April to October.

Contact: Phone (509) 923-2548 or write to P.O. Box 284, Pateros, WA 98846.

Directions: From Interstate 5 at Everett, turn east on U.S. 2 and drive 121 miles, then turn north on U.S. 97 and drive about 46 miles to Highway 153 (just south of Pateros). Drive two miles northwest on Highway 153 to Alta Lake Road, turn southwest on Alta Lake Road, and drive three miles to the resort.

Trip notes: This shorefront camp on Alta Lake offers horseback riding and a nearby 18-hole golf course. See the trip notes for Alta Lake State Park (campground number 45) for additional activities.

45 Alta Lake State Park

Location: On Alta Lake; map A4, grid f0.

Campsites, facilities: There are 11 primitive tent sites, 158 developed tent sites, and 31 sites for trailers or RVs up to 40 feet long. Picnic tables and fireplaces are provided. Flush toilets, piped water, showers, electricity, firewood, and sanitary services are available. A store, a cafe, and ice can be found within one mile. Some facilities are wheelchair accessible. Boat launching facilities are nearby. Leashed pets are permitted.

Reservations, fees: No reservations are accepted. Sites are $5–$16 per night. The campground is open year-round.

Contact: Phone (800) 233-0321 or (509) 923-2473, or write to Star Route 40, Pateros, WA 98846.

Directions: From Interstate 5 at Everett, turn east on U.S. 2 and drive 121 miles, then turn north on U.S. 97 and drive approximately 46 miles to Highway 153 (just south of Pateros). Drive two miles northwest on Highway 153 to Alta Lake Road, turn southwest on Alta Lake Road, and drive three miles to the park.

Trip notes: This state park is nestled among the pines along the shore of Alta Lake, where a half-mile-long swimming beach and boat launch are available. An 18-hole golf course and a riding stable are close by, and a nice one-mile hiking trail leads up to a scenic lookout.

46 Superstop RV Park and Marina

Location: On the Columbia River; map A4, grid f1.

Campsites, facilities: There are three tent sites and 12 sites for trailers or RVs of any length. Electricity, piped water, and sewer and cable TV hookups are provided. Flush toilets, bottled gas, sanitary services, a store, a restaurant, a laundry room, and ice are available. Boat docks and launching facilities are nearby. Leashed pets and motorbikes are permitted.

Reservations, fees: Reservations are accepted. Sites are $10–$16 per night. The campground is open year-round.

Contact: Phone (509) 923-2200, fax (509) 923-2726, or write to P.O. Box 147, Pateros, WA 98846.

Directions: From Interstate 5 at Everett, turn east on U.S. 2 and drive 121 miles, then turn north on U.S. 97 and drive about 47 miles to Pateros. The park is at the south end of town on the right.

Trip notes: This shorefront park and marina on the Columbia River is close to an 18-hole golf course, hiking trails, a riding stable, and tennis courts. Special note for RV campers: A full hookup gets you 10 percent off anything in the restaurant.

47 Bridgeport State Park

Location: On Rufus Woods Lake; map A4, grid f2.

Campsites, facilities: There are 14 sites for tents or self-contained RVs, and 20 sites with water and electrical hookups for trailers or RVs up to 45 feet long. Eight group campsites are also available. Piped water, fire grills, and picnic tables are provided. Flush toilets, showers, firewood, and a sanitary disposal station are available. A store, a cafe, and ice are located within one mile. Boat docks and launching facilities are nearby on both the upper and lower portions of the reservoir. Leashed pets are permitted.

Reservations, fees: No reservations are accepted. Sites are $10–$16 per night. The campground is open from April to late October.

Contact: Phone (800) 233-0321 or (509) 686-7231, or write to P.O. Box 846, Bridgeport, WA 98813.

Directions: From Interstate 5 south of Bellingham, turn east on Highway 20 and drive approximately 174 miles east. At Okanogan, turn south on U.S. 97 and drive 21 miles, then go south on Highway 17 and drive eight miles southeast to the park entrance.

Trip notes: Bridgeport State Park is located along the shore of Rufus Woods Lake, a reservoir on the Columbia River above the Chief Joseph Dam. Highlights include beach access and a boat launch. There are also hiking trails, but the parks department warns that rattlesnakes might be lurking in certain areas. Nearby recreation options include an 18-hole golf course.

㊽ Keller Ferry

Location: On Franklin Roosevelt Lake in Lake Roosevelt National Recreation Area; map A4, grid f8.

Campsites, facilities: There are 50 sites for tents, trailers, or RVs up to 16 feet long. Piped water, fire grills, and picnic tables are provided. Flush toilets, sanitary services, ice, and a playground are available. A cafe is located within one mile. Boat docks, launching facilities, fuel, and a marine dump station are also available. Leashed pets are permitted.

Reservations, fees: No reservations are accepted. Sites are $5–$10 per night; there is a $6 launch fee. The campground is open year-round, weather permitting.

Contact: Coulee Dam National Recreation Area, 1008 Crest Drive, Coulee Dam, WA 99116; (509) 633-9441.

Directions: From Interstate 90 at the town of Moses Lake, turn north on Highway 17 and drive 45 miles, then turn east on U.S. 2 and travel 34 miles to Wilbur. Turn north on Highway 21 and drive 14 miles to the campground.

Trip notes: This camp can be found along

the shore of Franklin Roosevelt Lake, a large reservoir created by the Grand Coulee Dam, about 15 miles west of camp. Waterskiing, fishing, and swimming are all options here.

㊾ Lakeshore Trailer Park and Marina

Location: On Lake Chelan; map A4, grid g0.

Campsites, facilities: There are 160 sites for trailers or RVs of any length. Electricity, piped water, sewer hookups, and picnic tables are provided. Flush toilets, sanitary services, and showers are available. A store, a cafe, a Laundromat, ice, a playground, and bottled gas can be found within one mile. Boat docks and launching facilities are nearby.

Reservations, fees: Reservations are accepted beginning December 15. Sites are $11–$24.50 per night. The campground is open year-round.

Contact: Phone (509) 682-8024, fax (509) 682-8248, or write to P.O. Box 1669, Chelan, WA 98816.

Directions: From Interstate 5 at Everett, turn east on U.S. 2 and drive 106 miles to the junction with U.S. 97. Turn north on U.S. 97 and drive 40 miles to Chelan. Turn north on Highway 150 (Manson Road) and drive one-half mile to the park on the left.

Trip notes: This municipal park and marina on Lake Chelan serves all members of the family, with fishing, swimming, boating, and hiking among the available activities. An 18-hole golf course, a miniature golf course, lighted tennis courts, and a visitor center are nearby. A trip worth taking is the ferry ride to one of several landings on the lake.

㊿ Steamboat Rock State Park

Location: On Banks Lake; map A4, grid g5.

Campsites, facilities: There are two primitive tent sites, five sites for tents or self-contained RVs, 100 sites with full hookups for trailers or RVs up to 60 feet long, and 13 boat-in campsites. Picnic tables and fire grills are provided. Flush toilets, a cafe, and a playground are available. Electricity, piped water, sewer hookups, and showers can be obtained for an extra fee. Some facilities are wheelchair accessible. Boat launching facilities are nearby. Leashed pets are permitted.

Reservations, fees: Contact Reservations Northwest at (800) 452-5687 ($6 reservation fee). Sites are $5–$16 per night. The campground is open year-round, with limited winter facilities.

Contact: Phone (800) 233-0321 or (509) 633-1304, or write to P.O. Box 352, Electric City, WA 99123.

Directions: From Seattle on Interstate 90, drive about 200 miles east to the town of Moses Lake. Turn north on Highway 17 and drive 45 miles. Turn east on U.S. 2 and drive five miles, then turn north on Highway 155 and drive 18 miles to the park on the left.

Trip notes: Steamboat Rock State Park is set along the shores of Banks Lake, a reservoir a few miles down from the Grand Coulee Dam. The park has a swimming beach, and fishing and waterskiing are popular. Horse trails are available in nearby Northrup Canyon. During the winter, the park is used by snowmobilers, cross-country skiers, and ice anglers.

⑤ Spring Canyon

Location: On Franklin Roosevelt Lake in Lake Roosevelt National Recreation Area; map A4, grid g6.

Campsites, facilities: There are 87 sites for tents, trailers, or self-contained RVs up to 26 feet long. Piped water, fire grills, and picnic tables are provided. Flush toilets, sanitary services, a cafe, and a playground are available. Some facilities are wheelchair accessible. Boat docks and launching facilities are available. Leashed pets are permitted.

Reservations, fees: No reservations are accepted. Sites are $5–$10 per night; there is a $6 launch fee. The campground is open year-round, weather permitting.

Contact: Lake Roosevelt National Recreation Area, 1008 Crest Drive, Coulee Dam, WA 99116; (509) 633-9441.

Directions: From Seattle on Interstate 90, drive about 200 miles east to the town of Moses Lake. Turn north on Highway 17 and drive 45 miles. Turn east on U.S. 2 and drive five miles, then turn north on Highway 155 and continue 26 miles to Grand Coulee. Turn east on Highway 174 and drive three miles to the campground entrance.

Trip notes: This large, developed campground is a popular vacation destination. Fishing for bass, walleye, trout, and sunfish are popular at the Franklin Roosevelt Lake. And, if you don't like to fish, try waterskiing. The campground is not far from the Grand Coulee Dam. Lake Roosevelt National Recreation Area offers numerous recreation options, such as programs conducted by rangers that include guided canoe trips, historical tours, campfire talks, and guided hikes. All programs are free of charge. This lake is known as a prime location to view bald eagles, especially in the winter months. Side trip options include visiting the Colville Tribal Museum in the town of Coulee Dam and touring the Grand Coulee Dam Visitor Center.

⑤ Lakeview Terrace Mobile Park 🚐🏕

Location: Near Franklin Roosevelt Lake; map A4, grid g7.

Campsites, facilities: There are 20 tent sites and 15 drive-through sites for trailers or RVs of any length. Electricity, piped water, sewer hookups, and picnic tables are provided. Flush toilets, showers, a laundry room, and a playground are available. Boat docks, launching facilities, and rentals are nearby. Pets and motorbikes are permitted.

Reservations, fees: Reservations are accepted. Sites are $15 per night. The campground is open year-round.

Contact: Phone (509) 633-2169 or write to Highway 174, Grand Coulee, WA 99133.

Directions: From Seattle on Interstate 90, drive about 200 miles east to the town of Moses Lake. Turn north on Highway 17 and drive 45 miles. Turn east on U.S. 2 and drive five miles, then turn north on Highway 155 and continue 26 miles to Grand Coulee. Turn east on Highway 174 and drive 3.5 miles east to the park entrance.

Trip notes: This pleasant resort is near Franklin Roosevelt Lake, which is created by the Grand Coulee Dam. It's a slightly less crowded option to the national park camps in the vicinity. See the trip notes for Spring Canyon (campground number 51) for water recreation options. A full-service marina and tennis courts are nearby.

53 Coulee Playland Resort and RV Park

Location: Near the Grand Coulee Dam; map A4, grid g5.

Campsites, facilities: There are 65 sites for tents, trailers, or RVs of any length. One yurt, which sleeps five, is also available. Electricity, piped water, sewer hookups, and picnic tables are provided. Flush toilets, sanitary services, a store, a laundry room, showers, firewood, ice, a playground, and a bait and tackle shop are available. Bottled gas and a cafe are located within one mile. Boat docks, launching facilities, and rentals are nearby. Pets and motorbikes are permitted.

Reservations, fees: Reservations are accepted. Sites are $14–$18 per night. The campground is open year-round, with limited winter facilities.

Contact: Phone (509) 633-2671 or write to P.O. Box 457, Electric City, WA 99123.

Directions: From Seattle on Interstate 90, drive about 200 miles east to the town of Moses Lake. Turn north on Highway 17 and drive 45 miles, then turn east on U.S. 2 and drive five miles. Turn north on Highway 155 and drive 26 miles to Electric City. The campground is just off the highway.

Trip notes: This park on North Banks Lake, south of the Grand Coulee Dam, is pretty and well treed, with spacious sites for both tents and RVs. The Grand Coulee Laser Light Show is just two miles away and well worth a visit. Hiking trails, marked bike trails, a full-service marina, and tennis courts are close by.

54 River Rue RV Park

Location: Near the Columbia River; map A4, grid h8.

Campsites, facilities: There are 86 sites for tents, trailers, or RVs. Rest rooms, showers, a sanitary dump, a pay phone, limited groceries, ice, snacks, RV supplies, fishing tackle, and LP gas are available. Recreational facilities include a playground, a sports field, and horseshoe pits. The facilities are wheelchair accessible. Leashed pets are permitted.

Reservations, fees: Reservations are recommended. Sites are $13–$18 per night. The campground is open from April through October.

Contact: Phone the park at (509) 647-2647 or write to HCR 11, Box 20, Wilbur, WA 99185.

Directions: From Spokane, drive west on U.S. 2 for about 66 miles (one mile past Wilbur). Turn north on Highway 174 and drive one-quarter of a mile. Turn north on Highway 21 and drive 13 miles to the park on the right.

Trip notes: This camp is located in high desert terrain, but it is surrounded by lots of trees. Several hiking trails leave from the campground. You can fish, swim, water-ski, or rent a houseboat at the Columbia River, which is a mile away. Another nearby side trip is the Grand Coulee Dam.

55 Blue Lake Resort

Location: On Blue Lake; map A4, grid i4.

Campsites, facilities: There are 30 tent sites and 56 sites for trailers or RVs of any length with full or partial hookups; six are drive-throughs. There are also 10 cabins which sleep up to four people. Electricity, piped water, sewer hookups, and picnic tables are provided. Flush toilets, sanitary services, firewood, showers, a store, ice, a roped swimming area, volleyball, and a playground are available. Boat docks, launching facilities, and rentals are nearby. Leashed pets and motorbikes are permitted.

Reservations, fees: Reservations are ac-

cepted. Sites are $14.50 per night; cabins are $34–$69 per night. The campground is open from April through September.

Contact: Phone (509) 632-5364 or write to 31199 Highway 17 North, Coulee City, WA 99115.

Directions: From Seattle on Interstate 90, drive about 200 miles east to exit 151. Turn right on Highway 283 North and drive 22 miles to the junction of Highway 17 and Highway 28. Turn left (north) on Highway 17 and drive approximately 15 miles to the park on the right.

Trip notes: Blue Lake Resort is in a desert-like area along the shore of Blue Lake between Sun Lakes State Park and Lake Lenore Caves State Park. Both are excellent side trips. Activities at Blue Lake include trout fishing, swimming, and boating. Tackle and boat rentals are available at the resort.

56 Sun Lakes State Park

Location: On Park Lake; map A4, grid i4.

Campsites, facilities: There are 174 sites for tents or self-contained RVs, 10 group campsites, and 18 sites with full hookups for trailers or RVs up to 50 feet long. Picnic tables are provided. Flush toilets, a sanitary disposal station, a cafe, a laundry room, ice, a swimming pool, electricity, piped water, sewer hookups, showers, and firewood are available. A store is located within one mile. Some facilities are wheelchair accessible. Boat docks, launching facilities, and rentals are nearby. Pets are permitted.

Reservations, fees: Contact Reservations Northwest at (800)452-5687 ($6 reservation fee). Sites are $11–$16 per night. The campground is open year-round.

Contact: Phone (800) 233-0321 or (509) 632-5583, or write to Star Route 1, P.O. Box 136, Coulee City, WA 99115.

Directions: From Seattle on Interstate 90, drive about 200 miles east to the town of Moses Lake. Turn north on Highway 17 and drive 38 miles to the park on your right.

Trip notes: Sun Lakes State Park is on the

shore of Park Lake, which is used primarily by boaters and water-skiers. The Lake Lenore Caves can be reached by a trail at the north end of the lake. Dry Falls and the interpretive center are also within the park boundaries. Nearby recreation possibilities include an 18-hole golf course, hiking trails, and a riding stable.

57 Coulee City Park

Location: On Banks Lake; map A4, grid i5.

Campsites, facilities: There are 100 tent sites and 60 sites for trailers or RVs up to 35 feet long; 32 are drive-throughs will full hookups. Electricity, piped water, sewer hookups, and picnic tables are provided. Flush toilets, sanitary services, showers, and a playground are available. Bottled gas, firewood, a store, a cafe, a Laundromat, and ice are located within one mile. Boat docks and launching facilities are nearby.

Reservations, fees: No reservations are accepted. Sites are $9–$12 per night. The campground is open from mid-April through September.

Contact: Phone (509) 632-5331 or write to P.O. Box 398, Coulee City, WA 99115.

Directions: From Seattle on Interstate 90, drive about 200 miles east to exit 176. Turn left one block and then right onto Highway 28. Drive through Ephrata and turn left on Highway 17 at Soap Lake. Drive north 25 miles, turn east on U.S. 2, and drive two miles to the park.

Trip notes: Coulee City Park is on the south shore of 30-mile-long Banks Lake, where boating, fishing, and waterskiing are popular. An 18-hole golf course is close by.

58 Sun Village Resort

Location: On Blue Lake; map A4, grid i4.

Campsites, facilities: There are six tent sites and 100 sites for trailers or RVs of any length; 40 are drive-throughs. Electricity, piped water, sewer hookups, and picnic tables are provided. Flush toilets, bottled gas, sanitary services, a store, a cafe, a laundry room, ice, and a playground are available. Showers and firewood can be obtained for an extra fee. Boat docks, launching facilities, and rentals are nearby. Leashed pets and motorbikes are permitted.

Reservations, fees: Reservations are accepted. Sites are $12–$16 per night. The campground is open from mid-April to October.

Contact: Phone (509) 632-5664, fax (509) 632-5360, or write to 33575 Park Lake Road NE, Coulee City, WA 99115.

Directions: From Seattle on Interstate 90, drive about 200 miles east to the town of Moses Lake. Turn north on Highway 17 and drive 36 miles to Blue Lake. Turn east on Park Lake Road (the south entrance) and drive one-half mile to the resort on the right.

Trip notes: Like Blue Lake Resort (campground number 55), this campground is along the shore of Blue Lake. The setting is hot desert, perfect for swimming and fishing. See the trip notes for Sun Lakes State Park (campground number 56) for information on the nearby state parks and other recreation options.

---

59 Sun Lakes State Park Resort 🚐

Location: Sun Lakes State Park; map A4, grid i4.

Campsites, facilities: There are 110 sites for trailers or RVs of any length; 64 are drive-throughs. Electricity, piped water, sewer hookups, and picnic tables are provided. Flush toilets, bottled gas, sanitary services, a store, showers, firewood, a cafe, a laundry room, ice, a playground, and a swimming pool are available. Boat docks, launching facilities, and rentals are nearby. Leashed pets are permitted.

Reservations, fees: Reservations are accepted. Sites are $16–$17 per night. The campground is open from mid-April to mid-October, weather permitting.

Contact: Phone (509) 632-5291 or write to 34228 Park Lake Road NE, Coulee City, WA 99115.

Directions: From Seattle on Interstate 90, drive about 200 miles east to exit 176. Turn left after one block and then right onto Highway 28. Drive through Ephrata, turn left on Highway 17 at Soap Lake, and drive 40 miles. At Park Lake Road (within Sun Lakes State Park), take a right and drive one mile east to the park.

Trip notes: This camp is run by the concessionnaire that operates within Sun Lakes State Park. It offers full facilities and is a slightly more developed alternative to the state campground. See the trip notes for Sun Lakes State Park (campground number 56).

---

60 Coulee Lodge Resort

Location: On Blue Lake; map A4, grid i4.

Campsites, facilities: There are 14 tent sites and 28 sites for trailers or RVs up to 35 feet long; 14 are drive-throughs. Electricity, piped water, sewer hookups, and picnic tables are provided. Flush toilets, bottled gas, sanitary services, a store, showers, firewood, a laundry room, boat docks, boat and jet ski rentals, launching facilities, and ice are available. A cafe is located within one mile. Some facilities are wheelchair accessible. Leashed pets and motorbikes are permitted.

Reservations, fees: Reservations are accepted. Sites are $12–$15 per night. The campground is open from mid-April to October.

Contact: Phone (509) 632-5565 or write to 33017 Park Lake Road NE, Coulee City, WA 99115.

Directions: From Seattle on Interstate 90, drive about 200 miles east to exit 176. Turn left after one block and then right onto Highway 28. Drive through Ephrata, turn left (north) on Highway 17 at Soap Lake, and drive 15 miles to the north end of Blue Lake Campground.

Trip notes: This is one of five camps in the general area and one of three in the immediate vicinity. Blue Lake offers plenty of summertime recreation options. See the trip notes for Sun Lakes State Park (campground number 56) for details.

Map A5

Washington State Map .... *page 6*
One inch equals approximately 20 miles.

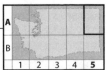

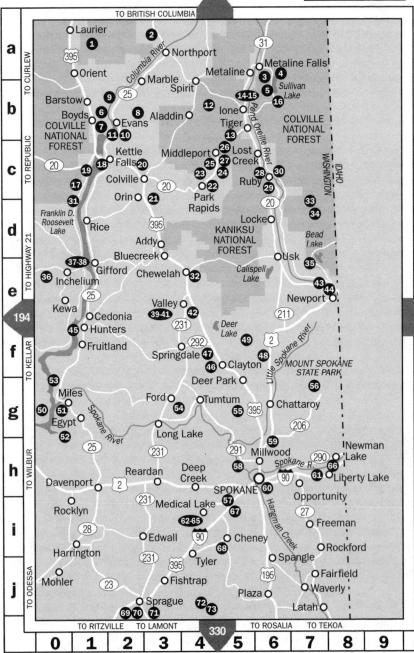

TO BRITISH COLUMBIA

a
Laurier
1
2
Northport
31
TO CURLEW
Orient
Marble
Spirit
Metaline
Metaline Falls
3 4
5   Sullivan Lake

b
Barstow
9
25
12
Ione
14-15
16
COLVILLE NATIONAL FOREST
Boyds
6
8 Aladdin
Tiger
Pend Oreille River
7
Evans
11 10
13
COLVILLE NATIONAL FOREST
Kettle Falls
Middleport
26
Lost Creek
IDAHO WASHINGTON

c
20
20
25
27
18
19
Colville
23
24
28 30
Ruby
29
17
Orin
21
22
Park Rapids
31
20
33
34

d
Franklin D. Roosevelt Lake
Rice
Addy
Locke
KANIKSU NATIONAL FOREST
Bead Lake
Bluecreek
395
TO HIGHWAY 21
37-38
Gifford
Chewelah
32
Calispell Lake
Usk
35

e
36 Inchelium
25
Valley
Newport
43 44
194
Kewa
39-41 42
231
Deer Lake
49
2
211

f
Cedonia
TO KELLAR
45 Hunters
Springdale
47
48
Fruitland
46 Clayton
MOUNT SPOKANE STATE PARK
Little Spokane River

g
53
Deer Park
56
Miles
Ford
Tumtum
50 51
54
55
395
Chattaroy
Egypt
52
Spokane River
Long Lake
206

h
231
291
Millwood
59
Newman Lake
Reardan
Deep Creek
58
Spokane R.
66
TO WILBUR
Davenport
2
SPOKANE
60
90
61 Liberty Lake
Rocklyn
57
Opportunity
28
Medical Lake
67
27
Freeman

i
62-65
Hangman Creek
Rockford
Harrington
231
Edwall
90
Cheney
Spangle
68
Fairfield
TO ODESSA
Mohler
23
395 Tyler
195
Waverly

j
Fishtrap
Plaza
Sprague
72 73
Latah
69 70 71
330
TO RITZVILLE   TO LAMONT   TO ROSALIA   TO TEKOA

0   1   2   3   4   5   6   7   8   9

Chapter A5 features:

---

❶ Pierre Lake

Location: On Pierre Lake in Colville National Forest; map A5, grid a1.

Campsites, facilities: There are 15 camp-

sites for tents, trailers, or RVs up to 24 feet long. Hand-pumped water, fire grills, and picnic tables are provided. Vault toilets, boat docks, and launching facilities are available on site. A convenience store and ice are located nearby (within seven miles). Leashed pets are permitted.

Reservations, fees: No reservations are accepted. There is no fee. The campground is open from mid-April to mid-October.

Contact: Colville National Forest, Kettle Falls Ranger District, Kettle Falls, WA 99141; (509) 738-6111 or fax (509) 738-7701.

Directions: From Spokane, turn north on U.S. 395 and drive 74 miles to Colville. Continue for about 25 miles north on U.S. 395 to Barstow. Turn north on County Road 4013 and drive nine miles to the campground.

Trip notes: Pierre Lake, a quiet, little-known jewel near the Canadian border, is the setting for this camp. It's only a short drive from U.S. 395, yet the campground gets relatively little use. Boating, fishing, and hiking are some of the recreation possibilities here.

❷ Sheep Creek

Location: On Sheep Creek; map A5, grid a3.

Campsites, facilities: There are 11 sites for tents or small trailers. Picnic tables, fire grills, and tent pads are provided. Vault toilets, piped water, and a group shelter are available. Leashed pets are permitted.

Reservations, fees: No reservations are accepted. There is no fee. The campground is open year-round.

Contact: Department of Natural Resources, Northeast Region, P.O. Box 190, Colville, WA 99114-0190; (509) 684-7474 or fax (509) 684-7484.

Directions: From Spokane, turn north on U.S. 395 and drive 84 miles to Kettle Falls. Turn north on Highway 25 and drive 33 miles to Northport. Continue one mile north on Highway 25, then turn left on Sheep Creek Road and travel four miles. Turn right into the campground.

Trip notes: This campground is in a forested area along Sheep Creek, about four miles from the Columbia River and very close to the Canadian border. It's a primitive camp, yet it has piped water. The fishing can be good nearby.

❸ Mill Pond

Location: Near Sullivan Lake in Colville National Forest; map A5, grid a6.

Campsites, facilities: There are 10 sites for tents, trailers, or RVs up to 21 feet long. Hand-pumped water, fire grills, and picnic tables are provided. Vault toilets are available. A trailer dump station is located within one mile. A small boat launch is available. Leashed pets are permitted.

Reservations, fees: For reservation and fee information, phone Sullivan Lake Ranger District at (509) 446-7500. The campground is open from late May to early September.

Contact: Colville National Forest, Sullivan Lake Ranger District, 12641 Sullivan Lake Road, Metaline Falls, WA 99153; (509) 446-7500 or fax (509) 446-7580.

Directions: From Spokane on Interstate 90, turn north on U.S. 2 and drive 48 miles to the junction with Highway 20 at the Washington/Idaho border. Turn west on Highway 20 and drive 48 miles northwest to Tiger, then turn north on Highway 31 and drive 15 miles to the town of Metaline Falls. Turn east on County Road 9345 and drive 4.5 miles to the campground.

Trip notes: Mill Pond Campground, located along the shore of a small reservoir just north of Sullivan Lake, is a good base camp for backpackers. A trail starts across the road and takes off into the backcountry. A wheelchair-accessible historical interpretive trail is located at the opposite end of the lake. There is also a pretty waterfall with a great view. All amenities are a short drive away in Metaline Falls. See the trip notes for East and West Sullivan Lakes (campground numbers 4 and 5) for other information about the area.

❹ East Sullivan

Location: On Sullivan Lake in Colville National Forest; map A5, grid a6.

Campsites, facilities: There are 38 sites for tents, trailers, or RVs up to 50 feet long. Piped water, fire grills, and picnic tables are provided. Vault toilets and a trailer dump station are available. Some facilities are wheelchair accessible. A boat dock and launching facilities are nearby. Leashed pets are permitted.

Reservations, fees: Some sites may be reserved by calling (800) 280-CAMP/2267 ($8.65 reservation fee). Contact the Sullivan Lake Ranger District at (509) 446-7500 for fee information. The campground is open from late May through August.

Contact: Colville National Forest, Sullivan Lake Ranger District, 12641 Sullivan Lake Road, Metaline Falls, WA 99153; (509) 446-7500 or fax (509) 446-7580.

Directions: From Spokane on Interstate 90, turn north on U.S. 2 and drive 48 miles to the junction with Highway 20 at the Washington/Idaho border. Turn west on Highway 20 and drive 48 miles northwest to Tiger, then turn north on Highway 31 and drive 15 miles to the town of Metaline Falls. Turn east on County Road 9345 and drive five miles. Turn east on Forest Service Road 22 and drive two-tenths of a mile to the campground.

Trip notes: This campground along the north shore of Sullivan Lake is a popular vacation destination, with boating, fishing, swimming, sailing, waterskiing, and hiking trails among the activities available. The beautiful Salmo-Priest Wilderness is located just three miles to the east. It gets light use, which means quiet, private trails. This is a prime place to view wildlife, including the rare Woodland caribou and Rocky Mountain bighorn sheep. A nearby grass airstrip provides an opportunity for fly-in camping.

❺ West Sullivan

Location: On Sullivan Lake in Colville National Forest; map A5, grid b6.

Campsites, facilities: There are six sites for tents, trailers, or RVs up to 30 feet long. Piped water, fire grills, and picnic tables are provided. Vault toilets are available. A trailer dump station is located within one mile. Some facilities are wheelchair accessible. Leashed pets are permitted.

Reservations, fees: Some sites may be re-

served by calling (800) 280-CAMP/2267 ($8.65 reservation fee). Contact the Sullivan Lake Ranger District at (509) 446-7500 for fee information. The campground is open from late May through August.

Contact: Colville National Forest, Sullivan Lake Ranger District, 12641 Sullivan Lake Road, Metaline Falls, WA 99153; (509) 446-7500 or fax (509) 446-7580.

Trip notes: This campground is set along the northwestern shore of Sullivan Lake and is a popular destination for boating, fishing, swimming, sailing, waterskiing, and hiking. A nearby grass airstrip provides the opportunity for fly-in camping.

❻ Whispering Pines RV Park

Location: On the Columbia River; map A5, grid b1.

Campsites, facilities: There are 15 tent sites and 42 sites for trailers or RVs of any length; 40 are drive-throughs. Electricity, sewer hookups, and picnic tables are provided. Flush toilets, sanitary services, a laundry room, a playground, piped water, showers, and firewood are available. Leashed pets are permitted.

Reservations, fees: Reservations are accepted. Sites are $14 per night. The campground is open year-round.

Contact: Phone (509) 738-2593 or write to P.O. Box 778, Kettle Falls, WA 99141.

Directions: From Spokane on Interstate 90, turn north on U.S. 395 and drive 84 miles to the town of Kettle Falls. Continue 6.5 miles north on U.S. 395. Turn east at the sign for the campground and drive 300 yards to the entrance.

Trip notes: This campground is a good layover for U.S. 395 RV cruisers. Located along the shore of the Columbia River, it's close to marked bike trails, a full-service marina, and tennis courts. A good side trip is to the Colville National Forest East Portal Interpretive Area, which is less than 10 miles away. To reach it, drive south to the junction of Highway 20 and go southwest for about six miles. Highlights include a nature trail and the Bangs Mountain

Auto Tour, a five-mile drive that takes you through old-growth forest to Bangs Mountain Vista overlooking the Columbia River–Kettle Falls area.

⑦ Kamloops

Location: On Franklin Roosevelt Lake in Lake Roosevelt National Recreation Area; map A5, grid b1.

Campsites, facilities: There are 14 tent sites. Picnic tables and fire grills are provided. Pit toilets are available, but there is no piped water. Boat docks are nearby. Leashed pets are permitted.

Reservations, fees: No reservations are accepted. Sites are $5–$10 per night. The campground is open year-round, weather permitting.

Contact: Lake Roosevelt National Recreation Area, 1008 Crest Drive, Coulee Dam, WA 99116; (509) 633-9441 or fax (509) 633-9332.

Directions: From Spokane on Interstate 90, turn north on U.S. 395 and drive 84 miles to the town of Kettle Falls. Continue seven miles west and then north on U.S. 395 to the campground.

Trip notes: This is one of the more primitive campgrounds located along Franklin Roosevelt Lake. It's located at Kamloops Island, an optimum area for waterskiing and fishing.

⑧ Williams Lake

Location: On Williams Lake; map A5, grid b2.

Campsites, facilities: There are eight sites for tents or small trailers. Picnic tables, fire grills, and tent pads are provided. Vault toilets, piped water, and a boat launch are available. Leashed pets are permitted.

Reservations, fees: No reservations are accepted. There is no fee. The campground is open year-round.

Contact: Department of Natural Resources, Northeast Region, P.O. Box 190, Colville, WA 99114-0190; (509) 684-7474 or fax (509) 684-7484.

Directions: From Spokane, turn north on U.S. 395 and drive 74 miles to Colville. Con-

tinue 1.5 miles north, then head north on Williams Lake Road and drive 13.7 miles. Turn left and then immediately right to the camp.

Trip notes: With a plethora of camps on nearby Franklin Roosevelt Lake, this secluded spot in a pretty, forested setting provides a less crowded alternative. It's set along the shore of Williams Lake, where the trout fishing is good. In winter, ice fishing is an option.

⑨ North Gorge

Location: On Franklin Roosevelt Lake in Lake Roosevelt National Recreation Area; map A5, grid b2.

Campsites, facilities: There are 10 sites for tents, trailers, or RVs. Piped water, fire grills, and picnic tables are provided. Pit toilets, boat docks, and launching facilities are available. Leashed pets are permitted.

Reservations, fees: No reservations are accepted. Sites are $5–$10 per night; there is a $6 launch fee. The campground is open year-round.

Contact: Lake Roosevelt National Recreation Area, 1008 Crest Drive, Coulee Dam, WA 99116; (509) 633-9441 or fax (509) 633-9332.

Directions: From Spokane on Interstate 90, turn north on U.S. 395 and drive 84 miles to the town of Kettle Falls. Turn north on Highway 25 and drive approximately 20 miles to the campground entrance.

Trip notes: This is the first of many campgrounds we discovered along the shore of 130-mile-long Franklin Roosevelt Lake, which was formed by damming the Columbia River at Coulee. Recreation options include waterskiing and swimming, plus fishing for walleye, trout, bass, and sunfish. During the winter, the lake level is drawn down and a unique trip is to walk along the barren lake's edge. See the trip notes for Kamloops (campground number 7) for more recreation information.

⑩ Evans

Location: On Franklin Roosevelt Lake in Lake Roosevelt National Recreation Area; map A5, grid b2.

Campsites, facilities: There are 46 sites for tents, trailers, or RVs up to 26 feet long. Piped water, fire grills, and picnic tables are provided. Flush toilets, a sanitary disposal station, a store, boat docks, launching facilities, and a playground are available. Some facilities are wheelchair accessible. Leashed pets are permitted.

Reservations, fees: No reservations are accepted. Sites are $5–$10 per night; there is a $6 launch fee. The campground is open year-round, with limited facilities in the winter.

Contact: Lake Roosevelt National Recreation Area, 1008 Crest Drive, Coulee Dam, WA 99116; (509) 633-9441 or fax (509) 633-9332.

Directions: From Spokane on Interstate 90, turn north on U.S. 395 and drive 84 miles to the town of Kettle Falls. Turn north on Highway 25 and drive eight miles to the campground entrance.

Trip notes: Like North Gorge, this campground is set along the shore of Franklin Roosevelt Lake. Fishing, swimming, and waterskiing are among the activities here. See the trip notes for Kamloops (campground number 7) for more information.

⑪ Marcus Island

Location: On Franklin Roosevelt Lake in Lake Roosevelt National Recreation Area; map A5, grid b2.

Campsites, facilities: There are 20 sites for tents, trailers, or RVs up to 20 feet long. Piped water, fire grills, and picnic tables are provided. Pit toilets and a boat dock are available. A store is located within one mile. Leashed pets are permitted.

Reservations, fees: No reservations are accepted. Sites are $5–$10 per night. The campground is open year-round, weather permitting.

Contact: Lake Roosevelt National Recreation Area, 1008 Crest Drive, Coulee Dam, WA 99116; (509) 633-9441 or fax (509) 633-9332.

Directions: From Spokane on Interstate 90, turn north on U.S. 395 and drive 84 miles to the town of Kettle Falls. Turn north on Highway 25 and continue four miles to the campground.

Trip notes: This campground just south of Evans (campground number 10) is quite similar to that camp, including a location nestled along the edge of Franklin Roosevelt Lake. Waterskiing, fishing, and swimming are the primary recreation options. See the trip notes for Kamloops (campground number 7) for information about the park and side trip options in the area.

⑫ Big Meadow Lake

Location: On Big Meadow Lake in Colville National Forest; map A5, grid b4.

Campsites, facilities: There are 16 sites for tents, trailers, or RVs up to 32 feet long. Fire grills, picnic tables, and vault toilets are provided, but there is no piped water. A boat launch, rest rooms, and a wheelchair-accessible nature trail and fishing pier are available. Leashed pets are permitted.

Reservations, fees: No reservations are accepted. There is no fee. The campground is open from May through September.

Contact: Colville National Forest, Colville Ranger District, 755 South Main Street, Colville, WA 99114; (509) 684-7010 or fax (509) 684-7280.

Directions: From Spokane on Interstate 90, turn north on U.S. 395 and drive 74 miles to Colville. Turn east on Highway 20 and drive one mile, then turn north on the Aladdin Highway and drive 20 miles to Meadow Creek Road. Turn east and travel six miles to the campground. Note: The road surface may be soft and/or rough, depending on the season.

Trip notes: Big Meadow Lake is at 3,400 feet with 71 surface acres. The camp, located in a beautiful scenic area, is quiet, remote, and relatively unknown. The Forest Service has provided a wildlife viewing platform and an environmental education lab near the campground.

⑬ Lake Leo

Location: On Lake Leo in Colville National Forest; map A5, grid b5.

Campsites, facilities: There are eight sites for tents, trailers, or RVs up to 15 feet long. Hand-pumped water and picnic tables are provided. Pit toilets and firewood are available. A boat ramp and launching facilities are nearby. Leashed pets are permitted.

Reservations, fees: No reservations are accepted. Sites are $5 per night. The campground is open from mid-May to mid-September.

Contact: Colville National Forest, Colville Ranger District, 755 South Main Street, Colville, WA 99114; (509) 684-7010 or fax (509) 684-7280.

Directions: From Spokane on Interstate 90, turn north on U.S. 395 and drive 74 miles to Colville. Turn east on Highway 20 and drive 23 miles to the campground.

Trip notes: Lake Leo is the northernmost and quietest camp on the chain of lakes in the immediate vicinity. Frater and Nile Lakes, both pretty small, are a mile north. In winter, there is a Nordic ski trail that starts adjacent to the camp. Fishing and boating are two options here.

⑭ Ione RV Park and Motel

Location: On the Pend Oreille River; map A5, grid b5.

Campsites, facilities: There are seven tent sites and 19 sites for trailers or RVs of any length. Electricity, piped water, sewer hookups, and picnic tables are provided. Flush toilets, sanitary services, showers, a laundry room, and a playground are available. A store, a cafe, and ice are located within one mile. Boat docks and launching facilities are nearby. Motorbikes are permitted.

Reservations, fees: Reservations are accepted. Sites are $10–$18 per night. The campground is open year-round.

Contact: Ione RV Park and Motel, P.O. Box 730, Ione, WA 99139; (509) 442-3213 or fax (509) 442-3503; e-mail: clarkd@10met.com.

Directions: From Spokane on Interstate 90, turn north on U.S. 395 and drive 74 miles to Colville. Turn east on Highway 20 and drive 36 miles, then turn north on Highway 31 and

drive four miles to Ione. The campground is located at the end of a bridge off Highway 31, two blocks south of Main Street.

Trip notes: This is a good layover for campers with RVs or trailers who want to stay in town. The park is on the shore of the Pend Oreille River, which offers pan fishing, swimming, and boating. There are several bike trails in the area as well.

⑮ Edgewater

Location: On the Pend Oreille River in Colville National Forest; map A5, grid b5.

Campsites, facilities: There are 23 sites for tents, trailers, or RVs up to 20 feet long. Piped water, fire grills, and picnic tables are provided. Vault toilets are available. A boat launch is nearby. Leashed pets are permitted.

Reservations, fees: No reservations are accepted. Contact the Sullivan Lake Ranger District at (509) 446-7500 for fee information. The campground is open from late May to early September.

Contact: Colville National Forest, Sullivan Lake Ranger District, 12641 Sullivan Lake Road, Metaline Falls, WA 99153; (509) 446-7500 or fax (509) 446-7580.

Directions: From Spokane on Interstate 90, turn north on U.S. 2 and drive 48 miles to the junction with Highway 20 at the Washington/Idaho border. Turn west on Highway 20 and drive 48 miles northwest to Tiger. Turn north on Highway 31 and drive three miles to County Road 9345 (one mile south of Ione). Turn east and drive two-tenths of a mile, then turn north on County Road 3669 and drive two miles. Turn west and proceed to the campground.

Trip notes: Edgewater can be found on the shore of the Pend Oreille River, about two miles upstream from the Box Canyon Dam. The camp is not far out of Ione, yet it has a primitive feel to it. Fishing is a popular activity here.

⑯ Noisy Creek

Location: On Sullivan Lake in Colville National Forest; map A5, grid b6.

Campsites, facilities: There are 19 sites for trailers or RVs up to 35 feet long. Piped water, fire grills, and picnic tables are provided. Vault toilets are available. Boat launching facilities are nearby. Leashed pets are permitted.

Reservations, fees: Some sites can be reserved by calling (800) 280-CAMP/2267 ($8.65 reservation fee). Contact the Sullivan Lake Ranger District at (509) 446-7500 for fee information. The campground is open from late May to early September.

Contact: Colville National Forest, Sullivan Lake Ranger District, 12641 Sullivan Lake Road, Metaline Falls, WA 99153; (509) 446-7500 or fax (509) 446-7580.

Directions: From Spokane on Interstate 90, turn north on U.S. 2 and drive 48 miles to the junction with Highway 20 at the Washington/Idaho border. Turn west on Highway 20 and drive 48 miles northwest to Tiger. Turn north on Highway 31 and drive three miles to County Road 9345 (one mile south of Ione). Turn east and drive nine miles to the campground.

Trip notes: This campground is situated in an idyllic setting, adjacent to where Noisy Creek pours into Sullivan Lake. Waterskiing is allowed on the 3.5-mile-long lake. A trail near camp heads east along Noisy Creek and then north up to Hall Mountain (elevation 6,323 feet), which is bighorn sheep country.

⑰ Lake Ellen

Location: On Lake Ellen in Colville National Forest; map A5, grid c1.

Campsites, facilities: There are 11 sites for tents, trailers, or RVs up to 22 feet long. Hand-pumped water and picnic tables are provided. Vault toilets and boat docks are available. Some facilities are wheelchair accessible. Leashed pets are permitted.

Reservations, fees: No reservations are accepted. There is no fee. The campground is open from mid-April to mid-October.

Contact: Colville National Forest, Kettle Falls Ranger District, Kettle Falls, WA 99141; (509) 738-6111 or fax (509) 738-7701.

Directions: From Spokane, turn north on U.S. 395 and drive approximately 87 miles.

Head west on Highway 20 for four miles to County Road 3. Turn left and drive south for 4.5 miles, then turn right on County Road 412 and drive five miles to the campground.

Trip notes: Fishing and swimming are permitted on this good-sized lake, located about three miles west of the Columbia River and the Lake Roosevelt National Recreation Area. See a Forest Service map for details.

⑱ Kettle Falls

Location: On Franklin Roosevelt Lake in Lake Roosevelt National Recreation Area; map A5, grid c1.

Campsites, facilities: There are 77 sites for tents, trailers, or RVs up to 26 feet long. Piped water, fire grills, and picnic tables are provided. Flush toilets, a sanitary disposal station, firewood, a cafe, and a playground are available. A store is located within one mile. Some facilities are wheelchair accessible. Boat docks, fuel, and launching facilities are available. Leashed pets are permitted.

Reservations, fees: No reservations are accepted. Sites are $5–$10 per night; there is a $6 launch fee. The campground is open year-round, with limited facilities in the winter.

Contact: Lake Roosevelt National Recreation Area, 1008 Crest Drive, Coulee Dam, WA 99116; (509) 633-9441 or fax (509) 633-9332.

Directions: From Spokane on Interstate 90, turn north on U.S. 395 and drive 84 miles to the town of Kettle Falls. Continue two miles west on U.S. 395 to the campground entrance.

Trip notes: This is a modern, developed campground that attracts fairly heavy use in the summer months. It's located along the shore of Franklin Roosevelt Lake, where waterskiing, swimming, and fishing are all options. In the summer, the rangers offer campfire programs in the evenings.

⑲ Canyon Creek

Location: Near the East Portal Historical Site in Colville National Forest; map A5, grid c1.

Campsites, facilities: There are 12 sites for tents, trailers, or RVs up to 30 feet long. Hand-pumped water, fire grills, and picnic tables are provided. Vault toilets are available. Some facilities are wheelchair accessible. Pets are permitted.

Reservations, fees: No reservations are accepted. There is no fee. The campground is open from mid-April to late October.

Contact: Colville National Forest, Kettle Falls Ranger District, Kettle Falls, WA 99141; (509) 738-6111 or fax (509) 738-7701.

Directions: From Spokane, turn north on U.S. 395 and drive approximately 87 miles. Head west on Highway 20 for 11 miles, then turn left and drive south on Forest Road 136 for one-third of a mile to the campground.

Trip notes: This roadside campground is located near the Bangs Mountain Auto Tour and within hiking distance of the East Portal Historical Site. It's a very pretty area not far from the Columbia River, which offers a myriad of recreation options.

⑳ Douglas Falls

Location: On Mill Creek; map A5, grid c2.

Campsites, facilities: There are 10 sites for tents or small trailers. Picnic tables, fire grills, and tent pads are provided. Vault toilets and piped water are available. A barrier-free vault toilet, trails, and picnic areas are also available. A baseball field is nearby. Leashed pets are permitted.

Reservations, fees: No reservations are accepted. There is no fee. The campground is open from April through November.

Contact: Department of Natural Resources, Northeast Region, P.O. Box 190, Colville, WA 99114-0190; (509) 684-7474 or fax (509) 684-7484.

Directions: From Spokane, turn north on U.S. 395 and drive 74 miles to Colville. Turn east on Highway 20, then take Aladdin Road north. Drive two miles, then continue straight for five miles. You'll see the parking area on the left.

Trip notes: This campground in a wooded area along Mill Creek near Douglas Falls, just

outside of town, is one of the best deals in the state, and a great camp for families or groups. It has piped water, a beautiful setting, easy access, a waterfall nearby, and even a baseball field, all for free.

㉑ Rocky Lake

Location: On Rocky Lake; map A5, grid d3.

Campsites, facilities: There are seven sites for tents or small trailers. Picnic tables, fire grills, and tent pads are provided. Vault toilets, piped water, and a boat launch are available. Leashed pets are permitted.

Reservations, fees: No reservations are accepted. There is no fee. The campground is open year-round.

Contact: Department of Natural Resources, Northeast Region, P.O. Box 190, Colville, WA 99114-0190; (509) 684-7474 or fax (509) 684-7484.

Directions: From Spokane, turn north on U.S. 395 and drive 74 miles to Colville. Turn east on Highway 20 and drive six miles east, then turn right on Artman-Gibson Road and continue three miles. Turn right again onto a one-lane gravel road and drive about one-half mile. Stay to the left and continue another two miles to the campground.

Trip notes: This isn't exactly paradise, but remarkable recreational diversity is just down the road. The campground is set on Rocky Lake, a shallow, weedy pond lined with a lot of rocks. But if you backtrack a bit on Rocky Lake Road, you'll see the entrance signs for the nearby Little Pend Oreille Habitat Management Area, a premium area for hiking, fishing, hunting, and photographing wildlife.

㉒ Flodelle Creek

Location: On Flodelle Creek; map A5, grid c4.

Campsites, facilities: There are eight sites for tents or small trailers. Picnic tables, fire grills, and tent pads are provided. Vault toilets and piped water are available. Leashed pets and motorbikes are permitted.

Reservations, fees: No reservations are ac-

cepted. There is no fee. The campground is open year-round.

Contact: Department of Natural Resources, Northeast Region, P.O. Box 190, Colville, WA 99114-0190; (509) 684-7474 or fax (509) 684-7484.

Directions: From Spokane, turn north on U.S. 395 and drive 74 miles to Colville. Go east on Highway 20 and drive 20 miles. Turn right on a two-lane gravel road and travel 300 yards, then turn left and drive 100 yards to the campground entrance.

Trip notes: This little-known campground is set along the banks of Flodelle Creek, where hiking, hunting, and fishing are quite good. It's advisable to obtain a detailed map of the area from the Department of Natural Resources. Motorbike trails are also available at this camp and are often used, so don't count on a particularly quiet spot.

㉓ Little Twin Lakes

Location: On Little Twin Lakes in Colville National Forest; map A5, grid c4.

Campsites, facilities: There are 20 sites for tents, trailers, or RVs up to 16 feet long. Fire grills and picnic tables are provided. There is no piped water. Pit toilets and firewood are available. Boat docks and launching facilities are located nearby. Leashed pets are permitted.

Reservations, fees: No reservations are accepted. There is no fee. The campground is open from mid-May to late September.

Contact: Colville National Forest, Colville Ranger District, 755 South Main Street, Colville, WA 99114; (509) 684-7010 or fax (509) 684-7280.

Directions: From Spokane, turn north on U.S. 395 and drive 74 miles to Colville. Turn east on Highway 20 and drive 12.5 miles, then turn northeast on County Road 4915 and drive 1.5 miles. Turn north on Forest Service Road 4939 and drive 4.5 miles to the campground.

Trip notes: Sites at this pretty, wooded campground on the shore of Little Twin Lakes have lake views and an unbeatable price. It's rare

to find such a nice spot on the water for free. See the trip notes for North Gorge (campground number 9) for more information.

㉔ Lake Gillette

Location: On Lake Gillette in Colville National Forest; map A5, grid c5.

Campsites, facilities: There are 14 sites for tents, trailers, or RVs up to 31 feet long. Piped water, fire grills, and picnic tables are provided. Vault toilets and sanitary services are available. A store and ice are located within one mile. Some facilities are wheelchair accessible. Boat docks, launching facilities, and rentals are nearby. Leashed pets are permitted.

Reservations, fees: No reservations are accepted. Sites are $5–$10 per night. The campground is open from mid-May to late September.

Contact: Colville National Forest, Colville Ranger District, 755 South Main Street, Colville, WA 99114; (509) 684-7010 or fax (509) 684-7280.

Directions: From Spokane on Interstate 90, turn north on U.S. 395 and drive 74 miles to Colville. Turn east on Highway 20 and drive 20 miles. Continue east on County Road 200 for one-half mile to the campground on the right.

Trip notes: This beautiful, popular camp is right on the shore of Lake Gillette. Like neighboring East Gillette Campground (campground number 25), it fills up fast in the summer. The camp is popular with off-road vehicle users.

㉕ East Gillette

Location: Near Lake Gillette in Colville National Forest; map A5, grid c5.

Campsites, facilities: There are 30 sites for tents, trailers, or RVs up to 31 feet long. Piped water, fire grills, and picnic tables are provided. Vault toilets and sanitary services are available. A store and ice are located within one mile. Some facilities are wheelchair accessible. Boat docks, launching facilities, and rentals are nearby. Leashed pets are permitted.

Reservations, fees: No reservations are

accepted. Sites are $5–$10 per night. The campground is open from mid-May to late September.

Contact: Colville National Forest, Colville Ranger District, 755 South Main Street, Colville, WA 99114; (509) 684-7010 or fax (509) 684-7280.

Directions: From Spokane on Interstate 90, turn north on U.S. 395 and drive 74 miles to Colville. Turn east on Highway 20 and drive 20 miles. Continue east on County Road 200 for one-half mile to the campground on the left.

Trip notes: This beautiful—and extremely popular—campground is near Lake Gillette, just south of Beaver Lodge Resort and Lake Thomas, one in a chain of seven lakes. There are a few hiking trails in the area. See the trip notes for Beaver Lodge Resort (campground number 27) for other recreation information. Be sure to make reservations early.

㉖ Lake Thomas

Location: On Lake Thomas in Colville National Forest; map A5, grid c5.

Campsites, facilities: There are 15 tent sites. Piped water, fire grills, and picnic tables are provided. Vault toilets and firewood are available. Sanitary services are located within one mile. Boat docks, launching facilities, and rentals are nearby. Leashed pets are permitted.

Reservations, fees: No reservations are accepted. Sites are $5 per night. The campground is open from mid-May to late September.

Contact: Colville National Forest, Colville Ranger District, 755 South Main Street, Colville, WA 99114; (509) 684-7010 or fax (509) 684-7280.

Directions: From Spokane on Interstate 90, turn north on U.S. 395 and drive 74 miles to Colville. Turn east on Highway 20 and drive 20 miles. Continue east on County Road 200 for one mile to the campground.

Trip notes: This camp on the shore of Lake Thomas is a less crowded alternative to the campgrounds at Lake Gillette. See the trip notes for Lake Gillette, East Gillette, and Beaver Lodge Resort (campground numbers 24, 25, and 27) for recreation information.

㉗ Beaver Lodge Resort

Location: On Lake Thomas; map A5, grid c5.

Campsites, facilities: There are 35 sites for trailers or RVs of any length. Several cabins are also available. Electricity, piped water, sewer hookups, and picnic tables are provided. Flush toilets, bottled gas, showers, firewood, a recreation hall, a store, a cafe, ice, and a playground are available. Sanitary services are located within one mile. Boat docks, launching facilities, and rentals are nearby. Leashed pets and motorbikes are permitted.

Reservations, fees: Reservations are accepted. Sites are $8–$14 per night; cabins are $40 per night. The campground is open year-round.

Contact: Phone (509) 684-5657 or write to 2430 Highway 20 East, Colville, WA 99114.

Directions: From Spokane on Interstate 90, turn north on U.S. 395 and drive 74 miles to Colville. Turn east on Highway 20 and drive 25 miles to the lodge on the right.

Trip notes: This developed camp is along the shore of Lake Gillette, one in a chain of seven lakes. Information is available at Little Pend Oreille at the southern end of the chain. Hiking trails and marked bike trails are close to the camp, and a Nordic ski trail can be found at Lake Leo at the northern end of the lake chain during the winter.

㉘ Blueside Resort

Location: On the Pend Oreille River; map A5, grid c6.

Campsites, facilities: There are 20 tent sites and 46 sites for trailers or RVs of any length; four are drive-throughs. There are also five cabins. Electricity, piped water, sewer hookups, and picnic tables are provided. Flush toilets, sanitary services, showers, a recreation hall, several sports fields, a store, a laundry room, ice, firewood, a playground, a swimming pool, boat docks, launching facilities, and boat fuel are available. Leashed pets and motorbikes are permitted.

Reservations, fees: Reservations are accepted. Sites are $12–$16 per night. The campground is open year-round, but only cabins are available in the winter.

Contact: Phone (509) 445-1327, fax (509) 445-1118, or write to 400041 Highway 20, Cusick, WA 99119.

Directions: From Spokane on Interstate 90, turn north on U.S. 2 and drive 48 miles to the junction with Highway 20 at the Washington/Idaho border. Turn west on Highway 20 and drive 37 miles to the park, located at milepost 400 on the right.

Trip notes: Trout fishing is excellent at this resort along the shore of the Pend Oreille River. The resort offers full facilities for anglers, including tackle, boat rentals, and a marina. The park is lovely, with grassy, shaded sites. Nearby recreation options include marked bike trails. The only other campground in the vicinity is the Outpost Resort (see next listing).

29 Outpost Resort

Location: On the Pend Oreille River; map A5, grid c6.

Campsites, facilities: There are 12 tent sites and 12 drive-through sites with full hookups for trailers or RVs of any length. There are also four cabins. Picnic tables are provided. Flush toilets, sanitary services, a store, a cafe, ice, electricity, piped water, sewer hookups, showers, boat docks, and launching facilities are available. Leashed pets and motorbikes are permitted.

Reservations, fees: Reservations are accepted. Sites are $10–$15 per night; cabins are $40–$60 per night. The campground is open year-round, with limited winter facilities.

Contact: Phone (509) 445-1317 or write to 405351 Highway 20, Cusick, WA 99119.

Directions: From Spokane on Interstate 90, turn north on U.S. 2 and drive 48 miles to the junction with Highway 20 at the Washington/Idaho border. Turn west on Highway 20 and drive 33 miles. The resort is between mile markers 405 and 406.

Trip notes: This comfortable campground in a pretty setting along the shore of the Pend Oreille River has fairly spacious sites. If you're cruising Highway 20, Blueside Resort (campground number 28) is located about five miles north, the nearest alternative if this camp is full.

30 Panhandle

Location: On the Pend Oreille River in Colville National Forest; map A5, grid c6.

Campsites, facilities: There are 11 sites for tents, trailers, or RVs up to 30 feet long. Piped water and picnic tables are provided. Vault toilets are available. Leashed pets are permitted.

Reservations, fees: No reservations are accepted. Sites are $8 per night. The campground is open from late May to late September.

Contact: Colville National Forest, Newport Ranger District, 315 North Warren Avenue, Newport, WA 99156; (541) 447-7300 or fax (541) 858-2402.

Directions: From Spokane on Interstate 90, turn north on U.S. 2 and drive 30 miles to the Metaline turnoff. Take Highway 211 West and drive for 15 miles to the junction of Highway 20. Cross Highway 20, driving through the town of Usk. Continue across the Pend Oreille River. Turn left after crossing the bridge and drive 15 miles north on Le Clerk Road to the campground on the left.

Trip notes: Here's a scenic spot to set up camp along the shore of the Pend Oreille River. This is a good base for a fishing or waterskiing trip. The campground is located directly across the river from the Outpost Resort (campground number 29). A network of hiking trails can be accessed by taking Forest Service roads to the east. See a Forest Service map for details.

31 Haag Cove

Location: On Franklin Roosevelt Lake in Lake Roosevelt National Recreation Area; map A5, grid d1.

Campsites, facilities: There are 18 sites for tents, trailers, or RVs up to 26 feet long. Piped water, fire grills, and picnic tables are provided. Pit toilets and boat docks are available. Leashed pets are permitted.

Reservations, fees: No reservations are accepted. Sites are $5–$10 per night. The campground is open year-round, weather permitting.

Contact: Lake Roosevelt National Recreation Area, 1008 Crest Drive, Coulee Dam, WA 99116; (509) 633-9441 or fax (509) 633-9332.

Directions: From Spokane on Interstate 90, turn north on U.S. 395 and drive 84 miles to the town of Kettle Falls. Turn west on Highway 20 and drive 12 miles to County Road 3. Turn south and drive five miles to the campground.

Trip notes: This campground is tucked away in a cove along the shore of Franklin Roosevelt Lake (Columbia River). A good side trip is to the Sherman Creek Habitat Management Area, located just north of camp. It's rugged and steep, but a good place to see and photograph wildlife.

㉜ The New 49er Motel and RV Park

Location: Near Chewelah; map A5, grid e4.

Campsites, facilities: There are 25 drive-through sites with full hookups for trailers or RVs up to 30 feet long. Electricity, piped water, sewer hookups, and picnic tables are provided. Flush toilets, sanitary services, showers, a spa, a recreation hall, ice, and a swimming pool are available. Bottled gas, a store, a cafe, and a Laundromat are located within one mile. Pets are permitted.

Reservations, fees: Reservations are accepted. Sites are $16.50 per night. The campground is open year-round.

Contact: Phone (509) 935-8613, fax (509) 935-8705, or write to South 311 Park Street, Chewelah, WA 99109.

Directions: From Spokane on Interstate 90, turn north on U.S. 395 and drive 44 miles to Chewelah. The park is on the south edge of town (follow the signs).

Trip notes: This is the heart of mining country. The park is in a mountainous setting next to a motel, with grassy sites. Nearby recreation options include an 18-hole golf course,

hiking trails, and marked bike trails. This is a good deal for RV cruisers—a rustic setting right in town.

㉝ Browns Lake

Location: On Browns Lake in Colville National Forest; map A5, grid d7.

Campsites, facilities: There are 18 sites for tents, trailers, or RVs up to 21 feet long. Hand-pumped water and picnic tables are provided. Vault toilets are available. A primitive boat launch is available for small boats such as canoes, row boats, and inflatables. Leashed pets are permitted.

Reservations, fees: No reservations are accepted. Sites are $8 per night, plus $4 per extra vehicle. The campground is open from late May to late September.

Contact: Colville National Forest, Newport Ranger District, 315 North Warren Avenue, Newport, WA 99156; (541) 447-7300 or fax (541) 858-2402.

Directions: From Spokane, turn north on U.S. 2 and drive for 30 miles to the Metaline cutoff (Highway 211). Take Highway 211 for 15 miles to the junction of Highway 20 at the town of Usk. From Usk, continue on Highway 20 across the Pend Oreille River. Turn east on County Road 3389 and drive for 6.5 miles, then turn north on Forest Service Road 5030 and continue three miles to the campground.

Trip notes: This campground is set along the shore of Browns Lake about five miles from South Skookum Lake. No motorized boats are permitted on the lake, and only fly-fishing is allowed. A hiking trail leaves the campground and ties into a wheelchair-accessible interpretive trail with beautiful views along way.

㉞ South Skookum Lake

Location: On South Skookum Lake in Colville National Forest; map A5, grid d7.

Campsites, facilities: There are 24 sites for tents, trailers, or RVs up to 30 feet long. Hand-pumped water and picnic tables are provided.

Vault toilets, a boat launch for small boats, and a wheelchair-accessible fishing dock are available. Leashed pets are permitted.

Reservations, fees: No reservations are accepted. Sites are $8 per night, plus $4 per extra vehicle. The campground is open from late May to late September.

Contact: Colville National Forest, Newport Ranger District, 315 North Warren Avenue, Newport, WA 99156; (541) 447-7300 or fax (541) 858-2402.

Directions: From Spokane, turn north on U.S. 2 and drive for 30 miles to the Metaline cutoff (Highway 211). Take Highway 211 for 15 miles to the junction of Highway 20. Cross Highway 20 to the town of Usk. From Usk, proceed across the Pend Oreille River and continue east on County Road 3389 for 7.5 miles to the campground.

Trip notes: The western shore of South Skookum Lake, at the foot of Kings Mountain (elevation 4,383 feet), is the site of this camp. A 1.3-mile-long hiking trail circles the water, and a spur trail has an overlook of the lake and a view of Kings Mountain.

㉟ Skookum Creek

Location: Near the Pend Oreille River; map A5, grid e7.

Campsites, facilities: There are 10 sites for tents or small trailers. Picnic tables, fire grills, and tent pads are provided. Vault toilets and piped water are available. Leashed pets are permitted.

Reservations, fees: No reservations are accepted. There is no fee. The campground is open year-round.

Contact: Department of Natural Resources, Northeast Region, P.O. Box 190, Colville, WA 99114-0190; (509) 684-7474 or fax (509) 684-7484.

Directions: From Spokane, turn north on U.S. 2 and drive 48 miles to Newport. Turn west on Highway 20 and drive 16 miles northwest to the town of Usk. Continue east across the bridge and turn right on LeClerc Road. Drive 2.5 miles, then turn left and drive about 400 yards to the campground on the left.

Trip notes: This campground is in a wooded area along Skookum Creek, about 1.5 miles from where it empties into the Pend Oreille River. It's a good canoeing spot, has piped water, and gets little attention. And you can't beat the price of admission.

㊱ Rainbow Beach Resort

Location: On Twin Lakes Reservoir; map A5, grid e0.

Campsites, facilities: There are three tent sites and 14 sites for trailers or RVs of any length; five are drive-throughs. Electricity, piped water, sewer hookups, and picnic tables are provided. Flush toilets, bottled gas, sanitary services, a shower, firewood, a recreation hall, a store, a laundry room, ice, and a playground are available. Boat docks, launching facilities, and rentals are nearby. Leashed pets are permitted.

Reservations, fees: Reservations are required. Sites are $8.50–$14 per night. The campground is open year-round.

Contact: Phone (509) 722-5901, fax (509) 722-5905, or write to HC 1, Box 146, Inchelium, WA 99138.

Directions: From Spokane on Interstate 90, turn north on U.S. 395 and drive 84 miles to the town of Kettle Falls. Turn east on Highway 20 and drive about five miles to the turnoff for Inchelium. Turn south and drive about 20 miles to Inchelium, then turn west on Bridge Creek–Twin Lakes County Road and drive two miles to Stranger Creek Road. Turn left and drive one-quarter of a mile to the resort on the right.

Trip notes: This quality resort is set along the shore of Twin Lakes Reservoir in the Colville Indian Reservation. Nearby recreation options include hiking trails, marked bike trails, a full-service marina, and tennis courts.

㊲ Clover Leaf

Location: On Franklin Roosevelt Lake in Lake Roosevelt National Recreation Area; map A5, grid e1.

Campsites, facilities: There are eight tent

sites. Piped water, fire grills, and picnic tables are provided. Pit toilets and a boat dock are available. Leashed pets are permitted.

Reservations, fees: No reservations are accepted. Sites are $5–$10 per night; there is a $6 launch fee. The campground is open year-round, with limited winter facilities.

Contact: Lake Roosevelt National Recreation Area, 1008 Crest Drive, Coulee Dam, WA 99116; (509) 633-9441 or fax (509) 633-9332.

Directions: From Spokane on Interstate 90, turn west on U.S. 2 and drive 34 miles, then turn north on Highway 25 and drive 61 miles. The campground is located about two miles south of Gifford.

Trip notes: This camp is small and quite primitive. In this particular area of Roosevelt Lake, waterskiing is not advised, but fishing is fine. See the trip notes for Kamloops and North Gorge (campground numbers 7 and 9) for recreation details.

⏰ Gifford

Location: On Franklin Roosevelt Lake in Lake Roosevelt National Recreation Area; map A5, grid e1.

Campsites, facilities: There are 47 sites for tents, trailers, or RVs up to 20 feet long. Piped water, fire grills, and picnic tables are provided. Pit toilets are available. Boat docks and launching facilities are nearby. Leashed pets are permitted.

Reservations, fees: No reservations are accepted. Sites are $5–$10 per night; there is a $6 launch fee. The campground is open year-round, with limited winter facilities.

Contact: Lake Roosevelt National Recreation Area, 1008 Crest Drive, Coulee Dam, WA 99116; (509) 633-9441 or fax (509) 633-9332.

Directions: From Spokane on Interstate 90, turn west on U.S. 2 and drive 34 miles, then turn north on Highway 25 and drive 60 miles. The campground is located about three miles south of Gifford.

Trip notes: Fishing and waterskiing are two of the draws at this camp on the shore of Franklin Roosevelt Lake (Columbia River). For a more detailed description of Roosevelt Lake,

see the trip notes for Kamloops and North Gorge (campground numbers 7 and 9).

⏰ Winona Beach Resort and RV Park

Location: On Waitts Lake; map A5, grid e3.

Campsites, facilities: There are 17 tent sites and 38 drive-through sites for trailers or RVs of any length. Electricity, piped water, sewer hookups, and picnic tables are provided. Flush toilets, showers, sanitary services, firewood, a recreation hall, a general store, a cafe, an antique store, and ice are available. Boat docks, launching facilities, and rentals are on site. Leashed pets and motorbikes are permitted.

Reservations, fees: Reservations are accepted. Sites are $12–$18 per night; a fee is charged for pets. The campground is open from April through October.

Contact: Phone (509) 937-2231, fax (509) 937-2215, or write to 33022 Winona Beach Road, Valley, WA 99181.

Directions: From Spokane on Interstate 90, turn north on U.S. 395 and drive 42 miles. Turn west at Valley exit 1 on Waitts Lake Road and and drive five miles to the resort.

Trip notes: This beautiful and comfortable resort on the shore of Waitts Lake has spacious sites and friendly folks. In the spring, the fishing for brown trout and rainbow trout can be quite good. The trout head to deeper water in the summer, and bluegill and perch are easier to catch.

⏰ Silver Beach Resort

Location: On Waitts Lake; map A5, grid e3.

Campsites, facilities: There are 53 sites for trailers or RVs of any length; two are drive-throughs. Electricity, piped water, sewer hookups, and picnic tables are provided. Flush toilets, bottled gas, sanitary services, a recreation hall, a store, showers, a restaurant, a laundry room, ice, a playground, boat docks, launching facilities, and boat rentals are available. Leashed pets are permitted.

Reservations, fees: Reservations are accepted. Sites are $13–$16 per night. The campground is open from late April through September.

Contact: Phone (509) 937-2811, fax (509) 937-2812, or write to 3323 Waitts Lake Road, Valley, WA 99181.

Directions: From Spokane on Interstate 90, turn north on U.S. 395 and drive 38 miles north to the Valley exit, then head west for six miles until you get to Waitts Lake. The resort is on the lake.

Trip notes: Silver Beach Resort offers grassy sites on the shore of Waitts Lake, where fishing and waterskiing are popular. See the trip notes for Winona Beach Resort and RV Park (campground number 39) for information about the lake.

㊶ Waitts Lake Resort

Location: On Waitts Lake; map A5, grid e3.

Campsites, facilities: There are 22 sites for tents, trailers, or RVs of any length; 13 have partial and five have full hookups. Electricity, piped water, and picnic tables are provided. Flush toilets, showers, a store, a restaurant, firewood, boat docks, boat rentals, launching facilities, and ice are available.

Reservations, fees: Reservations are required. Sites are $12.50–$16.50 per night. The campground is open from early April to late October.

Contact: Phone (509) 937-2400 or write to 3365 Waitts Lake Road, Valley, WA 99181.

Directions: From Spokane on Interstate 90, turn north on U.S. 395 and drive 42 miles. Turn north on Highway 232 and drive 1.5 miles, then go west on Highway 231 to Waitts Lake.

Trip notes: The shore of Waitts Lake is the home of this clean, comfortable resort, where lake views are available. See the trip notes for Winona Beach Resort and RV Park (campground number 39) for information about the lake.

㊷ Jump Off Joe Mobile Park and Resort

Location: On Jump Off Joe Lake; map A5, grid e4.

Campsites, facilities: There are 20 sites for tents and 19 sites for trailers or RVs. Rest rooms, showers, a pay phone, horseshoe pits, a recreation field, a store, and a barbecue are available. The camp also rents boats and has a boat ramp and dock. The facilities are wheelchair accessible. Leashed pets are permitted.

Reservations, fees: Reservations are recommended. Sites are $12–$15 per night. The campground is open from April through October.

Contact: Phone the resort at (509) 937-2133 or write to 3290 East Jump Off Joe Road, Valley, WA 99181.

Directions: From Spokane on Interstate 90, turn north on U.S. 395. Take the Jump Off Joe Road exit (three miles south of the town of Valley) and drive west on Jump Off Joe Road for 1.2 miles to the campground on the right.

Trip notes: Located on the edge of Jump Off Joe Lake, this wooded campground offers lake views and easy boating access. Recreational activities include boating, fishing, and swimming. Spokane and the Grand Coulee Dam are both within a short drive and provide excellent side trip options.

㊸ Pioneer Park

Location: On the Pend Oreille River in Colville National Forest; map A5, grid e8.

Campsites, facilities: There are 14 sites for tents, trailers, or RVs up to 24 feet long. Piped water and picnic tables are provided. Vault toilets are available. Boat docks, launching facilities, and rentals are nearby. Leashed pets are permitted.

Reservations, fees: No reservations are accepted. Sites are $8 per night. The campground is open from late May to late September.

Contact: Colville National Forest, Newport Ranger District, 315 North Warren Avenue, Newport, WA 99156; (541) 447-7300 or fax (541) 858-2402.

Directions: From Spokane, turn north on U.S. 2 and drive 41 miles to Newport. Continue across the Pend Oreille River and take an immediate left onto LeClerc Road. Travel two miles to the campground.

Trip notes: Pioneer Park Campground hails from the shore of Box Canyon Reservoir on the Pend Oreille River near Newport. The launch and adjoining parking area are suitable for larger boats. Waterskiing and water sports are popular here. There is a wheelchair-accessible interpretive trail with a boardwalk and beautiful views of the river. Signs along the way explain the history of Native Americans who once inhabited the area.

㊹ Old American Kampground

Location: Near the Pend Oreille River; map A5, grid e8.

Campsites, facilities: There are 25 tent sites and 50 sites for trailers or RVs of any length. Electricity, piped water, sewer hookups, and picnic tables are provided. Flush toilets, sanitary services, a laundry room, showers, bottled gas, boat docks, launching facilities, cable TV, and propane gas are available. Leashed pets and motorbikes are permitted.

Reservations, fees: Reservations are accepted. Sites are $10–$25 per night. The campground is open year-round.

Contact: Old American Kampground, 701 North Newport Avenue, Newport, WA 99156; (509) 447-3663 or fax (509) 447-0679; Web site: www.kmresorts.com.

Directions: From Spokane at Interstate 90, turn north on U.S. 2 and drive 48 miles to Newport. Turn north on Newport Avenue and drive one block to the campground at the end of the road.

Trip notes: Old American Kampground is near the Pend Oreille River, right in Newport at the Washington/Idaho border. The intersection of U.S. 2 and Highway 41 ia a major junction for this part of the country. The park is pretty, with river frontage and full facilities for boating and fishing. If you want a more secluded spot, Pioneer Park (campground number 43) is about a 15-minute drive away, on the east side of the river.

㊺ Hunters

Location: On Franklin Roosevelt Lake in Lake Roosevelt National Recreation Area; map A5, grid f1.

Campsites, facilities: There are 42 sites for tents, trailers, or RVs up to 26 feet long. Piped water, fire grills, and picnic tables are provided. Flush toilets, a store, and ice are available within one mile. Boat docks and launching facilities are nearby. Leashed pets are permitted.

Reservations, fees: No reservations are accepted. Sites are $5–$10 per night; there is a $6 launch fee. The campground is open year-round, with limited winter facilities.

Contact: Lake Roosevelt National Recreation Area, 1008 Crest Drive, Coulee Dam, WA 99116; (509) 633-9441 or fax (509) 633-9332.

Directions: From Spokane on Interstate 90, turn west on U.S. 2 and drive 34 miles, then turn north on Highway 25 and drive 47 miles to Hunter. Turn west on the signed access road and proceed to the campground.

Trip notes: This campground on a shoreline point along Roosevelt Lake (Columbia River) is a good spot for swimming, fishing, or waterskiing. See the trip notes for Kamloops and North Gorge (campground numbers 7 and 9) for further information on the area.

㊻ Shore Acres

Location: On Loon Lake; map A5, grid f4.

Campsites, facilities: There are 33 sites for trailers or RVs up to 30 feet long. Electricity, piped water, sewer hookups, and picnic tables are provided. Flush toilets, sanitary services, a store, showers, firewood, ice, a playground, boat docks, boat rentals, and launching facilities are available.

Reservations, fees: Reservations are

accepted. Sites are $16.50 per night. The campground is open from mid-April through September.

Contact: Phone (800) 900-2474 or (509) 233-2474, or write to 41987 Shore Acres Road, Loon Lake, WA 99148.

Directions: From Spokane on Interstate 90, turn north on U.S. 395 and drive 30 miles. Then turn west on Highway 292 and drive 1.5 miles to Shore Acres Road. Turn left and drive 1.5 miles to the park.

Trip notes: Located along the shore of Loon Lake, this campground has a long expanse of beach and is an alternative to Granite Point Rock across the lake (campground number 47). Note: If you're planning on visiting this park on a weekend, be aware of their policy of full-weekend reservations. You can't stay just a Friday or Saturday night—you have to reserve for the whole weekend. See the trip notes for Granite Point Rock for details about the fishing opportunities.

47 Granite Point Rock

Location: On Loon Lake; map A5, grid f4.

Campsites, facilities: There are 68 sites for trailers or RVs of any length. Electricity, piped water, sewer hookups, and picnic tables are provided. Flush toilets, showers, a recreation hall, a store, a cafe, a laundry room, ice, a playground, boat docks, boat rentals, and launching facilities are available. Bottled gas is located within one mile. Pets are not permitted.

Reservations, fees: Reservations are accepted. Sites are $15–$20 per night. The campground is open from mid-April to mid-September.

Contact: Phone (509) 233-2100 or write to 41000 Granite Point Road, Loon Lake, WA 99148.

Directions: From Spokane on Interstate 90, turn north on U.S. 395 and drive a total of 26 miles (eight miles past the town of Deer Park) to the campground.

Trip notes: This camp is on the shore of Loon Lake, a clear, clean, spring-fed lake with a sandy beach and swimming area. In the spring, the Mackinaw trout range from four to 30 pounds and can be taken by deep-water trolling (downriggers suggested). Easier to catch are the kokanee salmon and rainbow trout in the 12- to 14-inch class. A sprinkling of perch, sunfish, and bass come out of their hiding places when the weather heats up.

48 Jerry's Landing

Location: On Eloika Lake; map A5, grid f6.

Campsites, facilities: There are 20 drive-through sites for trailers or RVs of any length. Picnic tables are provided. Flush toilets, sanitary services, a store, ice, electricity, piped water, sewer hookups, showers, and firewood are available. Bottled gas is available within one mile. Boat docks, launching facilities, and rentals are nearby. Leashed pets and motorbikes are permitted.

Reservations, fees: Reservations are accepted. Sites are $14–$15 per night. The campground is open from April through September.

Contact: Phone (509) 292-2337 or write to North 41114 Lakeshore Drive, Elk, WA 99009.

Directions: From Spokane on Interstate 90, turn north on U.S. 2 and drive 23 miles, then head west on Oregon Road for one mile to the campground.

Trip notes: The shore of Eloika Lake is home to this camp in a lovely wooded setting with abundant wildlife. Trout fishing can be excellent as soon as the ice is off the lake in spring. During the hot days of summer, crappie fishing is good.

49 Pend Oreille County Park

Location: Near Newport; map A5, grid f5.

Campsites, facilities: There are 34 sites for tents and two sites for RVs or trailers. Rest rooms, showers, and a barbecue are provided. Leashed pets are permitted.

Reservations, fees: Reservations are accepted. Sites are $8 per night. The campground is open from Memorial Day to Labor Day.

Contact: Pend Oreille County Department of Public Works, P.O. Box 5065, Newport, WA 99156; (509) 447-4821.

Directions: From Spokane on Interstate 90, turn north on U.S. 2 and drive about 30 miles. After you cross the border between Spokane County and Pend Oreille County, look for signs and the county park entrance on the left.

Trip notes: This is the only campground around, and it's not a bad choice if you're looking for a layover spot. It's a good alternative to the often-crowded Mount Spokane State Park (campground number 56). There are many hiking trails and nature hikes on the grounds, and other nearby activities include fishing and hunting.

⑤ Seven Bays Resort and Marina

Location: On Franklin Roosevelt Lake; map A5, grid g0.

Campsites, facilities: There are 24 tent sites and 48 sites for trailers or RVs of any length; 28 have full hookups one is a drive-through. Electricity, piped water, sewer hookups, and picnic tables are provided. Flush toilets, bottled gas, sanitary services, showers, a store, a cafe, a laundry room, and ice are available. Boat docks and launching facilities are nearby. Leashed pets are permitted.

Reservations, fees: Reservations are accepted. Sites are $10–$15 per night. Senior discounts are available. The campground is open year-round.

Contact: Phone (509) 725-1676 or write to Route 1, P.O. Box 624, Davenport, WA 99122.

Directions: From Spokane on Interstate 90, turn west on U.S. 2 and drive 34 miles to Davenport. Turn north on Highway 25 and continue 23 miles to Miles, then turn south on Creston Road and drive five miles to the resort.

Trip notes: Lakeside sites and friendly folks are the highlights of this resort on the shore of Roosevelt Lake. This is an alternative to Fort Spokane and Hawk Creek (campground numbers 51 and 52). A full-service marina sets this spot apart from the others.

⑤ Fort Spokane

Location: On Franklin Roosevelt Lake in Lake Roosevelt National Recreation Area; map A5, grid g0.

Campsites, facilities: There are 67 sites for tents, trailers, or RVs up to 26 feet long. Piped water, picnic tables, and fire grills are provided. Flush toilets, sanitary services, and a playground are available. A store and ice are located within one mile. Some facilities are wheelchair accessible. Boat docks, launching facilities, and a marine dump station are nearby. Leashed pets are permitted.

Reservations, fees: No reservations are accepted. Sites are $5–$10 per night; there is a $6 launch fee. The campground is open year-round, with limited winter facilities.

Contact: Lake Roosevelt National Recreation Area, 1008 Crest Drive, Coulee Dam, WA 99116; (509) 633-9441 or fax (509) 633-9332.

Directions: From Spokane on Interstate 90, turn west on U.S. 2 and drive 34 miles, then turn north on Highway 25 and drive 26 miles to the campground.

Trip notes: Rangers offer evening campfire programs and guided daytime activities at this modern campground on the shore of Roosevelt Lake. This is one of 16 campgrounds on the 130-mile-long lake.

⑤ Hawk Creek

Location: On Franklin Roosevelt Lake in Lake Roosevelt National Recreation Area; map A5, grid g0.

Campsites, facilities: There are 25 sites for tents, trailers, or RVs up to 16 feet long. Picnic tables, fire grills, and piped water are provided. Pit toilets are available. Boat docks and launching facilities are nearby. Leashed pets are permitted.

Reservations, fees: No reservations are accepted. Sites are $5–$10 per night; there is a $6 launch fee. The campground is open year-round, with limited winter facilities.

Contact: Lake Roosevelt National Recreation Area, 1008 Crest Drive, Coulee Dam, WA 99116; (509) 633-9441 or fax (509) 633-9332.

Directions: From Spokane on Interstate 90, turn west on U.S. 2 and drive 34 miles, then turn north on Highway 25 and drive 23 miles to Miles. Turn west on Creston Road and drive 10 miles to the campground at the mouth of Hawk Creek.

Trip notes: This is a pleasant camping spot along the shore of Roosevelt Lake (Columbia River), adjacent to the mouth of Hawk Creek. The bay is a popular fishing area.

53 Porcupine Bay

Location: On Franklin Roosevelt Lake in Lake Roosevelt National Recreation Area; map A5, grid g0.

Campsites, facilities: There are 31 sites for tents, trailers, or RVs up to 20 feet long. Piped water, picnic tables, and fire grills are provided. Flush toilets and a playground are available. Boat docks and launching facilities are nearby. Some facilities are wheelchair accessible. Leashed pets are permitted.

Reservations, fees: No reservations are accepted. Sites are $5–$10 per night; there is a $6 launch fee. The campground is open year-round, weather permitting.

Contact: Lake Roosevelt National Recreation Area, 1008 Crest Drive, Coulee Dam, WA 99116; (509) 633-9441 or fax (509) 633-9332.

Directions: From Spokane on Interstate 90, turn west on U.S. 2 and drive 34 miles, then turn north on Highway 25 and drive 20 miles. At the sign for the Coulee Dam National Recreation Area, head north on the county road and you'll see the campground.

Trip notes: This is a good spot for campers with boats because of its proximity to a nearby dock and launch. A swimming beach is adjacent to the campground.

54 Long Lake Camp and Picnic Area

Location: On the Spokane River; map A5, grid g3.

Campsites, facilities: There are 12 sites for tents or small trailers. Picnic tables, fire grills, and tent pads are provided. Vault toilets and piped water are available. Most of the facilities are wheelchair accessible.

Reservations, fees: No reservations are accepted. There is no fee. The campground is open from April through September.

Contact: Department of Natural Resources, Northeast Region, P.O. Box 190, Colville, WA 99114-0190; (509) 684-7474 or fax (509) 684-7484.

Directions: From Spokane, turn west on U.S. 2 and drive 21 miles to Reardan. Drive north on Highway 231 for 14 miles, then turn right on Highway 291. Drive five miles and turn right into the campground.

Trip notes: This campground is located about 45 minutes from Spokane. Most of the facilities, including the swim area, are wheelchair accessible. Amenities include picnic areas, drinking water, and a scenic river view—and you can't beat the price. It's slightly more well known than many of the Department of Natural Resources camps.

55 Dragoon Creek

Location: Near the Little Spokane River; map A5, grid g5.

Campsites, facilities: There are 22 sites for tents or small trailers. Picnic tables, fire grills, and tent pads are provided. Vault toilets and piped water are available. Leashed pets are permitted.

Reservations, fees: No reservations are accepted. There is no fee. The campground is open from April through September.

Contact: Department of Natural Resources, Northeast Region, P.O. Box 190, Colville, WA 99114-0190; (509) 684-7474 or fax (509) 684-7484.

Directions: From Spokane, drive north on U.S. 395 for 16 miles. Turn left on Dragoon Creek Road and drive one-half mile to the campground entrance.

Trip notes: This spot is not far from U.S. 395, but it's quiet, rustic, and set along Dragoon Creek, a tributary to the Little Spokane River. The Department of Natural Resources offers a map that details the region. The area is forested and the camp has shaded sites.

56 Mount Spokane State Park

Location: On Mount Spokane; map A5, grid g7.

Campsites, facilities: There are two primitive tent sites and 12 sites for tents or self-contained RVs up to 30 feet long. Piped water, fire grills, and picnic tables are provided. Flush toilets and a cafe are available. A Laundromat is located within one mile. Leashed pets are permitted.

Reservations, fees: No reservations are accepted. Sites are $5–$10 per night. The campground is open year-round, with limited winter facilities.

Contact: Phone (509) 456-4169 or write to Route 1, P.O. Box 336, Mead, WA 99021.

Directions: From Interstate 90 at Spokane, turn east on U.S. 2 and drive about six miles northeast. Turn northeast on Highway 206 and drive 24 miles north to the park.

Trip notes: This is a prime hideaway on the slopes of Mount Spokane (5,878 feet). Its little brother, Mount Kit Carson (5,180 feet), sits alongside. Nearby recreation options include marked hiking trails, an equestrian trail, and tennis courts. In the winter Mount Spokane Ski Resort operates here. Don't miss the fantastic views at the wonderful Vista House restaurant. This is one of the better short trips available out of Spokane.

57 Overland Station

Location: Near Eloika Lake; map A5, grid i5.

Campsites, facilities: There are 40 tent sites and 32 sites for trailers or RVs of any length; 18 are drive-throughs. Electricity, piped water, sewer hookups, and picnic tables are provided. Flush toilets, showers, a store, a laundry room, ice, and a playground are available. Leashed pets and motorbikes are permitted.

Reservations, fees: No reservations are accepted. Sites are $13–$19.44 per night. The campground is open year-round.

Contact: Phone (509) 747-1703, fax (509)

244-6505, or write to 107 West Geiger Boulevard, Spokane, WA 99204.

Directions: On Interstate 90 in Spokane, drive about eight miles west and take exit 272. Drive one block east to the park on the right.

Trip notes: This is one of seven campgrounds located in the immediate Spokane area. A number of side trips will clue you in to the history of the area, including the Cheney Cowles Memorial Museum and the Museum of Native American Cultures. Riverfront Park is the site of the 1974 World Exposition, and it now offers a science center and planetarium, an opera house, a Japanese garden, a gondola ride, a carousel, an ice-skating rink, and a five-screen theater. The closest lake with good fishing is Eloika Lake, described in the trip notes for Jerry's Landing (campground number 48).

58 Riverside State Park

Location: Near Spokane; map A5, grid h5.

Campsites, facilities: There are two primitive tent sites and 101 sites for tents or self-contained RVs up to 45 feet long. Picnic tables and fire grills are provided. Flush toilets, showers, and firewood are available. A store, a restaurant, and ice are located within three miles. Boat launching facilities are located on the Spokane River about seven miles away at the reservoir. Leashed pets are permitted.

Reservations, fees: No reservations are accepted. Sites are $7–$11 per night. The campground is open year-round.

Contact: Riverside State Park, North 4427 Aubrey L. White Parkway, Spokane, WA 99205; (800) 233-0321 or (509) 456-3964.

Directions: From Spokane on Interstate 90, drive north on Division Street. Turn left on Mission Street. (Mission Street will become Maxwell Street and then Petett Drive.) The park entrance is on Petett Drive and the campground is two miles inside the park on the left, a total of five miles from Interstate 90.

Trip notes: This is a good option for people looking for a more rural alternative to the camps set on the outskirts of Spokane. The large state park provides an interpretive center, riding stables, and trails for hiking, horseback riding, and off-road vehicles. Nearby recreation options include an 18-hole golf course. A local point of interest is the unique Bowl and Pitcher Lava Formation in the river.

⑤⑨ Shadows Motel and Trailer Park

Location: In Spokane; map A5, grid h6.

Campsites, facilities: There are 10 tent sites and 25 sites for trailers or RVs of any length; 11 are drive-throughs. Electricity, piped water, and sewer hookups are provided. Flush toilets, sanitary services, showers, and a laundry room are available. Bottled gas, a store, a cafe, and ice are located within one mile. Leashed pets and motorbikes are permitted.

Reservations, fees: Reservations are accepted. Sites are $10–$20 per night. The campground is open year-round, with limited winter facilities.

Contact: Phone (509) 467-6951 or write to North 9025 Division, Spokane, WA 99218.

Directions: From Interstate 90 in Spokane, take the Division Street exit (exit 281) and drive six miles to North 9025 Division Street. The campground is located at the junction of U.S. 2 and U.S. 395.

Trip notes: This park is primarily a pit stop for highway cruisers. An 18-hole golf course, hiking trails, marked bike trails, and tennis courts are close by. See the trip notes for Overland Station (campground number 57) for information on attractions in Spokane.

⑥⓪ Trailer Inns RV Park

Location: In Spokane; map A5, grid h6.

Campsites, facilities: There are 97 sites for trailers or RVs of any length; 30 are drive-throughs. Electricity, piped water, sewer hookups, and picnic tables are provided. Flush toilets, bottled gas, showers, color TV, a laundry room, ice, and a playground are available. Sanitary services, a store, and a cafe are within

one mile. Leashed pets and motorbikes are permitted.

Reservations, fees: Reservations are accepted. Sites are $15–$21 per night. The campground is open year-round.

Contact: Phone (509) 535-1811 or write to 6021 East Fourth Avenue, Spokane, WA 99212.

Directions: From eastbound, take exit 285 (Sprague Avenue/Eastern Road) off Interstate 90 in Spokane and drive one-tenth of a mile on Eastern Road. Then turn west on Fourth Avenue and drive two blocks to the campground. From westbound, take exit 284 (Havana Street) and drive one block south on Havana Street. Turn east on Fourth Avenue and drive one mile.

Trip notes: This large RV park is a perfect layover on the way to Idaho. It's as close to a hotel as an RV park can get. Nearby recreation options include an 18-hole golf course, a racquet club, and tennis courts. See the trip notes for Overland Station (campground number 57) for information on attractions in Spokane.

⑥① KOA Spokane

Location: On the Spokane River; map A5, grid h7.

Campsites, facilities: There are 50 tent sites and 150 sites for trailers or RVs of any length; 109 are drive-throughs. Electricity and sewer hookups are available. Piped water and picnic tables are provided. Other amenities include flush toilets, sanitary services, showers, a recreation hall, a store, a laundry room, ice, a playground, and a swimming pool. A cafe is located within one mile. Leashed pets are permitted.

Reservations, fees: Reservations are accepted. Sites are $15–$25 per night. The campground is open from March through October.

Contact: Phone (509) 924-4722 or write to 3025 North Barker, Otis Orchards, WA 99027.

Directions: From Spokane, drive 13 miles east on Interstate 90 and take exit 293. Drive north on Barker Road for 1.25 miles to the campground.

Trip notes: This campground along the shore

of the Spokane River is close to an 18-hole golf course and tennis courts. See the trip notes for Overland Station (campground number 57) for information on attractions in Spokane.

⑥ Picnic Pines on Silver Lake

Location: On Silver Lake; map A5, grid i4.
Campsites, facilities: There are 10 tent sites and 29 drive-through sites for trailers or RVs of any length. Electricity, piped water, sewer hookups, and picnic tables are provided. Flush toilets, a recreation hall, a store, a bait shop, boat docks, boat rentals, launching facilities, a cafe, ice, and a playground are available. Bottled gas and a Laundromat are located within two miles. Leashed pets and motorbikes are permitted.
Reservations, fees: Reservations are accepted. Sites are $8–$12 per night. The campground is open year-round.
Contact: Phone (509) 299-3223 or write to South 9212 Silver Lake Road, Medical Lake, WA 99022.
Directions: From Interstate 90 west of Spokane, take exit 270 and drive three miles west on Medical Lake Road to Silver Lake Road. Turn left and drive one-half mile to the park.
Trip notes: This shorefront resort on Silver Lake caters primarily to RVs, though tent campers are welcome. Fishing can be excellent here. Nearby recreation options include marked bike trails, a full-service marina, and tennis courts. See the trip notes for West Medical Lake Resort (campground number 63) for further details.

⑥ West Medical Lake Resort

Location: On West Medical Lake; map A5, grid i4.
Campsites, facilities: There are 20 tent sites and 20 sites for trailers or RVs. Picnic tables are provided. Flush toilets, showers, a cafe, and ice are available. Electricity, piped water, and sewer hookups can be obtained for an extra fee. Boat docks, launching facili-

ties, and rentals are nearby. Leashed pets and motorbikes are permitted.
Reservations, fees: Reservations are required. Sites are $12–$14 per night. The campground is open from late April through September.
Contact: Phone (509) 299-3921 or write to P.O. Box 216, Medical Lake, WA 99022.
Directions: Take exit 264 off Highway 90 near Medical Lake and drive 4.5 miles north on Salnave Road, then turn west on Fancher and travel one-half mile to the resort.
Trip notes: This family-operated shorefront resort, one of five campgrounds on Medical Lake, is a popular spot for Spokane locals who make the half-hour drive. There are actually two lakes. West Medical is the larger of the two and also has the better fishing, with boat rentals available. Medical Lake is just a quarter-mile wide and a half-mile long, and boating is restricted to rowboats, canoes, kayaks, and sailboats. The lakes got their names from the wondrous medical powers once attributed to these waters.

⑥ Mallard Bay Resort

Location: On Medical Lake; map A5, grid i4.
Campsites, facilities: There are 50 sites for trailers or RVs of any length, plus two cabins. Electricity, piped water, and picnic tables are provided. Flush toilets, bottled gas, sanitary services, showers, a cafe, ice, swimming facilities with a diving board, and a playground are available. Boat docks, launching facilities, and rentals are nearby. Leashed pets and motorbikes are permitted.
Reservations, fees: Reservations are accepted. Sites are $13.95 per night; cabins are $32 per night. The campground is open from mid-April to late September.
Contact: Phone (509) 299-3830 or write to 14601 Salnave Road, Cheney, WA 99004.
Directions: From Interstate 90 west of Spokane, take exit 264 and drive two miles west on Salnave Road. Follow the signs to the resort.
Trip notes: This resort on the shore of Medical Lake is close to marked bike trails, a riding stable, and tennis courts. See the trip notes

for West Medical Lake Resort (campground number 63) for more details.

⑥⑤ Rainbow Cove Campground

Location: On Clear Lake; map A5, grid i4.

Campsites, facilities: There are five tent sites and 16 sites for trailers or RVs of any length. Electricity, piped water, sewer hookups, and picnic tables are provided. Showers, flush toilets, a cafe, ice, boat docks, boat rentals, and launching facilities are available. Leashed pets are permitted.

Reservations, fees: Reservations are accepted. Sites are $13.50 per night. The campground is open from mid-April to mid-October.

Contact: Phone (509) 299-3717 or write to South 12514 Clear Lake Road, Medical Lake, WA 99022.

Directions: From Interstate 90 west of Spokane, take exit 264 and drive west a very short distance on Salnave Road, then turn north on Clear Lake Road and follow the signs to the campground.

Trip notes: This pretty, wooded resort on the shore of Medical Lake is close to marked bike trails and tennis courts. See the trip notes for West Medical Lake Resort (campground number 63) for more details about the lake.

⑥⑥ Alpine Motel-RV and Tent Park of Spokane

Location: Near Spokane; map A5, grid h8.

Campsites, facilities: There are 110 sites for tents, trailers, or RVs. Restrooms, showers, a public phone, a Laundromat, a heated swimming pool, and ice are available. The facilities are wheelchair accessible. Leashed pets are permitted.

Reservations, fees: Reservations are recommended. Sites are $16–$20 per night. The campground is open year-round.

Contact: Phone the park at (509) 928-2700 or write to P.O. Box 363, Greenacres, WA 99016.

Directions: From Spokane, drive east on Interstate 90 for about 12 miles to Barker Road/Green Acres (exit 293). Travel north one-half block on Barker Road to the campground on the left.

Trip notes: This urban campground just outside of Spokane is primarily a layover camp, but could be a good base for those planning on visiting the Spokane area for a while. Recreational activities include swimming.

⑥⑦ Yogi Bear Camp Resort

Location: West of Spokane; map A5, grid i5.

Campsites, facilities: There are 168 sites for tents, trailers, or RVs up to 30 feet long, with full hookups, including electricity, water, sewer, cable TV, and modem-friendly phone service; 35 sites are drive-throughs. There are also fully equipped cabins that sleep up to five. Flush toilets, sanitary services, showers, firewood, propane, a laundry room, and a playground are available. Other amenities include a camp store; an activity center with an indoor pool, a spa, an exercise room, a game room, and a snack shack; a dog walk; and various sports facilities (volleyball, basketball, badminton). Leashed pets and motorbikes are permitted.

Reservations, fees: Reservations are accepted. Sites are $17–$24.50 per night; cabins are $45 per night. The campground is open year-round.

Contact: Phone (800) 494-7275, fax (509) 459-0148, or write to 7520 South Thomas Mallen Road, Cheney, WA 99204.

Directions: From Interstate 90 in Spokane, take exit 272 and drive one mile east on Westbow Road. Turn south on Thomas Mallen Road and drive one-half mile to the campground on the right.

Trip notes: Located in a wooded, rural area, yet just 10 minutes from downtown Spokane, this park is large and grassy, with towering ponderosa pines. Highlights include pretty hiking trails, an 18-hole golf course next door, and several other courses within 20 minutes of the resort. See the trip notes for Overland

Station (campground number 57) for details on the Spokane area.

68 Peaceful Pines Campground

Location: Near Turnbull National Wildlife Refuge; map A5, grid i5.

Campsites, facilities: There are 20 tent sites and 24 sites for trailers or RVs of any length. Electricity, piped water, sewer hookups, and picnic tables are provided. Flush toilets, sanitary services, and showers are available. A store, a cafe, and ice are located within one mile, and a Laundromat is within three miles. Leashed pets and motorbikes are permitted.

Reservations, fees: Reservations are accepted. Sites are $11.50–$14 per night. The campground is open year-round.

Contact: Phone (509) 235-4966 or write to 1231 West First Street, Cheney, WA 99004.

Directions: From Interstate 90 southwest of Spokane, take the Highway 270/Highway 904 exit. Drive six miles south to Cheney on Highway 904, then continue one mile to the campground.

Trip notes: This campground is a little-known, remote site just a short distance from Turnbull National Wildlife Refuge, an expanse of marsh and pine that is a significant stopover point for migratory birds on the Pacific Flyway. You can pick up a map and bird checklist at the refuge headquarters. This is a prime spot, only a 45-minute drive out of Spokane, yet relatively unknown.

69 Sprague Lake Resort

Location: On Sprague Lake; map A5, grid j2.

Campsites, facilities: There are 50 tent sites and 30 drive-through sites for trailers or RVs of any length. Electricity, piped water, sewer hookups, and picnic tables are provided. Flush toilets, sanitary services, a store, a laundry room, showers, ice, and a playground are available. Boat docks, launching facilities, and rentals are nearby. Leashed pets are permitted.

Reservations, fees: Reservations are accepted. Sites are $14–$17 per night. The campground is open from April through October.

Contact: Phone (509) 257-2864 or write to Route 1, P.O. Box 5, Sprague, WA 99032.

Directions: From Interstate 90 west of Spokane, take the Sprague Business Center exit. Follow the signs and drive two miles to the resort.

Trip notes: This developed campground is on the shore of Sprague Lake, about 35 miles from Spokane. It's a pleasant setting, clean and grassy.

70 Four Seasons Campground

Location: On Sprague Lake; map A5, grid j2.

Campsites, facilities: There are 25 tent sites and 30 drive-through sites for trailers or RVs. Electricity, piped water, sewer hookups, and picnic tables are provided. Flush toilets, sanitary services, showers, firewood, ice, a playground, a store with fishing tackle, a fish cleaning station, and a swimming pool are available. Boat docks, launching facilities, and rentals are nearby. Leashed pets and motorbikes are permitted.

Reservations, fees: Reservations are accepted. Sites are $12–$14 per night. The campground is open from mid-April through September, weather permitting.

Contact: Phone (509) 257-2332 or write to 2384 North Bob Lee Road, Sprague, WA 99032.

Directions: From Interstate 90 west of Spokane, take exit 245 and drive left (south) toward Sprague, following the signs to the lake and the campground.

Trip notes: This campground along the shore of Sprague Lake has spacious sites with plenty of vegetation. The fishing for rainbow trout is best in May and June, with some bass in spring and fall. Because there is an abundance of natural feed in the lake, the fish reach larger sizes here than in neighboring lakes. Perch, crappie, and catfish are abundant. In late July through August, a fair algae bloom is a turnoff for swimmers and water-skiers.

71 Last Roundup Motel, RV Park, and Campground 🚐 ⛺

Location: Near Sprague Lake; map A5, grid j3.
Campsites, facilities: There are 13 sites for trailers or RVs up to 40 feet long, plus a grass area for tents. Electricity, piped water, and sewer hookups are provided. Flush toilets, showers, a laundry room, and ice are available. Bottled gas, sanitary services, a store, and a cafe are located within one mile. Leashed pets and motorbikes are permitted.
Reservations, fees: Reservations are accepted. Sites are $10–$16 per night. The campground is open from April through October.
Contact: Phone (509) 257-2583, fax (509) 257-2615, or write to 312 East First Street, Sprague, WA 99032.
Directions: From Spokane, drive west on Interstate 90 for 35 miles to Sprague. Take exit 245 and drive one-half mile south on Highway 23 to Fourth Street. Turn west and drive one block to B Street. Turn north and drive three blocks to First Street. Turn east on First Street and drive one block to the park on the right.
Trip notes: Located just on the outskirts of Sprague, this camp is in a meadowlike, flat area with a rural feel and sunny, grassy sites. The best game in town is at nearby Sprague Lake.

72 Williams Lake Resort 🚐 ⛺

Location: On Williams Lake; map A5, grid j4.
Campsites, facilities: There are 15 tent sites and 60 sites for trailers or RVs of any length; seven are drive-throughs. Electricity, piped water, and picnic tables are provided. Flush toilets, bottled gas, sanitary services, firewood, a store, a cafe, a restaurant, showers, ice, a playground, boat docks, launching facilities, and boat rentals are available. Leashed pets and motorbikes are permitted.
Reservations, fees: Reservations are accepted. Sites are $12–$15 per night. The campground is open from mid-April to October.

Contact: Phone (800) 274-1540 or (509) 235-2391, or write to West 18617 Williams Lake Road, Cheney, WA 99004.
Directions: From Spokane, drive west on Interstate 90 for 10 miles to exit 270, turn south on Highway 904, and drive six miles to Cheney. Turn south on Cheney Plaza Road and drive 11.2 miles to Williams Lake Road. Turn west and drive 3.5 miles to the campground on the left.
Trip notes: This resort is on the shore of Williams Lake, which is just under three miles long and is popular for swimming and waterskiing. It's also one of the top fishing lakes in the region for rainbow and cutthroat trout. The lake is bordered in some areas by rocky cliffs. See the trip notes for Peaceful Pines Campground (number 68) for information on nearby Turnbull National Wildlife Refuge.

73 Bunkers Resort 🚐

Location: On Williams Lake; map A5, grid j4.
Campsites, facilities: There are 10 drive-through sites for trailers or RVs of any length. Electricity, piped water, and picnic tables are provided. Flush toilets, bottled gas, sanitary services, recreation hall, cabins, a restaurant, a store, a cafe, and ice are available. Boat docks, fishing docks, launching facilities, and rentals are nearby. Leashed pets are permitted.
Reservations, fees: Reservations are accepted. Sites are $10.50–$17.50 per night. The campground is open from mid-April to October.
Contact: Phone (509) 235-5212 or write to S36402 Bunker Landing Road, Cheney, WA 99004.
Directions: From Interstate 90 west of Spokane, take the Cheney exit and drive six miles south to Cheney. Turn south on Mullinex Road and drive 12 miles to the resort.
Trip notes: This campground is on the shore of Williams Lake. See the trip notes for Williams Lake Resort (campground number 72) for information on the lake, and the trip notes for Peaceful Pines Campground (number 68) for information on nearby Turnbull National Wildlife Refuge.

Map B1

One inch equals approximately 20 miles.

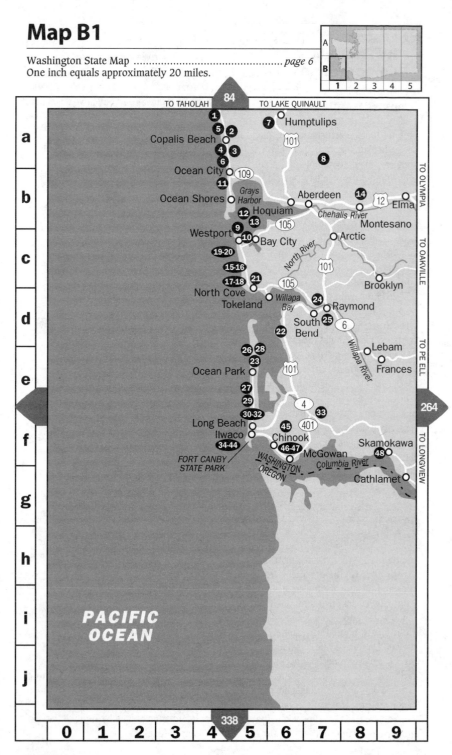

Chapter B1 features:

---

1 Pacific Beach State Park

Location: On the Pacific Ocean; map B1, grid a4.

Campsites, facilities: There are 33 tent sites and 31 sites for trailers or RVs up to 45 feet long. Picnic tables are provided. A sanitary disposal station, coin-operated showers, and toilets are available. Electricity and piped water are available for an extra fee. Some facilities are wheelchair accessible. Leashed pets are permitted.

Reservations, fees: Contact Reservations Northwest at (800) 452-5687 ($6 reservation fee). Sites are $10–$15 per night. The campground is open year-round.

Contact: Phone (800) 233-0321, call the state park at (360) 289-3553, or write to 148 State Route 115, Hoquiam, WA 98550.

Directions: From Interstate 5 south of Olympia, take exit 88 and turn west on U.S. 12. Drive 46 miles, then turn west on Highway 109 and drive 27 miles to Pacific Beach. The park is in town.

Trip notes: You can thank supply and demand for the popularity of this nine-acre beachfront campground In Pacific Beach.

Since there are no other coastal camps in the immediate vicinity, it tends to get crowded. Activities here include clamming, beachcombing, and surf fishing.

❷ Tidelands on the Beach

Location: Near Copalis Beach; map B1, grid a4.

Campsites, facilities: There are 100 tent sites and 55 sites for trailers or RVs of any length; 25 are drive-throughs. There are also three two-bedroom cabins. Electricity, piped water, sewer hookups, and picnic tables are provided. Sanitary services, toilets, firewood, coin-operated showers, and a playground are available. Bottled gas, a store, a cafe, and ice are located within one mile. Leashed pets are permitted.

Reservations, fees: Reservations are accepted. Sites are $10–$15 per night; cabins are $75 per night. The campground is open year-round.

Contact: Phone (360) 289-8963 or write to P.O. Box 36, Copalis Beach, WA 98535.

Directions: From Olympia, drive south on Interstate 5 to exit 4. Turn west on U.S. 12 and drive 46 miles. Turn west on Highway 109 and drive about 16 miles to the campground. It's located about one mile south of Copalis Beach between mileposts 20 and 21.

Trip notes: This wooded campground covering 47 acres has beach access, and though it's primarily an RV park, the sites are pleasant and grassy. Horseshoe pits and a sports field offer recreation possibilities. This a more remote option than the other sites in the area.

❸ Rod's Beach Resort

Location: Near Copalis Beach; map B1, grid a4.

Campsites, facilities: There are 80 sites for trailers or RVs of any length; 25 are drive-throughs. No tents are allowed. Electricity, piped water, sewer hookups, and cable TV are provided. There is also a motel at the site.

Sanitary services, toilets, showers, a recreation hall, a store, a cafe, ice, and a playground are available. Bottled gas is located within one mile. A swimming pool is available for an extra fee. Leashed pets are permitted.

Reservations, fees: Reservations are accepted. Sites are $12–$16 per night. The campground is open from March through October.

Contact: Phone the park at (360) 289-2222 or write to P.O. Box 507, 2961 State Route 109, Copalis Beach, WA 98535.

Directions: From Interstate 5 south of Olympia, take exit 88 and turn west on U.S. 12. Drive 46 miles, then turn west on Highway 109 and drive approximately 15.5 miles to the campground. It's located about 1.5 miles south of Copalis Beach at milepost 20.

Trip notes: A prime spot for RVers, this well-maintained, 10-acre park has large, grassy sites and a beach, plus nice sunsets. Access to the ocean and fishing are highlights.

❹ Driftwood Acres Ocean Camp

Location: In Copalis Beach; map B1, grid a4.

Campsites, facilities: There are 50 tent sites and 50 sites for trailers or RVs of any length. Piped water, sewer hookups, fire pits, and picnic tables are provided. Electricity, cable TV, showers, dump station, flush toilets, and firewood are available. Bottled gas, a store, a cafe, and ice are located within one mile. Leashed pets are permitted.

Reservations, fees: Reservations are accepted; call ahead for fees. The campground is open from Memorial Day weekend through Labor Day weekend.

Contact: Phone (360) 289-3484 or write to P.O. Box 216, Copalis Beach, WA 98535.

Directions: From Seattle on Interstate 5 heading south toward Olympia, take exit 104 and drive west on U.S. 101 (which becomes Highway 8 and then U.S. 12) to Aberdeen. Drive through Aberdeen into the town of Hoquiam. In Hoquiam, turn left and follow Highway 109 to the beaches. Turn north along the coast on Highway 109 to Copalis Beach.

Continue one-half mile north to the camp at milepost 21.5 on the left.

Trip notes: Spreading over some 150 acres, Driftwood Acres Ocean Camp has beach access and marked hiking trails. Additional facilities within five miles include an 18-hole golf course and a riding stable.

❺ Copalis Beach Surf and Sand

Location: In Copalis Beach; map B1, grid a4.

Campsites, facilities: There are seven tent sites and 50 sites for trailers or RVs of any length; 20 are drive-throughs. Electricity, piped water, sewer hookups, cable TV hookups, and picnic tables are provided. Sanitary services, laundry facilities, toilets, showers, a cafe, a lounge, and ice are available. Bottled gas and a store are located within one mile. Leashed pets are permitted.

Reservations, fees: Reservations are accepted. Sites are $15–$21.50 per night. The campground is open year-round.

Contact: Phone (360) 289-2707, fax (360) 289-4083, or write to P.O. Box 208, Copalis Beach, WA 98535.

Directions: From Seattle on Interstate 5 heading south toward Olympia, take exit 104 and drive west on U.S. 101 (which becomes Highway 8 and then U.S. 12) to Aberdeen. Drive through Aberdeen into the town of Hoquim. In Hoquim, turn left and follow Highway 109 to the beaches. Turn north along the coast on Highway 109 to Copalis Beach. Turn west on Heath Road and drive two-tenths of a mile to the campground.

Trip notes: Though not particularly scenic, this five-acre park is a decent layover for an RV vacation and will do the job if you're tired and ready to get off U.S. 101. It does have beach access. The surrounding terrain is flat and grassy.

❻ Riverside RV Resort

Location: Near Copalis Beach; map B1, grid a4.

Campsites, facilities: There are 15 tent sites and 53 sites with full hookups for trailers or RVs of any length; 20 are drive-throughs. Electricity, piped water, sewer hookups, and picnic tables are provided. Sanitary services, toilets, showers, hot tub, firewood, and a recreation hall are available. A store, a cafe, and ice are located within one mile. Leashed pets and motorbikes are permitted.

Reservations, fees: Reservations are accepted. Sites are $12–$15 per night. The campground is open year-round.

Contact: Phone (360) 289-2111 or write to P.O. Box 307, Copalis Beach, WA 98535.

Directions: From Seattle on Interstate 5 heading south toward Olympia, take exit 104 and drive west on U.S. 101 (which becomes Highway 8 and then U.S. 12) to Aberdeen. Drive through Aberdeen into the town of Hoquim. In Hoquim, turn left and follow Highway 109 to the beaches. Turn north along the coast on Highway 109 to Copalis Beach. The park is off the highway on the left.

Trip notes: River access is a bonus at this nice and exceptionally clean three-acre park. Salmon fishing is said to be excellent in the Copalis River, and a boat ramp is available nearby for anglers. Swimming and beachcombing are two other options.

❼ Riverview Recreation Area

Location: On the Humptulips River; map B1, grid a6.

Campsites, facilities: There are eight tent sites and six drive-through sites for trailers or RVs of any length. Picnic tables are provided. Flush toilets, showers, and firewood are available. A store, a cafe, and ice are within one mile. Electricity, piped water, and sewer hookups can be obtained for an extra fee. Boat launching facilities are located nearby at the Humptulips River. Leashed pets and motorbikes are permitted.

Reservations, fees: No reservations are accepted. Sites are $6–$15 per night. The campground is open year-round.

Contact: Phone the park at (360) 987-2216,

fax (360) 987-2335, or write to P.O. Box 97, Humptulips, WA 98552.

Directions: From Interstate 5 south of Olympia, take exit 88 and turn west on U.S. 12. Drive 46 miles, then turn north on U.S. 101 and drive 22 miles to Humptulips. Continue one-quarter of a mile west on Kirkpatrick Road to the park.

Trip notes: This five-acre camp is set at about 1,000 feet along the Humptulips River in a beautiful spot, with boating and fishing access not far from camp. It's a good layover if you're cruising U.S. 101, but it's also popular, so plan on arriving early.

❽ Schafer State Park

Location: On the Satsop River; map B1, grid a7.

Campsites, facilities: There are two primitive tent sites, 47 developed tent sites, and six sites with water and electric hookups for trailers or RVs up to 40 feet long. Picnic tables and fire grills are provided. A sanitary disposal station, toilets, and a playground are available. Water, showers, and firewood are also available for an additional charge. Some facilities are wheelchair accessible. Leashed pets are permitted.

Reservations, fees: No reservations are accepted. Sites are $5–$14 per night. The campground is open year-round, with limited winter facilities.

Contact: Phone (360) 482-3852 or write to Route 1, P.O. Box 87, Elma, WA 98541.

Directions: From Interstate 5 south of Olympia, take exit 88 and turn west on U.S. 12. Drive 32 miles to East Satsop Road (four miles east of Montesano). Turn north and drive eight miles to the park.

Trip notes: This heavily wooded, rural camp covers 119 acres along the East Fork of the Satsop River. There are good canoeing and kayaking spots, some with Class II and Class III rapids, along the Middle and West Forks of the Satsop. At one time this park was the Schafer Logging Company Park and was used by the employees and their families.

❾ Jolly Rogers RV Park

Location: Near Westport Harbor; map B1, grid c5.

Campsites, facilities: There are 25 sites with full hookups for trailers or RVs of any length. Sanitary services, toilets, coin-operated showers, and boat docks are available. Bottled gas, a store, a cafe, and laundry facilities are located within one mile. Leashed pets and motorbikes are permitted.

Reservations, fees: Reservations are accepted. Sites are $15 per night. The campground is open year-round.

Contact: Phone the park at (360) 268-0265, fax (360) 268-0435, or write to P.O. Box 342, Westport, WA 98595.

Directions: From Olympia, drive south on Interstate 5 to exit 88. Turn west on U.S. 12 and drive 46 miles. Turn south on Highway 105 and drive 22 miles southwest to Westport. Drive north to Point Chehalis on Neddie Rose Drive. The park is at the Westport Docks.

Trip notes: This camp covering one acre near Westport Harbor is your typical beachside RV park, with concrete sites and nearby beach access. It's a prime spot to watch ocean sunsets. Westport Light and Westhaven State Parks are nearby and offer day-use facilities along the ocean.

❿ Coho RV Park

Location: Near Westport Harbor; map B1, grid c5.

Campsites, facilities: There are 76 sites with full hookups for trailers or RVs of any length; six are drive-throughs. No tents are permitted. Sanitary services, cable TV, toilets, showers, laundry facilities, a meeting hall, and ice are available. Bottled gas, a store, and a cafe are within one mile. Boat docks, launching facilities, and fishing charters are located one block from this park. Pets are permitted.

Reservations, fees: Reservations are accepted. Sites are $14–$18 per night. The campground is open year-round.

Contact: Coho RV Park, P.O. Box 1087, Westport, WA 98595; (360) 268-0111 or fax (360) 268-9425; e-mail: coho@techline.com.

Directions: From Olympia, drive south on Interstate 5 and take exit 104. Turn west on U.S. 101 (which becomes Highway 8 and then U.S. 12) and drive 46 miles. Turn south on Highway 105 and drive 22 miles southwest to Westport. Turn northeast on Montesano Street (just south of town) and drive 3.5 miles to Nyhus Street. Turn northwest and drive 2.5 blocks to the campground on the left.

Trip notes: This two-acre park is one of 10 camping options in the immediate area. Nearby Westhaven and Westport Light State Parks are popular with rockhounds, scuba divers, and surf anglers. A full-service marina is within five miles of the campground.

⓫ Ocean City State Park

Location: Near Hoquiam; map B1, grid b5.

Campsites, facilities: There are three primitive tent sites, 149 developed tent sites, and 29 sites with full hookups for trailers or RVs up to 55 feet long. Picnic tables are provided, and sanitary services and toilets are available. An extra fee is charged for showers and firewood (in the summer). Some facilities are wheelchair accessible. Leashed pets are permitted.

Reservations, fees: Contact Reservations Northwest at (800) 452-5687 ($6 reservation fee). Sites are $10–$15 per night. The campground is open year-round.

Contact: Phone (800) 233-0321, call the state park at (360) 289-3553, or write to 148 State Route 115, Hoquiam, WA 98550.

Directions: From Interstate 5 south of Olympia, take exit 88 and turn west on U.S. 12. Drive 46 miles, then turn northwest on Highway 109 and drive 20 miles. Turn left on Highway 115 and drive 1.5 miles south to the park.

Trip notes: This 131-acre oceanfront camp is one of the choice spots in the area for tent campers. It's close to many interesting shops

and restaurants in town, and a short drive from an 18-hole golf course. Beachcombing, clamming, and fishing are possibilities at this park.

⓬ Totem RV and Trailer Park

Location: In Westport; map B1, grid b5.

Campsites, facilities: There are 10 tent sites and 76 sites for trailers or RVs of any length; 55 are drive-throughs. Electricity, piped water, sewer hookups, and picnic tables are provided. Sanitary services, toilets, showers, a store, laundry facilities, and ice are available. Bottled gas and a cafe are located next door. Boat docks, launching facilities, and fishing charters are nearby. Leashed pets and motorbikes are permitted.

Reservations, fees: Reservations are accepted. Sites are $13–$15 per night. The campground is open year-round.

Contact: Totem RV and Trailer Park, P.O. Box 1166, Westport, WA 98595; (360) 268-0025 or (888) TOTEMRV/868-3678; e-mail: andrn@techline.com.

Directions: From Olympia, drive south on Interstate 5 to exit 104. Turn west on U.S. 101 (which becomes Highway 8 and then U.S. 12) and drive 46 miles. Turn south on Highway 105 and drive 18 miles southwest to the turn-off for Westport. Drive north on the Highway 105 spur for four miles. Turn east on Dock Avenue and drive one block. Turn north on Nyhus Street and drive two blocks to the park on the left.

Trip notes: This two-acre park with large, graveled sites is close to Westhaven State Park, which offers day-use facilities. Marked bike trails, a full-service marina, and tennis courts are within five miles of the campground.

⓭ Holand Center

Location: In Westport; map B1, grid b5.

Campsites, facilities: There are 80 sites with full hookups for trailers or RVs up to 30 feet long. Picnic tables are provided. Toilets, laundry facilities, and showers are available. Bottled gas, a store, a cafe, and ice are located within one mile. Boat docks and launching facilities are nearby. Leashed pets are permitted.

Reservations, fees: Reservations are accepted. Sites are $16 per night. The campground is open year-round.

Contact: Phone (360) 268-9582, fax (360) 532-3818, or write to P.O. Box 1752, Westport, WA 98595.

Directions: From Olympia, drive south on Interstate 5 to exit 104. Turn west on U.S. 101 (which becomes Highway 8 and then U.S. 12) and drive 46 miles to Highway 105. Turn south and drive 22 miles to Westport. The park is at the corner of Highway 105 and Wilson Street.

Trip notes: This pleasant, 18-acre RV park is one of several in the immediate area. The sites are graveled and have ample space. There is no beach access from the park, but full recreational facilities are nearby.

14 Lake Sylvia State Park

Location: On Lake Sylvia; map B1, grid b8.

Campsites, facilities: There are two primitive tent sites and 35 sites for tents or self-contained RVs up to 30 feet long. Picnic tables and fire grills are provided. Piped water, a sanitary disposal station, toilets, a store, fishing supplies, a car-top boat launch, boat rentals, and a playground are available. An extra fee is charged for showers and firewood. A Laundromat and ice are located within one mile. Some facilities are wheelchair accessible. Leashed pets are permitted.

Reservations, fees: No reservations are accepted. Sites are $10–$14 per night. The campground is open year-round.

Contact: Phone (800) 233-0321 or (360) 249-3621, or write to P.O. Box 701, Montesano, WA 98563.

Directions: From Interstate 5 south of Olympia, take exit 88 and turn west on U.S. 12. Drive 36 miles to Montesano. Turn north at the sign for Lake Sylvia State Park and drive one mile to the camp.

Trip notes: A host of marked hiking trails highlight this 234-acre camp on the shore of Lake Sylvia. Additional recreation options include trout fishing and swimming. If Lake Sylvia is full, nearby camps are East Crossing (campground number 74 in Chapter A2) and Rainbow Cove (campground number 65 in Chapter A5).

15 Twin Harbors State Park

Location: On the Pacific Ocean; map B1, grid c5.

Campsites, facilities: There are 249 sites for tents, trailers, or RVs up to 35 feet long; 49 have full hookups. Picnic tables and fire grills are provided. Piped water, a sanitary disposal station, toilets, and a playground are available. A store, a cafe, and ice can be found within one mile. Firewood is available for an extra fee. Some facilities are wheelchair accessible. Leashed pets are permitted.

Reservations, fees: Contact Reservations Northwest at (800) 452-5687 ($6 reservation fee). Sites are $11–$16 per night. The campground is open year-round.

Contact: Phone (800) 233-0321 or (360) 268-9717, or write to Twin Harbors State Park, Westport, WA 98595.

Directions: From Interstate 5 south of Olympia, take exit 88 and turn west on U.S. 12. Drive 46 miles to the turnoff for Highway 105. Turn left and continue southwest for approximately 20 miles to the park entrance. The park is located three miles south of Westport.

Trip notes: Sprawling over 1,881 acres, this is one of the largest campgrounds on the coast, and therefore quite popular. The sites are very close together and often crammed to capacity in the summer months. Highlights include beach access and marked hiking trails, including the Shifting Sands Nature Trail. Fishing boats can be chartered nearby in Westport.

16 Pacific Motel and RV Park

Location: Near Twin Harbors; map B1, grid c5.

Campsites, facilities: There are 10 tent sites and 80 sites for trailers or RVs of any length; 32 are drive-throughs. Electricity, piped water, and sewer hookups are provided. Sanitary services, toilets, a recreation hall with a kitchen, cable TV, a public phone and fax, coin-operated showers, and a swimming pool are available. Bottled gas, a store, a cafe, a Laundromat, and ice are located within one mile. Boat docks and launching facilities are nearby. Leashed pets and motorbikes are permitted.

Reservations, fees: Reservations are accepted. Sites are $13–$18 per night. The campground is open year-round.

Contact: Phone (360) 268-9325 or write to 330 South Forrest, Westport, WA 98595.

Directions: From Interstate 5 south of Olympia, take exit 104 and turn west on U.S. 101 (which becomes Highway 8 and then U.S. 12). Drive 46 miles, then turn south on Highway 105 and drive 18 miles southwest. At the Highway 105 spur road turnoff to Westport, turn north and continue 1.7 miles to the park.

Trip notes: This five-acre park has grassy, shaded sites in a wooded setting. It's near Twin Harbors and Westport Light State Parks, both of which have beach access. Additional facilities found within five miles of the campground include a full-service marina.

⑰ Grayland Beach State Park

Location: On the Pacific Ocean; map B1, grid c5.

Campsites, facilities: There are three primitive tent sites and 60 full hookup sites for trailers or RVs up to 40 feet long. Picnic tables, toilets, and fire grills are provided. Showers are available for an extra fee. Some facilities are wheelchair accessible.

Reservations, fees: Contact Reservations Northwest at (800) 452-5687 ($6 reservation fee). Sites are $11–$16 per night. The campground is open year-round.

Contact: Grayland Beach State Park, c/o Twin Harbors State Park, Westport, WA 98595; (800) 233-0321 or (360) 268-9717.

Directions: From Interstate 5 south of Olympia, take exit 104 and turn west on U.S. 101 (which becomes Highway 8 and then U.S. 12).

Drive 46 miles to the turnoff for Highway 105. Turn left and continue southwest for approximately 22 miles to the park entrance. The park is just south of the town of Grayland.

Trip notes: This 411-acre oceanfront park has nearly 7,449 feet of excellent beach access, including a self-guided interpretive trail. It's one of the best parks in the immediate area and quite popular with out-of-towners, especially during the summer season. Recreation options include fishing, beachcombing, and kite flying. The campsites are relatively spacious for a state park, but they are not especially private.

⑱ Ocean Gate Resort

Location: In Grayland; map B1, grid c5.

Campsites, facilities: There are 20 tent sites and 24 drive-through sites for trailers or RVs of any length, as well as six cabins. Electricity, piped water, sewer hookups, and picnic tables are provided. Toilets, showers, and a playground are available. Bottled gas, a store, a cafe, laundry facilities, and ice can be found within one mile. Leashed pets and motorbikes are permitted.

Reservations, fees: Reservations are accepted. Sites are $11–$17 per night; cabins are $40–$85 per night for two people, plus $8 for each additional person per night. The campground is open year-round.

Contact: Phone (800) 473-1956 or (360) 267-1956, or write to P.O. Box 67, Grayland, WA 98547.

Directions: From Olympia, drive south on Interstate 5 to exit 104. Turn west on U.S. 101 (which becomes Highway 8 and then U.S. 12) and drive 46 miles. Turn south on Highway 105 and drive about 21 miles to the Y in the road. Take Highway 105 left toward Grayland. The park is in Grayland between mileposts 26 and 27.

Trip notes: This privately run, seven-acre park with beach access provides an alternative to the publicly run Grayland Beach State Park (campground number 17). Fishing and beachcombing are highlights.

⑲ Hammond Trailer Park

Location: In Westport; map B1, grid c5.

Campsites, facilities: There are 34 sites with full hookups for tents, trailers, or RVs of any length. Sanitary services, toilets, showers, cable TV, and laundry facilities are available. Bottled gas, a store, a cafe, and ice are within one mile. Boat docks, launching facilities, and boat rentals are nearby. Leashed pets are permitted.

Reservations, fees: Reservations are accepted. Sites are $12 per night. The campground is open year-round.

Contact: Phone (360) 268-9645 or write to P.O. Box 2134, 1845 South Montesano Road, Westport, WA 98595.

Directions: From Olympia, drive south on Interstate 5 to exit 104. Turn west on U.S. 101 (which becomes Highway 8 and then U.S. 12) and drive 46 miles. Turn south on Highway 105 and drive 22 miles to Westport. Turn north on Montesano Street and drive one-quarter of a mile to the park on the left.

Trip notes: Here's a good option for tent campers, since many of the parks in the area cater to RVs. The park covers five acres and has nearby beach access. A full-service marina is within five miles.

⑳ Islander RV Park

Location: On Grays Harbor; map B1, grid c5.

Campsites, facilities: There are 60 sites with full hookups for trailers or RVs up to 40 feet long; 30 are drive-throughs. Toilets, showers, a cafe, laundry facilities, ice, a swimming pool, and boat docks are available. Bottled gas, sanitary services, and a store are located within one mile. Leashed pets and motorbikes are permitted.

Reservations, fees: Reservations are accepted. Sites are $15–$20 per night. The campground is open year-round.

Contact: Phone (800) 322-1740 or (360) 268-9166, fax (360) 268-0902, or write to P.O. Box 488, Westport, WA 98595.

Directions: From Olympia, drive south on Interstate 5 to exit 104. Turn west on U.S. 101 (which becomes Highway 8 and then U.S. 12) and drive 46 miles. Turn south on Highway 105 and drive 22 miles to Westport. Turn east on Dock Avenue and drive three blocks. Turn north on Westhaven Drive and drive one-third of a mile, then turn east on Neddie Rose Avenue and drive one block to the park.

Trip notes: Located on Grays Harbor, this three-acre park isn't far from Westport Light and Westhaven State Parks, which offer oceanfront day-use facilities. On-site amenities at Islander RV Park include a restaurant, a motel, live music, dancing, and even fishing charters. A full-service marina is within five miles of the park.

㉑ Best Western Shores Motel and RV Park

Location: In Grayland; map B1, grid c5.

Campsites, facilities: There are 30 drive-through sites for trailers or RVs of any length. Electricity, piped water, sewer hookups, and picnic tables are provided. Flush toilets and a playground are available. An extra fee is charged for showers. Sanitary services, firewood, a store, and a cafe are located within one mile. Leashed pets are permitted.

Reservations, fees: Reservations are accepted. Sites are $12.50 per night. The campground is open year-round.

Contact: Phone (360) 267-6115 or write to P.O. Box 689, Grayland, WA 98547.

Directions: From Interstate 5 south of Olympia, take exit 104 and turn west on U.S. 101 (which becomes Highway 8 and then U.S. 12). Drive approximately 46 miles to the turnoff for Highway 105. Turn south and continue 22 miles southwest to Grayland. The RV park is located in town.

Trip notes: This is a small, private park designed for families. Beach access is not far, and Twin Harbors and Grayland Beach State Parks are just a few minutes away. This is an excellent layover for tourists who want to get off U.S. 101.

㉒ Happy Trails–Bay Center KOA

Location: On Willapa Bay; map B1, grid d6.

Campsites, facilities: There are 22 tent sites and 55 sites for trailers or RVs of any length, 11 with full and 44 with partial hookups; 15 sites are drive-throughs. There are also two cabins. Piped water and picnic tables are provided. Bottled gas, sanitary services, toilets, showers, a recreation hall, a store, laundry facilities, and ice are available. Electricity, sewer hookups, and firewood can be purchased for an extra fee. There is a cafe nearby. Boat docks and launching facilities are about three miles from camp on Willapa Bay. Leashed pets and motorbikes are permitted.

Reservations, fees: Reservations are accepted. Sites are $18–$23 per night; cabins are $34 per night. The campground is open from March through October.

Contact: Phone (360) 875-6344 or write to P.O. Box 315, Bay Center, WA 98527.

Directions: From Interstate 5 at Kelso, turn west on Highway 4 and drive 63 miles. Then turn north on U.S. 101 and drive about 10 miles, then take the Bay Center/Dike exit and drive three miles west to the campground.

Trip notes: This 11-acre camp on the shore of Willapa Bay has a trail leading to the beach. The campsites are graveled and shady.

㉓ Evergreen Court

Location: Near Leadbetter Point State Park; map B1, grid e5.

Campsites, facilities: There are eight tent sites and 34 sites for trailers or RVs of any length. Electricity, piped water, sewer hookups, cable TV, and picnic tables are provided. Sanitary services, toilets, showers, firewood, and a playground are available. A store, a cafe, and laundry facilities are within two miles. Leashed pets and motorbikes are permitted.

Reservations, fees: Reservations are accepted. Sites are $9–$12 per night. The campground is open year-round.

Contact: Phone the park at (360) 665-6351 or write to P.O. Box 488, Ocean Park, WA 98640.

Directions: From Interstate 5 at Longview, turn west on Highway 4 and drive 63 miles. Turn south on U.S. 101 and drive 13 miles to the junction with Highway 103. Turn north on Highway 103 and drive nine miles to the campground.

Trip notes: This five-acre, wooded campground with beach access is near Leadbetter Point State Park, a day-use park and natural area that adjoins a wildlife refuge. The trails at Leadbetter lead through the dunes and woods and provide opportunities for seeing both marine birds and waterfowl, especially in the spring and fall. There is also a boat launch. Within five miles of the campground are two nine-hole golf courses.

㉔ Timberland RV Park

Location: Near the Willapa River; map B1, grid d7.

Campsites, facilities: There is an area for dispersed tent camping and 24 drive-through sites for trailers or RVs of any length. Electricity, piped water, sewer hookups, cable TV, and picnic tables are provided. Toilets and showers are available. Bottled gas, sanitary services, a store, a cafe, laundry facilities, and ice are located within one mile. Boat docks can be found nearby where the Willapa River empties into Willapa Bay. Leashed pets and motorbikes are permitted.

Reservations, fees: Reservations are accepted. Sites are $9–$15 per night. The campground is open year-round.

Contact: Phone (360) 942-3325 or write to 850 Crescent, Raymond, WA 98577.

Directions: From Olympia, drive south on Interstate 5 to exit 104. Turn west on U.S. 101 (which becomes Highway 8 and then U.S. 12) and drive 46 miles to Hoquiam. Turn south on U.S. 101 and drive 21 miles to Raymond. At the junction of Highway 105 and U.S. 101, turn west on Highway 105 and drive six blocks. Turn south on Crescent Street and drive two blocks to the park at the end of the street.

Trip notes: The wooded shore of the Willapa River is the setting for this three-acre park, with fishing, hunting, clamming, and golfing among the nearby recreation options. The river is a popular spot during salmon or steelhead runs.

㉕ Southbend Mobile and RV Park

Location: On the Willapa River; map B1, grid d7.

Campsites, facilities: There are two tent sites and six drive-through sites for trailers or RVs of any length. Electricity, piped water, and sewer hookups are provided. Toilets, showers, a recreation hall, and a laundry room are available. Bottled gas, a store, a cafe, and ice are within one mile. Boat docks and launching facilities can be found nearby where the Willapa River empties into Willapa Bay. Pets and motorbikes are permitted.

Reservations, fees: Reservations are accepted. Sites are $15 per night. The campground is open year-round.

Contact: Phone (360) 875-5165 or write to P.O. Box 4, South Bend, WA 98586.

Directions: From Interstate 5 at Longview, turn west on Highway 4 and drive 63 miles, then turn north and drive about 20 miles to South Bend. Turn south on Central and proceed to the campground in town.

Trip notes: This small, wooded park covering two acres near the Willapa River makes a decent layover for tourists traveling U.S. 101. Additional facilities within five miles of the campground include an 18-hole golf course.

㉖ Ocean Park Resort

Location: On Willapa Bay; map B1, grid e5.

Campsites, facilities: There are seven tent sites and 70 sites for trailers or RVs of any length; 34 are drive-throughs. Electricity, piped water, sewer hookups, and picnic tables are provided. Bottled gas, toilets, a recreation hall, laundry facilities, ice, a playground, firewood, a hot tub, and a swimming pool are available. An extra fee is charged for showers. A store and a cafe can be found within one mile. Boat docks and launching facilities are located nearby on Willapa Bay. Leashed pets and motorbikes are permitted.

Reservations, fees: Reservations are accepted. Sites are $17 per night. The campground is open year-round.

Contact: Phone the park at (800) 835-4634 or (360) 665-4585, fax (360) 665-4130, or write to P.O. Box 339, Ocean Park, WA 98640.

Directions: From Interstate 5 at Portland, Oregon, turn northwest on Highway 30 and drive approximately 100 miles to Longview. Turn west on Highway 4 and drive 63 miles, then turn south on U.S. 101 and drive 13 miles to the junction with Highway 103. Turn north on Highway 103 and drive 11 miles to the town of Ocean Park, then turn east on 259th Street and drive two blocks to the park at the end of the road.

Trip notes: This wooded, 10-acre campground with access to the shoreline of Willapa Bay is primarily for RVs. The sites are grassy and shaded. To the north, Leadbetter Point State Park provides a side trip option.

㉗ Westgate Motor and Trailer Court

Location: Near Long Beach; map B1, grid e5.

Campsites, facilities: There are 39 sites for trailers or RVs of any length; 15 are drive-throughs. There are also six cabins. Electricity, piped water, and sewer hookups are provided. Rest rooms, showers, a recreation hall, and ice are available. A store, a cafe, and a Laundromat can be found within two miles. Boat docks and launching facilities are located nearby on Willapa Bay. Leashed pets are permitted.

Reservations, fees: Reservations are accepted. Sites are $17–$18 per night; cabins are $47.50–$65 per night. The campground is open year-round.

Contact: Phone the park at (360) 665-4211

or write to 20803 Pacific Highway, Ocean Park, WA 98640.

Directions: From Interstate 5 at Longview, turn west on Highway 4 and drive 63 miles, then turn south on U.S. 101 and drive 13 miles to the junction with Highway 103. Turn north on Highway 103 and drive 7.5 miles to the campground on the south edge of the town of Ocean Park.

Trip notes: Highlights of this very pretty and clean four-acre camp include beach access, oceanfront sites, and all the amenities. Additional facilities within five miles of the campground include an 18-hole golf course.

28 Ocean Aire

Location: Near Willapa Bay; map B1, grid e5.
Campsites, facilities: There are 46 drive-through sites for trailers or RVs of any length. No tents are allowed. Electricity, piped water, sewer hookups, and picnic tables are provided. Sanitary services, toilets, showers, laundry facilities, and ice are available. A store and a cafe can be found next door. Boat rentals are nearby on Willapa Bay. Leashed pets are permitted.

Reservations, fees: Reservations are accepted. Sites are $10–$15 per night. The campground is open year-round.

Contact: Phone (360) 665-4027 or write to P.O. Box 155, Ocean Park, WA 98640.

Directions: From Interstate 5 at Portland, Oregon, turn northwest on Highway 30 and drive approximately 100 miles to Astoria, Oregon. Turn north on U.S. 101 into Washington state. Continue north for about 10 miles to the junction with Highway 103. Turn north on Highway 103 and drive 11 miles to the town of Ocean Park, then turn east on 259th Street. Drive two blocks to the camp.

Trip notes: This camp covers two acres and has access to the shoreline of Willapa Bay. Additional facilities found within five miles of the campground include tennis courts. Leadbetter Point State Park, about eight miles north, is open for day use and provides footpaths for walking through the state-designated natural area and wildlife refuge.

29 Pegg's RV Park

Location: Near Long Beach; map B1, grid e5.
Campsites, facilities: There are six tent sites and 30 sites for trailers or RVs of any length. Electricity, piped water, cable TV, sewer hookups, and picnic tables are provided. Sanitary services, toilets, a recreation hall, laundry facilities, and ice are available. An extra fee is charged for showers. Bottled gas, a store, and a cafe can be found within one mile. Leashed pets and motorbikes are permitted.

Reservations, fees: Reservations are accepted. Sites are $16 per night. The campground is open from mid-April to mid-September.

Contact: Phone (360) 642-2451 or write to 15301 Pacific Highway, Long Beach, WA 98631.

Directions: From Interstate 5 at Portland, Oregon, turn northwest on Highway 30 and drive approximately 100 miles to Astoria, Oregon. Turn north on U.S. 101 into Washington state. Continue north for about 10 miles to the junction with Highway 103. Turn north on Highway 103 and drive 5.5 miles to the campground.

Trip notes: Pan fishing and beachcombing are two possible activities at this wooded three-acre campground with beach access. Additional facilities within five miles include an 18-hole golf course.

30 Ma and Pa's Pacific RV Park

Location: Near Long Beach; map B1, grid f5.
Campsites, facilities: There are 53 sites for trailers or RVs of any length. No tents are allowed. Electricity, piped water, sewer hookups, and picnic tables are provided. Toilets, laundry facilities, and ice are available. An extra fee is charged for showers. Bottled gas, a store, and a cafe can be found within one mile. Leashed pets are permitted.

Reservations, fees: Reservations are accepted. Sites are $16–$18.55 per night. The campground is open year-round.

Contact: Phone (360) 642-3253, fax (360) 642-5039, or write to 10515 Pacific Highway, Long Beach, WA 98631.

Directions: From Interstate 5 at Portland, Oregon, turn northwest on Highway 30 and drive approximately 100 miles to Astoria, Oregon. Turn north on U.S. 101 into Washington state. Continue north for about 10 miles to the junction with Highway 103. Turn north on Highway 103 and drive four miles to the campground.

Trip notes: This park on two acres with beach access has spacious concrete sites near the shore. Additional facilities found within five miles of the campground include an 18-hole golf course, marked bike trails, and a riding stable.

③ Cranberry Trailer Park

Location: Near Long Beach; map B1, grid f5.
Campsites, facilities: There are 20 sites for trailers or RVs of any length in this adult-only campground; two sites are drive-throughs. No tents are allowed. Electricity, piped water, and sewer hookups are provided. Sanitary services, toilets, showers, a recreation room, and ice are available. Bottled gas, a store, a cafe, and laundry facilities can be found within one mile. Leashed pets are permitted.

Reservations, fees: Reservations are accepted. Sites are $10–$12 per night. The campground is open from April through October, weather permitting.

Contact: Phone (360) 642-2027 or write to 1801 Cranberry Road, Long Beach, WA 98631.

Directions: From Interstate 5 at Portland, Oregon, turn northwest on Highway 30 and drive approximately 100 miles to Astoria, Oregon. Turn north on U.S. 101 into Washington state. Continue north for about 10 miles to the junction with Highway 103. Turn north on Highway 103 and drive 4.5 miles to Cranberry Road, then turn east and continue one-quarter of a mile to the campground.

Trip notes: This park covers two acres and has beach access. Additional facilities found within five miles of the campground include an 18-hole golf course, marked bike trails, and a riding stable.

③ Andersen's RV Park on the Ocean

Location: Near Long Beach; map B1, grid f5.
Campsites, facilities: There are 15 tent sites and 59 sites for trailers or RVs of any length. Electricity, piped water, sewer hookups, cable TV, and picnic tables are provided. Sanitary services, toilets, showers, a hall, laundry facilities, ice, propane, bottled gas, a fax machine, a horseshoe pit, and a playground are available. A store and cafe can be found within two miles. Leashed pets are permitted.

Reservations, fees: Reservations are accepted. Sites are $14–$18 per night. The campground is open year-round.

Contact: Phone (360) 642-2231 or (800) 645-6795, fax (360) 642-2231, or write to 1400 138th Street, Long Beach, WA 98631.

Directions: From Interstate 5 at Longview, turn west on Highway 4 and drive 63 miles, then turn south on U.S. 101 and drive 13 miles to the junction with Highway 103. Turn north on Highway 103 and drive five miles to the park.

Trip notes: A path through the dunes will get you to the beach in a flash from this five-acre camp set in a flat, sandy area with graveled sites. Recreation options include beach bonfires, beachcombing, surf fishing, and clamming (seasonal). Additional facilities found within five miles of the campground include a nine-hole golf course, a riding stable, and tennis courts.

③ Western Lakes

Location: Near Naselle; map B1, grid f7.
Campsites, facilities: There are three primitive tent sites. Picnic tables, fire grills, tent pads, and vault toilets are provided, but there is no piped water. Leashed pets are permitted.

Reservations, fees: No reservations are accepted. There is no fee. The campground is open year-round.

Contact: Department of Natural Resources, Central Region, 1405 Rush Road, Chehalis, WA 98532-8763; (360) 748-2383.

Directions: From Interstate 5 at Longview, turn west on Highway 4 and drive approximately 60 miles to milepost 3, just past Naselle. Turn north on C-Line Road and drive one mile (take the right fork to Naselle Youth Camp). Turn right on Road C-4000 and drive 1.4 miles, then turn left on Road C-2600 and drive one mile. Turn right on Road WA-WT-8520 and drive one-third of a mile to the campground.

Trip notes: You want quiet and solitude? You found it. This tiny, primitive campground is a jewel, set in a wooded area near Western Lakes, just outside of Naselle. It's a prime camp for travelers heading to the coast who want a day or two of privacy before they hit the crowds. There are some good hiking trails nearby.

34 The Beacon-Charters RV Park

Location: Near Fort Canby State Park; map B1, grid f5.

Campsites, facilities: There are 60 sites for trailers or RVs of any length. Electricity, piped water, and sewer hookups are provided. Toilets and ice are available. Showers can be obtained for an extra fee. Bottled gas, a store, a cafe, and a Laundromat are located within one mile. Boat docks and launching facilities are nearby. Leashed pets are permitted.

Reservations, fees: Reservations are accepted. Sites are $14–$16 per night. The campground is open year-round.

Contact: Phone (360) 642-2138 or write to P.O. Box 74, Ilwaco, WA 98624.

Directions: From Interstate 5 at Longview, turn west on Highway 4 and drive 63 miles, then turn south on U.S. 401, which becomes U.S. 101 at Astoria Bridge, and drive 15 miles to Ilwaco. The park is on the corner of Howerton and Elizabeth at the Port of Ilwaco.

Trip notes: This two-acre park at the Port of Ilwaco docks has riverside access and a view of the Columbia River. Highlights include fishing charters during the season (roughly from

mid-May through late September). Nearby Fort Canby State Park offers numerous hiking trails and an interpretive center on maritime and military history. Additional facilities within five miles of the campground include an 18-hole golf course.

35 Cove RV and Trailer Park

Location: Near Fort Canby State Park; map B1, grid f5.

Campsites, facilities: There are 43 sites for trailers or RVs of any length. Electricity, piped water, and sewer and cable TV hookups are provided. Sanitary services, toilets, coin-operated showers, and a laundry room are available. Bottled gas, a store, and a cafe are located within one mile. Boat docks, launching facilities, and rentals are nearby. Leashed pets are permitted.

Reservations, fees: Reservations are accepted. Sites are $12–$15 per night. The campground is open year-round.

Contact: Phone (360) 642-3689, fax (360) 642-3621, or write to P.O. Box 38, Ilwaco, WA 98624.

Directions: From Interstate 5 at Longview, turn west on Highway 4 and drive 63 miles, then turn south on U.S. 101 and drive 15 miles to Ilwaco. At the junction of Spruce Street SW and First Street, turn west on Spruce Street and drive one block, then turn south on Second Avenue SW and drive four blocks south to the campground.

Trip notes: This five-acre park located where the Pacific Ocean and the Columbia River meet has beach and fishing access nearby. Fish and clam cleaning facilities can be found in the park. A maritime museum, hiking trails, a full-service marina, and a riding stable are located within five miles of the camp.

36 Wildwood RV Park and Campground

Location: Near Fort Canby State Park; map B1, grid f5.

Campsites, facilities: There are 25 tent sites and 30 sites for trailers or RVs of any length at this campground for the age-50-and-over crowd. Electricity, piped water, sewer hookups, and picnic tables are provided. Sanitary services and toilets are available. Showers can be obtained for an extra fee. Bottled gas, firewood, a store, a cafe, laundry facilities, and ice are located within one mile. Leashed pets are permitted.

Reservations, fees: Reservations are accepted. Sites are $12–$17 per night. The campground is open from April through September.

Contact: Phone the park at (360) 642-2131 or write to Route 1, P.O. Box 76, Long Beach, WA 98631.

Directions: From Interstate 5 at Portland, Oregon, turn northwest on Highway 30 and drive approximately 100 miles to Astoria, Oregon. Turn north on U.S. 101 into Washington state. Continue north for about 10 miles to Sandridge Road (located one-half mile east of the junction with Highway 103). Turn north and drive three-quarters of a mile to the park.

Trip notes: This pretty, wooded park, for those age 50 and over, covers five acres and has beach access, pan fishing, and its own little pond. Additional facilities found within five miles of the campground include an 18-hole golf course, a full-service marina, and tennis courts. See the Beacon-Charters RV Park (campground number 34) for attractions at nearby Fort Canby State Park.

37 KOA Ilwaco

Location: Near Fort Canby State Park; map B1, grid f5.

Campsites, facilities: There are 50 tent sites and 114 drive-through sites for trailers or RVs of any length. Two cabins are also available. Electricity, piped water, and sewer and cable TV hookups are provided. Bottled gas, sanitary services, toilets, showers, a recreation hall, a store, laundry facilities, ice and a playground are available. Leashed pets are permitted.

Reservations, fees: Reservations are ac-

cepted; phone (800) 562-3258. Sites are $20–$26 per night; cabins are $40 per night. The campground is open from mid-May to mid-October.

Contact: Phone the park at (360) 642-3292 or write to P.O. Box 549, Ilwaco, WA 98624.

Directions: From Interstate 5 at Olympia, take the Highway 8 exit and drive west. Turn south on U.S. 101 and drive about nine miles to the junction of U.S. 101 Alternate. The campground is located at the junction.

Trip notes: This 17-acre camp is about nine miles from the beach. Pan fishing, horseshoe pits, and a recreation room provide possible activities. Additional facilities found within five miles of the campground include a maritime museum, hiking trails, and a nine-hole golf course.

38 Sou'Wester Lodge and Trailer Park

Location: In Seaview on the Long Beach Peninsula; map B1, grid f5.

Campsites, facilities: There are 10 tent sites and 60 sites for trailers or RVs of any length; five are drive-throughs. Electricity, piped water, and sewer hookups are provided. Toilets, showers, cable TV, and laundry facilities are available. Bottled gas, sanitary services, a store, a cafe, and ice are located within one mile. Boat launching facilities are nearby. Leashed pets and motorbikes permitted.

Reservations, fees: Reservations are accepted. Sites are $13.50–$25 per night. The campground is open year-round.

Contact: Phone the park at (360) 642-2542 or write to P.O. Box 102, Seaview, WA 98644.

Directions: From Interstate 5 at Portland, Oregon, turn northwest on Highway 30 and drive approximately 100 miles to Astoria, Oregon. Turn north on U.S. 101 and drive over the 4.25-mile Columbia River Bridge into Washington state. Turn left on U.S. 101 and drive to the traffic lights in the town of Ilwaco. Turn right and drive on U.S. 101 north for 1.6 miles to Seaview Beach Access (38th Place).

Turn left and drive toward the ocean. Look for the campground on the left.

Trip notes: This three-acre camp with beach access is one of the few sites in the immediate area that provides spots for tent camping. Fishing is a recreation option. Additional facilities found within five miles of the campground include an 18-hole golf course, a full-service marina, and a riding stable.

㉟ Fort Canby State Park

Location: On the Pacific Ocean; map B1, grid f5.

Campsites, facilities: There are four primitive tent sites, 190 developed tent sites, and 60 sites with full hookups for trailers or RVs up to 45 feet long. Picnic tables and fire grills are provided. A sanitary disposal station and toilets are available. Showers can be obtained for an extra fee. A store and a restaurant are located within one mile. Boat launching facilities are nearby. Leashed pets are permitted.

Reservations, fees: Contact Reservations Northwest at (800) 452-5687 ($6 reservation fee). Sites are $11–$16 per night. The campground is open year-round.

Contact: Phone (800) 233-0321 or (360) 642-3078, or write to P.O. Box 488, Ilwaco, WA 98624.

Directions: Drive to the small town of Ilwaco on U.S. 101. At the traffic light in town, turn west and drive three miles on the main road to the park entrance. Follow the signs to the campground areas.

Trip notes: This 1,881-acre park is the choice spot in the area for tent campers. There are two places to camp: a general camping area and the Lake O'Neil area, which offers sites right on the water. Highlights at the park include hiking trails and opportunities for surf, jetty, and ocean fishing. An interpretive center highlights the Lewis and Clark expedition and maritime and military history.

㊵ Oceanic RV Park

Location: In Long Beach; map B1, grid f5.

Campsites, facilities: There are 20 drive-through sites for trailers or RVs of any length. No tents are allowed. Electricity, piped water, and sewer hookups are provided. Toilets and showers are available. Bottled gas, sanitary services, a store, a cafe, a Laundromat, and ice are located within one mile. Boat docks, launching facilities, and rentals are nearby. Leashed pets are permitted.

Reservations, fees: Reservations are accepted. Sites are $11–$15 per night. The campground is open year-round.

Contact: Oceanic RV Park, P.O. Box 242, Long Beach, WA 98631; (360) 642-3836; e-mail: oceanic@aone.com.

Directions: From Interstate 5 at Portland, Oregon, turn northwest on Highway 30 and drive approximately 100 miles to Astoria, Oregon. Turn north on U.S. 101 into Washington state. Continue north for about 10 miles to the junction with Highway 103. Turn north on Highway 103 and drive two miles to Long Beach. The campground is at the south junction of Pacific Highway and Fifth Avenue.

Trip notes: This two-acre camp is within five miles of an 18-hole golf course, marked bike trails, and a full-service marina.

㊶ Sand-Lo Motel and RV Park

Location: Near Long Beach; map B1, grid f5.

Campsites, facilities: There are 15 sites for trailers or RVs of any length. Electricity, piped water, and cable TV and sewer hookups are provided. Sanitary services, toilets, showers, and laundry facilities are available. Bottled gas, a store, a cafe, and ice are located within one mile. Leashed pets and motorbikes are permitted.

Reservations, fees: Reservations are accepted. Sites are $17.75 per night. The campground is open year-round.

Contact: Phone (360) 642-2600 or write to P.O. Box 736, Long Beach, WA 98631.

Directions: From Interstate 5 at Longview, turn west on Highway 4 and drive 63 miles, then turn south on U.S. 101 and drive 13 miles to the junction with Highway 103. Turn north on Highway 103 and drive three miles to the park.

Trip notes: This tiny three-acre park with beach access is within five miles of an 18-hole golf course, a full-service marina, and a riding stable.

㊷ Driftwood RV Park and Cabins

Location: Near Long Beach; map B1, grid f5.

Campsites, facilities: There are 56 sites for trailers or RVs of any length; 22 are drive-throughs. Electricity, piped water, sewer hookups, and picnic tables are provided. Toilets, showers, laundry facilities, and cable TV are available. Bottled gas, a store, and a cafe can be found within one mile. Leashed pets are permitted.

Reservations, fees: Reservations are accepted. Sites are $17 per night. The campground is open from March through October.

Contact: Driftwood RV Park and Cabins, P.O. Box 296, 1512 North Pacific Highway, Long Beach, WA 98631; (360) 642-2711; e-mail: driftwd@aone.com.

Directions: From Interstate 5 at Portland, Oregon, turn northwest on Highway 30 and drive approximately 100 miles to Astoria, Oregon. Turn north on U.S. 101 into Washington state. Continue north for about 10 miles to the junction with Highway 103. Turn north on Highway 103 and drive two miles to the park on the right.

Trip notes: This two-acre park has grassy, shaded sites and beach access. Additional facilities within five miles of the campground include an 18-hole golf course and a full-service marina.

㊸ Anthony's Home Court RV Park

Location: In Long Beach; map B1, grid f5.

Campsites, facilities: There are 25 sites for trailers or RVs. Electricity, piped water, sewer hookups, and picnic tables are provided. Toilets, laundry facilities, ice, and cable TV are available. An extra fee is charged for showers.

Bottled gas, sanitary services, a store, and a cafe are located within one mile. Leashed pets are permitted.

Reservations, fees: Reservations are accepted. Sites are $15–$17 per night. The campground is open year-round.

Contact: Anthony's Home Court RV Park, P.O. Box 1532, Long Beach, WA 98631; (360) 642-2802; e-mail: djh@aone.com.

Directions: From Interstate 5 at Portland, Oregon, turn northwest on Highway 30 and drive approximately 100 miles to Astoria, Oregon. Turn north on U.S. 101 into Washington state. Continue north for about 10 miles to the junction with Highway 103. Turn north on Highway 103 and drive two miles to the park on the right.

Trip notes: This two-acre park with beach access is an alternative to Driftwood RV Park (campground number 42), which is just down the street. Additional facilities found within five miles of the campground include an 18-hole golf course, marked bike trails, and a riding stable.

㊹ Sand Castle RV Park

Location: In Long Beach; map B1, grid f5.

Campsites, facilities: There are 10 tent sites and 38 sites for trailers or RVs of any length. Electricity, piped water, sewer and cable TV hookups, and picnic tables are provided. Sanitary services, toilets, laundry facilities, and ice are available. An extra fee is charged for showers. Bottled gas, a store, and a cafe can be found within one mile. Boat docks, launching facilities, and rentals are nearby. Leashed pets and motorbikes permitted.

Reservations, fees: Reservations are accepted. Sites are $15–$20 per night. The campground is open year-round.

Contact: Phone (360) 642-2174, fax (360) 642-7122, or write to 1100 North Pacific Highway, Long Beach, WA 98631.

Directions: From Interstate 5 at Portland, Oregon, turn northwest on Highway 30 and drive approximately 100 miles to Astoria, Oregon. Turn north on U.S. 101 into Washington state. Continue north for about 10 miles to the junction with Highway 103. Turn north and drive two miles to the park on the right.

Trip notes: This very clean, though not particularly scenic, park covers two acres, has beach access, and is one of several in the immediate area. Additional facilities found within five miles of the campground include an 18-hole golf course, marked bike trails, a full-service marina, and a riding stable.

㊺ Chris' Campground and RV Park

Location: In Chinook; map B1, grid f6.

Campsites, facilities: There are 12 tent sites and 75 sites for trailers or RVs. Electricity and piped water are provided. A laundry room, a sanitary dump station, toilets, a store, and ice are available. Showers can be obtained for an extra fee. Bottled gas and a cafe are located within one mile. Boat docks and launching facilities are nearby on the Columbia River. Leashed pets are permitted.

Reservations, fees: Reservations are accepted. Sites are $12–$16 per night. The campground is open from April to late October.

Contact: Phone (360) 777-8475 or write to P.O. Box 204, Chinook, WA 98614.

Directions: From Longview, turn west on Highway 4 and drive 63 miles, then turn south on U.S. 101 and drive 20 miles to Chinook. This park is in Chinook.

Trip notes: This camp covers seven acres and has river access. Additional facilities found within five miles of the campground include a full-service marina. This park caters to anglers; a complete bait and tackle shop is located on the premises, and, in the months of April and May, the owner offers samples of free sturgeon bait and special discounts to all of his fishing customers. Nice folks.

㊻ River's End Campground and RV Park

Location: Near Fort Columbia State Park; map B1, grid f6.

Campsites, facilities: There are 24 tent sites and 54 sites for trailers or RVs of any length; 15 are drive-throughs. Electricity, piped water, sewer hookups, cable TV, and picnic tables are provided. Sanitary services, toilets, a recreation hall, laundry facilities, ice, and a playground are available. Showers and firewood can be obtained for an extra fee. Bottled gas, a store, and a cafe are located within one mile. Boat docks, launching facilities, and rentals are nearby on the Columbia River. Leashed pets and motorbikes permitted.

Reservations, fees: Reservations are accepted. Sites are $12–$16 per night. The campground is open from April to late October.

Contact: Phone (360) 777-8317 or write to P.O. Box 280, Chinook, WA 98614.

Directions: From Interstate 5 at Kelso, turn west on Highway 4 and drive 63 miles, then turn south on U.S. 101 and drive 20 miles to Chinook. The campground is at the north edge of town.

Trip notes: This wooded campground spreads over five acres and has riverside access. Salmon fishing is available here. Additional facilities found within five miles of the campground include marked bike trails and a full-service marina. Also nearby is Fort Columbia State Park, which has an interpretive center featuring the history of coastal artillery.

㊼ Mauch's Sundown RV Park

Location: Near Fort Columbia State Park; map B1, grid f6.

Campsites, facilities: There are 50 sites for trailers or RVs of any length at this adult-oriented park. Electricity, piped water, sewer hookups, and picnic tables are provided. Sanitary services, cable TV, toilets, firewood, laundry facilities, a store, propane gas, and ice are available. Showers can be obtained for an extra fee. A cafe is located within three miles. Boat docks and launching facilities are nearby on the Columbia River. Motorbikes are permitted.

Reservations, fees: Reservations are accepted. Sites are $8–$15 per night. The campground is open year-round.

Contact: Phone (360) 777-8713 or write to P.O. Box 129, Chinook, WA 98614.

Directions: From Astoria, Oregon, on Highway 30, drive north into Washington state for approximately eight miles to Chinook. The park is in town next to the Astoria Bridge.

Trip notes: Mauch's, an adults-only park, covers four acres, has riverside access, and is in a wooded, hilly setting with grassy sites. It's near Fort Columbia State Park, which has a newly renovated interpretive center featuring the history of coastal artillery.

48 Skamokawa Vista Park

Location: Near the Columbia River; map B1, grid f6.

Campsites, facilities: There are four tent sites and 30 sites for trailers or RVs of any length. Electricity, piped water, and picnic tables are provided. Six of the 21 RV sites offer direct water hookups. Flush toilets, a dump station, showers, firewood, tennis and basketball courts, and a playground are available. Bottled gas, a store, a cafe, and ice are located within one mile. Boat docks and launching facilities are nearby. Leashed pets and motorbikes are permitted.

Reservations, fees: Reservations are accepted. Sites are $10–$16 per night. The campground is open year-round.

Contact: Phone the park at (360) 795-8605 or write to P.O. Box 220, Skamokawa, WA 98647.

Directions: From Interstate 5 at Kelso, turn west on Highway 4 and drive 35 miles to Skamokawa. Continue one-half mile west on Highway 4 to the campground.

Trip notes: This camp covers 30 acres and has access to the Columbia River, where fishing, swimming, and boating are all options. Additional facilities found within five miles of the campground include a full-service marina and additional tennis courts.

Map B2

Washington State Map .... *page 6*
One inch equals approximately 20 miles.

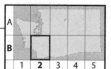

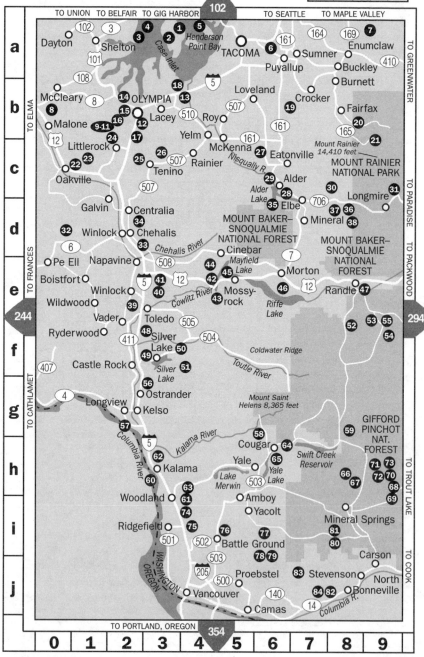

264

Chapter B2 features:

❶ Penrose Point State Park

Location: On Puget Sound; map B2, grid a3.

Campsites, facilities: There is one primitive tent site and 83 developed sites for tents or self-contained RVs up to 35 feet long. Picnic tables and fire grills are provided. A sanitary disposal station, coin-operated showers, and toilets are available. Some facilities are wheelchair accessible. Boat docks are nearby and can be used for overnight moorage for a fee. Leashed pets are permitted.

Reservations, fees: Contact Reservations Northwest at (800) 452-5687 ($6 reservation fee). Sites are $5–$11 per night. The campground is open year-round.

Contact: Phone (800) 233-0321 or (253) 884-2514, or write to 321-158th Avenue KPS, Lake Bay, WA 98439.

Directions: From Interstate 5 at Tacoma, drive 10 miles north on Highway 16, then turn west on Highway 302 and drive 5.25 miles. Go south on Key Peninsula Highway for 9.2 miles, through the towns of Key Center and Home. Turn left at Cornwall Road KPS and drive 1.25 miles. Turn left on 158th Avenue KPS and drive into the park.

Trip notes: This park on Carr Inlet in Puget Sound, overlooking Lake Bay, has a remote feel, but it's actually not far from Tacoma. Because of the circular driving route it takes to get here, a lot of people bypass it. The park is known for its excellent fishing, clamming, and oysters.

❷ Joemma Beach State Park

Location: On Puget Sound; map B2, grid a3.

Campsites, facilities: There are three primitive sites and 19 sites for tents, trailers, or RVs up to 35 feet long. Picnic tables, fire grills, and tent pads are provided. Vault toilets, piped water, boat launching facilities, and a dock are available. Leashed pets are permitted.

Reservations, fees: No reservations are accepted. Sites are $10 per night; there is a $3 launch fee. The campground is open from Memorial Day through Labor Day.

Contact: Phone (800) 233-0321 or (253) 265-3606, or write to 11101 56th Street NW, Gig Harbor, WA 98332.

Directions: From Tacoma, drive 10 miles north on Highway 16, then continue west for about 15 miles on Highway 302 to the town of Home. From the bridge in Home, follow Longbranch Road south for 1.3 miles, turn right on Whiteman Road and drive 2.3 miles, then turn right on Bay Road and drive one mile to the camp on the right.

Trip notes: This beautiful camp set along the shore of the peninsula is a less crowded alternative to Penrose Point State Park (campground number 1). Piped water and boating facilities make it a winner.

❸ Jarrell Cove State Park

Location: On Harstine Island; map B2, grid a3.

Campsites, facilities: There are 20 sites for tents or self-contained RVs up to 30 feet long. Picnic tables and fire grills are provided. Flush toilets and coin-operated showers are available. Some facilities are wheelchair accessible. Boat docks can be obtained for overnight moorage for a fee. Leashed pets are permitted.

Reservations, fees: No reservations are accepted. Sites are $10 per night; there is an $8–$11 moorage fee. The campground is open from April through October.

Contact: Phone (800) 233-0321 or (360) 426-9226, or write to East 391 Wingert Road, Shelton, WA 98584.

Directions: From Interstate 5 at Olympia, turn north on U.S. 101 and drive 22 miles to Shelton. Turn east on Highway 3 and drive about eight miles. Turn right on Spencer Lake Road and continue to the Harstine Bridge. Cross the bridge to Harstine Island and turn left at the stop sign. Continue four miles to the park on the left.

Trip notes: This wooded park is rarely crowded and offers a protected cove for boating and docking facilities. A private marina is nearby. Fishing here is excellent, and there is a nice beach for sunbathing or beachcombing.

❹ Jarrell Cove Marina

Location: Near Shelton; map B2, grid a3.

Campsites, facilities: There are four sites for trailers or RVs up to 27 feet long. Piped water, electricity, and picnic tables are provided. Bottled gas, toilets, showers, sanitary services, a store, a laundry room, barbecues, boat docks, and boat rentals are available. Leashed pets are permitted.

Reservations, fees: Reservations are accepted. Sites are $20 per night. The campground is open year-round.

Contact: Phone (360) 426-8823 or write to 220 East Wilson Road, Shelton, WA 98584.

Directions: From Interstate 5 at Olympia, turn north on U.S. 101 and drive 22 miles to Shelton. Turn east on Highway 3 and drive about eight miles. Turn right on Pickering Road and drive to the Harstine Bridge. Cross the bridge and continue north on North Island Drive. Turn west on Haskell Hill Road and drive one mile to the marina.

Trip notes: Marina and boat rentals are the big bonus here. The drive-through sites are ideal for pickup campers towing boats on trailers.

❺ Kopachuck State Park

Location: On Puget Sound; map B2, grid a4.

Campsites, facilities: There are two primitive tent sites and 41 developed sites for tents or self-contained RVs up to 35 feet long. Picnic tables and fire grills are provided. A sanitary disposal station, coin-operated showers, toilets, and boat buoys are available. Some facilities are wheelchair accessible. Leashed pets are permitted.

Reservations, fees: No reservations are accepted. Sites are $7–$11 per night. The

campground is open from March through October.

Contact: Phone (800) 233-0321 or (253) 265-3606, or write to 11101 56th Street NW, Gig Harbor, WA 98332.

Directions: From Interstate 5 at Tacoma, turn north on Highway 16 and drive seven miles. At the sign for Kopachuck State Park, turn west and drive five miles to the camp.

Trip notes: Located on Henderson Bay on Puget Sound near Tacoma, this is a nice, developed park with full facilities for tent campers. There is a large beach area for clamming or lounging. Fishing access is available by boat only. A boat launch is located not far from camp.

❻ Majestic Manor RV Park

Location: On the Puyallup River; map B2, grid a6.

Campsites, facilities: There are 12 tent sites and 118 sites for trailers or RVs of any length. Electricity, piped water, and sewer hookups are provided. Flush toilets, bottled gas, sanitary services, showers, a recreation hall, a store, laundry facilities, ice, and a swimming pool are available. A cafe is located within one mile. Leashed pets and motorbikes are permitted.

Reservations, fees: Reservations are accepted. Sites are $15–$20 per night. The campground is open year-round.

Contact: Phone (800) 348-3144 or (253) 845-3144, fax (253) 841-2248, or write to 7022 River Road, Puyallup, WA 98371.

Directions: From Interstate 5 near Tacoma, take exit 135 and drive four miles east on Highway 167 (River Road) to the park on the right.

Trip notes: This clean, pretty park along the Puyallup River caters to RVers. Nearby recreation options include an 18-hole golf course, a full-service marina, and tennis courts. For information on the attractions in Tacoma, see the trip notes for Dash Point State Park (campground number 127 in Chapter A2).

⑦ Kanaskat-Palmer State Park

Location: On the Green River; map B2, grid a9.

Campsites, facilities: There are 31 tent sites and 19 drive-through sites for trailers or RVs up to 35 feet long. Picnic tables are provided. Electricity, flush toilets, showers, and sanitary services are available. Some facilities are wheelchair accessible. Boat rentals can be found nearby on the Green River. Leashed pets are permitted.

Reservations, fees: No reservations are accepted. Sites are $11–$16 per night. The campground is open year-round, with limited facilities in the winter.

Contact: Phone (800) 233-0321 or (360) 886-0148, or write to 23700 Flaming Geyser, Auburn, WA 98002.

Directions: From Interstate 5 at Tacoma, turn east on Highway 410 and drive about 25 miles to Enumclaw. Turn northeast on Farman Road and drive 11 miles to the park on the left.

Trip notes: This wooded campground offers private campsites along the Green River. In summer, the river is ideal for rafting and kayaking. In winter, it attracts a nice run of steelhead. You can explore the area's hiking trails year-round.

⑧ Porter Creek

Location: On Porter Creek in Capitol Forest; map B2, grid b0.

Campsites, facilities: There are 14 primitive campsites for tents or small trailers. Picnic tables, fire grills, and tent pads are provided. There is no piped water. Vault toilets and horse-loading ramps are available. Leashed pets and motorbikes are permitted.

Reservations, fees: No reservations are accepted. There is no fee. The campground is open from April through October.

Contact: Department of Natural Resources, Central Region, 1405 Rush Road, Chehalis, WA 98532-8763; (360) 748-2383 or fax (360) 748-2387.

Directions: From Interstate 5 south of Olympia, turn west on U.S. 12 and drive 21 miles to Porter. Go northeast on Porter Creek Road for three miles, then continue straight for another one-half mile. The campground is on the left.

Trip notes: This primitive, rustic campground less than 20 miles from Olympia in Capitol Forest is managed by the Department of Natural Resources. Set along the shore of Porter Creek, it offers trails for hiking, horseback riding, or motorbiking.

⑨ Middle Waddell

Location: On Waddell Creek in Capitol Forest; map B2, grid b1.

Campsites, facilities: There are 24 sites for tents, trailers, or RVs. Picnic tables, fire grills, and tent pads are provided. Vault toilets are available, but there is no piped water. Leashed pets and motorbikes are permitted.

Reservations, fees: No reservations are accepted. There is no fee. The campground is open from April through October.

Contact: Department of Natural Resources, Central Region, 1405 Rush Road, Chehalis, WA 98532-8763; (360) 748-2383 or fax (360) 748-2387.

Directions: From Interstate 5 south of Olympia, take exit 95 and turn west on Highway 121. Drive four miles to Littlerock. Continue west for one mile and turn right on Waddell Creek Road. Drive three miles, turn left, and continue 100 yards to the campground on your left.

Trip notes: This wooded campground is nestled along Waddell Creek in Capitol Forest. The trails are used primarily for motorbikes, making for a rather noisy atmosphere. Remember, no piped water is available here.

⑩ Fall Creek

Location: On Fall Creek in Capitol Forest; map B2, grid b1.

Campsites, facilities: There are eight primitive campsites for tents or small trailers. Picnic tables, fire grills, and tent pads are provided. Vault toilets, piped water, and a horse-loading ramp are available, but there is no piped water. Leashed pets are permitted.

Reservations, fees: No reservations are accepted. There is no fee. The campground is open from April through October.

Contact: Department of Natural Resources, Central Region, 1405 Rush Road, Chehalis, WA 98532-8763; (360) 748-2383 or fax (360) 748-2387.

Directions: From Interstate 5 at Olympia, turn north on U.S. 101 and drive four miles. Take the Mud Bay exit and drive south on Delphi Road for six miles. Continue straight on Waddell Creek Road for three miles, then turn right and go 1.5 miles. Take the left fork and drive two miles on C-Line Road, then turn left onto Road C-4000 and drive 2.5 miles. Turn right and proceed 200 yards to the campground.

Trip notes: This wooded camp on Fall Creek in Capitol Forest is a good alternative to Middle Waddell (campground number 9), since the trails here are for hikers and horseback riders only. That means no motorbikes and a more peaceful setting.

⑪ Margaret McKenny

Location: In Capitol Forest; map B2, grid b1.

Campsites, facilities: There are 25 primitive sites for tents or small trailers; seven sites are walk-ins. Picnic tables, fire grills, and tent pads are provided. Pit toilets, a campfire circle, and a horse-loading ramp are available, but there is no piped water. Leashed pets are permitted.

Reservations, fees: No reservations are accepted. There is no fee. The campground is open from April through October.

Contact: Department of Natural Resources, Central Region, 1405 Rush Road, Chehalis, WA 98532-8763; (360) 748-2383 or fax (360) 748-2387.

Directions: From Interstate 5 south of Olympia, take exit 95 and turn west on Highway 121. Drive four miles to Littlerock. Continue west for one mile and turn right on Waddell Creek Road. Drive 2.5 miles, then turn left and drive about 200 yards to the campground.

Trip notes: This cool, scenic, streamside camp-

ground in Capitol Forest is managed by the Department of Natural Resources. Nearby trails can be used by hikers as well as horseback riders.

⑫ Olympia Campground

Location: Near Olympia; map B2, grid b2.

Campsites, facilities: There are 95 sites for tents, trailers, or RVs of any length; 40 are drive-throughs. Two cabins are also available. Piped water and picnic tables are provided. Flush toilets, bottled gas, a gas station, sanitary services, showers, a recreation hall, TV hookups, a store, laundry facilities, ice, a playground, a heated swimming pool in the summer, electricity, sewer hookups, and firewood are available. A cafe is located within one mile. Leashed pets and motorbikes are permitted.

Reservations, fees: Reservations are accepted. Sites are $18–$24 per night for two people, plus $3 for each additional person; cabins are $30 per night for four people. The campground is open year-round.

Contact: Phone (360) 352-2551 or write to 1441 83rd Avenue SW, Olympia, WA 98512.

Directions: From Olympia on Interstate 5, take exit 101 and drive east one-quarter mile east on Airdustrial Way. Turn right on Center Street and drive one mile. Turn right on 83rd Avenue and drive an eighth of a mile to the park on the left.

Trip notes: This wooded campground has all the comforts. Nearby recreation options include an 18-hole golf course, hiking trails, marked bike trails, and tennis courts.

⑬ Martin Way Motorhome and RV Park

Location: In Olympia; map B2, grid b4.

Campsites, facilities: There are 18 sites for trailers or RVs of any length in this adult-oriented campground; seven sites are drive-throughs. Electricity, piped water, and sewer and cable TV hookups are provided. Flush toilets, showers, and a laundry room are available. Bottled gas, sanitary services, a store, a cafe, and ice are located within one mile. No pets are allowed.

Reservations, fees: Reservations are accepted. Sites are $13–$20 per night. The campground is open year-round.

Contact: Phone (360) 491-6840 or write to 8103 Martin Way SE, Lacey, WA 98516.

Directions: From Interstate 5 in Olympia, take exit 111 and drive three-quarters of a mile south to Martin Way. Turn west and drive one-quarter mile to the park.

Trip notes: This park, oriented to campers 55 and older, is in urban Olympia. Nearby recreation options include an 18-hole golf course, a full-service marina, tennis courts, and the Nisqually National Wildlife Refuge, home to seven miles of foot trails and a great variety of plant and animal life.

⑭ Coach Post Mobile Home Park

Location: Near Olympia; map B2, grid b2.

Campsites, facilities: There are 20 drive-through sites for trailers or RVs of any length. Electricity, piped water, sewer and cable TV hookups, and picnic tables are provided. Flush toilets, showers, and a laundry room are available. Bottled gas, a store, a cafe, and ice are within a mile. Leashed pets are permitted.

Reservations, fees: Reservations are accepted. Sites are $25 per night. The campground is open year-round.

Contact: Phone (360) 754-7580 or write to 3633 Seventh Avenue SW, Olympia, WA 98512.

Directions: From U.S. 101 in Olympia, take the Black Lake exit and turn left at the fourth stoplight. Drive one mile on Seventh Avenue SW to the campground.

Trip notes: This wooded park is in a rural area just west of Olympia. An 18-hole golf course, a full-service marina, a riding stable, and tennis courts are close by.

⑮ Columbus Park

Location: On Black Lake; map B2, grid b2.

Campsites, facilities: There are 31 sites for trailers or RVs of any length. Electricity, piped water, and picnic tables are provided. Flush toilets, sanitary services, a store, a laundry room, ice, showers, firewood, a playground, boat docks, and launching facilities are available. Bottled gas and a cafe are within one mile. Leashed pets are permitted.

Reservations, fees: Reservations are recommended. Sites are $15 per night. The campground is open year-round.

Contact: Columbus Park, 5700 Black Lake Boulevard, Olympia, WA 98502; (360) 786-9460; e-mail: clmbusprk@aol.com.

Directions: From Interstate 5 in Olympia, take the U.S. 101 exit and drive 1.7 miles northwest, then continue south on Black Lake Boulevard for 3.5 miles to park on the left.

Trip notes: This spot in a wooded area along the shore of Black Lake is an option to Salmon Shores Resort (campground number 16). Nearby recreation possibilities include an 18-hole golf course and a full-service marina.

⑯ Salmon Shores Resort

Location: On Black Lake; map B2, grid b2.

Campsites, facilities: There are 20 tent sites and 45 sites for trailers or RVs of any length. Electricity, piped water, sewer hookups, and picnic tables are provided. Flush toilets, bottled gas, sanitary services, showers, a store, a laundry room, ice, firewood, and a playground are available. A cafe is located within one mile. Boat docks, launching facilities, and rentals are nearby on Black Lake. Leashed pets are permitted.

Reservations, fees: Reservations are accepted. Sites are $10–$14 per night. The campground is open year-round.

Contact: Phone (360) 357-8618 or write to 5446 Black Lake Boulevard, Olympia, WA 98512.

Directions: From Interstate 5 in Olympia, take the U.S. 101 exit and drive 1.7 miles northwest. Turn south on Black Lake Boulevard and drive 3.5 miles to the resort.

Trip notes: This resort on Black Lake is a

large, popular campground that comfortably accommodates tents and RVs alike. Sites are near the lakeshore. An 18-hole golf course, a full-service marina, and a riding stable are nearby. This is one of two camps in the immediate vicinity.

⑰ American Heritage Campground

Location: Near Olympia; map B2, grid b2.

Campsites, facilities: There are 23 tent sites and 72 sites for trailers or RVs of any length. Piped water and picnic tables are provided. Flush toilets, bottled gas, sanitary services, showers, a recreation hall, a group pavilion, recreation programs, a store, a cafe, a laundry room, ice, a playground, a heated swimming pool, electricity and sewer hookups, and firewood are available. Leashed pets and motorbikes are permitted.

Reservations, fees: Reservations are accepted. Sites are $18–$26 per night for two people, plus $3.50 for each additional person. The campground is open from Memorial Day through Labor Day weekend.

Contact: Phone (360) 943-8778 or write to 9610 Kimmie Street SW, Olympia, WA 98512.

Directions: From Olympia, drive five miles south on Interstate 5 to exit 99 and drive one-half mile east. Turn south on Kimmie Street and drive a quarter mile to the campground.

Trip notes: This spacious, wooded campground just off the highway is near lots of activities, including an 18-hole golf course, hiking trails, marked bike trails, and tennis courts. The park features novelty bike rentals, free wagon rides, and free nightly movies. It's exceptionally clean and very pretty, making for a pleasant layover on your way up or down Interstate 5.

⑱ Nisqually Plaza RV Park

Location: Near McAlister Creek; map B2, grid b3.

Campsites, facilities: There are 48 sites for trailers or RVs of any length; eight are drive-throughs. Electricity, piped water, sewer hookups, telephone, cable TV, and picnic tables are provided. Flush toilets, bottled gas, sanitary services, a store, a cafe, a laundry room, ice, a playground, and a swimming pool are available. Boat launching facilities are nearby. Leashed pets are permitted.

Reservations, fees: Reservations are accepted. Sites are $10–$20 per night. The campground is open year-round.

Contact: Phone (360) 491-3831 or write to 10220 Martin Way East, Olympia, WA 98503.

Directions: Heading north on Interstate 5 in Olympia, take exit 114 and turn right. Drive 200 feet and turn right onto Martin Way.

Trip notes: This campground is located on McAlister Creek, where salmon fishing and boating are popular. Nearby recreation opportunities include an 18-hole golf course and the Nisqually National Wildlife Refuge, which offers seven miles of foot trails for viewing a great variety of flora and fauna.

⑲ Rainbow Resort

Location: On Tanwax Lake; map B2, grid b6.

Campsites, facilities: There are seven tent sites and about 50 sites for trailers or RVs up to 40 feet long. Electricity, piped water, sewer hookups, and picnic tables are provided. Flush toilets, bottled gas, firewood, a recreation hall, showers, a store, a laundry room, a hot tub, ice, cable TV, boat docks, boat rentals, launching facilities, and a playground are available. A cafe is located within one mile. Small, leashed pets are permitted.

Reservations, fees: Reservations are accepted. Sites are $7–$14 per night. The campground is open year-round.

Contact: Phone (360) 879-5115 or write to 34217 Tanwax Lake Court East, Eatonville, WA 98328.

Directions: From Interstate 5 at Tacoma, drive 27 miles south on Highway 7, then turn east to Eatonville on Highway 161 and drive seven miles north to Tanwax Drive. Turn and drive east to the resort on Tanwax Lake.

Trip notes: This wooded park along the shore of Tanwax Lake has spacious, shady sites, with especially pretty spots for tents. Highlights include good fishing on the lake, a seasonal fish pond, and a nearby riding stable.

⑳ Evans Creek

Location: On Evans Creek in Mount Baker–Snoqualmie National Forest; map B2, grid b8.

Campsites, facilities: There are 27 tent sites. Picnic tables, hand-pumped water, and fire grills are provided. Vault toilets and firewood are available. Leashed pets are permitted.

Reservations, fees: No reservations are accepted. There is no fee. The campground is open from mid-June to late September.

Contact: Mount Baker–Snoqualmie National Forest, White River Ranger District, 857 Roosevelt Avenue East, Enumclaw, WA 98022; (360) 825-6585.

Directions: From Tacoma on Interstate 5, turn east on Highway 167 and drive nine miles, then continue 11 miles east on Highway 410 to Buckley. Drive 11 miles south on Highway 165 and turn left on Forest Service Road 7920. Drive 1.5 miles to the campground on the right.

Trip notes: This primitive campground is located close to Evans Creek in an off-road-vehicle area near the northwestern corner of Mount Rainier National Park. If you're looking for a quiet, secluded spot, this isn't it. The two nearby roads that lead into the park are secondary or gravel roads and provide access to several other primitive campgrounds and backcountry trails in the park. A national forest map details the back roads and hiking trails.

㉑ Ipsut Creek

Location: Near the Carbon River in Mount Rainier National Park; map B2, grid b8.

Campsites, facilities: There are 29 sites for tents and one group camp. Picnic tables are provided. Pit toilets and piped water are available. Leashed pets are permitted.

Reservations, fees: No reservations are accepted. There is no fee. The campground is open from Memorial Day to Labor Day.

Contact: Mount Rainier National Park, Tahoma Woods, Ashford, WA 98304; (360) 569-2211.

Directions: From Interstate 5 at Tacoma, turn east on Highway 512 and drive 12 miles. Turn right (east) on Highway 167 and drive one mile. Turn east on Highway 410 and drive 13 miles to Buckley. Turn southeast on Highway 165 and drive about 13 miles to the Carbon River Park entrance. The campground is five miles into the park. Note: The five-mile camp access road is closed to motor vehicles due to flood damage; only foot and bicycle traffic is permitted on this road.

Trip notes: This camp is at the end of Carbon River Road and at the beginning of several trails that lead into the backcountry of Mount Rainier National Park, past lakes, glaciers, waterfalls, and many other wonders. Obtain a map from the National Park Service for details, and get a wilderness permit if you plan to stay overnight in the backcountry.

㉒ North Creek

Location: On Cedar Creek; map B2, grid c1.

Campsites, facilities: There are five primitive sites for tents or small trailers. Picnic tables, fire grills, and tent pads are provided. Vault toilets and piped water are available. Leashed pets are permitted.

Reservations, fees: No reservations are accepted. There is no fee. The campground is open from April through October.

Contact: Department of Natural Resources, Central Region, 1405 Rush Road, Chehalis, WA 98532-8763; (360) 748-2383 or fax (360) 748-2387.

Directions: From Interstate 5 south of Olympia, turn west on U.S. 12 and drive 12 miles to Oakville. Continue 2.5 miles west on U.S. 12 to D-Line Road, then head east for two miles. Take the right fork and drive three miles. You'll see the camp on your right.

Trip notes: This little-known, wooded campground managed by the Department of Natural Resources is set along Cedar Creek. There are trails for hikers only. An option is visiting the Chehalis River, a short drive to the west. A canoe launch off U.S. 12 is available north of Oakville.

㉓ Sherman Valley

Location: On Cedar Creek in Capitol Forest; map B2, grid c1.

Campsites, facilities: There are five primitive sites for tents or small trailers and three walk-in sites. Picnic tables, fire grills, and tent pads are provided. Vault toilets and piped water are available. Leashed pets are permitted.

Reservations, fees: No reservations are accepted. There is no fee. The campground is open from April through October.

Contact: Department of Natural Resources, Central Region, 1405 Rush Road, Chehalis, WA 98532-8763; (360) 748-2383 or fax (360) 748-2387.

Directions: From Interstate 5 south of Olympia, turn west on U.S. 12 and drive 12 miles to Oakville. Continue 2.5 miles west on U.S. 12 to D-Line Road, then head east for 1.6 miles and take the fork on the right. Continue 4.5 miles to the campground on the right.

Trip notes: This is one of nine secluded camps located in Capitol Forest and managed by the Department of Natural Resources. Sherman Valley's pleasant, shady campsites are set along the shore of Porter Creek. Hiking trails can be found nearby.

㉔ Mima Falls Trailhead

Location: Near Mima Falls; map B2, grid c1.

Campsites, facilities: There are five primitive sites for tents or small trailers. Picnic tables, fire grills, and tent pads are provided. Vault toilets, piped water, and a horse-loading ramp are available. Leashed pets are permitted.

Reservations, fees: No reservations are accepted. There is no fee. The campground is open from April through October.

Contact: Department of Natural Resources,

Central Region, 1405 Rush Road, Chehalis, WA 98532-8763; (360) 748-2383 or fax (360) 748-2387.

Directions: From Interstate 5 south of Olympia, take the Highway 121 exit and drive four miles west to Littlerock. Continue west for one mile, then turn left on Mima Road and drive 1.5 miles. Turn right on Bordeaux Road and drive one-half mile. At Marksman Road, turn right and continue two-thirds of a mile. Turn left and proceed about 200 yards to the campground.

Trip notes: A highlight here is the excellent trail for hikers and horseback riders that leads to Mima Falls. The campground is very quiet and pretty, which, when combined with the piped water and free admission, makes this a first-rate choice.

㉕ Millersylvania State Park

Location: On Deep Lake; map B2, grid c2.

Campsites, facilities: There are four primitive tent sites, 135 developed tent sites, and 52 sites for trailers or RVs up to 45 feet long. Picnic tables and fire grills are provided. Flush toilets, a sanitary disposal station, a playground, electricity, piped water, showers, and firewood are available. A store, a restaurant, and ice are located within one mile. Some facilities are wheelchair accessible. Boat docks and launching facilities are nearby on Deep Lake. Leashed pets are permitted.

Reservations, fees: No reservations are accepted. Sites are $5–$14 per night. The campground is open year-round.

Contact: Phone (800) 233-0321 or (360) 753-1519, or write to 1224 Tilley Road South, Olympia, WA 98502.

Directions: From Interstate 5 south of Olympia, take exit 95 and drive east on Maytown Road. Turn north on Tilley Road and continue one-half mile to the park.

Trip notes: This popular park not too far from Olympia offers a host of activities, including swimming, trout fishing, hiking, and even a few gut-thumping fitness trails. The park is set along the shore of Deep Lake. Historic highlights are the groves of old-growth trees and the Civilian Conservation Corps buildings.

26 Offut Lake RV Resort

Location: On Offut Lake; map B2, grid c3.

Campsites, facilities: There are nine tent sites and 51 sites for trailers or RVs of any length; 35 sites have full hookups. There are also two cabins. Electricity, piped water, sewer hookups, and picnic tables are provided. Flush toilets, sanitary services, firewood, a recreation hall, a store, a laundry room, ice, coin-operated showers, boat docks, boat rentals, and a playground are available. Showers can be obtained for an extra fee. Leashed pets and motorbikes are permitted.

Reservations, fees: Reservations are accepted. Sites are $12–$17 per night. The campground is open year-round.

Contact: Phone (360) 264-2438 or write to 4005 120th Avenue SE, Tenino, WA 98589.

Directions: From Olympia, drive south on Interstate 5 for about seven miles and take the 101 Air Industrial Way exit. Turn east on Highway 507 and drive eight miles to exit 88A (Tenino). Turn north on Old Highway 99 and drive four miles. Turn east on Offut Lake Road and drive 1.5 miles to the resort.

Trip notes: This lovely wooded campground is on Offut Lake, just enough off the beaten track to provide a bit of seclusion. Fishing, swimming, and boating are favorite activities here. Anglers will find everything they need, including tackle and boat rentals, at the resort.

27 Henley's Silver Lake Resort

Location: Near Silver Lake; map B2, grid c6.

Campsites, facilities: There's an unlimited number of sites for tents and 30 sites for trailers or RVs; 15 sites have full hookups. There are also six cabins. Rest rooms, a sanitary dump, a public phone, snacks, boat rentals, a boat ramp, and a dock are available. Leashed pets are permitted except in the cabins.

Reservations, fees: Reservations for cabins and full-hookup RV sites only are accepted. Sites are $8–$11 per night; cabins are $55 a night. The campground is open from the first day of the fishing season in April through October, weather permitting.

Contact: Phone the resort at (360) 832-3580 or write to 40718 South Silver Lake Road East, Eatonville, WA 98328.

Directions: From Tacoma, drive south on Interstate 5 to Highway 7. Turn south on Highway 7 and drive about 20 miles to the yellow blinking light. Drive about 4.5 miles and you'll see a sign for the Silver Lake Recreation Area. Bear right and drive one-quarter mile to the resort on the left.

Trip notes: This full-facility resort is a perfect family vacation destination. It's one of the rare private campgrounds that caters to tent campers and RV cruisers. Silver Lake is beautiful and provides opportunities for boating and trout fishing. Highlights include a 250-foot boat dock and 50 rental rowboats.

28 Alder Lake Park

Location: On Alder Lake; map B2, grid c6.

Campsites, facilities: There 17 dry tent sites and 87 sites for trailers or RVs of any length, 37 with full hookups. Electricity and piped water are provided. Vault toilets are available. Boat docks and launching facilities are on Alder Lake.

Reservations, fees: Reservations are accepted. Sites are $8–$12 per night. The campground is open from Memorial Day through Labor Day.

Contact: Phone (360) 569-2778 or write 50324 School Road, Eatonville, WA 98330.

Directions: From Interstate 5 at Tacoma, drive 35 miles south on Highway 7 to Alder Lake. Turn left and proceed to the park.

Trip notes: This municipal park along the shore of Alder Lake has pretty campsites near the water and lots of trees and shrubbery. It's a very decent spot to spend a weekend, especially if you want to get off the highway and enjoy some peace and quiet. Of the two campgrounds on the lake (Eagle's Nest Motel-Alder Lake, campground number 29, is the other), this is the only one that allows tents. The Mount Rainier Scenic Railroad leaves from Elbe regularly and makes its way through the forests to Mineral Lake. It features open deck cars, live music, and restored passenger cars.

㉙ Eagle's Nest Motel-Alder Lake

Location: On Alder Lake; map B2, grid c6.

Campsites, facilities: There are 10 sites for trailers or RVs up to 25 feet long. Electricity, piped water, and sewer hookups are provided. Boat launching facilities are located on Alder Lake. Small, leashed pets are permitted.

Reservations, fees: Reservations are accepted. Sites are $15 per night. The campground is open year-round.

Contact: Phone (360) 569-2533 or write to 52120 Mountain Highway East, Eatonville, WA 98328.

Directions: From Interstate 5 at Tacoma, drive 29 miles south on Highway 7 and you'll see the turnoff for the park.

Trip notes: This wooded RV park overlooking Alder Lake is a cozy little spot with all the amenities. It's a smaller, more secluded option for RVs, yet still close to Tacoma. See Alder Lake Park (campground number 28) for information on the Mount Rainier Scenic Railroad.

㉚ Elbe Hills

Location: Near Elbe; map B2, grid c8.

Campsites, facilities: There are three primitive campsites for tents or small trailers. Picnic tables, fire grills, and tent pads are provided. Pit toilets and a group shelter are available, but there is no piped water. Leashed pets are permitted.

Reservations, fees: No reservations are accepted. There is no fee. The campground is open year-round.

Contact: Department of Natural Resources, South Puget Sound Region, P.O. Box 68, Enumclaw, WA 98022-0068; (360) 825-1631.

Directions: From Interstate 5 south of Olympia, take exit 68 and turn east on U.S. 12. Drive 30 miles, then turn north on Highway 7 and drive 17 miles to Elbe. Turn east on Highway 706 and drive six miles, then turn left on a dead-end road and continue three miles. Keep right and continue one-half mile, then turn left and drive about 100 yards to the four-wheel-drive trailhead.

Trip notes: Here's a spot for four-wheel-drive cowboys. The Department of Natural Resources manages this wooded campground and provides eight miles of trails for short wheelbase four-wheel-drive vehicles. Beware: Trucks often get stuck here or can't make it up the hills when it's wet and slippery.

㉛ Cougar Rock

Location: In Mount Rainier National Park; map B2, grid c9.

Campsites, facilities: There are 200 sites for tents or RVs up to 30 feet long. A group camp is also available. Picnic tables are provided. Flush toilets, piped water, a camp store (two miles away), and a sanitary disposal station are available. Some facilities are wheelchair accessible. Leashed pets are permitted.

Reservations, fees: Reservations are accepted. Sites are $10 per night. The campground is open from mid-May to mid-October.

Contact: Mount Rainier National Park, Tahoma Woods, Ashford, WA 98304; (360) 569-2211 or fax (360) 569-2170.

Directions: From Interstate 5 south of Olympia, take exit 68 and turn east on U.S. 12. Drive 30 miles, then turn north on Highway 7 and drive 17 miles to Elbe. Turn east on Highway 706 and drive about 12 miles to the park entrance, then go 11 miles to the campground entrance on the left, about two miles past the Longmire developed area.

Trip notes: Located at 3,180 feet, this park provides a recreation program, and trout fishing is allowed without a permit. See Gateway Inn and RV Park (campground number 36) for information on the nearby park sights and visitor centers.

⓷ Rainbow Falls State Park

Location: On the Chehalis River; map B2, grid d1.

Campsites, facilities: There are three primitive tent sites and 47 sites for tents or self-contained RVs up to 32 feet long. Picnic tables are provided. Flush toilets, piped water, a sanitary disposal station, showers, firewood, and a playground are available. Leashed pets are permitted.

Reservations, fees: No reservations are accepted. Sites are $5–$10 per night. The campground is open April through August.

Contact: Phone (800) 233-0321 or (360) 291-3767, or write to 4008 Highway 6, Chehalis, WA 98532.

Directions: From Interstate 5 at Chehalis, take exit 77 and travel 17 miles west on Highway 6 to the park entrance.

Trip notes: Although this campground is only about 20 minutes from Interstate 5, out-of-towners pass it every time. It's a nice spot, with a swinging bridge (built in 1934) over the Chehalis River. There is a pool at the base of Rainbow Falls for swimming and trout fishing, plus a playground for kids and 6.5 miles of hiking trails, including a self-guided nature trail through the old-growth forest.

⓸ Stan Hedwall Park

Location: On the Chehalis River; map B2, grid d2.

Campsites, facilities: There are 29 sites for trailers or RVs of any length. Electricity, piped water, and picnic tables are provided. Flush toilets, showers, sanitary services, and a playground are available. Bottled gas, a store, a cafe, and a Laundromat are located within one mile. Leashed pets are permitted.

Reservations, fees: Reservations are accepted. Sites are $10–$15 per night. The campground is open from March through October.

Contact: Phone (360) 748-0271 or write to P.O. Box 871, Chehalis, WA 98532.

Directions: Take exit 76 off Interstate 5 near

Chehalis and drive one-eighth mile south on Rice Road to the park.

Trip notes: This park along the Chehalis River is a possible layover for Interstate 5 travelers. Amenities include fishing and swimming access, a playground, and a recreation field. An 18-hole golf course and hiking trails are nearby.

⓺ Peppertree West RV Park

Location: In Centralia; map B2, grid d2.

Campsites, facilities: There are 20 tent sites and 42 sites for trailers or RVs of any length; 28 are drive-throughs. Flush toilets, sanitary services, showers, a recreation hall, a laundry room, ice, bottled gas, a store, and a cafe are available. Boat launching facilities are nearby. Leashed pets and motorbikes are permitted.

Reservations, fees: Reservations are accepted. Sites are $16–$20 per night. The campground is open year-round.

Contact: Phone (360) 736-1124 or write to 1208 Alder Street, Centralia, WA 98531.

Directions: From Olympia, drive south on Interstate 5 about 23 miles to exit 81 in Centralia. Go west on Melon Street, taking the first left, and drive to the park, which is in the southeast corner of Centralia.

Trip notes: If you're driving Interstate 5 and looking for a stopover, this spot is a good choice for tent campers or RVers. Surrounded by Chehalis Valley farmland, it's near an 18-hole golf course, hiking trails, and tennis courts.

⓻ Alder Lake

Location: On Alder Lake; map B2, grid d6.

Campsites, facilities: There are 27 sites for tents or small trailers. Picnic tables, fire grills, and tent pads are provided. Vault toilets, piped water, a group shelter, and a boat launch are available. Leashed pets are permitted.

Reservations, fees: No reservations are accepted. There is no fee. The campground is open year-round.

Contact: Department of Natural Resources, Central Region, 1405 Rush Road, Chehalis,

WA 98532-8763; (360) 748-2383 or fax (360) 748-2387.

Directions: From Interstate 5 south of Olympia, take exit 68 and turn east on U.S. 12. Drive 30 miles, then turn north on Highway 7 and drive 15 miles to Pleasant Valley Road (two miles south of Elbe). Turn right and drive 3.5 miles. Bear left on a paved, one-lane road for 100 yards and you'll see the campground on your right.

Trip notes: This campground is on the shore of Alder Lake in an area managed by the Department of Natural Resources. It's a nice, forested camp with good fishing nearby. Another recreation option is the Mount Rainier Scenic Railroad, which travels from Elbe through the forests to Mineral Lake.

36 Gateway Inn and RV Park

Location: Near Mount Rainier National Park; map B2, grid d8.

Campsites, facilities: There are 16 sites for trailers or RVs of any length; eight have full hookups. There are also nine cabins. Electricity, piped water, and picnic tables are provided. A restaurant and lounge are available. Leashed pets are permitted.

Reservations, fees: Reservations are accepted. Sites are $12–$15 per night; cabins are $59 per night for two people, plus $10 for each additional person. The campground is open year-round.

Contact: Phone (360) 569-2506 or write to 38820 Highway 706 East, Ashford, WA 98304.

Directions: From Interstate 5 south of Olympia, take exit 68 and turn east on U.S. 12. Drive 30 miles, then turn north on Highway 7 and drive 17 miles to Elbe. Turn east on Highway 706 and continue 12 miles to the campground on the right. This park is located near the southwestern entrance to Mount Rainier National Park.

Trip notes: This wooded park is very close to Mount Rainier, one of the most spectacular mountains in the hemisphere. After entering at the Nisqually (southwestern) entrance to Mount Rainier National Park and driving on Nisqually Paradise Road for about five miles, you'll find the Longmire Visitor Center, which offers general park information and exhibits on the plants and geology of the area. Continuing into the park for 10 more miles, you'll arrive at the Paradise Visitor Center, which has more exhibits and an observation deck. This is the only road into the park that's open year-round.

37 Mounthaven at Cedar Park

Location: Near Mount Rainier National Park; map B2, grid d8.

Campsites, facilities: There are 20 sites for trailers or RVs of any length. Electricity, piped water, and sewer hookups are provided. Flush toilets, showers, a laundry room, firewood, ice, and a playground are available. A cafe, a bakery, and a store are within one mile. Leashed pets are permitted.

Reservations, fees: Reservations are accepted. Sites are $20 per night. The campground is open year-round.

Contact: Phone (360) 569-2594 or write to 38210 Highway 706 East, Ashford, WA 98304.

Directions: From Interstate 5 south of Tacoma, take exit 127 onto Highway 512 and drive east two miles. Take the Mount Rainier/Pacific Avenue exit, turn right on Highway 7, and drive about 30 miles to Delbe. Highway 7 becomes Highway 706. Continue east on Highway 706 to about 4.5 miles past Ashford and the campground on the right. This park is located near the southwestern entrance to Mount Rainier National Park.

Trip notes: Two creeks run through this wooded campground near the Nisqually entrance to Mount Rainier National Park. See the trip notes for Gateway Inn and RV Park (campground number 36) for information about sights at the national park.

38 Sunshine Point

Location: In Mount Rainier National Park; map B2, grid d8.

Campsites, facilities: There are 18 sites for

tents or RVs up to 25 feet long. Picnic tables are provided. Piped water and pit toilets are available. Some facilities are wheelchair accessible. Leashed pets are permitted.

Reservations, fees: No reservations are accepted. Sites are $10 per night. The campground is open year-round.

Contact: Mount Rainier National Park, Tahoma Woods, Ashford, WA 98304; (360) 569-2211 or fax (360) 569-2170.

Directions: From Interstate 5 south of Olympia, take exit 68 and turn east on U.S. 12. Drive 30 miles, then turn north on Highway 7 and drive 17 miles to Elbe. Turn east on Highway 706 and drive 12 miles. The campground is just inside the park entrance.

Trip notes: This is one of five campgrounds in Mount Rainier National Park near the Nisqually entrance. Ipsut Creek and Cougar Rock (campground numbers 21 and 31 in this chapter) and White River and Ohanapecosh (campground numbers 20 and 30 in Chapter B3) are the others. Sunshine Point is the only one that's open year-round. See the trip notes for Gateway Inn and RV Park (campground number 36) for information about nearby sights and facilities.

㉟ River Oaks RV Park

Location: On the Cowlitz River; map B2, grid e2.

Campsites, facilities: There are 50 tent sites and 24 sites for trailers or RVs of any length. Piped water and picnic tables are provided. Flush toilets, electricity, showers, sanitary services, a laundry room, and ice are available. Bottled gas, a store, and a cafe are located within one mile. Boat launching facilities are nearby. Leashed pets and motorbikes are permitted.

Reservations, fees: Reservations are accepted. Sites are $12–$20 per night. The campground is open year-round.

Contact: Phone (360) 864-2895 or write to 491 Highway 506, Toledo, WA 98591.

Directions: From Interstate 5 near Castle Rock, drive one-half mile west on Highway 506.

Trip notes: This camp is set right on the Cowlitz River, with opportunities for swimming, boating, and fishing. Every spring the river is the site of a big smelt run, and they come thick. Using a dip net, you can fill a five-gallon bucket with just a couple of dips.

㊵ Frost Road Trailer Park

Location: Near Lewis and Clark State Park; map B2, grid e3.

Campsites, facilities: There are 15 tent sites and 21 sites for trailers or RVs of any length; six are drive-throughs. Electricity, piped water, sewer hookups, and picnic tables are provided. Flush toilets, sanitary services, showers, and a recreation hall are available. Pets are permitted.

Reservations, fees: Reservations are accepted. Sites are $9–$13 per night. The campground is open year-round.

Contact: Phone (360) 785-3616 or write to 762 Frost Road, Winlock, WA 98596.

Directions: From Olympia, drive south on Interstate 5 about 40 miles to exit 63 (near Winlock). Turn east on Highway 505 and drive about 3.5 miles to Henriot Road. Turn left and drive about one-quarter mile to a T where Henriot Road ends at Frost Road. Turn left on Frost Road and drive to the park at 762 Frost Road.

Trip notes: This is an excellent option to the campground at nearby Lewis and Clark State Park, which is often crowded to capacity. The campsites are wooded and quiet. See the trip notes for Lewis and Clark State Park (campground number 41) for recreation options.

㊶ Lewis and Clark State Park

Location: Near Chehalis; map B2, grid e3.

Campsites, facilities: There are 25 sites for tents or self-contained RVs. Picnic tables and fire grills are provided. Flush toilets, piped water, firewood, and a playground are available. Leashed pets are permitted.

Reservations, fees: No reservations are

accepted. Sites are $10 per night. The campground is open year-round.

Contact: Phone (800) 233-0321 or (360) 864-2643, or write to 4583 Jackson Highway, Winlock, WA 98596.

Directions: From Chehalis on Interstate 5, drive 12 miles southeast on Jackson Highway 99 and you'll see the park.

Trip notes: The highlight of this state park is an immense old-growth forest that contains some good hiking trails and a 1.5-mile nature trail. There is an interpretive center for Mount St. Helens, plus a kids' fishing pond stocked with trout.

⑫ Mayfield Lake County Park

Location: On Mayfield Lake; map B2, grid e4.
Campsites, facilities: There are 54 sites for tents, trailers, or self-contained RVs. Rest rooms, showers, a public phone, and a barbecue are available. A sanitary dump station is located nearby. Facilities are wheelchair accessible. Leashed pets are permitted.

Reservations, fees: Reservations are recommended. Sites are $11 per night.

Contact: Phone the park at (360) 985-2364 or write to 180 Beach Road, Mossyrock, WA 98564.

Directions: Drive 14 miles south of Centralia on Interstate 5 to the junction with U.S. 12 (exit 68), then drive east for 11 miles. You'll see signs for the campground on the left.

Trip notes: This popular park on the edge of Mayfield Lake is a less-developed option to Mayfield Lake Marina Resort (campground number 43). The camp has a relaxing atmosphere and comfortable, wooded sites. Recreational activities include waterskiing, fishing, swimming, and boating. A good side trip is touring nearby Mount St. Helens.

⑬ Mayfield Lake Marina Resort

Location: On Mayfield Lake; map B2, grid e4.
Campsites, facilities: There are 35 tent sites, 10 full-hookup sites, and 37 sites with electric-

ity only for trailers or RVs of any length. Picnic tables are provided. Flush toilets, sanitary services, showers, firewood, a store, and ice are available. A Laundromat is located within seven miles. Boat docks and launching facilities are available. Leashed pets are permitted.

Reservations, fees: Reservations are accepted. Sites are $11–$20 per night. The campground is open year-round.

Contact: Phone (360) 985-2357, fax (360) 985-2149, or write to 350 Hadaller Road, Mossyrock, WA 98564.

Directions: From Centralia, drive south on Interstate 5 for 14 miles to the exit for U.S. 12. Drive east on U.S. 12 for 15 miles to Winston Creek Road. Turn south and drive two miles to Hadaller Road. Turn right and drive one mile to the resort.

Trip notes: This resort is on the shore of Mayfield Lake. Nearby recreation options include fishing, swimming, and boating.

⑭ Harmony Lakeside RV Park

Location: Near Mayfield Lake; map B2, grid e4.
Campsites, facilities: There are 80 sites for trailers or RVs of any length; 48 are full-hookup sites, and the rest have water and electricity only. Flush toilets, sanitary services, showers, firewood, ice, boat docks, and launching facilities are available. Leashed pets and motorbikes are permitted.

Reservations, fees: Reservations are accepted. Sites are $18–$20 per night. The campground is open year-round.

Contact: Harmony Lakeside RV Park, 563 State Route 122, Silver Lake, WA 98585; (360) 983-3804; e-mail: maynardt@i-link-2.net; Web site: www.gocampingamerica.com/harmonylakeside.

Directions: From Centralia, drive south on Interstate 5 for 14 miles to the U.S. 12 turnoff (exit 68). Drive 21 miles east on U.S. 12 to Highway 122. Turn north and drive 2.5 miles to the park.

Trip notes: This park on Mayfield Lake offers numerous recreational activities, including fishing, swimming, and boating. Mayfield Lake Marina Resort and Ike Kinswa State Park are two nearby options (see campground numbers 43 and 45).

⑮ Ike Kinswa State Park 🚐 ⛺

Location: At Mayfield Lake; map B2, grid e5.
Campsites, facilities: There are two primitive tent sites, 60 developed tent sites, and 41 sites for trailers or RVs up to 60 feet long. Picnic tables and fire grills are provided. Flush toilets, a sanitary disposal station, a store, a cafe, a playground, piped water, showers, and firewood are available. Some facilities are wheelchair accessible. Boat docks and launching facilities are nearby. Leashed pets are permitted.
Reservations, fees: Contact Reservations Northwest at (800) 452-5687 ($6 reservation fee). Sites are $5–$16 per night. The campground is open year-round.
Contact: Phone (800) 233-0321 or (360) 983-3402, or write to 873 Harmony Road, Silver Lake, WA 98585.
Directions: From Interstate 5 south of Olympia, turn east on U.S. 12 and drive 18 miles to the entrance road on the left.
Trip notes: This campground covering 454 acres on the shore of Mayfield Lake is in the midst of a bonanza of recreational possibilities, including hiking trails, driftwood collecting, swimming, waterskiing, and boating. Fishing for rainbow and silver trout is a year-round affair here and can be quite good. Two fish hatcheries are located nearby. A spectacular view of Mount St. Helens can be found at a vista point 11 miles east. This is a very popular campground, and space is rarely available on summer weekends. Be sure to reserve at least a month in advance.

⑯ Redmon's RV Park 🚐

Location: Near Riffe Lake; map B2, grid e6.
Campsites, facilities: There are six drive-through sites for trailers or RVs of any length. Electricity, piped water, and sewer hookups

are provided. Flush toilets, bottled gas, sanitary services, a cafe, a store, and ice are available. Leashed pets are permitted.
Reservations, fees: Reservations are accepted. Sites are $20 per night. The campground is open year-round.
Contact: Phone (360) 498-5425 or write to 8136 Highway 12, Glenoma, WA 98336.
Directions: From Centralia, drive south on Interstate 5 for 14 miles to the exit for U.S. 12. Drive east on U.S. 12 for 50 miles to Glenoma. The park is in town on the highway.
Trip notes: This is a clean, comfortable campground in a beautiful setting. Side trips include visiting huge Riffe Lake to the southeast, or driving up Strawberry Mountain or to the edge of Mount St. Helens National Park (from Randle, head south on Highway 26).

⑰ Maple Grove Campground and RV Park 🚐 ⛺

Location: On the Cowlitz River; map B2, grid e8.
Campsites, facilities: There are 10 tent sites and about 64 drive-through sites for trailers or RVs of any length. Electricity, piped water, and picnic tables are provided. Flush toilets, sanitary services, firewood, a recreation hall, a store, a cafe, a laundry room, showers, bottled gas, ice, and a playground are available. Leashed pets are permitted.
Reservations, fees: Reservations are accepted. Sites are $10–$15 per night. The campground is open year-round, with limited winter facilities.
Contact: Phone (360) 497-2741 or write to P.O. Box 205, Randle, WA 98377.
Directions: From Interstate 5 south of Olympia, turn east on U.S. 12 and drive 48 miles to Randle. The park is in town on the highway.
Trip notes: This RV park along the shore of the Cowlitz River is close to hiking trails. For an excellent drive, from the park head along winding Highway 26, which starts at Randle and goes up to Strawberry Mountain (elevation 5,464 feet). It's a good lookout point toward Mount St. Helens to the west.

⓭ Fox Store and RV Park

Location: Near the Toutle River; map B2, grid f2.

Campsites, facilities: There are 37 sites for trailers or RVs of any length. Electricity, piped water, sewer hookups, and picnic tables are provided. Flush toilets, showers, firewood, and ice are available. Boat launching facilities are nearby. Leashed pets and motorbikes are permitted.

Reservations, fees: Reservations are accepted. Sites are $10–$15 per night. The campground is open year-round.

Contact: Phone (360) 274-6785 or write to 112 Burma Road, Castle Rock, WA 98611.

Directions: From Interstate 5 at Castle Rock, take exit 52 and drive 100 yards east to the park.

Trip notes: This wooded park is about 400 yards from the Toutle River and one-half mile from the Cowlitz River. Take your pick. Seaquest State Park and Silver Lake to the east provide two excellent, activity-filled side-trip options (see campground numbers 50 and 51 for more details).

⓮ Mount St. Helens RV Park

Location: Near Silver Lake; map B2, grid f2.

Campsites, facilities: There are approximately 90 sites for tents, trailers, or RVs. Cable TV, rest rooms, showers, a laundromat, a sanitary dump, a public phone, and ice are available. Horseshoes, a recreation hall, and a playground are also provided. The facilities are wheelchair accessible. Leashed pets are permitted.

Reservations, fees: No reservations are necessary, but they are recommended in the summer; call (360) 274-8522. Sites are $15–$17 per night. The campground is open year-round.

Contact: Phone (360) 274-8522 or write to 167 Schaffran Road, Castle Rock, WA 98611.

Directions: From Interstate 5 at Castle Rock, take exit 49. Turn east on Highway 504 and drive two miles to a sign on the right indicating the park to the left. Turn left at the sign onto Schaffran Road and drive to the park at the top of the hill.

Trip notes: Though this cozy park just outside of Castle Rock is close to the highway, it has a secluded feel. Fishing and boating are available nearby on Silver Lake. A good side trip is touring Mount St. Helens. The park is located only three miles from the Mount St. Helens Visitor Center.

⓯ Seaquest State Park

Location: Near Silver Lake; map B2, grid f3.

Campsites, facilities: There are four primitive tent sites and 92 sites for tents and self-contained RVs; 16 have full hookups. Piped water and picnic tables are provided. Flush toilets, a playground, six horseshoe pits, a ball field, a sanitary disposal station, showers, and firewood are available. A store is within one mile. Some facilities are wheelchair accessible. Leashed pets are permitted.

Reservations, fees: Contact Reservations Northwest at (800) 452-5687 ($6 reservation fee). Sites are $5–$16 per night. The campground is open year-round.

Contact: Phone (800) 233-0321 or (360) 274-8633, or write to P.O. Box 3030, Spirit Lake Highway, Castle Rock, WA 98611.

Directions: From Interstate 5 near Castle Rock, take exit 49 and drive seven miles east on Highway 504 to the park.

Trip notes: This state park is located across from Silver Lake, which is considered one of western Washington's premier bass, trout, and salmon fishing lakes. Other highlights include eight miles of hiking trails and the Mount St. Helens Interpretive Center, courtesy of the Forest Service. The park is popular for day use as well as camping; it's advisable to arrive early to claim a spot.

⓰ Silver Lake Motel and Resort

Location: On Silver Lake; map B2, grid f3.

Campsites, facilities: There are 13 tent

sites and 22 sites for trailers or RVs of any length. Electricity, piped water, sewer hook-ups, and picnic tables are provided. Flush toilets, a store, showers, ice, boat docks, boat rentals, launching facilities, and playground are available. Sanitary services and a cafe are within one mile. Leashed pets are permitted.

Reservations, fees: Reservations are accepted. Sites are $12–$20 per night. The campground is open year-round.

Contact: Phone (360) 274-6141, fax (360) 274-2183, or write to 3201 Spirit Lake Highway, Silver Lake, WA 98645.

Directions: From Interstate 5 near Castle Rock, take exit 49 and drive 6.5 miles east on Highway 504 to the park on the right.

Trip notes: This park is set along the shore of Silver Lake, one of Washington's better lakes for bass, trout, and salmon fishing. It's an excellent alternative to the more crowded campground at Seaquest State Park (campground number 50).

52 Iron Creek

Location: On the Cispus River in Gifford Pinchot National Forest; map B2, grid f8.

Campsites, facilities: There are 98 sites for tents, trailers, or RVs. Piped water and picnic tables are provided. Vault toilets and firewood are available. Some facilities are wheelchair accessible. Leashed pets are permitted.

Reservations, fees: Some sites can be reserved by calling (800) 280-CAMP/2267 ($8.65 reservation fee). Rates are $10 per night for a single site and $20 per night for a double site, plus $5 for each additional vehicle. The campground is open from mid-May to late October.

Contact: Gifford Pinchot National Forest, Randle Ranger District, P.O. Box 670, Randle, WA 98377; (360) 497-1100 or fax (360) 497-1102.

Directions: From Interstate 5 south of Olympia, take exit 68 and head east on U.S. 12. Drive 48 miles to Randle and take Highway 131 south. Drive one mile, then continue south for nine miles on Forest Service Road 25 to the campground entrance.

Trip notes: One of the more popular Forest Service campgrounds, this spot is set along the Cispus River near its confluence with Iron Creek. A Forest Service visitor center, which provides information about the Mount St. Helens–Mount Adams area, is nearby. The camp is located along the access route to the best eastside viewing areas for Mount St. Helens.

53 Tower Rock

Location: On the Cispus River in Gifford Pinchot National Forest; map B2, grid f8.

Campsites, facilities: There are 22 sites for tents, trailers, or RVs up to 21 feet long. Piped water and picnic tables are provided. Vault toilets and firewood are available. Leashed pets are permitted.

Reservations, fees: No reservations are accepted. Sites are $9 per night, plus $5 for each additional vehicle. The campground is open from mid-May to late September.

Contact: Gifford Pinchot National Forest, Randle Ranger District, P.O. Box 670, Randle, WA 98377; (360) 497-1100 or fax (360) 497-1102.

Directions: From Interstate 5 south of Olympia, take exit 68 and head east on U.S. 12. Drive 48 miles to Randle and take Highway 131 south. Drive one mile, then continue south on Forest Service Road 23 for 6.5 miles. Turn south on Forest Service Road 28 and drive 1.5 miles, then proceed two miles west on Forest Service Road 76 to the campground. A Forest Service map is essential.

Trip notes: This campground along the Cispus River is an option to nearby Iron Creek and North Fork (campground numbers 52 and 55). It has shaded and sunny sites, with lots of trees and plenty of room. Fishing is popular here.

54 Blue Lake Creek

Location: Near Blue Lake in Gifford Pinchot National Forest; map B2, grid f9.

Campsites, facilities: There are 11 sites for tents, trailers, or RVs up to 31 feet long. Picnic

tables are provided. Vault toilets and hand-pumped water are available. Firewood can be gathered outside of the campground area. Leashed pets are permitted.

Reservations, fees: No reservations are accepted. Sites are $8 per night, plus $5 for each additional vehicle. The campground is open from mid-May to late October.

Contact: Gifford Pinchot National Forest, Randle Ranger District, P.O. Box 670, Randle, WA 98377; (360) 497-1100 or fax (360) 497-1102.

Directions: From Interstate 5 south of Olympia, take exit 68 and head east on U.S. 12. Drive 48 miles to Randle and take Highway 131 south. Drive one mile, then continue south on Forest Service Road 23 for 15 miles to the campground.

Trip notes: This classic Washington hideaway along Blue Lake Creek is a good base camp for the 3.5-mile hike to Blue Lake. The trailhead is about one-half mile from the camp. Mountain biking is another option here.

⑤⑤ North Fork

Location: On the Cispus River in Gifford Pinchot National Forest; map B2, grid f9.

Campsites, facilities: There are 33 sites for tents, trailers, or RVs up to 31 feet long. Piped water and picnic tables are provided. Vault toilets and firewood are available. Leashed pets are permitted.

Reservations, fees: No reservations are accepted. Sites are $9 per night, plus $5 for each additional vehicle. The campground is open from mid-May to late September.

Contact: Gifford Pinchot National Forest, Randle Ranger District, P.O. Box 670, Randle, WA 98377; (360) 497-1100 or fax (360) 497-1102.

Directions: From Interstate 5 south of Olympia, take exit 68 and head east on U.S. 12. Drive 48 miles to Randle and take Highway 131 south. Drive one mile, then continue south for 11 miles on Forest Service Road 23 to the campground.

Trip notes: This campground along the North Cispus River offers fishing, as well as nature

trails, bike paths, and a scenic viewing area. A national forest map details the backcountry.

⑤⑥ Cedars RV Park

Location: Near the Coweeman River; map B2, grid g3.

Campsites, facilities: There are three tent sites and 25 full-hookup sites for trailers or RVs up to 36 feet in length; two are drive-throughs. Electricity, sewer and cable TV hookups, piped water, and picnic tables are provided. Flush toilets, showers, sanitary services, and a laundry room are available. There is a mini-mart 1.5 miles away. Pets and motorbikes are permitted.

Reservations, fees: No reservations are accepted. Sites are $11–$15 per night. The campground is open year-round.

Contact: Phone (360) 274-5136 or write to 115 Beauvais Road, Kelso, WA 98626.

Directions: Take exit 46 off Interstate 5 near Kelso and drive 100 feet east on Headquarters Road. Turn north on Bond Road and drive one-third mile, then turn east on Beauvais Road and go 50 feet to the park on the right.

Trip notes: This private park provides a good stopover for Interstate 5 travelers looking for a spot near Kelso. Campsites are graveled and shady. The nearby Coweeman River is a highlight, along with the park's natural setting.

⑤⑦ Oaks Trailer and RV Park

Location: In Commerce; map B2, grid g2.

Campsites, facilities: There are 62 drive-through sites for trailers or RVs up to 30 feet long. Electricity, piped water, and sewer hookups are provided. Flush toilets, sanitary services, showers, and a laundry room are available. Bottled gas, a store, and a cafe are located within one mile. Leashed pets are permitted.

Reservations, fees: Reservations are accepted. Sites are $16.50 per night. The campground is open year-round.

Contact: Phone (360) 425-2708, fax (360) 575-9987, or write to 636 California Way, Longview, WA 98632.

Directions: From Interstate 5 near Longview, take exit 36 and drive west on Highway 432 for 3.5 miles to Commerce. Drive one block south and then turn southeast to the park.

Trip notes: This park in an urban area near Longview is a good layover spot if you're heading south on Interstate 5 to Oregon or west on Highway 4 to the coast. An 18-hole golf course and a full-service marina are close by.

⑤⑧ Lake Merrill

Location: Near Mount St. Helens; map B2, grid g6.

Campsites, facilities: There are 11 tent sites. Picnic tables, fire grills, and tent pads are provided. Vault toilets, a wheelchair-accessible vault toilet and campsite, firewood, and hand-pumped water are available. Boat launching facilities are located on Lake Merrill. Leashed pets are permitted.

Reservations, fees: No reservations are accepted. There is no fee. The campground is open from May through September, weather permitting.

Contact: Department of Natural Resources, Southwest Region, P.O. Box 280, Castle Rock, WA 98611-0280; (360) 577-2025 or (360) 274-4196.

Directions: From Interstate 5 at Woodland, take exit 23 and drive 29 miles east on Highway 503 to Lewis River Road. Drive east and northeast on Lewis River Road to Forest Service Road 81. Turn left on Forest Service Road 81 and drive 4.5 miles. Turn left on the access road and continue to the campground.

Trip notes: This is the best choice in the area for campers seeking a quiet setting. The wooded campground is nestled on the shore of Lake Merrill, very near Mount St. Helens. It's a less-expensive and often less-crowded alternative to the more developed parks in the area. Note: A five-acre mud slide closed this camp; a two-year reconstruction is scheduled to be completed in mid-May of 1998.

⑤⑨ Lower Lewis River Falls

Location: On the Lewis River in Gifford Pinchot National Forest; map B2, grid g8.

Campsites, facilities: There are 42 sites for tents, trailers, or RVs up to 70 feet long. Composting toilets and hand-pumped water are available. Leashed pets are permitted.

Reservations, fees: No reservations are accepted. Rates are $9 per night for single sites, $18 per night for double sites, and $5 for each additional vehicle. The campground is open from May through September.

Contact: Gifford Pinchot National Forest, Mount St. Helens National Volcanic Monument, 42218 Yale Bridge Road, Amboy, WA 98601-0369; (360) 247-3900 or fax (360) 247-3901.

Directions: From Interstate 5 at Woodland, take exit 21 and drive east on Highway 503 to Lewis River Road. Drive east on Lewis River Road for seven miles. The road becomes Forest Service Road 90. Continue east on Forest Service Road 90 for 21 miles to the campground.

Trip notes: This is one of the great spots in the Pacific Northwest. The camp is set in the primary viewing area for three major waterfalls on the Lewis River. The spectacular Lewis River Trail is available for hiking or horseback riding, and there is a wheelchair-accessible loop. Several other hiking trails in the area branch off along backcountry streams. See a Forest Service map for details. The elevation is 1,400 feet.

⑥⓪ Louis Rasmussen RV Park

Location: On the Columbia River; map B2, grid h3.

Campsites, facilities: There are five tent sites and 22 sites for trailers or RVs of any length. Electricity, piped water, and sewer hookups are provided. Flush toilets, a dump station, and showers are available. Bottled gas, a store, a cafe, a Laundromat, and ice are located within one mile. Boat docks and launching facilities are nearby. Leashed pets and motorbikes are permitted.

Reservations, fees: Reservations are accepted. Sites are $9–$14 per night. The campground is open year-round.

Contact: Phone (360) 673-2626 or write to P.O. Box 70, Kalama, WA 98625.

Directions: From Interstate 5 near Kalama, take exit 30 and drive 100 feet west to Hendrickson Road. Turn south and drive one-half mile to the park.

Trip notes: This park in an urban area along the shore of the Columbia River is a perfect layover spot for Interstate 5 cruisers heading for Portland. Nearby recreation options include a full-service marina and tennis courts.

61 Woodland

Location: Near Woodland; map B2, grid i3.

Campsites, facilities: There are 10 campsites for tents or small trailers. Picnic tables, fire grills, and tent pads are provided. Vault toilets, piped water, firewood, and a children's playground are available. Some facilities are wheelchair accessible. Leashed pets are permitted.

Reservations, fees: No reservations are accepted. There is no fee. The campground is open from May to September.

Contact: Department of Natural Resources, Southwest Region, P.O. Box 280, Castle Rock, WA 98611-0280; (360) 577-2025 or (360) 274-4196.

Directions: From Interstate 5 at Woodland, take exit 21 and drive 100 yards east on Highway 503. Turn right to East CC Street and proceed to just south of the bridge. Turn right on County Road 1 and drive 300 yards, then turn left on County Road 38 and drive 2.5 miles to the campground on the left.

Trip notes: This is an optimum spot for people who are touring Washington on Interstate 5 but want a quiet setting along the way. The campground is nestled in a forest area that is managed by the Department of Natural Resources. It's private and wooded, yet is near the main highway and has playground equipment for the kids.

62 Camp Kalama Campground

Location: On the Kalama River; map B2, grid h3.

Campsites, facilities: There are 30 tent sites and 120 sites for trailers or RVs of any length; 17 are drive-throughs. Electricity, piped water, sewer and cable TV hookups, and picnic tables are provided. Flush toilets, bottled gas, sanitary services, a store, showers, firewood, a laundry, ice, boat launching facilities, and a playground are available. Leashed pets and motorbikes are permitted.

Reservations, fees: Reservations are accepted. Sites are $21 per night. The campground is open year-round.

Contact: Phone (800) 750-2456 or (360) 673-2456, fax (360) 673-2324, or write to 5055 North Meeker Drive, Kalama, WA 98625.

Directions: From Interstate 5 near Kalama, take exit 32 and drive one block south on the frontage road to the campground.

Trip notes: This option to Louis Rasmussen RV Park (campground number 60) has a more rustic setting and some accommodations for tent campers. It's set along the Kalama River, where fishing is popular. A full-service marina is nearby.

63 Lewis River RV Park

Location: On the Lewis River; map B2, grid h3.

Campsites, facilities: There are 90 sites for tents, trailers, or RVs of any length; five are drive-throughs. Electricity, piped water, sewer hookups, and picnic tables are provided. Flush toilets, firewood, sanitary services, showers, a bathhouse, a store, a laundry room, ice, and a swimming pool are available. Boat docks and launching facilities are nearby on the Lewis River. Leashed pets are permitted.

Reservations, fees: Reservations are accepted. Sites are $16–$18 per night. The campground is open year-round.

Contact: Phone (360) 225-9556 or write to 3125 Lewis River Road, Woodland, WA 98674.

Directions: From Castle Rock, drive about 38

miles south on Interstate 5 to exit 21 in Woodland, then go four miles east on Highway 503/Lewis River Road to the park.

Trip notes: This park is along the Lewis River, where the salmon and steelhead can run thick in season. It's a pleasant camp, with a choice of graveled or grassy shaded sites. An 18-hole golf course is nearby.

64 Lone Fir Resort 🚐 ⛺

Location: Near Yale Lake; map B2, grid h6.

Campsites, facilities: There are eight tent sites and 17 sites for trailers or RVs of any length. Electricity, piped water, sewer hookups, and picnic tables are provided. Flush toilets, a laundry room, a restaurant, showers, ice, and a swimming pool are available. Bottled gas, a store, and a cafe are within one mile. Boat docks and launching facilities are nearby. Pets and motorbikes are permitted.

Reservations, fees: Reservations are accepted. Sites are $13–$16 per night. The campground is open year-round.

Contact: Phone (360) 238-5210 or write to 16806 Lewis River Road, Cougar, WA 98616.

Directions: From Castle Rock, drive about 38 miles south on Interstate 5 to exit 21 in Woodland, then go 29 miles east on Highway 503/Lewis River Road to the resort. (You can see it from the highway.)

Trip notes: This private campground near Yale Lake (the smallest of four lakes in the area) is designed primarily for motor-home use, with grassy sites and plenty of shade trees. Mount St. Helens is a side trip option.

65 Volcano View Campground 🚐

Location: Near Mount St. Helens; map B2, grid h6.

Campsites, facilities: There are 47 sites for trailers or RVs of any length. Electricity, piped water, sewer hookups, and picnic tables are provided. Flush toilets, sanitary services, showers, firewood, a store, and ice are available. Pets are permitted.

Reservations, fees: Reservations are accepted. Sites are $12–$14 per night. The campground is open year-round.

Contact: Volcano View Campground, 438 Yale Bridge Road, Ariel, WA 98603; (360) 231-4329 or fax (360) 231-4429; e-mail: lread@worldaccessnet.com.

Directions: From Interstate 5 in Woodland, take exit 21 and drive 23 miles east to Jack's Restaurant, then turn south and go one mile to campground.

Trip notes: This campground with sites scattered along the edge of Yale Lake is close to Mount St. Helens, Lake Merrill, and Swift Creek Reservoir.

66 Paradise Creek 🚐 ⛺

Location: On Paradise Creek and the Wind River in Gifford Pinchot National Forest; map B2, grid h8.

Campsites, facilities: There are 42 sites for tents, trailers, or RVs up to 25 feet long. Hand-pumped well water, fire grills, and picnic tables are provided. Vault toilets are available. One toilet is wheelchair accessible. Leashed pets are permitted.

Reservations, fees: Some sites may be reserved by calling (800) 280-CAMP/2267 ($8.65 reservation fee). Sites are $9–$18 per night, plus $5 for each additional vehicle. The campground is open from mid-May to mid-November.

Contact: Gifford Pinchot National Forest, Wind River Ranger District, 1262 Hemlock Road, Carson, WA 98610; (509) 427-3200 or fax (509) 427-3215.

Directions: From Interstate 5 at Vancouver, Washington, turn east on Highway 14 and drive approximately 50 miles to Carson. Turn north on the Wind River Highway and drive 20 miles to the camp.

Trip notes: This alternative to the Beaver site (campground number 81) lies deeper in Gifford Pinchot National Forest at the confluence of Paradise Creek and the Wind River. Lava Butte is a short distance from the camp and is accessible by trail.

67 Falls Creek–Crest Horse Camp

Location: Near the Pacific Crest Trail in Gifford Pinchot National Forest; map B2, grid h8.

Campsites, facilities: There are six sites for tents, trailers, or RVs up to 15 feet long. Picnic tables and fire grills are provided. Pit toilets are available, but there is no piped water. Leashed pets are permitted.

Reservations, fees: No reservations are accepted. There is no fee. The campground is open from mid-June to late September.

Contact: Gifford Pinchot National Forest, Mount Adams Ranger District, 2455 Highway 141, Trout Lake, WA 98650; (509) 395-3400.

Directions: From Interstate 5 at Vancouver, Washington, turn east on Highway 14 and drive approximately 50 miles to Carson. Turn north on the Wind River Highway and drive six miles, then continue 15 miles north on Forest Service Road 65 to the campground.

Trip notes: This camp is set along the Race Track Trail adjacent to the Indian Heaven Wilderness.

68 Smokey Creek

Location: Near the Indian Heaven Wilderness in Gifford Pinchot National Forest; map B2, grid h9.

Campsites, facilities: There are three sites for trailers or RVs up to 22 feet long. Picnic tables are provided. Pit toilets are available, but there is no piped water. Leashed pets are permitted.

Reservations, fees: No reservations are accepted. There is no fee. The campground is open from June to late September.

Contact: Gifford Pinchot National Forest, Mount Adams Ranger District, 2455 Highway 141, Trout Lake, WA 98650; (509) 395-3400.

Directions: From Interstate 5 at Vancouver, Washington, turn east on Highway 14 and drive 66 miles. Turn north on Highway 141 and drive 25.5 miles to Forest Service Road 24 (5.5 miles southwest of the town of Trout Lake). Turn northwest and drive seven miles to the campground.

Trip notes: This primitive, little-used campground is set along Smokey Creek. A trail leading into the Indian Heaven Wilderness passes near the camp. Berry picking can be good here in season. See the trip notes for Tillicum and Saddle (campground numbers 71 and 73 in this chapter) and Walupt Horse Camp and Morrison Creek (campground numbers 62 and 68 in Chapter B3) for details on the recreation options in the immediate area.

69 Goose Lake

Location: On Goose Lake in Gifford Pinchot National Forest; map B2, grid h9.

Campsites, facilities: There are 25 tent sites and one site for trailers or RVs up to 18 feet long. Picnic tables and fire rings are provided. Vault toilets are available, but there is no piped water. A boat ramp is nearby. Leashed pets are permitted.

Reservations, fees: Reservations can be made by calling (800) 280-CAMP/2267 ($8.65 reservation fee). Sites are $9 per night, plus $5 for each additional vehicle. The campground is open from mid-June to late September.

Contact: Gifford Pinchot National Forest, Mount Adams Ranger District, 2455 Highway 141, Trout Lake, WA 98650; (509) 395-3400.

Directions: From Interstate 5 at Vancouver, Washington turn east on Highway 14 and drive 66 miles. Turn north on Highway 141 and drive 25.5 miles to Forest Service Road 24 (5.5 miles southwest of the town of Trout Lake). Continue west to Forest Service Road 60 and then continue west five more miles.

Trip notes: This campground is set at an elevation of 3,200 feet along the shore of Goose Lake and is the place for fishing and berry picking in the summer. The northern edge of Big Lava Bed and a nearby crater are adjacent to the camp.

70 Cultus Creek

Location: Near the Indian Heaven Wilderness in Gifford Pinchot National Forest; map B2, grid h9.

Campsites, facilities: There are 43 sites for

tents, trailers, or RVs up to 32 feet long. Piped water, picnic tables, and fire rings are provided. Vault toilets and firewood are available. Some facilities are wheelchair accessible. Leashed pets are permitted.

Reservations, fees: Reservations can be made by calling (800) 280-CAMP/2267 ($8.65 reservation fee). Rates are $9 per night for single sites, $18 per night for double sites, and $5 for each additional vehicle. The campground is open from June to September.

Contact: Gifford Pinchot National Forest, Mount Adams Ranger District, 2455 Highway 141, Trout Lake, WA 98650; (509) 395-3400.

Directions: From Interstate 5 at Vancouver, Washington, turn east on Highway 14 and drive 66 miles. Turn north on Highway 141 and drive 25.5 miles to Forest Service Road 24 (5.5 miles southwest of the town of Trout Lake). Continue 2.5 miles, then turn northwest and drive 12.5 miles to the campground.

Trip notes: Located at an elevation of 4,000 feet along Cultus Creek on the edge of the Indian Heaven Wilderness, this camp is close to trails that will take you into the backcountry, which has numerous small meadows and lakes among the stands of firs and pines. Horse trails can be found as well. The Pacific Crest Trail runs nearby. Evening programs are conducted by the campground hosts.

⑦ Tillicum

Location: Near Meadow Lake in Gifford Pinchot National Forest; map B2, grid h9.

Campsites, facilities: There are eight sites for tents only and 37 sites for tents, trailers, or RVs up to 18 feet long. Piped water, picnic tables, and fire rings are provided. Pit toilets and firewood are available. Leashed pets are permitted.

Reservations, fees: No reservations are accepted. There is no fee. The campground is open from mid-June to late September.

Contact: Gifford Pinchot National Forest, Mount St. Helens National Volcanic Monument, 42218 NE Yale Bridge Road, Amboy, WA 98601; (360) 247-3900 or fax (360) 247-3901.

Directions: From Interstate 5 at Vancouver, turn east on Highway 14 and drive 66 miles. Turn north on Highway 141 and drive 25.5 miles to Forest Service Road 24 (5.5 miles southwest of the town of Trout Lake). Turn northwest and drive 19 miles to the campground.

Trip notes: This pretty camp is primitive but well forested and within walking distance of a number of recreation options. A trail from the camp leads southwest past little Meadow Lake to Squaw Butte, then over to Big Creek. Give it a try; it's a nice hike, as well as an excellent ride for mountain bikers. This is a premium area for picking huckleberries in August and early September. The Lone Butte Wildlife Emphasis Area to the south provides a great side-trip opportunity.

⑫ Little Goose

Location: On Little Goose Creek in Gifford Pinchot National Forest; map B2, grid h9.

Campsites, facilities: There are 28 sites for tents, trailers, or RVs up to 18 feet long. Piped water, picnic tables, and fire rings are provided. Pit toilets are available. Leashed pets are permitted.

Reservations, fees: No reservations are accepted. There is no fee. The campground is open from June to late September.

Contact: Gifford Pinchot National Forest, Mount Adams Ranger District, 2455 Highway 141, Trout Lake, WA 98650; (509) 395-3400.

Directions: From Interstate 5 at Vancouver, turn east on Highway 14 and drive 66 miles. Turn north on Highway 141 and drive 25.5 miles to Forest Service Road 24 (5.5 miles south of the town of Trout Lake). Turn northwest and drive 10 miles to the campground.

Trip notes: This campground is near Little Goose Creek and the backcountry of the Indian Heaven Wilderness. See the trip notes for Tillicum and Saddle (campground numbers 71 and 73 in this chapter) and Walupt Horse Camp and Morrison Creek (campground numbers 62 and 68 in Chapter B3) for details of the area. Since this camp has piped water, it gets heavier use than most of the others in the immediate vicinity. Huckleberry picking is quite good in August and early September.

⑦ Saddle

Location: Near Mosquito Lakes in Gifford Pinchot National Forest; map B2, grid h9.

Campsites, facilities: There are 12 tent sites. Picnic tables and fire rings are provided. Pit toilets and firewood are available, but there is no piped water. Leashed pets are permitted.

Reservations, fees: No reservations are accepted. There is no fee. The campground is open from mid-June to late September.

Contact: Gifford Pinchot National Forest, Mount Adams Ranger District, 2455 Highway 141, Trout Lake, WA 98650; (509) 395-3400.

Directions: From Interstate 5 at Vancouver, Washington, turn east on Highway 14 and drive 66 miles. Turn north on Highway 141 and drive 25.5 miles to Forest Service Road 24 (5.5 miles south of the town of Trout Lake). Turn northwest and drive 19 miles. Take Forest Service Road 2480 north for one mile to the campground.

Trip notes: This rustic site receives relatively little use. There are two lakes nearby called Big and Little Mosquito Lakes, which are fed by Mosquito Creek. So, while we're on the subject, mosquito attacks in late spring and early summer can be like squadrons of World War II bombers moving in. The Pacific Crest Trail passes right by camp. The area is known for premium huckleberry picking in August and early September.

⑦ Paradise Point State Park

Location: On the East Fork of the Lewis River; map B2, grid i4.

Campsites, facilities: There are nine primitive tent sites and 70 sites for tents or self-contained RVs up to 45 feet long. Piped water, fire grills, and picnic tables are provided. Flush toilets, sanitary services, firewood, and showers are available. Boat launching facilities are located nearby on the East Fork of the Lewis River. Leashed pets are permitted.

Reservations, fees: Contact Reservations Northwest at (800) 452-5687 ($6 reservation fee). Sites are $5–$10 per night. The campground is open year-round.

Contact: Phone (800) 233-0321 or (360) 263-2350, or write to Route 1, P.O. Box 33914, Ridgefield, WA 98642.

Directions: From Vancouver, Washington, drive 15 miles north on Interstate 5. Take the Paradise Point State Park exit and follow the signs to the campground.

Trip notes: Good fishing is a bonus at this campground on the East Fork of the Lewis River. An 18-hole golf course and a two-mile hiking trail are some of the recreation possibilities. This is a good RV layover for I-5 travelers, but it does fill up quickly, so plan on arriving early in the day.

⑦ Big Fir Campground and RV Park

Location: Near Paradise Point State Park; map B2, grid i4.

Campsites, facilities: There are 33 tent sites and 37 sites for trailers or RVs of any length; three are drive-throughs. Electricity, piped water, sewer hookups, and picnic tables are provided. Flush toilets, sanitary services, showers, a store, and ice are available. Boat launching facilities are located within 1.5 miles. Leashed pets and motorbikes are permitted.

Reservations, fees: Reservations are accepted. Sites are $12–$18.50 per night. The campground is open year-round.

Contact: Phone (800) 532-4397 or (360) 887-8970, or write to 5515 NE 259th Street, Ridgefield, WA 98642.

Directions: Take the Ridgefield exit (exit 14) off Interstate 5 and drive four miles east to the campground on the right.

Trip notes: This campground is in a rural area not far from Paradise Point State Park. It's nestled in a wooded, hilly area with shaded gravel sites. See the trip notes for Paradise Point State Park (campground number 74) for details on the area.

76 Battle Ground Lake State Park

Location: On Battle Ground Lake; map B2, grid i5.

Campsites, facilities: There are 15 primitive tent sites and 35 sites for tents or self-contained RVs up to 50 feet long. Piped water, fire grills, and picnic tables are provided. Flush toilets, a sanitary disposal station, showers, a store, firewood, a restaurant, and a playground are available. Some facilities are wheelchair accessible. Boat launching facilities and rentals are nearby. Leashed pets are permitted.

Reservations, fees: Contact Reservations Northwest at (800) 452-5687 ($6 reservation fee). Sites are $5–$10 per night. The campground is open year-round.

Contact: Phone (800) 233-0321 or (360) 687-4621, or write to 17612 NE Palmer Road, Battle Ground, WA 98604.

Directions: From Vancouver, Washington, turn north on Highway 503 and drive approximately 15 miles until you get to the Battle Ground crossroads. Head east for three miles, then turn north and continue 1.5 miles to the lake.

Trip notes: This state park has horseback riding trails and some primitive campsites that will accommodate campers with horses. The lake is good for swimming and fishing, and it has a nice beach area; no motorized boats are allowed. If you're traveling on Interstate 5 and looking for a layover, this camp 15 minutes from the highway is ideal. In July and August, there are several local fairs and celebrations. Like many of the easy-access state parks on Interstate 5, it fills up quickly on weekends.

77 Sunset

Location: On the East Fork of the Lewis River in Gifford Pinchot National Forest; map B2, grid i6.

Campsites, facilities: There are six walk-in sites and 10 sites for tents, trailers, or RVs up to 22 feet long. Well water and picnic tables are provided. Pit toilets and firewood are available. Leashed pets are permitted.

Reservations, fees: No reservations are accepted. Sites are $9 per night, plus $5 for each additional vehicle. The campground is open year-round.

Contact: Gifford Pinchot National Forest, Mount St. Helens National Volcanic Monument, 42218 NE Yale Bridge Road, Amboy, WA 98601; (360) 247-3900 or fax (360) 247-3901.

Directions: From Interstate 5 at Vancouver, take exit 9 and drive north on Highway 502 for eight miles to Battle Ground, where Highway 502 becomes Highway 503/Main Street. Continue east on Main Street for one mile. Turn left on 142nd Avenue and proceed north to Sunset Falls Road (old County Road 12), just past Moulton Falls. Drive east for seven miles on Sunset Falls Road to the campground.

Trip notes: This campground is located at an elevation of 1,000 feet along the East Fork of the Lewis River. Fishing, hiking, huckleberry picking, and mushroom hunting are some of the favored pursuits of visitors.

78 Cold Creek

Location: On Cedar Creek; map B2, grid i6.

Campsites, facilities: There are six campsites for tents or small trailers. Picnic tables, fire grills, and tent pads are provided. Vault toilets and hand-pumped water are available. Leashed pets are permitted.

Reservations, fees: No reservations are accepted. There is no fee. The campground is open from May to September.

Contact: Department of Natural Resources, Southwest Region, P.O. Box 280, Castle Rock, WA 98611-0280; (360) 577-2025 or (360) 274-4196.

Directions: From Interstate 5 north of Vancouver, Washington, take exit 9 and drive east on NE 179th Street for 5.5 miles. Turn right on Highway 503 and drive 1.5 miles. Turn left on NE 159th Street and drive three miles, then turn right on 182nd Avenue. From there drive one mile, then turn left on NE

139th (Road L-1400) and continue eight miles. Turn left on Road L-1000 and drive three miles. Make another left and continue about one mile to the campground.

Trip notes: Okay, the directions are complicated, but few things worth remembering come easy, right? This campground is set in a forested area along Cedar Creek, with plenty of trails around for hiking and horseback riding. The camp gets minimal use, although it has piped water. A large shelter is available for groups, and makes this an ideal destination for families.

⑦ Rock Creek

Location: On Rock Creek; map B2, grid i6.

Campsites, facilities: There are 19 campsites for tents or small trailers. Picnic tables, fire grills, and tent pads are provided. Vault toilets, piped water, and a horse-loading ramp are available. Some facilities are wheelchair accessible. There is a campground host on site. Leashed pets are permitted.

Reservations, fees: No reservations are accepted. There is no fee. The campground is open year-round.

Contact: Department of Natural Resources, Southwest Region, P.O. Box 280, Castle Rock, WA 98611-0280; (360) 577-2025 or (360) 274-4196.

Directions: From Interstate 5 north of Vancouver, Washington, take exit 9 and drive east on NE 179th Street for 5.5 miles. Turn right on Highway 503 and drive 1.5 miles. Turn left on NE 159th Street and drive three miles, then turn right on 182nd Avenue and drive one mile. Turn left on NE 139th (Road L-1400) and drive eight miles, then turn left on Road L-1000 and drive 3.5 miles. (You'll pass Cold Creek Campground after three miles.) Turn left on Road L-1200 and proceed about 200 yards to the campground, which will be on your right.

Trip notes: Here's an alternative to Cold Creek (campground number 78). Also managed by the Department of Natural Resources, this camp can be found in a wooded area along Rock Creek. Hikers and horseback riders will

find plenty of trails nearby. For equestrians, the camp has the added bonus of facilities for horses.

⑧ Panther Creek

Location: On Panther Creek in Gifford Pinchot National Forest; map B2, grid i8.

Campsites, facilities: There are 33 sites for tents, trailers, or RVs up to 25 feet long. Hand-pumped well water and picnic tables are provided. Pit toilets are available. Leashed pets are permitted.

Reservations, fees: Some sites can be reserved by calling (800) 280-CAMP/2267 ($8.65 reservation fee). Sites are $9–$18 per night. The campground is open from mid-May to mid-October.

Contact: Gifford Pinchot National Forest, Wind River Ranger District, 1262 Hemlock Road, Carson, WA 98610; (509) 427-3200 or fax (509) 427-3215.

Directions: From Interstate 5 at Vancouver, Washington, turn east on Highway 14 and drive approximately 50 miles to Carson. Turn north on the Wind River Highway and drive nine miles, then turn east on Forest Service Road 6517 and travel 1.5 miles. Turn south on Forest Service Road 65 and drive 100 yards to the campground.

Trip notes: This campground along Panther Creek, several miles from the Wind River Ranger Station, is a good choice for those who enjoy fishing, hiking, and horseback riding.

⑧ Beaver

Location: On the Wind River in Gifford Pinchot National Forest; map B2, grid i8.

Campsites, facilities: There are 26 sites for tents, trailers, or RVs up to 25 feet long. Piped water, fire grills, and picnic tables are provided. Pit toilets are available. Two campsites are wheelchair accessible. Group camping facilities are also available. Leashed pets permitted.

Reservations, fees: Some sites can be reserved by calling (800) 280-CAMP/2267 ($8.65 reservation fee). Sites are $9–$18 per night;

group sites are $45 per night. The campground is open from mid-April to late September.

Contact: Gifford Pinchot National Forest, Wind River Ranger District, 1262 Hemlock Road, Carson, WA 98610; (509) 427-3200 or fax (509) 427-3215.

Directions: From Interstate 5 at Vancouver, Washington, turn east on Highway 14 and drive approximately 50 miles to Carson. Turn north on the Wind River Highway and drive 12 miles to the campground entrance.

Trip notes: This campground along the Wind River is a nice spot, with fishing access and pretty, shaded sites. Though small and remote, it has piped water—the perfect combination.

㉒ Beacon Rock State Park

Location: On the Columbia River; map B2, grid j7.

Campsites, facilities: There are 33 developed sites for tents or self-contained RVs up to 50 feet long. Picnic tables and fire grills are provided. Flush toilets, a sanitary disposal station, coin-operated showers, firewood to purchase, and a playground are available. Some facilities are wheelchair accessible. Boat docks, launching facilities, and rentals are nearby. Leashed pets are permitted.

Reservations, fees: No reservations are accepted. Sites are $10 per night; there is a $4 launch fee. The campground is open year-round, with limited winter facilities.

Contact: Phone (800) 233-0321 or (509) 427-8265, or write to 34841 State Route 14, Skamania, WA 98648.

Directions: From Interstate 5 at Vancouver, Washington, turn east on Highway 14 and drive 35 miles. The park straddles the highway; follow the signs to the campground.

Trip notes: This state park is set along the Columbia River with 14 miles of hiking trails heading inland. One trail leads to Beacon Rock, the second largest monolith in the world, which overlooks the Columbia River Gorge. If you like to fish, sturgeon are plentiful in the Columbia. Remember, there is a six-foot maximum size limit for Mr. Sturgeon.

㉘ Dougan Creek

Location: Near the Washougal River; map B2, grid j7.

Campsites, facilities: There are seven campsites for tents or small trailers. Picnic tables, fire grills, and tent pads are provided. Vault toilets and piped water are available. Leashed pets are permitted.

Reservations, fees: No reservations are accepted. There is no fee. The campground is open from mid-May to mid-September.

Contact: Department of Natural Resources, Southwest Region, P.O. Box 280, Castle Rock, WA 98611-0280; (360) 577-2025 or (360) 274-4196.

Directions: From Interstate 5 at Vancouver, Washington, turn east on Highway 14 and drive 20 miles. Turn north on Highway 140 and drive five miles to Washougal River Road. Turn right on Washougal River Road and drive about seven miles until you come to the end of the pavement and pass the picnic area on your left. The campground is just beyond the picnic area.

Trip notes: This campground located on Dougan Creek where it empties into the Washougal River is small and remote, but it has piped water and an on-site host. The camp is heavily forested and has pretty sites with river views.

㉞ Beacon Rock Resort

Location: On the Columbia River; map B2, grid j7.

Campsites, facilities: There are 20 sites for trailers or RVs of any length; three are drive-throughs. Electricity, piped water, sewer hookups, and picnic tables are provided. Flush toilets, bottled gas, showers, firewood, a store, a recreation hall, a laundry room, and ice are available. Boat launching facilities are located within one-quarter mile on the Columbia River. Leashed pets are permitted.

Reservations, fees: Reservations are accepted with a deposit. Sites are $10–$15 per night. The campground is open year-round.

Contact: Phone (509) 427-8473 or write to 62 Moorage Road, Skamania, WA 98648.

Directions: From Interstate 5 at Vancouver, Washington, turn east on Highway 14 and drive 34 miles. The park is in Skamania at the corner of Highway 14 and Moorage Road.

Trip notes: This trailer park is set along the Columbia River, a short distance from Beacon Rock State Park. See the trip notes for the state park (campground number 82) for details. Nearby recreation options include a nine-hole golf course four miles away and two 18-hole golf courses, eight and 12 miles away, respectively.

Map B3

Washington State Map .... *page 6*
One inch equals approximately 20 miles.

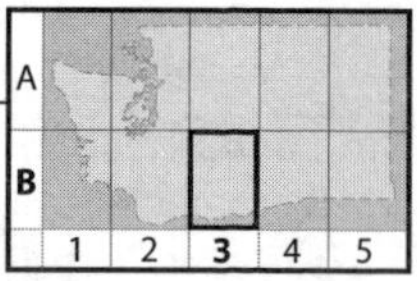

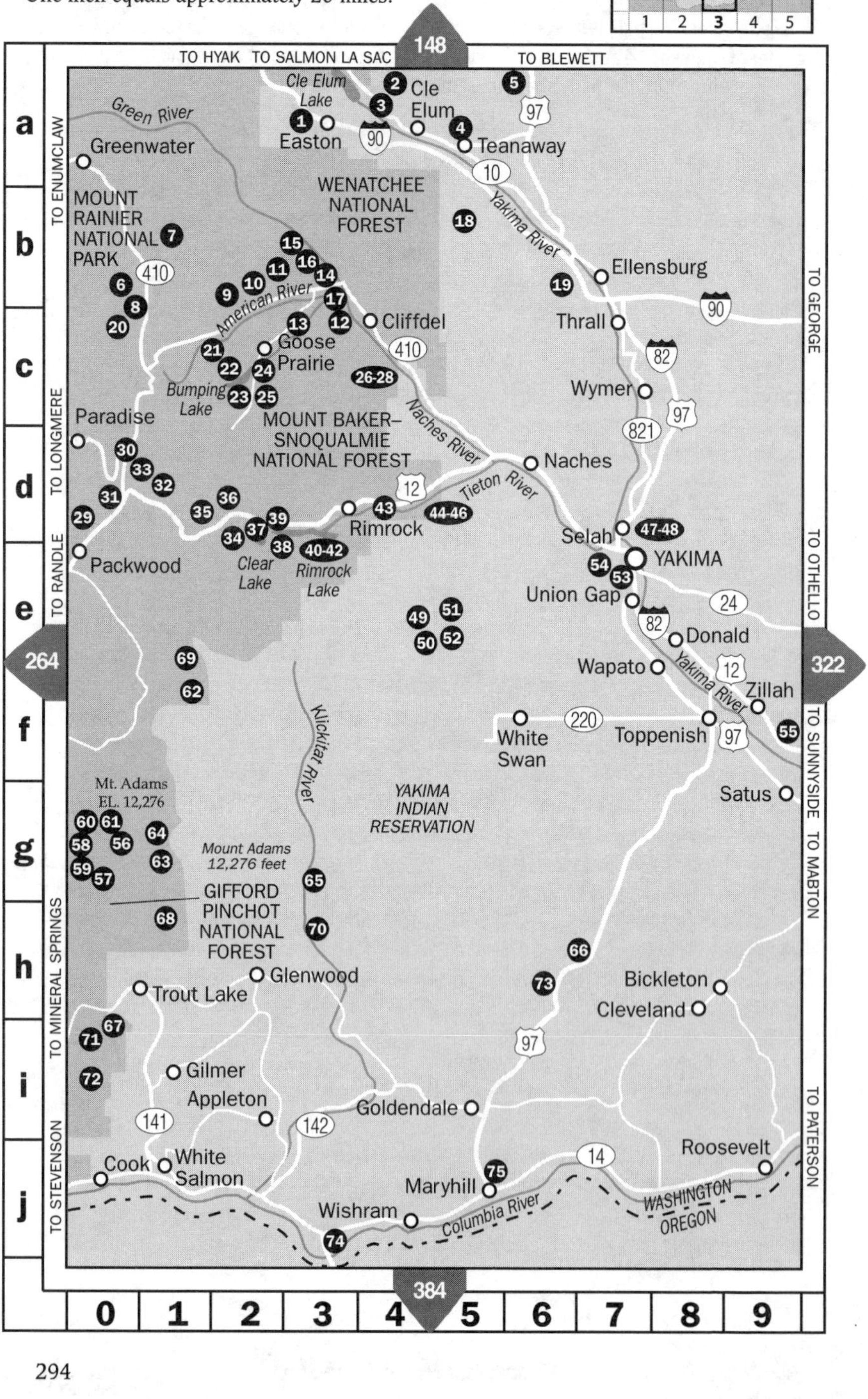

Chapter B3 features:

---

1 Lake Easton State Park

Location: On Lake Easton; map B3, grid a3.

Campsites, facilities: There are two primitive tent sites, 92 developed tent sites, and 45 sites for trailers or RVs up to 60 feet long. Picnic tables and fire grills are provided. Flush toilets, a sanitary disposal station, a playground, electricity, piped water, sewer hookups, showers, and firewood are available. A cafe and ice are located within one mile. Some facilities are wheelchair accessible. Boat launching facilities and floats are located on Lake Easton. Leashed pets are permitted.

Reservations, fees: Contact Reservations

Northwest at (800) 452-5687 ($6 reservation fee). Sites are $7–$16 per night. The campground is open from April 19 through October 16.

Contact: Phone (800) 233-0321 or (509) 656-2586, or write to P.O. Box 26, Easton, WA 98925.

Directions: From Interstate 5 at Seattle, turn east on Interstate 90 and drive approximately 68 miles to the park entrance, which is located one mile west of the town of Easton.

Trip notes: This campground offers a multitude of recreational opportunities. For starters, it's set along the shore of Lake Easton, with Kachess Lake and Keechelus Lake just a short drive away. The park provides opportunities for both summer and winter recreation, including swimming, fishing, boating, cross-country skiing, and snowmobiling. Nearby recreation options include an 18-hole golf course and hiking trails.

❷ Indian Camp

Location: On the Middle Fork of the Teanaway River; map B3, grid a4.

Campsites, facilities: There are nine campsites for tents or small trailers. Picnic tables, fire grills, and tent pads are provided. Pit toilets are available, but there is no piped water. Leashed pets are permitted.

Reservations, fees: No reservations are accepted. There is no fee. The campground is open year-round, weather permitting (heavy snows are generally expected from December through March).

Contact: Department of Natural Resources, Southeast Region, 713 East Bowers Road, Ellensburg, WA 98926-9341; (509) 925-8510 or fax (509) 925-8522.

Directions: From Seattle, turn east on Interstate 90 and drive 80 miles to Cle Elum. Take exit 85 and drive east on Highway 970 for 6.9 miles. Turn left on Teanaway Road and drive 7.3 miles, then turn left on West Fork Teanaway Road and drive six-tenths of a mile. Turn right on Middle Fork Teanaway Road and drive 3.9 miles to the campground, which will be on your left.

Trip notes: This campground along the Middle Fork of the Teanaway River is in a very primitive setting, with sunny, open sites along the water. Be sure to bring your own drinking water. Quiet and solitude are highlights of this little-used camp. It's an easy drive from here to trailheads accessing the Mount Stuart Range.

❸ McKean's Trailer Park

Location: Near the Yakima River; map B3, grid a4.

Campsites, facilities: There are 10 sites for trailers or RVs. Electricity, piped water, sewer hookups, and picnic tables are provided. A cafe is available. Bottled gas, sanitary services, a store, a Laundromat, and ice are located within one mile. Pets are permitted.

Reservations, fees: Reservations are recommended. Sites are $15 per night. The campground is open from March to late December.

Contact: Phone (509) 674-2254 or write to 327 Lincoln Street, Cle Elum, WA 98922.

Directions: From Interstate 5 at Seattle, turn east on Interstate 90 and drive approximately 80 miles to Cle Elum. The park is in Cle Elum at 1011 East First Street.

Trip notes: Cle Elum is Indian for "swift water," and this in-town camp is convenient for taking advantage of the waters of the Yakima River. You can rent rafts and canoes in Cle Elum and enjoy a 16-mile raft trip down the river to Thorp, where the rental company offers to pick you up and bring you back to Cle Elum. The Cle Elum Historical Telephone Museum is also in town. Lake Easton State Park and Trailer Corral are also located near the Yakima River.

❹ Trailer Corral

Location: On the Yakima River; map B3, grid a5.

Campsites, facilities: There are three tent sites and 24 sites for trailers or RVs of any length, plus six cabins. Electricity, piped water, sewer and cable TV hookups, and picnic tables are provided. Flush toilets, sanitary services, showers, firewood, laundry facilities, and ice are available. A store is located within one mile. Boat launching facilities are nearby. Leashed pets are permitted.

Reservations, fees: Reservations are accepted. Sites are $13–$17 per night. The campground is open year-round.

Contact: Phone (509) 674-2433 or write to 2781 Highway 970, Cle Elum, WA 98922.

Directions: From Interstate 5 at Seattle, turn east on Interstate 90 and drive approximately 80 miles to Cle Elum. Continue one mile east on Interstate 90 to exit 85, then head east on Highway 970 for one mile to the park on the left.

Trip notes: This wooded campground along the Yakima River offers a choice of grassy or graveled sites. See the trip notes for McKean's Trailer Park (campground number 3) for river rafting information. Nearby recreation options include an 18-hole golf course, marked hiking trails, and tennis courts.

⑤ Mineral Springs

Location: On Medicine Creek in Wenatchee National Forest; map B3, grid a6.

Campsites, facilities: There are five tent sites and seven sites for tents, trailers, or RVs up to 21 feet long. Piped water and picnic tables are provided. Vault toilets are available. Leashed pets are permitted.

Reservations, fees: No reservations are accepted. Sites are $8 per vehicle per night, with a two-vehicle limit. The campground is open from mid-April to late November.

Contact: Wenatchee National Forest, Cle Elum Ranger District, 830 West Second Street, Cle Elum, WA 98922; (509) 674-4411 or fax (509) 674-4794.

Directions: From Interstate 5 at Seattle, turn east on Interstate 90 and drive approximately 80 miles to Cle Elum. Take exit 86 to County Road 970 and drive east 12 miles, then turn northeast on U.S. 97 and drive about seven miles to the campground.

Trip notes: This campground at the confluence of Medicine and Swauk Creeks is one of five campgrounds along U.S. 97. Fishing, berry picking, and hunting are good in season in this area. In the winter, cross-country skiing and snowshoeing are two options.

⑥ Silver Springs

Location: In Mount Baker–Snoqualmie National Forest; map B3, grid b0.

Campsites, facilities: There are 16 tent sites and 40 sites for tents, trailers, or RVs up to 21 feet long. Picnic tables and fire grills are provided. Vault toilets, piped water, and firewood are available. Leashed pets are permitted.

Reservations, fees: Some sites can be reserved by calling (800) 280-CAMP/2267 ($8.65 reservation fee). Sites are $8–$10 per night. The campground is open from mid-May to late September.

Contact: Mount Baker–Snoqualmie National Forest, White River Ranger District, 857 Roosevelt Avenue East, Enumclaw, WA 98022; (360) 825-6585 or fax (360) 825-0660.

Directions: From Interstate 5 south of Tacoma, take exit 127 and turn east on Highway 512. Drive northeast until you hit Highway 167, then turn east and continue a short distance to Highway 410. Turn east and drive 15 miles to Enumclaw. From there, continue 31 miles southeast on Highway 410 and you'll see the campground entrance on your right.

Trip notes: This campground along the White River on the northeastern border of Mount Rainier National Park is a good alternative to the more crowded camps in the park. It's located in a beautiful section of old-growth forest and is very scenic. Hiking and fishing are among the recreational options. A Forest Service information center is nearby.

⑦ Corral Pass

Location: In Mount Baker–Snoqualmie National Forest; map B3, grid b1.

Campsites, facilities: There are 20 tent sites. Picnic tables and fire grills are provided. Vault toilets, a horse-loading ramp, and firewood are available, but there is no piped water. Leashed pets are permitted.

Reservations, fees: No reservations are accepted. There is no fee. The campground is open from July to late September.

Contact: Mount Baker–Snoqualmie National Forest, White River Ranger District, 857 Roosevelt Avenue East, Enumclaw, WA 98022; (360) 825-6585 or fax (360) 825-0660.

Directions: From Interstate 5 south of Tacoma, take exit 127 and turn east on Highway 512. Drive northeast until you hit Highway 167, then turn east and continue a short distance to Highway 410. Turn east and drive 15 miles to Enumclaw. From there, continue 31 miles southeast on Highway 410, then go six miles east on Forest Service Road 7174. It's a winding dirt road and not suitable for trailers or RVs.

Trip notes: This is the most remote of the campgrounds in the area. Set at 5,600 feet, it's primitive, quiet, and an ideal base camp for a hiking trip. Groups of horse-packers heading into the adjacent Norse Peak Wilderness frequent the camp. Several trails nearby lead to backcountry fishing lakes and streams. See a Forest Service map for details. In late summer and fall, visitors can find wild berries in the area.

❽ The Dalles

Location: In Mount Baker–Snoqualmie National Forest; map B3, grid b1.

Campsites, facilities: There are 19 tent sites and 26 sites for tents, trailers, or RVs up to 21 feet long. Picnic tables, fire grills, vault toilets, and piped water are provided. Firewood is available. There is a large shaded picnic area for day use. Leashed pets are permitted.

Reservations, fees: Some sites can be reserved by calling (800) 280-CAMP/2267 ($8.65 reservation fee). Sites are $8–$10 per night. The campground is open from mid-May to late September.

Contact: Mount Baker–Snoqualmie National Forest, White River Ranger District, 857 Roosevelt Avenue East, Enumclaw, WA 98022; (360) 825-6585 or fax (360) 825-0660.

Directions: From Interstate 5 south of Tacoma, take exit 127 and turn east on Highway 512. Drive northeast until you hit Highway 167, then turn east and continue a short distance to Highway 410. Turn east and drive 15 miles to Enumclaw. From there, continue 25.5 miles southeast on Highway 410 and you'll see the campground on your right.

Trip notes: This campground along the White River is close to a nature trail, and the White River entrance to Mount Rainier National Park is about 14 miles south on Highway 410. The camp sits amid a grove of old-growth trees; a particular point of interest is a huge old Douglas fir tree that is more than nine feet in diameter and 235 feet tall. This is one of the prettiest camps in the area.

❾ Pleasant Valley

Location: On the American River in Wenatchee National Forest; map B3, grid b2.

Campsites, facilities: There are 16 sites for tents, trailers, or RVs up to 32 feet long. Picnic tables and fire grills are provided. Hand-pumped water, a dump station, and vault toilets are available. Firewood is not provided but may be gathered. Leashed pets are permitted.

Reservations, fees: No reservations are accepted. Rates are $9 per night for single sites, $17 per night for double sites, and $5 for each additional vehicle. The campground is open from mid-June to late November.

Contact: Wenatchee National Forest, Naches Ranger District, 10061 Highway 12, Naches, WA 98937; (509) 653-2205 or fax (509) 653-2638.

Directions: From Yakima on Interstate 82, drive 13 miles northwest on U.S. 12 to Naches. From there, continue 4.5 miles west on U.S. 12, then drive 37 miles northwest on Highway 410 to the campground on the left.

Trip notes: This campground along the American River is a good base camp for a hiking trip. A trail from the camp follows Kettle Creek up to the American Ridge and

Kettle Lake in the William O. Douglas Wilderness. It joins another trail that follows the ridge and then drops down to Bumping Lake. A Forest Service map is essential. In the winter, the area is popular with cross-country skiers.

⑩ Pine Needle Group Camp

Location: On the American River in Wenatchee National Forest; map B3, grid b2.

Campsites, facilities: There are six group sites for tents, trailers, or RVs up to 21 feet long. Picnic tables are provided. Pit toilets are available, but there is no piped water. Firewood is not provided but may be gathered. Leashed pets are permitted.

Reservations, fees: Reservations are required. Sites are $40 per night. The campground is open from late April to mid-September.

Contact: Wenatchee National Forest, Naches Ranger District, 10061 Highway 12, Naches, WA 98937; (509) 653-2205 or fax (509) 653-2638.

Directions: From Yakima on Interstate 82, drive 13 miles northwest on U.S. 12 to Naches. From there, drive 4.5 miles west on U.S. 12, then 30.5 miles northwest on Highway 410 to the campground on the left.

Trip notes: This is a reservations-only group campground on the edge of the William O. Douglas Wilderness, along the American River. There are trails leading south into the backcountry at nearby camps; see a Forest Service map. The camp is easy to reach, rustic, and beautiful. Fishing access is available. For a side trip, visit Bumping Lake to the south, where boating, fishing, and swimming are all possible options.

⑪ Hells Crossing

Location: On the American River in Wenatchee National Forest; map B3, grid b3.

Campsites, facilities: There are 18 sites for tents, trailers, or RVs up to 16 feet long. Hand-pumped water and picnic tables are provided.

Vault toilets and a dump station are available. Firewood is not provided but may be gathered. Leashed pets are permitted.

Reservations, fees: No reservations are accepted. Rates are $9 per night for single sites, $18 per night for double sites, and $5 for each additional vehicle. The campground is open from late May to late November.

Contact: Wenatchee National Forest, Naches Ranger District, 10061 Highway 12, Naches, WA 98937; (509) 653-2205 or fax (509) 653-2638.

Directions: From Yakima on Interstate 82, drive 13 miles northwest on U.S. 12 to Naches. From there, drive 4.5 miles west on U.S. 12, then drive 33.5 miles northwest on Highway 410 to the campground on the right.

Trip notes: This campground lies along the American River. A steep trail from the camp leads up to Goat Peak and follows the American Ridge in the William O. Douglas Wilderness. Other trails join the ridgetop trail and connect with lakes and streams. A Forest Service map details the backcountry.

⑫ Sawmill Flat

Location: On the Naches River in Wenatchee National Forest; map B3, grid c3.

Campsites, facilities: There are 25 sites for tents, trailers, or RVs up to 24 feet long. Hand-pumped water and picnic tables are provided. Vault toilets, a dump station, an adirondack group shelter, and firewood are available. Some facilities are wheelchair accessible, including one campsite. Leashed pets are permitted.

Reservations, fees: No reservations are accepted. Rates are $9 per night for single sites, $17 per night for double sites, and $5 for each additional vehicle. The campground is open from April through November.

Contact: Wenatchee National Forest, Naches Ranger District, 10061 Highway 12, Naches, WA 98937; (509) 653-2205 or fax (509) 653-2638.

Directions: From Yakima on Interstate 82, drive 13 miles northwest on U.S. 12 to Naches. From there, drive 4.5 miles west on U.S. 12, then 23.5 miles northwest on Highway 410 to the campground on the left.

Trip notes: This campground on the Naches River near Halfway Flat offers fishing access and a hiking trail that leads west from Halfway Flat for several miles into the backcountry. Another trailhead is located at Boulder Cave to the south. See a Forest Service map for details.

⓭ Cedar Springs

Location: On the Bumping River in Wenatchee National Forest; map B3, grid c3.

Campsites, facilities: There are 15 sites for tents, trailers, or RVs up to 22 feet long. Picnic tables are provided. Hand-pumped water, vault toilets, a dump station, and firewood are available. Leashed pets are permitted.

Reservations, fees: No reservations are accepted. Rates are $9 per night for single sites, $18 per night for double sites, and $5 for each additional vehicle. The campground is open from late May to late November.

Contact: Wenatchee National Forest, Naches Ranger District, 10061 Highway 12, Naches, WA 98937; (509) 653-2205 or fax (509) 653-2638.

Directions: From Yakima on Interstate 82, drive 13 miles northwest on U.S. 12 to Naches. From there, drive 4.5 miles west on U.S. 12, then turn northwest on Highway 410 and drive 28.5 miles. Turn southwest on Forest Service Road 2000 and proceed one-half mile to the campground on the left.

Trip notes: The Bumping River is the locale of this camp. If you continue driving southwest for 11 miles on Forest Service Road 174, you'll get to Bumping Lake, where recreation options abound.

⓮ Little Naches

Location: On the Little Naches River in Wenatchee National Forest; map B3, grid b3.

Campsites, facilities: There are 21 sites for tents, trailers, or RVs up to 20 feet long and three double sites. Hand-pumped water, picnic tables, and fire grills are provided. Vault toilets, a dump station, and firewood are available. Leashed pets are permitted.

Reservations, fees: No reservations are accepted. Rates are $9 per night for single sites, $18 per night for double sites, and $5 for each additional vehicle. The campground is open from late May to late November.

Contact: Wenatchee National Forest, Naches Ranger District, 10061 Highway 12, Naches, WA 98937; (509) 653-2205 or fax (509) 653-2638.

Directions: From Yakima on Interstate 82, drive 13 miles northwest on U.S. 12 to Naches. From there, drive 4.5 miles west on U.S. 12, then turn northwest on Highway 410 and drive 25 miles. Turn and drive 100 yards northwest on Forest Service Road 1900 to the campground on the left.

Trip notes: This campground on the Little Naches River near the American River, 24 miles from Mount Rainier, is just one-tenth of a mile off the road, and the easy access is a major attraction for highway cruisers. Fishing access is available from camp.

⓯ Crow Creek

Location: On the Naches River in Wenatchee National Forest; map B3, grid b3.

Campsites, facilities: There are 15 sites for tents, trailers, or RVs up to 30 feet long. Picnic tables and fire grills are provided. Vault toilets and a dump station are available, but there is no piped water. Firewood is not provided but may be gathered. Leashed pets are permitted.

Reservations, fees: No reservations are accepted. Sites are $5 per night. The campground is open from mid-April to late November.

Contact: Wenatchee National Forest, Naches Ranger District, 10061 Highway 12, Naches, WA 98937; (509) 653-2205 or fax (509) 653-2638.

Directions: From Yakima on Interstate 82, drive 13 miles northwest on U.S. 12 to Naches. From there, drive 4.5 miles west on U.S. 12, then turn northwest on Highway 410 and drive 24.5 miles. Turn northwest on Forest

Service Road 1900 and continue 2.5 miles, then turn west on Forest Service Road 1902 and proceed one-half mile to the campground on the right.

Trip notes: This campground on the Naches River is popular with OHVers. A trail heading out from the camp leads into the backcountry and then forks in several directions. One route leads to the American River, another follows West Quartz Creek, and another goes along Fife's Ridge into the Norse Peak Wilderness. See a Forest Service map for details. There is good hunting and fishing in season in this area.

⓰ Kaner Flat

Location: Near the Naches River in Wenatchee National Forest; map B3, grid b3.

Campsites, facilities: There are 41 sites for tents, trailers, or RVs up to 30 feet long. Hand-pumped water and picnic tables are provided. Vault, composting, and flush toilets, a dump station, and firewood are available. Leashed pets are permitted.

Reservations, fees: No reservations are accepted. Sites are $9–$18 per night, and $5 for each additional vehicle. The campground is open from mid-April to late November.

Contact: Wenatchee National Forest, Naches Ranger District, 10061 Highway 12, Naches, WA 98937; (509) 653-2205 or fax (509) 653-2638.

Directions: From Yakima on Interstate 82, drive 13 miles northwest on U.S. 12 to Naches. From there, drive 4.5 miles west on U.S. 12, then turn northwest on Highway 410 and drive 25 miles. Turn northwest on Forest Service Road 1900 and drive 2.5 miles to the campground on the right.

Trip notes: This campground near the Naches River is on the site of a wagon trail camp on the Old Naches Trail, a route used in the 1800s by wagon trains, Native Americans, and the U.S. Cavalry on their way to west side markets. The Naches Trail is now used by motorcyclists and narrow clearance four-wheel-drive enthusiasts.

⓱ Indian Flat Group Camp

Location: On the American River in Wenatchee National Forest; map B3, grid b3.

Campsites, facilities: There are 11 sites for tents, trailers, or RVs up to 30 feet long. Piped water and picnic tables are provided. Pit toilets and firewood are available. Leashed pets are permitted.

Reservations, fees: Reservations are required. Sites are $40 per night. The campground is open from late May to mid-September.

Contact: Wenatchee National Forest, Naches Ranger District, 10061 Highway 12, Naches, WA 98937; (509) 653-2205 or fax (509) 653-2638.

Directions: From Yakima on Interstate 82, drive 13 miles northwest on U.S. 12 to Naches. From there, drive 4.5 miles west on U.S. 12, then drive 27 miles northwest on Highway 410 to the campground on the left.

Trip notes: This is a reservations-only group campground set along the American River. Fishing access is available. A trail from the camp leads into the backcountry, west along Fife's Ridge, and farther north to the West Quartz Creek drainage. A Forest Service map details the adventure possibilities.

⓲ Taneum

Location: On Taneum Creek in Wenatchee National Forest; map B3, grid b5.

Campsites, facilities: There are 14 sites for trailers or RVs up to 21 feet long. Picnic tables are provided. Piped water and firewood are available. Some facilities are wheelchair accessible. Leashed pets are permitted.

Reservations, fees: No reservations are accepted. Rates are $8 per night for single sites, $16 per night for double sites, and $5 for each additional vehicle, with a two-vehicle limit. The campground is open from May to late September.

Contact: Wenatchee National Forest, Cle Elum Ranger District, 830 West Second Street,

Cle Elum, WA 98922; (509) 674-4411 or fax (509) 674-4794.

Directions: From Interstate 5 at Seattle, turn east on Interstate 90 and drive approximately 80 miles to Cle Elum. Continue nine miles southeast on Interstate 90 to exit 93. Cross the freeway and drive south on Thorp Prairie Road for four miles. Cross back over the freeway to Taneum Road. Turn right and drive west for three miles to Forest Service Road 33. Continue west six miles to the campground on the left.

Trip notes: This rustic spot along Taneum Creek has been getting increased use in recent years due to off-road-vehicle displacement in other areas. Fishing is popular here in the summer, and in the winter months snowshoeing and cross-country skiing trails are available.

⑲ KOA Ellensburg

Location: On the Yakima River; map B3, grid b6.

Campsites, facilities: There are 50 tent sites and 100 sites for trailers or RVs of any length; 48 are drive-throughs. Piped water and picnic tables are provided. Flush toilets, sanitary services, showers, a recreation hall, a store, laundry facilities, ice, a playground, nightly movies, a seasonal wading pool, and a swimming pool are available. Electricity and sewer hookups can be obtained for an extra fee. Bottled gas and a cafe are located within one mile. Leashed pets and motorbikes are permitted.

Reservations, fees: Reservations are accepted. Sites are $17–$23 per night. The campground is open year-round.

Contact: Phone (509) 925-9319, fax (509) 925-8607, or write to 32 Thorp Highway South, Ellensburg, WA 98926.

Directions: From Seattle, go about 106 miles east on Interstate 90 to exit 106 near Ellensburg. You'll see the campground as you exit.

Trip notes: This is the only campground in a 25-mile radius, and it's exceptionally clean and scenic. It offers well-maintained, shaded campsites along the Yakima River. The Kittitas

County Historical Museum is in town at Third and Pine Streets, and then there's the town-sponsored Ellensburg Roundup every weekend during the summer. Nearby recreation options include an 18-hole golf course and tennis courts.

⑳ White River

Location: On the White River in Mount Rainier National Park; map B3, grid c0.

Campsites, facilities: There are 117 sites for tents or RVs up to 20 feet long. Picnic tables and fire grills are provided. Flush toilets and piped water are available. Some facilities are wheelchair accessible. Leashed pets are permitted.

Reservations, fees: No reservations are accepted. Sites are $8 per night. The campground is open from mid-June to mid-September.

Contact: Mount Rainier National Park, Tahoma Woods, Ashford, WA 98304; (360) 569-2211 or fax (360) 569-2170.

Directions: From Interstate 5 at Tacoma, turn east on Highway 512 and drive 12 miles. Go east on Highway 167 for one mile to the junction with Highway 410. Turn east on Highway 410 and drive to Enumclaw. Continue 27 miles southeast on Highway 410 to the White River entrance into the park. Take White River Road to the right and drive about seven miles to the campground.

Trip notes: This campground is set on the White River at 4,400 feet. A trail near camp leads a short distance (but vertically, it's a rise of 2200 feet) to the Sunrise Visitor Center. (Local rangers recommend that trailers be left at White River Campground and the 11-mile road trip to Sunrise be made by car.) From there, you can take several trails that lead to backcountry lakes and glaciers. This camp is often used by climbers planning to summit Mount Rainier.

㉑ Lodge Pole

Location: On the American River in Wenatchee National Forest; map B3, grid c2.

Campsites, facilities: There are 35 sites for tents, trailers, or RVs up to 20 feet long. Hand-pumped water and picnic tables are provided. Vault toilets, a dump station, and firewood are available. Leashed pets are permitted.

Reservations, fees: No reservations are accepted. Sites are $9 per night, and $5 for each additional vehicle. The campground is open from mid-June to mid-September.

Contact: Wenatchee National Forest, Naches Ranger District, 10061 Highway 12, Naches, WA 98937; (509) 653-2205 or fax (509) 653-2638.

Directions: From Yakima on Interstate 82, drive 13 miles northwest on U.S. 12 to Naches. From there, drive 4.5 miles west on U.S. 12, then turn northwest on Highway 410 and drive 40.5 miles to the campground on the right.

Trip notes: This campground is located along the American River about eight miles west of the western boundary of Mount Rainier National Park. See the trip notes for Gateway Inn and RV Park (campground number 36 in Chapter B2) for information on Mount Rainier. Fishing access is available nearby.

㉒ Bumping Crossing

Location: On the Bumping River in Wenatchee National Forest; map B3, grid c2.

Campsites, facilities: There are 12 sites for tents, trailers, or RVs up to 15 feet long. Picnic tables are provided. Vault toilets and firewood are available, but there is no piped water. A store, a cafe, and ice are located within one mile. Boat docks, launching facilities, and rentals are nearby on Bumping Lake. Leashed pets are permitted.

Reservations, fees: No reservations are accepted. There is no fee. The campground is open from late May to late November.

Contact: Wenatchee National Forest, Naches Ranger District, 10061 Highway 12, Naches, WA 98937; (509) 653-2205 or fax (509) 653-2638.

Directions: From Yakima on Interstate 82, drive 13 miles northwest on U.S. 12 to Naches. From there, drive 4.5 miles west on U.S. 12, then turn northwest on Highway 410 and drive 28.5 miles. Turn southwest on Forest Service Road 2000 and drive 10 miles to the campground on the right.

Trip notes: This campground on the Bumping River about a mile from the boat landing at Bumping Lake is a more primitive option to Bumping Lake and Boat Landing (campground number 23). It's a very good spot for a weekend trip, but remember to bring your own drinking water.

㉓ Bumping Lake and Boat Landing

Location: On Bumping Lake in Wenatchee National Forest; map B3, grid c2.

Campsites, facilities: There are 45 sites for tents, trailers, or RVs up to 30 feet long. Hand-pumped water and picnic tables are provided. Vault toilets and firewood are available. Boat docks, launching facilities, and rentals are nearby. Leashed pets are permitted.

Reservations, fees: No reservations are accepted. Sites are $11 per night, and $5 for each additional vehicle. The campground is open from mid-May to late November.

Contact: Wenatchee National Forest, Naches Ranger District, 10061 Highway 12, Naches, WA 98937; (509) 653-2205 or fax (509) 653-2638.

Directions: From Yakima on Interstate 82, drive 13 miles northwest on U.S. 12 to Naches. From there, drive 4.5 miles west on U.S. 12, then turn northwest on Highway 410 and drive 28.5 miles. Turn southwest on Forest Service Road 2000 and continue 11 miles to the campground on the right.

Trip notes: Woods and water, this spot has them both. A variety of water activities are allowed at Bumping Lake, including waterskiing, fishing, and swimming. Six campsites are adjacent to the boat facilities. There are also several hiking trails that go into the wilderness area surrounding the lake. This is one of the more developed camps in the area, with the added bonus of a boat ramp.

㉔ Soda Springs

Location: On the Bumping River in Wenatchee National Forest; map B3, grid c2.

Campsites, facilities: There are 26 sites for tents, trailers, or RVs up to 30 feet in length. Piped water and picnic tables are provided. Vault toilets, a dump station, firewood, several picnic shelters with fireplaces, and some wheelchair-accessible facilities are available. Leashed pets are permitted.

Reservations, fees: No reservations are accepted. Sites are $9 per night, and $5 for each additional vehicle. The campground is open from May to late November.

Contact: Wenatchee National Forest, Naches Ranger District, 10061 Highway 12, Naches, WA 98937; (509) 653-2205 or fax (509) 653-2638.

Directions: From Yakima on Interstate 82, drive 13 miles northwest on U.S. 12 to Naches. From there, drive 4.5 miles west on U.S. 12, then turn northwest on Highway 410 and drive 28.5 miles. Turn southwest on Forest Service Road 2000 and continue five miles to the campground on the left.

Trip notes: Highlights of this camp along Bumping Creek include natural mineral springs and a nature trail. Fishing access is available. A sheltered picnic area is provided.

㉕ Cougar Flat

Location: On the Bumping River in Wenatchee National Forest; map B3, grid c2.

Campsites, facilities: There are 12 sites for tents, trailers, or RVs up to 20 feet long. Hand-pumped water and picnic tables are provided. Vault toilets, a dump station, and firewood are available. Leashed pets are permitted.

Reservations, fees: No reservations are accepted. Sites are $9 per night, and $5 for each additional vehicle. The campground is open from late May to mid-September.

Contact: Wenatchee National Forest, Naches

Ranger District, 10061 Highway 12, Naches, WA 98937; (509) 653-2205 or fax (509) 653-2638.

Directions: From Yakima on Interstate 82, drive 13 miles northwest on U.S. 12 to Naches. From there, drive 4.5 miles west on U.S. 12, then turn northwest on Highway 410 and drive 28.5 miles. Turn southwest on Forest Service Road 2000 and continue six miles to the campground on the left.

Trip notes: One of several camps in the immediate vicinity, this spot along the Bumping River is close to good fishing, and a trail from the camp follows the river and then heads up the tributaries. See the Chapter B3 map for nearby camping options.

㉖ Squaw Rock Resort

Location: Near the Naches River; map B3, grid c4.

Campsites, facilities: There are 25 tent sites and 65 sites for trailers or RVs of any length. Electricity, piped water, and picnic tables are provided. Flush toilets, bottled gas, sanitary services, showers, a recreation hall, a store, a cafe, ice, a playground, and a swimming pool are available. Some sites have sewer hookups. Leashed pets are permitted.

Reservations, fees: Reservations are accepted. Sites are $18 per night. The campground is open year-round.

Contact: Phone (509) 658-2926, fax (509) 658-2927, or write to 15070 State Route 410, Naches, WA 98937.

Directions: From Yakima on Interstate 82, drive 13 miles northwest on U.S. 12 to Naches. From there, drive 4.5 miles west on U.S. 12, then turn northwest on Highway 410 and drive 15 miles to the campground on the left.

Trip notes: This park near the Naches River is close to a host of activities, including trout fishing, hiking trails, marked bike trails, and a riding stable. The park has a pool and hot tub. The nearby town of Naches, located southeast of the campground on Highway 410, offers all services.

㉗ Cottonwood

Location: On the Naches River in Wenatchee National Forest; map B3, grid c4.

Campsites, facilities: There are 18 sites for tents, trailers, or RVs up to 22 feet long. Piped water is available. Picnic tables are provided. Vault toilets, firewood, a sanitary disposal station, a store, a cafe, and ice are available nearby. Some facilities are wheelchair accessible. Leashed pets are permitted.

Reservations, fees: No reservations are accepted. Sites are $9 per night, and $5 for each additional vehicle. The campground is open from April through November.

Contact: Wenatchee National Forest, Naches Ranger District, 10061 Highway 12, Naches, WA 98937; (509) 653-2205 or fax (509) 653-2638.

Directions: From Yakima on Interstate 82, drive 13 miles northwest on U.S. 12 to Naches. From there, drive 4.5 miles west on U.S. 12, then turn northwest on Highway 410 and drive 17.5 miles to the campground on the left.

Trip notes: Pretty, shaded sites and river views are the main draw at this camp along the Naches River. Sawmill Flat, Little Naches, Crow Creek, Kaner Flat, and Halfway Flat (campground numbers 12, 14, 15, 16, and 28) provide nearby alternatives.

㉘ Halfway Flat

Location: On the Naches River in Wenatchee National Forest; map B3, grid c4.

Campsites, facilities: There are eight sites for tents, trailers, or RVs up to 27 feet long. Picnic tables are provided. Pit toilets, a dump station, and firewood are available, but there is no piped water. Leashed pets are permitted.

Reservations, fees: No reservations are accepted. Sites are $7 per night. The campground is open from April to late November.

Contact: Wenatchee National Forest, Naches Ranger District, 10061 Highway 12, Naches, WA 98937; (509) 653-2205 or fax (509) 653-2638.

Directions: From Yakima on Interstate 82,

drive 13 miles northwest on U.S. 12 to Naches. From there, drive 4.5 miles west on U.S. 12, then turn northwest on Highway 410 and drive 21 miles. Turn northwest on Forest Service Road 1704 and drive three miles to the campground on the left.

Trip notes: Fishing, hiking, and OHV opportunities abound at this campground along the Naches River. A trail leads from the campground into the backcountry of the William O. Douglas Wilderness, which can also be reached by car. Try hoofing it.

㉙ Packwood Trailer and RV Park

Location: In Packwood; map B3, grid d0.

Campsites, facilities: There are 15 tent sites and 57 sites for trailers or RVs of any length. Electricity, piped water, sewer hookups, and picnic tables are provided. Flush toilets, sanitary services, showers, bottled gas, a store, a cafe, and a laundry room are available. Leashed pets and motorbikes are permitted.

Reservations, fees: Reservations are accepted. Sites are $12.50–$17 per night. The campground is open year-round.

Contact: Phone (360) 494-5145, fax (360) 494-2841, or write to P.O. Box 309, Packwood, WA 98361.

Directions: From Interstate 5 south of Olympia, turn east on U.S. 12 and drive 65 miles to Packwood. The park is on the left side of the highway in town.

Trip notes: This is a pleasant campground suitable for both tent and RV campers. Groups are welcome. Mount Rainier National Park is just 25 miles north, and this camp is a good alternative if the park is full. Nearby recreation options include a riding stable and tennis courts.

㉚ Ohanapecosh

Location: On the Ohanapecosh River in Mount Rainier National Park; map B3, grid d0.

Campsites, facilities: There are 208 sites

for tents or RVs up to 30 feet long. Picnic tables are provided. Flush toilets, piped water, and a sanitary disposal station are available. Some facilities are wheelchair accessible. Pets are permitted.

Reservations, fees: Reservations are accepted. Sites are $12 per night. The campground is open from mid-May through September.

Contact: Mount Rainier National Park, Tahoma Woods, Ashford, WA 98304; (360) 569-2211 or fax (360) 569-2170.

Directions: From Interstate 5 south of Olympia, turn east on U.S. 12 and drive 65 miles to Packwood. Continue seven miles northeast on U.S. 12, then turn north on Highway 123 and drive five miles to the Ohanapecosh entrance to the park. The camp is next to the visitor center as you enter the park.

Trip notes: This campground along the Ohanapecosh River is near a visitor center with exhibits on the history of the forest, plus visitor information. Highway 706 heading west, and Highway 123 heading north, are closed by snowfall in winter.

🜺 La Wis Wis

Location: On the Cowlitz River in Gifford Pinchot National Forest; map B3, grid d0.

Campsites, facilities: There are 100 sites for tents, trailers, or RVs up to 24 feet long. Picnic tables are provided. Flush and vault toilets, piped water, and firewood are available. Leashed pets are permitted.

Reservations, fees: No reservations are accepted. Sites are $10–$16 per night. The maximum stay is 14 days. The campground is open from mid-May to late September.

Contact: Gifford Pinchot National Forest, Packwood Ranger District, Packwood, WA 98361; (360) 494-0600 or fax (360) 494-0602.

Directions: From Interstate 5 south of Olympia, take exit 68 and turn east on U.S. 12. Drive 65 miles to Packwood. Continue seven miles east on U.S. 12, then drive one-half mile west on Forest Service Road 1272.

Trip notes: This camp is ideally located for day trips to Mount Rainier and Mount St. Helens. It's set on the Cowlitz River, near the Ohanapecosh River in an old-growth forest. Hikers can explore the nature trails throughout the area. The entrance to Mount Rainier National Park and the Ohanapecosh Hot Springs is about seven miles south of the camp.

🜺 Soda Springs

Location: On Summit Creek in Gifford Pinchot National Forest; map B3, grid d1.

Campsites, facilities: There are six primitive tent sites. Picnic tables are provided. Vault toilets are available, but there is no piped water. Leashed pets are permitted.

Reservations, fees: No reservations are accepted. Sites are $6 per night. The campground is open from mid-June to early September.

Contact: Gifford Pinchot National Forest, Packwood Ranger District, Packwood, WA 98361; (360) 494-0600 or fax (360) 494-0602.

Directions: From Interstate 5 south of Olympia, take exit 68 and turn east on U.S. 12. Drive 65 miles to Packwood. Continue 10 miles northeast on U.S. 12, then turn north on Forest Service Road 45 and continue to Forest Service Road 4510. Drive seven miles to Forest Service Road 4510.052, the campground access road.

Trip notes: Set along Summit Creek, this is a good base camp for a backpacking expedition or daily hiking trips in the Cascade Range. There are several trails and lakes to choose from as destinations. Obtain a Forest Service map for details.

🜺 Summit Creek

Location: On Summit Creek in Gifford Pinchot National Forest; map B3, grid d1.

Campsites, facilities: There are six primitive tent sites. Picnic tables are provided. Vault toilets are available, but there is no piped water. Leashed pets are permitted.

Reservations, fees: No reservations are

accepted. Sites are $6 per night. The campground is open from mid-June to early September.

Contact: Gifford Pinchot National Forest, Packwood Ranger District, Packwood, WA 98361; (360) 494-0600 or fax (360) 494-0602.

Directions: From Interstate 5 south of Olympia, take exit 68 and turn east on U.S. 12. Drive 65 miles to Packwood. Continue 10 miles northeast on U.S. 12, then turn north on Forest Service Road 45 and continue to Forest Service Road 4510. Turn and drive about three miles to the campground.

Trip notes: This very primitive campground along Summit Creek is another good base camp for trips into the Cascade Range backcountry. See the trip notes for Soda Springs (campground number 32).

㉞ Clear Lake North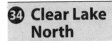

Location: On Clear Lake in Wenatchee National Forest; map B3, grid d2.

Campsites, facilities: There are 34 sites for tents, trailers, or RVs up to 22 feet long. Picnic tables are provided. Wheelchair-accessible vault toilets, a dump station, and firewood are available. There is no piped water at Clear Lake North, but there is hand-pumped water at Clear Lake South (campground number 37). Boat docks, launching facilities, and rentals are nearby. Leashed pets are permitted.

Reservations, fees: No reservations are accepted. Sites are $9 per night. The campground is open from mid-April to late November.

Contact: Wenatchee National Forest, Naches Ranger District, 10061 Highway 12, Naches, WA 98937; (509) 653-2205 or fax (509) 653-2638.

Directions: From Yakima on Interstate 82, drive 13 miles northwest on U.S. 12 to Naches. Continue 35.5 miles west on U.S. 12, then drive one mile south on County Road 1200. Continue one-half mile south on Forest Service Road 1200-840 to the campground.

Trip notes: This campground hails from an elevation of 3,100 feet along the shore of Clear Lake, which is the forebay for Rimrock Lake. No swimming is allowed, but you can fish. This camp is primitive and gets relatively little use.

㉟ White Pass Lake

Location: On Leech Lake in Wenatchee National Forest; map B3, grid d2.

Campsites, facilities: There are 16 sites for tents, trailers, or RVs up to 20 feet long. Picnic tables are provided. Vault toilets, a dump station, and firewood are available, but there is no piped water. A store, a cafe, a Laundromat, and ice are located within one mile. Boat docks and launching facilities are nearby. No motorized boats are allowed. Leashed pets are permitted.

Reservations, fees: No reservations are accepted. Sites are $7 per night. The campground is open from June to late November.

Contact: Wenatchee National Forest, Naches Ranger District, 10061 Highway 12, Naches, WA 98937; (509) 653-2205 or fax (509) 653-2638.

Directions: From Interstate 5 south of Olympia, take exit 68 and turn east on U.S. 12. Drive 65 miles to Packwood, then continue 19 miles northeast on U.S. 12. Turn north on the entrance road and drive 200 yards to Leech Lake.

Trip notes: This campground on the shore of Leech Lake at an elevation of 4,500 feet is near trails leading into the Goat Rocks Wilderness to the south and the William O. Douglas Wilderness to the north. A trailhead for the Pacific Crest Trail is also nearby. Beautiful Leech Lake is popular for fly fishing (the only type of fishing allowed here). White Pass Ski Area is located across the highway.

㊱ Dog Lake

Location: On Dog Lake in Wenatchee National Forest; map B3, grid d2.

Campsites, facilities: There are 11 sites for tents, trailers, or RVs up to 20 feet long. Picnic tables are provided. Vault toilets, a dump station, and firewood are available, but there is no piped water. Boat docks and launching facilities are nearby. Leashed pets are permitted, but no horses are allowed in the campground.

Reservations, fees: No reservations are accepted. Sites are $5 per night. The campground is open from late May to late November.

Contact: Wenatchee National Forest, Naches Ranger District, 10061 Highway 12, Naches, WA 98937; (509) 653-2205 or fax (509) 653-2638.

Directions: From Interstate 5 south of Olympia, take exit 68 and turn east on U.S. 12. Drive approximately 65 miles to Packwood. Continue 22 miles northeast on U.S. 12 to the campground.

Trip notes: This campground is on the shore of Dog Lake at 3,400 feet in elevation. Nearby trails lead into the William O. Douglas Wilderness. See a Forest Service map for details. Boating and fishing are two options here.

㊲ Clear Lake South

Location: In Wenatchee National Forest; map B3, grid d2.

Campsites, facilities: There are 23 sites for tents, trailers, or RVs up to 22 feet long. Hand-pumped water, picnic tables, a dump station, and vault toilets are available. Firewood is not provided but may be gathered. Boat docks, launching facilities, and rentals are nearby. Leashed pets are permitted.

Reservations, fees: No reservations are accepted. Sites are $9 per night. The campground is open from mid-April to late November.

Contact: Wenatchee National Forest, Naches Ranger District, 10061 Highway 12, Naches, WA 98937; (509) 653-2205 or fax (509) 653-2638.

Directions: From Yakima on Interstate 82, drive 13 miles northwest on U.S. 12 to Naches. From Naches, continue 35.5 miles west on U.S. 12, then drive one mile south on County Road 1200 to the campground.

Trip notes: This campground (elevation

3,100 feet) is located near the east shore of Clear Lake, which is the forebay for Rimrock Lake. Only fishing is allowed, which means no swimming. For winter travelers, several sno-parks in the area offer snowmobiling and cross-country skiing. There are many hiking trails to the north; see a Forest Service map.

㊳ Silver Beach Resort

Location: On Rimrock Lake; map B3, grid d3.

Campsites, facilities: There are 65 tent sites and 30 sites for trailers or RVs. Electricity, piped water, sewer hookups, and picnic tables are provided. A cafe, ice, boat docks, launching facilities, and boat rentals are available. A store and bottled gas are within nine miles. Pets and motorbikes are permitted.

Reservations, fees: Reservations are accepted. Sites are $10–$15 per night. The campground is open year-round, with limited winter facilities.

Contact: Phone (509) 672-2500 or write to 40350 Highway 12, Rimrock, WA 98937.

Directions: From Interstate 82 at Yakima, turn west on U.S. 12 and drive 40 miles to the resort on Rimrock Lake.

Trip notes: This resort along the shore of Rimrock Lake is one of several camps in the immediate area. It's very scenic, with beautiful lakefront sites. Hiking trails, marked bike trails, a full-service marina, and a riding stable are close by.

㊴ Indian Creek

Location: On Rimrock Lake in Wenatchee National Forest; map B3, grid d3.

Campsites, facilities: There are 39 sites for tents, trailers, or RVs up to 32 feet long. Piped water and picnic tables are provided. Vault toilets, a cafe, a store, a dump station, and ice are available. Firewood is not provided but may be gathered. Boat docks, launching facilities, and rentals are nearby. Leashed pets are permitted.

Reservations, fees: No reservations are accepted. Sites are $9–$11 per night. The campground is open from late May to mid-September.

Contact: Wenatchee National Forest, Naches Ranger District, 10061 Highway 12, Naches, WA 98937; (509) 653-2205 or fax (509) 653-2638.

Directions: From Yakima on Interstate 82, drive 13 miles northwest on U.S. 12 to Naches. Continue 31.5 miles west on U.S. 12 and you'll see the entrance.

Trip notes: Fishing, swimming, and waterskiing are among the activities at this shorefront campground on Rimrock Lake (elevation 3,000 feet). The camp is adjacent to Rimrock Lake Marina. Many excellent hiking trails to the north are routed into the William O. Douglas Wilderness.

④ South Fork

Location: On the South Fork of the Tieton River in Wenatchee National Forest; map B3, grid d3.

Campsites, facilities: There are 15 sites for tents, trailers, or RVs up to 20 feet long. Picnic tables are provided. Vault toilets, a dump station, and firewood are available, but there is no piped water. Boat docks are nearby. Leashed pets are permitted.

Reservations, fees: No reservations are accepted. Sites are $7 per night. The campground is open from late May to mid-September.

Contact: Wenatchee National Forest, Naches Ranger District, 10061 Highway 12, Naches, WA 98937; (509) 653-2205 or fax (509) 653-2638.

Directions: From Yakima on Interstate 82, drive 13 miles northwest on U.S. 12 to Naches. Continue 22.5 miles west on U.S. 12, then drive four miles south on County Road 1200. Turn south on Forest Service Road 1203 and drive one-half mile to the campground.

Trip notes: This campground at 5,000 feet along the South Fork of the Tieton River—less than a mile from where it empties into Rimrock Lake—is often a good spot for trout fishing and swimming. By traveling a bit farther south on Tieton River Road, you can see the huge Blue Slide, an enormous prehistoric rock and earth slide that has a curious blue tinge to it.

④ Peninsula

Location: On Rimrock Lake in Wenatchee National Forest; map B3, grid d3.

Campsites, facilities: There are 19 sites for tents, trailers, or RVs up to 20 feet long. Picnic tables are provided. Vault toilets and firewood are available, but there is no piped water. Boat docks and launching facilities are nearby. Leashed pets are permitted.

Reservations, fees: No reservations are accepted. There is no fee. The campground is open from mid-April to late November.

Contact: Wenatchee National Forest, Naches Ranger District, 10061 Highway 12, Naches, WA 98937; (509) 653-2205 or fax (509) 653-2638.

Directions: From Yakima on Interstate 82, drive 13 miles northwest on U.S. 12 to Naches. Continue 22.5 miles west on U.S. 12, then drive three miles south on County Road 1200. At Forest Service Road 1382, turn west and drive one more mile to the camp.

Trip notes: Swimming, fishing, and waterskiing are all allowed at Rimrock Lake (elevation 3,000 feet), where this shorefront camp is located. It's one of several on the lake. A nearby sno-park offers wintertime fun, including cross-country skiing and snowmobiling.

④ River Bend Group Camp

Location: On the Tieton River in Wenatchee National Forest; map B3, grid d3.

Campsites, facilities: There is one group camp that can accommodate up to 30 people and 10 vehicles. Piped water and picnic tables are provided. Vault toilets and firewood are available. Boat docks, launching facilities, and rentals are located on Rimrock Lake. Leashed pets are permitted.

Reservations, fees: Reservations are recommended. Sites are $35 per night. The campground is open from April to mid-September.

Contact: Wenatchee National Forest, Naches Ranger District, 10061 Highway 12, Naches, WA 98937; (509) 653-2205 or fax (509) 653-2638.

Directions: From Yakima on Interstate 82, drive 13 miles northwest on U.S. 12 to Naches. Continue 22 miles southwest on U.S. 12 to the campground.

Trip notes: This is a reservations-only group camp near Hause Creek at an elevation of 2,500 feet. It's set on the Tieton River about five miles from Rimrock Lake. Easy highway access and nice riverside sites are highlights. A sno-park is nearby.

⑭ Wildrose

Location: On the Tieton River in Wenatchee National Forest; map B3, grid d4.

Campsites, facilities: There are eight sites for tents, trailers, or RVs up to 22 feet long. Picnic tables are provided. Vault toilets, a dump station, and firewood are available, but there is no piped water. Leashed pets are permitted.

Reservations, fees: No reservations are accepted. Sites are $5 per night. The campground is open from April to late November.

Contact: Wenatchee National Forest, Naches Ranger District, 10061 Highway 12, Naches, WA 98937; (509) 653-2205 or fax (509) 653-2638.

Directions: From Yakima on Interstate 82, drive 13 miles northwest on U.S. 12 to Naches. Continue 20.5 miles southwest on U.S. 12 to the campground.

Trip notes: Located at an elevation of 2,400 feet along the Tieton River, Wildrose Campground is an alternative to South Fork, River Bend, Willows, Hause Creek, and Windy Point (campground numbers 40, 42, 44, 45, and 46). It's quite primitive and used slightly less than the others. If you're willing to do without the luxuries, it can serve as a good layover camp, with easy highway access.

⑭ Willows

Location: On the Tieton River in Wenatchee National Forest; map B3, grid d4.

Campsites, facilities: There are 16 sites for tents, trailers, or RVs up to 20 feet long. Picnic tables are provided. Hand-pumped water, vault toilets, a sanitary disposal service, and firewood are available. Leashed pets are permitted.

Reservations, fees: No reservations are accepted. Sites are $9 per night. The campground is open from April to late November.

Contact: Wenatchee National Forest, Naches Ranger District, 10061 Highway 12, Naches, WA 98937; (509) 653-2205 or fax (509) 653-2638.

Directions: From Yakima on Interstate 82, drive 13 miles northwest on U.S. 12 to Naches. Continue 20 miles southwest on U.S. 12 to the campground.

Trip notes: This primitive, beautiful, and easily accessible camp can be found on the Tieton River at 2,400 feet elevation. Rimrock Lake to the west provides many recreation options, and hiking trails leading into the William O. Douglas Wilderness are within driving distance.

⑭ Hause Creek

Location: On the Tieton River in Wenatchee National Forest; map B3, grid d4.

Campsites, facilities: There are 42 sites for tents, trailers, or RVs up to 30 feet long. Piped water and picnic tables are provided. Flush toilets, a dump station, and firewood are available. Some facilities are wheelchair accessible. Boat docks, launching facilities, and rentals are located on Rimrock Lake. Leashed pets are permitted.

Reservations, fees: No reservations are accepted. Sites are $9–$18 per night. The campground is open from late May to late November.

Contact: Wenatchee National Forest, Naches Ranger District, 10061 Highway 12, Naches, WA 98937; (509) 653-2205 or fax (509) 653-2638.

Directions: From Yakima on Interstate 82, drive 13 miles northwest on U.S. 12 to Naches. Continue 22 miles southwest on U.S. 12 to the campground.

Trip notes: Several creeks converge at the

site of this campground along the Tieton River (elevation 2,500 feet). The Tieton Dam, which creates Rimrock Lake, is just upstream. This is one of the larger, more developed camps in the area. Primitive alternatives include River Bend, Wildrose, and Willows (campground numbers 42, 43, and 44).

㊻ Windy Point

Location: On the Tieton River in Wenatchee National Forest; map B3, grid d4.

Campsites, facilities: There are 15 sites for tents, trailers, or RVs up to 22 feet long. Hand-pumped water and picnic tables are provided. Vault toilets, a sanitary disposal service, and firewood are available. Leashed pets are permitted.

Reservations, fees: No reservations are accepted. Sites are $9 per night. The campground is open from April to late November.

Contact: Wenatchee National Forest, Naches Ranger District, 10061 Highway 12, Naches, WA 98937; (509) 653-2205 or fax (509) 653-2638.

Directions: From Yakima on Interstate 82, drive 13 miles northwest on U.S. 12 to Naches. Continue 13 miles west on U.S. 12 to the campground.

Trip notes: This campground, located along the Tieton River at an elevation of 2,000 feet, is more isolated than the camps set westward toward Rimrock Lake. Piped water is a bonus. Fishing access is available.

㊼ Yakima Sportsman State Park

Location: On the Yakima River; map B3, grid d7.

Campsites, facilities: There are two primitive tent sites, 28 sites for tents or self-contained RVs, and 37 drive-through sites with full hookups for trailers or RVs of any length. Picnic tables and fire grills are provided. Flush toilets, sanitary services, and a playground are available. Showers and firewood can be obtained for an extra fee. A store and ice are within one mile. Leashed pets are permitted.

Reservations, fees: No reservations are accepted. Sites are $7–$16 per night. The campground is open year-round.

Contact: Phone (800) 233-0321 or (509) 575-2774, or write to Route 9, P.O. Box 498, Yakima, WA 98901.

Directions: From Yakima on Interstate 82, drive one mile east to the park.

Trip notes: Kayaking and rafting are possible at this park on the Yakima River. No swimming is allowed. There is also a fishing pond for children (no anglers over age 15 are allowed). Nearby recreation options include an 18-hole golf course and hiking trails. See the trip notes for KOA Yakima (campground number 48) for information on other points of interest in Yakima.

㊽ KOA Yakima

Location: On the Yakima River; map B3, grid d7.

Campsites, facilities: There are 50 tent sites and 90 drive-through sites for trailers or RVs of any length. Cabins are also available. Picnic tables are provided. Flush toilets, bottled gas, sanitary services, showers, a recreation hall, a store, laundry facilities, ice, a playground, electricity, piped water, sewer hookups, firewood, and boat rentals, including paddleboats, are available. A cafe is located within one mile. Leashed pets and motorbikes permitted.

Reservations, fees: Reservations are accepted. Sites are $20–$25 per night. The campground is open from March to mid-November.

Contact: Phone (800) 562-5773 or (509) 248-5882, or write to 1500 Keyes Road, Yakima, WA 98901.

Directions: From Interstate 82 at Yakima, take the Highway 24 exit and drive one-half mile east. Turn north on Keyes Road and drive 300 yards to the campground.

Trip notes: This campground along the Yakima River offers well-maintained, shaded sites and fishing access. Some points of interest in Yakima are the Yakima Valley Museum and the Yakima Trolley Lines, which offer rides on restored trolley cars originally built in 1906.

Indian Rock Paintings State Park is five miles west of Yakima on U.S. 12. Nearby recreation options include an 18-hole golf course, hiking trails, marked bike trails, and tennis courts.

49 Clover Flats

Location: Near the Goat Rocks Wilderness; map B3, grid e4.

Campsites, facilities: There are nine campsites for tents or small trailers. Picnic tables, fire grills, and tent pads are provided. Pit toilets and hand-pumped water are available. Leashed pets are permitted.

Reservations, fees: No reservations are accepted. There is no fee. The campground is open year-round, weather permitting (heavy snows are generally expected from December through March).

Contact: Department of Natural Resources, Southeast Region, 713 East Bowers Road, Ellensburg, WA 98926-9341; (509) 925-8510 or fax (509) 925-8522.

Directions: From Interstate 82 at Yakima, drive two miles south to Union Gap. Turn west on Ahtanum Road and drive to Tampico, then continue west on Road A-2000 (Middle Fork Road) for 18.5 miles to the campground. Note: The last few miles of Road A-2000 are very steep, with a 12 to 13 percent grade.

Trip notes: This campground is in the subalpine zone on the slope of Darland Mountain, which peaks at 6,982 feet. Trails connect the area with the Goat Rocks Wilderness, six miles to the west. Contact the Department of Natural Resources or Wenatchee National Forest for details. See the trip notes for Ahtanum Camp (campground number 52) for information on winter snowmobiling.

50 Tree Phones

Location: On the Middle Fork of Ahtanum Creek; map B3, grid e4.

Campsites, facilities: There are 14 campsites for tents or small trailers. Picnic tables, fire grills, and tent pads are provided. Pit toilets are available, but there is no piped water.

Saddlestock facilities are also available. Leashed pets and motorbikes are permitted.

Reservations, fees: No reservations are accepted. There is no fee. The campground is open year-round, weather permitting (heavy snows are expected from December through March).

Contact: Department of Natural Resources, Southeast Region, 713 East Bowers Road, Ellensburg, WA 98926-9341; (509) 925-8510 or fax (509) 925-8522.

Directions: From Interstate 82 at Yakima, drive two miles south to Union Gap. Turn west on Ahtanum Road and drive to Tampico, then continue west on Road A-2000 (Middle Fork Road) for 15 miles. Turn left and drive 100 yards to the campground.

Trip notes: This forested campground along the Middle Fork of Ahtanum Creek is close to hiking, motorbiking, and horseback riding trails. A shelter with a wood stove is available year-round for picnics. During the summer months, there are beautiful wildflower displays. See the trip notes for Ahtanum Camp (campground number 52) for snowmobiling information.

51 Snow Cabin

Location: On the North Fork of Ahtanum Creek; map B3, grid e5.

Campsites, facilities: There are eight campsites for tents or small trailers. Picnic tables, fire grills, and tent pads are provided. Pit toilets are available, but there is no piped water. Saddlestock facilities are available. Leashed pets are permitted.

Reservations, fees: No reservations are accepted. There is no fee. The campground is open year-round, weather permitting.

Contact: Department of Natural Resources, Southeast Region, 713 East Bowers Road, Ellensburg, WA 98926-9341; (509) 925-8510 or fax (509) 925-8522.

Directions: From Interstate 82 at Yakima, drive two miles south to Union Gap. Turn west on Ahtanum Road and drive to Tampico, then continue west on Road A-2000 (Middle Fork Road) for 9.5 miles to Ahtanum Camp. From there, take the North Fork Ahtanum Road (A-3000) and drive 4.5 miles. Keep left and drive 2.5 miles to the campground, which will be on your left.

Trip notes: Located in an area of old-growth timber, this place is popular with horse campers who use it to access old logging roads. There are cutthroat trout in Ahtanum Creek, and fishing is permitted.

⑤ Ahtanum Camp

Location: On Ahtanum Creek; map B3, grid e5.

Campsites, facilities: There are 11 campsites for tents or small trailers. Picnic tables, fire grills, and tent pads are provided. Pit toilets and piped water are available. Leashed pets are permitted.

Reservations, fees: No reservation are accepted. There is no fee. The campground is open year-round, weather permitting.

Contact: Department of Natural Resources, Southeast Region, 713 East Bowers Road, Ellensburg, WA 98926-9341; (509) 925-8510 or fax (509) 925-8522.

Directions: From Interstate 82 at Yakima, drive two miles south to Union Gap. Turn west on Ahtanum Road and drive to Tampico, then continue west on Road A-2000 (Middle Fork Road) for 9.5 miles to the campground, which will be on the left.

Trip notes: This campground on Ahtanum Creek is one of four primitive sites within 10 miles. For a good side trip, continue driving on Road A-2000 for 14 miles, where you'll reach the Darland Mountain viewpoint at 6,900 feet. The road gets very steep near the lookout and is not suitable for RVs or trailers. In the winter, this area offers 60 miles of groomed trails for snowmobilers. A snow shelter with firewood is provided at Tree Phones (campground number 50). Contact the Department of Natural Resources for a map.

⑤ Circle H RV Ranch

Location: In Yakima; map B3, grid e7.

Campsites, facilities: There are 12 tent sites and 51 sites for trailers or RVs of any length; nine are drive-throughs. Electricity, piped water, sewer hookups, and picnic tables are provided. Flush toilets, showers, a recreation hall, laundry facilities, a playground, and a swimming pool are available. Bottled gas, sanitary services, a store, a cafe, and ice are located within one mile. Leashed pets and motorbikes are permitted.

Reservations, fees: Reservations are accepted. Sites are $15–$19 per night. The campground is open year-round.

Contact: Phone (509) 457-3683, fax (509) 457-3683, or write to 1107 South 18th Street, Yakima, WA 98901.

Directions: From Interstate 82 in Yakima, take exit 34 and drive one block to South 18th Street. Turn north and drive one-quarter mile to the campground on the right.

Trip notes: This pleasant, clean park with a western flavor has comfortable, spacious sites. Nearby recreation options include an 18-hole golf course, hiking trails, marked bike trails, and a riding stable. See the trip notes for KOA Yakima (campground number 48) for information on points of interest in Yakima.

⑤ Trailer Inns RV Park

Location: In Yakima; map B3, grid e7.

Campsites, facilities: There are 152 sites for trailers or RVs of any length; 30 are drive-throughs. Electricity, piped water, sewer hookups, and picnic tables are provided. Flush toilets, bottled gas, sanitary services, showers, a recreation hall, a laundry room, ice, a swimming pool, a whirlpool, a sauna, a TV room with a 52-inch screen, a dog walk, an enclosed barbecue, and a playground are available. A store and a cafe are located within one mile. Leashed pets are permitted.

Reservations, fees: Reservations are accepted. Sites are $17–$21 per night. The campground is open year-round.

Contact: Phone (509) 452-9561 or write to 1610 North First Street, Yakima, WA 98901.

Directions: From Interstate 82 in Yakima, take exit 32 and drive three blocks south on North First Street to the park on the west side of the road.

Trip notes: Like the Trailer Inns RV Park in Spokane (campground number 60 in Chapter A5), this spot has many of the luxuries you'd find in a hotel, including a pool, a hot tub, a sauna, on-site security, and a large-screen TV. An 18-hole golf course, hiking trails, marked bike trails, and tennis courts are close by. See the trip notes for KOA Yakima (campground number 48) for information on some of the points of interest in Yakima.

55 Granger RV Park

Location: Near the Yakima River; map B3, grid f9.

Campsites, facilities: There are 45 tent sites and 25 drive-through sites for trailers or RVs of any length. Electricity, piped water, and sewer hookups are provided. Flush toilets, sanitary services, showers, and a laundry room are available. Bottled gas, a store, a cafe, and ice are located within one mile. Leashed pets are permitted.

Reservations, fees: Reservations are accepted. Sites are $15 per night. The campground is open year-round.

Contact: Phone (509) 854-1300 or write to P.O. Box 695, Granger, WA 98932.

Directions: From Yakima on Interstate 82, drive 25 miles south to Granger. Take the Highway 223 exit in Granger and you'll see the park on the left.

Trip notes: This park near the Yakima River has nice, grassy sites with lots of shade. Granger is known as "Washington's Fruit Basket," and tourists can pick their own fruits and vegetables from local farms. Several wineries in the area offer tours. A unique side trip can be made to the Toppenish Wildlife Refuge, which is particularly good for bird-watching. It's 15 miles away, south of Toppenish on U.S. 97. Call (509) 865-2405 for information.

56 Horseshoe Lake

Location: On Horseshoe Lake in Gifford Pinchot National Forest; map B3, grid g0.

Campsites, facilities: There are 11 sites for tents, trailers, or RVs up to 16 feet long. Picnic tables are provided. Pit toilets are available, but there is no piped water. Firewood may be gathered outside the campground area. Primitive launching facilities are located on the lake, but all gasoline motors are prohibited on the water. Leashed pets are permitted.

Reservations, fees: No reservations are accepted. There is no fee. The campground is open from mid-June to late September.

Contact: Gifford Pinchot National Forest, Randle Ranger District, P.O. Box 670, Randle, WA 98377; (360) 497-1100 or fax (360) 497-1102.

Directions: From Interstate 5 south of Olympia, take exit 68 and turn east on U.S. 12. Drive 48 miles to Randle and take U.S. 131 south. Drive one mile, then turn southeast on Forest Service Road 23 and continue 30 miles. Turn northeast on Forest Service Road 2329 and drive seven miles, then turn west and travel 1.5 miles on Forest Service Road 78 to the campground.

Trip notes: The shore of Horseshoe Lake is the site of this campground. A trail from the camp goes up nearby Green Mountain (elevation 5,000 feet). Another trail heads up the north flank of Mount Adams. See a Forest Service map for details. Berry picking is an option in the late summer months, and fishing and horseback riding are other available activities.

57 Takhlakh

Location: On Takhlakh Lake in Gifford Pinchot National Forest; map B3, grid g0.

Campsites, facilities: There are 54 sites for tents, trailers, or RVs up to 21 feet long. Piped water and picnic tables are provided. Vault toilets are available. Firewood may be gathered outside the campground area. Boat launching facilities are available in the day-use area, but all gasoline motors are prohibited on the lake. Some facilities are wheelchair accessible. Leashed pets are permitted.

Reservations, fees: Reservations are accepted. Sites are $9 per night, and $5 for each additional vehicle. The campground is open from mid-June to late September.

Contact: Gifford Pinchot National Forest, Randle Ranger District, P.O. Box 670, Randle, WA 98377; (360) 497-1100 or fax (360) 497-1102.

Directions: From Interstate 5 south of Olympia, take exit 68 and turn east on U.S. 12. Drive 48 miles to Randle and take Highway 131 south. Drive one mile, then turn southeast on Forest Service Road 23 and continue 30 miles. Turn northeast on Forest Service Road 2329 and drive two miles to the camp.

Trip notes: This campground is along the shore of Takhlakh Lake, one of five lakes in the area, all accessible by car. It's a beautiful place, but alas, mosquitoes abound until late July. A viewing area is available for visitors, while the more adventurous can go berry picking, fishing, and hiking.

🔵 Olallie Lake

Location: On Olallie Lake in Gifford Pinchot National Forest; map B3, grid g0.

Campsites, facilities: There are five sites for tents, trailers, or RVs up to 21 feet long. Picnic tables are provided. Pit toilets are available, but there is no piped water. Firewood may be gathered outside the campground area. Boat launching facilities are nearby, but all gasoline motors are prohibited on the lake. Leashed pets are permitted.

Reservations, fees: No reservations are accepted. Sites are $6 per night, and $4 for each additional vehicle. The campground is open from July to late September.

Contact: Gifford Pinchot National Forest, Randle Ranger District, P.O. Box 670, Randle, WA 98377; (360) 497-1100 or fax (360) 497-1102.

Directions: From Interstate 5 south of Olympia, take exit 68 and turn east on U.S. 12. Drive

48 miles to Randle and take Highway 131 south. Drive one mile, then turn southeast on Forest Service Road 23 and continue 30 miles. Turn northeast on Forest Service Road 2329 and drive one mile, then continue north on Forest Service Road 5601 for one-half mile to the campground. A Forest Service map is essential.

Trip notes: This campground is located at 4,000 feet on the shore of Olallie Lake, a small alpine lake that is one of several in the area fed by streams coming off the glaciers on nearby Mount Adams (elevation 12,276 feet). A word to the wise: Mosquitoes can be a problem in the spring and early summer. See the chapter about protection against insects at the beginning of this book.

🔵 Council Lake

Location: On Council Lake in Gifford Pinchot National Forest; map B3, grid g0.

Campsites, facilities: There are nine sites for tents, trailers, or RVs up to 15 feet long. Picnic tables are provided. Pit toilets are available, but there is no piped water. Firewood may be gathered outside the campground area. Boat launching facilities are available, but all gasoline motors are prohibited. Leashed pets are permitted.

Reservations, fees: No reservations are accepted. Sites are $6 per night, and $4 for each additional vehicle. The campground is open from July to mid-September.

Contact: Gifford Pinchot National Forest, Randle Ranger District, P.O. Box 670, Randle, WA 98377; (360) 497-1100 or fax (360) 497-1102.

Directions: From Interstate 5 south of Olympia, take exit 68 and turn east on U.S. 12. Drive 48 miles to Randle and take Highway 131 south. Drive one mile, then turn southeast on Forest Service Road 23 and continue 31 miles. Turn west on Forest Service Road 2334 and drive one mile to the campground.

Trip notes: This campground can be found at about 4,000 feet along the shore of Council Lake on the northwest flank of Mount Adams. It's one of three lakeside campgrounds in the area (the others are Takhlakh and Olallie Lake, campground numbers 57 and 58). This one offers access to trails for hikers, mountain bikers, and equestrians, although horses are not allowed in the campground.

⑥ Adams Fork

Location: On the Cispus River in Gifford Pinchot National Forest; map B3, grid g0.

Campsites, facilities: There are 24 sites for tents, trailers, or RVs up to 21 feet long. Hand-pumped water and picnic tables are provided. Vault toilets are available. Firewood may be gathered outside the campground area. Leashed pets are permitted.

Reservations, fees: No reservations are accepted. Sites are $9 per night, group sites are $11–$22 per night, and additional vehicles are $5 each. The campground is open from May to late October.

Contact: Gifford Pinchot National Forest, Randle Ranger District, P.O. Box 670, Randle, WA 98377; (360) 497-1100 or fax (360) 497-1102.

Directions: From Interstate 5 south of Olympia, take exit 68 and turn east on U.S. 12. Drive 48 miles to Randle and take Highway 131 south. Go one mile, then turn southeast on Forest Service Road 23 and drive 18 miles. Turn southeast on Forest Service Road 21 and drive five miles, then turn east and go 200 yards on Forest Service Road 56 to the campground.

Trip notes: This campground is set at 2,600 feet along the Upper Cispus River near Adams Creek and at the foot of Mount Adams. A nearby trail leads north to Blue Lake, about a half-mile walk from the camp.

⑥ Cat Creek

Location: On Cat Creek and the Cispus River in Gifford Pinchot National Forest; map B3, grid g0.

Campsites, facilities: There are five sites for tents, trailers, or RVs up to 15 feet long. Picnic tables and fire grills are provided. Pit toilets and firewood are available, but there is no piped water. Firewood may be gathered outside the campground area. Leashed pets are permitted.

Reservations, fees: No reservations are accepted. Sites are $6 per night, and $4 for each additional vehicle. The campground is open from mid-May to late October.

Contact: Gifford Pinchot National Forest, Randle Ranger District, P.O. Box 670, Randle, WA 98377; (360) 497-1100 or fax (360) 497-1102.

Directions: From Interstate 5 south of Olympia, take exit 68 and turn east on U.S. 12. Drive 48 miles to Randle and take Highway 131 south. Drive one mile, then turn southeast on Forest Service Road 23 and continue 18 miles. Turn east on Forest Service Road 21 and drive six miles to the campground.

Trip notes: This pretty camp is set along Cat Creek at its confluence with the Cispus River about 10 miles from the summit of Mount Adams. A trail starts less than a mile from the camp and leads up along Blue Lake Ridge to Blue Lake. See a Forest Service map for details.

⑥ Walupt Horse Camp

Location: Near the Goat Rocks Wilderness in Gifford Pinchot National Forest; map B3, grid f1.

Campsites, facilities: There are six sites for equestrians in tents, trailers, or RVs up to 18 feet long. Picnic tables and piped water are provided. Vault toilets and firewood are available. Leashed pets are permitted.

Reservations, fees: Reservations are required; phone (800) 280-CAMP/2267 ($8.65 reservation fee). Sites are $9 per night, and $5 for each additional vehicle. The campground is open from June through September, weather permitting.

Contact: Gifford Pinchot National Forest, Packwood Ranger District, Packwood, WA 98361; (360) 494-0600 or fax (360) 494-0602.

Directions: From Interstate 5 south of Olympia, take exit 68 and turn east on U.S. 12. Drive 62.5 miles to Forest Service Road 2100 (2.5 miles southwest of Packwood), then drive southeast on Forest Service Road 2100 for 16.5 miles. Head east on Forest Service Road 2160 for 3.5 miles to the campground.

Trip notes: Fishing access at Walupt Lake is just a mile from this camp. Several trails lead from the lake into the backcountry of the southern Goat Rocks Wilderness, which has 85 miles of trails that can be used by horses. If you have planned a multiday horse packing trip, you need to bring in your own feed for the horses. Feed must be pellets or processed grain only.

⑥ Killen Creek

Location: Near Mount Adams in Gifford Pinchot National Forest; map B3, grid g1.

Campsites, facilities: There are eight sites for tents, trailers, or RVs up to 21 feet long. Picnic tables are provided. Pit toilets are available, but there is no piped water. Firewood may be gathered outside the campground area. Leashed pets are permitted.

Reservations, fees: No reservations are accepted. There is no fee. The campground is open from July to late September.

Contact: Gifford Pinchot National Forest, Randle Ranger District, P.O. Box 670, Randle, WA 98377; (360) 497-1100 or fax (360) 497-1102.

Directions: From Interstate 5 south of Olympia, take exit 68 and turn east on U.S. 12. Drive 48 miles to Randle and take Highway 131 south. Drive one mile, then turn southeast on Forest Service Road 23 and continue 30 miles. Turn southeast on Forest Service Road 2329 and drive six miles, then continue 200 yards west on Forest Service Road 073 to the campground.

Trip notes: This campground along Killen Creek at the foot of Mount Adams (elevation 12,276 feet) marks the start of a three-mile trail that leads up the mountain and connects with the Pacific Crest Trail. It's worth the effort. Berry picking and horseback riding are two other summertime options.

⑥ Keene's Horse Camp

Location: On the South Fork of Spring Creek in Gifford Pinchot National Forest; map B3, grid g1.

Campsites, facilities: There are 13 sites for tents, trailers, or RVs up to 21 feet long. Picnic tables and fire grills are provided. Pit toilets and horse corrals are available, but there is no piped water. Firewood may be gathered outside the campground area. Leashed pets are permitted.

Reservations, fees: No reservations are accepted. There is no fee. The campground is open from July to late September.

Contact: Gifford Pinchot National Forest, Randle Ranger District, P.O. Box 670, Randle, WA 98377; (360) 497-1100 or fax (360) 497-1102.

Directions: From Interstate 5 south of Olympia, take exit 68 and turn east on U.S. 12. Drive 48 miles to Randle and take Highway 131 south. Drive one mile, then turn southeast on Forest Service Road 23 and continue 30 miles. Turn northeast on Forest Service Road 2329 and drive eight miles, then turn west on Forest Service Road 82 and drive 100 yards to the campground. A Forest Service map is essential.

Trip notes: This campground is set at 4,200 feet along the South Fork of Spring Creek on the northwest flank of Mount Adams (elevation 12,276 feet). The Pacific Crest Trail passes within a couple of miles of the camp. A number of trails lead from here into the backcountry and to several alpine meadows. The meadows are fragile, so walk along their outer edges.

⑥ Island Camp

Location: On Bird Creek; map B3, grid g3.

Campsites, facilities: There are six campsites for tents or small trailers. Picnic tables, fire grills, and tent pads are provided. Pit toilets are available, but there is no piped water. Leashed pets are permitted.

Reservations, fees: No reservations are accepted. There is no fee. The campground is open year-round.

Contact: Department of Natural Resources, Southeast Region, 713 East Bowers Road, Ellensburg, WA 98926-9341; (509) 925-8510 or fax (509) 925-8522.

Directions: From Yakima, drive 20 miles south on Interstate 82. Turn south on U.S. 97 and drive 53 miles to Goldendale. Turn west on Highway 142 and drive 34 miles to Glenwood. From the post office in Glenwood, drive 0.3 miles west, then turn right on Bird Creek Road and drive 0.9 miles. Turn left, cross over the cattleguard to Road K-3000 (Bird Creek Road), and drive 1.2 miles. Turn right on Road 5-4000 (gravel) and drive 1.3 miles. Turn left on Road K-4000 and drive 1.4 miles. Turn left on Road K-4200 and drive 0.2 miles to the camp.

Trip notes: This campground in a forested area along Bird Creek is close to lava tubes and blowholes. In the winter, the roads are used for snowmobiling. A snowmobile shelter with a wood stove is available year-round for picnics. See the trip notes for Maryhill State Park (campground number 75) for information on the nearby Klickitat Habitat Management Area.

66 Brooks Memorial State Park

Location: Near the Goldendale Observatory; map B3, grid h7.

Campsites, facilities: There are two primitive tent sites, 22 developed sites for tents or self-contained RVs, and 23 sites with water and electrical hookups for trailers or RVs up to 50 feet long. Picnic tables and fire grills are provided. Flush toilets, sanitary services, and a playground are available. Electricity, piped water, sewer hookups, and showers can be obtained for an extra fee. A store is located within one mile. Leashed pets are permitted.

Reservations, fees: No reservations are accepted. Sites are $7–$16 per night. The campground is open year-round, with limited winter facilities.

Contact: Phone (800) 233-0321 or (509) 773-5382, or write to 2465 Highway 97, Goldendale, WA 98620.

Directions: From Interstate 5 at Vancouver, Washington, turn east on Highway 14 and drive approximately 106 miles. Turn north on U.S. 97 and drive 11 miles to Goldendale.

Continue northeast on U.S. 97 for 15 miles to the park.

Trip notes: There is only one other campground (Maryhill State Park, campground number 75) within 25 miles of this forested park at an elevation of nearly 3,000 feet. Highlights include several miles of hiking trails, a 1.5-mile-long nature trail, and excellent fishing for trout in the nearby Klickitat River. An unusual side trip is bird-watching at Toppenish National Wildlife Refuge, 28 miles north of the park on U.S. 97; phone the refuge at (509) 865-2405 for details. If you like stargazing, the Goldendale Observatory is located just one mile north of Goldendale. It houses one of the largest telescopes in the world available for public use; phone (509) 773-3141 for hours of operation.

67 Peterson Prairie

Location: Near the town of Trout Lake in Gifford Pinchot National Forest; map B3, grid i0.

Campsites, facilities: There are 23 sites for tents, trailers, or RVs up to 32 feet long, and one group site. Piped water, picnic tables, and fire rings are provided. Vault toilets are available. Some facilities are wheelchair accessible. Leashed pets are permitted.

Reservations, fees: Reservations are necessary for the group site only; phone (800) 280-CAMP/2267 ($17.35 group reservation fee). Rates are $9 per night for individual sites and $32 per night for the group site. The campground is open from May to late September.

Contact: Gifford Pinchot National Forest, Mount Adams Ranger District, 2455 Highway 141, Trout Lake, WA 98650; (509) 395-3400 or fax (509) 395-3424.

Directions: From Interstate 5 at Vancouver, Washington, turn east on Highway 14 and drive 66 miles. Turn north on Highway 141 and drive 25.5 miles to Forest Service Road 24 (5.5 miles southwest of the town of Trout Lake). Continue west on Forest Service Road 24 for 2.5 miles to the campground.

Trip notes: Here's a good base camp if you want to have a short ride to town as well as access to the nearby wilderness areas. This is a prime spot for huckleberry picking, too. A sno-park in the area is open for winter recreation, with snowmobiling and cross-country skiing trails.

68 Morrison Creek

Location: On Morrison Creek in Gifford Pinchot National Forest; map B3, grid h1.

Campsites, facilities: There are 12 tent sites. Picnic tables and fire rings are provided in some sites. Vault toilets are available, but there is no piped water. Leashed pets are permitted.

Reservations, fees: No reservations are accepted. There is no fee. The campground is open from July to late September.

Contact: Gifford Pinchot National Forest, Mount Adams Ranger District, 2455 Highway 141, Trout Lake, WA 98650; (509) 395-3400 or fax (509) 395-3424.

Directions: From Interstate 5 at Vancouver, Washington, turn east on Highway 14 and drive 66 miles. Turn north on Highway 141 and drive 25 miles to County Road 17 (just 200 yards east of the town of Trout Lake). Turn north and drive two miles, then continue north on Forest Service Road 80 for 3.5 miles. Proceed six miles north on Forest Service Road 8040.

Trip notes: Here's a prime yet little-known spot. It's located along Morrison Creek at an elevation of 4,600 feet near the southern slopes of Mount Adams, which, at an elevation of 12,276 feet, is the second highest mountain in Washington (Rainier is higher). Nearby trails will take you to the snowfields and alpine meadows of the Mount Adams Wilderness.

69 Walupt Lake

Location: On Walupt Lake in Gifford Pinchot National Forest; map B3, grid e1.

Campsites, facilities: There are 44 sites for tents, trailers, or RVs up to 22 feet long. Picnic tables are provided. Piped water and pit and vault toilets are available. There is primitive boat access with a 10 mph speed limit; no waterskiing is allowed. Leashed pets are permitted.

Reservations, fees: No reservations are accepted. Sites are $9 per night, and $5 for each additional vehicle. The campground is open from mid-June to early September.

Contact: Gifford Pinchot National Forest, Packwood Ranger District, Packwood, WA 98361; (360) 494-0600 or fax (360) 494-0602.

Directions: From Interstate 5 south of Olympia, take exit 68 and turn east on U.S. 12. Drive 62.5 miles to Forest Service Road 21 (2.5 miles southwest of Packwood). Turn right and drive 16.5 miles southeast, then head east on Forest Service Road 2160 for 4.5 miles to the campground.

Trip notes: This is a good base camp for a multiday vacation. For starters, the camp is set along the shore of Walupt Lake. In addition, several nearby trails lead into the backcountry and to other smaller alpine lakes. See a Forest Service map for details.

70 Bird Creek

Location: Near the Mount Adams Wilderness; map B3, grid h3.

Campsites, facilities: There are eight campsites for tents or small trailers. Picnic tables, fire grills, and tent pads are provided. Pit toilets are available, but there is no piped water. Leashed pets are permitted.

Reservations, fees: No reservations are accepted. There is no fee. The campground is open from May to mid-October, weather permitting.

Contact: Department of Natural Resources, Southeast Region, 713 East Bowers Road, Ellensburg, WA 98926-9341; (509) 925-8510 or fax (509) 925-8522.

Directions: From Yakima, drive 20 miles south on Interstate 82. Turn south on U.S. 97 and drive 53 miles to Goldendale. Turn west on Highway 142 and drive 34 miles to Glenwood.

From the post office in Glenwood, drive 0.3 miles west, then turn right on Bird Creek Road and drive 0.9 miles. Turn left, cross over the cattleguard to Road K-3000 (Bird Creek Road), and drive 1.2 miles. Turn right on Road 5-4000 (gravel) and drive 1.3 miles. Turn left on Road K-4000 and stay left for the next two miles. Turn left into the campground.

Trip notes: This campground in a forested area along Bird Creek is one of two camps in the immediate area. (The other, also a primitive site, is Island Camp, campground number 65.) This spot lies just east of the Mount Adams Wilderness and is within three miles of Island Camp, where there are snowmobile trails. See the trip notes for Maryhill State Park (campground number 75) for information on the nearby Klickitat Habitat Management Area.

ⓘ Oklahoma

Location: On the White Salmon River in Gifford Pinchot National Forest; map B3, grid i0.

Campsites, facilities: There are 23 sites for tents, trailers, or RVs up to 22 feet long. Hand-pumped water, fire rings, and picnic tables are provided. Vault toilets are available. Some facilities are wheelchair accessible. Pets are permitted.

Reservations, fees: For reservations, phone (800) 280-CAMP/2267 ($8.65 reservation fee). Sites are $9 per night, and $5 for each additional vehicle. The campground is open from mid-May to mid-October.

Contact: Gifford Pinchot National Forest, Mount Adams Ranger District, 2455 Highway 141, Trout Lake, WA 98650; (509) 395-3400 or fax (509) 395-3424.

Directions: From Interstate 5 at Vancouver, Washington, turn east on Highway 14 and drive approximately 50 miles to Cook. Turn north on County Road 1800 and drive 14 miles to the campground entrance.

Trip notes: This campground is set along little White Salmon River. Fishing can be excellent in this area. As to why they named the camp "Oklahoma," who knows?

ⓘ Moss Creek

Location: On the White Salmon River in Gifford Pinchot National Forest; map B3, grid i0.

Campsites, facilities: There are 18 sites for tents, trailers, or RVs up to 32 feet long. Piped water, fire rings, and picnic tables are provided. Vault toilets are available. Some facilities are wheelchair accessible. Pets are permitted.

Reservations, fees: For reservations, phone (800) 280-CAMP/2267 ($8.65 reservation fee). Sites are $9 per night, and $5 for each additional vehicle. The campground is open from mid-May to late September.

Contact: Gifford Pinchot National Forest, Mount Adams Ranger District, 2455 Highway 141, Trout Lake, WA 98650; (509) 395-3400 or fax (509) 395-3424.

Directions: From Interstate 5 at Vancouver, Washington, go east on Highway 14 and drive 50 miles to Cook. Turn north on County Road 1800 and drive eight miles to the campground.

Trip notes: This campground on the White Salmon River is a short distance from Willard and Big Cedars County Park. Good fishing prospects can be found here, usually with few other people around. You get all the amenities, including nice, shaded sites.

ⓘ Pine Springs Resort

Location: Near Brooks Memorial State Park; map B3, grid h6.

Campsites, facilities: There are 11 tent sites and 21 sites for trailers or RVs. Cable TV, water, electricity and sewer hookups, a public phone, limited groceries, ice, snacks, RV supplies, and LP gas are available. Horseshoe pits are also provided. Leashed pets are permitted.

Reservations, fees: Reservations are recommended. Sites are $5–$12 per night. The campground is open March 1 through mid-November, weather permitting.

Contact: Phone the park at (509) 773-4434 or write to 2471 Highway 97, Goldendale, WA 98620.

Directions: From Interstate 5 at Vancouver, Washington, turn east on Highway 14 and drive approximately 100 miles, then turn north on U.S. 97 and drive 11 miles to Goldendale. Continue north on U.S. 97 for 11.5 miles. The park is next to Brooks Memorial State Park, between mileposts 24 and 25. The resort is located on the left.

Trip notes: This is an alternative to the state campground at Brooks Memorial State Park (campground number 66). It's a small, wooded camp with a stream running close by. Side trips include adjacent Brooks Memorial State Park, Goldendale Observatory State Park, and the Columbia River.

⑦ Horsethief Lake State Park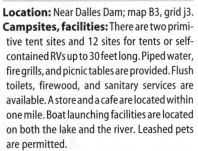

Location: Near Dalles Dam; map B3, grid j3.
Campsites, facilities: There are two primitive tent sites and 12 sites for tents or self-contained RVs up to 30 feet long. Piped water, fire grills, and picnic tables are provided. Flush toilets, firewood, and sanitary services are available. A store and a cafe are located within one mile. Boat launching facilities are located on both the lake and the river. Leashed pets are permitted.

Reservations, fees: No reservations are accepted. Sites are $5–$10 per night. The campground is open from April to late October.
Contact: Phone (800) 233-0321 or (509) 767-1159, or write to 50 Highway 97, Goldendale, WA 98620.
Directions: From Interstate 5 at Vancouver, Washington, turn east on Highway 14 and drive approximately 90 miles to the park entrance on the right.

Trip notes: This is a good spot to camp if you're driving along the Columbia River Highway. The state park sits along the shore of Horsethief Lake adjacent to the Dalles Dam. There are hiking trails and access to both the lake and the Columbia River. Nonpowered boats are allowed, and anglers can try for trout and bass. See the trip notes for Maryhill State Park (campground number 75) for information on other recreation options in the area.

⑦ Maryhill State Park

Location: On the Columbia River; map B3, grid j5.
Campsites, facilities: There are 20 tent sites (three primitive) and 50 sites with full hookups for trailers or RVs up to 50 feet long. Picnic tables are provided. Flush toilets, sanitary services, a store, and a cafe are available. Electricity, piped water, sewer hookups, showers, and firewood can be obtained for an extra fee. Some facilities are wheelchair accessible. Boat docks and launching facilities are nearby. Leashed pets are permitted.

Reservations, fees: Contact Reservations Northwest at (800) 452-5687 ($6 reservation fee). Sites are $11–$16 per night. Call for group camping information. The campground is open year-round.
Contact: Phone (800) 233-0321 or (509) 773-5007, or write to 50 Highway 97, Goldendale, WA 98620.
Directions: From Interstate 5 at Vancouver, Washington, turn east on Highway 14 and drive approximately 106 miles. The park is one mile north on U.S. 97.

Trip notes: Fishing, waterskiing, and windsurfing are among the possibilities at this park along the Columbia River. The climate here is very pleasant from March through mid-November. Two interesting places can be found near Maryhill: one is a replica of Stonehenge, located on a bluff overlooking the Columbia River, and the other is the Maryhill Museum; call (509) 773-3733 for details. A great side trip, 30 miles northwest, is the Klickitat Habitat Management Area. It's run by the Department of Fish and Game and has some primitive camping spots and a boat launch along the Klickitat River, where you can enjoy boating, fishing, hunting, or observing wildlife. To get there, drive 11 miles west of Goldendale on Highway 142, then continue northwest on Glendale Road for five miles and look for the headquarters on your left. The public areas beyond the wildlife refuge headquarters are easier to get to. Another treat at the refuge is Stinson Flat, a good steelhead spot.

Map B4

Washington State Map .... *page 6*
One inch equals approximately 20 miles.

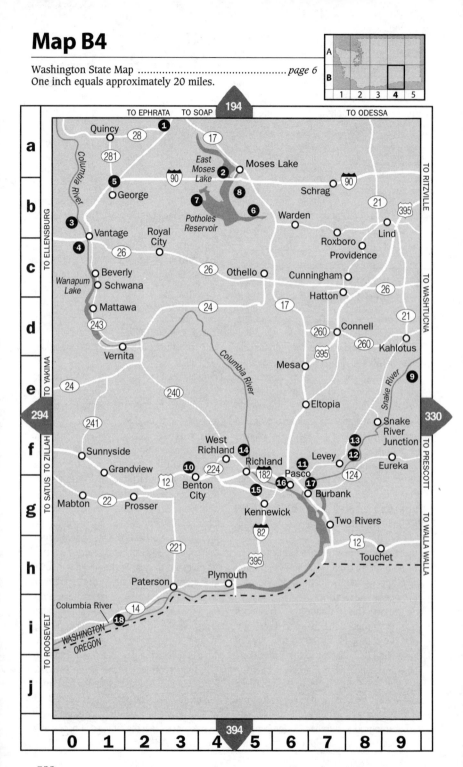

Chapter B4 features:

1 Oasis Park Resort

Location: Near Soap Lake; map B4, grid a3.

Campsites, facilities: There are 38 tent sites and 68 sites for trailers or RVs of any length; 10 are drive-throughs. Picnic tables, flush toilets, a golf course, bottled gas, sanitary services, a store, propane gas, a laundry room, ice, a swimming pool, and a fishing pond for children are provided. Electricity, piped water, sewer hookups, and showers are available. A cafe is located within one mile. Leashed pets and motorbikes are permitted.

Reservations, fees: Reservations are requested. Sites are $9–$15 per night. The campground is open year-round, with limited winter facilities.

Contact: Phone (509) 754-5102 or write to 2541 Basin Street SW, Ephrata, WA 98823.

Directions: From Seattle, drive about 180 miles east on Interstate 90 to exit 151 near the town of George. Turn west on Highway 283 (which becomes Highway 28) and drive five miles to Ephrata. Drive another 1.5 miles southwest on Highway 28 to the park.

Trip notes: This can be an extremely warm, arid area during the summer months, but, fortunately, Oasis Park Resort offers shaded sites. There are two fishing ponds at the resort: one has bass and crappie, while the other is for kids. Nearby recreation options include an 18-hole golf course. Mineral baths are located just a few miles north.

2 Big Sun Resort

Location: Near Moses Lake State Park; map B4, grid a4.

Campsites, facilities: There are 10 tent sites and 50 sites for trailers or RVs of any length; 19 are drive-throughs. Electricity, piped water, sewer hookups, and picnic tables are provided. Flush toilets, pay showers, a recreation hall, a laundry room, ice, and a playground are available. Sanitary services, a store, and a cafe are within one mile. Boat docks, launching facilities, and rentals are nearby. Leashed pets and motorbikes are permitted.

Reservations, fees: Reservations are accepted. Sites are $12–$17.50 per night. The campground is open year-round.

Contact: Phone (509) 765-8294, fax (509) 765-8874, or write to 2300 West Marina, Moses Lake, WA 98837.

Directions: From Seattle, drive about 170 miles east on Interstate 90 to exit 176. Drive one-half mile on Broadway to Burress Avenue. Turn west on Burress Avenue and drive one block, straight into the park.

Trip notes: This park is a short distance from Moses Lake State Park, which is open for day-use only. You'll find shady picnic spots with tables and fire grills, beach access, and moorage floats. Waterskiing is allowed on the lake.

3 KOA Vantage

Location: On the Columbia River; map B4, grid b0.

Campsites, facilities: There are 50 tent sites and 50 sites for trailers or RVs of any length. Piped water and picnic tables are provided. Electricity, sewer hookups, flush toilets, bottled gas, sanitary services, showers, a recreation hall, a laundry room, ice, a playground, and a swimming pool are available. A store and a cafe are located within one mile. Boat docks and launching facilities are nearby. Leashed pets and motorbikes are permitted.

Reservations, fees: Reservations are accepted. Sites are $15–$20 per night. The campground is open year-round.

Contact: Phone (509) 856-2230 or write to P.O. Box 1101, Vantage, WA 98950.

Directions: Drive 29 miles east of Ellensburg on Interstate 90 to Vantage, then take exit 136 and drive north for one-half mile to the park.

Trip notes: This campground offers pleasant, grassy sites overlooking the Columbia River, a short distance from the state park (see Ginkgo-Wanapum State Park, campground number 4). This is the only campground in the immediate area that provides space for tent camping. The next closest is 12 miles away at Shady Tree RV Park (campground number 5) in George.

❹ Ginkgo-Wanapum State Park

Location: On the Columbia River and Wanapum Lake; map B4, grid c0.

Campsites, facilities: There are 50 sites with full hookups for trailers or RVs up to 60 feet. Picnic tables, fire grills, and flush toilets are provided. Electricity, piped water, sewer hookups, showers, and firewood are available for an extra fee. Boat docks and launching facilities are nearby. Leashed pets are permitted.

Reservations, fees: No reservations are accepted. Sites are $16 per night. The campground is open from April through October.

Contact: Ginkgo-Wanapum State Park, Vantage, WA 98950; (800) 233-0321 or (509) 856-2700.

Directions: From Interstate 5 at Seattle, turn east on Interstate 90 and drive 108 miles to Ellensburg. Continue east on Interstate 90 for 29 miles, then take the Vantage exit and drive three miles south to the park on the right.

Trip notes: There are actually two separate parks here, Ginkgo State Park and Wanapum State Recreation Area. Camping is permitted only at Wanapum, which is seven miles south of the main entrance at Ginkgo. The recreation highlights are at Ginkgo, which is set along Wanapum Lake and the Columbia River. The park is the site of an ancient petrified forest, and there is an interpretive center and trail. Options include hiking, swimming, boating, waterskiing, and fishing. The campground at Wanapum is set up primarily for RVs, with full hookups, rest rooms, and showers.

❺ Shady Tree RV Park

Location: Near Frenchman Hills Lakes; map B4, grid b1.

Campsites, facilities: There are 30 tent sites and 44 drive-through sites for trailers or RVs of any length. Electricity, piped water, sewer hookups, and picnic tables are provided. Flush toilets, showers, and a laundry room are available. Sanitary services are located within 10 miles. Leashed pets and motorbikes are permitted.

Reservations, fees: No reservations are accepted. Sites are $16–$18 per night. The campground is open year-round.

Contact: Phone (509) 785-2851 or write to 1099 Highway 283 North, Quincy, WA 98848.

Directions: From Interstate 5 at Seattle, turn east on Interstate 90 and drive 108 miles to Ellensburg. Continue 41 miles east on Interstate 90 to exit 151. Proceed to the intersection of Highways 281 and 283 and you'll see the park.

Trip notes: This is an oasis in a desertlike area, with shade trees and grassy sites. A good side trip is to Frenchman Hills Lakes, bordered by sand dunes. Another option is Moses Lake State Park, which offers boating, swimming, and fishing.

❻ Mar-Don Resort

Location: Near Potholes Reservoir; map B4, grid b5.

Campsites, facilities: There are 300 sites for tents, trailers, or RVs of any length; seven are drive-throughs. Electricity, piped water, sewer hookups, and picnic tables are provided. Flush toilets, bottled gas, sanitary services, showers, a game room, a store, a laundry room, ice, a playground, boat moorage, boat rentals, and launching facilities are available. Leashed pets and motorbikes are permitted.

Reservations, fees: Reservations are recommended. Sites are $15–$18 per night. The campground is open year-round.

Contact: Phone (800) 416-2736 or (509) 346-2651, or write to 8198 Highway 262 Southeast, Othello, WA 99344.

Directions: From Seattle, drive about 180 miles east on Interstate 90 to exit 179 in the town of Moses Lake. Turn south on Highway 17 and drive 1.5 miles to Road M. Turn west and drive seven miles to Highway 262. Turn west and drive seven miles to the resort.

Trip notes: This park is located on Potholes Reservoir with opportunities for fishing, swimming, and boating. A marina, tackle, and boat rentals are all available. Hiking trails and marked bike trails are close by. There is also a 25-unit motel at the resort.

❼ Potholes State Park

Location: On Potholes Reservoir; map B4, grid b4.

Campsites, facilities: There are 126 sites for tents, trailers, or RVs up to 50 feet long; 60 have full hookups. Picnic tables and fire grills are provided. Flush toilets, sanitary services, a store, and a playground are available. Electricity, piped water, sewer hookups, showers, and firewood can be obtained for an extra fee. Boat launching facilities and rentals are nearby. Leashed pets are permitted.

Reservations, fees: Contact Reservations

Northwest at (800) 452-5687 ($6 reservation fee). Sites are $5–$16 per night. The campground is open from April through October.

Contact: Phone (800) 233-0321 or (509) 765-7271, or write to 6762 Highway 262 East, Othello, WA 99344.

Directions: From the town of Moses Lake on Interstate 90, take exit 179 and turn south on Highway 17. Drive about nine miles to the sign for the park, then turn right and continue 10 more miles to the park. The road is well signed.

Trip notes: This park is on Potholes Reservoir, where fishing is the highlight. Trout, walleye, crappie, and perch are among the species taken here. Waterskiing and hiking are two other options. There is a nice beach near the campground. A side trip to the Columbia Wildlife Refuge is recommended.

❽ Willows Trailer Village

Location: Near Moses Lake State Park; map B4, grid b5.

Campsites, facilities: There are 20 tent sites and 65 drive-through sites for trailers or RVs of any length. Electricity, piped water, sewer hookups, and picnic tables are provided. Flush toilets, bottled gas, showers, a store, a laundry room, and ice are available. Leashed pets and motorbikes are permitted.

Reservations, fees: No reservations are accepted. Sites are $12.50–$16.50 per night. The campground is open year-round.

Contact: Phone (509) 765-7531 or write 1347 Road M Southeast, Moses Lake, WA 98837.

Directions: From Seattle, drive about 180 miles east on Interstate 90 to exit 179 in the town of Moses Lake. Drive 2.5 miles south on Highway 17 to Road M. Turn southwest and drive 300 yards to the park.

Trip notes: One of four campgrounds in the area, this one has grassy, shaded sites along with horseshoe pits, barbecues, and a recreation field. See the trip notes for Big Sun Resort (campground number 2) for information on recreation spots in the vicinity.

9 Windust

Location: On Sacajawea Lake; map B4, grid e9.

Campsites, facilities: There is space for 30 tents, trailers, or RVs in open camping areas at both ends of the park. Piped water, picnic tables, and fire grills are provided. Flush toilets and a playground are available. Some facilities are wheelchair accessible. Boat docks and launching facilities are nearby. Leashed pets and motorbikes are permitted.

Reservations, fees: No reservations are accepted. Sites are $7 per night. The campground is open year-round, with no fee and limited facilities from October through March.

Contact: U.S. Army Corps of Engineers, Route 6, Box 693, Pasco, WA 99301; (509) 547-7781.

Directions: Take exit 102 off Interstate 82 and drive 12 miles east to Pasco. Drive five miles southeast on U.S. 12. Turn east on the Pasco/Kaholtus Highway and drive 28 miles to Burr Canyon Road. Turn right on Burr Canyon Road and drive six miles to the park.

Trip notes: Windust is the only game in town, with no other campgrounds within a 20-mile radius. The camp is along the shore of Sacajawea Lake near the Lower Monumental Dam on the Snake River. Swimming and fishing are popular.

10 Beach RV Park

Location: On the Yakima River; map B4, grid f3.

Campsites, facilities: There are 39 sites for trailers or RVs of any length; five are drive-throughs. Electricity, piped water, sewer hookups, and cable TV are provided. Flush toilets, showers, a laundry room, and ice are available. Bottled gas, sanitary services, a store, and a cafe are located within one mile. Boat launching facilities are nearby. Leashed pets and motorbikes are permitted.

Reservations, fees: Reservations are accepted. Sites are $18 per night. The campground is open year-round.

Contact: Phone (509) 588-5959 or write to

Route 3, P.O. Box 2094 C, Benton City, WA 99320.

Directions: From Interstate 82 west of Richland, take the Benton City exit and drive one block north, then turn west on Abby Street to the park at 113 Abby.

Trip notes: If you are heading west on Interstate 182 and it's getting late, you'd best stop here—the only option for a long stretch. This park along the shore of the Yakima River is a pleasant spot, with spacious RV sites and a large grassy area for tents. Nearby recreation options include an 18-hole golf course, a full-service marina, and tennis courts.

11 Arrowhead RV Park

Location: Near the Columbia River; map B4, grid f6.

Campsites, facilities: There are 35 tent sites and 80 sites for trailers or RVs of any length; 27 are drive-throughs. Electricity, piped water, sewer hookups, and picnic tables are provided. Flush toilets, showers, and a laundry room are available. A store and a cafe are located within one mile. Small pets and motorbikes are permitted.

Reservations, fees: Reservations are accepted. Sites are $20 per night for two people. The campground is open year-round.

Contact: Phone (509) 545-8206 or write to 3120 Commercial Avenue, Pasco, WA 99301.

Directions: Take exit 113 off Interstate 82 and drive nine miles to Pasco. This park is located on the eastern edge of Pasco at 3120 Commercial Street.

Trip notes: This is a decent layover spot in Pasco. Nearby recreation options include an 18-hole golf course, a full-service marina, and tennis courts.

12 Charbonneau Park

Location: On the Snake River; map B4, grid f8.

Campsites, facilities: There are 55 sites for tents, trailers, or RVs of any length; 17 are drive-throughs. Picnic tables and fire grills are provided. Flush toilets, sanitary services, showers, a playground, electricity, piped water, sewer hookups, and a primitive overflow camping area are available. Some facilities are wheelchair accessible. A marina with boat docks, launching facilities, and a marine dump station are nearby. Leashed pets are permitted.

Reservations, fees: No reservations are accepted. Sites are $12–$14 per night. The campground is open from April 1 to October 31 with full facilities; there are limited facilities the rest of the year. Park gates are locked from 10 P.M. to 6 A.M.

Contact: U.S. Army Corps of Engineers, Route 6, Box 693, Pasco, WA 99301-9165; (509) 547-7781.

Directions: Take exit 102 off Interstate 82 and drive 12 miles to Pasco. Drive six miles southeast of Pasco on U.S. 12, then drive eight miles northeast on Highway 124. Turn north on Sun Harbor Road and drive two miles to the park.

Trip notes: This shorefront camp along the Snake River, just above Ice Harbor Dam, is a good spot for fishing, boating, swimming, and waterskiing. The dam's visitor center (open daily from April through October) features exhibits and a fish-viewing room.

⑬ Fishhook Park

Location: On the Snake River; map B4, grid f8.

Campsites, facilities: There are 20 tent-only sites and 40 sites for tents, trailers, or RVs of any length; eight are drive-throughs. Picnic tables and fire grills are provided. Piped water, electricity, flush toilets, sanitary services, showers, telephone service, and a playground are available. Some facilities are wheelchair accessible. Boat docks and launching facilities are nearby. Leashed pets are permitted.

Reservations, fees: No reservations are accepted. Sites are $9–$13 per night. The campground is open from mid-May to mid-September. Park gates are locked from 10 P.M. to 6 A.M.

Contact: U.S. Army Corps of Engineers,

Route 6, Box 693, Pasco, WA 99301-9165; (509) 547-7781.

Directions: Take exit 102 off Interstate 82 and drive 12 miles to Pasco. Drive six miles southeast of Pasco on U.S. 12, then drive 16 miles northeast on Highway 124. Turn left on Fishhook Park Road and drive four miles to the park.

Trip notes: If you're driving along Highway 124 and you need a spot for the night, make the turn on Fishhook Park Road and check out this wooded camp along the Snake River. Some lawn area is provided, along with places to swim, fish, and water-ski.

⑭ Lloyd's Desert Gold RV Park

Location: Near the Columbia River; map B4, grid f5.

Campsites, facilities: There are 69 sites for trailers or RVs of any length; 18 are drive-throughs. Electricity, piped water, sewer hookups, and picnic tables are provided. Flush toilets, showers, bottled gas, sanitary services, a store, a laundry room, ice, and a swimming pool are available. A cafe is located within one mile. Boat docks and launching facilities are nearby on the Columbia River. Leashed pets are permitted.

Reservations, fees: Reservations are accepted. Sites are $17 per night. The campground is open year-round.

Contact: Phone (800) 788-GOLD/4653 or (509) 627-1000, or write to 611 SE Columbia Drive, Richland, WA 99352.

Directions: Take exit 102 off Interstate 82 and drive six miles to Richland. Take Columbia Drive west for one-quarter mile to 611 Columbia Drive Southeast.

Trip notes: This is a nice RV park about a mile from the Columbia River. Nearby recreation options include an 18-hole golf course, hiking trails, a full-service marina, and tennis courts. You can also visit the Department of Energy public information center at the Hanford Science Center. The park has a pool and spa if you just want to relax without going anywhere.

⑮ Columbia Park Campground

Location: On the Columbia River; map B4, grid g5.

Campsites, facilities: There are 22 tent sites and 100 sites for trailers or RVs; 26 are drive-throughs. Electricity, piped water, and picnic tables are provided. Flush toilets, sanitary services, ice, and a playground are available. Showers and firewood can be obtained for an extra fee. A store and a cafe are located within one mile. Boat docks and launching facilities are nearby. Leashed pets and motorbikes are permitted.

Reservations, fees: Reservations are accepted. Sites are $7–$11 per night. The campground is open year-round.

Contact: Phone (509) 783-3711 or write to 6601 SE Columbia, Kennewick, WA 99352.

Directions: From Spokane on U.S. 395 heading south, turn right on Interstate 182 and drive a few miles. Turn right on U.S. 395 and stay in the left lane (U.S. 395 becomes Highway 240). Continue on Highway 240 about one mile. Turn right into the campground.

Trip notes: This campground is in a grassy suburban area on the Columbia River, adjacent to Columbia Park. Nearby activities include waterskiing on the Columbia River, an 18-hole golf course, hiking trails, marked bike trails, and tennis courts. The sun can feel like a branding iron during the summer.

⑯ Greentree Mobile Home Park

Location: In Pasco; map B4, grid g6.

Campsites, facilities: There are 40 sites for trailers or RVs of any length. Electricity, piped water, and sewer hookups are provided. A laundry room and showers are available. Bottled gas, a store, a cafe, and ice are located within one mile. Boat docks, launching facilities, and rentals are nearby. Pets and motorbikes are permitted.

Reservations, fees: Reservations are accepted. Sites are $12–$14 per night. The campground is open year-round.

Contact: Phone (509) 547-6220 or write to 2103 North Fifth Avenue #69, Pasco, WA 99301.

Directions: Take exit 102 off Interstate 82 and drive 12 miles east to Pasco. Take exit 13 off Interstate 182 and you'll see the park on the southwest corner.

Trip notes: This park in urban Pasco is close to an 18-hole golf course, hiking trails, a full-service marina, and tennis courts. The Franklin County Historical Museum, which is located in town, and the Sacajawea State Park Museum and Interpretive Center, located three miles southeast of town, both offer extensive collections of Native American artifacts.

⑰ Hood Park

Location: On the Columbia River; map B4, grid g6.

Campsites, facilities: There are 68 sites for tents, trailers, or RVs of any length. Piped water, fire grills, and picnic tables are provided. Flush toilets, sanitary services, showers, electricity, a playground, and a primitive overflow camping area are available. A restaurant and convenience store are located within two miles. Some facilities are wheelchair accessible. Boat docks and launching facilities are nearby. Leashed pets are permitted.

Reservations, fees: No reservations are accepted. Sites are $12 per night, and $7 per night in the overflow area. The campground is open from mid-May to mid-September. The gates are locked from 10 P.M. to 6 A.M.

Contact: U.S. Army Corps of Engineers, Route 6, Box 693, Pasco, WA 99301-9165; (509) 547-7781.

Directions: Take exit 102 off Interstate 82 and drive 12 miles east to Pasco. Drive six miles southeast of Pasco on U.S. 12, then head east on Highway 124 to the campground.

Trip notes: A more developed, nearby alternative to Columbia Park Campground (campground number 15), this park has river access for swimming and boating. Other recreation options include basketball and horseshoes. McNary Wildlife Refuge and Sacajawea State Park are nearby.

18 Crow Butte State Park 🚐 ⛺

Location: On the Columbia River; map B4, grid i1.

Campsites, facilities: There are two primitive tent sites and 50 sites with full hookups for trailers or RVs up to 60 feet long. Fire grills and picnic tables are provided. Flush toilets, showers, and a sanitary disposal station are available. Some facilities are wheelchair accessible. Boat launching facilities are nearby. Leashed pets are permitted.

Reservations, fees: No reservations are accepted. Sites are $5–$16 per night. The campground is open year-round, with limited winter facilities.

Contact: Phone (800) 233-0321 or (509) 875-2644, or write to P.O. Box 217, Paterson, WA 99345.

Directions: From Interstate 5 at Vancouver, Washington, go east on Highway 14 and drive about 156 miles to the park on the right.

Trip notes: This state park along the Columbia River is the only campground in a 25-mile radius. Waterskiing, fishing, swimming, and hiking are among the possibilities here. The Umatilla National Wildlife Refuge is adjacent to the park and allows fishing and hunting in specified areas.

Map B5

Washington State Map .... *page 6*
One inch equals approximately 20 miles.

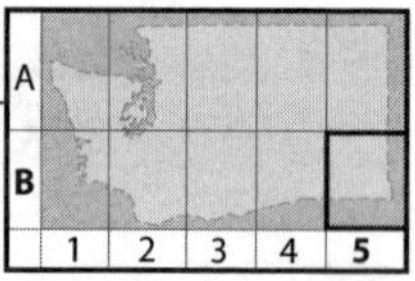

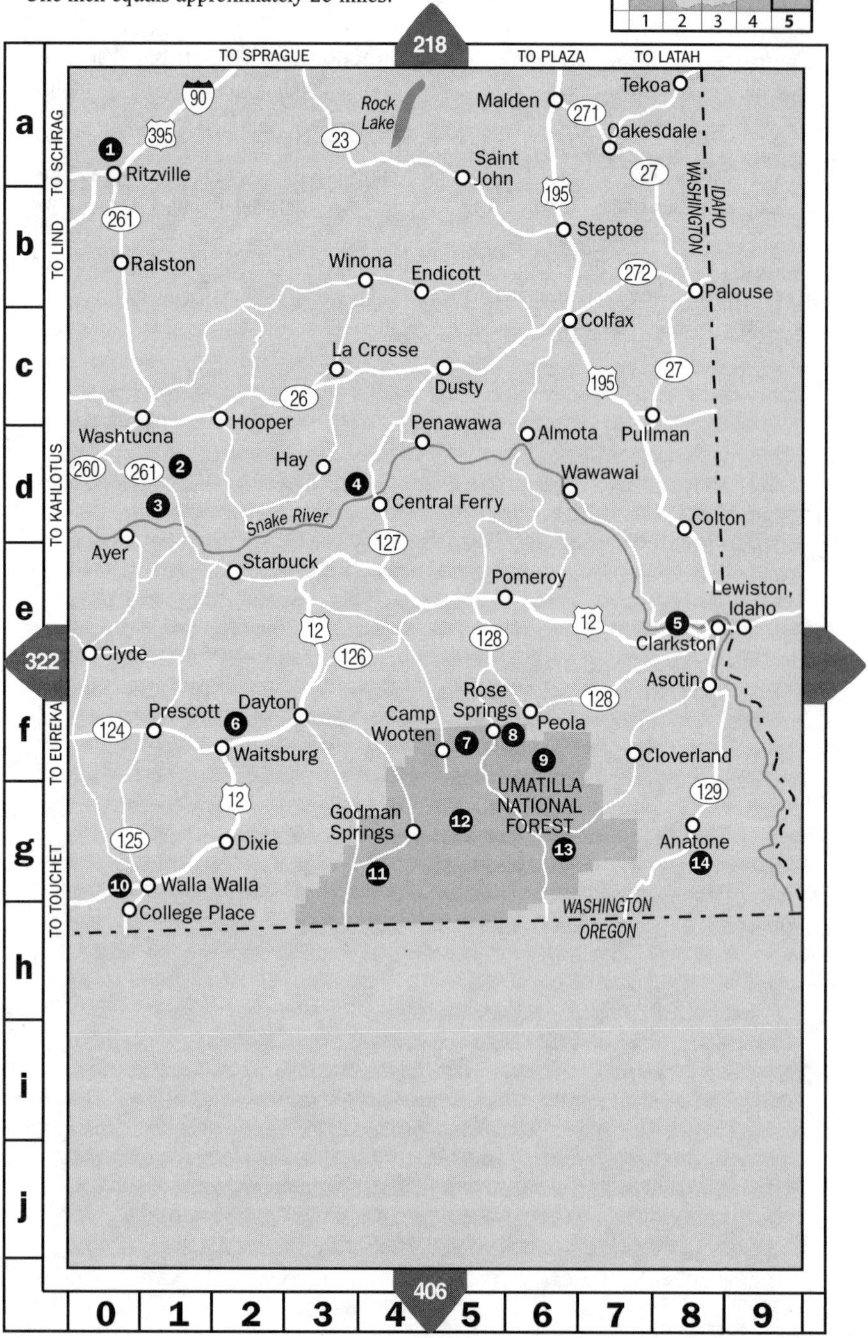

A
B
1 2 3 4 5

TO SPRAGUE   218   TO PLAZA   TO LATAH

a
TO SCHRAG
90
395
23
Rock Lake
Malden
271
Tekoa
Oakesdale
Saint John
❶
Ritzville
195
27

b
TO LIND
261
Ralston
Winona
Endicott
Steptoe
272
WASHINGTON
IDAHO
Palouse

c
La Crosse
Dusty
Colfax
195
27
26
Hooper

d
TO KAHLOTUS
Washtucna
260 261 ❷
Hay
❸
❹
Central Ferry
Penawawa
Almota
Wawawai
Pullman
Snake River
Colton

Ayer
Starbuck
127

e
322
Clyde
Pomeroy
128
12
12
❺
Clarkston
Lewiston, Idaho

f
TO EUREKA
124
Prescott
Dayton
❻
Waitsburg
126
Camp Wooten
Rose Springs
❼ ❽
Peola
❾
128
Asotin
Cloverland

g
TO TOUCHET
125
Dixie
Godman Springs
❶❷
UMATILLA NATIONAL FOREST
❶❸
129
Anatone
❶❹
❶❶
❶❷
12
❶⓪
Walla Walla
College Place
WASHINGTON
OREGON

h

i

j

0 1 2 3 4 5 6 7 8 9
406

Chapter B5 features:

1 Best Western Heritage Inn Motel and RV Park

Location: In Ritzville; map B5, grid a0.

Campsites, facilities: There are 30 drive-through sites for tents, trailers, or RVs of any length. Electricity, piped water, sewer hook-ups, and picnic tables are provided. Flush toilets, sanitary services, showers, a laundry room, ice, a playground, a sauna, and a swimming pool are available. Bottled gas, a store, and a cafe are located within one mile. Leashed pets and motorbikes are permitted.

Reservations, fees: Reservations are accepted. Sites are $20–$25 per night. The campground is open from mid-April to mid-October.

Contact: Phone (509) 659-1007 or write to 1513 Smitty's Boulevard, Ritzville, WA 99169.

Directions: From Interstate 90 at Spokane, turn west and drive 55 miles to Ritzville. Take exit 221 and you'll see the motel one-half block off the freeway.

Trip notes: If all you have is a tent, well, this is the only site to stake it within a radius of 25 miles. The nearest fishing is at Sprague Lake, 30 miles north on U.S. 395. Burroughs Historical Museum is a possible side trip in town. An 18-hole golf course and tennis courts are nearby.

2 Palouse Falls State Park

Location: On the Snake and Palouse Rivers; map B5, grid d1.

Campsites, facilities: There are 10 primi-tive campsites and 10 sites for tents, self-contained trailers, or RVs up to 40 feet long. Picnic tables and fire grills are provided. Pit toilets are available. Some facilities are wheelchair accessible. Leashed pets are permitted.

Reservations, fees: No reservations are accepted. Sites are $7 per night. The campground is open from April to late September, weather permitting.

Contact: Phone (800) 233-0321 or (509) 646-3252, or write to P.O. Box 157, Starbuck, WA 99359.

Directions: From Spokane, turn south on U.S. 195 and drive 59 miles. Turn east on Highway 26 and drive 17 miles southwest, then turn south on Highway 127 and continue southwest for 28 miles. Turn west on U.S. 12 and drive nine miles, then turn west again on Highway 261 and drive eight miles to Starbuck. Continue 14 miles northwest on Highway 261 to the park entrance, located seven miles northwest of Lyons Ferry.

Trip notes: You have to navigate a roundabout circuit of highways to get here, but this remote state park is well worth the trip. Set at the confluence of the Snake and Palouse Rivers, it's almost unknown and gets relatively little use even in the summer months. Spectacular 190-foot Palouse Falls is a sight not to miss. In recent years, a wheelchair-accessible trail has been completed. The park has shaded picnic facilities and an abundance of wildlife.

3 Lyon's Ferry State Park

Location: On the Snake River; map B5, grid d1.

Campsites, facilities: There are two primitive tent sites and 50 sites for tents or self-contained trailers or RVs. Picnic tables and fire grills are provided. Flush toilets, sanitary services, and showers are available. Some facilities are wheelchair accessible. Boat docks and launching facilities are nearby. Leashed pets are permitted.

Reservations, fees: No reservations are accepted. Sites are $10 per night. The campground is open from April through September.

Contact: Phone (800) 233-0321 or (509) 646-3252, or write to P.O. Box 157, Starbuck, WA 99359.

Directions: From Spokane, turn south on U.S. 195 and drive 59 miles. Turn east on Highway 26 and drive 17 miles southwest, then turn south on Highway 127 and continue southwest for 28 miles. Turn west on U.S. 12 and drive nine miles, then turn west again on Highway 261 and drive eight miles to Starbuck. Continue eight miles northwest on Highway 261 to the park on the right.

Trip notes: This state park at the confluence of the Snake and Palouse Rivers is loaded with activities, including fishing, hiking, swimming, waterskiing, and boating. A good side trip is a visit to beautiful Palouse Falls, located seven miles north.

❹ Central Ferry State Park

Location: On the Snake River; map B5, grid d4.

Campsites, facilities: There are eight primitive tent sites and 60 sites with full hookups for trailers or RVs up to 45 feet long. There is also one group camp accommodating up to 100 people. Picnic tables and fire grills are provided. Flush toilets, a sanitary service station, electricity, piped water, sewer hookups, a group fire ring, three horseshoe pit areas, and showers are available. A store and a restaurant are within two miles. Some facilities are wheelchair accessible. Boat docks, launching facilities, and a fishing pier are within the park. Leashed pets are permitted.

Reservations, fees: Contact Reservations

Northwest at (800) 452-5687 ($6 reservation fee). Sites are $15 per night. For group camp reservations, phone (509) 549-3551; group sites are $25 per night plus $1 per night per tent and $10 per night per RV. The campground is open from mid-March to mid-November.

Contact: Phone (800) 233-0321 or (509) 549-3551, or write to Route 3, P.O. Box 99, Pomeroy, WA 99347.

Directions: From Spokane, turn south on U.S. 195 and drive 59 miles. Turn east on Highway 26 and drive 17 miles southwest, then turn south on Highway 127 and continue southwest for 17 miles to the park entrance on the right.

Trip notes: This is the only campground within a 20-mile radius. It's located along the shore of the Snake River and has a beach. Waterskiing, sailing, boating, swimming, and fishing for bass and catfish are all options here.

❺ Chief Timothy State Park

Location: On the Snake River; map B5, grid e8.

Campsites, facilities: There are two primitive tent sites and 60 sites with water and electrical hookups for trailers or RVs of any length. Picnic tables and fire grills are provided. Flush toilets, sanitary services, and a playground are available. Electricity, piped water, sewer hookups, showers, and firewood can be obtained for an extra fee. Some facilities are wheelchair accessible. Boat docks and launching facilities are nearby. Leashed pets are permitted.

Reservations, fees: No reservations are accepted. Sites are $7–$16 per night. The campground is open year-round.

Contact: Phone (800) 233-0321 or (509) 758-9580, or write to Highway 12, Clarkston, WA 99403.

Directions: From Spokane, turn south on U.S. 195 and drive approximately 95 miles to the Washington/Idaho border. Turn south on Highway 128 and drive a short distance to U.S. 12, then turn west and drive to Clarkston.

Turn north at the sign for the park and proceed about eight miles.

Trip notes: This unusual state park is set on a bridged island in the Snake River, yet it's accessible to cars. All water sports are offered here, including fishing, swimming, boating, waterskiing, and sailing, plus docks for boating campers, a beach area, and an interpretive center focusing on the Lewis and Clark Expedition. Outfitters in Clarkston will take you sightseeing up the Grand Canyon of the Snake River. Call the Chamber of Commerce at (509) 758-7712 for details.

6 Lewis and Clark Trail State Park

Location: On the Lewis and Clark Trail; map B5, grid f2.

Campsites, facilities: There are four primitive tent sites and 30 sites for tents or self-enclosed trailers or RVs up to 28 feet long. Picnic tables and fire grills are provided. Flush toilets, showers, firewood, and sanitary services are available. A store, a cafe, and ice are located within one mile. Leashed pets are permitted.

Reservations, fees: No reservations are accepted. Sites are $7–$16 per night. The campground is open year-round.

Contact: Phone (800) 233-0321 or (509) 337-6457, or write to Route 1, P.O. Box 90, Dayton, WA 99328.

Directions: From Walla Walla on U.S. 12, turn east on U.S. 12 and drive 24 miles to the park entrance.

Trip notes: If it's getting late and you need to stop, consider this camp, the only one within 20 miles. It's not a bad choice, since it's set along the original Lewis and Clark Trail. During the summer, the rangers offer campfire programs, where they share the details of the site's history. The campground is in a forested, "prairie country" environment.

7 Tucannon

Location: In Umatilla National Forest; map B5, grid f5.

Campsites, facilities: There are 13 sites for tents, trailers, or RVs up to 15 feet long. Picnic tables and fire grills are provided. Vault toilets are available, but there is no piped water. Leashed pets are permitted.

Reservations, fees: No reservations are accepted. There is no fee. The campground is open from May to late November.

Contact: Umatilla National Forest, Pomeroy Ranger District, Route 1, Box 53-F, Pomeroy, WA 99347; (509) 843-1891 or fax (509) 843-4621.

Directions: From Spokane, turn south on U.S. 195 and drive 59 miles. Turn west on Highway 26 and drive 17 miles to Dusty, then turn south on Highway 127 and continue 28 miles to Dodge. Turn east on U.S. 12 and proceed 13 miles to Pomeroy. Turn south on County Road 101 and drive 17 miles, then head southwest on Forest Service Road 47 for four miles. Turn south on Forest Service Road 160 and drive 200 yards to the campground on the left.

Trip notes: For people willing to rough it, this backcountry camp in Umatilla National Forest is the place, with plenty of hiking, fishing, and hunting, all in a rugged setting. The camp is not far from the Tucannon River, which offers a myriad of options for vacationers.

8 Alder Thicket

Location: In Umatilla National Forest; map B5, grid f5.

Campsites, facilities: There are four sites for tents, trailers, or RVs up to 15 feet long. Picnic tables and fire grills are provided. Vault toilets are available, but there is no piped water. Leashed pets are permitted.

Reservations, fees: No reservations are accepted. There is no fee. The campground is open from mid-May to mid-November.

Contact: Umatilla National Forest, Pomeroy Ranger District, Route 1, Box 53-F, Pomeroy, WA 99347; (509) 843-1891 or fax (509) 843-4621.

Directions: From Spokane, turn south on U.S. 195 and drive 59 miles. Turn west on Highway 26 and drive 17 miles to Dusty, then turn south on Highway 127 and continue 28 miles to Dodge. Turn east on U.S. 12 and proceed 13 miles to Pomeroy. Turn south on Highway 128 and drive 10 miles south. At the fork continue straight to Forest Service Road 40 and continue 3.5 miles to the campground on the right.

Trip notes: This is probably the first time you've heard of this place. Hardly anybody knows about it, including people who live relatively nearby in Walla Walla. It's a prime base camp for a backcountry hiking adventure in summer or a jump-off point for a hunting trip in the fall. This is a very primitive camp, but it's great if you're looking for quiet and solitude.

⑨ Big Springs

Location: In Umatilla National Forest; map B5, grid f6.

Campsites, facilities: There are eight tent sites. Picnic tables are provided. Vault toilets are available, but there is no piped water. Leashed pets are permitted.

Reservations, fees: No reservations are accepted. There is no fee. The campground is open from mid-May to mid-November.

Contact: Umatilla National Forest, Pomeroy Ranger District, Route 1, Box 53-F, Pomeroy, WA 99347; (509) 843-1891 or fax (509) 843-4621.

Directions: From Spokane, turn south on U.S. 195 and drive 59 miles. Turn west on Highway 26 and drive 17 miles to Dusty, then turn south on Highway 127 and continue 28 miles to Dodge. Turn east on U.S. 12 and proceed 13 miles to Pomeroy. Turn south on Highway 128 and drive ten miles to the Y, then continue straight to Forest Service Road 40. Pass the national forest boundary and continue nine miles to the Clearwater lookout tower. Turn left on Forest Service Road 42 and continue for three miles, then turn left on Forest Service Road 4225 to the campground on the left. From Clarkston, drive on County Road 128 for 20 miles, then turn left on Iron Springs Road (Forest Service Road 42). Continue for about five miles, turning right on Forest Service Road 4225 to the campground on the right.

Trip notes: In the fall, Big Springs is used primarily by hunters, while, come summer, this nice, cool site is a possible base camp for a backpacking trip. Though quite primitive with little in the way of activity options, this is a perfect spot to get away from it all. It's advisable to obtain a Forest Service map.

⑩ Walla Walla Campground

Location: In Fort Walla Walla Park; map B5, grid g0.

Campsites, facilities: There are 49 tent sites and 21 sites for trailers or RVs up to 35 feet with partial hookups. An overflow area is also provided. Rest rooms, showers, water and electricity hookups, a phone, and a sanitary dump station are available. Leashed pets are permitted.

Reservations, fees: Reservations are accepted. Sites are $10–$15 per night. The campground is open year-round, with limited winter services.

Contact: Phone the park at (509) 527-3770 or write to Dalles Military Road, P.O. Box 1530, Walla Walla, WA 99362.

Directions: From U.S. 12 in Walla Walla, take the Highway 125 exit and drive approximately 2.5 miles south. Turn right on Dalles Military Road and continue one-half mile to the campground.

Trip notes: This 300-acre park feels rustic despite it's address within Walla Walla city limits. The campground is wooded with grassy sites. The park is divided by Garrison Creek, with the campground on one side and a picnic area, playground, and historical museum on the other. In May, the Balloon Stampede, a well-known hot air balloon festival, brings tourists in hordes, as does July's Mountain Man Rendezvous. Also in July, the drama department from the city college performs musicals at the park's amphitheater. This is the only campground we've found for miles, and it's a prime choice.

⑪ Godman

Location: Near the Wenaha-Tucannon Wilderness in Umatilla National Forest; map B5, grid g4.

Campsites, facilities: There are eight sites for tents, trailers, or RVs up to 15 feet long, plus one cabin that can accommodate up to eight people. Picnic tables and fire grills are provided. Vault toilets are available, but there is no piped water. Facilities are available for horses, including hitching rails and a spring. Leashed pets are permitted.

Reservations, fees: No reservations are accepted. There is no fee for the campsites, but cabins are $25 a night plus $5 per person. The campground is open from mid-June to late October; cabins are available year-round.

Contact: Umatilla National Forest, Pomeroy Ranger District, Route 1, Box 53-F, Pomeroy, WA 99347; (509) 843-1891 or fax (509) 843-4621.

Directions: From Spokane, turn south on U.S. 195 and drive 59 miles. Turn west on Highway 26 and drive 17 miles to Dusty, then turn south on Highway 127 and continue 28 miles to Dodge. Turn west on U.S. 12 and drive 24 miles to Dayton. Turn right on County Road 118 and drive 14 miles southeast, then head south on Forest Service Road 46 (Kendall Skyline Road) for 11 miles to the campground on the right.

Trip notes: This tiny, little-known spot bordering a wilderness area is primarily used as a base camp for backcountry expeditions. A trailhead provides access to the Wenaha-Tucannon Wilderness for both hikers and horseback riders. Horse facilities are available at the trailhead. In the winter, the trails and roads are used for snowmobiling.

⑫ Teal Spring

Location: In Umatilla National Forest; map B5, grid g5.

Campsites, facilities: There are eight sites for tents, trailers, or RVs up to 15 feet long.

Vault toilets are available, but there is no piped water. Picnic tables and fire grills are provided. Leashed pets are permitted.

Reservations, fees: No reservations are accepted. There is no fee. The campground is open from June to mid-November.

Contact: Umatilla National Forest, Pomeroy Ranger District, Route 1, Box 53-F, Pomeroy, WA 99347; (509) 843-1891 or fax (509) 843-4621.

Directions: From Spokane, turn south on U.S. 195 and drive 59 miles. Turn west on Highway 26 and drive 17 miles to Dusty, then turn south on Highway 127 and continue 28 miles to Dodge. Turn east on U.S. 12 and drive 13 miles to Pomeroy, then drive 10 miles south on Highway 128. At the Y, continue straight to Forest Service Road 40 and enter the national forest boundary. Drive nine miles to the Clearwater lookout tower; the campground turnoff is about a half mile past the tower on the right.

Trip notes: This is one of several small, primitive camps in the area. A Forest Service map details the backcountry roads, trails, and streams. Hunting is popular in the fall, and a snow shelter is available for winter use.

⑬ Wickiup

Location: In Umatilla National Forest; map B5, grid g6.

Campsites, facilities: There are five sites for tents, trailers, or RVs up to 15 feet long. Picnic tables and fire grills are provided. Vault toilets are available, but there is no piped water. A cold water spring can be found 100 yards from the campground. Leashed pets are permitted.

Reservations, fees: No reservations are accepted. There is no fee. The campground is open from mid-June to late October.

Contact: Umatilla National Forest, Pomeroy Ranger District, Route 1, Box 53-F, Pomeroy, WA 99347; (509) 843-1891 or fax (509) 843-4621.

Directions: From Spokane, turn south on U.S. 195 and drive 59 miles. Turn west on Highway 26 and drive 17 miles to Dusty, then turn south on Highway 127 and continue 28 miles to Dodge. Turn east on U.S. 12 and drive 13 miles to Pomeroy, then drive 10 miles south on Highway 128. At the Y, continue straight to Forest Service Road 40. At Troy Junction, about 17 miles, follow Forest Service Road 44 for three miles. Wickiup is at the intersection of Forest Service Roads 44 and 43. From Asotin, take the road leading west through Cloverland and onto Forest Service Road 43. Continue to the intersection at Forest Service Road 44, where the camp is located.

Trip notes: This is a primitive Forest Service campground that gets very little camping pressure. Most people have no idea it's even here; one forest ranger describes it as "little more than a wide spot in the road." However, it offers plenty of peace and quiet and is a good jump-off for summer backpacking trips or a fall hunting trip. A Forest Service map details backcountry roads and trails.

⑭ Fields Spring State Park

Location: Near Puffer Butte; map B5, grid g8.
Campsites, facilities: There are two primitive tent sites and 20 sites for tents or self-contained RVs up to 30 feet long. Piped water, picnic tables, and fire grills are provided. Flush toilets, a sanitary disposal station, and a playground are available. Showers and firewood can be obtained for an extra fee. A store, a restaurant, and ice are located within one

mile. Some facilities are wheelchair accessible. Leashed pets are permitted.

Reservations, fees: No reservations are accepted. Sites are $5–$10 per night. The campground is open year-round, with limited winter facilities.

Contact: Phone (800) 233-0321 or (509) 256-3332, or write to P.O. Box 86, Anatone, WA 99401.

Directions: From Spokane, turn south on U.S. 195 and drive approximately 95 miles to the Washington/Idaho border. Turn south on Highway 128 and drive a short distance to U.S. 12, then turn west and drive to Clarkston. Turn south on Highway 129 and drive 28.5 miles to the park entrance.

Trip notes: Just about nobody knows about this spot, and it's a good one. Tucked away in the southeast corner of the state, it's a designated environmental learning center. This park is noted for its variety of bird life and wildflowers. A hiking trail leads up to Puffer Butte at 4,500 feet, which offers a panoramic view of the Snake River Canyon, the Wallowa Mountains, and Idaho, Oregon, and Washington. Two day-use areas with boat launches, managed by the Department of Fish and Game, are within about 25 miles of the park. One is called the Snake River Access, 22.5 miles south of Asotin on Snake River Road; the other is the Grande Ronde River Access, 24 miles south of Asotin on the same road. During the winter, this state park is open for snowmobiling and cross-country skiing.

Oregon Campgrounds

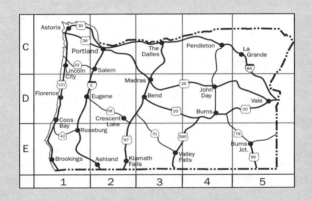

Map C1

Oregon State Map .... *page 6*
One inch equals approximately 20 miles.

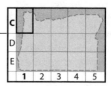

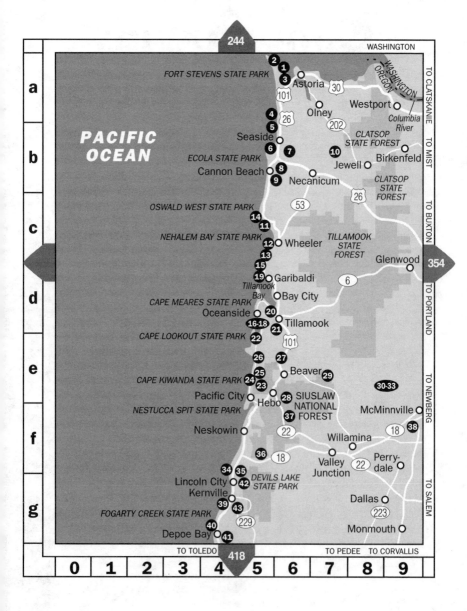

Chapter C1 features:

1 Astoria/ Warrenton Seaside KOA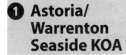

Location: Near Fort Stevens State Park; map C1, grid a6.

Campsites, facilities: There are 82 sites for tents, trailers, or RVs up to 55 feet. Cable TV, rest rooms, showers, security, a public phone, a laundry room, limited groceries, ice, snacks, RV supplies, LP gas, and a barbecue are available. Recreational facilities include a playground, a game room, a recreation field, horseshoes, a spa, and a heated swimming pool. Some facilities are wheelchair accessible. Leashed pets are permitted.

Reservations, fees: Reservations are recommended. Sites are $21–$30 per night. The campground is open year-round.

Contact: Phone the park at (503) 861-2606 or write to 1100 Ridge Road, Hammond, OR 97121.

Directions: From Portland, turn west on U.S. 26 and drive 73 miles to the junction with U.S. 101. Turn north and drive about 15 miles. One-quarter mile past the Camp Rilea Army Base, turn west at the sign for Fort Stevens State Park and follow the signs to Ridge Road. Turn and drive to the campground, located directly across from the state park.

Trip notes: This campground is nestled in a wooded area adjacent to Fort Stevens State Park, and tours of that historical military site can be arranged. This is an excellent option if the state park campground is full. A host of activities are available in the immediate area, including bicycling, hiking, deep-sea fishing, and beachcombing. See the trip notes for Fort Stevens State Park (campground number 2) for further details about the area.

2 Fort Stevens State Park

Location: At the mouth of the Columbia River; map C1, grid a5.

Campsites, facilities: There are 253 tent sites, 343 sites with full or partial hookups for trailers or RVs of any length, and a special camping area for hikers and bicyclists. Nine yurts are also available. Picnic tables and fire grills are provided. Flush toilets, a sanitary disposal station, showers, firewood, and a playground are available. Some facilities are wheelchair accessible. Boat docks and launching facilities are nearby. Leashed pets are permitted.

Reservations, fees: Contact Reservations Northwest at (800) 452-5687 ($6 reservation fee). Sites are $14–$19 per night, and $4 for hikers/bikers. The campground is open year-round.

Contact: Phone (800) 452-5687 or (503) 861-1671, or write to Hammond, OR 97121.

Directions: From Portland, turn west on U.S. 26 and drive 73 miles to the junction with U.S. 101. Turn north and drive about 15 miles. One-quarter mile past the Camp Rilea Army Base, turn west at the sign for Fort Stevens State Park and continue to the park.

Trip notes: This is a classic spot, set at the northern tip of Oregon, right where the Columbia River enters the Pacific Ocean. Fort Stevens State Park offers five miles of ocean frontage, three miles of Columbia River frontage, and several small lakes. Fishing is best out at the point, while swimming is best in the small lakes. Other highlights include an 8.5-mile bike trail and nine miles of hiking trails. The trailhead for the Oregon Coast Trail is here as well. History buffs will find a museum, tours of the fort and artillery batteries, and the remains of the *Peter Iredale* shipwreck.

❸ Kampers West Campground

Location: Near Fort Stevens State Park; map C1, grid a6.

Campsites, facilities: There are 10 tent sites and 210 sites for trailers or RVs of any length. Electricity, piped water, and picnic tables are provided. Flush toilets, bottled gas, sanitary services, showers, a laundry facilities, and ice are available. A store and a cafe

are within one mile. Leashed pets and motorbikes are permitted.

Reservations, fees: Reservations are accepted. Sites are $16.50–$21 per night. The campground is open year-round.

Contact: Phone (503) 861-1814, fax (503) 861-3620, or write to 1140 NW Warrenton Drive, Warrenton, OR 97146.

Directions: From Portland, turn west on U.S. 30 and drive 105 miles north and west to Astoria. Turn south on U.S. 101 and drive 6.5 miles to the Warrenton/Hammond Junction. Turn west on Warrenton and drive 1.5 miles to the campground on the right.

Trip notes: Located just four miles from Fort Stevens State Park, this privately run site offers full RV services. Nearby recreation possibilities include an 18-hole golf course, hiking trails, marked bike trails, and a riding stable.

❹ Bud's Campground

Location: On the Pacific Ocean; map C1, grid a5.

Campsites, facilities: There are eight sites for tents and 26 sites for trailers or RVs of any length. Electricity, piped water, sewer hookups, and picnic tables are provided. Flush toilets, showers, a store, laundry facilities, bottled gas, an automatic teller machine, and ice are available. A cafe is located within one mile. Boat docks, launching facilities, and rentals are nearby. Leashed pets and motorbikes are permitted.

Reservations, fees: Reservations are accepted. Sites are $12–$17 per night. The campground is open year-round.

Contact: Phone (800) 730-6855 or (503) 738-6855, or write to 4412 Highway 101 North, Gearhart, OR 97138.

Directions: From Interstate 5 at Portland, turn west on U.S. 26 and drive 73 miles. Turn north on U.S. 101 and drive about six miles to Gearhart. Continue one mile north on U.S. 101 to the campground on the left.

Trip notes: This private campground is set along the ocean, about three miles north of Seaside (see the trip notes for Pine Cove RV

Park and Venice RV Park, campground numbers 5 and 6). An 18-hole golf course, hiking trails, and a riding stable are close by.

❺ Pine Cove RV Park

Location: Near the Pacific Ocean; map C1, grid b5.

Campsites, facilities: There are 25 sites for trailers or RVs of any length, plus a grassy area for dispersed tent camping. Electricity, piped water, and sewer hookups are provided. Flush toilets, showers, and a laundry room are available. A store, a cafe, and ice are located within one mile. Leashed pets are permitted.

Reservations, fees: Reservations are accepted. Sites are $10–$15 per night. The campground is open year-round.

Contact: Phone (503) 738-5243 or write to 2481 Highway 101 North, Seaside, OR 97138.

Directions: From Interstate 5 at Portland, turn west on U.S. 26 and drive 73 miles to the junction with U.S. 101, then turn north on U.S. 101 and drive four miles to Seaside. Continue north about one mile. The park is located on the right at 2481 Highway 101 North.

Trip notes: This park and motel among the pines about a mile from Seaside is a good spot for fishing, both in the ocean and in the two rivers that run through town, where you can fish from the bridges. Crabbing in the ocean is good on calm spring days. Other activities nearby include an 18-hole golf course and hiking trails. See the trip notes for Venice RV Park (campground number 6) for more information about Seaside.

❻ Venice RV Park

Location: On the Neawanna River; map C1, grid b5.

Campsites, facilities: There are 31 drive-through sites for trailers or RVs of any length. Electricity, piped water, sewer and cable TV hookups, and picnic tables are provided. Flush toilets, showers, a laundry room, and ice are available. A store and a cafe are located within one mile. Leashed pets are permitted.

Reservations, fees: Reservations are accepted. Sites are $17–$19 per night. The campground is open year-round.

Contact: Phone (503) 738-8851 or write to 1032 24th Avenue, Seaside, OR 97138.

Directions: From Interstate 5 at Portland, turn west on U.S. 26 and drive 73 miles to the junction with U.S. 101, then turn north on U.S. 101 and drive four miles to Seaside. Drive to the north end of town, turn left (west) on 24th Avenue, and drive to the campground at 1032 24th Avenue.

Trip notes: This park along the Neawanna River—one of two rivers running through Seaside—is less than a mile from the beach. Seaside offers beautiful ocean beaches for fishing and surfing, moped and bike rentals, shops, and a theater. The city provides swings and volleyball nets on the beach. An 18-hole golf course is located nearby.

❼ Forest Lake Resort

Location: On the Necanicum River; map C1, grid b6.

Campsites, facilities: There are 25 tent sites and 33 sites for trailers or RVs of any length; 14 are drive-throughs. Electricity, piped water, sewer hookups, and picnic tables are provided. Flush toilets, showers, firewood, laundry facilities, and ice are available. Bottled gas, sanitary services, a store, and a cafe are located within one mile. Boat launching facilities are nearby. Leashed pets and motorbikes are permitted.

Reservations, fees: Reservations are accepted. Sites are $14–$20 per night. A 20 percent discount is offered in the winter. The campground is open year-round.

Contact: Phone (503) 738-6779 or write to HCR 63, Box 255, Seaside, OR 97138.

Directions: From Interstate 5 at Portland, turn west on U.S. 26 and drive 73 miles to the junction with U.S. 101, then turn north and drive just under one mile to the park.

Trip notes: This park is on the shore of the Necanicum River, which attracts a steelhead run every winter. The river is low during the summer but still provides many pools for swimming. Boating is allowed on the river. A small, scenic lake in the campground attracts wildlife. No swimming or boating is allowed on the campground lake, but it's stocked with trout, a practice that began in 1988. Nearby recreation options include an 18-hole golf course and a riding stable.

⑧ Sea Ranch Resort

Location: Near the Pacific Ocean; map C1, grid b6.

Campsites, facilities: There are 71 sites for tents, trailers, and RVs. Rest rooms, showers, a sanitary dump, and a public phone are available. Leashed pets are permitted.

Reservations, fees: Reservations are recommended. Sites are $17–$20 per night. The campground is open year-round.

Contact: Phone the resort at (503) 436-2815 or write to P.O. Box 214, Cannon Beach, OR 97110.

Directions: From Interstate 5 at Portland, turn west on U.S. 26 and drive 73 miles to the junction with U.S. 101, then turn south and drive three miles to the Cannon Beach exit. The resort is south three-tenths of a mile on the left.

Trip notes: This resort is in a wooded area with nearby access to the beach. Activities at the camp include stream fishing, swimming, and hunting, and you can go horseback riding on the seashore. The beach and the town of Cannon Beach are within walking distance of the resort.

⑨ RV Resort at Cannon Beach

Location: Near Ecola State Park; map C1, grid b6.

Campsites, facilities: There are 100 sites for trailers or RVs of any length; 10 are drive-throughs. Electricity, piped water, sewer hookups, and picnic tables are provided. Flush toilets, bottled gas, showers, firewood, a recreation hall, a store, a spa, a laundry room, ice,

a playground, and a swimming pool are available. Leashed pets are permitted.

Reservations, fees: Reservations are accepted. Sites are $23–$35 per night. The campground is open year-round.

Contact: Phone (503) 436-2231, fax (503) 436-1527, or write to P.O. Box 219, Cannon Beach, OR 97110.

Directions: From Interstate 5 at Portland, turn west on U.S. 26 and drive 73 miles to the junction with U.S. 101, then turn south and drive four miles to the Cannon Beach exit at milepost 29.5. Turn left (east) and drive 200 feet to the campground.

Trip notes: This private resort is located about seven blocks from one of the nicest beaches in the region. From the town of Cannon Beach you can walk for miles in either direction. Ecola State Park is just two miles north. Nearby recreational facilities include marked bike trails, a riding stable, and tennis courts.

⑩ Saddle Mountain State Park

Location: On Saddle Mountain; map C1, grid b7.

Campsites, facilities: There are 10 primitive tent sites. Picnic tables and fire grills are provided. Flush toilets and firewood are available. Leashed pets are permitted.

Reservations, fees: No reservations are accepted. Sites are $7–$14 per night. The campground is open from mid-April to late October.

Contact: Saddle Mountain State Park, Cannon Beach, OR 97110; (800) 452-5687 or (503) 861-1671.

Directions: From Portland, turn west on U.S. 26 and drive about 63 miles to Necanicum Junction. Turn north on the park entrance road and continue eight miles.

Trip notes: This is a good alternative to the many beachfront parks to the south. A 2.5-mile trail climbs to the top of Saddle Mountain, a great lookout on clear days. This park is a real find for the naturalist interested in rare and unusual varieties of plants, many of which have established themselves along the slopes of this isolated mountain.

⑪ Nehalem Bay State Park

Location: On the Pacific Ocean; map C1, grid c5.

Campsites, facilities: There are 283 sites for trailers or RVs of any length and a special camping area for hikers and bicyclists. There are also 10 yurts. Electricity, piped water, picnic tables, and fire grills are provided. Flush toilets, a sanitary disposal station, showers, and firewood are available. Some facilities are wheelchair accessible. Boat launching facilities are located nearby on Nehalem Bay. Leashed pets are permitted.

Reservations, fees: Contact Reservations Northwest at (800) 452-5687 ($6 reservation fee). Sites are $14–$17 per night, and $4 for hikers/bikers. The campground is open year-round.

Contact: Phone (503) 368-5943 or write to 8300-R Third Street Necarney, Nehalem, OR 97131.

Directions: From Portland, drive west on U.S. 26 for 73 miles, then turn south on U.S. 101 and drive 21 miles to Nehalem. Head west on the entrance road for 1.5 miles to the park.

Trip notes: This state park located on a sandy point separating the Pacific Ocean and Nehalem Bay offers six miles of beach frontage. The Oregon Coast Trail passes through the park. A horse camp with corrals and a 7.5-mile equestrian trail are available. There is also a 1.5-mile bike trail. An airport is adjacent to the park.

⑫ Jetty Fishery RV Park

Location: On Nehalem Bay; map C1, grid c5.

Campsites, facilities: There are 10 tent sites and 30 drive-through sites for trailers or RVs of any length. Electricity, piped water, and picnic tables are provided. Flush toilets, bottled gas, firewood, a store, showers, a cafe, ice, boat docks, launching facilities, and boat rentals are available. Leashed pets are permitted.

Reservations, fees: Reservations are accepted. Sites are $17 per night. The campground is open year-round.

Contact: Phone (503) 368-5746, fax (503) 368-5711, or write to 27550 Highway 101 North, Rockaway, OR 97136.

Directions: From Interstate 5 at Portland, turn west on U.S. 26 and drive 73 miles to the junction with U.S. 101, then turn south and drive 27 miles to the park entrance.

Trip notes: This small park is located at the base of a mile-long jetty, which extends out into Nehalem Bay and the ocean. Fishing and crabbing are good off the jetty, but sometimes the snags bite well, too. The small beach on the bay side of the jetty is a popular spot for kids. For boaters, a full-service marina is nearby.

⑬ Shorewood Travel Trailer Village 🚐

Location: On the Pacific Ocean; map C1, grid c5.

Campsites, facilities: There are 12 sites for trailers or RVs of any length. No tents are allowed. Electricity, piped water, and picnic tables are provided. Flush toilets, sanitary services, cable TV, showers, firewood, a laundry room, ice, and a playground are available. A store and a cafe are located within one mile. Leashed pets are permitted.

Reservations, fees: Reservations are accepted. Sites are $17–$19 per night. The campground is open year-round.

Contact: Phone (503) 355-2278 or write to 17600 Ocean Boulevard, Rockaway Beach, OR 97136.

Directions: From Interstate 5 at Portland, turn west on U.S. 26 and drive 73 miles to the junction with U.S. 101, then turn south and drive 30 miles to the town of Rockaway Beach. Drive one mile south of town to the Shorewood sign, then turn west and drive three blocks to the park.

Trip notes: This park is on an ideal beach for surf fishing for perch or beachcombing during low tides. The 1.5-mile hike to the Tillamook Bay jetty is a good side trip. An 18-hole golf course is located a short drive from the park.

⑭ Oswald West State Park

Location: On the Pacific Ocean; map C1, grid c5.

Campsites, facilities: There are 36 primitive walk-in tent sites. Wheelbarrows are available for campers to transport their supplies. Picnic tables and fire grills are provided. Piped water, flush toilets, and firewood are available. Leashed pets are permitted.

Reservations, fees: No reservations are accepted. Sites are $7–$14 per night. The campground is open from mid-March to late October.

Contact: Phone (800) 452-5687 or (503) 368-5943, or write to 8300-R Third Street Necarney, Nehalem, OR 97130.

Directions: From Portland, turn west on U.S. 26 and drive 73 miles, then turn south on U.S. 101 and travel four miles to Cannon Beach. Continue 10 miles south on U.S. 101 to the parking area. Walk one-quarter mile to the campground.

Trip notes: This state park is set along a dramatic section of the Oregon coast with rugged cliffs rising high above the ocean. This is not beach-walking territory, but the park does offer 15 miles of hiking trails, including the Oregon Coast Trail and a trail to the point of Cape Falcon, where campers can enjoy scenic views. A small beach and several fishing streams are nearby. The park is in a beautiful rain forest setting, with gigantic spruce and cedar trees.

⑮ Barview Jetty County Park

Location: Near Garibaldi; map C1, grid d5.

Campsites, facilities: There are 249 sites for tents or RVs of any length, 60 with full hookups. Electricity, piped water, sewer hookups, and picnic tables are provided. Flush toilets, a dump station, showers, and a playground are available. Bottled gas, a store, a cafe, and ice are located within one mile. Leashed pets are permitted.

Reservations, fees: Reservations are accepted; phone (503) 322-3522. Sites are $14–$18 per night, plus $2 for each additional vehicle, a $2 dump station fee, a $1 shower fee, and $5 for firewood. The campground is open year-round.

Contact: Phone (503) 322-3477, fax (503) 842-2721, or write to P.O. Box 633, Garibaldi, OR 97118.

Directions: From Interstate 5 at Portland, turn west on U.S. 26 and drive 73 miles to the junction with U.S. 101, then turn south and drive approximately 32 miles to Cedar Street (two miles north of Garibaldi). Turn west and drive one-quarter mile to the campground.

Trip notes: This park covering 160 acres is near the beach, adjacent to Tillamook Bay in a wooded area. The sites are set on grassy hills. Nearby recreation options include an 18-hole golf course, hiking trails, bike trails, surf and scuba fishing, and a full-service marina.

⑯ Happy Camp Resort

Location: On Netarts Bay; map C1, grid d5.

Campsites, facilities: There are 30 sites for trailers or RVs of any length. Electricity, piped water, and picnic tables are provided. Flush toilets, sanitary services, showers, sewer hookups, and cable TV are available. A store, a cafe, a Laundromat, bottled gas, ice, and firewood are located within one mile. Boat docks, launching facilities, and rentals are nearby. Leashed pets are permitted.

Reservations, fees: Reservations are accepted. Sites are $20 per night. The campground is open from February through November.

Contact: Phone (503) 842-4012 or write to P.O. Box 82, Netarts, OR 97143.

Directions: From Portland, turn west on U.S. 26 and drive 24 miles. Turn west on Highway 6 and drive 44 miles to Tillamook. Turn west on Netarts Highway/Third Street and drive seven miles to the campground entrance.

Trip notes: Netarts Bay offers sheltered waters, perfect for small boaters to take advantage of the excellent crabbing. Shoreliners can discover good crabbing and fair perch fishing. Crabbing gear, boat rentals, and crab cooking gear are available. The camp is set along the shore of the bay, a short drive from Cape Lookout State Park, Cape Meares State Park, and the national wildlife refuge.

⑰ Big Spruce Trailer Park 🚐

Location: On Netarts Bay; map C1, grid d5.
Campsites, facilities: There are 23 sites for trailers or RVs of any length; seven are drive-throughs. Electricity, piped water, sewer hookups, and picnic tables are provided. Flush toilets, bottled gas, cable TV, showers, and a laundry room are available. A store, a cafe, and ice are located within one mile. Boat docks and launching facilities are nearby. Leashed pets are permitted.
Reservations, fees: Reservations are accepted. Sites are $17.50–$19.50 per night. The campground is open year-round.
Contact: Phone (503) 842-7443 or write to 4850 Netarts Highway West, Tillamook, OR 97141.
Directions: From Portland, turn west on U.S. 26 and drive 24 miles. Turn west on Highway 6 and drive 44 miles to Tillamook. From Tillamook, drive 6.5 miles west on Netarts Highway/Third Street to the campground.
Trip notes: This trailer park is one block from the boat launch on Netarts Bay. See the trip notes for Happy Camp Resort (campground number 16) for details on the fishing here.

⑱ Bay Shore RV Park 🚐

Location: On Netarts Bay; map C1, grid d5.
Campsites, facilities: There are 53 sites for trailers or RVs of any length; 11 are drive-throughs. Electricity, piped water, sewer hookups, and picnic tables are provided. Flush toilets, bottled gas, showers, firewood, a recreation hall, a laundry room, and ice are available. A store and a cafe are within one mile. Boat docks, launching facilities, and rentals are nearby. Leashed pets are permitted.

Reservations, fees: Reservations are accepted. Sites are $10–$18 per night. The campground is open year-round.
Contact: Phone (503) 842-7774 or write to P.O. Box 218, Netarts, OR 97413.
Directions: From Portland, turn west on U.S. 26 and drive 24 miles. Turn west on Highway 6 and drive 44 miles to Tillamook. Turn west on Netarts Highway/Third Street and drive six miles to the park entrance.
Trip notes: This is one of three camps on the east shore of Netarts Bay. See the trip notes for Happy Camp Resort (campground number 16) for more information about the fishing here.

⑲ Biak-by-the-Sea Trailer Court 🚐

Location: On Tillamook Bay; map C1, grid d5.
Campsites, facilities: There are 45 drive-through sites for trailers or RVs of any length. Electricity, piped water, sewer hookups, and cable TV are provided. Flush toilets, showers, and laundry facilities are available. Bottled gas, a store, a cafe, and ice are located within one mile. Boat docks, launching facilities, and rentals are nearby. Leashed pets and motorbikes are permitted.
Reservations, fees: Reservations are accepted. Sites are $16 per night. The campground is open year-round.
Contact: Phone (503) 322-0111 or write to P.O. Box 916, Garibaldi, OR 97118.
Directions: From Portland, turn west on U.S. 26 and drive 24 miles. Turn west on Highway 6 and drive 44 miles to Tillamook. Turn north on U.S. 101 and drive 10 miles. Turn left on 10th Street and drive to the park on the left (just over the tracks).
Trip notes: This park along the shore of Tillamook Bay is a prime retreat for deep-sea fishing, crabbing, clamming, surf fishing, scuba diving, and beachcombing. The nearby town of Tillamook is home to a cheese factory and a historical museum. A good side trip is Cape Meares State Park, where you can hike through the national wildlife preserve and see how the seabirds nest along the cliffs.

⑳ Pacific Campground

Location: On Tillamook Bay; map C1, grid d5.

Campsites, facilities: There are 20 tent sites and 29 drive-through sites for trailers or RVs of any length. Electricity, piped water, sewer hookups, and picnic tables are provided. Flush toilets, cable TV, showers, firewood, and ice are available. A store and a cafe are located within one mile. Leashed pets (except in the tent area) and motorbikes are permitted.

Reservations, fees: Reservations are accepted. Sites are $10–$18 per night for two people, plus $1 for each additional person. The campground is open year-round.

Contact: Phone (503) 842-5201 or write to 1950 Suppress Road North, Tillamook, OR 97141.

Directions: From Portland, turn west on U.S. 26 and drive 24 miles. Turn west on Highway 6 and drive 44 miles to Tillamook. Turn north on U.S. 101 and drive 2.5 miles. The campground entrance is across from the Tillamook Cheese Factory.

Trip notes: This campground is located at the southern end of Tillamook Bay, not far from the Wilson River. The Tillamook Cheese Factory—the place for tasty tours—is just south of the park. An 18-hole golf course is also nearby. See the trip notes for Biak-by-the-Sea Trailer Court (campground number 19) for more information about the area.

㉑ Pleasant Valley RV Park

Location: On the Tillamook River; map C1, grid d5.

Campsites, facilities: There are 10 tent sites and 74 sites for trailers or RVs of any length, plus two cabins. Piped water and picnic tables are provided. Flush toilets, bottled gas, sanitary services, showers, firewood, a recreation hall, electricity, sewer hookups, cable TV, a store, a laundry room, ice, and a playground are available. Boat launching facilities are nearby. Leashed pets are permitted.

Reservations, fees: Reservations are accepted. Sites are $14–$19.50 per night; cabins are $25 per night. The campground is open year-round.

Contact: Phone (503) 842-4779 or (503) 842-2293, or write to 11880 Highway 101 South, Tillamook, OR 97141.

Directions: From Portland, turn west on U.S. 26 and drive 24 miles. Turn west on Highway 6 and drive 44 miles to Tillamook. Turn south on U.S. 101 and drive six miles to the campground entrance on the right.

Trip notes: This campground along the Tillamook River is very clean, with many recreation options in the immediate area.

㉒ Cape Lookout State Park

Location: Near Netarts Bay; map C1, grid e5.

Campsites, facilities: There are 189 tent sites, 53 sites with full hookups for trailers or RVs up to 60 feet long, and a special camping area for hikers and bicyclists. There are also six yurts. Picnic tables and fire grills are provided. Flush toilets, sanitary services, showers, and firewood are available. A restaurant is located within one mile. Some facilities are wheelchair accessible. Leashed pets are permitted.

Reservations, fees: Contact Reservations Northwest at (800) 452-5687 ($6 reservation fee). Sites are $15–$18 per night, and $4 for hikers/bikers. The campground is open year-round.

Contact: Phone (800) 452-5687 or (503) 842-4981, or write to 13000 Whiskey Creek Road West, Tillamook, OR 97141.

Directions: From Portland, turn west on U.S. 26 and drive 24 miles. Turn west on Highway 6 and drive 44 miles to Tillamook. Turn southwest on Netarts Road and drive 11 miles to the park entrance.

Trip notes: This unusual park offers an assortment of walks. One trail leads out along a ridge to headlands high above the ocean. Another walk will take you out through a variety of estuarine habitats along the five-mile sand spit that extends between the ocean and Netarts Bay. This is a paradise for bird-watchers, with 154 species to view. Fishing is another option here.

㉓ Webb Park

Location: Near the Pacific Ocean; map C1, grid e5.

Campsites, facilities: There are 30 sites for tents, trailers, or RVs. Toilets, piped water, showers, a sanitary dump, and a boat ramp are provided. Leashed pets are permitted.

Reservations, fees: No reservations are accepted. Sites are $10 per night. The campground is open year-round.

Contact: Phone the park at (503) 322-3477, call Tillamook County Parks at (503) 965-5001, or fax (503) 842-2721.

Directions: From Portland, turn west on U.S. 26 and drive 24 miles. Turn west on Highway 6 and drive 44 miles to Tillamook. Turn south on U.S. 101 and drive approximately 25 miles to the Pacific City exit. From Pacific City, turn north on Highway 30 and drive one mile to Cape Kiwanda. The camp is located on the right.

Trip notes: This public campground is an excellent alternative to the more crowded commercial RV parks off U.S. 101. It's not as developed, but offers a quiet, private setting and access to the ocean. Fishing and swimming are among your options here.

㉔ Cape Kiwanda RV Park

Location: On the Pacific Ocean; map C1, grid e5.

Campsites, facilities: There are 30 tent sites and 150 sites for trailers or RVs of any length. Electricity, piped water, sewer hookups, and picnic tables are provided. Flush toilets, sanitary services, showers, firewood, a recreation hall, laundry facilities, propane, a seafood market, a gift shop, an automatic teller machine, and a playground are available. Bottled gas, a store, a cafe, and ice are located within one mile. Boat docks, launching facilities, and rentals are nearby. Leashed pets and motorbikes are permitted.

Reservations, fees: Reservations are accepted. Sites are $14.50–$21 per night. The campground is open year-round.

Contact: Cape Kiwanda RV Park, P.O. Box 129, Pacific City, OR 97135; (503) 965-6230 or fax (503) 965-6412; e-mail: capekiwanda @oregoncoast.com.

Directions: From Portland, turn west on U.S. 26 and drive 24 miles. Turn west on Highway 6 and drive 44 miles to Tillamook. Turn south on U.S. 101 and drive 25 miles to the Pacific City exit. Drive three miles west toward Pacific City, then cross the bridge and travel one mile north and you'll see the park entrance.

Trip notes: This oceanfront park is a short distance from Cape Kiwanda State Park, which is open for day use only. Highlights at the park include a boat launch and hiking trails that lead out to the cape. A recreation option is four miles south at Nestucca Spit, where there is another day-use park. The point extends about three miles and is a good spot for bird-watching.

㉕ Raines Resort and RV Park

Location: On the Nestucca River; map C1, grid e5.

Campsites, facilities: There are 12 sites for trailers or RVs of any length. Electricity, piped water, sewer hookups, and picnic tables are provided. Flush toilets, sanitary services, showers, a store, and a laundry room are available. Bottled gas, a cafe, and ice are located within one mile. Boat docks, launching facilities, and rentals are nearby. Leashed dogs are permitted.

Reservations, fees: Reservations are accepted. Sites are $12–$15 per night. The campground is open year-round.

Contact: Phone (503) 965-6371 or write to P.O. Box 777, Pacific City, OR 97135.

Directions: From Portland, turn west on U.S. 26 and drive 24 miles. Turn west on Highway 6 and drive 44 miles to Tillamook. Turn south on U.S. 101 and drive 25 miles to Pacific City. Turn north on Brooten Road, drive 1.5

miles to Woods Bridge, and continue one block west to the park.

Trip notes: This campground is on the Nestucca River, which attracts a king salmon run from late August through Thanksgiving. A full-service marina is close by. Note: Tent campers and owners of small RVs may want to consider the free, primitive Bureau of Land Management campgrounds up the river. See the trip notes for Alder Glen, Elk Bend, Fan Creek, and Dovre (campground numbers 30 to 33).

26 Sand Beach

Location: In Siuslaw National Forest; map C1, grid e5.

Campsites, facilities: There are 101 sites for tents, trailers, or RVs up to 30 feet long. (If filled, the east and west parking lots provide additional sites for trailers or RVs.) Picnic tables and fire pits are provided. Piped water and flush toilets are available. Leashed pets are permitted.

Reservations, fees: Most sites are reservable by calling (800) 280-CAMP/2267 ($8.65 reservation fee). Sites are $12 per night. The campground is open from mid-May to early September.

Contact: Siuslaw National Forest, Hebo Ranger District, 31525 Highway 22, Hebo, OR 97122; (503) 392-3161 or fax (503) 392-4203.

Directions: On U.S. 101 southwest of Portland, drive to the little town of Pacific City. At the blinking red light, turn west and drive over the bridge. Make a sharp right, pass Cape Kiwanda, and drive about nine miles to the Sand Lake store. Turn left on Gallaway Road and drive to the campground at the end of the road.

Trip notes: This area is known for its large sand dunes, which are open to off-road vehicles. The campground is set along the shore of Sand Lake, which is actually more like an estuary since the ocean is just around the bend. This is the only coastal Forest Service campground for many miles, and it's quite popular. If you're planning a trip for midsummer, be sure to reserve far in advance. Entry permits are required for three-day weekends in the summer.

27 Camper Cove Park

Location: On Beaver Creek; map C1, grid e6.

Campsites, facilities: There are five tent sites and 15 drive-through sites for RVs up to 31 feet long, plus two cabins. Electricity, piped water, sewer hookups, and picnic tables are provided. Flush toilets, fire pits, a dump station, showers, firewood, a recreation hall, laundry facilities, and ice are available. Leashed pets are permitted.

Reservations, fees: Reservations are accepted. Sites are $12.50–$16.50 per night; call for cabin fees. The campground is open year-round.

Contact: Phone (503) 398-5334 or write to P.O. Box 42, Beaver, OR 97108.

Directions: From Portland, turn west on U.S. 26 and drive 24 miles. Turn west on Highway 6 and drive 44 miles to Tillamook. Turn south on U.S. 101 and drive 11.5 miles to the park entrance (2.5 miles north of Beaver).

Trip notes: This small, wooded campground along Beaver Creek is just far enough off the highway to provide quiet. The park can be used as a base camp for anglers, with steelhead and salmon fishing in season in the nearby Nestucca River. It gets crowded here, especially in the summer months, so be sure to make a reservation whenever possible.

28 Hebo Lake

Location: On Hebo Lake in Siuslaw National Forest; map C1, grid e6.

Campsites, facilities: There are 15 sites for tents, trailers, or RVs up to 18 feet long. Picnic tables and fire pits are provided. Piped water and vault toilets are available. Boats without motors are allowed on the lake. Leashed pets are permitted.

Reservations, fees: No reservations are accepted. Sites are $6 per night. The campground is open from May to mid-October.

Contact: Siuslaw National Forest, Hebo

Ranger District, 31525 Highway 22, Hebo, OR 97122; (503) 392-3161 or fax (503) 392-4203.

Directions: On U.S. 101 southwest of Portland, drive to the town of Hebo. Turn east on Highway 22 and drive one-quarter mile to Forest Service Road 14. Turn left (east) and drive for five miles to the campground.

Trip notes: This Forest Service campground along the shore of Hebo Lake is a secluded spot with sites nestled under trees. The trailhead for the eight-mile-long Pioneer-Indian Trail is located in the campground. The trail around the lake is barrier free.

㉙ Rocky Bend

Location: On the Nestucca River in Siuslaw National Forest; map C1, grid e7.

Campsites, facilities: There are six tent sites. Picnic tables and fire pits are provided, but there is no piped water. Vault toilets are available. No garbage service is provided, so you must pack out what you bring in. Leashed pets are permitted.

Reservations, fees: No reservations are accepted. There is no fee. The campground is open year-round.

Contact: Siuslaw National Forest, Hebo Ranger District, 31525 Highway 22, Hebo, OR 97122; (503) 392-3161 or fax (503) 392-4203.

Directions: On U.S. 101 southwest of Portland, drive to the tiny town of Beaver. Turn east on Blaine Road (keep right; Blaine Road turns into Nestucca Access Road) and drive 15.5 miles to the campground.

Trip notes: This campground along the Nestucca River is a little-known, secluded spot that provides guaranteed peace and quiet. There isn't much in the way of recreational activities out here, but hiking, fishing, clamming, and swimming are available along the coast, a relatively short drive away.

㉚ Alder Glen

Location: On the Nestucca River; map C1, grid e8.

Campsites, facilities: There are 11 sites for tents, trailers, or RVs up to 30 feet long. Fire

grills, vault toilets, and hand-pumped water are provided. Leashed pets are permitted.

Reservations, fees: No reservations are accepted. Sites are $6 per night, with a 14-day limit. The campground is open year-round, with limited winter facilities.

Contact: Bureau of Land Management, 4610 Third Street, Tillamook, OR 97141; (503) 842-7546.

Directions: On U.S. 101 southwest of Portland, drive to the tiny town of Beaver. Turn east on Blaine Road (keep right; Blaine Road turns into Nestucca Access Road) and drive 18 miles to the campground.

Trip notes: Set in a wooded spot along the beautiful Nestucca River, this campground is one of five on the scenic Nestucca River Scenic Backcountry Byway. The area is exceptionally lovely, with a wide variety of wildflowers and lush vegetation. Fishing is an option here, too.

㉛ Elk Bend

Location: On the Nestucca River; map C1, grid e8.

Campsites, facilities: There are three walk-in tent sites. Picnic tables, fire grills, pit toilets, and hand-pumped water are provided. Leashed pets are permitted.

Reservations, fees: No reservations are accepted. There is no fee, and there is a 14-day limit. The campground is open year-round, with limited winter facilities.

Contact: Bureau of Land Management, 4610 Third Street, Tillamook, OR 97141; (503) 842-7546.

Directions: On U.S. 101 southwest of Portland, drive to the tiny town of Beaver. Turn east on Blaine Road (keep right; Blaine Road turns into Nestucca Access Road) and drive 21 miles. Park in the lot and walk into the campground.

Trip notes: This camp just a few miles up the road from Alder Glen (campground number 30) offers the same facilities and attractions, but gets less use, presumably because campers must walk into it instead of driving (the sites are actually just below the parking lot). The camp doubles as a day-use picnic area.

Insider tip: The best campsite is set apart from the others about 100 yards down the river. It's private and secluded.

㉜ Fan Creek

Location: On the Nestucca River; map C1, grid e9.

Campsites, facilities: There are 11 sites for tents, trailers, or RVs up to 16 feet long. Fire grills, pit toilets, and hand-pumped water are provided. Leashed pets are permitted.

Reservations, fees: No reservations are accepted. Sites are $6 per night, with a 14-day limit. The campground is open year-round, with limited winter facilities.

Contact: Bureau of Land Management, 4610 Third Street, Tillamook, OR 97141; (503) 842-7546.

Directions: On U.S. 101 southwest of Portland, drive to the tiny town of Beaver. Turn east on Blaine Road (keep right; Blaine Road turns into Nestucca Access Road) and drive 24 miles to the campground.

Trip notes: The largest in the series of primitive camps along the Nestucca River, this site is popular with anglers. When fishing season comes around, the pools and falls along the Nestucca are choice spots for coho salmon, chinook salmon, steelhead, and trout. The camp is nestled in the trees with easy river access.

㉝ Dovre

Location: On the Nestucca River; map C1, grid e9.

Campsites, facilities: There are six tent sites and four sites for tents, trailers, or RVs up to 30 feet long. Fire grills, vault toilets, and hand-pumped water are provided. Leashed pets are permitted.

Reservations, fees: No reservations are accepted. Sites are $6 per night, with a 14-day limit. The campground is open year-round, with limited winter facilities.

Contact: Bureau of Land Management, 4610 Third Street, Tillamook, OR 97141; (503) 842-7546.

Directions: On U.S. 101 southwest of Portland, drive to the tiny town of Beaver. Turn east on Blaine Road (keep right; Blaine Road turns into Nestucca Access Road) and drive 26.5 miles to the campground.

Trip notes: This is the last campground you'll come across on the Nestucca River Scenic Backcountry Byway. It sits amid tall Douglas fir trees, wildflowers, and lush ground vegetation. In late summer and fall, visitors are treated to a show of brilliant red vine maple. The camp provides easy river access and is used heavily by anglers in the spring.

㉞ Tree N' Sea Trailer Park

Location: On the Pacific Ocean; map C1, grid f4.

Campsites, facilities: There are seven sites for trailers or RVs of any length. Electricity, piped water, and sewer hookups are provided. Flush toilets and showers are available. A store, a cafe, and a Laundromat are located within one mile. Leashed pets are permitted.

Reservations, fees: Reservations are recommended. Sites are $16–$22 per night. The campground is open year-round.

Contact: Phone (503) 996-3801 or write to 1015 Southwest 51st Street, Lincoln City, OR 97367.

Directions: From Portland, turn south on Highway 99 West and drive to Highway 18. Turn west on Highway 18 and drive 47 miles to U.S. 101. Turn south and drive five miles to Lincoln City. Turn west onto Southwest 51st Street and drive one block to the park.

Trip notes: This campground on the ocean in Lincoln City is a pleasant RV park that makes an adequate layover spot. See the trip notes for KOA Lincoln City and Devil's Lake State Park (campground numbers 35 and 42) for recreation options.

㉟ KOA Lincoln City

Location: On the Pacific Ocean; map C1, grid f5.

Campsites, facilities: There are 18 tent sites and 55 sites for trailers or RVs of any length; 14 are drive-throughs. Picnic tables are provided. Flush toilets, bottled gas, sanitary services, showers, firewood, a recreation hall, a store, a cafe, a laundry room, ice, and a playground are available. Electricity, piped water, and sewer and cable TV hookups cost extra. Boat launching facilities are nearby. Leashed pets are permitted.

Reservations, fees: Reservations are accepted. Sites are $18–$22 per night. The campground is open year-round.

Contact: Phone (503) 994-2961, fax (503) 994-9454, or write to 5298 NE Park Lane, Otis, OR 97368.

Directions: From Portland, turn south on Highway 99 West and drive to Highway 18. Turn west on Highway 18 and drive 47 miles. Turn south on U.S. 101 and drive five miles to Lincoln City. From Lincoln City, drive another 1.2 miles north on U.S. 101. Turn east on East Devil's Lake Road and drive one mile to the park.

Trip notes: This area offers opportunities for beachcombing, tidepooling, and fishing along a seven-mile stretch of beach. Two stops to consider if you're going into Lincoln City for supplies: the Premier Market, which has smoked salmon, and the Colonial Bakery, which carries the best pastries west of Paris. Nearby recreation options include an 18-hole golf course and tennis courts.

㊱ Lee's Evergreen RV Park

Location: On the Salmon River; map C1, grid f5.

Campsites, facilities: There are six sites for tents and 19 for trailers and RVs. Rest rooms, showers, a sanitary dump, a public phone, a laundry room, limited groceries, ice, RV supplies, and LP gas are available. Recreational facilities include a rec hall and horseshoes. Small leashed pets are permitted.

Reservations, fees: No reservations are accepted. Sites are $10–$17 per night. The campground is open year-round.

Contact: Phone (503) 994-3116 or write to P.O. Box 121, Otis, OR 97368.

Directions: From Salem, drive west on Highway 22 for 25 miles to Highway 18. Drive west on Highway 18 for about 25 miles toward Otis. Turn right at milepost 6. The camp is located on the right.

Trip notes: This wooded camp is set on the Salmon River, with opportunities for trout fishing. Nearby side trip options include H. B. Van Ouzer Forest Wayside and Devil's Lake State Park. Beach access is just a short drive west.

㊲ Castle Rock

Location: On Three Rivers in Siuslaw National Forest; map C1, grid f6.

Campsites, facilities: There are four tent sites. Piped water, picnic tables, and a vault toilet are provided. Leashed pets are permitted.

Reservations, fees: No reservations are accepted. There is no fee. The campground is open year-round.

Contact: Siuslaw National Forest, Hebo Ranger District, 31525 Highway 22, Hebo, OR 97122; (503) 392-3161 or fax (503) 392-4203.

Directions: On U.S. 101 southwest of Portland, drive to the tiny town of Hebo. Turn east on Highway 22 and drive five miles to the campground.

Trip notes: This tiny spot along Three Rivers provides an alternative for tent campers to the large beachfront RV parks popular on the Oregon coast. Fishing can be good here. Though primitive, this is a well-used camp that can fill up quickly.

㊳ Mulkey RV Park

Location: Near the South Yamhill River; map C1, grid f9.

Campsites, facilities: There are 70 sites for tents, trailers, or RVs of any length. Electricity, piped water, sewer hookups, and picnic tables are provided. Flush toilets, showers, a store, bottled gas, and a laundry are available. Leashed pets and motorbikes are permitted.

Reservations, fees: Reservations are recommended. Sites are $14–$18 per night. The campground is open year-round.

Contact: Phone (503) 472-2475 or write to 14325 SW Highway 18, McMinnville, OR 97128.

Directions: From Portland, turn south on Highway 99 and drive about 31 miles to McMinnville. Take Highway 18 southwest for 3.5 miles to the park entrance.

Trip notes: If you're in the area and looking for a camping spot, you'd best stop here—there are no other campgrounds within 30 miles. This wooded park is set near the South Yamhill River. Nearby recreation options include an 18-hole golf course, tennis courts, and the Western Deer Park and Arboretum, which has a playground.

㊟ Sea and Sand RV Park

Location: Near Siletz Bay; map C1, grid g4.

Campsites, facilities: There are 85 sites for trailers or RVs up to 35 feet long. Electricity, piped water, sewer and cable TV hookups, and picnic tables are provided. Flush toilets, showers, sanitary services, firewood, and a laundry room are available. A store, a cafe, and ice are located within one mile. Leashed pets are permitted.

Reservations, fees: Reservations are accepted. Sites are $18–$21 per night. The campground is open year-round.

Contact: Phone (503) 764-2313, fax (503) 764-2313, or write to 4985 Highway 101 North, Depoe Bay, OR 97341.

Directions: From Portland, turn south on Highway 99 West and drive southwest to Highway 18. Turn west on Highway 18 and drive 47 miles to U.S. 101. Turn south and drive five miles to Lincoln City. Drive another nine miles south to the campground entrance.

Trip notes: Beachcombing for fossils and agates is popular at this oceanfront park near Gleneden Beach on Siletz Bay. The sites have ocean views and pleasant terraces. The Siletz River and numerous small creeks are in the area.

㊵ Pirates Cove RV Park

Location: Near Depoe Bay State Park; map C1, grid g4.

Campsites, facilities: There are 105 sites for trailers or RVs of any length. Electricity, piped water, sewer hookups, and picnic tables are provided. Flush toilets, bottled gas, showers, a recreation hall, a store, a laundry room, ice, a playground, and a swimming pool are available. Leashed pets are permitted.

Reservations, fees: Reservations are accepted; phone (800) 452-2104. Sites are $17–$29 per night. The campground is open year-round.

Contact: Phone (541) 765-2302, fax (541) 765-2153, or write to P.O. Box 1278, Depoe Bay, OR 97341.

Directions: From Portland, turn south on Highway 99 West and drive southwest to Highway 18. Turn west on Highway 18 and drive 47 miles to U.S. 101. Turn south and drive five miles to Lincoln City. Drive 13 miles south. This park is located on U.S. 101 at the north edge of the town of Depoe Bay.

Trip notes: Perched on rock cliffs overlooking the ocean, this park has everything an ocean camper could want. Prime oceanfront sites are available, and this is an excellent spot for whale watching, especially in August, when they migrate north, and in January and February, when they return south. This is a scenic stretch of coastline, and some of the prime side trips include Depoe Bay State Park and Depoe Creek. Nearby recreation options include an 18-hole golf course, tennis courts, and a public aquarium.

㊶ Beverly Beach State Park

Location: On the Pacific Ocean; map C1, grid g4.

Campsites, facilities: There are 135 tent sites, 129 sites with full or partial hookups for trailers or RVs of any length, and a special camping area for hikers and bicyclists, as well as a reserved group area. There is also a village of 15 yurts. Picnic tables and fire grills are provided. Piped water, flush toilets, showers, and a sanitary disposal station are available. Some facilities are wheelchair accessible. Leashed pets are permitted.

Reservations, fees: Contact Reservations Northwest at (800) 452-5687 ($6 reservation fee). Sites are $16–$19 per night, and $4 for hikers/bikers. The campground is open year-round.

Contact: Phone (800) 452-5687 or (503) 265-9278, or write to 198 NE 123rd Street, Newport, OR 97365.

Directions: From Interstate 5 at Albany, turn west on U.S. 20 and drive 66 miles to Newport. Turn north on U.S. 101 and drive seven miles to the park entrance.

Trip notes: This beautiful campground is in a wooded, grassy area on the east side of U.S. 101. Like magic, you walk through a tunnel under the roadway and emerge on the beach. A one-mile hiking trail is available. Just a mile to the north is a small day-use state park called Devil's Punchbowl, named for an unusual bowl-shaped rock formation with caverns under it where the waves rumble about. For some great ocean views, head north one more mile to the Otter Crest Wayside.

42 Devil's Lake State Park

Location: On Devil's Lake; map C1, grid g5.
Campsites, facilities: There are 68 tent sites and 32 sites with full hookups for trailers or RVs of any length. A separate area for hikers and bikers is available. Picnic tables and fire grills are provided. Flush toilets, showers, and firewood are available. Some facilities are wheelchair accessible. Boat docks and launching facilities are nearby. Leashed pets are permitted.

Reservations, fees: Contact Reservations Northwest at (800) 452-5687 ($6 reservation fee). Sites are $16–$19 per night, and $4 for hikers/bikers. The campground is open from mid-April to late October.

Contact: Phone (503) 994-2002 or (800) 452-5687, or write to 1452 NE Sixth Street, Lincoln City, OR 97367.

Directions: From Portland, turn south on Highway 99 West and drive southwest to Highway 18. Turn west on Highway 18 and continue 47 miles to U.S. 101. Turn south and continue five miles to Lincoln City. Follow the signs to the park in town.

Trip notes: This is a take-your-pick deal. At Devil's Lake, you can boat, fish, or water-ski. An alternative is to head west and explore the seven miles of beaches. Lincoln City also has a number of arts and crafts galleries in town. Devil's Lake State Park is two miles east and offers facilities for day use only.

43 Sportsman's Landing RV Park

Location: On the Siletz River; map C1, grid g5.
Campsites, facilities: There are 30 sites for trailers or RVs of any length. Electricity, piped water, and sewer hookups are provided. Showers, a cafe, a barbecue area, and a laundry room are available. Boat launching and moorage facilities and a fishing dock are available. Leashed pets are permitted.

Reservations, fees: Reservations are accepted. Sites are $15 per night. The campground is open year-round.

Contact: Phone (541) 996-4225, fax (541) 994-4688, or write to 3804 Siletz Highway, Lincoln City, OR 97367.

Directions: From Portland, turn south on Highway 99 West and drive southwest to Highway 18. Turn west on Highway 18 and continue 47 miles to U.S. 101. Turn south and continue five miles to Lincoln City. Continue six miles south on U.S. 101, then drive 3.8 miles east on Highway 229 to the park entrance.

Trip notes: This park lies along the shore of the Siletz River, with full boating facilities and a restaurant that's world-famous for its Belgian waffles and crepes. If you head farther east on Highway 229, you'll discover several Forest Service roads that lead into the Siuslaw National Forest and provide access to a number of creeks. See a Forest Service map for details.

Map C2

Oregon State Map .... *page 6*
One inch equals approximately 20 miles.

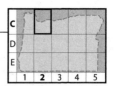

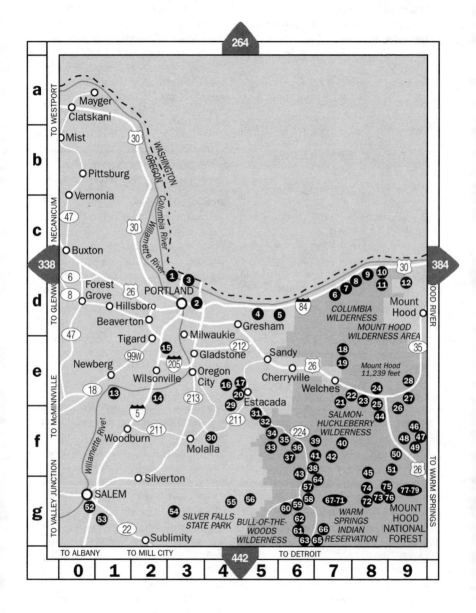

Chapter C2 features:

❶ Jantzen Beach RV Park 🚐

Location: Near the Columbia River; map C2, grid d3.

Campsites, facilities: There are 169 sites for trailers or RVs of any length. Electricity, piped water, sewer hookups, and picnic tables are provided. Flush toilets, showers, a recreation hall, a laundry room, ice, a playground, and a swimming pool are available. Bottled gas, a store, and a cafe are within one mile. Boat docks, launching facilities, and rentals are nearby. Leashed pets are permitted.

Reservations, fees: Reservations are accepted. Sites are $20–$22 per night. The campground is open year-round.

Contact: Phone (503) 289-7626, fax (503) 289-9220, or write to 1503 North Hayden Island Drive, Portland, OR 97217.

Directions: Take Interstate 5 about four miles north of Portland and look for the Jantzen Beach exit (exit 308). Then drive one-half mile west on Hayden Island Drive to the park on the right.

Trip notes: This RV campground is located near the banks of the Columbia River on the outskirts of Portland. Though close to the highway, the camp has a rural feel, with nice shady sites. An 18-hole golf course, a riding stable, and tennis courts are close by.

❷ Portland Meadows RV Park 🚐

Location: Near the Columbia River; map C2, grid d3.

Campsites, facilities: There are 32 sites with full hookups for trailers or RVs of any length. Electricity, piped water, and cable TV and sewer hookups are provided. Flush toilets, bottled gas, sanitary services, showers, a store, a cafe, a laundry room, and ice are available. Leashed pets under 20 pounds are permitted.

Reservations, fees: Reservations are accepted. Sites are $16–$18 per night. The campground is open year-round.

Contact: Phone (503) 285-1617, fax (503) 285-6041, or write to 222 Northeast Gertz Road, Portland, OR 97211.

Directions: Take the Columbia Boulevard exit off Interstate 5 in Portland. Drive one-half mile east, then turn north on Martin Luther King Boulevard (Union Avenue) and continue another half mile. Turn east on Gertz Road and proceed to the campground.

Trip notes: Many recreation opportunities are available in the Portland area. Numerous marinas on the Willamette and Columbia Rivers offer boat trips and rentals, and the city parks and nearby state parks have hiking, bicycling, and horseback riding possibilities; call (503) 238-7488 for more information. The Columbia River Highway (U.S. 30) is a scenic drive. If golf is your game, Portland has 18 public golf courses. The winter ski areas at Mount Hood are within an hour's drive.

❸ Fir Grove RV and Trailer Park 🚐

Location: Near the Columbia River; map C2, grid d3.

Campsites, facilities: There six sites for trailers or RVs of any length. Electricity, piped water, and sewer hookups are provided. Flush toilets, laundry facilities, and showers are available. Bottled gas, sanitary services, a store, a cafe, and a playground are located within one mile. Leashed pets and motorbikes are permitted.

Reservations, fees: Reservations are accepted. Sites are $20 per night. The campground is open year-round.

Contact: Phone (503) 252-9993 or write to 5541 Northeast 72nd Street, Portland, OR 97218.

Directions: In Portland off Interstate 205, take exit 23B and drive about 400 yards northeast on Columbia Boulevard, then one mile west on Northeast Killingsworth and you'll see the park entrance.

Trip notes: This park is near the banks of the Columbia River in the outskirts of Portland. See the trip notes for Portland Meadows RV Park (campground number 2) for information about the nearby recreation opportunities.

④ Crown Point RV Park

Location: Near the Columbia River; map C2, grid d5.

Campsites, facilities: There are 10 tent sites and 21 sites for trailers or RVs of any length. Electricity, piped water, and picnic tables are provided. Flush toilets, bottled gas, sanitary services, showers, a beauty shop, and a laundry room are available. There is a store and ice within one mile. Leashed pets are permitted.

Reservations, fees: Reservations are accepted. Sites are $18 per night. The campground is open year-round.

Contact: Phone (503) 695-5207 or write to 37000 East Historic Columbia River Highway, Corbett, OR 97019.

Directions: From Portland, drive east on Interstate 84 to exit 18, near Troutdale. Drive about 400 yards southeast on U.S. 30 (Crown Point Highway) to the park. (Note: This route includes a 10 percent grade. To avoid it, take the following route: From Portland, drive east on Interstate 84 to exit 18/Lewis and Clark State Park exit. Drive through the park for 7.3 miles on the Historic Columbia River Highway to the park on the right.)

Trip notes: This little park is located near the Columbia River along scenic U.S. 30. Crown Point State Park is nearby and is open during the day. It offers views of the Columbia River Gorge and the historic Vista House, a memorial built in 1918 to honor Oregon's pioneers. Multnomah Falls offers another possible side trip.

⑤ Oxbow County Campground

Location: On the Sandy River; map C2, grid d6.

Campsites, facilities: There are 45 sites for tents, trailers, or RVs up to 35 feet long. Picnic tables are provided. Piped water, pit toilets, firewood, barbecues, fire rings, and a playground are available. Boat launching facilities are nearby. Gates lock at sunset. No pets are permitted.

Reservations, fees: No reservations are accepted. Sites are $10–$13 per night. The campground is open year-round but is subject to flooding, so please call to confirm the status.

Contact: Phone (503) 663-4708 or write to 3010 Southeast Oxbow Parkway, Gresham, OR 97080.

Directions: From Portland, drive east on Interstate 84 to exit 17. Turn right (south) on Highway 257 and drive three miles to Division Street. Turn left and drive seven miles to the park.

Trip notes: This 1,000-acre park along the Sandy River, a short distance from the Columbia River Gorge, is a designated natural preservation area. Fishing, swimming, and nonmotorized boating are permitted here.

⑥ Ainsworth State Park

Location: Along the Columbia River Gorge; map C2, grid d7.

Campsites, facilities: There are 47 sites with full hookups for trailers or RVs of any length. Picnic tables and fire grills are provided. Flush toilets, showers, firewood, and a laundry room are available. Leashed pets are permitted.

Reservations, fees: No reservations are accepted. Sites are $14–$19 per night. The campground is open from mid-April to late October (or later, weather permitting).

Contact: Columbia River Gorge District, P.O. Box 100, Corbett, OR 97019; (503) 695-2361 or (800) 452-5687.

Directions: From Portland, turn east on Interstate 84 and drive 35 miles. Take the U.S. 30 exit and turn southwest; continue a short distance to the park. An alternate route is to take U.S. 30, a designated scenic highway, all the way from Portland (37 miles).

Trip notes: This state park is set along the scenic Columbia River Gorge. A two-mile section of the Columbia River Gorge Trail connects this park with John Yeon State Park, which is open during the day. Anglers should check out the Bonneville Fish Hatchery, home to an unusual giant sturgeon.

❼ Eagle Creek

Location: Near the Columbia Wilderness in Mount Hood National Forest; map C2, grid d7.
Campsites, facilities: There are 19 sites for tents, trailers, or RVs up to 20 feet long. Picnic tables and fire grills are provided. Piped water and flush toilets are available. Boat docks and launching facilities are nearby on the Columbia River. Leashed pets are permitted.
Reservations, fees: Reservations are required for groups. Sites are $8 per night. The campground is open from mid-May to October.
Contact: Columbia River Gorge National Scenic Area, 902 Wasco Avenue, Suite 200, Hood River, OR 97031; (541) 386-2333 or fax (541) 386-1916.
Directions: From Portland, turn east at exit 41 on Interstate 84 and drive approximately 43 miles to the campground, located two miles east of Bonneville.
Trip notes: This is a good base camp for a hiking trip. The Eagle Creek Trail leaves the campground and goes 13 miles to Wahtum Lake, where it intersects with the Pacific Crest Trail. There is a primitive campground at the 7.5-mile point. The upper seven miles of the trail pass through the Columbia Wilderness.

❽ Cascade Locks Marine Park

Location: In Cascade Locks; map C2, grid d8.
Campsites, facilities: There are 35 sites for tents, trailers, and RVs of any length. Picnic tables are provided. Flush toilets, sanitary services, showers, boat docks, launching facilities, and a playground are available. Bottled gas, a store, a cafe, a Laundromat, and ice are located within one mile. Leashed pets and motorbikes are permitted.
Reservations, fees: No reservations are accepted. Sites are $10 per night. The campground is open year-round, with limited winter facilities.
Contact: Phone (541) 374-8619, fax (541) 374-8428, or write to P.O. Box 307, Cascade Locks, OR 97014.
Directions: From Portland, turn east on Interstate 84 and drive approximately 44 miles to Cascade Locks. Take exit 44 and drive one mile east on Wanapa Street to the sign for the park on the left. Follow the signs to the park.
Trip notes: This public riverfront park covers 200 acres and offers a museum and boat rides. The salmon fishing is excellent here. Nearby recreation options include hiking trails and tennis courts.

❾ Herman Horse Camp

Location: Near the Pacific Crest Trail in Mount Hood National Forest; map C2, grid d8.
Campsites, facilities: There are seven sites for tents, trailers, or RVs up to 24 feet long. Piped water, fire grills, and picnic tables are provided. Stock handling facilities are available. Sanitary services, showers, a store, a cafe, a Laundromat, and ice are nearby. Leashed pets are permitted.
Reservations, fees: No reservations are accepted. Sites are $6 per night. The campground is open from mid-May to October.
Contact: Columbia River Gorge National Scenic Area, 902 Wasco Avenue, Suite 200, Hood River, OR 97031; (541) 386-2333 or fax (541) 386-1916.
Directions: From Portland, turn east on Interstate 84 and drive about 45 miles to the town of Cascade Locks. Continue east for 1.5 more miles to the campground entrance.
Trip notes: This campground is located about one-half mile from Herman Creek, not far from the Pacific Crest Trail. This is a particularly beautiful area, separated from Washington by the Columbia River. There are many recre-

ation options here, including biking, hiking, fishing, and boat trips.

⑩ Wyeth

Location: On Gordon Creek in Mount Hood National Forest; map C2, grid d8.

Campsites, facilities: There are 17 sites for tents, trailers, or RVs up to 32 feet long. Fire grills and picnic tables are provided. Piped water and flush toilets are available. Leashed pets are permitted.

Reservations, fees: No reservations are accepted. Sites are $8 per night. The campground is open from mid-May to October.

Contact: Columbia River Gorge National Scenic Area, 902 Wasco Avenue, Suite 200, Hood River, OR 97031; (541) 386-2333 or fax (541) 386-1916.

Directions: From Portland, turn east at exit 51 on Interstate 84 and drive about 45 miles to the town of Cascade Locks. Continue seven miles east to the Wyeth exit, then drive one-half mile on a county road (you'll see a sign) to the campground entrance.

Trip notes: This is a good layover spot for Columbia River corridor cruisers. The camp is set along Gordon Creek, near the Columbia. See the trip notes for Herman Horse Camp (campground number 9) for recreation details.

⑪ KOA Cascade Locks

Location: Near the Columbia River; map C2, grid d8.

Campsites, facilities: There are 25 sites for tents and 74 sites for trailers or RVs of any length, plus nine cabins. Electricity, piped water, sewer hookups, and picnic tables are provided. Flush toilets, bottled gas, sanitary services, showers, firewood, a hot tub, cable TV hookups, a recreation hall, a store, a laundry room, ice, a playground, and a heated swimming pool are available. The pool is open from May 20 through October 15, the hot tub from April through September. A cafe is lo-

cated within one mile. Leashed pets and motorbikes are permitted.

Reservations, fees: Reservations are accepted. Sites are $18–$23 per night; cabins are $30–$36 per night for two people. The campground is open from March 20 to October 20.

Contact: Phone (541) 374-8668 or write to Star Route, Box 660, Cascade Locks, OR 97014.

Directions: From Portland, turn east on Interstate 84 and drive about 44 miles to the town of Cascade Locks. Take exit 44 and travel two miles east on Forest Lane to the campground.

Trip notes: This is a good layover spot for RVers touring the Columbia River corridor. The campground offers level, shaded RV sites and grassy tent sites. Nearby recreation options include bike trails, hiking trails, and tennis courts. The 200-acre Cascade Locks Marine Park is nearby and offers everything from museums to boat trips.

⑫ Viento State Park

Location: Along the Columbia River Gorge; map C2, grid d9.

Campsites, facilities: There are 17 tent sites and 58 sites with water and electrical hookups for trailers or RVs up to 30 feet long. Picnic tables and fire grills are provided. Flush toilets, showers, firewood, and a laundry room are available. Leashed pets are permitted.

Reservations, fees: Reservations are accepted. Sites are $14–$19 per night. The campground is open from mid-April to late October (or later, weather permitting).

Contact: Columbia River Gorge District, P.O. Box 100, Corbett, OR 97019; (541) 374-8811 or (800) 452-5687.

Directions: From Portland, turn east on Interstate 84 and drive approximately 57 miles to the park entrance, located eight miles west of the town of Hood River.

Trip notes: This park along the Columbia River Gorge offers scenic hiking trails. Take the picturesque drive along old U.S. 30, which skirts the Columbia River. There are three other day-use state parks along Interstate 84 just west of Viento: Wygant, Vinzenz Lausmann, and Seneca Fouts. All are accessible by eastbound traffic only and offer quality hiking trails and scenic views.

⑬ Champoeg State Heritage Area

Location: On the Willamette River; map C2, grid e1.

Campsites, facilities: There are six tent sites and 48 sites with water and electrical hookups for trailers or RVs up to 50 feet long. There are also three group areas that accommodate a maximum of 25 tents each, an RV group site with 25 sites, and six yurts. Picnic tables and fire grills are provided. Flush toilets, a sanitary disposal station, showers, a group recreation hall for up to 60 people, and firewood are available. Some facilities are wheelchair accessible. Boat docking facilities are nearby. Leashed pets are permitted.

Reservations, fees: Contact Reservations Northwest at (800) 452-5687 ($6 reservation fee). Sites are $14–$18 per night. The campground is open year-round, with limited winter facilities.

Contact: Phone (800) 452-5687 or (503) 633-8170, or write to 7679 Champoeg Road NE, Saint Paul, OR 97137.

Directions: From Interstate 5 between Salem and Portland, take the Donald/Aurora exit and follow the signs for eight miles west to the park.

Trip notes: This state park along the banks of the Willamette River has an interpretive center, a botanical garden featuring native plants, and hiking and bike trails. In July, a pageant reenacting the early history of the area is staged Thursday through Sunday evenings. There is also a log cabin museum and the historic Newell House.

⑭ Isberg RV Park

Location: Near Aurora; map C2, grid e2.

Campsites, facilities: There are 84 sites for trailers or RVs of any length. Electricity, piped water, and sewer hookups are provided. Flush toilets, bottled gas, sanitary services, showers, a recreation hall, a store, a swimming pool, a laundry room, and ice are available. Leashed pets are permitted.

Reservations, fees: Reservations are accepted. Sites are $18–$22 per night. The campground is open year-round.

Contact: Phone (503) 678-2646, fax (503) 678-2724, or write to 21599 Dolores Way NE, Aurora, OR 97002.

Directions: Take Interstate 5 north for about seven miles from Woodburn, then take exit 278 at Aurora and drive east about 200 yards to the park.

Trip notes: This RV campground in a rural area just off the main highway offers a recreation room, a jogging trail, and a pitch-and-putt golf course. The setting is very pretty, thanks to lots of evergreen trees that shelter the camp from the highway. Portland and Salem are just 20 minutes away.

⑮ Trailer Park of Portland

Location: In Tualatin; map C2, grid e3.

Campsites, facilities: There are 100 drive-through sites for trailers or RVs of any length. Electricity, piped water, sewer hookups, and picnic tables are provided. Flush toilets, sanitary services, showers, a laundry room, and a playground are available. Bottled gas, a store, a cafe, and ice are within one mile. Leashed pets and motorbikes are permitted.

Reservations, fees: Reservations are accepted. Sites are $22 per night. The campground is open year-round.

Contact: Phone (503) 692-0225 or write to 6645 Southwest Nyberg Road, Tualatin, OR 97062.

Directions: Take Interstate 5 south from Portland to Tualatin, then take exit 289 and follow Highway 212 east for about one-quarter mile to the park.

Trip notes: This park just south of Portland

in a wooded setting has spacious sites, all with access to lawn areas. See the trip notes for Portland Meadows RV Park (campground number 2) for information about recreation possibilities in the area.

⑯ Barton Park

Location: Near the Clackamas River; map C2, grid e4.

Campsites, facilities: There are a total of 58 sites for tents, trailers, and RVs. Rest rooms, showers, a sanitary dump, a public phone, and a barbecue are available. Recreational facilities include horseshoe pits, a playground, and a boat ramp. Leashed pets are permitted.

Reservations, fees: Reservations are recommended. Sites are $10–$14 per night. The campground is open from May 1 through September.

Contact: Barton Park, (503) 637-3015. Clackamas County Parks Department, 902 Abernethy Road, Oregon City, OR 97045, (503) 655-8521 or fax (503) 650-3702.

Directions: From Portland, drive south on Interstate 205 for about 20 miles to the Clackamas/Estacada exit (Highway 212). Continue on Highway 212 to the Carver Road exit onto Highway 224. Turn right and cross the bridge over the Clackamas River. Turn left on Springwater Road and drive to the town of Springwater. Just outside of town, turn right on Barton Park Road and drive one-quarter mile to the park straight ahead.

Trip notes: Getting here is a bit of a maze, but the trip is well worth it. This camp, set on the Clackamas River, is surrounded by woods and tall trees. There is a swimming area in the stream, and the nearby Clackamas River provides good salmon fishing.

⑰ Milo McIver State Park

Location: On the Collawash River; map C2, grid e5.

Campsites, facilities: There are four primitive tent sites and 44 sites with water and electrical hookups for trailers or RVs of any

length. Picnic tables and fire grills are provided. Flush toilets, sanitary services, showers, and firewood are available. Facilities are wheelchair accessible. Boat launching facilities are nearby. Group facilities are available. Leashed pets are permitted.

Reservations, fees: Contact Reservations Northwest at (800) 452-5687 ($6 reservation fee). Sites are $9–$18 per night. The campground is open from mid-March to mid-November.

Contact: Phone (503) 630-7150, (503) 731-3411, or (800) 452-5687, or write to 24101 South Entrance Road, Estacada, OR 97023.

Directions: From Portland, turn east on U.S. 26 and drive approximately 25 miles, then turn south on Highway 211 and continue seven miles to the park.

Trip notes: Though not far from the Portland area, this park is far enough off the beaten track to provide a feeling of separation from the metropolitan area. It's set along the banks of the Collawash River and has a boat ramp. Trails for hiking are available, and a 4.5-mile equestrian trail is also accessible. A fish hatchery is a nearby point of interest.

⑱ McNeil

Location: On the Clear Fork of the Sandy River in Mount Hood National Forest; map C2, grid e7.

Campsites, facilities: There are 34 sites for tents, trailers, or RVs up to 22 feet long. Picnic tables and vault toilets are provided. There is no piped water. Leashed pets are permitted.

Reservations, fees: No reservations are accepted. Sites are $7 per night. The campground is open from May to late September.

Contact: Mount Hood National Forest, Zigzag Ranger District, 65000 East Highway 26, Welches, OR 97067; (503) 622-7674 or fax (503) 622-5622.

Directions: From Portland, drive 40 miles east on U.S. 26 to Zigzag. Turn northeast on County Road 18 and drive 4.5 miles, then go three-quarters of a mile northeast on Forest Service Road 1825 to the campground.

Trip notes: This campground is set along the

Clear Fork of the Sandy River. Several trails nearby provide access to the wilderness backcountry. See a Forest Service map for details.

⑲ Riley Horse Camp

Location: Near the Clear Fork of the Sandy River in Mount Hood National Forest; map C2, grid e7.

Campsites, facilities: There are 14 sites for tents, trailers, or RVs up to 16 feet long. Piped water, fire grills, vault toilets, and picnic tables are provided. Facilities for horses are available. Leashed pets are permitted.

Reservations, fees: Reserve some sites by calling (800) 280-CAMP/2267 ($8.65 reservation fee). Sites are $9 per night. The campground is open from May to late September.

Contact: Mount Hood National Forest, Zigzag Ranger District, 65000 East Highway 26, Welches, OR 97067; (503) 622-7674 or fax (503) 622-5622.

Directions: From Portland, drive 40 miles east on U.S. 26 to Zigzag. Turn northeast on County Road 18 and drive four miles, then proceed one mile east on Forest Service Road 1825. The campground is about 100 yards south on Forest Service Road 382.

Trip notes: Riley Horse Camp is close to McNeil (campground number 18) and offers the same opportunities, except Riley provides stock handling facilities. This is a popular base camp for horse packing trips into a nearby old-growth forest.

⑳ Lost Creek

Location: On Lost Creek in Mount Hood National Forest; map C2, grid e5.

Campsites, facilities: There are five walk-in sites for tents and nine sites for trailers or RVs up to 22 feet long. Facilities are wheelchair accessible. Well water, fire grills, vault toilets, and picnic tables are provided. Leashed pets are permitted.

Reservations, fees: Reserve some sites by calling (800) 280-CAMP/2267 ($8.65 reservation fee). Sites are $9–$18 per night. The campground is open from May to late September.

Contact: Mount Hood National Forest, Zigzag Ranger District, 65000 East Highway 26, Welches, OR 97067; (503) 622-7674 or fax (503) 622-5622.

Directions: From Portland, drive 40 miles east on U.S. 26 to Zigzag. Turn north on County Road 18/East Lolo Pass Road and drive 4.5 miles. Turn right on Forest Service Road 1825 and drive two miles to the campground on the right, just past the entrance to Riley Horse Camp.

Trip notes: This campground near McNeil and Riley (campground numbers 18 and 19) has some of the same opportunities. It's barrier free and offers an interpretive nature trail about one-mile long and a wheelchair-accessible fishing pier.

㉑ Green Canyon

Location: On the Salmon River in Mount Hood National Forest; map C2, grid e7.

Campsites, facilities: There are 15 sites for tents, trailers, or RVs up to 22 feet long. Picnic tables, well water, and fire grills are provided. Pit toilets are available. A store, a cafe, and ice are located within five miles. Some facilities are wheelchair accessible. Leashed pets are permitted.

Reservations, fees: No reservations are accepted. Sites are $9–$11 per night. The campground is open from May to late September.

Contact: Mount Hood National Forest, Zigzag Ranger District, 65000 East Highway 26, Welches, OR 97067; (503) 622-7674 or fax (503) 622-5622.

Directions: From Portland, drive 39 miles east on U.S. 26 to Forest Service Road 2618 (just north of Zigzag). Turn right and drive 4.5 miles south to the campground.

Trip notes: Few out-of-towners know about this winner. But the locals do, and they keep the place hopping in the summer. The camp is located along the banks of the Salmon River.

A long trail cuts through the site and parallels the river, passing through a magnificent old-growth forest. See a Forest Service map for details.

㉒ Toll Gate

Location: On the Zigzag River in Mount Hood National Forest; map C2, grid e7.

Campsites, facilities: There are 15 tent sites and nine sites for trailers or RVs up to 16 feet long. Picnic tables and fire grills are provided. Piped water and pit toilets are available. Leashed pets are permitted.

Reservations, fees: Reserve some sites by calling (800) 280-CAMP/2267 ($8.65 reservation fee). Sites are $9–$11 per night. The campground is open from late May to late September.

Contact: Mount Hood National Forest, Zigzag Ranger District, 65000 East Highway 26, Welches, OR 97067; (503) 622-7674 or fax (503) 622-5622.

Directions: From Portland, turn east on U.S. 26 and drive 40 miles to Zigzag. Continue 2.5 miles southeast on U.S. 26 to the campground entrance.

Trip notes: This campground along the banks of the Zigzag River near Rhododendron is extremely popular, and finding a site on a summer weekend can be next to impossible. Luckily, you can get a reservation. There are numerous hiking trails in the area. The nearest one to this campground leads east for several miles along the river.

㉓ Camp Creek

Location: Near the Zigzag River in Mount Hood National Forest; map C2, grid e8.

Campsites, facilities: There are 24 sites for tents, trailers, or RVs up to 22 feet long. Piped water, fire grills, and picnic tables are provided. Vault toilets are available. Leashed pets are permitted.

Reservations, fees: Reserve some sites by calling (800) 280-CAMP/2267 ($8.65 reservation fee). Sites are $9–$18 per night. The campground is open from late May to late September.

Contact: Mount Hood National Forest, Zigzag Ranger District, 65000 East Highway 26, Welches, OR 97067; (503) 622-7674 or fax (503) 622-5622.

Directions: From Portland, turn east on U.S. 26 and drive 40 miles to Zigzag. Continue southeast on U.S. 26 for about four miles to camp.

Trip notes: This campground is set along Camp Creek, not far from the Zigzag River. A hiking trail runs through camp and along the river, and another leads south to Still Creek. This campground, along with Toll Gate to the west (campground number 22), is very popular and you'll probably need a reservation.

㉔ Alpine

Location: Near the Pacific Crest Trail in Mount Hood National Forest; map C2, grid e8.

Campsites, facilities: There are 16 tent sites. Piped water, fire grills, vault toilets, and picnic tables are provided. Leashed pets are permitted.

Reservations, fees: No reservations are accepted. Sites are $7 per night. The campground is open from July to late September.

Contact: Mount Hood National Forest, Zigzag Ranger District, 65000 East Highway 26, Welches, OR 97067; (503) 622-7674 or fax (503) 622-5622.

Directions: From Portland, turn east on U.S. 26 and drive 55 miles to the small town of Government Camp. Continue east a short distance to Timberline Lodge Road (Forest Service Road 173), turn north, and proceed 4.5 miles to the campground.

Trip notes: This small campground is one mile from the Timberline Ski Area lodge on the south slopes of Mount Hood. It can get quite crowded here on weekends. The camp is managed by the same folks who run the lifts in winter. The Pacific Crest Trail can be accessed from the Timberline Lodge. Be sure to come prepared for very cold nights.

㉕ Still Creek

Location: On Still Creek in Mount Hood National Forest; map C2, grid e8.

Campsites, facilities: There are 27 sites for tents, trailers, or RVs up to 27 feet long. Picnic tables and fire grills are provided. Pit toilets and piped water are available. Leashed pets are permitted.

Reservations, fees: Reserve some sites by calling (800) 280-CAMP/2267 ($8.65 reservation fee). Sites are $9 per night. The campground is open from mid-June to late September.

Contact: Mount Hood National Forest, Zigzag Ranger District, 65000 East Highway 26, Welches, OR 97067; (503) 622-7674 or fax (503) 622-5622.

Directions: From Portland, drive 55 miles east on U.S. 26 to Government Camp. Continue one mile east on U.S. 26, then 500 yards south on Forest Service Road 2650.

Trip notes: This primitive camp near the junction of U.S. 26 and Highway 35 is located along Still Creek where it pours off the south slope of Mount Hood. Anglers should bring along their poles: the fishing in Still Creek can be excellent.

㉖ Grindstone

Location: Near Barlow Creek in Mount Hood National Forest; map C2, grid e9.

Campsites, facilities: There are two primitive sites for tents. Picnic tables and fire grills are provided. Vault toilets are available, but there is no piped water. Leashed pets are permitted.

Reservations, fees: No reservations are accepted. There is no fee. The campground is open from May to October.

Contact: Mount Hood National Forest, Hood River Ranger District, 6780 Highway 35, Mount Hood, OR 97041; (541) 352-6002 or fax (541) 352-7365.

Directions: From Portland, turn east on U.S. 26 and drive 55 miles to the town of Government Camp. Continue two miles east on U.S. 26, then 4.5 miles east on High-

way 35. From there, turn right and travel two miles southeast on Forest Service Road 3530 to the campground on the right.

Trip notes: This tiny campground along Barlow Creek, on Old Barlow Road, is a little-known and little-used spot. You won't find much out here but wind, water, and trees—but sometimes that's all you need.

㉗ Devil's Half Acre Meadow

Location: On Barlow Creek in Mount Hood National Forest; map C2, grid e9.

Campsites, facilities: There are five sites for tents, trailers, or RVs up to 16 feet long. Picnic tables and fire grills are provided. Firewood and pit toilets are available. There is no piped water. Leashed pets are permitted.

Reservations, fees: No reservations are accepted. There is no fee. The campground is open from May to October.

Contact: Mount Hood National Forest, Hood River Ranger District, 6780 Highway 35, Mount Hood, OR 97041; (541) 352-6002 or fax (541) 352-7365.

Directions: From Portland, turn east on U.S. 26 and drive 55 miles to the small town of Government Camp. Continue two miles east on U.S. 26, then drive 4.5 miles east on Highway 35. From there, go one mile southeast on Forest Service Road 3530.

Trip notes: This campground is a few miles upstream on Barlow Creek from Grindstone (campground number 26). Several hiking trails close to camp—including the Pacific Crest Trail—provide access to small lakes in the area. There are many historic points of interest in the vicinity.

㉘ Robinhood

Location: On the East Fork of the Hood River in Mount Hood National Forest; map C2, grid e9.

Campsites, facilities: There are 24 sites for tents or trailers up to 18 feet long. Piped water and picnic tables are provided. Leashed pets are permitted.

Reservations, fees: No reservations are accepted. Sites are $10 per night. The campground is open from mid-May to early September.

Contact: Mount Hood National Forest, Hood River Ranger District, 6780 Highway 35, Mount Hood, OR 97041; (541) 352-6002 or fax (541) 352-7365.

Directions: From Portland, turn east on Interstate 84 and drive 65 miles to the town of Hood River. Turn south on Highway 35 (exit 64) and drive 28 miles to the campground on the right.

Trip notes: This campground along the East Fork of the Hood River, at the base of Mount Hood, marks the start of a trail that follows the river north for about four miles, then joins a network of trails that provide access to the Mount Hood Wilderness. Fishing is another option here.

㉙ Metzler Park

Location: On Clear Creek; map C2, grid f4.

Campsites, facilities: There are 70 sites for tents, trailers, and RVs. Rest rooms, showers, a sanitary dump, a public phone, a playground, and a recreation field are available. Leashed pets are permitted.

Reservations, fees: Reservations are recommended; call (503) 655-8521. Sites are $10–$14 per night. The campground is open from May through September.

Contact: Metzler Park; (503) 630-4743. Clackamas County Parks Department, 902 Abernethy Road, Oregon City, OR 97045; (503) 655-8521 or fax (503) 650-3702.

Directions: From Portland, drive south on Interstate 205 for about 20 miles to the Clackamas/Estacada exit (Highway 212). Drive on Highway 212 to the Carver Road exit. Turn right and cross the bridge over the Clackamas River. Turn left on Springwater Road to the town of Springwater. Just outside of town, turn right on Metzler Park Road and drive three-quarters of a mile to the campground.

Trip notes: This county campground on a small stream not far from the Clackamas River is a hot spot for fishing, swimming, and pic-

nicking. Be sure to make your reservation early at this very popular park.

㉚ Feyrer Memorial Park

Location: On the Molalla River; map C2, grid f4.

Campsites, facilities: There are 60 sites for trailers and RVs. Rest rooms, showers, a sanitary dump, and a public phone are provided. There is also a playground and recreation field. Some facilities are wheelchair accessible. Leashed pets are permitted.

Reservations, fees: Reservations are recommended; call (503) 655-8521. Sites are $10–$14 per night. The campground is open from May through September.

Contact: Feyrer Memorial Park, (503) 829-6621. Clackamas County Parks Department, 902 Abernethy Road, Oregon City, OR 97045; (503) 655-8521 or fax (503) 650-3702.

Directions: From Interstate 5 at Salem, drive north on Highway 213 for about 30 miles to Molalla. From Molalla, drive east on Highway 211 for three miles to the campground on the right.

Trip notes: Located on the scenic Molalla River, this county park offers swimming and excellent salmon fishing. This is a superb option for weary Interstate 5 cruisers; the park is only 30 minutes off the highway and provides a peaceful, serene environment.

㉛ Promontory

Location: On North Fork Reservoir; map C2, grid f5.

Campsites, facilities: There are 58 sites for tents, trailers, or RVs up to 35 feet long. There are no RV hookups. Rest rooms, showers, limited groceries, ice, and snacks are provided. A playground, horseshoes, a boat ramp, a dock, and boat rentals are available. Leashed pets are permitted.

Reservations, fees: Reservations are recommended; phone (503) 630-7229. Sites are $14 per night. The campground is open from May 15 to November 1.

Contact: Phone the park at (503) 630-5152, or write to 40600 Southeast Highway 224, Estacada, OR 97023.

Directions: From Portland, drive south on Interstate 205 for about 20 miles to the Clackamas/Estacada exit (Highway 212). Travel on Highway 212 to Highway 224 and take the Carver/Estacada exit. From the town of Estacada, travel southeast for seven miles on Highway 224 to the campground on the right. There are prominent signs along the road indicating the directions to the camp.

Trip notes: This PG&E camp on North Fork Reservoir is part of a large recreation area and park. The water is calm and ideal for boating, and the trout fishing is excellent. This reservoir is actually a dammed-up overflow on the Clackamas River.

32 Lazy Bend

Location: On the Clackamas River in Mount Hood National Forest; map C2, grid f5.

Campsites, facilities: There are 21 sites for tents, trailers, or RVs up to 16 feet long. Picnic tables and fireplaces are provided. Piped water and flush toilets are available. Leashed pets are permitted.

Reservations, fees: Reserve some sites by calling (800) 280-CAMP/2267 ($8.65 reservation fee). Sites are $8 per night. The campground is open from late April through Labor Day.

Contact: Mount Hood National Forest, Estacada Ranger District, 595 NW Industrial Way, Estacada, OR 97023; (503) 630-6861 or fax (503) 630-2299.

Directions: From Interstate 5 south of Portland, take exit 288 and drive 12 miles east on Interstate 205 to Gladstone. Turn east on Highway 224 and drive 15 miles to Estacada. Continue 10.5 miles southeast on Highway 224 to the campground.

Trip notes: This campground is set along the banks of the Clackamas River, near the large North Fork Reservoir. It's far enough off the highway to provide a secluded, primitive feeling, though it gets its fair share of use on the weekends.

33 Fish Creek

Location: On the Clackamas River in Mount Hood National Forest; map C2, grid f5.

Campsites, facilities: There are 24 sites for tents, trailers, or RVs up to 16 feet long. Picnic tables and fire grills are provided. Vault toilets and hand-pumped water are available. Leashed pets are permitted.

Reservations, fees: Reserve some sites by calling (800) 280-CAMP/2267 ($8.65 reservation fee). Sites are $8 per night. The campground is open from late May to early September.

Contact: Mount Hood National Forest, Estacada Ranger District, 595 NW Industrial Way, Estacada, OR 97023; (503) 630-6861 or fax (503) 630-2299.

Directions: From Interstate 5 south of Portland, take exit 288 and drive 12 miles east on Interstate 205 to Gladstone. Turn east on Highway 224 and drive 15 miles to Estacada. Continue 15.5 miles southeast on Highway 224 to the campground.

Trip notes: This campground is located along the banks of the Clackamas River, not far from the Clackamas River Trail and North Fork Reservoir. Fishing is good in the Clackamas.

34 Armstrong

Location: On the Clackamas River in Mount Hood National Forest; map C2, grid f5.

Campsites, facilities: There are 12 sites for tents, trailers, or RVs up to 16 feet long. Picnic tables and fire rings are provided. Vault toilets and hand-pumped water are available. Some facilities are wheelchair accessible. Leashed pets are permitted.

Reservations, fees: Reserve some sites by calling (800) 280-CAMP/2267 ($8.65 reservation fee). Sites are $8 per night. The campground is open from late May to early September.

Contact: Mount Hood National Forest, Estacada Ranger District, 595 NW Industrial Way, Estacada, OR 97023; (503) 630-6861 or fax (503) 630-2299.

Directions: From Interstate 5 south of Port-

land, take exit 288 and drive 12 miles east on Interstate 205 Gladstone. Turn east on Highway 224 and drive 15 miles to Estacada. Continue 15 miles southeast on Highway 224 to the campground.

Trip notes: This campground is set along the banks of the Clackamas River and offers good fishing access. See Fish Creek (campground number 33) for more details on the area.

⑮ Lockaby

Location: On the Clackamas River in Mount Hood National Forest; map C2, grid f6.

Campsites, facilities: There are 30 sites for tents, trailers, or RVs up to 16 feet long. Picnic tables, fireplaces, hand-pumped water, and vault toilets are available. Leashed pets are permitted.

Reservations, fees: Reserve some sites by calling (800) 280-CAMP/2267 ($8.65 reservation fee). Sites are $9 per night. The campground is open from late May to early September.

Contact: Mount Hood National Forest, Estacada Ranger District, 595 NW Industrial Way, Estacada, OR 97023; (503) 630-6861 or fax (503) 630-2299.

Directions: From Interstate 5 south of Portland, take exit 288 and drive 12 miles east on Interstate 205 to Gladstone. Turn east on Highway 224 and drive 15 miles to Estacada. Continue 15 more miles southeast on Highway 224 to the campground.

Trip notes: This campground along the banks of the Clackamas River, next to Fish Creek and Armstrong (campground numbers 33 and 34), gets heavy use from anglers. Try to arrive early to ensure a choice spot.

⑯ Roaring River

Location: On the Roaring River in Mount Hood National Forest; map C2, grid f6.

Campsites, facilities: There are 19 sites for tents, trailers, or RVs up to 16 feet long. Picnic tables, fireplaces, hand-pumped water, and vault toilets are available. Leashed pets are permitted.

Reservations, fees: Reserve some sites by calling (800) 280-CAMP/2267 ($8.65 reservation fee). Sites are $9 per night. The campground is open from mid-May to mid-September.

Contact: Mount Hood National Forest, Estacada Ranger District, 595 NW Industrial Way, Estacada, OR 97023; (503) 630-6861 or fax (503) 630-2299.

Directions: From Interstate 5 south of Portland, take exit 288 and drive 12 miles east on Interstate 205 to Gladstone. Turn east on Highway 224 and drive 15 miles to Estacada. Continue 18 miles south on Highway 224 to the campground.

Trip notes: This campground at the confluence of the Roaring and Clackamas Rivers has to the Dry Ridge Trail and several other trails into the adjacent roadless area. See a Forest Service map for details.

⑰ Sunstrip

Location: On the Clackamas River in Mount Hood National Forest; map C2, grid f6.

Campsites, facilities: There are nine sites for tents, trailers, or RVs up to 15 feet long. Picnic tables, fireplaces, hand-pumped water, and vault toilets are available. Leashed pets are permitted.

Reservations, fees: Reserve some sites by calling (800) 280-CAMP/2267 ($8.65 reservation fee). Sites are $9 per night. The campground is open from late May to early September.

Contact: Mount Hood National Forest, Estacada Ranger District, 595 NW Industrial Way, Estacada, OR 97023; (503) 630-6861 or fax (503) 630-2299.

Directions: From Interstate 5 south of Portland, take exit 288 and drive 12 miles east on Interstate 205 for 12 miles to Gladstone. Turn east on Highway 224 and drive 15 miles to Estacada. Continue southeast about 19 miles on Highway 224 to the campground.

Trip notes: This campground on the banks of the Clackamas River offers fishing and rafting access. One of several camps along the Highway 224 corridor, Sunstrip is a favorite with rafting enthusiasts and can fill up quickly on weekends.

㉘ Alder Flat

Location: On the Clackamas River in Mount Hood National Forest; map C2, grid f6.

Campsites, facilities: There are six tent sites at this hike-in campground. Picnic tables and fire grills are provided. Vault toilets are available. There is no piped water. Leashed pets are permitted.

Reservations, fees: No reservations are accepted. There is no fee. The campground is open from late April to late September.

Contact: Mount Hood National Forest, Clackamas Ranger District, 61431 East Highway 224, Estacada, OR 97023; (503) 630-4256.

Directions: From Interstate 5 south of Portland, take exit 288 and drive 12 miles east on Interstate 205 to Gladstone. Turn east on Highway 224 and drive 15 miles to Estacada. Continue southeast for 26 miles to the Ripplebrook Ranger Station. Parking for the camp is about one-half mile west of the ranger station. Hike one mile to the campground.

Trip notes: This secluded hike-in campground is set along the banks of the Clackamas River. If you want peace and quiet and don't mind the short walk to get it, this is the spot. Be sure to pack out whatever you bring in.

㉙ Hideaway Lake

Location: Near the Rock Lakes Basin in Mount Hood National Forest; map C2, grid f7.

Campsites, facilities: There are nine sites for tents, small trailers, or camper vans. Picnic tables and fire grills are provided. Pit toilets are available. There is no piped water. Leashed pets are permitted.

Reservations, fees: No reservations are accepted. There is no fee. The campground is open from mid-June to late September.

Contact: Mount Hood National Forest, Estacada Ranger District, 595 NW Industrial Way, Estacada, OR 97023; (503) 630-6861 or fax (503) 630-2299.

Directions: From Interstate 5 south of Port-

land, take exit 288 and drive 12 miles east on Interstate 205 to Gladstone. Turn east on Highway 224 and drive 15 miles to Estacada. Continue southeast on Highway 224 for 27 miles, then go 7.5 miles east on Forest Service Road 57. From there, take Forest Service Road 58 and travel three miles north to Forest Service Road 5830. Turn northwest and drive 5.5 miles to the campground.

Trip notes: This is a jewel of a spot—a small, deep lake at an elevation of 3,800 feet. The campsites are separate and scattered around the water. At the north end of the lake, an 8.5-mile loop trail goes past a number of lakes in the Rock Lakes Basin, all of which support populations of rainbow and brook trout. If you don't want to make the whole trip in a day, you can camp overnight at Serene Lake. See a Forest Service map for information.

㊵ High Rock Springs

Location: Near the Rock Lakes Basin in Mount Hood National Forest; map C2, grid f7.

Campsites, facilities: There are seven tent sites. Picnic tables and fire grills are provided. Pit toilets are available. There is no piped water. Leashed pets are permitted.

Reservations, fees: No reservations are accepted. There is no fee. The campground is open from mid-June to late September.

Contact: Mount Hood National Forest, Estacada Ranger District, 595 NW Industrial Way, Estacada, OR 97023; (503) 630-6861 or fax (503) 630-2299.

Directions: From Interstate 5 south of Portland, take exit 288 and drive 12 miles east on Interstate 205 to Gladstone. Turn east on Highway 224 and drive 15 miles to Estacada. Continue southeast on Highway 224 for approximately 27 miles, then drive 7.5 miles east on Forest Service Road 57. Turn northeast on Forest Service Road 58 and travel 10.5 miles to the campground.

Trip notes: This small, remote campground is adjacent to High Rock Mountain. A half-mile climb earns a tremendous view of the surrounding area, including Mount Hood. About four miles east of the camp are trails that lead to some of the fishing lakes in the Rock Lakes Basin. In August and September, ripe huckleberries are yours for the picking.

㊶ Indian Henry

Location: On the Clackamas River in Mount Hood National Forest; map C2, grid f7.

Campsites, facilities: There are 86 sites for tents, trailers, or RVs up to 22 feet long. Picnic tables and fire grills are provided. Flush toilets, a sanitary dump station, and piped water are available. Some facilities are wheelchair accessible. Leashed pets are permitted.

Reservations, fees: Reserve some sites by calling (800) 280-CAMP/2267 ($8.65 reservation fee). Sites are $10 per night. The campground is open from late May to early September.

Contact: Mount Hood National Forest, Estacada Ranger District, 595 NW Industrial Way, Estacada, OR 97023; (503) 630-6861 or fax (503) 630-2299.

Directions: From Interstate 5 south of Portland, take exit 288 and drive 12 miles east on Interstate 205 to Gladstone. Turn east on Highway 224 and drive 15 miles to Estacada. Continue southeast on Highway 224 for 23 miles, then drive one-half mile southeast on Forest Service Road 4620.

Trip notes: One of the most popular campgrounds in the Estacada Ranger District, Indian Henry is located along the banks of the Clackamas River and has a wheelchair-accessible trail. Group campsites and an amphitheater are available. The nearby Clackamas River Trail has fishing access.

㊷ Lake Harriet

Location: In Mount Hood National Forest; map C2, grid f7.

Campsites, facilities: There are 13 sites for tents, trailers, or RVs up to 20 feet long. Picnic tables and fire grills are provided. Piped water and vault toilets are available. Some facilities are wheelchair accessible. Boat docks and

launching facilities are located on the lake. No horses are allowed in the campground. Leashed pets are permitted.

Reservations, fees: Reserve some sites by calling (800) 280-CAMP/2267 ($8.65 reservation fee). Sites are $9 per night. The campground is open from late April to late September.

Contact: Mount Hood National Forest, Estacada Ranger District, 595 NW Industrial Way, Estacada, OR 97023; (503) 630-6861 or fax (503) 630-2299.

Directions: From Portland, turn east on U.S. 26 and drive 55 miles to the small town of Government Camp. Continue 15 miles southeast on U.S. 26, then eight miles south on Forest Service Road 42. Turn west on Forest Service Road 57 and drive 16 miles to Forest Service Road 4630, then proceed two miles to the campground.

Trip notes: Formed by a dam on the Oak Grove Fork of the Clackamas River, this little lake is a popular spot during the summer. Rowboats and boats with small motors are permitted. The lake can provide good fishing for a variety of trout, including brown, brook, rainbow, and cutthroat.

㊸ Ripplebrook

Location: On the Oak Grove Fork of the Clackamas River in Mount Hood National Forest; map C2, grid f6.

Campsites, facilities: There are 13 sites for trailers or RVs up to 16 feet long. Picnic tables and fire grills are provided. Vault toilets are available, but there is no piped water. Leashed pets are permitted; horses are not allowed in the campground.

Reservations, fees: Reserve some sites by calling (800) 280-CAMP/2267 ($8.65 reservation fee). Sites are $9 per night. The campground is open from late April to late September.

Contact: Mount Hood National Forest, Estacada Ranger District, 595 NW Industrial Way, Estacada, OR 97023; (503) 630-6861 or fax (503) 630-2299.

Directions: From Interstate 5 south of Port-

land, take exit 288 and drive 12 miles east on Interstate 205 to Gladstone. Turn east on Highway 224 and drive 15 miles to Estacada. Continue 26.5 miles southeast on Highway 224 to the campground entrance.

Trip notes: Shaded sites with river views are a highlight at this campground along the banks of the Oak Grove Fork of the Clackamas River. This is one of the more popular camps in the area.

44 Trillium Lake

Location: On Trillium Lake in Mount Hood National Forest; map C2, grid f8.

Campsites, facilities: There are 55 sites for tents, trailers, or RVs up to 40 feet long. Picnic tables and fire grills are provided. Pit toilets and piped water are available. All sites are wheelchair accessible. Boat docks and launching facilities are available on the lake, but no motors are permitted. Leashed pets are permitted.

Reservations, fees: Reserve some sites by calling (800) 280-CAMP/2267 ($8.65 reservation fee). Sites are $10–$12 per night; multifamily sites are $20 per night. The campground is open from late May to late September.

Contact: Mount Hood National Forest, Zigzag Ranger District, 65000 East Highway 26, Welches, OR 97067; (503) 622-7674 or fax (503) 622-5622.

Directions: From Portland, turn east on U.S. 26 and drive 55 miles to the small town of Government Camp. Continue two miles southeast on U.S. 26, then drive south on Forest Service Road 2656 for 1.3 miles to the campground.

Trip notes: This campground is set along the shores of Trillium Lake, which is about one-half mile long and one-quarter mile wide. Fishing is good in the evening here, and the nearby boat ramp makes this an ideal camp for anglers. The lake is great for canoes, rafts, and small rowboats. Trillium Lake is an extremely popular vacation destination, so expect plenty of company. Reservations are highly recommended.

45 Meditation Point

Location: On Timothy Lake in Mount Hood National Forest; map C2, grid f8.

Campsites, facilities: There are four boat-in or walk-in tent sites. Picnic tables and fire grills are provided. Pit toilets are available. There is no piped water. Boat docks and launching facilities are nearby. Leashed pets are permitted.

Reservations, fees: No reservations are accepted. There is no fee. The campground is open from late May to mid-September.

Contact: Mount Hood National Forest, Zigzag Ranger District, 65000 East Highway 26, Welches, OR 97067; (503) 622-7674 or fax (503) 622-5622.

Directions: From Portland, turn east on U.S. 26 and drive 55 miles to the small town of Government Camp. Continue southeast on U.S. 26 for 15 miles, then drive eight miles south on Forest Service Road 42. Park at Pine Point Campground, located five miles west on Forest Service Road 57, and hike one mile or take a boat to the north shore of the lake.

Trip notes: Accessible only by foot or boat, this camp offers a more secluded location along Timothy Lake than Gone Creek, Hoodview, Oak Fork, and Pine Point. It's the only campground on the north shore of the lake, which means you'll get a quieter, less crowded environment, though you'll have to bring your own water. See the trip notes for Hoodview and Gone Creek (campground numbers 75 and 77) for details about the lake.

46 Barlow Creek

Location: On Barlow Creek in Mount Hood National Forest; map C2, grid f9.

Campsites, facilities: There are five sites for tents. Picnic tables and fire grills are provided. Vault toilets are available, but there is no piped water. Leashed pets are permitted.

Reservations, fees: No reservations are accepted. There is no fee. The campground is open from May through September.

Contact: Mount Hood National Forest, Hood

River Ranger District, 6780 Highway 35, Mount Hood, OR 97041; (541) 352-6002 or fax (541) 352-7365.

Directions: From Portland, turn east on U.S. 26 and drive 55 miles to the town of Government Camp. Drive another 12 miles east on U.S. 26. Turn north (left) on Forest Service Road 43 and drive five miles. Turn north (left) on Highway 35/30 and drive 1.5 miles to the campground on the right.

Trip notes: This campground is set along Barlow Creek on Old Barlow Road, which was the wagon trail for early settlers in this area. It is one of several primitive Forest Service camps in the immediate vicinity. There may not be much to do in these parts, but you sure can't beat the price.

㊼ Barlow Crossing

Location: On Barlow Creek in Mount Hood National Forest; map C2, grid f9.

Campsites, facilities: There are five sites for tents. Picnic tables and fire grills are provided. Pit toilets are available. There is no piped water. Leashed pets are permitted.

Reservations, fees: No reservations are accepted. There is no fee. The campground is open from mid-May through September.

Contact: Mount Hood National Forest, Hood River Ranger District, 6780 Highway 35, Mount Hood, OR 97041; (541) 352-6002 or fax (541) 352-7365.

Directions: From Portland, turn east on U.S. 26 and drive 55 miles to the town of Government Camp. Drive another 12 miles east on U.S. 26. Turn north (left) on Forest Service Road 43 and drive five miles. Turn north (left) on Highway 35/30 and drive one-half mile to the campground on the right.

Trip notes: This small roadside campground is set where Barlow Creek meets the White River. It's quiet, remote, little used, and an excellent fishing spot.

㊽ Frog Lake

Location: Near the Pacific Crest Trail in Mount Hood National Forest; map C2, grid f9.

Campsites, facilities: There are 33 sites for tents, trailers, or RVs up to 22 feet long. Hand-pumped water and picnic tables are provided. Vault toilets and firewood are available. Boat launching facilities are nearby. No motorized boats are allowed. Leashed pets are permitted.

Reservations, fees: Some sites may be reserved by calling (800) 280-CAMP/2267 ($8.65 reservation fee). Sites are $10–$12 per night, plus $5 for each additional vehicle. The campground is open from mid-June to mid-September.

Contact: Mount Hood National Forest, Hood River Ranger District, 6780 Highway 35, Mount Hood, OR 97041; (541) 352-6002 or fax (541) 352-7365.

Directions: From Portland, turn east on U.S. 26 and drive 55 miles to the town of Government Camp. Continue seven miles southeast on U.S. 26, then one mile southeast on Forest Service Road 2610. The camp is about 500 yards south on Forest Service Road 230.

Trip notes: This classic spot in the Cascade Range is on the shore of little Frog Lake, a short distance from the Pacific Crest Trail. Several other trails lead to nearby lakes. A possible day trip is Clear Lake to the south, which offers more recreation options.

㊾ White River Station

Location: On the White River in Mount Hood National Forest; map C2, grid f9.

Campsites, facilities: There are five sites for tents and RVs up to 16 feet long. Picnic tables and fire grills are provided. Vault toilets are available, but there is no piped water. Leashed pets are permitted.

Reservations, fees: No reservations are accepted. There is no fee. The campground is open from May through September.

Contact: Mount Hood National Forest, Barlow Ranger District, Bear Springs Work Center, 73558 Highway 216, Maupin, OR 97037; (541) 328-6211.

Directions: From Portland, turn east on U.S. 26 and drive 55 miles to the town of

Government Camp. Continue two miles east on U.S. 26, then drive two miles east on Highway 35. Turn south on Forest Service Road 48 and travel nine miles southeast, then turn east and drive one mile to Forest Service Road 3530. Turn south and drive one mile to the campground on the left.

Trip notes: This tiny campground is set along the White River on Old Barlow Road, an original wagon trail used by early settlers. One of several small, secluded camps in the area, White River Station is quiet and private, with good fishing prospects.

⑤⓪ Clear Lake

Location: Near the Pacific Crest Trail in Mount Hood National Forest; map C2, grid f9.

Campsites, facilities: There are 28 sites for tents, trailers, or RVs up to 32 feet long. Picnic tables, fire grills, hand-pumped water, firewood, and vault toilets are available. Boat launching facilities are nearby. Motorboats are allowed; the speed limit is 10 mph. Leashed pets are permitted.

Reservations, fees: Some sites may be reserved by calling (800) 280-CAMP/2267 ($8.65 reservation fee). Sites are $10–$12 per night, plus $5 for each additional vehicle. The campground is open from late May to early September.

Contact: Mount Hood National Forest, Hood River Ranger District, 6780 Highway 35, Mount Hood, OR 97041; (541) 352-6002 or fax (541) 352-7365.

Directions: From Portland, turn east on U.S. 26 and drive 55 miles to the town of Government Camp. Continue nine miles southeast on U.S. 26, then drive one mile south on Forest Service Road 2630 to the campground on the right.

Trip notes: This campground is along the shore of Clear Lake, a spot favored by anglers, swimmers, and windsurfers. The camp is wooded, with shady sites. A nearby trail heads north from the lake and provides access to the Pacific Crest Trail and Frog Lake, both good recreation options.

⑤① Little Crater

Location: On Little Crater Lake in Mount Hood National Forest; map C2, grid f9.

Campsites, facilities: There are 16 sites for tents, trailers, or RVs up to 22 feet long. Picnic tables and fire grills are provided. Vault toilets, firewood, and hand-pumped water are available. Leashed pets are permitted.

Reservations, fees: Some sites may be reserved by calling (800) 280-CAMP/2267 ($8.65 reservation fee). Sites are $9 per night, plus $5 for each additional vehicle. The campground is open from June to mid-September.

Contact: Mount Hood National Forest, Zigzag Ranger District, 65000 East Highway 26, Welches, OR 97067; (503) 622-7674 or fax (503) 622-5622.

Directions: From Portland, turn east on U.S. 26 and drive 55 miles to the town of Government Camp. Continue 15 miles southeast on U.S. 26, then drive six miles south on Forest Service Road 42. From there, proceed 2.5 miles northwest on Forest Service Road 58 to the campground.

Trip notes: This camp next to Crater Creek and scenic Little Crater Lake offers options for hikers and anglers alike—it's adjacent to the Pacific Crest Trail and about a mile from Timothy Lake. See the trip notes for Gone Creek (campground number 77) for more information about Timothy Lake.

⑤② Trailer Park Village

Location: Near the Willamette River; map C2, grid g0.

Campsites, facilities: There are 38 sites for trailers or RVs of any length. Electricity, piped water, and sewer hookups are provided. Flush toilets, showers, and a laundry room are available. Bottled gas, a store, a cafe, and ice are located within one mile. Pets are not permitted.

Reservations, fees: Reservations are accepted. Sites are $18 per night. The campground is open year-round.

Contact: Phone (503) 393-7424 or write to 4733 Portland Road NE, Salem, OR 97305.

Directions: From Interstate 5 at Salem, take Highway 99E about one-half mile east to the park.

Trip notes: This park is in the city of Salem, Oregon's capital. Several museums and parks are located in town, and the Willamette River flows nearby. Other recreation options include an 18-hole golf course, marked bike trails, and a full-service marina.

🚳 Salem Campground and RVs

Location: In Salem; map C2, grid g1.

Campsites, facilities: There are 30 tent sites and 190 sites with full hookups for trailers or RVs of any length, most of which are drive-throughs. Picnic tables are provided. Flush toilets, bottled gas, sanitary services, showers, a recreation hall, a store, a laundry room, ice, a playground, electricity, piped water, and sewer hookups are available. A cafe is located within one mile. Leashed pets and motorbikes are permitted.

Reservations, fees: Reservations are accepted. Sites are $13–$19 per night. The campground is open year-round.

Contact: Phone (800) 826-9605 or (503) 581-6736, fax (888) 827-9605, or write to 3700 Hagers Grove Road SE, Salem, OR 97301.

Directions: From Salem on Interstate 5, take exit 253. Drive east on Highway 22 about one-quarter mile. Turn right on Lancaster Drive, then right again on Hagers Grove Road and proceed to the park.

Trip notes: This park with shaded sites is just off Interstate 5 in Salem. A picnic area and a lake for swimming are within walking distance, and a nine-hole golf course, hiking trails, a riding stable, and tennis courts are nearby.

🚳 Silver Falls State Park

Location: Near Salem; map C2, grid g3.

Campsites, facilities: There are 50 tent sites and 54 sites with water and electrical hookups for trailers or RVs up to 60 feet long. Picnic tables and fire grills are provided. Flush toilets, sanitary services, showers, firewood, and a playground are available. Some facilities are wheelchair accessible. Leashed pets are permitted.

Reservations, fees: Reservations are accepted. Sites are $16–$18 per night. The campground is open from mid-April to late October.

Contact: Phone (503) 873-8681 or (800) 452-5687, or write to 20024 Silver Falls Highway SE, Sublimity, OR 97385.

Directions: From Interstate 5 at Salem, drive five miles east on Highway 22,, then turn east on Highway 214 and drive 15 miles to the park.

Trip notes: This is Oregon's largest state park, covering more than 8,000 acres. Numerous trails crisscross the area, including a seven-mile jaunt that meanders past 10 waterfalls over 100 feet high in the moist forest of Silver Creek Canyon. A horse camp and a 14-mile equestrian trail are available in the park. Fitness-conscious campers can check out the three-mile jogging trail or the four-mile bike trail. There is also a rustic nature lodge and group lodging facilities.

🚳 Shady Cove

Location: On the North Santiam River in Willamette National Forest; map C2, grid g4.

Campsites, facilities: There are 12 tent sites. Picnic tables, fire grills, and vault toilets are available. There is no piped water. Leashed pets are permitted.

Reservations, fees: No reservations are accepted. Sites are $5–$10 per night. The campground is open from mid-May to late September.

Contact: Willamette National Forest, Detroit Ranger District, HC 73, P.O. Box 320, Mill City, OR 97360; (503) 854-3366 or fax (503) 854-3520.

Directions: From Interstate 5 at Salem, take exit 253 and turn east on Highway 22. Drive

23 miles to Mehama, then turn left on Little North Santiam Road and drive 19 miles northeast to the campground.

Trip notes: This campground is on the Little North Santiam River in the midst of a heavily mined area. Some quality hiking trails are located off Forest Service roads to the south and east.

56 Elkhorn Valley

Location: On the Little North Santiam River; map C2, grid g5.

Campsites, facilities: There are 23 sites for tents, trailers, or RVs up to 18 feet long. Picnic tables, fire grills, vault toilets, and piped water are available. Leashed pets are permitted.

Reservations, fees: No reservations are accepted. Sites are $8 per night, with a 14-day limit. The campground is open from mid-May to late September.

Contact: Bureau of Land Management, 1717 Fabry Road SE, Salem, OR 97306; (503) 375-5646.

Directions: From Interstate 5 at Salem, take exit 253 and turn east on Highway 22. Drive 25 miles east, then turn northeast on North Fork Road and drive nine miles to the campground.

Trip notes: This pretty campground along the Little North Santiam River, not far from the North Fork of the Santiam River, has easy access and is only a short drive away from a major metropolitan area. This is an alternative to Shady Cove (campground number 55), which is located about 10 miles to the east.

57 Riverside

Location: On the Clackamas River in Mount Hood National Forest; map C2, grid g6.

Campsites, facilities: There are 16 sites for tents, trailers, or RVs up to 22 feet long. Picnic tables and fire grills are provided. Vault toilets and piped water are available. Leashed pets are permitted; no horses are allowed in the campground.

Reservations, fees: Some sites may be reserved by calling (800) 280-CAMP/2267 ($8.65

reservation fee). Sites are $9 per night. The campground is open from mid-May to late September.

Contact: Mount Hood National Forest, Estacada Ranger District, 595 NW Industrial Way, Estacada, OR 97023; (503) 630-6861 or fax (503) 630-2299.

Directions: From Interstate 5 south of Portland, take exit 288 and drive 12 miles east on Interstate 205 to Gladstone. Turn east on Highway 224 and drive 15 miles to Estacada. Continue southeast on Highway 224 for 27 miles, then drive 2.5 miles south on Forest Service Road 46 to the campground.

Trip notes: The banks of the Clackamas River are home to this campground. A trail worth hiking leaves the camp and follows the river for four miles north. Fishing is another option here, and several old Forest Service roads in the vicinity make excellent mountain biking trails.

58 Riverford

Location: On the Clackamas and Collawash Rivers in Mount Hood National Forest; map C2, grid g6.

Campsites, facilities: There are 10 sites for tents. Picnic tables and fire grills are provided. Vault toilets are available. There is no piped water at the campground; water is available at nearby Two Rivers Picnic Area. Leashed pets are permitted.

Reservations, fees: No reservations are accepted. Sites are $7 per night. The campground is open from late April to late September.

Contact: Mount Hood National Forest, Estacada Ranger District, 595 NW Industrial Way, Estacada, OR 97023; (503) 630-6861 or fax (503) 630-2299.

Directions: From Interstate 5 south of Portland, take exit 288 and drive 12 miles east on Interstate 205 to Gladstone. Turn east on Highway 224 and drive 15 miles to Estacada. Continue 27 miles southeast on Highway 224, then drive 3.5 miles south on Forest Service Road 46 to the campground.

Trip notes: Good fishing is a bonus around

this campground at the confluence of the Clackamas and Collawash Rivers.

⑤⑨ Raab

Location: On the Collawash River in Mount Hood National Forest; map C2, grid g6.

Campsites, facilities: There are 27 sites for tents, trailers, or RVs up to 22 feet long. Picnic tables and fire grills are provided. Pit toilets are available. There is no piped water in the campground; water is available one mile away at Two Rivers Picnic Area. Leashed pets are permitted.

Reservations, fees: Some sites may be reserved by calling (800) 280-CAMP/2267 ($8.65 reservation fee). Sites are $6 per night. The campground is open from late May to early September.

Contact: Mount Hood National Forest, Estacada Ranger District, 595 NW Industrial Way, Estacada, OR 97023; (503) 630-6861 or fax (503) 630-2299.

Directions: From Interstate 5 south of Portland, take exit 288 and drive 12 miles east on Interstate 205 to Gladstone. Turn east on Highway 224 and drive 15 miles to Estacada. Continue southeast on Highway 224 for 27 miles, then drive four miles south on Forest Service Road 46 to the campground.

Trip notes: This camp along the banks of the Collawash River, about a mile from its confluence with the Clackamas River, gets moderate use, but it's usually quiet and has a nice, secluded atmosphere.

⑥⓪ Kingfisher

Location: On the Hot Springs Fork of the Collawash River in Mount Hood National Forest; map C2, grid g6.

Campsites, facilities: There are 23 sites for tents, trailers, or RVs up to 16 feet long. Picnic tables and fireplaces are provided. Vault toilets and hand-pumped water are available. Leashed pets are permitted.

Reservations, fees: Some sites may be reserved by calling (800) 280-CAMP/2267 ($8.65 reservation fee). Sites are $9 per night. The

campground is open from late May to early September.

Contact: Mount Hood National Forest, Estacada Ranger District, 595 NW Industrial Way, Estacada, OR 97023; (503) 630-6861 or fax (503) 630-2299.

Directions: From Interstate 5 south of Portland, take exit 288 and drive 12 miles east on Interstate 205 to Gladstone. Turn east on Highway 224 and drive 15 miles to Estacada. Continue 26 miles southeast on Highway 224 to Forest Service Road 46. Turn right and drive 3.5 miles south on Forest Service Road 46, then three miles south on Forest Service Road 63. Turn west on Forest Service Road 70 and drive one mile to the campground.

Trip notes: This pretty campground along the banks of the Hot Springs Fork of the Collawash River is about three miles from Bagby Hot Springs, a Forest Service day-use area. It's an easy 1.5-mile hike to the hot springs from the day-use area. Fishing access is near the camp.

⑥① Humbug

Location: On the Breitenbush River in Willamette National Forest; map C2, grid g6.

Campsites, facilities: There are 21 sites for tents, trailers, or RVs up to 22 feet long. Picnic tables, fire grills, piped water, and vault toilets are available. Leashed pets are permitted.

Reservations, fees: No reservations are accepted. Sites are $8 per night. The campground is open from mid-April to late September.

Contact: Willamette National Forest, Detroit Ranger District, HC 73, P.O. Box 320, Mill City, OR 97360; (503) 854-3366 or fax (503) 854-3520.

Directions: From Interstate 5 at Salem, take exit 253 and turn east on Highway 22. Drive 52 miles to Detroit, then turn left on Forest Service Road 46 (Breitenbush Road) and travel five miles northeast to the campground.

Trip notes: Fishing and hiking are popular at this campground along the banks of the Breitenbush River about four miles from where it empties into Detroit Lake. The lake offers many other recreation opportunities.

62 Elk Lake

Location: Near the Bull of the Woods Wilderness in Willamette National Forest; map C2, grid g6.

Campsites, facilities: There are 14 primitive tent sites. Picnic tables, fire grills, and pit toilets are available. There is no piped water. Primitive launching facilities are available. Leashed pets are permitted.

Reservations, fees: No reservations are accepted. There is no fee. The campground is open from July to mid-September.

Contact: Willamette National Forest, Detroit Ranger District, HC 73, P.O. Box 320, Mill City, OR 97360; (503) 854-3366 or fax (503) 854-3520.

Directions: From Interstate 5 at Salem, take exit 253 and turn east on Highway 22. Drive 52 miles to Detroit, then turn left on Forest Service Road 46 (Breitenbush Road) and travel 4.5 miles. Continue 10 miles north on Forest Service Road 4696 (Elk Lake Road) to the campground. The road is extremely rough for the last two miles. High-clearance vehicles are recommended.

Trip notes: This remote campground is on the shore of Elk Lake, where boating, fishing, and swimming can be quite good in the summer. Several nearby trails provide access to the Bull of the Woods Wilderness. Please pack out your garbage.

63 Breitenbush Lake

Location: On Breitenbush Lake in Mount Hood National Forest; map C2, grid g6.

Campsites, facilities: There are 20 sites for tents or trailers. Picnic tables and fire grills are provided. Vault toilets are available. There is no piped water. A store and ice are located within five miles. Boat docks, launching facilities, and rentals are nearby. Leashed pets are permitted.

Reservations, fees: No reservations are

accepted. There is no fee. The campground is open from mid-June to late September.

Contact: Mount Hood National Forest, Estacada Ranger District, 595 NW Industrial Way, Estacada, OR 97023; (503) 630-6861 or fax (503) 630-2299.

Directions: From Interstate 5 south of Portland, take exit 288 and drive 12 miles east on Interstate 205 to Gladstone. Turn east on Highway 224 and drive 15 miles to Estacada. Continue 27 miles southeast on Highway 224, then drive 28.5 miles south on Forest Service Road 46. Turn east on Forest Service Road 4220 and drive 8.5 miles to the lake. Be aware that the access road to the lake is not maintained and can be pretty rough. Only high-clearance vehicles are recommended.

Trip notes: This lakeside campground is set at 5,500 feet on the western border of the Warm Springs Indian Reservation. Breitenbush is a large lake next to the Mount Jefferson Wilderness. Numerous trails provide access to other lakes in the area, and horses are allowed in areas specified by the Forest Service. The Pacific Crest Trail skirts the camp to the west. Ripe huckleberries can be found in these parts in late August and September.

64 Rainbow

Location: On the Oak Grove Fork of the Clackamas River in Mount Hood National Forest; map C2, grid g7.

Campsites, facilities: There are 17 sites for tents, trailers, or RVs up to 16 feet long. There is no piped water. Fire grills and picnic tables are provided. Vault toilets are available. Leashed pets are permitted.

Reservations, fees: Some sites may be reserved by calling (800) 280-CAMP/2267 ($8.65 reservation fee). Sites are $9 per night. The campground is open from late April to late September.

Contact: Mount Hood National Forest, Estacada Ranger District, 595 NW Industrial Way, Estacada, OR 97023; (503) 630-6861 or fax (503) 630-2299.

Directions: From Interstate 5 south of Port-

land, take exit 288 and drive 12 miles east on Interstate 205 to Gladstone. Turn east on Highway 224 and drive 15 miles to Estacada. Continue 27 miles southeast on Highway 224 to Forest Service Road 46. The camp is about 100 yards south on Forest Service Road 46.

Trip notes: This campground is set along the banks of the Oak Grove Fork of the Clackamas River not far from where it empties into the Clackamas River.

⑥⑤ Breitenbush

Location: On the Breitenbush River in Willamette National Forest; map C2, grid g7.
Campsites, facilities: There are 29 sites for tents, trailers, or RVs up to 22 feet long (longer trailers may be difficult to park and turn). Picnic tables and fire grills are provided. Piped water and vault toilets are available. Leashed pets are permitted.
Reservations, fees: No reservations are accepted. Sites are $8–$16 per night. The campground is open from mid-April to late September.
Contact: Willamette National Forest, Detroit Ranger District, HC 73, Box 320, Mill City, OR 97360; (503) 854-3366 or fax (503) 854-3520.
Directions: From Interstate 5 at Salem, take exit 253 and turn east on Highway 22. Drive 50 miles to Detroit. From Detroit, travel 10 miles north on Forest Service Road 46 to the campground.
Trip notes: Fishing access is a plus at this campground along the Breitenbush River. The South Breitenbush Gorge National Recreation Trail is three miles away. It's detailed on a map of Willamette National Forest. Breitenbush Hot Springs is just over a mile away. If this campground is crowded, try nearby Cleater Bend (campground number 66).

⑥⑥ Cleater Bend

Location: Near the Breitenbush River in Willamette National Forest; map C2, grid g7.
Campsites, facilities: There are nine sites for tents, trailers, or RVs up to 16 feet long. Picnic tables, fire grills, piped water, and

vault toilets are available. Leashed pets are permitted.
Reservations, fees: No reservations are accepted. Sites are $8 per night. The campground is open from mid-May to late September.
Contact: Williamette National Forest, Detroit Ranger District, HC 73, Box 320, Mill City, OR 97360; (503) 854-3366 or fax (503) 854-3520.
Directions: From Interstate 5 at Salem, take exit 253 and turn east on Highway 22. Drive 50 miles to Detroit. From Detroit, travel nine miles northeast on Forest Service Road 46 (Breitenbush Road) to the campground.
Trip notes: Creek views are a highlight of this camp on the banks of the Breitenbush River with pretty, shaded sites. The camp isn't far from Breitenbush (campground number 65); see those trip notes for area details.

⑥⑦ Camp Ten

Location: On Olallie Lake in Mount Hood National Forest; map C2, grid g7.
Campsites, facilities: There are seven sites for tents, trailers, or RVs up to 16 feet long. Picnic tables and fire grills are provided. Pit toilets are available. There is no piped water. Boat docks, launching facilities, boat rentals, and a store that sells fishing tackle and other supplies are nearby. Leashed pets are permitted.
Reservations, fees: No reservations are accepted. Sites are $6 per night. The campground is open from mid-June to late September.
Contact: Mount Hood National Forest, Estacada Ranger District, 595 NW Industrial Way, Estacada, OR 97023; (503) 630-6861 or fax (503) 630-2299.
Directions: From Interstate 5 south of Portland, take exit 288 and head east on Interstate 205 for 12 miles to Gladstone. Turn east on Highway 224 and drive 15 miles to Estacada. Continue southeast on Highway 224 for 27 miles, then drive south on Forest Service Road 46 for about 22 miles. From there, travel on Forest Service Road 4690 southeast for 8.2 miles. When you reach Forest Service

Road 4220, head south for six miles to the campground.

Trip notes: Here's another camp along the shore of Olallie Lake, a popular area. This one is on the western shore in the midst of the Olallie Lake Scenic Area, which is home to a number of pristine mountain lakes and a network of hiking trails. See a Forest Service map for trail locations. Boats without motors—including canoes, kayaks, and rafts—are permitted on the lake.

⑥⑧ Lower Lake

Location: Near Olallie Lake in Mount Hood National Forest; map C2, grid g7.

Campsites, facilities: There are nine walk-in tent sites. Picnic tables and fire grills are provided. Pit toilets are available. There is no piped water. Boat docks, launching facilities, and rentals are nearby at Olallie Lake. Leashed pets are permitted.

Reservations, fees: No reservations are accepted. There is no fee. The campground is open from mid-June to late September.

Contact: Mount Hood National Forest, Estacada Ranger District, 595 NW Industrial Way, Estacada, OR 97023; (503) 630-6861 or fax (503) 630-2299.

Directions: From Interstate 5 south of Portland, take exit 288 and head east on Interstate 205 for 12 miles to Gladstone. Turn east on Highway 224 and drive 15 miles to Estacada. Continue southeast on Highway 224 for 27 miles, then drive south on Forest Service Road 46 for about 22 miles. From there, travel on Forest Service Road 4690 southeast for 8.5 miles. When you reach Forest Service Road 4220, head south for 4.5 miles to the parking area. Hike one-half mile to the campground.

Trip notes: This sunny, open campground is along the shore of Lower Lake, a small, deep lake that's perfect for fishing and swimming. The camp is a short distance from Olallie Lake and near a network of trails that provide access to other nearby lakes. We advise you to obtain a Forest Ser-

vice map that details the backcountry roads and trails.

⑥⑨ Olallie Meadows

Location: Near Olallie Lake in Mount Hood National Forest; map C2, grid g7.

Campsites, facilities: There are five sites for tents, trailers, or RVs up to 16 feet long. Picnic tables and fire grills are provided. Pit toilets are available. There is no piped water. Boat docks, launching facilities, and rentals are located about three miles away on Olallie Lake. Leashed pets are permitted.

Reservations, fees: No reservations are accepted. There is no fee. The campground is open from mid-June to late September.

Contact: Mount Hood National Forest, Estacada Ranger District, 595 NW Industrial Way, Estacada, OR 97023; (503) 630-6861 or fax (503) 630-2299.

Directions: From Interstate 5 south of Portland, take exit 288 and head east on Interstate 205 for 12 miles to Gladstone. Turn east on Highway 224 and drive 15 miles to Estacada. Continue southeast on Highway 224 for 27 miles, then drive south on Forest Service Road 46 for about 22 miles. From there, travel on Forest Service Road 4690 southeast for 8.2 miles. When you reach Forest Service Road 4220, head south for 1.5 miles to the campground.

Trip notes: This campground is set at 4,500 feet in a large, peaceful meadow about three miles from Olallie Lake. The Pacific Crest Trail passes very close to camp. Horses are permitted only at specified campsites. See the trip notes for Paul Dennis (campground number 70) for area details.

⑦⓪ Paul Dennis

Location: On Olallie Lake in Mount Hood National Forest; map C2, grid g7.

Campsites, facilities: There are 15 sites for tents or small campers (trailers are not recommended) and three hike-in tent sites. Picnic tables and fire grills are provided. Pit toilets are available. There is no piped water. A store and ice are nearby. Boat docks, launching facilities, and rentals are located on Olallie Lake. Leashed pets are permitted.

Reservations, fees: No reservations are accepted. Sites are $6 per night. The campground is open from mid-June to late September.

Contact: Mount Hood National Forest, Estacada Ranger District, 595 NW Industrial Way, Estacada, OR 97023; (503) 630-6861 or fax (503) 630-2299.

Directions: From Interstate 5 south of Portland, take exit 288 and head east on Interstate 205 for 12 miles to Gladstone. Turn east on Highway 224 and drive 15 miles to Estacada. Continue southeast on Highway 224 for 27 miles, then drive south on Forest Service Road 46 for about 22 miles. From there, travel on Forest Service Road 4690 southeast for 8.2 miles. When you reach Forest Service Road 4220, head south for 6.2 miles to the campground.

Trip notes: This campground is along the north shore of Olallie Lake. From here, you can see the reflection of Mount Jefferson (10,497 feet). Boats with motors are not permitted on the lake. A trail from camp leads to Nep-Te-Pa Lake, Monon Lake, and Long Lake, which lies just east of the border of the Warm Springs Indian Reservation. It's advisable to obtain a Forest Service map.

71 Peninsula

Location: On Olallie Lake in Mount Hood National Forest; map C2, grid g7.

Campsites, facilities: There are 35 sites for tents, trailers, or RVs up to 22 feet long, and six walk-in tent sites. Picnic tables and fire grills are provided. Vault toilets are available. There is no piped water. Some facilities are wheelchair accessible. Boat docks, launching facilities, and rentals are nearby. Leashed pets are permitted.

Reservations, fees: No reservations are accepted. Sites are $6 per night. The campground is open from mid-June to late September.

Contact: Mount Hood National Forest, Estacada Ranger District, 595 NW Industrial Way, Estacada, OR 97023; (503) 630-6861 or fax (503) 630-2299.

Directions: From Interstate 5 south of Portland, take exit 288 and head east on Interstate 205 for 12 miles to Gladstone. Turn east on Highway 224 and drive 15 miles to Estacada. Continue southeast on Highway 224 for 27 miles, then drive south on Forest Service Road 46 for about 22 miles. From there, travel on Forest Service Road 4690 southeast for 8.2 miles. When you reach Forest Service Road 4220, head south for 6.5 miles to the campground.

Trip notes: Peninsula, the largest of several campgrounds along Olallie Lake, is on the south shore. The amphitheater is near camp, and, during the summer, rangers present campfire programs. Boats without motors are permitted on the lake. Numerous smaller lakes in the area can be reached from trails nearby. See the trip notes for Paul Dennis (campground number 70) for details.

72 Shellrock Creek

Location: On Shellrock Creek in Mount Hood National Forest; map C2, grid g8.

Campsites, facilities: There are five sites for tents, trailers, or RVs up to 16 feet long. Picnic tables and fire grills are provided. Vault toilets are available. There is no piped water. Leashed pets are permitted.

Reservations, fees: No reservations are accepted. Sites are $7 per night. The campground is open from mid-June to early September.

Contact: Mount Hood National Forest, Estacada Ranger District, 595 NW Industrial Way, Estacada, OR 97023; (503) 630-6861 or fax (503) 630-2299.

Directions: From Portland, turn east on

U.S. 26 and drive 55 miles to the small town of Government Camp. Continue 15 miles southeast on U.S. 26, then eight miles south on Forest Service Road 42. Turn west on Forest Service Road 57 and drive 15 miles to Forest Service Road 58. The campground is one mile north on Forest Service Road 58.

Trip notes: This quiet little campground is at a nice spot on Shellrock Creek, good for "sneak fishing" for trout. It's advisable to obtain a Forest Service map that details the backcountry roads and trails.

(73) Oak Fork

Location: On Timothy Lake in Mount Hood National Forest; map C2, grid g8.

Campsites, facilities: There are 47 sites for tents, trailers, or RVs up to 32 feet long. Picnic tables and fire grills are provided. Hand-pumped water, firewood, and vault toilets are available. A boat ramp and launching facilities are nearby. Leashed pets are permitted.

Reservations, fees: Some sites may be reserved by calling (800) 280-CAMP/2267 ($8.65 reservation fee). Sites are $10–$12 per night. The campground is open from June through mid-September.

Contact: Mount Hood National Forest, Zigzag Ranger District, 65000 East Highway 26, Welches, OR 97067; (503) 622-7674 or fax (503) 622-5622.

Directions: From Portland, drive 55 miles east on U.S. 26 to the town of Government Camp. Continue southeast on U.S. 26 for 15 miles, then drive eight miles south on Forest Service Road 42. Turn right on Forest Service Road 57 and drive three miles to the park on the right.

Trip notes: This camp is set along the south shore of Timothy Lake, just east of Hoodview and Gone Creek; see campground numbers 75 and 77 for more details.

(74) Pine Point

Location: On Timothy Lake in Mount Hood National Forest; map C2, grid g8.

Campsites, facilities: There are 25 sites for tents, trailers, or RVs up to 31 feet long (10 single sites, 10 double sites, and five group sites). Picnic tables and fire grills are provided. Piped water, firewood , a wheelchair-accessible fishing pier, and vault toilets are available. A boat ramp and launching facilities are nearby. Leashed pets are permitted.

Reservations, fees: Some sites may be reserved by calling (800) 280-CAMP/2267 ($8.65 reservation fee). Sites are $10–$35 per night, depending on the type of campsite, plus $5 for each additional vehicle. The campground is open from late May to mid-September.

Contact: Mount Hood National Forest, Zigzag Ranger District, 65000 East Highway 26, Welches, OR 97067; (503) 622-7674 or fax (503) 622-5622.

Directions: From Portland, turn east on U.S. 26 and drive 55 miles to the small town of Government Camp. Continue southeast on U.S. 26 for 15 miles, then drive eight miles south on Forest Service Road 42. Turn right on Forest Service Road 57 and drive four miles to the campground on the right.

Trip notes: One of five camps on Timothy Lake, this spot is located on the southwest shore and has lake access. The trail that leads around the lake and to the Pacific Crest Trail is just outside of the camp. See the trip notes for Gone Creek (campground number 77) for boating and fishing details.

(75) Hoodview

Location: On Timothy Lake in Mount Hood National Forest; map C2, grid g9.

Campsites, facilities: There are 43 sites for tents, trailers, or RVs up to 31 feet long. Picnic tables and fire grills are provided. Piped water, firewood, and vault toilets are available. A boat ramp is nearby. Leashed pets are permitted.

Reservations, fees: Some sites may be reserved by calling (800) 280-CAMP/2267 ($8.65 reservation fee). Sites are $10–$12 per night, plus $5 for each additional vehicle. The campground is open from mid-May to mid-September.

Contact: Mount Hood National Forest, Zigzag Ranger District, 65000 East Highway 26, Welches, OR 97067; (503) 622-7674 or fax (503) 622-5622.

Directions: From Portland, turn east on U.S. 26 and drive 55 miles to the town of Government Camp. Continue southeast on U.S. 26 for 15 miles, then drive eight miles south on Forest Service Road 42. Turn right on Forest Service Road 57 and continue three miles to the campground on the right.

Trip notes: Here's another camp along the south shore of Timothy Lake. A trail out of camp branches south for a few miles, and if followed to the east, eventually leads to the Pacific Crest Trail. See the trip notes for Gone Creek (campground number 77) for boating and fishing information.

76 Summit Lake

Location: On Summit Lake in Mount Hood National Forest; map C2, grid g9.

Campsites, facilities: There are six tent sites. Fire grills and picnic tables are provided. Vault toilets and piped water are available. There is no piped water. No motorboats are allowed. Leashed pets are permitted.

Reservations, fees: No reservations are accepted. There is no fee. The campground is open from late May through September.

Contact: Mount Hood National Forest, Clackamas Ranger District, (503) 834-2275. Estacada Ranger Station, 595 NW Industrial Way, Estacada, OR 97023.

Directions: From Portland, turn east on U.S. 26 and drive 55 miles to the town of Government Camp. Continue southeast on U.S. 26 for 15 miles, then drive 12 miles south on Forest Service Road 42. Head west on Forest Service Road 141 (a dirt road) for one mile to the campground on the left.

Trip notes: This is an idyllic setting in a remote area along the western slopes of the Cascade Range. Located on the shore of little Summit Lake, the camp is primitive but a jewel. It's a perfect alternative to the more crowded camps at Timothy Lake—and you can access all the same recreation options by driving just a short distance north.

77 Gone Creek

Location: On Timothy Lake in Mount Hood National Forest; map C2, grid g9.

Campsites, facilities: There are 45 sites for tents, trailers, or RVs up to 31 feet long. Piped water, fire grills, and picnic tables are provided. Vault toilets and firewood are available. A boat ramp is nearby. Leashed pets are permitted.

Reservations, fees: Some sites may be reserved by calling (800) 280-CAMP/2267 ($8.65 reservation fee). Sites are $10–$12 per night, plus $5 for each additional vehicle. The campground is open from mid-May to mid-September.

Contact: Mount Hood National Forest, Zig-zag Ranger District, 65000 East Highway 26, Welches, OR 97067; (503) 622-7674 or fax (503) 622-5622.

Directions: From Portland, turn east on U.S. 26 and drive 55 miles to the town of Government Camp. Continue southeast on U.S. 26 for 15 miles, then drive eight miles south on Forest Service Road 42. Turn right on Forest Service Road 57 and drive one mile west to the campground on the right.

Trip notes: This campground set along the south shore of Timothy Lake at 3,200 feet is one of four camps at the lake. Timothy Lake provides good fishing for brook trout, cutthroat trout, rainbow trout, and kokanee salmon. Boats with motors are allowed, but a 10 mph speed limit keeps it quiet. Several trails in the area—including the Pacific Crest Trail—provide access to several small mountain lakes.

78 Joe Graham Horse Camp

Location: Near Clackamas Lake in Mount Hood National Forest; map C2, grid g9.

Campsites, facilities: There are 14 sites for tents, trailers, horse trailers, or RVs up to 28 feet long; nine have corrals. Picnic tables, hitching posts, and fire grills are provided. Piped water, vault toilets, and firewood are available. Leashed pets are permitted.

Reservations, fees: Some sites may be reserved by calling (800) 280-CAMP/2267 ($8.65 reservation fee). Sites are $9 per night, plus $5 for each additional vehicle. The campground is open from mid-May to mid-September.

Contact: Mount Hood National Forest, Zigzag Ranger District, 65000 East Highway 26, Welches, OR 97067; (503) 622-7674 or fax (503) 622-5622.

Directions: From Portland, turn east on U.S. 26 and drive 55 miles to the town of Government Camp. Continue southeast on U.S. 26 for 15 miles, then drive eight miles south on Forest Service Road 42 to the campground on the left.

Trip notes: This campground, named for a forest ranger, is just north of tiny Clackamas Lake and is one of two campgrounds in the area that allows horses; see the trip notes for Clackamas Lake (campground number 79) for additional information. Timothy Lake (the setting for the Gone Creek, Hoodview, Oak Fork, Pine Point, and Meditation Point sites) provides a nearby alternative to the northwest. The Pacific Crest Trail is located just east of camp.

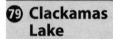 Clackamas Lake

Location: Near the Clackamas River in Mount Hood National Forest; map C2, grid g9.

Campsites, facilities: There are 46 sites for tents, trailers, horse trailers, or RVs up to 16 feet long; 19 have corrals. Piped water, fire grills, and picnic tables are provided. Vault toilets and firewood are available. Boat docks and launching facilities are nearby at Timothy Lake. Leashed pets are permitted.

Reservations, fees: Some sites may be reserved by calling (800) 280-CAMP/2267 ($8.65 reservation fee). Sites are $9 per night, plus $5 for each additional vehicle. The campground is open from June to mid-September.

Contact: Mount Hood National Forest, Zigzag Ranger District, 65000 East Highway 26, Welches, OR 97067; (503) 622-7674 or fax (503) 622-5622.

Directions: From Portland, turn east on U.S. 26 and drive 55 miles to the town of Government Camp. Continue southeast on U.S. 26 for 15 miles, then drive eight miles south on Forest Service Road 42/Skyline Road, about 500 feet past the Clackamas Lake Historic Ranger Station. Turn east (left) on Forest Service Road 4270 and drive one-half mile to the campground on the left.

Trip notes: Clackamas Lake is small and shallow, but not far from the Clackamas River. The Pacific Crest Trail passes nearby, and Timothy Lake is little more than a one-mile hike from camp. See the trip notes for Gone Creek (campground number 77) for information on Timothy Lake.

Map C3

One inch equals approximately 20 miles.

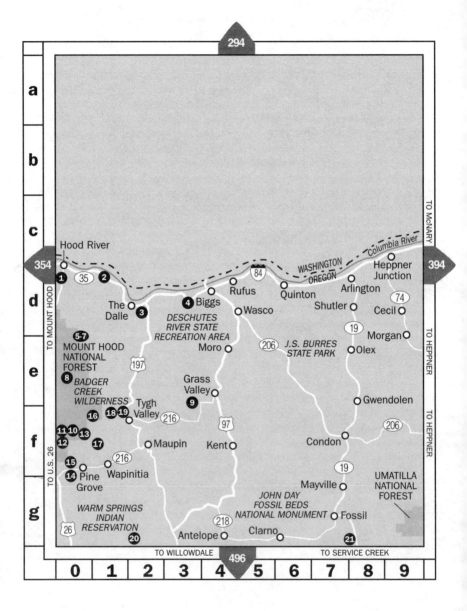

Chapter C3 features:

1 Tucker Park

Location: On the Hood River; map C3, grid d0.

Campsites, facilities: There are five tent sites and 29 sites for tents, trailers, or RVs of any length. Picnic tables are provided. Electricity, piped water, flush toilets, showers, firewood, and a playground are available. A store, a cafe, a Laundromat, and ice are located within one mile. Leashed pets and motorbikes are permitted.

Reservations, fees: No reservations are accepted. Sites are $13–$14 per night. The campground is open from April through October.

Contact: Phone (541) 386-4477 or write to 2440 Dee Highway, Hood River, OR 97031.

Directions: From Portland, turn east on Interstate 84 and drive about 65 miles to the town of Hood River, then travel four miles south on Highway 281 to the park.

Trip notes: This county park along the banks of the Hood River is just far enough out of the way to be missed by most of the tourist traffic. Recreation includes trout fishing and swimming.

2 Memaloose State Park

Location: In the Columbia River Gorge; map C3, grid d1.

Campsites, facilities: There are 67 tent sites and 43 sites with full hookups for trailers or RVs of any length. Picnic tables and fire grills are provided. Flush toilets, sanitary services, showers, and firewood are available. Some facilities are wheelchair accessible. Leashed pets and motorbikes are permitted.

Reservations, fees: Contact Reservations Northwest at (800) 452-5687 ($6 reservation fee). Sites are $13–$19 per night. The campground is open from mid-April to late October.

Contact: Columbia River Gorge District, P.O. Box 100, Corbett, OR 97019; (541) 478-3008 or (800) 452-5687.

Directions: This park is accessible only to westbound traffic on Interstate 84. From The Dalles, drive 11 miles west on Interstate 84 to the signed turnoff. The park is located about 75 miles east of Portland.

Trip notes: This park borrows its name from ancient Native Americans, who used a nearby offshore island as a sacred burial ground. Set along the scenic Columbia River Gorge, it makes a prime layover spot for campers cruising the Oregon-Washington border. This popular camp receives a good deal of traffic, so plan on arriving early to claim a spot.

3 Lone Pine RV Park

Location: Near the Columbia River; map C3, grid d2.

Campsites, facilities: There are 22 drive-through sites for trailers or RVs of any length. Electricity, piped water, and sewer hookups are provided. Flush toilets, showers, a cafe, a laundry room, ice, and a playground are available. Bottled gas and sanitary services are located within one mile. Boat docks and launching facilities are nearby. Leashed pets are permitted.

Reservations, fees: Reservations are accepted. Sites are $20 per night. The campground is open from mid-April through September.

Contact: Phone (541) 296-9133 or write to 335 U.S. 197, The Dalles, OR 97058.

Directions: From Portland, turn east on Interstate 84 and drive approximately 90 miles to The Dalles. Take exit 87 to U.S. 197 and follow it to the park.

Trip notes: This private park isn't far from the Columbia River, where fishing, boating, and swimming are options. The area gets hot weather and occasional winds shooting through the river canyon during summer months. Nearby recreation possibilities include an 18-hole golf course and tennis courts.

❹ Deschutes River State Recreation Area 🚐 ⛺

Location: On the Deschutes River; map C3, grid d3.

Campsites, facilities: There are 34 primitive sites for tents, trailers, or self-contained RVs up to 30 feet long. There is also a group area for RVs and tents. Picnic tables and fire grills are provided. Piped water and flush toilets are available. Leashed pets are permitted.

Reservations, fees: No reservations are accepted. Sites are $10–$13 per night. The campground is open from mid-April to late October.

Contact: Phone (541) 739-2322 or (800) 452-5687, or write to 89600 Biggs-Rufus Highway, Wasco, OR 97065.

Directions: From Portland, turn east on Interstate 84 and drive approximately 90 miles

to The Dalles. Continue 12 miles east on Interstate 84, then take exit 97 at Celilo and turn south on Highway 206. Drive five miles to the park.

Trip notes: This park along the Deschutes River near where it enters the Columbia River offers bicycling and hiking trails and good steelhead fishing in season. There's a small day-use state park called Heritage Landing across the river, which has a boat ramp and rest room facilities. The U.S. Army Corps of Engineers offers a free train ride and tour of the dam at The Dalles during the summer. Good rafting is a bonus here. For 25 miles upstream, the river is mostly inaccessible by car.

❺ Knebal Springs

Location: Near Knebal Springs in Mount Hood National Forest; map C3, grid e0.

Campsites, facilities: There are five sites for tents and small trailers or RVs. Piped water, picnic tables, and fire grills are provided. Pit toilets and horse loading and tending facilities are available. Leashed pets are permitted.

Reservations, fees: No reservations are accepted. There is no fee. The campground is open from June to early October.

Contact: Mount Hood National Forest, Barlow Ranger District, P.O. Box 67, Dufur, OR 97021; (541) 467-2291 or fax (541) 467-2271.

Directions: From Portland, turn east on Interstate 84 and drive approximately 90 miles. Take exit 87 and turn south on U.S. 197. Drive 13 miles south to Dufur, then turn right on Dufur Valley Road and drive 12 miles west. Continue on Forest Service Road 44 and go west to Forest Service Road 4430. Turn north and travel four miles, then drive southwest on Forest Service Road 1720 for one mile to the campground.

Trip notes: This spot is in a semiprimitive area near Knebal Springs, an ephemeral water source. A trail from the camp provides access to a network of other trails in the area. A Forest Service map is advised.

⑥ Eightmile Crossing

Location: On Eightmile Creek in Mount Hood National Forest; map C3, grid e0.

Campsites, facilities: There are 24 sites for tents, trailers, or RVs up to 30 feet long. No piped water is available. Picnic tables and fire grills are provided. Pit toilets are available. Leashed pets are permitted.

Reservations, fees: No reservations are accepted. There is no fee. The campground is open from June to mid-October.

Contact: Mount Hood National Forest, Barlow Ranger District, P.O. Box 67, Dufur, OR 97021; (541) 467-2291 or fax (541) 467-2271.

Directions: From Portland, turn east on Interstate 84 and drive approximately 90 miles. Take exit 87 and turn south on U.S. 197. Drive 13 miles south to Dufur, then turn right on Dufur Valley Road and drive 12 miles west. Continue on Forest Service Road 44 and go west to Forest Service Road 4430. Turn north and travel one-half mile to the campground.

Trip notes: This campground beside Eightmile Creek gets relatively little camping pressure. It's pretty and shaded, with sites scattered along the banks of the creek. From the day-use area, you can access a nice hiking trail that runs along Eightmile Creek. The fishing can be good here, so bring your gear.

⑦ Pebble Ford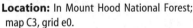

Location: In Mount Hood National Forest; map C3, grid e0.

Campsites, facilities: There are three sites for tents, trailers, or RVs up to 15 feet long. Picnic tables and fire grills are provided. Pit toilets are available. There is no piped water. Leashed pets are permitted.

Reservations, fees: No reservations are accepted. There is no fee. The campground is open from July to early October.

Contact: Mount Hood National Forest, Barlow Ranger District, P.O. Box 67, Dufur, OR 97021; (541) 467-2291 or fax (541) 467-2271.

Directions: From Portland, turn east on Interstate 84 and drive approximately 90 miles.

Take exit 87 and turn south on U.S. 197. Drive 13 miles south to Dufur, then turn right on Dufur Valley Road and drive 12 miles west. Continue on Forest Service Road 44 and drive five miles west. Turn south on Forest Service Road 130 and travel one-half mile to the campground.

Trip notes: This is just a little camping spot by the side of the gravel Forest Service road. Primitive and quiet, it's an alternative to the better-known Eightmile Crossing (campground number 6). There are some quality hiking trails in the area if you're willing to travel a bit to the trailheads.

⑧ Badger Lake

Location: On Badger Lake in Mount Hood National Forest; map C3, grid e0.

Campsites, facilities: There are four sites for tents only, accessible only by high-clearance vehicles. Picnic tables and fire grills are provided. Pit toilets are available. There is no piped water. Leashed pets are permitted.

Reservations, fees: No reservations are accepted. There is no fee. The campground is open from July to early October.

Contact: Mount Hood National Forest, Barlow Ranger District, P.O. Box 67, Dufur, OR 97021; (541) 467-2291 or fax (541) 467-2271.

Directions: From Portland, turn east on Interstate 84 and drive 65 miles to the town of Hood River. Turn south on Highway 35 (exit 64) and drive 37 miles, then turn left onto Forest Service Road 48 and drive 16 miles to Forest Service Road 4860. Turn north and drive eight miles to Forest Service Road 140, then drive four miles to the lake. The last two miles on this primitive road require a high-clearance vehicle.

Trip notes: This high-country campground is set along the shore of Badger Lake. Boating is permitted, if you can manage to get a boat in here. No trailers are allowed on campground roads. The camp is adjacent to the Badger Creek Wilderness, and numerous trails provide access to the backcountry. The nearest trail heads out of camp northeast along Badger Creek for several miles.

❾ Beavertail

Location: On the Deschutes River; map C3, grid e3.

Campsites, facilities: There are 21 sites for tents, trailers, or RVs up to 30 feet long. Picnic tables and fire grills are provided. Vault toilets are available. There is no piped water. Boat launching facilities are nearby. Leashed pets are permitted.

Reservations, fees: No reservations are accepted. Sites are $3 per night, with a 14-day stay limit. The campground is open year-round.

Contact: Bureau of Land Management, P.O. Box 550, Prineville, OR 97754; (541) 416-6700 or fax (541) 416-6798.

Directions: From Portland, turn east on U.S. 26 and drive approximately 68 miles. Turn east on Highway 216 and drive 26 miles, then turn south on U.S. 197 and drive three miles to Maupin. Turn north on Deschutes River Road and drive 17 miles northeast to the campground.

Trip notes: This isolated campground is set along the banks of the Deschutes River on Bureau of Land Management property with fishing and rafting options. The Deschutes is one of the classic trout streams in the Pacific Northwest. It's a small, pretty spot, with roomy sites, lots of trees, and river views.

❿ Bonney Meadows

Location: In Mount Hood National Forest; map C3, grid f0.

Campsites, facilities: There are five sites for tents and small trailers or RVs. Picnic tables and fire grills are provided. Pit toilets are available. There is no piped water. Leashed pets are permitted.

Reservations, fees: No reservations are accepted. There is no fee. The campground is open from July to early October.

Contact: Mount Hood National Forest, Barlow Ranger District, P.O. Box 67, Dufur, OR 97021; (541) 467-2291 or fax (541) 467-2271.

Directions: From Portland, turn east on Interstate 84 and drive 91 miles. Take exit 87 and turn south on U.S. 197. Drive 31 miles to Tygh Valley, then turn west and head toward Wamic. From Wamic, drive six miles west on County Road 226, then continue south and west on Forest Service Road 48 for 14 miles. Next, drive two miles north on Forest Service Road 4890, then continue four miles north on Forest Service Road 4891 to the campground.

Trip notes: This high-elevation, primitive campground is located on the east side of the Cascade Range. As a result, there is little water in the area—and also very few people, so you're liable to have the place all to yourself. Several trails are available, one of which travels 1.5 miles up to a group of small lakes. See a Forest Service map for details.

⓫ Keeps Mill

Location: On Clear Creek in Mount Hood National Forest; map C3, grid f0.

Campsites, facilities: There are five sites for tents. The road to the campground is not good for trailers. Picnic tables and fire grills are provided. Vault toilets are available. There is no piped water. Leashed pets are permitted.

Reservations, fees: No reservations are accepted. There is no fee. The campground is open from May through September.

Contact: Mount Hood National Forest, Barlow Ranger District, (541) 328-6211. Bear Springs Work Center, 73558 Highway 216, Maupin, OR 97037.

Directions: From Portland, turn east on U.S. 26 and drive 55 miles to Government Camp. Continue east for 25 miles, then turn east on Highway 216. Travel three miles and turn north on Forest Service Road 2120. Travel three miles to the end of the road.

Trip notes: This small, pretty campground is located at the confluence of Clear Creek and the White River. Many hiking trails are in the area. A map of Mount Hood National Forest detailing the back roads and trails is strongly advised.

⑫ Clear Creek Crossing

Location: On Clear Creek in Mount Hood National Forest; map C3, grid f0.

Campsites, facilities: There are five sites for tents. Picnic tables and fire grills are provided. Vault toilets are available. There is no piped water. Leashed pets are permitted.

Reservations, fees: No reservations are accepted. There is no fee. The campground is open from May through September.

Contact: Mount Hood National Forest, Barlow Ranger District, (541) 328-6211. Bear Springs Work Center, 73558 Highway 216, Maupin, OR 97037.

Directions: From Portland, turn east on U.S. 26 and drive 55 miles to the small town of Government Camp. Take Highway 26 east and drive 25 miles to the Highway 216. Turn east (left) on Highway 216 and drive three miles. Turn north on Forest Service Road 2130 and drive another three miles. Turn east on Forest Service Road 260 and drive one-half mile directly into the campground.

Trip notes: This campground along the banks of Clear Creek is a secluded, little-known spot in Mount Hood National Forest. Fishing and hiking are two recreation options here.

⑬ Rock Creek Reservoir

Location: On Rock Creek Reservoir in Mount Hood National Forest; map C3, grid f0.

Campsites, facilities: There are 33 sites for tents, trailers, or RVs up to 22 feet long. Picnic tables and fire grills are provided. Pit toilets, piped water, and firewood are available. Some of the facilities are wheelchair accessible. There are boat docks nearby, but no motorboats are allowed on the reservoir. Leashed pets are permitted.

Reservations, fees: Some sites may be reserved by calling (800) 280-CAMP/2267 ($8.65 reservation fee). Sites are $9–$11 per night. The campground is open from mid-April to early October.

Contact: Mount Hood National Forest, Barlow Ranger District, P.O. Box 67, Dufur, OR 97021; (541) 467-2291 or fax (541) 467-2271.

Directions: From Portland, turn east on Interstate 84 and drive 91 miles. Take exit 87 and turn south on U.S. 197. Drive 31 miles to Tygh Valley, then turn west and head toward Wamic. From Wamic, drive six miles west on County Road 226, then continue west on Forest Service Road 48 for one mile. The campground is located about 200 yards west on Forest Service Road 4820.

Trip notes: Fishing is excellent and the environment is perfect for canoes or rafts at this campground along the shore of Rock Creek Reservoir. No hiking trails are in the immediate vicinity, but there are many old Forest Service roads that are ideal for walking or mountain biking.

⑭ Bear Springs

Location: On Indian Creek in Mount Hood National Forest; map C3, grid f0.

Campsites, facilities: There are 21 sites for tents, trailers, or RVs up to 32 feet long. Piped water, fire grills, and picnic tables are provided. Vault toilets and firewood are available. Leashed pets are permitted.

Reservations, fees: Some sites may be reserved by calling (800) 280-CAMP/2267 ($8.65 reservation fee). Sites are $8 per night, plus $5 for each additional vehicle. The campground is open from June through September.

Contact: Mount Hood National Forest, Barlow Ranger District, (541) 328-6211. Bear Springs Work Center, 73558 Highway 216, Maupin, OR 97037.

Directions: From Portland, turn east on U.S. 26 and drive 55 miles to the small town of Government Camp. Continue southeast on U.S. 26 for 25 miles, then turn east on Highway 216 and drive five miles. Turn east (right) on Reservation Road and look for the campground on the right.

Trip notes: This campground is set along the banks of Indian Creek on the border of the Warm Springs Indian Reservation. The Bear

Springs Work Center is near the camp, and rangers will be happy to supply maps and answer your questions about the area. There are a few good hiking trails nearby along U.S. 26; see a Forest Service map for details.

⓯ McCubbins Gulch

Location: In Mount Hood National Forest; map C3, grid f0.

Campsites, facilities: There are five sites for tents and RVs. Picnic tables and fire grills are provided. Pit toilets available. There is no piped water. Leashed pets are permitted.

Reservations, fees: No reservations are accepted. There is no fee. The campground is open from May through September.

Contact: Mount Hood National Forest, Barlow Ranger District, (541) 328-6211. Bear Springs Work Center, 73558 Highway 216, Maupin, OR 97037.

Directions: From Portland, turn east on U.S. 26 and drive 55 miles to the small town of Government Camp. Continue southeast on U.S. 26 for 25 miles, then turn east on Highway 216. Continue on Highway 216 for six miles, then make a sharp left onto Forest Service Road 2110 and continue for 1.5 miles. Look for the campground entrance on the right side.

Trip notes: This is a small, primitive camp along a small creek that offers decent fishing and OHV recreation. Though out of the way, the camp is heavily used, so claim a spot early in the day. To the south is the Warm Springs Indian Reservation. A nearby camping option is Bear Springs (campground number 14).

⓰ Forest Creek

Location: On Forest Creek in Mount Hood National Forest; map C3, grid f1.

Campsites, facilities: There are eight sites for tents, trailers, or RVs up to 16 feet long. No piped water is available. Picnic tables and fire grills are provided. Pit toilets are available. Leashed pets are permitted.

Reservations, fees: No reservations are accepted. There is no fee. The campground is open from July to early October.

Contact: Mount Hood National Forest, Barlow Ranger District, P.O. Box 67, Dufur, OR 97021; (541) 467-2291 or fax (541) 467-2271.

Directions: From Portland, turn east on Interstate 84 and drive 91 miles. Take exit 87 and turn south on U.S. 197. Drive 31 miles to Tygh Valley, then turn west and head toward Wamic. From Wamic, drive six miles west on County Road 226, then continue south and west on Forest Service Road 48 for 12.5 miles. From there drive one mile southeast on Forest Service Road 4885, then go south for one-quarter mile on Forest Service Road 3530 to the campground.

Trip notes: Reached by walking across a small bridge, this very old camp along Forest Creek on the original Barlow Trail was once used by early settlers. By venturing a few miles north on the network of Forest Service roads, you can access a number of trails that lead into the Badger Creek Wilderness. See a Forest Service map for specific roads and trails.

⓱ Bonney Crossing

Location: On Badger Creek in Mount Hood National Forest; map C3, grid f1.

Campsites, facilities: There are eight sites for tents, trailers, or RVs up to 16 feet long. Picnic tables and fire grills are provided. Pit toilets are available. There is no piped water. Leashed pets are permitted.

Reservations, fees: No reservations are accepted. Sites are $5 per night. The campground is open from mid-April to mid-October.

Contact: Mount Hood National Forest, Barlow Ranger District, P.O. Box 67, Dufur, OR 97021; (541) 467-2291 or fax (541) 467-2271.

Directions: From Portland, turn east on Interstate 84 and drive 91 miles. Take exit 87 and turn south on U.S. 197. Drive 31 miles to Tygh Valley, then turn west and head toward Wamic. From Wamic, drive six miles west on County Road 226, then continue west on Forest Service Road 48 for one mile. From there, drive 200 yards west on Forest Service

Road 4810 to Forest Service Road 4811 and then east on Forest Service Road 271 to the campground.

Trip notes: This campground along Badger Creek is the trailhead for the Badger Creek Trail, which provides access to the Badger Creek Wilderness. The camp gets fairly light use and is usually very quiet. Fishing is available in the creek.

⑱ Pine Hollow Lakeside Resort

Location: On Pine Hollow Reservoir; map C3, grid f1.

Campsites, facilities: There are 35 tent sites and 75 sites for trailers or RVs. Electricity, piped water, and picnic tables are provided. Flush toilets, bottled gas, sanitary services, showers, firewood, a store, a cafe, a laundry room, and ice are available. Boat docks, launching facilities, and rentals are nearby. Leashed pets are permitted.

Reservations, fees: Reservations are accepted. Sites are $14–$17 per night. The campground is open from mid-March through October.

Contact: Phone (541) 544-2271 or write to 34 North Mariposa Drive, Wamic, OR 97063.

Directions: From Portland, turn east on Interstate 84 and drive 91 miles. Take exit 87 and turn south on U.S. 197. Drive south to the Tygh Valley Road exit, then drive 4.5 miles west on Wamic Market Road to Ross Road and follow it north 3.5 miles to the campground.

Trip notes: This resort on the shore of Pine Hollow Reservoir is the best game in town for RV campers, with shaded lakefront sites. Year-round fishing, boating, swimming, and waterskiing are some recreation options here.

⑲ Wasco County Fairgrounds

Location: On Badger Creek; map C3, grid f1.

Campsites, facilities: There are 50 tent sites and 100 drive-through sites for trailers or RVs of any length. Electricity, piped water, and picnic tables are provided. Flush toilets, a dump station, sanitary services, and showers are available. A store, a cafe, and ice are located within one mile. Leashed pets are permitted.

Reservations, fees: Reservations are accepted. Sites are $10–$12 per night. The campground is open from February through November.

Contact: Phone (541) 483-2288 or write to 81849 Fairground Road, Tygh Valley, OR 97063.

Directions: From Portland, turn east on Interstate 84 and drive 91 miles. Take exit 87 and turn south on U.S. 197. Drive south to the Tygh Valley Road exit, then drive northwest for about two miles. The campground is located on Fairgrounds Road.

Trip notes: This county campground is set near the confluence of Badger and Tygh Creeks. Hiking trails, marked bike trails, and tennis courts are close by.

⑳ Kah-Nee-Ta Resort

Location: On the Warm Springs Indian Reservation; map C3, grid g2.

Campsites, facilities: There are 50 drive-through sites for trailers or RVs of any length. Electricity, piped water, cable TV, and sewer hookups are provided. Flush toilets, bottled gas, sanitary services, showers, a cafe, laundry facilities, ice, a playground, a spa with a therapist and mud baths, and an Olympic-sized, spring-fed swimming pool with a 140-foot water slide are available. Some facilities are wheelchair accessible. Leashed pets and motorbikes are permitted, but some areas are restricted.

Reservations, fees: Reservations are accepted. Sites are $32 per night; call for special winter rates. The campground is open year-round.

Contact: Phone (541) 553-1112, fax (541) 302-6622, or write to P.O. Box K, Warm Springs, OR 97761.

Directions: From Portland, turn east on

U.S. 26 and drive about 105 miles to Warm Springs. Drive 11 miles northeast on Highway 3 to Kah-Nee-Ta and the resort on the right.

Trip notes: This is the only public camp on the east side of the Warm Springs Indian Reservation; there are no other camps within 30 miles. The Warm Springs River runs nearby, with opportunities for fishing. Recreation options in the area include an 18-hole golf course, mini-golf, biking and hiking trails, a riding stable, and tennis courts.

㉑ Shelton Wayside

Location: Near Fossil; map C3, grid g8.

Campsites, facilities: There are 36 primitive sites for tents, trailers, or RVs up to 30 feet long. Picnic tables and fire grills are provided. Piped water, firewood, and vault toilets are available. Pets are permitted.

Reservations, fees: No reservations are accepted. Sites are $7 per night. The campground is open from mid-April to late October.

Contact: Clyde Holliday State Recreation Site, P.O. Box 9, Canyon City, OR 97820; (800) 452-5687 or (541) 575-2773.

Directions: From Interstate 84 at Biggs, take exit 104 and turn south on U.S. 97. Drive 57 miles, then turn east on Highway 218 and drive 44 miles to Fossil. Turn southeast on Highway 19 and drive 10 miles to the park on the right.

Trip notes: This is a good layover if you're stuck in the area with no place to camp for the night; there are no campgrounds on major roadways for an hour's drive in any direction. The closest alternatives are primitive sites (Bull Prairie and Fairview, campground numbers 16 and 17 in Chapter C4), accessible by Forest Service roads. There is a nice two-mile hiking trail at the park.

Map C4

Oregon State Map .... *page 6*
One inch equals approximately 20 miles.

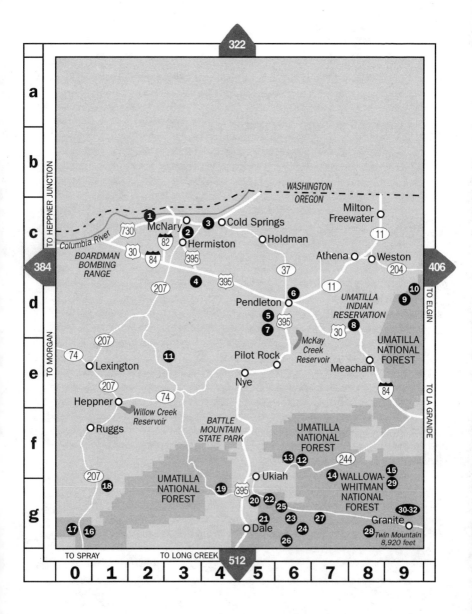

Chapter C4 features:

① Shady Rest Mobile Home Park

Location: On the Columbia River; map C4, grid c2.

Campsites, facilities: There are 26 drive-through sites for trailers or RVs of any length. Electricity, piped water, and sewer hookups are provided. Flush toilets, showers, a laundry room, and a swimming pool are available. A store, a cafe, and ice are located within one mile. Boat docks and launching facilities are nearby. Leashed pets are permitted.

Reservations, fees: Reservations are accepted. Sites are $17 per night. The campground is open year-round.

Contact: Phone (541) 922-5041 or write to Route 1, P.O. Box 240, Umatilla, OR 97882.

Directions: From Interstate 84 west of Pendleton, take exit 188 and drive six miles north on U.S. 395 to Hermiston. Continue five miles northwest on U.S. 395 to the junction with Interstate 82 and drive to Umatilla. Turn west on U.S. 730 and drive one-half mile to the park on the right at milepost 182.

Trip notes: This campground is along the Columbia River in a grassy area surrounded by trees. Nearby recreation options include a golf course, a marina, and tennis courts.

② Dun-Rollin Trailer Park

Location: Near the Columbia River; map C4, grid c3.

Campsites, facilities: There are 15 sites for trailers or RVs of any length. Electricity, piped water, and sewer hookups are provided. Flush toilets, sanitary disposal services, showers, laundry facilities, and a playground are available. Bottled gas, a store, a cafe, and ice are located within one mile. Leashed pets and motorbikes are permitted.

Reservations, fees: Reservations are accepted. Sites are $15 per night. The campground is open year-round.

Contact: Phone (541) 567-6918 or write to 445 East Jennie, Hermiston, OR 97838.

Directions: From Interstate 84 west of Pendleton, take exit 188 and drive six miles north on U.S. 395 to Hermiston. Continue one-quarter mile north on U.S. 395 to Jennie, then drive one-half mile east to the park on the left.

Trip notes: This RV park is not far from the Columbia River and the Cold Springs National

Wildlife Refuge. A golf course, bike paths, a marina, and tennis courts are close by.

❸ Hat Rock Campground

Location: Near the Columbia River; map C4, grid c4.

Campsites, facilities: There are eight tent sites and 72 sites for trailers or RVs of any length, 15 with full and 57 with partial hookups. Electricity, piped water, sewer hookups, and picnic tables are provided. Flush toilets, sanitary disposal services, showers, a store, a cafe, a laundry room, a swimming pool, and ice are available. Boat docks and launching facilities are nearby. Leashed pets are permitted.

Reservations, fees: Reservations are accepted. Sites are $14–$15 per night. The campground is open year-round.

Contact: Phone the campground at (541) 567-4188 or the Hat Rock Store at (541) 567-0917, or write to 82280 Hatrock Road, Hermiston, OR 97838.

Directions: From Interstate 84 west of Pendleton, take exit 188 and drive six miles north on U.S. 395 to Hermiston. Turn northeast on U.S. 730 and drive one mile. Turn north on the state park access road and continue one-half mile to the park on the left.

Trip notes: This campground is not far from Hat Rock State Park, a day-use area with a boat launch along the banks of the Columbia River. The campground itself is very pretty, with lots of trees and close access to the river and fishing.

❹ Fort Henrietta RV Park

Location: On the Umatilla River; map C4, grid d3.

Campsites, facilities: There are seven sites for trailers or RVs and an area for dispersed tent camping. Rest rooms, showers, and a sanitary dump are provided. Some of the facilities are wheelchair accessible. The camp is within walking distance of two restaurants. Licensed, leashed pets are permitted.

Reservations, fees: No reservations are accepted. Sites are $15 per night. The campground is open year-round.

Contact: Phone the park at (541) 376-8411, fax (541) 376-8218, or write to P.O. Box 9, Echo, OR 97826.

Directions: From Interstate 84 west of Pendleton, take exit 188 and drive one mile southeast on Echo Highway. Cross the railroad tracks, turn south on Dupont Street, and drive three-tenths of a mile to Main Street. The park is one block west on Main Street on the left side.

Trip notes: The park is located in the historic community of Echo along the Umatilla River. The river provides some good trout fishing. This is a quiet, pleasant layover spot for travelers cruising Interstate 84.

❺ Shadeview Mobile Home Park

Location: Near the Umatilla River; map C4, grid d5.

Campsites, facilities: There are 14 sites for trailers or RVs of any length. Electricity, piped water, and sewer hookups are provided. Flush toilets and showers are available. Bottled gas, sanitary disposal services, a store, a cafe, a Laundromat, and ice are located within one mile. Pets are permitted.

Reservations, fees: Reservations are accepted. Sites are $13 per night. The campground is open year-round.

Contact: Phone (541) 276-0688 or write to 1417 Southwest 37th Street, Pendleton, OR 97801.

Directions: From Pendleton on Interstate 84, turn south on U.S. 395 and drive one mile, then travel one-quarter mile west on Southgate Place. The park is one block north on 37th Street.

Trip notes: This park is near the Umatilla River, where a levee offers walking and fishing opportunities. Nearby recreation options include marked bike trails and tennis courts. The Cold Springs National Wildlife Refuge, eight miles east of Hermiston, is home to a large variety of waterfowl.

⑥ Brooke RV Court 🚐

Location: Near the McKay Creek National Wildlife Refuge; map C4, grid d6.

Campsites, facilities: There are 43 sites for trailers or RVs of any length. Electricity, piped water, sewer hookups, and picnic tables are provided. Flush toilets, cable TV, showers, a laundry room, and ice are available. Bottled gas, sanitary disposal services, a store, and a cafe are located within one mile. Small leashed pets are permitted.

Reservations, fees: Reservations are accepted. Sites are $17 per night. The campground is open year-round.

Contact: Phone (541) 276-5353 or write to 5 Northeast Eighth Street, Pendleton, OR 97801.

Directions: From Pendleton on Interstate 84, take exit 213 and drive 2.3 miles. Turn right on South Eighth Street and drive two blocks past the bridge to where the road dead-ends at the park.

Trip notes: This pleasant, riverside suburban park in Pendleton is also on the historic Oregon Trail. Waterfowl can be observed at the McKay Creek National Wildlife Refuge seven miles south of Pendleton. The Pendleton Mills and outlet are in town. Other nearby recreation opportunities include a golf course, bike paths, and tennis courts.

⑦ Brooke RV-West 🚐

Location: Near the McKay Creek National Wildlife Refuge; map C4, grid d5.

Campsites, facilities: There are 40 drive-through sites with full hookups for trailers or RVs up to 60 feet long. Electricity, piped water, sewer hookups, and picnic tables are provided. Flush toilets, cable TV, showers, a laundry room, and ice are available. Bottled gas, sanitary disposal services, a store, and a cafe are within one mile. Some facilities are wheelchair accessible. Leashed pets are permitted.

Reservations, fees: Reservations are accepted. Sites are $17 per night. The campground is open from March to mid-November.

Contact: Phone (541) 276-5353 or (888) 276-

5353, or write to 601 Airport Road, Pendleton, OR 97801.

Directions: From Pendleton on Interstate 84, take exit 207 and turn left into the park.

Trip notes: See the trip notes for Brooke RV Court (campground number 6).

⑧ Emigrant Springs State Heritage Area 🚐

Location: Near the Umatilla Indian Reservation; map C4, grid d8.

Campsites, facilities: There are 33 tent sites and 18 sites with full hookups for trailers or RVs of any length. Also for rent are a totem bunkhouse, a cabin, and two covered camper wagons. Picnic tables and fire grills are provided. Flush toilets, showers, firewood, a laundry room, some horse facilities, a community building with a kitchen, and a playground are available. Leashed pets are permitted.

Reservations, fees: Contact Reservations Northwest at (800) 452-5687 ($6 reservation fee). Sites are $13–$20 per night; the totem bunkhouse is $20 per night. The campground is open from May through October.

Contact: Phone (541) 983-2277 or write to P.O. Box 85, Meacham, OR 97859.

Directions: From Pendleton, drive 26 miles southeast on Interstate 84 to the park on the right.

Trip notes: This wooded state park offers group camping areas and a display on the Oregon Trail. This is a good layover for people driving Interstate 84. It's just south of the Umatilla Indian Reservation.

⑨ Umatilla Forks 🚐

Location: Along the Umatilla River in Umatilla National Forest; map C4, grid d9.

Campsites, facilities: There are seven tent sites and eight sites that can accommodate tents, trailers, or RVs. Piped water, picnic tables, fire grills, and vault toilets are provided. Leashed pets are permitted.

Reservations, fees: No reservations are

accepted. There is no fee. The campground is open from April to October.

Contact: Umatilla National Forest, Walla Walla Ranger District, 1415 West Rose Street, Walla Walla, WA 99362; (509) 525-6290 or fax (509) 522-6000.

Directions: From Pendleton, drive east on Umatilla River Road for 33 miles to the campground. Umatilla River Road eventually becomes Forest Service Road 32.

Trip notes: This camp is located between the South and North Forks of the Umatilla River, set at 2,400 feet. Recreation opportunities include hiking and fishing. The camp provides the rare combination of piped water with no fee, and has an added bonus of being relatively unknown, making it a prime spot.

⑩ Woodward

Location: Near Langdon Lake in Umatilla National Forest; map C4, grid d9.

Campsites, facilities: There are 18 sites for tents, trailers, or RVs. Piped water, picnic tables, fire grills, and vault toilets are provided. A picnic shelter is available by reservation. Leashed pets are permitted.

Reservations, fees: No reservations are accepted. Sites are $5 per night. The campground is open from mid-June to mid-September.

Contact: Umatilla National Forest, Walla Walla Ranger District, 1415 West Rose Street, Walla Walla, WA 99362; (509) 525-6290 or fax (509) 522-6000.

Directions: From Pendleton on Interstate 84, turn north on Highway 11 and drive approximately 27 miles to Weston. Turn east on Highway 204 and drive 17 miles. The campground is located just off the highway, near Langdon Lake.

Trip notes: This campground is located near privately owned Langdon Lake. A flat trail circles the camp.

⑪ Cutsforth County Park

Location: On Willow Creek; map C4, grid e3.

Campsites, facilities: There are 35 sites for tents, trailers, or RVs up to 30 feet. Rest rooms, showers, horseshoes, and a playground are provided. Some facilities are wheelchair accessible. Leashed pets are permitted.

Reservations, fees: No reservations are accepted. Sites are $5–$8 per night. The campground is open from May 15 to November 20.

Contact: Lexington Public Works, P.O. Box 428, Lexington, OR 97839; (541) 989-9500.

Directions: From Interstate 84 west of Pendleton, exit on Highway 207/Heppner Highway and drive 30 miles to Lexington. Turn left on Highway 74 and drive 10.5 miles. Turn left on Willow Creek Road and drive for 23 miles to the park.

Trip notes: Though just a short jaunt from the interstate, this park is secluded and private. It's set beside a small, wheelchair-accessible pond in a quiet, wooded area. Trout fishing is available in the stocked ponds. See the trip notes for Anson Wright County Park (campground number 18) for details on the area.

⑫ Lane Creek

Location: On Camus Creek in Umatilla National Forest; map C4, grid f6.

Campsites, facilities: There are eight sites for tents, trailers, or RVs up to 45 feet long. No piped water is available. Picnic tables and fire grills are provided. Vault toilets are available. Leashed pets are permitted.

Reservations, fees: No reservations are accepted. There is no fee. The campground is open year-round, with no winter maintenance (November through March).

Contact: Umatilla National Forest, John Day Ranger District, P.O. Box 158, Ukiah, OR 97880; (541) 427-3231 or fax (541) 276-5026.

Directions: From Pendleton on Interstate 84, turn south on U.S. 395 and drive 50 miles to Ukiah. Turn east on Highway 244 and travel nine miles to the campground.

Trip notes: This campground is set at 3,850 feet along Camus Creek just inside the forest boundary, with easy access to all the amenities of town. Highlights include a hot springs and good hunting and fishing. A Forest Service map details the back roads.

⑬ Bear Wallow Creek

Location: On Bear Wallow Creek in Umatilla National Forest; map C4, grid f6.

Campsites, facilities: There are eight sites for tents, trailers, or RVs up to 30 feet long. No piped water is available. Picnic tables and fire grills are provided. Vault toilets are available. Leashed pets are permitted.

Reservations, fees: No reservations are accepted. There is no fee. The stay limit is 14 days. The campground is open year-round, with no winter maintenance (November through March).

Contact: Umatilla National Forest, North Fork John Day Ranger District, P.O. Box 158, Ukiah, OR 97880; (541) 427-3231 or fax (541) 276-5026.

Directions: From Pendleton on Interstate 84, turn south on U.S. 395 and drive 50 miles to Ukiah. Turn east on Highway 244 and drive 10 miles to the camp.

Trip notes: Set near the confluence of Bear Wallow and Camus Creeks at an elevation of 3,900 feet, this is one of three camps off Highway 244. The others are Lane Creek and Frazier (campground numbers 12 and 14). Bear Wallow Creek Camp is primarily used in the fall by hunters. It's quiet, primitive, and free. A three-quarter-mile interpretive trail meanders next to Bear Wallow Creek, highlighting steelhead habitat. The trail is wheelchair accessible.

⑭ Frazier

Location: On Frazier Creek in Umatilla National Forest; map C4, grid f7.

Campsites, facilities: There are 21 sites for tents, trailers, or RVs up to 30 feet long. Picnic tables, fire grills, and vault toilets are available. There is no piped water. Some facilities are wheelchair accessible. An all-terrain-vehicle loading ramp is available. Leashed pets are permitted.

Reservations, fees: No reservations are accepted. There is no fee. The campground is open year-round, with no winter maintenance (November through March).

Contact: Umatilla National Forest, North Fork John Day Ranger District, P.O. Box 158, Ukiah, OR 97880; (541) 427-3231 or fax (541) 276-5026.

Directions: From Pendleton on Interstate 84, turn south on U.S. 395 and drive 50 miles to Ukiah. Turn east on Highway 244 and drive 16 miles, then go one-half mile south on Forest Service Road 5226.

Trip notes: This campground set at 4,300 feet along the banks of Frazier Creek is a popular hunting area that also has some fishing. It's advisable to obtain a map of Umatilla National Forest. There are nearly 100 miles of all-terrain-vehicle and motorcycle trails at the nearby Winom-Frazier Off-Highway-Vehicle Complex. Lehman Hot Springs provides a nearby side trip option.

⑮ Spool Cart

Location: On the Grande Ronde River in Wallowa-Whitman National Forest; map C4, grid f9.

Campsites, facilities: There are 16 sites for tents, trailers, or RVs up to 22 feet long. Picnic tables and fire grills are provided. Firewood and vault toilets are available. There is no piped water. Leashed pets are permitted.

Reservations, fees: No reservations are accepted. There is no fee. The campground is open from late May to late November.

Contact: Wallowa-Whitman National Forest, LaGrande Ranger District, 3502 Highway 30, LaGrande, OR 97850; (541) 963-7186 or fax (541) 962-8580.

Directions: From LaGrande, drive nine miles northwest on Interstate 84, then 13 miles southwest on Highway 244. Turn south and drive seven miles on Forest Service Road 51 to the campground on the right.

Trip notes: This campground on the banks of the Grande Ronde River gets its name from the large cable spools that were left on a cart at the site for some years. Hilgard Junction

State Park to the north provides numerous recreation options, and the Oregon Trail Interpretive Park is nearby. It's advisable to obtain a map of Wallowa-Whitman National Forest that details the back roads and other side trips.

⑯ Bull Prairie

Location: On Bull Prairie Lake in Umatilla National Forest; map C4, grid g0.

Campsites, facilities: There are 25 sites for tents, trailers, or RVs up to 31 feet long. Picnic tables and fire grills are provided. Piped water, sanitary disposal services, firewood, and vault toilets are available. Boat docks and launching facilities are on site. Pets are permitted.

Reservations, fees: No reservations are accepted. Sites are $6 per night. The campground is open from May to October.

Contact: Umatilla National Forest, Heppner Ranger District, P.O. Box 7, Heppner, OR 97836; (541) 676-9187 or fax (541) 676-2105.

Directions: From Interstate 5 at Albany, turn east on U.S. 20 and drive 100 miles to Sisters. Turn east on Highway 126 and drive 39 miles to Prineville, then continue east on U.S. 26 for 48 miles to the Highway 207 turnoff. Drive north on Highway 207 approximately 50 miles to Forest Service Road 2039 (paved). Turn right and drive three miles northeast to the campground.

Trip notes: This campground is set along the shore of Bull Prairie Lake. Boating (no motors permitted), swimming, fishing, and hunting are some of the options here. This spot attracts little attention from out-of-towners, yet offers plenty of recreation opportunities, making it an ideal vacation destination for many.

⑰ Fairview

Location: Near Bull Prairie Lake in Umatilla National Forest; map C4, grid g0.

Campsites, facilities: There are five sites for trailers or RVs up to 16 feet long. Picnic tables and fire grills are provided. Firewood and vault toilets are available. There is no piped water. Boat docks and launching facilities are nearby at Bull Prairie Lake. Leashed pets are permitted.

Reservations, fees: No reservations are accepted. There is no fee. The campground is open from May to late October.

Contact: Umatilla National Forest, Heppner Ranger District, P.O. Box 7, Heppner, OR 97836; (541) 676-9187 or fax (541) 676-2105.

Directions: From Interstate 5 at Albany, turn east on U.S. 20 and drive 100 miles to Sisters. Turn east on Highway 126 and drive 39 miles to Prineville, then continue east on U.S. 26 for 48 miles to the Highway 207 turnoff. Drive north on Highway 207 approximately 49 miles. Turn west on Forest Service Road 400 and drive 500 yards to the campground.

Trip notes: This campground adjacent to Fairview Springs near Mahogany Butte is a small, primitive site known by very few people. Located in a remote area at 4,300 feet, it's primarily used as a base camp by hunters.

⑱ Anson Wright County Park

Location: On Chapin Creek; map C4, grid g1.

Campsites, facilities: There are 30 sites for tents, trailers, or RVs up to 30 feet. Rest rooms, showers, a barbecue, and a playground are provided. Some facilities are wheelchair accessible. Leashed pets are permitted.

Reservations, fees: No reservations are accepted. Sites are $5–$8 per night. The campground is open from May 16 to November 16.

Contact: Morrow County Public Works, P.O. Box 428, Lexington, OR 97839; (541) 989-9500.

Directions: From Interstate 84 west of Pendleton, take exit 182. Turn southwest on Highway 207 and drive 46 miles to the park access road (signed). Continue south for 21 miles to the park.

Trip notes: Set within wooded hills on a small stream, this county park offers visitors prime trout fishing in several stocked ponds as well as hiking opportunities. There is a wheelchair-accessible fishing pond. Attractions in the area include the Pendleton Mills, Emigrant Springs State Park, Hardman Ghost Town (24 miles away), and the Columbia River.

⑲ Divide Well

Location: In Umatilla National Forest; map C4, grid g4.

Campsites, facilities: There are six primitive tent sites. Picnic tables and a vault toilet are provided, but there is no piped water. Leashed pets are permitted.

Reservations, fees: No reservations are accepted. There is no fee. The campground is open year-round, with no winter maintenance (November through March).

Contact: Umatilla National Forest, North Fork John Day Ranger District, P.O. Box 158, Ukiah, OR 97880; (541) 427-3231 or fax (541) 276-5026.

Directions: From Pendleton on Interstate 84, turn south on U.S. 395 and drive 50 miles to Ukiah. Turn west on Forest Service Road 53 and drive 10 miles, then turn left on Forest Service Road 5312 and drive six miles. Turn right on Forest Service Road 5320 and travel one mile, then turn right on Forest Service Road 5327 and continue one-half mile to the campground. A Forest Service map is recommended.

Trip notes: This primitive, remote campground set at 4,700 feet can serve as a good base camp for a hunting trip. Mule deer and Rocky Mountain elk are abundant in the surrounding pine forest. Potamus Point Scenic Overlook, offering a spectacular view of the John Day River drainage, is 11 miles south of the camp on Forest Service Road 5316.

⑳ Ukiah-Dale Forest State Recreation Site

Location: On the North Fork of the John Day River; map C4, grid g5.

Campsites, facilities: There are 27 primitive sites for tents, trailers, or self-contained RVs up to 40 feet long. Picnic tables and fire grills are provided. Piped water, fire-

wood, and vault toilets are available. Pets are permitted.

Reservations, fees: No reservations are accepted. Sites are $7–$13 per night. The campground is open from mid-April to late October.

Contact: Phone (541) 983-2277 or (800) 452-5687, or write to P.O. Box 85, Meacham, OR 97859.

Directions: From Pendleton on Interstate 84, turn south on U.S. 395 and drive 48 miles to Ukiah. Continue three miles south on U.S. 395 to the park.

Trip notes: Fishing is a prime activity at this campground near the banks of the North Fork of the John Day River. It's a good layover for visitors cruising U.S. 395 looking for a spot for the night. Emigrant Springs State Park near Pendleton is a possible side trip.

㉑ Tollbridge

Location: On the North Fork of the John Day River in Umatilla National Forest; map C4, grid g5.

Campsites, facilities: There are seven sites for tents, trailers, or RVs up to 31 feet long. Picnic tables and fire grills are provided. Piped water and a vault toilet are available. Leashed pets are permitted.

Reservations, fees: No reservations are accepted. There is no fee. The stay limit is 14 days. The campground is open year-round, with no winter maintenance (November through March).

Contact: Umatilla National Forest, North Fork John Day Ranger District, P.O. Box 158, Ukiah, OR 97880; (541) 427-3231 or fax (541) 276-5026.

Directions: From Pendleton on Interstate 84, turn south on U.S. 395 and drive 62 miles to Forest Service Road 55 (one mile north of Dale). Turn left and drive one-half mile southeast, then 100 yards on Forest Service Road 10 to the campground.

Trip notes: This small, secluded campground (elevation 3,800 feet) lies at the confluence of Desolation Creek and the North Fork of the John Day River, and is adjacent to the Bridge

Creek Wildlife Area. Hunting and fishing are two options here.

㉒ Drift Fence

Location: Near Ross Springs in Umatilla National Forest; map C4, grid g5.

Campsites, facilities: There are five sites for tents, trailers, or RVs up to 16 feet long. There is no piped water. A vault toilet and picnic tables are available. Leashed pets are permitted.

Reservations, fees: No reservations are accepted. There is no fee. The campground is open year-round.

Contact: Umatilla National Forest, North Fork John Day Ranger District, P.O. Box 158, Ukiah, OR 97880; (541) 427-3231 or fax (541) 276-5026.

Directions: From Pendleton on Interstate 84, turn south on U.S. 395 and drive 50 miles to Ukiah. Turn east on Forest Service Road 52 and drive seven miles to the campground.

Trip notes: Hunting is a highlight at this campground set at 4,200 feet, with an abundance of elk and deer in the area. The camp is adjacent to Blue Mountain National Forest Scenic Byway. The Bridge Creek Interpretive Trail, located three miles northwest of the campground off Forest Service Road 52, leads to a viewpoint where elk may be seen roaming in the Bridge Creek area.

㉓ Gold Dredge Camp

Location: On the North Fork of the John Day River in Umatilla National Forest; map C4, grid g6.

Campsites, facilities: There are eight sites for trailers or RVs. No piped water or fire grills are provided, but vault toilets and picnic tables are available. Leashed pets are permitted.

Reservations, fees: No reservations are accepted. There is no fee. The campground is open year-round, with no winter maintenance (November through March).

Contact: Umatilla National Forest, North Fork John Day Ranger District, P.O. Box 158,

Ukiah, OR 97880; (541) 427-3231 or fax (541) 276-5026.

Directions: From Pendleton on Interstate 84, turn south on U.S. 395 and drive 62 miles to Forest Service Road 55 (one mile north of Dale). Turn left and drive six miles to the crossroads. Continue east on Forest Service Road 5506 for 2.5 miles to the campground.

Trip notes: Hunting and fishing are among the possibilities at this campground along the banks of the North Fork of the John Day River, a federally certified Wild and Scenic river. By traveling to the end of Forest Service Road 5506, you can access a trail that heads into the adjacent North Fork John Day Wilderness.

㉔ Oriental Creek

Location: On the North Fork of the John Day River in Umatilla National Forest; map C4, grid g6.

Campsites, facilities: There are seven primitive tent sites. Pit toilets and picnic tables are available, but there is no piped water. One toilet is wheelchair accessible. Leashed pets are permitted.

Reservations, fees: No reservations are accepted. There is no fee. The campground is open year-round, with no winter maintenance (November through March).

Contact: Umatilla National Forest, North Fork John Day Ranger District, P.O. Box 158, Ukiah, OR 97880; (541) 427-3231 or fax (541) 276-5026.

Directions: From Pendleton on Interstate 84, turn south on U.S. 395 and drive 62 miles to Forest Service Road 55 (one mile north of Dale). Turn left and drive six miles to the crossroads. Continue east on Forest Service Road 5506 for six miles to the campground. This road is not recommended for trailers.

Trip notes: This campground is set at 3,500 feet along the banks of the North Fork of the John Day River. Nearby trails provide access to the North Fork John Day Wilderness. Hunting and fishing are two possible activities here. No motorbikes are permitted in the wilderness area.

㉕ Driftwood

Location: On the North Fork of the John Day River in Umatilla National Forest; map C4, grid g6.

Campsites, facilities: There are seven sites for tents and trailers. A vault toilet and picnic tables are provided, but there is no piped water. Leashed pets are permitted.

Reservations, fees: No reservations are accepted. There is no fee. The campground is open year-round, with no winter maintenance (November through March).

Contact: Umatilla National Forest, North Fork John Day Ranger District, P.O. Box 158, Ukiah, OR 97880; (541) 427-3231 or fax (541) 276-5026.

Directions: From Pendleton on Interstate 84, turn south on U.S. 395 and drive 62 miles to Forest Service Road 55 (one mile north of Dale). Turn left and drive six miles to the crossroads. Continue east on Forest Service Road 5506 for one mile.

Trip notes: This tiny campground is located on the banks of the North Fork of the John Day River at an elevation of 2,500 feet. Recreational opportunities include hunting, fishing, swimming, rafting, and float tubing.

㉖ Welch Creek

Location: On Desolation Creek in Umatilla National Forest; map C4, grid g6.

Campsites, facilities: There are five primitive tent sites. Picnic tables and a vault toilet are provided, but there is no piped water. Leashed pets are permitted.

Reservations, fees: No reservations are accepted. There is no fee. The campground is open year-round, with no winter maintenance (November through March).

Contact: Umatilla National Forest, North Fork John Day Ranger District, P.O. Box 158, Ukiah, OR 97880; (541) 427-3231 or fax (541) 276-5026.

Directions: From Pendleton on Interstate 84, turn south on U.S. 395 and drive 62 miles to Forest Service Road 55 (one mile north of Dale). Turn left and drive one mile, then turn right on Forest Service Road 10 and continue 13 miles to the campground.

Trip notes: This primitive camp, located on the banks of Desolation Creek, is remote and out of the way. Hunting and fishing are popular here.

㉗ Big Creek Meadows

Location: On Big Creek in Umatilla National Forest; map C4, grid g7.

Campsites, facilities: There are four primitive tent sites. A picnic table and a vault toilet are provided, but there is no piped water. Leashed pets are permitted.

Reservations, fees: No reservations are accepted. There is no fee. The campground is open year-round, with no winter maintenance (November through March).

Contact: Umatilla National Forest, North Fork John Day Ranger District, P.O. Box 158, Ukiah, OR 97880; (541) 427-3231 or fax (541) 276-5026.

Directions: From Pendleton on Interstate 84, turn south on U.S. 395 and drive 50 miles to Ukiah. Turn east on Forest Service Road 52 and drive 22 miles. Turn right on Forest Service Road 5225 and travel a short distance, then turn right on Forest Service Road 5225-020 and continue one-half mile to the camp.

Trip notes: This primitive campground is located at an elevation of 5,100 feet on the banks of Big Creek. The North Fork John Day Wilderness is located about one-quarter mile away. Fishing and hunting are among the activities here.

㉘ North Fork John Day

Location: On the North Fork of the John Day River in Umatilla National Forest; map C4, grid g8.

Campsites, facilities: There are eight sites for tents, trailers, or RVs up to 22 feet long. Picnic tables and fire grills are provided. Vault toilets are available. There is no piped water. Leashed pets are permitted.

Reservations, fees: No reservations are accepted. There is no fee. The stay limit is 14 days. The campground is open year-round, with no winter maintenance (November through March).

Contact: Umatilla National Forest, North Fork John Day Ranger District, P.O. Box 158, Ukiah, OR 97880; (541) 427-3231 or fax (541) 276-5026.

Directions: From Pendleton on Interstate 84, turn south on U.S. 395 and drive 50 miles to Ukiah. Turn east on Forest Service Road 52 and travel 36 miles to the campground.

Trip notes: This campground along the banks of the North Fork of the John Day River is an ideal base camp for a wilderness backpacking trip. A horse-handling area is also available for wilderness users. Trails from camp lead into the North Fork John Day Wilderness. The camp is located at the intersection of Elkhorn and Blue Mountain National Forest Scenic Byways. No motorbikes are permitted in the wilderness.

㉙ River

Location: On the Grande Ronde River in Wallowa-Whitman National Forest; map C4, grid g9.

Campsites, facilities: There are six sites for tents or trailers. Picnic tables and fire grills are provided. Vault toilets are available. There is no piped water. Leashed pets are permitted.

Reservations, fees: No reservations are accepted. There is no fee. The campground is open from late May to late November.

Contact: Wallowa-Whitman National Forest, LaGrande Ranger District, 3502 Highway 30, LaGrande, OR 97850; (541) 963-7186 or fax (541) 962-8580.

Directions: From LaGrande, drive nine miles northwest on Interstate 84, then 13 miles southwest on Highway 244. From there, continue 11 miles south on Forest Service Road 51.

Trip notes: This campground is along the banks of the Grande Ronde River. See the trip notes for Spool Cart (campground number 15) for more information.

㉚ Anthony Lake

Location: On Anthony Lake in Wallowa-Whitman National Forest; map C4, grid g9.

Campsites, facilities: There are 37 sites for tents, trailers, or RVs up to 22 feet long. Piped water, fire grills, and picnic tables are provided. Vault toilets are available. Some facilities are wheelchair accessible. Boat launching facilities are nearby. Leashed pets are permitted.

Reservations, fees: No reservations are accepted. Sites are $5 per night. The campground is open from July to late September.

Contact: Wallowa-Whitman National Forest, Baker Ranger District, P.O. Box 907, Baker City, OR 97814; (541) 523-4476 or fax (541) 523-1965.

Directions: From Interstate 84 at Baker City, turn north on U.S. 30 and drive 13 miles to Haines. Drive 17 miles northwest on County Road 1146, then nine miles west on Forest Service Road 73.

Trip notes: This campground is adjacent to Anthony Lake, where boating without motors is permitted. Several smaller lakes, within two miles by car or trail, are ideal for trout fishing from a raft, float tube, or canoe. The trailhead for the Elkhorn Crest Trail is near here.

㉛ Grande Ronde Lake

Location: On Grande Ronde Lake in Wallowa-Whitman National Forest; map C4, grid g9.

Campsites, facilities: There are eight sites for tents, trailers, or RVs up to 16 feet long. Picnic tables and fire grills are provided. Piped water and vault toilets are available. Boat docks and launching facilities are nearby. Leashed pets are permitted.

Reservations, fees: No reservations are accepted. Sites are $3 per night. The campground is open from July to mid-September.

Contact: Wallowa-Whitman National Forest,

Baker Ranger District, P.O. Box 907, Baker City, OR 97814; (541) 523-4476 or fax (541) 523-1965.

Directions: From Interstate 84 at Baker City, turn north on U.S. 30 and drive 13 miles to Haines. Drive 17 miles northwest on County Road 1146, then 9.5 miles west on Forest Service Road 73. The camp is one-half mile northwest on Forest Service Road 43.

Trip notes: This campground is located at an elevation of 7,200 feet along the shore of Grande Ronde Lake, a small lake where the trout fishing can be good. Several trails are to the south near Anthony Lake. A map of Wallowa-Whitman National Forest details the possibilities.

⏳ Mud Lake

Location: On Mud Lake in Wallowa-Whitman National Forest; map C4, grid g9.

Campsites, facilities: There are three tent sites and five sites for trailers or RVs up to 16 feet long. Picnic tables and fire grills are provided. Piped water and vault toilets are available. Boat docks and launching facilities are located nearby at Anthony Lake. Leashed pets are permitted.

Reservations, fees: No reservations are accepted. Sites are $3 per night. The campground is open from July to mid-September.

Contact: Wallowa-Whitman National Forest, Baker Ranger District, P.O. Box 907, Baker City, OR 97814; (541) 523-4476 or fax (541) 523-1965.

Directions: From Interstate 84 at Baker City, turn north on U.S. 30 and drive 13 miles to Haines. Drive 17 miles northwest on County Road 1146, then nine miles west on Forest Service Road 73.

Trip notes: This campground is on the shore of small Mud Lake, where the trout fishing can be fairly good. The campground is tiny and pleasant, with lots of vegetation and relatively little use. Bring your mosquito repellent.

Map C5

One inch equals approximately 20 miles.

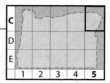

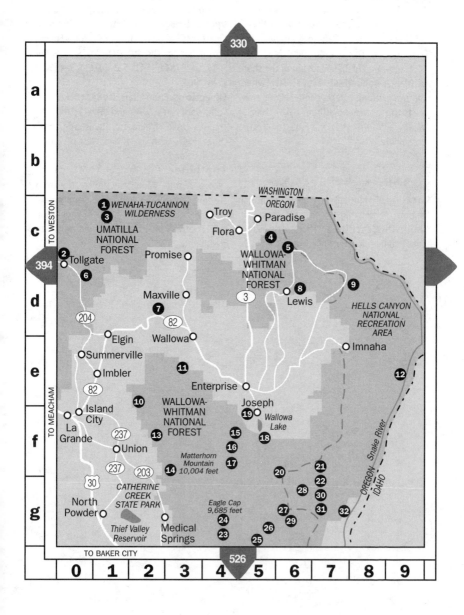

Chapter C5 features:

1 Mottet

Location: Near the South Fork of the Walla Walla River in Umatilla National Forest; map C5, grid b2.

Campsites, facilities: There are seven sites for tents, trailers, or RVs. Picnic tables and fire grills are provided. Springwater and vault toilets are available. Trash must be packed out; no garbage facilities are provided. Leashed pets are permitted.

Reservations, fees: No reservations are accepted. There is no fee. The campground is open from July to mid-October.

Contact: Umatilla National Forest, Walla Walla Ranger District, 1415 West Rose Street, Walla Walla, WA 99362; (509) 522-6290 or fax (509) 522-6000.

Directions: From Pendleton on Interstate 84, turn north on Highway 11 and drive approximately 27 miles to Weston. Turn east on Highway 204 and drive 17.5 miles to Forest Service Road 64. Turn left and drive about 15 miles on Forest Service Road 64 to Forest Service Road 6403. Turn left and drive about two miles to the campground.

Trip notes: This campground is set at 5,200 feet in a nice spot, adjacent to a trailhead that leads down to the South Fork of the Walla Walla River. Located far from the beaten path, it's quite primitive and relatively unknown, so you're almost guaranteed privacy.

2 Target Meadows

Location: Near the South Fork of the Walla Walla River in Umatilla National Forest; map C5, grid c0.

Campsites, facilities: There are 19 sites for tents, trailers, or RVs. Piped water, picnic tables, fire grills, and vault toilets are provided. Leashed pets are permitted.

Reservations, fees: No reservations are accepted. Sites are $5 per night. The campground is open from mid-June to mid-September.

Contact: Umatilla National Forest, Walla Walla Ranger District, 1415 West Rose Street, Walla Walla, WA 99362; (509) 522-6290 or fax (509) 522-6000.

Directions: From Pendleton on Interstate 84, turn north on Highway 11 and drive approximately 27 miles to Weston. Turn east on Highway 204 and drive 17.5 miles to Forest Service Road 64. Turn left and drive one-half mile to Forest Service Road 6401. Turn north and drive two miles. The camp is located about 1,000 yards north on spur road 050.

Trip notes: This quiet campground with shady sites and a sunny meadow is set at 4,800 feet, adjacent to the Burnt Cabin Trailhead, which leads to the South Fork of the Walla Walla River.

❸ Jubilee Lake

Location: On Jubilee Lake in Umatilla National Forest; map C5, grid c1.

Campsites, facilities: There are 51 sites for tents, trailers, or RVs up to 27 feet long, with some drive-through sites. Picnic tables and fire grills are provided. Piped water, firewood, and flush toilets are available. Some facilities are barrier-free. Boat docks and launching facilities are nearby. Leashed pets are permitted.

Reservations, fees: No reservations are accepted. Sites are $10 per night, plus $5 for each additional vehicle. The campground is open from mid-June through September.

Contact: Umatilla National Forest, Walla Walla Ranger District, 1415 West Rose Street, Walla Walla, WA 99362; (509) 522-6290 or fax (509) 522-6000.

Directions: From Pendleton on Interstate 84, turn north on Highway 11 and drive approximately 27 miles to Weston. Turn east on Highway 204 and drive 17.5 miles to Forest Service Road 64. Turn left and drive 12 miles northeast. The camp is 700 yards south on Forest Service Road 250.

Trip notes: This campground along the shore of Jubilee Lake (elevation 4,800 feet) is a good area for swimming, fishing, and hiking. Boats are permitted, but only electric motors are allowed. A 2.5-mile trail loops around the lake and is designated to provide different levels of handicapped accessibility. Fishing access is available along the trail.

❹ Coyote

Location: Near Coyote Springs in Wallowa-Whitman National Forest; map C5, grid c5.

Campsites, facilities: There are 29 sites for tents, trailers, or RVs up to 22 feet long. Picnic tables and fire grills are provided. Vault toilets are available, but there is no piped water. A

spring is located within one-quarter mile. Leashed pets are permitted.

Reservations, fees: No reservations are accepted. There is no fee. The campground is open from mid-May to December.

Contact: Wallowa-Whitman National Forest, Wallowa Valley Ranger District, (541) 426-5546. Wallowa Mountains Visitor Center, 88401 Highway 82, Enterprise, OR 97828.

Directions: From LaGrande on Interstate 84, turn north on Highway 82 and drive 62 miles north and east to Enterprise. Turn north on Highway 3 and drive 15 miles, then 25 miles northeast on Forest Service Road 46 to the campground.

Trip notes: This campground set at 4,800 feet, adjacent to Coyote Springs, is the largest of the three primitive camps in the vicinity, offering open sites and privacy.

❺ Dougherty

Location: Near Dougherty Springs in Wallowa-Whitman National Forest; map C5, grid c6.

Campsites, facilities: There are 12 sites for tents, trailers, or RVs up to 22 feet long. Picnic tables and fire grills are provided. Vault toilets are available, but there is no piped water. Leashed pets are permitted.

Reservations, fees: No reservations are accepted. There is no fee. The campground is open from June to late November.

Contact: Hells Canyon National Recreation Area, (541) 426-5546. Wallowa Mountains Visitor Center, 88401 Highway 82, Enterprise, OR 97828.

Directions: From LaGrande on Interstate 84, turn north on Highway 82 and drive 62 miles north and east to Enterprise. Turn north on Highway 3 and drive 15 miles, then 30 miles northeast on Forest Service Road 46.

Trip notes: This wooded, primitive campground (elevation 5,000 feet) adjacent to Dougherty Springs is one in a series of remote camps set near natural springs. Hells Canyon National Recreation Area to the east provides many recreation options.

❻ Woodland

Location: In Umatilla National Forest; map C5, grid d0.

Campsites, facilities: There are seven sites for tents, trailers, or RVs. Picnic tables, fire grills, and vault toilets are provided, but there is no piped water. No garbage facilities are provided, so campers must pack out their own trash. Leashed pets are permitted.

Reservations, fees: No reservations are accepted. There is no fee. The campground is open from mid-June to mid-September.

Contact: Umatilla National Forest, Walla Walla Ranger District, 1415 West Rose Street, Walla Walla, WA 99362; (509) 522-6290 or fax (509) 522-6000.

Directions: From Pendleton on Interstate 84, turn north on Highway 11 and drive approximately 27 miles to Weston. Turn east on Highway 204 and drive 23 miles. The campground is located just off the highway.

Trip notes: This primitive camp with easy highway access can be a perfect spot for Interstate 84 cruisers looking for a short detour. See a Forest Service map for details about the recreation options within driving distance.

❼ Minam State Park

Location: Near the Grande Ronde River; map C5, grid d2.

Campsites, facilities: There are 12 primitive sites for tents, trailers, or self-contained RVs of any length. Picnic tables and fire grills are provided. Piped water and pit toilets are available. Leashed pets are permitted.

Reservations, fees: No reservations are accepted. Sites are $11 per night; weekly rates are available from October through mid-May. The campground is open from mid-April to late October.

Contact: Phone (541) 432-8855 or (800) 452-5687, or write to 72214 Marina Lane, Joseph, OR 97846.

Directions: From Pendleton, turn east and drive 54 miles on Interstate 84 to LaGrande. Take exit 261 and turn north on Highway 82.

Drive 16 miles to Elgin, then continue 15 miles to the park entrance road. Turn north and drive one-half mile to the park.

Trip notes: Morning and evening trout fishing can be decent at this campground along the banks of the Minam River in Minam State Park. This is a good launch point to float the Wild and Scenic Grande Ronde River. The park is small and pretty, and well worth the detour off Interstate 84.

❽ Vigne

Location: On Chesnimnus Creek in Wallowa-Whitman National Forest; map C5, grid d6.

Campsites, facilities: There are seven sites for tents, trailers, or RVs up to 22 feet long. Picnic tables and fire grills are provided. Piped water and vault toilets are available. Leashed pets are permitted.

Reservations, fees: No reservations are accepted. There is no fee. The campground is open from mid-April to late November.

Contact: Wallowa-Whitman National Forest, Wallowa Valley Ranger District; (541) 426-5546. Wallowa Mountains Visitor Center, 88401 Highway 82, Enterprise, OR 97828.

Directions: From LaGrande on Interstate 84, turn north on Highway 82 and drive 62 miles north and east to Enterprise. Turn north on Highway 3 and drive 15 miles, then 10 miles northeast on Forest Service Road 46. Turn east on Forest Service Road 4625 and continue 10 miles to the campground.

Trip notes: This campground along the banks of Chesnimnus Creek has pretty, shaded riverside sites. Fishing is a recreation possibility here, along with exploring a few of the many hiking trails in the area. See a Forest Service map for details. This is the only Forest Service camp in the area that has piped water.

❾ Buckhorn

Location: Near Buckhorn Overlook in Wallowa-Whitman National Forest; map C5, grid d7.

Campsites, facilities: There are six sites for tents or trailers. Picnic tables and fire grills are provided. Vault toilets are available, but there is no piped water. Leashed pets are permitted.

Reservations, fees: No reservations are accepted. There is no fee. The campground is open from June to late November.

Contact: Hells Canyon National Recreation Area, (541) 426-5546. Wallowa Mountains Visitor Center, 88401 Highway 82, Enterprise, OR 97828.

Directions: From LaGrande on Interstate 84, turn north on Highway 82 and drive 62 miles to Enterprise. Continue three miles on Highway 82, then drive 32 miles northeast on County Road 772. Continue 10 miles on Forest Service Road 46 to the campground.

Trip notes: Set at 5,200 feet elevation, adjacent to Buckhorn Springs, this small, primitive, and obscure camp gets little use. The elevation offers a spectacular view of the Imnaha River drainage.

⑩ Hot Lake RV Resort

Location: On Hot Lake; map C5, grid e2.

Campsites, facilities: There are 100 wide sites for tents, trailers, or RVs. Rest rooms, showers, laundry facilities, groceries, a sanitary dump station, a public phone, a swimming pool, a hot spa, ice, and RV supplies are available. Some facilities are wheelchair accessible. Leashed pets are permitted.

Reservations, fees: Reservations are recommended. Sites are $20 per night. The campground is open year-round.

Contact: Phone the park at (541) 963-5253, fax (541) 962-6272, or write to 65182 Hot Lake Lane, LaGrande, OR 97850.

Directions: From the south end of LaGrande at the junction of Interstate 84 and Highway 203, take exit 265. Drive southeast on Highway 203 for five miles to Foothill Road. The resort is on Foothill Road, three-tenths of a mile west on the left.

Trip notes: This camp is located on the shore of Hot Lake, where fishing, boating, hunting, and swimming are all possible. It's also on the historic Old Oregon Trail. Attractions in the

area include Hilgard Junction State Park and Wallowa-Whitman National Forest.

⑪ Boundary

Location: Near the Eagle Cap Wilderness in Wallowa-Whitman National Forest; map C5, grid e3.

Campsites, facilities: There are eight primitive tent sites. Leashed pets are permitted.

Reservations, fees: No reservations are accepted. There is no fee. The campground is open from mid-June to November.

Contact: Wallowa-Whitman National Forest, Eagle Cap Ranger District, (541) 426-5546. Wallowa Mountains Visitor Center, 88401 Highway 82, Enterprise, OR 97828.

Directions: From LaGrande on Interstate 84, turn north on Highway 82 and drive 46 miles to Wallowa. Turn south on Forest Service Road 8250 and drive eight miles, then go three-quarters of a mile south on Forest Service Road 8250-040 to the camp.

Trip notes: This pretty, private campground is set along the banks of Bear Creek. Nearby trails provide access to the Eagle Cap Wilderness. This is another in a series of little-known primitive sites in the area.

⑫ Saddle Creek

Location: Near the Hells Canyon Wilderness in Wallowa-Whitman National Forest; map C5, grid e9.

Campsites, facilities: There are seven sites for tents. Picnic tables and fire grills are provided. Vault toilets are available, but there is no piped water. Leashed pets are permitted. Note: RVs and trailers are not recommended on the access road.

Reservations, fees: No reservations are accepted. There is no fee. The campground is open from July to mid-November.

Contact: Hells Canyon National Recreation Area, (541) 426-5546. Wallowa Mountains Visitor Center, 88401 Highway 82, Enterprise, OR 97828.

Directions: From LaGrande on Interstate 84, turn north on Highway 82 and drive 62 miles to Enterprise. Continue south on Interstate 82 for six miles to Joseph. Turn east on Highway 350 and drive 30 miles to the small town of Imnaha. Go straight up the hill on Forest Service Road 4240 and drive 19 miles to the campground.

Trip notes: This campground is set at 6,900 feet in a wooded environment. Nearby trails provide access to Saddle Creek and Hells Canyon National Recreation Area.

⑬ Moss Springs

Location: Near the Eagle Cap Wilderness in Wallowa-Whitman National Forest; map C5, grid f2.

Campsites, facilities: There are 11 tent and trailer sites. Picnic tables and fire grills are provided. Horse facilities and vault toilets are available. Leashed pets are permitted.

Reservations, fees: No reservations are accepted. There is no fee. The campground is open from June to mid-October.

Contact: Wallowa-Whitman National Forest, LaGrande Ranger District, 3502 Highway 30, LaGrande, OR 97850; (541) 963-7186 or fax (541) 962-8580.

Directions: From Interstate 84 at LaGrande, turn east on Highway 237 and drive 15 miles to Cove. Drive 1.5 miles southeast of Cove on County Road 237, then eight miles east on Forest Service Road 6220 to the camp entrance at the end of the road.

Trip notes: A trailhead at this camp provides access to the Eagle Cap Wilderness, a good jump-off point for a multiday backpacking trip. Obtain a map of Wallowa-Whitman National Forest for detailed trail information. This camp is also a popular spot with horse packers. A loading ramp is provided.

⑭ North Fork Catherine Trailhead

Location: Near the Eagle Cap Wilderness in Wallowa-Whitman National Forest; map C5, grid f3.

Campsites, facilities: There are six sites for tents or trailers. Picnic tables and fire grills are provided. Vault toilets are available. There is no piped water. Leashed pets are permitted.

Reservations, fees: No reservations are accepted. There is no fee. The campground is open from June to late October.

Contact: Wallowa-Whitman National Forest, LaGrande Ranger District, 3502 Highway 30, LaGrande, OR 97850; (541) 963-7186 or fax (541) 962-8580.

Directions: From LaGrande on Interstate 84, travel 14 miles southeast on Highway 203 to Union. Drive 10 miles southeast of Union on Highway 203, then four miles east on Forest Service Road 7785. The camp is 3.5 miles northeast on Forest Service Road 7785.

Trip notes: This campground long the North Fork of Catherine Creek is located at a trailhead that provides access to various lakes and streams in the Eagle Cap Wilderness. It's a good starting point for a hiking trip. A national forest map details the possibilities.

⑮ Hurricane Creek

Location: Near the Eagle Cap Wilderness in Wallowa-Whitman National Forest; map C5, grid f4.

Campsites, facilities: There are eight tent sites. Picnic tables and fire grills are provided. Firewood and vault toilets are available, but there is no piped water. Leashed pets are permitted.

Reservations, fees: No reservations are accepted. There is no fee. The campground is open from mid-June to late October.

Contact: Wallowa-Whitman National Forest, Eagle Cap Ranger District, (541) 426-5546. Wallowa Mountains Visitor Center, 88401 Highway 82, Enterprise, OR 97828.

Directions: From Interstate 84 at LaGrande, turn north on Highway 82 and drive 62 miles to Enterprise. Continue six miles south to Joseph. The campground is located 3.5 miles southwest of Joseph on Forest Service Road 8205.

Trip notes: This campground along Hurricane Creek at the edge of the Eagle Cap Wilderness is a good place to begin a backcountry backpacking trip. There is no access for RVs, providing more of a wilderness environment. Obtaining maps of the area from the ranger district is essential.

⓰ Shady

Location: On the Lostine River in Wallowa-Whitman National Forest; map C5, grid f4.

Campsites, facilities: There are 12 sites for tents, trailers, or RVs up to 16 feet long. Vault toilets are available, but there is no piped water. Picnic tables and fire grills are provided. Leashed pets are permitted.

Reservations, fees: No reservations are accepted. There is no fee. The campground is open from mid-June to November.

Contact: Wallowa-Whitman National Forest, Eagle Cap Ranger District, (541) 426-5546. Wallowa Mountains Visitor Center, 88401 Highway 82, Enterprise, OR 97828.

Directions: From Interstate 84 at LaGrande, turn north on Highway 82 and drive 52 miles to Lostine. Drive 15 miles south of Lostine on Forest Service Road 8210.

Trip notes: This campground along the banks of the Lostine River is close to trails that provide access to the Eagle Cap Wilderness, a beautiful and pristine area that's perfect for an extended backpacking trip.

⓱ Two Pan

Location: On the Lostine River in Wallowa-Whitman National Forest; map C5, grid f4.

Campsites, facilities: There are eight tent or trailer sites. Vault toilets are available, but there is no piped water. Picnic tables and fire grills are provided. Leashed pets are permitted.

Reservations, fees: No reservations are accepted. There is no fee. The campground is open from mid-June to November.

Contact: Wallowa-Whitman National Forest, Eagle Cap Ranger District, (541) 426-5546. Wallowa Mountains Visitor Center, 88401 Highway 82, Enterprise, OR 97828.

Directions: From Interstate 84 at LaGrande,

turn north on Highway 82 and drive 52 miles to Lostine. Drive 17 miles south of Lostine on Forest Service Road 8210 to the campground.

Trip notes: This campground lies at the end of a Forest Service road on the banks of the Lostine River. Adjacent trails provide access to numerous lakes and streams in the Eagle Cap Wilderness. At 5,600 feet, this is a prime jump-off spot for a multiday wilderness adventure.

⓲ Wallowa Lake State Park

Location: On Wallowa Lake; map C5, grid f5.

Campsites, facilities: There are 89 tent sites and 121 full-hookup sites for trailers or RVs of any length, plus group campsites. Electricity, piped water, sewer hookups, and picnic tables are provided. Flush toilets, sanitary disposal services, showers, and firewood are available. A store, a cafe, and ice are located within one mile. Some facilities are wheelchair accessible. Boat docks, launching facilities, and rentals are nearby. Leashed pets are permitted.

Reservations, fees: Contact Reservations Northwest at (800) 452-5687 ($6 reservation fee). Sites are $16–$19 per night. The campground is open from mid-April to late October.

Contact: Phone (800) 452-5687 or (541) 432-8855, or write to 72214 Marina Lane, Joseph, OR 97846.

Directions: From Pendleton on Interstate 84, turn east and drive approximately 54 miles to LaGrande. Take exit 261 and turn north on Highway 82. Drive 68 miles to Joseph, then continue six miles south on Highway 82 to the south shore of the lake and the campground.

Trip notes: The shore of scenic Wallowa Lake is the site of this campground. Highlights include a pretty one-mile nature trail and trailheads provide access into the Eagle Cap Wilderness. A marina is nearby for boaters and anglers. Picnicking, swimming, and wildlife viewing are a few of the other activities available to visitors.

⑲ Mountain View Motel and Trailer Park

Location: Near Wallowa Lake; map C5, grid f5.

Campsites, facilities: There are 10 tent sites and 27 sites for trailers or RVs of any length; three are drive-throughs. Electricity, piped water, sewer hookups, and picnic tables are provided. Flush toilets and showers are available. Bottled gas, a store, a cafe, and a Laundromat are located within one mile. Leashed pets are permitted.

Reservations, fees: Reservations are accepted. Sites are $10–$15 per night. The campground is open year-round.

Contact: Phone (541) 432-2982 or write to 83450 Joseph Highway, Joseph, OR 97846.

Directions: From LaGrande on Interstate 84, turn north on Highway 82 and drive 62 miles to Enterprise. Continue four miles southeast on Highway 82 to the campground, located 1.5 miles north of Joseph.

Trip notes: This park is not far from Wallowa Lake. Nearby recreational facilities include a golf course, hiking trails, bike paths, and a riding stable.

⑳ Lick Creek

Location: On Lick Creek in Wallowa-Whitman National Forest; map C5, grid g6.

Campsites, facilities: There are seven tent sites and five sites for trailers or RVs up to 30 feet long. Picnic tables and fire grills are provided. Vault toilets are available, but there is no piped water. Leashed pets are permitted.

Reservations, fees: No reservations are accepted. There is no fee. The campground is open from mid-June to late November.

Contact: Hells Canyon National Recreation Area, (541) 426-5546. Wallowa Mountains Visitor Center, 88401 Highway 82, Enterprise, OR 97828.

Directions: From Interstate 84 at LaGrande, turn north on Highway 82 and drive 62 miles to Enterprise. Continue six miles south to Joseph, then drive 7.5 miles east on Highway 350. Turn south on Forest Service Road 39 and continue 15 miles to the campground.

Trip notes: This campground along the banks of Lick Creek in Hells Canyon National Recreation Area is secluded and pretty.

㉑ Blackhorse

Location: On the Imnaha River in Wallowa-Whitman National Forest; map C5, grid f7.

Campsites, facilities: There are 16 sites for tents, trailers, or RVs up to 30 feet long. Picnic tables and fire grills are provided. Piped water, firewood, and vault toilets are available. Leashed pets are permitted.

Reservations, fees: No reservations are accepted. There is no fee. The campground is open from June to late November.

Contact: Hells Canyon National Recreation Area, (541) 426-5546. Wallowa Mountains Visitor Center, 88401 Highway 82, Enterprise, OR 97828.

Directions: From Interstate 84 at LaGrande, turn north on Highway 82 and drive 62 miles to Enterprise. Continue six miles south to Joseph, then drive 7.5 miles east on Highway 350. Turn south on Forest Service Road 39 and continue 29 miles to the campground.

Trip notes: This campground along the banks of the Imnaha River in Hells Canyon National Recreation Area is in a secluded section of Wallowa-Whitman National Forest at an elevation of 4,000 feet.

㉒ Ollokot

Location: On the Imnaha River in Wallowa-Whitman National Forest; map C5, grid g7.

Campsites, facilities: There are 12 sites for tents, trailers, or RVs up to 30 feet long. Picnic tables and fire grills are provided. Piped water and vault toilets are available. Leashed pets are permitted.

Reservations, fees: No reservations are ac-

cepted. There is no fee. The campground is open from June to late November.

Contact: Hells Canyon National Recreation Area, (541) 426-5546. Wallowa Mountains Visitor Center, 88401 Highway 82, Enterprise, OR 97828.

Directions: From Interstate 84 at LaGrande, turn north on Highway 82 and drive 62 miles to Enterprise. Continue six miles south to Joseph, then drive 7.5 miles east on Highway 350. Turn south on Forest Service Road 39 and continue 30 miles.

Trip notes: This campground, on the banks of the Imnaha River in Hells Canyon National Recreation Area at an elevation of 4,000 feet, is a primitive alternative to the other camps in the immediate area. For those seeking a little more solitude, this could be the spot.

㉓ Tamarack

Location: On Eagle Creek in Wallowa-Whitman National Forest; map C5, grid g4.

Campsites, facilities: There are 12 tent sites and 12 sites for trailers or RVs up to 22 feet long. Picnic tables and fire grills are provided. Piped water, firewood, and vault toilets are available. Leashed pets are permitted.

Reservations, fees: No reservations are accepted. There is no fee. The campground is open from June to late October.

Contact: Wallowa-Whitman National Forest, Pine Ranger District, General Delivery, Halfway, OR 97834; (541) 742-7511 or fax (541) 742-6705.

Directions: From Interstate 84 at Baker City, drive 23 miles northeast on Highway 203 to the town of Medical Springs. From Medical Springs, travel 15.5 miles southeast on Forest Service Road 67 to the bridge across Eagle Creek. The camp is 300 yards east on Forest Service Road 77.

Trip notes: Located on the banks of Eagle Creek in a beautiful area with lush vegetation and abundant wildlife, this camp is a good spot for a fishing and hiking trip in a remote setting.

㉔ Two Color

Location: On Eagle Creek in Wallowa-Whitman National Forest; map C5, grid g4.

Campsites, facilities: There are 14 sites for tents and six sites for trailers or RVs up to 22 feet long. Picnic tables and fire grills are provided. Piped water and vault toilets are available. Leashed pets are permitted.

Reservations, fees: No reservations are accepted. There is no fee. The campground is open from mid-June to late October.

Contact: Wallowa-Whitman National Forest, LaGrande Ranger District, 3502 Highway 30, LaGrande, OR 97850; (541) 963-7186 or fax (541) 962-8580.

Directions: From Interstate 84 at Baker City, drive 23 miles northeast via Interstate 84 and Highway 203 to the town of Medical Springs. From Medical Springs, go 15.5 miles southeast on Forest Service Road 6700, then 1.5 miles northeast on Forest Service Road 7755 to the park entrance on the right.

Trip notes: This campground is along the banks of Eagle Creek, about a mile north of Tamarack (see campground number 23 for more details).

㉕ Eagle Forks

Location: On Eagle Creek in Wallowa-Whitman National Forest; map C5, grid g5.

Campsites, facilities: There are seven tent sites and five sites for trailers or RVs up to 21 feet long. Picnic tables and fire grills are provided. Firewood, piped water, and vault toilets are available. Leashed pets are permitted.

Reservations, fees: No reservations are accepted. There is no fee. The campground is open from June to late October.

Contact: Wallowa-Whitman National Forest, Pine Ranger District, General Delivery, Halfway, OR 97834; (541) 742-7511 or fax (541) 742-6705.

Directions: From Interstate 84 at Baker City, drive four miles north, then turn east on Highway 86 and drive 36 miles to Richland.

From Richland, travel 11 miles north to New Bridge via a county road and Forest Service Road 7735.

Trip notes: This campground, located at the confluence of Little Eagle Creek and Eagle Creek, has a trail that follows the creek northwest for five miles, making for a prime day hike, though the spot attracts few people. It's quite pretty as well and perfect for a weekend getaway or an extended layover.

㉖ McBride

Location: On Brooks Ditch in Wallowa-Whitman National Forest; map C5, grid g5.

Campsites, facilities: There are 11 tent sites and eight sites for trailers or RVs up to 16 feet long. Picnic tables and fire grills are provided. Piped water and vault toilets are available. Leashed pets are permitted.

Reservations, fees: No reservations are accepted. There is no fee. The campground is open from mid-May to late October.

Contact: Wallowa-Whitman National Forest, Pine Ranger District, General Delivery, Halfway, OR 97834; (541) 742-7511 or fax (541) 742-6705.

Directions: From Interstate 84 at Baker City, drive four miles north, then turn east on Highway 86 and drive 52 miles to Halfway. Continue six miles northwest of Halfway on Highway 413, then drive 2.5 miles west on Forest Service Road 7710 to the campground.

Trip notes: This campground along the banks of Brooks Ditch is little used, primitive, and obscure. Though not particularly scenic, it will work as a quick, free layover spot.

㉗ Twin Lakes

Location: Near Twin Lakes in Wallowa-Whitman National Forest; map C5, grid g6.

Campsites, facilities: There are six tent sites. Picnic tables and fire grills are provided. Firewood and vault toilets are available, but there is no piped water. Leashed pets are permitted.

Reservations, fees: No reservations are ac-

cepted. There is no fee. The campground is open from July to mid-September.

Contact: Hells Canyon National Recreation Area, (541) 426-4978. Wallowa Mountains Visitor Center, 88401 Highway 82, Enterprise, OR 97828.

Directions: From Interstate 84 at Baker City, drive four miles north, then turn east on Highway 86 and drive 52 miles to Halfway. From Halfway, drive five miles north on County Road 733, then 24 miles north on Forest Service Road 66 to the campground.

Trip notes: This campground is nestled between the little Twin Lakes, both of which offer excellent fishing. Nearby trails provide access to backcountry lakes and streams. See a Forest Service map for details.

㉘ Hidden

Location: On the Imnaha River in Wallowa-Whitman National Forest; map C5, grid g6.

Campsites, facilities: There are 10 tent sites and three tent or trailer sites. Picnic tables and fire grills are provided. Piped water, firewood, and vault toilets are available. Leashed pets are permitted.

Reservations, fees: No reservations are accepted. There is no fee. The campground is open from June to late November.

Contact: Hells Canyon National Recreation Area, (541) 426-4978. Wallowa Mountains Visitor Center, 88401 Highway 82, Enterprise, OR 97828.

Directions: From Interstate 84 at LaGrande, turn north on Highway 82 and drive 62 miles to Enterprise. Continue six miles south to Joseph, then drive 7.5 miles east on Highway 350. Turn south on Forest Service Road 39 and go 29 miles, then proceed seven miles southwest on Forest Service Road 3960.

Trip notes: River views and spacious sites can be found at this campground in an exceptionally pretty spot along the banks of the Imnaha River in the Hells Canyon National Recreation Area. It's essential to obtain a map of Wallowa-Whitman National Forest that details back roads and hiking trails.

㉙ Fish Lake

Location: On Fish Lake in Wallowa-Whitman National Forest; map C5, grid g6.

Campsites, facilities: There are 10 tent sites and five sites for trailers or RVs up to 22 feet long. Picnic tables and fire grills are provided. Springwater, firewood, and vault toilets are available. Boat launching facilities are nearby. Leashed pets are permitted.

Reservations, fees: No reservations are accepted. There is no fee. The campground is open from mid-June to late October.

Contact: Wallowa-Whitman National Forest, Pine Ranger District, General Delivery, Halfway, OR 97834; (541) 742-7511 or fax (541) 742-6705.

Directions: From Interstate 84 at Baker City, drive four miles north, then turn east on Highway 86 and drive 52 miles to Halfway. From Halfway, drive five miles north on County Route 733, then 18.5 miles north on Forest Service Road 66.

Trip notes: This pretty, well-forested camp with comfortable sites along the shore of Fish Lake makes a good base for a fishing trip. Side trip options include hiking on nearby trails that lead to mountain streams.

㉚ Evergreen

Location: On the Imnaha River in Wallowa-Whitman National Forest; map C5, grid g7.

Campsites, facilities: This is a group campsite for tents, trailers, or RVs up to 31 feet long. Vault toilets are available, but there is no piped water. Picnic tables and fire grills are provided. Leashed pets are permitted.

Reservations, fees: No reservations are accepted. There is no fee. The campground is open from June to late November.

Contact: Hells Canyon National Recreation Area, (541) 426-4978. Wallowa Mountains Visitor Center, 88401 Highway 82, Enterprise, OR 97828.

Directions: From Interstate 84 at LaGrande, turn north on Highway 82 and drive 62 miles to Enterprise. Continue six miles south to Joseph. Take Highway 350 east from Joseph

for 7.5 miles, then continue 29 miles south on Forest Service Road 39. The camp is eight miles southwest on Forest Service Road 3960.

Trip notes: This campground can be found along the banks of the Imnaha River in Hells Canyon National Recreation Area. It's one of seven camps in the vicinity.

㉛ Indian Crossing

Location: On the Imnaha River in Wallowa-Whitman National Forest; map C5, grid g7.

Campsites, facilities: There are 14 sites for tents, trailers, or RVs up to 30 feet long. Piped water, picnic tables, and fire grills are provided. Vault toilets and horse facilities are available. Leashed pets are permitted.

Reservations, fees: No reservations are accepted. There is no fee. The campground is open from June to late November.

Contact: Hells Canyon National Recreation Area, (541) 426-5546. Wallowa Mountains Visitor Center, 88401 Highway 82, Enterprise, OR 97828.

Directions: From Interstate 84 at LaGrande, turn north on Highway 82 and drive 62 miles to Enterprise. Continue six miles south to Joseph. From Joseph, drive 7.5 miles east on Highway 350, then 29 miles south on Forest Service Road 39. The campground is 10 miles southwest on Forest Service Road 3960 at the end of the road.

Trip notes: The trailhead for the Eagle Cap Wilderness is near this camp. Obtain a Forest Service map for side trip possibilities.

㉜ Lake Fork

Location: On Lake Fork Creek in Wallowa-Whitman National Forest; map C5, grid g7.

Campsites, facilities: There are 10 sites for tents, trailers, or RVs up to 22 feet long. Picnic tables and fire grills are provided. Piped water and vault toilets are available. Leashed pets are permitted.

Reservations, fees: No reservations are accepted. Sites are $4 per night. The campground is open from June to late November.

Contact: Hells Canyon National Recreation Area, (541) 426-4978. Wallowa Mountains Visitor Center, 88401 Highway 82, Enterprise, OR 97828.

Directions: From Baker City on Interstate 84, drive four miles north, then turn east on Highway 86 and travel 62 miles. Proceed eight miles north on Forest Service Road 39, then turn left and continue one-half mile to the campground.

Trip notes: This campground along the banks of Lake Fork Creek is an ideal jump-off point for a backpacking trip. A trail from camp follows the creek west for about 10 miles to Fish Lake, then continues on to several smaller lakes.

Map D1

Oregon State Map .... *page 6*
One inch equals approximately 20 miles.

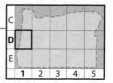

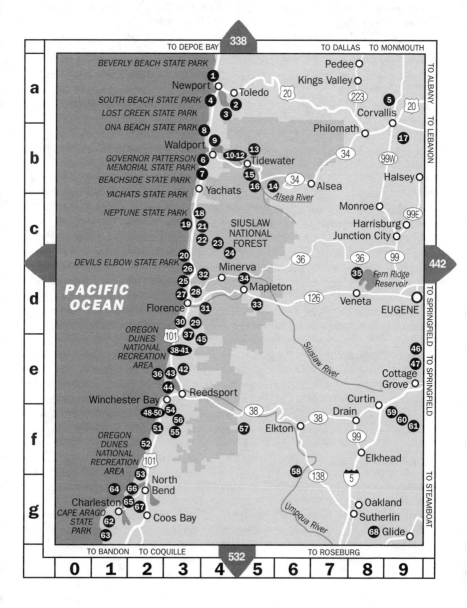

Chapter D1 features:

1 Agate Beach RV Park

Location: Near the Pacific Ocean; map D1, grid a4.

Campsites, facilities: There are 32 sites for trailers or RVs of any length. Electricity, piped water, sewer hookups, and picnic tables are provided. Flush toilets, sanitary services, showers, and a laundry room are available. A store and ice are located within one mile. Leashed pets are permitted.

Reservations, fees: Reservations are accepted. Sites are $16–$17 per night. The campground is open year-round.

Contact: Phone (541) 265-7670 or write to 6138 North Coast Highway, Newport, OR 97365.

Directions: From Interstate 5 at Albany, turn west on U.S. 20 and drive 66 miles to Newport. Turn north on U.S. 101 and drive three miles to the park on the north end of town.

Trip notes: This park is a short distance from Agate Beach Wayside, a small state park with beach access. Agate hunting can be good. Sometimes the agates are covered by a layer of sand and you have to dig a bit. But other times, wave action will clear the sand, unveiling the agates at low tides.

❷ Harbor Village RV Park 🚐

Location: On Yaquina Bay; map D1, grid a4.

Campsites, facilities: There are 140 sites for trailers or RVs of any length. Electricity, piped water, sewer hookups, and picnic tables are provided. Flush toilets, showers, and a laundry room are available. Bottled gas, a store, and a cafe are within one mile. Boat docks, launching facilities, and rentals are nearby. One leashed pet per site is permitted.

Reservations, fees: Reservations are accepted. Sites are $15 for two people per night. The campground is open year-round.

Contact: Phone (541) 265-5088, fax (541) 265-5895, or write to 923 SE Bay Boulevard, P.O. Box 6, Newport, OR 97365.

Directions: From Interstate 5 at Albany, turn west on U.S. 20 and drive 65.5 miles. Turn south on John Moore Road and drive one-half mile to the bay. Turn left on Bay Boulevard and you'll see the entrance to the trailer park on the left.

Trip notes: This park is near the shore of Yaquina Bay in a wooded area. See the trip notes for Newport Marina and RV Park (campground number 3) for information on attractions in Newport. Nearby recreation options include clamming, crabbing, deep-sea fish-

ing, an 18-hole golf course, hiking trails, and a full-service marina.

❸ Newport Marina and RV Park 🚐

Location: On Yaquina Bay; map D1, grid a4.

Campsites, facilities: There are 115 sites for trailers or RVs. Electricity, piped water, and sewer hookups are provided. Flush toilets, showers, cable TV, a store, a laundry room, and ice are available. A marina with boat docks and launching facilities is nearby. Leashed pets are permitted.

Reservations, fees: Reservations are accepted. Sites are $21.40 per night. The campground is open year-round.

Contact: Phone (541) 867-3321, fax (541) 867-3352, or write to 600 SE Bay Boulevard, Newport, OR 97365.

Directions: From Interstate 5 at Albany, turn west on U.S. 20 and drive 66 miles to Newport. Turn south on U.S. 101 and travel one-quarter mile, then go one-half mile east on Marine Science Drive and you'll see the park entrance on the left.

Trip notes: This park is set along the shore of Yaquina Bay near Newport, a resort town that offers a variety of attractions. Among them are ocean fishing, a museum and aquarium at the nearby Hatfield Marine Science Center, the Undersea Garden, the Waxworks, Ripley's Believe It or Not, and the Lincoln County Historical Society Museum. Nearby recreation options include an 18-hole golf course, hiking trails, a full-service marina, and tennis courts.

❹ South Beach State Park 🚐 ⛺

Location: On the Pacific Ocean; map D1, grid a4.

Campsites, facilities: There are 244 sites for trailers or RVs of any length, and a special primitive camping area for hikers and bicyclists. There are also three group sites and 10 yurts. Electricity, water hookups, fire grills, and picnic tables are provided. Flush toilets, a sanitary disposal station, showers, and firewood are available. Some facilities are wheelchair accessible. Leashed pets are permitted.

Reservations, fees: Contact Reservations Northwest at (800) 452-5687 ($6 reservation fee). Sites are $15–$19 per night; yurts are $25; the group fee is $50; and the fee for hikers/bicyclists is $4. The campground is open year-round.

Contact: Phone the park at (541) 867-4715 or write to 5580 South Coast Highway, South Beach, OR 97366.

Directions: From Interstate 5 at Albany, turn west on U.S. 20 and drive 66 miles to Newport. Turn south on U.S. 101 and drive two miles to the park entrance on the right.

Trip notes: This park along the beach offers opportunities for beachcombing, fishing, and hiking. In fact, the Oregon Coast Trail passes right through the park. A primitive hike-in campground is also available. See the trip notes for Newport Marina and RV Park (campground number 3) for information on attractions in Newport.

⑤ Corvallis Motorhome Park

Location: In Corvallis; map D1, grid a8.

Campsites, facilities: There are 27 sites for trailers or RVs. Electricity, piped water, and sewer hookups are provided. Flush toilets, showers, a store, a cafe, a laundry room, and ice are available. Bottled gas and sanitary services are located within one mile. Pets are permitted.

Reservations, fees: Reservations are accepted. Sites are $15 per night. The campground is open year-round.

Contact: Phone (541) 752-2334, fax (541) 757-2390, or write to 200 Northwest 53rd Street, Corvallis, OR 97330.

Directions: From U.S. 20 at Corvallis, continue 2.5 miles west on U.S. 20, then turn north on 53rd Street and travel 1.3 miles to the park on the right.

Trip notes: This is a decent layover spot on

your way to and from the coast. Nearby recreation options include an 18-hole golf course, hiking trails, and a riding stable.

⑥ Beachside State Park

Location: Near Alsea Bay; map D1, grid b3.

Campsites, facilities: There are 50 sites for tents, 32 sites with water and electrical hookups for trailers or RVs up to 30 feet long, and a special camping area for hikers and bicyclists. Picnic tables and fire grills are provided. Flush toilets, showers, and firewood are available. Some facilities are wheelchair accessible. Leashed pets are permitted.

Reservations, fees: Contact Reservations Northwest at (800) 452-5687 ($6 reservation fee). Sites are $16–$19 per night, and $4–$5 per night for hikers/bicyclists. The campground is open year-round.

Contact: Phone (541) 563-3220 or write to P.O. Box 693, Waldport, OR 97394.

Directions: From Interstate 5 at Albany, turn west on U.S. 20 and drive 66 miles to Newport. Turn south on U.S. 101 and drive 16 miles to Waldport. Continue four miles south on U.S. 101 to the park entrance at milepost 158.

Trip notes: This state park offers about nine miles of beach and is not far from Alsea Bay and the Alsea River. See the trip notes for Waldport/Newport KOA and Kozy Kove Marina (campground numbers 9 and 14) for more information on the fishing opportunities in the area.

⑦ Tillicum Beach

Location: On the Pacific Ocean in Siuslaw National Forest; map D1, grid b3.

Campsites, facilities: There are 61 sites for tents, trailers, or RVs up to 40 feet long. Picnic tables and fire grills are provided. Flush toilets and piped water are available. Leashed pets are permitted.

Reservations, fees: No reservations are accepted. Sites are $12 per night. The campground is open year-round.

Contact: Concessionaire, (541) 822-3799. Siuslaw National Forest, Waldport Ranger District, P.O. Box 400, Waldport, OR 97394; (541) 563-3211 or fax (541) 563-3124.

Directions: From Interstate 5 at Albany, turn west on U.S. 20 and drive 66 miles to Newport. Turn south on U.S. 101 and drive 14 miles to Waldport. Continue 4.5 miles south on U.S. 101 to the campground entrance on your right.

Trip notes: Ocean-view campsites are a big draw at this campground along the water, just south of Beachside State Park. Nearby Forest Service roads provide access to streams in the mountains east of the beach area. A Forest Service map details the possibilities. Since it's just off the highway, this camp fills up very quickly in the summer, so expect crowds.

❽ Seal Rock Trailer and RV Cove

Location: Near Seal Rock State Park; map D1, grid b3.

Campsites, facilities: There are 26 sites for trailers or RVs of any length; two are drive-throughs. Electricity, piped water, sewer hookups, and picnic tables are provided. Flush toilets, a dump station, and showers are available. Firewood, a store, a cafe, and ice are located within one mile.

Reservations, fees: Reservations are accepted. Sites are $13–$24 per night. The campground is open year-round.

Contact: Phone (541) 563-3955 or write to P.O. Box 71, Seal Rock, OR 97376.

Directions: From Interstate 5 at Albany, turn west on U.S. 20 and drive 66 miles to Newport. Turn south on U.S. 101 and drive 10 miles to the town of Seal Rock. Continue one-quarter mile south on U.S. 101 to the park entrance on the left.

Trip notes: This trailer park is on the rugged coastline near Seal Rock State Park (open for day use only), where you may find seals, sea lions, and a variety of birds.

❾ Waldport/ Newport KOA

Location: On Alsea Bay; map D1, grid b4.

Campsites, facilities: There are 12 tent sites and 75 sites for trailers or RVs of any length, plus five cabins. Electricity, piped water, and sewer hookups are provided. Flush toilets, showers, and a recreation hall are available. Bottled gas, sanitary services, a store, a cafe, a Laundromat, and ice are located within one mile. Boat docks, launching facilities, and rentals are nearby. Leashed pets are permitted.

Reservations, fees: Reservations are accepted. Sites are $18–$26 per night. The campground is open year-round.

Contact: Phone (541) 563-2250, fax (541) 563-4098, or write to P.O. Box 397, Waldport, OR 97394.

Directions: From Interstate 5 at Albany, turn west on U.S. 20 and drive 66 miles to Newport. Turn south on U.S. 101 and drive to milepost 155 at the north end of the Alsea Bay Bridge. The park is located on the west side of the bridge.

Trip notes: This pretty park set amid pine trees is within walking distance to the beach, the bay, and downtown Waldport—and to top it off, the campsites have beautiful ocean views. Alsea Bay's sandy and rocky shorelines make this area a favorite with anglers. The crabbing and clamming can also be quite good. Ona Beach State Park, about five miles north on U.S. 101, offers more fishing and a boat ramp along Beaver Creek. It's open for day use only. Other nearby recreation options include hiking trails, marked bike trails, the Oregon Coast Aquarium, and a marina.

❿ Drift Creek Landing

Location: On the Alsea River; map D1, grid b4.

Campsites, facilities: There are 60 drive-through sites for trailers or RVs of any length. Electricity, piped water, and sewer hookups are provided. Flush toilets, private telephone service, cable TV, bottled gas, showers, a recreation hall, a store, a cafe, a laundry room, boat docks, boat rentals, and launching facilities are available. Leashed pets are permitted.

Reservations, fees: Reservations are accepted. Sites are $13–$18 per night. The campground is open year-round.

Contact: Phone (541) 563-3610 or write to 3851 Highway 34, Waldport, OR 97394.

Directions: From Interstate 5 at Albany, turn west on U.S. 20 and drive 66 miles to Newport. Turn south on U.S. 101 and drive 14 miles to Waldport. Turn east on Highway 34 and travel 3.5 miles to the campground.

Trip notes: This campground is along the shore of the Alsea River in a heavily treed and mountainous area. The Oregon Coast Aquarium is 15 miles away, and an 18-hole golf course is located nearby. For more information on the area, see the trip notes for Waldport/Newport KOA (campground number 9).

⓫ Fishin' Hole Trailer Park

Location: On the Alsea River; map D1, grid b4.

Campsites, facilities: There are 16 tent sites and 26 sites for trailers or RVs of any length. Electricity, piped water, sewer hookups, and picnic tables are provided. Flush toilets, showers, a cafe, a laundry room, boat docks, boat rentals, and launching facilities are available. Leashed pets are permitted.

Reservations, fees: Reservations are accepted; call (800) 597-2853. Sites are $13 per night. The campground is open year-round.

Contact: Phone (541) 563-3401 or write to 3911 Highway 34, Waldport, OR 97394.

Directions: From Interstate 5 at Albany, turn west on U.S. 20 and drive 66 miles to Newport. Turn south on U.S. 101 and drive 14 miles to Waldport. Turn east on Highway 34 and drive four miles to the entrance on the left.

Trip notes: This is one of several campgrounds along the shore of the Alsea River. For information on the area, see the trip notes for Waldport/Newport KOA (campground number 9).

⓬ Chinook Trailer Park

Location: On the Alsea River; map D1, grid b5.

Campsites, facilities: There are 22 sites for trailers or RVs of any length. Electricity, piped water, and sewer hookups are provided. Flush toilets, showers, and a laundry room are available. Bottled gas, a store, a cafe, and ice are within one mile. Boat docks are nearby. Leashed pets and motorbikes are permitted.

Reservations, fees: Reservations are accepted. Sites are $16 per night. The campground is open year-round.

Contact: Phone (541) 563-3485 or write to 3299 Highway 34, Waldport, OR 97394.

Directions: From Interstate 5 at Albany, turn west on U.S. 20 and drive 66 miles to Newport. Turn south on U.S. 101 and drive 14 miles to Waldport. Turn east on Highway 34 and drive 3.5 miles to the park entrance.

Trip notes: This trailer park is along the shore of the Alsea River. For more information on the area, see the trip notes for Waldport/Newport KOA (campground number 9).

⓭ Taylor's Landing

Location: On the Alsea River; map D1, grid b5.

Campsites, facilities: There are six tent sites and 28 sites for trailers or RVs of any length. Electricity, piped water, cable TV, sewer hookups, and picnic tables are provided. Flush toilets, bottled gas, showers, a cafe, and a laundry room are available. Boat docks, launching facilities, and rentals are nearby. Leashed pets and motorbikes are permitted.

Reservations, fees: Reservations are accepted. Sites are $10–$18 per night. The campground is open year-round.

Contact: Phone (541) 528-3388 or write to 7264 Alsea Highway 34, Waldport, OR 97394.

Directions: From Interstate 5 at Albany, turn west on U.S. 20 and drive 66 miles to Newport. Turn south on U.S. 101 and drive 14 miles to

Waldport. Turn east on Highway 34 and drive seven miles to the entrance on the right.

Trip notes: This campground is along the Alsea River. For more information on the area, see the trip notes for Waldport/Newport KOA and Kozy Kove Marina (campground numbers 9 and 14).

⑭ Kozy Kove Marina

Location: On the Alsea River; map D1, grid b5.

Campsites, facilities: There are 10 sites for tents and 25 sites for trailers or RVs of any length. Cable TV, electricity, piped water, sewer hookups, and picnic tables are provided. Flush toilets, bottled gas, sanitary services, showers, a store, a cafe, a laundry room, and ice are available. Boat docks, launching facilities, and rentals are nearby. There are boat ramps on site. Leashed pets and motorbikes are permitted.

Reservations, fees: Reservations are accepted. Sites are $7.50–$15.50 per night. The campground is open year-round.

Contact: Phone (541) 528-3251, fax (541) 563-3825, or write to 9464 Alsea Highway, Tightwater, OR 97390.

Directions: From Interstate 5 at Albany, turn west on U.S. 20 and drive 66 miles to Newport. Turn south on U.S. 101 and drive 14 miles to Waldport. Turn east on Highway 34 and drive 9.5 miles to the campground entrance on the left.

Trip notes: This campground is on the Alsea River about 10 miles east of Waldport. Nearby Forest Service roads provide access to the various creeks and streams in the surrounding mountains. Consult a Siuslaw National Forest map for details.

⑮ Canal Creek

Location: On Canal Creek in Siuslaw National Forest; map D1, grid b5.

Campsites, facilities: There are seven sites for tents only and 10 sites for tents or small RVs, plus a group area. Picnic tables and fire

grills are provided. Hand-pumped water and vault toilets are available. The group site has a picnic shelter and a play area. Leashed pets are permitted.

Reservations, fees: No reservations are accepted. Sites are $7 per night. The campground is open year-round.

Contact: Siuslaw National Forest, Waldport Ranger District, P.O. Box 400, Waldport, OR 97394; (541) 563-3211 or fax (541) 563-3124.

Directions: From Interstate 5 at Albany, turn west on U.S. 20 and drive 15 miles to Philomath. Turn south on Highway 34 and drive 52 miles to Forest Service Road 3462. Turn south and go four miles to the camp.

Trip notes: This pleasant little campground is just off the beaten path in a large, wooded, open area along Canal Creek. It feels remote, yet has easy access and is close to the coast and all the amenities. The climate here is relatively mild, with 13 degrees Fahrenheit being the coldest winter temperature recorded in recent years. On the other hand, there is the rain—lots of it.

⑯ Blackberry

Location: On the Alsea River in Siuslaw National Forest; map D1, grid b5.

Campsites, facilities: There are 32 sites for tents, trailers, or RVs. Picnic tables and fire grills are provided. Piped water and flush toilets are available. There is no firewood. A boat ramp is on site. Leashed pets are permitted.

Reservations, fees: No reservations are accepted. Sites are $7 per night. The campground is open from May through October. Note: Phone ahead to make sure this site is open; it may close without notice.

Contact: Siuslaw National Forest, Waldport Ranger District, P.O. Box 400, Waldport, OR 97394; (541) 563-3211 or fax (541) 563-3124.

Directions: From Interstate 5 at Albany, turn west on U.S. 20 and drive 15 miles to Philomath. Turn south on Highway 34 just past Philomath and drive 41 miles to the campground entrance.

Trip notes: This is a good base camp for a fishing trip on the Alsea River. The Forest Service provides boat launches and picnic areas at several spots along this stretch of river. Often there will be a "camp host," who can give you inside information on nearby recreational opportunities.

⑰ Willamette City Park

Location: On the Willamette River; map D1, grid b9.

Campsites, facilities: There are 10 sites for tents, trailers, or RVs of any length. Vault toilets, piped water, a covered outdoor kitchen area, picnic tables, and a small playground are available. Bottled gas, a store, a cafe, a Laundromat, and ice are within one mile. There is a dump station in the center of town, three miles away. Boat docks and launching facilities are located two miles away. Leashed pets are permitted.

Reservations, fees: No reservations are accepted. Sites are $8 per night. The campground is open year-round to self-contained RVs and from March through October to tents, trailers, and RVs.

Contact: Corvallis Department of Parks and Recreation, P.O. Box 1083, Corvallis, OR 97339; (541) 757-6918.

Directions: From U.S. 20 at Corvallis, drive one mile south on Highway 99W, then proceed one-half mile east on SE Goodnight Road to the park.

Trip notes: This 40-acre city park is on the banks of the Willamette River, just outside Corvallis. The camping area is actually a large clearing near the entrance to the park, which has been left in its natural state. There are trails leading down to the river, and the bird-watching is good here.

⑱ Cape Perpetua

Location: On Cape Creek in Siuslaw National Forest; map D1, grid c3.

Campsites, facilities: There are 37 sites for tents, trailers, or RVs up to 22 feet long, plus one group site that can accommodate 100 campers. Picnic tables and fire grills are provided. Flush toilets, piped water, and sanitary services are available. Leashed pets are permitted.

Reservations, fees: Reservations are required for the group site; phone (541) 822-3799. Individual sites are $12 per night; call for group site rates. The campground is open from mid-May to late September.

Contact: Concessionaire, (541) 822-3799. Siuslaw National Forest, Waldport Ranger District, P.O. Box 400, Waldport, OR 97394; (541) 563-3211 or fax (541) 563-3124.

Directions: From Interstate 5 at Albany, turn west on U.S. 20 and drive 66 miles to Newport. Turn south on U.S. 101 and drive 23 miles to Yachats. Continue three miles south on U.S. 101 to the entrance on the left.

Trip notes: This Forest Service campground is set along Cape Creek in the Cape Perpetua Scenic Area. The visitor information center provides hiking and driving maps to guide you through this spectacular region, and you can also watch a movie about the area. Maps highlight the tidepool and picnic spots. The coastal cliffs are perfect for whale watching from December through March. Neptune State Park is just south and offers additional rugged coastline vistas.

⑲ Sea Perch

Location: Near Cape Perpetua; map D1, grid c3.

Campsites, facilities: There are four tent sites and 14 drive-through sites for tents, trailers, or RVs of any length. Electricity, piped water, sewer hookups, and picnic tables are provided. Flush toilets, bottled gas, sanitary services, showers, firewood, a recreation hall, a store, a cafe, a laundry room, ice, and a beach are available. Leashed pets and motorbikes are permitted.

Reservations, fees: Reservations are accepted. Sites are $16–$22.50 per night. The campground is open year-round.

Contact: Phone (541) 547-3505 or write to 95480 Highway 101, Yachats, OR 97498.

Directions: From Interstate 5 at Albany, turn west on U.S. 20 and drive 66 miles to Newport. Turn south on U.S. 101 and drive 6.5 miles to the campground at milepost 171 on the right.

Trip notes: Sea Perch is right in the middle of one of the most scenic areas on the Oregon coast. This private camp just south of Cape Perpetua has sites on the beach and lawn areas, plus its own shell museum. For more information on the area, see the trip notes for Cape Perpetua (campground number 18).

⑳ Carl G. Washburne State Park

Location: On the Pacific Ocean; map D1, grid c3.

Campsites, facilities: There are six primitive walk-in sites, two tent sites, and 58 sites with full hookups for trailers or RVs up to 45 feet long. A special area is available for hikers and bicyclists. Picnic tables are provided. Flush toilets, showers, and firewood are available. Leashed pets are permitted.

Reservations, fees: No reservations are accepted. Sites are $15–$19 per night, and $4 per night for hikers/bicyclists. The campground is open year-round.

Contact: Carl G. Washburne State Park, Florence, OR 97439; (800) 452-5687 or (541) 547-3416.

Directions: From Interstate 5 at Eugene, turn west on Highway 126 and drive 61 miles to Florence. Turn north on U.S. 101 and drive 12.5 miles, then go one-quarter mile west on the park entrance road.

Trip notes: This park is located in a unique area with a variety of exciting side trips close at hand. Short hikes lead from the campground to a two-mile-long beach, extensive tide pools along the base of the cliffs, and a three-mile trail to Heceta Head Lighthouse. The inland sections of the park are frequented by elk, which are commonly spotted by camp-

ers. Just three miles south of the park are the Sea Lion Caves, where an elevator takes visitors down into the cavern for an insider's view of the life of a sea lion.

㉑ Rock Creek

Location: On Rock Creek in Siuslaw National Forest; map D1, grid c4.

Campsites, facilities: There are 16 sites for tents, trailers, or RVs up to 22 feet long. Fire grills and picnic tables are provided. Flush toilets and piped water are available. Leashed pets are permitted.

Reservations, fees: No reservations are accepted. Sites are $12 per night. The campground is open from late May to mid-September.

Contact: Concessionaire, (541) 822-3799. Siuslaw National Forest, Waldport Ranger District, P.O. Box 400, Waldport, OR 97394; (541) 563-3211 or fax (541) 563-3124.

Directions: From Interstate 5 at Albany, turn west on U.S. 20 and drive 66 miles to Newport. Turn south on U.S. 101 and drive 23 miles to Yachats. Continue south on U.S. 101 for 10 miles to the campground entrance on your left.

Trip notes: This little, out-of-the-way campground is set along Rock Creek, just one-quarter mile from the ocean. It's a premium spot for coastal-highway travelers, although it can get packed very quickly. An excellent side trip is Cape Perpetua, a designated scenic area located a few miles up the coast. The cape offers beautiful ocean views and a visitor center that will supply you with information on nature trails, picnic spots, tide pools, and where to find the best viewpoints in the area.

㉒ Lanham Bike Camp

Location: In Siuslaw National Forest; map D1, grid c4.

Campsites, facilities: There are six primitive hike-in/bike-in tent sites. Picnic tables and fire grills are provided. There is no piped water here, but it can be obtained at Rock Creek. Leashed pets are permitted.

Reservations, fees: No reservations are accepted. There is no fee. The campground is open year-round.

Contact: Siuslaw National Forest, Waldport Ranger District, P.O. Box 400, Waldport, OR 97394; (541) 563-3211 or fax (541) 563-3124.

Directions: From Interstate 5 at Albany, turn west on U.S. 20 and drive 66 miles to Newport. Turn south and drive 23 miles to Yachats. Continue south on U.S. 101 for 10 miles, pass Rock Creek Campground, and hike or bike in from there.

Trip notes: This very primitive camp is a good layover spot for cyclists working their way along the coast highway—and you can't beat the price. See the trip notes for Rock Creek (campground number 21) for area information.

㉓ Tenmile Creek

Location: Near Cummins and Rock Creeks in Siuslaw National Forest; map D1, grid c4.

Campsites, facilities: There are four sites for tents, small trailers, or RVs. Fire grills and picnic tables are provided. Vault toilets are available, but there is no piped water. Leashed pets are permitted.

Reservations, fees: No reservations are accepted. There is no fee. The campground is open year-round.

Contact: Siuslaw National Forest, Waldport Ranger District, P.O. Box 400, Waldport, OR 97394; (541) 563-3211 or fax (541) 563-3124.

Directions: From Interstate 5 at Eugene, turn west on Highway 126 and drive 61 miles to Florence. Turn north on U.S. 101, drive about 20 miles, turn east on Forest Service Road 56, and drive 5.5 miles to the campground.

Trip notes: This small, secluded spot is only 15 or 20 minutes from the highway, yet it remains a virtual secret. A map of Siuslaw National Forest details the surrounding backcountry. Bring drinking water or a water filter. If you're going to stick around for a while, plan

on spending a day at Cape Perpetua. It's spectacularly scenic, with great hiking trails and perfect viewpoints for whale watching.

㉔ North Fork Siuslaw

Location: On the North Fork of the Siuslaw River in Siuslaw National Forest; map D1, grid c4.

Campsites, facilities: There are five tent sites. Picnic tables and fire grills are provided. Pit toilets are available, but there is no piped water. Leashed pets are permitted.

Reservations, fees: No reservations are accepted. There is no fee in winter; sites are $5 per night in summer. The campground is open year-round.

Contact: Siuslaw National Forest, Mapleton Ranger District, Mapleton, OR 97453; (541) 268-4473 or (541) 268-4476.

Directions: From Interstate 5 at Eugene, turn west on Highway 126 and drive 50 miles to County Road 5070/North Fork (located one mile east of Florence). Turn right and drive 12 miles northeast to the campground.

Trip notes: Little known and little used, this camp along the North Fork of the Siuslaw River is the ideal hideaway. A dirt road opposite the camp follows Wilhelm Creek for about two miles. A newly constructed trail through old-growth forest is nearby. See a Forest Service map for other side trip possibilities.

㉕ Alder Dune

Location: Near Alder Lake in Siuslaw National Forest; map D1, grid d3.

Campsites, facilities: There are 39 sites for tents, trailers, or RVs up to 30 feet long. Picnic tables and fire grills are provided. Flush toilets and piped water are available. Leashed pets are permitted.

Reservations, fees: No reservations are accepted. Sites are $12 per night. The campground is open from mid-May through mid-September.

Contact: Siuslaw National Forest, Mapleton

Ranger District, Mapleton, OR 97453; (541) 268-4473 or (541) 268-4476.

Directions: From Interstate 5 at Eugene, turn west on Highway 126 and drive 61 miles to Florence. Turn north on U.S. 101 and drive eight miles to the campground on the left.

Trip notes: This campground is located near four lakes—Alder Lake, Sutton Lake, Dune Lake, and Mercer Lake (the largest). A boat launch is available at Sutton Lake. An option is exploring the expansive sand dunes in the area by foot. There is no off-road-vehicle access here. See the trip notes for Lane County Harbor Vista Park (campground number 27) for other information on the area.

㉖ Sutton

Location: Near Sutton Lake in Siuslaw National Forest; map D1, grid d3.

Campsites, facilities: There are 80 sites for tents, trailers, or RVs up to 30 feet long, some with partial hookups. There are also group sites. Picnic tables and fire grills are provided. Flush toilets and piped water are available. A boat ramp is nearby. Leashed pets are permitted.

Reservations, fees: Reservations are necessary for group sites only. Rates are $12 per night for single sites, and $40–$100 for group sites. The campground is open year-round.

Contact: Siuslaw National Forest, Mapleton Ranger District, Mapleton, OR 97453; (541) 268-4473 or (541) 268-4476.

Directions: From Interstate 5 at Eugene, turn west on Highway 126 and drive 61 miles to Florence. Turn north on U.S. 101 and drive six miles, then go 1.5 miles northwest on Forest Service Road 794/Sutton Beach Road and you'll see the campground entrance.

Trip notes: This campground is located adjacent to Sutton Creek, not far from Sutton Lake. Holman Vista on Sutton Beach Road provides a beautiful view of the dunes and ocean. Wading and fishing are both popular. A hiking trail system leads from the camp out to the dunes. There is no off-road-vehicle access here. An alternative camp is Alder Dune to the north (campground number 25).

㉗ Lane County Harbor Vista Park

Location: Near Florence; map D1, grid d3.

Campsites, facilities: There are 38 sites for tents, trailers, or RVs up to 60 feet long. Picnic tables are provided. Flush toilets, sanitary services, showers, piped water, and a playground are available. Pets and motorbikes are permitted.

Reservations, fees: Reservations are accepted. Sites are $11–$15 per night. The campground is open year-round.

Contact: Phone (541) 997-5987 or write to 87658 Harbor Vista Road, Florence, OR 97439.

Directions: From Interstate 5 at Eugene, turn west on Highway 126 and drive 61 miles to Florence. From Florence, travel three miles north on Rhododendron Drive, then take Harbor Vista Road to the campground at 87658 Harbor Vista Road.

Trip notes: This county park located out among the dunes near the entrance to the harbor offers a great lookout point from the observation deck. A number of side trips are available, including Darlington State Park, Jessie M. Honeyman Memorial State Park (see the trip notes for Jessie M. Honeyman, campground number 30), and the Indian Forest, just four miles north of Florence. Florence also has displays of Native American dwellings and crafts.

㉘ B & E Wayside Mobile and RV Park

Location: Near Florence; map D1, grid d3.

Campsites, facilities: There are 24 sites for trailers or RVs of any length. Electricity, piped water, sewer hookups, and picnic tables are provided. Flush toilets, sanitary services, showers, and a laundry room are available. Bottled gas, a store, a cafe, and ice are located within two miles. Boat launching facilities are nearby. Leashed pets are permitted.

Reservations, fees: Reservations are ac-

cepted. Sites are $18 per night. The campground is open year-round.

Contact: Phone (541) 997-6451 or write to 3760 Highway 101 North, Florence, OR 97439.

Directions: From Interstate 5 at Eugene, turn west on Highway 126 and drive 61 miles to Florence. Turn north on U.S. 101 and drive 1.8 miles to the park on the right.

Trip notes: This park is clean and quiet. See the trip notes for Lane County Harbor Vista Park and Port of Siuslaw RV and Marina (campground numbers 27 and 31) for side trip ideas. Nearby recreation options include two golf courses and a riding stable (two miles away).

㉙ Lakeshore Trailer Park

Location: On Woahink Lake; map D1, grid d3.

Campsites, facilities: There are 20 sites for trailers or RVs of any length; six are drive-throughs. Electricity, piped water, and sewer hookups are provided. Flush toilets, cable TV, showers, and a laundry room are available. A cafe is located within one mile. Boat docks are nearby. Leashed pets are permitted.

Reservations, fees: Reservations are accepted. Sites are $17 per night. The campground is open year-round.

Contact: Lakeshore Trailer Park, 83763 Highway 101, Florence, OR 97439; (541) 997-2741; e-mail: lakeshor@presys.com.

Directions: From Interstate 5 at Eugene, turn west on Highway 126 and drive 61 miles to Florence. Turn south on U.S. 101 and drive four miles to the park on the left at milepost 195.

Trip notes: Here's a prime area for vacationers. This park is set along the shore of Woahink Lake, a popular spot to fish for trout, perch, catfish, crappie, bluegill, and bass. It's adjacent to Jessie M. Honeyman Memorial State Park and the Oregon Dunes National Recreation Area. Off-road-vehicle access to the dunes is four miles northeast of the park. Hiking trails through the dunes can be found at Honeyman Memorial State Park. If you set out across the dunes off the trail, note your path. People hiking off-trail commonly get lost here.

㉚ Jessie M. Honeyman Memorial State Park

Location: Near Cleowax Lake; map D1, grid d3.

Campsites, facilities: There are 382 sites for tents, trailers, or RVs up to 60 feet long, and a special camping area for hikers and bicyclists. There are also four yurts. Picnic tables and fire grills are provided. Flush toilets, sanitary services, showers, and firewood are available. Some facilities are wheelchair accessible. Boat docks and launching facilities are nearby. Leashed pets are permitted.

Reservations, fees: Contact Reservations Northwest at (800) 452-5687 ($6 reservation fee). Sites are $16–$20 per night, and $4 for hikers/bicyclists. The campground is open year-round.

Contact: Phone (541) 563-3220 or write to 84505 Highway 101, Florence, OR 97439.

Directions: From Interstate 5 at Eugene, turn west on Highway 126 and drive 61 miles to Florence. Turn south on U.S. 101 and drive three miles to the park entrance.

Trip notes: This popular state park is located along the shore of Cleowax Lake and adjacent to the dunes of the Oregon Dunes National Recreation Area. The dunes here are quite impressive, with some reaching to 500 feet. The three lakes in the park offer facilities for boating, fishing, and swimming. A one-mile hiking trail with access to the dunes is available in the park.

㉛ Port of Siuslaw RV and Marina

Location: On the Siuslaw River; map D1, grid d4.

Campsites, facilities: There are 84 sites for tents, trailers, or RVs of any length. Electricity, piped water, sewer hookups, and picnic tables are provided. Flush toilets, cable TV, sanitary services, showers, a laundry room, and ice are available. A cafe is located within one mile. Boat docks and launching facilities are nearby. Leashed pets are permitted.

Reservations, fees: Reservations are accepted. Sites are $16–$18 per night. The campground is open year-round.

Contact: Phone (541) 997-3040 or write to P.O. Box 1638, Florence, OR 97439.

Directions: From Interstate 5 at Eugene, turn west on Highway 126 and drive 61 miles to Florence. In Florence, turn off U.S. 101 and drive about one-half mile east on First Street to Harbor Street and the marina.

Trip notes: This public resort can be found along the Siuslaw River in a grassy, urban setting. Anglers with boats will find that the U.S. 101 bridge support pilings make good spots for crabbing and fishing for perch and flounder.

❸❷ Mercer Lake Resort

Location: On Mercer Lake; map D1, grid d4.

Campsites, facilities: There are 13 sites for trailers or RVs of any length; four are drive-throughs. Electricity, piped water, cable TV, sewer hookups, and picnic tables are provided. Flush toilets, sanitary services, showers, a store, a laundry room, and ice are available. Boat docks, launching facilities, and rentals are nearby. Leashed pets are permitted.

Reservations, fees: Reservations are accepted. Sites are $15–$19 per night. The campground is open year-round.

Contact: Mercer Lake Resort, 88875 Bay Berry, Florence, OR 97439; (541) 997-3633 or fax (541) 997-5096; e-mail: patty@presys.com.

Directions: From Interstate 5 at Eugene, turn west on Highway 126 and drive 61 miles to Florence. Turn north on U.S. 101 and drive five miles, then go one mile east on Mercer Lake Road. Turn left on Bay Berry Lane and proceed to the campground.

Trip notes: This resort is set along the shore of Mercer Lake, one of a number of lakes that have formed among the ancient dunes in this area.

❸❸ Archie Knowles

Location: On Knowles Creek in Siuslaw National Forest; map D1, grid d5.

Campsites, facilities: There are nine sites for tents, trailers, or RVs up to 16 feet long. Picnic tables and fire grills are provided. Flush toilets and piped water are available. Leashed pets are permitted.

Reservations, fees: No reservations are accepted. Sites are $10 per night. The campground is open from May to late September.

Contact: Siuslaw National Forest, Mapleton Ranger District, Mapleton, OR 97453; (541) 268-4473 or (541) 268-4476.

Directions: From Interstate 5 at Eugene, turn west on Highway 126 and drive 44 miles to the entrance, three miles east of Mapleton.

Trip notes: This little campground along Knowles Creek about three miles east of Mapleton is rustic yet offers proximity to the highway. Staff at the ranger station in Mapleton can provide maps and information and answer any questions.

❸❹ Maple Lane Trailer Park-Marina

Location: On the Siuslaw River; map D1, grid d5.

Campsites, facilities: There are two tent sites and 46 sites with full hookups for trailers or RVs of any length. Electricity, piped water, and sewer hookups are provided. Flush toilets, bottled gas, sanitary services, and showers are available. A store, a cafe, and ice are located within one mile. A bait and tackle shop is open during the fishing season. Boat docks and launching facilities are on site. Small pets (under 15 pounds) are permitted.

Reservations, fees: Reservations are accepted. Sites are $7–$14 per night. The campground is open year-round.

Contact: Phone (541) 268-4822 or write to 10730 Highway 126, Mapleton, OR 97453.

Directions: From Interstate 5 at Eugene, turn

west on Highway 126 and drive 47 miles to Mapleton. The park is located on Highway 126 behind the Forest Service station.

Trip notes: This park along the shore of the Siuslaw River in Mapleton is close to boat rentals and hiking trails. The general area is surrounded by Siuslaw National Forest land. A Forest Service map details nearby backcountry side trip options.

㉟ Fern Ridge Shores

Location: On Fern Ridge Reservoir; map D1, grid d8.

Campsites, facilities: There are 61 sites for trailers and RVs up to 40 feet long. Rest rooms, showers, a sanitary dump station, security, a public phone, and ice are available. Recreational facilities include horseshoes, a field, a boat ramp, and a dock. Some facilities are wheelchair accessible. Two leashed pets per site are permitted.

Reservations, fees: Reservations are recommended. Sites are $20–$25 per night. The campground is open year-round.

Contact: Fern Ridge Shores, 29652 Jeans Road, Veneta, OR 97487; (541) 935-2335 or fax (541) 935-5417.

Directions: From Interstate 5 at Eugene, drive 10 miles west on Highway 126 to Veneta. From the junction of Highway 126 (West 11th Street) and Beltline Road, drive west for 7.6 miles on Highway 126 to Ellmaker Road. Turn north on Ellmaker Road and continue 1.1 miles to Jeans Road. Then turn east and continue 1.3 miles to the park on the right.

Trip notes: This camp is in a wooded area along the shore of Fern Ridge Reservoir, where swimming, boating, and bass fishing are among the pastimes. This is a friendly, family-oriented park that makes a great vacation destination, as well as an excellent layover for travelers cruising Interstate 5.

㊱ Carter Lake

Location: On Carter Lake in Oregon Dunes National Recreation Area; map D1, grid e2.

Campsites, facilities: There are 23 sites for tents, trailers, or RVs up to 35 feet long. Picnic tables and fire grills are provided. Piped water and flush toilets are available. Leashed pets are permitted.

Reservations, fees: No reservations are accepted. Sites are $14 per night. The campground is open from mid-May through September.

Contact: Oregon Dunes National Recreation Area, 855 Highway 101, Reedsport, OR 97467; (541) 271-3611 or fax (541) 750-7244.

Directions: From Interstate 5 at Eugene, turn west on Highway 126 and drive 61 miles to Florence. Turn south on U.S. 101 and drive 8.5 miles. Turn west on Forest Service Road 1084 and drive 200 yards to the camp.

Trip notes: This campground is on the north shore of Carter Lake. Boating, swimming, and fishing are permitted on this long, narrow lake, which is set among dunes overgrown with vegetation. The nearby Taylor Dunes Trail is an easy half-mile wheelchair-accessible trail to the dunes past Taylor Lake. Hiking is allowed in the dunes, but there is no off-road-vehicle access here. If you want off-road access, head north one mile to Siltcoos Road, turn west, and drive 1.3 miles to Driftwood II (campground number 38).

㊲ Woahink Lake RV Resort

Location: On Woahink Lake; map D1, grid e3.

Campsites, facilities: There are 38 sites for trailers or RVs of any length. No tent camping is allowed. Rest rooms, showers, cable TV, a public phone, and a laundry room are available. Recreational facilities include horseshoe pits, a recreation hall, a game room, and a boat dock. One large or two small leashed pets per site are permitted.

Reservations, fees: Reservations are recommended; call (800) 659-6454. Sites are $19 per night. The campground is open year-round.

Contact: Woahink Lake RV Resort, 83570 Highway 101 South, Florence, OR 97439; (541)

997-6454, fax (541) 902-0481; e-mail: wohink@presys.com.

Directions: From Interstate 5 at Eugene, turn west on Highway 126 and drive 61 miles to Florence. Turn south on U.S. 101 and drive 5.1 miles to the camp on the right.

Trip notes: One of several RV parks in the Florence area, this camp is located on Woahink Lake, where trout fishing is an option. Nearby Oregon Dunes National Recreation Area is a good side trip.

⑧ Driftwood II

Location: Near Siltcoos Lake in Oregon Dunes National Recreation Area; map D1, grid e3.

Campsites, facilities: There are 69 sites for tents, trailers, or RVs up to 50 feet long. Picnic tables and fire grills are provided. Piped water and flush and vault toilets are available. A sanitary disposal station is located within five miles. Some facilities are wheelchair accessible. Boat docks, launching facilities, and rentals can be found about four miles away on Siltcoos Lake. Leashed pets are permitted.

Reservations, fees: Some sites may be reserved by calling (800) 280-CAMP/2267 ($8.65 reservation fee). Sites are $13 per night. The campground is open year-round.

Contact: Oregon Dunes National Recreation Area, 855 Highway 101, Reedsport, OR 97467; (541) 271-3611 or fax (541) 750-7244.

Directions: From Interstate 5 at Eugene, turn west on Highway 126 and drive 61 miles to Florence. Turn south on U.S. 101 and drive seven miles, then go 1.5 miles west on Siltcoos Beach Road to the campground.

Trip notes: This is primarily a campground for off-road vehicles. It's set near the ocean in Oregon Dunes National Recreation Area and has off-road-vehicle access. Several small lakes, the Siltcoos River, and Siltcoos Lake are nearby.

⑨ Lagoon

Location: Near Siltcoos Lake in Oregon Dunes National Recreation Area; map D1, grid e3.

Campsites, facilities: There are 39 sites for tents, trailers, or RVs up to 35 feet long. Picnic tables and fire grills are provided. Piped water and flush and vault toilets are available. A telephone and sanitary services are located within five miles. Boat docks, launching facilities, and rentals are nearby on Siltcoos Lake. Leashed pets are permitted.

Reservations, fees: No reservations are accepted. Sites are $13 per night. The campground is open year-round.

Contact: Oregon Dunes National Recreation Area, 855 Highway 101, Reedsport, OR 97467; (541) 271-3611 or fax (541) 750-7244.

Directions: From Interstate 5 at Eugene, turn west on Highway 126 and drive 61 miles to Florence. Turn south on U.S. 101 and drive seven miles, then go 1.3 miles west on Siltcoos Beach Road to the campground.

Trip notes: One of several campgrounds in the area, this one is along the lagoon about one mile from Siltcoos Lake. The Lagoon Trail is a prime spot for wildlife viewing.

⑩ Tyee

Location: On the Siltcoos River in Oregon Dunes National Recreation Area; map D1, grid e3.

Campsites, facilities: There are 16 sites for tents, trailers, or RVs up to 30 feet long. Picnic tables and fire grills are provided. Piped water and vault toilets are available. A store, boat docks, launching facilities, and rentals are nearby. Leashed pets are permitted.

Reservations, fees: No reservations are accepted. Sites are $15 per night. The campground is open from April through November.

Contact: Oregon Dunes National Recreation Area, 855 Highway 101, Reedsport, OR 97467; (541) 271-3611 or fax (541) 750-7244.

Directions: From Interstate 5 at Eugene, turn west on Highway 126 and drive 61 miles to Florence. Turn south on U.S. 101 and drive six miles to the Westlake turnoff and you'll see the campground.

Trip notes: This campground along the shore of the Siltcoos River is an option to Driftwood II and Lagoon (campground numbers 38 and 39). Swimming, fishing, and waterskiing are permitted at the nearby lake. Off-road-vehicle access to the dunes is available from Driftwood II, and there are hiking trails in the area.

41 Waxmyrtle

Location: Near Siltcoos Lake in Oregon Dunes National Recreation Area; map D1, grid e3.

Campsites, facilities: There are 54 sites for tents, trailers, or RVs up to 35 feet long. Picnic tables and fire grills are provided. Piped water and flush toilets are available. Boat docks, launching facilities, and rentals are nearby on Siltcoos Lake. Leashed pets are permitted.

Reservations, fees: No reservations are accepted. Sites are $13 per night. The campground is open from late May to mid-October.

Contact: Oregon Dunes National Recreation Area, 855 Highway 101, Reedsport, OR 97467; (541) 271-3611 or fax (541) 750-7244.

Directions: From Interstate 5 at Eugene, turn west on Highway 126 and drive 61 miles to Florence. Turn south on U.S. 101 and drive seven miles, then go 1.3 miles west on Siltcoos Beach Road to the campground on your left.

Trip notes: One of three camps in the immediate vicinity, Waxmyrtle is adjacent to Lagoon and less than a mile from Driftwood II (campground numbers 39 and 38). The camp is near the Siltcoos River and a couple of miles from Siltcoos Lake, a good-sized lake with boating facilities where you can water-ski, fish, and swim. Hiking trails can also be found in the area.

42 Tahkenitch Landing

Location: Near Tahkenitch Lake in Oregon Dunes National Recreation Area; map D1, grid e3.

Campsites, facilities: There are 27 sites for tents, trailers, or RVs up to 30 feet long. Picnic tables are provided. Vault toilets, boat launching facilities, and a floating dock are available, but there is no piped water. Leashed pets are permitted.

Reservations, fees: No reservations are accepted. Sites are $12 per night. The campground is open year-round.

Contact: Oregon Dunes National Recreation Area, 855 Highway 101, Reedsport, OR 97467; (541) 271-3611 or fax (541) 750-7244.

Directions: From Interstate 5 at Eugene, turn west on Highway 126 and drive 61 miles to Florence. Turn south on U.S. 101 and drive 14 miles to the campground on the east side of the road.

Trip notes: This camp overlooking Tahkenitch Lake has easy access for fishing and swimming. There is no piped water here, but water, a boat ramp, and a dock are available nearby at Tahkenitch Lake.

43 Tahkenitch

Location: Near Tahkenitch Lake in Oregon Dunes National Recreation Area; map D1, grid e3.

Campsites, facilities: There are 34 sites for tents, trailers, or RVs up to 30 feet long. Picnic tables and fire grills are provided. Piped water and flush and vault toilets are available. Boat docks and launching facilities are on the lake across the highway. Leashed pets are permitted.

Reservations, fees: No reservations are accepted. Sites are $14 per night. The campground is open year-round.

Contact: Oregon Dunes National Recreation Area, 855 Highway 101, Reedsport, OR 97467; (541) 271-3611 or fax (541) 750-7244.

Directions: From Interstate 5 at Eugene, turn west on Highway 126 and drive 61 miles to Florence. Turn south on U.S. 101 and drive 14 miles. The campground entrance is on the right.

Trip notes: This campground is located in a wooded area across the highway from Tahkenitch Lake, which has numerous coves and backwater areas for fishing and swimming. A hiking trail close to the camp goes through the dunes out to the beach, as well as to Threemile Lake. If this camp is filled, Tahkenitch Landing (campground number 42) provides nearby space.

㊹ Surfwood Campground and RV Park

Location: On Winchester Bay; map D1, grid e3.

Campsites, facilities: There are 22 tent sites and 141 sites for trailers or RVs; 64 are drive-throughs. Electricity, piped water, sewer hookups, and picnic tables are provided. Flush toilets, sanitary services, showers, firewood, a store, a laundry room, ice, a playground, and a seasonal pool are available. Boat docks and launching facilities are within a half mile. Leashed pets and motorbikes are permitted.

Reservations, fees: Reservations are accepted. Sites are $12–$16 per night. The campground is open year-round.

Contact: Phone (541) 271-4020 or write to 75381 Highway 101, Reedsport, OR 97467.

Directions: From Interstate 5 south of Eugene, take exit 162 and drive 57 miles west on Highway 38 to Reedsport. Turn south on U.S. 101 and drive 2.5 miles to the park, located one-half mile north of Winchester Bay.

Trip notes: Fishing is the focal point at this park located half a mile from the marina at Winchester Bay. Hiking is another option, with trails heading west across the dunes to the ocean and east to lakes in wooded areas. An elk preserve can be found adjacent to Highway 38 some 10 miles to the east. The campground itself has pull-through sites separated by shrubs, which creates privacy.

㊺ Darlings Resort

Location: On Siltcoos Lake; map D1, grid e4.

Campsites, facilities: There are 42 sites for trailers or RVs of any length; 18 have full hookups. Electricity, piped water, sewer hookups, and picnic tables are provided. Flush toilets, showers, firewood, a store, a tavern, boat docks, boat rentals, launching facilities, and a laundry room are available. Leashed pets are permitted.

Reservations, fees: Reservations are accepted. Sites are $14–$18 per night. The campground is open year-round.

Contact: Phone (541) 997-2841 or write to 4879 Darling Loop, Florence, OR 97439.

Directions: From Interstate 5 at Eugene, turn west on Highway 126 and drive 61 miles to Florence. Turn south on U.S. 101 and drive five miles, then go one-half mile east on North Beach Road to the resort.

Trip notes: This park can be found in a rural area along the north shore of Siltcoos Lake, adjacent to the extensive Oregon Dunes National Recreation Area. An access point to the dunes for hikers and off-road vehicles is just across the highway. The lake has a full-service marina.

㊻ KOA Sherwood Forest

Location: Near Eugene; map D1, grid e9.

Campsites, facilities: There are 20 tent sites and 100 sites for trailers or RVs of any length. Electricity, piped water, sewer hookups, and picnic tables are provided. Flush toilets, sanitary services, showers, a recreation hall, a store, a laundry room, ice, a playground, and a swimming pool are available. Bottled gas and a cafe are within one mile. Pets and motorbikes are permitted.

Reservations, fees: Reservations are accepted. Sites are $17–$21 per night. The campground is open year-round.

Contact: Phone (541) 895-4110 or write to 298 East Oregon Avenue, Creswell, OR 97426.

Directions: From Interstate 5 south of Eugene, take the Creswell exit and drive west on Oregon Avenue for one-half block to the campground at 298 East Oregon Avenue.

Trip notes: Located 10 miles south of Eugene, this is a fairly good layover for RV travelers heading north on Interstate 5. Nearby recreational facilities include a golf course and tennis courts.

㊼ Taylor's Travel Park

Location: Near the Willamette River; map D1, grid e9.

Campsites, facilities: There are 10 tent sites and 20 sites for trailers or RVs of any length. Electricity, piped water, sewer hookups, and picnic tables are provided in the summer months. Flush toilets, sanitary services, showers, and a playground are available. Bottled gas, a store, a cafe, a Laundromat, and ice are within one mile. Leashed pets and motorbikes are permitted.

Reservations, fees: Reservations are accepted. Sites are $12 per night. The campground is open year-round, with limited winter facilities.

Contact: Phone (541) 895-4715 or write to 82149 Davisson Road, Creswell, OR 97426.

Directions: From Interstate 5 south of Eugene, take the Creswell exit, then drive one-quarter mile west on Oregon Avenue and 1.2 miles south on Highway 99. Turn left on Davisson Road and drive one-half mile south to the park.

Trip notes: An alternative to KOA Sherwood Forest (campground number 46), this spot is close to the Coast Fork of the Willamette River. Nearby recreational offerings include a golf course and a full-service marina (15 miles away).

⑱ Umpqua Lighthouse State Park

Location: On the Umpqua River; map D1, grid f2.

Campsites, facilities: There are 44 tent sites and 22 sites with full hookups for trailers or RVs up to 45 feet long. Piped water and picnic tables are provided. Flush toilets, showers, and firewood are available. Boat docks and launching facilities are on the Umpqua River. Leashed pets are permitted.

Reservations, fees: Contact Reservations Northwest at (800) 452-5687 ($6 reservation fee). Sites are $9–$17 per night. The campground is open year-round.

Contact: Umpqua Lighthouse State Park, 10965 Cape Arago Highway, Coos Bay, OR 97420; (800) 452-5687 or (541) 271-4118.

Directions: From Interstate 5 south of Eugene, take exit 162 and turn west on Highway 38. Drive 57 miles to Reedsport, then turn south on U.S. 101 and drive six miles to the park entrance.

Trip notes: This park is near the mouth of the Umpqua River, an unusual area where the dunes are as high as 500 feet. Hiking trails lead out from the park and south into Umpqua Dunes Scenic Area. The park offers more than two miles of beach access on the ocean and half a mile along the Umpqua River. The adjacent lighthouse is still in operation and provides a good side trip opportunity.

⑲ Discovery Point RV Park

Location: On Winchester Bay; map D1, grid f2.

Campsites, facilities: There are 15 tent sites and 50 sites for trailers or RVs of any length; 14 are drive-throughs. Electricity, piped water, sewer hookups, and picnic tables are provided. Flush toilets, showers, a store, a laundry room, and ice are available. Sanitary services and bottled gas are located within one mile. Boat docks and launching facilities are nearby. Leashed pets and motorbikes are permitted.

Reservations, fees: Reservations are accepted. Sites are $18–$20 per night. The campground is open year-round.

Contact: Phone (541) 271-3443, fax (541) 271-9357, or write to HC 81, P.O. Box 242, Reedsport, OR 97467.

Directions: From Interstate 5 south of Eugene, take exit 162 and turn west on Highway 38. Drive 57 miles to Reedsport, then turn south on U.S. 101 and drive to the Windy Cove exit near Winchester Bay. Continue 1.5 miles west to the resort.

Trip notes: This resort is on the shore of Winchester Bay in a fishing village near the mouth of the Umpqua River. For details on nearby recreation options, see the trip notes for Surfwood Campground and RV Park (campground number 44).

⑤⓪ Windy Cove County Park

Location: On the Pacific Ocean; map D1, grid f2.

Campsites, facilities: There are 29 tent sites and 40 sites with full hookups for trailers or RVs up to 60 feet long. Electricity, piped water, sewer hookups, and picnic tables are provided. Flush toilets, showers, and cable TV are available. Bottled gas, sanitary services, a store, a cafe, a Laundromat, and ice are located within one mile. Boat docks, launching facilities, and rentals are nearby. Pets and motorbikes are permitted.

Reservations, fees: No reservations are accepted. Sites are $14.70 per night. The campground is open year-round.

Contact: Phone (541) 271-5634 or write to P.O. Box 1265, Winchester Bay, OR 97467.

Directions: From Interstate 5 south of Eugene, take exit 162 and turn west on Highway 38. Drive 57 miles to Reedsport, then turn south on U.S. 101 and drive five miles to Winchester Bay. Take the Windy Cove exit and proceed to the park on the left.

Trip notes: This county park is actually comprised of two parks, Windy Cove "A" and "B." Set near ocean beaches and sand dunes, both also offer other nearby recreational facilities, including an 18-hole golf course and tennis courts.

⑤① Seadrift Motel and RV Park

Location: Near Tenmile Lake; map D1, grid f2.

Campsites, facilities: There are 42 drive-through sites for trailers or RVs of any length, plus a 10-unit motel in the park. Picnic tables are provided. Flush toilets, sanitary services, showers, a clubhouse, grounds security, and cable TV are available. A store, a cafe, and a Laundromat are located within one mile. Boat docks, launching facilities, and rentals are nearby. Leashed pets are permitted.

Reservations, fees: Reservations are ac-

cepted. Call (541) 271-3611 for fee information. The campground is open year-round.

Contact: Oregon Dunes National Recreation Area, 855 Highway 101, Reedsport, OR 97467; (541) 271-3611 or fax (541) 750-7244.

Directions: From Interstate 5 south of Eugene, take exit 162 and turn west on Highway 38. Drive 57 miles to Reedsport, then turn south on U.S. 101 and drive 12 miles. The campground entrance is on the right.

Trip notes: This campground is located along Eel Creek, near both Eel Lake and Tenmile Lake and 12 miles north of Coos Bay. Waterskiing is allowed on Tenmile Lake but not on Eel Lake. Nearby hiking trails lead into the Umpqua Dunes Scenic Area. Access for off-road vehicles is available at Spinreel.

⑤② Spinreel

Location: On Tenmile Creek in Oregon Dunes National Recreation Area; map D1, grid f2.

Campsites, facilities: There are 36 sites for tents, trailers, or RVs up to 40 feet long. Piped water and flush toilets are available. Picnic tables and fire grills are provided. Firewood, a store, and a Laundromat are nearby. Boat docks, launching facilities, and rentals are located on Tenmile Lake. Leashed pets are permitted.

Reservations, fees: No reservations are accepted. Sites are $13 per night. The campground is open year-round.

Contact: Oregon Dunes National Recreation Area, 855 Highway 101, Reedsport, OR 97467; (541) 271-3611 or fax (541) 750-7244.

Directions: From Coos Bay on U.S. 101, drive 10 miles north on U.S. 101 and you'll see a sign directing you to Spinreel Campground. Drive one mile northwest to the campground.

Trip notes: This campground, primarily for off-road-vehicle enthusiasts, is at the outlet of Tenmile Lake in the Oregon Dunes National Recreation Area. A boat launch is located near the camp. Other recreational opportunities include hiking trails and off-road-vehicle access to the dunes. Off-road-vehicle rentals are available adjacent to the camp.

⑤ Bluebill

Location: On Bluebill Lake in Oregon Dunes National Recreation Area; map D1, grid g2.

Campsites, facilities: There are 18 sites for tents, trailers, or RVs up to 30 feet long. Picnic tables and fire grills are provided. Flush toilets and piped water are available. Leashed pets are permitted.

Reservations, fees: No reservations are accepted. Sites are $13 per night. The campground is open from May through November.

Contact: Oregon Dunes National Recreation Area, 855 Highway 101, Reedsport, OR 97467; (541) 271-3611 or fax (541) 750-7244.

Directions: From Coos Bay on U.S. 101, drive 1.5 miles north on U.S. 101, then a mile west on Horsfall Dunes and Beach Access Road. From there, drive two miles northwest on Horsfall Road and you'll see the campground entrance.

Trip notes: This campground gets very little camping pressure. It's next to little Bluebill Lake, which sometimes dries up during the summer. A one-mile trail goes around the lake bed. The camp is a short distance from Horsfall Lake, which is surrounded by private property. If you continue west on the Forest Service road, you'll come to a picnicking and parking area near the beach that has off-road-vehicle access to the dunes at the Horsfall day-use area or Horsfall Beach.

⑤ William M. Tugman State Park

Location: On Eel Lake; map D1, grid f3.

Campsites, facilities: There are 115 sites with water and electrical hookups for trailers or RVs up to 50 feet long, and a special camping area for hikers and bicyclists. Electricity, piped water, and picnic tables are provided. Flush toilets, sanitary services, showers, firewood, and a laundry room are available. Some facilities are wheelchair accessible. Boat docks and launching facilities are nearby. Leashed pets are permitted.

Reservations, fees: Contact Reservations Northwest at (800) 452-5687. Sites are $9–$19 per night, and $4 for hikers/bicyclists. The campground is open year-round.

Contact: Sunset Bay State Park, 10965 Cape Arago Highway, Coos Bay, OR 97420; (541) 888-4902 or (800) 233-0321.

Directions: From Interstate 5 south of Eugene, take exit 162 and turn west on Highway 36. Drive 57 miles to Reedsport, then turn south on U.S. 101 and drive eight miles to the park entrance on the left.

Trip notes: This campground is set along the shore of Eel Lake, which offers almost five miles of shoreline for swimming and trout fishing. A boat ramp is available, but there is a 10 mph speed limit for boats. Oregon Dunes National Recreation Area is across the highway. Hiking is available just a few miles north at Umpqua Lighthouse State Park.

⑤ North Lake Resort and Marina

Location: On Tenmile Lake; map D1, grid f3.

Campsites, facilities: There are 100 sites for trailers or RVs of any length. Picnic tables are provided. Flush toilets, bottled gas, sanitary services, showers, firewood, a store, ice, a playground, electricity, piped water, and sewer hookups are available. A cafe and a Laundromat are located within one mile. Boat docks, launching facilities, and rentals are nearby. Leashed pets are permitted.

Reservations, fees: Reservations are accepted. Sites are $14–$20 per night. The campground is open year-round.

Contact: Phone (541) 759-3515, fax (541) 759-3326, or write to 2090 North Lake Avenue, Lakeside, OR 97449.

Directions: From Interstate 5 south of Eugene, turn west on Highway 36. Drive 57 miles to Reedsport, turn south on U.S. 101, and drive 11 miles. Take the Lakeside exit and go three-quarters of a mile east to North Lake Avenue, then go one-half mile east to the resort.

Trip notes: This resort along the shore of Tenmile Lake is wooded and secluded, a perfect layover spot for U.S. 101 travelers. The lake has a full-service marina, and bass fishing can be good here.

56 Eel Creek

Location: Near Eel Lake in Oregon Dunes National Recreation Area; map D1, grid f3.

Campsites, facilities: There are 52 sites for tents, trailers, or RVs up to 35 feet long. Picnic tables and fire grills are provided. Piped water and flush and vault toilets are available. Boat docks, launching facilities, and rentals are nearby. Leashed pets are permitted.

Reservations, fees: No reservations are accepted. Sites are $14 per night. The campground is open year-round.

Contact: Oregon Dunes National Recreation Area, 855 Highway 101, Reedsport, OR 97467; (541) 271-3611 or fax (541) 750-7244.

Directions: From Interstate 5 at Eugene, turn west on Highway 126 and drive 61 miles to Florence. Turn south on U.S. 101 and drive about 33 miles to the entrance on your right.

Trip notes: This campground along Eel Creek is near both Eel and Tenmile Lakes. Waterskiing is allowed at Tenmile Lake, but not at Eel Lake. Nearby trails access the Umpqua Dunes Scenic Area, where you'll find spectacular scenery in an area closed to off-road vehicles. Off-road access is available at Spinreel (campground number 52).

57 Loon Lake Lodge Resort

Location: On Loon Lake; map D1, grid f5.

Campsites, facilities: There are 24 sites for tents, trailers, or RVs up to 32 feet. Facilities include a public phone, security, ice, an adult room, a game room, and snacks. A boat ramp, dock, marina, and rentals are also available. Leashed pets are permitted.

Reservations, fees: Reservations are recommended. Sites are $16 per night. The campground is open year-round.

Contact: Phone the park at (541) 599-2244, fax (541) 599-2274, or write to 9011 Loon Lake Road, Reedsport, OR 97467.

Directions: From Interstate 5 south of Eugene, take exit 162. Drive west on Highway 99 for about six miles to Highway 38. Drive west

on Highway 38 to the County Road 3 exit (milepost 13.5). Drive south on County Road 3 for 8.2 miles to the resort on the right.

Trip notes: This resort is nestled among the trees on pretty Loon Lake. It's not a long drive from either U.S. 101 or Interstate 5, making it an ideal layover spot for travelers eager to get off the highway. The lake offers good bass fishing, swimming, and boating.

58 Tyee

Location: On the Umpqua River; map D1, grid f6.

Campsites, facilities: There are 15 sites for tents, trailers, or RVs up to 25 feet long. Piped water, fire grills, and picnic tables are provided. Vault toilets and firewood are available. A store is located within one mile. Leashed pets are permitted.

Reservations, fees: No reservations are accepted. Sites are $7 per night, plus $3 for each additional vehicle. The campground is open from mid-May to October 5.

Contact: Bureau of Land Management, 777 NW Garden Valley Boulevard, Roseburg, OR 97470; (541) 440-4930.

Directions: From Interstate 5 north of Roseburg, take exit 136. Turn west on Highway 138 and drive 12 miles. Cross Bullock Bridge, turn right on County Road 57, and drive one-half mile to the campground entrance.

Trip notes: Here's a classic spot, set along the Umpqua River with great fishing in season, yet very few people know of it. The camp isn't far from Interstate 5 and it's the only campground in the immediate vicinity.

59 Pass Creek County Park

Location: Near Roseburg; map D1, grid f9.

Campsites, facilities: There are 10 tent sites and 30 sites for trailers or RVs up to 30 feet long. Electricity, piped water, sewer hookups, and picnic tables are provided. Flush toilets, showers, and a playground are available. A store, a cafe, a Laundromat, and ice are within one mile. Leashed pets are permitted.

Reservations, fees: No reservations are accepted. Sites are $11–$14 per night. The campground is open from March through October.

Contact: Phone (541) 942-3281 or write to P.O. Box 81, Curtin, OR 97428.

Directions: From Roseburg, drive 35 miles north on Interstate 5, then take exit 163 and go to the park entrance (well signed).

Trip notes: This decent layover spot for travelers on Interstate 5 can be found in a wooded, hilly area with many shaded sites. There are no other campgrounds in the immediate area, so if it's late and you need a place to stay, grab this one.

60 Pine Meadows

Location: On Cottage Grove Reservoir; map D1, grid f9.

Campsites, facilities: There are 92 sites for tents, trailers, or RVs of any length, with some drive-through sites. Picnic tables and fire rings are provided. Flush toilets, sanitary services, showers, and a swimming area are available. A boat dock, launching facilities, and a mini-market are nearby. Leashed pets and street-legal motorbikes are permitted.

Reservations, fees: No reservations are accepted. Sites are $10–$12 per night. The campground is open from mid-May to September 14th.

Contact: U.S. Army Corps of Engineers, Recreation Information, Cottage Grove, OR 97424; (541) 942-8657, (541) 942-5631, or fax (541) 942-1305.

Directions: From Interstate 5 south of Cottage Grove, take exit 170, then drive three miles south on London Road. Turn left on Reservoir Road and drive two miles to the park entrance.

Trip notes: This campground is set near the banks of Cottage Grove Reservoir, where boating, fishing, waterskiing, and swimming are among the recreation options. It's an easy hop from Interstate 5, but a lot of campers don't realize it.

61 Primitive Group Campground

Location: On Cottage Grove Reservoir; map D1, grid f9.

Campsites, facilities: There are three group sites, each consisting of five individual walk-in sites. Picnic tables, vault toilets, piped water, sanitary services, and fire rings are available. Boat docks, launching facilities, and a mini-market are nearby. Leashed pets and street-legal motorbikes are permitted.

Reservations, fees: Reservations are required; call (541) 942-8657 beginning May 18. Sites are $30 per night. The campground is open from May 22 to September 8.

Contact: U.S. Army Corps of Engineers, Recreation Information, Cottage Grove, OR 97424; (541) 942-8657, (541) 942-5631, or fax (541) 942-1305.

Directions: From Interstate 5 south of Cottage Grove, take exit 170. Turn south on London Road and drive three miles. Turn left on Reservoir Road and drive 2.5 miles to the park entrance.

Trip notes: This campground on Cottage Grove Reservoir is open to boating, fishing, waterskiing, and swimming. See the trip notes for neighboring Pine Meadows (campground number 60) for more information.

62 Sunset Bay State Park

Location: Near Sunset Bay; map D1, grid g1.

Campsites, facilities: There are 106 sites for tents or self-contained RVs, 29 sites with full hookups for trailers or RVs up to 47 feet long, and a separate area for hikers and bicyclists. There are also four yurts. Picnic tables and fire grills are provided. Flush toilets, showers, and firewood are available. A restaurant is located within 2.5 miles. Some facilities are wheelchair accessible. Leashed pets are permitted.

Reservations, fees: Contact Reservations Northwest at (800) 452-5687 ($6 reservation fee). Sites are $15–$19 per night; yurts are $25 per night for the first five people and $5 per additional person; and sites for hikers/bicyclists are $2–$4 per night. The campground is open from May through September.

Contact: Phone (541) 888-4902 or write to 10965 Cape Arago Highway, Coos Bay, OR 97420.

Directions: From Coos Bay on U.S. 101, take the Charleston exit and proceed 12 miles southwest on the Cape Arago Highway to the park entrance on the left.

Trip notes: This campground is near Sunset Bay, a small, enclosed, well-protected bay with a nice beach for swimming. The camp is very popular, offering easy access from U.S. 101. Hiking, swimming, and boating are just a few of the options here. Other highlights include beautiful views of sandstone cliffs, expansive floral gardens, and offshore reefs.

⑥③ Bastendorff Beach Park

Location: Near Cape Arago State Park; map D1, grid g1.

Campsites, facilities: There are 25 tent sites and 56 sites for trailers or RVs. Rest rooms, showers, a sanitary dump, a public phone, and a barbecue are provided. Horseshoe pits, a playground, basketball courts, and a picnic area are also available. The facilities are wheelchair accessible. Leashed pets are permitted.

Reservations, fees: Reservations are accepted; call (800) 676-7563. Sites are $13–$15 per night. The campground is open year-round.

Contact: Phone the park at (541) 888-5353, or write to 181 South Broadway, Coos Bay, OR 97420.

Directions: From Coos Bay on U.S. 101, take the Charleston exit and proceed to Charleston. Turn southwest on Cape Arago Highway and drive two miles, following the signs to the park.

Trip notes: This campground provides access to the ocean and a small lake. Nearby activities include sand dune buggy riding, clamming, crabbing, fishing, swimming, and boating. A nice side trip is to Shore Acres State Park and Botanical Gardens, about 2.5 miles away.

⑥④ Charleston Marina RV Park

Location: On Coos Bay; map D1, grid g1.

Campsites, facilities: There are 108 sites for tents, trailers, or RVs of any length. Cable TV, rest rooms, showers, a sanitary dump, a public phone, a laundry room, and LP gas are available. A boat dock and ramp, a marina, and a playground are provided. The facilities are wheelchair accessible. Leashed pets are permitted.

Reservations, fees: Reservations are recommended. Sites are $17 per night. The campground is open year-round.

Contact: Phone the park at (541) 888-9512, fax (541) 888-6111, or write to P.O. Box 5433, Charleston, OR 97420.

Directions: From U.S. 101 at Coos Bay, take the Charleston exit and turn west on the Cape Arago Highway. Drive nine miles and cross the Charleston/South Slough Bridge to Boat Basin Drive. Drive north on Boat Basin Drive for two blocks to Kingfisher Drive. Travel east for one block on Kingfisher Drive to the campground on the left.

Trip notes: This large, developed park and marina is located near Charleston on the Pacific Ocean. Recreational activities in and near the campground include hiking, swimming, clamming, crabbing, boating, huckleberry and blackberry picking, and fishing for tuna, salmon, and halibut.

⑥⑤ Oceanside RV Park

Location: Near the Pacific Ocean; map D1, grid g1.

Campsites, facilities: There are 10 tent sites and 20 sites for trailers or RVs. Rest rooms, showers, a sanitary dump, a public phone, a fish cleaning station, and LP gas are available. There is also some fishing equipment. The facilities are wheelchair accessible. Leashed pets are permitted.

Reservations, fees: Reservations are recommended. Sites are $8–$18 per night. The campground is open year-round.

Contact: Oceanside RV Park, 9838 Cape Arago Highway, Charleston, OR 97420; (541) 888-2598, (800) 570-2598; e-mail: oceanside @harborside.com.

Directions: From U.S. 101 north of Coos Bay, take the Charleston Harbor exit and drive west on Charleston Harbor Highway for 8.5 miles to the west end of the Charleston Bridge. Turn west on Cape Arago Highway and drive 1.8 miles to the campground on the right.

Trip notes: This is one of several private, developed parks in the Charleston area. The park is within walking distance of the Pacific Ocean, with opportunities for swimming, fishing, clamming, crabbing, and boating. A marina is 1.5 miles away.

66 Horsfall

Location: In Oregon Dunes National Recreation Area; map D1, grid g2.

Campsites, facilities: There are 70 sites for trailers or RVs up to 50 feet in length. Piped water, coin-operated showers, and flush toilets are available. Leashed pets are permitted.

Reservations, fees: Some sites may be reserved by calling (800) 280-CAMP/2267 ($8.65 reservation fee). Sites are $10 per night. The campground is open year-round.

Contact: Oregon Dunes National Recreation Area, 855 Highway 101, Reedsport, OR 97467; (541) 271-3611 or fax (541) 750-7244.

Directions: From Coos Bay on U.S. 101, drive 1.5 miles north on U.S. 101, then turn west on Horsfall Road and drive about one mile. Turn on the campground access road and drive one-half mile to the campground.

Trip notes: This campground is actually a nice, large paved area for parking RVs. It's the staging area for off-road-vehicle access into the southern section of Oregon Dunes National Recreation Area.

67 Kelley's RV Park

Location: Near Coos Bay; map D1, grid g2.

Campsites, facilities: There are 38 sites for trailers or RVs of any length; three are drive-throughs. Electricity, piped water, sewer hook-ups, and picnic tables are provided. Flush toilets and a laundry room are available. Bottled gas, a store, and a cafe are located within one mile. Boat docks and launching facilities are nearby. Leashed pets are permitted.

Reservations, fees: Reservations are accepted. Sites are $15–$16 per night. The campground is open year-round.

Contact: Phone (541) 888-6531 or write to 555 South Empire Boulevard, Coos Bay, OR 97420.

Directions: In Coos Bay, take the Charleston exit off U.S. 101 and go 4.5 miles to the park at 555 South Empire Boulevard.

Trip notes: This RV park is in the town of Coos Bay, well known for its salmon, deep-sea fishing, and lumber. Nearby recreation options include a full-service marina.

68 Whistler's Bend

Location: On the North Umpqua River; map D1, grid g8.

Campsites, facilities: There are 23 sites for tents, trailers, or RVs up to 30 feet long. Group camping is available. Picnic tables and fire grills are provided. Piped water, flush toilets, showers, and a playground are available. Boat launching facilities are nearby. Leashed pets are permitted.

Reservations, fees: No reservations are accepted. Sites are $8 per night, plus $3 for each additional vehicle; call for group camping fees. The campground is open year-round.

Contact: Phone (541) 673-4863 or write to 2828 Whistlers Park Road, Roseburg, OR 97470.

Directions: From Roseburg on Interstate 5, travel 15 miles east on Highway 138 to the signed cutoff to the park. Turn left and drive three miles to the end of the road and the park entrance.

Trip notes: This county park along the banks of the North Umpqua River is an idyllic spot because it's just a 20-minute drive from Interstate 5, yet it gets little pressure from outsiders.

Map D2

Oregon State Map .... *page 6*
One inch equals approximately 20 miles.

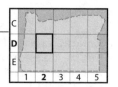

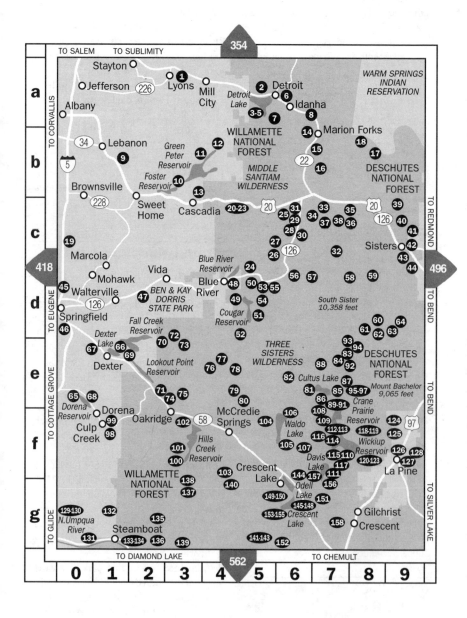

Chapter D2 features:

---

❶ John Neal Memorial Park 🚐 ⛺

Location: On the North Santiam River; map D2, grid a3.

Campsites, facilities: There are 40 sites for tents, trailers, and self-contained RVs. Rest rooms and piped water are provided. Recreational facilities include a boat ramp, a playground, horseshoes, a barbecue, and a recreation field. Leashed pets are permitted.

Reservations, fees: No reservations are accepted. Sites are $8 per night. The campground is open from May through October.

Contact: Linn County Parks Department, 3010 Ferry Street SW, Albany, OR 97321; (541) 967-3917 or fax (541) 924-0202.

Directions: From Interstate 5 at Salem, drive east on Highway 22 for about 20 miles to Lyons. From the junction of Highway 22 and the Mehama-Lyons exit, drive south for one mile on Mehama-Lyons to Highway 226. Turn east and drive for 1.5 miles to 13th Street. Follow the signs to the campground.

Trip notes: Set on the banks of the North Santiam River, this camp offers good boating and trout fishing possibilities. Other options include exploring lakes and trails in the adjacent national forest land or visiting Silver Falls State Park.

❷ Detroit Lake State Park

Location: On Detroit Lake; map D2, grid a5.

Campsites, facilities: There are 134 tent sites and 177 sites with full or partial hookups for trailers or RVs up to 60 feet long. Fire grills and picnic tables are provided. Flush toilets, showers, and firewood are available. Boat docks and launching facilities are nearby. Leashed pets are permitted.

Reservations, fees: Contact Reservations Northwest at (800) 452-5687 ($6 reservation fee). Sites are $12–$22 per night. The campground is open from March through November.

Contact: Phone the park at (541) 851-3406 or write to P.O. Box 549, Detroit, OR 97342.

Directions: From Interstate 5 at Salem, take exit 253 and turn east on Highway 22. Drive 50 miles to the park entrance, located two miles west of Detroit.

Trip notes: This campground is set at 1,600 feet along the shore of Detroit Lake, where fishing, swimming, and waterskiing are permitted. The park offers a fishing dock and a moorage area, and a boat ramp and bathhouse are available nearby at the Mongold Day Use Area. The lake is crowded on the opening day of trout season in late April because it's heavily stocked.

❸ Piety Island Boat-In

Location: On Detroit Lake in Willamette National Forest; map D2, grid a5.

Campsites, facilities: There are 12 tent sites on this island campground, which is accessible by boat only. Picnic tables and fire grills are provided. Pit toilets are available. Boat docks, launching facilities, and rentals are nearby. Leashed pets are permitted.

Reservations, fees: No reservations are ac-

cepted. There is no fee. The campground is open from May to late September.

Contact: Willamette National Forest, Detroit Ranger District, HC 73, Box 320, Mill City, OR 97360; (503) 854-3366 or fax (503) 854-3520.

Directions: From Interstate 5 at Salem, take exit 253 and turn east on Highway 22. Drive about 45 miles to Detroit Lake. Continue east on Highway 22 along the north side of the lake. There is a boat ramp about three miles west of the town of Detroit. Launch your boat and head southeast to the island in the middle of the lake. The campground is located on the east side of the island.

Trip notes: If you want to get away from the crowds at Detroit Lake State Park, this camp provides that possibility for boaters. Other campgrounds along the shore have piped water. The Detroit Ranger Station, located on the north shore of the lake, can answer questions about the area and provide maps that detail nearby hiking trails.

❹ Southshore

Location: On Detroit Lake in Willamette National Forest; map D2, grid a5.

Campsites, facilities: There are eight walk-in tent sites and 23 sites for tents, trailers, or RVs up to 22 feet long. Fire grills and picnic tables are provided. Vault toilets and hand-pumped water are available. Boat launching facilities are nearby at a day-use area. Leashed pets are permitted.

Reservations, fees: No reservations are accepted. Sites are $8–$16 per night. The campground is open from mid-April to late September.

Contact: Willamette National Forest, Detroit Ranger District, HC 73, Box 320, Mill City, OR 97360; (503) 854-3366 or fax (503) 854-3520.

Directions: From Interstate 5 at Salem, take exit 253 and turn east on Highway 22. Drive 52 miles to Detroit. Continue 2.5 miles southeast on Highway 22, then four miles west on Forest Service Road 10 (Blow Out Road) to the camp.

Trip notes: This popular camp is along the south shore of Detroit Lake, where fishing, swimming, and waterskiing are some of the recreation options. The Stahlman Point Trailhead is about one-half mile from camp.

⑤ Hoover

Location: On Detroit Lake in Willamette National Forest; map D2, grid a5.

Campsites, facilities: There are 34 sites for tents, trailers, or RVs up to 32 feet long. Picnic tables and fire grills are provided. Flush toilets and piped water are available. Some facilities are wheelchair accessible. Boat docks and launching facilities are nearby. Leashed pets are permitted.

Reservations, fees: No reservations are accepted. Sites are $10–$20 per night. The campground is open from mid-April to mid-October.

Contact: Willamette National Forest, Detroit Ranger District, HC 73, Box 320, Mill City, OR 97360; (503) 854-3366 or fax (503) 854-3520.

Directions: From Interstate 5 at Salem, take exit 253 and turn east on Highway 22. Drive 52 miles to Detroit. Continue 2.5 miles southeast on Highway 22, then one mile northwest on Forest Service Road 10 (Blow Out Road) to the campground.

Trip notes: This campground is along the eastern arm of Detroit Lake, near the mouth of the Santiam River. There is a wheelchair-accessible fishing area and nature trail. See the trip notes for Southshore (campground number 4) for other recreation options.

⑥ Upper Arm

Location: On Detroit Lake in Willamette National Forest; map D2, grid a6.

Campsites, facilities: There are five tent sites. Fire grills and picnic tables are provided. Pit toilets are available. There is no piped water. Boat docks, launching facilities, and rentals are nearby. Leashed pets are permitted.

Reservations, fees: No reservations are accepted. There is no fee. The campground is open from mid-April to late October.

Contact: Willamette National Forest, Detroit Ranger District, HC 73, Box 320, Mill City, OR 97360; (503) 854-3366 or fax (503) 854-3520.

Directions: From Interstate 5 at Salem, take exit 253 and turn east on Highway 22. Drive 50 miles to Detroit, then turn left on Forest Service Road 46 (Breitenbush Road) and travel one mile northeast to the campground.

Trip notes: This little campground is set along the shore of the narrow upper arm of Detroit Lake, close to where the Breitenbush River empties into it. It's the smallest and most primitive camp in the area, but also one of the most heavily used. Expect crowds and arrive as early as possible to claim a spot.

⑦ Hoover Group Camp

Location: On Detroit Lake in Willamette National Forest; map D2, grid a5.

Campsites, facilities: There are nine sites for tents, trailers, or RVs up to 15 feet long. This is a group camp that will accommodate up to 70 people. Piped water and picnic tables are provided. Vault toilets and a group picnic shelter are available. Boat docks, launching facilities, and rentals are nearby. Leashed pets are permitted.

Reservations, fees: Reservations are required; call (800) 280-CAMP/2267 ($17.35 reservation fee). Group sites are $120 per night, with a two-night minimum for weekend reservations. The campground is open from mid-April to mid-October.

Contact: Willamette National Forest, Detroit Ranger District, HC 73, Box 320, Mill City, OR 97360; (503) 854-3366 or fax (503) 854-3520.

Directions: From Interstate 5 at Salem, take exit 253 and turn east on Highway 22. Drive 52 miles to Detroit. Continue 2.5 miles southeast on Highway 22, then one-half mile northwest on Forest Service Road 10 (Blow Out Road) to the campground.

Trip notes: This is a perfect spot for a family reunion or club trip. Detroit Lake offers a myriad of activities, including hiking, fishing, swimming, and boating, just to name a few.

The campground has nice, open sites and direct access to the lake.

❽ Whispering Falls 🚐 ⛺

Location: On the Santiam River near Detroit Lake in Willamette National Forest; map D2, grid a6.

Campsites, facilities: There are 16 sites for tents, trailers, or RVs up to 22 feet long. Picnic tables and fire grills are provided. Piped water and flush toilets are available. A cafe is located within five miles. Leashed pets are permitted.

Reservations, fees: No reservations are accepted. Sites are $10 per night. The campground is open from mid-April to late September.

Contact: Willamette National Forest, Detroit Ranger District, HC 73, Box 320, Mill City, OR 97360; (503) 854-3366 or fax (503) 854-3520.

Directions: From Interstate 5 at Salem, take exit 253 and turn east on Highway 22. Drive 52 miles to Detroit. Continue eight miles east on Highway 22 to the campground.

Trip notes: This popular campground is on the banks of the Santiam River. If the campsites at Detroit Lake (campground number 2) are crowded, this provides a more secluded option and it's only about a 10-minute drive from the lake. By driving 4.5 miles east on Forest Service Road 2243, you can access a good hiking trail that runs along Cheat Creek.

❾ Waterloo County Campground 🚐 ⛺

Location: On the Santiam River; map D2, grid b1.

Campsites, facilities: There are 60 sites for tents, trailers, or RVs; 50 have partial hookups. Piped water, fire pits, and picnic tables are provided. Rest rooms with showers are available. Boat ramps are located in the surrounding day-use area. Leashed pets are permitted.

Reservations, fees: Reservations are rec-

ommended for groups; phone (541) 967-3917. Sites are $12–$13 per night; group sites are $8 per person per night; there is a $5 fee for each additional vehicle. Senior discounts are available. The campground is open from April through October.

Contact: Linn County Parks Department, 3010 Ferry Street SW, Albany, OR 97321; (541) 967-3917 or fax (541) 924-0202.

Directions: From Interstate 5 at Albany, drive east on U.S. 20 for about 20 miles, through Lebanon. Turn north at the Waterloo exit and drive approximately two miles to the camp on the right. The camp is on the south side of the Santiam River.

Trip notes: There is more than a mile of Santiam River frontage in this campground. Swimming, fishing, picnicking, and field sports are options here.

❿ Sunnyside County Park 🚐 ⛺

Location: On Foster Lake; map D2, grid b3.

Campsites, facilities: There are 162 sites for tents, trailers, or RVs. Electricity, flush toilets, showers, and a sanitary dump station are provided. Picnic areas, volleyball courts, a boat ramp, and moorage are available. Firewood can be obtained for a fee. Leashed pets are permitted.

Reservations, fees: Reservations are recommended for groups; phone (541) 967-3917. Sites are $12–$13 per night; group sites are $8 per person per night; there is a $5 fee for each additional vehicle. Senior discounts are available. The campground is open from April through October.

Contact: Linn County Parks Department, 3010 Ferry Street SW, Albany, OR 97321; (541) 967-3917 or fax (541) 924-0202.

Directions: From Interstate 5 at Albany, take the U.S. 20 exit and drive east about 35 miles, through Lebanon and Sweet Home, to the Quartzville Road exit. Turn north and drive one mile on Quartzville Road to the campground on the right. The camp is on the south side of Foster Reservoir.

Trip notes: This is Linn County's most popular park. Recreation options include boating, fishing, waterskiing, and swimming.

⓫ Whitcomb Creek County Park

Location: On Green Peter Reservoir; map D2, grid b3.

Campsites, facilities: There are 39 tent, trailer, or RV sites. Picnic tables are provided. Leashed pets are permitted.

Reservations, fees: Reservations are recommended for groups; phone (541) 967-3917. Sites are $9 per night. The campground is open from April through October.

Contact: Linn County Parks Department, 3010 Ferry Street SW, Albany, OR 97321; (541) 967-3917 or fax (541) 924-0202.

Directions: From Interstate 5 at Albany, take the U.S. 20 exit and drive east about 35 miles to the Quartzville Road exit. Turn northeast and drive 10 miles on Quartzville Road to the campground on the right.

Trip notes: This camp is on the north shore of Green Peter Reservoir in a wooded area with lots of ferns, which gives it a rainforest feel. Recreation options include swimming, hiking, and picnicking. Two boat ramps are located on the reservoir about a mile from camp.

⓬ Yellowbottom

Location: On Quartzville Creek; map D2, grid b4.

Campsites, facilities: There are 21 tent sites and 10 drive-through sites for trailers or RVs up to 28 feet long. Picnic tables and fire grills are provided. Piped water and vault toilets are available. Leashed pets are permitted.

Reservations, fees: No reservations are accepted. Sites are $8 per night, with an 18-day stay limit. The campground is open from mid-May to late September.

Contact: Bureau of Land Management, 1717 Fabry Road SE, Salem, OR 97306; (503) 375-5646.

Directions: From Interstate 5 at Albany, take exit 233 and turn east on U.S. 20. Drive 26 miles to Sweet Home, then turn northeast on Quartzville Road and proceed 21 miles to the campground.

Trip notes: This campground along the banks of Quartzville Creek is always missed by out-of-town visitors. It's located on the edge of Willamette National Forest and the Middle Santiam Wilderness. Though primitive, the camp is perfect for a quiet getaway weekend.

⓭ Cascadia State Park

Location: On the Santiam River; map D2, grid b4.

Campsites, facilities: There are 25 primitive sites for tents, trailers, or self-contained RVs up to 35 feet long. Picnic tables and fire grills are provided. Piped water, vault toilets, and firewood are available. A store is located within one mile. Some facilities are wheelchair accessible. Leashed pets are permitted.

Reservations, fees: No reservations are accepted. Sites are $9–$12 per night. The campground is open from March through October.

Contact: Phone (800) 452-5687 or (541) 851-3406, or write to P.O. Box 549, Detroit, OR 97542.

Directions: From Interstate 5 at Albany, turn east on U.S. 20 and drive 40 miles to the park on the left.

Trip notes: The highlight of this 258-acre park along the banks of the Santiam River is a scenic waterfall, with a two-mile hiking trail leading to it. Fishing is also available.

⓮ Riverside

Location: On the Santiam River in Willamette National Forest; map D2, grid b6.

Campsites, facilities: There are 37 sites for tents, trailers, or RVs up to 21 feet long. Picnic tables and fire grills are provided. Piped water and pit toilets are available. Leashed pets are permitted.

Reservations, fees: No reservations are accepted. Sites are $8 per night. The campground is open from late April to late September.

Contact: Willamette National Forest, Detroit

Ranger District, HC 73, Box 320, Mill City, OR 97360; (503) 854-3366 or fax (503) 854-3520.

Directions: From Interstate 5 at Salem, take exit 253 and turn east on Highway 22. Drive 50 miles to Detroit. Continue 14 miles southeast on Highway 22 to the campground.

Trip notes: This campground is set along the banks of the Santiam River, where the fishing can be good. A point of interest is the Marion Forks Fish Hatchery, located just a few miles south. The Mount Jefferson Wilderness is directly to the east in Willamette National Forest.

⑮ Marion Forks

Location: On the Santiam River in Willamette National Forest; map D2, grid b7.

Campsites, facilities: There are 15 sites for tents, trailers, or RVs up to 22 feet long. Picnic tables and fire grills are provided. Pit toilets and piped water are available. Leashed pets are permitted.

Reservations, fees: No reservations are accepted. Sites are $8 per night. The campground is open from mid-May to mid-October.

Contact: Willamette National Forest, Detroit Ranger District, HC 73, Box 320, Mill City, OR 97360; (503) 854-3366 or fax (503) 854-3520.

Directions: From Interstate 5 at Salem, take exit 253 and turn east on Highway 22. Drive 50 miles to Detroit. Continue 16 miles southeast on Highway 22 to the campground.

Trip notes: This campground is along Marion Creek, adjacent to the Marion Forks Fish Hatchery. A Forest Service guard station and a restaurant are across Highway 22. There are some quality hiking trails in the area; see a Forest Service map for trailhead locations.

⑯ Big Meadows

Location: Near Mount Jefferson Wilderness in Willamette National Forest; map D2, grid b7.

Campsites, facilities: There nine sites for tents, trailers, or RVs. Picnic tables, fire grills, and four horse corrals are provided at each site. Hand-pumped water and vault toilets are available. Leashed pets are permitted.

Reservations, fees: No reservations are accepted. Sites are $9 per night. The campground is open from mid-April to mid-September, weather permitting.

Contact: Willamette National Forest, Detroit Ranger District, HC 73, Box 320, Mill City, OR 97360; (503) 854-3366 or fax (503) 854-3520.

Directions: From Interstate 5 at Salem, take exit 253 and turn east on Highway 22. Drive 52 miles to Detroit. Continue southeast on Highway 22 for 27 miles to Big Meadows Road (Forest Service Road 2267). Turn left and drive one mile, then turn left again onto Forest Service Road 2257 and drive one-half mile to the campground.

Trip notes: This is one of the newer and most popular campgrounds in the area. Built by the Forest Service with the support of a horse club, it's used heavily by equestrians taking pack trips into Big Meadows and the adjacent Mount Jefferson Wilderness. If you're not a horse lover, you may want to stick with Riverside (campground number 14) or Marion Forks (campground number 15).

⑰ Jack Creek

Location: Near Mount Jefferson Wilderness in Deschutes National Forest; map D2, grid b8.

Campsites, facilities: There is an area for dispersed tent, trailer, or RV camping with access to some picnic tables and fire grills. Vault toilets are available. There is no piped water. Leashed pets are permitted.

Reservations, fees: No reservations are accepted. There is no fee. The campground is open from mid-April to mid-October.

Contact: Deschutes National Forest, Sisters Ranger District, P.O. Box 249, Sisters, OR 97759; (541) 549-2111 or fax (541) 549-7746.

Directions: From Interstate 5 at Albany, turn east on U.S. 20 and drive approximately 87 miles. At the sign for Camp Sherman, turn north and drive about five miles. Continue northwest on Forest Service Roads 12 and 1230 to the campground.

Trip notes: A more primitive option to the other camps in the area, this campground is set along the banks of Jack Creek. No fishing is permitted here in order to protect the bull trout habitat.

⑱ Sheep Springs Horse Camp

Location: Near the Mount Jefferson Wilderness in Deschutes National Forest; map D2, grid b8.

Campsites, facilities: There are 11 sites for tents, trailers, or RVs up to 20 feet long. Hand-pumped water and fire grills are provided. Vault toilets and box stalls for horses are available.

Reservations, fees: Reservations are required; phone (541) 822-3799. Sites are $9 per night, plus $5 per extra vehicle. The campground is open from late May to mid-October.

Contact: Deschutes National Forest, Sisters Ranger District, P.O. Box 249, Sisters, OR 97759; (541) 549-2111 or fax (541) 549-7746.

Directions: From Interstate 5 at Albany, turn east on U.S. 20 and drive approximately 87 miles. At the sign for Camp Sherman, turn north and drive about five miles. Travel four miles north of Camp Sherman on Forest Service Road 1420, then one mile north on Forest Service Road 12. From there, drive 1.5 miles northwest on Forest Service Road 1260 to the campground.

Trip notes: This equestrian camp is located near the trailhead for the Metolius-Windigo Horse Trail, which heads northeast into the Mount Jefferson Wilderness and south to Black Butte. Contact the Forest Service for details and maps of the backcountry.

⑲ Diamond Hill RV Park

Location: In the Willamette Valley; map D2, grid c0.

Campsites, facilities: There are 20 tent sites and 65 sites for trailers or RVs of any length. Electricity, piped water, sewer hookups, and picnic tables are provided. Flush toilets, bottled gas, sanitary services, showers, firewood, a store, a laundry room, ice, a playground, and a swimming pool are available. A cafe is located within one mile. Small leashed pets and motorbikes are permitted.

Reservations, fees: Reservations are accepted. Sites are $15–$19 per night. The campground is open year-round.

Contact: Phone (541) 995-9279 or write to 32917 Diamond Hill Drive, Harrisburg, OR 97446.

Directions: Drive 15 miles north of Eugene on Interstate 5, then take exit 209. The campground is about one block away on the west side of the highway.

Trip notes: This private campground is located in the center of the Willamette Valley, just off the highway. It's a great layover spot if you're cruising up or down Interstate 5. Eugene Kamping World (campground number 45), 10 miles south, is the closest camp.

⑳ Trout Creek

Location: On the South Santiam River in Willamette National Forest; map D2, grid c4.

Campsites, facilities: There are 24 sites for tents, trailers, or RVs up to 22 feet long. Six of the sites will accommodate RVs up to 36 feet long. Picnic tables and fire grills are provided. Hand-pumped water and vault toilets are available. Leashed pets are permitted.

Reservations, fees: No reservations are accepted. Sites are $8 per night, plus $5 for each additional vehicle. The campground is open from May through October.

Contact: Willamette National Forest, Sweet Home Ranger District, 3225 Highway 20, Sweet Home, OR 97386; (541) 367-5168 or fax (541) 367-5506.

Directions: From Interstate 5 at Albany, take exit 233 and drive 26 miles east on U.S. 20 to the town of Sweet Home. Continue 20 miles east on U.S. 20 to the campground entrance on the right.

Trip notes: This campground is set along the banks of the South Santiam River, about seven miles east of Cascadia. Fishing and swimming are some of the possibilities here. The Trout Creek Trail, located just across the highway, is routed into the Menagerie Wilderness. The Walton Ranch Elk Viewing Area is immediately west of the campground, and at the Trout Creek Trailhead you'll also find a short trail leading to an elk-viewing platform.

㉑ Yukwah

Location: On the Santiam River in Willamette National Forest; map D2, grid c4.

Campsites, facilities: There are 19 sites for tents, trailers, or RVs up to 31 feet long. Picnic tables and fire grills are provided. Hand-pumped water, vault toilets, a large picnic area, and a fishing platform are available. Leashed pets are permitted.

Reservations, fees: No reservations are accepted. Sites are $8 per night, plus $5 for each additional vehicle. The campground is open from May through October.

Contact: Willamette National Forest, Sweet Home Ranger District, 3225 Highway 20, Sweet Home, OR 97386; (541) 367-5168 or fax (541) 367-5506.

Directions: From Interstate 5 at Albany, take exit 233 and drive 26 miles east on U.S. 20 to the town of Sweet Home. Continue 19 miles east on U.S. 20 to the campground.

Trip notes: This campground is a quarter of a mile east of Trout Creek Campground (number 20) and offers the same recreation possibilities. There is a half-mile-long, compacted surface nature trail at the camp that's barrier-free.

㉒ Fernview

Location: On the Santiam River in Willamette National Forest; map D2, grid c5.

Campsites, facilities: There are 11 sites for tents, trailers, or small RVs. Picnic tables and fire grills are provided. Hand-pumped water and vault toilets are available. Leashed pets are permitted.

Reservations, fees: No reservations are accepted. Sites are $8 per night, plus $5 for each additional vehicle. The campground is open from May to mid-September.

Contact: Willamette National Forest, Sweet

Home Ranger District, 3225 Highway 20, Sweet Home, OR 97386; (541) 367-5168 or fax (541) 367-5506.

Directions: From Interstate 5 at Albany, take exit 233 and drive 26 miles east on U.S. 20 to the town of Sweet Home. Continue 23 miles east on U.S. 20 to the campground entrance on the right.

Trip notes: This campground is set at the confluence of Boulder Creek and the Santiam River, just south of the Menagerie Wilderness. Just across U.S. 20 lies the Rooster Rock Trail, which leads to—where else?—Rooster Rock, the site of an old lookout tower.

㉓ House Rock

Location: On the Santiam River in Willamette National Forest; map D2, grid c5.

Campsites, facilities: There are 17 tent sites. Picnic tables and fire grills are provided. Vault toilets and hand-pumped water are available. Leashed pets are permitted.

Reservations, fees: No reservations are accepted. Sites are $8–$10 per night, plus $5 for each additional vehicle. The campground is open from May through October.

Contact: Willamette National Forest, Sweet Home Ranger District, 3225 Highway 20, Sweet Home, OR 97386; (541) 367-5168 or fax (541) 367-5506.

Directions: From Interstate 5 at Albany, take exit 233 and drive 26 miles east on U.S. 20 to the town of Sweet Home. From Sweet Home, continue 26.5 miles east on U.S. 20, then turn right on Forest Service Road 2044 and travel southeast for a short distance to the campground.

Trip notes: This campground is set at the confluence of Sheep Creek and the South Santiam River. Trout fishing can be good, particularly during summer evenings. The camp is located in the midst of an old-growth forest and is surrounded by huge, majestic evergreens. History buffs should explore the short loop trail out of camp, which passes by House Rock, a historic shelter for Native Americans, and continues to the Historic Old Santiam Wagon Road.

㉔ Mona

Location: Near Blue River Reservoir in Willamette National Forest; map D2, grid c5.

Campsites, facilities: There are 23 sites for tents, trailers, or RVs up to 21 feet long. Picnic tables and fire grills are provided. Piped water and flush toilets are available. Some facilities are wheelchair accessible. Leashed pets are permitted.

Reservations, fees: No reservations are accepted. Sites are $10–$19 per night. The campground is open from mid-May to late September.

Contact: Willamette National Forest, Blue River Ranger District, P.O. Box 199, Blue River, OR 97413; (541) 822-3317 or fax (541) 822-3783.

Directions: From Interstate 5 at Springfield, turn east on Highway 126 and drive 37 miles to the town of Blue River. Continue east for three miles on Highway 126, then head north on Forest Service Road 15 for three miles to the campground.

Trip notes: This campground is along the shore of Blue River Reservoir, close to where the Blue River joins it. A boat ramp is located across the river from the campground. After launching a boat, campers can ground it near the campsite. This camp is extremely popular when the reservoir is full.

㉕ Lost Prairie

Location: On Hackleman Creek in Willamette National Forest; map D2, grid c6.

Campsites, facilities: There are eight tent sites and two sites for trailers or RVs up to 22 feet long. Picnic tables and fire grills are provided. Hand-pumped water and vault toilets are available. Some facilities are wheelchair accessible. Leashed pets are permitted.

Reservations, fees: No reservations are accepted. Sites are $7 per night. The campground is open from May through October.

Contact: Willamette National Forest, Sweet Home Ranger District, 3225 Highway 20, Sweet Home, OR 97386; (541) 367-5168 or fax (541) 367-5506.

Directions: From Interstate 5 at Albany, take exit 233 and drive 26 miles east on U.S. 20 to the town of Sweet Home. Continue 40 miles east on U.S. 20 to the camp on the right.

Trip notes: This campground is set along the banks of Hackleman Creek at 3,300 feet. Three excellent hiking trails can be found within five miles of the camp: Hackleman Old-Growth Grove, Cone Peak, and Iron Mountain. The latter two offer spectacular wildflower viewing in the late spring and early summer. This camp is an alternative to nearby Fish Lake (campground number 31).

㉖ Olallie

Location: On the McKenzie River in Willamette National Forest; map D2, grid c5.

Campsites, facilities: There are 17 sites for tents, trailers, or RVs up to 30 feet long. Picnic tables and fire grills are provided. Vault toilets and hand-pumped water are available. Leashed pets are permitted.

Reservations, fees: No reservations are accepted. Sites are $6 per night, plus $3 for each additional vehicle. The campground is open from late May to early September.

Contact: Willamette National Forest, McKenzie Ranger District, 57600 McKenzie Highway, McKenzie Bridge, OR 97413; (541) 822-3381 or fax (541) 822-3854.

Directions: From Interstate 5 at Eugene, turn east on Highway 126 and drive 47 miles to the town of McKenzie Bridge. Continue 11 miles northeast on Highway 126 to the campground.

Trip notes: This campground along the banks of the McKenzie River offers opportunities for boating, fishing, and hiking. Other bonuses include easy access from Highway 126 and a jump-off point into the Willamette National Forest. A Forest Service map details back roads and trails.

㉗ Trailbridge

Location: On Trailbridge Reservoir in Willamette National Forest; map D2, grid c5.

Campsites, facilities: There are 20 sites for tents and 21 sites for trailers or RVs. Picnic tables and fire grills are provided. Piped water, vault and flush toilets, and firewood are available. Boat ramps are nearby. Leashed pets are permitted.

Reservations, fees: No reservations are accepted. Sites are $6 per night, plus $3 for each additional vehicle. The campground is open from late April to early September.

Contact: Willamette National Forest, McKenzie Ranger District, 57600 McKenzie Highway, McKenzie Bridge, OR 97413; (541) 822-3381 or fax (541) 822-3854.

Directions: From Interstate 5 near Springfield, take the Highway 126 exit and turn east. Drive 47 miles to the town of McKenzie Bridge. Continue northeast on Highway 126 for 13 miles, then turn southwest at the turnoff at the north end of Trailbridge Reservoir and continue 200 yards to the campground.

Trip notes: This campground is set along the shore of Trailbridge Reservoir, where boating, fishing, and hiking are recreation options. It's an exceptional spot for car campers. Highway 126 east of McKenzie Bridge is a designated scenic route, providing a pleasant trip to the camp. A good side trip is to take the beautiful 40-minute drive east to the little town of Sisters. To the south you can see the Three Sisters Mountains (all over 10,000 feet), and you'll cross the Pacific Crest Trail as well. From this camp, there is access to the McKenzie River National Recreation Trail.

㉘ Lakes End

Location: On Smith Reservoir in Willamette National Forest; map D2, grid c6.

Campsites, facilities: There are 17 boat-in tent sites. Picnic tables and fire grills are provided. Pit toilets are available, but there is no piped water. Boat docks are nearby. Leashed pets are permitted.

Reservations, fees: No reservations are accepted. There is no fee. The campground is open from late May to early September.

Contact: Willamette National Forest, McKenzie Ranger District, 57600 McKenzie Highway, McKenzie Bridge, OR 97413; (541) 822-3381 or fax (541) 822-3854.

Directions: From Interstate 5 near Springfield, take the Highway 126 exit and turn east. Drive 47 miles to the town of McKenzie Bridge. Continue northeast on Highway 126 for 13 miles, then drive three miles north on Forest Service Road 1477 to the boat ramp. Travel by boat for another two miles to the north end of Smith Reservoir and the campground.

Trip notes: This secluded boat-in campground is set along the shore of Smith Reservoir. It's one of the few boat-in campgrounds in the entire state. You'll find no cars, no traffic, and most likely no people. The trout fishing in this reservoir can be exceptionally good.

㉙ Ice Cap

Location: On Carmen Reservoir in Willamette National Forest; map D2, grid c6.

Campsites, facilities: There are 11 tent sites and 11 sites for tents, trailers, or RVs up to 16 feet long. Picnic tables and fire grills are provided. Piped water and flush toilets, boat launching facilities, and boat rentals are about two miles away at Clear Lake Resort. Leashed pets are permitted.

Reservations, fees: No reservations are accepted. Sites are $9 per night, plus $5 for each additional vehicle. The campground is open from late May to early September.

Contact: Willamette National Forest, McKenzie Ranger District, 57600 McKenzie Highway, McKenzie Bridge, OR 97413; (541) 822-3381 or fax (541) 822-3854.

Directions: From Interstate 5 near Springfield, take the Highway 126 exit and turn east. Drive 47 miles to the town of McKenzie Bridge. Continue northeast on Highway 126 for 19 miles, then drive 200 yards southwest on the entrance road to the campground.

Trip notes: This campground is set on a hill above Carmen Reservoir, which was created by a dam on the McKenzie River. The McKenzie River National Recreation Trail passes by camp, and Koosah Falls and Sahalie Falls are nearby. Clear Lake, a popular local vacation destination, is a short drive away.

⑳ Coldwater Cove

Location: On Clear Lake in Willamette National Forest; map D2, grid c6.

Campsites, facilities: There are 35 sites for tents, trailers, or RVs up to 30 feet long. Picnic tables and fire grills are provided. Hand pumps for water and vault toilets are available. Some facilities are wheelchair accessible. Boat docks, launching facilities, rowboats, a store, a cafe, and cabin rentals are available nearby at Clear Lake Resort. Leashed pets are permitted.

Reservations, fees: Reserve some sites by calling (800) 280-CAMP/2267 ($8.65 reservation fee). Sites are $10 per night, plus $5 for each additional vehicle. The campground is open from late May to early September.

Contact: Willamette National Forest, McKenzie Ranger District, 57600 McKenzie Highway, McKenzie Bridge, OR 97413; (541) 822-3381 or fax (541) 822-3854.

Directions: From Interstate 5 near Springfield, take the Highway 126 exit and turn east. Drive 47 miles to the town of McKenzie Bridge. Continue northeast on Highway 126 for 14 miles, then turn east on Forest Service Road 1372 and continue to the campground.

Trip notes: This campground is on the south shore of Clear Lake, a spring-fed lake formed by a natural lava dam and the source of the McKenzie River. No motors are permitted on the lake, making it ideal for anglers in rowboats or canoes. The northern section of the McKenzie River National Recreation Trail passes by the camp.

㉛ Fish Lake

Location: Near Clear Lake in Willamette National Forest; map D2, grid c6.

Campsites, facilities: There are eight sites for tents, trailers, or RVs up to 16 feet long. Picnic tables and fire grills are provided. Piped water and vault toilets are available. Leashed pets are permitted.

Reservations, fees: No reservations are accepted. Sites are $6 per night, plus $3 for each

additional vehicle. The campground is open from late May to early September.

Contact: Willamette National Forest, McKenzie Ranger District, 57600 McKenzie Highway, McKenzie Bridge, OR 97413; (541) 822-3381 or fax (541) 822-3854.

Directions: From Interstate 5 near Springfield, take the Highway 126 exit and turn east. Drive 47 miles to the town of McKenzie Bridge. Continue northeast on Highway 126 for 23 miles, then drive 200 yards southwest on the entrance road to the campground.

Trip notes: This campground is on the shore of Fish Lake, though the "lake" usually dries up by the middle of the summer. An interpretive display is set up at the guard station nearby. Across the road is a trail that follows the Old Santiam Wagon Road and the northern trailhead for the McKenzie River National Recreation Trail. The Clear Lake picnic area is two miles south off Highway 126.

㉜ Scott Lake

Location: On Scott Lake in Willamette National Forest; map D2, grid c7.

Campsites, facilities: There are 12 walk-in tent sites. Picnic tables are provided. Pit toilets are available, but there is no piped water. Leashed pets are permitted.

Reservations, fees: No reservations are accepted. There is no fee. The campground is open from late June to early September.

Contact: Willamette National Forest, McKenzie Ranger District, 57600 McKenzie Highway, McKenzie Bridge, OR 97413; (541) 822-3381 or fax (541) 822-3854.

Directions: From Interstate 5 at Eugene, turn east on Highway 126 and drive 54 miles to the junction with Highway 242. Head east on Highway 242 for 14.5 miles to Forest Service Road 1532 and turn left to the campground. Highway 242 is not recommended for trailers; the speed limit is 35 mph and the maximum vehicle length is 35 feet.

Trip notes: This campground offers hike-in sites (only about an eighth of a mile from the road) set around Scott Lake at an elevation of 4,800 feet. Only nonmotorized boats are allowed on the lake. Trails leading out from camp provide access to several small lakes in the Mount Washington Wilderness.

㉝ Big Lake

Location: On Big Lake in Willamette National Forest; map D2, grid c7.

Campsites, facilities: There are 49 sites for tents, trailers, or RVs up to 16 feet long. Picnic tables and fire grills are provided. Piped water, and vault and flush toilets are available. Boat ramps and launching facilities are nearby. Leashed pets are permitted.

Reservations, fees: Reserve some sites by calling (800) 280-CAMP/2267 ($8.65 reservation fee). Sites are $10 per night, plus $5 for each additional vehicle. The campground is open from late June to early September.

Contact: Willamette National Forest, McKenzie Ranger District, 57600 McKenzie Highway, McKenzie Bridge, OR 97413; (541) 822-3381 or fax (541) 822-3854.

Directions: From Interstate 5 at Albany, take exit 233 and turn east on U.S. 20. Go 74 miles to the convergence of Highways 20, 126, and 22. Continue east on Highway 126 for five miles to Forest Service Road 2690, then turn south and continue for 3.5 miles to the campground.

Trip notes: This jewel of a spot on the north shore of Big Lake at 4,650 feet offers a host of activities, including fishing, swimming, waterskiing, and hiking. Big Lake has heavy motorized boat use. One of the better hikes is the five-mile wilderness loop trail that heads out from the south shore of the lake and cuts past a few small lakes before returning. It's quite heavily traveled, however, and requires a regulatory permit from the Forest Service to use.

㉞ Big Lake West Campground

Location: On Big Lake in Willamette National Forest; map D2, grid c7.

Campsites, facilities: There are 11 walk-in sites (only 200 feet from the road). Fire pits

and picnic tables are provided. Piped water and vault toilets are available. Leashed pets permitted.

Reservations, fees: Reserve some sites by calling (800) 280-CAMP/2267 ($8.65 reservation fee). Sites are $8 per night, plus $4 for each additional vehicle. The campground is open from mid-June to early September.

Contact: Willamette National Forest, McKenzie Ranger District, 57600 McKenzie Highway, McKenzie Bridge, OR 97413; (541) 822-3381 or fax (541) 822-3854.

Directions: From Interstate 5 at Albany, take exit 233 and turn east on U.S. 20. Go 74 miles to the convergence of Highways 20, 126, and 22. Continue east on Highway 126 for five miles to Forest Service Road 2690, then turn south and drive for 4.3 miles to the campground.

Trip notes: This spot west of the Big Lake Campground has many of the same attractions, but the walk-in sites offer some seclusion and quiet. The Mount Washington Wilderness and Patjens Lake access trails can be reached from here. See Big Lake (campground number 33) for some hiking options from the south shore of the lake.

㉟ Scout Lake

Location: On Scout Lake in Deschutes National Forest; map D2, grid c7.

Campsites, facilities: There are 13 sites for tents, trailers, or RVs up to 40 feet long. Picnic tables and fire grills are provided. Vault toilets and piped water are available. Leashed pets are permitted in the campground only (not in the day-use area).

Reservations, fees: Reservations are accepted. Sites are $7–$18 per night. The campground is open from mid-April to late September.

Contact: Deschutes National Forest, Sisters Ranger District, P.O. Box 249, Sisters, OR 97759; (541) 549-2111 or fax (541) 549-7746.

Directions: From Interstate 5 at Albany, take exit 233 and turn east on U.S. 20. Drive 74 miles to the convergence of Highways 20, 126, and 22. Continue east on Highway 126 for 12 miles to Suttle Lake Forest Road, then head west. Drive south of Suttle Lake on Forest Service Road 2066 for a short distance to the campground.

Trip notes: This campground about half a mile from Suttle Lake is a good spot for swimming and hiking. The camp is available for groups, but reservations need to be made in advance. Call the ranger district for details.

36 South Shore

Location: On Suttle Lake in Deschutes National Forest; map D2, grid c7.

Campsites, facilities: There are 38 sites for tents, trailers, or RVs up to 40 feet long. Picnic tables and fire grills are provided. Piped water and vault toilets are available. Boat docks, launching facilities, and rentals are nearby. Leashed pets are permitted.

Reservations, fees: Some reservations are accepted; phone (800) 280-CAMP/2267 ($8.65 reservation fee). Sites are $10–$12 per night, plus $5 for each additional vehicle. The campground is open from mid-April to late September.

Contact: Deschutes National Forest, Sisters Ranger District, P.O. Box 249, Sisters, OR 97759; (541) 549-2111 or fax (541) 549-7746.

Directions: From Interstate 5 at Albany, take exit 233 and turn east on U.S. 20. Go 74 miles to the convergence of Highways 20, 126, and 22. Continue east on Highway 126 for 12 miles to Suttle Lake Forest Road, then head west and proceed a short distance to the campground.

Trip notes: This campground is located at 3,400 feet on the south shore of Suttle Lake, where waterskiing is permitted. A hiking trail winds around the lake, and a stable and horseback riding rentals are nearby. Fishing and windsurfing are other popular activities.

37 Link Creek

Location: On Suttle Lake in Deschutes National Forest; map D2, grid c7.

Campsites, facilities: There are 33 sites for tents, trailers, or RVs up to 40 feet long. Picnic tables and fire grills are provided. Piped water and vault toilets are available. Boat docks,

launching facilities, and rentals are nearby. Leashed pets are permitted.

Reservations, fees: Some reservations are accepted; phone (800) 280-CAMP/2267 ($8.65 reservation fee). Sites are $10–$12 per night, plus $5 for each additional vehicle. The campground is open from mid-April to late September.

Contact: Deschutes National Forest, Sisters Ranger District, P.O. Box 249, Sisters, OR 97759; (541) 549-2111 or fax (541) 549-7746.

Directions: From Interstate 5 at Albany, take exit 233 and turn east on U.S. 20. Go 74 miles to the convergence of Highways 20, 126, and 22. Continue east on Highway 126 for 12 miles to Suttle Lake Forest Road, then head west. Drive a short distance to the campground.

Trip notes: This campground is located at the west end of Suttle Lake. See the trip notes for South Shore (campground number 36) for recreation details.

38 Blue Bay

Location: On Suttle Lake in Deschutes National Forest; map D2, grid c7.

Campsites, facilities: There are 25 sites for tents, trailers, or RVs up to 30 feet long. Picnic tables and fire grills are provided. Piped water and vault toilets are available. Boat docks, launching facilities, and rentals are nearby. Leashed pets are permitted.

Reservations, fees: Some reservations are accepted; phone (800) 280-CAMP/2267 ($8.65 reservation fee). Sites are $10–$12 per night, plus $5 for each additional vehicle. The campground is open from mid-April to late September.

Contact: Deschutes National Forest, Sisters Ranger District, P.O. Box 249, Sisters, OR 97759; (541) 549-2111 or fax (541) 549-7746.

Directions: From Interstate 5 at Albany, take exit 233 and turn east on U.S. 20. Go 74 miles to the convergence of Highways 20, 126, and 22. Continue east on Highway 126 for 12 miles to Suttle Lake Forest Road, then head west. Drive a short distance to the campground.

Trip notes: This campground is set along the south shore of Suttle Lake. See the trip notes for South Shore (campground number 36) for recreation details.

㊴ KOA Sisters

Location: On Branchwater Lake; map D2, grid c9.

Campsites, facilities: There are 64 sites for tents, trailers, or RVs. Air-conditioning, electric heat, cable TV, rest rooms, showers, a sanitary dump, security, a public phone, a laundry room, limited groceries, ice, snacks, RV supplies, LP gas, and a barbecue are available. Recreational facilities include a sports field, a playground, a game room, horseshoes, a spa, and a heated swimming pool. Some facilities are wheelchair accessible. Leashed pets are permitted.

Reservations, fees: Reservations are recommended. Sites are $19–$23 per night. The campground is open year-round.

Contact: Phone the park at (541) 549-3021, fax (541) 549-8144, or write to 67667 Highway 20 West, Bend, OR 97701.

Directions: From Interstate 5 at Albany, turn east on U.S. 20 and drive 100 miles to Sisters. Continue approximately four miles southeast to the park on the right side of the highway.

Trip notes: This park is located amid wooded mountains outside of Sisters at an elevation of 3,200 feet. Branchwater Lake offers swimming and good trout fishing. See the trip notes for Belknap Springs Lodge (campground number 40) for information about the surrounding area.

㊵ Belknap Springs Lodge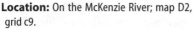

Location: On the McKenzie River; map D2, grid c9.

Campsites, facilities: There are seven sites for tents and 40 sites for trailers or RVs with electrical and water hookups. There is also a lodge with 12 rooms and five cabins available. Rest rooms, showers, a sanitary dump, and a public phone are provided. Recreational facilities include a heated swimming pool, a recreation field, horseshoes, and a recreation hall. Some facilities are wheelchair accessible.

Leashed pets are permitted, except in the lodge or the cabins.

Reservations, fees: Reservations are recommended. Rates per night are $12–$18 for campsites, $60–$90 for lodge rooms, and $35–$90 for cabins. The campground is open year-round.

Contact: Phone the park at (541) 822-3512, fax (541) 822-3327, or write to P.O. Box 2001, McKenzie Bridge, OR 97413.

Directions: From Interstate 5 at Albany, turn east on U.S. 20 and drive 100 miles to Sisters. From the junction of Highway 242 and Highway 126 (in Sisters), drive east on Highway 126 for one mile to Belknap Springs Road. The lodge is north three-tenths of a mile on Belknap Springs Road. For an alternate route, from Hoodoo on Highway 126, drive west for 28 miles to the park.

Trip notes: This beautiful park is located in a wooded, mountainous area on the McKenzie River. Trout fishing can be excellent here. If you're looking for hiking opportunities, check out the Three Sisters and Mount Washington Wilderness Areas, both accessible by driving west of Sisters on Highway 242. These are exceptionally scenic and pristine expanses of forest and well worth exploring. The Pacific Crest Trail runs north and south through both wilderness areas.

㊶ Riverside

Location: On the Metolius River in Deschutes National Forest; map D2, grid c9.

Campsites, facilities: There are 16 tent sites. Picnic tables and fire grills are provided. Vault toilets and hand-pumped water are available. Leashed pets are permitted.

Reservations, fees: No reservations are accepted. Sites are $6 per night. The campground is open from mid-April through September.

Contact: Deschutes National Forest, Sisters Ranger District, P.O. Box 249, Sisters, OR 97759; (541) 549-2111 or fax (541) 549-7746.

Directions: From Interstate 5 at Albany, turn east on U.S. 20 and drive approximately 87 miles. At the sign for Camp Sherman, turn north and drive about five miles. From the store in Camp Sherman, drive two miles south on Forest Service Road 900 to the campground.

Trip notes: This campground is set along the banks of the Metolius River, less than a mile from Metolius Springs at the base of Black Butte. It's just far enough off the highway to be missed by most other people.

㊷ Indian Ford

Location: On Indian Ford Creek in Deschutes National Forest; map D2, grid c9.

Campsites, facilities: There are 25 sites for tents, trailers, or RVs up to 40 feet long. Picnic tables and fire grills are provided. Vault toilets and hand-pumped water are available. Leashed pets are permitted.

Reservations, fees: No reservations are accepted. Sites are $9 per night, plus $5 for each additional vehicle. The campground is open from May through September.

Contact: Deschutes National Forest, Sisters Ranger District, P.O. Box 249, Sisters, OR 97759; (541) 549-2111 or fax (541) 549-7746.

Directions: From Interstate 5 at Albany, turn east on U.S. 20 and drive 95 miles to the campground, located five miles northwest of Sisters.

Trip notes: This campground is on the banks of Indian Ford Creek. On the north side of nearby Black Butte is the spring that feeds the Metolius River. Aspen trees provide great bird-watching opportunities within the campground.

㊸ Cold Springs

Location: On Trout Creek in Deschutes National Forest; map D2, grid c9.

Campsites, facilities: There are 23 sites for tents, trailers, or RVs up to 40 feet long. Picnic tables and fire grills are provided. Vault toilets and piped water are available. Leashed pets are permitted.

Reservations, fees: No reservations are accepted. Sites are $9 per night, plus $5 for each

additional vehicle. The campground is open from May through September.

Contact: Deschutes National Forest, Sisters Ranger District, P.O. Box 249, Sisters, OR 97759; (541) 549-2111 or fax (541) 549-7746.

Directions: From Interstate 5 at Albany, turn east on U.S. 20 and drive 100 miles to Sisters. Turn southwest on Highway 242 and drive five miles to the camp.

Trip notes: This wooded campground is located at 3,400 feet at the source of little Trout Creek. It's just far enough off the main drag to be missed by many campers. Spring and early summer are the times for great bird-watching in the area's abundant aspen.

㊹ Circle 5 Trailer Park

Location: Near Sisters; map D2, grid c9.

Campsites, facilities: There are 10 tent sites and 22 drive-through sites for trailers or RVs of any length. Electricity, piped water, sewer hookups, cable TV, and picnic tables are provided. Flush toilets, bottled gas, sanitary services, showers, and a laundry room are available. A store, a cafe, and ice are located within one mile. Leashed pets are permitted.

Reservations, fees: Reservations are accepted. Sites are $10–$19 per night. The campground is open year-round.

Contact: Phone (541) 549-3861 or write to Box 1360, Sisters, OR 97759.

Directions: From Interstate 5 at Albany, turn east on U.S. 20 and drive 100 miles to Sisters. Continue one-half mile southeast on U.S. 20 to the park entrance on the left.

Trip notes: This motor-home camp is just outside Sisters, within walking distance of the town. The sites are cool and shady. Nearby recreation options include a riding stable and tennis courts.

㊺ Eugene Kamping World

Location: Near the Willamette River; map D2, grid d0.

Campsites, facilities: There are 30 tent sites and 114 drive-through sites for trailers or RVs of any length. Electricity, piped water, sewer hookups, and picnic tables are provided. Flush toilets, bottled gas, sanitary services, showers, a recreation hall, cable TV, a miniature golf course, a store, a laundry room, ice, and a playground are available. A cafe is located within one mile. Small leashed pets are permitted.

Reservations, fees: Reservations are accepted. Sites are $16–$21 per night. The campground is open year-round.

Contact: Phone (541) 343-4832, fax (541) 343-3008, or write to 90932 South Stuartway, Coburg, OR 97408.

Directions: Drive seven miles north of Eugene on Interstate 5. Take the Coburg exit (exit 199) and go 400 yards west to the campground access. Turn left and drive up the driveway.

Trip notes: Eugene is one of Oregon's major cities, but it offers many riverside parks and hiking opportunities. Both the Willamette and McKenzie Rivers run right through town. The McKenzie, in particular, provides good trout fishing. Recreation options near this campground include a golf course and tennis courts.

㊻ Eugene Mobile Village 🚐

Location: Near the Willamette River; map D2, grid d0.

Campsites, facilities: There are 30 drive-through sites for trailers or RVs of any length. Electricity, piped water, and sewer hookups are provided. Flush toilets, sanitary services, showers, and a laundry room are available. Bottled gas, a store, a cafe, and ice are located within one mile. Leashed pets are permitted.

Reservations, fees: Reservations are accepted. Sites are $17 per night. The campground is open year-round.

Contact: Phone (541) 747-2257 or write to 4750 Franklin Boulevard, Eugene, OR 97403.

Directions: In Eugene, take exit 189 off Interstate 5, then proceed one mile on Franklin Boulevard to the park on the left.

Trip notes: This RV park is in Eugene, a mile away from the Willamette River. (See the trip notes for Eugene Kamping World, number 45, for more information.) The camp is wooded but close to many attractions. Nearby recreation options include a golf course, bike paths, a full-service marina, and tennis courts.

㊼ Vida-Lea Mobile Lodge 🚐

Location: On the McKenzie River; map D2, grid d2.

Campsites, facilities: There are 13 drive-through sites for trailers or RVs of any length in this adult-only campground. Electricity, piped water, and sewer hookups are provided. Flush toilets, sanitary services, showers, and a laundry room are available. Boat docks and launching facilities are nearby. Leashed pets (one per unit) and motorbikes are permitted.

Reservations, fees: Reservations are accepted. Sites are $16 per night. The campground is open year-round.

Contact: Phone (541) 896-3898 or write to 44221 McKenzie Highway, Leaburg, OR 97489.

Directions: From Interstate 5 at Eugene, turn east on Highway 126 and drive 16 miles to Leaburg. Continue three miles east on Highway 126 to the park.

Trip notes: This private resort is on the banks of the scenic McKenzie River. Ben and Kay Dorris State Park, which is open for day use, is about six miles east of the campground on Highway 126 and is also set along the McKenzie River. Nearby recreation options include a golf course, hiking trails, and bike paths.

㊽ Lazy Days 🚐

Location: On the McKenzie River; map D2, grid d4.

Campsites, facilities: There are 24 drive-through sites for trailers or RVs of any length. Electricity, piped water, sewer hookups, and picnic tables are provided. Flush toilets, bottled gas, telephones, storage lockers, showers, cable TV, firewood, and a laundry room are available. Boat launching facilities are nearby. Leashed pets are permitted.

Reservations, fees: Reservations are accepted. Sites are $15 per night for a maximum of four campers per site. The campground is open year-round.

Contact: Phone (541) 822-3889 or write to 52511 McKenzie, Blue River, OR 97413.

Directions: From Interstate 5 at Eugene, turn east on Highway 126 and drive 37 miles to the town of Blue River. Continue 1.5 miles east on Highway 126 to the park on the left.

Trip notes: This RV park is set along the banks of the McKenzie River, not far from Blue River Reservoir. Covering about 1,400 acres, the lake offers opportunities for fishing, swimming, and waterskiing. A golf course and several restaurants are nearby.

㊾ Patio RV Park

Location: Near the South Fork of the McKenzie River; map D2, grid d4.

Campsites, facilities: There are 60 sites for trailers or RVs of any length in this adult-only campground. Electricity, piped water, sewer hookups, and picnic tables are provided. Flush toilets, bottled gas, sanitary services, showers, firewood, a recreation hall, and a laundry room are available. A store, a cafe, and ice are within one mile. Leashed pets are permitted.

Reservations, fees: Reservations are accepted. Sites are $18–$20 per night. The campground is open year-round, weather permitting.

Contact: Phone (541) 822-3596, fax (541) 822-3783, or write to 55636 McKenzie, Blue River, OR 97413.

Directions: From Interstate 5 at Springfield, turn east on Highway 126 and drive 37 miles to the town of Blue River. Continue east for six miles on Highway 126, then drive two miles east on McKenzie River Drive to the park on the right.

Trip notes: This RV park is near the banks of the South Fork of the McKenzie River, not far from Cougar Lake, which offers opportunities for fishing, swimming, and waterskiing. Nearby

recreation options include a golf course, hiking trails, and bike paths.

㊿ Delta

Location: On the McKenzie River in Willamette National Forest; map D2, grid d5.

Campsites, facilities: There are 38 sites for tents, trailers, or RVs up to 21 feet long. Picnic tables and fire grills are provided. Hand-pumped water and vault toilets are available. Some facilities are wheelchair accessible. Leashed pets are permitted.

Reservations, fees: No reservations are accepted. Sites are $10–$19 per night. The campground is open from mid-May to late September.

Contact: Willamette National Forest, Blue River Ranger District, P.O. Box 199, Blue River, OR 97413; (541) 822-3317 or fax (541) 822-3783.

Directions: From Interstate 5 at Springfield, turn east on Highway 126 and drive 37 miles to the town of Blue River. Continue east on Highway 126 for another five miles. Turn south (right) on Forest Service Road 19 (Aufderheide Scenic Byway). Drive one-quarter mile, then turn right on Forest Service Road 400 and continue one mile to the campground.

Trip notes: This popular campground is along the banks of the McKenzie River in a stand of old-growth Douglas fir. The Delta Old Growth Nature Trail, a half-mile wheelchair-accessible interpretive trail, is routed through the campground. There is an amphitheater in the camp as well. Blue River and Cougar Reservoirs are nearby, both of which offer trout fishing, waterskiing, and swimming.

⓷ Slide Creek

Location: On Cougar Reservoir in Willamette National Forest; map D2, grid d5.

Campsites, facilities: There are 16 sites for tents, trailers, or RVs. Picnic tables and fire grills are provided. Hand-pumped water and vault toilets are available. A boat ramp is available. Leashed pets are permitted.

Reservations, fees: No reservations are accepted. Sites are $10–$19 per night. The campground is open from mid-May to mid-September.

Contact: Willamette National Forest, Blue River Ranger District, P.O. Box 199, Blue River, OR 97413; (541) 822-3317 or fax (541) 822-3783.

Directions: From Interstate 5 at Springfield, turn east on Highway 126 and drive 37 miles to the town of Blue River. Continue east for five miles, then travel south on Forest Service Road 19 (Aufderheide Scenic Byway) for 11 miles. Take the Eastside Road 500 for 1.5 miles along the east side of Cougar Reservoir to the campground.

Trip notes: This campground is on the banks of Cougar Reservoir, which covers about 1,300 acres and offers opportunities for fishing and swimming. The pretty lakeside camp is quite popular, so plan to arrive early on weekends.

🔢 French Pete

Location: On the South Fork of the McKenzie River in Willamette National Forest; map D2, grid d5.

Campsites, facilities: There are 17 sites for tents, trailers, or RVs. Picnic tables and fire grills are provided. Hand-pumped water and vault toilets are available. Some facilities are wheelchair accessible. Leashed pets are permitted.

Reservations, fees: No reservations are accepted. Sites are $10–$19 per night. The campground is open from mid-May to mid-September.

Contact: Willamette National Forest, Blue River Ranger District, P.O. Box 199, Blue River, OR 97413; (541) 822-3317 or fax (541) 822-3783.

Directions: From Interstate 5 near Springfield, take the Highway 126 exit and turn east. Drive 37 miles to the town of Blue River. Continue east for five miles on Highway 126, then turn south on Forest Service Road 19 (Aufderheide Scenic Byway) and travel 12 miles to the campground.

Trip notes: This quiet, wooded campground is on the banks of the South Fork of the McKenzie River and French Pete Creek. A trail

across the road from the campground provides access to the Three Sisters Wilderness. Two more primitive camps (Homestead and Frissell Crossing, campground numbers 77 and 78) are a few miles southeast on the same road.

🔢 McKenzie Bridge

Location: On the McKenzie River in Willamette National Forest; map D2, grid d5.

Campsites, facilities: There are 20 sites for tents, trailers, or RVs up to 35 feet long. Picnic tables and fire grills are provided. Vault toilets and hand-pumps for water are available. Leashed pets are permitted.

Reservations, fees: Some sites may be reserved by calling (800) 280-CAMP/2267 ($8.65 reservation fee). Sites are $9 per night, plus $5 for each additional vehicle. The campground is open from late May to early September.

Contact: Willamette National Forest, McKenzie Ranger District, 57600 McKenzie Highway, McKenzie Bridge, OR 97413; (541) 822-3381 or fax (541) 822-3854.

Directions: From Interstate 5 near Springfield, take the Highway 126 exit and turn east. Drive 46 miles to the campground, located one mile west of the town of McKenzie Bridge.

Trip notes: This campground is along the banks of the McKenzie River, near the town of McKenzie Bridge. There is good evening fly-fishing for trout during summer on this stretch of river.

🔢 Horse Creek Group Camp

Location: On Horse Creek in Willamette National Forest; map D2, grid d5.

Campsites, facilities: There are eight tent sites and 13 sites for trailers or RVs up to 21 feet long. Picnic tables and fire grills are provided. Hand-pumped water and vault toilets are available. Leashed pets are permitted.

Reservations, fees: Reservations are required; call (800) 280-CAMP/2267 ($17.35 reservation fee). Sites are $40–$60 per night.

The campground is open from March through September.

Contact: Willamette National Forest, McKenzie Ranger District, 57600 McKenzie Highway, McKenzie Bridge, OR 97413; (541) 822-3381 or fax (541) 822-3854.

Directions: From Interstate 5 near Springfield, take the Highway 126 exit and turn east. Drive 47 miles to the town of McKenzie Bridge. Turn south on Horse Creek Road and drive three miles to the campground.

Trip notes: This campground reserved for groups is on the banks of Horse Creek, near the town of McKenzie Bridge. A possible side trip is Harris Wayside State Park, with hiking trails and wildlife viewing; the park is available for day use only.

55 Paradise

Location: On the McKenzie River in Willamette National Forest; map D2, grid d5.

Campsites, facilities: There are 64 sites for tents, trailers, or RVs up to 40 feet long. Picnic tables and fire grills are provided. Flush toilets, piped water, and firewood are available. Leashed pets are permitted.

Reservations, fees: Reserve some sites by calling (800) 280-CAMP/2267 ($8.65 reservation fee). Sites are $10 per night, plus $5 for each additional vehicle. The campground is open from late May to early September.

Contact: Willamette National Forest, McKenzie Ranger District, 57600 McKenzie Highway, McKenzie Bridge, OR 97413; (541) 822-3381 or fax (541) 822-3854.

Directions: From Interstate 5 near Springfield, take the Highway 126 exit and turn east. Drive 47 miles to the town of McKenzie Bridge. Continue 3.5 miles east on Highway 126 to the campground.

Trip notes: This campground along the banks of the McKenzie River may be right off the highway, but it's in a rustic, streamside setting with access to the McKenzie River National Recreation Trail. Trout fishing can be good here. See the trip notes for McKenzie Bridge (campground number 53) for other options.

56 Limberlost

Location: On Lost Creek in Willamette National Forest; map D2, grid d6.

Campsites, facilities: There are 12 sites for tents or small trailers (no longer than 35 feet). Picnic tables and fire grills are provided. Pit toilets are available, but there is no piped water. Leashed pets are permitted.

Reservations, fees: No reservations are accepted. Sites are $6 per night, plus $3 for each additional vehicle. The campground is open from late May to early September.

Contact: Willamette National Forest, McKenzie Ranger District, 57600 McKenzie Highway, McKenzie Bridge, OR 97413; (541) 822-3381 or fax (541) 822-3854.

Directions: From Interstate 5 near Springfield, take the Highway 126 exit and turn east. Drive 47 miles to the town of McKenzie Bridge. Continue four miles east on Highway 126, then drive 1.5 miles on Highway 242 to the camp. Note: Highway 242 is spectacularly scenic, but also very narrow, winding, and steep. RVs and trailers are discouraged (there is a 35-foot length limit on Highway 242).

Trip notes: Hidden and secluded, this little campground is set along Lost Creek about two miles from where it empties into the McKenzie River. It's a good base camp for a trout fishing trip.

57 Alder Springs

Location: In Willamette National Forest; map D2, grid d6.

Campsites, facilities: There are six tent sites. No piped water is available. Picnic tables and fire grills are provided. Pit toilets are available. Leashed pets are permitted.

Reservations, fees: No reservations are accepted. There is no fee. The campground is open from late May to early September.

Contact: Willamette National Forest, McKenzie Ranger District, 57600 McKenzie Highway, McKenzie Bridge, OR 97413; (541) 822-3381 or fax (541) 822-3854.

Directions: From Interstate 5 near Springfield, take the Highway 126 exit and turn east.

Drive 47 miles to the town of McKenzie Bridge. Continue east on Highway 126 for seven miles, then head east on Highway 242 for eight miles to the campground. Note: Highway 242 is spectacularly scenic, but also very narrow, winding, and steep. RVs and trailers are discouraged (there is a 35-foot length limit on Highway 242).

Trip notes: Good hiking possibilities are a highlight of this remote campground at elevation 3,600 feet. A map of Willamette National Forest details the nearby back roads and trails. The Three Sisters Wilderness is located just south of the highway.

58 Lava Camp Lake

Location: Near the Pacific Crest Trail in Deschutes National Forest; map D2, grid d7.

Campsites, facilities: There are 10 sites for tents, trailers, or RVs up to 22 feet long. Picnic tables and fire grills are provided. Pit toilets are available. There is no piped water. Leashed pets are permitted.

Reservations, fees: No reservations are accepted. There is no fee. The campground is open from June through September, weather permitting.

Contact: Deschutes National Forest, Sisters Ranger District, P.O. Box 249, Sisters, OR 97759; (541) 549-2111 or fax (541) 549-7746.

Directions: From Interstate 5 at Albany, take exit 233 and turn east on U.S. 20. Drive 100 miles to Sisters. Turn southwest on Highway 242 and drive 17 miles west to the campground.

Trip notes: This wooded campground is set at 5,200 feet in the McKenzie Pass, not far from the Pacific Crest Trail. Other trails provide hiking possibilities as well. A map of Deschutes National Forest details back roads, trails, and streams.

59 Whispering Pine Horse Camp

Location: Near the Trout Creek Swamp in Deschutes National Forest; map D2, grid d8.

Campsites, facilities: There are nine primitive sites for tents, trailers, or RVs. Picnic tables and fire grills are provided. Pit toilets are available. There is no piped water. Leashed pets are permitted.

Reservations, fees: No reservations are accepted. Sites are $6 per night, plus $3 for each additional vehicle. The campground is open from June to September.

Contact: Deschutes National Forest, Sisters Ranger District, P.O. Box 249, Sisters, OR 97759; (541) 549-2111 or fax (541) 549-7746.

Directions: From Interstate 5 at Albany, take exit 233 and turn east on U.S. 20. Drive 100 miles to Sisters. Turn southwest on Highway 242 and drive 11 miles on that road and Forest Service Road 1018 to the campground.

Trip notes: This wooded campground (elevation 4,400 feet) near Trout Creek Swamp is pretty, isolated, and private. Be sure to bring your own water. It's primarily set up as a horse camp with corrals. Although generally not crowded, the camp is gaining in popularity and groups of horse users occasionally fill it up.

60 Todd Lake

Location: On Todd Lake in Deschutes National Forest; map D2, grid d8.

Campsites, facilities: There are 11 hike-in tent sites. Picnic tables and fire grills are provided. Vault toilets are available. There is no piped water. Leashed pets are permitted.

Reservations, fees: No reservations are accepted. There is no camping fee, but there is a $25 annual trail pass or $5 per day trailhead parking fee. The campground is open from July to October.

Contact: Deschutes National Forest, Bend–Fort Rock Ranger District, 1230 NE Third Street, Bend, OR 97701; (541) 388-5664 or fax (541) 383-5531; Web site: www.empnet.com/dnf.

Directions: From Interstate 5 at Albany, turn east on U.S. 20 and drive 122 miles to Bend. Drive 25 miles west on Cascade Lakes Highway (Highway 46), then about one mile north on Forest Service Road 370. Hike one-half mile to the campground.

Trip notes: This is one of numerous camps in the area that offer a pristine mountain experience, yet can be reached by car. Small Todd Lake Campground is on the shore of an alpine lake at 6,200 feet. It's popular for canoeing and offers great views.

(61) Devil's Lake

Location: On Devil's Lake in Deschutes National Forest; map D2, grid d8.

Campsites, facilities: There are nine walk-in tent sites. Picnic tables and fire grills are provided. Vault toilets are available. There is no piped water. Leashed pets are permitted.

Reservations, fees: No reservations are accepted. There is no fee. The campground is open from July through September, weather permitting.

Contact: Deschutes National Forest, Bend–Fort Rock Ranger District, 1230 NE Third Street, Bend, OR 97701; (541) 388-5664 or fax (541) 383-5531; Web site: www.empnet.com/dnf.

Directions: From Interstate 5 at Albany, turn east on U.S. 20 and drive 122 miles to Bend. From Bend, travel 27 miles west on Cascade Lakes Highway (Highway 46). Walk 200 yards to the campground.

Trip notes: This walk-in campground is set along the shore of a scenic alpine lake with aqua-jade water. Devil's Lake is a popular rafting and canoeing spot, and there are several trailheads that lead from the lake into the wilderness.

(62) Soda Creek

Location: Near Sparks Lake in Deschutes National Forest; map D2, grid d8.

Campsites, facilities: There are four tent sites and eight sites for tents, trailers, or RVs up to 22 feet long. Picnic tables and fire grills are provided. Vault toilets are available. There is no piped water. Leashed pets are permitted.

Reservations, fees: No reservations are accepted. There is no fee. The campground is open from July through September, weather permitting.

Contact: Deschutes National Forest, Bend–Fort Rock Ranger District, 1230 NE Third Street, Bend, OR 97701; (541) 388-5664 or fax (541) 383-5531; Web site: www.empnet.com/dnf.

Directions: From Interstate 5 at Albany, turn east on U.S. 20 and drive 122 miles to Bend. From Bend, drive 25 miles west on Cascade Lakes Highway (Highway 46), then about 100 yards south on Forest Service Road 400 to the campground.

Trip notes: This campground is located on the road to Sparks Lake, nestled between two meadows in a pastoral setting. Boating—particularly canoeing—is ideal here. Only fly-fishing is permitted.

(63) Three Creeks Lake

Location: On Three Creeks Lake in Deschutes National Forest; map D2, grid d9.

Campsites, facilities: There are 10 sites for tents, trailers, or RVs up to 30 feet long. Picnic tables and fire grills are provided. Vault toilets are available. There is no piped water. Boat docks, launching facilities, and rentals are nearby. Boats with motors are not allowed. Leashed pets are permitted.

Reservations, fees: No reservations are accepted. Sites are $6 per night, plus $3 for each additional vehicle. The campground is open from mid-June to mid-September, weather permitting.

Contact: Deschutes National Forest, Sisters Ranger District, P.O. Box 249, Sisters, OR 97759; (541) 549-2111 or fax (541) 549-7746.

Directions: From Interstate 5 at Albany, turn east on U.S. 20 and drive 100 miles to Sisters. Turn south on Forest Service Road 16 and travel 18 miles to the campground.

Trip notes: This wooded campground is set along the south shore of Three Creeks Lake in a pretty spot at 6,400 feet in elevation. Fishing, swimming, hiking, and nonmotorized boating are the highlights. Also see the trip notes for Driftwood (campground number 64).

64 Driftwood

Location: On Three Creeks Lake in Deschutes National Forest; map D2, grid d9.

Campsites, facilities: There are 12 tent sites and five sites for tents, trailers, or RVs up to 16 feet long. Picnic tables and fire grills are provided. Pit toilets are available. There is no piped water. Boat docks, launching facilities, and rentals are nearby. Boats with motors are not allowed. Leashed pets are permitted.

Reservations, fees: No reservations are accepted. Sites are $6 per night, plus $3 for each additional vehicle. The campground is open from mid-June to mid-September, weather permitting.

Contact: Deschutes National Forest, Sisters Ranger District, P.O. Box 249, Sisters, OR 97759; (541) 549-2111 or fax (541) 549-7746.

Directions: From Interstate 5 at Albany, turn east on U.S. 20 and drive 100 miles to Sisters. Turn south on Forest Service Road 16 and travel 18 miles to the camp.

Trip notes: This wooded campground at an elevation of 6,400 feet is often blocked by snowdrifts until July 4. Although it's on the lakeshore hidden from outsiders, the area can get very crowded. The campground is full most weekends from July 4 to Labor Day. Fishing, swimming, hiking, and nonmotorized boating are some of the recreation options.

65 Schwarz Park

Location: On Dorena Lake; map D2, grid e0.

Campsites, facilities: There are 80 sites for trailers or RVs of any length. Picnic tables and fire rings are provided. Flush toilets, sanitary services, and showers are available. A mini-market is within one mile. Boat launching facilities are located on the lake, about two miles upstream. Leashed pets and street-legal motorbikes are permitted.

Reservations, fees: No reservations are accepted for individual sites, which are $10 per night. Reservations for group sites are taken beginning April 27; group sites are $50–$95 per night. There is a $4 fee for each additional

vehicle. The campground is open from April 24 through September 28.

Contact: U.S. Army Corps of Engineers, Recreation Information, Cottage Grove, OR 97424; (541) 942-5631 or (541) 942-1418.

Directions: From Interstate 5 south of Eugene, take exit 174 in Cottage Grove, then drive four miles east on Row Road to the campground entrance.

Trip notes: This large campground is set below Dorena Lake on the Row River, where fishing, swimming, boating, and waterskiing are among the recreation options. The Row River Trail parallels Dorena Lake's north shoreline for 6.2 miles. This paved trail is excellent for walking, bike riding, and shoreline access.

66 Dolly Varden

Location: On Fall Creek in Willamette National Forest; map D2, grid e1.

Campsites, facilities: There are three sites for tents and two sites for tents, trailers, or RVs up to 16 feet long. Picnic tables and fire grills are provided. Vault toilets are available. There is no piped water. Leashed pets are permitted.

Reservations, fees: No reservations are accepted. Sites are $8 per night, plus $3 for each additional vehicle. The campground is open from May to mid-September.

Contact: Willamette National Forest, Lowell Ranger District, 60 Pioneer Street, Lowell, OR 97452; (541) 937-2129 or fax (541) 937-2032.

Directions: From Interstate 5 south of Eugene, take exit 188 and turn east on Highway 58. Drive about 25 miles to Lowell, then drive two miles north on County Road 6220. Turn east on County Road 6240 and drive a short distance to Forest Service Road 18 (Fall Creek Road), then continue east to the campground. The total distance on the two roads is about 10 miles.

Trip notes: This pretty campground is adjacent to Fall Creek and is at the lower trailhead for the scenic, 14-mile Fall Creek National Recreation Trail, which follows the creek and ranges between 960 and 1,385 feet in elevation.

⑥⑦ Dexter Shores Motorhome and RV Park

Location: Near Lookout Point Reservoir; map D2, grid e1.

Campsites, facilities: There are five tent sites and 56 sites for trailers or RVs. Electricity, piped water, sewer, cable TV, and telephone hookups, and picnic tables are provided. Flush toilets, sanitary services, showers, firewood, a laundry room, and a playground are available. Bottled gas, a cafe, and ice are within one mile. Boat docks and launching facilities are nearby. Leashed pets and motorbikes permitted.

Reservations, fees: Reservations are accepted. Sites are $15–$20 per night. The campground is open year-round.

Contact: Phone (541) 937-3711, fax (541) 937-1724, or write to P.O. Box 70, Dexter, OR 97431.

Directions: From Interstate 5 south of Eugene, take exit 188 and go east on Highway 58. Drive 11.5 miles, turn south on Lost Creek Road, then turn left on Dexter Road and drive one-half block east to the park on the right.

Trip notes: If you're traveling on Interstate 5, this RV park is well worth the 15-minute drive out of Springfield. It's across the street from Dexter Point Reservoir, where fishing and boating are permitted, and within walking distance of Lookout Point. Swimming, sailing, windsurfing, and waterskiing are allowed on nearby Dexter and Fall Creek Lakes.

⑥⑧ Baker Bay County Park

Location: On Dorena Lake; map D2, grid e1.

Campsites, facilities: There are 52 sites for tents, trailers, or self-contained RVs up to 35 feet long, plus two group sites. Picnic tables and fire grills are provided. Piped water and sanitary services are available. A store is lo-

cated within two miles. Boat docks and launching facilities are nearby. Leashed pets are permitted.

Reservations, fees: Reservations are accepted for group sites only. Single sites are $12 per night, and group sites are $35 per night. The campground is open from late April to October.

Contact: Lane County Recreation Department, 35635 Shoreview Drive, Dorena, OR 97434; (541) 942-7669.

Directions: From Interstate 5 south of Eugene, take exit 174 (Dorena Lake exit) in Cottage Grove, then drive six miles east on Shore View Drive to the campground entrance on the left.

Trip notes: This campground is along the shore of Dorena Lake, where fishing, waterskiing, canoeing, swimming, and boating are among the recreation options.

⑥⑨ Winberry

Location: On Winberry Creek in Willamette National Forest; map D2, grid e2.

Campsites, facilities: There are five sites for tents and two sites for trailers or RVs up to 16 feet long. Picnic tables and fire grills are provided. Hand-pumped water and vault toilets are available. Leashed pets are permitted.

Reservations, fees: No reservations are accepted. Sites are $8–$10 per night, plus $3 for each additional vehicle. The campground is open from late May to mid-September.

Contact: Willamette National Forest, Lowell Ranger District, 60 Pioneer Street, Lowell, OR 97452; (541) 937-2129 or fax (541) 937-2032.

Directions: From Interstate 5 south of Eugene, take exit 188 and turn east on Highway 58. Drive about 15 miles to Lowell, then drive two miles north on County Road 6220. Turn on County Road 6245 (Winberry Road) and drive six miles southeast, then continue 3.5 miles on Forest Service Road 1802 to the campground.

Trip notes: This campground is located on Winberry Creek. A little inside knowledge: On the map, Lookout Point Reservoir appears to be about three miles away, but to get there, you have to drive nine miles to Lowell, at the north end of the reservoir. The closest hiking option is just downstream from the campground on Forest Service Road 1802-150. Be cautious—there is poison oak at the top of the ridge.

(70) Big Pool

Location: On Fall Creek in Willamette National Forest; map D2, grid e2.

Campsites, facilities: There are three tent sites and two sites for tents, trailers, or RVs up to 16 feet long. Picnic tables and fire grills are provided. Vault toilets are available. There is no piped water. Leashed pets are permitted.

Reservations, fees: No reservations are accepted. Sites are $8 per night, plus $5 for each additional vehicle. The campground is open from May to mid-September.

Contact: Willamette National Forest, Lowell Ranger District, 60 Pioneer Street, Lowell, OR 97452; (541) 937-2129 or fax (541) 937-2032.

Directions: From Interstate 5 south of Eugene, take exit 188 and turn east on Highway 58. Drive about 25 miles to Lowell. Turn north on County Road 6220 and drive two miles, then go 10 miles east on County Road 6240 and 1.5 miles on Forest Service Road 18 (Fall Creek Road) to the campground.

Trip notes: This campground along Fall Creek at about 1,000 feet is quiet, secluded, and primitive. The scenic Fall Creek National Recreation Trail passes the camp on the other side of the creek. See the trip notes for Dolly Varden (campground number 66) for more details on the area.

(71) Black Canyon

Location: On the Middle Fork of the Willamette River in Willamette National Forest; map D2, grid e2.

Campsites, facilities: There are 72 sites for tents, trailers, or RVs up to 22 feet long. Picnic tables and fire grills are provided. Piped water, vault toilets, and firewood are available. Sanitary services, a cafe, and a Laundromat are within five miles. Some of the facilities are wheelchair accessible. Launching facilities are nearby at the south end of Lookout Point Reservoir. Leashed pets are permitted.

Reservations, fees: No reservations are accepted. Sites are $10–$12 per night, plus $5 for each additional vehicle. The campground is open from May to late October.

Contact: Willamette National Forest, Lowell Ranger District, 60 Pioneer Street, Lowell, OR 97452; (541) 937-2129 or fax (541) 937-2032.

Directions: From Interstate 5 south of Eugene, take exit 188 and drive 27 miles southeast on Highway 58. The camp is located six miles west of Oakridge.

Trip notes: This campground is along the banks of the Middle Fork of the Willamette River, not far from Lookout Point Reservoir, where fishing and boating are popular. The camp is pretty and wooded, with comfortable sites. Weekend programs are offered in the amphitheater in July and August.

(72) Bedrock

Location: On Fall Creek in Willamette National Forest; map D2, grid e3.

Campsites, facilities: There are 20 sites for tents, trailers, or RVs up to 22 feet long. Picnic tables and fire grills are provided. Vault toilets and hand-pumped water are available. Leashed pets are permitted.

Reservations, fees: No reservations are accepted. Sites are $9–$11 per night, plus $3 for each additional vehicle. The campground is open from May to late October.

Contact: Willamette National Forest, Lowell Ranger District, 60 Pioneer Street, Lowell, OR 97452; (541) 937-2129 or fax (541) 937-2032.

Directions: From Interstate 5 south of Eugene, take exit 188 and turn east on Highway 58. Drive about 25 miles to Lowell. Turn north on County Road 6220 and drive two miles, then 10 miles east on County Road 6240 and six miles on Forest Service Road 18 (Fall Creek Road) to the campground.

Trip notes: This campground along the banks of Fall Creek is one of the access points for the scenic Fall Creek National Recreation Trail.

See the trip notes for Dolly Varden (campground number 66) for trail information. The campground is also adjacent to the Jones Trail, which heads north for about six miles before joining a Forest Service road.

(73) Puma Creek

Location: On Fall Creek in Willamette National Forest; map D2, grid e3.

Campsites, facilities: There are 11 sites for tents, trailers, or RVs up to 16 feet long. Picnic tables and fire grills are provided. Vault toilets and hand-pumped water are available. Leashed pets are permitted.

Reservations, fees: No reservations are accepted. Sites are $9 per night, plus $3 for each additional vehicle. The campground is open from May to late October.

Contact: Willamette National Forest, Lowell Ranger District, 60 Pioneer Street, Lowell, OR 97452; (541) 937-2129 or fax (541) 937-2032.

Directions: From Interstate 5 south of Eugene, take exit 188 and turn east on Highway 58. Drive about 25 miles to Lowell. Turn north on County Road 6220 and drive two miles, then 10 miles east on County Road 6240 and 6.5 miles east on Forest Service Road 18 (Fall Creek Road) to the campground.

Trip notes: This campground is set along the banks of Fall Creek, across from the Fall Creek National Recreation Trail. It's one of four camps in the immediate area. See the trip notes for Dolly Varden (campground number 66) for more information.

(74) Shady Dell Group Camp

Location: On the Middle Fork of the Willamette River in Willamette National Forest; map D2, grid e3.

Campsites, facilities: There are group sites only for tents, trailers, or RVs up to 15 feet long. Picnic tables and fire grills are provided. Hand-pumped water, vault toilets, and firewood are available. Sanitary services, a cafe, and a Laundromat are available within five miles. Some of the facilities are wheelchair accessible. Leashed pets are permitted.

Reservations, fees: No reservations are accepted. Sites are $40 per night. The campground is open from May to late October.

Contact: Willamette National Forest, Lowell Ranger District, 60 Pioneer Street, Lowell, OR 97452; (541) 937-2129 or fax (541) 937-2032.

Directions: From Interstate 5 south of Eugene, take exit 188 and drive 28 miles southeast on Highway 58. The camp is located five miles west of Oakridge.

Trip notes: This campground is on the banks of the Middle Fork of the Willamette River, across from Lookout Point Reservoir, a long, narrow lake adjacent to Highway 58. Noteworthy here is a stand of old-growth cedars.

(75) Salmon Creek Falls

Location: On Salmon Creek in Willamette National Forest; map D2, grid e3.

Campsites, facilities: There are 14 sites for tents, trailers, or RVs up to 24 feet long. Picnic tables and fire grills are provided. Hand-pumped water and vault toilets are available. A store, a cafe, a Laundromat, and ice are available within five miles. Leashed pets are permitted.

Reservations, fees: No reservations are accepted. Sites are $10–$12 per night, plus $4 for each additional vehicle. The campground is open from late April to mid-October.

Contact: Willamette National Forest, Oakridge/Rigdon Ranger Districts, 49098 Salmon Creek Road, Oakridge, OR 97463; (541) 782-2283 or fax (541) 782-5306.

Directions: From Interstate 5 south of Eugene, take exit 188 and drive 35 miles southeast on Highway 58 to Oakridge. Turn left and drive 3.5 miles northeast on Forest Service Road 24 (Salmon Creek Road) to the campground.

Trip notes: This pretty campground along the banks of Salmon Creek at an elevation of

1,500 feet is just far enough from Highway 58 to be missed by most campers. Highlights include sunny and shaded sites and easy access, plus wild thimbleberries and hazelnuts to pick in the summer. The camp is adjacent to Salmon Creek Falls.

(76) Kiahanie

Location: On the West Fork of the Willamette River in Willamette National Forest; map D2, grid e4.

Campsites, facilities: There are 19 sites for tents, trailers, or RVs up to 24 feet long. Picnic tables and fire grills are provided. Hand-pumped water and vault toilets are available. Leashed pets are permitted.

Reservations, fees: No reservations are accepted. Sites are $8 per night, plus $4 for each additional vehicle. The campground is open from late April through October.

Contact: Willamette National Forest, Oakridge/Rigdon Ranger Districts, 49098 Salmon Creek Road, Oakridge, OR 97463; (541) 782-2283 or fax (541) 782-5306.

Directions: From Interstate 5 south of Eugene, take exit 188 and drive 35 miles southeast on Highway 58 to Oakridge. Continue two miles to Westfir. Head 19 miles northeast on Forest Service Road 19 (Aufderheide Scenic Byway) to the campground.

Trip notes: We almost hate to reveal it, but this is one heck of a spot for fly-fishing (the only kind allowed). This remote campground is set along the West Fork of the Willamette River, a designated Wild and Scenic River. If you want beauty and quiet, you came to the right place. An even more remote campground is farther north on Forest Service Road 19 at Box Canyon Horse Camp (campground number 80).

(77) Homestead

Location: On the South Fork of the McKenzie River in Willamette National Forest; map D2, grid e4.

Campsites, facilities: There are eight sites for tents, trailers, or RVs. Picnic tables and fire grills are provided. Vault toilets are available, but there is no piped water. Leashed pets are permitted.

Reservations, fees: No reservations are accepted. There is no fee. The campground is open from mid-May to mid-September.

Contact: Willamette National Forest, Blue River Ranger District, P.O. Box 199, Blue River, OR 97413; (541) 822-3317 or fax (541) 822-3783.

Directions: From Interstate 5 at Eugene, turn east on Highway 126 and go 37 miles to the town of Blue River. Drive east for five miles, then go south on Forest Service Road 19 (Aufderheide Scenic Byway) 17 miles to the camp.

Trip notes: This quiet little campground is set along the banks of the South Fork of the McKenzie River. It's primitive, little-known, and free. Frissell Crossing (campground number 78) is nearby and has water available from a hand pump.

(78) Frissell Crossing

Location: Near the Three Sisters Wilderness in Willamette National Forest; map D2, grid e4.

Campsites, facilities: There are 12 sites for tents, trailers, or RVs. Picnic tables and fire grills are provided. Hand-pumped water and vault toilets are available. Leashed pets are permitted.

Reservations, fees: No reservations are accepted. Sites are $7–$14 per night. The campground is open from mid-May to mid-September.

Contact: Willamette National Forest, Blue River Ranger District, P.O. Box 199, Blue River, OR 97413; (541) 822-3317 or fax (541) 822-3783.

Directions: From Interstate 5 at Eugene, turn east on Highway 126 and go 37 miles to the town of Blue River. Drive east for five miles, then go 23 miles south on Forest Service Road 19 (Aufderheide Scenic Byway) to the camp.

Trip notes: This campground (elevation 2,600 feet) is on the banks of the South Fork of the McKenzie River, adjacent to a trailhead that provides access to the backcountry of the Three Sisters Wilderness. This is the only camp in the immediate area that has drinking water. Homestead (campground number 77) provides a free, primitive alternative.

(79) Blair Lake

Location: On Blair Lake in Willamette National Forest; map D2, grid e4.

Campsites, facilities: There are six walk-in tent sites. Picnic tables are provided. Hand-pumped water, fire rings, and a pit toilet are available. Leashed pets are permitted.

Reservations, fees: No reservations are accepted. Sites are $4 per night, plus $4 for each additional vehicle. The campground is open from June to mid-October.

Contact: Willamette National Forest, Oakridge/Rigdon Ranger Districts, 49098 Salmon Creek Road, Oakridge, OR 97463; (541) 782-2283 or fax (541) 782-5306.

Directions: From Interstate 5 south of Eugene, take exit 188 and turn east on Highway 58. Drive 35 miles to the town Oakridge, then travel one mile east on County Road 149. Turn left on Forest Service Road 24 and drive eight miles northeast, then go seven miles on Forest Service Road 1934. This is a gravel road that is not recommended for RVs or trailers.

Trip notes: This campground set at 4,800 feet along the shore of little Blair Lake is popular with equestrians. The sites are pretty, well shaded, and close to the lake. Wildflowers and huckleberries abound in season. Boats without motors are permitted, and fishing is good.

(80) Box Canyon Horse Camp

Location: Near Chucksney Mountain in Willamette National Forest; map D2, grid e5.

Campsites, facilities: There are 12 sites for tents, trailers, or RVs that allow horse and rider to camp close together. Picnic tables, fire grills, and corrals are provided. A manure disposal site and vault toilets are available. There is no piped water. Leashed pets are permitted.

Reservations, fees: No reservations are accepted. There is no fee. The campground is open from mid-May to mid-September.

Contact: Willamette National Forest, Blue River Ranger District, P.O. Box 199, Blue River, OR 97413; (541) 822-3317 or fax (541) 822-3783.

Directions: From Interstate 5 at Eugene, turn east on Highway 126 and drive 37 miles to the town of Blue River. Continue east for five miles, then drive 30 miles south on Forest Service Road 19 (Aufderheide Scenic Byway) to the campground.

Trip notes: Only 80 miles from Eugene, this unusual, secluded campground offers trails into several wilderness areas, including the Chucksney Mountain Trail, Crossing-Way Trail, and Grasshopper Trail. It's a good base camp for a backpacking trip.

(81) West Cultus

Location: On Cultus Lake in Deschutes National Forest; map D2, grid e6.

Campsites, facilities: There are 12 boat-in or hike-in tent sites. Picnic tables and fire grills are provided. Vault toilets are available. There is no piped water. Boat docks and launching facilities are available on site; boat rentals are located at the adjacent Cultus Lake Resort. Leashed pets are permitted.

Reservations, fees: No reservations are accepted. There is no camping fee, but there is a $25 annual trail pass or $5 per day trailhead parking fee. The campground is open from June to late September, weather permitting.

Contact: Deschutes National Forest, Bend–Fort Rock Ranger District, 1230 NE Third Street, Bend, OR 97701; (541) 388-5664 or fax (541) 383-5531; Web site: www.empnet.com/dnf.

Directions: From Interstate 5 at Albany, turn east on U.S. 20 and drive 122 miles to Bend. Turn southwest on Cascade Lakes Highway (Highway 46) and drive 45 miles. Turn west on Forest Service Road 4635 and travel 1.5 miles to the parking area, then travel by boat about three miles to the west shore of the lake or hike the trail around the lake.

Trip notes: This campground set at 4,700 feet along the west shore of Cultus Lake is accessible by boat or trail only. It's about three miles by trail from the parking area to the campground. This is a good spot for water-skiing, fishing, and swimming. Trails branch out from the campground and provide access to numerous small backcountry lakes.

(82) Irish and Taylor

Location: Near the Pacific Crest Trail in Deschutes National Forest; map D2, grid e6.

Campsites, facilities: There are six tent sites. Picnic tables and fire grills are provided. Pit toilets are available. There is no piped water. Leashed pets are permitted.

Reservations, fees: No reservations are accepted. There is no fee. The campground is open from mid-June to mid-September.

Contact: Deschutes National Forest, Bend–Fort Rock Ranger District, 1230 NE Third Street, Bend, OR 97701; (541) 388-5664 or fax (541) 383-5531; Web site: www.empnet.com/dnf.

Directions: From Interstate 5 at Albany, turn east on U.S. 20 and drive 122 miles to Bend. Turn southwest on Cascade Lakes Highway (Highway 46) and drive 43 miles, then go 3.5 miles southwest on Forest Service Road 4630. The camp is 6.5 miles west on Forest Service Road 600. This is a rough road (only high-clearance vehicles), but it's worth the ride.

Trip notes: Little-known, beautiful, and free, this remote campground is set between two small lakes, about a mile from the Pacific Crest Trail. Other nearby trails provide access into the backcountry.

(83) Point

Location: On Elk Lake in Deschutes National Forest; map D2, grid e7.

Campsites, facilities: There are eight sites for tents, trailers, or RVs up to 22 feet long, but be advised the sites are uneven and difficult for RVs. Picnic tables and fire grills are provided. Vault toilets and piped water are available. Boat docks and launching facilities are on site. Boat rentals, a store, a restaurant, gas, and propane are located at Elk Lake Resort, one mile away. Leashed pets are permitted.

Reservations, fees: No reservations are accepted. Sites are $9 per night, plus $3–$5 per additional vehicle. The campground is open from late May to late September, weather permitting.

Contact: Deschutes National Forest, Bend–Fort Rock Ranger District, 1230 NE Third Street, Bend, OR 97701; (541) 388-5664 or fax (541) 383-5531; Web site: www.empnet.com/dnf.

Directions: From Interstate 5 at Albany, turn east on U.S. 20 and drive 122 miles to Bend. Turn southwest on Cascade Lakes Highway (Highway 46) and drive 33 miles to the campground entrance.

Trip notes: This hidden campground is along the shore of Elk Lake, where fishing and hiking can be good. A map of the Deschutes National Forest details the trails.

(84) Elk Lake

Location: On Elk Lake in Deschutes National Forest; map D2, grid e7.

Campsites, facilities: There are 23 sites for tents, trailers, or RVs up to 22 feet long, but be advised the sites are uneven and difficult for RVs. Picnic tables and fire grills are provided. Vault toilets and piped water are available. Boat docks and launching facilities are on site. Boat rentals can be obtained nearby. Leashed pets are permitted.

Reservations, fees: No reservations are accepted. Sites are $9 per night, plus $3–$5 per additional vehicle. The campground is open from June through September, weather permitting.

Contact: Deschutes National Forest, Bend–Fort Rock Ranger District, 1230 NE Third Street, Bend, OR 97701; (541) 388-5664 or fax (541) 383-5531; Web site: www.empnet.com/dnf.

Directions: From Interstate 5 at Albany, turn east on U.S. 20 and drive 122 miles to Bend. Turn southwest on Cascade Lakes Highway (Highway 46) and drive 33 miles to Elk Lake. The campground is on the southwest side of the lake.

Trip notes: This campground is on the shore

of Elk Lake, adjacent to a private resort (Elk Lake Resort). See the trip notes for Point (campground number 83) for recreation options.

⑧⑤ Cultus Lake

Location: On Cultus Lake in Deschutes National Forest; map D2, grid e7.

Campsites, facilities: There are 54 boat-in sites for tents. Picnic tables and fire grills are provided. Piped water and vault toilets are available. Boat docks and launching facilities are on site. Boat rentals are nearby. Leashed pets are permitted.

Reservations, fees: No reservations are accepted. Sites are $9 per night, plus $3–$5 per additional vehicle. The campground is open from June to October.

Contact: Deschutes National Forest, Bend–Fort Rock Ranger District, 1230 NE Third Street, Bend, OR 97701; (541) 388-5664 or fax (541) 383-5531; Web site: www.empnet.com/dnf.

Directions: From Interstate 5 at Albany, turn east on U.S. 20 and drive 122 miles to Bend. Turn southwest on Cascade Lakes Highway (Highway 46) and drive 45 miles. Turn west on Forest Service Road 4635 and travel 1.5 miles to the campground.

Trip notes: This camp along the east shore of Cultus Lake is a popular spot for windsurfing, waterskiing, swimming, fishing, and hiking.

⑧⑥ Little Cultus Lake

Location: On Little Cultus Lake in Deschutes National Forest; map D2, grid e7.

Campsites, facilities: There are 10 sites for tents, trailers, or RVs up to 22 feet long. Picnic tables and fire grills are provided. Hand-pumped water, vault toilets, and a boat launch are available. Leashed pets are permitted.

Reservations, fees: No reservations are accepted. Sites are $5 per night, plus $3–$5 per additional vehicle. The campground is open from late May to late September, weather permitting.

Contact: Deschutes National Forest, Bend–

Fort Rock Ranger District, 1230 NE Third Street, Bend, OR 97701; (541) 388-5664 or fax (541) 383-5531; Web site: www.empnet.com/dnf.

Directions: From Interstate 5 at Albany, turn east on U.S. 20 and drive 122 miles to Bend. Turn southwest on Cascade Lakes Highway (Highway 46) and drive 45 miles. Turn west on Forest Service Road 4635, drive one-half mile to Forest Service Road 4630, and turn left. Drive 1.5 miles to Forest Service Road 600, then turn left and drive one mile to the campground.

Trip notes: This campground along the shore of Little Cultus Lake has campsites that aren't clearly marked. It's a popular spot for swimming, fishing, boating (speed restricted), and hiking. Nearby trails access numerous backcountry lakes, and the Pacific Crest Trail passes about six miles west of the camp.

⑧⑦ Lava Lake

Location: On Lava Lake in Deschutes National Forest; map D2, grid e7.

Campsites, facilities: There are 43 sites for tents, trailers, or RVs up to 22 feet long. Picnic tables and fire grills are provided. Vault toilets, piped water, showers, a laundry room, a fish cleaning station, and sanitary disposal services are available. Boat docks and launching facilities are on site. Boat rentals are nearby. Leashed pets are permitted.

Reservations, fees: No reservations are accepted. Sites are $10 per night, plus $3–$5 per additional vehicle. The campground is open from April 20 through October, weather permitting.

Contact: Deschutes National Forest, Bend–Fort Rock Ranger District, 1230 NE Third Street, Bend, OR 97701; (541) 388-5664 or fax (541) 383-5531; Web site: www.empnet.com/dnf.

Directions: From Interstate 5 at Albany, turn east on U.S. 20 and drive 122 miles to Bend. Turn southwest on Cascade Lakes Highway (Highway 46) and drive 38 miles to the entrance to Lava Lake. The campground is on the lake.

Trip notes: This well-designed campground is on the shore of pretty Lava Lake. Mount

Bachelor and the Three Sisters are in the background, making a classic picture. Boating and fishing are popular here.

⑧⑧ Cultus Corral Horse Camp

Location: Near Cultus Lake in Deschutes National Forest; map D2, grid e7.

Campsites, facilities: There are 11 sites for tents, trailers, or RVs of any length. Picnic tables, fire grills, and four-horse corrals are provided. Hand-pumped water, vault toilets, and a corral are available. Leashed pets are permitted.

Reservations, fees: No reservations are accepted. Sites are $5 per night, plus $3–$5 per additional vehicle. The campground is open from June to October.

Contact: Deschutes National Forest, Bend–Fort Rock Ranger District, 1230 NE Third Street, Bend, OR 97701; (541) 388-5664 or fax (541) 383-5531; Web site: www.empnet.com/dnf.

Directions: From Interstate 5 at Albany, turn east on U.S. 20 and drive 122 miles to Bend. Turn southwest on Cascade Lakes Highway (Highway 46) and drive 43 miles. Turn right on Forest Service Road 4630 and travel a quarter mile to the campground entrance.

Trip notes: This campground is about one mile from Cultus Lake, near many trails that provide access to backcountry lakes. The Pacific Crest Trail passes about 10 miles from the camp, making this a good base camp for a backpacking trip.

⑧⑨ Cow Meadow

Location: On the Deschutes River in Deschutes National Forest; map D2, grid e7.

Campsites, facilities: There are 20 sites for tents, trailers, or RVs up to 16 feet long. Picnic tables and fire grills are provided. Vault toilets are available. There is no piped water. Boat docks and a launch are nearby at Crane Prairie Campground. Leashed pets are permitted.

Reservations, fees: No reservations are accepted. Sites are $5 per night, plus $3–$5 per additional vehicle. The campground is open from May to mid-October.

Contact: Deschutes National Forest, Bend–Fort Rock Ranger District, 1230 NE Third Street, Bend, OR 97701; (541) 388-5664 or fax (541) 383-5531; Web site: www.empnet.com/dnf.

Directions: From Interstate 5 at Albany, turn east on U.S. 20 and drive 122 miles to Bend. Turn southwest on Cascade Lakes Highway (Highway 46) and drive 44 miles. Turn east on Forest Service Road 620 and drive to the end of the road and the campground, about two miles. Note: The entrance road can be muddy.

Trip notes: This campground is set along the Deschutes River, near the north end of Crane Prairie Reservoir. It's a pretty spot and the price is right.

⑨⓪ Crane Prairie

Location: On Crane Prairie Reservoir in Deschutes National Forest; map D2, grid e7.

Campsites, facilities: There are 146 sites for tents, trailers, or RVs. Picnic tables and fire grills are provided. Piped water and vault toilets are available. Boat docks, launching facilities, and a fish cleaning station are available on site. Boat rentals, showers, gas, and laundry facilities are located nearby. Leashed pets are permitted.

Reservations, fees: No reservations are accepted. Sites are $10 per night, plus $3–$5 per additional vehicle. The campground is open from April 20 through October, weather permitting.

Contact: Deschutes National Forest, Bend–Fort Rock Ranger District, 1230 NE Third Street, Bend, OR 97701; (541) 388-5664 or fax (541) 383-5531; Web site: www.empnet.com/dnf.

Directions: From Interstate 5 at Albany, turn east on U.S. 20 and drive 122 miles to Bend. Turn south on U.S. 97 and drive 20 miles to County Road 42. Turn west and drive 21 miles to Forest Service Road 4270. Turn north and drive 4.5 miles to the campground entrance.

Trip notes: This campground along the north shore of Crane Prairie Reservoir is a good spot for fishing, boating, and hiking.

(91) Crane Prairie Resort

Location: On Crane Prairie Reservoir; map D2, grid e7.

Campsites, facilities: There are 20 sites for trailers or RVs. Electricity, piped water, sewer hookups, and picnic tables are provided. Bottled gas, firewood, a store, and ice are available. Boat docks, launching facilities, and rentals are nearby. Leashed pets are permitted.

Reservations, fees: Reservations are accepted. Sites are $10–$15 per night. The campground is open from late April to mid-October.

Contact: Phone (541) 385-2173 or write to P.O. Box 322, LaPine, OR 97739.

Directions: From Interstate 5 at Albany, turn east on U.S. 20 and drive 122 miles to Bend. From Bend, travel 48 miles southwest on Highway 46 (Cascade Lakes Highway). Turn on Forest Service Road 4270 and drive seven miles to the resort entrance.

Trip notes: This resort is set along the north shore of popular Crane Prairie Reservoir, a good spot for canoeing and fishing. No waterskiing is permitted.

(92) Little Fawn Group Camp

Location: On Elk Lake in Deschutes National Forest; map D2, grid e8.

Campsites, facilities: There are 18 sites for tents, trailers, or RVs up to 22 feet long. Picnic tables, hand-pumped water, and fire grills are provided. Vault toilets are available. Boat docks, launching facilities, and rentals are nearby on the southwest shore of the lake. Leashed pets are permitted.

Reservations, fees: Reservations are required for the group sites. Individual sites are $8 per night, and group sites are $50 per night, plus $3–$5 per additional vehicle. The campground is open from June through September, weather permitting.

Contact: Deschutes National Forest, Bend–Fort Rock Ranger District, 1230 NE Third Street, Bend, OR 97701; (541) 388-5664 or fax (541) 383-5531; Web site: www.empnet.com/dnf.

Directions: From Interstate 5 at Albany, turn east on U.S. 20 and drive 122 miles to Bend. Turn southwest on Cascade Lakes Highway (Highway 46) and drive 31 miles, then two miles southeast on Forest Service Road 470. The campground is on the east side of Elk Lake.

Trip notes: Choose between sites on the water's edge or nestled nearby in the forest at this campground along the eastern shore of Elk Lake. A play area for children can be found at one of the lake's inlets. See the trip notes for Point (campground number 83) for recreation options.

(93) Mallard Marsh

Location: On Hosmer Lake in Deschutes National Forest; map D2, grid e7.

Campsites, facilities: There are 15 sites for tents, trailers, or RVs up to 22 feet long. Picnic tables and fire grills are provided. Vault toilets and hand-pumped water are available. Boat launching facilities are nearby. Leashed pets are permitted.

Reservations, fees: No reservations are accepted. Sites are $5 per night, plus $3–$5 per additional vehicle. The campground is open from late May to late September.

Contact: Deschutes National Forest, Bend–Fort Rock Ranger District, 1230 NE Third Street, Bend, OR 97701; (541) 388-5664 or fax (541) 383-5531; Web site: www.empnet.com/dnf.

Directions: From Interstate 5 at Albany, turn east on U.S. 20 and drive 122 miles to Bend. Turn southwest on Cascade Lakes Highway (Highway 46) and drive 31 miles, then two miles southeast on Forest Service Road 4625 to the camp.

Trip notes: This quiet campground is on the shore of Hosmer Lake, which is stocked with brown trout and Atlantic salmon and reserved for catch-and-release fly-fishing only. The lake is ideal for canoeing. You'll get a pristine, quality angling experience.

94 South

Location: On Hosmer Lake in Deschutes National Forest; map D2, grid e8.

Campsites, facilities: There are 23 sites for tents, trailers, or RVs up to 22 feet long. Picnic tables and fire grills are provided. Vault toilets, hand-pumped water, and boat launch facilities are available. Leashed pets are permitted.

Reservations, fees: No reservations are accepted. Sites are $5 per night, plus $3–$5 per additional vehicle. The campground is open from late May to late September, weather permitting.

Contact: Deschutes National Forest, Bend–Fort Rock Ranger District, 1230 NE Third Street, Bend, OR 97701; (541) 388-5664 or fax (541) 383-5531; Web site: www.empnet.com/dnf.

Directions: From Interstate 5 at Albany, turn east on U.S. 20 and drive 122 miles to Bend. Turn southwest on Cascade Lakes Highway (Highway 46) and drive 31 miles, then three miles southeast on Forest Service Road 4625 to the camp.

Trip notes: This campground is along the shore of Hosmer Lake. See the trip notes for Mallard Marsh (campground number 93) for recreation details.

95 Little Lava Lake

Location: Near Lava Lake in Deschutes National Forest; map D2, grid e8.

Campsites, facilities: There are 10 sites for tents, trailers, or RVs up to 22 feet long. Picnic tables and fire grills are provided. Vault toilets and piped water are available. Boat docks and rentals are nearby. Launching facilities are on site. Leashed pets are permitted.

Reservations, fees: No reservations are accepted. Sites are $5 per night, plus $3–$5 per additional vehicle. The campground is open from June to late September, weather permitting.

Contact: Deschutes National Forest, Bend–Fort Rock Ranger District, 1230 NE Third Street, Bend, OR 97701; (541) 388-5664 or fax (541) 383-5531; Web site: www.empnet.com/dnf.

Directions: From Interstate 5 at Albany, turn east on U.S. 20 and drive 122 miles to Bend. Turn southwest on Cascade Lakes Highway (Highway 46) and drive 38 miles to the entrance to Lava Lake. The campground is on Little Lava Lake.

Trip notes: The campsites at this popular campground are not well marked, but the camping area is near the lakeshore. Boating, fishing, swimming, and hiking are some of the recreation options.

96 Mile

Location: On the Deschutes River in Deschutes National Forest; map D2, grid e8.

Campsites, facilities: There are 10 sites for tents, trailers, or RVs up to 22 feet long. Picnic tables and fire grills are provided. Vault toilets are available. There is no piped water. Leashed pets are permitted.

Reservations, fees: No reservations are accepted. There is no fee. The campground is open from late May to late September, weather permitting.

Contact: Deschutes National Forest, Bend–Fort Rock Ranger District, 1230 NE Third Street, Bend, OR 97701; (541) 388-5664 or fax (541) 383-5531; Web site: www.empnet.com/dnf.

Directions: From Interstate 5 at Albany, turn east on U.S. 20 and drive 122 miles to Bend. Turn southwest on Cascade Lakes Highway (Highway 46) and drive 40 miles to the campground.

Trip notes: This quiet campground is set along the banks of the Deschutes River in a quiet, primitive spot. Fishing and hiking are among your options here. See a Forest Service map for trail locations.

97 Deschutes Bridge

Location: On the Deschutes River in the Deschutes National Forest; map D2, grid e8.

Campsites, facilities: There are 12 sites for tents, trailers, or RVs up to 22 feet long. Picnic tables and fire grills are provided. Piped water and vault toilets are available. Leashed pets are permitted.

Reservations, fees: Reservations are required only for groups; phone (541) 382-9443. Individual sites are $7 per night, and group sites are $50 per night (up to 75 people), plus $3–$5 per additional vehicle. The campground is open from June to October.

Contact: Deschutes National Forest, Bend–Fort Rock Ranger District, 1230 NE Third Street, Bend, OR 97701; (541) 388-5664 or fax (541) 383-5531; Web site: www.empnet.com/dnf.

Directions: From Interstate 5 at Albany, turn east on U.S. 20 and drive 122 miles to Bend. Turn southwest on Cascade Lakes Highway (Highway 46) and drive 41 miles to the campground.

Trip notes: This wooded campground is on the banks of the Deschutes River in a beautiful, lush green spot. It's slightly more developed than the nearby Mile site (campground number 96).

98 Sharps Creek

Location: On Sharps Creek; map D2, grid f1.

Campsites, facilities: There are 10 sites for tents, trailers, or RVs up to 30 feet long. Picnic tables and fire pits are provided. Piped water, vault toilets, and firewood are available. Leashed pets are permitted.

Reservations, fees: No reservations are accepted. Sites are $5 per night, with a 14-day stay limit, plus $3 for each additional vehicle. The campground is open from mid-May through September, weather permitting.

Contact: Bureau of Land Management, P.O. Box 10266, Eugene, OR 97401; (541) 683-6600.

Directions: From Interstate 5 at Cottage Grove, take exit 174, then travel 18 miles east on Row River Road and four miles south on Sharps Creek Road to the campground.

Trip notes: Like the nearby Rujada site (campground number 99), this camp on the banks of Sharps Creek is just far enough off the beaten path to be missed by most campers. It's quiet, primitive, and remote, and there are not many recreation options in the immediate area, though swimming and fishing at

Cottage Grove Reservoir are just a short drive away.

99 Rujada

Location: On Layng Creek in Umpqua National Forest; map D2, grid f1.

Campsites, facilities: There are 11 sites for tents, trailers, or RVs up to 30 feet long. Picnic tables and fire pits are provided. Flush toilets and piped water are available. Some facilities are wheelchair accessible. Leashed pets are permitted.

Reservations, fees: No reservations are accepted. Sites are $5 per night. The campground is open from late May to late September.

Contact: Umpqua National Forest, Cottage Grove Ranger District, 78405 Cedar Park Road, Cottage Grove, OR 97424; (541) 942-5591.

Directions: From Cottage Grove on Interstate 5, take exit 174 and head east on Row River Road for 19 miles. Turn left on Forest Service Road 17 (Layng Creek Road) and drive two miles to the campground on the right.

Trip notes: This campground is on the banks of Layng Creek, right at the national forest border. There's a good swimming spot about two miles upstream from its confluence with the Row River, and those with time and patience can fish in the creek. By continuing east on Forest Service Road 17, you can access a trailhead that leads one-half mile to beautiful Spirit Falls, a spectacular 60-foot waterfall. A bit farther east is another easy trail to Moon Falls, even more awe-inspiring at 125 feet.

100 Sand Prairie

Location: On the Willamette River in Willamette National Forest; map D2, grid f3.

Campsites, facilities: There are 20 sites for tents, trailers, or RVs up to 22 feet long. Picnic tables and fire grills are provided. Vault and flush toilets and piped water are available. Some of the facilities are wheelchair accessible. A boat launch is nearby on Hills Creek Reservoir. Leashed pets are permitted.

Reservations, fees: No reservations are ac-

cepted. Sites are $10 per night, plus $4 per additional vehicle. The campground is open from mid-April to mid-November.

Contact: Willamette National Forest, Rigdon Ranger District, 49098 Salmon Creek Road, Oakridge, OR 97463; (541) 782-2283 or fax (541) 782-5306.

Directions: From Interstate 5 south of Eugene, drive 38 miles southeast on Highway 58 (two miles past Oakridge), then one-half mile on County Road 360. Then drive 11 miles south on Forest Service Road 21.

Trip notes: This peaceful campground is in a forest of old-growth trees along the Middle Fork of the Willamette River, just south of Hills Creek Reservoir at the trailhead for the Middle Fork Trail. This 30-mile trail is nearly complete.

101 Packard Creek

Location: On Hills Creek Reservoir in Willamette National Forest; map D2, grid f3.

Campsites, facilities: There are 33 sites for tents, trailers, or RVs up to 30 feet long. Picnic tables and fire grills are provided. Piped water, vault toilets, and firewood are available. Some facilities are wheelchair accessible. Boat docks and launching facilities are nearby. Leashed pets are permitted.

Reservations, fees: No reservations are accepted. Sites are $10–$12 per night, plus $4 per additional vehicle. The campground is open from mid-May to mid-September.

Contact: Willamette National Forest, Rigdon Ranger District, 49098 Salmon Creek Road, Oakridge, OR 97463; (541) 782-2283 or fax (541) 782-5306.

Directions: From Interstate 5 south of Eugene, drive 38 miles southeast on Highway 58 (two miles past Oakridge), then one-half mile southeast on County Road 360. The camp is five miles south on Forest Service Road 21.

Trip notes: The campground is set at 1,600 feet along the west shore of Hills Creek Reservoir, a 2,900-acre reservoir where fishing and boating are popular. No boats with motors are permitted on the Larison Cove arm of the lake.

102 Blue Pool

Location: On Salt Creek in Willamette National Forest; map D2, grid f3.

Campsites, facilities: There are 24 sites for tents, trailers, or RVs up to 18 feet long. Picnic tables and fire grills are provided. There is no potable water, but vault and flush toilets are available. Leashed pets are permitted.

Reservations, fees: No reservations are accepted. Sites are $7–$9 per night, plus $4 per additional vehicle. The campground is open from late April to mid-October.

Contact: Willamette National Forest, Rigdon Ranger District, 49098 Salmon Creek Road, Oakridge, OR 97463; (541) 782-2283 or fax (541) 782-5306.

Directions: From Interstate 5 south of Eugene, drive 45 miles southeast on Highway 58 to the campground.

Trip notes: This campground is set along Salt Creek at 2,000 feet. With its proximity to the highway and easy access to the creek, it's a decent layover spot. Volleyball and good fishing are among the highlights, and McCredie Hot Springs is half a mile away.

103 Sacandaga

Location: On the Willamette River in Willamette National Forest; map D2, grid f4.

Campsites, facilities: There are 16 sites for tents, trailers, or RVs up to 21 feet long. Picnic tables and fire grills are provided, and vault toilets and firewood are available. There is no piped water. Leashed pets are permitted.

Reservations, fees: No reservations are accepted. There is no fee. The campground is open from mid-April to mid-November.

Contact: Willamette National Forest, Oakridge/Rigdon Ranger Districts, 49098 Salmon Creek Road, Oakridge, OR 97463; (541) 782-2283 or fax (541) 782-5306.

Directions: From Interstate 5 south of Eugene, take exit 188 and turn east on Highway 58. Drive 38 miles southeast (two miles past Oakridge), then go one-half mile on County Road 360. From there, continue 25 miles southeast on Forest Service Road 21. The camp is on the right.

Trip notes: This primitive campground sits on a bluff overlooking the Willamette River. It's adjacent to historic Rigdon Meadows, the site of a stagecoach station in pioneer days.

104 Skookum Creek

Location: Near the Three Sisters Wilderness in Willamette National Forest; map D2, grid f5.

Campsites, facilities: There are eight walk-in tent sites, two of which are wheelchair accessible. Picnic tables and fire grills are provided. Hand-pumped water, hitching rails, and pit toilets are available. Leashed pets are permitted.

Reservations, fees: No reservations are accepted. Sites are $5 per night, plus $5 for each additional vehicle. The campground is open from mid-May to mid-November.

Contact: Willamette National Forest, Oakridge/Rigdon Ranger Districts, 49098 Salmon Creek Road, Oakridge, OR 97463; (541) 782-2283 or fax (541) 782-5306.

Directions: From Interstate 5 at Eugene, turn east on Highway 126 and drive 37 miles to the town of Blue River. Continue east for five miles to Forest Service Road 19 (Aufderheide Scenic Byway). Turn right and drive 30 miles south to Box Canyon. From there, drive south for three miles on Forest Service Road 1957 to the campground.

Trip notes: Popular with equestrians, this remote campground is near the border of the Three Sisters Wilderness. The Erma Bell Lakes Trailhead at the camp provides access to numerous lakes and other trails in the backcountry. This is a primitive, little-known spot.

105 Shadow Bay

Location: On Waldo Lake in Willamette National Forest; map D2, grid f6.

Campsites, facilities: There are 92 sites for tents, trailers, or RVs up to 30 feet long. Picnic tables and fire grills are provided. Piped water and flush toilets are available. Boat launching facilities are nearby. Pets are permitted.

Reservations, fees: No reservations are accepted. Sites are $8–$10 per night, plus $5 for each additional vehicle. The campground is open from July through September, weather permitting.

Contact: Willamette National Forest, Oakridge/Rigdon Ranger Districts, 49098 Salmon Creek Road, Oakridge, OR 97463; (541) 782-2283 or fax (541) 782-5306.

Directions: From Interstate 5 south of Eugene, take exit 188 and travel 59 miles southeast on Highway 58. Turn left and drive 5.5 miles north on Forest Service Road 5897, then two miles west on Forest Service Road 5896 to the camp.

Trip notes: This camp at an elevation of 5,400 feet is tucked away along the southeast shore of Waldo Lake, which has the special distinction of being one of the three purest lakes in the world. Trivia buffs note: Of those three lakes, two are in Oregon (the other is Crater Lake) and the third is in Siberia. For hikers, a trail circles the lake and intersects several other trails that provide access to the Waldo Lake Wilderness. The camps on this lake are in a great location and spectacularly lovely, but have one drawback—they are infested by mosquitoes in June and July. Bring bug repellent and netting if you want a peaceful trip.

106 North Waldo

Location: On Waldo Lake in Willamette National Forest; map D2, grid f6.

Campsites, facilities: There are 58 sites for tents, trailers, or RVs up to 30 feet long. Picnic tables and fire grills are provided. Piped water and flush toilets are available. Boat launching facilities are available. Pets are permitted.

Reservations, fees: No reservations are accepted. Sites are $10 per night, plus $5 for each additional vehicle. The campground is open from July through September, weather permitting.

Contact: Willamette National Forest, Oakridge/Rigdon Ranger Districts, 49098 Salmon Creek Road, Oakridge, OR 97463; (541) 782-2283 or fax (541) 782-5306.

Directions: From Interstate 5 south of Eugene, take exit 188 and travel 59 miles southeast on Highway 58. Turn left and drive 10.5 miles north on Forest Service Road 5897, then two miles west on Forest Service Road 5898 to the entrance road to the campground.

Trip notes: Mosquitoes are especially bad news here in July. See the trip notes for Shadow Bay (campground number 105) for detailed information about Waldo Lake.

(107) North Davis Creek

Location: Near Wickiup Reservoir in Deschutes National Forest; map D2, grid f6.

Campsites, facilities: There are 17 sites for tents, trailers, or RVs up to 22 feet long. Picnic tables and fire grills are provided. Hand-pumped water and vault toilets are available. Boat docks and launching facilities are nearby. Leashed pets are permitted.

Reservations, fees: No reservations are accepted. Sites are $7 per night, plus $3–$5 per additional vehicle. The campground is open from May to late October.

Contact: Deschutes National Forest, Bend–Fort Rock Ranger District, 1230 NE Third Street, Bend, OR 97701; (541) 388-5664 or fax (541) 383-5531; Web site: www.empnet.com/dnf.

Directions: From Interstate 5 south of Eugene, take exit 188 and turn east on Highway 58. Drive 73 miles, then turn east on County Road 61. Drive three miles, then continue north on Cascade Lakes Highway (Highway 46) for about 13 miles to the campground.

Trip notes: This remote, secluded campground set along a western channel of Wickiup Reservoir receives little use. The area was logged in 1987 because of a pine beetle infestation. In late summer, the reservoir level tends to drop.

(108) Quinn River

Location: On Crane Prairie Reservoir in Deschutes National Forest; map D2, grid f7.

Campsites, facilities: There are 41 sites for tents, trailers, or RVs up to 30 feet long. Picnic tables and fire grills are provided. Hand-pumped water and vault toilets are available. Boat launch facilities are available. Leashed pets are permitted.

Reservations, fees: No reservations are accepted. Sites are $9 per night, plus $3–$5 per additional vehicle. The campground is open from late April to mid-October.

Contact: Deschutes National Forest, Bend–Fort Rock Ranger District, 1230 NE Third Street, Bend, OR 97701; (541) 388-5664 or fax (541) 383-5531; Web site: www.empnet.com/dnf.

Directions: From Interstate 5 at Albany, turn east on U.S. 20 and drive 122 miles to Bend. Turn south on U.S. 97 and drive 20 miles to County Road 42. Turn west and drive 25 miles to Cascade Lakes Highway (Highway 46). Turn north and drive four miles to the campground.

Trip notes: This campground is set along the western shore of Crane Prairie Reservoir, a popular spot for anglers. A large parking lot is available for boats and trailers.

(109) Rock Creek

Location: On Crane Prairie Reservoir in Deschutes National Forest; map D2, grid f7.

Campsites, facilities: There are 32 sites for tents, trailers, or RVs up to 22 feet long. Picnic tables and fire grills are provided. Hand-pumped water, a fish cleaning station, and vault toilets are available. Boat launching facilities are on site and boat docks are nearby. Leashed pets are permitted.

Reservations, fees: No reservations are accepted. Sites are $9 per night, plus $3–$5 per additional vehicle. The campground is open from April 20 through October, weather permitting.

Contact: Deschutes National Forest, Bend–Fort Rock Ranger District, 1230 NE Third Street, Bend, OR 97701; (541) 388-5664 or fax (541) 383-5531; Web site: www.empnet.com/dnf.

Directions: From Interstate 5 at Albany, turn east on U.S. 20 and drive 122 miles to Bend. Turn south on U.S. 97 and drive 20 miles to County Road 42. Turn west and drive 25 miles. Turn north on Cascade Lakes Highway (Highway 46) and drive three miles to the campground.

Trip notes: This campground along the west shore of Crane Prairie Reservoir is an alternative to Quinn River (campground number 108).

110 North Twin Lake

Location: On North Twin Lake in Deschutes National Forest; map D2, grid f7.

Campsites, facilities: There are 10 sites for tents, trailers, or RVs up to 22 feet long. Picnic tables and fire grills are provided. Vault toilets are available. There is no piped water. Boat docks, launching facilities, and rentals are nearby. Leashed pets are permitted.

Reservations, fees: No reservations are accepted. Sites are $5 per night, plus $3–$5 per additional vehicle. The campground is open from June to late September, weather permitting.

Contact: Deschutes National Forest, Bend–Fort Rock Ranger District, 1230 NE Third Street, Bend, OR 97701; (541) 388-5664 or fax (541) 383-5531; Web site: www.empnet.com/dnf.

Directions: From Interstate 5 at Eugene, take exit 188 and turn east on Highway 58. Drive 73 miles, then turn east on County Road 61. Continue three miles. Turn north on Highway 46. Keep going for 18 miles and turn east on County Road 42. Travel five miles, turn south on Forest Service Road 4260, and drive one-half mile to the campground.

Trip notes: This campground on the shore of North Twin Lake is a popular weekend spot for families. It's small and fairly primitive, but has lake access and a pretty setting. Only non-motorized boats are permitted.

111 Lava Flow

Location: On Davis Lake in Deschutes National Forest; map D2, grid f7.

Campsites, facilities: There are 12 sites for tents, trailers, or RVs up to 22 feet long. Picnic tables and fire grills are provided. Vault toilets and firewood (to be gathered from the surrounding area) are available. There is no piped water. A boat launch is nearby. Leashed pets are permitted.

Reservations, fees: No reservations are accepted. There is no fee. The campground is open from late May to late October, weather permitting.

Contact: Deschutes National Forest, Crescent Ranger District, P.O. Box 208, Crescent, OR 97733; (541) 433-2234.

Directions: From Interstate 5 south of Eugene, take exit 188 and then turn east on Highway 58. Drive 86 miles and turn east on County Road 61. Drive three miles, then continue nine miles north on Forest Service Road 46. The camp is located two miles north on Forest Service Road 850.

Trip notes: This campground is set along the northeast shore of Davis Lake, a very shallow lake that provides good duck hunting during the fall. Fishing is decent in early summer.

112 West South Twin

Location: On Wickiup Reservoir in Deschutes National Forest; map D2, grid f7.

Campsites, facilities: There are 24 sites for trailers or RVs up to 22 feet long. Picnic tables and fire grills are provided. Piped water and flush toilets are available. Boat launching facilities are on site, and boat rentals are nearby. Leashed pets are permitted.

Reservations, fees: No reservations are accepted. Sites are $10 per night, plus $3–$5 per additional vehicle. The campground is open from mid-May to mid-October, weather permitting.

Contact: Deschutes National Forest, Bend–Fort Rock Ranger District, 1230 NE Third Street, Bend, OR 97701; (541) 388-5664 or fax (541) 383-5531; Web site: www.empnet.com/dnf.

Directions: From Interstate 5 south of Eugene, take exit 188 and turn east on Highway 58. Drive 73 miles, then turn east on County Road 61. Continue three miles, then turn north on Cascade Lakes Highway (Highway 46). Travel another 18 miles to County Road 42. Turn and go east for five miles, then head south for two miles on County Road 42 and 1.5 miles on Forest Service Road 4260.

Trip notes: This camp is set on Wickiup Reservoir near the western shore of South Twin Lake, a major access point to the Wickiup Reservoir. It's a popular angling spot with very good kokanee salmon fishing.

⑬ Gull Point

Location: On Wickiup Reservoir in Deschutes National Forest; map D2, grid f7.

Campsites, facilities: There are 79 sites for tents, trailers, or RVs up to 30 feet long. There are also two sites available for groups of up to 25 people. Picnic tables and fire grills are provided. Piped water, a sanitary dump station, and flush and vault toilets are available. Boat launching facilities are on site. Leashed pets are permitted.

Reservations, fees: Reservations are only accepted for group sites. Individual sites are $10 per night, and group sites are $40 per night, plus $3–$5 per additional vehicle. The campground is open from mid-April through October, weather permitting.

Contact: Deschutes National Forest, Bend–Fort Rock Ranger District, 1230 NE Third Street, Bend, OR 97701; (541) 388-5664 or fax (541) 383-5531; Web site: www.empnet.com/dnf.

Directions: From Interstate 5 south of Eugene, take exit 188 and turn east on Highway 58. Drive 73 miles to County Road 61. From here, turn east and drive three miles. Turn north on Cascade Lakes Highway (Highway 46). Continue 18 miles to County Road 42. Turn east and continue for five miles to Forest Service Road 4260. Turn south and drive three miles to the campground.

Trip notes: This campground is in an open setting with sparse vegetation on the north

shore of Wickiup Reservoir. You'll find good fishing for kokanee salmon here.

⑭ Twin Lakes RV Resort

Location: On Wickiup Reservoir; map D2, grid f7.

Campsites, facilities: There are 120 sites for tents, trailers, and RVs of any length; 22 have full hookups. There are also 14 cabins. Rest rooms, showers, a sanitary dump, a private phone, a laundry room, limited groceries, a full-service restaurant, ice, snacks, some RV supplies, LP gas, and a barbecue are available. A boat ramp, rentals, and a dock are provided; no motors are permitted on South Twin Lake. Leashed pets are permitted.

Reservations, fees: Reservations are recommended. Sites are $12–$18 per night, and cabins are $62–$94 per night. The campground is open from April 25 to October 15.

Contact: Phone the park at (541) 593-6526, fax (541) 410-4688, or write to P.O. Box 3550, Sun River, OR 97707.

Directions: From Interstate 5 south of Eugene, take exit 188 and turn east on Highway 58. Drive 86 miles, then turn north on U.S. 97 and drive 26 miles to LaPine. Continue 2.5 miles northeast on U.S. 97, then 11 miles west on County Road 43. Continue another four miles west on County Road 42 to the Twin Lakes Resort sign. Turn south and drive to the resort, two miles ahead.

Trip notes: This resort is a popular family vacation destination, with a full-service marina and all the amenities, including beach areas. Recreational activities range from hiking to fishing, swimming, and boating on Wickiup Reservoir.

⑮ Sheep Bridge

Location: Near Wickiup Reservoir in Deschutes National Forest; map D2, grid f7.

Campsites, facilities: There are 18 sites for tents, trailers, or RVs up to 22 feet long. Picnic tables and fire grills are provided. Hand-pumped water and vault toilets are available. Leashed pets are permitted.

Reservations, fees: No reservations are accepted. Sites are $5 per night, plus $3–$5 per additional vehicle. The campground is open from April through October, weather permitting.

Contact: Deschutes National Forest, Bend–Fort Rock Ranger District, 1230 NE Third Street, Bend, OR 97701; (541) 388-5664 or fax (541) 383-5531; Web site: www.empnet.com/dnf.

Directions: From Interstate 5 south of Eugene, take exit 188 and turn east on Highway 58. Drive 73 miles to County Road 61. From here, turn east and drive three miles. Turn north on Cascade Lakes Highway (Highway 46). Continue 18 miles to County Road 42. Turn east and continue for five miles to Forest Service Road 4260. From here, the camp is one-half mile down on the west side of the road.

Trip notes: This campground is set along the channel north of Wickiup Reservoir in an open, treeless area that has minimal privacy and is dusty in summer.

⑯ South Twin Lake

Location: On South Twin Lake in Deschutes National Forest; map D2, grid f7.

Campsites, facilities: There are 24 sites for tents, trailers, or RVs up to 22 feet long. Picnic tables and fire grills are provided. Piped water and flush toilets are available. Boat docks, launching facilities, boat rentals, showers, and laundry facilities are nearby. Leashed pets are permitted.

Reservations, fees: No reservations are accepted. Sites are $12 per night, plus $3–$5 per additional vehicle. The campground is open from mid-April through October, weather permitting.

Contact: Deschutes National Forest, Bend–Fort Rock Ranger District, 1230 NE Third Street, Bend, OR 97701; (541) 388-5664 or fax (541) 383-5531; Web site: www.empnet.com/dnf.

Directions: From Interstate 5 south of Eugene, take exit 188 and turn east on High-

way 58. Drive 73 miles to County Road 61. From here, turn east and drive three miles. Turn north on Cascade Lakes Highway (Highway 46). Continue 18 miles to County Road 42. Turn east and continue for five miles to Forest Service Road 4260, then turn south and drive 1.5 miles to the campground.

Trip notes: This campground is on the shore of South Twin Lake, a popular spot for swimming, fishing, and boating (non-motorized only).

⑰ Reservoir

Location: On Wickiup Reservoir in Deschutes National Forest; map D2, grid f7.

Campsites, facilities: There are 28 sites for tents, trailers, or RVs up to 22 feet long. Picnic tables and fire grills are provided. Boat launching facilities and vault toilets are available, but there is no piped water. Leashed pets are permitted.

Reservations, fees: No reservations are accepted. Sites are $5 per night, plus $3–$5 per additional vehicle. The campground is open from May to late October, weather permitting.

Contact: Deschutes National Forest, Bend–Fort Rock Ranger District, 1230 NE Third Street, Bend, OR 97701; (541) 388-5664 or fax (541) 383-5531; Web site: www.empnet.com/dnf.

Directions: From Interstate 5 south of Eugene, take exit 188 and turn east on Highway 58. Drive 73 miles to County Road 61. Turn east and continue for three miles. Turn north on Cascade Lakes Highway (Highway 46). Drive 11 miles and turn east on Forest Service Road 44. Proceed 1.5 miles to the camp.

Trip notes: This campground is set along the south shore of Wickiup Reservoir, where the kokanee salmon fishing is good. The camp is best in early summer, before the lake level drops. Because of a pine beetle infestation, the area was logged in 1987.

⑱ Fall River

Location: On the Fall River in Deschutes National Forest; map D2, grid f8.

Campsites, facilities: There are 12 sites for tents, trailers, or RVs up to 22 feet long. Picnic tables and fire grills are provided. Vault toilets are available. There is no piped water. Leashed pets are permitted.

Reservations, fees: No reservations are accepted. Sites are $5 per night, plus $3–$5 per additional vehicle. The campground is open from mid-April through October, weather permitting.

Contact: Deschutes National Forest, Bend–Fort Rock Ranger District, 1230 NE Third Street, Bend, OR 97701; (541) 388-5664 or fax (541) 383-5531; Web site: www.empnet.com/dnf.

Directions: From Interstate 5 at Albany, turn east on U.S. 20 and drive 122 miles to Bend. From Bend, travel 16.5 miles south on U.S. 97, then 15 miles southwest on County Road 42 to the campground.

Trip notes: This campground is on the Fall River, where fishing is restricted to fly-fishing only. Check the regulations for other restrictions.

⑪⑨ Pringle Falls

Location: On the Deschutes River in Deschutes National Forest; map D2, grid f8.

Campsites, facilities: There are seven sites for tents, trailers, or RVs up to 22 feet long. Picnic tables and fire grills are provided. Vault toilets are available. There is no piped water. Leashed pets are permitted.

Reservations, fees: No reservations are accepted. Sites are $5 per night, plus $3–$5 per additional vehicle. The campground is open from April through September, weather permitting.

Contact: Deschutes National Forest, Bend–Fort Rock Ranger District, 1230 NE Third Street, Bend, OR 97701; (541) 388-5664 or fax (541) 383-5531; Web site: www.empnet.com/dnf.

Directions: From Interstate 5 at Albany, turn east on U.S. 20 and drive 122 miles to Bend. Turn south on U.S. 97 and drive 27.5 miles to County Road 43 (2.5 miles north of LaPine). Turn west and drive seven miles. The camp is about one-half mile northeast on Forest Service Road 4360.

Trip notes: This pretty campground along the Deschutes River, fairly close to Pringle Falls, is a popular canoe launching point.

⑫⓪ Wickiup Butte

Location: On Wickiup Reservoir in Deschutes National Forest; map D2, grid f8.

Campsites, facilities: There are 12 sites for tents, trailers, or RVs up to 22 feet long. Picnic tables and fire grills are provided. Vault toilets are available. There is no piped water. Boat launching facilities are nearby. Leashed pets are permitted.

Reservations, fees: No reservations are accepted. Sites are $5 per night, plus $3–$5 per additional vehicle. The campground is open from May to late October, weather permitting.

Contact: Deschutes National Forest, Bend–Fort Rock Ranger District, 1230 NE Third Street, Bend, OR 97701; (541) 388-5664 or fax (541) 383-5531; Web site: www.empnet.com/dnf.

Directions: From Interstate 5 south of Eugene, take exit 188 and turn east on Highway 58. Drive 86 miles, then turn north on U.S. 97 and drive 26 miles to LaPine. Continue 2.5 miles northeast on U.S. 97, then seven miles west on County Road 43. The camp is located another seven miles west on Forest Service Road 44.

Trip notes: This campground is set along the southeast shore of Wickiup Reservoir, where kokanee salmon fishing is good during the early summer. See the trip notes for Reservoir (campground number 117) for information on the lake environment.

⑫① Riverview Trailer Park

Location: On the Little Deschutes River; map D2, grid f8.

Campsites, facilities: There are 15 tent sites and 19 sites for trailers or RVs of any length. Electricity, cable TV, well water, sewer hookups, and picnic tables are provided. Flush toilets, showers, a recreation hall, and a laundry room are available. Small, leashed pets are permitted.

Reservations, fees: Reservations are accepted. Sites are $11–$17 per night. The campground is open year-round.

Contact: Phone (541) 536-2382 or write to 52731 Huntington Road, LaPine, OR 97739.

Directions: From Interstate 5 south of Eugene, take exit 188 and turn east on Highway 58. Drive 86 miles, then turn north on U.S. 97 and drive 26 miles to LaPine. Continue 2.5 miles northeast on U.S. 97, then one mile west on County Road 43. The camp is one mile north on Huntington Road on the left.

Trip notes: This campground is set along the bank of the Little Deschutes River, which offers excellent trout fishing. It's missed by a lot of highway travelers; they just plain don't know about it.

122 Hidden Pines RV Park

Location: On the Little Deschutes River; map D2, grid f8.

Campsites, facilities: There are two tent sites and 18 sites for trailers or RVs of any length; four are drive-throughs. Electricity, piped water, cable TV hookups, sewer hookups, and picnic tables are provided. Flush toilets, sanitary services, showers, firewood, a laundry room, and ice are available. Bottled gas, a store, and a cafe are all within eight miles. No pets are allowed.

Reservations, fees: Reservations are accepted. Sites are $12–$17 per night. The campground is open from April to mid-October.

Contact: Hidden Pines RV Park, 52158 Elderberry Lane, LaPine, OR 97739; (541) 536-2265; e-mail: hdnpnsrvpk@aol.com.

Directions: From Interstate 5 south of Eugene, take exit 188 and turn east on Highway 58. Drive 86 miles, then turn north on U.S. 97 and drive 26 miles to LaPine. Continue 2.5 miles north on U.S. 97, then 2.5 miles west at Wickiup Junction. The camp is one-half mile south on Pine Forest and 400 yards east on Wright Avenue.

Trip notes: So you think you've come far enough, eh? If you want a spot in a privately run RV park two miles from the bank of the Little Deschutes River, you've found it.

123 Bull Bend

Location: On the Deschutes River in Deschutes National Forest; map D2, grid f8.

Campsites, facilities: There are 12 sites for tents, trailers, or RVs. Picnic tables and fire grills are provided. Vault toilets are available. There is no piped water. Leashed pets are permitted.

Reservations, fees: No reservations are accepted. Sites are $5 per night, plus $3–$5 per additional vehicle. The campground is open from April through September, weather permitting.

Contact: Deschutes National Forest, Bend–Fort Rock Ranger District, 1230 NE Third Street, Bend, OR 97701; (541) 388-5664 or fax (541) 383-5531; Web site: www.empnet.com/dnf.

Directions: From Interstate 5 south of Eugene, take exit 188 and turn east on Highway 58. Drive 86 miles, then turn north on U.S. 97 and drive 26 miles to LaPine. Continue 2.5 miles northeast on U.S. 97, then eight miles west on County Road 43. The camp is 1.5 miles southwest on Forest Service Road 4370.

Trip notes: This campground is on the inside of a major bend in the Deschutes River. A mini float trip can be made by starting at the upstream end of camp, floating around the bend, and then taking out at the downstream end of camp.

124 Big River

Location: On the Deschutes River in Deschutes National Forest; map D2, grid f9.

Campsites, facilities: There are five tent sites and eight sites for tents, trailers, or RVs up to 22 feet long. There is also one group site that can accommodate up to 60 people. Picnic tables and fire grills are provided. Vault toilets are available. There is no piped water. Boat launching facilities are on site. Leashed pets are permitted.

Reservations, fees: Reservations are only accepted for the group site. Individual sites are $5 per night, and the group site is $50 per night, plus $3–$5 per additional vehicle. The campground is open from April through September.

Contact: Deschutes National Forest, Bend–Fort Rock Ranger District, 1230 NE Third Street, Bend, OR 97701; (541) 388-5664 or fax (541) 383-5531; Web site: www.empnet.com/dnf.

Directions: From Interstate 5 at Albany, turn east on U.S. 20 and drive 122 miles to Bend. From Bend, drive 16.5 miles south on U.S. 97, then five miles southwest on County Road 42 to the campground.

Trip notes: This is a good spot along the banks of the Deschutes River in a nice location. Rafting, fishing, and boating using motors are permitted. Access is easy.

125 Lapine State Park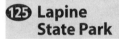

Location: On the Deschutes River; map D2, grid f9.

Campsites, facilities: There are 145 sites with full or partial hookups for trailers or RVs of any length. Picnic tables are provided. Flush toilets, sanitary services, showers, and firewood are available. Some facilities are wheelchair accessible. Leashed pets are permitted.

Reservations, fees: Contact Reservations Northwest at (800) 452-5687 ($6 reservation fee). Sites are $9–$16 per night. The campground is open year-round.

Contact: High Desert Management Unit, 62976 O.B. Riley Road, Bend, OR 97701; (800) 233-0321 or (541) 388-6055.

Directions: From Interstate 5 south of Eugene, take exit 188 and turn east on Highway 58. Drive 86 miles, then turn north on U.S. 97 and drive 26 miles to LaPine. Continue eight miles north on U.S. 97. Turn west on State Recreation Road and continue three miles.

Trip notes: This state park is set along the banks of the Deschutes River, where trout fishing and canoeing are excellent. The park is the home of Oregon's appropriately named Big Tree, the largest ponderosa pine in the

state. A half-mile long hiking trail and cross-country skiing are also available.

126 Highlander Motel and Trailer Park

Location: Near the Little Deschutes River; map D2, grid f9.

Campsites, facilities: There are 30 sites for trailers or RVs up to 35 feet long; 16 are drive-throughs. Electricity, piped water, and sewer hookups are provided. Flush toilets, bottled gas, sanitary services, showers, a store, a cafe, and ice are available. A Laundromat is located within one mile. Leashed pets are permitted.

Reservations, fees: Reservations are accepted. Sites are $13 per night. The campground is open year-round.

Contact: Phone (541) 536-2131 or write to P.O. Box 322, LaPine, OR 97739.

Directions: From Interstate 5 south of Eugene, take exit 188 and turn east on Highway 58. Drive 86 miles, then turn north on U.S. 97 and drive 26 miles to LaPine. The campground is located at the north edge of town.

Trip notes: This campground is near the Little Deschutes River. A golf course and tennis courts are close by.

127 Prairie

Location: On Paulina Creek in Deschutes National Forest; map D2, grid f9.

Campsites, facilities: There are 16 sites for tents, trailers, or RVs up to 30 feet long. Picnic tables and fire grills are provided. Piped water, firewood, and vault toilets are available. Leashed pets are permitted.

Reservations, fees: No reservations are accepted. Sites are $9 per night, plus $3–$5 per additional vehicle. The campground is open from mid-May through October, weather permitting.

Contact: Deschutes National Forest, Bend–Fort Rock Ranger District, 1230 NE Third Street, Bend, OR 97701; (541) 388-5664 or fax (541) 383-5531; Web site: www.empnet.com/dnf.

Directions: From Interstate 5 south of Eugene, take exit 188 and turn east on Highway 58. Drive 86 miles, then turn north on U.S. 97 and drive 26 miles to LaPine. Continue five miles northeast on U.S. 97, then three miles southeast on County Road 21 to the campground.

Trip notes: This camp along the banks of Paulina Creek is near the trailhead for the Peter Skene Ogden National Recreation Trail.

128 McKay Crossing

Location: On Paulina Creek in Deschutes National Forest; map D2, grid f9.

Campsites, facilities: There are 10 sites for tents, trailers, or RVs up to 22 feet long. Picnic tables and fire grills are provided. Vault toilets are available. There is no piped water. Leashed pets are permitted.

Reservations, fees: No reservations are accepted. Sites are $7 per night, plus $3–$5 per additional vehicle. The campground is open from June to late October.

Contact: Deschutes National Forest, Bend–Fort Rock Ranger District, 1230 NE Third Street, Bend, OR 97701; (541) 388-5664 or fax (541) 383-5531; Web site: www.empnet.com/dnf.

Directions: From Interstate 5 south of Eugene, take exit 188 and turn east on Highway 58. Drive 86 miles, then turn north on U.S. 97 and drive 26 miles to LaPine. Continue five miles northeast on U.S. 97, then three miles southeast on County Road 21. The camp is two miles east on Forest Service Road 2120.

Trip notes: This pleasant little campground is set along the banks of Paulina Creek. A nearby trail travels east for six miles to Paulina Lake (also reachable by car). See the trip notes for Paulina Lake (campground number 36 in Chapter D3) for recreation alternatives in the area.

129 Rock Creek

Location: On Rock Creek; map D2, grid g0.

Campsites, facilities: There are 17 sites for tents, trailers, or RVs up to 30 feet long. Picnic tables and fire grills are provided. Vault toi-

lets, piped water, and firewood are available. Leashed pets are permitted.

Reservations, fees: No reservations are accepted. Sites are $7 per night, with a 14-day stay limit, plus $3 for each additional vehicle. The campground is open from May 20 to mid-October.

Contact: Bureau of Land Management, 777 NW Garden Valley Boulevard, Roseburg, OR 97470; (541) 440-4930 or fax (541) 440-4948.

Directions: From Interstate 5 at Roseburg, drive 22 miles east on Highway 138 to Rock Creek Road. Turn north and drive seven miles to the campground.

Trip notes: This campground on the banks of Rock Creek in a relatively obscure spot is sparse and primitive, but supplies all the necessities at a reasonable price. It's not well known, either, so you're likely to have privacy as a bonus.

130 Millpond

Location: On Rock Creek; map D2, grid g0.

Campsites, facilities: There are 12 sites for tents, trailers, or RVs up to 30 feet long. Picnic tables and fire grills are provided. Flush and vault toilets, piped water, firewood, a ball field, and a group shelter are available. Some facilities are wheelchair accessible. Leashed pets are permitted.

Reservations, fees: No reservations are accepted. Sites are $8 per night, with a 14-day stay limit, plus $3 for each additional vehicle. The campground is open from May through October.

Contact: Bureau of Land Management, 777 NW Garden Valley Boulevard, Roseburg, OR 97470; (541) 440-4930.

Directions: From Interstate 5 at Roseburg, drive 22 miles east on Highway 138 to Rock Creek Road. Turn north and drive five miles to the campground.

Trip notes: This campground along the banks of Rock Creek is the first camp you'll see along Rock Creek Road, which accounts for its relative popularity in this area. Like Rock Creek Campground (number 129), it's primitive and remote.

131 Susan Creek

Location: On the North Umpqua River; map D2, grid g0.

Campsites, facilities: There are 31 sites for trailers or RVs up to 35 feet long. Picnic tables and fire grills are provided. Flush toilets, piped water, showers, and firewood are available. Some facilities and trails are wheelchair accessible. Leashed pets are permitted.

Reservations, fees: No reservations are accepted. Sites are $10 per night, with a 14-day stay limit, plus $3 for each additional vehicle. The campground is open from May 20 to October 5.

Contact: Bureau of Land Management, 777 NW Garden Valley Boulevard, Roseburg, OR 97470; (541) 440-4930.

Directions: From Interstate 5 at Roseburg, travel 30 miles east on Highway 138 to the campground.

Trip notes: This popular campground along the banks of the North Umpqua Wild and Scenic River is a good base camp for a fishing trip. The setting is pretty, with lots of trees and river access. Highlights include hiking trails and opportunities for white-water rafting and kayaking.

132 Scaredman

Location: On Canton Creek; map D2, grid g1.

Campsites, facilities: There are nine sites for tents, trailers, or RVs up to 25 feet long. Picnic tables and fire grills are provided. Vault toilets are available. There is no piped water. Leashed pets are permitted.

Reservations, fees: No reservations are accepted. There is no fee. The stay limit is 14 days. The campground is open year-round.

Contact: Bureau of Land Management, 777 NW Garden Valley Boulevard, Roseburg, OR 97470; (541) 440-4930.

Directions: From Interstate 5 at Roseburg, drive 40 miles east on Highway 138 to Steamboat. From Steamboat, drive three miles north on Canton Creek Road to the campground.

Trip notes: This small campground along the banks of Canton Creek is virtually unknown to out-of-towners. It's very primitive, offering little but cleared-out areas for tents and a chance to swim, but it's also private and secluded.

133 Island

Location: On the Umpqua River in Umpqua National Forest; map D2, grid g1.

Campsites, facilities: There are seven sites for tents, trailers, or RVs up to 24 feet long. Picnic tables and fire grills are provided. Vault toilets are available. There is no piped water. Leashed pets are permitted.

Reservations, fees: No reservations are accepted. Sites are $5 per night. The campground is open year-round.

Contact: Umpqua National Forest, North Umpqua Ranger District, 18782 North Umpqua Highway, Glide, OR 97443; (541) 496-3532 or fax (541) 496-3534.

Directions: From Roseburg on Interstate 5, take exit 120 and drive 40 miles east on Highway 138. The campground is located on the right off the highway, just past a little settlement called Steamboat.

Trip notes: This campground is set along the banks of the Umpqua River at a spot popular for both rafting and fishing (you can't keep any fish under 20 inches long). A hiking trail that leads east and west along the river is accessible by driving a short distance west. See a Forest Service map for details.

134 Canton Creek

Location: Near the Umpqua River in Umpqua National Forest; map D2, grid g2.

Campsites, facilities: There are five sites for tents, trailers, or RVs up to 22 feet long. Picnic tables and fire grills are provided. Piped water and flush toilets are available. Leashed pets are permitted.

Reservations, fees: No reservations are accepted. Sites are $7 per night. The campground is open from mid-May to late October.

Contact: Umpqua National Forest, North

Umpqua Ranger District, 18782 North Umpqua Highway, Glide, OR 97443; (541) 496-3532 or fax (541) 496-3534.

Directions: From Roseburg on Interstate 5, take exit 120 and drive about 39 miles east on Highway 138 to Steamboat. Turn left on Forest Service Road 38 and proceed about 400 yards to the campground.

Trip notes: This campground at the confluence of Canton and Steamboat Creeks, less than a mile from the North Umpqua River, gets little overnight use, but there are lots of day swimmers in July and August. No fishing is permitted on Steamboat or Canton Creeks because they are spawning areas for steelhead and salmon. Steamboat Falls is six miles north on Forest Service Road 38. See the trip notes for Island (campground number 133) for other area details.

135 Steamboat Falls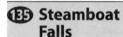

Location: On Steamboat Creek in Umpqua National Forest; map D2, grid g2.

Campsites, facilities: There are 11 sites for tents, trailers, or RVs up to 24 feet long. Picnic tables, vault toilets, and fire grills are provided. There is no piped water. Leashed pets are permitted.

Reservations, fees: No reservations are accepted. Sites are $5 per night. The campground is open year-round, with no fee from November through late May.

Contact: Umpqua National Forest, North Umpqua Ranger District, 18782 North Umpqua Highway, Glide, OR 97443; (541) 496-3532 or fax (541) 496-3534.

Directions: From Roseburg on Interstate 5, take exit 120 and drive east on Highway 138 to Steamboat. Turn left and drive six miles northeast on Forest Service Road 38. The camp is one mile farther on Forest Service Road 3810.

Trip notes: This campground is on the banks of Steamboat Creek, at beautiful Steamboat Falls, which features a fish ladder that provides passage for steelhead and salmon on their upstream migratory journey. No fishing

is permitted in Steamboat Creek. Other camping options are Island and Canton Creek (campground numbers 133 and 134).

136 Boulder Flat

Location: On the North Umpqua River in Umpqua National Forest; map D2, grid g2.

Campsites, facilities: There are 11 sites for tents, trailers, or RVs up to 24 feet long. Picnic tables and fire grills are provided. Vault toilets are available. There is no piped water. A store, propane, and ice are located within five miles. A raft launch is on site. Leashed pets are permitted.

Reservations, fees: No reservations are accepted. Sites are $5 per night. The campground is open year-round.

Contact: Umpqua National Forest, North Umpqua Ranger District, 18782 North Umpqua Highway, Glide, OR 97443; (541) 496-3532 or fax (541) 496-3534.

Directions: From Roseburg on Interstate 5, take exit 120 and drive 54 miles east on Highway 138 to the campground.

Trip notes: This campground is set along the banks of the North Umpqua River at the confluence of Boulder Creek. Across the river from the campground, a trail follows Boulder Creek north for 10.5 miles through the Boulder Creek Wilderness, a climb in elevation from 2,000 to 5,400 feet. Access to the trail is at Soda Springs Dam, two miles east of the camp. It's a good thumper for backpackers. A little over a mile to the east are some huge, dramatic pillars of volcanic rock, colored with lichen.

137 Campers Flat

Location: On the Willamette River in Willamette National Forest; map D2, grid g3.

Campsites, facilities: There are five sites for tents, trailers, or RVs up to 21 feet long. Picnic tables and fire grills are provided. Hand-pumped water, vault toilets, and firewood are available. Leashed pets are permitted.

Reservations, fees: No reservations are accepted. Sites are $8 per night, plus $4 for each additional vehicle. The campground is open from mid-May to mid-September.

Contact: Willamette National Forest, Rigdon Ranger District, 49098 Salmon Creek Road, Oakridge, OR 97463; (541) 782-2283 or fax (541) 782-5306.

Directions: From Interstate 5 south of Eugene, drive 38 miles southeast on Highway 58 (two miles past Oakridge), then one-half mile on County Road 360. Turn south onto Forest Service Road 21 and drive 20 miles to the camp.

Trip notes: This pretty, open camp on the Middle Fork of the Willamette River is well known and liked by locals, so expect a lot of company.

138 Secret

Location: On the Willamette River in Willamette National Forest; map D2, grid g3.

Campsites, facilities: There are six sites for tents, trailers, or RVs up to 15 feet long. Picnic tables and fire grills are provided. Vault toilets are available, but there is no piped water. Leashed pets are permitted.

Reservations, fees: No reservations are accepted. Sites are $6 per night, plus $4 for each additional vehicle. The campground is open from mid-May to mid-September.

Contact: Willamette National Forest, Rigdon Ranger District, 49098 Salmon Creek Road, Oakridge, OR 97463; (541) 782-2283 or fax (541) 782-5306.

Directions: From Interstate 5 south of Eugene drive southeast on Highway 58 two miles past Oakridge, then one-half mile on County Road 360. Turn south on Forest Service Road 21 and drive 18 miles to the camp.

Trip notes: This campground in a nice setting on the Middle Fork of the Willamette River attracts many locals, making it a very busy spot.

139 Toketee Lake

Location: On Toketee Lake in Umpqua National Forest; map D2, grid g3.

Campsites, facilities: There are 33 sites for tents, trailers, or RVs up to 22 feet long. Vault toilets are available, but there is no piped water. Picnic tables and fire grills are provided. Boat docks and launching facilities are nearby. Leashed pets are permitted.

Reservations, fees: Reservations are accepted. Sites are $5 per night. The campground is open from mid-April to late October.

Contact: Umpqua National Forest, Diamond Lake Ranger District, 2020 Toketee Ranger Station Road, Idleyld Park, OR 97447; (541) 498-2531 or fax (541) 498-2515.

Directions: From Roseburg on Interstate 5, take exit 120 and drive about 60 miles east on Highway 138. Then go one mile on Forest Service Road 34, past the lake, to the campground.

Trip notes: This campground is just north of Toketee Lake. The North Umpqua River Trail passes near camp and continues north along the river for many miles. Diehard hikers can also take it west, where it meanders for a while before heading north into the Boulder Creek Wilderness. Toketee Lake offers many recreation options, and a worthwhile point of interest is Toketee Falls, located just west of the lake turnoff. Another is Umpqua Hot Springs, a few miles northeast of the camp.

140 Indigo Springs

Location: Near the Willamette River in Willamette National Forest; map D2, grid g4.

Campsites, facilities: There are three sites for tents, trailers, or RVs up to 16 feet long. Picnic tables and fire grills are provided. Vault toilets and firewood are available. There is no piped water. Leashed pets are permitted.

Reservations, fees: No reservations are accepted. There is no fee. The campground is open from mid-April to mid-November.

Contact: Willamette National Forest, Rigdon Ranger District, 49098 Salmon Creek Road, Oakridge, OR 97463; (541) 782-2283 or fax (541) 782-5306.

Directions: From Interstate 5 south of Eugene, take exit 188 and turn east on Highway 58. Drive 38 miles southeast (two miles past Oakridge), then one-half mile on County Road 360. From there, continue 29 miles southeast on Forest Service Road 21. The camp is on the left.

Trip notes: This campground sits along the bank of Indigo Creek, not far from its confluence with the Middle Fork of the Willamette River. The camp gets it name from several large springs in the area.

⑭ East Lemolo

Location: On Lemolo Lake in Umpqua National Forest; map D2, grid g5.

Campsites, facilities: There are 15 sites for tents or small RVs. No piped water is available. Picnic tables and fire rings are provided. Vault toilets are available. Boat docks, launching facilities, and rentals are nearby. Leashed pets are permitted.

Reservations, fees: Reservations are accepted. Sites are $5 per night. The campground is open from mid-May to late October.

Contact: Umpqua National Forest, Diamond Lake Ranger District, 2020 Toketee Ranger Station Road, Idleyld Park, OR 97447; (541) 498-2531 or fax (541) 498-2515.

Directions: From Roseburg on Interstate 5, take exit 120 and drive 74 miles east on Highway 138, then three miles north on Forest Service Road 2610. The campground is located about two miles east on Forest Service Road 2666.

Trip notes: This campground is on the southeastern shore of Lemolo Lake, where boating and fishing are some of the recreation possibilities. Boats with motors are allowed. The North Umpqua River and its adjacent trail are just beyond the north shore of the lake. If you hike for two miles northwest of the lake, you can reach spectacular Lemolo Falls.

⑭ Poole Creek

Location: On Lemolo Lake in Umpqua National Forest; map D2, grid g5.

Campsites, facilities: There are 59 sites for tents, trailers, or RVs up to 22 feet long. Picnic tables and fire grills are provided. Piped water and vault toilets are available. Boat docks, launching facilities, and rentals are nearby. Leashed pets are permitted.

Reservations, fees: Reserve the group sites by calling (800) 280-CAMP/2267 ($8.65 reservation fee). Sites are $6–$8 per night. The campground is open from late April to late October.

Contact: Umpqua National Forest, Diamond Lake Ranger District, 2020 Toketee Ranger Station Road, Idleyld Park, OR 97447; (541) 498-2531 or fax (541) 498-2515.

Directions: From Roseburg on Interstate 5, take exit 120 and drive 72 miles east on Highway 138, then four miles north on Forest Service Road 2610 to the campground.

Trip notes: This campground on the western shore of Lemolo Lake isn't far from Lemolo Lake Resort, which is open for recreation year-round. This is by far the most popular Forest Service camp at the lake. See the trip notes for East Lemolo (campground number 141) for more information.

⑭ Lemolo Lake Resort

Location: On Lemolo Lake; map D2, grid g5.

Campsites, facilities: There are three tent sites and 32 sites for trailers or RVs of any length; 27 are drive-throughs. There are also 10 cabins. Electricity, piped water, sewer hookups, and picnic tables are provided. Flush toilets, bottled gas, sanitary disposal services, showers, a store, a cafe, a laundry room, a lounge, boat docks, boat rentals, launching facilities, and ice are available. Leashed pets and motorbikes are permitted.

Reservations, fees: Reservations are accepted. Sites are $10–$17 per night. The campground is open from March through October, weather permitting.

Contact: Phone (541) 793-3300 or write to HC 60, P.O. Box 79B, Idleyld Park, OR 97447.

Directions: From Roseburg on Interstate 5, take exit 138 and drive approximately 80 miles east on Highway 138, then go five miles north on Lemolo Lake Road (Bird's Point Road) to the resort.

Trip notes: This resort is on the western shore of Lemolo Lake and offers recreation opportunities year-round. See the trip notes for East Lemolo (campground number 141) for more details.

144 Trapper Creek

Location: On Odell Lake in Deschutes National Forest; map D2, grid f6.

Campsites, facilities: There are 32 sites for tents, trailers, or RVs up to 22 feet long. Picnic tables and fire grills are provided. Piped water and vault toilets are available. Firewood may be gathered from the surrounding area. A store, a Laundromat, and ice are within one mile. Leashed pets are permitted.

Reservations, fees: No reservations are accepted. Sites are $10–$12 per night, plus $5 for each additional vehicle. The campground is open from June through September.

Contact: Deschutes National Forest, Crescent Ranger District, P.O. Box 208, Crescent, OR 97733; (541) 433-2234.

Directions: From Interstate 5 south of Eugene, turn east on Highway 58 and drive approximately 61 miles to the turnoff for Odell Lake. Turn southwest on Forest Service Road 5810 and drive 1.25 miles to the campground.

Trip notes: The west end of Odell Lake is the setting for this camp. Boat docks and rentals are nearby at the Shelter Cove Resort (campground 145).

145 Shelter Cove Resort

Location: On Odell Lake; map D2, grid g6.

Campsites, facilities: There are 11 tent sites and 58 drive-through sites for trailers or RVs up to 30 feet long, plus eight cabins. Electricity and picnic tables are provided. Flush toilets, showers, a store, a cafe, and ice are available. Boat docks, launching facilities, and rentals are nearby. Leashed pets are permitted.

Reservations, fees: Reservations are recommended. Sites are $9–$14 per night, and cabins are $60–$130 per night. The campground is open year-round.

Contact: Phone (541) 433-2548 or write to West Odell Lake Road, Cascade Summit, OR 97425.

Directions: From Interstate 5 south of Eugene, drive southeast on Highway 58 to Odell Lake. Take the West Odell Road turnoff at the north end of Odell Lake, then drive 2.5 miles south on West Odell Road to the camp.

Trip notes: This private resort along the north shore of Odell Lake offers opportunities for hiking, fishing, and swimming. A general store and tackle shop are available.

146 Simax Group Camp

Location: On Crescent Lake in Deschutes National Forest; map D2, grid g6.

Campsites, facilities: There are three group campsites for 30 to 40 campers each. Flush toilets, showers, picnic tables, fireplaces, and a group shelter that accommodates 50 campers are available. Facilities are wheelchair accessible. Leashed pets are permitted.

Reservations, fees: Reservations are required. Rates are $60 per night for Site A (the most accessible) and $85 per night for Sites B and C. Site B is the most difficult to access and only tents are advised; Site C is best for RVs. The group shelter fee is $25 per day. The campground is generally open from Memorial Day through Labor Day.

Contact: Deschutes National Forest, Crescent Ranger District, P.O. Box 208, Crescent, OR 97733; (541) 433-2234 or fax (541) 433-3224.

Directions: From Interstate 5 south of Eugene, take exit 188 and turn east on Highway 58. Drive about 70 miles to the town of Crescent Lake. Turn west on Forest Service Road 60 and go one mile. Turn south on Forest Service Road 6005 and drive one more mile to the campground entrance.

Trip notes: This is a new camp on Crescent Lake with trails to day-use beaches. See neighboring Spring and Contorta (campground numbers 154 and 155) for more details.

⑭ Crescent Lake

Location: On Crescent Lake in Deschutes National Forest; map D2, grid g6.

Campsites, facilities: There are 47 sites for tents, trailers, or RVs up to 35 feet long. Picnic tables and fire grills are provided. Piped water, vault toilets, and boat launching facilities are available. Firewood may be gathered from the surrounding area. Leashed pets are permitted.

Reservations, fees: No reservations are accepted. Sites are $10–$12 per night, plus $5 for each additional vehicle. The campground is open from mid-May to late October.

Contact: Deschutes National Forest, Crescent Ranger District, P.O. Box 208, Crescent, OR 97733; (541) 433-2234 or fax (541) 433-3224.

Directions: From Interstate 5 south of Eugene, drive approximately 70 miles southeast on Highway 58 to the town of Crescent Lake. From Crescent Lake, drive three miles southwest on Forest Service Road 60 to the campground.

Trip notes: This campground is set along the north shore of Crescent Lake. Boat docks, launching facilities, and rentals are also nearby at Crescent Lake Resort, adjacent to the campground. A trail from camp heads into the Diamond Peak Wilderness and also branches north to Odell Lake.

⑭ Odell Creek

Location: On Odell Lake in Deschutes National Forest; map D2, grid g6.

Campsites, facilities: There are 22 sites for tents, trailers, or RVs up to 22 feet long. Picnic tables and fire grills are provided. Vault toilets are available, but there is no piped water. Firewood may be gathered from the surrounding area. Leashed pets are permitted.

Reservations, fees: No reservations are accepted. Sites are $5 per night, plus $3 for each additional vehicle. The campground is open from mid-May to late September.

Contact: Deschutes National Forest, Crescent Ranger District, P.O. Box 208, Crescent, OR 97733; (541) 433-2234 or fax (541) 433-3224.

Directions: From Interstate 5 south of Eugene, drive southeast on Highway 58 to Odell Lake. At the east end of the lake, take Forest Service Road 680 and drive 400 yards to the campground.

Trip notes: You can fish, swim, and hike at this campground along the east shore of Odell Lake. A trail from the nearby Crater Buttes trailhead heads southwest into the Diamond Peak Wilderness and provides access to several small lakes in the backcountry. Boat docks, launching facilities, and rentals are nearby at the Odell Lake Lodge, adjacent to the campground.

⑭ Sunset Cove

Location: On Odell Lake in Deschutes National Forest; map D2, grid g6.

Campsites, facilities: There are 26 sites for tents, trailers, or RVs up to 22 feet long. Picnic tables and fire grills are provided. Piped water, vault toilets, a boat launch, and fish cleaning facilities are available. Firewood may be gathered from the surrounding area. Leashed pets are permitted.

Reservations, fees: No reservations are accepted. Sites are $10 per night, plus $5 for each additional vehicle. The campground is open from mid-May to mid-October.

Contact: Deschutes National Forest, Crescent Ranger District, P.O. Box 208, Crescent, OR 97733; (541) 433-2234 or fax (541) 433-3224.

Directions: From Interstate 5 south of Eugene, turn southeast on Highway 58 and drive approximately 72 miles to the campground.

Trip notes: This campground is on the northeast shore of Odell Lake. Boat docks and rentals are available nearby at the Shelter Cove Resort (campground number 145).

⑮ Princess Creek

Location: On Odell Lake in Deschutes National Forest; map D2, grid g6.

Campsites, facilities: There are 46 sites for tents, trailers, or RVs up to 22 feet long. Picnic tables and fire grills are provided. Piped water and vault toilets are available. Firewood may be gathered from the surrounding area. Showers, a store, a Laundromat, boat launching facilities, and ice are within five miles. Leashed pets are permitted.

Reservations, fees: No reservations are accepted. Sites are $10–$12 per night, plus $5 for each additional vehicle. The campground is open from mid-May through September.

Contact: Deschutes National Forest, Crescent Ranger District, P.O. Box 208, Crescent, OR 97733; (541) 433-2234 or fax (541) 433-3224.

Directions: From Interstate 5 south of Eugene, turn southeast on Highway 58 and drive approximately 68 miles to the campground.

Trip notes: This campground is on the northeast shore of Odell Lake. See the trip notes for Odell Creek (campground number 148) for recreation details. Boat docks and rentals are available nearby at the Shelter Cove Resort (campground number 145).

151 Gold Lake

Location: On Gold Lake in Willamette National Forest; map D2, grid g7.

Campsites, facilities: There are 20 sites for tents, trailers, or RVs up to 22 feet long. Picnic tables and fire grills are provided. Hand-pumped water and vault toilets are available. Boat docks and launching facilities are nearby. Leashed pets are permitted.

Reservations, fees: No reservations are accepted. Sites are $10 per night, plus $5 for each additional vehicle. The campground is open from June through September.

Contact: Willamette National Forest, Oakridge/Rigdon Ranger Districts, 49098 Salmon Creek Road, Oakridge, OR 97463; (541) 782-2283 or fax (541) 782-5306.

Directions: From Interstate 5 south of Eugene, take exit 188 and drive 61 miles southeast on Highway 58. Turn left on Forest Service Road 500 and drive two miles northeast to the campground.

Trip notes: This campground is set along the shore of Gold Lake, where swimming and boating (for boats without motors) are permitted. Fishing is also allowed, but is limited to fly-fishing. A trail at the camp provides access to numerous small lakes to the west and Waldo Lake to the north. In summer, wildflowers and huckleberries abound.

152 Inlet

Location: On Lemolo Lake in Umpqua National Forest; map D2, grid g6.

Campsites, facilities: There are 14 sites for tents, trailers, or RVs up to 22 feet long. Vault toilets are available, but there is no piped water. Picnic tables and fire grills are provided. Boat docks, launching facilities, and rentals are nearby. Leashed pets are permitted.

Reservations, fees: Reservations are accepted. Sites are $5 per night. The campground is open from mid-May to late October.

Contact: Umpqua National Forest, Diamond Lake Ranger District, 2020 Toketee Ranger Station Road, Idleyld Park, OR 97447; (541) 498-2531 or fax (541) 498-2515.

Directions: From Roseburg on Interstate 5, take exit 120 and drive 74 miles east on Highway 138, then three miles north on Forest Service Road 2610. The camp is about three miles east on Forest Service Road 2666.

Trip notes: This campground on the eastern inlet of Lemolo Lake is just across the road from the North Umpqua River Trail, which is routed east into the Oregon Cascades Recreation Area and the Mount Thielsen Wilderness. See the trip notes for East Lemolo (campground number 141) for more recreation details.

153 Timpanogas

Location: On Timpanogas Lake in Willamette National Forest; map D2, grid g6.

Campsites, facilities: There are 11 sites for tents, trailers, or RVs up to 21 feet long. Picnic tables and fire grills are provided. Hand-pumped water, vault toilets, and firewood are available. Boat docks are nearby, but no boats with motors are allowed. Leashed pets are permitted.

Reservations, fees: No reservations are accepted. Sites are $6 per night, plus $3 for each additional vehicle. The campground is open from mid-June to mid-October.

Contact: Willamette National Forest, Rigdon Ranger District, 49098 Salmon Creek Road, Oakridge, OR 97463; (541) 782-2283 or fax (541) 782-5306.

Directions: From Interstate 5 south of Eugene, take exit 188 and turn east on Highway 58. Drive 38 miles southeast (two miles past Oakridge), then one-half mile on County Road 360. Turn southeast on Forest Service Road 21 and drive 38 miles to the campground.

Trip notes: This remote campground is on the shore of Timpanogas Lake in the Oregon Cascades Recreation Area. A trailhead adjacent to camp provides access into the backcountry. A hike-in campground, located about two miles away at Indigo Lake, has five primitive sites and pit toilets. It's accessible by trail from this camp.

154 Spring

Location: On Crescent Lake in Deschutes National Forest; map D2, grid g6.

Campsites, facilities: There are 68 sites for tents, trailers, or RVs up to 22 feet long. Picnic tables and fire grills are provided. Piped water, vault toilets, boat launching facilities, and firewood (to be gathered from the surrounding area) are available. Leashed pets are permitted.

Reservations, fees: No reservations are accepted. Sites are $10–$12 per night, plus $5 for each additional vehicle. The campground is open from June through September.

Contact: Deschutes National Forest, Crescent Ranger District, P.O. Box 208, Crescent, OR 97733; (541) 433-2234 or fax (541) 433-3224.

Directions: From Interstate 5 south of Eugene, take exit 188 and turn east on Highway 58. Drive approximately 70 miles to the town of Crescent Lake. Drive eight miles west on Forest Service Road 60, then turn northeast on the entrance road to the campground.

Trip notes: This campground is on the southern shore of Crescent Lake. See the trip notes

for Contorta (campground number 155) for more information.

155 Contorta

Location: On Crescent Lake in Deschutes National Forest; map D2, grid g6.

Campsites, facilities: There is an area for dispersed camping for tents, trailers, or RVs up to 22 feet long. There is no piped water. Picnic tables and vault toilets are provided. Boat docks and launching facilities are located a mile away at Spring Campground. Leashed pets are permitted.

Reservations, fees: No reservations are accepted. There no fee. The campground is open from June to late September.

Contact: Deschutes National Forest, Crescent Ranger District, P.O. Box 208, Crescent, OR 97733; (541) 433-2234 or fax (541) 433-3224.

Directions: From Interstate 5 south of Eugene, take exit 188 and turn east on Highway 58. Drive approximately 70 miles to the turnoff, which is just past Odell Lake at Crescent Lake Junction. Drive 11 miles southwest on Forest Service Road 60, then one mile on Forest Service Road 280 to the campground.

Trip notes: This campground is on the southern shore of Crescent Lake, where swimming, boating, and waterskiing are among the summer pastimes. A number of trails from the nearby Windy-Oldenburg Trailhead provide access to lakes in the Diamond Peak Wilderness and Oregon Cascades Recreation Area. A parking area for snowmobiles and cross-country skiers is at the north end of the lake.

156 East Davis Lake

Location: On Davis Lake in Deschutes National Forest; map D2, grid g7.

Campsites, facilities: There are 33 sites for tents, trailers, or RVs up to 22 feet long. Picnic tables, fire grills, hand-pumped water, and vault toilets are provided. Firewood may be gathered from the surrounding area. Boat launching facilities are nearby at Lava Flow Campground. Leashed pets are permitted.

Reservations, fees: No reservations are accepted. Sites are $8 per night, plus $4 for each additional vehicle. The campground is open from May to late October.

Contact: Deschutes National Forest, Crescent Ranger District, P.O. Box 208, Crescent, OR 97733; (541) 433-2234 or fax (541) 433-3224.

Directions: From Interstate 5 south of Eugene, take exit 188 and turn east on Highway 58. Drive 73 miles, then turn east on County Road 61 and drive three miles. Continue 6.5 miles north on Forest Service Road 46. The camp is 1.5 miles west on Forest Service Road 46855.

Trip notes: This campground is nestled in the woods along the south shore of Davis Lake. Recreation options include fishing, boating, and hiking. Boat launching facilities are available at West Davis Lake (campground number 157).

⑮⑦ West Davis Lake

Location: On Davis Lake in Deschutes National Forest; map D2, grid g7.

Campsites, facilities: There are 25 sites for tents, trailers, or RVs up to 22 feet long. Picnic tables and fire grills are provided. Hand-pumped water, vault toilets, and firewood (to be gathered from the surrounding area) are available. Leashed pets are permitted.

Reservations, fees: No reservations are accepted. Sites are $8 per night, plus $4 for each additional vehicle. The campground is open from May to late October.

Contact: Deschutes National Forest, Crescent Ranger District, P.O. Box 208, Crescent, OR 97733; (541) 433-2234 or fax (541) 433-3224.

Directions: From Interstate 5 south of Eugene, take exit 188 and turn east on Highway 58. Drive 73 miles, then turn east on County Road 61. Drive three miles, then continue three miles north on Forest Service Road 46. Travel four miles on Forest Service Road 4660, then 1.5 miles on Forest Service Road 4669 to the campground.

Trip notes: Spacious sites and easy access to the water are highlights of this campground on the south shore of Davis Lake.

⑮⑧ Crescent Creek

Location: On Crescent Creek in Deschutes National Forest; map D2, grid g7.

Campsites, facilities: There are 10 sites for tents, trailers, or RVs up to 22 feet long. Picnic tables and fire grills are provided. Hand-pumped water and vault toilets are available. Firewood may be gathered from the surrounding area. Leashed pets are permitted.

Reservations, fees: No reservations are accepted. Sites are $8 per night, plus $4 for each additional vehicle. The campground is open from May to late October.

Contact: Deschutes National Forest, Crescent Ranger District, P.O. Box 208, Crescent, OR 97733; (541) 433-2234 or fax (541) 433-3224.

Directions: From Interstate 5 at Eugene, take exit 188 and turn east on Highway 58. Drive 73 miles, then turn east on County Road 61 and drive 3.5 miles to the campground.

Trip notes: This is one of the Cascade's classic hidden campgrounds, set along the banks of Crescent Creek at 4,500 feet. The buzz words here are pretty, developed, and private.

Map D3

Oregon State Map .... *page 6*
One inch equals approximately 20 miles.

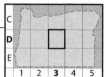

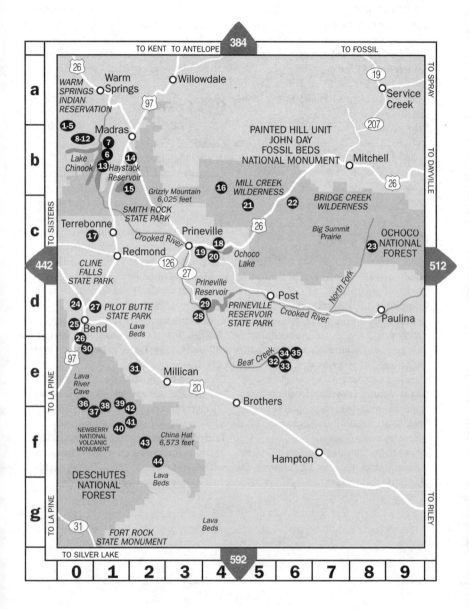

Chapter D3 features:

❶ Black Butte Motel and RV Park

Location: Near the Metolius River; map D3, grid a0.

Campsites, facilities: There are 19 sites with full hookups and 12 sites with partial hookups for trailers or RVs of any length. Electricity, piped water, sewer hookups, and picnic tables are provided. Flush toilets, showers, firewood, and a laundry room are available. Bottled gas, sanitary services, a store, a cafe, and ice are located within one block. Leashed pets and motorbikes are permitted.

Reservations, fees: Reservations are accepted. Sites are $17–19 per night. The campground is open year-round.

Contact: Black Butte Motel and RV Park, 25635 SW Forest Service Road 1419, Camp Sherman, OR 97730; (541) 595-6514 or fax (541) 595-5971; e-mail: cdog@outlawnet.com.

Directions: From Interstate 5 at Albany, turn east on U.S. 20 and drive approximately 87 miles. At the sign for Camp Sherman, turn north and drive about five miles. Turn east on Forest Service Road 1419 and drive one-quarter mile to the park on the right.

Trip notes: This RV park offers a choice of graveled or grassy sites in a clean, scenic environment. See the trip notes for Camp Sherman (campground number 8) for more area information.

❷ Cold Springs Resort and RV Park

Location: On the Metolius River; map D3, grid a0.

Campsites, facilities: There are 45 sites with full hookups for trailers or RVs of any length, plus two cabins on the river. Fire pits, picnic tables, and patios are provided. Rest rooms, showers, laundry facilities, firewood, and a riverfront picnic facility are available. Bottled gas, a store with groceries, fishing and sport supplies, a cafe, a Laundromat, a post office, and ice are located within one-quarter mile. Leashed pets are permitted.

Reservations, fees: Reservations are accepted. Sites are $18–$20 per night; cabins are $88–$129 per night, depending on the season and the number of people. The campground is open year-round.

Contact: Phone (541) 595-6271, fax (541) 595-1400, or write to 25615 Cold Springs Resort Lane, Camp Sherman, OR 97730.

Directions: From Interstate 5 at Albany, turn east on U.S. 20 and drive approximately 87 miles. At the sign for Camp Sherman, turn north and drive about five miles. Turn right at the stop sign and drive about 300 feet. Turn right on Cold Springs Resort Lane and drive through the forest and the meadow, crossing Cold Springs Creek, to the resort.

Trip notes: This pretty, wooded RV park on the Metolius River with an acre of riverfront lawn is world-famous for its fly fishing. Nearby recreation options include a golf course, swimming, boating, waterskiing, windsurfing, hiking and biking trails, a riding stable, and tennis courts. Winter activities range from alpine and nordic skiing to sledding, snowmobiling, and winter camping. There is a private bridge from the resort to Camp Sherman (campground number 8), and the towns of Sisters and Bend are nearby (15 miles and 35 miles, respectively).

❸ Allen Springs

Location: On the Metolius River in Deschutes National Forest; map D3, grid a0.

Campsites, facilities: There are four tent sites and 12 sites for tents, trailers, or RVs up to 22 feet long. Picnic tables and fire grills are provided. Vault toilets and piped water are available. A store, a cafe, a Laundromat, and ice are located within five miles. Leashed pets are permitted.

Reservations, fees: No reservations are accepted. Sites are $10 per night, plus $5 for each additional vehicle. The campground is open from May through September; there is no fee from October through April, when no water is available.

Contact: Deschutes National Forest, Sisters Ranger District, P.O. Box 249, Sisters, OR 97759; (541) 549-2111 or fax (541) 549-7746.

Directions: From Interstate 5 at Albany, turn east on U.S. 20 and drive approximately 87 miles. At the sign for Camp Sherman, turn north and drive about five miles. From Camp Sherman, travel five miles north on Forest Service Road 14 to the campground.

Trip notes: This campground is along the banks of the Metolius River, where fishing and hiking can be good. For an interesting side trip, head to the Wizard Falls Fish Hatchery about a mile away.

❹ Pioneer Ford

Location: On the Metolius River in Deschutes National Forest; map D3, grid a0.

Campsites, facilities: There are two tent sites and 18 sites for tents, trailers, or RVs up to 40 feet long. Piped water and fire grills are provided. Vault toilets and firewood are available. Leashed pets are permitted.

Reservations, fees: No reservations are accepted. Sites are $10 per night, plus $5 for each additional vehicle. The campground is open from April through September.

Contact: Deschutes National Forest, Sisters Ranger District, P.O. Box 249, Sisters, OR 97759; (541) 549-2111 or fax (541) 549-7746.

Directions: From Interstate 5 at Albany, turn east on U.S. 20 and drive approximately 87 miles. At the sign for Camp Sherman, turn north and drive about five miles. From Camp Sherman, travel approximately seven miles north on Forest Service Road 14 to the campground entrance.

Trip notes: This campground is along the banks of the Metolius River. See the trip notes for Camp Sherman (campground number 8) for recreation options.

⑤ Lower Bridge

Location: On the Metolius River in Deschutes National Forest; map D3, grid a0.

Campsites, facilities: There are 12 sites for tents, trailers, or RVs up to 22 feet long. Picnic tables and fire grills are provided. Vault toilets and piped water are available. Leashed pets are permitted.

Reservations, fees: No reservations are accepted. Sites are $10 per night, plus $5 for each additional vehicle. The campground is open year-round, with limited services and no fee in the off-season (October through March).

Contact: Deschutes National Forest, Sisters Ranger District, P.O. Box 249, Sisters, OR 97759; (541) 549-2111 or fax (541) 549-7746.

Directions: From Interstate 5 at Albany, turn east on U.S. 20 and drive approximately 87 miles. At the sign for Camp Sherman, turn north and drive about five miles. From Camp Sherman, travel nine miles north on Forest Service Road 14 to the entrance road to the campground.

Trip notes: This campground is set along the banks of the Metolius River. See the trip notes for Camp Sherman (campground number 8) for details about the area.

⑥ Perry South

Location: On Lake Billy Chinook in Deschutes National Forest; map D3, grid b1.

Campsites, facilities: There are four tent sites and 59 sites for tents, trailers, or RVs up to 40 feet long. Picnic tables and fire grills are provided. Hand-pumped water, vault toilets, boat docks, and launching facilities are available. Leashed pets are permitted.

Reservations, fees: No reservations are accepted. Sites are $9 per night, plus $5 for each additional vehicle. The campground is open from May through September.

Contact: Deschutes National Forest, Sisters Ranger District, P.O. Box 249, Sisters, OR 97759; (541) 549-2111 or fax (541) 549-7746.

Directions: From Interstate 5 at Albany, turn east on U.S. 20 and drive 100 miles to Sisters.

Continue 20 miles east on Highway 126 to Redmond, then turn north on U.S. 97 and drive about 10 miles to Culver. From Culver, drive 25 miles west and north on County Road 64 to the campground entrance.

Trip notes: This campground is set near the shore of the Metolius arm of Lake Billy Chinook. See the trip notes for KOA Madras/Culver and Crooked River Ranch RV Park (campground numbers 14 and 17) for recreation details. The lake borders the Warm Springs Indian Reservation.

⑦ Monty

Location: On the Metolius River in Deschutes National Forest; map D3, grid b1.

Campsites, facilities: There are 20 sites for tents, trailers, or RVs up to 22 feet long. Picnic tables and fire grills are provided. Firewood and vault toilets are available. There is no piped water. Boat docks and launching facilities are nearby at Perry South (campground number 6). Leashed pets are permitted.

Reservations, fees: No reservations are accepted. There is no fee. The campground is open from May through September.

Contact: Deschutes National Forest, Sisters Ranger District, P.O. Box 249, Sisters, OR 97759; (541) 549-2111 or fax (541) 549-7746.

Directions: From Interstate 5 at Albany, turn east on U.S. 20 and drive 100 miles to Sisters. Continue 20 miles east on Highway 126 to Redmond, then turn north on U.S. 97 and drive about 10 miles to Culver. From Culver, drive 30 miles west and north on County Road 64 to the campground entrance.

Trip notes: Trout fishing can be good at this remote campground along the banks of the Metolius River near where it empties into Lake Billy Chinook. Warm Springs Indian Reservation is across the river.

⑧ Camp Sherman

Location: On the Metolius River in Deschutes National Forest; map D3, grid b1.

Campsites, facilities: There are 15 sites for tents, trailers, or RVs up to 40 feet long. Picnic

tables and fire grills are provided. Vault toilets and piped water are available. Leashed pets are permitted.

Reservations, fees: No reservations are accepted. Sites are $10 per night, plus $5 for each additional vehicle. The campground is open year-round, with limited services and no fee in the off-season (October through March).

Contact: Deschutes National Forest, Sisters Ranger District, P.O. Box 249, Sisters, OR 97759; (541) 549-2111 or fax (541) 549-7746.

Directions: From Interstate 5 at Albany, turn east on U.S. 20 and drive approximately 87 miles. At the sign for Camp Sherman, turn north and drive about five miles. From the store in Camp Sherman, travel one-half mile north on Forest Service Road 1419 to the campground.

Trip notes: Camp Sherman is set along the banks of the Metolius River, where you can fish for wild trout. This place is for expert fly anglers seeking a quality fishing experience. It's advisable to obtain a map of the Deschutes National Forest that details back roads, trails, and streams. This is one of five camps in the immediate area.

❾ Allingham

Location: On the Metolius River in Deschutes National Forest; map D3, grid b1.

Campsites, facilities: There are 10 sites for tents, trailers, or RVs up to 40 feet long. Picnic tables and fire grills are provided. Vault toilets and piped water are available. Leashed pets are permitted.

Reservations, fees: No reservations are accepted. Sites are $10 per night, plus $5 for each additional vehicle. The campground is open from April through September.

Contact: Deschutes National Forest, Sisters Ranger District, P.O. Box 249, Sisters, OR 97759; (541) 549-2111 or fax (541) 549-7746.

Directions: From Interstate 5 at Albany, turn east on U.S. 20 and drive approximately 87 miles. At the sign for Camp Sherman, turn north and drive about five miles. From the store in Camp Sherman, travel one mile north to the campground.

Trip notes: This campground along the banks of the Metolius River is one of five camps in the immediate area. See the trip notes for Camp Sherman (campground number 8) for area details.

❿ Smiling River

Location: On the Metolius River in Deschutes National Forest; map D3, grid b1.

Campsites, facilities: There are 37 sites for tents, trailers, or RVs up to 22 feet long. A few sites can accommodate RVs up to 40 feet in length. Picnic tables and fire grills are provided. Vault toilets and piped water are available. Leashed pets are permitted.

Reservations, fees: No reservations are accepted. Sites are $10 per night, plus $5 for each additional vehicle. The campground is open from May through September.

Contact: Deschutes National Forest, Sisters Ranger District, P.O. Box 249, Sisters, OR 97759; (541) 549-2111 or fax (541) 549-7746.

Directions: From Interstate 5 at Albany, turn east on U.S. 20 and drive approximately 87 miles. At the sign for Camp Sherman, turn north and drive about five miles. From the store in Camp Sherman, travel one mile north to the campground.

Trip notes: Here's another camp along the banks of the Metolius River. See the trip notes for Camp Sherman (campground number 8) for more details.

⓫ Pine Rest

Location: On the Metolius River in Deschutes National Forest; map D3, grid b1.

Campsites, facilities: There are eight tent sites. Picnic tables and fire grills are provided. Vault toilets and piped water are available. Leashed pets are permitted.

Reservations, fees: No reservations are accepted. Sites are $10 per night, plus $5 for each additional vehicle. The campground is open from April through September.

Contact: Deschutes National Forest, Sisters Ranger District, P.O. Box 249, Sisters, OR 97759; (541) 549-2111 or fax (541) 549-7746.

Directions: From Interstate 5 at Albany, turn east on U.S. 20 and drive approximately 87 miles. At the sign for Camp Sherman, turn north and drive about five miles. From the store in Camp Sherman, travel 1.5 miles north to the campground.

Trip notes: This campground is set along the banks of the Metolius River. See the trip notes for Camp Sherman (campground number 8) for more information.

⑫ Gorge

Location: On the Metolius River in Deschutes National Forest; map D3, grid b1.

Campsites, facilities: There are 18 sites for tents, trailers, or RVs up to 22 feet long. Picnic tables and fire grills are provided. Vault toilets and piped water are available. Leashed pets are permitted.

Reservations, fees: No reservations are accepted. Sites are $10 per night, plus $5 for each additional vehicle. The campground is open from April through September.

Contact: Deschutes National Forest, Sisters Ranger District, P.O. Box 249, Sisters, OR 97759; (541) 549-2111 or fax (541) 549-7746.

Directions: From Interstate 5 at Albany, turn east on U.S. 20 and drive approximately 87 miles. At the sign for Camp Sherman, turn north and drive about five miles. From the store in Camp Sherman, travel two miles north to the camp.

Trip notes: Here is another of the camps set along the banks of the Metolius River. See the trip notes for Camp Sherman (campground number 8) for more details.

⑬ The Cove Palisades State Park

Location: On Lake Billy Chinook; map D3, grid b1.

Campsites, facilities: There are 95 tent sites and 178 sites with full or partial hookups for trailers or RVs up to 60 feet long, plus three cabins. Picnic tables and fire grills are provided. Flush toilets, sanitary services, show-

ers, firewood, a store, and ice are available. Some facilities are wheelchair accessible. Boat docks, launching facilities, and rentals are nearby. Leashed pets are permitted.

Reservations, fees: Contact Reservations Northwest at (800) 452-5687 ($6 reservation fee). Sites are $16–$20 per night; cabins are $45–$65 per night. The campground is open year-round.

Contact: Phone (800) 452-5687 or (541) 546-3412, or write to Route 1, P.O. Box 60 CP, Culver, OR 97734.

Directions: From Interstate 5 at Portland, turn east on U.S. 26 and drive 118 miles southeast to Madras. Turn south on U.S. 97 and drive nine miles to Culver, then head west on the entrance road for five miles.

Trip notes: This park is a mile away from the shore of Lake Billy Chinook, where some lakeshore cabins are available. Colorful rock formations rise from the canyon walls, and exceptional views can be had from the park. Swimming, fishing, hiking, and boating are just a few of your options here. Houseboats are available in the nearby marina.

⑭ KOA Madras/ Culver

Location: Near Lake Billy Chinook; map D3, grid b2.

Campsites, facilities: There are 31 tent sites and 68 drive-through sites for trailers or RVs of any length. Electricity, piped water, sewer hookups, and picnic tables are provided. Flush toilets, bottled gas, sanitary services, showers, firewood, a recreation hall, a store, a cafe, a laundry room, ice, a playground, and a swimming pool are available. Boat docks and launching facilities are nearby. Leashed pets and motorbikes are permitted.

Reservations, fees: Reservations are accepted; phone (800) 563-1992. Sites are $16–$21 per night. The campground is open year-round.

Contact: Phone (541) 546-3046 or write to 2435 Southwest Jericho Lane, Culver, OR 97734.

Directions: From Portland, turn east on U.S. 26 and drive 118 miles to Madras, then turn south on U.S. 97 and drive nine miles. Continue one-half mile east on Jericho Lane to the campground.

Trip notes: This campground is about three miles from Lake Billy Chinook, a steep-sided reservoir formed where the Crooked River, Metolius River, Deschutes River, and Squaw Creek all merge. Like much of the country east of the Cascades, this is a high desert area.

⓯ Haystack Reservoir

Location: On Haystack Reservoir in Crooked River National Grassland; map D3, grid b2.

Campsites, facilities: There are 24 sites for tents, trailers, or RVs up to 22 feet long. Picnic tables and fire grills are provided. Flush toilets and piped water are available. A store, a cafe, and ice are located within five miles. Boat docks, launching facilities, and rentals are nearby. Leashed pets are permitted.

Reservations, fees: No reservations are accepted. Sites are $8 per night, plus $3 for each additional vehicle. The campground is open from mid-May through September.

Contact: Crooked River National Grassland, 813 SW Highway 92, Madras, OR 97741; (541) 416-6640 or fax (514) 416-6694.

Directions: From Interstate 5 at Portland, turn east on Interstate 84 and drive 91 miles. Turn south on U.S. 97 and drive 90 miles to Madras. Continue south on U.S. 97 for nine miles, then turn southeast on County Road 100 and drive three miles. Turn north on Forest Service Road 96 and continue one-half mile to the campground.

Trip notes: This campground can be found along the shore of Haystack Reservoir, where waterskiing, swimming, and fishing are some of the recreation options. The camping and fishing crowds are relatively light.

⓰ Whistler Spring

Location: In Ochoco National Forest; map D3, grid b4.

Campsites, facilities: There is a large area for dispersed tent camping. A picnic table and

a vault toilet are provided. There is no piped water. Horses are welcome. Leashed pets are permitted.

Reservations, fees: No reservations are accepted. There is no fee. The campground is open from late May to late October.

Contact: Ochoco National Forest, Prineville Ranger District, P.O. Box 490, Prineville, OR 97754; (541) 416-6500.

Directions: From Prineville on U.S. 26, turn north on McKay Road and drive 12 miles, then drive 18 miles northeast on Forest Service Road 27. Turn south on Forest Service Road 2700-500 and drive one-quarter mile to the campground.

Trip notes: This is a trailhead camp for a trail heading into the Mill Creek Wilderness. The area is extremely popular with rock hounds, who search for thunder eggs, jasper, and agates (digging is forbidden in wilderness areas, however). Though primitive, this is a pretty camp that guarantees quiet and privacy.

⓱ Crooked River Ranch RV Park

Location: Near Smith Rock State Park; map D3, grid c0.

Campsites, facilities: There are 17 tent sites and 88 sites for trailers or RVs of any length; 15 are drive-throughs. Electricity, piped water, and sewer hookups are provided. Flush toilets, sanitary services, showers, a store, a cafe, laundry facilities, ice, a playground, and a swimming pool are available. Leashed pets are permitted.

Reservations, fees: Reservations are accepted. Sites are $11–$17 per night. The campground is open from April through October.

Contact: Phone (541) 923-1441, fax (541) 548-0278, or write to P.O. Box 1448, Crooked River Ranch, OR 97760.

Directions: From Interstate 5 at Albany, turn east on U.S. 20 and drive approximately 100 miles to Sisters. Turn east on Highway 126 and continue 20 miles to Redmond. Turn north on U.S. 97 and drive six miles, then turn west on Lower Bridge Road at Terrebonne and follow the signs for 7.5 miles.

Trip notes: This campground is a short distance from Smith Rock State Park, which contains unusual, colorful volcanic formations overlooking the Crooked River Canyon. Lake Billy Chinook to the north is a good spot for waterskiing and fishing for bass and panfish. The park has a basketball court and a softball field; nearby recreation options include a golf course and tennis courts.

18 Crystal Corral RV Park

Location: Near Ochoco Lake State Park; map D3, grid c4.

Campsites, facilities: There are 20 tent sites and 24 sites for trailers or RVs of any length. Electricity, piped water, and sewer hookups are provided. Flush toilets, bottled gas, showers, a store, a cafe, a laundry room, and ice are available. Boat docks, launching facilities, and rentals are nearby. Leashed pets (one per site) and motorbikes are permitted.

Reservations, fees: Reservations are accepted. Sites are $8–$16 per night. The campground is open year-round.

Contact: Phone (541) 447-5932 or write to 11777 NE Ochoco Highway, Prineville, OR 97754.

Directions: From Interstate 5 at Portland, turn east on U.S. 26 and drive approximately 147 miles to Prineville. Continue eight miles east on U.S. 26 to the park on the left.

Trip notes: This RV park isn't far from Ochoco Lake State Park, where boating and fishing are among the activities.

19 Ochoco Lake State Park

Location: On Ochoco Lake; map D3, grid c4.

Campsites, facilities: There are 22 primitive sites for tents, trailers, or self-contained RVs up to 30 feet long, and a special area for hikers and bicyclists. Picnic tables and fire grills are provided. Piped water, firewood, and flush toilets are available. Boat launching facilities are nearby. Leashed pets are permitted.

Reservations, fees: No reservations are accepted. Sites are $7–$14 per night, and $4 for hikers/bikers. The campground is open year-round.

Contact: Phone (800) 452-5687 or (541) 447-4363, or write to Prineville Reservoir Route, 916777 Parkland Drive, Prineville, OR 97754.

Directions: From Interstate 5 at Portland, turn east on U.S. 26 and drive approximately 147 miles to Prineville. Continue seven miles east on U.S. 26 to the park entrance.

Trip notes: This is one of the nicer camps along U.S. 26 in eastern Oregon. The state park is on the shore adjacent to Ochoco Lake, where boating and fishing are popular pastimes. Some quality hiking trails can be found in the area.

20 Lakeshore RV Park and Store

Location: On Ochoco Lake; map D3, grid c4.

Campsites, facilities: There are 19 sites for tents and 43 sites for trailers or RVs up to 45 feet long. Air-conditioning, electric heat, cable TV, rest rooms, showers, a sanitary dump, a public phone, limited groceries, ice, and RV supplies are available. Recreational facilities include a recreation hall, a playground, a marina, a boat dock, a ramp, and boat rentals. Some facilities are wheelchair accessible. Small leashed pets are permitted.

Reservations, fees: Reservations are recommended. Sites are $18 per night. The campground is open year-round.

Contact: Phone the park at (541) 447-6059, fax (541) 447-6059, or write to 12333 NE Ochoco Highway, Prineville, OR 97754.

Directions: From Interstate 5 at Portland, drive about 147 miles east on U.S. 26 to Prineville. Continue eight miles to the park on the left.

Trip notes: Set on grassy hills on beautiful Ochoco Lake, this park offers many recreational opportunities, including hunting, trout fishing, swimming, and boating. It's a more developed option to the nearby state park campground.

㉑ Wildcat

Location: On the East Fork of Mill Creek in Ochoco National Forest; map D3, grid c5.

Campsites, facilities: There are 17 sites for tents, trailers, or RVs up to 30 feet long. Picnic tables and fire grills are provided. Piped water and vault toilets are available. Leashed pets are permitted.

Reservations, fees: No reservations are accepted. Sites are $8 per night, plus $3 for each additional vehicle. The campground is open from mid-April to late October.

Contact: Ochoco National Forest, Prineville Ranger District, P.O. Box 490, Prineville, OR 97754; (541) 416-6500.

Directions: From Interstate 5 at Albany, take exit 233 and turn east on U.S. 20. Drive 74 miles, then turn east on Highway 126 and continue 65 miles to Prineville. Turn east on U.S. 26 and drive nine miles, then turn northeast on Forest Service Road 33 and continue about 10.5 miles to the campground.

Trip notes: This campground along the East Fork of Mill Creek is near a trailhead that provides access into the Mill Creek Wilderness. Stein's Pillar and Twin Pillars, popular rock climbing spots, are nearby. Ochoco Lake and Ochoco Lake State Park to the south provide side trip possibilities.

㉒ Walton Lake

Location: On Walton Lake in Ochoco National Forest; map D3, grid c6.

Campsites, facilities: There are 30 sites for tents, trailers, or RVs up to 31 feet long. Picnic tables and fire grills are provided. Piped water and vault toilets are available. Boat launching facilities are nearby. Leashed pets are permitted.

Reservations, fees: No reservations are accepted. Sites are $6 per night. The campground is open from June to late September.

Contact: Ochoco National Forest, Big Summit Ranger District, 348855 Ochoco Ranger District, Prineville, OR 97754-9612; (541) 416-6645.

Directions: From Interstate 5 at Albany, take exit 233 and turn east on U.S. 20. Drive 74 miles, then turn east on Highway 126 and continue 65 miles to Prineville. Go 16.5 miles east on U.S. 26, then 14 miles northeast on County Route 123. Turn north on Forest Service Road 23, proceed to the Ochoco Ranger Station, and go seven miles to the campground.

Trip notes: This campground is along the shore of Walton Lake, where fishing and swimming are popular; only boats without motors are allowed. Hikers can explore a nearby trail that leads south to Round Mountain.

㉓ Deep Creek

Location: On the North Fork of the Crooked River in Ochoco National Forest; map D3, grid c8.

Campsites, facilities: There are six sites for tents, trailers, or RVs up to 22 feet long. Picnic tables and fire grills are provided. Vault toilets are available, but there is no piped water. Leashed pets are permitted.

Reservations, fees: No reservations are accepted. There is no fee. The campground is open from June to mid-October.

Contact: Ochoco National Forest, Big Summit Ranger District, 348855 Ochoco Ranger District, Prineville, OR 97754-9612; (541) 416-6645.

Directions: From Interstate 5 at Albany, take exit 233 and turn east on U.S. 20. Drive 74 miles, then turn east on Highway 126 and continue southeast for 65 miles to Prineville. Continue 16.5 miles east on U.S. 26, then 8.5 miles northeast on County Route 23. Turn southeast on Forest Service Road 42 and drive 23.5 miles to the campground.

Trip notes: This camp is small and gets little use, but it's in a nice spot—the confluence of Deep Creek and the North Fork of the Crooked River. Highlights include pretty, shady sites and river access. Fishing is possible here.

㉔ Tumalo State Park

Location: On the Deschutes River; map D3, grid d0.

Campsites, facilities: There are 64 sites for tents, 21 sites with full hookups for trailers or RVs up to 44 feet long, a special camping area for hikers and bicyclists, and two tepees. Electricity, piped water, sewer hookups, fire grills, and picnic tables are provided. Flush toilets, showers, firewood, and a playground are available. A store, a cafe, and ice are located within one mile. Leashed pets are permitted.

Reservations, fees: Contact Reservations Northwest at (800) 452-5687 ($6 reservation fee). Sites are $9–$19 per night, and $4 for hikers/bikers. The campground is open year-round.

Contact: High Desert Management Unit, 62976 O.B. Riley Road, Bend, OR 97701; (800) 452-5687 or (541) 388-6055.

Directions: From Interstate 5 at Albany, turn east on U.S. 20 and drive approximately 117 miles to the park entrance (located five miles west of Bend). Drive one mile west to the campground on the left.

Trip notes: Trout fishing can be good at this camp along the banks of the Deschutes River. The swimming area is safe and ideal for schoolchildren, and boating is also an option here. See the trip notes for Bend Keystone RV Park (campground number 26) for more recreation information.

㉕ Scandia RV and Mobile Park

Location: Near the Deschutes River; map D3, grid d0.

Campsites, facilities: There are 60 sites for tents, trailers, or RVs of any length; seven are drive-throughs. Electricity, piped water, picnic tables, cable TV, and sewer hookups are provided. Flush toilets, showers, and a laundry room are available. Bottled gas, sanitary services, a store, a cafe, and ice are located within one mile. Leashed pets are permitted.

Reservations, fees: Reservations are accepted. Sites are $20 per night. The campground is open year-round.

Contact: Phone (541) 382-6206, fax (541) 382-4087, or write to 61415 South Highway 97, Bend, OR 97701.

Directions: From Interstate 5 at Albany, turn east on U.S. 20 and drive 122 miles to Bend. Travel one-half mile south of Bend on U.S. 97 and you'll see the trailer park entrance.

Trip notes: This park near the Deschutes River is close to a golf course, a stable, bike paths, and tennis courts. See the trip notes for Bend Keystone RV Park (campground number 26) for additional recreation information.

㉖ Bend Keystone RV Park

Location: Near the Deschutes River; map D3, grid e0.

Campsites, facilities: There are 29 sites for trailers or RVs of any length. Electricity, cable TV, piped water, and sewer hookups are provided. Flush toilets, showers, and a laundry room are available. Bottled gas, sanitary services, a store, a cafe, and ice are located within one mile. Cats are permitted.

Reservations, fees: Reservations are accepted. Sites are $16 per night. The campground is open year-round.

Contact: Phone (541) 382-2335 or write to 305 Northeast Burnside, Bend, OR 97701.

Directions: From Interstate 5 at Albany, turn east on U.S. 20 and drive 122 miles to Bend. Turn south on U.S. 97 and drive one-half mile to the turnoff for the park.

Trip notes: Bend is a popular spot to use as a home base. The 100-mile Deschutes Forest Highway Loop connects here. Several state parks are within an hour's drive, and several city-managed parks provide access to the Deschutes River. Good side trips include the Oregon High Desert Museum, just six miles south of Bend on U.S. 97. A few miles farther is the Lava River Cave and the Lava Butte Geological Area.

㉗ Bend Kampground

Location: Near Bend; map D3, grid d1.

Campsites, facilities: There are 40 tent sites and 74 sites for trailers or RVs of any length; 40 are drive-throughs. Piped water and picnic tables are provided. Electricity, sewer hookups, flush toilets, showers, a laundry room, a store, a deli, ice, firewood, a playground, a swimming pool, a recreation room, bottled gas, and a sanitary disposal station are available. Leashed pets are permitted.

Reservations, fees: Reservations are accepted. Sites are $16–$22 per night. The campground is open year-round.

Contact: Phone (541) 382-7738 or write to 63615 North Highway 97, Bend, OR 97701.

Directions: From Interstate 5 at Albany, turn east on U.S. 20 and drive 122 miles to Bend. Travel two miles north of Bend on U.S. 97 and you'll see the campground entrance.

Trip notes: Recreation options near this camp include a golf course, hiking trails, bike paths, and tennis courts. See the trip notes for Bend Keystone RV Park (campground number 26) for additional recreation information.

28 Prineville Reservoir Resort

Location: On Prineville Reservoir; map D3, grid d3.

Campsites, facilities: There are 71 sites for trailers or RVs of any length; four are drive-throughs. Electricity, piped water, fire pits, and picnic tables are provided. Flush toilets, bottled gas, sanitary disposal services, showers, firewood, a store, a cafe, a laundry room, and ice are available. Boat docks, launching facilities, and rentals are nearby. Leashed pets are permitted.

Reservations, fees: Reservations are accepted. Sites are $11–$17 per night. The campground is open from mid-March to mid-October, weather permitting.

Contact: Phone (541) 447-7468 or write to 1300 PLR, Prineville, OR 97754.

Directions: From Interstate 5 at Albany, turn east on U.S. 20 and drive 100 miles to Sisters. Turn east on Highway 126 and drive 39 miles to Prineville. Turn east on U.S. 26 and drive one mile, then drive one mile south on Combs Flat Road. The camp is 18 miles south on Juniper Canyon Road.

Trip notes: This resort is on the shore of Prineville Reservoir, a good spot for water sports and fishing. The mostly shaded sites are a combination of dirt and gravel, and there is easy access to the reservoir.

29 Prineville Reservoir State Park

Location: On Prineville Reservoir; map D3, grid d4.

Campsites, facilities: There are 25 tent sites and 75 sites with partial hookups for trailers or RVs up to 40 feet long. There are also three camper cabins. Electricity, piped water, sewer hookups, and picnic tables are provided. Flush toilets, showers, and firewood are available. Boat docks and launching facilities are nearby. Pets are permitted.

Reservations, fees: Reservations are accepted. Sites are $16–$20 per night. The campground is open year-round.

Contact: Phone (800) 452-5687 or (541) 447-4363, or write to 916777 Parkland Drive, Prineville, OR 97754.

Directions: From Interstate 5 at Portland, turn east on U.S. 26 and drive approximately 147 miles to Prineville. Continue one mile east on U.S. 26, then turn south on Combs Flat Road and drive one mile. Continue 16 miles southeast on Prineville Reservoir Road to the park.

Trip notes: This state park is set along the shore of Prineville Reservoir. Swimming, boating, fishing, and waterskiing are among the activities here. The nearby boat docks and ramp are a bonus. This is one of two campgrounds on the lake; the other is Prineville Reservoir Resort (RVs only), campground number 28.

30 Crown Villa RV Park

Location: Near Bend; map D3, grid e0.

Campsites, facilities: There are 124 sites for trailers or RVs of any length; 106 have full hookups and 18 have partial hookups. Electricity, piped water, sewer hookups, and picnic tables are provided. Flush toilets, showers, cable TV, a laundry room, bottled gas, ice, a sanitary disposal station, and a playground are available. A store and a cafe are located within one mile. Leashed pets are permitted.

Reservations, fees: Reservations are accepted. Sites are $17–$27 per night. The campground is open year-round.

Contact: Phone (541) 388-1131 or write to 60801 Brosterhous Road, Bend, OR 97702.

Directions: From Interstate 5 at Albany, turn east on U.S. 20 and drive 122 miles to Bend. Travel two miles south of Bend on U.S. 97, then head east on Brosterhous Road to the park at 60801 Brosterhous Road.

Trip notes: This RV park offers large, grassy sites. Nearby recreation options include horseback riding and golf. See the trip notes for Bend Keystone RV Park (campground number 26) for additional recreation information.

③ Swamp Wells Horse Camp

Location: Near the Arnold Ice Caves in Deschutes National Forest; map D3, grid e2.

Campsites, facilities: There are five primitive sites for tents, trailers, or RVs up to 22 feet long. Picnic tables and fire grills are provided. There is no piped water. Leashed pets are permitted.

Reservations, fees: No reservations are accepted. There is no fee. The campground is open from April to late November.

Contact: Deschutes National Forest, Bend-Fort Rock Ranger District, 1230 NE Third Street, Bend, OR 97701; (541) 388-5664 or fax (541) 383-5531.

Directions: From Interstate 5 at Albany, turn east on U.S. 20 and drive 122 miles to Bend. From Bend, travel 1.5 miles south on U.S. 97, then six miles east on Forest Service Road 18. The camp is five miles south on Forest Service Road 1810, then three miles southeast on 1816. You'll be traveling on a dirt road, but a well-marked one.

Trip notes: After looking at the map, this campground may appear to be quite remote, but it's actually in an area that has been heavily logged. This is a good place for horseback riding, and trails heading south reenter the forested areas. The system of lava tubes nearby at the Arnold Ice Caves is fun to explore. A Forest Service map details trail options.

③ Antelope Flat Reservoir

Location: On Antelope Flat Reservoir in Ochoco National Forest; map D3, grid e5.

Campsites, facilities: There are 25 sites for tents, trailers, or RVs up to 30 feet long. Picnic tables and fire grills are provided. Hand-pumped water and vault toilets are available. Boat launching facilities are nearby. Leashed pets are permitted.

Reservations, fees: No reservations are accepted. Sites are $8 per night, plus $3 for each additional vehicle. The campground is open from early May to late October.

Contact: Ochoco National Forest, Prineville Ranger District, P.O. Box 490, Prineville, OR 97754; (541) 416-6500.

Directions: From Interstate 5 at Albany, take exit 233 and turn east on U.S. 20. Drive 74 miles, then turn east on Highway 126 and continue southeast for 65 miles to Prineville. Turn south on County Road 380 and drive 30 miles southeast, then 11 miles south on Forest Service Road 17. The camp is 300 yards east on Forest Service Road 1700-600.

Trip notes: This pretty spot along the west shore of Antelope Flat Reservoir has wide sites and easy access to the lake. Fishing can be good, and boating with motors is permitted. This is also a good lake for canoes.

③ Double Cabin

Location: On Double Cabin Creek in Ochoco National Forest; map D3, grid e6.

Campsites, facilities: There are five sites for tents, trailers, or small RVs. Picnic tables, fire grills, and a vault toilet are provided. There is no piped water. Leashed pets are permitted.

Reservations, fees: No reservations are accepted. There is no fee. The campground is open from mid-May to late October.

Contact: Ochoco National Forest, Prineville Ranger District, P.O. Box 490, Prineville, OR 97754; (541) 416-6500.

Directions: From Interstate 5 at Albany, take exit 233 and turn east on U.S. 20. Drive 74 miles, then turn east on Highway 126 and continue southeast for 65 miles to Prineville. Turn south on County Road 380 and drive 30 miles southeast, then turn south on Forest Service Road 17 and drive 10 miles. Turn east on Forest Service Road 16 and drive five miles, then turn north on Forest Service Road 1600-350 and drive one-quarter mile to the campground.

Trip notes: This primitive camp is close to some nice side trips. For one, go back to Forest Service Road 16 and travel one-quarter mile farther up the road to beautiful little Double Cabin Pond. You'll pass old beaver dams on the way. Hikers can enjoy breathtaking views by trudging up the ridge to the north of the camp.

㉞ Elkhorn

Location: Near Drake Creek in Ochoco National Forest; map D3, grid e6.

Campsites, facilities: There are four sites for tents, trailers, or small RVs. Picnic tables, fire grills, and a vault toilet are provided. There is no piped water. Leashed pets are permitted.

Reservations, fees: No reservations are accepted. There is no fee. The campground is open from mid-May to late October.

Contact: Ochoco National Forest, Prineville Ranger District, P.O. Box 490, Prineville, OR 97754; (541) 416-6500.

Directions: From Interstate 5 at Albany, take exit 233 and turn east on U.S. 20. Drive 74 miles, then turn east on Highway 126 and continue southeast for 65 miles to Prineville. Turn south on County Road 380 and drive 34 miles, then go five miles southeast on Forest Service Road 16 to the campground.

Trip notes: Set near Drake Creek and Miller Lake, this wooded camp is an alternative to Wiley Flat (campground number 35). The area is popular for rockhounding, with moss agates the most sought-after stones. A designated collecting area is three-quarters of a mile north on Forest Service Road 1690, about 1.5 miles west of Elkhorn Campground.

㉟ Wiley Flat

Location: On Wiley Creek in Ochoco National Forest; map D3, grid e6.

Campsites, facilities: There are five sites for tents, trailers, or RVs up to 30 feet long. Picnic tables and fire grills are provided. Vault toilets are available, but there is no piped water. Leashed pets are permitted.

Reservations, fees: No reservations are accepted. There is no fee. The campground is open from mid-June to late October.

Contact: Ochoco National Forest, Prineville Ranger District, P.O. Box 490, Prineville, OR 97754; (541) 416-6500.

Directions: From Interstate 5 at Albany, take exit 233 and turn east on U.S. 20. Drive 74 miles, then turn east on Highway 126 and continue southeast for 65 miles to Prineville. Turn south on County Road 380 and drive 34 miles, then go 10 miles southeast on Forest Service Road 16. The camp is one mile west on Forest Service Road 1600-400.

Trip notes: This campground is set along Wiley Creek in a nice, hidden spot with minimal crowds. A map of Ochoco National Forest details nearby access roads. A good gut-thumping hike is the trip to Tower Point Lookout. It's one mile north of the camp—and a 1,000-foot climb straight up. Double Cabin (campground number 33) provides a nearby, but more primitive, alternative.

㊱ Paulina Lake

Location: On Paulina Lake in Deschutes National Forest; map D3, grid e0.

Campsites, facilities: There are 69 sites for trailers or RVs up to 30 feet long. Picnic tables and fire grills are provided. Flush toilets, showers, and a laundromat are located within five miles. Piped water is available. Boat docks, launching facilities, and rentals are nearby. Leashed pets are permitted.

Reservations, fees: No reservations are accepted. Sites are $11–$13 per night, plus $3–$5 for each additional vehicle. The campground is open from late May to late October.

Contact: Deschutes National Forest, Bend-Fort Rock Ranger District, 1230 NE Third Street, Bend, OR 97701; (541) 388-5664 or fax (541) 383-5531.

Directions: From Interstate 5 south of Eugene, take exit 188 and turn east on Highway 58. Drive 86 miles, then turn north on U.S. 97 and drive 26 miles to LaPine. Continue five miles northeast, then go 13 miles east on County Road 21 to the campground.

Trip notes: This campground is set along the south shore of Paulina Lake at 6,300 feet. The recreation options here include boating, sailing, fishing, and hiking. Nearby trails provide access to the remains of volcanic activity, including craters and obsidian flows.

㊲ Chief Paulina Horse Camp

Location: On Paulina Lake in Deschutes National Forest; map D3, grid f1.

Campsites, facilities: There are 14 sites for tents, trailers, or RVs up to 30 feet long. Picnic tables and fire grills are provided. Piped water and vault toilets are available. Boat docks and rentals are nearby. Leashed pets are permitted.

Reservations, fees: Reservations are required. Sites are $11 per night, plus $3–$5 per additional vehicle. The entire camp can be reserved for $45 a night. The campground is open from late May to late October, weather permitting.

Contact: Deschutes National Forest, Bend-Fort Rock Ranger District, 1230 NE Third Street, Bend, OR 97701; (541) 388-5664 or fax (541) 383-5531.

Directions: From Interstate 5 south of Eugene, take exit 188 and turn east on Highway 58. Drive 86 miles, then turn north on U.S. 97 and drive 26 miles to LaPine. Continue five miles northeast, then go 15 miles east on County Road 21 to the campground.

Trip notes: This campground is near the south shore of Paulina Lake. Horse trails and a vista point are close by. See the trip notes for Paulina Lake (campground number 36) for additional recreation information.

㊳ Little Crater

Location: Near Paulina Lake in Deschutes National Forest; map D3, grid f1.

Campsites, facilities: There are 50 sites for tents, trailers, or RVs up to 30 feet long. Picnic tables and fire grills are provided. Piped water and vault toilets are available. Boat docks, launching facilities, and rentals are nearby. Leashed pets are permitted.

Reservations, fees: No reservations are accepted. Sites are $11–$13 per night, plus $3–$5 per additional vehicle. The campground is open from late May to late October.

Contact: Deschutes National Forest, Bend-Fort Rock Ranger District, 1230 NE Third Street, Bend, OR 97701; (541) 388-5664 or fax (541) 383-5531.

Directions: From Interstate 5 south of Eugene, take exit 188 and turn east on Highway 58. Drive 86 miles, then turn north on U.S. 97 and drive 26 miles to LaPine. Continue five miles northeast, then go 15 miles east on County Road 21 to the campground.

Trip notes: This campground is near the east shore of Paulina Lake in Newberry Crater, a caldera. See the trip notes for Paulina Lake (campground number 36) for more information.

㊴ Cinder Hill

Location: On East Lake in Deschutes National Forest; map D3, grid f1.

Campsites, facilities: There are 110 sites for tents, trailers, or RVs up to 30 feet long. Picnic tables and fire grills are provided. Piped water and flush and vault toilets are available. Boat docks, launching facilities, and rentals are nearby. Leashed pets are permitted.

Reservations, fees: No reservations are accepted. Sites are $11–$13 per night, plus $3–$5 per additional vehicle. The campground is open from late May to late October.

Contact: Deschutes National Forest, Bend-Fort Rock Ranger District, 1230 NE Third Street, Bend, OR 97701; (541) 388-5664 or fax (541) 383-5531.

Directions: From Interstate 5 south of Eugene, take exit 188 and turn east on Highway 58. Drive 86 miles, then turn north on U.S. 97 and drive 26 miles to LaPine. Continue five miles northeast, then go 18 miles east on County Road 21 to the campground.

Trip notes: This campground can be found along the northeast shore of East Lake at an elevation of 6,400 feet. Boating, fishing, and hiking are among the recreation options here.

⑳ East Lake

Location: On East Lake in Deschutes National Forest; map D3, grid f1.

Campsites, facilities: There are 29 sites for tents, trailers, or RVs up to 30 feet long. Picnic tables and fire grills are provided. Piped water and flush and vault toilets are available. Boat docks, launching facilities, and rentals are nearby. Leashed pets are permitted.

Reservations, fees: No reservations are accepted. Sites are $11–$13 per night, plus $3–$5 per additional vehicle. The campground is open from late May to late October.

Contact: Deschutes National Forest, Bend-Fort Rock Ranger District, 1230 NE Third Street, Bend, OR 97701; (541) 388-5664 or fax (541) 383-5531.

Directions: From Interstate 5 south of Eugene, take exit 188 and turn east on Highway 58. Drive 86 miles, then turn north on U.S. 97 and drive 26 miles to LaPine. Continue five miles northeast, then go 17 miles east on County Road 21 to the campground.

Trip notes: This campground is set along the south shore of East Lake. Boating and fishing are popular here, and hiking trails provide access to signs of former volcanic activity in the area.

㊶ Hot Springs

Location: Near East Lake in Deschutes National Forest; map D3, grid f1.

Campsites, facilities: There are 42 sites for tents, trailers, or RVs up to 30 feet long. Picnic tables and fire grills are provided. Piped water and vault toilets are available. Boat docks, launching facilities, and rentals are nearby. Leashed pets are permitted.

Reservations, fees: No reservations are accepted. Sites are $11–$13 per night, plus $3–$5 per additional vehicle. The campground is open from late May to late October.

Contact: Deschutes National Forest, Bend-Fort Rock Ranger District, 1230 NE Third Street, Bend, OR 97701; (541) 388-5664 or fax (541) 383-5531.

Directions: From Interstate 5 south of Eugene, take exit 188 and turn east on Highway 58. Drive 86 miles, then turn north on U.S. 97 and drive 26 miles to LaPine. Continue five miles northeast, then go 17.5 miles east on County Road 21 to the campground.

Trip notes: This campground lies across the road from East Lake. See the trip notes for East Lake (campground number 40) for additional recreation information.

㊷ East Lake Resort and RV Park

Location: On East Lake; map D3, grid f1.

Campsites, facilities: There are 32 sites for tents, trailers, or RVs of any length. Electricity, piped water, and picnic tables are provided. Flush toilets, bottled gas, showers, barbecues, firewood, a store, a cafe, a laundry room, ice, boat launching facilities, boat rentals, and a playground are available. A dump station is nearby. Leashed pets are permitted.

Reservations, fees: Reservations are accepted. Sites are $15 per night. The campground is open from mid-May to mid-October, weather permitting.

Contact: Phone (541) 536-2230 or write to P.O. Box 95, LaPine, OR 97739.

Directions: From Interstate 5 south of

Eugene, take exit 188 and turn east on Highway 58. Drive 86 miles, then turn north on U.S. 97 and drive 26 miles to LaPine. Continue six miles northeast, then go 18 miles east on East Lake–Paulina Lake Road, which deadends at the campground.

Trip notes: This resort is in a wooded, mountainous setting with shaded sites on the east shore of East Lake. Opportunities for fishing, boating, and swimming abound.

43 China Hat

Location: In Deschutes National Forest; map D3, grid f2.

Campsites, facilities: There are 14 sites for tents, trailers, or RVs up to 30 feet long. Picnic tables and fire grills are provided. Vault toilets are available. There is no piped water. Leashed pets are permitted.

Reservations, fees: No reservations are accepted. There is no fee. The campground is open from May to late October, weather permitting.

Contact: Deschutes National Forest, Bend-Fort Rock Ranger District, 1230 NE Third Street, Bend, OR 97701; (541) 388-5664 or fax (541) 383-5531.

Directions: From Interstate 5 south of Eugene, take exit 188 and go east on Highway 58. Drive 86 miles, then turn north on U.S. 97 and drive 26 miles to LaPine. Drive east on Forest Service Road 22 for about 30 miles, then north for six miles on Forest Service Road 18.

Trip notes: This remote campground is set at 5,100 feet in a rugged, primitive area. Hunters use it as a base camp in the fall. Hiking and bird-watching opportunities are a highlight.

44 Cabin Lake

Location: In Deschutes National Forest; map D3, grid f2.

Campsites, facilities: There are 14 sites for tents, trailers, or RVs up to 30 feet long. Picnic tables and fire grills are provided. Vault toilets are available. There is no piped water. Leashed pets are permitted.

Reservations, fees: No reservations are accepted. There is no fee. The campground is open from mid-May to late October.

Contact: Deschutes National Forest, Bend-Fort Rock Ranger District, 1230 NE Third Street, Bend, OR 97701; (541) 388-5664 or fax (541) 383-5531.

Directions: From Interstate 5 south of Eugene, take exit 188 and turn east on Highway 58. Drive 86 miles, then turn north on U.S. 97 and drive 26 miles to LaPine. Continue about 30 miles east on Forest Service Road 22, then south on Forest Service Road 18 for six miles to the campground.

Trip notes: This remote campground set at 4,500 feet is adjacent to an 80-plus-year-old bird blind—a great place to watch birds. The spot is primitive and secluded, receiving little use even in the busy summer months.

Map D4

One inch equals approximately 20 miles.

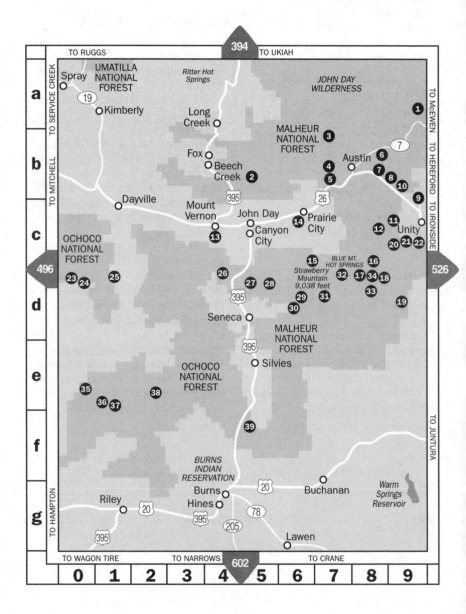

Chapter D4 features:

---

① McCully Forks

Location: On McCully Creek in Wallowa-Whitman National Forest; map D4, grid a9.

Campsites, facilities: There are six tent sites. Picnic tables and fire grills are provided. Vault toilets are available. There is no piped water. Leashed pets are permitted.

Reservations, fees: No reservations are accepted. There is no fee. The campground is open from late May to late October.

Contact: Wallowa-Whitman National Forest, Baker Ranger District, P.O. Box 907, Baker City, OR 97814; (541) 523-4476 or fax (541) 523-1965.

Directions: From Interstate 84 at Baker City, travel southwest on Highway 7 to the 410 junction. Turn right and travel six miles northwest on Highway 410. The campground is located three miles past Sumpter.

Trip notes: Here's an easy-access campground along the banks of McCully Creek that's tiny, free, and primitive. Recreational gold-panning is allowed in the creek (within the campground only). The camp gets moderately heavy use and is often full on weekends.

② Magone Lake

Location: On Magone Lake in Malheur National Forest; map D4, grid b5.

Campsites, facilities: There three sites for tents and 18 sites for trailers or RVs up to 16 feet long; four are drive-throughs. There is a separate group camping site designed for six families and a picnic shelter that can accommodate 50 to 100 people. Some facilities are wheelchair accessible, including two of the campsites. Picnic tables and fire grills are provided. Piped water, composting toilets, a boat ramp, and a beach area are available. Boat docks and launching facilities are nearby. Leashed pets are permitted.

Reservations, fees: No reservations are required, except for the group site and picnic shelter; call the ranger district for current fees. The campground is open from May through November, weather permitting.

Contact: Malheur National Forest, Long Creek Ranger District, P.O. Box 849, John Day, OR 97845; (541) 575-2110 or fax (541) 575-3001.

Directions: From John Day, travel eight miles west on U.S. 26, then drive nine miles north on U.S. 395. Turn northeast on Forest Service Road 36 and drive eight miles. The camp is two miles north on Forest Service Road 3618.

Trip notes: This campground is set along the shore of little Magone Lake. A 1.8-mile trail rings the lake, and the portion extending from the beach area to the campground (about a quarter mile) is barrier-free. A half-mile trail is routed to Magone Slide, an unusual geological formation. See a Forest Service map for other trails in the area. Swimming, fishing, sailing, and canoeing are some of the popular activities at this lake. An easy-access bike trail can be found within a quarter mile of the campground.

❸ Olive Lake

Location: On Olive Lake in Umatilla National Forest; map D4, grid b7.

Campsites, facilities: There are 24 sites for tents, trailers, or RVs up to 31 feet long (four can handle up to 45 feet). Vault toilets are available, but there is no piped water. Picnic tables and fire grills are provided. Boat docks and launching facilities are available. Leashed pets are permitted.

Reservations, fees: No reservations are accepted. There is no fee; the stay limit is 14 days. The campground is open from June to mid-October, weather permitting.

Contact: Umatilla National Forest, North Fork John Day Ranger District, P.O. Box 158, Ukiah, OR 97880; (541) 427-3231 or fax (541) 276-5026.

Directions: From Pendleton on Interstate 84, turn south on U.S. 395 and drive 62 miles to Forest Service Road 55 (one mile north of Dale). Turn right and drive one-half mile, then turn right on Forest Service Road 10 and continue for 26 miles to the park on the right.

Trip notes: This campground is set at 6,100 feet along the shore of Olive Lake, located between two sections of the North Fork John Day Wilderness. Nearby trails provide access to the wilderness. Motorbikes and mountain bikes are not permitted there.

❹ Middle Fork

Location: On the Middle Fork of the John Day River in Malheur National Forest; map D4, grid b7.

Campsites, facilities: There are 10 sites for tents, trailers, or RVs up to 20 feet long. Picnic tables and fire grills are provided. Vault toilets are available. There is no piped water. Leashed pets are permitted.

Reservations, fees: No reservations are accepted. There is no fee. The campground is open from May through November, weather permitting.

Contact: Malheur National Forest, Long Creek Ranger District, P.O. Box 849, John Day, OR 97845; (541) 575-2110 or fax (541) 575-3001.

Directions: From Prairie City on U.S. 26, travel 15 miles northeast on U.S. 26, then one mile north on Highway 7 to its junction with County Road 20. The camp is five miles northwest on County Road 20.

Trip notes: Scattered along the banks of the Middle Fork of the John Day River, this rustic spot is easy to reach off a paved road. Besides wildlife-watching and berry picking, the main activity at this camp is fishing, so bring along your fly rod.

❺ Dixie

Location: Near Dixie Summit in Malheur National Forest; map D4, grid b7.

Campsites, facilities: There are 11 sites for tents, trailers, or RVs up to 20 feet long. Picnic tables, vault toilets, and fire grills are provided. Hand-pumped well water is available. A store, a cafe, gas, and ice are available within six miles. Leashed pets are permitted.

Reservations, fees: No reservations are accepted. There is no fee. The campground is open from May through November, weather permitting.

Contact: Malheur National Forest, Long Creek Ranger District, P.O. Box 849, John Day, OR 97845; (541) 575-2110 or fax (541) 575-3001.

Directions: From Prairie City on U.S. 26, travel 11 miles northeast on U.S. 26, then one-half mile north on Forest Service Road 365 to the campground.

Trip notes: This campground is set at Dixie Summit (elevation 5,300 feet) near Bridge Creek, where you can toss in a fishing line. The camp is just off U.S. 26, close enough to provide easy access.

⑥ Antlers Guard Station

Location: On the North Fork of the Burnt River in Wallowa-Whitman National Forest; map D4, grid b8.

Campsites, facilities: There is one four-bed cabin. Picnic tables and fire grills are provided. Piped water and vault toilets are available. Leashed pets are permitted.

Reservations, fees: No reservations are accepted. There is no fee. It's open from May to mid-September.

Contact: Wallowa-Whitman National Forest, Unity Ranger District, P.O. Box 907, Baker City, OR 97814; (541) 448-3351 or fax (541) 523-1479.

Directions: From Interstate 84 at Pendleton, take exit 304, turn south (left) on Highway 7, and drive 20 miles to Whitney. Turn south on County Road 529 and drive three miles along the North Fork of the Burnt River to the cabin site.

Trip notes: This spot is just off U.S. 26 and is a staging site for ATV trails.

⑦ Oregon

Location: Near Austin Junction in Wallowa-Whitman National Forest; map D4, grid b8.

Campsites, facilities: There are 11 sites for tents, trailers, or RVs up to 28 feet long. Picnic tables and fire grills are provided. Piped water and vault toilets are available. Leashed pets are permitted.

Reservations, fees: No reservations are accepted. There is no fee. The campground is open from May to mid-September.

Contact: Wallowa-Whitman National Forest, Unity Ranger District, P.O. Box 907, Baker City, OR 97814; (541) 448-3351 or fax (541) 523-1479.

Directions: From Interstate 84 at Pendleton, take Baker City exit 304 and drive 32 miles on Highway 7 to Austin Junction. Turn east on U.S. 26 and drive 20 miles to the campground.

Trip notes: This campground is just off U.S. 26 and is a staging site for ATV trails.

⑧ Yellow Pine

Location: On Road Creek in Wallowa-Whitman National Forest; map D4, grid b8.

Campsites, facilities: There are 21 sites for tents, trailers, or RVs up to 28 feet long. Picnic tables and fire grills are provided. Piped water, a waste disposal station, and vault toilets are available. Leashed pets are permitted.

Reservations, fees: No reservations are accepted. There is no fee. The campground is open from late May to mid-September.

Contact: Wallowa-Whitman National Forest, Unity Ranger District, P.O. Box 907, Baker City, OR 97814; (541) 448-3351 or fax (541) 523-1479.

Directions: From Interstate 84 at Pendleton, take exit 209 and turn south on U.S. 395. Drive 120 miles, then turn east on U.S. 26 and drive 47 miles to the campground (11 miles northwest of Unity).

Trip notes: Highlights of this camp include easy access and good recreation potential, including hiking trails. One half-mile-long, wheelchair-accessible trail connects to the preceding camp.

⑨ Unity Lake State Recreation Site

Location: On Unity Reservoir; map D4, grid b9.

Campsites, facilities: There are 21 sites with water and electrical hookups for tents or RVs up to 60 feet long, and a separate area for hikers and bicyclists. Picnic tables and fire grills are provided. Piped water, flush toilets, showers, a sanitary disposal station, and firewood are available. Some facilities are wheelchair accessible. Boat docks and launching facilities are nearby. Leashed pets are permitted.

Reservations, fees: No reservations are accepted. Sites are $15–$20 per night, and $4 for hikers/bikers. The campground is open from mid-April to late October.

Contact: Phone (800) 452-5687 or (541) 575-2773, or write to P.O. Box 9 Canyon City, OR 97820.

Directions: From Pendleton on Interstate 84, take exit 209 and turn south on U.S. 395. Drive 120 miles, then turn east on U.S. 26 and drive 56 miles. Turn north (left) on Highway 245 and drive three miles to the park on the left.

Trip notes: This easy-to-reach camp along the east shore of Unity Reservoir is a popular spot when the weather is good. Campers can choose from hiking, swimming, boating, fishing, picnicking, or enjoying the scenic views.

⑩ Wetmore

Location: On the Middle Fork of the Burnt River in Wallowa-Whitman National Forest; map D4, grid b9.

Campsites, facilities: There are 16 sites for tents, trailers, or RVs up to 28 feet long. Picnic tables and fire grills are provided. Piped water, firewood, and vault toilets are available. Some facilities are wheelchair accessible. Leashed pets are permitted.

Reservations, fees: No reservations are accepted. There is no fee. The campground is open from late May to mid-September.

Contact: Wallowa-Whitman National Forest, Unity Ranger District, P.O. Box 907, Baker City, OR 97814; (541) 448-3351 or fax (541) 523-1479.

Directions: From Interstate 84 at Pendleton, take exit 209 and turn south on U.S. 395. Drive 120 miles, then turn east on U.S. 26 and drive 48 miles to the campground (10 miles northwest of Unity).

Trip notes: This campground near the Middle Fork of the Burnt River is a nice base camp for a fishing or hiking trip. The stream can provide good trout fishing. Trails are detailed on a map of Wallowa-Whitman National Forest. In addition, an excellent half-mile, wheelchair-accessible trail passes through old-growth forest.

⑪ Amelia

Location: Near Table Rock Lookout in Wallowa-Whitman National Forest; map D4, grid b8.

Campsites, facilities: There are four sites for tents, trailers, or RVs up to 28 feet long. Picnic tables and fire grills are provided. A vault toilet is available. Leashed pets are permitted.

Reservations, fees: No reservations are accepted. There is no fee. The campground is open from May to mid-September.

Contact: Wallowa-Whitman National Forest, Unity Ranger District, P.O. Box 907, Baker City, OR 97814; (541) 448-3351 or fax (541) 523-1479.

Directions: From Interstate 84 at Pendleton, take exit 304 and drive 32 miles on Highway 7 to Austin Junction. Turn east on U.S. 26 and drive 23 miles to Unity. Turn west on Highway 600, then turn left on Forest Service Road 6005 and left again on Forest Service Road 6010. Drive to the wilderness trail sign and the campground. (Forest Service Road 6010 is very narrow and rough.)

Trip notes: A trail leads from camp to the Monument Rock Wilderness and is closed to motorized and mechanized vehicles. This difficult 2.6-mile trail is for hikers and horseback riders. Scenic areas on the route are Mine Ridge, Bullrun Rock, and Bullrun Mountain.

⑫ Table Rock

Location: Near Table Rock Lookout in Wallowa-Whitman National Forest; map D4, grid b8.

Campsites, facilities: There are four sites for tents, trailers, or RVs up to 28 feet long. Picnic tables and fire grills are provided. A vault toilet is available. Leashed pets are permitted.

Reservations, fees: No reservations are accepted. There is no fee. The campground is open from May to mid-September.

Contact: Wallowa-Whitman National Forest, Unity Ranger District, P.O. Box 907, Baker City, OR 97814; (541) 448-3351 or fax (541) 523-1479.

Directions: From Pendleton on Interstate 84, take Baker City exit 304 and drive 32 miles on Highway 7 to Austin Junction. Turn east on U.S. 26 and drive 23 miles to Unity. Turn west on Highway 600 and take, in succession, Forest Service Roads 6005, 6010, 6005.030, 6005.035, and 6005.045 to the wilderness trail sign and the campground. (Note that these roads are primitive and narrow. From Unity, it's about 10 miles to the campground. A Forest Service map is recommended.)

Trip notes: Table Rock Campground has a trail that leads from camp to the Monument Rock Wilderness and is closed to motorized and mechanized vehicles. This difficult 2.2-mile trail is for hikers and horseback riders. Scenic areas on the route are the Elkhorn Range, the Greenhorn Range, Deardorf Mountain, Glacier Mountain, and the Strawberry Mountain Range.

⑬ Clyde Holliday State Recreation Site

Location: Near the John Day River; map D4, grid c4.

Campsites, facilities: There are 30 sites for trailers or RVs up to 60 feet long. Electricity, picnic tables, and fire grills are provided. Piped water, firewood, sanitary disposal services, showers, and flush toilets are available. Some facilities are wheelchair accessible. Leashed pets are permitted.

Reservations, fees: No reservations are accepted. Sites are $14–$19 per night. The campground is open from March through November.

Contact: Phone (800) 452-5687 or (541) 575-2773, or write to P.O. Box 9, Canyon City, OR 97820.

Directions: From John Day at the intersection of U.S. 395 and U.S. 26, travel seven miles west on U.S. 26 to the park on the left.

Trip notes: This state park near the John Day River is a popular fishing spot, with river access for visitors. In John Day, don't miss Kam Wah Chung, a Chinese herbalist's office from the 1880s that's now a museum administered by the state Parks Department.

⑭ Depot Park

Location: On the John Day River; map D4, grid c6.

Campsites, facilities: There are 20 sites for tents, trailers, or RVs up to 35 feet. Rest rooms, showers, a sanitary dump, and a public phone are provided. Leashed pets are permitted.

Reservations, fees: No reservations are accepted. Sites are $13 per night. The campground is open from May 1 to October 31.

Contact: Prairie City Hall, P.O. Box 370, Prairie City, OR 97869; (541) 820-3605.

Directions: From the junction of U.S. 26 and Main Street in Prairie City, drive south on Main Street for one-half mile to the park (signed).

Trip notes: This urban park on grassy flatlands has access to the John Day River, a good trout fishing spot. The camp is a more developed alternative to the many Forest Service campgrounds in the area. Nearby attractions include the Strawberry Mountain Wilderness (prime hiking trails) and Clyde Holliday State Recreation Site.

⑮ Strawberry

Location: On Strawberry Creek in Malheur National Forest; map D4, grid c7.

Campsites, facilities: There are 11 sites for tents. Picnic tables and fire grills are provided. Piped water and vault toilets are available. Leashed pets are permitted.

Reservations, fees: No reservations are accepted. Call the ranger district for current fee information. The campground is open from June to mid-October.

Contact: Malheur National Forest, Prairie City Ranger District, P.O. Box 337, Prairie City, OR 97869; (541) 820-3311 or fax (541) 820-4503.

Directions: From John Day at the intersection of U.S. 395 and U.S. 26, travel 13 miles east on U.S. 26. Drive one-half mile southeast on County Road 62 to County Road 60. Turn south on County Road 60, drive 8.5 miles to Forest Service Road 6001, and then drive 2.5 miles to the campground on the left.

Trip notes: This campground is set along the

banks of Strawberry Creek at 5,700 feet in elevation. Nearby trails provide access to the Strawberry Mountain Wilderness, Strawberry Lake, and Strawberry Falls. It's a pretty area with hiking and hunting options. Fishing in Strawberry Creek is another possibility.

⑯ Elk Creek

Location: On Elk Creek in Malheur National Forest; map D4, grid c8.

Campsites, facilities: There are five tent sites. Picnic tables and fire grills are provided. Vault toilets are available. There is no piped water. Leashed pets are permitted.

Reservations, fees: No reservations are accepted. There is no fee. The campground is open from mid-May to mid-November.

Contact: Malheur National Forest, Prairie City Ranger District, P.O. Box 337, Prairie City, OR 97869; (541) 820-3311 or fax (541) 820-4503.

Directions: From Pendleton on Interstate 84, take exit 209 and turn south on U.S. 395. Drive 120 miles, then turn east on U.S. 26 and drive 21 miles to Prairie City. Turn southeast on County Road 62 and drive 8.5 miles, then travel 16 miles southeast on Forest Service Road 13. The camp is 1.5 miles south on Forest Service Road 16.

Trip notes: This tiny, pretty camp at the confluence of the North and South Forks of Elk Creek (elevation 5,000 feet) has lots of hunting and fishing opportunities. It's advisable to obtain a map of Malheur National Forest that details the backcountry roads. North Fork Malheur (campground number 33) is an alternate camp in the area.

⑰ Mammoth

Location: On the South Fork of the Burnt River in Wallowa-Whitman National Forest; map D4, grid c8.

Campsites, facilities: There are two sites for tents, trailers, or RVs up to 28 feet long. Picnic tables and fire grills are provided. Vault toilets are available. Leashed pets are permitted.

Reservations, fees: No reservations are accepted. There is no fee. The campground is open from May to mid-September.

Contact: Wallowa-Whitman National Forest, Unity Ranger District, P.O. Box 907, Baker City, OR 97814; (541) 448-3351 or fax (541) 523-1479.

Directions: From Pendleton on Interstate 84, take Baker City exit 304 and drive 32 miles on Highway 7 to Austin Junction. Turn east on U.S. 26 and drive 23 miles to Unity. Turn west on Highway 600, west again on Forest Service Road 6005, and west a final time on Forest Service Road 2640. (The camp is nine miles from Unity.)

Trip notes: The South Fork of the Burnt River is a nice trout creek with, according to the local ranger, "good evening bites for anglers who know how to sneak-fish." The camp is private and scenic.

⑱ Long Creek

Location: On Long Creek Reservoir in Wallowa-Whitman National Forest; map D4, grid d8.

Campsites, facilities: There are three sites for tents, trailers, or RVs up to 28 feet long. Picnic tables and fire grills are provided. A vault toilet is available. Leashed pets are permitted.

Reservations, fees: No reservations are accepted. There is no fee. The campground is open from May to mid-September.

Contact: Wallowa-Whitman National Forest, Unity Ranger District, P.O. Box 907, Baker City, OR 97814; (541) 448-3351 or fax (541) 523-1479.

Directions: From Pendleton on Interstate 84, take exit 304, turning south (left) on Highway 7. Drive 32 miles to Austin Junction, then turn east on U.S. 26 and drive 23 miles to Unity. Drive through Unity, turn south on Forest Service Road 1680, and drive nine miles to the campground on the left.

Trip notes: This small, little-known campground boasts good trout fishing in Long Creek Reservoir.

⑲ Eldorado

Location: On East Camp Creek in Wallowa-Whitman National Forest; map D4, grid d9.

Campsites, facilities: There are six sites for tents, trailers, or RVs up to 28 feet long. Picnic tables and fire grills are provided. Vault toilets are available. Leashed pets are permitted.

Reservations, fees: No reservations are accepted. There is no fee. The campground is open from May to mid-September.

Contact: Wallowa-Whitman National Forest, Unity Ranger District, P.O. Box 907, Baker City, OR 97814; (541) 448-3351 or fax (541) 523-1479.

Directions: From Pendleton on Interstate 84, take exit 304, turning south (left) on Highway 7. Drive 32 miles to Austin Junction, then turn east on U.S. 26 and drive 23 miles to Unity. Drive through Unity, and continue another 10 miles on U.S. 26. Turn south on the signed campground access road and drive three miles to the campground.

Trip notes: Trout fishing in spring and early summer at East Camp Creek is a draw here. The campground is also convenient for fishing at Murray Reservoir.

⑳ Elk Creek No. 2

Location: On the South Fork of the Burnt River in Wallowa-Whitman National Forest; map D4, grid c8.

Campsites, facilities: There is one group area for up to six tents, trailers, or RVs up to 28 feet long. Picnic tables and fire grills are provided. Vault toilets are available. There is no piped water. Leashed pets are permitted.

Reservations, fees: No reservations are accepted. There is no fee. The campground is open from late May to mid-September.

Contact: Wallowa-Whitman National Forest, Unity Ranger District, P.O. Box 907, Baker City, OR 97814; (541) 448-3351 or fax (541) 523-1479.

Directions: From Pendleton on Interstate 84, take exit 209 and turn south on U.S. 395. Drive 120 miles, then turn east on U.S. 26 and drive 58 miles to Unity. In Unity, turn southwest on

Forest Service Road 6005 (South Fork Road) and drive 10 miles to the campground.

Trip notes: This small, obscure camp along the banks of the South Fork of the Burnt River is a good base for fishing and hiking.

㉑ South Fork

Location: On the South Fork of the Burnt River in Wallowa-Whitman National Forest; map D4, grid c9.

Campsites, facilities: There are 14 sites for tents, trailers, or RVs up to 28 feet long. Picnic tables and fire grills are provided. Piped water and vault toilets are available. Leashed pets are permitted.

Reservations, fees: No reservations are accepted. There is no fee. The campground is open from late May to mid-September.

Contact: Wallowa-Whitman National Forest, Unity Ranger District, P.O. Box 907, Baker City, OR 97814; (541) 448-3351 or fax (541) 523-1479.

Directions: From Pendleton on Interstate 84, take exit 209 and turn south on U.S. 395. Drive 120 miles, then turn east on U.S. 26 and drive 58 miles to Unity. From Unity, drive six miles southwest on Forest Service Road 6005 (South Fork Road) to the campground.

Trip notes: This campground is set along the banks of the South Fork of the Burnt River, a nice trout creek with good evening bites for anglers who know how to sneak-fish. It's a gem of a spot, with piped water, privacy, and scenery—all for free.

㉒ Stevens Creek

Location: On the South Fork of the Burnt River in Wallowa-Whitman National Forest; map D4, grid c9.

Campsites, facilities: There is one group area for up to six tents, trailers, or RVs of any length. Picnic tables and fire grills are provided, but there is no piped water. Vault toilets are available. Leashed pets are permitted.

Reservations, fees: No reservations are accepted. There is no fee. The campground is open from late May to mid-September.

Contact: Wallowa-Whitman National Forest, Unity Ranger District, P.O. Box 907, Baker City, OR 97814; (541) 448-3351 or fax (541) 523-1479.

Directions: From Pendleton on Interstate 84, take exit 209 and turn south on U.S. 395. Drive 120 miles, then turn east on U.S. 26 and drive 58 miles to Unity. Turn south on Forest Service Road 6005 (South Fork Road) and drive seven miles to the campground.

Trip notes: This campground along the banks of the South Fork of the Burnt River is an option to the other small camps along the river. The trout fishing is good here. See the trip notes for South Fork (campground number 21) for more information.

㉓ Wolf Creek

Location: On Wolf Creek in Ochoco National Forest; map D4, grid d0.

Campsites, facilities: There are 11 sites for tents, trailers, or RVs up to 22 feet long. Picnic tables and fire grills are provided, but there is no piped water. Vault toilets are available. Leashed pets are permitted.

Reservations, fees: No reservations are accepted. Sites are $7 per night, with a 14-day stay limit. The campground is open from May to early November.

Contact: Ochoco National Forest, Paulina Ranger District, 71500 Beaver Creek Road, Paulina, OR 97751; (541) 416-6679 or fax (541) 416-6679.

Directions: From Interstate 5 at Albany, take exit 233 and turn east on U.S. 20. Drive 74 miles, then turn east on Highway 126 and continue southeast for 65 miles to Prineville. Turn south on County Road 380 and drive 55 miles to Paulina. Continue 3.5 miles east on County Road 380, then go 6.5 miles north on County Road 113. The camp is 1.5 miles north on Forest Service Road 42.

Trip notes: This campground is set along the banks of Wolf Creek, a nice stream that runs through Ochoco National Forest. It's a quality spot. Some excellent hiking trails can be found to the northeast in the Black Canyon Wilderness.

㉔ Sugar Creek

Location: On Sugar Creek in Ochoco National Forest; map D4, grid d0.

Campsites, facilities: There are 17 sites for tents, trailers, or RVs up to 21 feet long. Picnic tables and fire grills are provided. Well water and vault toilets are available. Some facilities are wheelchair accessible. Leashed pets are permitted.

Reservations, fees: No reservations are accepted. Sites are $7 per night, with a 14-day stay limit. The campground is open from June to early November.

Contact: Ochoco National Forest, Paulina Ranger District, 71500 Beaver Creek Road, Paulina, OR 97751; (541) 416-6679 or fax (541) 416-6679.

Directions: From Interstate 5 at Albany, take exit 233 and turn east on U.S. 20. Drive 74 miles, then turn east on Highway 126 and continue southeast for 65 miles to Prineville. Turn south on County Road 380 and drive 55 miles to Paulina. Continue 3.5 miles east on County Road 380, then 6.5 miles north on County Road 113. The camp is two miles east on Forest Service Road 58.

Trip notes: This campground on the banks of Sugar Creek is small, quiet, and remote. There is a covered group shelter in the new day-use area and a wheelchair-accessible trail.

㉕ Frazier

Location: On Frazier Creek in Ochoco National Forest; map D4, grid d1.

Campsites, facilities: There are six sites for tents, trailers, or RVs up to 21 feet long. Picnic tables and fire grills are provided. Vault toilets are available. There is no piped water. Leashed pets are permitted.

Reservations, fees: No reservations are accepted. There is no fee. The stay-limit is 14 days. The campground is open from June to early November.

Contact: Ochoco National Forest, Paulina Ranger District, 71500 Beaver Creek Road, Paulina, OR 97751; (541) 416-6679 or fax (541) 416-6679.

Directions: From Interstate 5 at Albany, take exit 233 and turn east on U.S. 20. Drive 74 miles, then turn east on Highway 126 and continue southeast for 65 miles to Prineville. Turn south on County Road 380 and drive 55 miles to Paulina. Continue 3.5 miles east on County Road 380, then go two miles north on County Road 113. Turn east on County Road 135 and drive 10 miles, then six miles on Forest Service Road 58. Continue for two miles on Forest Service Road 58-500.

Trip notes: This small, remote, and little-used camp is set at an elevation of 4,300 feet. Some dirt roads adjacent to the camp are good for mountain biking in summer and cross-country skiing and snowmobiling in winter. It's advisable to obtain a map of Ochoco National Forest.

26 Starr

Location: On Starr Ridge in Malheur National Forest; map D4, grid d4.

Campsites, facilities: There are five tent sites and eight sites for trailers or RVs up to 25 feet long. Picnic tables and fire grills are provided. Vault toilets are available. There is no piped water. Leashed pets are permitted.

Reservations, fees: No reservations are accepted. There is no fee. The campground is open from early May to November.

Contact: Malheur National Forest, Bear Valley Ranger District, P.O. Box 849, John Day, OR 97845; (541) 575-3000 or fax (541) 575-3419.

Directions: From John Day at the intersection of U.S. 395 and U.S. 26, travel 15 miles south on U.S. 395 to the campground.

Trip notes: This good layover spot for travelers on U.S. 395 happens to be adjacent to Starr Ski Bowl, which is popular in winter for skiing and sledding. The camp itself doesn't offer much in the way of recreation, but to the northeast is the Strawberry Mountain Wilderness, which has a number of trails, lakes, and streams.

27 Wickiup

Location: On Wickiup Creek in Malheur National Forest; map D4, grid d5.

Campsites, facilities: There are eight sites for tents, trailers, or RVs up to 16 feet long. Picnic tables and fire grills are provided. Piped water, vault toilets, and horse corrals are available. Leashed pets are permitted.

Reservations, fees: No reservations are accepted. Call the ranger district for fee information. The campground is open from early May to November.

Contact: Malheur National Forest, Bear Valley Ranger District, P.O. Box 849, John Day, OR 97845; (541) 575-3000 or fax (541) 575-3419.

Directions: From John Day at the intersection of U.S. 395 and U.S. 26, travel 10 miles south on U.S. 395 and eight miles southeast on Forest Service Road 15 to the campground.

Trip notes: This campground is along the banks of Wickiup Creek at a historic site, with many original structures still in place. There is good fishing in the creek. To the north are many trails that are routed into the Strawberry Mountain Wilderness.

28 Canyon Meadows

Location: On Canyon Meadows Reservoir in Malheur National Forest; map D4, grid d5.

Campsites, facilities: There are 15 sites for tents, trailers, or RVs up to 16 feet long. Picnic tables and fire grills are provided. Piped water and vault toilets are available. Leashed pets are permitted.

Reservations, fees: No reservations are accepted. There is no fee. The campground is open from mid-May to late October.

Contact: Malheur National Forest, Bear Valley Ranger District, P.O. Box 849, John Day, OR 97845; (541) 575-3000 or fax (541) 575-3419.

Directions: From John Day at the intersection of U.S. 395 and U.S. 26, drive 10 miles south on U.S. 395, then nine miles southeast on Forest Service Road 15. The camp is five miles northeast on Forest Service Road 1520.

Trip notes: This campground is on the shore of Canyon Meadows Reservoir, where non-motorized boating, plus swimming, sailing, fishing, and hiking, are recreation options. There are several hiking trails nearby that lead north into the Strawberry Mountain Wilderness.

㉙ Indian Springs

Location: Near the Strawberry Mountain Wilderness in Malheur National Forest; map D4, grid d6.

Campsites, facilities: This is a primitive campground with no designated sites. No piped water or pit toilets are available. Leashed pets are permitted.

Reservations, fees: No reservations are accepted. There is no fee. The campground is open from June to mid-October.

Contact: Malheur National Forest, Bear Valley Ranger District, P.O. Box 849, John Day, OR 97845; (541) 575-3000 or fax (541) 575-3419.

Directions: From John Day at the intersection of U.S. 395 and U.S. 26, travel 10 miles south on U.S. 395, then east on Forest Service Road 15 for about 15 miles to Forest Service Road 16. Turn left and drive 2.5 miles, then turn left on Forest Service Road 1640 and continue seven miles north on a gravel and then dirt road to the campground.

Trip notes: This campground is located at Indian Springs, a pretty spot near Bear Creek. A side trip option is to drive the 77-mile loop around the Strawberry Mountain Wilderness. A map of Malheur National Forest details the back roads. Backpackers and hikers will find many trailheads along the Forest Service road.

㉚ Parish Cabin

Location: On Little Bear Creek in Malheur National Forest; map D4, grid d6.

Campsites, facilities: There are three tent sites and 16 sites for tents, trailers, or RVs up to 32 feet long. Picnic tables and fire grills are provided. Piped water, vault toilets, and horse facilities are available. Some facilities are barrier-free. Leashed pets are permitted.

Reservations, fees: No reservations are accepted. Call the ranger district for fee information. The campground is open from mid-May to late November.

Contact: Malheur National Forest, Bear Valley Ranger District, P.O. Box 849, John Day, OR 97845; (541) 575-3000 or fax (541) 575-3419.

Directions: From John Day at the intersection of U.S. 395 and U.S. 26, travel 10 miles south on U.S. 395, then 16 miles southeast on Forest Service Road 15. Turn onto Forest Service Road 16 and drive one-quarter mile to the campground.

Trip notes: This campground along the banks of Little Bear Creek is in a pretty spot that's not heavily used. Fishing is available in the creek. See a Forest Service map for hiking trails in the area.

㉛ Big Creek

Location: Near the Strawberry Mountain Wilderness in Malheur National Forest; map D4, grid d7.

Campsites, facilities: There are 15 sites for tents, trailers, or RVs up to 16 feet long. Picnic tables and fire grills are provided. Hand-pumped water and vault toilets are available. Leashed pets are permitted.

Reservations, fees: No reservations are accepted. Call the ranger district for current fee information. The campground is open from mid-May to mid-November.

Contact: Malheur National Forest, Prairie City Ranger District, P.O. Box 337, Prairie City, OR 97869; (541) 820-3311 or fax (541) 820-4503.

Directions: From John Day at the intersection of U.S. 395 and U.S. 26, travel 10 miles south on U.S. 395, then southeast on Forest Service Road 15 for 16 miles. Turn east and drive eight miles on Forest Service Road 16 (which becomes Forest Service Road 815). Continue one-half mile north on Forest Service Road 815 to the campground.

Trip notes: This campground is set along the banks of Big Creek. Nearby Forest Service roads provide access into the Strawberry Mountain Wilderness. Fishing and mountain biking are other recreational options. In the appropriate seasons, elk, bear, coyote, and deer are hunted here.

32 Trout Farm

Location: Near Prairie City in Malheur National Forest; map D4, grid d7.

Campsites, facilities: There are six sites for tents, trailers, or RVs up to 21 feet long. Picnic tables and fire grills are provided. Piped water and vault toilets are available. Leashed pets are permitted.

Reservations, fees: No reservations are accepted. Call the ranger district for current fee information. The campground is open from June to mid-October.

Contact: Malheur National Forest, Prairie City Ranger District, P.O. Box 337, Prairie City, OR 97869; (541) 820-3311 or fax (541) 820-4503.

Directions: From Pendleton on Interstate 84, take exit 209 and turn south on U.S. 395. Drive 120 miles, then turn east on U.S. 26 and drive 21 miles to Prairie City. Turn southeast on County Road 62 and drive 15 miles to the entrance on the right.

Trip notes: This campground is on the Upper John Day River, which provides good trout fishing with easy access for people who don't wish to travel off paved roads. A picnic shelter is available for family picnics, and a small pond at the campground has a wheelchair-accessible trail.

33 North Fork Malheur

Location: On the North Fork of the Malheur River in Malheur National Forest; map D4, grid d8.

Campsites, facilities: There are five tent or trailer sites. Picnic tables and fire grills are provided. Vault toilets are available. There is no piped water. Leashed pets are permitted.

Reservations, fees: No reservations are accepted. There is no fee. The campground is open from mid-May to mid-November.

Contact: Malheur National Forest, Prairie City Ranger District, P.O. Box 337, Prairie City, OR 97869; (541) 820-3311 or fax (541) 820-4503.

Directions: From Pendleton on Interstate 84, take exit 209 and turn south on U.S. 395. Drive 120 miles, then turn east on U.S. 26 and drive 21 miles to Prairie City. Turn southeast on County Road 62 and drive 8.5 miles, then 16 miles southeast on Forest Service Road 13. Drive two miles south on Forest Service Road 16, then take the left fork (Forest Service Road 1675) and drive two miles to the camp.

Trip notes: This secluded campground is set along the banks of the North Fork of the Malheur River, a designated Wild and Scenic River. Hiking trails and dirt roads provide additional access to the river and backcountry streams. It's essential to obtain a Forest Service map. Good fishing, hunting, and mountain biking opportunities abound in the area.

34 Little Crane

Location: On Little Crane Creek in Malheur National Forest; map D4, grid d8.

Campsites, facilities: There are five tent and trailer sites. Picnic tables and fire grills are provided. Vault toilets are available. There is no piped water. Leashed pets are permitted.

Reservations, fees: No reservations are accepted. There is no fee. The campground is open from June to mid-November.

Contact: Malheur National Forest, Prairie City Ranger District, P.O. Box 337, Prairie City, OR 97869; (541) 820-3311 or fax (541) 820-4503.

Directions: From Pendleton on Interstate 84, take exit 209 and turn south on U.S. 395. Drive 120 miles, turn east on U.S. 26, and go 21 miles to Prairie City. Turn southeast on County Road 62 and drive 8.5 miles, then 16 miles southeast on Forest Service Road 13. The camp is 5.5 miles south on Forest Service Road 16.

Trip notes: Small, primitive, quiet, and private all describe this camp along the banks of Little Crane Creek. The stream is good for sneak-fishing for trout. There are also some nice hiking trails in the area, the closest one at the North Fork of the Malheur River, detailed on a Forest Service map.

35 Delintment Lake

Location: On Delintment Lake in Ochoco National Forest; map D4, grid e0.

Campsites, facilities: There are 24 sites for tents, trailers, or RVs up to 30 feet long. Picnic tables and fire grills are provided. Hand-pumped water and vault toilets are available. Some facilities are wheelchair accessible. A fishing dock and launching facilities are located in the campground. Leashed pets are permitted.

Reservations, fees: No reservations are accepted. Sites are $6 per night, plus $3 per extra vehicle. The campground is open from May through October.

Contact: Ochoco National Forest, Snow Mountain Ranger District, HC 74, P.O. Box 12870, Hines, OR 97738; (541) 573-4300 or fax (541) 573-4398.

Directions: From the intersection of U.S. 395 and U.S. 20 at Burns, turn south on U.S. 20 and drive three miles, then turn north on County Road 127 (which turns into Forest Service Road 47) and drive about 10 miles. Turn left on Forest Service Road 41 and travel about 30 miles to the campground.

Trip notes: Not many people know about this one set along the shore of Delintment Lake, originally a beaver pond which was gradually developed into a lake covering 57 acres. Here's a secret: Rainbow trout here average 12 to 18 inches.

36 Emigrant Creek

Location: Near Emigrant Creek in Ochoco National Forest; map D4, grid e1.

Campsites, facilities: There are seven sites for tents, trailers, or RVs up to 30 feet long. Picnic tables and fire grills are provided, but there is no piped water. Vault toilets are available. Leashed pets are permitted.

Reservations, fees: No reservations are accepted. There is no fee. The campground is open from May through October.

Contact: Ochoco National Forest, Snow Mountain Ranger District, HC 74, P.O. Box 12870, Hines, OR 97738; (541) 573-4300 or fax (541) 573-4398.

Directions: From the intersection of U.S. 395 and U.S. 20 at Burns, turn south on U.S. 20 and

drive three miles. Turn northwest on Forest Service Road 47 and drive 25 miles, then go another 10 miles west on Forest Service Road 43 to the campground.

Trip notes: One of three camps in the immediate area, this spot is on the border of Ochoco and Malheur National Forests in a meadow near Emigrant Creek. Several nearby back-country dirt roads are good for mountain biking. See a Forest Service map for details.

37 Falls

Location: On Emigrant Creek in Ochoco National Forest; map D4, grid e1.

Campsites, facilities: There are five sites for tents, trailers, or RVs up to 30 feet long. Picnic tables and fire grills are provided. Hand-pumped water and vault toilets are available. Leashed pets are permitted.

Reservations, fees: No reservations are accepted. Sites are $6 per night, plus $2 per extra vehicle. The campground is open from May through October.

Contact: Ochoco National Forest, Snow Mountain Ranger District, HC 74, P.O. Box 12870, Hines, OR 97738; (541) 573-4300 or fax (541) 573-4398.

Directions: From the intersection of U.S. 395 and U.S. 20 at Burns, turn south on U.S. 20 and drive three miles. Turn northwest on Forest Service Road 47 and drive 25 miles. The camp is another 8.5 miles west on Forest Service Road 43.

Trip notes: This small, quiet spot is set along the banks of Emigrant Creek, not far from Emigrant Creek Campground (see number 36). Fishing access to the creek is available nearby.

38 Yellowjacket

Location: On Yellowjacket Lake in Malheur National Forest; map D4, grid e2.

Campsites, facilities: There are 20 sites for tents, trailers, or RVs up to 22 feet long. Picnic tables, hand-pumped well water, and pit or vault toilets are available. A boat launch is nearby. Leashed pets are permitted.

Reservations, fees: No reservations are accepted. There is no fee. The campground is open from late May to mid-October.

Contact: Ochoco National Forest, Burns Ranger District, HC 74, P.O. Box 12870, Hines, OR 97738; (541) 573-4300 or fax (541) 573-4398.

Directions: Travel one mile south of Burns on U.S. 20, then northwest for 32 miles on Forest Service Road 47. Turn right on Forest Service Road 37 and drive two miles. Turn right on Forest Service Road 3745 and drive one mile to the campground.

Trip notes: This campground is along the shore of Yellowjacket Lake, where fishing can be very good in the summer. Boats without motors are encouraged. The price of the camp is definitely a bonus.

39 Idlewild

Location: In Divine Canyon in Malheur National Forest; map D4, grid f5.

Campsites, facilities: There are 26 sites for tents, trailers, or RVs up to 30 feet long. Picnic tables, fire grills, and picnic sites are provided. Piped water, a group shelter, and vault toilets are available. Some facilities are wheelchair accessible. Leashed pets are permitted.

Reservations, fees: No reservations are accepted. There is no fee. The campground is open from late May to mid-October.

Contact: Ochoco National Forest, Burns Ranger District, HC 74, P.O. Box 12870, Hines, OR 97738; (541) 573-4300 or fax (541) 573-4398.

Directions: From Burns on U.S. 20, travel 17 miles north on U.S. 395 to the campground on the right.

Trip notes: This campground is set in Divine Canyon, a designated sno-park in the winter that's popular with locals for snowmobiling and cross-country skiing. Several trailheads start here, including the Divine Summit Interpretive Loop Trail and the Idlewild Loop Trail. It's also a popular spot for visitors traveling up U.S. 395 and in need of a stopover, since it provides easy access and a pretty setting. See a Forest Service map for backcountry roads that make great mountain biking trails.

Map D5

Oregon State Map .... *page 6*
One inch equals approximately 20 miles.

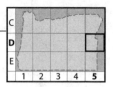

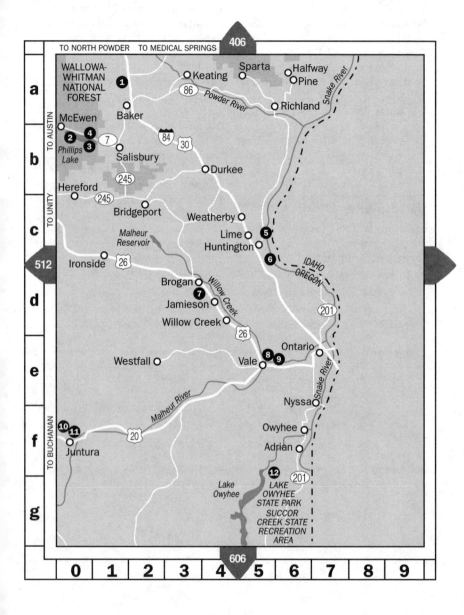

Chapter D5 features:

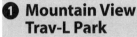

1 Mountain View Trav-L Park

Location: In Baker City; map D5, grid a2.

Campsites, facilities: There are 11 tent sites and 69 full-hookup sites for trailers or RVs of any length; most are pull-throughs. Electricity, piped water, sewer hookups, cable TV hookups, and picnic tables are provided. Flush toilets, sanitary disposal services, showers, a laundry room, ice, a playground, and a swimming pool are available. Bottled gas, a store, and a cafe are located within one mile. Leashed pets and motorbikes are permitted.

Reservations, fees: Reservations are accepted; call (800) 323-8899 and ask for Best Holiday. Sites are $14–$17.95 per night. The campground is open year-round, with limited winter facilities.

Contact: Phone (541) 523-4824 or write to 2845 Hughes Lane, Baker City, OR 97814.

Directions: From Interstate 84 at Baker City, take exit 304 and drive 1.5 miles west on Campbell Street. Take a right and drive one mile north on 10th Street to Hughes Lane. The camp is one block east on Hughes Lane.

Trip notes: This grassy campground is "the gateway to camping on the Oregon Trail," complete with an Oregon Trail Interpretive Center for those with a historical bent. The park is clean and cool, with spacious sites and many recreation options nearby.

2 Southwest Shore

Location: On Phillips Lake in Wallowa-Whitman National Forest; map D5, grid b0.

Campsites, facilities: There are 20 sites for tents, trailers, or RVs up to 24 feet long. Fire grills and vault toilets are available. There is no piped water. A boat ramp is located adjacent to the campground. Leashed pets are permitted.

Reservations, fees: No reservations are accepted. There is no fee. The campground is open from May to mid-November.

Contact: Wallowa-Whitman National Forest, Baker Ranger District, P.O. Box 907, Baker City, OR 97814; (541) 523-4476 or fax (541) 523-1965.

Directions: From Interstate 84 at Baker City, drive southwest on Highway 7 for 24 miles (just past Phillips Lake). Turn south on Hudspath Lane and drive two miles. Turn southeast on Forest Service Road 2220 and drive 2.5 miles to the campground entrance.

Trip notes: This campground is set along the south shore of Phillips Lake, a four-mile-long reservoir created by the Mason Dam on the Powder River. It's one of two primitive camps on the lake. The boat ramp is usable only when water is high in the reservoir.

3 Millers Lane

Location: On Phillips Lake in Wallowa-Whitman National Forest; map D5, grid b1.

Campsites, facilities: There are seven sites for tents, trailers, or RVs up to 20 feet long. Picnic tables and fire grills are provided. Firewood and vault toilets are available. There is no piped water. A boat ramp is located at Southwest Shore Campground. Leashed pets are permitted.

Reservations, fees: No reservations are ac-

cepted. There is no fee. The campground is open from May to mid-November.

Contact: Wallowa-Whitman National Forest, Baker Ranger District, P.O. Box 907, Baker City, OR 97814; (541) 523-4476 or fax (541) 523-1965.

Directions: From Interstate 84 at Baker City, drive southwest on Highway 7 for 24 miles (just past Phillips Lake). Turn south on Hudspath Lane and drive two miles. Turn southeast on Forest Service Road 2220 and drive 3.5 miles to the campground entrance.

Trip notes: This small campground is situated along the south shore of Phillips Lake, a long, narrow reservoir that's the largest in the region. Millers Lane is one of two primitive camps on the lake.

❹ Union Creek

Location: On Phillips Lake in Wallowa-Whitman National Forest; map D5, grid b1.

Campsites, facilities: There are 58 sites for tents, trailers, or RVs up to 32 feet long. Electricity, piped water, sewer hookups, and picnic tables are provided. Flush toilets, firewood, and ice are available. There is a small concession stand for packaged goods and fishing tackle. Some facilities are wheelchair accessible. Boat docks and launching facilities are adjacent to the campground. Leashed pets are permitted.

Reservations, fees: No reservations are accepted. Sites are $10–$16 per night. The campground is open from mid-April to mid-November.

Contact: Wallowa-Whitman National Forest, Baker Ranger District, P.O. Box 907, Baker City, OR 97814; (541) 523-4476 or fax (541) 523-1965.

Directions: From Interstate 84 at Baker City, travel southwest on Highway 7 for 20 miles to the campground.

Trip notes: This campground along the north shore of Phillips Lake is easy to reach, yet missed by most travelers on Interstate 84. It's the largest of three camps on the lake, and the only one with piped water.

❺ Farewell Bend State Recreation Area

Location: On the Snake River; map D5, grid c5.

Campsites, facilities: There are 47 primitive tent sites and 93 sites with partial hookups for trailers or RVs of any length. There are also four tepees and two covered wagons. Piped water, barbecues, and picnic tables are provided. Flush toilets, sanitary disposal services, showers, and firewood are available. Boat launching facilities are nearby. Leashed pets are permitted.

Reservations, fees: Contact Reservations Northwest at (800) 452-5687 ($6 reservation fee). Sites are $12–$16 per night; tepees or covered wagons are $25 a night. The campground is open year-round, with limited winter facilities.

Contact: Farewell Bend State Recreation Area, Star Route, Huntington, OR 97907; (800) 452-5687 or (541) 869-2365.

Directions: From Ontario (near the Oregon/Idaho border), travel 25 miles northwest on Interstate 84 to the park entrance on the right side of the road.

Trip notes: This campground along the banks of the majestic Snake River is known as the "catfish capital" of Oregon. It's the site of a historic wagon train camp, and an exhibit on the Oregon Trail details its history. Recreation options include boating, swimming, and picnicking.

❻ Spring

Location: On the Snake River; map D5, grid c5.

Campsites, facilities: There are 44 sites for tents, trailers, or RVs. Picnic tables and fire grills are provided. Piped water, sanitary disposal services, and vault toilets are available. Boat launching facilities are nearby. Leashed pets are permitted.

Reservations, fees: No reservations are accepted. Sites are $4 per night, with a 14-day stay limit. The campground is open from March through October and some off-season weekends.

Contact: Bureau of Land Management, 3165 10th Street, Baker City, OR 97814; (541) 523-1256.

Directions: From the Oregon/Idaho border, drive northwest on Interstate 84 to Huntington. Turn northeast on Snake River Road and drive 3.5 miles to the campground.

Trip notes: This campground along the banks of the Snake River Reservoir is one of two camps in or near Huntington. A more developed alternative is Farewell Bend State Recreation Area (see campground number 5), which offers showers and all the other luxuries a camper could want. Fishing and hunting opportunities are nearby.

❼ Brogan Trailer Park and Camp

Location: Near Willow Creek; map D5, grid d3.

Campsites, facilities: There are four tent sites and 24 drive-through sites for trailers or RVs of any length. Electricity, piped water, sewer hookups, and picnic tables are provided. Flush toilets, showers, laundry facilities, and ice are available. Bottled gas, a store, and a cafe are located within one mile. Leashed pets are permitted.

Reservations, fees: Reservations are accepted. Sites are $6–$10 per night. The campground is open from April through December.

Contact: Phone (541) 473-3062 or write to 3029 Sixth Street, Brogan, OR 97903.

Directions: From Interstate 84 at Ontario, turn west on U.S. 20/26 and drive 12 miles to Vale. Turn northwest on U.S. 26 and drive 24 miles to Brogan. The campground is in town on the left.

Trip notes: This rural campground is on the inner edge of the West's Great Basin, a high-desert area that extends to Idaho. Nearby side trips include Willow Creek, which runs along U.S. 26, and Malheur Reservoir, northwest of Brogan.

❽ Prospector Travel Trailer Park

Location: In Vale; map D5, grid e5.

Campsites, facilities: There are 10 tent sites and 28 drive-through sites for trailers or RVs of any length, plus a separate area for tents. Picnic tables are provided. Flush toilets, bottled gas, sanitary disposal services, showers, a laundry room, and ice are available. A store and a cafe are located within one mile. Leashed pets and motorbikes are permitted.

Reservations, fees: Reservations are accepted. Sites are $5 per person and $16–$20 per RV a night. The campground is open year-round, weather permitting.

Contact: Phone (541) 473-3879, fax (541) 473-2338, or write to 511 North 11th Street East, Vale, OR 97918.

Directions: From Interstate 84 at Ontario, turn west on U.S. 20/26 and drive 12 miles to Vale. Turn north on U.S. 26 and drive one-half mile, then go one block east on Hope Street to the campground on the left.

Trip notes: This is one of two camps (Westerner Trailer Park, campground number 9, is the other) for travelers in the Vale area. This one is more comfortable for tents, with a specifically designated grassy area. It claims to be a fishing and hunting paradise, and even has a fish and game cleaning room.

❾ Westerner Trailer Park

Location: On Willow Creek; map D5, grid e5.

Campsites, facilities: There are 10 sites for tents, trailers, or RVs of any length. Electricity, piped water, cable TV, sewer hookups, and picnic tables are provided. Flush toilets, showers, a laundry room, and ice are available. Bottled gas, a store, a cafe, and a swimming pool are located within two blocks. Leashed pets and motorbikes are permitted.

Reservations, fees: Reservations are accepted. Sites are $10 per night. The campground is open year-round.

Contact: Phone (541) 473-3947 or write to 317 A Street East, Vale, OR 97918.

Directions: From Interstate 84 at Ontario, turn west on U.S. 20/26 and drive 12 miles to Vale. The campground is located on the left at the junction of U.S. 20 and U.S. 26.

Trip notes: This campground on the banks of Willow Creek is a good layover spot for travelers heading to or from Idaho on U.S. 20. See the trip notes for Prospector Travel Trailer Park (campground number 8) for more information.

⑩ Chukar Park

Location: Near the North Fork of the Malheur River; map D5, grid f0.

Campsites, facilities: There are 18 sites for tents, trailers, or RVs up to 30 feet long. Picnic tables and fire grills are provided. Piped water and vault toilets are available. Leashed pets are permitted.

Reservations, fees: No reservations are accepted. Sites are $4 per night, with a 14-day stay limit. The campground is open from mid-April through November.

Contact: Bureau of Land Management, 100 Oregon Street, Vale, OR 97918; (541) 473-3144.

Directions: From Interstate 84 at Ontario, turn west on U.S. 20 and drive 73 miles to Juntura. Continue six miles northwest of Juntura on Beulah Reservoir Road to the campground.

Trip notes: This campground is set along the banks of the North Fork of the Malheur River. The area in general provides habitat for chukar, an upland game species. Hunting can be good in season during the fall, but requires much hiking in rugged terrain.

⑪ Oasis RV Park

Location: In Juntura; map D5, grid f0.

Campsites, facilities: There are 14 sites for trailers or RVs of any length; eight are drive-throughs. Electricity, piped water, and sewer hookups are provided. Flush toilets, showers, a cafe, and ice are available. Bottled gas and a store are located within one mile. Leashed pets are permitted.

Reservations, fees: No reservations are accepted. Sites are $12 per night. The campground is open year-round.

Contact: Phone (541) 277-3605 or write to P.O. Box 277, Juntura, OR 97911.

Directions: From Interstate 84 at Ontario, turn west on U.S. 20 and drive 73 miles to Juntura. The park is located in town.

Trip notes: One of the only camps in the area, this RV park is close to Chukar State Park. See the trip notes for Chukar Park (campground number 10) for more details.

⑫ Lake Owyhee State Park

Location: On Owyhee Lake; map D5, grid f5.

Campsites, facilities: There are seven sites for tents or self-contained RVs, and 33 sites with water and electrical hookups for trailers or RVs of any length. There are also two tepees. Picnic tables and fire grills are provided. Flush toilets, a sanitary disposal station, and showers are available. Boat docks and launching facilities are available nearby. Leashed pets are permitted.

Reservations, fees: No reservations are accepted. Sites are $14–$15 per night. The campground is open from April 12 through October.

Contact: Phone (800) 452-5687 or (541) 339-2331, or write to 3012 Island Avenue, LaGrande, OR 97850.

Directions: From Interstate 84 at Ontario (near the Oregon/Idaho border), turn south on Highway 201. Drive 19 miles to Owyhee Junction, then turn southwest on Owyhee Lake Road and drive 28 miles to the road's end and the entrance to the park.

Trip notes: This state park is set along the shore of Owyhee Lake, a good lake for waterskiing in the day and fishing for warm-water species in the morning and evening. Owyhee is famous for its superb bass fishing. Other highlights include views of unusual geological formations and huge rock pinnacles from the park. Leslie Gulch provides the only other camping option at the lake.

Map E1

One inch equals approximately 20 miles.

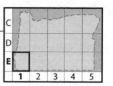

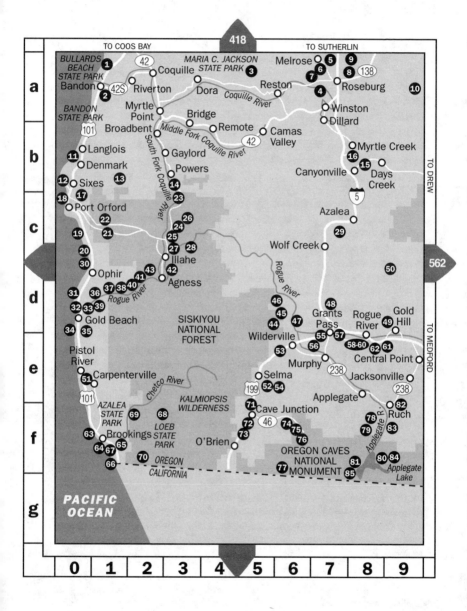

Chapter E1 features:

❶ Bullards Beach State Park

Location: On the Coquille River; map E1, grid a1.

Campsites, facilities: There are 192 sites with full or partial hookups for trailers or RVs up to 64 feet long. Seven yurts are also available, one of which is wheelchair accessible. Each yurt can sleep five people. Other options include a special area for horses, as well as an area reserved for hikers and bicyclists. Piped water, picnic tables, and fire grills are provided. Flush toilets, a sanitary disposal station, showers, firewood, a yurt meeting hall, and a loading ramp for horses are available. Some facilities are wheelchair accessible. Boat docks and launching facilities are located in the park on the Coquille River. Leashed pets are permitted.

Reservations, fees: Contact Reservations Northwest at (800) 452-5687 ($6 reservation fee). Sites are $16–$19 per night; yurts are $25 per night; and sites for hikers/bicyclists are $4 per night. The campground is open year-round.

Contact: Phone (800) 452-5687 or (541) 347-2209, or write to P.O. Box 25, Bandon, OR 97411.

Directions: In Coos Bay, drive south on U.S. 101 for about 22 miles to the park on the right (located two miles north of Bandon).

Trip notes: The Coquille River is the centerpiece of this park, which has good fishing in season for both boaters and crabbers, with four miles of shore access. If fishing isn't your thing, the park also has several hiking trails. A historic lighthouse built in 1896 provides a side trip option. Equestrians can explore the seven-mile horse trail.

❷ Bandon RV Park

Location: Near Bandon State Park; map E1, grid a1.

Campsites, facilities: There are 40 sites for trailers or RVs of any length; some are drive-throughs. Electricity, piped water, cable TV, and sewer hookups are provided. Flush toilets, sanitary services, showers, and a laundry room are available. Bottled gas and a store are located within one mile. Boat docks and launching facilities are nearby. Leashed pets are permitted.

Reservations, fees: Reservations are accepted; phone (800) 393-4122. Sites are $16.75–$18.50 per night. The campground is open year-round.

Contact: Phone (541) 347-4122 or write to 935 Southeast Second Street, Bandon, OR 97411.

Directions: From U.S. 101 at Coos Bay, drive 23 miles south to Bandon. Bandon RV Park is on U.S. 101, one block south of the Highway 42S junction.

Trip notes: This in-town RV park is a good base for many adventures. Rock hounds will enjoy combing for agates and other semiprecious stones hidden along the beaches, while kids can explore the West Coast Game Park Walk-Through Safari petting zoo seven miles south of town. Bandon State Park, four miles south of town, has a nice wading spot in the creek at the north end of the park. Nearby recreation opportunities include an 18-hole golf course, a riding stable, and tennis courts.

❸ Park Creek

Location: Near Coquille; map E1, grid a5.

Campsites, facilities: There are 15 sites for tents, small trailers, or camping vans. Picnic tables and fire grills are provided. Vault toilets are available. There is no piped water. Leashed pets are permitted.

Reservations, fees: No reservations are accepted. There is no fee, but the stay limit is 14 days. The campground is open year-round.

Contact: Bureau of Land Management, 1300 Airport Lane, North Bend, OR 97459; (541) 756-0100.

Directions: From Interstate 5 south of Roseburg, turn west on Highway 42 and drive approximately 64 miles to Coquille. Turn east on Coquille Fairview Road and travel 7.5 miles to Fairview. Turn right on Coos Bay Wagon Road. Drive 3.5 miles, turn east (left) on Middle

Creek Access Road, and proceed 11 miles to the campground.

Trip notes: Want to be by yourself? You came to the right place. This pretty little campground is set along Park Creek in the middle of nowhere. It's very primitive, so don't forget your drinking water.

❹ Wildlife Safari RV Park

Location: Near Roseburg; map E1, grid a7.

Campsites, facilities: There are 18 drive-through sites for self-contained trailers or RVs. Electricity, a gift shop, and a cafe are available. There is no piped water. Leashed pets and motorbikes are permitted.

Reservations, fees: No reservations are accepted. Sites are $8–$10 per night. The campground is closed in the winter.

Contact: Wildlife Safari RV Park, P.O. Box 1600, Winston, OR 97496; (541) 679-6761 or fax (541) 679-9210; e-mail: maserith.com/safari.

Directions: From Interstate 5 south of Roseburg, take exit 119 and drive 3.5 miles southwest on Highway 42 to the park at the end of the road.

Trip notes: This park is part of the Wildlife Safari Park in Winston (near Roseburg), which offers a walk-through petting zoo. Nearby recreation options include an 18-hole golf course, hiking trails, and marked bike trails.

❺ John P. Amacher County Park

Location: On the Umpqua River; map E1, grid a7.

Campsites, facilities: There are 10 sites for tents and 20 sites with full or partial hookups for trailers or RVs up to 30 feet long. Electricity, piped water, sewer hookups, and picnic tables are provided. Flush toilets, showers, and a playground are available. Bottled gas, a store, a cafe, a Laundromat, and ice are located within one mile. Boat launching facilities are nearby. Leashed pets and motorbikes are permitted.

Reservations, fees: No reservations are accepted. Sites are $11–$14 per night. The campground is open year-round.

Contact: Phone (541) 672-4901, fax (541) 440-6248, or write to P.O. Box 800, Winchester, OR 97495.

Directions: From Roseburg, drive five miles north on Interstate 5. Take exit 129, turning south on Old Highway 99, and drive one-quarter mile to the park on the right, just across Winchester Bridge.

Trip notes: This prime layover spot for Interstate 5 RV cruisers is in a wooded county park along the banks of the North Umpqua River, just far enough off the beaten track to be missed by most out-of-towners. An 18-hole golf course and tennis courts are close by.

❻ Twin Rivers Vacation Park

Location: Near the Umpqua River; map E1, grid a7.

Campsites, facilities: There are 11 tent sites and 72 sites for trailers or RVs of any length; 35 are drive-throughs with full hookups. Electricity, piped water, cable TV, sewer hookups, and picnic tables are provided. Flush toilets, bottled gas, showers, firewood, a store, a laundry room, ice, and a playground are available. Boat launching facilities are nearby. Leashed pets and motorbikes are permitted.

Reservations, fees: Reservations are accepted. Sites are $15–$20 per night. The campground is open year-round.

Contact: Phone (541) 673-3811 or write to 433 River Forks Park, Roseburg, OR 97470.

Directions: From Roseburg on Interstate 5, take exit 125 and travel west for five miles. Turn south on Old Garden Valley Road and drive 1.5 miles to the end of the road and the entrance to the campground.

Trip notes: This wooded campground near the Umpqua River is the only camp in Roseburg with tent as well as RV sites. Nearby recreation options include a golf course, a county park, and bike paths.

⑦ Douglas County Fairgrounds RV

Location: Near the Umpqua River; map E1, grid a6.

Campsites, facilities: There are 50 sites for tents, trailers, or RVs of any length with partial hookups. Tent camping is limited to two nights. Electricity, piped water, and picnic tables are provided. Flush toilets, sanitary services, showers, and a playground are available. A store, a cafe, a Laundromat, and ice are located within one mile. Leashed pets are permitted.

Reservations, fees: No reservations are accepted. Sites are $15 per night, with a 14-day stay limit and a $2 dump station fee. The campground is open year-round, except one week in August during the county fair. Phone ahead to confirm that they're open.

Contact: Phone (541) 957-7010, fax (541) 440-6023, or write to 2110 Southwest Frear Street, Roseburg, OR 97470.

Directions: From Interstate 5 in Roseburg, take exit 123 and drive south, following signs to the campground.

Trip notes: This county park is near the Umpqua River, one of Oregon's prettiest rivers. There is often good fishing in season. A golf course, bike paths, and tennis courts are nearby.

⑧ Alameda Avenue Trailer Park

Location: Near the Umpqua River; map E1, grid a7.

Campsites, facilities: There are 35 sites for trailers or RVs up to 30 feet long. Electricity, piped water, and sewer hookups are provided. Flush toilets, sanitary services, showers, and a laundry room are available. Bottled gas, a store, a cafe, and ice are located within one mile. Leashed pets are permitted.

Reservations, fees: Reservations are accepted. Sites are $15 per night. The campground is open year-round.

Contact: Phone (541) 672-2348 or write to 581 NE Alameda Avenue, Roseburg, OR 97470.

Directions: In Roseburg, take the Garden Valley exit off Interstate 5 and travel east to Business Route 99. Drive one-quarter mile north to Northeast Alameda Avenue. The park is on the left.

Trip notes: Alameda Avenue Trailer Park, one of four parks in Roseburg, is near the Umpqua River. A golf course, bike paths, and tennis courts are among the recreation possibilities in the area.

⑨ Mount Nebo Trailer Park

Location: Near the Umpqua River; map E1, grid a7.

Campsites, facilities: There are 26 sites for trailers or RVs up to 45 feet long; four are drive-throughs. Electricity, piped water, and sewer hookups are provided. Flush toilets, sanitary services, showers, and a laundry room are available. Bottled gas, a store, and a cafe are within one mile. Leashed pets are permitted.

Reservations, fees: Reservations are accepted. Sites are $17 per night. The campground is open year-round.

Contact: Phone (541) 673-4108 or write to 2071 NE Stephens Street, Roseburg, OR 97470.

Directions: From Interstate 5 at Roseburg, take exit 125 and drive northeast to Stephens Street. Turn north and drive less than a mile to the park on the right.

Trip notes: This is an option for RVers stopping in Roseburg. The park is near the Umpqua River and close to a golf course, bike paths, and tennis courts.

⑩ Cavitt Creek

Location: On Cavitt Creek; map E1, grid a9.

Campsites, facilities: There are eight sites for trailers or RVs up to 20 feet long. Picnic tables and fire grills are provided. Pit toilets and piped water are available. Leashed pets are permitted.

Reservations, fees: No reservations are accepted. Sites are $7 per night, plus $3 for each additional vehicle, with a 14-day stay limit. The campground is open year-round.

Contact: Bureau of Land Management, 777

NW Garden Valley Boulevard, Roseburg, OR 97470; (541) 440-4930.

Directions: From Interstate 5 at Roseburg, drive 18 miles east on Highway 138 to Glide. From Glide, travel seven miles southeast on Little River Road, then three miles south on Cavitt Creek Road to the campground.

Trip notes: Wooded, primitive, and private describe this camp along the banks of Cavitt Creek about three miles from its confluence with the Little River. The swimming hole beneath Cavitt Creek Falls is a local favorite. If you want to get deeper into the woods, the following camps provide options farther down the same road: Coolwater and White Creek (campground numbers 2 and 3 in Chapter E2) and Wolf Creek (campground number 23 in Chapter D4).

⓫ KOA Bandon– Port Orford

Location: Near the Elk River; map E1, grid b0.

Campsites, facilities: There are 46 tent sites and 26 drive-through sites for trailers or RVs of any length. Cabins are also available. Picnic tables are provided. Flush toilets, bottled gas, sanitary services, showers, firewood, a recreation hall, a store, a laundry room, ice, a playground, electricity, piped water, and sewer hookups are available. Pets and motorbikes are permitted.

Reservations, fees: Reservations are accepted. Sites are $16.50–$20.50 per night; cabins are $29 per night. The campground is open year-round.

Contact: Phone (541) 348-2358 or write to 46612 Highway 101, Langlois, OR 97450.

Directions: From U.S. 101 at Coos Bay, turn south and drive approximately 50 miles to the campground at milepost 286, on the right.

Trip notes: This spot is considered to be just a layover camp, but it offers large, secluded sites nestled among big trees and coastal ferns. The Elk and Sixes Rivers, where the fishing can be good, are minutes away, and Cape Blanco State Park is just a few miles down the road.

⓬ Cape Blanco State Park

Location: Between the Sixes and Elk Rivers; map E1, grid b0.

Campsites, facilities: There are 58 sites with water and electrical hookups for tents, trailers, or RVs up to 70 feet long. Other options are a special camp for horses, a camping area reserved for hikers and bicyclists, and one primitive group site that can accommodate 25 people. Picnic tables, piped water, electrical hookups, and fire grills are provided. Firewood, flush toilets, showers, and a sanitary disposal station are available. Some facilities are wheelchair accessible. Leashed pets are permitted.

Reservations, fees: Contact Reservations Northwest at (800) 452-5687 ($6 reservation fee). Sites are $15–$18 per night; yurts are $25 per night; and sites for hikers/bicyclists are $4 per night. The campground is open year-round.

Contact: Humbug Mountain State Park, P.O. Box 1345, Port Orford, OR 97465; (541) 332-6774.

Directions: From Coos Bay, turn south on U.S. 101 and drive approximately 46 miles to Cape Blanco Road. Turn northwest and drive five miles to the campground on the left.

Trip notes: This large park is named for the white ("blanco") chalk appearance of the sea cliffs, which rise 200 feet above the ocean. Sea lions inhabit the offshore rocks, and trails and a road lead to the black sand beach below the cliffs. Another highlight is the good access to the Sixes River, which runs for more than two miles through the meadows and forests of the park. Of historical interest are the lighthouse and Hughes House Museum, both located within the park. Trails for horseback riding are also available.

⓭ Sixes River

Location: On the Sixes River; map E1, grid b1.

Campsites, facilities: There are 20 sites for tents, trailers, or RVs up to 30 feet long. Picnic

tables and fire grills are provided. Pit toilets are available. There is no piped water. Leashed pets are permitted.

Reservations, fees: No reservations are accepted. Sites are $5 per night, plus $3 for each additional vehicle, with a 14-day stay limit. The campground is open year-round.

Contact: Bureau of Land Management, 1300 Airport Lane, North Bend, OR 97459; (541) 756-0100.

Directions: From U.S. 101 at Coos Bay, turn south and drive about 40 miles to Sixes. Turn east on Sixes River Road and drive 11.5 miles to the campground. The last half mile is an unpaved road.

Trip notes: Set along the banks of the Sixes River, this is a primitive, secluded campground for people who want quiet and a free, rustic spot. Cape Blanco State Park provides a camping or side trip option.

⑭ Powers County Park

Location: Near the South Fork of the Coquille River; map E1, grid b3.

Campsites, facilities: There are 40 sites for tents, trailers, or RVs. Rest rooms, showers, a sanitary dump, and a public phone are provided. Other facilities include a boat ramp, horseshoes, a playground, and a recreation field. Leashed pets are permitted.

Reservations, fees: No reservations are accepted. Sites are $9–$11 per night. The campground is open year-round.

Contact: Phone the park at (541) 439-2791 or write to P.O. Box 12, Powers, OR 97466.

Directions: From Interstate 5 south of Roseburg, take exit 120 and turn west on Highway 42. Drive about 50 miles to the Powers Highway exit (before Myrtle Point). Drive west on Powers Highway for 19 miles to the park on the right.

Trip notes: This private and secluded public park in a wooded, mountainous area is a great stop for travelers going from Interstate 5 to the coast. A small pond at the park provides a spot for visitors to boat, swim, and fish for trout.

⑮ Charles V. Stanton Park

Location: On the South Umpqua River; map E1, grid b8.

Campsites, facilities: There are 20 tent sites and 20 sites for trailers or RVs up to 30 feet long. Electricity, piped water, sewer hookups, and picnic tables are provided. Flush toilets, showers, and a playground are available. Bottled gas, sanitary disposal services, a store, a cafe, a Laundromat, and ice are located within one mile. Leashed pets and motorbikes are permitted.

Reservations, fees: No reservations are accepted. Sites are $11–$14 per night. The campground is open year-round.

Contact: Phone (541) 839-4483 or write to 1540 Stanton Park Road, Canyonville, OR 97417.

Directions: Take exit 99 off Interstate 5 in Canyonville (follow the sign), then drive one mile north on the frontage road to the campground on the right.

Trip notes: This campground set along the banks of the South Umpqua River is an all-season spot with a nice beach for swimming in the summer, good steelhead fishing in the winter, and wild grape picking in the fall.

⑯ Surprise Valley RV Park

Location: On the South Umpqua River; map E1, grid b8.

Campsites, facilities: There are 15 tent sites and 25 drive-through sites for trailers or RVs of any length. Electricity, piped water, sewer hookups, and picnic tables are provided. Flush toilets, showers, and a laundry room are available. Leashed pets are permitted.

Reservations, fees: No reservations are accepted. Sites are $10–$15 per night. The campground is open year-round.

Contact: Phone (541) 839-6634 or write to P.O. Box 909, Canyonville, OR 97417.

Directions: From Interstate 5 at Canyonville, drive three miles north to exit 102, then one mile east on Gazley Road to the campground.

Trip notes: This RV park is near the South Umpqua River about two miles from a gambling casino. If you desire a more remote setting, the following sites are the answer: Dumont Creek, Boulder Creek, and Camp Comfort (campground numbers 16, 17, and 18 in Chapter E2).

⑰ Elk River Campground

Location: Near the Elk River; map E1, grid c0.

Campsites, facilities: There are 70 sites for tents, trailers, or RVs up to 60 feet long. Rest rooms, showers, a sanitary dump, a public phone, and a laundry room are available. Recreational facilities include a sports field, horseshoes, a recreation hall, and a boat ramp. Some facilities are wheelchair accessible. Leashed pets are permitted.

Reservations, fees: Reservations are recommended. Sites are $12–$14 per night. The campground is open year-round.

Contact: Phone the park at (541) 332-2255, fax (541) 332-6033, or write to 93363 Elk River Road, Port Orford, OR 97465.

Directions: From the north end of Port Orford, continue north on U.S. 101 for 1.5 miles to Elk River Road (milepost 297). Turn east on Elk River Road and drive 1.8 miles to the campground on the left.

Trip notes: This quiet and restful camp is an excellent base for fall and winter fishing on the Elk River, which is known for its premier salmon fishing. A one-mile private access road goes to the river, so guests get their own personal fishing hole.

⑱ Port Orford Trailer Village

Location: Near the Elk and Sixes Rivers; map E1, grid c0.

Campsites, facilities: There are seven tent sites and 49 sites for trailers or RVs of any length; two are drive-throughs. Electricity, piped water, sewer hookups, and picnic tables are provided. Flush toilets, bottled gas, sanitary services, showers, a recreation hall, a laundry room, and ice are available. Boat docks and launching facilities are nearby. Pets and motorbikes are permitted.

Reservations, fees: Reservations are accepted. Sites are $17 per night. The campground is open year-round.

Contact: Phone (541) 332-1041 or write to P.O. Box 697, Port Orford, OR 97465.

Directions: From U.S. 101 at Coos Bay, turn south and drive approximately 50 miles to Port Orford. Drive one block east on Madrona Avenue, then one-half mile north on Port Orford Loop on the left side to the campground.

Trip notes: The hosts make you feel at home at this friendly mom-and-pop campground in Port Orford. An informal group campfire and happy hour is scheduled each evening. Other nice touches include a small gazebo where you can get coffee each morning and a patio where you can sit. Fishing is good during the fall and winter on the nearby Elk and Sixes Rivers, and the campground has a smokehouse, a freezer, and a cleaning table.

⑲ Humbug Mountain State Park

Location: Near the Pacific Ocean; map E1, grid c0.

Campsites, facilities: There are 78 tent sites and 30 sites with full hookups for trailers or RVs up to 55 feet long. A special camping area is provided for hikers and bicyclists. Fire grills and picnic tables are provided. Flush toilets, showers, and firewood are available. Leashed pets are permitted.

Reservations, fees: Contact Reservations Northwest at (800) 452-5687 ($6 reservation fee). Sites are $15–$18 per night; the camping area for hikers/bicyclists is $4 per night. The campground is open year-round.

Contact: Phone (541) 332-6774 or write to P.O. Box 1345, Port Orford, OR 97465.

Directions: From Coos Bay, turn south on U.S. 101 and drive 50 miles to Port Orford. Continue six miles south on U.S. 101 to the park entrance on the left.

Trip notes: Humbug Mountain State Park is

named after the mountain that towers almost 2,000 feet above the nearby coastline. A three-mile trail leads to its peak. This is a special place because both the Pacific Ocean and nearby Brush Creek are accessible, and you can fish in either. Another highlight of the park: beautiful evening sunsets.

⑳ Arizona Beach Campground

Location: Near Gold Beach; map E1, grid c0.
Campsites, facilities: There are 48 tent sites and 78 sites for trailers or RVs of any length; seven are drive-throughs. There is also a motel on the grounds. Electricity, piped water, sewer hookups, and picnic tables are provided. Flush toilets, bottled gas, sanitary services, showers, firewood, a store, a laundry room, and a playground are available. Leashed pets and motorbikes are permitted.
Reservations, fees: Reservations are accepted. Sites are $14–$20 per night, and the motel is $39–$79 per night. The campground is open year-round.
Contact: Phone (541) 332-6491 or write to P.O. Box 621, Gold Beach, OR 97444.
Directions: From U.S. 101 at the town of Gold Beach, drive 14 miles north to the campground on the right.
Trip notes: This pleasant campground offers grassy, tree-lined sites along half a mile of ocean beach frontage. A creek runs through the campground, and you can swim at the mouth of it in the summer. Elk and deer roam nearby. An 11-unit motel is available for campers who need some cleanup time.

㉑ Laird Lake

Location: On Laird Lake in Siskiyou National Forest; map E1, grid c1.
Campsites, facilities: There are undeveloped, dispersed tent sites, with no designated spaces. There is no piped water. Leashed pets are permitted.
Reservations, fees: No reservations are accepted. There is no fee. The campground is open year-round.

Contact: Siskiyou National Forest, Powers Ranger District, Powers, OR 97466; (541) 439-3011 or fax (541) 439-7704.
Directions: From U.S. 101 at Coos Bay, turn south and drive 47 miles to County Road 208 (three miles north of Port Orford). Turn right and drive 7.5 miles southeast, then take Forest Service Road 5325 southeast and drive 15.5 miles to the campground. The road is paved for 11 miles and rock-surfaced for the last 4.5 miles to the campground.
Trip notes: This secluded campground is set along the shore of Laird Lake in a very private and scenic spot. Most campers have no idea such a place exists in the area. This can be just what you're looking for if you're tired of fighting the crowds for the more developed camps along U.S. 101.

㉒ Butler Bar

Location: On the Elk River in Siskiyou National Forest; map E1, grid c1.
Campsites, facilities: There are nine sites for tents, trailers, or RVs up to 16 feet long. Picnic tables and fire grills are provided. Hand-pumped water and pit toilets are available. Leashed pets are permitted.
Reservations, fees: No reservations are accepted. There is no fee. The campground is open year-round.
Contact: Siskiyou National Forest, Powers Ranger District, Powers, OR 97466; (541) 439-3011 or fax (541) 439-7704.
Directions: From U.S. 101 at Coos Bay, turn south and drive 47 miles to County Road 208 (three miles north of Port Orford). Turn right and drive 7.5 miles southeast, then take Forest Service Road 5325 southeast and drive 11 miles to the campground. The road is paved all the way to the camp.
Trip notes: This campground set back from the shore of the Elk River is surrounded by old-growth forest, with some reforested areas nearby. Across the river is the Grassy Knob Wilderness, but it has no trails and is generally too rugged to hike. For fishing enthusiasts, the Elk River has native trout and steelhead in the winter.

23 Myrtle Grove

Location: On the South Fork of the Coquille River in Siskiyou National Forest; map E1, grid c3.

Campsites, facilities: There are five tent sites. Picnic tables and fire grills are provided. Pit toilets are available. There is no piped water. Leashed pets are permitted.

Reservations, fees: No reservations are accepted. There is no fee. The campground is open year-round.

Contact: Siskiyou National Forest, Powers Ranger District, Powers, OR 97466; (541) 439-3011 or fax (541) 439-7704.

Directions: From U.S. 101 south of Coos Bay, turn west on Highway 42 and drive 20 miles, then turn south on Highway 242 and drive approximately 18 miles to Powers. Continue south on County Road 90 for 4.3 miles, then drive 4.5 miles south on Forest Service Road 33, and you'll see the campground. The road is paved all the way to the camp.

Trip notes: This Forest Service campground is located along the South Fork of the Coquille River, a little downstream from Daphne Grove (campground number 24) and in similar surroundings. The Big Tree Recreation Site, home to a huge Port Orford cedar, is a few miles away. A prime hike can be made on the trail that runs adjacent to Elk Creek. (The road to Big Tree may be closed due to slides, so be sure to check with the ranger district in advance.)

24 Daphne Grove

Location: On the South Fork of the Coquille River in Siskiyou National Forest; map E1, grid c3.

Campsites, facilities: There are 15 sites for tents, trailers, or RVs up to 35 feet long. Picnic tables and fire grills are provided. Vault toilets and hand-pumped water are available. Some facilities are wheelchair accessible. Leashed pets are permitted.

Reservations, fees: No reservations are accepted. Sites are $6 per night from late May to late September, and free the rest of the year. The campground is open year-round, with limited winter facilities.

Contact: Siskiyou National Forest, Powers Ranger District, Powers, OR 97466; (541) 439-3011 or fax (541) 439-7704.

Directions: From Interstate 5 south of Roseburg, take exit 120 and drive 55 miles east on Highway 42. Turn south on Highway 242 and drive to Powers. Continue 4.5 miles southeast on County Road 90, then 10.5 miles south on Forest Service Road 33, and you'll see the campground entrance.

Trip notes: This prime spot along the South Fork of the Coquille River, surrounded by old-growth Douglas fir and cedar, is far enough out of the way to attract little attention. The road is paved all the way to, as well as in, the campground, a plus for RVs and "city cars."

25 Rock Creek

Location: Near the South Fork of the Coquille River in Siskiyou National Forest; map E1, grid c3.

Campsites, facilities: There are seven sites for tents, trailers, or RVs. Picnic tables, hand-pumped water, and fire grills are provided. Vault toilets and firewood are available. Leashed pets are permitted.

Reservations, fees: No reservations are accepted. Sites are $5 per night from late May to late September, and free the rest of the year. The campground is open year-round, with limited winter facilities.

Contact: Siskiyou National Forest, Powers Ranger District, Powers, OR 97466; (541) 439-3011 or fax (541) 439-7704.

Directions: From Interstate 5 south of Roseburg, take exit 120 and drive 55 miles east on Highway 42. Turn south on Highway 242 and drive to Powers. Continue 4.5 miles southeast on County Road 90 to Forest Service Road 33. Go south for 13 miles, then 1.5 miles southwest on Forest Service Road 3347 to the campground. The road is paved all the way.

Trip notes: This little-known camp surrounded by old-growth forest and some reforested areas is set along Rock Creek, just upstream from its confluence with the South Fork of the Coquille River. A good side trip here is the one-mile climb to Azalea Lake, which is stocked with trout. There are some hike-in campsites at the lake, but they have no piped drinking water. In July, the azalea are spectacular.

26 Squaw Lake

Location: On Squaw Lake in Siskiyou National Forest; map E1, grid c3.

Campsites, facilities: There are seven partially developed sites for tents, trailers, or RVs up to 21 feet. Pit toilets are available. There is no piped water. Leashed pets are permitted.

Reservations, fees: No reservations are accepted. There is no fee. The campground is open year-round.

Contact: Siskiyou National Forest, Powers Ranger District, Powers, OR 97466; (541) 439-3011 or fax (541) 439-7704.

Directions: From Interstate 5 south of Roseburg, take exit 120 and drive 55 miles east on Highway 42. Turn south on Highway 242 and drive to Powers. Continue 4.5 miles southeast on County Road 90. At Forest Service Road 33 drive south for 12.5 miles, then southeast on Forest Service Road 3348 for 4.5 miles. Turn east on Forest Service Road 3342 and drive one mile to the campground. The road is paved for all but the last half mile.

Trip notes: This campground along the shore of five-acre Squaw Lake is set in rich, old-growth forest. The trailheads for the Panther Ridge Trail and Coquille River Falls Trail are a 10-minute drive from the campground. It's strongly advised that you obtain a Forest Service map detailing the backcountry roads and trails.

27 Illahe

Location: On the Rogue River in Siskiyou National Forest; map E1, grid c3.

Campsites, facilities: There are 14 sites for tents, trailers, or RVs up to 21 feet long. Piped water, fire rings, and picnic tables are provided. Flush toilets are available. A store is

located within five miles. Boat docks are nearby. Leashed pets are permitted.

Reservations, fees: No reservations are accepted. Sites are $6 per night, plus $2 for each additional vehicle. The campground is open from mid-May to mid-October.

Contact: Siskiyou National Forest, Gold Beach Ranger District, 29279 Ellensburg Avenue, Gold Beach, OR 97444; (541) 247-3600 or fax (541) 247-3617.

Directions: From the town of Gold Beach on U.S. 101, take Agness–Gold Beach Road east for 30 miles to the turnoff to Agness. From Agness, travel five miles north on County Road 375 to the campground entrance.

Trip notes: This quiet and isolated camping area has great hiking opportunities, yet boating and fishing are just a mile away at Foster Bar (campground number 42). It's a pretty spot hidden from the majority of tourists.

28 Tucker Flat

Location: On the Rogue River; map E1, grid c4.

Campsites, facilities: There are 10 primitive tent sites. Picnic tables and fire grills are provided. Pit toilets and bear-proof trash cans are available. There is no piped water. Leashed pets are permitted.

Reservations, fees: No reservations are accepted. There is no fee. The campground is open from May to late October, weather permitting.

Contact: Bureau of Land Management, 3040 Biddle Road, Medford, OR 97504; (541) 770-2200.

Directions: From Interstate 5 near Grants Pass, take exit 61 and travel 20 miles west on Merlin-Galice Access Road to the Grave Creek Bridge (the second bridge over the Rogue River). Turn left after crossing the bridge onto BLM Road 34-8-1. Continue 16 miles, turn left onto BLM Road 32-8-31, and drive for another seven miles. Turn left onto BLM Road 32-9-14.2 and go 15 miles. The campground is just around the corner from the Rogue River Ranch.

Trip notes: This campground is set in the Zane Grey Bureau of Land Management tract, which covers 18,460 acres of rugged country, with steep canyons and many small waterfalls. The Rogue River passes through the tract, and the Rogue River Trail runs alongside the river for 26 miles. A riding stable is located nearby.

㉙ Meadow Wood RV Resort and Camp

Location: In Glendale; map E1, grid c7.

Campsites, facilities: There are 25 tent sites and 34 drive-through sites for trailers or RVs of any length; 11 sites have full hookups. Electricity, piped water, and picnic tables are provided. Flush toilets, bottled gas, sanitary disposal services, showers, firewood, a recreation hall, a store, a laundry room, ice, a playground, and a heated swimming pool are available. Leashed pets are permitted.

Reservations, fees: Reservations are accepted. Sites are $12–$20 per night. The campground is open year-round.

Contact: Phone (541) 832-3114, fax (541) 832-2454, or write to 869 Autumn Lane, Glendale, OR 97442.

Directions: Traveling southbound on Interstate 5, take exit 86 north of Glendale and drive three miles south on the frontage road to Barton Road. Turn east and drive two-tenths of a mile. Drive south on Autumn Lane for three-quarters of a mile to the park. Traveling northbound on Interstate 5, take exit 83 and travel two-tenths of a mile east. Turn south on Autumn Lane and drive three-quarters of a mile to the camp.

Trip notes: This is a good option for RVers looking for a camping spot along Interstate 5. All the amenities are available. Nearby attractions include an old ghost town, gold panning, and Wolf Creek Tavern.

㉚ Honeybear Campground

Location: Near Gold Beach; map E1, grid d0.

Campsites, facilities: There are 20 tent sites and 65 sites for trailers or RVs of any length; 20 are drive-throughs with partial hookups. Picnic tables are provided. Flush toilets, electricity, piped water, cable TV, sanitary services, showers, firewood, a recreation hall, a restaurant, a store, a laundry room, ice, and a playground are available. Leashed pets and motorbikes are permitted.

Reservations, fees: Reservations are accepted. Sites are $14.95–$17.95 per night. The campground is open year-round, weather permitting.

Contact: Phone (541) 247-2765 or write to P.O. Box 97, Ophir, OR 97464.

Directions: From U.S. 101 at the town of Gold Beach, drive nine miles north to Ophir Road. The campground is two miles north on the right side of Ophir Road.

Trip notes: This campground offers wooded sites with ocean views. The owners have built a huge, authentic chalet that contains a German deli, a recreation area, and a big dance floor. On summer nights, they hold dances with live music.

㉛ Nesika Beach Trailer Park

Location: Near Gold Beach; map E1, grid d0.

Campsites, facilities: There are six tent sites and 32 sites for trailers or RVs of any length. Electricity, piped water, cable TV, sewer hookups, and picnic tables are provided. Flush toilets, sanitary services, showers, a store, a laundry room, and ice are available. There is a cafe within walking distance. Pets and motorbikes are permitted.

Reservations, fees: Reservations are accepted. Sites are $12–$15 per night. The campground is open year-round.

Contact: Phone (541) 247-6077 or write to 32887 Nesika Road, Gold Beach, OR 97444.

Directions: Take U.S. 101 six miles north of the town of Gold Beach to Nesika Road. Turn left and drive one-half mile west to the campground on the right.

Trip notes: This campground next to Nesika Beach is a good layover spot for U.S. 101 cruisers. An 18-hole golf course is close by.

⚃ Ireland's Ocean View RV Park

Location: On the Pacific Ocean; map E1, grid d0.

Campsites, facilities: There are 32 sites for trailers or RVs up to 40 feet. Tent camping is permitted only in combination with an RV. Cable TV, phones, showers, rest rooms, a laundry room, a recreation room, horseshoe pits, and picnic areas are available. Leashed pets are permitted.

Reservations, fees: Reservations are recommended. Sites are $13.50–$20 per night. The campground is open year-round.

Contact: Phone the park at (541) 247-0148 or write to 29272 Ellensburg Avenue, P.O. Box 727, Gold Beach, OR 97444.

Directions: This camp is in the town of Gold Beach on U.S. 101. The camp is located across from the U.S. Forest Service office.

Trip notes: One of the newest RV parks in the area, this spot is on the beach in the quaint little town of Gold Beach, only one mile from the famous Rogue River. Recreation options include beachcombing, fishing, and boating. Great ocean views are possible from the observatory/lighthouse.

⚄ Indian Creek Recreation Park

Location: On the Rogue River; map E1, grid d0.

Campsites, facilities: There are 25 tent sites and 100 sites for trailers or RVs of any length. Electricity, piped water, sewer and cable TV hookups, and picnic tables are provided. Flush toilets, showers, firewood, a recreation hall, a store, a sauna, a cafe, a laundry room, ice, and a playground are available. Bottled gas is located within two miles. Boat docks, launching facilities, and rentals are nearby. Leashed pets and motorbikes are permitted.

Reservations, fees: Reservations are accepted. Sites are $15–$22 per night. The campground is open year-round.

Contact: Phone (541) 247-7704 or write to 94680 Jerry's Flat Road, Gold Beach, OR 97444.

Directions: In the town of Gold Beach on U.S. 101, look for Jerry's Flat Road and drive one-half mile east to the campground.

Trip notes: This campground is along the Rogue River on the outskirts of the town of Gold Beach. Nearby recreation options include a riding stable, riding trails, and boat trips on the Rogue.

⚅ Oceanside RV Park

Location: On the Pacific Ocean; map E1, grid d0.

Campsites, facilities: There are 90 sites for trailers or RVs of any length; 20 are drive-throughs. Electricity, piped water, sewer hookups, and picnic tables are provided. Flush toilets, showers, cable TV, a small store, and ice are available. Bottled gas, sanitary services, a store, a cafe, and a Laundromat are located within two miles. Boat docks, launching facilities, and rentals are nearby. Leashed pets and motorbikes are permitted.

Reservations, fees: Reservations are recommended in the summer. Sites are $15–$20 per night. The campground is open year-round.

Contact: Phone (541) 247-2301 or write to P.O. Box 1107, Gold Beach, OR 97444.

Directions: This park is in Gold Beach, at the south jetty of the Port of Gold Beach.

Trip notes: Set right on the ocean, this park is close to beachcombing terrain, marked bike trails, and boating facilities.

㉟ Hunter Creek RV Park

Location: On Hunter Creek; map E1, grid d0.

Campsites, facilities: There are 60 sites for tents, trailers, or RVs. Rest rooms, showers, a public phone, a laundry room, limited groceries, RV supplies, LP gas, a playground, and a game room are available.

Reservations, fees: Reservations are recommended. Sites are $13–$16 per night. The campground is open year-round.

Contact: Phone the park at (541) 247-2322, fax (541) 247-0578, or write to P.O. Box 1227, 28555 Hunter Creek Loop, Gold Beach, OR 97444.

Directions: From U.S. 101 at the south end of the town of Gold Beach, turn east on Hunter Creek Road and drive seven-tenths of a mile southeast. The campground is located on the left side of the road.

Trip notes: This camp set amidst wooded mountains on a small stream in the town of Gold Beach is preferred by tent campers over the other camps in town since it's a bit more private and secluded. For anglers, steelhead fishing can be excellent from January through March.

36 Fairgrounds RV Resort

Location: On the Rogue River; map E1, grid d1.

Campsites, facilities: There are 45 sites for trailers or RVs up to 35 feet long; two are drive-throughs. Electricity, piped water, sewer hookups, and picnic tables are provided. Flush toilets, bottled gas, sanitary services, showers, firewood, a recreation hall, a store, a laundry room, and ice are available. Boat docks and launching facilities are nearby. Leashed pets and motorbikes are permitted.

Reservations, fees: Reservations are accepted. Sites are $17–$29.50 per night. The campground is open year-round.

Contact: Fairgrounds RV Resort, 96526 North Bank Rogue Road, Gold Beach, OR 97444; (541) 247-4541 or fax (541) 247-4504; e-mail: fourseasons@harborside.com.

Directions: Drive one mile north of the town of Gold Beach on U.S. 101, then three miles northeast on Rogue River Road. Follow the signs on North Bank Rogue Road to the campground.

Trip notes: This resort along the shore of the Rogue River is close to a nine-hole golf course and boat trips on the Wild and Scenic Rogue—using anything from a raft to a jet boat. The sites are well kept, with nice lawns and lots of trees.

37 Kimball Creek Bend

Location: On the Rogue River; map E1, grid d1.

Campsites, facilities: There are 13 tent sites and 56 sites for trailers or RVs of any length; 18 are drive-throughs. Electricity, piped water, sewer hookups, and picnic tables are provided. Flush toilets, bottled gas, sanitary services, showers, a recreation hall, a store, a laundry room, ice, and a playground are available. Boat docks and launching facilities are nearby. Leashed pets are permitted.

Reservations, fees: Reservations are accepted; phone (888) 814-0633. Sites are $17–$25.50 per night. The campground is open year-round.

Contact: Phone (541) 247-7580 or write to 97136 North Bank Rogue Road, Gold Beach, OR 97444.

Directions: From the town of Gold Beach, drive one mile north on U.S. 101, then 3.5 miles northeast on Rogue River Road to North Bank Rogue Road and head 4.5 miles to the campground.

Trip notes: This campground on the scenic Rogue River is just far enough from the coast to provide quiet and its own distinct character. Nearby recreation options include an 18-hole golf course, hiking trails, and boating facilities.

38 Lucky Lodge RV Park

Location: On the Rogue River; map E1, grid d1.

Campsites, facilities: There are four tent sites and 32 full hookup sites for trailers or RVs of any length; most are drive-throughs. Electricity, piped water, sewer hookups, and picnic tables are provided. Flush toilets, bottled gas, sanitary services, showers, firewood, a recreation hall, and a laundry room are available. Boat docks and rentals are located within eight miles. Leashed pets are permitted.

Reservations, fees: Reservations are accepted. Sites are $17 per night. The campground is open year-round.

Contact: Phone (541) 247-7618 or write to 32040 Watson Lane, Gold Beach, OR 97444.

Directions: Drive one mile north of Gold Beach on U.S. 101. At Rogue River Road, continue 3.5 miles northeast to North Bank Rogue Road and follow it 4.5 more miles to the park.

Trip notes: This is a good layover spot for U.S. 101 travelers who want to get off the highway circuit. It's set on the shore of the river and offers opportunities for fishing, boating, and swimming. Nearby recreation options include hiking trails.

❸❾ Anglers Trailer Village

Location: On the Rogue River; map E1, grid d1.

Campsites, facilities: There are 36 sites with full hookups for trailers or RVs of any length and an area that can accommodate about three tents. Electricity, piped water, cable TV, and sewer hookups are provided. Flush toilets, showers, a recreation hall, and a laundry room are available. Leashed pets are permitted.

Reservations, fees: Reservations are accepted. Sites are $15 per night. The campground is open year-round.

Contact: Phone (541) 247-7922 or write to 95706 Jerry's Flat Road, Gold Beach, OR 97444.

Directions: In Gold Beach on U.S. 101, turn east at the south end of the Rogue River Bridge, then drive 3.5 miles north on Jerry's Flat Road to the campground.

Trip notes: This is one of seven campgrounds on the lower Rogue River near Gold Beach. It's best used as an overnight layover.

❹⓿ Lobster Creek

Location: On the Rogue River in Siskiyou National Forest; map E1, grid d2.

Campsites, facilities: There are six sites for tents, trailers, or RVs up to 21 feet long. Fire rings and picnic tables are provided. Flush toilets and piped water are available. A boat launch is also available. Leashed pets are permitted.

Reservations, fees: No reservations are accepted. Sites are $6 per night, plus $2 for each additional vehicle. Camping is also permitted on a gravel bar area for $3 per night. The campground is open from mid-May to mid-October.

Contact: Siskiyou National Forest, Gold Beach Ranger District, 29279 Ellensburg Avenue, Gold Beach, OR 97444; (541) 247-3600 or fax (541) 247-3617.

Directions: From the town of Gold Beach on U.S. 101, take County Road 595 (which becomes Forest Service Road 33) about 10 miles northeast to the campground on the left.

Trip notes: This small campground on a river bar along the Rogue River, about a 15-minute drive from Gold Beach, makes a good base for a fishing trip.

❹❶ Quosatana

Location: On the Rogue River in Siskiyou National Forest; map E1, grid d2.

Campsites, facilities: There are 42 sites for tents, trailers, or RVs up to 32 feet long. Piped water, fire grills, and picnic tables are provided. Flush toilets, a sanitary disposal station, and a boat ramp are available. Some facilities are wheelchair accessible. Leashed pets are permitted.

Reservations, fees: No reservations are accepted. Sites are $8 per night, plus $3 for each additional vehicle. The campground is open year-round.

Contact: Siskiyou National Forest, Gold Beach Ranger District, 29279 Ellensburg Avenue, Gold Beach, OR 97444; (541) 247-3600 or fax (541) 247-3617.

Directions: From the town of Gold Beach on U.S. 101, drive on County Road 595 (which becomes Forest Service Road 33) for 13 miles northeast to the campground on the left.

Trip notes: This campground is set along the banks of the Rogue River, upstream from the much smaller Lobster Creek (campground number 40). Ocean access is just a short drive away, and the quaint town of Gold Beach offers a decent side trip. Nearby Otter Point State Park (day use only) has further recreation options. This is a good base camp for a hiking or fishing trip.

㊷ Foster Bar

Location: On the Rogue River in Siskiyou National Forest; map E1, grid d3.

Campsites, facilities: There are several dispersed sites for tents, trailers, or RVs up to 16 feet long, though access is difficult for RVs and trailers. Fire rings and picnic tables are provided. Pit toilets and boat launching facilities are available, but there is no piped water. Leashed pets are permitted.

Reservations, fees: No reservations are accepted. There is no fee. The campground is open year-round.

Contact: Siskiyou National Forest, Gold Beach Ranger District, 29279 Ellensburg Avenue, Gold Beach, OR 97444; (541) 247-3600 or fax (541) 247-3617.

Directions: From the town of Gold Beach on U.S. 101, take Agness–Gold Beach Road east for 30 miles to the turnoff to Agness. Turn right on Illahe-Agness Road and drive three miles to the campground.

Trip notes: This camping area is located on the banks of the Rogue River at a popular put-in spot for the eight-mile inner tube ride to Agness. Life jackets are mandatory because of rough rapids. Hiking opportunities are good and you can also fish from the river bar. Illahe and Agness RV Park provide nearby camping options (see campground numbers 27 and 43).

㊸ Agness RV Park

Location: On the Rogue River; map E1, grid d2.

Campsites, facilities: There are 81 sites for trailers or RVs of any length; 43 are drive-throughs. Electricity, piped water, sewer hookups and picnic tables are provided. Flush toilets, sanitary services, showers, and a laundry room are available. A store, a cafe, bottled gas, and ice are located within 100 yards. Boat launching facilities are nearby. Pets and motorbikes are permitted.

Reservations, fees: Reservations are accepted. Sites are $15 per night. The campground is open year-round.

Contact: Phone (541) 247-2813 or write to 4215 Agness Road, Agness, OR 97406.

Directions: From Gold Beach on U.S. 101, drive 28 miles east on Jerry's Flat Road and you'll see the entrance to the campground on the left.

Trip notes: This is a destination campground on the scenic Rogue River in the middle of the Siskiyou National Forest. Fishing is the main focus here. Boating is sharply limited because the nearest pullout is 12 miles downstream. It's advisable to obtain a Forest Service map detailing the backcountry.

㊹ Sam Brown and Sam Brown Horse Camp

Location: Near Grants Pass in Siskiyou National Forest; map E1, grid d5.

Campsites, facilities: There are 37 sites for tents, trailers, or RVs of any length at Sam Brown and seven equestrian tent sites with small corrals across the road at Sam Brown Horse Camp. At Sam Brown, picnic tables, fire grills, hand-pumped water, and vault toilets are provided. Firewood, a picnic shelter, and an amphitheater are available. Many sites are wheelchair accessible.

Reservations, fees: No reservations are accepted. Sam Brown sites are $2 per night. Sam Brown Horse Camp sites are $5 per night. There is a $2 charge for each additional vehicle at both camps. The campground is open from late May to mid-October.

Contact: Siskiyou National Forest, Galice Ranger District, 200 NE Greenfield Road, Grants Pass, OR 97526; (541) 471-6500 or fax (541) 471-6514.

Directions: From Grants Pass, drive 3.5 miles north on Interstate 5, then take exit 61 and turn northwest on County Road 2-6. Drive 12.5 miles, then turn left on Forest Service Road 25 and head southwest for 14 miles to the campground.

Trip notes: This campground is located in an isolated area near Grants Pass along Briggs

Creek in a valley of venerable pine and Douglas fir. Many sites lie in the shade of the old-growth trees, and many others are set right on the banks of the creek. There are several hiking and horseback riding trails in the vicinity. An amphitheater is available for small group presentations.

㊺ Big Pine

Location: On Myers Creek in Siskiyou National Forest; map E1, grid d5.

Campsites, facilities: There are 14 tent sites. Picnic tables and fire grills are provided. Vault toilets, hand-pumped water, and firewood are available. The facilities are wheelchair accessible. Leashed pets are permitted.

Reservations, fees: No reservations are accepted. Sites are $5 per night. The campground is open from late May to mid-October.

Contact: Siskiyou National Forest, Galice Ranger District, 200 NE Greenfield Road, Grants Pass, OR 97526; (541) 471-6500 or fax (541) 471-6514.

Directions: From Grants Pass, drive 3.5 miles north on Interstate 5, then take exit 61 and turn northwest on County Road 2-6. Drive 12.5 miles, then turn left on Forest Service Road 25 and head southwest for 12.8 miles to the campground.

Trip notes: This little campground is near the banks of Myers Creek, amid a valley of old-growth pine and Douglas fir. Many sites are right on the creek, and all are shaded. One of the world's tallest ponderosa pine trees is located in the campground, and there is a wheelchair-accessible nature trail. It's advisable to obtain a national forest map.

㊻ Bend o' the River RV Park

Location: On the Rogue River; map E1, grid d6.

Campsites, facilities: There are five tent sites and 25 sites for trailers or RVs of any length. Electricity, piped water, sewer hookups, and picnic tables are provided. Flush toilets, sanitary disposal services, showers, firewood, a cafe, a store, a laundry room, and ice are available. Leashed pets are permitted.

Reservations, fees: Reservations are accepted. Sites are $7–$15 per night. The campground is open year-round.

Contact: Phone (541) 479-2547 or write to 7501 Lower River Road, Grants Pass, OR 97526.

Directions: Take exit 58 off Interstate 5 in Grants Pass, then drive south on Sixth Street to G Street (which becomes Upper River Road and then Lower River Road). The park is located seven miles west on Lower River Road.

Trip notes: This campground is set along the banks of the Rogue River. It's a pretty spot far enough out of Grants Pass to have its own unique feel.

㊼ White Horse

Location: On the Rogue River; map E1, grid d7.

Campsites, facilities: There are 45 sites for tents, trailers, or RVs up to 35 feet long; eight have full hookups. Piped water and picnic tables are provided. Rest rooms, showers, a public phone, fire grills, horseshoes, a reservable picnic shelter, and a playground are available. Leashed pets are permitted.

Reservations, fees: Reservations are accepted. Sites are $14–$19 per night, plus $3 for each additional vehicle. The campground is open year-round, but only to self-contained RVs in the winter.

Contact: Josephine County Parks, 125 Ringuetle Street, Grants Pass, OR 97527; (541) 474-5285 or fax (541) 474-5288.

Directions: From Interstate 5 at Grants Pass, drive in town to the junction of Sixth and G Streets. Turn west on G Street and drive one mile (G Street turns into Upper River Road). Continue for seven miles on Upper River Road to the campground on the left.

Trip notes: This pleasant county park on the banks of the Rogue River is one of several parks in the Grants Pass area that provides opportunities for trout fishing, swimming, hiking, and boating. Take your pick.

48 Grants Pass Overniters

Location: Near Grants Pass; map E1, grid d7.

Campsites, facilities: There are eight tent sites and 42 drive-through sites for trailers or RVs of any length. Electricity, piped water, sewer hookups, and picnic tables are provided. Flush toilets, showers, a laundry room, ice, and a swimming pool are available. A store is located within one mile. Pets and motorbikes are permitted.

Reservations, fees: Reservations are accepted. Sites are $12–$16 per night. The campground is open year-round.

Contact: Phone (541) 479-7289 or write to 5941 Highland Avenue, Grants Pass, OR 97526.

Directions: From Grants Pass, drive three miles north on Interstate 5 to exit 61E, then drive north on the frontage road to the park.

Trip notes: This wooded park is set in a rural area just outside Grants Pass. There are several other campgrounds in the area.

49 Lazy Acres RV

Location: On the Rogue River; map E1, grid d9.

Campsites, facilities: There are 60 sites with full hookups for trailers or RVs of any length and 15 dry tent camping sites. Electricity, piped water, sewer hookups, and picnic tables are provided. Flush toilets, bottled gas, cable TV, a dump station, a playground, and a laundry room are available. Boat docks are nearby. Leashed pets are permitted.

Reservations, fees: No reservations are accepted. Sites are $12–$15 per night. The campground is open year-round.

Contact: Phone (541) 855-7000 or write to 1550 Second Avenue, Gold Hill, OR 97525.

Directions: In Gold Hill on Interstate 5, take the South Gold Hill exit and drive one-quarter mile north, then 1.2 miles west on Second Avenue to the campground on the left.

Trip notes: This wooded campground on the Rogue River is less scenic than KOA Medford–Gold Hill (campground number 62), but it offers the same recreation options.

50 Elderberry Flat

Location: On Evans Creek; map E1, grid d9.

Campsites, facilities: There are 10 primitive tent sites. Picnic tables and fire grills are provided. Wheelchair-accessible vault toilets are available, but there is no piped water. Leashed pets are permitted.

Reservations, fees: No reservations are accepted. There is no fee. The campground is open from late May to early November.

Contact: Bureau of Land Management, 3040 Biddle Road, Medford, OR 97501; (541) 770-2200.

Directions: From Interstate 5, take the City of Rogue River exit into town. Turn right on East Evans Creek Road and drive 18 miles to West Fork Evans Creek Road. Turn left and drive nine miles to the campground.

Trip notes: Virtually unknown, this campground on the banks of Evans Creek is only about a 30-minute drive from Interstate 5. It's small, primitive, and private—a perfect layover spot for weary highway cruisers who want to get away from the crowds for a while.

51 Whaleshead Beach Resort

Location: Near the Pacific Ocean; map E1, grid e0.

Campsites, facilities: There are 115 sites for tents, trailers, or RVs of any length. Ten cabins are also available. Cable TV, restrooms, showers, a public phone, a laundry room, limited groceries, ice, snacks, RV supplies, and LP gas are available. There is a sanitary dump station six miles away. Recreational facilities include horseshoe pits, a recreation hall, and a game room. Some facilities are wheelchair accessible. Leashed pets are permitted.

Reservations, fees: Reservations are recommended. Sites are $15–$25 per night. Cabins are $65–$130 per night. The campground is open year-round.

Contact: Phone the park at (541) 469-7446, fax (541) 469-7447, or write to 19921 Whaleshead Road, Brookings, OR 97415.

Directions: From the north end of the Chetco

River Bridge in Brookings, drive 8.5 miles north on U.S. 101. The campground is on the right at milepost 349.5.

Trip notes: This resort, about a quarter of a mile from the beach, is set in a forested area with a small stream nearby. Activities at and around the camp include ocean and river fishing, jet boat trips, whale watching excursions, and a golf course (30 minutes away).

52 Lake Selmac

Location: On Lake Selmac; map E1, grid e5.

Campsites, facilities: There are 81 sites for tents, trailers, or RVs up to 32 feet long. Piped water and picnic tables are provided. Facilities include rest rooms, showers, a sanitary dump, a public phone, snacks, a barbecue, horseshoes, a playground, a recreation field, and a boat ramp and dock. Facilities are wheelchair accessible. Leashed pets are permitted.

Reservations, fees: Reservations are recommended. Sites are $12–$17 per night, plus $5 for each additional vehicle. The campground is open year-round, with limited winter service.

Contact: Josephine County Parks, 125 Ringuetle Street, Grants Pass, OR 97527; (541) 474-5285.

Directions: From Interstate 5 at Grants Pass, take exit 58 and drive southwest on U.S. 199 for 23 miles to Selma. The camp is located in town (well signed).

Trip notes: Nestled in a wooded, mountainous area, this park offers swimming, hiking, boating, and good trout fishing on beautiful Lake Selmac. See the trip notes for Lake Selmac RV Resort (campground number 54) for details about the area.

53 Grants Pass/ Redwood KOA

Location: Near Grants Pass; map E1, grid e6.

Campsites, facilities: There are 40 sites for tents, trailers, or RVs. Rest rooms, showers, a sanitary dump, security, a public phone, a laundry room, limited groceries, ice, RV supplies, LP gas, and a barbecue are available.

There is also a recreation hall, a playground, and a recreation field. Leashed pets are permitted.

Reservations, fees: Reservations are recommended. Sites are $17–$22 per night. The campground is open year-round.

Contact: Phone the park at (541) 476-6508 or write to 13370 Redwood Highway, Wilderville, OR 97543.

Directions: From Interstate 5 at the south end of Grants Pass, turn southwest on U.S. 199 and drive 14 miles. The campground is located on the right at milepost 14.5.

Trip notes: This KOA campground along a stream in the hills outside of Grants Pass is popular with bird-watchers. It's a perfect layover spot for travelers who want to get away from the highway for a while. For an interesting side trip, drive south down scenic U.S. 199 to Cave Junction or Illinois River State Park.

54 Lake Selmac RV Resort

Location: On Lake Selmac; map E1, grid e6.

Campsites, facilities: There are 18 tent sites and 25 sites for trailers or RVs of any length. Electricity, piped water, sewer hookups, and picnic tables are provided. Flush toilets, bottled gas, sanitary services, showers, firewood, a store, a cafe, a laundry room, ice, and a playground are available. Boat docks, launching facilities, and rentals are nearby. Horseback riding trails are available in the summer. Pets and motorbikes are permitted.

Reservations, fees: Reservations are accepted. Sites are $11–$15 per night. The campground is open year-round, with limited winter facilities.

Contact: Phone (541) 597-4989, fax (541) 597-4989, or write to 2700 Lakeshore Drive, Selma, OR 97538.

Directions: From Interstate 5 at Grants Pass, turn southwest on U.S. 199 and drive approximately 25 miles to Selma. Take the Lake Selmac exit and drive two miles east on Lakeshore Drive to the resort on the left.

Trip notes: This resort is along the shore of Lake Selmac near a golf course. About 30 miles away is Oregon Caves National Monument, where you can take an unusual, 75-minute guided tour. The caves consist of a series of amazing caverns connected by a long, winding trail. Dress warmly; it can be cold and clammy. To reach the caves, drive 20 miles east of Cave Junction on Highway 46. The road gets narrow near the end and is not recommended for trailers.

55 Rogue Valley Overniters

Location: Near the Rogue River; map E1, grid e7.

Campsites, facilities: There are 110 sites for tents, trailers, and RVs; 26 are drive-throughs. Electricity, piped water, cable TV, and sewer hookups are provided. Flush toilets, sanitary disposal services, showers, and a laundry room are available. Bottled gas, a store, a cafe, and ice are available within one mile. Leashed pets are permitted.

Reservations, fees: Reservations are accepted. Sites are $19–$20 per night. The campground is open year-round.

Contact: Phone (541) 479-2208 or write to 1806 Northwest Sixth Street, Grants Pass, OR 97526.

Directions: Take exit 58 off Interstate 5 in Grants Pass, then follow Sixth Street south for about 400 yards to the campground.

Trip notes: This park is just off the freeway in Grants Pass, the jump-off point for trips down the Rogue River. The summer heat in this part of Oregon can surprise visitors in late June and early July.

56 Schroeder

Location: On the Rogue River; map E1, grid e7.

Campsites, facilities: There are two tent sites and 28 sites for trailers and RVs. Rest rooms, showers, and a public phone are available. Recreational facilities include horseshoes, a recreation field, a barbecue, a playground, and a boat ramp. Leashed pets are permitted.

Reservations, fees: Reservations are ac-

cepted. Sites are $12–$17 per night. The campground is open year-round.

Contact: Josephine County Parks, 125 Ringuetle Street, Grants Pass, OR 97527; (541) 474-5285.

Directions: From Interstate 5 at Grants Pass, take exit 58 and drive four miles west on U.S. 199 to the campground.

Trip notes: Trout fishing, swimming, and boating are among the possibilities at this camp along the Rogue River. Just a short jog off the highway, it makes an excellent layover for Interstate 5 travelers. It's not a highly publicized camp, so many tourists pass by it in favor of the more commercial camps in the area.

57 River Park RV Resort

Location: On the Rogue River; map E1, grid e7.

Campsites, facilities: There are three tent sites and 47 sites for trailers or RVs. Cable TV, rest rooms, showers, a sanitary dump, a public phone, laundry facilities, and ice are available. Leashed pets are permitted.

Reservations, fees: Reservations are recommended. Sites are $18–$20 per night. The campground is open year-round.

Contact: Phone the park at (800) 677-8857 or (541) 479-0046, fax (541) 471-1448, or write to 2956 Rogue River Highway, Grants Pass, OR 97527.

Directions: From Interstate 5 at Grants Pass, take exit 55 and drive on Sixth Street across the Rogue River. Turn left on Parkdale and drive one block. Turn left on Highway 99 and drive two miles to the park on the left.

Trip notes: This park has a quiet, serene riverfront setting, yet is close to all the conveniences of a small city. Highlights here include 700 feet of Rogue River frontage for trout fishing and swimming. It's one of several parks in the immediate area.

58 Circle W Campground

Location: On the Rogue River; map E1, grid e8.

Campsites, facilities: There are 25 sites for trailers or RVs of any length; four are drive-throughs. Electricity, piped water, sewer hookups, and picnic tables are provided. Flush toilets, sanitary disposal services, showers, a store, a laundry room, ice, bottled gas, and a playground are available. A cafe and a boat dock are located nearby. Leashed pets are permitted.

Reservations, fees: Reservations are accepted. Sites are $15–$21 per night. The campground is open year-round.

Contact: Phone (541) 582-1686 or write to 8110 Rogue River Highway, Grants Pass, OR 97527.

Directions: Take the Rogue River exit (exit 48) off Interstate 5, then drive one mile west on Highway 99 to the campground.

Trip notes: This campground along the Rogue River is close to chartered boat trips down the Rogue, a golf course, and tennis courts. Fishing and swimming access are available from the campground.

⑤⑨ Have a Nice Day Campground

Location: On the Rogue River; map E1, grid e8.

Campsites, facilities: There are 16 tent sites and 30 sites for trailers or RVs of any length; three are drive-throughs. Electricity, piped water, sewer hookups, and picnic tables are provided. Flush toilets, sanitary disposal services, showers, a laundry room, and a playground are available. A store and a cafe are located within one mile. Boat docks and launching facilities are nearby. Leashed pets and motorbikes are permitted.

Reservations, fees: Reservations are accepted. Sites are $17 per night. The campground is open year-round, with limited winter facilities.

Contact: Phone (541) 582-1421 or write to 7275 Rogue River Highway, Grants Pass, OR 97527.

Directions: Take exit 48 off Interstate 5, cross the river, and travel 1.5 miles west on Highway 99.

Trip notes: This campground with grassy, shaded sites is set along the Rogue River, where fishing, swimming, and boating are options.

⑥⓪ Riverfront Trailer Park

Location: On the Rogue River; map E1, grid e8.

Campsites, facilities: There are 22 sites for trailers or RVs of any length; 19 have full and three have partial hookups. Electricity, piped water, sewer and cable TV hookups, and picnic tables are provided. Flush toilets, sanitary disposal services, showers, a laundry room, and ice are available. Bottled gas, a store, and a cafe are located within one mile. Fishing docks, boat docks, and launching facilities are nearby. Small, leashed pets are permitted.

Reservations, fees: Reservations are accepted. Sites are $20 per night. The campground is open year-round.

Contact: Phone (541) 582-0985 or write to 7060 Rogue River, Grants Pass, OR 97527.

Directions: From Interstate 5 south of Grants Pass, turn west at exit 48 and drive two miles on Highway 99 to the park.

Trip notes: This spot is convenient to good fishing, swimming, and boating on the Rogue River.

⑥① Valley of the Rogue State Park

Location: On the Rogue River; map E1, grid e8.

Campsites, facilities: There are 21 sites for tents or self-contained RVs and 152 sites with full or partial hookups for trailers or RVs up to 75 feet long. Picnic tables and fire grills are provided. Flush toilets, sanitary disposal services, showers, firewood, a laundry room, a meeting hall, and group campsites are available. A restaurant is nearby. Some facilities are wheelchair accessible. Boat launching facilities are nearby. Leashed pets are permitted.

Reservations, fees: Contact Reservations Northwest at (800) 452-5687 ($6 reservation fee). Sites are $13–$18 per night. (Weekly and monthly rates are available in the winter months.) The campground is open year-round, with limited winter facilities.

Contact: Phone (541) 582-1118 or write to 3792 North River Road, Gold Hill, OR 97525.

Directions: From Grants Pass, turn south on Interstate 5 and travel 12 miles. Turn right at exit 45B and drive to the park on the right.

Trip notes: With easy highway access, this popular spot along the banks of the Rogue River is often filled to near capacity during the summer months. Recreation options include fishing, hiking, swimming, and boating. A large picnic shelter is available for groups.

62 KOA Medford– Gold Hill

Location: On the Rogue River; map E1, grid e8.

Campsites, facilities: There are 12 tent sites and 53 sites for trailers or RVs of any length; 27 are drive-throughs. Electricity, piped water, sewer hookups, and picnic tables are provided. Flush toilets, bottled gas, sanitary disposal services, showers, firewood, a store, a laundry room, ice, a playground, and a swimming pool are available. A cafe is located within one mile, and boat launching facilities are within five miles. Leashed pets and motorbikes are permitted.

Reservations, fees: Reservations are accepted. Sites are $15–$20 per night. The campground is open year-round.

Contact: Phone (541) 855-7710 or write to P.O. Box 320, Gold Hill, OR 97525.

Directions: In Gold Hill on Interstate 5, take the South Gold Hill exit (exit 40) and drive 400 yards to Blackwell Road. The camp is approximately another 400 yards south on the right.

Trip notes: This campground along the banks of the Rogue River is near a golf course, bike paths, tennis courts, and the Oregon Vortex. It's one of the many camps located between Gold Hill and Grants Pass.

63 Harris Beach State Park

Location: On the Pacific Ocean; map E1, grid f1.

Campsites, facilities: There are 66 sites for tents or self-contained RVs, and 86 sites with full or partial hookups for trailers or RVs up to 50 feet long. There are four yurts, each accommodating five people, and a special camping area for hikers and bicyclists. Picnic tables and fire grills are provided. Electricity, piped water, sewer and cable TV hookups, flush toilets, sanitary services, showers, and firewood are available. Some facilities are wheelchair accessible. Leashed pets are permitted.

Reservations, fees: Contact Reservations Northwest at (800) 452-5687 ($6 reservation fee). Sites are $12–$20 per night; yurts are $25 per night; and sites for hikers/bikers are $4 per night. The campground is open year-round.

Contact: Phone (800) 452-5687 or (541) 469-2021, or write to 1655 Highway 101, Brookings, OR 97415.

Directions: From Brookings on U.S. 101, drive two miles north to the park entrance on the left.

Trip notes: Beachcombing, hiking, and fishing are a few of the activities available at this campground along the beach. Goat Rock, a migratory bird sanctuary, is just offshore, and there are numerous trout streams in the area. For details, pick up a Siskiyou National Forest map in Brookings at 555 Fifth Street. In the fall and winter, the nearby Chetco River attracts good runs of salmon and steelhead, respectively.

64 Port of Brookings Harbor Beachfront RV Park

Location: On the Pacific Ocean; map E1, grid f1.

Campsites, facilities: There are 25 tent sites and 138 spaces for trailers or RVs of any length. Rest rooms, showers, a sanitary dump, a public phone, a laundry room, ice, horseshoes, and a marina with a boat ramp, a boat dock, and snacks are available. The facilities are wheelchair accessible. Leashed pets are permitted.

Reservations, fees: Reservations are recommended. Sites are $9–$18 per night. The campground is open year-round.

Contact: Phone the park at (541) 469-5867, or (800) 441-0856 in Oregon, or write to 16035 Boat Basin Road, Brookings, OR 97415.

Directions: From Brookings, drive approximately 2.5 miles south on U.S. 101 to Benham Lane. Drive west on Benham Lane for six-tenths of a mile to Boat Basin Road. The park is one block north on the left side.

Trip notes: Located just past the Oregon/California border on the Pacific Ocean, this park is a great layover spot. Oceanfront sites are available, and recreational activities include boating, fishing, and swimming. Nearby Harris Beach State Park makes a good side trip, with beach access and hiking trails.

65 At Rivers Edge RV Resort

Location: On the Chetco River; map E1, grid f1.

Campsites, facilities: There are 110 sites for trailers or RVs of any length; 15 are drive-throughs. Electricity, piped water, and sewer hookups are provided. Flush toilets, bottled gas, sanitary services, showers, a recreation hall with exercise equipment, a laundry room, a small boat launch, and cable TV are available. Leashed pets and motorbikes are permitted.

Reservations, fees: Reservations are accepted. Sites are $20–$25 per night. The campground is open year-round.

Contact: Phone (541) 469-3356 or write to 98203 South Bank Chetco Road, Brookings, OR 97415.

Directions: From Brookings on U.S. 101, drive 1.5 miles east on South Bank Chetco River Road and follow the signs to the park.

Trip notes: This campground along the banks of the Chetco River offers complete fishing services, including guided salmon and

steelhead trips on the Chetco in the fall and winter. Deep-sea trips for salmon or rockfish are available in the summer. Other amenities include bait, tackle, and a free fishing class for campers, plus a beach for sunbathing and swimming.

66 Chetco RV Park

Location: Near the Chetco River; map E1, grid f1.

Campsites, facilities: There are 117 drive-through sites for trailers or RVs of any length. Electricity, piped water, sewer hookups, and picnic tables are provided. Flush toilets, sanitary services, showers, a recreation hall, a laundry room, and ice are available. Boat docks, launching facilities, and rentals are nearby. Small pets are permitted.

Reservations, fees: Reservations are accepted. Sites are $15–$18 per night. The campground is open year-round.

Contact: Phone (541) 469-3863, fax (541) 469-4025, or write to 16117 Highway 101 South, Brookings, OR 97415.

Directions: In Brookings, drive one mile south of the Chetco River Bridge on U.S. 101 and you'll see the park entrance.

Trip notes: This park is near both the Chetco River, known for its winter steelhead run, and the beach. Whale watching is good from January through May. The nature trails located a short drive up the river road are a nice side trip.

67 Sea Bird RV

Location: On the Pacific Ocean; map E1, grid f1.

Campsites, facilities: There are 60 sites for trailers or RVs of any length; nine are drive-throughs. Electricity, piped water, sewer hookups, and picnic tables are provided. Flush toilets, sanitary services, showers, a recreation hall, and a laundry room are available. Boat docks, launching facilities, and rentals are nearby. Leashed pets and motorbikes are permitted.

Reservations, fees: Reservations are ac-

cepted. Sites are $16 per night. The campground is open year-round.

Contact: Phone (541) 469-3512 or write to P.O. Box 1026, Brookings, OR 97415.

Directions: From Brookings, drive a quarter mile south of the Chetco River Bridge on U.S. 101 and you'll see the park entrance.

Trip notes: This is one of several campgrounds set along the beach here. Nearby recreation options include marked bike trails, a full-service marina, and tennis courts.

68 Little Redwood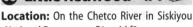

Location: On the Chetco River in Siskiyou National Forest; map E1, grid f2.

Campsites, facilities: There are 12 sites for tents, trailers, or RVs up to 16 feet long. Picnic tables and fire grills are provided. Piped water and vault toilets are available. Leashed pets are permitted.

Reservations, fees: No reservations are accepted. Sites are $6 per night, plus $3 for each additional non-towed vehicle. The campground is open from late May to mid-September.

Contact: Siskiyou National Forest, Chetco Ranger District, 555 Fifth Street, Brookings, OR 97415; (541) 469-2196 or fax (541) 469-2196.

Directions: From Brookings, drive one-half mile south on U.S. 101 to County Road 784 (North Bank Chetco River Road). Turn northeast and drive 7.5 miles. At Forest Service Road 1376, proceed six miles to the campground.

Trip notes: This campground is set among old-growth fir trees near the banks of the Chetco River. The primary water sport here in the summer is swimming, but trout fishing can be worth a try, too. The camp is also on the main western access route to the Kalmiopsis Wilderness, which is about 20 miles away.

69 Loeb State Park

Location: Near the Chetco River; map E1, grid f2.

Campsites, facilities: There are 53 sites with water and electrical hookups for trailers

or RVs up to 50 feet long. Picnic tables and fire grills are provided. Flush toilets and firewood are available. Leashed pets are permitted.

Reservations, fees: No reservations are accepted. Sites are $13–$15 per night. (Weekly and monthly rates are available from November through March.) The campground is open year-round.

Contact: Harris Beach State Park, 1655 Highway 101, Brookings, OR 97415; (541) 469-2021.

Directions: From Brookings on U.S. 101, drive eight miles northeast on North Bank Road to the park entrance on the right.

Trip notes: This park is located in a canyon formed by the Chetco River and is adjacent to Siskiyou National Forest. Highlights include a beautiful myrtlewood grove and a short spur trail that leads to the Forest Service's Redwood Nature Trail. A Forest Service map details other nearby trailheads.

70 Winchuck

Location: On the Winchuck River in Siskiyou National Forest; map E1, grid f2.

Campsites, facilities: There are 15 sites for tents, trailers, or RVs of any length. Picnic tables and fire grills are provided. Vault toilets and piped water are available. Leashed pets are permitted.

Reservations, fees: No reservations are accepted. Sites are $6 per night, plus $3 for each additional non-towed vehicle. The campground is open from late May to mid-September.

Contact: Siskiyou National Forest, Chetco Ranger District, 555 Fifth Street, Brookings, OR 97415; (541) 469-2196 or fax (541) 469-2196.

Directions: From Brookings, drive 5.5 miles south on U.S. 101, then six miles east on County Road 896. From there, take Forest Service Road 1107 one mile east to the campground.

Trip notes: This forested campground is on the banks of the Winchuck River, an out-of-the-way stream that out-of-towners don't know exists. It's quiet, remote, and not that far from the coast, although it feels like an inland spot. The camp was recently reconstructed and now offers clean, spacious sites.

(71) Kerby Trailer Park and Campground

Location: Near the Illinois River; map E1, grid f5.

Campsites, facilities: There are 13 sites for trailers and RVs; five have full and nine have partial hookups. Electricity, piped water, sewer hookups, and picnic tables are provided. Flush toilets, bottled gas, showers, and a laundry room are available. A store and ice are located within 1.5 miles. Pets and motorbikes are permitted.

Reservations, fees: Reservations are accepted. Sites are $10–$11 per night. The campground is open from May through late October.

Contact: Phone (541) 592-2897 or write to P.O. Box 256, Kerby, OR 97531.

Directions: From Interstate 5 at Grants Pass, turn south on U.S. 199 and drive approximately 26 miles to Kerby. This campground is about 400 yards south of Kerby on U.S. 199.

Trip notes: This small campground is near the Illinois River, a good stream during the summer for swimming. See the trip notes for Lake Selmac RV Resort (campground number 54) for side trip information. Other recreation options include an 18-hole golf course, hiking trails, and tennis courts.

(72) Shady Acres

Location: On the Illinois River; map E1, grid f5.

Campsites, facilities: There are four tent sites and 21 sites for trailers or RVs of any length; four are drive-throughs. Electricity, piped water, sewer hookups, and picnic tables are provided. Cable TV can be obtained for a fee. Flush toilets, bottled gas, sanitary services, showers, a laundry room, and firewood are available. A store, a cafe, and ice are within one mile. Small, leashed pets are permitted.

Reservations, fees: Reservations are accepted. Sites are $14 per night. The campground is open year-round.

Contact: Phone (541) 592-3702 or write to 27550 Redwood Highway, Cave Junction, OR 97523.

Directions: From Interstate 5 at Grants Pass, turn southwest on U.S. 199 and drive approximately 30 miles to Cave Junction. Continue one mile south on U.S. 199 and you'll see the entrance to the park.

Trip notes: This park is in a forested area near the banks of the Illinois River. See the trip notes for Lake Selmac RV Resort (campground number 54) for information on Oregon Caves National Monument.

(73) Town and Country RV Park

Location: On the Illinois River; map E1, grid f5.

Campsites, facilities: There are 51 sites for tents, trailers, or RVs. Cable TV, showers, rest rooms, a sanitary dump, a public phone, a laundry room, and ice are available. Horseshoe pits, a clubhouse, and a playground are also provided. Leashed pets are permitted.

Reservations, fees: Reservations are recommended. Sites are $15 per night. The campground is open year-round.

Contact: Phone the park at (541) 592-2656 or write to 28288 Redwood Highway, Cave Junction, OR 97523.

Directions: From Interstate 5 at Grants Pass, take exit 55 and turn south on U.S. 199. Drive about 35 miles to Cave Junction. From the junction of U.S. 199 and Highway 46, continue two miles south on U.S. 199. The campground is on the right.

Trip notes: This park on the Illinois River provides good opportunities for swimming, fishing, and boating (no motors are permitted). Nearby side trips include Oregon Caves National Monument (21 miles) and Grants Pass (31 miles). Crescent City is located 50 miles away.

74 Country Hills Resort

Location: Near Oregon Caves National Monument; map E1, grid f6.

Campsites, facilities: There are 12 tent sites and 20 sites for trailers or RVs of any length; two are drive-throughs. There are also six cabins. Picnic tables are provided. Flush toilets, showers, firewood, a small store, a laundry room, and ice are available. Leashed pets are permitted.

Reservations, fees: Reservations are accepted. Sites are $12–$15 per night; cabins are $45–$56 per night. The campground is open year-round.

Contact: Phone (541) 592-3406, fax (541) 592-3406, or write to 7901 Caves Highway, Cave Junction, OR 97523.

Directions: From Interstate 5 at Grants Pass, take exit 55 and turn south on U.S. 199. Drive 26 miles to the town of Cave Junction. Turn east on Highway 46 and drive eight miles to the campground.

Trip notes: Lots of sites at this wooded camp border Sucker Creek, a popular spot for swimming and fishing. See the trip notes for Lake Selmac RV Resort (campground number 54) for information about the nearby Oregon Caves National Monument.

75 Grayback

Location: Near Oregon Caves National Monument in Siskiyou National Forest; map E1, grid f6.

Campsites, facilities: There are 37 sites for tents, trailers, or RVs up to 22 feet long. Picnic tables and fire grills are provided. Flush toilets and piped water are available. Facilities are wheelchair accessible. Leashed pets are permitted.

Reservations, fees: Some sites can be reserved by calling (541) 591-3400 ($8.65 reservation fee). Sites are $12 per night. The campground is open from May through October.

Contact: Siskiyou National Forest, Illinois Valley Ranger District, P.O. Box 389, Cave Junc-

tion, OR 97523; (541) 592-2166 or fax (541) 592-6545.

Directions: From Interstate 5 at Grants Pass, take exit 58 and turn south on U.S. 199. Drive 33 miles to the town of Cave Junction, then turn east on Highway 46 and drive 12 miles to the campground.

Trip notes: This wooded campground along the banks of Sucker Creek has sites with ample shade and is a good choice if you're planning to visit Oregon Caves National Monument, which is about 10 miles away. The camp is in a grove of old-growth firs and is a prime place for bird-watching. A half-mile barrier-free trail cuts through the camp.

76 Cave Creek

Location: Near Oregon Caves National Monument in Siskiyou National Forest; map E1, grid f6.

Campsites, facilities: There are 18 tent sites. Piped water, vault toilets, and picnic tables are provided. Showers are located within eight miles. Leashed pets are permitted.

Reservations, fees: For reservation and fee information, phone (541) 592-3400. The campground is open from June through September.

Contact: Siskiyou National Forest, Illinois Valley Ranger District, P.O. Box 389, Cave Junction, OR 97523; (541) 592-2166 or fax (541) 592-6545.

Directions: From Interstate 5 at Grants Pass, take exit 58 and turn south on U.S. 199. Drive 33 miles to the town of Cave Junction, then turn east on Highway 46 and drive 16 miles. Turn right on Forest Service Road 4032 and drive one mile south to the campground.

Trip notes: No campground is closer to Oregon Caves National Monument than this Forest Service camp, a mere four miles away. There is even a trail out of camp that leads directly to the caves. See the trip notes for Lake Selmac RV Resort (campground number 54) for details on the monument. The camp lies in a grove of old-growth timber along the banks of Cave Creek, a small stream with some trout fishing opportunities. The sites are shaded, and an abundance of wildlife can be spotted in the area. Hiking opportunities abound.

(77) Bolan Lake

Location: On Bolan Lake in Siskiyou National Forest; map E1, grid f6.

Campsites, facilities: There are 12 sites for tents, trailers, or RVs up to 16 feet long. Picnic tables and fire grills are provided. Pit toilets and firewood are available, but there is no piped water. Leashed pets are permitted.

Reservations, fees: No reservations are accepted. There is no fee. The campground is open from July through October.

Contact: Siskiyou National Forest, Illinois Valley Ranger District, P.O. Box 389, Cave Junction, OR 97523; (541) 592-2166 or fax (541) 592-6545.

Directions: From Cave Junction, take County Road 12 eight miles southeast, then go 14 miles southeast on County Road 4007. The camp is at Forest Service Road 408. Note: It's not advisable to pull large trailers or RVs on the access road; it's very narrow and rough.

Trip notes: Very few out-of-towners know about this camp with pretty, shaded sites along the shore of 15-acre Bolan Lake. A trail from the lake leads up to a fire lookout and ties into miles of other trails. See a Forest Service map for trailhead locations. This spot is truly a bird-watcher's paradise, with a variety of species to view. The fishing can be good here as well.

(78) Jackson

Location: On the Applegate River in Rogue River National Forest; map E1, grid f8.

Campsites, facilities: There are 10 sites for tents, trailers, or RVs up to 20 feet long. Piped water and flush toilets are available. Firewood is available for purchase. Leashed pets are permitted.

Reservations, fees: No reservations are accepted. Sites are $7 per night, plus $3.50 for each additional vehicle. The campground is open from May through October.

Contact: Rogue River National Forest, Rogue River Ranger District, 2990 North Pacific Highway, Medford, OR 97501; (541) 770-5146.

Directions: From Interstate 5 south of Medford, take the Jacksonville exit and drive the few miles to Jacksonville. Turn southwest on Highway 238 and drive eight miles, then turn southwest on County Road 10 and continue for nine miles to the camp on the right. Jackson is directly across from Flumet Flat Campground.

Trip notes: This camp is located at 1,500 feet elevation nestled in an old mining area. It's right on the Applegate River, with a swimming hole and good trout fishing.

(79) Flumet Flat

Location: On the Applegate River in Rogue River National Forest; map E1, grid f8.

Campsites, facilities: There are 34 sites for tents, trailers, or RVs up to 40 feet long. Picnic tables and fire grills are provided. Piped water and flush toilets are available. Showers, a store, a cafe, a laundry room, and ice are available nearby at McKee Bridge. Firewood can be purchased. Leashed pets are permitted.

Reservations, fees: Reservations are available for groups only. Sites are $7 per night, plus $3.50 for each additional vehicle. The campground is open year-round.

Contact: Rogue River National Forest, Rogue River Ranger District, 2990 North Pacific Highway, Medford, OR 97501; (541) 770-5146.

Directions: From Interstate 5 south of Medford, take the Jacksonville exit and drive the few miles to Jacksonville. Turn southwest on Highway 238 and drive eight miles, then turn southwest on County Road 10 and continue for nine miles. Turn southwest on Forest Service Road 1095 and proceed one mile to the campground.

Trip notes: This campground is set along the banks of the Applegate River about six miles north of Applegate Reservoir. The Gin-Lin Nature Trail, named for the Chinese miner who struck it rich in local gold mines, is nearby. The camp has a large parklike lawn area with facilities for volleyball, badminton, and horseshoes.

And thanks to a low elevation of 1,500 feet, the swimming hole is actually relatively warm.

(80) French Gulch

Location: On Applegate Reservoir in Rogue River National Forest; map E1, grid f8.

Campsites, facilities: There are nine walk-in sites for tents. Picnic tables and fire grills are provided. Hand-pumped water, firewood, and vault toilets are available. Boat docks and launching facilities are within one to two miles. Leashed pets are permitted.

Reservations, fees: No reservations are accepted. Sites are $6 per night, plus $3 for each additional vehicle. The campground is open from May through October.

Contact: Rogue River National Forest, Rogue River Ranger District, 2990 North Pacific Highway, Medford, OR 97501; (541) 770-5146.

Directions: From Interstate 5 south of Medford, take the Jacksonville exit and drive the few miles to Jacksonville. Turn southwest on Highway 238 and drive eight miles, then turn south on County Road 10 and continue for 14 miles. Drive 1.5 miles east on Forest Service Road 1075 and park. A short walk is required.

Trip notes: This campground along the shore of Applegate Reservoir is a popular summer fishing spot for Ashland anglers. It's also a good boat-in campground when the lake level allows; the launch ramp is not far from the camp.

(81) Watkins

Location: On Applegate Reservoir in Rogue River National Forest; map E1, grid f8.

Campsites, facilities: There are 14 walk-in sites for tents. Picnic tables, hand-pumped water, and fire grills are provided. Vault toilets and firewood are available. Boat docks and launching facilities are within one mile. Leashed pets are permitted.

Reservations, fees: No reservations are accepted. Sites are $6 per night, plus $3 for each additional vehicle. The campground is open from May through October.

Contact: Rogue River National Forest, Rogue River Ranger District, 2990 North Pacific Highway, Medford, OR 97501; (541) 770-5146.

Directions: From Interstate 5 south of Medford, take the Jacksonville exit and drive a few miles to Jacksonville. Turn southwest on Highway 238 and drive eight miles, then turn southwest on County Road 10 and continue for 17 miles.

Trip notes: Located on the southwest shore of Applegate Reservoir, this campground, like Carberry (campground number 85), is small and quite primitive, but it's pretty and offers all the same recreation options. Few campers know about this spot, so it usually doesn't fill up quickly.

(82) Cantrall-Buckley Park

Location: On the Applegate River; map E1, grid f9.

Campsites, facilities: There are 25 sites for tents, trailers, and RVs up to 25 feet long. Rest rooms, showers, and a public phone are provided. Recreational facilities include horseshoes, a playground, a recreation field, and a barbecue.

Reservations, fees: Group reservations are accepted. Sites are $10 per night. The campground is open from May to mid-October.

Contact: Jackson County Parks, 400 Antelope Road, White City, OR 97503; (541) 776-7001 or fax (541) 826-8360.

Directions: From Interstate 5 at Medford, turn west on Highway 238 and drive 18 miles to Hamilton Road. Turn south on Hamilton Road and drive one mile to the camp (signed).

Trip notes: This county park outside of Medford offers pleasant, shady sites in a wooded setting. The Applegate River, which has good trout fishing, runs nearby.

(83) Beaver Sulphur

Location: On Beaver Creek in Rogue River National Forest; map E1, grid f9.

Campsites, facilities: There are 10 sites for tents. Picnic tables and fire grills are provided.

Vault toilets and hand-pumped water are available. Leashed pets are permitted.

Reservations, fees: No reservations are accepted. Sites are $4 per night, plus $2 per extra vehicle. The campground is open from May to December.

Contact: Rogue River National Forest, Star Ranger District, 6941 Upper Applegate Road, Jacksonville, OR 97530; (541) 899-1812 or fax (541) 858-2401.

Directions: From Interstate 5 south of Medford, take the Jacksonville exit and drive a few miles to Jacksonville. Turn southwest on Highway 238 and drive eight miles, then turn southwest on County Road 10 and continue nine miles. Turn east on Forest Service Road 20 and proceed three miles to the campground.

Trip notes: Tiny and hidden, this camp along the banks of Beaver Creek, about nine miles from Applegate Reservoir, has pretty, shaded sites and easy access to the creek. Fishing is a possibility. A Forest Service map will detail the roads and trails in the area.

84 Squaw Lake

Location: On Squaw Lake in Rogue River National Forest; map E1, grid f9.

Campsites, facilities: There are 17 walk-in sites for tents and two family group sites that can accommodate up to 10 people each. Picnic tables and fire grills are provided. Vault toilets and hand-pumped water are available. Leashed pets are permitted.

Reservations, fees: Reservations are required; phone (541) 899-1812. Sites are $5 per night. The campground is open year-round.

Contact: Rogue River National Forest, Star Ranger District, 6941 Upper Applegate Road, Jacksonville, OR 97530; (541) 899-1812 or fax (541) 858-2401.

Directions: From Interstate 5 south of Medford, take the Jacksonville exit and drive

the few miles to Jacksonville. Turn southwest on Highway 238 and drive eight miles, then turn southwest on County Road 10 and continue for 14 miles. Turn south on Forest Service Road 1075 and drive eight miles to the campground.

Trip notes: Numerous trails crisscross the area around this camp on the shore of Squaw Lake. The setting is more intimate than the larger Applegate Reservoir to the west. This spot is also more popular, and it's the only campground in the district that requires reservations. Be sure to call ahead for a space.

85 Carberry

Location: On Applegate Reservoir in Rogue River National Forest; map E1, grid g8.

Campsites, facilities: There are 10 walk-in sites for tents. Space is available in the parking lot for trailers or RVs. Picnic tables and fire grills are provided. Vault toilets and hand-pumped water are available. Boat docks and launching facilities are within two miles. Leashed pets are permitted.

Reservations, fees: No reservations are accepted. Sites are $6 per night, plus $3 for each additional vehicle. The campground is open from May through October.

Contact: Rogue River National Forest, Rogue River Ranger District, 2990 North Pacific Highway, Medford, OR 97501; (541) 770-5146.

Directions: From Interstate 5 south of Medford, take the Jacksonville exit and drive a few miles to Jacksonville. Turn southwest on Highway 238 and drive eight miles, then turn southwest on County Road 10 and continue 18 miles. A short walk is required.

Trip notes: You'll find recreational opportunities aplenty at this campground on the southwest shore of Applegate Reservoir, including fishing, boating, and swimming. This is a smaller and more primitive alternative to French Gulch (campground number 80).

Map E2

One inch equals approximately 20 miles.

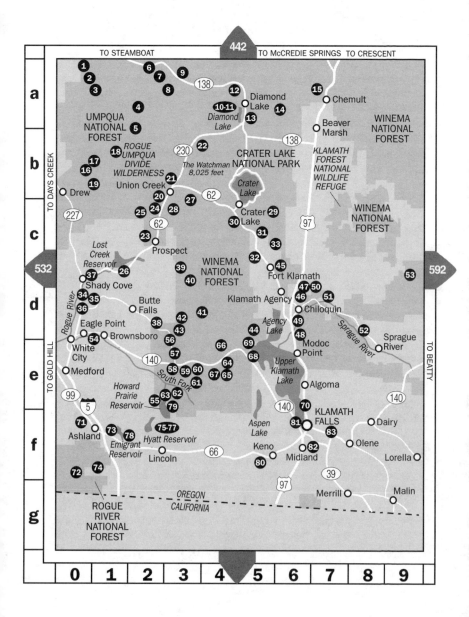

Chapter E2 features:

❶ Wolf Creek

Location: On the Little River in Umpqua National Forest; map E2, grid a0.

Campsites, facilities: There are seven sites for tents, trailers, or RVs up to 30 feet long and one group site. Picnic tables and fire grills are provided. Flush toilets and piped water are available. Some facilities are wheelchair accessible. Leashed pets are permitted.

Reservations, fees: Reservations are required for groups. Individual sites are $7 per night, and the group site is $70 per night. The campground is open from mid-May through September.

Contact: Umpqua National Forest, North Umpqua Ranger District, 18782 North Umpqua Highway, Glide, OR 97443; (541) 496-3532 or fax (541) 496-3534.

Directions: From Roseburg on Interstate 5, take exit 120 and drive 18 miles east on Highway 138 to Glide. From Glide, travel 12 miles southeast on County Road 17 to the campground.

Trip notes: Close to civilization with easy access, this pretty camp is located at the entrance to the national forest along the banks of the Little River near the Wolf Creek Civilian Conservation Center. If you want to get deeper into the interior of the Cascades, Hemlock Lake and Lake of the Woods (campground numbers 4 and 5) are about 21 and 15 miles east, respectively.

❷ Coolwater

Location: On the Little River in Umpqua National Forest; map E2, grid a0.

Campsites, facilities: There are seven sites for tents, trailers, or RVs up to 24 feet long. Picnic tables and fire grills are provided. Vault toilets and hand-pumped water are available. Leashed pets are permitted.

Reservations, fees: No reservations are accepted. Sites are $5 per night, with no fee from November to May 20. The campground is open year-round.

Contact: Umpqua National Forest, North Umpqua Ranger District, 18782 North Umpqua Highway, Glide, OR 97443; (541) 496-3532 or fax (541) 496-3534.

Directions: From Roseburg on Interstate 5, take exit 120 and drive 18 miles east on Highway 138 to Glide. From Glide, travel 17 miles southeast on County Road 17 to the campground.

Trip notes: This campground along the banks of the Little River doesn't get much use. Fishing and swimming are two options here. Scenic Grotto Falls can be reached by traveling north on Forest Service Road 2703 (across the road from the camp). Near the falls is Emile Grove, home of a thicket of old-growth Douglas firs and the huge "Bill Taft Tree," named after the former president.

❸ White Creek

Location: On the Little River in Umpqua National Forest; map E2, grid a0.

Campsites, facilities: There are three sites for tents, trailers, or RVs up to 31 feet long. Picnic tables and fire grills are provided. Vault toilets and hand-pumped well water are available. Leashed pets are permitted.

Reservations, fees: No reservations are accepted. Sites are $5 per night, with no fee from November through May 20. The campground is open year-round

Contact: Umpqua National Forest, North Umpqua Ranger District, 18782 North Umpqua Highway, Glide, OR 97443; (541) 496-3532 or fax (541) 496-3534.

Directions: From Roseburg on Interstate 5, take exit 120 and drive 18 miles east on Highway 138 to Glide. From Glide, continue for 17 miles on Little River Road to Forest Service Road 2792 (Red Butte Road). Proceed one-quarter mile to the campground.

Trip notes: Hiking and fishing are two of the recreation options at this campground set at the confluence of White Creek and the Little River. See the trip notes for Coolwater (campground number 2) for other details about the area.

➍ Hemlock Lake

Location: On Hemlock Lake in Umpqua National Forest; map E2, grid a2.

Campsites, facilities: There are 13 sites for tents, trailers, or RVs up to 35 feet long. Picnic tables and fire grills are provided. Vault toilets are available, but there is no piped water. Boat docks and launching facilities are nearby. No motors are allowed on the lake. Leashed pets are permitted.

Reservations, fees: No reservations are accepted. Sites are $5 per night, with no fee from November through May 20. The campground is open year-round.

Contact: Umpqua National Forest, North Umpqua Ranger District, 18782 North Umpqua Highway, Glide, OR 97443; (541) 496-3532 or fax (541) 496-3534.

Directions: From Roseburg on Interstate 5, take exit 120 and drive 18 miles east on Highway 138 to Glide. Travel on County Road 17 east from Glide for 16.5 miles, then drive 15.5 miles east on Forest Service Road 27 to the campground.

Trip notes: This is a little-known jewel of a spot. For starters, it's set along the shore of Hemlock Lake. An eight-mile loop trail called the Yellow Jacket Loop is just south of the campground. For finishers, another trail leaves camp and heads north for about three miles to the Lake of the Woods Campground. From there, it's just a short hike to either Hemlock Falls or Yakso Falls, both spectacularly scenic.

➎ Lake of the Woods

Location: On Lake of the Woods in Umpqua National Forest; map E2, grid b2.

Campsites, facilities: There are 11 sites for tents, trailers, or RVs up to 35 feet long. Picnic tables and fire grills are provided. Flush toilets and hand-pumped well water are available. Leashed pets are permitted.

Reservations, fees: No reservations are accepted. Sites are $7 per night. The campground is open from June to late October.

Contact: Umpqua National Forest, North Umpqua Ranger District, 18782 North Umpqua Highway, Glide, OR 97443; (541) 496-3532 or fax (541) 496-3534.

Directions: From Roseburg on Interstate 5, take exit 120 and drive 18 miles east on Highway 138 to Glide. Travel on County Road 17 east from Glide for 16.5 miles, then drive 11 miles east on Forest Service Road 27 to the campground.

Trip notes: The shore of little Lake of the Woods is the setting of this camp, which makes a nice home base for several good hikes. One of them leaves the camp and heads south for about three miles to the Hemlock Lake Campground. Two other nearby trails provide short, scenic hikes to either Hemlock Falls or Yakso Falls.

➏ Apple Creek

Location: On the Umpqua River in Umpqua National Forest; map E2, grid a2.

Campsites, facilities: There are eight sites for tents, trailers, or RVs up to 21 feet long. Picnic tables and fire grills are provided. Vault toilets are available. There is no piped water. Leashed pets are permitted.

Reservations, fees: No reservations are accepted. Sites are $5 per night, with no fee from November through May 20. The campground is open year-round.

Contact: Umpqua National Forest, North Umpqua Ranger District, 18782 North Umpqua Highway, Glide, OR 97443; (541) 496-3532 or fax (541) 496-3534.

Directions: From Interstate 5 at Roseburg, take exit 120 and travel east on Highway 138 for about 43 miles. The camp is next to the highway.

Trip notes: This campground is along the banks of the Umpqua River at a popular spot for rafting and fly-fishing. The North Umpqua River Trail runs east and west along the river for many miles. This camp is pretty, small, and primitive, with easy highway access. If it's full, try Horseshoe Bend (campground number 7).

❼ Horseshoe Bend

Location: On the Umpqua River in Umpqua National Forest; map E2, grid a2.

Campsites, facilities: There are 24 sites for tents, trailers, or RVs up to 35 feet long and one group site. Picnic tables, fire grills, piped water, and flush toilets are provided. A Laundromat, a store, gas, and propane are available one mile east. Some facilities are wheelchair accessible; the camp is partially modified for the disabled. Raft launching facilities are nearby. Leashed pets are permitted.

Reservations, fees: Reservations are accepted for the group site only. Individual sites are $10 per night, and the group site is $65 per night. The campground is open from mid-May to late September.

Contact: Umpqua National Forest, North Umpqua Ranger District, 18782 North Umpqua Highway, Glide, OR 97443; (541) 496-3532 or fax (541) 496-3534.

Directions: From Roseburg on Interstate 5, take exit 120 and drive 47 miles east on Highway 138, then turn right at the signed entrance and follow the road south a short distance to the campground.

Trip notes: This campground is in the middle of a big bend in the North Umpqua River. Rafting and fly-fishing are both popular here. See the trip notes for Apple Creek (campground number 6) for area information.

❽ Twin Lakes

Location: On Big Twin Lake in Umpqua National Forest; map E2, grid a3.

Campsites, facilities: There are four hike-in tent sites. Picnic tables and fire pits are provided. A pit toilet is available. There is no piped water. Leashed pets are permitted.

Reservations, fees: No reservations are accepted. There is no fee. The campground is open from mid-June to late October, weather permitting.

Contact: Umpqua National Forest, North Umpqua Ranger District, 18782 North Umpqua Highway, Glide, OR 97443; (541) 496-3532 or fax (541) 496-3534.

Directions: From Roseburg on Interstate 5, take exit 120 and drive 14 miles east to Glide. From the North Umpqua Ranger Station, take Highway 138 east for 33 miles to Marsters Bridge. Cross the bridge and turn right on Forest Service Road 4770. Follow Forest Service Road 4770 for 10 miles to the trailhead for Twin Lakes Trail No. 1500. It's a 1.25-mile hike to the campground.

Trip notes: If you can find it, you'll love it. This remote place of quiet and great beauty is known by few and gets little use, so you may have the whole camp to yourself. The camp is set at 5,100 feet along the shore of Big Twin Lake, which covers 14 acres and is 48 feet deep. Area highlights include some excellent hiking trails and two trail shelters. One trail leads to Twin Lakes Mountain (elevation 5,879 feet).

❾ Whitehorse Falls

Location: On the Clearwater River in Umpqua National Forest; map E2, grid a3.

Campsites, facilities: There are five tent sites. Picnic tables and fire grills are provided. Vault toilets are available, but there is no piped water. Leashed pets are permitted.

Reservations, fees: Reservations are accepted. Sites are $5 per night. The campground is open from June to late October.

Contact: Umpqua National Forest, Diamond Lake Ranger District, 2020 Toketee Ranger Station Road, Idleyld Park, OR 97447; (541) 498-2531 or (541) 498-2515.

Directions: From Roseburg on Interstate 5, take exit 120 and drive 67 miles east on Highway 138 to the campground.

Trip notes: This campground is along the Clearwater River, one of the coldest streams in Umpqua National Forest. Even though the camp is adjacent to the highway, the setting is primitive. Pretty Clearwater Falls, a few miles east, is a good side trip option. Fishing, hiking, rafting, and swimming are among the other recreation possibilities.

⑩ Broken Arrow

Location: On Diamond Lake in Umpqua National Forest; map E2, grid a4.

Campsites, facilities: There are 148 sites for tents, trailers, or RVs up to 35 feet long. Picnic tables and fire grills are provided. Flush toilets, showers, and piped water are available. Some facilities are wheelchair accessible. Boat docks, launching facilities, and rentals are nearby. Leashed pets are permitted.

Reservations, fees: Reservations are accepted for groups only; call (800) 280-CAMP/2267 ($8.65 reservation fee). Individual sites are $9–$12 per night. The campground is open from late May to mid-September.

Contact: Umpqua National Forest, Diamond Lake Ranger District, 2020 Toketee Ranger Station Road, Idleyld Park, OR 97447; (541) 498-2531 or (541) 498-2515.

Directions: From Roseburg on Interstate 5, take exit 120 and drive 80 miles east on Highway 138. Turn on Forest Service Road 4795 and drive to the campground.

Trip notes: This campground is set at 5,200 feet near the south shore of Diamond Lake, the largest natural lake in Umpqua National Forest. Boating, fishing, swimming, hiking, and bicycling keep visitors busy here. Diamond Lake is adjacent to the Mount Thielsen Wilderness, Crater Lake National Park, and Mount Bailey, all of which offer a variety of recreation opportunities year-round. Diamond Lake is quite popular with anglers because of its good trout trolling, particularly in early summer.

⑪ Thielsen View

Location: On Diamond Lake in Umpqua National Forest; map E2, grid a4.

Campsites, facilities: There are 60 sites for tents, trailers, or RVs up to 30 feet long. Picnic tables and fire grills are provided. Piped water and vault toilets are available. Some facilities are wheelchair accessible. Boat docks, launching facilities, and rentals are nearby. Leashed pets are permitted.

Reservations, fees: No reservations are accepted. Sites are $9–$12 per night. The campground is open from late May to late September.

Contact: Umpqua National Forest, Diamond Lake Ranger District, 2020 Toketee Ranger Station Road, Idleyld Park, OR 97447; (541) 498-2531 or (541) 498-2515.

Directions: From Roseburg on Interstate 5, take exit 120 and drive 80 miles east on Highway 138. Then turn south onto Forest Service Road 4795 and drive to the campground.

Trip notes: This campground is along the west shore of Diamond Lake. See the trip notes for Broken Arrow (campground number 10) for information on recreation opportunities.

⑫ Clearwater Falls

Location: On the Clearwater River in Umpqua National Forest; map E2, grid a4.

Campsites, facilities: There are nine tent sites. Picnic tables and fire grills are provided. Vault toilets are available, but there is no piped water. Leashed pets are permitted.

Reservations, fees: Reservations are accepted. Sites are $5 per night. The campground is open from mid-May to late October.

Contact: Umpqua National Forest, Diamond Lake Ranger District, 2020 Toketee Ranger Station Road, Idleyld Park, OR 97447; (541) 498-2531 or (541) 498-2515.

Directions: From Roseburg on Interstate 5, take exit 120 and drive 70 miles west on Highway 138. At Forest Service Road 4785, head south to the campground.

Trip notes: The main attraction at this campground along the banks of the Clearwater River is the cascading section of stream called Clearwater Falls. See the trip notes for Whitehorse Falls (campground number 9) for area details.

⑬ Diamond Lake

Location: On Diamond Lake in Umpqua National Forest; map E2, grid a5.

Campsites, facilities: There are 238 sites for tents, trailers, or RVs up to 35 feet long.

Picnic tables and fire grills are provided. Flush toilets, showers, piped water, and firewood are available. Boat docks, launching facilities, and rentals are nearby. Leashed pets are permitted.

Reservations, fees: Some sites can be reserved by calling (800) 280-CAMP/2267 ($8.65 reservation fee). Sites are $10–$20 per night. The campground is open from late April to late October.

Contact: Umpqua National Forest, Diamond Lake Ranger District, 2020 Toketee Ranger Station Road, Idleyld Park, OR 97447; (541) 498-2531 or (541) 498-2515.

Directions: From Roseburg on Interstate 5, take exit 120 and drive 78 miles east on Highway 138. Turn at the sign for Diamond Lake Resort and follow the road (keep straight; don't turn toward the resort) to the campground.

Trip notes: This extremely popular camp along the east shore of Diamond Lake has all the luxuries: flush toilets, showers, and piped water. See the trip notes for Broken Arrow (campground number 10) for recreation information.

⑭ Digit Point

Location: On Miller Lake in Winema National Forest; map E2, grid a6.

Campsites, facilities: There are 64 sites for tents, trailers, or RVs up to 30 feet long. Picnic tables and fire grills are provided. Piped water, a sanitary disposal station, and flush toilets are available. Boat docks and launching facilities are nearby. Leashed pets are permitted.

Reservations, fees: No reservations are accepted. Sites are $8 per night. The campground is open from Memorial Day to mid-October.

Contact: Winema National Forest, Chemult Ranger District, P.O. Box 150, Chemult, OR 97731; (541) 365-7001 or fax (541) 365-7019.

Directions: From Interstate 5 south of Eugene, take exit 188 and turn east on Highway 58. Drive 86 miles, then turn south on U.S. 97 and drive seven miles to Forest Service Road 9772 (one mile north of Chemult). Turn right and drive 12 miles west to the campground.

Trip notes: This campground is on the shore of Miller Lake, a popular spot for boating, fishing, and swimming. Nearby trails provide access to the Mount Thielsen Wilderness and the Pacific Crest Trail.

⑮ Corral Spring

Location: In Winema National Forest; map E2, grid a7.

Campsites, facilities: There are six sites for tents, trailers, or RVs up to 22 feet long. Picnic tables and fire grills are provided. Vault toilets are available, but there is no piped water. A store, a cafe, a Laundromat, and ice are located within five miles. Leashed pets are permitted.

Reservations, fees: No reservations are accepted. There is no fee. The campground is open from mid-May to late October.

Contact: Winema National Forest, Chemult Ranger District, P.O. Box 150, Chemult, OR 97731; (541) 365-7001 or fax (541) 365-7019.

Directions: From Interstate 5 south of Eugene, take exit 188 and turn east on Highway 58. Drive 86 miles, then turn south on U.S. 97 and drive 6.5 miles to Forest Service Road 9774 (2.5 miles north of Chemult). Turn right and drive two miles west to the campground.

Trip notes: This campground next to Corral Spring is primitive, remote, and quiet.

⑯ Dumont Creek

Location: On the South Umpqua River in Umpqua National Forest; map E2, grid b0.

Campsites, facilities: There are five sites for tents, trailers, or RVs up to 16 feet long. Picnic tables and fire grills are provided. Vault toilets are available, but there is no piped water. Leashed pets are permitted.

Reservations, fees: No reservations are accepted. There is no fee. The campground is open from late May to late October.

Contact: Umpqua National Forest, Tiller Ranger District, 27812 Tiller Trail Highway, Tiller, OR 97484; (541) 825-3201 or fax (541) 825-3259.

Directions: From Interstate 5 at Canyonville (exits 99 or 100), travel 25 miles east on County Road 1 to Tiller. Turn left on County Road 46 and drive six miles northeast. The camp is 5.5 miles northeast on Forest Service Road 28.

Trip notes: This campground along the banks of the South Umpqua River and Dumont Creek is quiet, primitive, and remote. Boulder Creek (campground number 17), just a few miles east, provides an option. A good side trip is nearby South Umpqua Falls, a beautiful, wide waterfall featuring a fish ladder and a platform so you can watch the fish struggle upstream.

⑰ Boulder Creek

Location: On the South Umpqua River in Umpqua National Forest; map E2, grid b1.

Campsites, facilities: There are 12 sites for tents, trailers, or RVs up to 15 feet long. Picnic tables and fire grills are provided. Vault toilets are available, but there is no piped water. Leashed pets are permitted.

Reservations, fees: No reservations are accepted. There is no fee. The campground is open from late May to late October.

Contact: Umpqua National Forest, Tiller Ranger District, 27812 Tiller Trail Highway, Tiller, OR 97484; (541) 825-3201 or fax (541) 825-3259.

Directions: From Interstate 5 at Canyonville (exits 99 or 100), travel 25 miles east on County Road 1 to Tiller. Turn left on County Road 46 and drive six miles northeast. The camp is seven miles northeast on Forest Service Road 28.

Trip notes: This campground is on the banks of the South Umpqua River near Boulder Creek. See the trip notes for Dumont Creek (campground number 16) for information on the area.

⑱ Camp Comfort

Location: On the South Umpqua River in Umpqua National Forest; map E2, grid b1.

Campsites, facilities: There are five sites for tents, trailers, or RVs up to 15 feet long. Picnic tables and fire grills are provided. Vault toilets are available, but there is no piped water. Leashed pets are permitted.

Reservations, fees: No reservations are accepted. There is no fee. The campground is open from late May to late October.

Contact: Umpqua National Forest, Tiller Ranger District, 27812 Tiller Trail Highway, Tiller, OR 97484; (541) 825-3201 or fax (541) 825-3259.

Directions: From Interstate 5 at Canyonville (exits 99 or 100), travel 25 miles east on County Road 1 to Tiller. Turn left on County Road 46 and drive six miles northeast. Continue about 18 miles northeast on Forest Service Road 28 to the campground.

Trip notes: This campground is on the banks of the South Umpqua River, deep in the Umpqua National Forest. Trailheads providing access to the Rogue–Umpqua Divide Wilderness can be found at the ends of the Forest Service roads west of the camp. A good side trip is South Umpqua Falls, which you pass on the drive to the camp.

⑲ Cover

Location: On Jackson Creek in Umpqua National Forest; map E2, grid b1.

Campsites, facilities: There are seven sites for tents, trailers, or RVs up to 16 feet long. Picnic tables and fire grills are provided. Vault toilets are available, but there is no piped water. Leashed pets are permitted.

Reservations, fees: No reservations are accepted. There is no fee. The campground is open from late May to late October.

Contact: Umpqua National Forest, Tiller Ranger District, 27812 Tiller Trail Highway, Tiller, OR 97484; (541) 825-3201 or fax (541) 825-3259.

Directions: From Interstate 5 at Canyonville (exits 99 or 100), travel 25 miles east on County Road 1 to Tiller. Turn left on County Road 46 and drive five miles northeast. Turn right on Forest Service Road 29 and drive 12 miles east to the campground.

Trip notes: If you want quiet, this camp along the banks of Jackson Creek is the right place, since hardly anyone knows about it. If you head east to Forest Service Road 30 and follow it south, you can access a major trail into the Rogue–Umpqua Divide Wilderness. Be sure not to miss the world's largest sugar pine tree, a few miles west of camp.

⑳ Union Creek

Location: Near the Upper Rogue River in Rogue River National Forest; map E2, grid b2.

Campsites, facilities: There are 75 sites for tents, trailers, or RVs up to 30 feet long. Picnic tables and fire grills are provided. Potable piped water and vault toilets are available. Firewood can be purchased. A store and a restaurant are within walking distance. Leashed pets are permitted.

Reservations, fees: No reservations are accepted. Sites are $8 per night, plus $4 per second vehicle a night. The campground is open from mid-May to mid-October.

Contact: Rogue Recreation, 2990 North Pacific Highway, Medford, OR 97501; (541) 770-5146 or (541) 560-3400, or fax (541) 865-2795.

Directions: From Medford on Interstate 5, travel 56 miles north on Highway 62 to the campground on the left.

Trip notes: One of the most popular camps in the district, this spot is more developed than the nearby camps of Mill Creek, River Bridge, and Natural Bridge. It's set along the banks of Union Creek where it joins the Upper Rogue River. The Upper Rogue River Trail passes near camp. Interpretive programs are offered in the summer, and a convenience store and a restaurant are within walking distance.

㉑ Farewell Bend

Location: On the Upper Rogue River in Rogue River National Forest; map E2, grid b3.

Campsites, facilities: There are 61 sites for tents, trailers, or RVs up to 40 feet long. Picnic tables, fire grills, and fire rings are provided. Potable piped water, firewood for purchase, and flush toilets are available. Some facilities

are wheelchair accessible. Leashed pets are permitted.

Reservations, fees: No reservations are accepted. Sites are $10 per night, plus $5 per extra vehicle a night. The campground is open from late May to late October.

Contact: Rogue Recreation, 2990 North Pacific Highway, Medford, OR 97501; (541) 770-5146 or (541) 560-3400, or fax (541) 865-2795.

Directions: From Medford on Interstate 5, travel 59 miles north on Highway 62 to the campground on the left.

Trip notes: This extremely popular campground is along the banks of the Upper Rogue River near the Rogue River Gorge. A quarter-mile barrier-free trail leads from camp to the Rogue Gorge Viewpoint and is definitely worth the trip. The Upper Rogue River Trail passes near camp. It attracts a lot of the campers who also visit Crater Lake.

㉒ Hamaker

Location: Near the Upper Rogue River in Rogue River National Forest; map E2, grid b4.

Campsites, facilities: There are 10 sites for tents, trailers, or RVs up to 30 feet long. Picnic tables, fire grills, and stoves are provided. Potable pumped water and vault toilets are available. Firewood can be purchased. Leashed pets are permitted.

Reservations, fees: No reservations are accepted. Sites are $6 per night, plus $3 per extra vehicle a night. The campground is open from late May to late October.

Contact: Rogue Recreation, 2990 North Pacific Highway, Medford, OR 97501; (541) 770-5146 or (541) 560-3400, or fax (541) 865-2795.

Directions: From Medford on Interstate 5, travel 57 miles northeast on Highway 62 and then 11 miles north on Highway 230. Continue about 600 yards east on Forest Service Road 6530 to the campground.

Trip notes: Set at 4,000 feet near the Upper Rogue River, this is a beautiful little spot high in a mountain meadow. Wildflowers and wildlife abound in the spring and early summer. This is one of the least-used camps in the area, and a prime camp for Crater Lake visitors.

㉓ River Bridge

Location: On the Upper Rogue River in Rogue River National Forest; map E2, grid c2.

Campsites, facilities: There are six sites for tents, trailers, and RVs up to 30 feet long. Picnic tables and fireplaces are provided. Vault toilets are available. There is no piped water. Leashed pets are permitted.

Reservations, fees: No reservations are accepted. There is no fee. The campground is open from April to November.

Contact: Rogue River National Forest, Prospect Ranger District, 47201 Highway 62, Prospect, OR 97536; (541) 560-3400 or fax (541) 560-3444.

Directions: From Medford on Interstate 5, travel 42 miles northeast on Highway 62. Turn left and drive one mile north on Forest Service Road 6210 to the campground on the left.

Trip notes: This campground along the banks of the Upper Rogue River is particularly scenic, with private and secluded sites and river views. This is a calmer part of the Wild and Scenic Upper Rogue, though no swimming or rafting is recommended. The Upper Rogue River Trail passes by the camp and follows the river for many miles to the Pacific Crest Trail in Crater Lake National Park.

㉔ Natural Bridge

Location: On the Upper Rogue River Trail in Rogue River National Forest; map E2, grid c2.

Campsites, facilities: There are 17 sites for tents, trailers, or RVs up to 30 feet long. Picnic tables and fire grills are provided. Vault toilets are available, but there is no piped water. Leashed pets are permitted.

Reservations, fees: No reservations are accepted. There is no fee. The campground is open from early May to early November.

Contact: Rogue River National Forest, Prospect Ranger District, 47201 Highway 62,

Prospect, OR 97536; (541) 560-3400 or fax (541) 560-3444.

Directions: From Medford on Interstate 5, travel 54 miles north on Highway 62. Turn left and drive one mile west on Forest Service Road 300 to the camp on the left.

Trip notes: Expect lots of company in the midsummer months at this popular camp, which is located where the Upper Rogue River runs underground. The Upper Rogue River Trail passes by the camp and follows the river for many miles to the Pacific Crest Trail in Crater Lake National Park. There is an interpretive area and a spectacular geological viewpoint adjacent to the camp. A quarter-mile barrier-free trail is also available.

㉕ Abbott Creek

Location: On Abbott and Woodruff Creeks in Rogue River National Forest; map E2, grid c2.

Campsites, facilities: There are 25 sites for tents, trailers, or RVs up to 20 feet long. Picnic tables and fire grills are provided. Potable pump water and vault toilets are available. Firewood can be purchased. Leashed pets are permitted.

Reservations, fees: No reservations are accepted. Sites are $6 per night, plus $3 per extra vehicle a night. The campground is open from late May to late October.

Contact: Rogue Recreation, 2990 North Pacific Highway, Medford, OR 97501; (541) 770-5146 or (541) 560-3400, or fax (541) 865-2795.

Directions: From Medford on Interstate 5, travel 47 miles northeast on Highway 62. Turn left and drive 3.5 miles northwest on Forest Service Road 68 to the camp on the left.

Trip notes: Set at the confluence of Abbott and Woodruff Creeks about two miles from the Upper Rogue River, this is a better camp for visitors with children than some of the others along the Rogue River. Abbott Creek is small and tame compared to the roaring Rogue. The kids probably still won't be tempted to dip their toes, however, because the water usually runs at a body-numbing 42 degrees, even in the summer.

26 Joseph P. Stewart State Park

Location: On Lost Creek Lake; map E2, grid d1.

Campsites, facilities: There are 50 sites for tents or self-contained RVs and 151 sites with water and electrical hookups for trailers or RVs of any length. Picnic tables and fire grills are provided. Flush toilets, sanitary disposal services, showers, firewood, and a playground are available. Some facilities are wheelchair accessible. Boat launching facilities are nearby. Leashed pets are permitted.

Reservations, fees: No reservations are accepted. Sites are $13–$14 per night. The campground is open from mid-April to late October.

Contact: Phone (800) 452-5687 or (541) 560-3334, or write to 35251 Highway 62, Trail, OR 97524.

Directions: From Interstate 5 at Medford, drive 34 miles northeast on Highway 62 to the campground.

Trip notes: This state park is on the shore of Lost Creek Lake, a reservoir with a marina, a beach, and boat rentals. The park is home to 5.5 miles of hiking trails and a six-mile bike path. This nice spot gets attention from Oregonians in the area but is missed by most other people.

27 Huckleberry Mountain

Location: Near Crater Lake National Park in Rogue River National Forest; map E2, grid c3.

Campsites, facilities: There are 27 primitive sites for tents, trailers, or RVs up to 21 feet long. Picnic tables and fireplaces are provided. Hand-pumped water and vault toilets are available. Leashed pets are permitted.

Reservations, fees: No reservations are accepted. There is no fee. The campground is open from June to late October.

Contact: Rogue River National Forest, Prospect Ranger District, 47201 Highway 62, Prospect, OR 97536; (541) 560-3400 or fax (541) 560-3444.

Directions: From Medford on Interstate 5,

turn north on Highway 62 and drive 35 miles to Prospect. From Prospect, continue 17.5 miles northeast on Highway 62, then four miles south on Forest Service Road 60. Note: The access road is quite rough; trailers are not recommended.

Trip notes: Here's a prime hideaway for Crater Lake visitors. Set at an elevation of 5,400 feet, this camp about 15 miles from the entrance to Crater Lake National Park really does get overlooked by highway travelers, so you have a good shot at privacy and quiet. The camp is located at the site of an old 1930s Civilian Conservation Corps camp, and the Forest Service has even refurbished the original fireplaces to keep the historic aura intact.

28 Mill Creek

Location: Near the Upper Rogue River in Rogue River National Forest; map E2, grid c3.

Campsites, facilities: There are eight sites for tents, trailers, or RVs up to 25 feet long. Picnic tables and fire grills are provided. Vault toilets are available, but there is no piped water. Leashed pets are permitted.

Reservations, fees: No reservations are accepted. There is no fee. The campground is open from April to November.

Contact: Rogue River National Forest, Prospect Ranger District, 47201 Highway 62, Prospect, OR 97536; (541) 560-3400 or fax (541) 560-3444.

Directions: From Medford on Interstate 5, travel 47 miles northeast on Highway 62, then one mile east on Forest Service Road 30 to the campground.

Trip notes: This campground along the banks of Mill Creek, about two miles from the Upper Rogue River, has beautiful, private sites and is heavily vegetated. It's one in a series of remote, primitive camps near Highway 62 missed by out-of-towners and is an excellent choice for tenters.

29 Lost Creek

Location: Near the Crater Lake Pinnacles in Crater Lake National Park; map E2, grid c5.

Campsites, facilities: There are eight sites for tents. Picnic tables and fire grills are provided. Piped water and some vault toilets are available. Leashed pets and motorbikes are permitted (on paved roads only).

Reservations, fees: Reservations are not accepted. Sites are $5 per night. The campground is open from mid-July to mid-September.

Contact: Crater Lake National Park, P.O. Box 7, Crater Lake, OR 97604; (541) 594-2211.

Directions: From Interstate 5 at Medford, turn east on Highway 62 and drive 77 miles to the Annie Springs junction. Take Rim Drive around the lake to the Pinnacles, then turn left and drive five miles to the campground.

Trip notes: In good weather, this is a prime spot in Crater Lake National Park—you avoid most of the crowd driving the Rim Road. This primitive campground is set near little Lost Creek and the Pinnacles, a series of spires. The only trail access down to Crater Lake is at Cleetwood Cove. Some of the park facilities are open in the winter for cross-country skiing along the unplowed roadways. Winter access to the park is available only from the south and west on Highway 62 to Rim Village.

㉚ Mazama

Location: Near the Pacific Crest Trail in Crater Lake National Park; map E2, grid c5.

Campsites, facilities: There are 198 sites for tents, trailers, or RVs up to 32 feet long. Picnic tables and fire grills are provided. Piped water, flush toilets, sanitary disposal services, showers, a laundry room, gas pumps, a store, firewood, and ice are available. Some facilities are wheelchair accessible. Leashed pets and motorbikes are permitted (on paved roads only).

Reservations, fees: No reservations are accepted. Sites are $13–$14 per night. The campground is open from mid-June to early October.

Contact: Phone (541) 830-8700, fax (541) 830-8514, or write to P.O. Box 2704, White City, OR 97503.

Directions: From Medford on Interstate 5, turn east on Highway 62 and drive 77 miles to the Annie Springs entrance. The campground is just past the entrance.

Trip notes: This is one of two campgrounds at Crater Lake; the other is Lost Creek (campground number 29). The Pacific Crest Trail passes near the camp, but the only trail access down to Crater Lake is at Cleetwood Cove. Some of the park facilities are open in the winter for cross-country skiing along the unplowed roadways. Winter access to the park is available only from the west on Highway 62 to Rim Village.

㉛ Crater Lake Camp and RV Park

Location: Near Crater Lake National Park; map E2, grid c5.

Campsites, facilities: There is an area for dispersed tent camping and 24 sites for trailers or RVs of any length. Two sites are drive-throughs; eight sites have full hookups and the remaining 16 have partial hookups. There are two cabins. Electricity, piped water, sewer hookups, and picnic tables are provided. Flush toilets, showers, firewood, a store, a laundry room, ice, a swimming pool, and a playground are available. Leashed pets and motorbikes are permitted.

Reservations, fees: Reservations are accepted. Sites are $12–$18 per night; cabins are $35 per night. The campground is open from mid-May to October.

Contact: Phone (541) 381-2275 or write to P.O. Box 490, Fort Klamath, OR 97626.

Directions: From Medford on Interstate 5, turn north on Highway 62 and drive 88 miles north and east to the campground at milepost 85.

Trip notes: This campground is located near the south entrance to Crater Lake National Park, the nearest private park in the area. Traffic is heavy during the summer months, but this can be a good option to the packed national park camps. The campground features tepees and trout ponds for fishing.

㉜ Fort Klamath Lodge and RV Park 🚐 ⛺

Location: On the Wood River; map E2, grid c5.

Campsites, facilities: There are five tent sites and 11 sites for trailers or RVs of any length. Electricity, piped water, sewer hookups, and picnic tables are provided. Flush toilets, bottled gas, showers, and a laundry room are available. A store and ice are located within one mile. Leashed pets and motorbikes are permitted.

Reservations, fees: Reservations are accepted. Sites are $10–$12 per night. The campground is open from April through September.

Contact: Phone (541) 381-2234 or write to P.O. Box 428, Fort Klamath, OR 97626.

Directions: From Interstate 5 at Medford, take the Jackson County Airport exit and drive five miles north to White City. Turn east on Highway 140 and drive 74 miles to Klamath Falls. From Klamath Falls, travel 21 miles north on U.S. 97, then 14.5 miles north on Highway 62. The campground is 1.5 miles northwest of Fort Klamath.

Trip notes: This campground is on the banks of the Wood River, just outside Fort Klamath, the site of numerous military campaigns in the late 1800s against the Modoc Indians.

㉝ Jackson F. Kimball State Park 🚐 ⛺

Location: On the Wood River; map E2, grid c6.

Campsites, facilities: There are six primitive sites for tents, trailers, or self-contained RVs up to 45 feet long. Picnic tables and fire grills are provided. Firewood and vault toilets are available, but there is no piped water. Leashed pets are permitted.

Reservations, fees: No reservations are accepted. Sites are $7 per night. The campground is open from mid-April to late October.

Contact: Phone (800) 452-5687 or (541) 388-6211, or write to 63030 O. B. Riley Road, Suite A, Bend, OR 97701.

Directions: From Interstate 5 at Medford, take the Jackson County Airport exit and drive five miles north to White City. Turn east on Highway 140 and drive 74 miles to Klamath Falls. Turn north on U.S. 97 and drive 24 miles, then 13 miles north on Highway 62 to Fort Klamath. From Fort Klamath, drive three miles north on Highway 232.

Trip notes: This primitive state campground near the Wood River is another nice spot just far enough off the main drag to remain a secret. A nice hiking trail leads to the headwaters of the Wood River, which has decent fishing.

㉞ Fly-Casters RV Park 🚐

Location: On the Rogue River; map E2, grid d0.

Campsites, facilities: There are 47 sites for trailers or RVs of any length; two are drive-throughs. Electricity, piped water, sewer hookups, and picnic tables are provided. Flush toilets, bottled gas, showers, and a laundry room are available. A store, a cafe, and ice are located within one mile. Boat launching facilities are nearby. Leashed pets are permitted.

Reservations, fees: Reservations are accepted. Sites are $14–$29 per night. The campground is open year-round.

Contact: Phone (541) 878-2749, fax (541) 878-2742, or write to P.O. Box 699, Shady Cove, OR 97539.

Directions: From Interstate 5 at Medford, drive north on Highway 62 for 23 miles and you'll see the camp along the highway. It's 2.7 miles south of the junction of Highways 62 and 227.

Trip notes: This spot along the banks of the Rogue River is a good base camp for RVers who want to fish or hike. The county park in Shady Cove offers picnic facilities and a boat ramp. Lost Creek Lake is about a 15-minute drive northeast.

㉟ Shady Trails RV Park and Camp

Location: On the Rogue River; map E2, grid d0.

Campsites, facilities: There are 10 tent sites and 40 sites for trailers or RVs of any length. Electricity, piped water, sewer hookups, and picnic tables are provided. Flush toilets, cable TV, bottled gas, sanitary disposal services, showers, a store, ice, and a playground are available. A cafe is located within one mile. Boat launching facilities are nearby. Pets and motorbikes are permitted.

Reservations, fees: Reservations are accepted. Sites are $16–$20 per night. The campground is open year-round.

Contact: Phone (541) 878-2206 or write to 1 Meadow Lane, Shady Cove, OR 97539.

Directions: From Interstate 5 at Medford, drive 23 miles north on Highway 62 to the campground.

Trip notes: This park is set along the banks of the Rogue River in a wooded, mountainous area, with many shaded sites. Recreation options include fishing on the Rogue River or exploring Casey State Park.

㊱ Rogue River RV Park

Location: On the Rogue River; map E2, grid d0.

Campsites, facilities: There are 70 sites for tents, trailers, or RVs up to 60 feet long. Free cable TV, rest rooms, showers, a sanitary dump station, security, a public phone, laundry facilities, limited groceries, ice, and RV supplies are available. Other facilities include a barbecue pavilion, green lawns, horseshoe pits, nearby restaurants, and a boat ramp. The facilities are wheelchair accessible. Leashed pets under 35 pounds are permitted.

Reservations, fees: Reservations are recommended. Sites are $10–$19 per night. The campground is open year-round.

Contact: Phone the park at (800) 775-0367 or (541) 878-2404 or write to 21800 Crater Lake Highway 62, Shady Cove, OR 97539.

Directions: From Interstate 5 at Medford, turn north on Highway 62 and drive 20 miles northeast. The park is located on the right.

Trip notes: This resort provides access to mountain lakes, the surrounding wilderness, and the Rogue River. The beautiful setting is lush and heavily wooded. Activities on the river include riverbank fishing, rafting, and guided trips. Hunting facilities and winter sports are also available at the resort.

㊲ Bear Mountain RV Park

Location: On the Rogue River; map E2, grid d1.

Campsites, facilities: There are some tent sites and 37 drive-through sites for trailers or RVs of any length; 30 have full hookups and seven have partial hookups. Electricity, piped water, sewer hookups, and picnic tables are provided. Flush toilets, bottled gas, sanitary disposal services, showers, a laundry room, ice, and a playground are available. A store and a cafe are located within one mile. Boat docks and launching facilities are nearby. Leashed pets and motorbikes are permitted.

Reservations, fees: Reservations are accepted. Sites are $12–$16 per night. The campground is open year-round.

Contact: Phone (541) 878-2400 or write to 27301 Highway 62, Trail, OR 97541.

Directions: From Interstate 5 at Medford, drive north on Highway 62. From the junction of Highways 62 and 227, continue east on Highway 62 for 2.5 more miles to the campground.

Trip notes: This campground is in an open, grassy area on the Rogue River about six miles from Lost Creek Lake, where boat ramps and picnic areas are available for day use. The campsites are spacious and shaded.

㊳ Whiskey Springs

Location: Near Willow Lake in Rogue River National Forest; map E2, grid d2.

Campsites, facilities: There are 34 sites for

tents, trailers, or RVs up to 30 feet long. Picnic tables and fire grills are provided. Potable piped water and vault toilets are available. Firewood can be purchased. Boat docks, launching facilities, and rentals are within 1.5 miles. Some facilities are wheelchair accessible. Leashed pets are permitted.

Reservations, fees: No reservations are accepted. Sites are $6 per night, plus $3 per extra vehicle a night. The campground is open from late May through September.

Contact: Rogue Recreation, 2990 North Pacific Highway, Medford, OR 97501; (541) 770-5146 or (541) 560-3400, or fax (541) 865-2795.

Directions: From Medford on Interstate 5, travel 15 miles northeast on Highway 62. Turn right and drive 18 miles east on Butte Falls Highway to the town of Butte Falls. From Butte Falls, travel nine miles southeast on Butte Falls Highway/County Road 30. Turn left on Forest Service Road 3317 and drive 300 yards to the campground on the left.

Trip notes: This campground at Whiskey Springs, near Fourbit Creek, is one of the larger, more developed backwoods Forest Service camps in the area. A wheelchair-accessible nature trail is nearby.

㊴ Imnaha

Location: Near the Sky Lakes Wilderness in Rogue River National Forest; map E2, grid d3.

Campsites, facilities: There are four sites for tents. Picnic tables and fire grills are provided. Vault toilets are available, but there is no piped water. Leashed pets are permitted.

Reservations, fees: No reservations are accepted. There is no fee. The campground is open year-round.

Contact: Rogue River National Forest, Butte Falls Ranger District, P.O. Box 227, Butte Falls, OR 97522; (541) 865-2700 or fax (541) 865-2795.

Directions: From Medford on Interstate 5, travel 35 miles northeast on Highway 62 to Prospect, then drive 12 miles east on Forest Service Road 37 to the campground.

Trip notes: This campground along Imnaha

Creek is a good base camp for a wilderness trip. Trailheads at the ends of the nearby Forest Service roads lead east into the Sky Lakes Wilderness.

㊵ South Fork

Location: On the South Rogue River in Rogue River National Forest; map E2, grid d3.

Campsites, facilities: There are six sites for tents, trailers, or RVs up to 15 feet long. Picnic tables, well water, and fire grills are provided. Vault toilets are available. Leashed pets are permitted.

Reservations, fees: No reservations are accepted. Sites are $3 per night. The campground is open year-round.

Contact: Rogue River National Forest, Butte Falls Ranger District, P.O. Box 227, Butte Falls, OR 97522; (541) 865-2700 or fax (541) 865-2795.

Directions: From Medford on Interstate 5, travel 15 miles north on Highway 62, then 32 miles east on Forest Service Road 34 to the campground.

Trip notes: This campground is set along the South Rogue River. To the east, trails at the ends of the nearby Forest Service roads provide access to the Sky Lakes Wilderness. A map of Rogue River National Forest details all back roads, trails, and waters.

㊶ Parker Meadows

Location: On Parker Meadow in Rogue River National Forest; map E2, grid d3.

Campsites, facilities: There are eight sites for tents, trailers, or RVs up to 15 feet long. Picnic tables and fire grills are provided. Pumped water and vault toilets are available. Leashed pets are permitted.

Reservations, fees: No reservations are accepted. Sites are $3 per night. The campground is open from mid-June to late September.

Contact: Rogue River National Forest, Butte Falls Ranger District, P.O. Box 227, Butte Falls, OR 97522; (541) 865-2700 or fax (541) 865-2795.

Directions: From Medford on Interstate 5, travel 14 miles northeast on Highway 62, then 18 miles east to Butte Falls. Continue 10 miles southeast of Butte Falls on County Road 30, then 11 miles northeast on Forest Service Road 37 to the campground.

Trip notes: Fantastic views of nearby Mount McLoughlin are among the highlights of this camp set at 5,000 feet in a beautiful meadow. Trailheads at the ends of the Forest Service roads lead into the Sky Lakes Wilderness. This is a nice spot, complete with water.

㊷ Snowshoe

Location: Near Snowshoe Butte in Rogue River National Forest; map E2, grid d3.

Campsites, facilities: There are five sites for tents, trailers, or RVs. Picnic tables and fire grills are provided. Vault toilets are available. There is no piped water. Leashed pets are permitted.

Reservations, fees: No reservations are accepted. There is no fee. The campground is open year-round.

Contact: Rogue River National Forest, Butte Falls Ranger District, P.O. Box 227, Butte Falls, OR 97522; (541) 865-2700 or fax (541) 865-2795.

Directions: From Medford on Interstate 5, travel 14 miles northeast on Highway 62, then 18 miles east to Butte Falls. Travel nine miles southeast of Butte Falls on County Road 30, then five miles northeast on Forest Service Road 3065 to the campground.

Trip notes: If you're in search of peace and quiet, this nice, secluded spot located at 4,000 feet near Snowshoe Butte is missed by many.

㊸ Fourbit Ford

Location: On Fourbit Creek in Rogue River National Forest; map E2, grid d3.

Campsites, facilities: There are seven sites for tents. Picnic tables and fire grills are provided. Potable pumped water and vault toilets are available. A store, a cafe, and ice are located within five miles. Boat docks, launching facilities, and rentals are nearby. Leashed pets are permitted.

Reservations, fees: No reservations are accepted. Sites are $6 per night, plus $3 per extra vehicle a night. The campground is open from late May to late September.

Contact: Rogue Recreation, 2990 North Pacific Highway, Medford, OR 97501; (541) 770-5146 or (541) 560-3400, or fax (541) 865-2795.

Directions: From Medford on Interstate 5, travel 15 miles northeast on Highway 62. Turn left and drive 18 miles east on Butte Falls Highway to the town of Butte Falls. In Butte Falls, turn left and drive nine miles southeast on County Road 30. Turn left on Forest Service Road 3065 and drive one mile to the campground on the left.

Trip notes: This campground along Fourbit Creek is one in a series of hidden spots tucked away near County Road 30.

㊹ Rocky Point Resort

Location: On Upper Klamath Lake; map E2, grid d5.

Campsites, facilities: There are five tent sites and 28 sites for trailers or RVs of any length; five are drive-throughs. Electricity, piped water, sewer hookups, and picnic tables are provided. Flush toilets, sanitary disposal services, showers, firewood, a recreation hall, a store, a cafe, a laundry room, ice, and a playground are available. Boat docks, launching facilities, and rentals are nearby. Leashed pets are permitted.

Reservations, fees: Reservations are accepted. Sites are $14–$18 per night. The campground is open year-round.

Contact: Phone (541) 356-2287, fax (541) 356-2222, or write to Harriman Route, 28121 Rocky Point Road, Klamath Falls, OR 97601.

Directions: From Interstate 5 at Medford, take the Jackson County Airport exit and drive five miles north to White City. Turn east on Highway 140 and drive approximately 47 miles, then drive three miles north on Rocky Point Road to the campground.

Trip notes: This camp a mile past Harriman Springs on Upper Klamath Lake has opportunities for fishing, boating, and swimming. See the trip notes for Harriman Springs Resort and Marina (campground number 69) for more details about the area.

⑤ Crater Lake Resort

Location: On the Wood River; map E2, grid d6.

Campsites, facilities: There are some tent sites and 23 sites for trailers or RVs of any length; 10 have full hookups and 13 have partial hookups. Electricity, piped water, sewer hookups, and picnic tables are provided. Flush toilets, showers, a recreation hall, a laundry room, and a trout pool are available. Bottled gas, a store, a cafe, and ice are within one mile. Leashed pets and motorbikes are permitted.

Reservations, fees: Reservations are accepted. Sites are $12–$16 per night. The campground is open from mid-April to mid-October.

Contact: Crater Lake Resort, P.O. Box 457, Fort Klamath, OR 97626; (541) 381-2349; e-mail: cratrlkrst@aol.com.

Directions: From Interstate 5 at Medford, take the Jackson County Airport exit and drive five miles north to White City. Turn east on Highway 140 and drive 74 miles to Klamath Falls. From Klamath Falls, travel 21 miles north on U.S. 97, then 12.5 miles north on Highway 62 to the campground, just before Fort Klamath.

Trip notes: This campground is on the banks of the Wood River, just outside Fort Klamath, the site of numerous military campaigns against the Modoc Indians in the late 1800s.

⑥ Walt's Cozy Camp

Location: On the Williamson River; map E2, grid d6.

Campsites, facilities: There are 20 tent sites and 34 sites for trailers or RVs of any length; six are drive-throughs. Electricity, piped water, sewer hookups, and picnic tables are provided.

Flush toilets, showers, firewood, a store, a cafe, a laundry room, and ice are available. Leashed pets and motorbikes are permitted.

Reservations, fees: Reservations are accepted. Sites are $8–$12 per night. The campground is open from April to mid-October.

Contact: Phone (541) 783-2537 or write to P.O. Box 243, Chiloquin, OR 97624.

Directions: From Interstate 5 at Medford, take the Jackson County Airport exit and drive five miles north to White City. Turn east on Highway 140 and drive 79 miles to U.S. 97, then turn north and drive 25 miles to Chiloquin. Continue three miles to the campground.

Trip notes: This campground along the banks of the Williamson River near Collier Memorial State Park is one of three camps in the immediate area. For a more remote setting, Potter's Trailer Park and Head of the River (campground numbers 52 and 53) are to the east.

⑦ Collier Memorial State Park

Location: On the Williamson River; map E2, grid d6.

Campsites, facilities: There are 18 sites for tents or self-contained RVs and 50 sites with full hookups for trailers or RVs up to 60 feet long. Picnic tables and fire grills are provided. Flush toilets, sanitary disposal services, showers, firewood, a laundry room, a playground, and a day-use hitching area are available. Some facilities are wheelchair accessible. Leashed pets are permitted.

Reservations, fees: No reservations are accepted. Sites are $12–$16 per night. The campground is open from mid-April to late October.

Contact: Phone (800) 452-5687 or (541) 388-6211, or write to 63030 O. B. Riley Road, Suite A, Bend, OR 97701.

Directions: From Interstate 5 at Medford, take the Jackson County Airport exit and drive five miles north to White City. Turn east on Highway 140 and drive 79 miles to Klamath Falls. Turn north on U.S. 97 and drive 30 miles to the park entrance.

Trip notes: This campground is set at the

confluence of Spring Creek and the Williamson River, both of which are superior trout streams. A nature trail is also available. An open-air museum detailing Oregon's logging history is in the park, and pioneer log cabins still stand nearby.

⑱ Agency Lake Resort

Location: On Upper Klamath Lake; map E2, grid e6.

Campsites, facilities: There are 15 tent sites and 18 sites for trailers or RVs of any length, plus four cabins. Electricity, piped water, sewer hookups, and picnic tables are provided. Flush toilets, showers, a store, ice, boat docks, launching facilities, and marine gas are available. Leashed pets and motorbikes are permitted.

Reservations, fees: Reservations are accepted. Sites are $8–$16 per night, and cabins are $45 per night. The campground is open year-round.

Contact: Phone (541)783-2489 or write to 3700 Modoc Point Road, Chiloquin, OR 97624.

Directions: From Interstate 5 at Medford, take the Jackson County Airport exit and drive five miles north to White City. Turn east on Highway 140 and drive approximately 74 miles to Klamath Falls, then turn north on U.S. 97 and drive about 30 miles to Chiloquin. Turn west at the Modoc Point sign, drive four miles north to milepost 4, and follow the signs to the campground.

Trip notes: This campground is on Upper Klamath Lake in an open, grassy area with some shaded sites. See the trip notes for Rocky Point Resort (campground number 44) for more information.

⑲ Waterwheel Camp and RV Park

Location: On the Williamson River; map E2, grid d6.

Campsites, facilities: There are six tent sites and 28 sites for trailers or RVs of any

length; 22 are drive-throughs. Electricity, piped water, sewer hookups, and picnic tables are provided. Flush toilets, bottled gas, sanitary disposal services, showers, firewood, a store, a laundry room, ice, and a playground are available. A cafe is located within one mile. Boat docks and launching facilities are nearby. Leashed pets and motorbikes are permitted.

Reservations, fees: Reservations are accepted. Sites are $15–$19 per night. The campground is open year-round.

Contact: Phone (541) 783-2738 or write to 200 Williamson River Drive, Chiloquin, OR 97624.

Directions: From Interstate 5 at Medford, take the Jackson County Airport exit and drive five miles north to White City. Turn east on Highway 140 and drive approximately 74 miles to Klamath Falls, then turn north on U.S. 97 and drive about 30 miles to the park, located one-half mile south of Chiloquin.

Trip notes: This rural campground along the banks of the Williamson River is close to hiking trails. Fishing can be excellent here, with a boat ramp and fishing tackle right at the camp.

⑳ Williamson River

Location: Near Collier Memorial State Park in Winema National Forest; map E2, grid d7.

Campsites, facilities: There are three tent sites and seven sites for trailers or RVs up to 30 feet long. Picnic tables and fire grills are provided. Hand-pumped well water and vault toilets are available. Some facilities are wheelchair accessible. A restaurant is located within five miles. Leashed pets are permitted.

Reservations, fees: No reservations are accepted. Sites are $5 per night, plus $2 for each additional vehicle. The campground is open from May 15 to November 25, weather permitting.

Contact: Winema National Forest, Chiloquin Ranger District, 38500 Highway 97 North, Chiloquin, OR 97624; (541) 783-4001 or fax (541) 783-4009.

Directions: From Interstate 5 at Medford, take the Jackson County Airport exit and drive five miles north to White City. Turn east on Highway 140 and drive 79 miles to U.S. 97, then turn north and drive 25 miles to Chiloquin. Continue 5.5 miles north on U.S. 97, then drive one mile northeast on Forest Service Road 9730 to the campground.

Trip notes: Another great little spot is discovered, this one with excellent trout fishing along the banks of the Williamson River. A map of Winema National Forest details the back roads and trails. Collier Memorial State Park provides a nearby side trip option.

51 Williamson River Resort

Location: On the Williamson River; map E2, grid d7.

Campsites, facilities: There are eight sites for trailers or RVs of any length. Electricity, piped water, and picnic tables are provided. Bottled gas, sanitary disposal services, a store, and ice are available. A cafe is located within one mile. Boat docks, launching facilities, and rentals are nearby. Leashed pets are permitted.

Reservations, fees: Reservations are accepted. Sites are $10 per night; The campground is open year-round.

Contact: Phone (541) 783-2071 or write to 31900 Modoc Point Road, Chiloquin, OR 97624.

Directions: From Interstate 5 at Medford, take the Jackson County Airport exit and drive five miles north to White City. Turn east on Highway 140 and drive approximately 74 miles to Klamath Falls, then turn north on U.S. 97 and drive about 29.5 miles to Chiloquin. Turn on Modoc Point Road and continue 5.5 miles to the park.

Trip notes: This little RV park is along the banks of the Williamson River. The Williamson is one of Oregon's famous fishing streams, attracting anglers from many miles away, and can be fished by drift boat. A boat ramp is available at Camp 52, but you can also just put on your waders and wander out into the stream.

52 Potter's Trailer Park

Location: On the Sprague River; map E2, grid d8.

Campsites, facilities: There are 17 tent sites and 23 full-hookup sites for trailers or RVs of any length. Electricity, piped water, telephones, sewer hookups, and picnic tables are provided. Flush toilets, showers, firewood, a recreation hall, a store, a cafe, a laundry room, and ice are available. Pets and motorbikes are permitted.

Reservations, fees: Reservations are accepted. Sites are $15 per night. The campground is open year-round, with limited winter facilities.

Contact: Phone (541) 783-2253 or write to 11700 Sprague River Road, Chiloquin, OR 97624.

Directions: From Interstate 5 at Medford, take the Jackson County Airport exit and drive five miles north to White City. Turn east on Highway 140 and drive approximately 74 miles to Klamath Falls, then turn north on U.S. 97 and drive 24 miles to Chiloquin. Turn east on Sprague River Highway and continue 12 miles to the resort.

Trip notes: This camp is on the banks of the Sprague River. For the most part, the area east of Klamath Lake doesn't get much attention. But if you want to check out a relatively close spot that's out in booger country, try Head of the River (campground number 53).

53 Head of the River

Location: On the Williamson River in Winema National Forest; map E2, grid d9.

Campsites, facilities: There are five sites for tents, trailers, or RVs up to 30 feet long. Picnic tables and fire pits are provided. Vault toilets are available. There is no piped water. Leashed pets are permitted.

Reservations, fees: No reservations are accepted. There is no fee. The campground is open from Memorial Day through late November.

Contact: Winema National Forest, Chiloquin Ranger District, 38500 Highway 97 North, Chiloquin, OR 97624; (541) 783-4001 or fax (541) 783-4009.

Directions: From Interstate 5 at Medford, take the Jackson County Airport exit and drive five miles north to White City. Turn east on Highway 140 and drive 79 miles to U.S. 97, then turn north and drive 25 miles to Chiloquin. Turn and drive five miles northeast on County Road 858/Sprague River Highway. Turn northeast on County Road 600/Williamson River Highway and drive 27 miles. Turn north on Forest Service Road 4648 and drive one mile to the campground.

Trip notes: Almost nobody knows about this small, lonely spot. The only camp for miles around, it's set along the headwaters of the Williamson River, where the fishing can be excellent.

⑤⑭ Medford Oaks Campark

Location: Near Eagle Point; map E2, grid e1.

Campsites, facilities: There are 60 sites for tents, trailers, or RVs of any length. Rest rooms, showers, a sanitary dump, a public phone, a laundry room, limited groceries, ice, RV supplies, and LP gas are available. Recreational facilities include a seasonal heated swimming pool, movies, horseshoe pits, Ping-Pong, a recreation field for baseball and volleyball, and a playground. One leashed pet per campsite is permitted, subject to management's approval.

Reservations, fees: Reservations are recommended. Sites are $8–$11 per night. Group rates are available. The campground is open year-round.

Contact: Phone the park at (541) 826-5103, fax (541) 826-5984, or write to 7049 State Highway 140, Eagle Point, OR 97524.

Directions: From Interstate 5 at Medford, turn north on Highway 62 and drive five miles to Highway 140. Turn east on Highway 140 and drive 6.8 miles to the campground on the left.

Trip notes: This park is in a quiet rural setting among the trees. Just a short hop off Inter-

state 5, it's an excellent choice for travelers heading south to California. The campground is located along the shore of a pond that provides good pan fishing.

⑤⑤ Lily Glen Campground

Location: On Howard Prairie Lake; map E2, grid e2.

Campsites, facilities: There are 20 sites for tents, trailers, or RVs, with no hookups. Picnic tables, piped water, and vault toilets are available. Leashed pets are permitted.

Reservations, fees: Only reservations for groups are accepted. Sites are $12 per night. The campground is open year-round.

Contact: Jackson County Parks, 400 Antelope Road, White City, OR 97503; (541) 776-7001 or fax (541) 826-8360.

Directions: From Interstate 5 at Medford, turn east on Dead Indian Memorial Road and drive 21 miles to the campground.

Trip notes: Set along the shore of Howard Prairie Lake, this campground is a secluded, primitive getaway. Trout fishing is available. Tubb Springs Wayside State Park and the nearby Rogue River National Forest are possible side trips.

⑤⑥ Willow Lake Resort

Location: On Willow Lake; map E2, grid e3.

Campsites, facilities: There are 37 tent sites and 45 drive-through sites for trailers or RVs up to 30 feet long. Electricity, piped water, sewer hookups, and picnic tables are provided. Flush toilets, sanitary disposal services, showers, firewood, a store, a cafe, LP gas, ice, and a playground are available. Leashed pets are permitted.

Reservations, fees: Reservations are accepted. Sites are $12–$16 per night. The campground is open year-round.

Contact: Jackson County Parks, 400 Antelope Road, White City, OR 97503; (541) 776-7001 or fax (541) 826-8360.

Directions: From Medford on Interstate 5,

travel 15 miles northeast on Highway 62, then 25 miles east on Butte Falls Highway. Go two miles southeast on Willow Lake Road to the campground.

Trip notes: This campground is on the shore of Willow Lake close to hiking trails and a small marina.

⑤⑦ Willow Prairie

Location: Near Fish Lake in Rogue River National Forest; map E2, grid e3.

Campsites, facilities: There are 10 sites for tents, trailers, or RVs up to 15 feet long. Picnic tables and fire grills are provided. Pumped water and vault toilets are available. A store, a cafe, and ice are located within five miles. Boat docks, launching facilities, and rentals are nearby. Leashed pets are permitted.

Reservations, fees: Reservations are required. Sites are $6 per night. The campground is open from late May to late September.

Contact: Rogue River National Forest, Butte Falls Ranger District, P.O. Box 227, Butte Falls, OR 97522; (541) 865-2700 or fax (541) 865-2795.

Directions: From Medford on Interstate 5, travel 31.5 miles east on Highway 140, then 1.5 miles north on Forest Service Road 37. The camp is one mile west on Forest Service Road 3738.

Trip notes: This spot near the origin of the west branch of Willow Creek is primarily used as a horse camp. A map of Rogue River National Forest details the back roads and can help you get here. Fish Lake is four miles south.

⑤⑧ North Fork

Location: Near Fish Lake in Rogue River National Forest; map E2, grid e3.

Campsites, facilities: There are five tent sites and four sites for trailers or RVs up to 24 feet long. Picnic tables and fire grills are provided. Vault toilets and hand-pumped water are available. Boat docks, launching facilities, and rentals are nearby. Some facilities are wheelchair accessible, including a barrier-free vault toilet. Leashed pets are permitted.

Reservations, fees: No reservations are accepted. There is no fee, but donations are accepted. The campground is open from early May to early November.

Contact: Rogue River National Forest, Ashland Ranger District, 645 Washington Street, Ashland, OR 97520; (541) 482-3333 or fax (541) 858-2402.

Directions: From Interstate 5 at Medford, take the Jackson County Airport exit (the last Medford exit) and drive five miles north to White City. Turn east on Highway 140 and drive 31.5 miles, then go half a mile south on Forest Service Road 37 to the campground.

Trip notes: Here's a small, pretty campground with easy access from the highway and close proximity to Fish Lake. It's fairly popular, so reserve your spot early. Excellent fly-fishing can be found along the Fish Lake Trail, which leads directly out of camp.

⑤⑨ Fish Lake

Location: On Fish Lake in Rogue River National Forest; map E2, grid e3.

Campsites, facilities: There are 19 sites for tents, trailers, or RVs up to 40 feet long. Picnic tables and fire grills are provided. Piped water, flush toilets, a wheelchair-accessible picnic shelter, a store, a cafe, and ice are available. Firewood can be purchased. Boat docks, launching facilities, and rentals are nearby. Leashed pets are permitted.

Reservations, fees: No reservations are accepted. Sites are $10 per night, plus $5 per extra vehicle a night. The campground is open from mid-May to mid-October.

Contact: Rogue Recreation, 2990 North Pacific Highway, Medford, OR 97501; (541) 770-5146 or (541) 560-3400, or fax (541) 865-2795.

Directions: From Interstate 5 at Medford, take the Jackson County Airport exit (the last Medford exit) and drive five miles north to White City. Turn east on Highway 140 and drive 30 miles to the campground on the right.

Trip notes: Boating, fishing, hiking, and bicycling are among the recreation options at this campground on the north shore of Fish Lake. Easy one-mile access to the Pacific Crest

Trail is also available. If this campground is full, Doe Point and Fish Lake Resort (campground numbers 60 and 61) are nearby.

⑥⓪ Doe Point

Location: On Fish Lake in Rogue River National Forest; map E2, grid e3.

Campsites, facilities: There are five walk-in tent sites and 25 sites for tents, trailers, or RVs up to 40 feet long. Picnic tables and fire grills are provided. Potable piped water, flush toilets, a store, a cafe, and ice are available. Firewood can be purchased. Boat docks, launching facilities, and rentals are nearby. Leashed pets are permitted.

Reservations, fees: No reservations are accepted. Sites are $10 per night, plus $5 per extra vehicle a night. The campground is open from mid-May to mid-October.

Contact: Rogue Recreation, 2990 North Pacific Highway, Medford, OR 97501; (541) 770-5146 or (541) 560-3400, or fax (541) 865-2795.

Directions: From Interstate 5 at Medford, take the Jackson County Airport exit (the last Medford exit) and drive five miles north to White City. Turn east on Highway 140 and drive 30 miles to the campground on the right.

Trip notes: This campground is along the north shore of Fish Lake, nearly adjacent to Fish Lake Campground. Doe Point is slightly preferable because it's densely vegetated, offering shaded, well-screened sites. Privacy, rare at many campgrounds, can be found here. Recreation options include boating, fishing, hiking, and bicycling, plus an easy one-mile access trail to the Pacific Crest Trail.

⑥① Fish Lake Resort

Location: On Fish Lake; map E2, grid e3.

Campsites, facilities: There are five tent sites and 45 sites for trailers or RVs up to 30 feet long, plus 10 cabins. Electricity, piped water, sewer hookups, and picnic tables are provided. Flush toilets, bottled gas, sanitary disposal services, showers, a recreation hall, a store, a cafe,

a laundry room, ice, boat docks, boat rentals, and launching facilities are available. Leashed pets and motorbikes are permitted.

Reservations, fees: Reservations are accepted. Sites are $12–$18 per night; call for cabin fees. The campground is open year-round, weather permitting.

Contact: Phone (541) 949-8500 or write to P.O. Box 40, Medford, OR 97501.

Directions: From Interstate 5 at Medford, take the Jackson County Airport exit (exit 30) and drive five miles north to White City. Turn east on Highway 140 and drive 30 miles to Fish Lake Road. Turn south and drive half a mile to the camp.

Trip notes: This campground along Fish Lake is privately operated under permit by the Forest Service and offers a resort-type feel, catering primarily to families. Hiking, bicycling, fishing, and boating are some of the activities here. This is the largest and most developed of the three camps at Fish Lake. It's also the only one open year-round, though the snow keeps away all but the most rugged campers. Cozy cabins are available for rental, however, and the resort is quite active in winter, with opportunities for cross-country skiing, ice fishing, and snowmobiling.

⑥② Daley Creek

Location: On Daley Creek in Rogue River National Forest; map E2, grid e3.

Campsites, facilities: There are five tent sites and two sites for trailers or RVs up to 24 feet long. Picnic tables and fire grills are provided, but there is no piped water. Some facilities are wheelchair accessible, including two camping units and a barrier-free vault toilet. Leashed pets are permitted.

Reservations, fees: No reservations are accepted. There is no fee, but donations are accepted. The campground is open from early May to early November.

Contact: Rogue River National Forest, Ashland Ranger District, 645 Washington Street, Ashland, OR 97520; (541) 482-3333 or fax (541) 858-2402.

Directions: From Ashland, drive 22 miles

northeast on Dead Indian Memorial Road, then go 1.5 miles north on Forest Service Road 37 to the campground.

Trip notes: This campground along the banks of Daley Creek is a primitive and free alternative to some of the more developed spots in the area. The Beaver Dam Trail heads right out of camp, leading along the creek. Fishing can be decent downstream from here.

⑥ Beaver Dam

Location: On Beaver Dam Creek in Rogue River National Forest; map E2, grid e3.

Campsites, facilities: There are two primitive tent sites and two sites for trailers or RVs up to 18 feet long. Picnic tables and fire grills are provided. Vault toilets are available, but there is no piped water. Leashed pets are permitted.

Reservations, fees: No reservations are accepted. There is no fee, but donations are accepted. The campground is open from early May to early November.

Contact: Rogue River National Forest, Ashland Ranger District, 645 Washington Street, Ashland, OR 97520; (541) 482-3333 or fax (541) 858-2402.

Directions: From Ashland, drive 22 miles northeast on Dead Indian Memorial Road, then go 1.5 miles north on Forest Service Road 37 to the campground.

Trip notes: This pretty and shaded spot adjacent to Daley Creek Campground is quiet and rustic, with unusual vegetation along the creekside for botany fans. The trailhead for the Beaver Dam Trail is also here.

⑥ Aspen Point

Location: On Lake of the Woods in Winema National Forest; map E2, grid e4.

Campsites, facilities: There are 60 sites for tents, trailers, or RVs up to 55 feet long. Picnic tables and fire grills are provided. Piped water and flush toilets are available. Boat docks, launching facilities, and rentals are nearby. Leashed pets are permitted.

Reservations, fees: Reservations can be

made by calling (800) 280-CAMP/2267 ($8.65 reservation fee). Sites are $8–$10 per night. The campground is open from late May to late September.

Contact: Winema National Forest, Klamath Ranger District, 1936 California Avenue, Klamath Falls, OR 97601; (541) 885-3400 or fax (541) 885-3452.

Directions: From Interstate 5 at Medford, take the Jackson County Airport exit and drive five miles north to White City. Turn east on Highway 140 and drive approximately 41.5 miles to Forest Service Road 3704. Drive one-half mile, then proceed 100 yards west at the signed entrance.

Trip notes: This campground is near the north shore of Lake of the Woods, adjacent to Lake of the Woods Resort. A hiking trail just north of camp leads north for several miles, wandering around Fourmile Lake and extending into the Sky Lakes Wilderness. Other trails nearby head into the Mountain Lakes Wilderness. Fishing, swimming, boating, and waterskiing are among the activities here.

⑥ Sunset

Location: Near Lake of the Woods in Winema National Forest; map E2, grid e4.

Campsites, facilities: There are 67 sites for tents, trailers, or RVs up to 55 feet long. Picnic tables and fire grills are provided. Piped water and flush toilets are available. Some facilities are wheelchair accessible. Boat docks, launching facilities, and rentals are nearby. Leashed pets are permitted.

Reservations, fees: Reservations can be made by calling (800) 280-CAMP/2267 ($8.65 reservation fee). Sites are $8–$10 per night. The campground is open from June to mid-September.

Contact: Winema National Forest, Klamath Ranger District, 1936 California Avenue, Klamath Falls, OR 97601; (541) 885-3400 or fax (541) 885-3452.

Directions: From Interstate 5 at Medford, take the Jackson County Airport exit and drive five miles north to White City. Turn east on Highway 140 and drive approximately 41.5

miles to Forest Service Road 3704. Turn south and drive two miles. The camp is one-half mile west on Forest Service Road 3738.

Trip notes: This campground near the eastern shore of Lake of the Woods is fully developed and offers a myriad of recreation options. It's popular for both fishing and rafting.

66 Fourmile Lake

Location: At Fourmile Lake in Winema National Forest; map E2, grid e4.

Campsites, facilities: There are 25 sites for tents, trailers, or RVs up to 22 feet long. Picnic tables and fire grills are provided. Hand-pumped well water and vault toilets are available. Leashed pets are permitted.

Reservations, fees: No reservations are accepted. Sites are $5–$10 per night. The campground is open from June to late September.

Contact: Winema National Forest, Klamath Ranger District, 1936 California Avenue, Klamath Falls, OR 97601; (541) 885-3400 or fax (541) 885-3452.

Directions: From Interstate 5 at Medford, take the Jackson County Airport exit and drive five miles north to White City. Turn east on Highway 140 and drive approximately 40 miles, then continue six miles north on Forest Service Road 3661 to the campground.

Trip notes: This beautiful spot is the only camp on the shore of Fourmile Lake. Several nearby trails provide access to the Sky Lakes Wilderness. The Pacific Crest Trail passes about two miles from camp.

67 Lake of the Woods Resort

Location: On Lake of the Woods; map E2, grid e4.

Campsites, facilities: There are 27 sites for tents, trailers, or RVs up to 35 feet long, plus eight cabins that can accommodate from three to eight people. Rest rooms, showers, a sanitary dump, a public phone, a laundry room, ice, snacks, a restaurant, a lounge, and LP gas bottles are available. There is also a boat ramp, dock, marina, rentals, and a barbecue. Leashed pets are permitted.

Reservations, fees: Reservations are recommended. Sites are $14–$16 per night, and cabins are $58.30–$84.80 per night. The campground is open from mid-May through September, weather permitting.

Contact: Phone the resort at (541) 949-8300 or write to 950 Harriman Route, Klamath Falls, OR 97601.

Directions: From Interstate 5 at Medford, turn north on Highway 62 and drive five miles, then turn east on Highway 140 and drive approximately 41 miles to Lake of the Woods Road. Turn south and continue to the resort on the right.

Trip notes: Located on beautiful Lake of the Woods, this resort offers fishing (four kinds of trout, catfish, bass) and boating in a secluded forest setting. It's a family-oriented campground with all the amenities. In the winter, snowmobiling and cross-country skiing are popular (you can rent equipment at the resort). Attractions in the area include the Mountain Lakes Wilderness and the Pacific Crest Trail.

68 Odessa

Location: Near Klamath Lake in Winema National Forest; map E2, grid e5.

Campsites, facilities: There are five tent sites. Picnic tables and fire grills are provided. Vault toilets are available, but there is no piped water. Leashed pets are permitted.

Reservations, fees: No reservations are accepted. There is no fee. The campground is open year-round, weather permitting.

Contact: Winema National Forest, Klamath Ranger District, 1936 California Avenue, Klamath Falls, OR 97601; (541) 885-3400 or fax (541) 885-3452.

Directions: From Interstate 5 at Medford, take the Jackson County Airport exit and drive five miles north to White City. Turn east on Highway 140 and drive approximately 57.5 miles, then go one mile northeast on Forest Service Road 3639 to the campground.

Trip notes: This campground is along Odessa

Creek, near the shore of Upper Klamath Lake. Boating and fishing are allowed, but not waterskiing. The lake can provide excellent fishing for rainbow trout on both flies and Rapalas.

⑥⑨ Harriman Springs Resort and Marina

Location: On Upper Klamath Lake; map E2, grid e5.

Campsites, facilities: There are six tent sites and 12 sites for trailers or RVs; eight are drive-throughs. There are also four cabins, two with kitchens. Electricity, piped water, sewer hookups, and picnic tables are provided. Flush toilets, showers, firewood, a restaurant, a lounge, a laundry room, ice, boat docks, boat and canoe rentals, and launching facilities are available. Bottled gas, sanitary disposal services, and a store are located within one mile. Leashed pets and motorbikes are permitted.

Reservations, fees: Reservations are accepted. Sites are $14–$18 per night, and cabins are $48–$58 per night. The campground is open year-round.

Contact: Phone (541) 356-2331, fax (541) 356-2232, or write to 26661 Rocky Point Road, Klamath Falls, OR 97601.

Directions: From Interstate 5 at Medford, take the Jackson County Airport exit and drive five miles north to White City. Turn east on Highway 140 and drive approximately 47 miles. Turn right on Rocky Point Road and drive about two miles to the campground on the right.

Trip notes: This resort is on the shore of Pelican Bay at the north end of Upper Klamath Lake, adjacent to the Upper Klamath National Wildlife Refuge. Trout fishing is good, especially from a canoe.

⑦⓪ Oregon 8 RV Park

Location: On Upper Klamath Lake; map E2, grid e6.

Campsites, facilities: There are 10 tent sites and 29 drive-through sites for trailers or RVs of any length. Electricity, piped water, cable TV, sewer hookups, and picnic tables are provided. Flush toilets, showers, a recreation hall, a laundry room, ice, and a swimming pool are available. Bottled gas, a store, and a cafe are located within one mile. Leashed pets and motorbikes are permitted.

Reservations, fees: Reservations are accepted. Sites are $10–$15 per night. The campground is open year-round, with limited winter facilities.

Contact: Phone (541) 882-0482 or write to 5225 Highway 97 North, Klamath Falls, OR 97601.

Directions: From Interstate 5 at Medford, turn north on Highway 62 and drive five miles, then turn east on Highway 140 and drive 74 miles to Klamath Falls. From Klamath Falls, travel 3.5 miles north on U.S. 97 to the campground.

Trip notes: This campground is near Hanks Marsh on the southeast shore of Upper Klamath Lake, within 50 miles of Crater Lake. Nearby recreation options include a golf course, bike paths, and a marina.

⑦① Jackson Hot Springs

Location: Near Ashland; map E2, grid f0.

Campsites, facilities: There are 30 tent sites and 20 drive-through sites for trailers or RVs of any length. Electricity, piped water, sewer hookups, and picnic tables are provided. Flush toilets, showers, a cafe, a laundry room, ice, and a swimming pool are available. Bottled gas is located within one mile. No pets are permitted.

Reservations, fees: No reservations are accepted. Sites are $13–$18 per night. The campground is open year-round.

Contact: Phone (541) 482-3776 or write to 2253 Highway 99 North, Ashland, OR 97520.

Directions: Near Ashland, take exit 19 off Interstate 5 and travel west for one-quarter mile to the stoplight. Turn right and drive 500 feet to the campground.

Trip notes: This campground has mineral

hot springs that empty into a swimming pool, not a hot pool (76 degrees). Hot mineral baths are available in private rooms. Nearby recreation options include a golf course, hiking trails, bike paths, and tennis courts.

⑫ Wrangle

Location: Near the Pacific Crest Trail in Rogue River National Forest; map E2, grid f0.

Campsites, facilities: There are five sites for tents. Picnic tables and fire grills are provided. Vault toilets, hand-pumped water, and a community kitchen are available. Leashed pets are permitted.

Reservations, fees: No reservations are accepted. There is no fee. The campground is open from early June to late October.

Contact: Rogue River National Forest, Star Ranger District, 6941 Upper Applegate Road, Jacksonville, OR 97530; (541) 899-1812 or fax (541) 858-2401.

Directions: From Interstate 5 at Ashland, travel three miles north on Highway 99 to Talent, then drive south on Forest Service Road 22 for 17 miles until it ends at Forest Service Road 20. Head west on Forest Service Road 20 for 4.5 miles. The entrance road to the campground is on the right.

Trip notes: This campground is set at the headwaters of Wrangle Creek in the Siskiyou Mountains. The Pacific Crest Trail passes near camp. A map of Rogue River National Forest details hiking trails and streams, as well as backcountry roads. Dutchman Peak Lookout, built in the late 1920s and featured in the historical register, is located within five miles. This is a lovely campground, and unusual with its combination of drinking water and no fee.

⑬ Glenyan Campground of Ashland

Location: Near Emigrant Lake; map E2, grid f1.

Campsites, facilities: There are 68 sites for tents, trailers, or RVs of any length; 12 have full and 38 have partial hookups. Electricity,

piped water, sewer hookups, and picnic tables are provided. Flush toilets, bottled gas, sanitary disposal services, showers, firewood, a recreation hall, a store, a laundry room, ice, a playground, and a swimming pool are available. Leashed pets are permitted.

Reservations, fees: Reservations are accepted. Sites are $17.50–$22 per night. The campground is open year-round.

Contact: Phone (541) 488-1785 or write to 5310 Highway 66, Ashland, OR 97520.

Directions: From Interstate 5 at Ashland, turn east on Highway 66 and drive 3.5 miles to the campground on the right.

Trip notes: This campground within seven miles of Ashland offers shady sites near Emigrant Lake. Recreation options in the area include a golf course, hiking trails, bike paths, and tennis courts. It's an easy jump from Interstate 5 at Ashland.

⑭ Mount Ashland

Location: On the Pacific Crest Trail in Klamath National Forest; map E2, grid f1.

Campsites, facilities: There are eight sites for tents, trailers, or RVs up to 15 feet long. Picnic tables and fire grills are provided. Vault toilets are available, but there is no piped water. Leashed pets are permitted.

Reservations, fees: No reservations are accepted. There is no fee. The campground is open from July to late October.

Contact: Klamath National Forest, Scott River Ranger District, 1312 Fairlane Road, Yreka, CA 96097; (530) 468-5351. (Yes, the address and phone number are correct.)

Directions: From Ashland, travel 12 miles south on Interstate 5. Turn west on County Road 993 and drive one mile. Turn on Forest Service Road 20 and drive nine miles to the campground.

Trip notes: Set at 6,000 feet along the Pacific Crest Trail, this beautiful site is heavily wooded and has abundant wildlife. On clear days, there are great lookouts, particularly to the south where California's 14,000-foot Mount Shasta is an awesome sight.

⑦ Hyatt Lake

Location: On Hyatt Lake; map E2, grid f3.
Campsites, facilities: There are 10 tent sites and 36 sites for tents, trailers, or RVs up to 35 feet in length. Picnic tables and fire grills are provided. Piped water, showers, flush toilets, a sanitary disposal station, and a boat ramp are available. Leashed pets are permitted.
Reservations, fees: No reservations are accepted. Sites are $10 per night, with a 14-day stay limit. The campground is open April 26 through October, weather permitting.
Contact: Bureau of Land Management, 3040 Biddle Road, Medford, OR 97504; (541) 482-2031.
Directions: From Interstate 5 at Ashland, drive 16 miles east on Highway 66, then four miles north on East Hyatt Lake Road. Turn left into the campground.
Trip notes: This campground is on the south end of Hyatt Lake, which has grown into a good fishing spot. Nearby recreation options include a marina and a swimming beach. The Pacific Crest Trail passes right by the camp entrance.

⑦ Hyatt Lake Resort

Location: On Hyatt Lake; map E2, grid f2.
Campsites, facilities: There are 13 tent sites and 22 sites for trailers or RVs of any length; four are drive-throughs. There are also four cabins with no kitchen facilities; each sleeps four. Electricity, piped water, sewer hookups, and picnic tables are provided. Flush toilets, sanitary disposal services, showers, a store, a cafe, a laundry room, ice, a playground, and boat rentals are available. Boat docks and launching facilities are nearby. Leashed pets and motorbikes are permitted.
Reservations, fees: Reservations are accepted. Sites are $12–$17 per night; call for cabin fees (monthly rates are available). The campground is open from April through October.

Contact: Phone (541) 482-3331 or write to 7979 Hyatt Prairie Road, Ashland, OR 97520.
Directions: From Interstate 5 at Ashland, drive 17 miles east on Highway 66, then three miles northeast on Hyatt Lake Road. The camp is one mile farther on Hyatt Prairie Road.
Trip notes: This campground is set along the shore of Hyatt Lake, where hiking and fishing are some of the recreation options. This is a scaled-down option to the resort at adjacent Howard Prairie Lake. The Pacific Crest Trail is just half a mile away.

⑦ Camper's Cover

Location: On Hyatt Lake; map E2, grid f2.
Campsites, facilities: There are 23 sites for trailers or RVs up to 30 feet long; seven are drive-throughs. Electricity, piped water, sewer hookups, and picnic tables are provided. Flush toilets, showers, firewood, a store, a cafe, and ice are available. Boat docks are nearby. Leashed pets are permitted.
Reservations, fees: Reservations are accepted. Sites are $14.50 per night. The campground is open year-round.
Contact: Phone (541) 482-1201 or write to 7900 Hyatt Prairie Road, Ashland, OR 97520.
Directions: From Interstate 5 at Ashland, drive 18 miles east on Highway 66, then three miles northeast on Hyatt Lake Road. The camp is 2.5 miles farther on Hyatt Prairie Road.
Trip notes: This campground is along the shore of Hyatt Lake, with the Pacific Crest Trail passing about a mile away.

⑦ Emigrant Campground

Location: On Emigrant Lake; map E2, grid f2.
Campsites, facilities: There are 42 sites for tents, trailers, and self-contained RVs, plus an overflow area. Two group camp areas and the picnic and barbecue areas can be reserved. Rest rooms, showers, a sanitary dump, a public phone, a laundry room, snacks, and a barbecue are available. Recreational facilities include horseshoe pits, a playground, and a

recreation field. A boat ramp is provided. Some facilities are wheelchair accessible. Pets are permitted in designated areas only.

Reservations, fees: Reservations are only accepted for the group camps and picnic areas. Sites are $14 per night. Children 15 and under are free, and pets are $1 per night. The campground is open from mid-March to mid-October.

Contact: Jackson County Parks, 400 Antelope Road, White City, OR 97503; (541) 776-7001 or fax (541) 826-8360.

Directions: From Interstate 5 at Ashland, turn southeast on Highway 66 and drive five miles to the campground.

Trip notes: This campground nestled among the trees along Emigrant Lake has an unusual "no turn away" policy, so you're just about guaranteed a site. Emigrant Lake is a well-known recreational area, and activities at this park include swimming, hiking, boating, waterskiing, and fishing. There are also two super water slides. The park has its own swimming cove. Side trip possibilities include exploring nearby Mount Ashland, where a ski area operates in the winter, and visiting the world-renowned Shakespeare Festival in Ashland.

⑦ Howard Prairie Lake Resort

Location: On Howard Prairie Lake; map E2, grid f3.

Campsites, facilities: There are 300 sites for tents, trailers, or RVs of any length. Electricity, piped water, sewer hookups, 24-hour security, and picnic tables are provided. Flush toilets, bottled gas, sanitary disposal services, showers, firewood, a store, a cafe, a laundry room, boat docks, boat rentals, moorage, and launching facilities are available. Leashed pets are permitted.

Reservations, fees: No reservations are accepted. Sites are $12–$17 per night. The campground is open from mid-April through October.

Contact: Phone (541) 482-1979, fax (541)

773-3130, or write to 3249 Hyatt Prairie Road, Ashland, OR 97520.

Directions: From Interstate 5 at Ashland, take Highway 66 east to Dead Indian Memorial Road, go 19 miles east to Howard Prairie Road, and drive five miles south to the reservoir.

Trip notes: This wooded campground is along the shore of Howard Prairie Lake, where hiking, swimming, fishing, and boating are among the recreation options. This is one of the largest campgrounds within more than a hundred miles.

⑧⑩ Topsy

Location: On the Upper Klamath River; map E2, grid f5.

Campsites, facilities: There are 15 sites for trailers or RVs up to 40 feet long. Picnic tables and fire grills are provided. Pit toilets and piped water are available. Facilities are wheelchair accessible. Boat launching facilities are nearby. Leashed pets are permitted.

Reservations, fees: No reservations are accepted. Sites are $7 per night, with a 14-day stay limit. The campground is open from mid-May through Labor Day.

Contact: Bureau of Land Management, 2795 Anderson Avenue, Building 25, Klamath Falls, OR 97603; (541) 883-6916 or fax (541) 884-2097.

Directions: From Klamath Falls, travel west for 14.5 miles on Highway 66. Turn south on Topsy Road and travel 1.5 miles to the campground.

Trip notes: This campground is on the Upper Klamath River, which is a good spot for trout fishing and a top river for rafters (experts only). There is Class IV and V white water at Caldera, Satan's Gate, Hell's Corner, and Three Rocks. The area is good for mountain biking, too.

⑧⑪ KOA Klamath Falls

Location: On Upper Klamath Lake; map E2, grid f6.

Campsites, facilities: There are 18 tent

sites and 73 sites for trailers or RVs of any length; 37 are drive-throughs. Electricity, piped water, sewer hookups, and picnic tables are provided. Flush toilets, bottled gas, sanitary disposal services, showers, a recreation hall, a store, a laundry room, ice, a playground, and a swimming pool are available. A cafe is located within one mile. Boat docks and launching facilities are nearby. Leashed pets and motorbikes are permitted.

Reservations, fees: Reservations are accepted; call (800) 562-9036. Sites are $17–$22 per night. The campground is open year-round, with limited winter facilities.

Contact: Phone (541) 884-4644 or write to 3435 Shasta Way, Klamath Falls, OR 97603.

Directions: From Interstate 5 at Medford, turn north on Highway 62 and drive five miles, then turn east on Highway 140 and drive 74 miles to Klamath Falls. From Klamath Falls, travel 1.5 miles northwest on U.S. 97, then one block west on Shasta Way.

Trip notes: This campground is along the shore of Upper Klamath Lake, near the marina. Hiking trails and tennis courts are nearby. This is a good base camp if you plan to explore the Crater Lake area.

⑧② Tingley Lake Estates

Location: On Tingley Lake; map E2, grid f6.

Campsites, facilities: There are six tent sites and 10 sites for trailers or RVs of any length; three have full and seven have partial hookups. Electricity, piped water, sewer hookups, and picnic tables are provided. Telephone and cable TV hookups, flush toilets, sanitary disposal services, showers, a laundry room, boat docks, and a playground are available. A store, a cafe, and ice are located within two miles. Leashed pets are permitted.

Reservations, fees: Reservations are accepted. Sites are $14–$16 per night. The

campground is open year-round, weather permitting, with limited winter services.

Contact: Phone (541) 882-8386 or write to 11800 Tingley Road, Klamath Falls, OR 07603.

Directions: From Interstate 5 at Medford, turn north on Highway 62 and drive five miles, then turn east on Highway 140 and drive 74 miles to Klamath Falls. From Klamath Falls, drive seven miles southwest on U.S. 97, then two miles east on Old Midland Road. The camp is half a mile south on Tingley Road.

Trip notes: This privately operated RV park provides a layover for travelers crossing the Oregon border on U.S. 97. Tingley Lake has opportunities for bass fishing, boating, and swimming.

⑧③ Wiseman's Mobile Court and RV 🚐

Location: Near Upper Klamath Lake; map E2, grid f7.

Campsites, facilities: There are 17 sites for trailers or RVs of any length. Electricity, piped water, and sewer hookups are provided. Flush toilets, sanitary disposal services, showers, and laundry facilities are available. Bottled gas is located within one mile. Leashed pets are permitted.

Reservations, fees: Reservations are accepted. Sites are $16 per night. The campground is open year-round.

Contact: Phone (541) 884-4327 or write to 6800 South Sixth Street, Klamath Falls, OR 97603.

Directions: From Interstate 5 at Medford, turn north on Highway 62 and drive five miles, then turn east on Highway 140 and drive 74 miles to Klamath Falls. Continue 4.5 miles east on Highway 140 to the park.

Trip notes: This is a suburban RV park with the barest essentials. It's a decent layover spot if you need a quick place to stay.

Map E3

One inch equals approximately 20 miles.

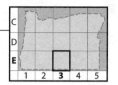

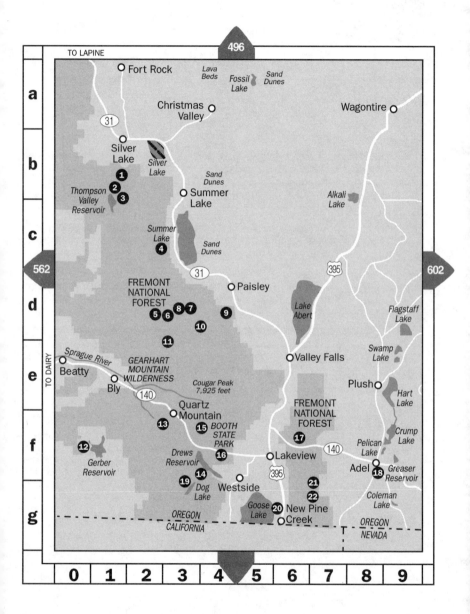

TO LAPINE

496

O Fort Rock

Lava Beds

Fossil Lake

Sand Dunes

a

31

Christmas Valley O

Wagontire O

O Silver Lake

b

Silver Lake

❶

Thompson Valley Reservoir

❷

❸

Sand Dunes

O Summer Lake

Alkali Lake

Summer Lake

c

❹

Sand Dunes

562

31

395

602

FREMONT NATIONAL FOREST

O Paisley

d

❺ ❻ ❽ ❼

❾

❿

Lake Abert

Flagstaff Lake

⓫

Swamp Lake

Sprague River

e

O Beatty

GEARHART MOUNTAIN WILDERNESS

O Valley Falls

TO DAIRY

O Bly

140

Cougar Peak 7,925 feet

O Plush

Hart Lake

Quartz Mountain

FREMONT NATIONAL FOREST

⓭

⓯

BOOTH STATE PARK

Crump Lake

f

⓬

⓱

140

Pelican Lake

Gerber Reservoir

Drews Reservoir

⓰

O Lakeview

O Adel ⓲

Greaser Reservoir

⓮

395

❿⓳

Coleman Lake

Dog Lake

O Westside

㉑

g

OREGON CALIFORNIA

Goose Lake

㉒

㉒

New Pine Creek

OREGON NEVADA

㉒⓴ O

| 0 | 1 | 2 | 3 | 4 | 5 | 6 | 7 | 8 | 9 |

Chapter E3 features:

❶ Silver Creek Marsh

Location: Near Silver Creek in Fremont National Forest; map E3, grid b1.

Campsites, facilities: There are 17 tent sites. Picnic tables and fire grills are provided. Well water, firewood, vault toilets, and hitching trails and corrals for horses are available. Leashed pets are permitted.

Reservations, fees: No reservations are accepted. There is no fee. The campground is open from May to late October.

Contact: Fremont National Forest, Silver Lake Ranger District, P.O. Box 129, Silver Lake, OR 97638; (541) 576-2107 or fax (541) 576-7587.

Directions: From Interstate 5 south of Eugene, take exit 188 and turn east on Highway 58. Drive 86 miles, then turn north on U.S. 97 and drive 26 miles. Turn east on Highway 31 and go 48 miles to Forest Service Road 27 (one mile west of the town of Silver Lake). Turn south and drive 10 miles. The camp is 200 yards southwest of Forest Service Road 27.

Trip notes: A trailhead and terminus for segments of the National Recreational Trail are located at this small, quiet, and primitive camp that gets little attention.

❷ Thompson Reservoir

Location: On Thompson Reservoir in Fremont National Forest; map E3, grid b1.

Campsites, facilities: There are 19 sites for tents, trailers, or RVs up to 22 feet long, plus a separate group camping area. Picnic tables and fire grills are provided. Hand-pumped water and vault toilets are available. Boat launching facilities are nearby. Leashed pets are permitted.

Reservations, fees: No reservations are accepted. There is no fee. The campground is open from May to mid-November.

Contact: Fremont National Forest, Silver Lake Ranger District, P.O. Box 129, Silver Lake, OR 97638; (541) 576-2107 or fax (541) 576-7587.

Directions: From U.S. 395 at the town of Valley Falls, turn west on Highway 31 and drive 73 miles to the town of Silver Lake. Continue one mile west on Highway 31, then 14 miles south on Forest Service Road 27. The camp is one mile east on Forest Service Road 287.

Trip notes: Located on the north shore of Thompson Reservoir, this camp is simple and pretty, with shaded sites close to the water. Fishing and boating are permitted. See trip notes for East Bay (campground number 3).

❸ East Bay

Location: On Thompson Reservoir in Fremont National Forest; map E3, grid c1.

Campsites, facilities: There are 17 sites for tents, trailers, or RVs. Picnic tables and fire grills are provided. Well water and vault toilets are available. The facilities are wheelchair accessible. Boat launching facilities are nearby. Leashed pets are permitted.

Reservations, fees: No reservations are accepted. Sites are $6 per night. The campground is open from May to mid-November.
Contact: Fremont National Forest, Silver Lake Ranger District, P.O. Box 129, Silver Lake, OR 97638; (541) 576-2107 or fax (541) 576-7587.
Directions: From U.S. 395 at the town of Valley Falls, turn west on Highway 31 and drive 73 miles to the town of Silver Lake. Continue one-half mile west on Highway 31, then drive 13 miles south on Forest Service Road 28. Proceed 1.5 miles west on Forest Service Road 014 to the campground.
Trip notes: This campground on the east shore of Thompson Reservoir has been re-vamped and improved, with paved roads and sites and better toilet facilities. It's still a long way from home, so be sure to bring all of your supplies with you. A day-use area is adjacent to the camp. Silver Creek Marsh (campground number 1) is an even more primitive setting along a stream.

④ Dairy Point

Location: On Dairy Creek in Fremont National Forest; map E3, grid c3.
Campsites, facilities: There are four sites for tents or trailers. Picnic tables, fire grills, a vault toilet, and hand-pumped water are provided. All garbage must be packed out. Leashed pets are permitted.
Reservations, fees: No reservations are accepted. There is no fee. The campground is open from April 15 through October.
Contact: Fremont National Forest, Paisley Ranger District, P.O. Box 67, Paisley, OR 97636; (541) 943-3114 or fax (541) 943-4479.
Directions: From U.S. 395 at the town of Valley Falls, turn west on Highway 31 and drive 22 miles to Paisley. Continue one-half mile west on Highway 31, then turn left on Mill Street and continue to Forest Service Road 33. Drive 19.8 miles, then turn right on Forest Service Road 28 and drive 2.3 miles to the campground.
Trip notes: This campground, elevation 5,800 feet, is located next to the Dairy Creek Bridge. The setting is beautiful and peaceful,

with a towering backdrop of mountains. Fishing and inner tubing are popular activities at Dairy Creek.

⑤ Sandhill Crossing

Location: On the Sprague River in Fremont National Forest; map E3, grid d2.
Campsites, facilities: There are five sites for tents, trailers, or RVs; some are drive-throughs. Picnic tables, fire grills, vault toilets, and hand-pumped water are provided. All garbage must be packed out. Leashed pets are permitted.
Reservations, fees: No reservations are accepted. There is no fee. The campground is open from April 15 through October.
Contact: Fremont National Forest, Paisley Ranger District, P.O. Box 67, Paisley, OR 97636; (541) 943-3114 or fax (541) 943-4479.
Directions: From U.S. 395 at the town of Valley Falls, turn west on Highway 31 and drive 22 miles to Paisley. Continue one-half mile west on Highway 31, then turn left on Mill Street and go to Forest Service Road 33. Drive 19.8 miles, then turn right on Forest Service Road 28 and drive 11 miles. Turn left on Forest Service Road 3411 and drive eight miles to the campground.
Trip notes: If you're looking for a combination of beauty and solitude, you've found it. This camp is located at 6,100 feet on the banks of the Wild and Scenic Sprague River, where fishing is superior. The camp is popular with anglers and hunters in the fall.

⑥ Lee Thomas

Location: On the North Fork of the Sprague River in Fremont National Forest; map E3, grid d3.
Campsites, facilities: There are seven sites for tents, trailers, or RVs up to 16 feet long. Picnic tables and fire grills are provided. Well water and vault toilets are available. Pack out all garbage. Leashed pets are permitted.
Reservations, fees: No reservations are accepted. There is no fee. The campground is open from April to late October.

Contact: Fremont National Forest, Paisley Ranger District, P.O. Box 67, Paisley, OR 97636; (541) 943-3114 or fax (541) 943-4479.

Directions: From U.S. 395 at the town of Valley Falls, turn west on Highway 31 and drive 22 miles to Paisley. Continue one-half mile west on Highway 31, then turn left on Mill Street and go to Forest Service Road 33. Drive 19.8 miles, then turn right on Forest Service Road 28 and drive 11 miles. Turn left on Forest Service Road 3411 and proceed five miles to the campground.

Trip notes: Nestled along the North Fork of the Sprague River in the interior of Fremont National Forest, this small, cozy camp is a genuine hideaway, with all the necessities provided.

❼ Campbell Lake

Location: On Campbell Lake in Fremont National Forest; map E3, grid d3.

Campsites, facilities: There are 15 sites for tents, trailers, or RVs up to 16 feet long. Picnic tables and fire grills are provided. Well water and vault toilets are available. A boat launch is adjacent to the camp. Boats with electric motors are permitted, but gas motors are prohibited. All garbage must be packed out. Leashed pets are permitted.

Reservations, fees: No reservations are accepted. There is no fee. The campground is open from July to late September.

Contact: Fremont National Forest, Paisley Ranger District, P.O. Box 67, Paisley, OR 97636; (541) 943-3114 or fax (541) 943-4479.

Directions: From U.S. 395 at the town of Valley Falls, turn west on Highway 31 and drive 22 miles to Paisley. Continue one-half mile west on Highway 31, then turn left on Mill Street and go to Forest Service Road 33. Drive 19.8 miles, then turn right on Forest Service Road 28 and drive 10 miles. Turn left on Forest Service Road 033 and proceed to the campground.

Trip notes: This campground on the shore of Campbell Lake is near Deadhorse Lake Campground (see number 8). Both camps are very busy and are full most weekends in July and August. No boats with gas motors are permitted on Campbell Lake. Good side trips are available in Fremont National Forest. A Forest Service map details the back roads.

❽ Deadhorse Lake

Location: On Deadhorse Lake in Fremont National Forest; map E3, grid d3.

Campsites, facilities: There are five hike-in sites, 10 sites for tents, trailers, or RVs up to 16 feet long, and a separate area for group camping. Picnic tables and fire grills are provided. Well water and vault toilets are available. A boat launch is nearby. Boats with electric motors are permitted, but gas motors are prohibited. All garbage must be packed out. Leashed pets are permitted.

Reservations, fees: No reservations are accepted. There is no fee. The campground is open from July through September.

Contact: Fremont National Forest, Paisley Ranger District, P.O. Box 67, Paisley, OR 97636; (541) 943-3114 or fax (541) 943-4479.

Directions: From U.S. 395 at the town of Valley Falls, turn west on Highway 31 and drive 22 miles to Paisley. Continue one-half mile west on Highway 31, then turn left on Mill Street and go to Forest Service Road 33. Drive 19.8 miles, then turn right on Forest Service Road 28 and drive 10 miles. Turn left on Forest Service Road 033 and proceed to the campground.

Trip notes: The shore of Deadhorse Lake is home to this camp. A hiking trail winds around the perimeter of the lake, hooking up with other trails along the way. One original Civilian Conservation Corps canoe is left in the lake, a relic of the 1930s. Good side trips are nearby in Fremont National Forest.

❾ Marsters Spring

Location: On the Chewaucan River in Fremont National Forest; map E3, grid d4.

Campsites, facilities: There are 10 sites for tents, trailers, or RVs up to 22 feet long. Picnic

tables and fire grills are provided. Well water and vault toilets are available. Leashed pets are permitted.

Reservations, fees: No reservations are accepted. There is no fee. The campground is open from April to mid-November.

Contact: Fremont National Forest, Paisley Ranger District, P.O. Box 67, Paisley, OR 97636; (541) 943-3114 or fax (541) 943-4479.

Directions: From U.S. 395 at the town of Valley Falls, turn west on Highway 31 and drive 22 miles to Paisley. Continue one-half mile west on Highway 31, then turn left on Mill Street and drive to Forest Service Road 33. Turn south and drive seven miles to the campground.

Trip notes: This pretty campground is on the banks of the Chewaucan River, a good fishing area. It's the largest of several popular camps in this river corridor.

⑩ Happy Camp

Location: On Dairy Creek in Fremont National Forest; map E3, grid d4.

Campsites, facilities: There are nine sites for tents, trailers, or RVs up to 16 feet long. Picnic tables and fire grills are provided. Piped water and vault toilets are available. Leashed pets are permitted.

Reservations, fees: No reservations are accepted. There is no fee. The campground is open from mid-May to late October.

Contact: Fremont National Forest, Paisley Ranger District, P.O. Box 67, Paisley, OR 97636; (541) 943-3114 or fax (541) 943-4479.

Directions: From U.S. 395 at the town of Valley Falls, turn west on Highway 31 and drive 22 miles to Paisley. Continue one-half mile west on Highway 31, then turn left on Mill Street and go to Forest Service Road 33. Drive 19.8 miles, then turn right on Forest Service Road 28 and drive two miles. Continue 2.4 miles on Forest Service Road 047 to the campground.

Trip notes: Here's a pleasant spot with open sites along Dairy Creek. The camp houses some old Depression-era Civilian Conservation Corps shelters, preserved in their original state. Horseshoe pits are provided.

⑪ Corral Creek

Location: Near the Gearhart Mountain Wilderness in Fremont National Forest; map E3, grid e3.

Campsites, facilities: There are six sites for tents, trailers, or RVs up to 16 feet long. Picnic tables and fire grills are provided. Vault toilets are available. There is no potable water. Hitching posts and corrals for horses are provided. Leashed pets are permitted.

Reservations, fees: No reservations are accepted. There is no fee. The campground is open from mid-May to late October.

Contact: Fremont National Forest, Bly Ranger District, P.O. Box 25, Bly, OR 97622; (541) 353-2427.

Directions: From Interstate 5 at Medford, turn north on Highway 62 and drive five miles. Turn east on Highway 140 and drive 79 miles to Klamath Falls. Continue 53 miles east on Highway 140 to the town of Bly, then head northeast on Forest Service Road 3660 for about 16 miles to the junction of Forest Service Road 34. Turn right on Forest Service Road 012 and drive to the campground.

Trip notes: Set along Corral Creek, this camp is adjacent to a trailhead that provides access into the Gearhart Mountain Wilderness, making it a prime base camp for a backpacking trip. Access is also available from camp to the Palasade Rocks, a worthwhile side trip. Another option is Quartz Mountain Snowpark, which is located 14 miles east of the campground.

⑫ Gerber Reservoir

Location: On Gerber Reservoir; map E3, grid f0.

Campsites, facilities: There are 50 sites for tents, trailers, or RVs up to 30 feet long. Picnic tables and fire grills are provided. Piped water, firewood, a sanitary dump station, vault toilets, a boat ramp, a boat dock, launching facilities, and a fish cleaning station are available. Leashed pets are permitted.

Reservations, fees: No reservations are

accepted. Sites are $7 per night. The campground is open from May to mid-October.

Contact: Bureau of Land Management, P.O. Box 151, Lakeview, OR 97630; (541) 947-2177 or fax (541) 947-2143.

Directions: From Interstate 5 at Medford, turn north on Highway 62 and drive five miles, then turn east on Highway 140 and drive 40 miles to Dairy. Turn south on Highway 70 and drive seven miles to Bonanza. Turn east on East Langell Valley Road and drive for 11 miles. Turn left on Gerber Road and drive eight miles to the campground.

Trip notes: This camp can be found at an elevation of 4,800 feet alongside the west shore of Gerber Reservoir. Almost nobody has heard of Gerber, since it's out in the middle of nowhere. And that's just how we like it, right? Recreation options include swimming, fishing, boating, and hiking.

⑬ Lofton Reservoir

Location: On Lofton Reservoir in Fremont National Forest; map E3, grid f2.

Campsites, facilities: There are 26 sites for tents, trailers, or RVs up to 22 feet long. Picnic tables and fire grills are provided. Well water and vault toilets are available. Boat docks and launching facilities are nearby. Leashed pets are permitted.

Reservations, fees: No reservations are accepted. There is no fee. The campground is open from mid-May to late October.

Contact: Fremont National Forest, Bly Ranger District, P.O. Box 25, Bly, OR 97622; (541) 353-2427.

Directions: From Interstate 5 at Medford, turn north on Highway 62 and drive five miles, then turn east on Highway 140 and drive 74 miles to Klamath Falls. Continue 54 miles east on Highway 140 to Bly. From Bly, continue 13 miles southeast on Highway 140, then seven miles south on Forest Service Road 3715. From there, go 1.5 miles northeast on Forest Service Road 3715A to the campground.

Trip notes: This remote campground is on the shore of Lofton Reservoir. Other lakes are

nearby and are accessible by Forest Service roads. This area marks the beginning of the Great Basin, a high-desert area that extends to Idaho.

⑭ Drews Creek

Location: Near Lakeview in Fremont National Forest; map E3, grid f3.

Campsites, facilities: There are five sites for tents, trailers, or RVs. Picnic tables, fire grills, vault toilets, and piped water are provided. All garbage must be packed out. Leashed pets are permitted.

Reservations, fees: No reservations are accepted. There is no fee. The campground is open from early June to mid-October.

Contact: Fremont National Forest, Lakeview Ranger District, HC 64, Box 60, Lakeview, OR 97630; (541) 947-3334 or fax (541) 947-6315.

Directions: From Lakeview, travel 10 miles west on Highway 140, then turn left on County Road 1-13. Drive four miles, then turn right and drive six miles on County Road 1-11D and Forest Service Road 4017 to the campground.

Trip notes: Located along Drews Creek at 4,900 feet, this is an exceptionally beautiful campground. Wild roses grow near the creek, and there are several unmarked trails that lead to nearby hills where campers can enjoy scenic views. This is a great spot for a family trip, with horseshoe pits, an area for baseball, and a large group barbecue. Fishing is available in nearby Dog Lake, which also provides facilities for boating. Waterskiing is another option at Drews Reservoir, two miles to the west.

⑮ Cottonwood Meadows

Location: On Cottonwood Meadow Lake in Fremont National Forest; map E3, grid f4.

Campsites, facilities: There are 21 sites for tents, small trailers, or RVs. Picnic tables and fire grills are provided. Piped water and vault toilets are available. Boat docks are nearby. Electric motors are allowed, but gasoline motors are prohibited on the lake. Leashed pets are permitted.

Reservations, fees: No reservations are accepted. There is no fee. The campground is open from early June to late October.

Contact: Fremont National Forest, Lakeview Ranger District, HC 64, Box 60, Lakeview, OR 97630; (541) 947-3334 or fax (541) 947-6315.

Directions: From Lakeview, travel 24 miles west on Highway 140, then eight miles northeast on Forest Service Road 3870.

Trip notes: This campground along the shore of Cottonwood Meadow Lake is one of the better spots in the vicinity for fishing and hiking. Boats with electric motors are allowed on the lake, but gas motors are prohibited. Three hiking trails wind around the lake, and facilities for horses include hitching posts, feeders, water, and corrals.

⑯ Junipers Reservoir RV Resort

Location: On Junipers Reservoir; map E3, grid f4.

Campsites, facilities: There are 15 tent sites and 40 sites for trailers or RVs. Rest rooms, showers, a sanitary dump station, a public phone, modem access, a laundry room, and ice are available. Recreational facilities include a rec hall, a volleyball court, and horseshoe pits. Some of the facilities are wheelchair accessible. Leashed pets are permitted.

Reservations, fees: Reservations are recommended. Sites are $16–$19 per night. The campground is open from May to mid-October.

Contact: Phone the park at (541) 947-2050 or write to HC 60, P.O. Box 1994A, Lakeview, OR 97630.

Directions: From Burns on U.S. 20, drive approximately 135 miles south on U.S. 395 to Lakeview. From the junction of U.S. 395 and Highway 140 (in Lakeview), drive west on Highway 140 for 10 miles. The resort is on the right at milepost 86.5.

Trip notes: This resort on an 8,000-acre cattle ranch is in a designated Oregon Wildlife Viewing Area, and campers may catch glimpses of seldom-seen species. There are many nature walking trails at the park, and driving tours are

offered for guests. Fishing for catfish is good in the vicinity (though not at the reservoir), and the summer climate is mild and pleasant.

⑰ Mud Creek

Location: On Mud Creek in Fremont National Forest; map E3, grid f6.

Campsites, facilities: There are seven sites for tents, trailers, or RVs up to 16 feet long. Piped water, picnic tables, fire grills, and vault toilets are available. Leashed pets are permitted.

Reservations, fees: No reservations are accepted. There is no fee. The campground is open from June to mid-October.

Contact: Fremont National Forest, Lakeview Ranger District, HC 64, Box 60, Lakeview, OR 97630; (541) 947-3334 or fax (541) 947-6315.

Directions: From Lakeview, drive about five miles north on U.S. 395, then eight miles east on Highway 140. The camp is seven miles north on Forest Service Road 3615.

Trip notes: This remote camp is in an isolated stand of lodgepole pines along the banks of Mud Creek. Drake Peak (8,405 feet) is nearby. There are no other camps in the immediate vicinity.

⑱ Adel Store and Park

Location: In Adel; map E3, grid f8.

Campsites, facilities: There are eight sites for trailers or RVs of any length. Electricity, piped water, and sewer hookups are provided. A store, a cafe, and ice are available. Leashed pets and motorbikes are permitted.

Reservations, fees: No reservations are accepted. Sites are $15 per night. The campground is open from April through October, weather permitting.

Contact: Phone (541) 947-3850 or write to P.O. Box 45, Adel, OR 97620.

Directions: From Lakeview, drive about five miles north on U.S. 395, then turn east on Highway 140 and drive 28 miles to Adel. The RV park is in town.

Trip notes: This is the only game in town, so

you'd better grab it while you can. Recreation options in the area include hang gliding, rockhounding, or visiting Hart Mountain National Antelope Refuge, 40 miles north of Adel.

⑲ Dog Lake

Location: On Dog Lake in Fremont National Forest; map E3, grid g3.

Campsites, facilities: There are eight sites for tents, trailers, or RVs up to 16 feet long. Piped water, picnic tables, and fire grills are provided. Vault toilets are available. A boat launch is nearby. Leashed pets are permitted.

Reservations, fees: No reservations are accepted. There is no fee. The campground is open from mid-April to mid-October.

Contact: Fremont National Forest, Lakeview Ranger District, HC 64, Box 60, Lakeview, OR 97630; (541) 947-3334 or fax (541) 947-6315.

Directions: From Lakeview, travel 10 miles west on Highway 140, then turn left on County Road 1-13. Drive four miles, then turn right on County Road 1-11D and drive to Forest Service Road 4017. Continue 12 miles on Forest Service Road 4017.

Trip notes: This campground is on the west shore of Dog Lake, where fishing and boats with motors are permitted. Dog Lake is a warm-water and cold-water fishery. Prospects for seeing waterfowl and eagles are good, too.

⑳ Goose Lake State Park

Location: On Goose Lake; map E3, grid g6.

Campsites, facilities: There are 48 sites with water and electrical hookups for trailers or RVs up to 50 feet long. Picnic tables and fire grills are provided. Flush toilets, showers, a dump station, and firewood are available. Boat launching facilities are nearby. Leashed pets are permitted.

Reservations, fees: No reservations are accepted. Sites are $7–$20 per night. The campground is open from mid-April to late October.

Contact: Phone (800) 452-5687 or (541) 947-3111, or write to the park at P.O. Box 207, New Pine Creek, OR 97635.

Directions: From the junction of U.S. 395 and Highway 140 at Lakeview, turn south on U.S. 395 and drive 14 miles. Turn west at the park entrance road and drive one mile to the campground.

Trip notes: This park is on the east shore of unusual Goose Lake, which lies half in Oregon and half in California. Waterfowl from the Pacific Flyway frequent this out-of-the-way spot. Boating is popular here.

㉑ Willow Creek

Location: On Willow Creek in Fremont National Forest; map E3, grid g7.

Campsites, facilities: There are eight sites for tents, trailers, or RVs up to 22 feet long. Picnic tables and fire grills are provided. There is no piped water. Vault toilets are available. Leashed pets are permitted.

Reservations, fees: No reservations are accepted. There is no fee. The campground is open from June to mid-October.

Contact: Fremont National Forest, Lakeview Ranger District, HC 64, Box 60, Lakeview, OR 97630; (541) 947-3334 or fax (541) 947-6315.

Directions: From Lakeview, travel about five miles north on U.S. 395, then eight miles east on Highway 140. Turn right on Forest Service Road 3915 and drive nine miles, then turn right on Forest Service Road 4011 and continue to the campground.

Trip notes: This campground is along the banks of Willow Creek, not far from a dirt road that heads north to Burnt Creek. A hiking trail accesses the Crane Mountain Trail. Pick up a Forest Service map that details the back roads.

㉒ Deep Creek

Location: On Deep Creek in Fremont National Forest; map E3, grid g7.

Campsites, facilities: There are two sites for tents and four sites for trailers or RVs up to 22 feet long. Picnic tables and fire grills are provided. Vault toilets are available. There is no piped water. Leashed pets are permitted.

Reservations, fees: No reservations are

accepted. There is no fee. The campground is open from June to mid-October.

Contact: Fremont National Forest, Lakeview Ranger District, HC 64, Box 60, Lakeview, OR 97630; (541) 947-3334 or fax (541) 947-6315.

Directions: From Lakeview, travel about five miles north on U.S. 395, then eight miles east on Highway 140. Turn right on Forest Service Road 3915 and drive 14 miles, then turn right on Forest Service Road 4015 and drive one mile to the campground.

Trip notes: Shaded by huge ponderosa pine and quaking aspen, this pretty, little-used campground on the banks of Deep Creek is the place if you're after privacy. Magnificent spring wildflowers are a highlight here.

Map E4

One inch equals approximately 20 miles.

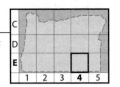

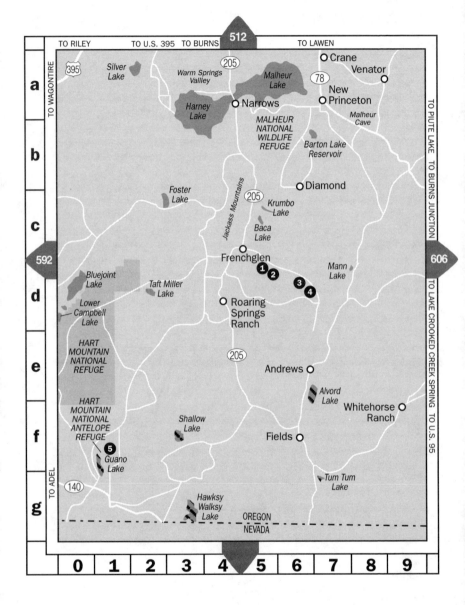

Chapter E4 features:

❶ Steens Mountain Resort

Location: On the Blitzen River; map E4, grid d5.

Campsites, facilities: There are 99 sites for tents, trailers, or RVs, plus five cabins. Rest rooms, showers, a sanitary dump station, a public phone, laundry facilities, and ice are available. Leashed pets are permitted.

Reservations, fees: Reservations are recommended. Sites are $10–$16 per night; cabins are $49 per night. The campground is open year-round.

Contact: Phone the park at (541) 493-2415 or write to North Loop Road, Frenchglen, OR 97738.

Directions: From Burns on U.S. 20, turn south on Highway 205 and drive about 60 miles to Frenchglen. Turn east on Steens Mountain Road and drive three miles to the resort.

Trip notes: The self-proclaimed "gateway to the Steens Mountains," this resort has a great view of the surrounding gorges, providing excellent photographic opportunities. Hiking and hunting are other possibilities in the area. Fishing is available on the Blitzen River, with easy access from the camp.

❷ Page Springs

Location: Near Malheur National Wildlife Refuge; map E4, grid d5.

Campsites, facilities: There are 36 sites for tents, trailers, or RVs up to 24 feet long. Picnic tables and fire grills are provided. Piped water, firewood, and vault toilets are available. Some facilities are wheelchair accessible. Leashed pets are permitted.

Reservations, fees: No reservations are ac-

cepted. Sites are $4 per vehicle per night. The campground is open year-round.

Contact: Bureau of Land Management, HC 74-12533, Highway 20 West, Burns, OR 97738; (541) 573-4400 or fax (541) 573-4411.

Directions: From Burns on U.S. 20, turn south on Highway 205 and drive about 60 miles to Frenchglen, then drive three miles east on Steens Mountain Road to the campground.

Trip notes: This campground is adjacent to Page Springs and the Malheur National Wildlife Refuge. The Frenchglen Hotel is administered by the state parks department and offers overnight accommodations and food. Activities include hiking on the trails in the area, plus bird-watching, fishing, hunting, and sight-seeing.

❸ Fish Lake

Location: On Fish Lake; map E4, grid d6.

Campsites, facilities: There are 23 sites for tents, trailers, or RVs up to 24 feet long. Picnic tables and fire grills are provided. Piped water, firewood, and vault toilets are available. Boat launching facilities are nearby. Some facilities are wheelchair accessible. Leashed pets are permitted.

Reservations, fees: No reservations are accepted. Sites are $4 per vehicle a night. The campground is open from June through October, weather permitting.

Contact: Bureau of Land Management, HC 74-12533, Highway 20 West, Burns, OR 97738; (541) 573-4400 or fax (541) 573-4411.

Directions: From Burns on U.S. 20, turn south on Highway 205 and drive about 60 miles to Frenchglen, then go 16 miles east on Steens Mountain Road to the campground.

Trip notes: The shore of little Fish Lake is the setting for this primitive but pretty camp, elevation 7,400 feet. Not known to many, it can make an excellent weekend getaway spot for backpacking and sight-seeing. Fishing is an option, made easier by the boat ramp near camp.

④ Jackman Park

Location: Near Malheur National Wildlife Refuge; map E4, grid d7.

Campsites, facilities: There are six primitive sites for tents, trailers, or RVs up to 24 feet long. Picnic tables are provided. Firewood, hand-pumped water, and pit toilets are available. Leashed pets are permitted.

Reservations, fees: No reservations are accepted. Sites are $4 per vehicle a night. The campground is open from July to late October, weather permitting.

Contact: Bureau of Land Management, HC 74-12533, Highway 20 West, Burns, OR 97738; (541) 573-4400 or fax (541) 573-4411.

Directions: From Burns on U.S. 20, turn south on Highway 205 and drive about 60 miles to Frenchglen, then drive 20 miles east on Steens Mountain Road to the campground.

Trip notes: Set at 8,100 feet in the eastern Oregon desert, this is one of four camps in the area. Page Springs is nearby (see campground number 2) and the Adel Store (for supplies) is about 15 miles northeast at the southeastern end of the Malheur National Wildlife Refuge.

⑤ Hart Antelope Refuge

Location: Near Adel; map E4, grid f1.

Campsites, facilities: There are 12 primitive sites for tents, trailers, or RVs up to 20 feet long. Pit toilets are provided, but there is no drinking water. Leashed pets are permitted.

Reservations, fees: No reservations are accepted. There is no fee. The campground is open from May to November, with limited facilities in the winter.

Contact: Phone (541) 947-3315, fax (541) 947-4414, or write to P.O. Box 111, Lakeview, OR 97630.

Directions: From Lakeview, drive about five miles north on U.S. 395, then turn east on Highway 140 and drive 28 miles to Adel. At the sign for the Hart Antelope Refuge, turn north and drive 43 miles northeast on a paved, then gravel road to the refuge headquarters. The campground is four miles beyond this point. The road is often impassable in the winter.

Trip notes: This unusual refuge offers canyons and hot springs. There is no drinking water at the campground, but it can be obtained at the headquarters, which you pass on the way in. Some of Oregon's largest antelope herds roam this large area. The nearest place for supplies is in Adel at the Adel Store.

Map E5

Oregon State Map .... *page 6*
One inch equals approximately 20 miles.

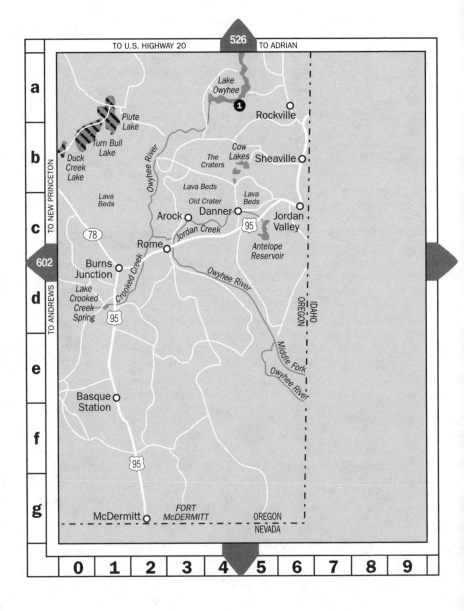

Chapter E5 features:

1 Leslie Gulch

Location: On Owyhee Lake; map E5, grid a5.

Campsites, facilities: There are eight undeveloped sites for tents, trailers, or RVs up to 20 feet long. Picnic tables are provided. Vault toilets are available. There is no piped water. Boat launching facilities are available on site. Leashed pets are permitted.

Reservations, fees: No reservations are accepted. There is no fee. The campground is open from April to November.

Contact: Bureau of Land Management, 100 Oregon Street, Vale, OR 97918; (541) 473-3144 or fax (541) 473-6213.

Directions: From Homedale, Idaho, drive south on U.S. 95 to the Leslie Gulch Recreation Area turnoff (McBride Creek Road) and travel west for 25 miles to the campground.

Trip notes: This campground is on the eastern shore of Owyhee Lake, not far from the Oregon/Idaho border. Warm-water fishing, waterskiing, and hiking are among the recreation options in this high desert area. Lake Owyhee State Park provides the other nearby recreation destination. There are no other campgrounds located within a one-hour drive.

Index

Index

Index

Index

About the Author

Tom Stienstra has made it his life work to explore the West—camping, hiking, fishing, and boating—searching for the best of the outdoors and writing about it.

He is the outdoors writer for the *San Francisco Examiner,* which distributes his column on the New York Times News Service. He is also the author of 15 books and the associate editor of *Western Outdoor News.*

In 1994 and 1997, he was named the National Outdoor Writer of the Year, newspaper division, by the Outdoor Writers Association of America, and in 1990, 1992, and 1997, he was named the California Outdoor Writer of the Year.

His books with Foghorn Outdoors are the best-selling outdoor guidebooks in the country.

Other Foghorn titles include:

California Camping

California Hiking (with Ann Marie Brown)

California Fishing

California Boating and Water Sports

Tom Stienstra's Outdoor Getaway Guide: Northern California

Easy Camping in Northern California

Epic Trips of the West

Acknowledgements

Michael Hodgson, author of *Facing The Extreme* (with Ruth Anne Kocour) and technical editor of *Outdoor Retailer,* reviewed all the equipment and technical information for this edition.

The following state and federal resource experts provided critical late-breaking information regarding changes in reservations services, fees, and recreational services:

Michael Dombeck, Linda Feldman, and Dick Patterson, U.S. Forest Service Headquarters, Washington, D.C.

Matt Mathes, U.S. Forest Service, Pacific Region headquarters, San Francisco, California

Kathy Burdett, National Park Service, Washington, D.C.

Oregon

Janet Kirsch, Deschutes National Forest, Crescent Ranger District

Vicki English and Kate Goosens, Deschutes National Forest, Sisters Ranger District

Donna Gress, Fremont National Forest, Bly Ranger District

Catherine Callaghan, Fremont National Forest, Lakeview Ranger District

Rich Carver, Fremont National Forest, Silver Lake Ranger District

Robin Murray, Malheur National Forest, Bear Valley Ranger District

Carole Holly, Malheur National Forest, Prairie City Ranger District

Kim Paulk, Mount Hood National Forest, Mount Hood Ranger District

Pam Duncan, Mount Hood National Forest, Barlow Ranger District

Dennis Beechler, Mount Hood National Forest, Bear Springs Ranger District

Larry Reed, Mount Hood National Forest, Estacada Ranger District

Jill Lowen, Crooked River National Grassland

Linda Rock, Ochoco National Forest, Prineville Ranger District

Jeri Ledgerwood, Ochoco National Forest, Snow Mountain Ranger District

Chris Dent, Rogue River National Forest, Prospect Ranger District

Steve Johnson, Rogue river National Forest, Ashland Ranger District

Don McLennan, Siskiyou National Forest, Illinois Valley Ranger District

Mary Stansell, Siskiyou National Forest, Gold Beach Ranger District

Chery Lyda, Siskiyou National Forest, Galice Ranger District

Carol Johnson, Siuslaw National Forest, Hebo Ranger District

Ron Murphy, Umpqua National Forest, North Umpqua Ranger District

Terry Klingenberg, Umpqua National Forest, Diamond Lake Ranger District

JoAnne Perkins, Umpqua National Forest, Cottage Grove Ranger District

Lori Depew, Umpqua National Forest, Tiller Ranger District

Sue Womack, Wallowa-Whitman National Forest, Eagle Cap Ranger District

Robin Rose, Wallowa-Whitman National Forest, Baker Ranger District

Rose Parks, Wallowa-Whitman National Forest, LaGrande Ranger District

Lupe Wilson, Willamette National Forest, Sweet Home Ranger District

Chris Jenson, Willamette National Forest, Rigdon Ranger District

Ray Crist, Willamette National Forest, Detroit Ranger District

Larry Lassiter, Willamette National Forest, Lowell Ranger District

Dave Graham, Willamette National Forest, McKenzie Ranger District

Judith Parker, Winema National Forest, Chemult Ranger District

Jeanie Sheehan, Winema National Forest, Klamath Ranger District

Dan Hand, Lake Roosevelt National Recreation Area

Jim Villani, Oregon Dunes National Recreation Area

Gregg Morgan, Bureau of Land Management, Roseburg District Office

Mark Eddings, U.S. Army Corps of Engineers

Julie McCann, Clackamas County Parks

Frank Howard, Oregon State Parks

Washington

Keith Warfield, Colville National Forest, Republic Ranger District

Penny Miller, Colville National Forest, Colville Ranger District

Kim Dirienz, Colville National Forest, Sullivan Ranger District

Kathy Wallis, Colville National Forest, Newport Ranger District

Linda Kimmel, Gifford Pinchot National Forest, Packwood Ranger District

Linda Nolan, Mount St. Helens National Volcanic Monument

Lois Dechand, Gifford Pinchot National Forest, Mount Adams Ranger District

Roger Lembrick, Gifford Pinchot National Forest, Wind River Ranger District

Pam Young, Mount Baker–Snoqualmie National Forest, Skyomish Ranger District

Eli Warren, Mount Baker–Snoqualmie National Forest, Mount Baker Ranger District

Diane Holz, Mount Baker–Snoqualmie National Forest, Darrington Ranger District

Willa Bedient, Okanogan National Forest, Tonasket Ranger District

Jim Archambeault, Okanogan National Forest, Methow Valley Ranger District

Donna Scheibe, Umatilla National Forest, Walla Walla Ranger District

Susan Peterson, Wenatchee National Forest, Lake Wenatchee Ranger District

Heide Gocke, Wenatchee National Forest, Entiat Ranger District

Mike Ames, Wenatchee National Forest, Cle Elum Ranger District

Dave Hays, U.S. Army Corps of Engineers

Linda Burnett, Washington State Parks

Donna Rahier, Mount Rainier National Park

Editor in Chief	*Donna Leverenz*
Editors	*Jean Linsteadt* *Karin Mullen*
Production Coordinator	*Kyle Morgan*
Production Assistants	*Jean-Vi Lenthe* *Mark Aver*
Research Editor	*Janet Connaughton*
Cover Photo	*Dave Rosenberg* *Tony Stone Images*

Leave No Trace

Leave No Trace, Inc., is a program dedicated to maintaining the integrity of outdoor recreation areas through education and public awareness. Foghorn Press is a proud supporter of this program and its ethics.

Here's how you can Leave No Trace:

Plan Ahead and Prepare
- Learn about the regulations and special concerns of the area you are visiting.
- Visit the backcountry in small groups.
- Avoid popular areas during peak-use periods.
- Choose equipment and clothing in subdued colors.
- Pack food in reusable containers.

Travel and Camp with Care
On the trail:
- Stay on designated trails. Walk single file in the middle of the path.
- Do not take shortcuts on switchbacks.
- When traveling cross-country where there are no trails, follow animal trails or spread out your group so no new routes are created. Walk along the most durable surfaces available, such as rock, gravel, dry grasses, or snow.
- Use a map and compass to eliminate the need for rock cairns, tree scars, or ribbons.
- If you encounter pack animals, step to the downhill side of the trail and speak softly to avoid startling them.

At Camp:
- Choose an established, legal site that will not be damaged by your stay.
- Restrict activities to areas where vegetation is compacted or absent.
- Keep pollutants out of the water by camping at least 200 feet (about 70 adult steps) from lakes and streams.
- Control pets at all times, or leave them at home with a sitter. Remove dog feces.

Pack It In and Pack It Out
- Take everything you bring into the wild back out with you.
- Protect wildlife and your food by storing rations securely. Pick up all spilled foods.

- Use toilet paper or wipes sparingly; pack them out.
- Inspect your campsite for trash and any evidence of your stay. Pack out all trash—even if it's not yours!

Properly Dispose of What You Can't Pack Out
- If no refuse facility is available, deposit human waste in catholes dug six to eight inches deep at least 200 feet from water, camps, or trails. Cover and disguise the catholes when you're finished.
- To wash yourself or your dishes, carry the water 200 feet from streams or lakes and use small amounts of biodegradable soap. Scatter the strained dishwater.

Keep the Wilderness Wild
- Treat our natural heritage with respect. Leave plants, rocks, and historical artifacts as you found them.
- Good campsites are found, not made. Do not alter a campsite.
- Let nature's sounds prevail; keep loud voices and noises to a minimum.
- Do not build structures or furniture or dig trenches.

Minimize Use and Impact of Fires
- Campfires can have a lasting impact on the backcountry. Always carry a lightweight stove for cooking, and use a candle lantern instead of building a fire whenever possible.
- Where fires are permitted, use established fire rings only.
- Do not scar the natural setting by snapping the branches off live, dead, or downed trees.
- Completely extinguish your campfire and make sure it is cold before departing. Remove all unburned trash from the fire ring and scatter the cold ashes over a large area well away from any camp.

For more information, call 1-800-332-4100.

FOGHORN ✖ OUTDOORS

Founded in 1985, Foghorn Press has quickly become one of the country's premier publishers of outdoor recreation guidebooks. Through its unique Books Building Community program, Foghorn Press supports community environmental issues, such as park, trail, and water ecosystem preservation.

Foghorn Press books are available throughout the United States in bookstores and some outdoor retailers. If you cannot find the title you are looking for, visit Foghorn's Web site at www.foghorn.com or call 1-800-FOGHORN.

The Complete Guide Series

- *Pacific Northwest Hiking* (648 pp) $20.95—New 2nd edition
- *Washington Fishing* (528 pp) $20.95—New 2nd edition
- *California Camping* (768 pp) $20.95—New 10th anniversary edition
- *California Hiking* (688 pp) $20.95—New 3rd edition
- *California Waterfalls* (408 pp) $17.95
- *California Fishing* (768 pp) $20.95—New 4th edition
- *California Golf* (864 pp) $20.95—New 7th edition
- *California Beaches* (640 pp) $19.95
- *California Boating and Water Sports* (608 pp) $19.95
- *California In-Line Skating* (480 pp) $19.95
- *Tahoe* (678 pp) $20.95—New 2nd edition
- *Alaska Fishing* (448 pp) $20.95—New 2nd edition
- *New England Hiking* (416 pp) $18.95
- *New England Camping* (520 pp) $19.95
- *Utah and Nevada Camping* (384 pp) $18.95
- *Southwest Camping* (544 pp) $17.95
- *Baja Camping* (288 pp) $14.95—New 2nd edition
- *Florida Camping* (672 pp) $20.95—New!

The National Outdoors Series

- *America's Secret Recreation Areas—Your Recreation Guide to the Bureau of Land Management's Wild Lands of the West* (640 pp) $17.95
- *America's Wilderness—The Complete Guide to More Than 600 National Wilderness Areas* (592 pp) $19.95
- *The Camper's Companion—The Pack-Along Guide for Better Outdoor Trips* (464 pp) $15.95
- *Wild Places: 20 Journeys Into the North American Outdoors* (305 pp) $15.95

A book's page length and availability are subject to change.

For more information, call 1-800-FOGHORN,
e-mail: foghorn@well.com, or write to:
Foghorn Press
340 Bodega Avenue
Petaluma, CA 94952

Chapter Reference Map

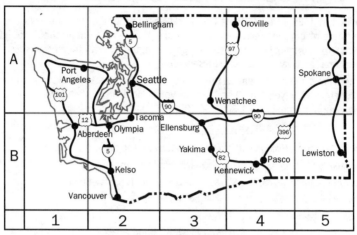

Washington map page 83

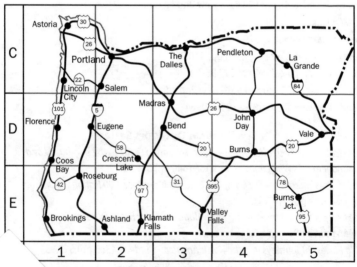

Oregon map page 337